The Literature of the Sages
Second Part

Compendia Rerum Iudaicarum ad Novum Testamentum

SECTION TWO

THE LITERATURE OF THE JEWISH PEOPLE
IN THE PERIOD OF THE SECOND TEMPLE AND THE TALMUD

1. MIKRA
Text, Translation, Reading and Interpretation of the Hebrew Bible
in Ancient Judaism and Early Christianity
Editors: M.J. Mulder, H. Sysling

2. JEWISH WRITINGS OF THE SECOND TEMPLE PERIOD
Apocrypha, Pseudepigrapha, Qumran Sectarian Writings, Philo, Josephus
Editor: M.E. Stone

3a. THE LITERATURE OF THE SAGES
FIRST PART: Oral Tora, Halakha, Mishna, Tosefta, Talmud,
External Tractates
Editor: S. Safrai. Executive editor: P.J. Tomson

3b. THE LITERATURE OF THE SAGES
SECOND PART: Midrash and Targum, Liturgy, Poetry, Mysticism, Contracts,
Inscriptions, Ancient Science and the Languages of Rabbinic Literature
Editors: S. Safrai, Z. Safrai, J. Schwartz, P.J. Tomson

Published under the auspices of the
Foundation Compendia Rerum Iudaicarum ad Novum Testamentum,
Amsterdam

The Literature of the Sages

Second Part:
Midrash and Targum
Liturgy, Poetry, Mysticism
Contracts, Inscriptions, Ancient Science
and the Languages of Rabbinic Literature

Edited by
Shmuel Safrai ז"ל, Zeev Safrai,
Joshua Schwartz, Peter J. Tomson

2006

Fortress Press

Contents

Section Three: Contracts, Inscriptions, Ancient Science

Section Four: The Languages of Rabbinic Literature

Foreword

In 1974 the editors of the first Compendia volume opened their General Introduction with the statement that "The *Compendia Rerum Iudaicarum ad Novum Testamentum* is designed as a historical work on the relationship of Judaism and Christianity." Within this design, the ideological overtones of which were never muted, the present volume is a – long awaited – tailpiece of considerable importance. After the two introductory volumes of Section One (1974 and 1976), with their orientation on the history and social culture of Judaism in the period of the formation of the New Testament, Section Two set out to explore the fundamental texts of that period with a volume on the Hebrew Bible in Ancient Judaism and Early Christianity (1988), and another on the Jewish writings of the Second Temple Period which did not find a place in the canon of the Hebrew Bible nor in the corpus of later rabbinic Judaism (1984). The third volume of Section Two, devoted to the literature of the Sages of classical rabbinic Judaism, began to appear in 1987 (vol. 3a). Now, in the year 2006, this beginning is completed with the present volume (vol. 3b). Instead of deploring the delay, the Foundation chooses to express its great satisfaction with the fact that this point is now reached in such an impressive way, and that so much profit could be gained from the progress in the many areas of the study of rabbinic literature made within the past years.

Equally satisfying is the fact that in the meantime no less than five monograph volumes have appeared in Compendia's Section Three devoted to Jewish traditions in early Christian literature.

The Foundation is most grateful to Prof. Peter J. Tomson and his co-editors Profs. Zeev Safrai and Joshua Schwartz, for having accepted the burden to give shape and coherence to a subject of such dimensions, and to complete what Prof. Shmuel Safrai, who passed away in 2004, started so many years ago.

In the same spirit of respect and gratitude the Foundation wishes to honour the memory of Mr. R.A. (Bob) Levisson, who became president of the Foundation in January 1984, energetically promoted the appearance of the previous volumes of this Section, and remained active until his death in 2001, and likewise the memory of Herman E. Oving, for many years a faithful and vigilant treasurer, who passed away in the year 2000.

It is the conviction of the Board of the Compendia Foundation that this volume, which explores such vital aspects of rabbinic literature and thought, has the potential to contribute to the aims of the Foundation, and to scholarship in general, for a long time to come.

Albert van der Heide, president

Introduction

Section two of the Compendia, entitled *The Literature of the Jewish People in the Period of the Second Temple and the Talmud*, is based on three pillars: *Mikra*, or the Hebrew Bible as understood in ancient Judaism and early Christianity; *Jewish Writings of the Second Temple Period*; and *The Literature of the Sages*. Prof. Shmuel Safrai, who was among the founding editors of the Compendia, took on the responsibility for the third project and was appointed editor of the volume to appear on rabbinic literature.

Much thought was given to the content of the planned volume and to the order of the chapters. The guiding principle was based on the known or approximate date of 'final' editing of the various corpora as well as on the division of the literature of the sages into such categories as Oral Tora, halakha, aggada, midrash, targum, prayer and much more. A number of general and methodological chapters were also planned to set the tone for the work. It was soon found that the scope of the project was enormous, and expediency dictated that the work be divided into two volumes. The first one, which appeared in 1987, contains chapters on Oral Tora and halakha, as well as Mishna, Tosefta, the Palestinian and Babylonian Talmuds, and external tractates. The second volume was to deal with midrash, aggada, targum, liturgical texts, and a number of auxiliary subjects.

The overall idea was to give a scholarly and imaginative presentation of the range of texts preserved by rabbinic Judaism or in its vicinity – texts that at the same time were thought to reflect the great variety of Jewish life both within the ambit of rabbinic tradition and beyond it. As to such sources, Safrai never tired of underlining the importance of 'real life' documents such as inscriptions, contracts, and archaeological finds. Not only does this approach carry the reader well beyond the accepted time limits of ancient Judaism – being a primary context for the New Testament writings – but also into little studied and sometimes obscure corners of rabbinic literature. The last item to be added to the list of documents discussed in the book certainly did not belong in the latter category, but had simply been all the time overlooked by the editors. It was during the last editorial meeting with Prof. Safrai, conducted in his home a month before he died, that he brought up the idea and exclaimed: 'The Passover Haggada, of course! How could we forget it!'

The second part of the project, which we present now to the reader, was, unfortunately and for many reasons, a long time in the making. Prof. Safrai passed away in July 2003 and did not live to see its completion. The present editors, who were privileged to have been among his students, have made every effort to continue the project in keeping with his academic and research guidelines, although obviously each and every author had total and complete methodological autonomy and at times may not agree with other authors or with Shmuel Safrai himself.

Safrai believed that the background to the New Testament was to be found in ancient Judaism and that this Jewish background existed in a wide array of sources, and especially in the literature of the sages, extending throughout a rather long period and far beyond the first century. In this Safrai was not unique, but rather he continued a scholarly tradition that had begun to search out the roots of early Christianity in Judaism rather than in the Greco-Roman world. While this trend had its ups and downs in terms of academic popularity, it became increasingly popular in Jewish circles with the advent of *Wissenschaft des Judentums*. While Christian academic circles were notably slower to adopt this point of view and often kept disagreeing over its attendant methodologies, the rich subject matter of rabbinic literature and its evident parallels with the New Testament and other early Christian writings eventually increased the popularity of this literature also in these circles. In more recent decades, the discovery and scholarly exploitation of the Dead Sea scrolls was particularly helpful in this respect, a fact Safrai fully recognized although he left the study of these documents largely to his long-time friend, colleague, and co-founder of the Compendia, David Flusser.

The use of rabbinic literature for the understanding of the New Testament was not without its problems, especially as strides were made in the methodologies associated with rabbinic literature as well as with the New Testament. It became clear that historical traditions in the literature of the sages could not be accepted at face value and that attestations were problematic. For Safrai, however, the literary formulation of a rabbinic work or the conclusion of its editorial process did not belie the fact that many traditions in such literature might have been early, even with direct influence on the New Testament world or at least representing a common tradition, thus providing scholars of the New Testament with many additional sources.

Identifying such traditions was not a simple matter, however, and it became increasingly unpopular to even attempt to do so among scholars of rabbinic literature, talmudists and historians, whether they doubted the historicity of texts and the relevance of 'late' texts for 'earlier' times or not, and especially in the case of midrash and aggada, main topics of the present volume. Matters were not helped by the sometime simplistic use of rabbinic literature by New Testament scholars. Nor did exaggerated statements of the non-historical and 'ideological' character of the rabbinic documents by scholars reacting to this historical naivety assist in advancing the sober approach that is needed here. Safrai at times found himself standing almost alone in withstanding the pressure to sever any unambiguous ties between rabbinic literature and the New Testament. However, during the course of time it has become clear that certain parts of the New Testament can be understood only in relation to rabbinic thought, that 'background' is relative, and that *la longue durée* might apply to religious and literary phenomena. Indeed, it has become increasingly accepted to see some type of 'chain of tradition' which allows for the use of 'later' material or at least provides better methodologies for interpreting 'earlier' material. The present editors, following Shmuel Safrai's lead, refrained from restricting the chronological time frame and leave it for the reader of the individual chapters to judge the relevance of some of the later material for the New Testament and its world. As the reader will note, the present articles represent 'state of the art' in terms of methodological and literary issues, providing the reader – scholar and layman – with the understanding necessary to examine the relevance, or lack of such, of the literature of the sages for the world of the New Testament.

If, however, when all is said and done, the literature of the sages is problematical for the purpose at hand as defined by the *Compendia* and usage depends on methodologies concerning which there is still disagreement, sometimes still strident, then why bother? Why should the scholar of the New Testament just not make do with the literature that is clearly contemporaneous with the New Testament? Why not concentrate on the Apocrypha and Pseudepigrapha and on Qumran, or on Josephus and Philo? These questions and subsequently the answers to them, helped form Shmuel Safrai's methodological modus vivendi. Thus, while there might be a good deal of Second Temple literature closer in time to the New Testament, the literature of the sages provides information that these other types of literature do not. It is the literature of the sages which provides, for instance, detailed information on the family, agriculture, education, and everyday life, and Safrai wrote a series of chapters on such matters in the first section of the *Compendia*, using for the most part rabbinic literature as his primary source material. Furthermore it is possible to point out an important popular phenomenon in both literatures, i.e. in the parable, a genre unique to the New Testament and to the literature of the sages which does not appear in other Second Temple literature.

Relevant information or material for comparison with the New Testament might be found both in halakhic literature as well as in midrash and aggada. Regarding halakha, it should of course be pointed out that the fact that the concomitant topics of everyday life are discussed in rabbinic literature in no way relates to the question of whether rabbinic halakha was normative in New Testament times or not. Rather, the question is whether the halakhic descriptions of everyday life, custom and practice represent actual or 'common' behaviour of some sort – and Safrai felt that they did and thus might reflect such life among Jesus and his disciples as well as in early Christianity of the Land of Israel. This was also the case regarding *realia* mentioned or dealt with in aggadic literature, which was usually much later than halakhic literature. Safrai felt that even in this case, the descriptions or traditions might reflect life during the time of Jesus and whether this was normative behaviour or not was not the central issue, although this issue should not be ignored.

Indeed, just as life in the Second Temple period was far from being monolithic in nature and homogenous in practice, the social realities described in rabbinic literature were manifold and reflect different and sometimes even competing and contradictory social realities. This led Safrai to understand that while Jesus and his disciples may have been closest in outlook to the Pharisees, they were particularly similar to the personalities described in rabbinic literature as the 'early *hasidim*' and Safrai saw Jesus and his movement as reflections in the mirror of ancient hasidism, a group close to the world of the sages, but not identical to it.[1] This, ironically, again showed the importance of rabbinic literature for understanding the socio-religious world of Jesus. The ancient hasidic movement is described only in that literature, but it also shows that this literature, in spite

---

[1] See e.g. S. Safrai, 'Hassidic Teaching'; idem, 'Hassidim ve-anshei maase'; idem, 'Yeshu veha-tenua he-hassidit'.

of its wealth of detail and descriptions, reflects phenomena that were not common to other literatures, thus making rabbinic literature, being unique in this point, more suspect in the view of those who tended to limit its historicity and relevance for the study of the history of ancient Judaism. The unique nature of rabbinic literature also highlighted the continued need for caution. Ultimately, however, both for Safrai and for the editors of this volume, it was never claimed that it is necessary to *prove* a connection between this or that literature or tradition in rabbinic literature and Second Temple times or the New Testament, but rather to show the *probability* of such and to show that a certain 'proximity' existed between the literatures and traditions, all the while bearing in mind the unique aspects of both literatures and traditions. Beyond that, each author and reader could draw his or her own conclusions. This is both the strong point as well as the weakness of the methodologies described above. Establishing just the realm of probability made it difficult to arrive at clear-cut conclusions regarding many of the seemingly similar issues or to establish clear-cut comparisons. In the view of many scholars, much remained overly dependent on subjective academic proclivities of scholars. But perhaps a more adequate way of saying this is that we are dealing with an inescapable margin of uncertainty, and the share of scholarly wisdom is soberly and honestly to delineate this uncertainty while avoiding to fall in the trap of historical scepticism.

These matters are especially poignant for the present volume which deals with midrash and aggada as well as with a number of fields tangential or auxiliary to rabbinic literature and its study. Firstly, very often there has not yet been a systematic presentation of textual work on this literature; much still remains to be done at the basic level of establishing a critical text. To what extent are midrash and aggada, and their tradition histories, able to aid the scholar of history or of ancient Judaism at all, and this is meant in the widest sense of the word? Is there history in the legend or is there legend in the legend? And are the texts usable in any form for the study of ancient society or the New Testament? It is impossible to even begin to reach any conclusions on the use of these literatures in general and for the New Testament in particular before one understands their nature, their texts and their traditions, and furthering this is indeed one of the prime motives and goals of the present volume, as it was of the first one. Needless to say, dealing with the above, in any form or fashion, made manifold demands on any scholar who would attempt to tie it all together in terms of a clear and coherent historical presentation. Few are the scholars capable of dealing with rabbinic literature from all standpoints, from literature, to history, to religion and to everyday life, and Shmuel Safrai was one of those few. Here lies the legacy that Shmuel Safrai has bequeathed to the readers of the *Compendia* as well as to scholarship in general.

Let us now proceed to a general overview of the volume. The 20 chapters of the book are divided into four sections which reflect the wide array of literature and literary phenomena not dealt with in the first volume. The first section deals with Midrash and Targum. Two studies, that of Menahem I. Kahana and of Myron B. Lerner, on the Halakhic Midrashim and on the works of Aggadic Midrash and the Esther Midrashim, respectively, are almost book-length and represent outstanding original contributions to Talmudics which will probably remain reference studies for a good many years to come. They are especially important regarding textual history and literary criticism, the sine qua non for any use of this material for any purposes of a historical nature. Both Kahana and Lerner take the reader through detailed tours of the 'state of the art', describing previous studies in their fields, the history of textual criticism on their relative topics as well as provide detailed descriptions and studies of the works included in the fields under discussion. Marc Hirshman provides an overview of aggadic midrash, dealing with terminology and especially with midrash as creative exegesis within its social setting. Chaim Milikowsky provides a neat scholarly description on Seder Olam Rabba. Zeev Safrai discusses the terminology of targumic literature and describes the extant Targums and their relationship to the Tora.

This opening section represents a direct continuation of the first volume, presenting studies on central documents of rabbinic Judaism. It also complements the 'midrashic genre' of the New Testament. The following sections of the volume reflect the willingness of the editors to see influence in genres of rabbinic literature of a seemingly more peripheral nature or of parallel non-rabbinic literary traditions. Thus, the next section deals with liturgy, poetry and mysticism, all literary genres of importance in the world of the New Testament. Joseph Tabory deals with Jewish prayer in general as well as with the Passover Haggada, both topics that connect quite clearly to the reality of the New Testament. He describes Second Temple period liturgies as well as post-70 CE liturgies and blessings. While the subject of Vered Noam's contribution may only be tangentially connected to the section, her study of Megillat Taanit presents a first translation of this text and its *scholion* into English together with an important commentary on its history and structure, proving once again the importance of textual study independent of historical research. Ezra Fleischer and Joseph Yahalom study additional expressions of liturgy, with the first study devoted to *piyyut* and the second to Aramaic and Hebrew mourning poems and eulogies. These sensitive expressions of liturgical emotion are found in large part outside of the corpus of rabbinic literature, but are contemporary to a number of genres and literatures of the of rabbis. Finally, Michael Swartz shows the power of mystical esoteric texts describing visionary experiences and magic ritual. He discusses seminal works or genre including Merkava literature, Hekhalot literature and Sefer Yetsira.

The third section deals with contracts, inscriptions and ancient science, documents more than others reflective of 'real life'. Mordechai A. Friedman studies contracts in rabbinic literature as well as in other literatures. In addition to providing examples and discussions of 'talmudic contracts', Friedman also deals with parallel material in the Elephantine Papyri, the documents of the Judean Desert, and last but not least the Cairo Geniza. Jonathan Price and Haggai Misgav discuss Greek and Jewish inscriptions both in terms of their historical contribution as well as regarding their relationship to rabbinic literature. While inscriptions obviously lack the complexity and sophistication of rabbinic literature, they often provide a bird's eye view of real life of real people. 'Science' is dealt with by Samuel Kottek in his article on medicine, by Zeev Safrai in regard of geography and cosmography and by Avraham Ofir Shemesh studying both real and folkloristic elements of biology as they appear in rabbinic literature. Yuval Harari deals with the world

XV

of the occult and the relationship of the sages to it. While this may not be considered 'science' in terms of the modern usage of the word, it was very much so in the ancient world for both Jew and non-Jew. Sorcery, demons, divination, astrology and the like were not just concepts in the world of the New Testament, but were integral parts of everyday life and belief for many.

The last section of the book deals with the languages of rabbinic literature. Moshe Bar-Asher offers a concise but rich description of Mishnaic Hebrew, and Yohanan Breuer of Talmudic Aramaic, while Daniel Sperber deals with Greek in rabbinic literature. Not only do these technical studies illuminate important and interesting aspects of rabbinic literature, but they also relate to the critical question of languages in relation to Jesus, the first century CE and the New Testament. Understanding the languages of rabbinic literature may often provide the key to further understanding of the New Testament and its linguistic milieu, whether in terms of 'official' languages such as Hebrew, 'vernaculars' such as Aramaic, or 'foreign' languages such as Greek or Latin. The use of languages and borrowings can often serve as a cultural barometer.

Thus we hope the volume will fulfil multiple purposes, even if not equally much in all of its parts. Thus, it is firstly intended to give an overview of rabbinic scholarship and to contribute to its advancement. Secondly, along with its first part, it is meant to offer the reader a faithful and detailed picture of rabbinic literature in its wealth of forms and contents. Thirdly, with this picture in mind and precisely in view of the methodological problems we have mentioned, we are confident that the volume will assist the reader in more adequately assessing important aspects of the cultural and ideological background of the New Testament world.

Joshua Schwartz
Zeev Safrai
Peter Tomson

Note on Orthography and Acknowledgments

Orthography is never simple in an English work citing Hebrew, Aramaic and Greek sources, and their transcriptions. We have aimed at an intelligent and never ruthlessly systematic approach, taking into account specific requirements raised by the text in question. We have not of course applied the following rules to quotations from other modern works and their titles.

As to the transcription of Hebrew, the spelling of biblical names remains as accepted in English. Other names as cited in rabbinic literature and related sources are transliterated using a simple anglo-based system aimed at producing modern Israeli pronunciation. The scholar will know to distinguish.

The same system is used for other Hebrew and Aramaic words in general, though here the net result is not fully uniform either. In chapters with a linguistic or archaeological orientation, enhanced diacritical precision is applied when necessary.

Transliterated technical terms are italicised when they remain rare, but only a first time when they recur frequently.

As a rule, technical terms are capitalised when they concern literary documents, but otherwise are printed in lower case.

Slight variations in the bibliographical system are due to conventions particular to specialised disciplines such as linguistics and archaeology

We are indebted to the following persons for their work on translations from the authors' Hebrew: Edward Levin, ch. 1; Yoel Lerner, chs. 8, 19; Irvin B. Fishel, ch. 9; Jeffrey Green, ch. 10; Miriam Schlusselberg, appendix ch. 4; Esther Vantu, ch. 16; Geoffrey Herman, ch. 17; Michael Weitzman, ch. 18.

The indices have been prepared with great acuity by Tom Franken.

Section One
Midrash and Targum

Chapter One

The Halakhic Midrashim

Menahem I. Kahana

1. Introduction

CHARACTERISTICS OF HALAKHIC MIDRASH

The Collections

The Halakhic Midrashim[1] contain both halakhic and aggadic (i.e., non-legal) material from the Tannaic period arranged according to the order of verses in the Tora. This stands in contrast with other the major compositions of this period, Mishna and Tosefta, in which the material is arranged by subject. Halakhic Midrashim were composed on four of the five books of the Tora: Exodus, Leviticus, Numbers, and Deuteronomy. There is only a single whole extant Halakhic Midrash on each of these four books: Mekhilta de-Rabbi Yishmael on Exodus (MekRY),[2] Sifra on Leviticus,[3] Sifrei on Numbers (SifNum),[4] and Sifrei on Deuteronomy (SifDeut).[5] Three other Midrashim have been partially reconstructed from Geniza fragments and from citations by Rishonim (medieval authorities): Mekhilta de-Rabbi Shimon bar Yohai on Exodus (MekRSbY),[6] Sifrei Zuta on Numbers (SifZNum),[7] and Mekhilta on Deuteronomy (MekDeut).[8] Passages from an additional Tannaic midrash on the book of Deuteronomy, known as Sifrei Zuta on Deuteronomy (SifZDeut), were recently discovered.[9]

In his fundamental study of the Halakhic Midrashim, D. Hoffmann drew a clear and persuasive distinction between the midrashic schools of R. Akiva and R. Yishmael as to their homiletical method, midrashic terminology, and names of major sages mentioned, as well as by the body of midrashim themselves.[10] Hoffmann similarly demonstrated that the Tannaic Midrash collections on the Tora that have come down to us represent, in practice, these two schools, with

---

[1] Capitalised 'Halakhic Midrashim' shall be used here to indicate the written collections, while a 'halakhic midrash' or 'halakhic midrashim' denote one or more basic units of what can also mean the genre, 'halakhic midrash'. Similarly, we shall speak of 'a Midrash' indicating a collection that contains many 'midrashim'.

[2] Citations in this survey follow ms Oxf 151 (completing abbreviations and correcting obvious errors, based on the other texts; similar procedure is followed for the other Midrashim). References follow the edition by Horovitz and Rabin.

[3] Citations follow ms Vat 66. References for the *dibburim* of *Nedava* and *Hova* follow the Finkelstein edition, the rest the Weiss edition.

[4] Citations follow ms Vat 32; references follow the edition by Horovitz.

[5] Citations follow ms Vat 32, references the edition by Finkelstein.

[6] Citations and references follow the Epstein – Melamed edition.

[7] Citations and references follow the Horovitz edition.

[8] Citations follow Hoffmann, *Midrasch Tannaim*, and the Geniza fragments published by Schechter and Kahana. I followed accepted practice for the names of the above Midrashim; for alternative names for Halakhic Midrashim see Epstein, 'Mechilta and Sifrei in the Works of Maimonides', 102-113, and the following descriptions of each individual Midrash.

[9] Citations and references follow the Kahana edition (*Sifrei Zuta*). For the midrashic work *Baraita de-Melekhet ha-Mishkan* not discussed in this survey, see Kirschner, *Baraita*.

[10] See below, 'The Schools of R. Yishmael and of R. Akiva'.

one Midrash from the school of R. Akiva and a second from R. Yishmael's for each of the books of the Tora except Genesis:

(1) from the school of R. Akiva: MekRSbY, the major portion of Sifra, SifZNum, and SifDeut;

(2) from the school of R. Yishmael: MekRY, several additions appended to Sifra, SifNum, and MekDeut.

Other scholars, most prominently J.N. Epstein, developed and expanded upon the distinctions between these two schools, while at the same time defining the unique character of each of the specific Tannaic Halakhic Midrashim.

A re-examination of the Halakhic Midrashim taking into consideration additional passages from the three Halakhic Midrashim rediscovered in the Geniza and the new passages from SifZDeut teaches that, alongside the common elements of the Midrashim belonging to each school, the differences must be given greater prominence. The four Midrashim from the school of R. Yishmael are marked by a relatively high degree of uniformity. Those from the school of R. Akiva, in contrast, are not homogeneous and can be divided into two subcategories that differ from each other in many aspects:

(1a) MekRSbY, Sifra, and SifDeut, representing the classic school of midrash of R. Akiva and bear a marked proximity to the Mishna;

(1b) SifZNum and SifZDeut, exhibiting a pronounced linguistic and contentual singularity with very tenuous ties to the Mishna of R. Yehuda the Prince.

This division, by itself, raises the possibility that the two groups of Halakhic Midrashim from the school of R. Akiva are merely random representatives of the literary production of two academies that originally included two parallel midrashic redactions for each of the Pentateuchal books from Exodus to Deuteronomy. First of all, it is improbable that redactors of a school of midrash on the Tora would begin their work with the Book of Numbers or would content themselves with Midrashim on Exodus, Leviticus, and Deuteronomy. It is more likely that additional Halakhic Midrashim have existed which have not been preserved. Support for this hypothesis may be brought from midrashim that were transferred verbatim from one collection to another. Thus, for example, SifZNum and SifZDeut contain midrashim on Exodus and Leviticus that derive from collections of what we term 'the Sifrei Zuta school' (see below). Further remnants of collections of the halakhic midrash of the Tannaim can be discerned in the many baraitot preserved in the other rabbinic works, most importantly, the Tosefta and the two Talmuds.

The above evidence teaches that the literature of halakhic midrash was originally much more extensive and richer than the extant works would indicate. Such a perception must make us wary of unequivocal conclusions on the basis of the limited data that we possess and that represent merely the tip of the iceberg. However, an awareness of our limitations does not exempt us from attempting a considered evaluation of the body of data known to us in view of the nature and method of the Halakhic Midrashim.

The Term Halakhic Midrash

The accepted name in Hebrew scholarly literature for the Tannaic Midrashim on the Tora, *Midreshei ha-Halakha*, is somewhat misleading, since as we said these Midrashim also contain aggadic material, a fact that is especially striking in MekRY and in SifDeut, half of whose exegeses are of an aggadic nature.[11] Nonetheless, the name *Midreshei ha-Halakha* is defensible, since almost all the legal material mentioned in the Tora is included in them, while only scant non-halakhic material, such as narratives, genealogical lists, ethical exhortations, and the like, is the subject of orderly midrashic exposition.[12] Criteria have not been formulated that would explain why certain aggadic passages were included in the Halakhic Midrashim, while others are not subject to such exegetical treatment. The clear linkage of the Tannaic Midrashim to the legal material in the Tora can be learned from the fact that three out of the eight extant Halakhic Midrashim (MekRY, SifNum, and SifZNum) start with the first legal topic appearing in the appropriate biblical book, and not with the beginning of the book itself. This also explains the absence of any Halakhic Midrash on the Book of Genesis, which is mostly concerned with non-legal topics.[13] It is note-worthy within this context that the source of most of the aggadic material incorporated in the Halakhic Midrashim is not identical with that of the halakhic material, thus strongly indicating that the basic redactions of the sages from each of the two schools contained passages that were principally halakhic.[14]

Literary Nature and Relation to Early Midrash

In the Halakhic Midrashim, a sharp distinction is drawn between the biblical text and its interpretation by the sages. The typical passage opens with a lemma consisting of one or more words from the biblical verse, followed by a presentation of the interpretation. The quote and its interpretation comprise a basic literary unit known as a *midrash* or *drasha*.[15] Generally speaking, the order of the biblical verses is followed.[16]

---

[11] The approximate percentages of aggadic material are: SifDeut 55%(!); MekRY 45%; SifNum 25%; Sifra 5%. The incomplete preservation of the other Midrashim precludes any estimation of the extent of aggadic material, but they, too, do include it.

[12] A detailed listing of biblical verses expounded appears below, in the description of each separate Midrash.

[13] Mirsky, 'Midrash Tannaim le-Bereshit' sought to prove that the redactors of Genesis Rabba possessed a Tannaic midrash to Genesis, but his proofs are unconvincing. It cannot be ruled out that a Tannaic Midrash to Genesis was redacted in some form, but no independent fragment of such a Tannaic work has come down to us.

[14] See below, 'Aggada'.

[15] Cf n1 above. For the development of the terms *darash* and *midrash* from the Bible through the Apocrypha and the Judean Desert scrolls to rabbinic literature see Bacher, *Terminologie*, s.v. דרש; Heinemann, 'Le-hitpathut'; Segal, 'Miscellanies', 194; Fraenkel, *Methodology*, 11-12; Gertner, 'Terms'.

[16] On rare occasions do the Midrashim diverge from the biblical order. See, e.g., the exposition of Exod 22:15, 'If a man seduces a virgin who is not betrothed', MekRSbY p207f, that places the

The Halakhic Midrashim are written in mishnaic Hebrew, in a concise and focused style. They occasionally contain simple explanations of the biblical language in terms of rabbinic language and vocabulary,[17] or paraphrases.[18] More often, the Midrashim exceed the simple interpretation and derive or support laws and ideas from Scripture[19] employing midrash methods.[20] Addition-

exposition of the words בתולה (virgin) and אשר לא ארשה (who is not betrothed) before that of the phrase וכי יפתה איש (if a man seduces). Similarly, the exposition of the parallel verse in Deut 22:28, 'If a man meets a virgin (נערה בתולה) who is not betrothed', in SifDeut 244 (p273f), in which the interpretation of the words בתולה and אשר לא ארשה precedes the exposition of the word נערה. These two apparently originated in the covert controversy against the methodology of R. Akiva (in accordance with the tradition in MekRY p308), with which the redactors of these Midrashim desired to begin.

[17] See, e.g., the midrash in SifNum 8 (p14); 142 (p189): '"a tenth of an ephah" – one of ten from an ephah'. The commentaries on SifNum were hard-pressed to explain what this midrash adds; in fact, however, it adds nothing new, but merely translates the biblical עשירית into the Mishnaic wording of אחד מעשרה. Similarly, the exposition of SifDeut 118 (p177) (and likewise, MekRSbY p44): 'על כן, accordingly – מפני כן, therefore.' For a more extensive discussion of this phenomenon, cf Lieberman, *Hellenism*, 49-51; Gottlieb, 'Midrash as Philology'.

[18] Several of these elementary midrashim are preserved only in the best mss, while scribes of other versions apparently regarded them as unnecessary verbosity. See. e.g., the midrash in MekRY p22 that is extant only in a Geniza fragment in Oxf (ms Heb. 18.10; the addition in the Geniza fragment appears within brackets, < >): '"In this manner you shall eat it: your loins girded" (Exod 12:11) < – your loins girded, your sandals on your feet, and your staff in your hand> like journeyers.' See Elias, *Ha-Mekhilta*, 94; cf Sifra, Emor 13:11 (101c) according to ms Vat 66 and other mss: '"And you shall make proclamation on the same day: you shall hold a holy convocation" (Lev 23:21) < – sanctify it>.'

[19] Extensive scholarly polemics has been going on as to whether the sages learned new halakhot from their study of verses, or found support in them for known laws. Most likely, at times they acted in one way, and at other times, the other. See, e.g., Safrai, 'Halakha', 155-163. A significant contribution to the innovative element in Tannaic midrash was made by Halbertal, *Revolutions*. However, he frequently did not make full use of the good mss that are currently available, or did not distinguish with sufficient precision between the different Midrashim (for a straightforward example, see Halbertal, 130-132, the discussion concerning the law of minors in an עיר נדחת ('a city led astray'), in which he disregarded Epstein's close reading of the Geniza fragment: Epstein, *Studies*, 136: '[From here they said,] the children *are left alive*.' He similarly did not take into account that the exposition in SifDeut 94 (p155/4-5), is not part of SifDeut, but rather a folio that crept in from MekDeut (see Epstein, *Prolegomena*, 572, 707, 718). These reservations, however, do not detract from the convincing nature of the principal thesis he raised and many of his analyses. To the contrary, at times additional proofs may be brought in support of his arguments. Compare, e.g., Halbertal, 59-62, regarding the concept of 'דרוש, provide a midrashic explanation and receive reward' in relation to the stubborn and rebellious son, on Kahana, *Sifrei Zuta*, 315; similarly Halbertal, 16-17, concerning 'who is sick with her impurity' (Lev 15:33), on a reference in my edition of *Sifrei Zuta*, 372, in which I sought to find contentual connection between three or four halakhot that the sources explicitly present as derived by R. Akiva.

[20] It should be noted, incidentally, that the usual view that Epstein held that midrash does not create halakha (see, e.g., Halbertal, op cit., 14) is too simplistic. Admittedly, Epstein, *Prolegomena*, 511, writes: 'Generally speaking, midrash supports the halakha, but does not create it. Support for the halakha is brought from Scripture; halakha is not found or created by exposition.' This decisive formulation, however, cannot easily be reconciled with what he writes in other places in this book, such as what he says about R. Akiva (71): 'But R. Akiva is the first Tanna who left his mark on the

7

ally, the simple interpretation is sometimes followed by extensive discussion of halakhic and aggadic topics that only indirectly bear on the verse.[21]

Most of the midrashim are unattributed, but it also happens that the name of an author is mentioned at their beginning or end. Frequently, a number of anonymous explanations are offered for a single biblical expression; they may also be presented with an explicit Tannaic disagreement regarding its meaning. In many instances, reasons and proofs are appended to reinforce the sages' understanding of the passage. Some of the reasoning is formulated by way of dialogue, during the course of which several alternative interpretations are suggested, and explanations are presented as to why a certain interpretation is to be accepted, and others not. Frequently, other verses are cited as proof texts for the interpretation that is offered in the basic midrash. At times, this implies the midrashic understanding of the proof text as interpreted elsewhere, not its simple meaning.[22] Also, verses may be brought to resolve a contradiction between different verses or to clarify a new teaching that is understood from verses and expressions that are mentioned in the Bible more than once. The explanations are usually founded on fine distinctions in the content of the biblical text, its individual words, or sometimes even its letters. All this is underlaid by the basic acceptance of the authority of the Bible and its sacred text as

Mishna: not only did he innovate and derive hundreds of halakhot based on his casuistry, he also examined the received tradition and amended it, correcting it by his considered thought; [he] "expounded and concurred with the halakha", or did not concur.' Or, idem, 80: 'But there are also instances in which he refuted שמועה (tradition) or עדות (testimony), expounded on his own, and did not agree with the 'halakha.' It should be recalled that the *Prolegomena* were not written by Epstein, but edited from notes of his lessons by his faithful student E.Z. Melamed; see Lieberman's correct remarks, *Siphre Zutta*, 135f, concerning the care that must therefore be taken. Cf below, 'History of Reseach', near n290.

[21] See, e.g., SifZNum, p333/18-334/16, on which Horovitz writes (p333 *s.v.* ללי): 'It seems the exposition lists all the clauses belonging to the law of the one who kills.' In rare instances, the midrash also systematically collects a series of halakhot that are not derived from the biblical text. See, e.g., the summation of the laws of inheritance derived by logical inference (*kal va-homer*) in SifNum 134 (p178/13-179/6), that were attached to the exposition of Num 27:8. (These laws conclude with an exposition related to the topic under discussion, based on Num 27:11. Later on SifNum resumes expounding the verses in their proper order and when coming to v11 merely refers to the above exposition, see p179/16: '"And he shall possess it" – regarding the matter we mentioned').

[22] See, e.g., the 'Mekhilta de-arayot' in Sifra, Aharei 85d: 'Rabbi says, It is revealed and known before the One who spoke and brought the world into being that they would be torn away [i.e., they would sin] concerning illicit sexual relations, as it is said, "Moses heard the people weeping..." (Num 11:10).' The proof from this verse is not founded on the simple meaning but rather on its midrashic meaning, as is explained in the exposition of the verse in its proper place, according to the school of R. Yishmael (SifNum 90, p91): '"Moses heard the people weeping throughout their families" – R. Nehorai would say, This teaches that Israel grieved when Moses instructed them *to desist from illicit sexual relations*.' (The corrector of ms Vat 66 was unaware of this and added the verse from Num 25:6 to the cited passage in Sifra!). Weiss correctly wrote in his commentary, *ad loc.*: 'It therefore seems that at times the rabbis relied on the accepted interpretation of the biblical text, and rendered the verse in accordance with the intent of this interpretation, as if it were the simple meaning, because they relied on what was known to them.'

a divine text and a profound belief in the exclusive legitimacy of the interpretation of Scripture that accords with Pharisaic halakha.

The above literary qualities are unique to the Tannaic midrashim. Earlier Jewish literature contains glimmerings of this sort of midrash method, but in the Halakhic Midrashim it appears for the first time in a consistent and developed way.[23] Signs of the attempt to resolve the tension between the absolute authority of the Tora and the need for its actualization and harmonization can already be found in the Bible itself, especially in Chronicles, where it takes the form of a paraphrastic reformulation of the biblical verses themselves.[24] The same is true of the Temple Scroll, in which disparate Tora passages discussing the same topic are brought together along with their interpretation and specification in the line with the laws and views prevalent among the Judean Desert sect.[25] All of this is done by way of rewriting the words of the Tora as a command of God in the first person, and this sharply contrasts with the distinction Tannaic literature makes between the verse and its interpretation.[26] The *pesher* literature from Qumran provides another example of verses being quoted in lemmas alongside their interpretation, but this concerns philosophic, ethical, or political actualizations of the books of the Prophets, not legal Tora passages, as is characteristically the case in the Halakhic Midrashim.[27] A rare instance of early Pharisaic midrash apparently consisting of verses quoted and their adjoining interpretation by means of other verses can be found in the homiletical expansion of the verse, 'My father was a fugitive Aramean' (Deut 26:5) from the Pesah Haggada.[28] Also, the New Testament contains a number of instances of a verse being quoted with its halakhic interpretation or exposition as also the

---

[23] For a characterization of rabbinic midrash, cf Porton, *Understanding Rabbinic Midrash*, 8-11.

[24] Cf Zunz, *Vorträge*, 13-36 (= Hebrew, 7-20); Seeligman, 'The Beginnings of the Midrash'; Fishbane, *Biblical Interpretation in Ancient Israel*.

[25] The phenomenon of the concentration of Scriptural verses on a single topic along with their interpretation and completion is paralleled by a similar phenomenon within several tractates of the Mishna. For a comparison of the methodology of these mishnayot with that of the *Temple Scroll* and the drawing of conclusions concerning the development of their exegetical methods cf Goldberg, 'The Early and the Late Midrash'.

[26] See Yadin, *Temple Scroll*, vol 1, 71-88. On occasion completions similar to those in the Tannaic Midrashim are incorporated in the Temple Scroll. See, e.g., Halivni, *Midrash, Mishna and Gemara*, 30-34, regarding, '"If a man seduces a virgin who is not betrothed" – who is suitable for him, in terms of the law.' In this interpretation based on the assumed implausibility that the midrashic completion teaches only elementary matters, Halivni was influenced by the nature of later talmudic exposition, as opposed to early Tannaic midrash, that at times adds nothing to the literal meaning. See above, nn17, 18; and cf Kahana, *Sifrei Zuta*, 165f n8.

[27] For the exegetical-interpretive nature of the Pesharim, see Horgan, *Pesharim*; Nitzan, *Pesher Habakkuk*, 29-80. For a comprehensive review of hints of Halakhic Midrashim in Qumran, see Fraade, 'Looking for Legal Midrash'.

[28] For the reconstruction of this early midrash, that apparently was already current during the Second Temple period, and for a summary of the scholarly literature on the subject, see Tabory, *Passover Ritual*, 350-359; for a reconstruction of the exposition of the fifth verse, see Kahana, *Sifrei Zuta*, 423f.

mention of alternative interpretations and their rejection,[29] but, obviously, these do hardly compare with the systematic midrash of the Tora in the literature of the Halakhic Midrashim.

As compared with the writings of the Judean Desert sect, the literature of the Halakhic Midrashim on the whole exhibit a characteristic independence from the Bible. (1) Unlike the Judean Desert scrolls, it does not present its interpretation as the absolute and unequivocal word of God, but rather as reasoned human interpretation of the Tora that exposes the philological and theological difficulties emerging from Scripture.[30] (2) In contrast with a consistent and uniform conception of the scrolls, the Halakhic Midrashim openly present disagreeing views of sages from several generations in one collective redaction.[31] (3) The Halakhic Midrashim are written in pithy rabbinic language, while the scrolls employ a language closely resembling that of the Bible both in grammar and in its lofty and dramatic style. (4) The halakhic specification of biblical law is vastly more developed in the Halakhic Midrashim than in the scrolls. (5) In many instances the content of the halakhot set forth in Tannaic literature is more removed from the simple meaning than in the scrolls.[32] In this context it is noteworthy that in the other branch of Tannaic literature, Mishna

---

[29] See, e.g., Kremers, 'Die Auslegung der Bibel'; Flusser, 'Midrash ha-Tanakh ba-Berit ha-Hadasha', 305-312.

[30] At times this human interpretation is presented as a manifestation of the word of God. See, e.g., SifDeut 41 (p86): 'Whence do you say that if a person heard something from an Israelite minor, he is to regard this as if he heard it from a sage, as it is said, ...and not as one who hears from a [single] sage, but as one who hears from sages, as it is said..., and not as one who hears from sages, but as one who hears from the Sanhedrin, as it is said..., and not as one who hears from the Sanhedrin, but as one who hears from Moses, as it is said..., and not as one who hears from Moses, but as one who hears from the mouth of the Lord, as it is said....' For a discussion of this fundamental dilemma, see Fraade, *From Tradition to Commentary*, 79-83.

[31] Glimmerings of the elements of the discussions among and disagreements between sages that are so common in Tannaic literature can be found in the book of Ecclesiastes, that is centered around human indecision, and not a message unequivocally transmitted by the Lord to His emissaries as in most of the books of the Bible. The sages were undecided regarding the inclusion of Ecclesiastes in the biblical canon, since they discovered that it contained contradictions and things that tend to heresy. See LevR 28.1 (p648) and the parallels listed there; cf Lieberman, *Studies*, 53-59. The talmudic sources interpret the heretical statements in Ecclesiastes and resolve its inconsistencies, but no *positive reason* was offered for the inclusion of Ecclesiastes among the books of the Bible. Possibly, the reason may be related to the fundamental legitimacy that this book imparts to human thought, in which the rabbis found support for their own methodology? S.D. Luzzatto already indicated the later linguistic usages in Ecclesiastes, some of which correspond to the language of Mishnaic Hebrew. For a summary of the scholarly literature see Vargon, 'Identity and Period', 368 n11.

[32] Obviously, generalizations should be avoided, and there certainly is a vast disparity between the biblical law and that of the Judean Desert scrolls. For the most part, however, this difference is less than the broad and profound gap between the biblical law and the Pharisaic halakha set forth in rabbinic literature. For a summation of the unique characteristics of the Halakhic Midrashim as compared to the Judean Desert literature and the allegorical commentary of Philo, see Fraade, *From Tradition to Commentary*, 1-23.

and Tosefta, the halakha is arranged in a topical order independent from the sequence of Tora verses.[33]

The greater literary independence of the writings of the Tannaim may be explained both by their relative lateness and by the overall view of the sages regarding their own authority and power. Since we have not as yet uncovered written halakhic documents of Pharisaic orientation from the period of the Judean Desert,[34] we can not make out the main reasons for these differences. But whatever the cause, the formulation of the Tannaic midrash collections seems to have ensued from several factors. (1) The canonization of the biblical literature and the idea that no books were to be added created the need of compositions clearly distinguishing between the Bible and its interpretation by the sages. (2) The consolidation and sanctification of a practically uniform Bible text caused its interpretation to be based, inter alia, on a close reading of its details.[35] (3) The multiplication of halakhic details that had no basis in the simple meaning of Scripture and the increasing gap between biblical law and Pharisaic halakha furthered the need to create a new codex of halakha and of midrash.[36] (4) The external polemics against the legitimacy of Pharisaic halakha and the argument that it was only a 'taught by the precept of men' (cf. Mark 7:13) led to an enhancement of the midrash methods that lessened the gap between Scripture and halakha, while at the same time reinforcing the need to demonstrate the link between the halakhot and the verses in independent works. (5) The internal polemics between the Tannaic schools also intensified the need for the redaction of the midrash.[37]

---

[33] See Goldberg, 'The Mishna', 222-235.

[34] Such documents might never be discovered, since, in the early period, the Pharisees prohibited the commitment to writing of Oral Tora. See the summational article by Sussmann, in Sussmann – Rosenthal, *Talmudic Studies*, vol 3, 209-384.

[35] For the nature of this non-Massoretic version see below, 'Authority of the Bible'.

[36] Testimony of rare and surprising candor that reveals this gap is to be found in mHag 1:8 and parallels; tEr 8:23 (p138); tHag 1:9 (p379, from which this quote): '[The rules concerning] the absolution of vows hang in the air, for they have nothing from which to draw support; the laws of Sabbath, *hagigot* [festival-offerings], and misappropriations of Temple property are like mountains suspended on a hair: sparse Scripture and many laws, they have not from what to draw support. ...[The rules regarding] civil litigation, Temple service, purity [laws], and forbidden sexual relations, and added to them the laws concerning valuations, things that are declared *herem*, and things declared Temple property: for these there is abundant midrash and halakha; they have from what to draw support; Abba Jose ben Hanan says, these are eight corners of the Tora, the substance of halakha.' See Lieberman, *Tosefta Ki-Fshutah*, Eruvin, 470: 'As regards the matter at hand, this is very difficult, for it cannot be said that Abba Yose ben Hanan came to exclude the laws of vows and the laws of the Sabbath.' Lieberman then refers to the Bavli's emendation of the Mishna, 'and it is they (הן הן) that are the essentials of the Tora', to read: 'both these and these (הן והן) are the essentials of the Law,' which he questions, based on several parallels. Lieberman concludes: 'much further study is required'; cf *Tosefta Ki-Fshutah*, Hagiga, 1286. With due respect, I think there is no difficulty here, rather a trenchant statement that frankly reveals the problematic nature of finding biblical support for numerous halakhot in several realms of Jewish religious law.

[37] Another possibility is that external governmental prohibitions against Tora study, and the fear that this would result in the Tora being forgotten, spurred the process of a new summation of the

Authority of the Bible

As we said, in the Halakhic Midrashim, the Tora and all of its verses are perceived as the authoritative and obligatory word of God,[38] and this belief made for the creation of midrash based on close reading of the minutest details of words and letters of the text. The sages of the Halakhic Midrashim openly combat the argument that Moses forged the Tora[39] or that he wrote certain verses of his own volition,[40] while also rejecting the Samaritan version of the Tora as a corruption of the original.[41]

In no instance in the Halakhic Midrashim or other rabbinic sources do we find sages arguing among themselves about the version of the Bible on which to base their exposition.[42] Nevertheless, the Halakhic Midrashim do contain echoes of the awareness of more than one version of a passage, both in explicit testimonies[43] and in expositions that instruct, 'Do not read X but Y' – when the second version does in fact exist in another textual tradition, and this is therefore not to be viewed as mere wordplay.[44] There are also midrashim that may incorporate two alternative textual traditions.[45] This awareness makes the ab-

---

halakhot, either redaction by subject, as in the Mishna, or redaction by the order of the verses in the Tora, as in the Halakhic Midrashim. To be precise, the general explanations cited above are applicable to a relatively long period; better knowledge of the time of redaction of the Halakhic Midrashim might enable a more correct understanding of the surrounding circumstances.

[38] See SifNum 112 (p121): 'He said, I accept upon myself the entire Tora, except this – he has spurned the word of the Lord.'

[39] See e.g. SifDeut 26 (p36); 102 (p161).

[40] See SifNum 112 (p121): '[He said] [Moses] spoke the entire Tora from the mouth of the Holy One, blessed be He, but this thing Moses said from himself – he has spurned the word of the Lord.' This is especially pronounced Deuteronomy, that is presented by Scripture as a speech by Moses, while SifDeut repeatedly emphasizes: '[Moses] said to them, It is not from myself that I speak to you, rather, I speak to you from the Holy One, blessed be He.' See SifDeut 5 (p13) and references by Finkelstein *ad loc.*, l. 1.

[41] See SifDeut 56 (p123).

[42] Lieberman, *Hellenism*, 47.

[43] E.g. SifDeut 356 (p423): 'Three books were found in the Temple Court. ...In one it is written, "The eternal God is your dwelling place מעון" (Deut 33:27), and in two it is written, "The eternal God is your dwelling place מעונה". The rabbis canceled the first, and upheld the [other] two...' See Talmon, 'Three Scrolls'; see also MekRY p50, the list of things that were written for King Ptolemy, and the discussion by Geiger, *Urschrift*, 282-287; Tov, *Criticism*, 34f.

[44] E.g. SifNum 98 (p97): '"וישטחו להם שטוח And they spread them out for themselves" (Num 11:32) – R. Joshua ben Korha says, Do not say [i.e., read] thusly, rather, וישחטו להן שחוט [and they slaughtered for themselves], teaching that they required [ritual] slaughtering.' Indeed, the version of the Samaritan Tora on this verse reads: וישחטו להם שחוטה, while a similar version is reflected in LXX ms Vat. For a discussion of this and other examples, see Talmon, 'Aspects,' 126-132.

[45] E.g. the midrash in MekRY *Mishpatim* 10 (p284): '"[But if the ox has been accustomed to gore in the past, and its owner has been warned] but has not kept it in ישמרנו" (Exod 21:29) – R. Eliezer says, There is no שמירה for [the ox] other than the knife.' This may possibly be understood as an interpretation following the MT, ישמרנו, along with that of LXX, ישמידנו, 'has not destroyed it'. See this suggested methodology, within a discussion of this and other expositions, by Rosenthal, 'Methodical Approach'.

sence of open disagreement on the issue all the more pronounced. It should not surprise us, however, because controversies regarding the text of the Bible would be liable to undercut the very basis of Tannaic exegesis.

As regards the biblical text underlying Halakhic Midrashim, it should be emphasized that it is not absolutely identical with the Massoretic text, the details of which were finally formulated only in the medieval period. Here and there the Halakhic Midrashim cite a different version that accords with the Septuagint, the Samaritan Tora, or the Peshitta. We also find midrashim based on a non-Massoretic version that prove this was the consensual biblical text possessed by the Tannaim-exegetes.[46] An awareness of the phenomenon is of importance both for an examination of the textual versions of the Bible and for a proper understanding of the midrash itself.[47]

Development of Exegetical Methods

The first Tannaic testimony about the midrashic methods applied to the Tora concerns Hillel:[48] 'Hillel expounded seven exegetical methods (מידות) before the elders of Bathyra...' These comprise, in practice, basic methods of clarifying a given verse by examining other verses containing:

(1) a law either more of less severe than the one under discussion (קל וחומר, *kal va-homer* or *a minori ad majus*);

(2) analogy (גזירה שווה, *gezera shava* or 'comparison of similar expressions');

(3) a law that is specified in one place but gets support from elsewhere (בנין אב, *binyan av* or 'prototype');

(4) two verses that contradict one another (שני כתובים, *shenei ketuvim*);[49]

(5) a general formulation along with one or more individual cases (כלל ופרט,[50] *kelal u-ferat* or 'general and particular');

---

[46] See Aptowitzer, *Schriftwort.*

[47] This phenomenon is especially expressed in the good mss. Less reliable versions adapted the text of the quotation to the MT; the traditional commentaries of the Halakhic Midrashim also ignored this, as a general rule. See Kahana, 'Biblical Text'; Buchner, 'Relationship'.

[48] Following Sifra, chap. 1, p. 9 (according to the addendum page in ms Vat 66). Cf tSan 7:11 (p427); ARN a37 (p110).

[49] The Constantinople printed edition of Sifra changed the wording of this hermeneutical rule, that the editors did not understand, and attached it to the preceding rule: ובנין אב משני כתובים. Similar emendations were made in the parallels in the Tosefta and in Avot de-R. Natan. See below, in comparison with the hermeneutical rules of R. Yishmael.

[50] Thus the correct version, that is documented in most of the texts. Finkelstein established the version ופרט וכלל in his edition on the basis of ms Vat 31, under the influence of foreign considerations. See Finkelstein, *Sifra on Leviticus*, vol 1, 123; cf Kahana, 'Development of *Kelal u-Ferat*', 214.

(6) a rare word or phenomenon that is explicated by instances in other places (כיוצא בו במקום אחר[51], *ka-yotse bo be-makom aher* or 'similarly, in another place');[52]

(7) a matter understood by its context (דבר למד מעינינו, *davar lamed me-inyano*).[53]

A later list of thirteen midrash methods appears in the beginning of Sifra in the name of R. Yishmael.[54] In addition to their greater number, these methods are characterized by their extended meaning, their detail, and their greater sophistication. For example, Hillel's *shenei ketuvim* is given a specific interpretation: 'Two texts that refute one another, until a third text comes and decides between them.'[55] Likewise, *davar lamed me-inyano*, the method of 'understand-

---

[51] This is the correct reading, in accordance with most of the Sifra mss, and not וכשיוצא, 'and similarly', as Finkelstein maintains in his edition, based solely on the unique version of ms Vat 31 (and he did not realize that the scribe of the ms. himself corrected his version and erased the letter *shin* by writing a dot above it!).

[52] All commentators encountered difficulty with this rule (see recently, Finkelstein's gloss, *Sifra on Leviticus*). We clearly should prefer the above interpretation proposed by my late teacher, Prof. E.S. Rosenthal (already set forth by R. Hillel in his commentary on Sifra, 'according to one interpretation', but rejected by him). The interpretation is understandable from the common phrase in Halakhic Midrashim, 'Like this כיוצא בו, you say.' In both these instances כיוצא has the meaning of 'similarly' (for this singular meaning of יוצא see Sharvit, 'Studies', 119; Mishor, 'Yotze'). See, e.g., SifNum, *piska* 69, p. 64, with an exposition of the dot above the word רחוקה (Num 9:10): '"...Or is afar off רחוקה on a journey" – vocalization over [the letter] ה, that even if close by and he is unclean, he shall not observe the Paschal sacrifice with them' (i.e., the meaning of the dot is erasure, as was the accepted method of erasure in antiquity, see Lieberman, *Hellenism*, 43-46). SifNum follows this with a lengthy list of instances of 'like this כיוצא בו, you say' in other places, in which dots in the biblical text are similarly understood, ending with the conclusion that this explanation is to be adopted in this case, as well: 'Here, too, you say "or is afar off on a journey" [with] a dot over the ה, [meaning] <that even> if close by and he is unclean, he shall not observe the Paschal sacrifice with them.'

[53] For the connection between the hermeneutical principles of Hillel and the methods of deduction common in the Hellenistic world, see Daube, 'Methods'; Lieberman, *Hellenism*, 47-68; see also below.

[54] A. Schwartz wrote several detailed studies of the hermeneutical rules, cf his summational 'Hauptergebnisse'. Schwartz successfully analyzed the internal development of several hermeneutical principles, but his apologetic attempts to illuminate their sublime logic and to idealize the Israelite spirit they reflect, along with his sketch of their gradual inner decline that lessened the value of the Jewish people in the eyes of non-Jewish intellectuals, do not meet the demands of modern philology.

[55] As concerns the diversity of the function of the third verse, that at times seemingly joins one of the other two verses and forms a majority of two against one, while in other instances teaches of a compromise, see Friedman, *Sifra*, 24-27; cf the detailed discussion: Henshke, 'Rabbis' Approach'. It should be noted that only a small portion of the *shenei ketuvim* expositions in Halakhic Midrashim make use of a third, decisive verse; the majority of these expositions present the seeming contradiction implicit in the two verses in the formula: 'One verse says X, and the other says Y; how are the two verses to be resolved,' followed by a proposal for resolving the two verses that is not based on a third 'decisive' verse, but that explains each verse as reflective of a different reality. The contradiction between these two verses is usually only seeming, and serves as a methodical introduction to suggested exegetical resolution; on the other hand, patent contradic-

ing from context', was supplemented: 'and something that is learned from a later reference in the same passage'. Additional methods were specified, such as Hillel's *binyan av*, that R. Yishmael developed into: 'A prototypical inference from a single verse, and a prototypical inference from two verses'. The method of *kelal u-ferat* was especially developed, as it was divided into subsections, with an accompanying explanation of their meanings, thus for example: 'General and particular; particular and general; general, particular, and general – [the law] is discussed only in accordance with the subject of the particular case; [...] everything that was in the general statement that is specified, that does so to teach [a law], is not specified only to teach of itself [i.e., the specific case], but rather to teach of all that is encompassed by the general statement.'

Furthermore, at times we witness a development of the meaning of exegetical methods that were identically formulated in the lists of Hillel and R. Yishmael. An outstanding example of this phenomenon is the method of *gezera shava*, whose primary meaning, as proposed by Lieberman, is a comparison between two analogous matters.[56] It was related of Hillel that he expounded a *gezera shava* before the elders of Bathyra, based on a single word that appears in two similar passages and bears directly upon the law learned from it.[57] In the later Tannaic period, however, the *gezera shava* became an almost arbitrary comparison between halakhot taught on two different matters, based on the same or proximate word that appeared in both laws, and for the most part without any relation to the literal meaning of these words. By means of the transformation of this method it was now possible to prove anything, therefore compelling the sages to limit its possible uses.[58]

---

tions between two verses are generally not openly presented in the Halakhic Midrashim, and the means of their resolution – the placing of each verse in a different reality – is, in most instances, not highlighted.

[56] See Lieberman, *Hellenism*, 58-62, who explains the term *gezera shava* in the sense of: comparison to the equal, and notes the both logically and etymologically parallel term used by Greek rhetoricians (σύγκρισις πρὸς ἴσον), with references to a small number of talmudic sources in which this early meaning is preserved.

[57] tPes 4:13 (p165) and parallels: 'Once the fourteenth [of Nisan] fell on the Sabbath. Hillel the Elder was asked, What is the law of the Paschal sacrifice: does it override the Sabbath? He replied: ...Just as the *tamid*, regarding which it was stated "at its set time", overrides the Sabbath, so, too, the Paschal sacrifice, regarding which it was stated "at its set time", overrides the Sabbath.'

[58] See, e.g., the view of R. Yishmael that a *gezera shava* may be derived only from unencumbered words, from which no other exposition has been drawn (see following section); or the rule that 'a person may not derive a *gezera shava* on his own authority', that yPes 6:1, 33a already ascribes to the elders of Bathyra, Hillel's disputants. Cf the restrictions transmitted in the name of the Amora R. Abba bar Mamal *ib.*: 'A person may expound a *gezera shava* in support of his tradition, and he may not expound a *gezera shava* to contradict his tradition. ...A person may derive a *kal va-homer* on his own authority, but he may not derive a *gezera shava* on his own authority. Consequently, a refutation may be based on a *kal va-homer*, but a refutation may not be based on a *gezera shava*.' A hint of the force of this hermeneutical principle and its distance from the simple meaning also appears in the writings of the medieval sages, a majority of whom regarded expositions learned by

15

An additional baraita containing examples of each of the thirteen methods was appended to the baraita of R. Yishmael at the beginning of Sifra. Most of the traditional commentators based their interpretation on this explanatory baraita. It would seem, however, that it is at variance with the baraita of R. Yishmael as to the meaning of several items,[59] and that it reflects more fully developed methods from the late Tannaic period.[60] The method of *kelal u-ferat* is an outstanding example of this change. According to the initial meaning of this baraita, *ke-ein ha-perat*, 'similar to the particular statement', is to be employed for diverse instances of generalizations and specifications, without regard for their order of appearance in the verse: a generalization followed by a specification; and a specification followed by a generalization; and a generalization followed by a specification once again followed by a generalization. In contrast with this understanding, reflections of which can be found in a number of locations throughout the talmudic literature, the explanatory baraita regards each of these three possibilities to be a different rule, as is more common in talmudic literature: '*Kelal u-ferat* – when there is a general and a particular statement, the general statement includes only what is specified in the particular statement; *perat u-khelal* – the general statement is made an addition to the particular statement; *kelal u-ferat u-khelal* – you may discuss it only in accordance with the particular statement.' This explanation facilitates an almost certain reconstruction of the original count of the thirteen methods, that the explanatory baraita sets at fifteen or sixteen.[61]

The development of the exegetical methods was paralleled by the formation of a school headed by R. Akiva, who preferred to base midrashim on precise readings of certain words and letters in the verse, and not to rely upon general exegetical rules,[62] thus resulting in a widening of the gap between the midrash and the simple meaning of Scripture.

The gradual formulation process of complicated and developed hermeneutical methods ever more distant from the early midrash methods continued in the Amoraic period. For example, in most of their midrashim, the Amoraim

---

means of a *gezera shava* as a tradition from Sinai (מסורת למשה מסיני). See the summation of the subject in *Talmudic Encyclopedia*, vol 5, 546-564; see also Gilat, 'The Development of the Gezera Shavah', in id., *Studies*, 265-272.

[59] See, e.g., the example of בנין אב מכתוב אחד, 'a prototypical inference from a single verse', that relates to two subjects that are discussed in a single portion, and the example of בנין אב משני כתובים, 'a prototypical inference from two verses' that relates to two subjects discussed in two portions. This differs from the common original meaning of these hermeneutical principles in the Tannaic Midrashim. See Kahana, 'Development of *Kelal u-Ferat*', 176-181.

[60] Finkelstein also noted this phenomenon in his commentary on the hermeneutical rules in *Sifra on Leviticus*, vol 1, 187-189. Several of his proofs, however, do not withstand critical examination. See Kahana, 'Development of *Kelal u-Ferat*', 179 n22.

[61] See the detailed discussion in Kahana ib.; see also (*ad loc.*) my critical discussion of the views of other scholars on this issue, primarily Schwartz, 'Quantitätsrelation'; de Vries, *Studies in the Literature*, 161-164; Chernick, 'Formal Development'; idem, *Hermeneutical Studies*.

[62] For more detailed treatment, see below, 'Distinct Exegetical Methods'.

applied the *kelal u-ferat* method to verses in which the *kelal* no longer represents a biblical word of general content, and the *perat* does not denote a word that details the generalization.[63] The main reason for this can apparently be traced to the ongoing attempt to find biblical proof texts for increasing numbers of halakhot that had not initially been derived from Scripture.[64]

THE SCHOOLS OF R. YISHMAEL AND OF R. AKIVA

Distinct Exegetical Methods

One of the important achievements of research into the Halakhic Midrashim is the delineation of the methodological difference between R. Yishmael and R. Akiva,[65] and in its wake, the distinction between the two chief types of halakhic midrash.[66]

Some of the methodological differences between the two rabbis are already portrayed in Tannaic sources, and their consequential disagreement on a number of topics is also presented in Amoraic sources. Only modern scholars, however, methodically collected the disagreements as these are dispersed throughout talmudic literature. The reconstruction of the differences between R. Yishmael and R. Akiva and their schools was made on the basis of four levels of evidence: (1) dicta transmitted in the name of R. Yishmael or R. Akiva; (2) views talmudic sources attribute to the schools of the two Tannaim, such as תנא דבי ר' ישמעאל, 'A scholar of the school of Yishmael (says),' or, תני ר' שמעון בר יוחי, 'R. Shimon bar Yohai (a disciple of R. Akiva) taught'; (3) analysis of the differences between Halakhic Midrashim belonging to the two schools: (4) disagreements between R. Yishmael and R. Akiva as reconstructed by the Talmuds. These strata generally complete one another, and careful comparison has allowed scholars to reach well-founded conclusions. At times, however, the evidence about the disagreements between R. Yishmael

---

[63] For detailed discussion of the development of this hermeneutical principle see Chernick, 'Formal Development'. As regards the increase in the number of hermeneutical principles, see the additional list of thirty-two rules attributed to R. Eliezer the son of R. Yose ha-Gelili. This list, however, apparently was formulated only in the Geonic period, and therefore exceeds the purview of this survey. See Zucker, 'Pitron'.

[64] See below, 'Relation to Other Works', on the Halakhic Midrashim and the Talmuds.

[65] For a description of R. Akiva's actions and methods, see Finkelstein, *Akiba*; Safrai, *Akiva*; Goldin, 'Profile'. For a comprehensive discussion of the traditions regarding R. Yishmael, see Porton, *Rabbi Yishmael*. In the first three volumes the author collected the traditions of R. Yishmael in various sources, and the fourth volume contains a summation, in which he relates to the literary forms in which R. Yishmael's dicta were presented (chap. 3); R. Yishmael's relations with other Sages (chap. 4); R. Yishmael's opinions (chap. 5); R. Yishmael as exegete (chap. 6); and the historical reliability of the traditions concerning his personality and opinions (chap. 7). For a critical discussion of Porton's conclusions, see below, n161.

[66] The first methodical and comprehensive study was written by Hoffmann, 'Einleitung' [1888]. The latest exhaustive research on this issue was conducted by Epstein, *Prolegomena*, 501-746. Cf the slightly different approach of Albeck, *Untersuchungen*; idem, *Introduction*, 79-143.

17

and R. Akiva that emerges from the different levels is inconsistent and we should be wary of some of the generalizations and harmonizations voiced by the talmudic sources.[67]

R. Yishmael's midrash is generally more moderate than R. Akiva's, and his expositions are also less distant from the simple meaning of the verse.[68] R. Yishmael also relies upon more *middot*, interpretive rules, and comparisons between different verses, in contrast with R. Akiva's tendency to focus upon the individual verse and draw conclusions regarding its meanings from specific words and letters.[69] The two Tannaim frequently employ different midrash methods to reach identical halakhic conclusions, while in some instances they differ both regarding the midrash and its halakhic outcome. The following examples may help clarify the two approaches as to the exposition of 'super-fluous' words and particles and the duplication of verbs, nouns, verses, or entire passages.

In one instance R. Akiva derives a halakha from the exposition of a letter *vav* that he considers to be superfluous, a legal conclusion vigorously opposed by R. Yishmael. bSan 51b reads:

"And if the daughter (ובת) of a priest defiles herself through harlotry [it is her father whom she defiles; she shall be put to the fire]" (Lev 21:9 – this refers to a maiden (נערה) who is betrothed (ארוסה)... – the opinion of R. Yishmael. R.

---

[67] Most scholars did not stress sufficiently the gap that can exist between the various Tannaic strata and therefore drew erroneous conclusions; see, e.g. below, n70. Harris, *How Do We Know*, chaps. 2-3, correctly accentuated the speculative element in the reconstruction of the disagreement between R. Yishmael and R. Akiva in the Bavli and especially the Yerushalmi. Unfortunately, Harris did not engage in a systematic examination of the midrashic methods in Tannaic literature itself as reflected in the Halakhic Midrashim and also evident in the baraitot cited in Amoraic literature (see discussion below). The lack of this central element in Harris's book significantly detracts from his conclusions that play down the disagreement between the schools of R. Yishmael and R. Akiva during the Tannaic period and present them in an unbalanced fashion. His conclusions are consequently flawed in his presentation of the innovative nature of the conceptions of the Amoraim in the Talmuds (see also below n292). Porton, *Rabbi Yishmael*, took care to devote a separate discussion to the traditions of R. Yishmael in each of the Tannaic and Amoraic compositions, but the picture that he draws is plagued by many flaws (see below n161).

[68] Several scholars regard R. Yishmael as a commentator who employs simplistic interpretive methods. This view was expressed most forcefully by Heschel, *Theology*, who depicts R. Yishmael as a commentator who is consistently faithful to the simple meaning (see his general description, Introduction, xli-lvi, that is exemplified in many chapters of his book). In contrast, it should be stressed that in many instances R. Yishmael's expositions, as well, are not simplistic, and several of the hermeneutical methods by which the Tora is expounded are by no means simplistic, certainly not in the modern scholarly sense of this term, and at times are not even the *peshat* (simple meaning) as this is understood by the Tannaim themselves (which they define with the terms דברים ככתבן, ממש, כמשמעו, and the like). Notwithstanding this, R. Yishmael's exegetical method is less extreme than that of R. Akiva, and many of his interpretations are indeed more literal.

[69] This general and fundamental difference between R. Yishmael and R. Akiva, that is indirectly implied by most scholars of halakha (see, e.g., Epstein, *Prolegomena*, 521f, 536), was especially developed by my teacher Prof. Avraham Goldberg in his lectures. For an example of this, see Epstein, *ib.* 562f; Lieberman, *Tosefta Ki-Fshutah*, Bava Kamma, 58.

18

Akiva says: Whether betrothed or married (נשואה), she is taken out to be burnt. ...R. Akiva said to him: Yishmael, my brother, "daughter" (בת) [*bat*], "and if the daughter" (ובת) – I am expounding [I learn out of the *vav* that prefixes the word *bat*]. He [R. Yishmael] replied: And because of your *bat u-vat* exposition [of the superfluous *vav*], shall this one be taken out to be burnt?[70]

As regards another exposition based on a seemingly unnecessary *vav*, according to R. Eliezer: 'R. Yishmael said to him, My master, why, you tell Scripture to be silent until I expound (!). R. Eliezer replied: Yishmael, you are a mountain palm.'[71]

R. Akiva, in the footsteps of his teachers, also consistently expounded the particles אך (but) and רק (only) as exclusionary, and את and גם (also) as inclusory. R. Yishmael, as well, esteemed R. Akiva's erudition in these expositions.[72] At times R. Akiva was even more adept at this than his teachers, as is related in *bPes* 22b and parallels:

---

[70] This is the only instance that contains explicit testimony of R. Akiva's exposition of the letter *vav*, while in a number of places in the Talmud this exposition is regarded as his general method (unlike the unattributed passage in bSan 51b, that takes pains to explain the need for the *vav*, also in accordance with R. Yishmael!). A number of additional unattributed expositions of the *vav* were also ascribed to R. Akiva; cf bYev 68b; ySot 8:10, 23a. As a result of this perception, the Talmuds occasionally explained R. Akiva's expositions as based on his exposition of the letter *vav*, even in instances in which his explanation was, in fact, grounded in some other Scriptural issue. Cf his extreme exposition in mSot 5:1 (ms K): 'As the water puts her to the proof, so does it put him to the test, as it is said, "And it shall come (ובאו) ...and it shall come (ובאו) ". As she is forbidden to the husband, so is she forbidden to the paramour, as it is said, "if she has defiled herself (אם ניטמאה)": she has defiled herself (ניטמאה), opinion of R. Akiva.' Both Bavli and Yerushalmi understood R. Akiva's exposition to be based on the seemingly superfluous *vav* in ובאו and in וניטמאה. See an expansion of this idea in Epstein, *Mavo*, 81-84, who adopts the interpretation of the two Talmuds. R. Akiva, however, patently based his exposition on the repetitious wording, not on the letter *vav*. This is proven from the Palestinian manuscripts that read: ניטמא ניטמאה...ובאו ובאו, not באו ובאו...ניטמאה וניטמאה, as in the emended version of the Talmuds that follows from their interpretation. This is also stated explicitly in the parallel in SifNum 7 (p12): 'R. Akiva says: Why does Scripture use "she has defiled herself", *three times*? This means: defiled in relation to her husband, defiled in relation to her paramour, and defiled regarding [the consumption of] *terumot*.' We therefore should be wary of the reconstruction by the Talmuds of the views of R. Akiva and R. Yishmael.

[71] Sifra, *Negaim* 13:2 (68b). I.e., just as the palm that grows in the mountains bears no fruit, you, too, do not have the ability to expound.

[72] See GenR 1:14 (p12) and parallels: 'R. Yishmael asked R. Akiva: He said, Because you were the attendant of Nahum of Gimzo twenty-two years, אכים [and] רקים [the words *akh, rak*] exclude; אתים [and] גמים [the words *et, gam*] include. This את that is written here, what does it signify?' It should not be concluded from this that R. Yishmael never based an exposition on the preposition את. To the contrary, on this problematic verse, that is related to the controversy with the Gnostics, it was specifically R. Yishmael who derived his explanation from this word, as is stated expressly in the continuation of the midrash, in accordance with all the mss, and in the independent parallel in bHag 12a (following the common conception that only R. Akiva bases expositions on the preposition את, several scholars have suggested emending this midrash. See Kahana, 'Critical Editions', 520-524; cf also below, n104).

Shimon ha-Amsoni (...) would interpret every את in the Tora. When he came to "You must revere [את] the Lord your God" (Deut 10:20), he refrained [from teaching this]. His pupils said to him, Master, what will be with all the אתים that you have expounded?[73] He replied: Just as I received reward for interpreting, so, too, do I receive reward for refraining from it. Until R. Akiva came and expounded: "You must revere [את] the Lord your God" – to include Tora scholars.

R. Yishmael and R. Akiva similarly dissented in the interpretation of the repetition of a verb and infinitive that commonly occurs in the Bible, as in SifNum 112, p121:

"...That person shall utterly be cut off " (*hikaret tikaret*, Num 15:31) *<hikaret>* in this world, *tikaret* in the world to come – opinion of R. Akiva. <R.> Yishmael said to him: Because it [also] says, "That person shall be cut off" (*venikhretah*, ib. 15:30), do I understand that there are three cuttings off, in three worlds!? What does Scripture teach by *hikaret tikaret*? That the Tora speaks in human language.[74]

This dispute is already characterized by the Palestinian Talmud (*Shabbat* 19:2, 17a and parallels) as a consistent disagreement between R. Yishmael and R. Akiva:

To this point, it has been interpreted in accordance with R. Akiva, who said that [these] wordings are inclusory. As regards [the opinion of] R. Yishmael, who said that [these are] wordings of [simple] repetition, and the Tora enlarged in its usual manner: *halokh halakhta*; *nikhsof nikhsafta*; *gunov gunavt[i]* [...].

---

[73] Attention should be paid to the severe and unforgiving attitude of the pupils to the midrashim they express in this question. According to the pupils, the failure of an exposition based on the usage of את teaches of the failure of the entire method, with the inescapable conclusion that all other expositions of this preposition that had been put forth in the past by Shimon ha-Amsoni are to be similarly rejected.

[74] The version of ms Vat is corrupted here, and the textual emendations in <brackets> were made in accordance with a majority of the other textual versions. See also bKer 11a, the disagreement concerning the interpretation of 'but has not been redeemed (והפדה לא נפדתה, Lev 19:20)'. R. Akiva expounds this literally, as referring to a special reality, while R. Yishmael, in contrast, argues that 'the Tora spoke in the language of man'. It should be stressed that the expression 'the Tora spoke in the language of man' appears in Tannaic and Amoraic sources only in relation to the rejection of midrashim based on verb-infinitive repetition and on the repetition of the biblical phrase איש איש at the beginning of a topic. 'The language of man' in this source is not the Mishnaic language common in the Tannaic period, since it completely lacks the mode of emphasis employing verb-infinitive repetition or inclusionary repetition, such as איש איש. See Bendavid, *Biblical Hebrew*, 133, 472, 506. It therefore is plausible that R. Akiva expounded these biblical forms because he sensed their uniqueness in comparison with rabbinic language. On the other hand, emphasis by means of a verb and an accompanying infinitive continued to appear in Akkadian, Syriac, and talmudic Aramaic, and so it is not inconceivable that when R. Yishmael spoke of 'the language of man', his intent was to these languages. Cf the different formulation in the unattributed passage in the Yerushalmi cited immediately following: 'The Tora enlarged in its usual manner.'

A similar conception in the explanation of the repetition of biblical nouns and of synonyms is to be found in a midrash from the school of R. Yishmael:

> "He shall abstain from wine and strong drink" (Num 6:3) – but wine is strong drink, and strong drink is wine? Rather, the Tora spoke two synonyms. And likewise, you say that *shehita* (slaughtering) is *zeviha* (sacrificing) ... *kemitza* is *harama* [both terms meaning taking up in one's hand] ... *amuka* is *shefela* (deep, low) ... *ot* is *mofet* (sign, wonder) ... rather, the Tora spoke two synonyms.[75]

A similar situation is created by the concluding verses of biblical passages that R. Yishmael regards as literary repetitions and not to be expounded.[76] In contrast to R. Akiva, he adopted a similar approach regarding the repetition of entire passages (see below).

R. Akiva's far-reaching way of expounding might also explain the assertion by the Mishna: 'When R. Akiva died, exegetes ceased.'[77] Noteworthy in this context is the aggadic tradition in *bMen* 29b that the Holy One, blessed be He, said to Moses: 'At the end of a number of generations there will be a man, Akiva son of Yosef by name, who will expound on every tip [of the letters in the Tora] mounds and mounds of halakhot.'[78]

R. Yishmael opposed the minute exposition of biblical verses practiced by R. Akiva and based his own exegeses primarily on general hermeneutical rules and comparison of different verses, as is demonstrated by his thirteen midrash methods described above. In addition to those rules, other principles were prevalent in the school of R. Yishmael, one of which relates to topics that are repeated in the Tora:[79]

---

[75] SifNum 23 (p27). yOrla 1:2, 60d attributes this approach to R. Yishmael himself: '...for R. Yishmael there said that *havaya* is the same as *hakama* [both referring to existence]; *shevira* is the same as *nefitza* [both referring to breaking], *geula* is the same as *pediya* [both referring to redemption, in the sense of reclamation].' In contrast, see the different approach of the exposition of Deut 13:2: 'And he gives you a sign or portent' in SifDeut 83 (p149; Akivan): '"A sign" – in heaven; "a portent" – on earth.'

[76] See his view in SifNum 152 (p197); 157 (p212): הפסיק הענין 'This ended the topic'. Epstein, *Prolegomena*, 535, refers to the similar method of R. Yonatan, a pupil of R. Yishmael, who, by explaining the literary repetitions in the end of the topic as כחותם הדברים 'concludes the subject', opposes expositions based on repetition resulting from the conclusion of sections.

[77] mSot 9:15. The citations follow ms K and other good manuscripts; see *Dikdukei Soferim ha-Shalem*, Sota, 349f. The omission of this dictum in the printed versions led a majority of scholars to ignore it in their discussions of R. Akiva as exegete.

[78] In practice, we do not know of any laws that R. Akiva derived from the tips of the letters, and this was most likely an extreme characterization of his hermeneutical method. Cf bEr 21b: 'R. Hisda said in the name of Mar Ukva: This teaches that it is possible to pile up mounds of laws on every tip.' See also the wording of LevR 19 (p413): 'The tips of R. Eliezer and the tips of R. Joshua,' that is understood by the *Arukh* as the exposition of letter tips by R. Eliezer and by R. Joshua. See the gloss by Margulies *ad loc*. (my thanks to Marc Hirshman, who drew my attention to this).

[79] The quotation is from an unattributed exposition in SifNum 2 (p4), Yishmaelian: the parallel bSot 3a expressly attributes it, תנא דבי ר' ישמעאל.

> This is a rule for expounding the Tora: Every passage that was stated in one place but lacks one element, and was taught again in another place, was repeated only for the element that was omitted.[80] R. Akiva says, Every occurrence of לאמר (saying) must be expounded.[81]

This apparently indicates that the school of R. Yishmael maintained that expositions are not to be founded on repetition of similar verses in two passages. The problem with this is that on occasion the Halakhic Midrashim of R. Yishmael do employ such repetitions as a basis of exposition, whence it may be assumed that there was no unanimity on this point in the school of R. Yishmael.[82] At any rate, the incompleteness of our information regarding the opinions of R. Yishmael and R. Akiva on this cardinal issue exemplifies our limited knowledge about the ideas of the Tannaim.

A hermeneutical rule of R. Yishmael that has escaped scholarly attention relates to the tension between the simple meaning of the verse and the sages' sense of reason and correctness. R. Akiva resolves the tension by means of an extreme midrash that removes the verse from its literal meaning and interprets it in accord with an opinion that seemed fitting to the Tannaim. R. Yishmael, in contrast, will candidly present the inconsistency between reason and the verse's meaning following his hermeneutical rules, and presents a compromise that allows both to coexist. The sole extant example that explicitly sets this forth discusses the time of death of the woman accused of adultery who drank the 'water of bitterness'. According to the Tannaic understanding of the description in the Tora (Num 5:27), the woman will die immediately after drinking the water, while several Tannaim think that if she possessed prior merits, her death is postponed for a certain period of time.[83] The element of 'merit' delaying death that runs counter to the simple meaning was expounded by R. Akiva from the expression, 'a meal-offering of remembrance' (Num 5:15).[84] R. Yishmael, who opposed this exegesis, felt duty-bound to interpret the phrase

---

[80] That is, the section was written a second time, to complete something in it. A number of additional expositions in Yishmaelian Halakhic Midrashim allude to this cardinal principle for explaining the need for repeated passages. See MekRY Pisha 16 (p53); Mishpatim 6 (p269); Midrash Tannaim on Deut 15:12 (p85). Cf Sifra Nedava 15:2 (p97); Behukotai 12:9 (115a).

[81] As could be expected, R. Akiva disagrees with R. Yishmael, and apparently maintains that both passages must be expounded in their entirety; however, his exact intent when speaking of the passage that includes the wording לאמר is unclear.

[82] Cf Hoffmann, 'Einleitung' [1888], 7; Horovitz, Introduction, *Siphre d'be Rab*, x; Epstein, *Prolegomena*, 532.

[83] See mSot 3:4-5 and parallels; cf the views of Tannaim who are totally opposed to the principle of 'merit'.

[84] SifNum 8 (p14): '"A meal-offering of remembrance" (Num 5:15) – R. Akiva says this one [i.e., the remembrance] also is for the good, as it says, "but if the woman has not defiled herself" (v28). All that I know is a remembrance of sin. Whence [do we know that it is also] a remembrance of merit? Scripture teaches: "a meal-offering of remembrance" – in all respects.'

differently using his *kelal u-ferat* rule.[85] On the other hand, he also concluded, based on a *kal va-homer*, that if the water had the power to recall a previous iniquity, it certainly was capable of recalling a prior merit.[86] This led to his formulation of an interpretive rule:

> This is a good rule for the interpretation of the Tora, that every *kelal u-ferat* that is deficient in [human] logic – both [the *kelal u-ferat* and logic] are accepted, and the logical inference is not placed in an inferior position. How are both to be accepted, without the logical inference being placed in an inferior position? If she was impure, she is immediately punished; and if she possessed merit, the merit suspends her [punishment].

The tension between the simple meaning of Scripture and the halakha is the subject of a similar disagreement between R. Yishmael and R. Akiva. The latter, as is his wont, explains the Tora in a manner that conforms with the halakha. R. Yishmael, in contrast, pointedly indicates the instances in which there is a disparity between the two:

> R. Yishmael says: In three places the halakha supersedes the biblical text: the Tora said: "Cover it *with earth*" (Lev 17:13), but the halakha said, With anything that brings forth vegetation; the Tora said: "You shall take *an awl*" (Deut 15:17), but the halakha said, With anything; the Tora said: "And he writes here *a bill* of divorce" (Deut 24:1), but the halakha said, With anything.[87]

It nonetheless should be stressed that in many instances R. Yishmael as well uses his hermeneutical method to expound the Tora and harmonize it with the halakha.

Another realm with a rather characteristic differential between R. Yishmael and R. Akiva relates to the bounds of the applicability of the *middot*, that R. Yishmael limits, while R. Akiva expands. A few examples: R. Yishmael permits the use of *gezera shava* only if it is 'vacated from one side', while R. Akiva maintains that 'we learn from *gezera shava* even if it is not vacated';[88]

---

[85] '"A meal-offering of remembrance" is the generalization; "a remembrance of sin" is the specification; the generalization only includes what is in the specification.' – This, indeed, is the simple meaning of the verse.

[86] 'Which [divine] attribute is greater, the attribute of bestowing good, or that attribute of exacting punishment? Let us say, the attribute of bestowing good [this conclusion is derived from Exod 20:5-6, in which it is stated that the Lord "...visits the guilt of the fathers upon the children, *upon the third and fourth generation* of those who reject Me", in comparison with "showing kindness *to the thousandth generation* of those who love Me"]. If the attribute of exacting punishment is diminished, then it is "a remembrance of sin"; if the attribute of bestowing good <is the greater>, then it is "a remembrance of merit".'

[87] MidrTann Deut 24:1 (p154) and parallels. See Henshke, 'Two Subjects'.

[88] That is to say, R. Yishmael is of the opinion that a *gezera shava* is to be employed only if one of the two words on which it is based is free, i.e., it has not been used in other expositions. R. Akiva, in contrast, maintains that this hermeneutical method may also be used for two words that have already been put to other exegetical use. See the detailed discussion by Epstein, *Prolegomena*, 522.

R. Yishmael negates the possibility of expounding *lamed min ha-lamed* (a deduced meaning from a deduced meaning), while R. Akiva allows for such a possibility;[89] and where R. Yishmael is of the opinion, 'Punishments are not derived from logic',[90] other sages including R. Akiva assert they are, according to one tradition.[91]

R. Yishmael and R. Akiva also differ regarding the permissibility of expounding certain topics in public. R. Ba, in the name of Rav Yehuda, attributes the mishna, 'The forbidden sexual relationships may not be expounded before three persons,' solely to R. Akiva, and as opposed to the opinion of R. Yishmael.[92] Sifra (from the school of R. Akiva) accordingly did not include expositions regarding the forbidden sexual relationships in the portions of *Aharei* (Lev 18:7-23) and *Kedoshim* (Lev 20:10-21), while in these portions the second Halakhic Midrash on Leviticus (from the school of R. Yishmael) did contain such expositions; some of these were then inserted in certain Sifra manuscripts.[93]

Several explanations were offered for the reason behind this disagreement.[94] I maintain that R. Akiva's position is to be understood in light of his far-reaching midrash and of his fear that publicizing such expositions that appeal to human cravings was liable to result in licentious behavior and, in the words of the Bavli on this mishna, 'may come to permit that which is prohibited'.[95] In contrast, R. Yishmael with his more moderate exegetical method, did

---

[89] That is, according to R. Yishmael, everything that is not specified in the Tora, but rather is learned by exposition, cannot serve as the basis for an additional exposition. R. Akiva, on the other hand, permits founding a new exposition on a previous one. See Epstein, *Prolegomena*, 524.

[90] In other words, a person is not punished for violating a law that is learned by a *kal va-homer*. See Epstein, *Prolegomena*, 525. Further study is needed to clarify the legal ramifications, both theoretical and practical, of this principle.

[91] The disagreement as to whether the *kelal u-ferat* method is to be employed (according to R. Yishmael), or that of *ribui u-miut* (as R. Akiva suggests) seemingly reflects a similar difference. See Epstein, *Prolegomena*, 527. It is highly doubtful, however, whether the view ascribed by the Talmuds to R. Akiva on this issue actually reflects his original opinion. See the persuasive reservations of Chernick, 'Ribbuyim and Miutim'. Cf an additional rule stated in the name of R. Yishmael, specifically: 'An amplification following an amplification teaches of a restriction' (see Epstein, *Prolegomena*, 530; his discussion needs to be completed and corrected).

[92] mHag 2:1; yHag 2:1, 77a.

[93] For details see below, the description of Sifra.

[94] See bHag 12a; cf Albeck, addenda to mHag in his *Mishna*, p511; Lieberman, *Tosefta Ki-Fshutah*, Hagiga, 1286f.

[95] bHag 11b. A similar fear may underlie the law in mMeg 4:10 and parallels that prohibits the public expounding of biblical passages such as the story of Reuben and of David and Amnon. For the prohibition that applies specifically to public reading, see Fraade, 'Rabbinic Views', 256-265. For the exposure of the few laws that could seemingly be inferred from these passages, along with another explanation of this law, namely, the desire not to publicize the sins of the forefathers of the Israelite nation, see Henshke, 'What Should Be Omitted'.

not fear publicly expounding the passage of forbidden sexual relationships, presenting its prohibitions and concessions based on his hermeneutical rules.[96]

In the same comment on the quoted mishna, R. Ba in the name of Rav Yehuda similarly attributes the halakha, 'The Story of Creation is not expounded before two', as following the view of R. Akiva exclusively, in opposition to R. Yishmael. The dispute is also reflected in the disagreement in Genesis Rabba between the two Tannaim concerning the legitimacy of expounding the word את in Gen 1:1. R. Akiva explains the word as intended to prevent the Gnostic interpretation that 'heaven and earth also are divinities', and therefore no exposition is to be learned from it, while R. Yishmael has no qualms in expounding the word in this problematic verse.[97] Genesis Rabba also contains a similar disagreement between the two Tannaim over expounding את in two other verses that are likely to be understood as supporting the view of the heretics.[98] Here as well, the dispute is based on their methodological difference. R. Yishmael was not wary of expounding these verses, while R. Akiva was apprehensive that publicly expounding such sensitive verses using his far-reaching method would support the expositions of the heretics,[99] and he therefore refrained from doing so.[100]

As regards the third halakha in the mishna we quoted, that the *Merkava* section (i.e., concerning the divine throne-chariot in Ezek 1) may not be expounded before a single person, the Yerushalmi rejects the possibility that this too is the opinion of R. Akiva and establishes that it is a view universally held. This is an anonymous opinion and might represent only the view of a redactor who was not aware of other traditions.[101] That is to say, taking into account the confirmed attribution of the first two sections in the mishna to R. Akiva and

---

[96] A prime example of this is to be found in the *kelal u-ferat* exposition cited in the beginning of the 'Mekhilta de-arayot', Sifra Aharei 86b, whose sole purpose is to prevent any possibility of an erroneous exposition. See Kahana, 'Kelal u-Ferat', 183f.

[97] GenR 1,14 (p12). The Gnostic background of the interpretation attacked by R. Akiva was first examined by Joel, *Blicke*, 168f; cf Urbach, *Sages*, 76, 184f. For the evolution of the interpretations of this exposition and the attempts to proofread it, see Kahana, 'Critical Editions', 523 n13.

[98] For the disagreement in GenR p206 concerning the exposition of the verse, 'I have gained a male child with the help of the Lord' (Gen 4:1) and its Gnostic background, see Kahana, 'Critical Editions', 520-524. For a more extensive examination of these expositions, including a proposal to understand the disagreement in GenR p574 on the verse, 'God was with the boy' (Gen 21:20), on the background of the identification in the Heikhalot literature of Metatron as a boy, see Segal, *Two Powers*, 74-83.

[99] See MekRY p112 for the trenchant polemic by R. Akiva against several expositions of R. Pappus that tended towards Gnostic heresy and the discussion of these expositions by Altman, 'Gnostic Background', 385; Kahana, 'Critical Editions', 499-515.

[100] For an expansion of the disagreement of R. Yishmael and R. Akiva concerning the exposition of the Creation story and the approach of the redactor of GenR to this charged issue, see Kahana, 'Redaction'. A similar fundamental approach is expressed in Nahmanides' objections to using aggadic dicta in the Jewish-Christian polemic in which he participated, due to his unwillingness to provide an opening for extreme Christian expositions. See Fox, 'Nahmanides'.

[101] See Halperin, *Merkabah*, 29.

not to R. Yishmael, it is not inconceivable that the third section is to be so ascribed.[102] However this deserves a separate discussion.[103] Regardless of this question, in light of the above we cannot accept the opinion of Heschel that R. Yishmael was a rationalist who vigorously opposed esoteric expositions of the Tora and matters that cannot be attained by the intellect.[104] More generally, one should avoid associating the predilection for the simple meaning with religious rationalism.[105]

The Division into Schools

The discovery of the differing exegetical methods of R. Yishmael and of R. Akiva led scholars to divide the Halakhic Midrashim into two corresponding schools. The classification was based on the differences in the following realms:

---

[102] Several traditions that ascribe to R. Yishmael expositions concerning the vision of the Merkava in the first chapter of Ezekiel remain in the talmudic literature. See, e.g., MidrProv 20 (ed Visotsky p144); MidrPs 1:2 (p2, textual variants; the parallels give another attribution, but the unattributed parallel in MidrTann Deut 3:27, p19, apparently originating in the Yishmaelian MekDeut, confirms MidrPs). See also several expositions of the Merkava verses that were incorporated in Yishmaelian Midrashim, such as SifNum 115 (p126); MidrTann Deut 3:23 (p15). The Hekhalot literature also ascribes much material to R. Yishmael (although scholars disagree on his identification) and to R. Natan, one of the outstanding sages of the school of R. Yishmael, echoes of which may possibly be found in the basic tradition that R. Yishmael expounded the Merkava vision.

[103] I gave a preliminary discussion of this issue in a lecture delivered in Jerusalem in 1987, marking the fifth anniversary of Gershom Scholem's death.

[104] Heschel's proofs often rely upon the 'corrected' version of midrashim (such as the disagreement between R. Yishmael and R. Akiva in GenR (p12), in which the identities of the disputants are exchanged; see Heschel, *Theology*, Introduction, xxxv; cf above n72), and anachronistic explanations of Tannaic dicta under the influence of the conceptions of modern critical exegesis. He similarly labors to find differences between the schools of R. Akiva and R. Yishmael in aggada (see p10f), basing his arguments on shared midrashic material in Halakhic Midrashim that does not specifically reflect one of these schools (see below, 'Aggada'). Cf the general and forceful critical comment by Urbach, *Sages*, 695 n20. It should be emphasized, however, that Heschel's book should not be disparaged, since it contains a considerable number of sound insights and convincing scholarly discoveries that should be pursued further.

[105] E.g. Sifra Aharei 2:8 (81a) (Akivan), that interprets the word לעזאזל as 'to the harsh place in the mountains', unlike the interpretation attributed to תנא דבי ר' ישמעאל in bYom 67b: '*Azazel* – because it atones for the episode of Uza and Azael.' That is to say, the school of R. Yishmael, specifically, had to base its interpretation on the primordial myth of Uza and Azael, two angels who descended from heaven, desired the daughters of man, and corrupted the earth, as is described in detail in the Hekhalot literature (see Scholem, 'Havdala', 274f). See also 'Mekhilta de-Miluim' (Yishmaelian) appended to Sifra (43c): 'Even though God is willing to grant atonement for your sins, you must be given over into the mouth of the Satan.' And cf the rational discussion in mYom 6:8, 'Whence did they know that the he-goat had reached the wilderness?' – in contrast with R. Yishmael's explanation based on the miraculous sign of the thread of crimson wool that is appended to this mishna (see Epstein, *Mavo*, 960).

(1) the *midrash methods* described above, including those prevalent in the compositions from the school of R. Yishmael;[106]

(2) *midrash terminology*: certain terms and introductory formulas are shared by all Halakhic Midrashim, while other terms are characteristic of either school; some of these singular terms are essential to the particular school's method,[107] while others are merely alternative terms to which the redactors were accustomed;[108]

---

[106] Both midrash schools make frequent use of several of the straightforward hermeneutical methods, such as *kal va-homer* and *gezera shava* (although the emphasis that the word of the *gezera shava* is 'free', as we could expect, appears only in the school of R. Yishmael). Other methods, such as *kelal u-ferat*, *perat u-kelal*, and *kelal u-ferat u-kelal*, appear only in Yishmaelian Midrashim. Others again that are common in the school of R. Yishmael do appear, with slightly different terminology, in the Akivan works. See, e.g., the principle in the baraita of R. Yishmael (Sifra p4): 'Everything included in a generalization and then specified in order to teach a law, does not do so for its specific case, but rather teaches regarding the entire general category;' it is formulated in similar fashion in the Midrashim from the school of R. Yishmael: 'X, that was in the generalization, and was then specified, did so to teach regarding the generalization' (such as MekRY p27, p64; SifNum, p2, p39; MidrTann p59, p92). However, in the Akivan Midrashim it is formulated differently: 'X was in a generalization. Why was it then specified? In order to draw an inference regarding it' (such as MekRSbY p39, p147; Sifra Nedava p87, Tsav 3:1, 31a; SifDeut, p184, p257), and similarly in the language of the Mishna, also Akivan (mBM 2:5). Needless to say, the most reliable mss of the Midrashim must be used to examine this question, devoting special effort to a clarification of the text of extinct Midrashim. See, e.g., MekRSbY p169/1, that seemingly employs the hermeneutical rule: 'X was in a generalization, and was then specified in order to advance another similar deduction; it was specified to teach of a leniency, and not of a stringency'; a closer study, however, indicates that MekRSbY is not the source of the exposition; see below, description of MekRSbY.

[107] Cf terms that appear only in Yishmaelian Midrashim, such as זו מידה בתורה, 'This is a hermeneutical principle in the Tora'; מידות מי"ג, 'Go and learn from the thirteen hermeneutical methods'; מופנה להקיש ולדון הימנו גזירה שוה (but see the exceptional case in MekRSbY 41/4). Cf also the typically Yishmaelian question at the beginning of *parashot*: זו פרשה נאמרה למה, 'Why was this *parasha* stated?' clarifying the general innovation of the *parasha*. In contrast, the Akivan Midrashim formulate the idea of expounding a seemingly superfluous letter that is characteristic of this school in the singular fashion of first citing the word without the letter in question, and then citing it in its complete form.

[108] See, e.g.:

	Yishmaelian	Akivan
question of meaning	למה נאמר	מה תלמוד לומר
proposed conclusion	מגיד, נמצינו למדים	מלמד
rejection of proposed conclusion	או, שומע אני	יכול
exclusion (מיעוט)	להוציא	פרט ל-
inclusion (ריבוי)	להביא	לרבות

For additional terms characteristic of each school see Epstein, *Prolegomena*, 568; Albeck, *Introduction*, 93-102; Kahana, *Sifrei zuta*, 44-53; many more terms could be added. It should not be overlooked, however, that for a number of terms the difference between the two schools is not absolute, even if expressing the term that is in more common usage by each of the schools. Other terms are limited to specific Halakhic Midrashim, most conspicuously SifZNum and SifZDeut; see their description, below.

(3) *names of central sages*: the compositions from the school of R. Yishmael cite many dicta of R. Yishmael himself and of students from his school, headed by R. Yoshia, R. Yonatan, R. Natan, and R. Yitshak; these sages receive scant mention in Halakhic Midrashim of R. Akiva and in the Mishna that also belongs to the Akivan texts. Conversely, Halakhic Midrashim of the school of R. Akiva particularly mention several of his leading pupils;[109] in other instances, a document is distinguished by the name it gives to a particular rabbi;[110]

(4) *typical expositions* that consistently appear a number of times in a school's text, or expositions that employ an interpretive principle typical of either school;[111]

(5) *anonymous dicta* whose attribution to the heads of either school is indicated by the parallels in the talmudic literature.[112]

As we stated in the beginning, the fundamental classification made on the basis of these criteria remains valid, though a comprehensive and more precise examination based on the same criteria teaches that the Akivan texts are to be further divided into two subgroups.

---

[109] See the detailed description immediately following.

[110] Outstanding is the use by Akivan Midrashim of 'R. Shimon', while Yishmaelian Midrashim cite 'R. Shimon ben Yohai'. The difference might relate to the fact that R. Shimon was an outstanding Akivan scholar, so stating his private name sufficed to identify him. The school of R. Yishmael, in contrast, sought to avoid confusion between him and other rabbis with the same first name, and therefore added his father's name.

[111] Cf the question when observance of the commandments became obligatory for the Israelites when entering the Land of Israel: immediately (the Akivan view), or only after fourteen years of 'taking possession and dwelling', as the Yishmaelian school had it. This consistent difference between the two schools finds expression in various midrashim, as listed by Epstein, *Prolegomena*, 539-542, 567f. Cf also Kahana, *Prolegomena*, 304-311. For additional parallelisms, see Epstein, *ib.*, 585-587; Albeck, *Introduction*, 87, and many more.

[112] Although this criterion was considerably amplified by Hoffmann and after him Epstein, we should register a reservation, since the Halakhic Midrashim also contain unattributed midrashim that the parallels ascribe to sages of the opposing school. Scholars have not compiled orderly lists of this phenomenon, thus impeding an assessment of the relative weight of the unattributed dicta. Even in the instances in which comparative lists of unattributed teachings were drawn up, such as תנא דבי ר' ישמעאל in MekRY in comparison with תני ר' שמעון בן יוחי, they are not always accurate. See criticism by Albeck, *Untersuchungen*, 112-114, 121-133; idem, *Introduction*, 129-133. In general, we should avoid the attribution of dicta to specific sages on the basis of parallels that are the product of different redactors, since they often reflect exchanged traditions, some of which are also dependent upon the redactor's concealed halakhic tendencies (cf the discussion on the contradictory controversies in Melamed, *Introduction*, 365-369), or other orientations of conscious opposition to certain sages. Cf Lieberman, *Siphre Zutta*, 90, who attacked 'the method accepted by contemporary scholars' regarding unattributed dicta. Relying on the names of sages cited explicitly in each Midrash seems to be a more reliable method of school identification (see below).

Names of the Sages

A study of the names of dominant sages mentioned in the Halakhic Midrashim will likely yield important information about the date and sources of each individual document. It will also clarify the division of the Midrashim by school and their relation to Mishna and Tosefta. Previous scholars did draw up lists of Tannaim who appear in each document and drew important conclusions concerning the sages characteristic of each of the two schools.[113] Up until the present, however, this aspect of the Halakhic Midrashim has not been the subject of a comprehensive examination. Also, while scholars have put much energy in trying to determine the authorship of unattributed dicta, especially in order to identify the redactors of the Halakhic Midrashim,[114] they have neglected to some extent the comparative study of the names of dominant sages explicitly mentioned.

We will begin with a table of the twenty central Tannaim in descending order in the four complete Halakhic Midrashim,[115] comparing also the Mishna.[116] The table includes only sages mentioned in the halakhic portions of the documents, since only they clearly reflect the division into the schools of R. Yishmael and of R. Akiva.[117]

---

[113] See, e.g., Weiss, *Dor Dor ve-Dorshav*, vol 2, 201-212; Epstein, *Prolegomena*, 572-581; Neusner, *Babylonia*, vol 1, 192-220.

[114] For several methodological objections, see above, n112.

[115] The table does not include data from Halakhic Midrashim that are not preserved in their entirety, because there is no certainty that the extant sections accurately reflect the whole midrash. See below n133 for the list of sages in MekRSbY.

[116] The number in parentheses following each name is the total number of appearances of this name in the Midrashim and in the Mishna. Usually, all the instances of the names of sages were counted, and only in isolated instances did I omit the mention of the sage's name that is not accompanied by a new dictum (such as the recurring mention of 'Akiva' and 'Tarfon' in the teaching by R. Tarfon in SifNum, p70). The total number of appearances of the sages in a specific composition is therefore also dependent upon the manner in which their teachings are presented (such as 'the words of R. X;' 'that R. X says'), or the manner in which disagreement or consent with a certain view is presented (such as 'They said to R. X'). Another problem is raised by the textual variants in names of sages difficult to distinguish (such as commonly, 'Eliezer' – 'Elazar'). However these limitations concern a relatively small number of cases and cannot detract from the general picture. I used the 'Maagarim' CD-ROM of the Academy of the Hebrew language in Jerusalem in drawing up these lists.

[117] See below, 'Aggada'.

	MekRY[118]	SifNum[119]	Sifra[120]	SifDeut[121]	Mishna[122]
1	R. Yishmael (85)	R. Yishmael (55)	R. Yehuda (181)	R. Yehuda (54)	R. Yehuda (678)
2	R. Akiva (50)	R. Akiva (51)	R. Shimon (163)	R. Akiva (35)	R. Meir (369)
3	R. Eliezer (42)	R. Yoshia (44)	R. Akiva (130)	R. Shimon (33)	R. Shimon (367)
4	R. Yoshia (37)	R. Natan (38)	R. Yose (58)	R. Eliezer (33)	R. Yose (366)
5	R. Natan (37)	R. Eliezer (35)	R. Eliezer (57)	R. Yose ha-Gelili (21)	R. Akiva (335)
6	R. Yonatan (36)	R. Yonatan (34)	R. Meir (56)	R. Yishmael (14)	Beit Shammai (326)
7	Rabbi (36)	Rabbi (33)	Rabbi (50)	Rabbi (11)	R. Eliezer (319)
8	R. Yitshak (22)	R. Shimon (28)	R. Yose ha-Gelili (40)	R. Eliezer ben Yaakov (11)	Beit Hillel (317)
9	R. Yose ha-Gelili (22)	R. Yehuda (20)	R. Elazar (40)	R. Yose (8)	R. Yoshua (195)
10	R. Shimon (20)	Abba Hanin (19)	R. Yishmael (37)	Beit Hillel (7)	R. Elazar (106)

[118] Horovitz-Rabin p1-74, p218-348 (excluding the aggadic material in the portion of *Beshalah*, and the portion of *Yitro* until the beginning of the Ten Commandments). The text follows ms Oxf 151, with minor emendations.

[119] Horovitz p1-72/4, p106-168, p174-223 (excluding the aggadic material in the portions of *Behaalotekha* and *Balak*). The text follows a new edition I am preparing based on ms Vat 32 with minor emendations.

[120] Finkelstein p11-220 (*Nedava* and *Hova*); Weiss fol. 29-40c, 43c-85c l. 18, 86c l. 13-91c l. 26, 93c l. 13-115 (excluding the baraita of the thirteen *middot*, 'Mekhilta de-Miluim', and 'Mekhilta de-arayot' in the portions of *Aharei* and *Kedoshim*). The text follows ms Vat 66 with minor emendations; the passages from the portions of *Behar* and *Behukotai* that are missing from this ms follow ms Vat 31.

[121] Finkelstein p122/11-322 (excluding the aggadic material in the portions of *Devarim* to *Ekev*, and *Nitzavim* until *Vezot haberakha*, and similarly the Yishmaelian marginal annotations added in the halakhic material, in small print in ed Finkelstein). Text following ms Vat 32 with minor emendations.

[122] Text following ms K with minor emendations.

11	R. Yehuda (14)	R. Yose ha-Gelili (11)	R. Yoshua (26)	Beit Shammai (7)	Rabban Gamaliel (105)
12	R. Yehuda ben Bathyra (13)	Isi ben Akiva (10)	R. Yose ben Yehuda (210	R. Elazar ben Azariah (7)	Rabban Shimon ben Gamaliel (103)
13	R. Meir (12)	R. Meir (9)	Beit Hillel (19)	R. Yose ben Yehuda (6)	R. Yishmael (78)
14	R. Elazar ben Azariah (11)	R. Tarfon (9)	Beit Shammai (18)	R. Elazar (6)	R. Tarfon (66)
15	R. Yose (9)	R. Yehuda ben Bathyra (9)	R. Elazar ben Azariah (15)	R. Meir (5)	R. Elazar ben Azariah (43)
16	Abba Hanin (8)	R. Yitshak (8)	R. Tarfon (15)	R. Yoshua (4)[123]	R. Yohanan ben Nuri (41)
17	R. Aha ben Yoshia (6)	R. Elazar (8)	R. Elazar ben Shimon (15)		Rabbi (36)
18	R. Eliezer ben Jacob (5)	R. Elazar ha-Kappar (6)	R. Eliezer ben Jacob (14)		R. Yose ha-Gelili (27)
19	R. Shimon ben Elazar (4)	R. Shimon ben Elazar (5)	R. Yohanan ben Nuri (13)		Ben Azzai (27)
20	R. Yoshua (4) Rabban Yohanan ben Zakkai (4)	R. Elazar ben Azariah (5) Ben Azzai (5)	Rabban Shimon ben Gamaliel (13) Ben Azzai (13)		Rn Yohanan ben Zakkai (26) R. Dosa ben Harkinas (26)[124]

[123] The other sages in the halakhic portion of SifDeut appear only 3 or fewer times, and accordingly have not been noted.

[124] The name 'R. Eliezer ben Yaakov' appears in the Mishna 42 times, but at times it can hardly be determined if this is the older or the younger one, and I therefore did not include him.

A study of the table indicates the high degree of similarity between the Tannaim mentioned in MekRY and in SifNum (Yishmaelian),[125] and the strong similarity between the Tannaim mentioned in Sifra and those in SifDeut (Akivan).[126] There also is a considerable affinity between the Akivan Midrashim and the Mishna, which belongs to the same school.[127]

In the Yishmaelian collections, R. Yishmael enjoys prominent standing and in fact heads the list, to be followed by R. Akiva; the differential between them in MekRY is considerable (85-50) and small in SifNum (55-51).[128] In the Akivan collections, in contrast, R. Yishmael's standing is much lower in comparison to R. Akiva. In Sifra the disparity is extremely broad: Akiva is no. 3 with 130 mentions, and Yishmael no. 10 with 37. There is a slightly smaller differential in SifDeut: Akiva 2nd (35)[129] – Yishmael 6th (14).[130] Compare the even greater difference between the two Tannaim in the Mishna: Akiva 5th (335) – Yishmael 13th (78). The proportion in the Tosefta is similar: Akiva 8th (324) – Yishmael 16th (82).

A similar picture emerges from an examination of the leading pupils of the two schools. As all modern scholars have stressed, R. Yoshia, R. Natan, and R. Yonatan occupy a central position in the Yishmaelian Midrashim,[131] but are completely absent from Sifra, SifDeut, and the Mishna.[132] The same is true for other rabbis from the school of R. Yishmael: R. Yitshak, Abba Hanin (who transmits the dicta of R. Eliezer), R. Aha ben R. Yoshia, Isi ben Akiva, Isi ben Yehuda, and Isi ben Menahem.

---

[125] Of the 20 major sages, 17 are common to both Midrashim, and only 3 are different in each Midrash.

[126] All 16 of the sages rabbis mentioned at least 4 times in SifDeut are included in the list of 20 major sages in Sifra.

[127] A total of 18 of the 20 major sages in Sifra and the Mishna are shared by both sources, and only 2 are different (R. Yose ben R. Yehuda and R. Elazar ben R. Shimon in Sifra, cf below n134; and the two Patriarchs, Rabban Gamaliel and Rabban Yohanan ben Zakkai, in the Mishna).

[128] In addition, 'pupil of R. Yishmael' appears 3 times in MekRY, and twice in SifNum.

[129] The first number gives the place in the list of sages, the number in parentheses the number of mentions. Incidentally, attention should be paid to the fact that Halakhic Midrashim are of different lengths, and we should be wary of comparisons of the absolute number of rabbis in the various midrashim. A comparison of the total number of rabbis in each midrash according to the Venice 1545-1546 edition, in which the four midrashim were printed in uniform fashion, reveals the absence of any great differences in this realm, and that the average number of rabbis mentioned on each page is similar (MekRY – 21, Sifra – 20, SifNum and SifDeut – 19.5).

[130] For a similar phenomenon in MekRSbY, the third Midrash belonging to this classic school see below n133; the same is true for the Midrashim from the second school of R. Akiva: R. Yishmael occupies eleventh place in the halakhic material in SifZNum with 7 dicta, while his name has not come to light in SifZDeut. See Kahana, *Sifrei Zuta*, 60-64.

[131] MekRY: R. Yoshia and R. Natan 4-5 (37), R. Yonatan 6 (36); SifNum: R. Yoshia 3 (44), R. Natan 4 (38), R. Yonatan 5 (34).

[132] For the two dicta of R. Natan that were added to the Mishna from baraitot, see Epstein, *Mavo*, 975. On the other hand, R. Natan appears in the Tosefta (that on occasion also includes Yishmaelian material) in the nineteenth place, with 63 teachings. See also the 4 dicta of R. Natan in MekRSbY, that reflect the somewhat variegated nature of this Midrash (see description below).

On the other side of the divide, R. Yehuda, pupil of R. Akiva, occupies first place in Sifra and SifDeut (from the school of R. Akiva), with a wide margin separating him from the rabbis who come after him: R. Akiva and R. Shimon[133] his pupil.[134] A similar phenomenon infuses the Mishna and the Tosefta, in which the number of dicta by R. Yehuda is much greater than the number of teachings of the pupils of R. Akiva who come after him: R. Shimon, R. Meir, and R. Yose.[135] It is also of interest to compare the senior standing of R. Yehuda and R. Shimon in the Akivan collections with the well-known dictum of R. Yohanan in *B.T. Sanhedrin* 86a: 'An anonymous [teaching in] Sifra is from R. Yehuda, an anonymous [teaching in] Sifrei is from R. Shimon, and it is all taught in accordance with the views of R. Akiva.'[136] In contrast, the standing of R. Akiva's pupils: R. Yehuda, R. Shimon, R. Meir, and R. Yose is much weaker in the Yishmaelian collections.[137]

The table of names also reflects certain distinctions between the collections belonging to the same school, as well as accentuating the common traits. For example, among the leading pupils of the school of R. Yishmael, R. Yitshak enjoys a higher standing in MekRY, while Isi ben Akiva's position is stronger in SifNum[138] Correspondingly, among the outstanding pupils of R. Akiva, the status of R. Meir and R. Yose is higher in Sifra than in SifDeut[139] There is also a marked difference regarding the names of sages in the two subgroups of R. Akiva. See, for example, the relatively strong standing of R. Elazar ben

---

[133] Sifra: R. Yehuda 1 (181), R. Shimon 2 (163), R. Akiva 3 (130); SifDeut: R. Yehuda 1 (54), R. Akiva 2 (35), R. Shimon 3-4 (33). These three head the list of sages in the extant halakhic sections from MekRSbY (Epstein-Melamed, p9 l. 12-44, p145 l. 22-224, with addition of several names included in as yet unpublished Geniza fragments): R. Yehuda 1 (32), R. Akiva 2 (30), R. Shimon 3 (21). They are followed, in appearances similar to other Akivan Midrashim: R. Yose ha-Gelili 4 (20), R. Eliezer 5 (18), Rabbi [Yehuda ha-Nasi] 6 (12), R. Eliezer ben Yaakov and R. Yishmael 7-8 (10), R. Yose 9 (8), Beit Hillel and Beit Shammai 10-11 (6), R. Meir, R. Elazar ben Azaria, Ben Azzai, and R. Nehemia 12-15 (5), R. Yose ben R. Yehuda and R. Natan 16-17 (4). The other sages appear three or fewer times. R. Akiva and his disciples also occupy a central position in the second Akivan school; see details in Kahana, *Sifrei Zuta*, 60-64.

[134] See also the relatively numerous expositions by the sons of R. Yehuda and R. Shimon: R. Yose ben R. Yehuda in Sifra 12 (21), and in SifDeut 13 (6); R. Elazar ben R. Shimon in Sifra 17 (15). These two sages are also frequently cited in the Tosefta (R. Yose ben R. Yehuda 14 [112], R. Elazar ben R. Shimon 18 [69]), but they are not included in the list of the first 20 sages of the Mishna.

[135] Mishna: R. Yehuda 1 (678!), R. Meir 2 (369), R. Shimon 3 (367), R. Yose 4 (366), R. Akiva 5 (335); Tosefta: R. Yehuda 1 (920!), R. Shimon 2 (568), R. Yose 3 (544), R. Meir 4 (508).

[136] It should be noted that the scholars who concentrated on the unattributed material in the Halakhic Midrashim devoted a lengthy examination to the unattributed dicta of R. Yehuda and R. Shimon (see, e.g., Epstein, *Prolegomena*, 656-661, 705f), but without considering these obvious and impressive data.

[137] MekRY: R. Shimon 10 (22), R. Yehuda 11 (14), R. Meir 13 (12), R. Yose 15 (9); SifNum: R. Shimon 8 (28), R. Yehuda 9 (20), R. Meir 13 (9), while R. Yose is mentioned only twice.

[138] R. Yitshak: MekRY 8 (22), SifNum 16 (8); Isi ben Akiva: SifNum 12 (10), while he does not appear in the halakhic portions of MekRY.

[139] R. Yose: Sifra 4 (58), SifDeut 9 (8); R. Meir: Sifra 6 (56), SifDeut 15 (5).

Shimon in SifZNum,[140] or the eight sages that are mentioned exclusively in this midrash.[141]

Attention should also be paid to the important position occupied by R. Eliezer, both in the Yishmaelian and the Akivan collections;[142] R. Yose ha-Gelili also is quite prominent in all Midrashim.[143] The number of explicit mentions of sages, however, is not always an indicator of the degree to which their teachings are put to use. See, for example, the frequent mention of Rabbi in all Midrashim,[144] with the exception of SifZDeut (and SifDeut), from which he is absent. In his discussion of the issue Lieberman concluded that the redactor of SifZNum possessed the dicta of Rabbi and of R. Natan and incorporated them in his text, but intentionally omitted any mention of their names due to his opposition to the Patriarchate.[145]

Names of sages are also instructive as regards another important realm: the date of material cited in the name of specific sages in the different works. See the following table:[146]

generation of Tannaim	MekRY	SifNum	Sifra	SifDeut	Mishna	Tosefta
1 and before	2	3	6	6	20	13
2	17	7	8	11	12	9
3	37	36	27	29	19	14
4	34	41	48	42	47	49
5	9.5	12.6	10.4	10.2	2	14.7
6	0.5	0.4	0.6	1.8	0.04	0.3
	100%	100%	100%	100%	100%	100%

The table reveals that the amount of material transmitted in the Mishna in the name of first-generation Tannaim (20%) is considerably greater than in the

---

[140] SifZNum 9 (10), in contrast with Sifra 17 (15), SifDeut (0), Mishna (2), Tosefta 17 (69).

[141] Details in Lieberman, *Siphre Zutta*, 81. Similarly, the appearance of the Tanna R. Helbo in SifZDeut; see Kahana, *Sifrei Zuta*, 62f.

[142] MekRY 3 (42), SifNum 5 (35), MekRSbY 5 (18), Sifra 5 (57), SifDeut 3-4 (33), SifZNum 3 (19), SifZDeut (3). Cf his similar standing in the Mishna: 7 (319) and in the Tosefta: 5 (386).

[143] MekRY 9 (22), SifNum 11 (11), MekRSbY 4 (20), Sifra 8 (40), SifDeut 5 (21), SifZNum 10 (9), SifZDeut (1), in contrast with his lower standing in the Mishna and the Tosefta (Mishna 18 [27], Tosefta 24 [40]); and a considerable percentage of his teachings in the Mishna and the Tosefta are actually midrashic.

[144] MekRY 7 (36), SifNum 7 (33), MekRSbY 6 (12), Sifra 7 (50), SifDeut 7 (11), and intriguingly, also in the Tosefta 10 (288), while Rabbi appears much less frequently in the Mishna: 17 (36).

[145] See Lieberman, *Siphre Zutta*, 83-91. Cf also below, the description of SifZNum

[146] The following data refer to all the sages appearing in the Halakhic Midrashim, both in the halakhic and the aggadic material. Individual sages of indeterminate time were not taken into account. My thanks to my pupil S. Toledano who constructed the table (the data for the sixth generation are relatively precise, while the other data were rounded off a bit).

Halakhic Midrashim (Sifra and SifDeut, Akivan: 6%; MekRY and SifNum, Yishmaelian: only 2-3%).[147] On the other hand, the material transmitted in the Mishna in the name of fifth-generation Tannaim is extremely meager (2%) in comparison to the Halakhic Midrashim (10-12%). These data seemingly indicate that the material of Tannaic attribution in the Mishna on the whole is somewhat earlier than in the Halakhic Midrashim.

Also noteworthy is the minimal amount of sixth-generation material in the Mishna, where we find only two dicta from the sons of Rabbi, Rabban Gamaliel and R. Shimon. The material from this generation of Tannaim in the Halakhic Midrashim, however, is greater and in addition to the sons of Rabbi includes R. Hiyya, R. Hoshaia, R. Benaya, R. Simai, R. Abba (= Rav), and others. This datum reinforces the hypothesis also suggested by other data that the Halakhic Midrashim were redacted after the Mishna.[148]

Redaction of the Schools' Material

The redactors of the Halakhic Midrashim did not limit themselves to teachings by sages clearly identified with their own school but frequently cited sages from the other one as well. Generally, they would begin by material from their own school and follow this up, in dialectical fashion, by material from the other school, either mentioning its author or anonymously by way of דבר אחר, 'another interpretation'.[149] Thus, precedence was afforded for the most part to Yishmaelian material in Halakhic Midrashim of this school, to be followed by the teachings from the school of R. Akiva, while the Akivan collections first present the dicta of their own school, and only afterwards the Yishmaelian dicta. The opinions from the other school are usually presented in the terminology of the school to which the redactors belonged,[150] and only in very rare

---

[147] A characteristic reflection of this phenomenon can be found in the standing of Beit Hillel and Beit Shammai. They occupy a central position in the Mishna: Beit Shammai 6 (326), Beit Hillel 8 (317), while their standing in the Halakhic Midrashim is considerably weaker. This is especially pronounced in MekRY and SifNum, each of which contains only 2 or 3 mentions of Beit Hillel or Beit Shammai. Nor do Beit Hillel and Beit Shammai enjoy especially strong standing in the main stream of the school of R. Akiva: Sifra 13-14 (18-19), SifDeut 10-11 (7), and most of the material cited in their name is, in practice, taken from the Mishna. More dicta in the name of Beit Hillel and Beit Shammai appear only in the Sifrei Zuta school: SifZNum 6-7 (12), SifZDeut 3-4 (7), based on traditions that are not known from the Mishna. See Lieberman, *Siphre Zutta*, 82f; Kahana, *Sifrei Zuta*, 60-64, 86.

[148] Also noteworthy is the disparity reflected in the Halakhic Midrashim in the references to sixth-generation Tannaim. See especially the paucity of material in SifNum (0.4%) in comparison with SifDeut (1.8%), a datum that might possibly teach of the slightly earlier redaction of the former; see also below, description of SifNum.

[149] See Hoffmann, 'Einleitung' [1888], 24. Cf the more comprehensive work by Goldberg, 'Leshonot'.

[150] See, e.g., MekRY *Mishpatim* 17 (p308), that attributes to R. Akiva the expression: 'An expression free to be used as a basis for the *gezera shava*,' in accordance with the thinking of R. Yishmael and his school, but in contrast with the view of R. Akiva himself (see above, n88, 107), as

instances in the corresponding terminology of the other school.[151] Furthermore, at times we discern a slanted way of editing, with the redactors presenting the views of sages from the other school in a partial and fragmentary manner in order to tip the scales in favor of their own conception. This tendency was not noted by earlier scholars, and we will offer an example from each of the two schools.

Let us begin with the school of R. Akiva. As was mentioned above, R. Akiva and his school expound verb-infinitive repetition, as also the repetition of the words: איש איש, 'any man', to which R. Yishmael and his school objected on the grounds that 'the Tora speaks in human language.' An explicit disagreement on this point is preserved once in the Halakhic Midrashim: in SifNum (Yishmaelian).[152] There are an additional five times in the Bavli, each of which has a parallel in Akivan collections, Sifra[153] and SifDeut,[154] but without ever mentioning the phrase, 'the Tora speaks in human language'. The omission is especially striking in the three parallels in Sifra that cite the views of the sages opposing the midrashim based on 'redundant' wording, but without giving for a reason that 'the Tora speaks in human language'. In the two additional disagreements in SifDeut, the view opposing the 'redundant' wording midrash is not cited at all. It is likely that the consistent omission from

was already noted by Finkelstein, *Sifra*, vol 1, 176. Additional examples of this could be provided by a comparison of baraitot in the Halakhic Midrashim with the parallels in which the same material is presented in different terminology. See, e.g., Albeck, *Introduction*, 101f. Albeck concluded from this that it was not yet the schools of Tannaim that did employed a fixed terminology but only the redactors (who, in his opinion, were active in a later period). See my own view below n161 and 260.

[151] See, e.g., MekRY Kaspa 5 (p335f), the exposition of the verse, 'You shall not boil a kid in its mother's milk.' To the question, 'Why is [this law] stated in three places,' MekRY first offers the answer of R. Yishmael himself. This is followed, respectively, by the answers of R. Yoshia and R. Yonatan (two outstanding Yishmaelian scholars), Abba Hanin in the name of R. Eliezer (a chain of transmission characteristic of the school of R. Yishmael), and R. Shimon ben Elazar (not clearly identified with either school). MekRY then cites the views of Akivan sages: R. Shimon ben Yohai, R. Akiva himself, and R. Yose ha-Gelili, in the ordinary way. The formulation, however, of R. Akiva's answer, in all the textual versions including an excellent Geniza fragment, employs the terminology of the school of R. Akiva: 'Why is it stated in three places? [Once] to exclude (פרט -ל) wild animals, [once] to exclude (פרט ל-) cattle, and [once] to exclude (פרט ל-) fowl.' The wording פרט ל- appears dozens of times in texts from the school of R. Akiva, but this is its sole appearance in MekRY. Apparently, the teachings by R. Akiva and R. Yose ha-Gelili were incorporated in MekRY in a relatively late phase from Akivan Midrashim in which the view of these Tannaim appears in the identical wording. See MekRSbY p219 (according to MidrGad), and SifDeut 104 (p163; see textual variants). Support for this hypothesis can be found in the exposition introduced by דבר אחר included in MekRY following the dictum of R. Shimon ben Yohai that apparently concluded the original Yishmaelian expositions. For the single occurrence of -פרט ל in SifNum 115 (p125), probably another addition under Akivan influence, see Kahana, *Prolegomena*, 226.

[152] See above, 'The Schools of R. Yismael and of R. Akiva', at n74.

[153] bNid 32b and parallels = Sifra Zavim beg. *parasha* 1 (74d); bZev 108b = Sifra Aharei 10:2 (84a); bKer 11a = Sifra Kedoshim 5:2 (89c).

[154] Cf bKid 17a and parallels with SifDeut 119 (p178); bKet 67b, with SifDeut 116 (p175).

Akivan collections of the argument that 'the Tora speaks in human language' ensued from their redactors' intentional disregard of the principle, possibly because it stands in stark opposition to a central principle of their own.[155]

The tendentiousness in the Yishmaelian collections is seen in the dating of the dedication of the Tabernacle in the wilderness, a matter which involves some detail. The Tora describes the ceremony in two ways. Exod 29 and Lev 8-9 tell of the consecration of *the priests* for service in the Tabernacle during the *seven* days of consecration, with its climax on the *eighth* day. Num 7, in contrast, speaks of the dedication with the sacrifices of the *chieftains* over the course of *twelve* days. Exod 40:17 provides additional information: 'In the first month [Nisan] of the second year [of the exodus], on the first of the month, the Tabernacle was set up.' Several Tannaim connected this with their identification of the people who were unclean and could not offer the Paschal sacrifice at its proper time (Num 9:1-14).

The school of R. Yishmael offered the following reconstruction of events. The seven days of dedication began on 23 Adar. On the eighth day of this count, 1 Nisan, the Tabernacle was erected, and on the same day fire descended from heaven and Nadab and Abihu, the sons of Aaron, died; from that day until 12 Nisan, the chieftains offered their sacrifices.[156] As regards the people who were unclean and therefore unable to celebrate the Passover at the proper time, SifNum 69 (p63) offers the following exposition:

> "But there were some men who were unclean by reason of a corpse, etc." (Num 9:6). Who were these? The bearers of the coffin of Joseph, the opinion of R. Yishmael. R. Akiva says: Mishael and Elzaphan, who became unclean for Nadab and Abihu. R. Yitshak says, אין, צריך, that is not possible:[157] if they were the coffin-bearers of Joseph, they could have become clean; and if Mishael and Elizaphan, they could have become clean. Then who were they? They had become unclean for a *met mitzva* [a corpse of unknown identity, whose burial is incumbent upon all], as it is said, "...And could not offer the Paschal sacrifice at its proper time [literally, on that day]" – they could not offer it on that day, but they could do so on the following day. Consequently, their seventh day was the eve of Passover.

R. Yitshak, one of the outstanding rabbis of the school of R. Yishmael, therefore rejected the identification of R. Akiva and maintained that Mishael and

---

[155] The printed editions of Sifra Kedoshim 10:1 (91a) read: 'R. Yose says, The Tora spoke *as the language of man*, in many languages, and all require explanation.' This statement seemingly contradicts the above, but in actuality the words 'as the language of man' are absent from ms Vat 66 and the other mss and commentaries of the Rishonim *ad loc.*, and are a later addition solely of the printed version. This was already noted by Harris, *How Do We Know*, 276 n20.

[156] See SifNum 44 (p49). Cf Sifra 'Mekhilta de-Miluim' fol. 42d-43c (Yishmaelian), that rejects the alternative possibility that the 'eighth day' is the eighth of Nisan.

[157] That is, 'We cannot or may not interpret thusly.' This special meaning of the phrase אין צריך appears in additional places such as SifDeut 16 (p27). For צריך = יכול (is possible), see Lieberman, *Tosefta Ki-Fshutah*, Zeraim, vol 2, 785 n35.

Elizaphan who had incurred seven day uncleanness by bringing out their dead cousins (Num 19:11) had sufficient time to become clean before Passover. He based his argument on the conception mentioned above, that they had incurred uncleanness on 1 Nisan. A precise reading of the phrase 'on that day' teaches that the uncleanness had been incurred on 8 Nisan, and therefore specifically on 'that day', namely, 14 Nisan, the seventh and last day of their uncleanness, they could not become clean, but they could on the following day, as individuals who cleaned themselves from uncleanness they had incurred for a *met mitzvah*.

A study of the parallels in bSuk 25a-b and bPes 90b (according to the mss) teaches that, according to R. Akiva:

> They were Mishael and Elizaphan, the seventh day of whose [uncleanness] fell on the eve of Passover, as it is said, "and could not offer the Paschal sacrifice on that day" – on that day they could not, but on the next day they could.[158]

Thus it was according to R. Akiva that the seven days of dedication began on *Rosh Hodesh* Nisan (1 Nisan), and the eighth day, on which Mishael and Elizaphan became unclean, was 8 Nisan, in opposition to the reconstruction of these events by the school of R. Yishmael. But not only did the exposition in SifNum (Yishmaelian) not provide the reasoning of R. Akiva's exposition in accordance with his midrash method, it also ended the dispute by citing the opinion of R. Yitshak who rejected R. Akiva's argument on the basis of the contrary conventions of the school of R. Yishmael, even though his own view was founded on the exposition of 'on that day', in agreement with R. Akiva's exposition in the Bavli![159]

In conclusion, the redactors of the Halakhic Midrashim were no neutral editors of the sources they possessed.[160] That they belonged to the schools

---

[158] The citation is from bSuk 25a-b following two Yemenite mss: JTS EMC 270; Oxf 2677 (with my thanks to Menahem Katz for drawing my attention to this). As regards bPes, see the references of Rabinovitz, *Dikdukei Soferim*, 278, letter נ; and the commentary by Hoffmann, *Leviticus*, on Lev 8:1. The version of the printed edition and several mss of the Bavli was emended in accordance with SifNum, under the influence of Rashi, whose comment bears closer study.

[159] A conception similar to that held by R. Akiva, that the seven days of dedication began on Nisan 1, already appears in the Temple Scroll; see Yadin, *Temple Scroll*, vol 1, 93-95. It is not inconceivable that opposition was voiced in the school of R. Yishmael to this simplistic interpretation, not only because of the difficulty ensuing from the different depiction in Num 7, but also in the wake of the rabbinic aversion for the method of the Judean Desert sect, that celebrated Nisan 1 each year; see Yadin, *ib.*, 89-91.

[160] In many of his recent studies, J. Neusner has stressed the redactors' influence in fashioning the extant talmudic material. Beyond engaging in methodical discussions and gathering data regarding several individual compositions, however, Neusner did not significantly advance the study of the practices and tendencies of the redactors of talmudic literature. While correctly maintaining that each book must be examined individually, his skepticism concerning the possibility to learn of historical reality from the literature results, among other reasons, from the scant attention he pays to comparative study of parallels. Such a study requires an in-depth journey into the contents of the ramified and complex talmudic material itself; but Neusner's fear of delving into this realm appar-

themselves can be learned from the common midrash methods employed in their works; from the midrashic terms used, in part intrinsically linked to their midrash method; from the ordering principle giving precedence to sages of their own school; and from tendentious adaptations of midrashim from the other school.[161]

ently also influenced the path taken by his research and his methodological conclusions. It would seem, in contrast with Neusner, that especially a study of the parallels produced by the various redactors will aid us in disclosing the practice and orientation of each individual talmudic composition. It is only in this manner that scholarly Talmud research will progress, both for a better understanding of talmudic literature in detail and in general and for enriching our knowledge of historical reality in the talmudic period. Cf following footnote.

[161] The position that the redactors of the Midrashim were affiliated in one way or another to the schools is held by Hoffmann, Epstein, and others. In opposition, Albeck asserts that the redactors of the Midrashim, who in his opinion were active in a later period, did not themselves belong to either school, nor did they choose to cite the expositions of certain sages and omit the views of their opponents. Even Albeck, however, tends to agree that the redactors of MekRY and SifNum used more sources from the school of R. Yishmael than did the redactors of Sifra and SifDeut. See his *Untersuchungen*, 121-139; *Introduction*, 129-133. Since we do not possess the sources available to the redactors of the Halakhic Midrashim, we have difficulty in assessing the degree of redactional involvement in the adaption of this material. The resolution of this issue is also dependent on the question of the estimated time of the redaction; from this perspective, the position championed by Hoffmann, Epstein, and others seems more plausible. See below n260. In either event, the aggregate of data summarized above teaches that the extant Halakhic Midrashim are to be ascribed to either the school of R. Yishmael or to that of R. Akiva, in contrast with the view set forth by Albeck.

Porton, *Rabbi Ishmael* vol 4, takes forceful issue with the reconstruction of the disagreement between R. Yishmael and R. Akiva by Hoffmann, Epstein, and others. He asserts that an exhaustive study of R. Yishmael's midrashic method does not indicate any consistent difference with R. Akiva (160-211). He further maintains that we cannot reconstruct the original views of R. Yishmael since they have often come down to us in contradictory and uneven traditions. He also rejects the notion that Midrashim such as MekRY and SifNum were redacted by the pupils of R. Yishmael, specifically, claiming instead that the redactors of all Halakhic Midrashim were influenced by the more dominant school of R. Akiva, as were the redactors of the Mishna, the Tosefta, and the Talmuds. These editors cited only those dicta of R. Yishmael's that were of interest to them; and at times they even created artificial disagreements between the two Tannaim. In light of this Porton rules out any possibility of determining which traditions were spoken by R. Yishmael himself, and which were merely attributed to him (218-225). Space does not permit a detailed discussion of Porton's thesis. Generally speaking, his argument is based on erroneous data concerning the baraita of the thirteen rules attributed to R. Yismael and on superficial characterization of disagreements between R. Yishmael and R. Akiva (many of which he did not understand properly). He was unaware of R. Yishmael's methodical preference for deriving the law from fixed interpretive rules, in contrast with R. Akiva who preferred to rely upon ad hoc distinctions deduced from duplications and superfluous letters in the verse discussed (see above discussion). Nor did Porton do justice to R. Yishmael's moderate midrash as compared with R. Akiva's more developed method. Instead, he took pains to refute the popular view, to which Hoffmann and Epstein did not subscribe, that R. Yishmael seeks the simple meaning of the text while R. Akiva engages in homiletical interpretations, and on the basis of this misunderstanding he attempted to upset the entire applecart. Also, Porton's rejection of the accepted division of the Midrashim by the two schools did not follow a considered discussion of the arguments advanced by the scholars who support such a classification. Nonetheless Porton's book contains interesting insights and

CONTENT

A comprehensive discussion of the vast subject material of the Halakhic Midrashim would exceed the purview of the current essay. We have chosen four areas of halakha and thought that are to be regarded solely as examples of such within the Halakhic Midrashim. For further indications see the section 'History of Research and Future Challenges', below.

Early Halakha

By far the greatest part of halakhic material in the Halakhic Midrashim resembles parallel Tannaic material in Mishna, Tosefta, and talmudic baraitot. Moreover, as we noted, the Halakhic Midrashim quote more dicta from later Tannaim than does the Mishna.[162] At the same time, they preserve traces of halakhot that differ from the Pharisaic halakha transmitted in most talmudic sources. Some of these reflect the views of Tannaim that, for whatever reason, have not come down to us in the other collections, while another portion seems to reflect the earlier halakha from the Second Temple period.[163]

As to the reasons for the preservation of early halakhot in the Halakhic Midrashim, the following observations present themselves: (1) the highly developed dialectics of the Halakhic Midrashim that include methodical discussion of alternative interpretations of Scripture and a reasoned acceptance of one interpretation over another, with the rejected interpretation occasionally representing the early halakha; (2) the diversity of sources used by the redactors of the Halakhic Midrashim, some of which have not reached us in an orderly form, such as the form of the 'Mishna' used by the school of R. Yishmael or that used by the Akivan subschool of Sifrei Zuta; (3) the attempt of later redactors to adapt early midrashim they possessed to the accepted halakha of their time; (4) the inferior standing of the Halakhic Midrashim in comparison with the Mishna, which paradoxically led to a more faithful preservation of original versions and traditions. Conversely, the halakhic authority of the Mishna and its orderly interpretation by the Amoraim and later authorities often resulted in the emendation and adaptation of its versions and traditions to the reigning halakha in a later period.

The traditional commentators of the Halakhic Midrashim generally sought to obscure the remnants of non-normative halakha in favor of the more com-

---

original and illuminating perspectives, if accompanied by a careful examination of the sources themselves.

[162] See above, 'Names of the Sages'.

[163] The antiquity of these halakhot does not necessarily indicate the lateness of the normative halakha of the sages. To the contrary, as Sussmann emphasizes ('History of Halakha', 12f, esp 64f), the new finds from the Judean Desert scrolls teach that the Pharisaic halakha is not necessary a later development in relation to the Sadducean halakha. 'We now see that both existed side by side, and struggled with each other from early times.'

mon and well-known halakha brought in the Mishna and the Talmuds.[164] Geiger was the first scholar to systematically reveal the early halakha in the Halakhic Midrashim.[165] Finkelstein discussed the topic in a number of studies attempting to prove that Sifra contains remnants of an early Second Temple Midrash on Leviticus,[166] as also that SifDeut preserves early halakhot following Beit Shammai[167] along with more ancient fragments from the Second Temple period,[168] even from the time of the Prophets (!).[169] These studies represent major scholarly advances by raising the proper questions and proposing fertile insights, although a not inconsiderable portion of their conclusions is not based on close study of the language of the collections nor supported by the evidence from Qumran which became available only recently.

Any solid reconstruction of early halakha and its historical reality as reflected in the Halakhic Midrashim must rely upon evidence of various categories: (1) a better understanding of the midrashic material based on the assumption that it may differ from the later, normative halakha; (2) halakhic evidence preserved in external sources such as the Apocrypha, the Judean Desert scrolls, Philo, and Josephus; (3) the names of early sages or of sages who preserved a relatively large number of early halakhot, such as Beit Shammai or R. Eliezer; (4) early language and terminology preserved in the midrashic material; (5) halakhot that are fundamentally close to the simple meaning of the biblical texts, keeping in mind that these laws were actually observed in the early period; (6) an adequate model of the development of the halakha based on a comprehensive knowledge of the relevant historical periods. Our conclusions should be based on a combination of these categories of evidence.

The Halakhic Midrashim seemingly preserve more remains of early halakhic views that were rejected than of those that were accepted. For example, in interpreting the verse: 'And you shall teach them diligently to your children, and you shall talk of them' (Deut 6:7), SifDeut 34 (p61) discusses the question of which passages are to be recited in the daily recitig of the *Shema* and con-

---

[164] Cf the fundamental assertion by Friedmann in his commentary on MekRY, Mishpatim 4, 80b, concerning the question of whether or not a matter of life and death overrides the Temple service: 'Meir Ish-Shalom said, all the commentators of the Mekhilta raised questions concerning this formula, and proofread it. ...I wonder about the manner in which they proofread books, and because a dictum or subject seems doubtful to us and is opposed to all that we have become accustomed to, shall we go and erase from books? ...This halakha is ancient and rejected ...and we have proofs that such was the old Mishna.' For the matter at hand, and especially the difficulty raised by the superior versions, cf Kahana, *Two Mekhiltot*, 110 n. 11.

[165] See Geiger, *Urschrift*; idem, *Kevutzat maamarim*. It is noteworthy that despite the rudimentary nature of the *Wissenchaft des Judentums* at the time and his personal interest in such studies to justify his Reform worldview, much of what he said there is still relevant.

[166] See the summation in Finkelstein's introduction, *Sifra*, vol 1, 21-71. Cf my critique, below n401.

[167] See his article, 'Hashpaat Beit Shammai'. Cf my criticism, below n515.

[168] See, e.g., his article, 'An Old Baraita in Sifrei on Deuteronomy'.

[169] See esp Finkelstein, *New Light*, 1-34.

cludes: 'These [verses] must be recited, but the Ten Commandments need not be recited.' SifDeut 35 (p63) contains a parallel discussion in its exposition of the verse, 'Bind them as a sign on your hand' (Deut 6:8), as to the question which verses are to be written in the *tefillin*. It concludes: 'These [verses] are to be bound [i.e., written in the *tefillin*], but the Ten Commandments are not to be bound.' The Mishna (Tam 5:1) speaks of the priests' recitating of the Ten Commandments in the Temple together with the reading of the *Shema*, and evidence of their inclusion together outside the Temple, as well, is preserved in the Nash Papyrus. As regards *tefillin*, Yadin published copies from the Qumran caves that included the Ten Commandments.[170] Also noteworthy in this context is the Samaritan practice of writing the Ten Commandments on the doorposts of their houses.[171] The reason given by the Talmuds for ceasing the recitation of the Ten Commandments is 'the insinuation of the *minim*; so that they would not say that these alone [the Ten Commandments] were given to Moses at Sinai.'[172] These *minim* were apparently Christian sects who raised such claims.[173] It follows that the opposition by the midrash in SifDeut to including the Ten Commandments in *Shema* and *tefillin* does reflect an early halakha enjoining just that.[174]

In other instances, an early halakha is reflected in an interpretive supposition that does not seem purely hypothetical. See, for example, the understanding in Sifra that Yom Kippur is meant in Lev 23:32, 'A sabbath of complete rest [*shabbat shabbaton*] shall it [*hu*] be for you, and you shall afflict your souls':

> Whence do we know that eating, drinking, bathing, anointing, the wearing of shoes, and sexual relations are forbidden on Yom Kippur? Scripture teaches, *shabbaton*: cease. Or, we could think that all of these are forbidden on the Sabbath? Scripture teaches, *hu*: all these are prohibited on *hu* [Yom Kippur], and they are not all prohibited on the Sabbath.[175]

---

[170] See Yadin, *Tefillin*; also Habermann, 'Phylacteries' for additional external evidence.

[171] See Gaster, 'Samaritan Phylacteries', 135f; Naveh, 'Inscriptions', 304.

[172] yBer 1:8, 3a. Cf bBer 12a.

[173] See, e.g., Irenaeus, Adv. haer. 4.16.3: '...God, who prepares man for His friendship through the medium of the Decalogue ...God, however, standing in no need of anything from man. And therefore does Scripture say, "These words the Lord spoke to all the assembly of the children of Israel in the mount, and He added no more"' – i.e., ולא הוסיף; cf Deut 5:19, 'The Lord spoke those words to your whole congregation at the mountain ...with a mighty voice, and He added no more (ולא יסף).' For the exchange יסף-הוסיף that is reflected also in the Samaritan Targum, see the summation of the research literature by Kister, 'Contribution', 355f.

[174] See summation of material and additional literature by Urbach, 'Ten Commandments'. However, he adopted a different approach in his interpretation of the exposition in Sifrei and in his general thesis concerning the time of the controversy.

[175] Sifra Emor 14:4 (102a).

As Kasher has noted, the rejection of the view that one is to fast on the Sabbath was directed against conceptions that advocated this.[176] The custom of fasting on the Sabbath is evidenced by depictions of Jewish Sabbath observance by Greek and Roman writers from the first century BCE to the first century CE, such as Suetonius, Trogus, Pompeius, Martialis, Petronius, and other testimonies.[177]

Another category of early halakhot preserved in the Halakhic Midrashim is embedded in positive conclusions that the later redactors sought to obscure or change by adding a new midrashic stratum. See, for example, SifDeut 140 (p193): "'The Feast of Booths" [you shall observe for seven days; Deut 16:13] – להדיוט, for the commoner. Whence do we learn [that there is a commandment] also לגבוה, for the high one? Scripture teaches: "The Feast of Booths *to the Lord*" (Lev 23:34).' As several of the commentators observed, the word גבוה, 'high', here refers to the Lord in the Temple. In fact, Neh 8:16 states: 'They made themselves booths on their roofs, in their courtyards [cf. להדיוט], in the courtyards of the House of God [cf. לגבוה].' The Temple Scroll also contains the express command to build *sukkot* in the Temple courtyards.[178] However, the immediate continuation of the midrash in SifDeut teaches otherwise: 'If so, why does Scripture say, "You shall observe"? – When you erect a booth, I account it for you as if you had made it לגבוה.' לגבוה here does not have the same meaning as above, and it seems the redactors of the midrash added this part of the exposition from another source in order to give contemporary significance to the verse, 'The Feast of Booths you shall observe for seven days' – לגבוה, even without the Temple.[179]

An exposition by R. Yishmael concerning the purity of the priest who burns the red heifer contains an instructive example of the preservation of early midrash:

> "טהור [איש], A pure person [must gather the ashes]" (Num 19:9) – why was this stated? If [the verse] had not stated it, I could deduce this logically. If the sprinkler [of the purification water] is clean, then will not the gatherer [of the heifer's ashes used for preparing the water] be clean? Therefore Scripture teaches, "pure" – from any impurity. And which is this? The *tevul yom* (who bathed but must await sunset to be fully pure).[180]

---

[176] See Kasher, *Tora Shelemah*, vol 14 (Beshala), Miluim, 310-321. Several of his proofs, however, do not withstand the test of historical criticism; see also below.

[177] See the well-founded article by Gilat, 'Fasting' (= *Studies*, 109-122), to which we should add the arguments by Kasher and his proof from Sifra (see previous note).

[178] See Yadin, *Temple Scroll*, vol 2, 179f.

[179] Cf the parallel exposition in Sifra Emor 12:3 (102b), that also indicates the linguistic difference between the verses in Leviticus and Deuteronomy, and explains: 'How so? The חגיגה is for Heaven, and [the commandment of] סוכה for the commoner.' That is, the חגיגה festival-offering is for Heaven, while the commandment of סוכה is for the commoner in Israel.

[180] SifNum 124 (p157).

The first interpretation, '"pure" – from any impurity', seemingly corresponds to the views of the Sadducees, who disagreed with the Pharisaic sages and maintained that the red heifer ceremony was to be performed only by those who not only had bathed but for whom the sun had set and thus were fully clean.[181] Such a 'Sadducee' midrash is explicit in a Qumran fragment that reads pertaining to those participating in the red heifer ceremony: איש טהור מכול טמאת ערב, '...a person cleansed of any evening-impurity [impurity that is removed by the onset of the evening]'.[182] Similarly, the Damascus Covenant lays down: איש טהור, מכול טומאתו אשר יעריב א]ת השמש[, '...a person cleaned of all his impurity by the setting [of the sun]'.[183] Accordingly, SifNum quoted an early exposition that was contrary to the Pharisaic position, and only afterwards did it limit itself to *tevul yom* impurity, in accordance with the Pharisaic view.[184]

In summation, it should be stressed that most of the halakhot in the Halakhic Midrashim are paralleled in the other Tannaic sources. On occasion, they also preserve remnants of an earlier stage of development, though we should not automatically attribute every exceptional view in the Halakhic Midrashim to such an early stage, since it may also reflect a disagreement among the Tannaim themselves. Nor is every alternative interpretation set forth in the Halakhic Midrashim necessarily a surviving remnant of early halakha, since it may be no more than a hypothetical interpretation or one that is implied by the simple meaning of the biblical text but is opposed by the midrash.

Aggada

The differences between the Yishmaelian and the Akivan collections find marked expression in the halakhic material that forms the core of this literature.[185] The differences are considerably narrower, however, in the aggadic passages, which scholarly research has shown to originate in all likelihood in shared early material.[186] Parallel collections frequently contain aggadic expositions of very similar order, content, and style. Notwithstanding this, the differences clearly indicate that they contain two different redactions of early material, not a divergence resulting from copying by different scribes. The two

---

[181] See mPar 3:7; cf 4QMMT 2:13-16.
[182] 4Q277, 1, l. 1-3.
[183] See J.M. Baumgarten, DJD XVIII (1996), 131, 173.
[184] Kister discussed this fine example in his article: 'Studies in 4QMiqsat Ma'ase Ha-Tora', 332-334; see the details there.
[185] See above, 'The Term Halakhic Midrash'.
[186] See Hoffman, *Mechilta*, ix; Albeck, *Untersuchungen*, 154; Epstein, *Prolegomena*, 738f. Finkelstein devoted a number of articles to this issue; see esp. 'Studies in the Tannaitic Midrashim', in which he attempted to demonstrate that the two *Mekhiltot* on Exodus drew upon a common written source for their aggadic sections. The four proofs that he brought to this end, however, do not withstand the test of critical examination; see Kahana, *Two Mekhiltot*, 27f.

midrashic schools often differ in their specific interpretations of expressions and words, they adopt differing approaches to specific biblical passages,[187] and more comprehensive differences of opinion between the two are not unknown.[188]

Despite the high degree of similarity in the aggadic material, most scholars have sought to apply to it the accepted school division.[189] However, although certain data would seem to point in this direction,[190] clear-cut differences in hermeneutical methods, exegetical terms, and names of sages are mostly to be found in the halakhic portions. Accordingly, the common aggadic material of the Halakhic Midrashim was quite probably not produced in the schools of R. Yishmael or of R. Akiva; however, it is plausible that in the process of inserting the material in the collections, the schools' redactors occasionally left their mark, as well.[191]

As to proportion, the aggadic material in MekRY and MekDeut (Yishmaelian) is notably larger than its counterpart in MekRSbY and SifDeut (Akivan). Moreover, the aggada incorporated in these two Yishmaelian collections is frequently superior in style and content to the parallel material in the Akivan ones.[192] On the other hand, the reader is struck by the considered thought invested in the aggadic material by the redactors of SifDeut and especially MekRSbY, who apparently sought to reformulate the secondary material that they received.[193]

---

[187] See, e.g., Goldberg, 'Dual Exegeses', which uncovers the differing approaches of the two Midrashim regarding the conduct of Aaron and his sons following the death of Nadab and Abihu. MekRY and MekRSbY exhibit analogous dissimilarities regarding Moses' entreaties to enter to Land of Israel (see Kahana, *Two Mekhiltot*, 264-274); likewise, the disparate approach of SifNum and SifZNum regarding Moses' response to the initiative taken by the chieftains in the dedication of the Tabernacle (see below, description of SifZNum, n487).

[188] See, e.g., the emphasis on the universal dimension of the Tora in the Yishmaelian aggada, in contrast with the obscuring of this element in its Akivan counterpart (see detailed treatment below, 'Attitude towards Non-Jews').

[189] See the summation of the various opinions in Kahana, *Two Mekhiltot*, 19-23.

[190] See, e.g., the different attitude of the two schools to the 'Mishna', that finds expression also in the aggadic sections. See Kahana, 'Notes', 237-240.

[191] As regards some term or other, or the chance appellation of a sage, following the prevalent practice in one of the schools. See Kahana, *Two Mekhiltot*, 23-24, 337-341; idem, *Sifre Zuta*, 92-96.

[192] For a detailed illustration of these differences, with a comparative study of selected passages in MekDeut and SifDeut, see Kahana, 'New Fragments', 496-507; idem, 'Citations', 24-31; idem, 'Pages', 176-179, and a summary of the findings in my book *Two Mekhiltot*, 377-379. For an exemplification of a similar phenomenon in selected portions of MekRY as compared with MekRSbY, see Kahana, *Two Mekhiltot*, 201f, 376f. Obviously, nothing definite can be established on this point, and there are also examples to the contrary, in which the aggadic material that was appended to the Midrashim of the school of R. Akiva is preserved in a more complete and original fashion; see, e.g., *Two Mekhiltot*, 365.

[193] See the summary of the finds regarding MekRSbY in Kahana, *Two Mekhiltot*, 370-377; see also below, the description of MekRSbY.

The two Halakhic Midrashim on Numbers contain similar aggadic material, but there is no textual evidence from Geniza fragments of SifZNum, which makes any reliable comparison impossible. A preliminary examination of the fragmentary aggadic citations from SifZNum in Yalkut Shimoni and Midrash ha-Gadol indicates a rather large difference vis-à-vis the aggadot of SifNum, and the characteristics marking the relationship between them differ from the common features exhibited by the dual midrashim on Exodus and Deuteronomy. The aggadic material incorporated in SifZNum (Akivan) is often more detailed than its parallels in SifNum (Yishmaelian). These initial findings are not surprising once we realize that SifZNum represents an independent midrashic branch of the school of R. Akiva whose aggadic material possesses unique features as compared with the aggadic material in MekRSbY and Sif-Deut, which represent the other branch of this school.[194]

Finally, it should be noted that this analysis of aggadic material in the Halakhic Midrashim relates to the larger units covering entire Tora portions, not aggadic expositions of isolated verses that are incorporated as an integral part of the halakhic material from both schools.

Polemic against Minim

At times the midrash of the Halakhic Midrashim, which may be taken to represent the views of the Pharisees, attacks some other sect who regarded the Tora as a sacred and authoritative source but interpreted it in their own way or who disagreed with the Tannaim over the divine origin of the Tora. In a few instances, such a controversy is overtly present, but usually it is concealed and its identification requires information from other sources as to the opinions combated.

The recent discoveries of the Judean Desert scrolls and of the Gnostic archives at Nag Hammadi, along with the modern research of Samaritan and early Christian literature, have advanced the study of the polemic against non-Jewish or non-Pharisaic views in Tannaic literature including the Halakhic Midrashim,[195] but this study is still in its infancy. Many rabbinic expositions directed against such sects have not yet been discerned, and even the identity of the various minim has not always been satisfactorily defined.

Several of the admonitions and invectives in the Tora were understood by the Halakhic Midrashim as directed against individuals and sects that professed such nonaccepted views. Two examples:

---

[194] The aggadic material preserved from SifZDeut, as well, fundamentally resembles its parallels in MekDeut and SifDeut, but the extant short fragments from it do not enable us to characterize its singular nature. See Kahana, *Sifrei Zuta*, 92-93.

[195] For a comprehensive study of the references to the sects in rabbinic literature, see Sussmann, 'History of Halakha', 40-60.

"Because he has spurned the word of the Lord" (Num 15:31) – this refers to a Sadducee; "and violated His commandment" – this is the *apikoros* [a certain kind of heretic]. Another explanation: "Because he has spurned the word of the Lord" – this refers to the one who perverts the accepted [Pharisaic] interpretation of the Tora; "and violated His commandment" – this is the one who violates the covenant in the flesh [i.e., who undoes circumcision]. (SifNum 112, p121)

'"Vengeance will I wreak on My foes" (Deut 32:41) – this refers to the Cutheans; "and will recompense those that hate Me" – these are the *minim* [heretics].' (SifDeut 331, p381)

In some instances, the words of the Tora are perceived as refuting heretical views:

"I the Lord am your God" (Exod 20:2) – why was this stated? Because He was revealed at the sea as a mighty warrior who wages war. (...) He was revealed on Mount Sinai as a compassionate elder (...) so as not to give the non-Jewish peoples a pretext to say that these are two entities, rather "I the Lord am your God" – I am in Egypt, I am at the sea, I am at Sinai. (MekRY bahodesh 5, p219)

"But the following, which do bring up the cud or have true hoofs which are cleft through, you may not eat" (Deut 14:7) – R. Akiva said, Was Moses a hunter or an archer? Rather, this is the answer to those who say that the Tora is not from Heaven. (SifDeut 102, p161)

"See, then, that I, I am He" (Deut 32:39) – this is the answer to the one who says that there is no Kingship in Heaven. (...) "There is no God beside Me" – this is the answer to the one who says that there are two powers in Heaven (...) "I deal death and give life" – this is the answer to the one who says that there is kingship in Heaven, but it does not possess the power to kill or give life, nor to maltreat or act beneficently. (MekDeut)[196]

In addition to manifest polemics, the Halakhic Midrashim also contend with the various sects in a veiled or indirect fashion. See, for example, the diverse proofs assembled by the Tannaim to the effect that the phrase ממחרת השבת, 'the day after the sabbath' in Lev 23:15 is to be understood as the day following the *festival*, not the day after 'the Sabbath' in its usual meaning of the seventh day.[197] While this is not stated, the rejected interpretation was championed by the Boethusians, as is stated in the Bavli, as also by the Samaritans and the members of the Judean Desert sect.[198] A similar phenomenon is to be found in the midrash on the phrase in Exod 12:2, 'This month shall mark for you the beginning of the months,' with the meaning of lunar month. The goal of the midrash is to find a foothold in the Tora for the lunar calendar of the Pharisees, in contrast with the solar calendar used, for example, by the members of the

---

[196] MekDeut, following a fragment published in Kahana, 'Pages', 190; cf Marmorstein, *Religions-geschichtliche Studien*, 68; Segal, *Two Powers*, 84-85; Basser, *Midrashic Interpretations*, 240-244.
[197] Sifra emor 12 (100d).
[198] bMen 61a. See Haran, 'Mi-mokhorat ha-shabbat'; Yadin, *Temple Scroll*, vol 1, 116-119.

Judean Desert sect.[199] It is noteworthy that in most of these examples the redactor collected the views of many Tannaim, each teaching in his own way how the Pharisaic opinion is to be read from the Bible. This phenomenon is seen in many points of contention between the Pharisaic sages and their opponents.[200]

A frequent motif in the Halakhic Midrashim emphasizes that, despite Israel's sins and their exile from their land, they still remain God's children.[201] Thus for example: "'[So that they do not defile the camp] of those in whose midst I dwell" (Num 5:3) – so beloved is Israel that even though they may be unclean, the Divine Presence rests among them.'"[202] We could reasonably hear in this and similar midrashim an echo of the controversy with Christians who claimed that the God had abandoned Israel. Indeed the Bavli cites an express disagreement between a *min*, apparently a Christian, and a Palestinian Amora:

> A certain *min* said to R. Hanina: Now you are surely unclean, for it is written: "Her uncleanness clings to her skirts" (Lam 1:9).[203] He replied: Come and see what is written concerning them: "Which abides with them in the midst of their uncleanness" (Lev 16:16) - even at the time when they are unclean, the Divine Presence dwells among them.[204]

Along with such expositions whose patent polemical orientation was already noted by Rishonim and traditional midrash commentators, there are also midrashim whose polemical bent is revealed only in light of the discovery of opposing views in Qumran literature. A single expanded example will suffice to illustrate the phenomenon. The question at issue is what offerings require a libation to accompany it. We read in SifNum 107 (p106f):

---

[199] MekRY bo 2 (p6). See Talmon, 'Calendar Reckoning'. Cf Sussmann, 'History of Halakha', 30-31. At times knowledge of this calendar enables us to correctly understand expositions that the commentators had difficulty in explaining. See, e.g., MekRY Bo 2 (p8; following the version of YalShim, Midrash Hakhamim, and apparently also the Geniza fragment T-S C4.6): "'The beginning of the months" – do I hear the restriction to two months? Scripture teaches: "of the months of the year".' (The version of the printed edition reads after the first supposition: 'Whence for the other months'; mss Oxf and Munich retain only the question מנין, 'whence'). The formal supposition of the midrash, deducing from the plural language of חודשים, 'months', that Nisan is the beginning of only two months, is preposterous. But perhaps the intent is to exclude the calendar of the sect, since in the calendar of the latter, the first day of Nisan marked the beginning of a three-month period (Nisan + two other months), to be followed by a leap day that inaugurated a second three-month season.

[200] See, e.g., the lengthy list in MekRY Ki tisa (p340) and parallels, of Tannaim who brought proofs that a matter of life and death overrides the Sabbath. Cf Herr, 'Problem of War'.

[201] Cf Urbach, *Sages*, 525-541.

[202] SifNum 1 (p4).

[203] See the entire context in Lamentations: 'Jerusalem has greatly sinned, therefore she is become a mockery. ...Her uncleanness clings to her skirts, she gave no thought to her future; she has sunk appallingly; she has no comforter [= Messiah?]'.

[204] bYom 56b-57a. See Levertoff, *Midrash Sifre*, 1 n3, who referred to this parallel in the Bavli, but himself continued the Jewish-Christian polemic by identifying 'Israel' in this midrash with 'the Church' (!).

"And will make an offering by fire" [Num 15:3] – do I infer that whatever is offered as an offering by fire requires a libation? Scripture teaches, [only] "a burnt-offering" (...)

Now I know only that this is the case for a burnt-offering. How do we know that it includes peace-offerings? Scripture teaches, "a sacrifice".

Is the implication that one brings [a libation] with these, and, similarly, with a sin-offering or a guilt-offering? Scripture teaches: "...in fulfilment of a vow explicitly uttered or as a freewill offering". I have encompassed [within the requirement of libations] only sacred things that are brought on account of a vow or a freewill offering. (...)

Is the implication that one brings [a libation] with an obligatory burnt-offering brought on the Festivals, and that one brings [a libation] with an obligatory sin-offering brought on the Festivals? Scripture teaches: "And if it is an animal from the herd (*ben bakar*) that you offer to the Lord as a burnt-offering or as a sacrifice..." (Num 15:8) – "*ben bakar*" was included in the general rule, but was singled out from the general rule to teach about the general rule [itself]. Just as an animal from the herd is brought on account of a vow or a freewill offering and requires libations, so, too, everything that is brought on account of a vow or a freewill offering requires libations. Thus a sin-offering and a guilt-offering are excluded, for they are not brought on account of a vow or a freewill offering, and therefore do not require libations.

The forced exposition of *ben bakar* that was included in the general rule but singled out from the generalization returns in the same section, SifNum 107 (p109), in the exposition of Num 15:8 itself. Intriguingly, the exposition appears a third time, in similar format and with similar content, in SifNum 34 (p39) regarding the libation of the Nazirite sacrifice:

"And its libations" (Num 6:17) – these are for the burnt-offering and the peace-offering. Are they also for the sin-offering and the guilt-offering? Logic would dictate that since a *metsora* [person suffering from a skin affliction or 'leper'] shaves off his hair and brings an offering, and a Nazirite shaves off his hair and brings an offering, if I deduce that the sin-offering and the guilt-offerings of the *metsora* require libations, so, too, should the sin-offering and guilt-offering of the Nazirite require libations. Scripture teaches: "He shall offer the ram as a sacrifice of well-being to the Lord, together with the basket of unleavened cakes" (*ib.*) – "the ram" was included in the general rule, but was singled out from the generalization to teach about the general rule [itself]. What distinguishes the ram is that it is brought on account of a vow or a thanksgiving offering, and requires libations; so, too, whatever is brought on account of a vow or a thanksgiving offering requires libations. Excluded are the sin-offering and the guilt-offering, that are not brought on account of a vow or a thanksgiving offering, and [therefore] do not require libations.

A number of other midrashic passages teach us that the school of R. Akiva deduced that the sin-offering and the guilt-offering do not require libations.[205] Such, indeed, is the ruling of mMen 9:6: 'All the offerings of an individual or of the congregation require libations, except for (...) a sin-offering and a guilt-offering; but the sin-offering and the guilt-offering of the *metsora* require libations.' This law, however, is not specified in the section of the libations in Num 15 nor in any other place in the Tora. To the contrary, just as the law of the *metsora* in Lev 14 expressly states that his sin-offering and guilt-offering require libations, so the simple meaning of Num 6:14-17 would imply that the sin-offering of the Nazirite requires libations, as do the burnt-offering and the peace-offerings mentioned in proximity to this law. The law seems indicated also by other verses such as Num 28:15, 'And there shall be one goat as a sin-offering to the Lord, to be offered in addition to the regular burnt-offering and its libation.'[206]

In contrast to the above Pharisaic view, however, the Temple Scroll consistently teaches that libations are to be brought with the sin-offering as well.[207] We logically conclude that the diverse homiletical reasons given by midrashic literature to justify the Pharisaic approach merely echo the polemic against the Dead Sea sectarians.[208]

Along with our disclosure of the polemic in the Halakhic Midrashim against the diverse sects, it should be recalled that many conceptual emphases followed from *internal* developments and do not relate to external polemics.[209] In general, the dividing line between the different sects was not always so clear, and several Tannaim did not fear to adopt opinions in halakha and thought close to other sects. See, for example, characterization of the Boethusian approach in the scholion of Megillat Taanit:

> The Boethusians would say: "Eye for eye, tooth for tooth" (Exod 21:24) – if a
> person knocked out his fellow's tooth, his own tooth shall be knocked out; if he

---

[205] SifZNum p245: '"With their meal-offerings and their libations" – why did I exclude the sin-offering, for it is brought only for atonement?' See also the exclusion of the sin-offering and the guilt-offering in SifZNum p281; in another baraita from the school of R. Akiva in bMen 90b; and via the possible use of *kelal u-ferat u-khelal* in bMen 91a. Another explanation for the exclusion is given by ySot 2:1, 17d: 'R. Shimon ben Yohai taught: Why did they say that all the sin-offerings and guilt-offerings in the Tora do not require libations? So that the offering of a sinner would not appear to be adorned.'

[206] Cf the emphasis placed by Rashi in his commentary on the verse: '"Its libation" does not refer to the goat, for there are no libations for a sin-offering'. See also Num 29:11.

[207] See Yadin, *Temple Scroll*, vol 1, 143-146; cf also Jub 7:3-5.

[208] Yadin already discussed the controversy itself. Unlike what Yadin states, however, the proof for the Pharisaic polemic consists of the intensive and multifaceted occupation with this topic in the Tannaic sources mentioned above (the majority of which went unnoticed by Yadin), and is not to be inferred from 'the lengthy discussion in bMen 90b-91b', as Yadin puts it, which was merely a scholastic Amoraic discussion, that apparently was no longer aware of the realistic dimension of the polemic in the past.

[209] See, e.g., the emphasis of this point by Urbach, *Sages*, 527.

blinded his fellow, he shall be blinded, and both shall be equal [in their disability]. "And they shall spread out the garment before the elders of the town" (Deut 22:17) – a whole garment.[210]

Talmudic sources teach that the Tanna R. Eliezer, among the disciples of Beit Shammai, similarly interpreted the verses.[211] Likewise, in the realm of aggada and theology, see the series of midrashim by R. Pappias that are close to the views held by the Gnostics.[212]

Attitude toward Non-Jews

Along with the attitude of the Halakhic Midrashim toward the *minim* or non-Pharisaic Jews, we should also pay attention to their attitude to non-Jews as individuals and as peoples. In a very large number of expositions, the Tannaim are excessive both in praising the singular traits of Israel and its merits and in disparaging non-Jews and their halakhic inferiority. Notwithstanding this, in a few instances the Halakhic Midrashim also contain expositions that exhibit a positive attitude to non-Israelites. See, for example, the exposition of Deut 33:3 that appears three times in SifDeut 344 (p400f): "'Lover, indeed, of the people" (Deut 33:3) – this teaches that the Holy One, blessed be He, loves Israel, which is not the case for every nation and kingdom,' and similar expositions in the parallel in MekDeut. In addition to these ethnocentric sentiments, however, MekDeut surprisingly contains the following midrash: "'Lover, indeed, of the people" – this teaches that the love with which the Holy One, blessed be He, loved Israel, was similarly directed by Him toward the non-Jewish peoples.'[213] MekDeut concurrently presents several additional midrashim of universal bent that emphasize the initial desire of the Holy One 'to bequeath the world to the [non-Jewish] nations' and to give the Tora to all peoples of the world and not specifically to Israel. The parallel expositions in SifDeut, in contrast, make a consistent effort to blur the universal message of the expositions that stress the standing of God as the Creator of all the world's denizens; instead, they accentuate the initial choice of the Holy One, blessed be He, of Israel alone.[214]

---

[210] Megillat Taanit, in its interpretation of the date Tammuz 4. The quotation follows ms א, ed Noam, *Megillat Ta'anit*, 78.

[211] See bBK 84a: 'It was taught: R. Eliezer said: "Eye for eye" is to be understood literally'; SifDeut 238 (p270), "'And they shall spread out the garment" – ...R. Eliezer says, The matter is as it is written' (thus ms Vat 32, and other textual witnesses; the version 'R. Eliezer *ben Jaakov*' that Finkelstein included in his edition is an emendation inspired by the parallel in bKet 46a). For an extensive discussion of the characterization of the Boethusians by Megillat Taanit and the parallels, see Rosenthal, 'The Oral Law', 448-455; Noam, *Megillat Ta'anit*, 206-216.

[212] MekRY Masekhta deshirata 6 (p112f); MekRSbY p68. See Kahana, 'Critical Editions', 499-515.

[213] For a detailed discussion of this exposition, see Kahana, 'Pages', 180-185.

[214] For their details, see Kahana, 'Pages', 200f. For the halakhic and theological background reflected in this polemic, cf my article, 'Relation'.

A similar emphasis on the Tora's initial belonging to all humankind is found in additional Yishmaelian Midrashim, SifNum and MekRY. This was shown by Hirshman in a detailed and persuasive study of these works and their attitude to non-Jews and their wisdom,[215] indicating also the relative obscuring in MekRSbY of the universalism of MekRY.[216] Further study must be devoted to the question whether the universalist orientation of R. Yishmael's school is also reflected in its halakhic rulings,[217] along with a comparison of the attitude toward non-Jews in the Halakhic Midrashim with that of talmudic literature as a whole.[218]

RELATION TO OTHER WORKS

Aramaic Targums and Other Translations

The Aramaic Targums on the Tora that were meant to be recited in public[219] incorporate a considerable amount of midrashic material corresponding to the

---

[215] See Hirshman, *Tora*; see also idem, 'Rabbinic Universalism', 101-115.

[216] See, e.g., the comparison he conducted (Hirshman, *Tora*, 38-42), between the developed preface to the Sinai revelation in MekRY p204-206 and its parallel in MekRSbY p137. For the general theme of the exposition in MekRY, see *ib.* p97. It would seem that we could indicate additional topics in which the exposition in MekRSbY obscured the ideas of MekRY. See, e.g., the two added interpretations that appear only in MekRSbY, one praising Israel: 'I teach that they worshiped Me out of love'; and the other that is disparaging of the non-Jewish peoples: 'I gave them seven commandments, and they could not uphold them.' (Cf the exposition of MidrGad *ad loc.*: 'They came to the wilderness of Sinai, where enmity descended for the entire world, for their non-observance of the Tora'. Melamed, in the n. MekRSbY p136, mentions that this explanation originated in bShab 89a, but the wording in bis not totally congruent with the exposition in Midr-Gad, and it is not inconceivable that this exposition, with its extreme anti-Gentile sentiment, has its origin in MekRSbY). Conversely, the two expositions in MekRY on the verse 'I answered you from the secret place of thunder' (Ps 81:8), that is not understood in its simple meaning but as the converse reality of 'thundering at the whole world for your sake', do not appear in MekRSbY. The latter likewise omits the exposition on Balaam's positive response to the giving of the Tora to Israel, and even the expansion of the motif of Israel's unique response is greatly limited in Mek-RSbY. (The expositions of R. Yose ben Dormaskit and R. Yehuda ben Lakish in MekRSbY, 136/20-137/5, are lacking in context. This seemingly demonstrates the secondary nature of Mek-RSbY, and its dependence upon the shared material that is preserved in MekRY. It should be recalled, however, that the reconstruction of ed Melamed *ad loc.* is not based on a direct manuscript version, but only on an abridged collection of MekRSbY. See the description of Codex 9 in Kahana, *Manuscripts*, 57.)

[217] Based on an analysis of the strict halakhot concerning idolatry in the Yishmaelian 'Mekhilta de-arayot', Hirshman (*Tora*, 60) concluded that specifically because of the openness of the Tora to all, according to this school, those Gentiles who stubbornly continue to engage in idolatry are doomed to perdition. This issue, however, should be re-examined on the basis of a more comprehensive comparison of the attitude to individual idolaters or Gentiles and non-Jewish nations reflected in the Yishmaelian Midrashim with the Akivan ones. An examination of the relationship between the halakhic and aggadic materials also requires further study. See the reservation in my article, 'Pages', 185; I intend to discuss this at length elsewhere.

[218] See, e.g., Porton, *Goyim*; Feldman, *Jew and Gentile*.

[219] For a summation, see Fraade, 'Targum'.

teachings included in the Halakhic Midrashim.[220] Sometimes the Targums help in clarifying a midrash as to its literal meaning[221] or certain cryptic allusions. An example of the latter is found in the puzzling midrash in MekRY (p148) on Exod 15:16, "'Till Your people cross over, O Lord" – until they cross the sea, until they cross the Jordan, until they cross the brooks of Arnon.' A similar interpretation involving the brooks of Arnon appears in all Aramaic Targums on the verse. Likewise, Deut 3:24, 'Who can do such works and mighty acts as Yours?' is expounded in MekRY (p182) and parallels: "'Such works" – at the sea; "and mighty acts" – at the brooks of Arnon.' The miracles at the Reed Sea and the Jordan River are mentioned in the Tora and are common knowledge, but the one at the Arnon is not. It is found, however, in an extensive tradition in Targums Neofiti, Pseudo-Yonatan, and others on Num 21:14, 'and the brooks: the Arnon' – to the effect that the mountains on both sides of the Arnon drew near to each other and crushed the enemies of Israel who were hiding in these mountains.[222]

In other places the Targums aid in uncovering problems that also troubled the Halakhic Midrashim. A fine example is presented by the consistent deviation from the simple meaning by the various Targums on Num 10:31, involving Moses' request to Jethro: 'Please do not leave us, inasmuch as you know where we should camp in the wilderness and can be our guide (לעיניים והיית לנו, lit., be eyes for us].' Unlike the literal translation of the Peshitta ('be eyes for us') and the simple rendition in the Vulgate ('that you may be a *ductor*, guide, for us'), other translations offer nonliteral interpretations:

LXX: καὶ ἔσῃ ἐν ἡμῖν πρεσβύτης, "And you shall be an elder among us."

Onkelos: "And the mighty deeds that were done for us you have seen with your eyes."

Ps-Yonatan: "And you taught us legal procedure, and you are as dear to us as the pupil of the eye."

Neofiti: "Since you know the miracles that the Lord has performed for us in every place we have encamped or while traveling in the wilderness, you shall be testimony for us."

---

[220] Many examples of this were listed in Geiger, *Urschrift*, although his perception of Ps-Yon as an early Targum should be emended (see below). For the mention of תרגום in halakhic midrash, see Fraade, 'Scripture'.

[221] E.g., the exposition of Num 18:8, 'I grant them to you למשחה', in SifNum 117 (p135): 'משחה [lit., anointing] means only greatness'. This reflects one of the meanings of משח or Aramaic רבי. Onkelos, Neofiti, and Ps-Yon render למשחה as לרבו. See also Rosenthal, 'Givat ha-Mivtar,' 346.

[222] See also the Geniza fragment of MekRY p182 that replaces ארנון with ארנונה, similar to the wording of the Targums *ad loc.* and in other places, and in the *Onomasticon* of Eusebius; see Kahana, *Two Mekhiltot*, 86.

Most of the interpretations put forth by the Targums and other translations also appear in SifNum 80 (p76f), and some also contain an attempt to base the homiletical interpretation on the words of the verse:

> "Inasmuch as you know where we should camp" – he said to him, If someone else who had not seen the miracles and wonders in the wilderness were to leave [us] and go his own way, this would not be unseemly. But you, who has seen, should you leave and go your own way? "Please do not leave us" [cf. Onkelos, Neofiti].

> R. Yehuda says, You, who have seen the grace that was given to our fathers in Egypt (...), you shall leave and go your own way? "Please do not leave us."

> Another interpretation: "...And can be our guide" – is it not enough for you that you should sit with them [Israel] in the Sanhedrin and be our guide in the teachings of the Tora? [Cf. LXX and Ps-Yonatan]

> Another interpretation: "...And can be our guide" – is it not enough for us that on every matter that is hidden from our eyes, you shall illuminate our eyes for us?

> Another interpretation: You shall be as beloved to us as the orb of the eye [cf. Ps-Yonatan].

The deviation from the simple meaning of the text – namely, that Moses asked Jethro to aid them by his familiarity with the ways of the wilderness and be their guide – in the Targums and SifNum (and apparently also SifZNum p265) is most likely founded in the problem why Moses needed Jethro's services to start with, since the pillar of cloud showed them the way.[223] The problem is aggravated by the nearby detailed depiction of the activity of the cloud and the journeying and encampment in the wilderness by the sign of the Lord (Num 9:15-23). It could seem that Moses suffered from a lack of faith at this juncture,[224] which the exegetes and targumists then would have sought to conceal, or, they would go look for the 'real' reason of the biblical expression, assuming the Bible couldn't mean such things.

Each Aramaic Targum must be examined separately for the question of which came first, the Halakhic Midrashim or the Targum. Early material informing the language of the midrashim in the Halakhic collections is sometimes found embedded in Neofiti, the Fragmentary Targum, and Onkelos.[225] On the other hand, Neofiti and the Fragmentary Targum occasionally contain homiletical expansions that would seem to originate in the Halakhic Midra-

---

[223] This was already indicated by Geiger, *Urschrift*, 224.

[224] The request by Moses is not immediately followed by Jethro's reply, rather, v33 relates that in addition to the cloud, 'the Ark of the Covenant of the Lord traveled in front of them to seek out a resting place for them'; see there.

[225] Such as the language of MekRY and MekRSbY: 'Moses' hands שוברות Amalek', that is derived from the language of the Targum: 'מתגברין prevail the house of Amalek', that was changed to the euphemistic 'מתברין was broken the house of Amalek'; see Kahana, *Two Mekhiltot*, 255-257.

shim.[226] Although Pseudo-Yonatan is closely and consistently linked to the Halakhic Midrashim, it would appear that its author did not possess early midrash material[227] but rather used several of the currently extant Halakhic Midrashim[228] in order to supplement the material of Neofiti and the Fragmentary Targum that we know was available to him. Proofs of his use of the Halakhic Midrashim can be brought from corruptions that are best explained as errors made by its redactor when rendering these documents.[229] We would be hard-pressed to find strong connections with the Halakhic Midrashim and other ancient Bible translations such as the Septuagint, the Peshitta, and the Vulgate. The primary relevance of these documents for the study of the Tannaic midrashim lies in the non-Massoretic biblical versions they represent and which occasionally confirm the biblical text underlying the Halakhic Midrashim.[230]

Mishna and Tosefta

In the Halakhic Midrashim, the order of halakhot follows the biblical text, and these documents are primarily concerned with demonstrating the close connection between the Tannaic halakha and the Bible. In addition, we saw the Halakhic Midrashim also expound many aggadic passages. The Mishna, in contrast, orders the Tannaic halakha by subject, with the linkage to the Bible generally not presented. Moreover, the aggadic material in the Mishna is very limited in comparison to the Halakhic Midrashim. Notwithstanding these differences, there clearly is a mutual relationship between the Halakhic Midrashim and mishnaic literature. Along with exposition, the Halakhic Midrashim contain a considerable number of quoted mishnayot and baraitot,[231] frequently

---

[226] See, e.g., Neofiti on Num 12:1, and many similar examples.

[227] As the view maintained by Geiger and other scholars.

[228] The use of MekRY by Ps-Yon is certain (see the summation of the literature in Shinan, *Embroidered Targum*, 173-176), and it frequently draws upon SifNum, as well. Ps-Yon uses SifDeut in orderly fashion only in the former's rendition of Deut 1. For its likely use in several expositions of MekDeut, see Henshke, 'Relationship', 206-209. Its application in the other Midrashim requires further study.

[229] See Maori, 'Aramaic Targums', 9-12; Kahana, *Two Mekhiltot*, 361f; Henshke, 'Pseudo-Jonatan', 187-199.

[230] See above, 'Authority of the Bible'. A systematic discussion of the relationship between the Peshitta and the Midrashim was conducted by Maori, *Peshitta*, who properly established and developed methodological criteria for distinguishing between the various factors that caused the Peshitta to deviate from the MT. These standards enabled him to isolate the interpretive-midrashic elements that apparently came under the influence of the Jewish interpretive tradition (see 15-20). The book's main drawback, however, lies in the author's almost total disregard of the chronological dimension. The composition of the Peshitta is dated to the second or third centuries, and care should be taken in the uncovering of its Jewish sources in sources that are preserved in works redacted only in and after the Amoraic period, that are central to Maori's book.

[231] See the collection and characterization of this material in Epstein, *Mavo*, 728-751; Melamed, *Relationship*, 9-181.

cited with set introductory formulae such as מיכן אמרו, 'Hence they said'; מיכן אתה אומר, 'Hence where do you say'; אמרו, 'They said', and the like. In other instances the material is brought without such an introduction.[232] We also find midrashic reasoning for a halakha incorporated in the Mishna,[233] as well as short homiletic units characteristic of the Akivan school of midrash.[234] It also happens that the 'abstract' halakhic formulation of the Mishna is an adaptation of early midrashic material.[235]

An examination of the mishnayot and baraitot in the Halakhic Midrashim teaches of an important distinction between MekRSbY, Sifra, and SifDeut, from the central school of R. Akiva, and the Yishmaelian collections. The Akivan works make frequent use of the extant Mishna, often seek to link it with the verses and their interpretation, and generally cite it verbatim.[236] In MekRY and SifNum (Yishmaelian), on the other hand, מיכן אמרו, 'Hence they said', is not so common, and when the Mishna is cited, this is not done in its actual language but rather by way of paraphrase and abbreviation. Nor do these works contain many quotations of baraitot and of Tosefta passages introduced with 'Hence they said'.[237]

---

[232] For an analysis of the process by which quotations from the Mishnaic literature were incorporated in the Halakhic Midrashim, see Epstein, *Mavo*, 747-751. Cf the critical notes in Kahana, 'Marginal Annotations', 69-74. See also Halivni, *Midrash*, 59-63; this issue requires further study.

[233] See the detailed listing of this material: Melamed, *Relationship*, 182-189. For a characterization of the homiletical method of the midrashim in the Mishna as compared with the early midrash in the *Temple Scroll*, see also Goldberg, 'Early and Late'.

[234] See, e.g., the two midrashic expansions in mShab 9 and mSot 5, that revolve around the expositions of R. Akiva himself; or the exposition of a verb-infinitive duplication in mBM 2:9. The midrashic terminology in the Mishna, as well, is usually close to the school of R. Akiva. See, e.g., the seven occurrences of יכול, 'possibly' (as compared with a single instance of שומע אני, 'I hear'); מלמד, 'this teaches', 6 cases; מגיד, 'this teaches', 0; פרט ל-, 'except for', 3, להוציא, 'excluding', 0. For the methodology of R. Yehuda ha-Nasi himself, who generally adopts R. Akiva's method, see De Vries, 'Rabbi's Methodology in the Halakhic Midrashim', in *Studies*, 130-141.

[235] See the examples in Kahana, 'Searching Examination', 118-122; SifZDeut, p88, 242-244, 370f.

[236] See Epstein, *Mavo*, 728-733 (for a rejection of the opposite possibility, that the Mishna quotes Sifra, see below, section on Sifra).

[237] Epstein, *Mavo*, 733; cf the more extreme formulation in idem, *Prolegomena*, 468: 'Sifrei on Numbers, that is not Akivan, but Yishmaelian, does not make use of our Mishna, from the teaching of Rabbi'. Melamed, in contrast, somewhat moderates the sharp distinction between the two schools; see his summation in *Relationship*, 181: 'We have clearly shown that the redactors of the Yishmaelian Midrashim, as well, were frequently occupied with our Mishna and our Tosefta. ...They also walk in the set paths and lanes of their fellows from the school of R. Akiva'. Some of Melamed's proofs are based on very short sentences, the origin of which cannot be determined. In other instances, Melamed ignored certain textual changes between the Mishna and the quotations in Yishmaelian Midrashim, or did not give sufficient consideration to the good mss of MekRY and SifNum, that often preserved versions different from our Mishna that were 'corrected' and adapted in most texts (see, e.g., Kahana, *Prolegomena*, 184-191). It nonetheless seems that the Yishmaelian Midrashim do, in fact, cite our Mishna on occasion, along with other sources that they cite (probably including the 'Mishna of R. Yishmael'). The Akivan Midrashim, for the most part, frequently cite the extant Mishna.

The difference resounds through the versions headed by ms Vatican 32 that include SifNum and SifDeut. The abbreviation, וכולה מתניתין..., '...etc. from the Mishna', is quite prevalent in SifDeut in which the Mishna is frequently cited verbatim, but totally absent from SifNum where it is generally not cited in its original language.[238] The disparity between the Yishmaelian collections and the Mishna is also pronounced in the case of sages identified with this school who are not mentioned in the Mishna.[239] To these indicators we should perhaps add the captivating find that the term *mishna* itself appears only in the Akivan Midrashim and is totally absent from the Yishmaelian ones.[240]

It would therefore appear that the Akivan redactors of MekRSbY, Sifra, and SifDeut related to the extant Mishna, also formulated in the Akivan school as an authoritative source, while the Yishmaelian editors of MekRY and Sif-Num did not recognize the supreme authority of our Mishna. An exception is the Sifrei Zuta branch that belongs to the school of R. Akiva but is notedly singular in a number of realms; a decisive majority of the mishnayot it cites are considerably different from our Mishna.[241] Lieberman has suggested that this reflects the opposition by its redactors to Rabbi's court and teachings.[242]

The Tosefta was redacted following the Mishna and is based in great measure on halakhic sources from the school of R. Akiva. It contains a bit more midrashic material on halakhic and aggadic topics than the Mishna,[243] a portion of which was even taken from Yishmaelian midrash sources.[244] In contrast with the Mishna, it also occasionally mentions prominent Yishmaelian sages.[245] Additional study of the individual Halakhic Midrashim is required to determine whether their redactors had knowledge of the extant Tosefta[246] or whether they made use of other collections that included similar baraitot.

---

[238] Epstein, *Mavo*, 732, 737, 746, and Melamed, *Relationship*, 86-87, viewed this abridgment as being the work of copyists. This abbreviation, however, should more plausibly be attributed to the later redactors. See Kahana, 'Notes', 239 n28.

[239] See above, 'Names of Sages'; also, above n110 re. 'R. Shimon' vs. 'R. Shimon ben Yohai'.

[240] See detailed description of material in Kahana, 'Notes', 237-240.

[241] For the *mishnayot* of SifZNum, see Epstein, *Prolegomena*, 745; Lieberman, *Siphre Zutta*, 11-64. For the mishnayot of SifZDeut, see Kahana, *Sifrei Zuta*, 85-88.

[242] See Lieberman, *Siphre Zutta*, 83-91.

[243] Melamed, *Relationship*, 189 observes that the Tosefta contains some 190 midrashic baraitot, as compared with the approximately 90 in the Mishna. It should be noted, however, that the Tosefta is larger than the Mishna.

[244] Such as two large fragments in tShevu; see Epstein, 'Remnants from the School of Rabbi Yishmael on the Book of Leviticus', in *Studies*, vol 2, 108-124.

[245] E.g.: R. Natan (63 times); R. Yoshia (3 times); R. Yitshak (3 times); R. Yonatan (1 time).

[246] The conclusion of Melamed, *Relationship*, 181.

The Talmuds

Thousands of quotations in Bavli[247] and Yerushalmi[248] teach us that the Amoraim drew upon collections of halakhic midrash on the Tora. Most of the citations in the Bavli are from the school of R. Akiva,[249] but there are also a large number of passages from R. Yishmael's school and other sources. About 40 percent of the quotations in the Talmud are of material that is not found in the extant Halakhic Midrashim,[250] and some of it was unquestionably taken from other Yishmaelian and Akivan collections and additional extinct sources.

The remaining 60 percent of citations common to the Talmuds and the Halakhic Midrashim apparently indicate that the Amoraim possessed collections akin to the extant collections. The mutual parallels are not completely congruent: the dissimilarity between the Halakhic Midrashim and the Yerushalmi is smaller than that between the Midrashim and the Bavli. Exceptional in this respect is Sifra, very many midrashim of which are cited by the Bavli in their original language,[251] as well as MekRSbY, with a considerable number of its expositions cited by the Bavli.[252] Some of these incongruencies ensue from differing traditions and transmissions of the material, while in other instances interpretive glosses and additions, along with numerous abridgements and adaptations, were attached to the talmudic baraitot, notably in the Bavli, but also in the Yerushalmi.[253] We may conclude with certainty that the Halakhic Midrashim generally reflect the teachings of the Tannaim in a better and more faithful manner than the parallel materials in the Talmuds.[254]

The Amoraim often appended their explanations and clarifications to the baraitot paralleling the Halakhic Midrashim; needless to say, these ancient comments are of incalculable value for a full understanding of the Tannaic dicta. The midrashim were not always given a literal interpretation by the Amoraim, however, and several of the general perceptions in the Talmuds

---

[247] See their listing, by their order in the Pentateuch, in Melamed, *Halakhic Midrashim in the Babylonian Talmud*. In his introduction, 35f, Melamed reached a total of some 2,270 midrashim.

[248] See listing in Melamed, *Halakhic Midrashim in the Palestinian Talmud*, who reports of approximately 1,130 midrashic baraitot on Exodus-Deuteronomy in the Yerushalmi (the book was published posthumously by the author's children; the introduction is based on his own writing in idem, *Introduction*, 275-294).

[249] See Melamed, *Halakhic Midrashim in the Babylonian Talmud*, 35f.

[250] This calculation is based on Melamed's detailed summation concerning the number of preserved Midrashim, for each of the books of the Tora, in the two Talmuds.

[251] See below, section on Sifra, n397.

[252] See Melamed, *Halakhic Midrashim in the Babylonian Talmud*, 36; see also below, the description of MekRSbY.

[253] See their characterization and typology in Melamed, *loc. cit.* Many examples of local adaptations of the Halakhic Midrashim in talmudic baraitot are to be found in a long series of specific monographs by different scholars.

[254] This important conclusion opposes the conception of a majority of traditional Halakhic Midrashim commentaries (both Rishonim and Aharonim), who generally preferred the traditions of the Bavli.

concerning the methods of the schools of R. Yishmael, R. Akiva, and other sages are inconsistent with the views of these Tannaim themselves.[255]

Not only did the specific exegetical and halakhic views held by the Amoraim influence their interpretation of midrashic baraitot, but in addition, they differ with the Halakhic Midrashim in their view of the hermeneutical methods. This especially concerns the tendency common to redactors from both schools to base several halakhot on one single biblical expression, while they may also find support for a single halakha in a number of verses. One of the obvious assumptions in the Talmuds, in contrast, involves each biblical expression to contain the foundation of a unique midrash and the same law not to be derived from more than one biblical passages.[256] The full development of the interpretive potential of the verses that followed from this assumption – which the Amoraim ascribed to the Tannaim themselves – led to the shedding of the literal meaning of many Tannaic expositions in the Talmud.[257]

The developed homiletical methodology of the Amoraim along with their strengthened belief in the singular nature of each verse gave rise to another development in their biblical midrash. They took another step forward in extending the Akivan method, increasingly focusing on the details of the verse and basing ever-growing numbers of halakhot and their particulars on Scrip-

---

[255] Cf above n70 for the exposition of the *vav* by R. Akiva; similarly, regarding the accepted principle in the Bavli that R. Akiva expounded ריבוי ומיעוט of the biblical text, that R. Shimon 'interpreted the reason of Scripture', and other principles the Talmuds ascribe to Tannaim, but that are not in Tannaic literature itself.

[256] See the teaching by Abaye in bSan 34a: 'One verse may convey several meanings, *but a single teaching cannot be derived from several different verses.*' A close reading reveals that the immediately following dictum, 'as taught in the school of R. Yishmael', contains no source for the second part of Abaye's statement; and likewise in the parallel bShab 88b. This fundamental difference between the Halakhic Midrashim and the Talmuds was especially developed by Albeck, *Untersuchungen*, 1-21; *Introduction*, 84-93.

[257] Several Amoraim, as well, probably disagreed with this hermeneutical principle. Cf the dictum by R. Yonatan in yBer 2, 4c and parallels: 'Everything that is not elucidated should be supported by several places.' On the other hand, several Tannaim may have already championed a principle that would later be prevalent in the Talmud. The subject needs a thorough investigation of the views of Tannaim and Amoraim who differ from this principle and of the redaction of their teachings in the Halakhic Midrashim, the Aggadic Midrashim, and the Talmuds. This complex subject is hindered by the question of the reliability of the traditions in the diverse sources. For a general example, cf three dicta by Ben Azzai. In MekRY p70 he derives a *gezera shava* from the wording of the law of the firstling: 'You shall set apart (והעברת) for the Lord every first issue of the womb' (Exod 13:12) and of the law of animal tithes: '...All that passes (יעבור) under the shepherd's staff' (Lev 27:32): in both instances sanctity is imparted to the animal only during its mother's lifetime, not after she has died. In MekRSbY p42 he learns another law from the same *gezera shava*, i.e., that sanctity is imparted to an animal with a permanent defect. And in SifDeut (p143), based on a limitation from the word רק, he establishes the distinction that the animal whose mother has died is exempt from animal tithes. The question then is whether these three midrashim may be combined, leading to the conclusion that Ben Azzai learned two laws from the same midrash (the motherless animal and the animal with a defect) while, on the other hand, he derives the same law (the motherless animal) from two different midrashim; or, perhaps, are these alternate traditions?

ture, while at the same time further distancing these from the simple meaning of the verse. This topic, however, deserves a broad scholarly inquiry[258] that exceeds the purview of the current discussion.[259]

TIME AND PLACE OF REDACTION

It seems we should accept the predominant scholarly view that the final redaction of the Halakhic Midrashim was conducted in the Land of Israel, in the first or second generation following the redaction of the Mishna, that is, in the middle of the third century CE. An earlier dating cannot be proposed, because the latest sages mentioned in most Halakhic Midrashim belong to these generations. Nor should a date be assigned at the end of the Amoraic period, somewhere in the fifth century, as some have suggested on the basis of quite weak evidence,[260] and certainly we should reject the dating of several Halakhic Midrashim to the eighth century.[261]

---

[258] Cf the *sugya* in bSan 4a-b that 'the Massora is determinant', that is, there is a basis for the exposition of the deficient biblical spelling, unlike the usual vocalization of the word (an analysis of this tendentious *sugya* would exceed the available space). For the interpretive method of the Tannaim, see Naeh, 'Did the Tannaim'. For an Amoraic development of the *kelal u-ferat* rule, see above, n63; cf above, n70. A short summary of hermeneutical methods in the period of the Amoraim was drawn up by de Vries, *Studies* , 22-30.

[259] For the question of the use of the classic Aggadic Midrashim in material from the Halakhic ones, see Hoffmann, 'Einleitung' [1888], 76; Albeck, *Einleitung und Register*, 58-64; idem, 'Midrash Vayikra Rabba', 28-30; Lieberman, 'Hazanut Yannai', 229-234. For the use of other Aggadic Midrashim cf Friedmann, *Seder Eliahu Rabba*, Introduction, 60 (it would appear from the large quotes from SifNum and MekRY in Seder Eliyahu that its redactor possessed these works; the same might be true also of SifZNum and other Midrashim). Especially noteworthy are Halakhic Midrashim that preserved versions of nonextant ones. Cf Kahana, *Two Mekhiltot*, 355-359 for a lengthy midrash quotation in LamR version A, that reflects an earlier tradition of MekRSbY and enables us to follow the gradual evolution of the tradition in the extant MekRSbY. See below, the description of SifZDeut for its use by Sefer Pitron Tora and Midrash Hadash.

[260] See Weiss, *Dor Dor*, vol 2, chap. 24 p210-212; and esp Albeck, *Untersuchungen*, 87-120; idem, *Introduction*, 102-143. Cf Albeck's similar conclusions regarding the Tosefta, *ib.*, 54-72; idem, *Mehkarim ba-baraita*. His argument was based especially on the conjecture that the Talmuds were not cognizant of our Halakhic Midrashim (and the Tosefta), a notion he deduced from a number of Amoraic dicta that are the equivalent of (but do not mention) baraitot in the Halakhic Midrashim, as well as from complex talmudic deliberations on problems that are explicitly resolved in the Halakhic Midrashim. He cannot assume the Talmud would devote such serious effort to these issues if the Halakhic Midrashim had been available. Albeck's position was subjected to a detailed and well-reasoned critique by A. Goldberg, 'Chanokh Albeck'. His main arguments against Albeck are: (1) it cannot be concluded from the dictum of an Amora that is equivalent to a Tannaic source that he or his fellows did not possess it, because the Talmud often brings baraitot as the dicta of Amoraim. Cf the many dicta of R. Yohanan that are equivalent word for word (!) to baraitot (תניא כוותיה דר' יוחנן, 'It was taught in accordance with R. Yohanan'; תניא נמי הכי 'it has similarly been taught...'). Such dicta teach that R. Yohanan based his opinion on baraitot, but did not always see fit to emphasize this, or that over the course of time his teachings were related without mentioning this detail, whether unintentionally or consciously (for the construction of the *sugya*); (2) the Talmud's struggling with difficult baraitot while not mentioning baraitot from the

The language of the Halakhic Midrashim closely resembles that of the Mishna, and lacks any influences of the Galilean Aramaic typical of the *beit midrash* in the fifth century, at least in Galilee. The basic character of the Halakhic Midrashim as well reinforces the view that they reflect a transitional period between the Mishna, that as we saw is quoted verbatim in several of these documents, and the Talmuds. This transitional aspect is especially pronounced in the element of dialectic reasoning that is more fully developed in the Halakhic Midrashim than in the Mishna, but had still not reached the peak of development to be reached in the Talmuds, even in the Yerushalmi. On the other hand, the fact that the Halakhic Midrashim preserve the views of the Tannaim better and more authentically than the Talmuds[262] poses a very major obstacle for the conjecture that they were redacted about the same time as the Yerushalmi, after a lengthy period of 'hibernation' in which they underwent hardly any change. The same conclusion is suggested by the fact that the more developed hermeneutical method of the Amoraim is not discernible in the Halakhic Midrashim.

Nor is it to be assumed, and this should be stressed, that the various Halakhic Midrashim were redacted at the same time. Rather, the time of redaction of each individual collection must be separately discussed. At first glance, a slightly earlier date could be suggested for SifNum, which makes no mention of sixth-generation Tannaim, except for a single narrative that speaks of R. Hiyya.[263] This hypothesis could be strengthened by the brevity and relative scarcity of its associative expositions as compared with other Halakhic Midrashim. It would appear, though, that after its initial redaction an additional stratum from the 'school of Rabbi' was added.[264] Contrastingly, most scholars

---

Halakhic Midrashim that would likely resolve problems raised in the Talmud, does not necessarily teach that the latter baraitot were not before the Amoraim, because the Talmud may be interested in the difficult source out of the desire to construct an interpretive *sugya*, or for a halakhic reason, i.e., to rule against the baraita from the Halakhic Midrashim. Such goals were no less important for the redactors of the Talmud than the understanding of the baraitot themselves. We should add to Goldberg's arguments that even if we were to assume that the redactors of the Talmuds and/or some of the Amoraim had no knowledge of our Halakhic Midrashim, this should not be a reason for assigning a later date to the redaction of the latter. Clearly, not all the Amoraim in their different academies were familiar with all the collections of Tannaic baraitot, and an Amora's lack of knowledge of a certain baraita is no proof of its nonexistence. See e.g., a similar argument in the response to Albeck by Epstein, 'Rejoinder' (= *Studies*, vol 2, 177); idem, *Prolegomena*, 564f.

[261] See Wacholder, 'Date', who maintains that MekRY is a non-authentic Midrash whose redactor utilized all the talmudic and midrashic literature he possessed, as well as material he invented. In this respect, he further equates (119) MekRSbY with MekRY, while leaving open the question of the time of redaction and originality of the other Halakhic Midrashim. The truth be told, Wacholder's claims lack any scholarly foundation, as I demonstrated in a detailed critique that appears as an appendix to my article, 'Critical Editions', 515-520. I later learned that some of these issues had already been tackled by Stemberger, 'Datierung'. Cf also Boyarin, 'Status'.

[262] See above, 'Relation to Other Works: The Talmuds'.

[263] SifNum 115 (p129).

[264] See below, description of SifNum

have maintained that MekRSbY is the latest of Halakhic Midrashim, basing themselves on its expansions, the use they think it made of other Halakhic Midrashim, and the developed nature they found its halakhot and exegeses to possess; but such a conclusion seems to lack a firm basis.[265]

Most scholars correctly think that all of the Tannaic Halakhic Midrashim were redacted in the Land of Israel. This conclusion is supported by the similarity of their language to that of Mishna and Tosefta, which were also completed in the Land of Israel, and by the stronger affinity of their material with its parallels in the Yerushalmi and the Palestinian Aggadic Midrashim, as compared to the frequent differences with the Babylonian baraitot.[266] Even more compelling is the internal evidence. For example, the transferal of literary units from one place to another is usually unaccompanied by any attempt to adapt them to their new position, and this accords with the common strategy of the redactors of Tannaic and Amoraic literature in the Land of Israel. The redactors of the Bavli, in contrast, frequently sought to have their displaced *sugyot* conform to their new position. Also, the division of the Pentateuch into portions following Palestinian reading practice is noticeable in the redacted form of the Halakhic Midrashim.[267]

All this also applies to the midrashim belonging to the school of R. Yishmael, though some scholars thought these were redacted in Babylonia on the basis of the assumption that most of the leading Tannaim from this school, such as R. Yoshia, R. Yonatan, R. Natan, and R. Yitshak, were Babylonians.[268] A re-examination of the subject revealed that several of these, such as R. Yoshia, were not,[269] and that others seemingly immigrated to the Land of Israel.[270]

---

[265] See below, description of MekRSbY.

[266] See, e.g., Hoffmann, 'Einleitung' [1888], 34, 69f; Epstein, *Prolegomena*, 677, 710; Albeck, *Introduction*, 143.

[267] For the biblical units that are expounded in SifDeut and always open with the beginning of the Palestinian *seder*, see Kahana, 'New Fragments', 495 n64. The same holds true for the first exposition of MekRSbY, that is based on the beginning of two Palestinian *sedarim*. See Kahana, *Two Mekhiltot*, 386. In other instances, only an awareness of the Palestinian division into *sedarim* enables us to correctly understand expositions in the Halakhic Midrashim, such as MekRY Bo 15 (p52 = SifNum 123, p151): 'There are portions ...with specification at the beginning and generalization at the end: "But you shall be to Me a kingdom of priests and a holy nation" (Exod 19:6) – specification; "these are the words that you shall speak to the children of Israel" (*ib.*) – generalization.' The verse in Exodus seemingly does not begin a new topic, and only the knowledge that it begins a Palestinian *seder* (15) clarifies the exposition. The original division of the Halakhic Midrashim, as well, does not accord with the Babylonian *parshiyot* division (see details in the description of the different Halakhic Midrashim), and an original literary unit of a Halakhic Midrash sometimes contains verses from two Babylonian Tora portions; cf SifNum, *piska* 131 (p173); Kahana, *Prolegomena*, 13f.

[268] See Weiss, *Dor Dor*, vol 2, 203-205; and esp. Halevy, *Dorot ha-Rishonim*, vol 1, section 5, 678f. Cf Neusner, *Babylonia*, vol 1, 128-135, 179-187.

[269] For R. Yoshia, see Epstein, *Prolegomena*, 570 n179. I. Gafni conducted a critical discussion of Halevy's theory of the 'Babylonian Tannaim' in his book *Jews of Babylonia*, 81-91. Cf the observation by Porton, *Rabbi Ishmael*, vol 4, 56, that the Bavli does not contain more traditions by R. Yishmael and his disciples than the Yerushalmi. This datum obligates us, in his opinion, to re-

Especially impressive is the statement by R. Yonatan – who was (unjustifiably) considered in the past to be a Babylonian Tanna – which is incorporated in a passage in MekDeut that extols the obligation to reside in the Land of Israel and vehemently opposes leaving it even for the purpose of Tora study: 'I vow never to leave the Land [of Israel].'[271] The evidence thus suggests a Palestinian redaction for all the Halakhic Midrashim.[272]

At present we do not possess sufficient data for a more precise location of the *batei midrash* of R. Yishmael and R. Akiva, nor of locations or regions in which the various Halakhic Midrashim were redacted. The question is obviously related to the difficulties in identifying the last redactors of the collections, to which most scholars have devoted lengthy inquiries without reaching convincing conclusions.[273] This is finely demonstrated by the discussions of leading scholars of the past century concerning the identity of the redactor of SifZNum and the venue of his activity. Epstein was the first to conclude that R. Hiyya redacted SifZNum in Sepphoris,[274] to which Albeck objected,[275] leading Epstein to change his view, albeit for other reasons,[276] and to attribute the final arrangement of SifZNum to Sepphoris to Bar Kappara.[277] In turn, Lieberman discussed this at length, and based on other considerations determined that although Bar Kappara redacted SifZNum, he did so in Lydda, not in Sepphoris.[278] But then after all this scholarly activity, a basalt lintel was uncovered in Dabura in the Golan that decisively bore the inscription:[279]

זה בית מדרשו שהלרבי אליעזר הקפר

This is the *beit midrash* of Rabbi Eliezer ha-Kappar

---

evaluate the supposition that R. Yishmael's disciples went to Babylonia during the Bar Kokhba revolt and remained there. If they really had been active in Babylonia in the Tannaic period, we would expect to find a larger number of their traditions in the Bavli.

[270] This apparently is the position taken by Epstein, *Prolegomena*, 520.

[271] See the detailed discussion in Kahana, 'Importance of Dwelling'. For a critique of Halevy's general conception concerning the premier standing of the Tora center in Babylonia and the connection between this notion and Halevy's anti-Zionist stance, see the view of Prof. E.S. Rosenthal I cited *ib.*, 512 n25. Cf also Rosenthal's illuminating article, 'Tradition and Innovation', 362-365.

[272] The manner of transmission of the Halakhic Midrashim and their distribution in Babylonia is a separate issue. See Kahana, *Two Mekhiltot*, 386ff; below, the description of MekRSbY.

[273] See, e.g., the detailed researches by Epstein, *Prolegomena*, 646-655, 709, 728-735, 744-755, in which he also relates to the views of other scholars.

[274] See Epstein, 'Sifrei Zutta' (= idem, *Studies*, vol 2, 145-147).

[275] See Albeck, 'Neuere Ausgaben', 404-410.

[276] See Epstein, 'A Rejoinder', 233 (= idem, *Studies*, vol 2, 174).

[277] See Epstein, *Prolegomena*, 745; see also the gloss by Melamed *ib.*

[278] See Lieberman, *Siphre Zutta*, 92-124.

[279] See, also for the orthography, Orman, 'Jewish Inscriptions', 406-408; Naveh, *On Stone and Mosaic*, 25f. Further study is required to determine if it concerns the father, R. Eliezer ha-Kappar, or his son who bore the same name and was known as 'Bar Kappara'.

Accordingly, the entire issue requires re-examination. It is to be hoped that future archaeological and literary finds will aid in solving these knotty questions.

HISTORY OF RESEARCH AND FUTURE CHALLENGES

The first steps in the systematic research of the Halakhic Midrashim were taken in the late eighteenth and early the nineteenth centuries by scholars of the *Wissenschaft des Judentums*: A. Geiger, L. Zunz, Z. Frankel, I.H. Weiss, M. Friedmann, and others.[280] They focussed on three main realms: (1) a historical description of the development of talmudic and midrashic literature as a whole; (2) the manner in which halakha and midrash were studied and developed in antiquity;[281] and (3) a reinterpretation of the various Halakhic Midrashim.[282]

In the late nineteenth and early twentieth centuries the study of the Halakhic Midrashim intensified, with works by I. Lewy, D. Hoffmann, S. Schechter, H.S. Horovitz, and others.[283] They focussed on three other activities: (1) describing the schools of R. Yishmael and R. Akiva and classifying the Halakhic Midrashim by this division;[284] (2) publishing critical editions of the major Halakhic Midrashim based on the manuscripts;[285] (3) reconstructing lost Halakhic Midrashim using Yalkut Shimoni, Midrash ha-Gadol, Geniza fragments, and other sources.[286]

Modern scholars of the Halakhic Midrashim, most prominently J.N. Epstein, Ch. Albeck, S. Lieberman, and L. Finkelstein, continued the publication of the Halakhic Midrashim while conducting up-to-date studies in a diverse range of related subjects.[287] Except for Finkelstein, however, these scholars

---

[280] For a description of the methodology and activity of Geiger, Frankel, and Weiss, see Harris, *How Do We Know*; for Frankel's activity, Albeck's introduction to his re-edition of Zunz, *Vorträge*; cf Fraenkel, *Methodology*, 542-548.

[281] For the study of the two realms by these and other scholars, see Sussmann, 'History of Halakha', 12-15.

[282] The edition by Weiss of MekRY and Sifra, and by Friedmann of MekRY, SifNum, SifDeut, the beginning of Sifra, and 'Baraita de-Malekhet ha-Mishkan'.

[283] For a description of the methodology and activity of these scholars, see Urbach, 'Zacharias Frankel, Israel Lewy, Saul Horovitz: Three Talmud Teachers of the Breslau Seminary', in *Studies*, 851-862; Harris, *How Do We Know*, 229-234 (Hoffmann); Sussman, 'Schechter'.

[284] See esp. Hoffmann, 'Einleitung' [1888], the introductions by Horovitz to SifNum and SifZNum. Cf the important work by Bacher, *Terminologie* (for an assessment of his activity, see Fraenkel, *Methodology*, 551-553).

[285] The editions by Horovitz of SifNum and MekRY, and his preparations for a new edition of SifDeut.

[286] The discovery of citations from MekRSbY and other Midrashim in MidrGad by I. Lewy; the publication of fragments from MekRSbY, SifZNum, and MekDeut by Schechter; the publication of MekRSbY and MidrTann by Hoffmann; and the publication of SifZNum by Horovitz.

[287] For a detailed portrayal of the activity of these and additional scholars, see Kahana, *Two Mekhiltot*, 16-19.

invested most of their energy in studying the Mishna and Tosefta,[288] somewhat neglecting the Halakhic Midrashim.

As regards the development of research methodology, it should be stressed that the orderly critical inquiry into rabbinic literature took its first steps in the rabbinical seminaries of the three religious movements – Orthodox, Conservative, and Reform – leading at times to apologetic colorations in accordance with the religious-pedagogic notions of the respective movements.[289] These proclivities came to the fore in studies examining such questions as whether the Halakhic Midrashim reflect ancient, long accepted halakhot or whether the sages also crafted new halakhot based on their midrash. This cardinal question had direct implications for the areas of belief, thought, and lifestyle that divided those same movements in the present.[290] Within this context, we cannot disregard the establishment of the Talmud Department of the Hebrew University in Jerusalem whose founder, J.N. Epstein, had been educated both as a talmudist and a philologist and significantly advanced the application of the philological and historical method in the study of rabbinic literature,[291] while at the same time insisting on the fashioning of the Hebrew University as an independent academic institution.[292]

Before presenting the challenges facing the research of the Halakhic Midrashim, we must underline the inferior status of this field of study as compared with the Mishna. There are many reasons why this is so. The Mishna is arranged by subject, which facilitates its systematic study and comprehension. The order of halakhot in the Halakhic Midrashim, on the other hand, follows the biblical verses to which they relate, and they are mostly presented in an irregular, partial, and fragmentary manner. In addition, the student of halakhic midrash must constantly examine the question of the connection between the verse and its exegesis, a question the answer to which is in many cases quite complex. To this we must add the fact that the Mishna has reached us in its entirety, was closely explained and complemented in the Tosefta, and for most

[288] See the monumental study by Epstein, *Mavo*; the orderly and lucid commentary on the Mishna by Albeck; and the qualitatively and quantitatively outstanding enterprise by Lieberman in editing and interpreting the Tosefta *Ki-Fshutah*, 'according to its simple meaning'.

[289] Harris, *How Do We Know* revealed this in a fine and persuasive manner. It should nonetheless be stressed, correcting some unbalance in Harris, that these Tora scholars along with their ideological agenda also acted as critical researchers blessed with impressive innovative abilities; see below, n292.

[290] See the summational research by Urbach, 'Derasha', in which he also revealed the apologetic aspects. Cf above n20.

[291] For a characterization of Epstein's methodological contribution, together with an assessment of the scholarly enterprise of his outstanding pupil S. Lieberman, see the instructive article by Rosenthal, 'Ha-moreh'.

[292] See Sussmann, 'Epstein'. Cf the unseemly portrayal of Epstein by Harris, *How Do We Know* 262, ignoring Epstein's scholarly independence and the force of his methodological and contentual discoveries. Had Harris bothered to depict the hermeneutical methods during the Tananitic period itself (see above n67), he would probably have afforded Epstein his deserved place in the study of the subject.

of its tractates has been interpreted in regular fashion by the Amoraim in both Talmuds. The Mishna was then augmented by numerous commentaries by the Geonim and the Rishonim, and, in terms of scholarly research, its lot is relatively better than the Halakhic Midrashim. In contrast, significant portions of the Halakhic Midrashim have not survived, there are no orderly commentaries on them by the Amoraim and Geonim, and only some of them were commented on by the Rishonim. Consequently, we often have great difficulty in understanding even their simple meaning.

Progress in research in the field depends, first and foremost, on the sustained effort to discover lost portions in the libraries throughout the world, along with the publication of new critical editions of all Halakhic Midrashim. Since the first modern editions, new manuscripts were uncovered for most of the Midrashim, Yalkutim and other collections that quote passages from the Halakhic Midrashim, as well as several very helpful commentaries by Rishonim and Aharonim (pre-modern scholars) that were previously unknown. Oriental text versions are of especial importance, primarily the many fragments from the Cairo Geniza, whose existence was not known to the editors of the early editions. The Oriental manuscripts often preserve the more original version of the Halakhic Midrashim, where other texts corrupted them, or intentionally 'corrected' them in order to ease the difficulties they posed or to harmonize them with the better known and more authoritative parallels in the Mishna and the Bavli.

The methodology of the critical editing of talmudic sources has also advanced by great strides in determining the text and presenting textual variants.[293] In contrast with the earlier editions whose text in many difficult passages is based on adaptations of secondary textual witnesses or parallels, the new editions should be based on the reliable manuscripts of each of the Midrashim. The critical apparatus must more accurately present the linguistic and contentual variants in each of the primary textual witnesses, to enable other scholars to reconstruct both the original version of the midrash and its development into the different versions.

On the basis of more authoritative editions of the Halakhic Midrashim, detailed commentaries should be written for each collection. Such commentaries must draw upon scholarly achievements which were made in the fields of Talmud, linguistics, history, rabbinic thought, literature, and the like. In terms of methodology, they must contend with the difficulties faced by earlier editors and commentators by determining the original version of the expositions and the significance of the textual variants, reconstructing the biblical text referred to (if different from the Massoretic text), clarifying midrash terminology in

---

[293] See reviews of the Horovitz and Lauterbach editions of MekRY by Melamed, 'Horovitz-Rabin'; Lieberman, 'Mekhilta de-Rabbi Yishmael'; Kahana, *Two Mekhiltot*, 47-112. See a review of the Horovitz edition of SifNum in Kahana, *Prolegomena*, 277-294. See reviews of the Finkelstein edition of SifDeut by Epstein, 'Finkelstein'; Lieberman, 'Siphre zu Deuteromium'.

view of the schools' division, elucidating the peculiarities of biblical and mishnaic Hebrew, and paying attention to the historical circumstances in the Land of Israel in the time of the Tannaim and to the halakhic and intellectual attitudes that obtained.

Beyond the first level of proper and literal understanding of the midrashim, the attempt should be made to grasp the relation between midrash and verse in view of the questions that occupied the Tannaim. They could be trying to explain the lexical or contentual meaning of the Bible as such, or they could be seeking to lend the verses a new meaning taking inspiration from their halakhic practices, their concepts and beliefs, or the internal and external controversies in which they engaged. Several dimensions should be kept in mind here: the broader biblical context envisaged by the midrash teachers; the multiple relations existing between midrash, targum, and halakha; the literary structure of larger midrash units whose analysis may yield clues to their message; and the typical way of each sage following his own midrash tradition as well as the expositional tendencies of major Tannaim over larger sections of midrash literature.

The study of the Halakhic Midrashim must also adopt critical viewpoints neglected by early and recent midrash commentators, such as distinguishing between the teachers of the midrashim and their editors; analyzing the ways the editors transferred midrashim from their original place to a new one without change; examining the diverse sources available to the editors and the way these are represented in the extant collections; distinguishing more sharply between the different branches of the schools of R. Yishmael and R. Akiva as regards terminology, hermeneutical methods, Mishna tradition, and theological and halakhic attitude; and isolating foreign elements, marginal annotations, and interpretive glosses that entered the Halakhic Midrashim after their initial redaction.

New editions accompanied by critical commentaries will provide the foundation for a renewed discussion of all the basic issues pertaining to these documents, only some of which were examined in the present introduction. They will also facilitate an overall elucidation of their literary and contentual nature in comparison with the other sections of talmudic literature and with Jewish and non-Jewish literature at large.

Preparatory work in several of these realms has been undertaken in recent years. There is the production of a CD-ROM of Tannaic literature by the Historical Dictionary Project of the Academy of the Hebrew Language in Jerusalem; the systematic collection of the extant halakhic midrash fragments in libraries throughout the world, especially from the Geniza; the publication of all Geniza fragments (apart from Sifra); preparations for the new scholarly edition of several Midrashim;[294] a linguistic analysis of the superior manu-

---

[294] For a detailed treatment of these areas, see below, the descriptions of the different Midrashim.

67

scripts;[295] the development of literary approaches that will aid in the analysis of the halakhic and aggadic passages in the Halakhic Midrashim;[296] and an orderly and detailed commentary of several passages from the Halakhic Midrashim.[297] It is to be hoped that these will yield fruits that will continue to meet the scholarly challenges we have listed.

II. Description of the Collections

MEKHILTA DE-RABBI YISHMAEL

The Mekhilta de-Rabbi Yishmael (MekRY) is a midrash from the school of R. Yishmael on the Book of Exodus. The word *mekhilta* means 'measure'.[298] Its attribution to R. Yishmael, first found with R. Shmuel ben Hofni and R. Nissim Gaon, possibly ensued from the reference to R. Yishmael as the first sage in the exposition of לאמר, 'to say' and 'This month shall mark for you' (Exod 12:1-2) at the beginning of the work.[299] An exposition for the entire narrative section of Exod 1-11 is lacking, and the work opens with the first laws in Exod 12:1, continuing with uninterrupted exposition of the legal and narrative passages until 23:19, and concluding with the exposition of two short legal passages on the Sabbath in Exod 31 and 35. All this teaches of the close link of MekRY with the legal material in Exodus. Yet the criteria for which verses in Exodus are subject to an exposition and which are not remain unclear, since expositions on of lengthy narrative sections are included, while a number of legal passages are skipped.[300]

MekRY is divided into nine *masekhtot*: Pasha (Exod 12:1-13:16); Vayehi beshalah (13:17-14:31); Shirata (15:1-21); Vayasa (15:22-17:7); Amalek (17:8-18:27); Bahodesh or Debiri (19:1-20:26); Nezikin (21:1-22:23); Kaspa (22:24-29); and Shabta (31:12-17; 35:1-3). Each *masekhta* is divided into a

---

[295] See, e.g., Kutscher, 'Geniza Fragments'; Bar-Asher, 'Preliminary Study'; Naeh, 'Tannaic Hebrew'.

[296] See esp. Boyarin, *Intertextuality*; Fraade, *Tradition*. Cf Hartman and Budick, *Midrash*; Fraade, 'Interpreting Midrash'.

[297] See esp. Goldin, Song; Basser, Midrashic Interpretations; Kahana, *Two Mekhiltot*.

[298] See Lauterbach, 'Name'; and a more precise treatment: Epstein, 'Mekhilta and Sifrei', 343-357. See also *ib.* for additional Amoraic and Geonic names of MekRY, such as 'Mekhilta ve-eleh shemot', 'Mekhilta de-Erets Yisrael', and 'Sifrei'.

[299] Ed. Horovitz, 4, 6. In this context Melamed, *Introduction*, 182 mentions other Midrashim named after the first Rabbi appearing in them, including MekRSbY (for the phenomenon, see also Danzig, *Introduction*, 53, 713). Although the earlier expositions in MekRY mention other rabbis (Rabbi, R. Elazar ben Zadok, and R. Natan) before R. Yishmael, they do not do so in reference to the explanation of the verses from Exodus for which there are expositions (the attribution of MekRY to the midrashic school of R. Yishmael is an innovation solely by scholars in recent generations, see above, 'The Collections'; and it is only by chance that this conclusion corresponds with the name given the Midrash by several Rishonim).

[300] The explanations offered for this by Geiger, *Urschrift*, 279, and Epstein, *Prolegomena*, 549, are extremely forced. See Kahana, *Two Mekhiltot*, 25-26.

number of *parashiyyot*, each of which in turn is divided into halakhot, numbered with the letters of the *alef-bet*. The end of each parasha contains a summation of the number of halakhot it contains; the *masekhtot* conclude by mentioning and summing up the parashiyyot as well, and the entire Midrash ends with a summation of the *masekhtot*. These summations are presented by means of allusions to each parasha in Aramaic, that is also the language of the division into *masekhtot*, parashiyyot, and halakhot.[301]

Two critical editions of MekRY, that do not refer to each other, have been published, one by H.S. Horovitz, posthumously edited and completed by I.A. Rabin (Frankfurt, 1931); the other by J.Z. Lauterbach, in three volumes (Philadelphia, 1934-1935). These editions were favorably received by E.Z. Melamed, who reviewed the Horovitz edition,[302] and S. Lieberman, who evaluated the Lauterbach edition.[303]

Horovitz established the printed edition as the basis for his edition, at times emending and completing it in accordance with other textual versions. In the critical apparatus he provided a detailed listing of variants from the two complete manuscripts, Oxford 151 and Munich 117;[304] from the Leghorn 1801 edition, that is based, inter alia, on the emendations by Soliman Ohana; from the many quotations in Yalkut Shimoni and Midrash Hakhamim[305] that include most of MekRY; and from other indirect testimonies, primarily Lekah Tov, Sekhel Tov, Tanhuma, and Sefer ve-Hizhir. Horovitz added a concise but thorough critical commentary, with references to the parallels.

The Lauterbauch edition is more eclectic. In determining the text, the editor generally preferred the common version of the two manuscripts. In addition to the textual versions that were available to Horovitz, Lauterbauch used a few pages from the Geniza, ms Rome Casanatensa H 2736 for Masekhta de-Shirata, and ms Oxford 2637 for Yalkut Shimoni. The variant readings are listed in an extremely selective way; parallels are listed in an additional sec-

---

[301] For this entire subject, see Lauterbach, 'Arrangement'. The division is preserved in its entirety only in the Geniza fragments. It was abbreviated in the Western mss and in the printed editions, and following them, even in the critical edition by Horovitz, it was also corrupted in several places. It is not inconceivable that the division of MekRY, like that of the other Halakhic Midrashim, was not made by the redactors of the Midrashim, but only in a later period. This supposition could explain, among other questions, the lack of correlation between the different forms of division in the Halakhic Midrashim and their affiliation to the various schools. Thus, e.g., the division of MekRY (Yishmaelian) resembles that of Sifra (Akivan); cf below, section on Sifra. Notwithstanding this, some of the elements for the division of MekRY are very early. See LevR 24:5 (p558): 'R. Yohanan in the name of R. Shimon ben Yohai: Moses dictated to us three portions, and each contains sixty commandments, namely: *Parashat pesahim, Parashat nezikin,* and *Parashat kedoshim tiheyu.*'
[302] *Tarbiz* 6 (1935) 112-123 (Hebr.).
[303] *Kiryath Sepher* 12 (1935) 54-65 (Hebr.).
[304] ms Munich was published in a facsimile edition, with an introduction describing its nature: Goldin, *Munich.*
[305] The ms that formerly belonged to S. Halberstam, A. Epstein, and V. Aptowitzer is currently in the library of the Jewish Theological Seminary in New York (JTS ms 4937).

tion. The edition also contains an English translation, a lengthy introduction, and important indices of Scriptural passages and names of persons and places.[306]

Both editions suffer from the lack of a preliminary comprehensive discussion regarding the character of the various textual traditions and their mutual relations. Consequently, the editors were unaware of the direct dependence of the Venice 1545 edition on the Constantinople 1515 (?) edition, as pointed out by Melamed;[307] of the common source of the Ashkenazic mss Finkelstein concluded on;[308] and especially of the relative superiority of ms Oxford first noted by Lieberman.[309] The lack of a comprehensive evaluation of the textual versions is also apparent in the tendency of the editors to base the text of MekRY, especially its difficult passages, on the adapted and emended versions of Midrash Hakhamim, a Midrash by an Italian sage from the fifteenth century who relied in great measure upon the MekRY, but, as the title of the work implies, not on a specific textual version.[310]

Additional versions of MekRY have come to light after the publication of the two editions. Especially noteworthy are ms Vatican 299[311] that preserves about half of our text, and some eighty pages from the Cairo Geniza.[312] The importance of the latter lies in the Oriental, early textual traditions many of them reflect, which are generally superior to the Ashkenazic tradition represented by the manuscripts underlying the two critical editions. In many instances, the better version is preserved only in the Geniza fragments.[313] In other

[106] Lauterbach added a commentary to passages in the MekRY in his edition only in a few instances, while he interpreted isolated passages separately. See, e.g., his article, 'Me-Biurei ha-Mekhilta'.

[307] *Tarbiz* 6 (1935), 498-509 (Hebr).

[308] See Finkelstein, 'Mekilta'. In this basic article Finkelstein sought to delineate the stemma of the MekRY texts, and he drew several important conclusions pertaining to the shared origin of the Western textual versions. For corrections and addenda to this article, see Kahana, *Two Mekhiltot*, 66f, 106-110.

[109] See his concise comment in his review, 56. This is clearly implied by a systematic examination of these texts; see Kahana, *Two Mekhiltot*, 57-62. The inferiority of the printed version to the mss is attested by Melamed in his critique of the Horovitz edition, which he accompanies with examples from a number of realms.

[310] The discovery of two pages from the MekRY in the bindings of books in the Modena library teaches that many emendations of the text of Midrash Hakhamim were not made by its author, but previously. See Kahana, *Two Mekhiltot*, 48-49; idem, 'Pages of Halakhic Midrashim'.

[311] This was first noted by Finkelstein, 'Mekhilta', 6 n4.

[312] See the detailed description in Kahana, *Manuscripts*, 41-49 (after the publication of the book, an additional four pages were discovered in the Storico Communale di Modena: no. 23 and no. 30.1. Transcriptions of all the fragments see Kahana, *Genizah Fragments*, 1-152. Many citations from MekRY were also incorporated in Yemenite Midrashim, such as Midrash he-Hafets, Midrash ha-Beiur, and others. For the nature and importance of these Midrashim, that were not used by the editors, see Kahana, 'Yemenite Midrashim'.

[313] See Boyarin, 'Hidden Light'; Kahana, 'Critical Editions', 489-515; idem, *Two Mekhiltot*, 66-110; Elias, 'Ha-Mekhilta'. Cf Abramson, 'Four Matters', 8; Lieberman, 'New *Piska*'; Boyarin,

places the Oriental Geniza version confirms the shared reading of the Ashkenazic manuscripts, also for very difficult readings that could point to intentional intervention in the original textual tradition of the MekRY by its later
redactors or copyists.[314]

In the Middle Ages, commentaries were written on MekRY by several
Rishonim,[315] only one of which is partially extant, ms Mantua 36.[316] The first
printed editions were followed by a number of short emendations and commentaries based on manuscripts[317] and by a number of lengthy commentaries
by Aharonim that relied solely on the printed version, along with quotations
appearing in Yalkut Shimoni.[318] The most important of the latter are Shevut
Yehuda by R. Yehuda Najar and Berurei ha-Middot by R. Yitshak Elijah Landau. They were closely followed by two scholarly commentaries: Middot
Sofrim by Isaac Hirsch Weiss, and Meir Ayin by Meir Friedmann (Ish Shalom). Friedmann's work laid the foundation for the editions by Horovitz and
Lauterbach. After the publication of these two editions, *Masekhta de-Shirata*
was the subject of a new commentary.[319] Also, a new edition of *Parshat
Amalek* appeared which included a detailed argument in favor of the originality
of the aggadic material in MekRY as compared with MekRSbY.[320]

'Towards the Talmudic Lexicon' (for the phrase קיום נפש in the Geniza instead of פקוח נפש, see
Kister, 'Plucking', 356f).

[314] See, e.g., MekRY Masekhta de-nezikin 4, p263f, the discussion of the halakhic hierarchy of
Sabbath observance, the Temple service, matters of life-and-death, the execution of a death sentence, and the burial of a *met mitzva* (a corpse of unknown identity, whose burial is incumbent
upon all), and the question of which overrides which. The three Western mss: Vat, Oxf, and
Munich, and a fragment from the Eastern Geniza (T-S C4.7) contain a contradiction between the
declarations by the Mekhilta at the beginning of the discussion and the proofs brought in their
support in the continuation of the discussion, on the one hand, and the conclusions that are presented at the end of the discussion, on the other. The consistent recurrence of this phenomenon
(three times) rules out its being a chance corruption by copyists. Furthermore, since there were
disagreements on these issues, both in the Tannaic period and later, between Rabbanites and
Karaites, the question of who produced this spotty extant version, and when, requires further
study.

[315] See the testimonies regarding the commentaries by R. Samuel he-Hasid and R. Meir ben Kalonymus in Urbach, *Sages*, 194, 365, 418; cf Kahana, *Two Mekhiltot*, 39 n1.

[316] For this commentary, that also was unavailable to the editors, see Ta-Shema, 'Unpublished
Franco-German Commentary'.

[317] R. Meir Benvenist, *Ot Emet* (Salonika, 1565), that was used by the editors, and also: commentaries and glosses by R. Soliman Ohana that were preserved in ms JTS Rab. 2404 and margins of
the Venice 1545 edition in the Lenin Library in Moscow, Guenzburg Collection no. 811; glosses
and interpretations by the pupil of R. Bezalel Ashkenazi(?), JTS Rab. 2946 (see Lieberman,
'About Two MSS', 105-112; Benayahu, 'The Glosses', 47-114). See also Kahana, *Two Mekhiltot*,
40 n3 (in the meantime, the commentary by R. Eliezer Nahum has been published: Jerusalem
2000).

[318] See the comprehensive list in Kahana, *Two Mekhiltot*, 39f.

[319] Goldin, *Song*.

[320] See Kahana, *Two Mekhiltot*.

The overall nature of MekRY and its sources has been examined and described by the scholars,[321] along with long lists of monographs examining its diverse sources,[322] its attitude toward the Mishna[323] and to MekRSbY,[324] its narrative traditions,[325] its conceptual worlds,[326] and other topics.[327]

MEKHILTA DE-RABBI SHIMON BEN YOHAI

The Mekhilta de-Rabbi Shimon ben Yohai (MekRSbY), an Akivan Midrash on the Book of Exodus, is attributed to R. Shimon ben Yohai because of his exposition at the beginning of the book.[328] The work was known to a considerable number of Rishonim,[329] subsequently was lost, and then partially recovered by modern scholars. M. Friedmann (Ish Shalom) was the first to collect the quotations from MekRSbY known in his time,[330] and his list was complemented with a number of items by D. Hoffmann in his pioneering study of the Tannaic midrashim.[331] Israel Lewy then discovered that large portions of the midrash had been cited by R. David ha-Adani in Midrash ha-Gadol on Exodus,[332] and S. Schechter published a few fragments from MekRSbY itself that he uncovered in the Cairo Geniza.[333] The first edition of MekRSbY was published by Hoffmann (Frankfurt, 1905), based on Midrash ha-Gadol and a small number of the

---

[321] See the detailed introduction at the beginning of the edition by Friedmann, *Mechilta*, Introduction; Hoffmann, 'Einleitung' [1888], 36-45; Albeck, *Untersuchungen*, 91-96; idem, *Introduction*, 106-112; Epstein, *Prolegomena*, 548-587. See also the introduction by Lauterbach to his edition, esp. the list of later rabbis that it mentions, xx n15, and his hypothesis that R. Yohanan participated in one of its redactions (xxvi). For a new discussion of the question of the time of its redaction, see above, 'Time and Place of Redaction'; Kahana, *Two Mekhiltot*, 380-387.

[322] See, e.g., Finkelstein, *Sifra*, vol 5, 194*-211*. Cf above, n151.

[323] See Ginzberg, 'Al ha-yahas'.

[324] See, e.g., Yehuda, 'Two Mekhilot'.

[325] See, e.g., Boyarin, *Intertextuality*.

[326] See Kadushin, *Conceptual Approach*. Kadushin did not examine the unique nature of MekRY, but merely used it to illustrate his general conception regarding the study of rabbinic thought.

[327] See the additional references in Strack and Stemberger, *Einleitung*, 274-280; Kahana, *Two Mekhiltot*, 25-46.

[328] For the practice of naming a Midrash according to the first Tanna mentioned, see above, section on MekRY, n299. Several *Rishonim* knew the Midrash by other names, such as 'Mekhilta de-sanya', after the beginning in the section of the סנה (the burning bush) in Exod 3:2; 'Mekhilta'; 'Sifrei'; 'Sifrei de-vei Rav', and others. See Epstein, *Studies*, vol 2, 180-189; Abramson, 'New Fragment', 362.

[329] Kasher, *Sefer ha-Rambam*, 11-14, compiled a list of some 25 sages who relied upon MekRSbY.

[330] See the introduction to the Vienna 1870 edition of MekRY, xlix-lv, and the Addenda, 119-124 (cf the critical attitude by Weiss, *Dor Dor*, vol 2, 205, who deprecated the efforts invested by Friedmann in the location of quotations from MekRSbY, writing that 'in our opinion, this is merely a waste of time'!). Friedmann was preceded by R. Abraham, the son of the Vilna Gaon, who mentioned in his book (*Rav pealim*, 82) several quotations from MekRSbY by Nahmanides. For the positions of Zunz and Landauer, see Kahana, *Two Mekhiltot*, 117 n1.

[331] See Hoffmann, 'Einleitung' [1888], 45-51.

[332] See Lewy, 'Ein Wort', 2 ff.

[333] Schechter, 'Geniza Fragments', 443-445; 776f.

Geniza fragments identified by Schechter. The next edition, published by J.N. Epstein and E. Melamed in 1955, is based on 95 MekRSbY leaves or fragments of leaves discovered in the Geniza. The rest of the midrash was reconstructed using four manuscripts of Midrash ha-Gadol.[334] Four additional MekRSbY fragments were subsequently published,[335] transcriptions of all the new Geniza fragments came to light,[336] as was a new edition of parashat Amalek of MekRSbY based on newly discovered manuscripts.[337]

The introduction to the Epstein-Melamed edition contains a description of the MekRSbY manuscripts and their main distinguishing features, but the principles guiding the editors were not presented, nor was an orderly description of the critical symbols included.[338] The manuscripts were copied in an admirably accurate manner, and only in rare instances the transcription, that was based on photographs, should be corrected on the basis of the original manuscripts. It should be noted, however, that the largest manuscript of MekRSbY on whose basis some 65 pages were published is an inferior text written in thirteenth-century Spain. About another 15 pages are not actual MekRSbY manuscripts but are surviving fragments from two copies of abridged midrashic collections of the work. Consequently, the textual tradition of MekRSbY set forth in the major portion of the edition is not an especially reliable one and is plagued by many copyist's corruptions and mistakes.

The editors correctly noted the striking disparity between the certain MekRSbY fragments discovered in the Geniza and the doubtful passages that they printed in smaller type. Most of the doubtful reconstructions, encompassing about one third of the edition, were based on Midrash ha-Gadol, and the editors were forced to complete the rest based on the parallel material in MekRY, Sifra, *Midrash Tannaim*, and other Midrashim. Obviously, error could hardly be avoided in such a complex labor of reconstruction, and in his review of the edition, Margulies referred to a few passages that were incorporated within the text on the basis of Midrash ha-Gadol, yet do not originate in MekRSbY but in Mishnat Rabbi Eliezer, Avot de-Rabbi Natan, or the Babylonian Talmud.[339] A similar situation holds for the completion of missing passages in the Geniza fragments on the basis of Midrash ha-Gadol (printed within brackets, in nor-

---

[334] In the 1969 reprinting of this edition some of the corrections and addenda were moved from the appendices to within the text (in the editor's handwriting), with the addition of several new corrections that were based on a Genizah fragment published by Sarfatti, and Margulies' criticism of the edition. For a more detailed description of the stages in the discovery of MekRSbY, see Kahana, *Two Mekhiltot*, 117-119.

[335] See Sarfatti, '*Keta*', 176, and the comment by Z. Ben-Hayyim, *ib.* 177f; Abramson, 'New Fragment'; Glick, 'Another Fragment'; Kahana, 'Another Page'.

[336] See Kahana, *Genizah Fragments*, 153-186.

[337] See Kahana, *Two Mekhiltot*, 151-197.

[338] For a summation, see Kahana, *Two Mekhiltot*, 120.

[339] See Margulies, 'Mekhilta'.

mal type), whose origin in MekRSbY is extremely doubtful.[340] On the other hand, several other passages from Midrash ha-Gadol were omitted whose origin in MekRSbY has now been proven by new quotations from MekRSbY by several Rishonim, such as R. Hafets ben Yatsliah and the Karaite authority Yeshua ben Yehuda.[341]

MekRSbY begins with a lengthy exposition concerned with a single topic: the choosing of Moses as the agent who shall redeem Israel, and Moses' response to this election. The exposition is composed of two developed literary units (pp. 1-4/3; 4/3-7/9), each of which is focused on the beginning of the Palestinian *seder* with which it opens: Exod 3:1[342] and Exod 6:2, the only two lemmas in these units.[343] The phenomenon of the construction of an entire exposition around the opening verses of a Palestinian *seder* is very rare in the Tannaic Midrashim,[344] but frequent in the Amoraic Midrashim and in the Tan-

---

[340] For an interesting example, see the exposition of the verse 'If he did not do it by design' (Exod 21:13), p169 in the reconstruction of l. 1 in accordance with ms Firkovich, 4a: 'Something th[at was first implied in a generalization and afterwards was specified to add another provision similar to the generalization is specified for leniency, and not for stringency].' This is one of the thirteen hermeneutical principals by which the Tora is explained (see Sifra, ed Finkelstein p4). In fact, except for the explanatory baraita in Sifra *ad loc.* (p7), this is the only instance of this hermeneutical method that is preserved in the talmudic literature. A new reading of ms Firkovich teaches that vague taces from the second letter of l. 1 also are present, but this apparently is not the letter י, as in Melamed's reconstruction following MidrGad: ... ה]יה בכלל... Hoffman comments in his edition of MekRSbY (125) that this example appears with greater detail in the explanation in MidrGad of the thirteen hermeneutical rules at the beginning of its exposition of Leviticus, that he himself published, 'Ein Midrash', 67. Kasher, *Tora Sheleimah* on this verse (para. 247), notes that this example appears also in the commentary by R. Saadia Gaon on this midrashic principle. A study of the other hermeneutical principles in MidrGad Lev *ib.* teaches that R. David ha-Adani made use of Saadia's commentary on the *middot* (A. Steinsaltz, in his edition of MidrGad on Leviticus, was unaware of this, and mentioned that he had not found their source). Moreover, R. Saadia Gaon did not base the majority of his interpretation of the hermeneutical principles on examples that he found in rabbinic literature, but rather on illustrations that he formulated (for the authorship by R. Saadia Gaon of the commentary attributed to him, see my article, 'Kelal u-Ferat', n2, n7). It would therefore appear that the example of this hermeneutical principle mentioned in MidrGad on Exod 21:13 cited above is not in the joint reconstruction of MekRSbY by Hoffmann and Melamed, but rather in the commentary by Saadia (for the use of MidrGad in other passages from the commentary of R. Saadia Gaon on the Tora, see Tobi, 'Midrash ha-Gadol', 317-319).

[341] Cf Kahana, *Two Mekhiltot*, 122.

[342] The beginning of MekRSbY was established by the editors here on the basis of the passage cited by Soliman Ohana. See also the reference (p1 n1) to the evidence in the list of books in the Geniza: '...כתב אבדתאה, A book that begins, "And Moses was herdsman..." (Exod 3:1).' MekRSbY's beginning here is also proven from a Geniza fragment in the JTS Library in New York, that the editors did not possess (ENA 909.23), in which the beginning of the Midrash is preserved.

[343] This fact was unknown to Epstein, who wrote in a general formulation: 'A midrash on the portion of *Shemot* and *Vaera*' (*Prolegomena*, 549). Melamed seemingly concurred with Epstein, and therefore added a marginal reference in his edition to the verses from Exodus that are the subject of exposition there, even though not lemmas.

[344] A clear example of this is to be found in SifDeut 304-305 (p323-327); MidrTann p178-180, that focus upon the exposition of Deut 31:14 (with which *seder* 25 opens) and that are concerned with Moses' request at the end of his life to enter the Land, and God's response. For the literary and

huma versions. The deficient extant documentation prevents our determining if MekRSbY included additional expositional units on Exod 6-11. At any rate, Midrash ha-Gadol preserved expositions that apparently originated in Mek-RSbY from the legal subjects in Exod 12:1 onwards. Indeed, starting with verse 3 in this chapter, MekRSbY is documented in a Geniza fragment published by Abramson.[345] MekRSbY continues to expound the verses in their order at least until Exod 23:19,[346] after which the exact scope of the Midrash is unclear. Based on Midrash ha-Gadol, Melamed reconstructed MekRSbY on Exod 23:20-24:10, and selected verses from chaps. 30, 31, 34, and 35 of Exodus in his edition, but several of these quotations clearly do not originate in MekRSbY.[347] This issue requires further study.[348]

The Epstein-Melamed edition does not include a commentary; also, the parallels were listed only partially. Many comments on the midrashim in MekRSbY appear in the edition by Hoffmann and in Kasher's glosses in Tora Sheleimah, but these cannot fulfil the need for an orderly and detailed critical commentary of MekRSbY as a whole.

Research into MekRSbY is presented in Epstein's general essay on the work which Melamed published by way of introduction; it pays special attention to the question of the redactors. Melamed added his own discussion concerning terminology and vocabulary, the names of sages cited, the method of quoting sources, and characteristic hermeneutical methods. The second edition contains an additional short chapter on 'Mishna and Baraita Quotations in Mekhilta de-Rabbi Shimon ben Yohai',[349] and the appendixes include various subject indexes that aid in the further study of this work.

Most scholars concur that the halakhic portion of MekRSbY was redacted fairly late. This opinion was first expressed by Epstein, who wrote at the end of his Introduction: 'The Mekhilta de-R. Shimon ben Yohai, from the school of R. Akiva, is the latest of all Halakhic Midrashim. It often quotes verbatim from Sifra, Sifrei, and Tosefta, and many halakhot are incidentally connected with the midrash. All this points to a late date.' Based on an orderly study of the section of the Hebrew slave in the two Mekhiltot, Z.A. Yehuda concluded

---

contentual relationship between these expositions and the opening exposition of MekRSbY, see Kahana, *Two Mekhiltot*, 384.

[345] See above, n335.

[346] Geniza fragments preserve documentation of MekRSbY until Exod 22:24 (see the Epstein-Melamed edition, 212), but Yeshua ben Yehuda continues to bring direct quotations from MekRSbY until Exod 23:17, and MekRSbY is clearly the source of the halakhic expositions in Midr-Gad on the following two verses (v18-19).

[347] See, e.g., the expositions on p221/30-222/7 that originate in MekRY p340-343, and not in MekRSbY. Cf the different reconstruction in ed Hoffman, 160-166 that also contains several passages from MekRY.

[348] See, e.g., Tosafot in bMen 66b, s.v. כנף: 'In Sifrei, in the portion of "You shall bring forward" (Exod 28:1), the version is...' This may be a corruption (cf Sifra Nedava 13, p96), but it might also originate in a lost text from MekRSbY, that, as was noted above (n328), is also called 'Sifrei'.

[349] A concise formulation of Melamed's conclusions, *Relationship*, 94-104.

that MekRSbY was redacted after MekRY.[350] B. de Vries took this premise a step further and asserted that 'Mekhilta de-Rabbi Shimon ben Yohai contains a reworking of baraitot from Mekhilta de-Rabbi Yishmael, not a parallel source or one in common.'[351] H.I. Levine examined several halakhic topics in Mek-RSbY, reaching the even more far-reaching conclusion that 'the activity by the redactor of Mekhilta de-R. Shimon ben Yohai closely resembles that of the Amoraim in the area of interpretating the Mishna. Like them, he clarifies the halakhic concepts in the Mishna, expands on it, draws parallels to it, and examines the relationship between one mishna and another by the use of certain interpretations [of mishnayot or baraitot].' On the basis of this analysis, Levine wrote that, apparently, 'the redactor of MekRSbY was himself an Amora,' while emphasizing that further study of these specific details is required before conclusions can be drawn regarding MekRSbY as a whole.[352] An investigation of Levine's proofs teaches that almost all are based on tenuous speculation, not on hard evidence as to the text of the sources available to the redactor of Mek-RSbY and the nature of his editing activities. Objections could also be raised concerning the quality of De Vries's proofs of the use MekRSbY made of MekRY. An examination of the singular character of MekRSbY therefore requires further study that would have to include a new and consistent examination of its terminology, of the names of sages it mentions, and of its prevalent hermeneutical methods, since at extremely rare times these seem to include several elements typical of the other school, that of R. Yishmael.[353]

As we said earlier, the aggadic material in MekRSbY fundamentally resembles the parallel material in MekRY. An orderly examination of the parallel aggadic material of parashat Amalek teaches of the primacy of the tradition in MekRY. MekRSbY apparently was fashioned by redactors who sought to inform the expositions with a more developed literary and theological nature that was rather independent from the rigid linkage to the verses. Along with the theological development of several of the expositions of this section, the work occasionally exhibits stylistic hyperbole, exegetical diffusion, a tendency to attribute anonymous midrashim to specific sages, and possibly even the attempt to artificially rewrite disputes. Some of the expositions exhibit a simplification of content bordering on popularization, stressing themes centered on the basics of religious life such as the importance of obeying God's word, observance of the commandments and avoidance of sin, the standing of prayer, and the good end that awaits Israel, along with the tribulations that shall befall its enemies.[354]

---

[350] Yehudah, 'Hebrew Slave'.

[351] See his article, 'Use'.

[352] See Levine, *Studies*, 191.

[353] I gave a preliminary discussion of this topic in a lecture at the Thirteenth World Congress of Jewish Studies, Jerusalem 2001, which I intend to publish shortly.

[354] See the extensive treatment, Kahana, *Two Mekhiltot*, 201-363, and the summary, 364-376.

A comprehensive description of the aggadic material of the two Mekhiltot would require a detailed examination such as has not been conducted to date. Nonetheless, a partial examination of a number of *parashiyyot* in MekRSbY uncovered finds similar to those made in parashat Amalek.[355] The literary nature of the first aggadic unit, that appears not in MekRY, somehow resembles the genre of Tanhuma; it also reflects the literary development characteristic of the aggadic material of MekRSbY and its rather late time of creation. The same is true for some of the aggadic material incorporated in the halakhic sections[356] and part of the halakhic material found in the aggadic passages.[357]

A Gaonic response (probably by Rav Sherira and Rav Hai) attributes a quotation from MekRSbY to the teaching of the rabbis that is available in the 'other *sifrei de-vei Rav*' (i.e., all Halakhic Midrashim except Sifra), 'and thus all the *tannaim* learned, without exception'. It then continues to compare it with a citation from MekRY which is termed 'Mekhilta de-Erets Yisrael'. This led scholars to conclude that MekRSbY was the primary Mekhilta taught at the time by the 'tannaim' (i.e., the teachers of baraitot) in Babylonia, while MekRY was more widespread in the Land of Israel; it was not studied in Babylonia (at least not in the yeshiva of Pumbeditha), and the Geonim cited it from a written book.[358] This could possibly relate to the manner in which MekRSbY was transmitted, and, in fact, the Bavli frequently quotes midrashim similar or identical to the work.[359] In either event, the history of its transmission is to be separated from the question of the venue of its redaction, and there is no reason to move the latter from the Land of Israel to Babylonia.[360]

---

[355] See idem, 376-379.

[356] See Milikowsky, 'Parallels', in which he indicates a problematic exposition in MekRSbY, that resulted from the combination by the redactor of MekRSbY of a passage from Seder Olam (or from another similar source) with an additional source.

[357] See Kahana, *Two Mekhiltot*, 282-287, the discussion regarding the law in MekRSbY of the firstborn of an unclean beast, that was adapted in MekRY under the influence of the later halakha.

[358] See Hoffmann, 'Einleitung' [1888], 36, 41; Epstein, *Studies*, vol 2, 104f; idem, the introduction to MekRSbY p13f; Lieberman, *Tosefta Ki-Fshutah*, Bava Kamma, 45. Cf Kahana, *Two Mekhiltot*, 386 n140, concerning the wording of MekRY in one place, in relation to the leading of prayer by the Reader: עוברין לפני התיבה, following the prevalent Palestinian phrase, in contrast with the rather more Babylonian formulation in the corresponding passage in MekRSbY: שיורדין לפני התיבה.

[359] See the summation by Melamed, *Halachic Midrashim in the Babylonian Talmud*, 36: 'In its citation of midrashim on Exodus, the Bavli is closer to MekRSbY than to MekRY. Even in passages taken from MekRY, the wording of the Bavli is not identical with that of the extant MekRY. This is not the case for the relationship between the Bavli and MekRSbY: in most instances, the wording in both is congruent.' See, however, what Melamed wrote in his introduction, 31, on the need to examine the relation of each individual tractate to the extant Halakhic Midrashim (cf his book *Halakhic Midrashim in the Palestinian Talmud*, in which the approximate same number of expositions in MekRY and in MekRSbY are listed as parallels for the expositions of the Yerushalmi).

[360] See Kahana, *Two Mekhiltot*, 386; cf idem, 'Importance of Dwelling'.

SIFRA

Sifra is an Akivan Midrash on Leviticus. The Aramaic word *sifra*, meaning 'book' or 'the book' and thus commonly used in Babylonia,[361] most likely attests to its centrality and importance.[362] In the Land of Israel it was called *Torat kohanim*, corresponding to the name given to the Pentateuchal book.

According to most scholars, Sifra contains Akivan expositions on Lev 1:1-7:38; 10:8-18:6; 18:19; 18:24-20:5; 20:22-27:34.[363] Several textual versions contain additional Yishmaelian expositions on Lev 8:1-10:7; 18:1-7; 18:18; 18:28; 20:6-22 (see below).

The division of Sifra is complicated. It was originally divided into nine sections, as is indicated both by a statement of the Tanna R. Shimon son of R. Yehuda ha-Nasi to Bar Kappara[364] and by the testimony of Geonim and Rishonim.[365] In the textual documents, however, the original, Akivan part of the work is divided into eleven or twelve *megillot* or *dibburim*: Nedava or Vayikra (Lev 1:1-3:17); Hova or Nefesh (4:1-5:26); Tsav (6:1-7:38); Sheratsim (10:8-12:8); Negaim (13:1-59); Metsora (14:1-57); Zavim (15:1-33); Aharei (16:1-18:30, with omissions); Kedoshim (19:1-20:27, with omissions); Emor (21:1-24:23); Sinai (25:1-26:2); Behukotai (26:3-27:34, with omissions). The increase of the number of units is probably due to the division of the Babylonian Tora portions that was added to the original division.

Several proposed reconstructions of the original nine parts of Sifra were put forth in the past.[366] A satisfactory solution was found only recently by S. Naeh, who managed to base the precise delineation of the nine sections on the

---

[361] The name 'Sifra' or 'Sifra de-vei Rav' already appears in the Bavli and in the Geonic literature. See Epstein, *Prolegomena*, 645. The Bavli calls the other Halakhic Midrashim שאר ספרי דבי רב.

[362] The importance of this Midrash apparently ensued from the large number of halakhot that it contains. The premier importance of Leviticus is reflected in the longstanding practice to begin the study of the Tora with it, and not with Genesis.

[363] The attribution of the expositions in Behukotai (Lev 26:3 ff.) is doubtful. Epstein, *Prolegomena*, 691-697, spoke of several of its aggadic expositions, some of which disagree with the rest of Sifra, and some of which accord with the school of R. Yishmael. He also asserted, however, that 'in its halakhic part, the portion of Behukotai differs from the rest of Sifra.' He further noted that ms Vat 31 ends with '*megilta* nine' at the end of Behar, from which he concluded that the original division of Sifra into nine units did not include the portion of Behukotai. The reconstruction of the initial division of Sifra (see immediately below) does not support the latter conclusion by Epstein. His statement regarding the aggadic material in Behukotai, as well, is questionable, since, as was mentioned above ('Aggada'), the attribution of all the aggadic material in the Halakhic Midrashim to either the Yishmaelian or the Akivan school is extremely difficult. The majority of the halakhic material in *Behukotai* most likely is to be assigned to the school of R. Akiva, but this question requires further study (cf recently Stemberger, 'Eigenart und Redaktion').

[364] 'I taught him two-thirds of a third of Torat kohanim' (bKid 33a; see there).

[365] Such as: NumR 18,21: 'And nine chapters of Torat kohanim'; Halakhot Gedolot (ed Warsaw) 143d, 'And nine *dibburim* of Torat kohanim,' or, in the wording of the colophon of Sifra in ms Vat 31: סליק[ו] תשע גולי האריׄ, 'nine *megillot* of Sifra were finished'. See the extensive discussion in Naeh, 'Structure, A', 483-491.

[366] See, e.g., Epstein, *Prolegomena*, 699; Melamed, *Introduction*, 189.

division that were accurately preserved in ms Parma.[367] He also showed that the key to the division is not contentual, but follows from the more or less equal size of these nine units that not without reason are known as *megillot*, literally: 'scrolls'. Along with the name of the work as a whole, 'Sifra', this attests to its early reduction to writing.[368]

Each *megilla* or *dibbur* is divided into *parashiyyot*[369] that are further split into perakim or chapters, and these into halakhot,[370] with the numerical total appended at the end of each unit of the *parashiyyot*, perakim, and halakhot it contains.[371] The hierarchical division is not preserved in some textual versions, but in my opinion we should not view that as the remainder of an early alternative division, rather as a something for which the copyists are responsible.[372]

---

[367] See Naeh, 'Structure, A'.

[368] See *ib.*, 494-512. It should be stressed that Naeh's proofs relate to the writing of Sifra in Babylonia, while the question of the time of the initial composition of Sifra and the other Halakhic Midrashim where they were redacted, in the Land of Israel, still requires study. See Sussmann, *Talmudic Studies*, vol 3, 373-375.

[369] This division, too, might be of early origin. See the dictum by R. Yitshak in CantR 6,9.2: '"There are sixty queens" (Song 6:8) – these are the sixty tractates of halakhot [= the Mishna]. "And eighty concubines" – these are the eighty *parashiyyot* in Torat kohanim.' This latter number does not correspond to the number of *parashiyyot* in the extant Sifra, and R. Yitshak might possibly refer to Leviticus itself, not to its Midrash. See Naeh, 'Structure, A', 584; idem, 'Structure, B', 78-82.

[370] For the details, see Naeh, 'Structure, B', 71 ff. The editor of the printed edition did not understand that the perakim are part of the parasha, and counted them separately within each parasha or dibbur. Consequently, the system of references according to the printed editions, that is accepted to the present in the scholarly literature as well, distinguishes between the independent number of the *parashot* and that of the *perakim*.

[371] The division of the Sifra closely resembles that of MekRY (see above). The latter, as well, is divided into nine units (albeit called *masekhtot*, 'tractates'), that in turn are divided into *parashiyyot*, and these (without *perakim*), into halakhot. Likewise, a number of sentences in Aramaic that found their way into Sifra could possibly be regarded as remnants of Aramaic summations of the *parashiyyot* allusions (see Naeh, 'Structure, B', 90f; see also ms London 341 of Sifra, fol. 148a, 210a), similar to the summations that are preserved in their entirety in MekRY.

[372] Naeh, 'Structure, B', 78-87, described at length the nature of the division of Sifra; he believes that the non-hierarchical division is the first one. See his arguments, primarily the methodic argument: 'I do not find any clear reason why the scribes would have likely deleted the division signs in a systematic manner.' In my opinion, however, we can rely concerning this question as well on the testimony of the reliable Sifra manuscripts, primarily ms Vat 66 and most of the Geniza copies (that are supported by mss Vat 31 and Parma, and by other textual versions), in which the hierarchical division is preserved. It is also difficult to accept Naeh's proposal that the prevalent division in the second-rate manuscripts, such as ms Oxf and ms London, reflect the original division, especially since in a number of places they, too, retain the hierarchical division. The unoriginal division tradition of these manuscripts comes to the fore in SifNum and SifDeut (see below, their descriptions); and, as was noted above, the lack of division allusions in large portions of the Ashkenaz-French manuscripts is to be regarded as nothing more than a copyists' omission.

Sifra is quoted to this day according to the edition that I.H. Weiss published almost a century and a half ago in Vienna (1862).[373] It is based on the Venice printed edition with corrections from Yalkut Shimoni, along with an apparatus of references to the parallels and short interpretive notes. In the absence of a fullblown critical edition of Sifra, great weight must also be given to two facsimile editions of Sifra manuscripts: the one of ms Vatican 66 published in New York in 1957 with an introduction by Finkelstein, and the copy of ms Vatican 31 published by Makor (Jerusalem, 1972).

A commentary on Sifra, almost to the end of *dibbura de-Nedava*, was published in Breslau in 1915 from the posthumous legacy of R. Meir Friedmann (Ish Shalom), who drew upon several manuscripts. In 1983-1990 L. Finkelstein published a four-volume critical edition of the first two *dibburim* of Sifra (Nedava and Hova), consisting of an introductory volume, a text volume that includes references to the parallels and a concise interpretation, a volume of textual variants, and a volume with extensive commentary. Finkelstein was already at an advanced age when preparing the commentary, and he unfortunately did not live to complete it. A fifth volume sent to press close to Finkelstein's death in 1992 contains indexes to the four preceding volumes, along with a collection of Finkelstein's scholarly articles on the Halakhic Midrashim.

The text of Finkelstein's edition is based on ms Vatican 66,[374] unquestionably the best text of Sifra, and, in fact, the most accurate extant codex of the Halakhic Midrashim. The manuscript is of Oriental origin, most likely Babylonia, and dated to the tenth[375] or ninth[376] century. It preserves many remnants of pure Tannaic idiom,[377] original terminology,[378] traces of the incorporation of the foreign units from the school of R. Yishmael,[379] and most importantly, an abundance of good readings.[380] The manuscript has supralinear 'Babylonian'

---

[373] Due to this fact, that indicates the relative backwardness of the study of this Halakhic Midrashim, it will be discussed below fairly extensively.

[374] Finkelstein meticulously, and properly, placed his corrections and additions within brackets within the text. Some of his corrections, however, in which he proposed changing the rare linguistic forms and singular style of ms Vat 66, are superfluous. In the places where the original pages of the ms are missing, his proposals for the text appear in smaller letters, based on other textual versions, not necessarily the best of them, without explicit mention of the version on which his edition is based. For the flaws in the edition that result from these editorial decisions, see, e.g., Kahana, 'Kelal u-Ferat', 174 n5.

[375] As is surmised by M. Lutzki in the introduction to the photocopy edition, 70.

[376] As is postulated by M. Beit Arie (for the uniqueness of the ms, see Beit-Arie, *Hebrew Codicology*, 41).

[377] See Naeh, 'Tannaic Hebrew'; idem, 'Notes'.

[378] See, e.g., Wajsberg, 'Difference', 147-152, who took note of the original distinction between the terms תלמוד and תלמוד לומר, that was consistently preserved in ms Vat 66, but not in the other complete textual versions of the Halakhic Midrashim.

[379] See Haneman, 'Linguistic Tradition'.

[380] See. e.g., the examples analyzed by Finkelstein in his introduction to the facsimile edition; Naeh, 'Tannaic Hebrew', 316-354; idem, 'Did the Tannaim', 419-448.

vocalization[381] added by another scribe, who in many instances also corrected the first hand to follow his own tradition and textual version.[382] In a separate volume, Finkelstein listed the textual variants from all Sifra manuscripts:[383] ms Breslau 108 (currently in the Jewish Theological Seminary library in New York: JTS Rab. 2171), which is relatively close to ms Vatican 66; the Constantinople 1523 (?) printed edition, which comprises most of the portion of Vayikra and apparently also reflects an Oriental textual tradition; the Italian MSS. Vatican 31 and Parma 139; the Venice printed edition; ms Oxford 151 and ms London 341, which present the Franco-Askenazic textual tradition;[384] pages from a Yemenite ms. possessed by Rabbi Y. Kapah; many Geniza pages (photo reproductions of which appear at the beginning of the introductory volume);[385] and the versions of the major secondary textual witnesses in the Yalkutim and medieval commentaries and Midrashim.[386] To supplement the edition, attention should be paid to a considerable number of Geniza fragments and other Sifra pages, mainly from Eastern Europe, that were identified after its publication.[387]

Three Sifra commentaries by Rishonim have been published – one by

---

[381] See Yeivin, *Hebrew Language Tradition*, 203f.

[382] See Naeh, 'Tannaic Hebrew', 18.

[383] The references in the textual variant volume to the text volume were made on the basis of the corrupted division of the printed versions (see above, n370), that was added by the editor in brackets to the text volume, as well. It is unfortunate that the editor did not add at the top of the pages of the variants volume references to the corresponding pages in the text volume; this method of marking could have facilitated finding one's way in the variants volume. The text volume also should have had orderly references to the biblical verses from Leviticus that are expounded, as Finkelstein did in his edition of SifDeut

[384] At the beginning of Sifra, the scribe of ms London makes a few references to versions in an additional manuscript that he calls 'another Torat kohanim'. See fol. 139a, 139b, 141b, 142a. This fact is of major importance, because in the continuation of Sifra, as well, the scribe sometimes includes two versions, side by side, without drawing attention to this. For the similar practice by this scribe in the copying of SifNum, see Kahana, *Prolegomena*, 25.

[385] The list of signs at the beginning of the edition lacks a listing of the markings of the Geniza fragments. To complement most of these data, see Kahana, *Manuscripts*, 66 ff. The only fragment that I could not identify at the time was ג, a photograph of which did not appear in the edition. In the meantime, I succeeded in locating it in the JTS library in New York, aided by Danzig, *Catalogue*, and his markings, as JTS ENA 2941.5-7, 35-36.

[386] The description of the direct textual versions presented above is slightly different from the description of the stemma of the textual versions in the introductory volume of the Finkelstein edition, 71ff, esp the table p119.

[387] See the detailed listing, Kahana, *Manuscripts*, 66-88, to which should be added: (a) eight parchment pages in Karlsruhe (= ms Vat 66, 42/11-51/18, 70/18-72/18, 80/5-84/4, 100/13-108/12, 182/2-185/9, 194/17-197/11); (b) a single parchment page in London, BL Or. 10797.2 belonging to Codex 7 (= ms Vat 66, 109/17-110/15, 111/7-112/3); (c) two parchment pages in Modena 30.2 belonging to Codex 13 (= ms Vat 66, 226/16-229/13, 253/22-256/6); (d) a single parchment page containing two written columns that is preserved in Vienna: Oester-Nationalbibliothek Wien, Hebr. Frag. C. 8 (= ms Vat 66, 228/1-239/3) (my thanks to B. Richler and E. Shevat for drawing my attention to the above four fragments); (e) a single paper page in JTS Rab. 1872, pp. 47-48 (= ms Vat 66, 370/22-371/4, 411/5-413/10).

Rabad (R. Abraham ben David of Posquieres),[388] one by Rabbenu Hillel,[389] and the one attributed to R. Samson of Sens[390] – and a relatively large number of commentaries by Aharonim.[391] To these we should add the commentaries on Sifra still in manuscript form, several of which are being published in the Shoshana edition,[392] and many testimonies of extinct Sifra commentaries.[393] All

---

[388] The commentary by Rabad published by Weiss in his edition was reprinted, based on several mss, in the new edition of Sifra commentaries published by A. Shoshana. Three volumes have been published to date: *Baraita de-R. Yishmael* (1991), *Dibura de-Hoba* (1992), *Dibura de-Nedaba*, vol 1 (1998).

[389] Ed. S. Koleditzky, Jerusalem 1961.

[390] For various proposed identifications of the author of the commentary, see ed. Shoshana, *Hovah*, 10-12.

[391] See the detailed listing in ed. Finkelstein, vol 1, 13-21 (Finkelstein's comments in para. 3 are to be corrected in accordance with Naeh, 'Structure, B', 95-98 and Shama, *Mekhilta de-arayot*, 26-28, who demonstrated that the author of *Korban Aharon* made use of a manuscript of Sifra).

[392] (1) The commentary attributed to R. Samuel in ms Munich 59; (2) the commentary by R. Hayyim Havraya; (3) the commentary and emendments by R. Soliman Ohana; (4) the emendments by R. Benjamin ha-Kohen on Sifra and *Korban Aharon* – see their description in ed. Shoshana *loc. cit.* To these we should add: (5) the commentary by R. Hayyim Kafusi in ms Moscow-Guenzburg 19; (6) the commentary by R. Meir Benveniste (the author of *Ot Emet*) in ms Moscow-Guenzburg 112; (7) the commentary and emendments by R. Israel on Sifra and Sifrei. (The commentary that was written on a copy of the Venice printed edition was formerly possessed by the book dealer Naphtali Kaplan of Jerusalem, who gave it to me to examine. It is based in great measure on the commentary and glosses of R. Soliman Ohana, to whom R. Israel explicitly alludes at times ['this I found,' and the like], while frequently adding his own interpretation. He used, inter alia, 'Pesikta' [= Midrash Lekah Tov, Venice printing], Yalkut Shimoni, Ha-Mizrahi, and other printed books, as well as manuscripts of *Rabad* and Rabbenu Hillel, but he apparently did not possess a manuscript of Sifra itself. In one place he states, 'And I wrote its interpretation in my commentary on the Tora' [Sifra, Behukotai 57c]. I made this identification on the basis of a number of places in which he writes 'And it seems to me, Israel.' It would appear that he is R. Israel Benjamin, one of the leading pupils of R. Joseph Ibn Tabul of Egypt, who immigrated to the Land of Israel together with his fellow R. Samuel Ibn Sid, and who was known as an outstanding Tora scholar [see, e.g., his writ of approval at the beginning of the books *Or ha-Hammah* and *Zoharei Hammah*]. R. Israel Benjamin employs similar language: 'It appears to me, Israel' also in some of his glosses and comments on his prayerbook, his Festival prayerbook, and in Kabbalistic writings (see Benayahu, 'Ezra of Pano', 823; *ib.*, 'Sefer Beit Vaad', 139f]. This fact, to which Prof. Benayahu drew my attention, strengthens the hypothesis that R. Israel Benjamin authored the commentary to Sifra;) (8) the commentary by R. Yitshak Aaron ben Meir (Tazria to Behukotai) in ms Jerusalem Nat. and Un. Lib. 8° 98; (9) pages from a commentary in Judeo-Arabic (Shemini, end of chap. 9, to the beginning *parasha* 8) in fragment JTS ENA 2715.46, see its entry in Danzig, *Catalogue*; (10) pages from a commentary on Sifra or on Leviticus that cites Sifra, in the fragment JTS ENA 3382.8, see Danzig, *Catalogue*, the entries for this fragment, 3011.6; (11) for a fragment from the commentary by R. Hananel ben Samuel on Sifra, see Fenton, 'Judaeo-Arabic Commentary', 32f. As regards the Oxford Geniza fragment ms Heb. e 108.27-33 that was mentioned by Fenton (and his erroneous recording of 'c' in place of 'e'), E. Shevat drew my attention to additional leaves from this commentary in the Oxford Geniza fragment ms Heb. d 34.69-77 and ms Heb. e 110.1-8. Further study is required to determine whether this is a commentary on Sifra, or a commentary on Leviticus that frequently quotes and discusses passages from Sifra.

[393] (1) A commentary cited in the Geonic commentary on the Order of Toharot, ed. Epstein, see introduction, 46, 90, 92, and more; (2) the commentary by R. Meir ben Kalonymus, see A. Ep-

in all, we have manuscript evidence of fifty copies of Sifra and more than forty commentaries on the midrash. These figures greatly exceed the number of textual copies and commentaries available for the other Halakhic Midrashim[394] and reflect the premier standing of this work in the Middle Ages. It was very commonly studied in the past, and was an unparalleled tool for the comprehension of difficult topics relating to sacred objects and the purity laws. The fate of the critical publication of Sifra, on the other hand, has not been as positive, and it is to be hoped that this failing will be remedied in the not too distant future.[395]

Sifra is singular in the paucity of aggadic material it contains, the lengthy deliberations of many expositions, the extensive use made of the extant Mishna,[396] and the great proximity to the parallel baraitot in the Bavli, whose sages apparently possessed a Midrash very similar to the extant Sifra.[397] A brief

stein, 'Das talmudische Lexicon', 451; (3) the commentary by R. Samuel he-Hasid, see Urbach, *Tosafists*, 194; (4) the commentary of R. Simhah of Speyer, see Urbach, *Tosafists*, 418; (5) the commentary by R. Moses ben R. Hisdai, that is mentioned by R. Hayyim Or Zaru'a, see Sifra, ed. Shoshana, Hovah, p. 12; (6) the commentary by R. Mordecai ben Joseph, that is mentioned in *Sha'arei Ziyyon*, see Ta-Shma, 'Lost Books', 222; (7) the commentary by ר"ש, see Aptowitzer, *Sefer Rabiyah*, Introduction, 264; (8) the commentary by R. Abraham Zutra, see Lieberman, *Tosefta Ki-Fshutah*, Berakhot, Introduction, 14 n. 3; (9) the commentary by R. Yitshak ben R. Melchizedek, see the commentary by Rabbenu Hillel, Introduction, para. 5; (10) the commentary by R. Isaiah di Trani, see Wertheimer, *Rabbi Isaiah*, Introduction, 60; (11) a commentary mentioned in the list of books from the Geniza by R. Joseph Rosh ha-Seder, see Abramson, 'Rabbi Joseph', 84; (12) a commentary mentioned in the commentary by R. Moses Ibn Musa on the thirteen hermeneutical principles, see Higger, *Ginzberg Jubilee Volume*, Hebrew Section, 95, 114, and more; (13) a commentary possessed by *Maharil* (Jacob ben Moses Moellin), see Dinari, *Rabbis of Germany*, 150.

[394] Kahana, *Manuscripts*, 25.

[395] For additional studies discussing selected passages from Sifra, see, e.g. Geiger, 'Devarim ahadim al ha-Sifra', in *Kevutsat maamarim*, 165-172; Finkelstein, *Sifra*, vol 5, 3-39, 145-174; Fraade, 'Scripture'.

[396] Epstein, *Mavo*, 723-729, brought several proofs for the use by Sifra of the Mishna. Melamed, *Relationship*, discusses this in detail; see his summary p9, that Sifra contains some 400 quotations, about 320 from the Mishna, approximately 90 from the Tosefta, and only about 15 taken from other collections of mishnayot. Reichman has recently attempted to prove the opposite thesis that the Mishna was possessed by Sifra. See Reichman, *Mishna und Sifra*. His argument, however, cannot stand up to a critical examination; to the contrary, a number of vigorous proofs in defense of Epstein's position can be brought from a number of the quotations that he discusses. See, e.g., Kahana, *Sifrei Zuta*, 379 n6. See the review of the book by Stemberger, 'Ronen Reichman'. Cf Neusner, 'Sifra's Critique'; idem, 'Sifra and the Problem'; Stemberger, 'Sifra-Tosefa-Yerushalmi'.

[397] See Melamed, *Halakhic Midrashim in the Babylonian Talmud*, 35f. Cf the summation in his *Introduction*, 261: 'The baraitot of the Halakhic Midrashim in the bavli number approximately 2,300. About half of this number (1,100) are expositions on Leviticus. Some 800 of the latter are from *Torat kohanim*, and only about 300 are from other halakhic midrash collections on Leviticus, that are lost.' See also Naeh, 'Structure, B', 74 n. 85, who refers to three places in the Bavli with lengthy passages taken from Sifra, whose extent is congruous with the units of the Sifra according to our division. One cites the *parasha* in its entirety, even though its end is not relevant to the issue discussed by the Talmud, from which he concluded that the extant division of Sifra also may have been known to the redactors of the Babylonian Talmud; see *ad loc*. For the close association

attempt at identifying the final redactors of Sifra was made by Epstein.[398] According to Finkelstein, the redactors of the extant Sifra drew on an early Midrash on Leviticus that had been used by the Tora scholars who instructed the priests in the work of the Temple and the sacrifices. Based on this assumption, Finkelstein attempted to resolve a long line of difficult expositions, in which the redactors would have cited the early Midrash verbatim, adding a later stratum to make it conform to their approach.[399] This view suits Finkelstein's general stance in the study of Halakhic Midrashim,[400] but it seems that many of his proofs can be refuted.[401] Brown, on the other hand, asserts that along with the ancient midrashim, Sifra also contains expositions reflective of a version later than their parallels in the two Talmuds, but his proofs are unconvincing.[402]

Although, as noted, the core midrash of Sifra is Akivan, it was augmented in a later period by several lengthy passages from the school of R. Yishmael that apparently came from a Halakhic Midrash that went lost. Let us review them:

(1) The baraita of thirteen hermeneutical rules at the beginning of Sifra. This baraita appears in all the textual versions, and there is evidence that it had this opening position already in the Geonic period.[403] The positioning of the baraita at the beginning of Sifra could reflect the ancient practice of beginning the study of the Tora with Leviticus. The baraita is composed of several

between the Bavli, specifically (and not the Yerushalmi) to the Yishmaelian 'Mekhilta de-arayot' see Shama, *Mekhilta de-arayot*, 22. For a contrasting view, see the comment by Melamed, *Halakhic Midrashim in the Babylonian Talmud*, 35 n12 regarding the Akivan main portion of Sifra: 'I learned from a comparison of the quotations with the version of the Yerushalmi that in most places it copies verbatim the exact wording of the extant Torat kohanim, while the version of the Bavli differs from it, either slightly or greatly.' For an illustration of this phenomenon, see Melamed, *Introduction*, 290-292.

[398] See Epstein, *Prolegomena*, 646-663. For the tradition that 'an unattributed [teaching in] Sifra is [that of] R. Yehuda', see above, 'Names of the Sages': the analysis of the findings that R. Yehuda is the most frequently mentioned sage in Sifra and in the other classical works from the school of R. Akiva.

[399] See his edition, vol 1, 21-71; idem, 'Core'.

[400] See above (Early Halakha), and below, section on SifDeut

[401] For an example, see his discussion of Sifra, Kedoshim chap. 7:7-9, 90d. He believes that the changed location of the exposition that is concerned with the question of post-Destruction halakha results from the absence of the exposition in the early Sifra and its post-Destruction insertion in the Sifra of revised redaction, in various places taken from the marginal glosses. In actuality, however, this is merely a simple correction of the order of the expositions in the Ashkenaz textual versions, that was inspired by the parallel in bYev 6a ff.

[402] See Brown, 'Literary Analysis'. In my humble opinion, all that can be deduced from the examples he brings in support of his position is that the redactors of the Sifra were cognizant of the Mishna and other baraitot, and sought to include them during the course of its expositions of the verses, a point on which scholarly opinion is unanimous.

[403] See, e.g., Zucker, 'Two Anti-Karaite Passages', 8, who demonstrated that this was already so prior to R. Saadia Gaon. See also Finkelstein, *Sifra*, vol 1, 186f, since it appears in the list of books from the Geniza and in the Seder Rav Amram Gaon.

sources: (a) the count of the thirteen hermeneutical methods, according to R. Yishmael; (b) the exemplification of these rules in the Scholion that does not always correspond to the original meaning of these principles in the initial baraita;[404] (c) the seven hermeneutical rules of Hillel that were inserted in the middle of the rule of *shenei ketuvim*.[405]

(2) *Mekhilta de-Miluim*[406] which includes expositions of the narrative of the dedication of the Tabernacle at the end of the portion of Tsav and the beginning of Shemini (Lev 8:1-10:7). Several Sifra versions lack this Mekhilta[407] or have only part of it,[408] while in one Geniza fragment it apparently was placed elsewhere than at the end of Tsav.[409] The inner division signs of the Mekhilta de-Miluim in the reliable manuscripts differ from the main body of Sifra.[410] The Mekhilta also contains several terms from the school of R. Yishmael[411] and several contentual matters characteristic of this school.[412] The full version of Mekhilta de-Miluim comprises two cycles of expositions on Lev 9:1 ('On the eighth day'), and two such cycles on Lev 9:22-10:7. Several manuscripts, however, lack the first cycle on 9:22-10:7,[413] and the beginning of the second cycle does not appear in one manuscript.[414] The second cycle of expositions on

[404] See above, 'Development of Exegetical Methods'.

[405] See ed. Finkelstein, vol 2, 9, n. on l. 33. The hermeneutical rule of *shenei ketuvim* is the only one to receive two examples in the Scholion, at least one of which, as well, was probably added from some other source.

[406] Or, 'Aggadat Miluim', 'Tosefta shel parashat Miluim', and similar appellations used by some Rishonim.

[407] ms Breslau and the commentary by Rabbenu Hillel (its omission from this manuscript was already observed by Finkelstein, who was the first scholar to base the discussion of the source of 'Mekhilta de-Miluim' on the finds in the manuscripts; see Finkelstein, 'Sources', 237).

[408] ms Vat 31 contains only the first part, until the end of the portion of Tsav, and similarly in ms Parma, but in the latter the entire 'Mekhilta de-Miluim' was completed, at the end of the manuscript, by another scribe. For the partial omissions in other textual versions, see below, n413, 414.

[409] See Kahana, *Manuscripts*, 69, the description of Cambridge Geniza fragment T-S C 5.4.

[410] Haneman, 'Linguistic Tradition', 85f, commented that ms Vat 66 lacks the subtitles at the beginning and end of 'Mekhilta de-Miluim', and the division into *parashot* and *perakim* also is absent, in contrast with the main body of Sifra. To this we may add that in a Geniza fragment of Musery Collection VI 153.2 the division sign of 'פס' 'סל' (= סליק פסוקא, end of verse), that is characteristic of the alternate division system employed by MekRSbY and SifNum, appears in the first cycle of expositions on Lev 9:22-10:7.

[411] See Hoffmann, 'Einleitung' [1888], 29; Albeck, *Untersuchungen*, 83; Epstein, *Prolegomena*, 641.

[412] See, e.g., the expositions relating to the time of the Tabernacle dedication, that correspond to the method of the school of R. Yishmael in SifNum, and that run counter to the view of R. Akiva (see above, 'Redaction of the Schools Material').

[413] ms Vat 66, the completion in ms Parma, Codex no. 3 of the Geniza fragments (Cambridge T-S NS 252.4 + T-S C 5.9; see Kahana, *Manuscripts*, 68), and also T-S C 5.14. This was most probably the version in the original manuscript, that was completed with the Geniza fragment: Cambridge T-S 329.347; see Kahana, *Manuscripts*, 87.

[414] T-S NS 329.347; for its writing as a *pinkas* (i.e., pages connected lengthwise), and its nature as complementing another Codex, see Kahana, *Manuscripts*, 87.

Lev 9:22 ff. is markedly associated with the school of R. Yishmael, while the first one lacks any clear indicators of its origin.[415]

(3) *Mekhilta de-arayot*.[416] The original Akivan Sifra does not expound the prohibitions of incestuous and other forbidden sexual relations in Aharei (Lev 18:7-18, 20-23)[417] and Kedoshim (Lev 20:10-21). This is understandable, as scholars have noted, in light of R. Akiva's opposition to the public expounding of the passage containing these prohibitions.[418] Several versions of Sifra add a second set of expositions on Lev 18:1-7 in Aharei[419] and expositions on the sexual prohibitions in Lev 20:6-22 in Kedoshim. The end of this unit is an exposition of Lev 18:18 + 28 in a different order from Scripture. These units obviously did not originally belong to the Akivan Sifra, as is also attested by their absence from most versions[420] and from their inclusion at an improper place in some others.[421] The usual division markers of Sifra are missing from these sections in MSS. Vatican 66 and Oxford.[422] The hermeneutical method, the names of sages, and the midrashic terms in these two units patently teach

---

[415] See Epstein, *Prolegomena*, 641: 'The second version, based on its style and the Tannaim mentioned in it, ...is closer to the school of R. Yishmael than the former, that is entirely aggada, and of a late style.' Goldberg, 'Dual Exegeses', 115-118, on the other hand, concluded that only the second cycle of expositions on Lev 9:22-10:7 is Yishmaelian, while the rest of the unit, from the beginning of 'Mekhilta de-Miluim', is an integral part of the original Akivan Midrash. In my opinion, the proofs concisely mentioned above strengthen the major scholarly view that 'Mekhilta de-Miluim' is foreign to Sifra. See also above ('Aggada') regarding the weak connection between the aggadic material in the Halakhic Midrashim to the schools of R. Yishmael and R. Akiva.

[416] Or, in the wording of Rabbenu Hillel, 'Megillat arayot'.

[417] That is to say, all the verses that detail the laws of forbidden sexual relationships, except for Lev 18:19, 'Do not come near a woman during her period of uncleanness to uncover her nakedness,' that apparently was expounded because of its connection to a central halakha that is unrelated to forbidden incestuous marriages.

[418] See above, 'Distinct Exegetical Methods'.

[419] The only verse expounded in the second cycle in addition to those in the first cycle is v7: 'Your father's nakedness, that is, the nakedness of your mother, you shall not uncover,' the exposition of which is part of the *kelal u-ferat* exposition that began in v. 6. Consequently, the section of *arayot* itself was actually not included in this addition, as well.

[420] Ed. Venice and mss Vat 31, Breslau, London, and Parma. Geniza fragment Oxf ms Heb. d 54.2-10 lacks the section of *arayot* in the *parasha* of Aharei, but it is not inconceivable that the section of *arayot* was included in the *parasha* of Kedoshim, that has been lost.

[421] mss Vat 66, Oxf, and the commentaries of Rabbenu Hillel, Rabad, and that attributed to R. Samson of Sens. For their exact location in all the textual versions, see Shama, *Mekhilta de-arayot*, 9-17. To which should be added one page in JTS Rab. 1872, p47f, that includes the beginning of 'Mekhilta de-arayot' in the *parasha* of Aharei, after the end of the *parasha* of Kedoshim of the school of R. Akiva.

[422] In addition to these direct textual versions, 'Mekhilta de-arayot' is also preserved in Codex no. 1 of the Geniza fragments (Paris, Alliance III C 17 + New York JTS ENA 960.29-30). See Kahana, *Manuscripts*, 66-68, and the manuscripts available to the author of *Korban Aharon* (see above, n391); see Shama, *Mekhilta de-arayot*, 26-28. Quotations from this Mekhilta also appear in YalShim, in the three above medieval commentaries, and in other compositions. See Lieberman, *Palestinian Talmudic Literature*, 538, who notes that 'Mekhilta de-arayot' was already written together with Sifra in the time of R. Hai Gaon.

of their origin in the second midrash on Leviticus from the school of R. Yish-mael,[423] which apparently adopted R. Yishmael's permissive stance regarding the public exposition of the sexual prohibitions.

Along with these large units, Sifra also incorporates several short midrashim from the school of R. Yishmael.[424] All these remains indicate the past existence of a Tannaic midrash on Leviticus from the school of R. Yish-mael. This conclusion is supported by a long series of halakhic midrashim on Leviticus from the school of R. Yishmael preserved in the Talmuds.[425] More-over the *paytan* Yannai probably possessed such a midrashic work.[426] To the present, unfortunately, no direct remnant of this lost Midrash has been found.

SIFREI NUMBERS

Sifrei Numbers (SifNum) is a Midrash of the school of R. Yishmael. The Ara-maic word *sifrei* means 'books', and this name is also given to the Halakhic Midrashim on Deuteronomy and, in the past, to one on Exodus.[427] SifNum comprises midrashim on eleven biblical units: Num 5:1-7:19; 7:84-8:4; 8:23-9:14; 10:1-10; 10:29-12:16; 15:1-41; 18:1-19:22; 25:1-14; 26:52-56; 27:1-31:24; 35:9-34. A comparison of the verses that are expounded with those that are not teaches that most of the legal passages are covered, while a majority of the narrative sections are disregarded. This is not an absolute criterion, since

---

[423] This was already sensed by Frankel, *Darkhei ha-Mishna*, 147, and following him, by Fried-mann, in the introduction to this commentary on the Mekhilta, lxv. For a systematic discussion of the topic, see Hoffmann, 'Einleitung' [1888], 29f; Epstein, *Prolegomena*, 340. The conclusion drawn by these scholars, that was based mainly on the version of the printed edition and of Yal-Shim, is reinforced by a study of the mss. A forceful example of this is provided by the exposition of Lev 20:9 in the beginning of 'Mekhilta de-arayot', Sifra Kedoshim 9:5 (91d). The version of ed. Weiss is: 'איש - what does Scripture teach by איש איש [if any man]? To include (לרבות) the daughter, the *tumtum* [person of indeterminate sex], and the *androginos* [hermaphrodite].' The exposition of the repetitive language איש איש and the term לרבות are characteristic of the school of R. Akiva. This version, however, is adapted on the basis of bSan 66a, while ms Vat 66 contains a completely different exposition that is free of Akivan elements: '"If any man curses his father or his mother" (Lev 20:9) – this teaches only regarding the man; whence [do we learn also] the woman, the *tumtum*, and the *androginos*? Scripture teaches: "He who curses his father or his mother shall be put to death" (Exod 21:17).'

[424] See Epstein, *Prolegomena*, 639, 682-691 (see above, n363, regarding the *parasha* of Behuko-tai).

[425] See Melamed, *Halachic Midrashim in the Babylonian Talmud*, 35f. See the details in the in-dented material (Yishmaelian), 161-331; idem, *Palestinian Talmud*, 45-100.

[426] See Lieberman, 'Hazanut Yannai', 229-234 (= idem, *Palestinian Talmudic Literature*, 131-136). The other proofs advanced by scholars who sought to find traces of the Yishmaelian Midrash in the midrashim on Leviticus are not convincing. See Rabinovitz, *Ginze Midrash*, 51-59. And similarly, the fragment published by Ginzberg, *Geniza Studies*, vol 1, 67-83, that seemingly contains only abridgments from the extant Sifra, as is correctly noted by Zucker, 'Teguvot', 396-398.

[427] See Epstein, *Studies*, vol 2, 183-189. SifNum is additionally named 'Sifrei de-vei Rav', 'Sifrei Rabbati', 'Sefer Vayedaber', 'Mekhilta/Makhalah Vayedaber', and others. See Epstein, *ib.*

several narrative sections, such as the complaint by the people in the wilderness, or the act of Phinehas at Shittim, are expounded, while several halakhic topics are not, such as the commandment to dispossess the inhabitants of the land and the destruction of the cult places (*bamot*). It is difficult to determine the criteria for the inclusion of expositions in SifNum.

SifNum was formerly divided into two books, each named after their beginning. The first was called *Sefer vayedaber*, after the initial word of the first verse expounded in Num 5:1, 'The Lord spoke [*vayedaber*] to Moses,'[428] and the second apparently was named *Sefer zot*, because it opened with the words 'This is [*zot*] the statute of the Tora' (Num 19:2).[429] This rare division of the portions in Numbers (Bamidbar-Korah in one unit, and Hukat-Massaei in the other, instead of the usual Bamidbar-Shelah and Korah-Massaei) is reflected in a testimony from the Cairo Geniza regarding the commentary by R. Shmuel ben Hofni on 'the book of *Zot hukat ha-Tora*'.[430] Each of the two books is divided into secondary topics, which are further divided into 'baraitot'. The numerical sum of baraitot is listed at the end of each subject, in the interim division of each of the two books, and at the conclusion of each of the two books themselves.[431] Another division of SifNum is by verses (סליק פסוקא, 'end of verse'),[432] but this would seem to be a later apportionment.[433] The division according to the Babylonian Tora portions in several inferior manuscripts is not original.[434]

A critical edition of SifNum was published by H.S. Horovitz in Leipzig, 1917. The body of the edition is based on the *editio princeps*, Venice 1546, with corrections and additions from MSS. Vatican 32 and London 341 and numerous citations from SifNum in Yalkut Shimoni, Midrash Hakhamim, the commentary on SifNum by Rabbenu Hillel, and several medieval midrashim. The edited text is accompanied by a critical apparatus and a concise running

---

[428] Or, possibly, the calling of the entire Book of Numbers by this name, based on the first verse in the book.

[429] See Kahana, *Prolegomena*, 122-125.

[430] See Abramson, *Center and Periphery*, 73f. Cf Kahana, *Prolegomena, ib.*

[431] Traces of the original division into subjects and baraitot remain especially in ms Vat. See Kahana, *Prolegomena*, 125f.

[432] This expression is corrupted in the printed versions of SifNum, in which it appears as סליק פיסקא, 'end of *piska*'. The numerical count of the *piskaot* was first added in the printed edition of SifNum containing the commentary *Zera Avraham* (Dyhrenfurth 1811); the references to SifNum and SifDeut in the scholarly literature follow this division.

[433] A proof for the relative lateness of the division into verses may be brought from the absence in the good manuscripts of the סליק פסוקא. notation at the end of several subjects, such at the end of the section of *halla* (p116), an omission that most likely was due to the alternate notation there for the baraitot. The notation for the conclusion of the פסוקא at the end of the section of the *nahalot* (land holdings) (p179, l. 18) is absent from all the textual versions; ms Vat has, in its stead, the summation י"ב ברייתא.

[434] In one place (131, p173) a single literary unit contains verses from two Babylonian Tora portions. For a discussion of the forced attempt by ms Berlin and Midrash Hakhamim to add, in the middle of the exposition, a title for the portion of *Pinhas*, see Kahana, *Prolegomena*, 13f.

commentary which also indicates parallels. The edition begins with a lengthy introduction that includes, inter alia, a characterization of the hermeneutical method of SifNum. It is the first critical edition of any work from Tannaic literature; only following its completion did Horovitz, who was 'marvelously erudite and a profound thinker',[435] begin preparing his editions of MekRY and SifDeut.

Unavoidably, however, this pioneer edition has limitations. Additional primary textual versions of SifNum were discovered after the publication of Horovitz's edition: most importantly ms Oxford 151; ms Berlin Tübingen 1594.33;[436] eight leaves of ms Firkovich II A 269; Yalkut Talmud Tora by R. Yaakov ben Hananel Sikili that quotes extensive portions of SifNum; several commentaries on SifNum by Rishonim; midrashim by Rishonim who made use of SifNum, and more.[437] In determining the text of SifNum, Horovitz relied heavily upon the reworked and emended text of Midrash Hakhamim that he considered to be the best textual version of SifNum, while ms Vatican, the oldest manuscript of SifNum, was regarded by him to be a manuscript of lesser quality. This erroneous appraisal of the manuscripts ensued primarily from his confusion between the textual versions of SifNum and its parallels, and also from his unawareness of several basic principles of talmudic philology that were developed only after the publication of his edition. Note should also be taken of his selective listing of variants and the harmonizing tendency evident in many of his interpretations.[438]

As was mentioned above, the best manuscript of SifNum is Vatican 32. This is expressed in various features it possesses, such as: traces of the early division of SifNum; remnants of Tannaic language; rare or difficult words that were emended in other textual versions; original terminology; the special style of the expositions; a particular version of the Mishna, where other textual versions frequently emended in accordance with the extant Mishna; baraitot that were not reworked in accordance with their parallels in Bavli; surviving remnants of early halakhot; a version of the Bible different from the Massoretic text; and a more marked form of foreign elements contained in the text.[439] Along with its authentic readings, ms Vatican also contains many cases

---

[435] Following Lieberman, *Siphre Zutta*, 4.

[436] ms Berlin was already used by Kuhn, who devoted a special appendix to the description and listing of its textual variants, in comparison with ed. Horovitz, as an appendix to Kuhn's translation to German of SifNum See Kuhn, *Sifre zu Numeri*, 703-775.

[437] See the details in my work, *Prolegomena*, that is based on the Ph.D. dissertation that I wrote under the supervision of Prof. E.S. Rosenthal. After the publication of the book, I received additional leaves of SifNum; see Kahana, *Manuscripts*, 89-94. For transcriptions of all the fragments see Kahana, *Genizah fragments*, 187-213. More citations from SifNum were also uncovered in various works still in manuscripts, such as the commentary by the Karaite sage Yeshua ben Yehuda on Numbers, and the Midrash by R. Samuel ben Nissim Masnut. A comprehensive survey of this material will appear in a new edition of SifNum that I am currently preparing.

[438] See the detailed discussion in Kahana, *Prolegomena*, 277-294.

[439] See Kahana, *Prolegomena*, 116-227.

of *homoioteleuton*, interchanged letters, and even a small number of emendations and adaptations. Obviously, other textual versions must be employed as well, both in order to reconstruct the original readings of SifNum, and to study their evolution in the Middle Ages.[440]

A number of Rishonim composed commentaries on SifNum, most of which also cover SifDeut. Most important are the commentaries of Rabbenu Hillel,[441] the one attributed to Rabad,[442] the commentary in ms Mantua 36,[443] and that by R. Soliman Ohana.[444] Outstanding commentaries by Aharonim on SifNum are those by R. David Pardo, R. Meir Friedmann (Ish Shalom), and R. Naphtali Zvi Yehuda Berlin (the 'Netziv').[445]

---

[440] For the genealogy of the textual versions, see *ib.*, 229f. and the summational table, 276. For support for the hypothesis that the source of Yalkut Talmud Tora is indeed Sephardic, see Kahana, 'Midrashic Fragments', 44f.

[441] This commentary was published twice by S. Koleditzky. The first edition (Jerusalem 1948) was based on ms Sassoon, that is fragmentary and very corrupted. The second edition (Jerusalem 1985) follows ms Vienna, a ms that was emended in accordance with the Venice printed version of Sifrei. Consequently, both editions suffer from numerous flaws. See the detailed analysis, Kahana, 'Commentary of Rabbenu Hillel'.

[442] I discussed the textual versions of this commentary and its great importance in *Prolegomena*, 77-81; and in 'Manuscripts Commentaries', 96-100, before asking my colleague Prof. H.W. Basser to publish the critical edition. See Basser, *Pseudo-Rabad, Numbers* and idem, *Pseudo-Rabad, Deuteronomy*, in which he succeeded in deciphering most of the commentator's references and allusions. Unfortunately, the edition is frequently plagued by inaccurate transcriptions of the version in the manuscripts. Basser was also excessive in the radical addenda and emendations that he added on his own (correctly placing them within brackets), that are often unnecessary. In the editor's introduction to the commentary on Numbers he took note of several new points that I had previously overlooked. On the other hand, several of Basser's observations in his introduction should be corrected. It is our hope that he will be able to complete his original plan to publish a new and corrected edition of this important commentary.

[443] See its description in my *Prolegomena*, 70-76; idem, 'Manuscripts Commentaries', 100-105; cf Ta-Shema, 'Unpublished Franco-German Commentary'. Many textual variants from this manuscript, along with some of its halakhic discussions, were published in the second edition of Rabbenu Hillel's commentary on Sifrei. See also Herskovitz, *Sefer ha-Perushim*, Introduction, 17, who proposes that R. Avigdor Zarfati is the author of the commentary on Sifrei in ms Mantua. Several of the proofs that he brought for the suggested attribution of the commentary on Sifrei are intriguing and should be examined, but his proposal to view Zarfati also as the author of the commentary on MekRY, GenR, and LevR is tenuous. It would seem that the editor drew heavily upon my article and the article by Ta-Shema mentioned above, although, for reasons known only to him, without mentioning this.

[444] For its descriptions, see Kahana, *Prolegomena*, 82-85; idem, 'Manuscripts Commentaries', 107-110.

[445] For a listing of these and other commentaries, see Kahana, 'Manuscripts Commentaries', to which we should add: (1) the commentary on Sifrei by R. Eliezer Nahum, based on the author's autograph in the Institute of Oriental Studies in St. Peterburg, that I published: *Rabbi Eliezer Nahum*; (2) the commentary on Sifrei attributed to R. Benjamin (see above, section on Sifra, n392, no. [7]); (3) four leaves from a medieval commentary on SifNum (see Fenton, 'Découverte', 97-101); (4) fragments from the Arabic commentary on SifNum by R. Hananel ben Shmuel (see Fenton, 'Judaeo-Arabic Commentary', 32f [it perhaps is a commentary on Numbers; see above, section on Sifra, n392 no. 10]); (5) the commentary by Raban (R. Eliezer ben Joel of Bonn) on

An exceptional feature of SifNum is the number of foreign elements it incorporates, some of which are inserted in the middle of expositions, interrupting the flow, while the placement of others does not follow the order of the Pentateuch.[446] Some of these foreign elements are cited in the name of R. Yehuda ha-Nasi or 'Rabbi', or are attributed to him in talmudic parallels.[447] Moreover most of Rabbi's dicta in SifNum that do fit in the course of the expositions are presented as a last opinion concluding the exposition. This leads us to believe that the initial redaction of SifNum was followed by the insertion of another stratum from 'the school of Rabbi'.[448] Attention should also be paid to the fact that SifNum barely contains expositions in the name of Tannaim from the generation after R. Yehuda the Prince.[449] This may indicate a rather early date of redaction. The brevity of the expositions in SifNum in comparison with other Halakhic Midrashim and the relative paucity of associative expansions in this Midrash would seem to support this surmise.[450]

SIFREI ZUTA NUMBERS

Sifrei Zuta Numbers (SifZNum) is an Akivan Midrash. Aramaic *zuta* means 'small', corresponding to the name *Sifrei Rabbati*, 'the larger *Sifrei*' given to SifNum by several Rishonim. The Geniza fragments of SifZNum, however, do not confirm the limited scope of the Midrash as compared to SifNum,[451] so the name may possibly attest to its rarity.[452] The exact extent of SifZNum has not been determined. However, like SifNum, it clearly opened with an exposition

---

Sifrei to which his grandson Raviyah (Rabbi Eliezer ben Yaakov) attests (see *Sefer Raviyah*, ed. Dablitsi, 39 [the editor proposes emending this as if it were the commentary by Rabbenu Hillel]; 43 [the passages he cites are from SifDeut]). My thanks to my student R. Reiner for drawing my attention to this reference.

[446] For a number of examples of this phenomenon, that Horovitz ands Epstein already noted, see Kahana, *Prolegomena*, 217-227.

[447] See Epstein, *Mavo*, 749-751; Kahana, 'Marginal Annotations'.

[448] The phenomenon that R. Yehuda ha-Nasi's dicta are usually cited at the end of an exposition was already observed by Goldberg, 'Leshonot davar aher', 104. Goldberg, however, explained this differently, namely, the general method of Halakhic Midrashim to include the views of the rabbis of the other school at the end of the expositions. Cf Kahana, 'Marginal Annotations', 79-84.

[449] R. Elazar, the son of R. Elazar ha-Kappar, is mentioned a single time, SifNum p46; R. Hiyya, a single time (p129; the variant readings there, 'Rabbi' or 'R. Meir', apparently are not original), and R. Yose ben Eliezer or Elazar, who is mentioned on p82, is possibly the grandson of R. Shimon ben Yohai (Samuel bar Nahmani, who is mentioned on p69, is not the prominent Amora, but a Tanna; see Kahana, 'Midrashic Fragments', 53f). Cf above, 'Names of the Sages', near the end.

[450] For an expanded discussion of SifNum, that includes a study of its terminology, hermeneutical method, connection to other Halakhic Midrashim, and its redaction, see Borner-Klein, *Der Midrasch Sifre*.

[451] The scope of the SifZNum Geniza fragment of Matot and Massaei is approximately equivalent to that of the parallel material in SifNum, while the extent of the SifZNum Geniza fragment of *Hukat* is about one third longer than that of SifNum on the same Tora portion.

[452] Other names for this Midrash are 'Sifrei', 'Zutei', 'Sifrei Yerushalmi', 'Sifrei shel panim aherot', 'Mekhilta', 'Makhalah', and others. See Epstein, *Prolegomena*, 741.

of the first law in Num 5:2,[453] skipped Num 31:25-35:8,[454] again just like Sif-Num, and as a general rule included expositions on the same verses as Sif-Num.[455] In any event, the fragmentary preservation of the work does not allow us to estimate its original scope.[456]

The Midrash was originally divided into several large subunits, each of which encompassed several topics. The larger units, whose scope and names are not known to us, were divided into numbered *parashiyyot*.[457]

Zunz was the first scholar to collect material about Rishonim quoting SifZNum and about the different names of the work;[458] following him, Brüll[459] and others thoroughly discussed the Midrash.[460] Schechter successfully identified and published a Geniza fragment consisting of two leaves from SifZNum on the Tora portions of Matot and Massaei.[461] At the same time B. Koenigsberger began to reconstruct the Midrash in orderly fashion, but he was able to publish only two instalments, from the portion of Bamidbar to that of Behaa-

---

[453] As is demonstrated from the list of books discovered in a Cambridge Geniza fragment (T-S Loan 149), that includes '...כתאב מכלה ואבתדאה, The book of Halakhic Midrash, beginning: Since it is said, "She shall not touch any consecrated thing" (Lev 12:4) – one would think, that this includes tithes' (cf Mann, *Texts and Studies*, vol 1, 645). The beginning of SifZNum at this place is also inferred by the name given the Midrash by R. Natan ben Yehiel in the *Arukh*: מדרש פנים אחרים של וישלחו (based on Num 5:2, 'to remove, וישלחו from camp'); this is also the first quotation from SifZNum in YalShim. See also the reference in 'Index of Derashot of Maimonides', in J.L. Maimon, *Rabbenu Moshe ben Maimon*, 11: "'If anyone who has become unclean fails to cleanse himself" (Num 19:20) – at the beginning of Sifrei Zutei' (= ed. Horovitz, p1 l. 16).

[454] As in the Geniza fragment of the portions of Matot and Massaei.

[455] See its scattered expositions that are cited in YalShim and MidrGad.

[456] Epstein, *Prolegomena*, 600, seemingly sought to offer a proof for his surmise that *piska* 131 from the portion of Balak in SifNum is 'apparently taken from the school of R. Akiva' by writing: 'Sifrei Zuta does not contain any exposition on this portion.' The commentary by Rabbenu Hillel on this *piska*, however, explicitly states: 'Thus it is taught in Sifrei Zuta: the chieftain of Pharaoh came to him at night' (and so in ed. S. Koleditzky [Jerusalem, 1985], 182, that is based on ms Vienna. This quotation is omitted from ms Frankfurt, that was used by Horovitz, and from ms Sassoon, on which Koleditzky based his first edition of the commentary by Rabbenu Hillel, and therefore was overlooked by Epstein). For the phenomenon of passages from SifZNum that were not cited by YalShim because of their similarity to expositions in SifNum, see Lieberman, *Siphre Zutta*, 10 n36.

[457] The Geniza fragment of the portion of Hukat includes a subdivision from 'parash[a] 8' to 'parash[a] 13'. The beginning of the portion of Hukat and the accompanying division sign (parasha 7?) are not preserved, but parasha 1 of this unit clearly began with another topic that preceded that of the red heifer. In the second Geniza fragment from Matot and Massaei, the beginning of the topic of the cities of refuge is marked as 'parash[a] 12', and the notation of 'parash[a] 13' appears in the continuation of the same topic. The place where the *parasha* begins is unclear, but the presence of parashiyyot with the same numbers in the portion of Hukat, as well, patently indicates that SifZNum was originally divided into several subunits ('*masekhtot*', as in MekRY? '*megillot*', as in Sifra?).

[458] See Zunz-Albeck, *Vorträge*, 267.

[459] See Brull, 'Der kleine Sifre'.

[460] See the literature listed in Epstein, *Prolegomena*, 741; Lieberman, *Siphre Zutta*, 3f.

[461] Schechter, 'Fragment of Sifre Zutta'.

lotekha.[462] The first reconstruction of SifZNum as a whole was made by Horovitz, initially with notes in German,[463] subsequently in Hebrew, with an independent critical apparatus and an extensive commentary that also indicates parallels. The second edition published in Leipzig in 1917 together with Horovitz's edition of SifNum also includes an introduction that describes the unique nature of the Midrash.

Horovitz based his reconstruction on the explicit quotations of 'zutei' in Yalkut Shimoni; passages in Midrash ha-Gadol that he asserted were copied from SifZNum;[464] the Geniza fragment published by Schechter; quotations incorporated in Numbers Rabba on Naso; and citations in the writings of the Rishonim. After the appearance of Horovitz's edition, Epstein published a fragment of five leaves from SifZNum on the passage of the red heifer that he identified in material sent to him from St. Petersburg.[465] Also published were a small number of citations from SifZNum that were recognized in the writings of the Rishonim,[466] to which we may add several further quotations.[467] The Horovitz edition must also be revised in accordance with ms Oxford 2637 of Yalkut Shimoni,[468] the manuscripts of Midrash ha-Gadol on Numbers,[469] and the manuscripts and *editio princeps* of Numbers Rabba.[470] On the other hand, the Horovitz edition should be rid of a rather large number of passages from Midrash ha-Gadol he included and which did not in fact originate in SifZNum but in SifNum,[471] MekRSbY, the Mishna, Avot de-R. Natan, the two Talmuds, Tanhuma, Mishnat R. Eliezer, Pirkei de-R. Eliezer, the Mishne Tora of Maimonides, and additions made by the author of Midrash ha-Gadol on his

[462] First instalment: Frankfurt 1894; second instalment: Pleschen 1907 (the editor was of the opinion that SifZNum also included passages from the portion of Bamidbar, but see above, n453).

[463] This edition was initially published in successive instalments in *MGWJ* 50-54 (1906-1910), later in a single volume: Horovitz, *Sifre Zutta* (1910).

[464] Horovitz printed the doubtful passages from MidrGad in small letters; he marked the passages that are preserved only there with an initial circle, and the certain passages that appear only in YalShim, with an initial hyphen.

[465] Epstein, 'Sifrei Zutta'. New transcriptions of SifZNum fragments see Kahana, *Genizah fragments*, 214-226.

[466] See Lieberman, *Siphre Zutta*, 6f; Kahana, 'To Whom', 261-264; idem, *Prolegomena*, 65f, 72f.

[467] See, e.g., the citations from *Sefer ha-Mitzvot* by R. Hefetz ben Yatzliah, and esp *Midrash Hadash* published by Mann, *The Bible as Read*, that consistently quotes SifZNum in its sermons on Numbers; see Kahana, *Sifrei Zuta*, 38 n11.

[468] This manuscript is superior to the *editio princeps* of YalShim (Salonika 1526-1527) that was used by Horovitz.

[469] Horovitz's edition followed a single manuscript, while now it is possible to make use of two editions of MidrGad on Numbers, each of which is based on different manuscripts: ed. S. Fisch, vol 1 (London 1958), vol 2 (Jerusalem 1963); and the edition of Z.M. Rabinovitz (Jerusalem 1967).

[470] Horovitz used the later and corrected Romm edition (Vilna 1878). For the *editio princeps* published in Constantinople 1512, and the manuscripts of this Midrash, see Kahana, *Prolegomena*, 107-112.

[471] MidrGad on Numbers made considerable use of SifNum, as Rabinovitz correctly observed in the introduction to his edition, 7. Horovitz was undecided on this issue; see his introduction to SifNum, xix; consequently, he included several passages from SifNum in his edition of SifZNum.

monides, and additions made by the author of Midrash ha-Gadol on his own account.[472]

SifZNum became the subject of two traditional commentaries[473] and of modern studies written by three major scholars: Epstein,[474] Albeck,[475] and Lieberman, who devoted an entire book to this Midrash.[476]

Although SifZNum is of Akivan vintage, it is distinguished from the classic Midrashim of this school in a number of realms: (1) it makes use of a relatively large number of unique terms;[477] (2) it mentions the names of several Tannaim who do not appear elsewhere;[478] (3) it often uses a style absent from the other sources, as well as rhetorical and poetical language;[479] (4) it includes a large quantity of halakhot not documented in other sources as well as otherwise unknown disagreements of Beit Hillel and Beit Shammai;[480] and (5) it consistently quotes a Mishna version that does not correspond to the extant Mishna.[481]

Scholars have also noted that Rabbi's name is absent from this work.[482] Lieberman drew this distinction sharper into focus by noting that halakhot of Rabbi (R. Yehuda the Prince) and of R. Natan do appear in SifZNum, but without attribution.[483] Lieberman additionally indicated 'clear allusions' against the Patriarchate in the expositions of SifZNum. In light of this evidence, he concluded that the redactor of SifZNum was in conflict with the Patriarchate of R. Yehuda the Prince, did not acknowledge the superior authority of his Mishna, and intentionally refrained from mentioning both his name and that of R. Natan, who was the son of the Exilarch – thus 'punishing' both leaders, the Nasi in the land of Israel and the Exilarch in Babylonia.[484] It should be noted that the innuendos against the court of the Nasi identified by Lieberman are not unambiguous. Nor is the omission of R. Natan from SifZNum unique to this

---

[472] See Epstein, *Mavo*, 741; idem, *Prolegomena*, 745; Lieberman, *Siphre Zutta*, 12f, 83f, 108, 142; Kahana, *Sifrei Zuta*, 42f.

[473] Jaskowicz, *Sifre Zuta* (that also includes a Hebrew translation for Horovitz's introductions to SifNum and SifZNum that were written in German); Garbus, *Sifre Zuta*.

[474] See his introduction to a passage from the section of the red heifer that he published, and idem, *Prolegomena*, 741-746.

[475] Albeck, 'Zu den neueren', 404-410; idem, *Untersuchungen*, 148-151.

[476] Lieberman, *Siphre Zutta*.

[477] See Horovitz, Introduction, xvi; Epstein, *Prolegomena*, 741-746; Albeck, 'Zu den neueren', 404-410.

[478] See Lieberman, *Siphre Zutta*, 81.

[479] As is maintained by Lieberman, *Siphre Zutta*, 75-80, 116-122. For the issue of the poetical wordings, cf Kahana, *Sifrei Zuta*, 79-80.

[480] See Lieberman, *Siphre Zutta*, 64-74, 116-122.

[481] See Epstein, *Mavo*, 739-746; Lieberman, *Siphre Zutta*, 11-64.

[482] See Hoffmann, 'Einleitung' [1888], 63; Epstein, *Prolegomena*, 745.

[483] See Lieberman, *Siphre Zutta*, 83-87.

[484] See *ib.*, 87-91.

Midrash; to the contrary, the feature is characteristic of all Akivan Midra-shim.[485]

It is also noteworthy that while the material in the lengthy aggadic sections of SifZNum basically resembles the parallel material in SifNum, it usually is a bit more detailed. On rare occasions does the aggadic material contain traces of the singular terms and sages characteristic of the halakhic material of the work,[486] and in a number of passages it is even possible to identify a consistent approach that noticeably differs from the aggadic material in SifNum.[487]

The exceptional character of SifZNum has challenged scholars into trying to identify its final redactor,[488] but it seems that only the discovery of new passages from this Midrash and other ones redacted by the same school will advance the discussion.

SIFREI DEUTERONOMY

Sifrei on Deuteronomy (SifDeut) is basically a Midrash of the school of R. Akiva. It encompasses six sections from Deuteronomy: 1:1-30; 3:23-29; 6:4-9; 11:10-26:15; 31:14; 32:1-34:12 (the end of Deuteronomy). Each of the initial verses of the six units also begins a Palestinian *seder*,[489] but the principle that guided the redactors of SifDeut in including expositions on these sections is unclear.

The *editio princeps* divides SifDeut into *piskaot* (סליק פיסקא, 'end of *piska*'), like the division of the printed edition of SifNum. Most manuscripts contain a division into verses (סליק פסוקא, 'end of verse'). In a number of places, there is an alternative division into chapters (סליק פירקא, 'end of chap-ter'), and rather frequently, the unclear abbreviation 'פ appears. In most of the complete manuscripts, however, the division is irregular, as it the case in Sif-Num; and no division markers are preserved in Geniza fragments from a num-ber of codices.[490] Some of the added notations of *piskaot* in the relatively com-

---

[485] See above, 'Names of the Sages'. Further study should be devoted to the question of whether they, too, exhibit the phenomenon of expressing unattributed views, as is the practice in SifZNum; see Horovitz in his introduction to SifZNum, xix; Lieberman, *Siphre Zutta*, 89.

[486] See Epstein, *Prolegomena*, 743; Kahana, *Sifrei Zuta*, 94-96.

[487] See, e.g., the consistent approach of SifZNum, 250-253, in favor of the independent enterprise of the chieftains at the dedication of the Sanctuary, and against Moses, who hesitated to accept their offering. The parallel exposition of SifNum (p51-53), in contrast, expresses its reservations at the initiative of the chieftains, while fully justifying the response by Moses.

[488] See above, 'Time and Place of Redaction'.

[489] *Sedarim* 1, 4, 6, 10, 25, 26; see also above, n267, for the reflection of the Palestinian division of the Halakhic Midrashim into *sedarim*. The fifth unit is actually an exposition of only the first verse in *seder* 25 (31:14), as is common in the Palestinian Aggadic Midrashim in the Amoraic period.

[490] Slightly more than half of the *piskaot* that are marked in the printed version are marked in ms Vat 32 (of the 305 end of *piska* markers until the beginning of Haazinu, where the manuscript leaves off, some 170 division markers appear in ms Vat (most consisting of the abbreviated mark-ing 'פ, the minority with פסוקא 'סל, 'end of verse', or one of its abbreviations: 'פסו, 'פס, and in one instance: סליק פירקא, 'end of chapter'). The division marks are relatively numerous in ms Berlin, as

plete division of the printed edition disrupt the flow of the expositions.[491] At the same time, SifDeut preserves remnants of a presumably earlier division into 'baraitot',[492] as also of a later division into the Babylonian weekly Tora portions.[493]

Most scholars regard the central unit of SifDeut, that uninterruptedly expounds the legal passages in Deut 12:1-26:15 (*piskaot* 59-303), as Akivan. It is also accepted that the expositions of the *Shema* passages (Deut 6:4-9 and 11:13-21; *piskaot* 31-36 and 41-47) contain clear signs pointing to the school of R. Yishmael. The affiliation, however, of the aggadic sections in the first and last parts of SifDeut is the subject of disagreement. Hoffmann initially thought that the entire first part of the Midrash (*piskaot* 1-58) is Yishmaelian, and the last part (*piskaot* 304-357) Akivan.[494] He later changed his opinion and attributed the last aggadic section beginning with *piska* 304 also to the school of R. Yishmael.[495] This view was fundamentally also held by Epstein, though he considered the Yishmaelian aggada section at the beginning of SifDeut as

---

well (mostly ס' פ'). In ms London, in contrast, SifDeut contains only eleven division markers: five instances of סליק פסוקא, in full or in abbreviated form at the beginning of the Midrash: the end of *piskaot* 1, 25 (before the beginning of Vaethanan), 30 (before the beginning of 'Hear, O Israel'), 39, 52 (end of *Ekev*); one פרשה in the portion of *Reeh* (end of *piska* 96); and five instances of סליק פסוקא in the portions of Ki tetsei and Ki tavo (end of *piskaot* 287, 291, 295, 296, 301). ms Oxf contains ten division markers, the majority in places similar to those in ms London: three סליק פירקא, in full or in abbreviation, in the beginning of the Midrash (end of *piskaot* 1, 25, 30); two adjoining letters פ' in the portion of *Reeh* (end of *piska 'ot* 96, 98); four סל' פס' or פס' in the portion of *Ki tetse* (end of *piskaot* 287, 291, 295, 296); and one סל' פיר' in Ki tavo (end of *piska* 301). No division markers are preserved in most of the Geniza fragments (see the description of Codices no. 3, 5, 6, 7, 8, 10, 11 in Kahana, *Manuscripts*, 100-105). One Codex (no. 9) contains a single instance of סלק פירק', and another Codex (no. 13), a solitary instance of סליק פסוקא The Spanish Codex no. 1, in contrast, marks these divisions in orderly fashion with סל' פס'. The Yemenite Codices (nos. 4, 12, 14) expressly mark the end of each verse withסליק פסקא or פס (cf also below, the description of MekDeut, n522, for a description of the סל' פס division in the Yemenite codex of MekDeut).

[491] See, e.g., סליק פיסקא, p378, l. 10, that interrupts the exposition of R. Yehuda in the middle.

[492] See the three interim summations in ms Vat: p84 l. 6, before the beginning of the expositions of 'If, then, you obey': ב}{ב' א' עד הכא צ'א מראשיה {ב}בריאתא, 'From the beginning to here, 91 {*b*}*baraita*' (the initial *bet* was erased, apparently by the scribe; possibly, the doubling of the *bet* marked a letter accentuated by a *dagesh* [the copying from the Finkelstein edition is not accurate]); p244, at the end of *Shoftim*: '63 *baraita*'; p. 322, at the end of *Ki tavo*: '9 *baraita*'. Cf the similar summaries preserved in the topic conclusions in SifNum (see the description above). ms Berlin of SifDeut contains such a division in two almost regular cycles at the beginning of SifDeut The first unit (Deut 1:1-30) contains 42 sections, followed by an additional cycle of 66 sections, that ends in the middle of *Ekev* (p. 86 l. 4); see Kahana, *Prolegomena*, 14 n13. (Two remnants of this division also remained in Codex no. 2, that was reconstructed from bookbindings in Modena and in Nonantola; see Kahana, *Manuscripts*, 100.) This division is not exactly the same as the division into 'baraitot' in ms Vat, since it lists, until the beginning of 'If, then, you obey,' 104 sections, and not 91, as is attested by ms Vat.

[493] This is also the case for ms Vat, the best manuscript, that copied the words והיה עקב and שפטים.

[494] See Hoffmann, 'Einleitung' [1888], 66f.

[495] See Hoffmann, 'Zur Einleitung in den Midrasch Tannaim', 307.

encompassing only *piska'ot* 1-54. Epstein placed the changeover between the schools at the end of *piska* 54 on the basis of a Geniza fragment of the (Yishmaelian) MekDeut discovered by Schechter; it resembles SifDeut *piska* 54 but beginning with *piska* 55 completely diverges from it.[496] Goldberg reexamined the question and concluded that the aggadic sections at the beginning of Sif-Deut (*piskaot* 1-54, excluding the *Shema* passages) and at its end are from the school of R. Akiva, in accordance with his view that all the longer aggadic sections in the Halakhic Midrashim belong to this school.[497] At this point we recall the observation made in the section 'Aggada' above that most of the characteristics of the two schools do not find expression in the aggadic material and that the parallel aggadic material has a great similarity, especially so in SifDeut and MekDeut.[498] In light of this, the 'seam' at the beginning of *piska* 55 is to be viewed as a transition from the aggadic material that does not belong to either school to the halakhic material from the school of R. Akiva.

L. Finkelstein published a critical edition of SifDeut[499] in Berlin in 1939, a month after the outbreak of World War II.[500] He based his edition on five almost complete primary textual witnesses that contain both SifNum and Sif-Deut, i.e. the *editio princeps* and four manuscripts;[501] furthermore using six short Geniza fragments,[502] Midrash Hakhamim, Yalkut Shimoni, and additional secondary versions. As regards the text, Finkelstein writes in his introduction: 'For the most part, I chose the versions of ms Rome, rejecting it only where it was clear that another version was superior.'[503] In regard to the spelling in the edition, Finkelstein explained in his introduction: 'The text of *Sifrei* was writ-

---

[496] See Epstein, *Studies*, vol 2, 125f; idem, *Prolegomena*, 625-630. Cf the view of Albeck that *piskaot* 31-54 in SifDeut are similar to MekRY and SifNum, *Untersuchungen*, 84; idem, *Introduction*, 95 n32.

[497] See Goldberg, 'School of Rabbi Akiva'.

[498] See Kahana, 'New Fragments', 486f.

[499] As Finkelstein attests in his introduction, he spent fifteen years on the preparation of his edition. See his articles that preceded the edition: Finkelstein, 'Prolegomena to an Edition'; idem, 'Improved Readings'; 'Maimonides' (= Finkelstein, *Sifra*, vol 5, 53*-152*).

[500] Most of the copies of this edition remained in Germany and were lost, and consequently, until 1969, when a second edition of the book was published, many scholars were forced to continue using the Friedmann (Ish-Shalom) edition of SifDeut as a basis for their research.

[501] mss Vat and London, that were also used by Horovitz in the preparation of his edition of Sif-Num, and mss Oxf and Berlin, that were not available to him. Unfortunately, the ends of mss Vat, Oxf, and Berlin are not complete, and for the last part of his edition Finkelstein according relied only on the two other textual versions. For the passages of 'Hear, O Israel,' and 'If, then, you obey,' Finkelstein also referred to ms Rome Casanatensa, that contains Halakhic Midrashim fragments whose biblical verses are integrated in the daily prayer.

[502] Two of them (T-S C 2.62; T-S C 2.181) are actually passages from MekDeut, and not SifDeut. See Kahana, 'New Fragments', 488f; idem, 'Pages', 19-21. Finkelstein also used a fragment from the Landenburg Library, that I was unsuccessful in locating (for a description of the fragment, see K. Darmstädter, *Israelitisches Gemeindeblatt*, Jan. 21, 1927, 4f).

[503] For a detailed description of method and conception concerning the critical editing of sources, see his entire introduction to his edition; cf his article, 'The Mekhilta', 52-54 (= Finkelstein, *Sifra*, vol 5, 50*-52*).

ten in the Land of Israel, obviously in Palestinian spelling, or to be more precise, in Galilean spelling. Many times a *yod* or a *vav* was added as an aid to
vocalization, and the plural is usually marked with a *nun* in place of a *mem*.
For the convenience of the reader, I did not pay attention to these fine points
and seemingly superfluous letters. In the main, I printed words in their usual
spelling, although from the aspect of, and for the study of, Hebrew spelling, as
well as for pronunciation, [not even] the crowns of letters nor the 'point of a
yod' should be waived.'[504] To aid the reader, the critical apparatus also lists
textual versions that support Finkelstein's text, not only the versions that differ
from it. In the commentary and parallel references section, Finkelstein made
use of Horovitz's literary estate, citing him verbatim within brackets.

The instalments first published were reviewed by Epstein[505] and Lieberman.[506] Epstein harshly criticized Finkelstein's eclecticism in determining the
text, incorporating without any indication readings from Midrash ha-Gadol
originating from MekDeut and other parallels, as also the emendations of its
editor, as against all textual witnesses. Epstein similarly faulted Finkelstein's
method of spelling that frequently diverges from all manuscripts. Apart from
these methodological objections, Epstein discussed a large number of detailed
topics, textual versions, and interpretations. In conclusion, he stressed that,
despite all drawbacks, 'at long last we have a text of *Sifrei* for a foundation on
which to build; both the project and the builder are to be congratulated'. Lieberman's criticism is more sympathetic. He, too, complained that Finkelstein
edited a text at variance with the manuscripts, but emphasized the important
contribution and the various advantages of the edition, such as the small number of corruptions in relation to the size of the book, the attention paid to the
mutual relations between the manuscripts, the large number of quotations from
the literature of the Rishonim, the numerous references to talmudic and extra-
talmudic parallels, and the up-to-date references to scholarly literature.

A facsimile edition of Finkelstein's work was published in New York in
1969. In the introduction he notes, with refreshing candour: 'I would still like
to correct the mistakes that arose during the copying of the changes; and also
the textual version, where I was so audacious as to emend the text in opposition to all the accepted versions, which should not be done, but I was childish
at the time.' He also directed the reader to quotations from SifDeut in Yalkut
Talmud Tora and Pseudo-Rabad that became available to him after his work
was already in the stage of being published.

---

[504] See his further comments that his plan was 'to explain in detail in the introduction the nature of
each manuscript, its orientation, and its special traits. I am boyed by the hope that, God willing, I
will shortly succeed in publishing a special booklet that will contain all this material', but this was
not to be.

[505] Epstein, 'Finkelstein' (= Epstein, *Studies*, vol 2, 889-906).

[506] Lieberman, 'Siphre zu Deuteronomium' (= Lieberman, *Palestinian Talmudic Literature*, 566-
578). In his review, Lieberman mentions the article by Epstein; the seemingly earlier date of
Lieberman's article ensues from the delay in publication of *Kiryath Sepher*.

All this compels the reader of Finkelstein's edition constantly and thoroughly to check the critical apparatus and the commentary in order to reconstruct the manuscript versions and to examine the editor's considerations in determining the text. Most of the primary and secondary textual witnesses of SifDeut and of its commentaries also include SifNum,[507] as is the case for ms Vatican 32, the best version of SifNum and SifDeut. Although Finkelstein wrote he preferred its readings, in practice he digressed from it many times, and in particular, he did not base his text on it in most of the problematic passages where this definitely should be done.[508] Furthermore, new texts of SifDeut have been discovered, in addition to the list of addenda that Finkelstein included at the beginning of his second edition. The most important are: some 25 leaves from the Cairo Geniza; 13 leaves in ms JTS Rab. 2392; 10 leaves from Yemen in the Yehudah Nachum collection;[509] and copious citations from SifDeut in the Yemenite midrash in ms Cincinnati 2026.[510]

In several manuscripts of SifDeut, in the central section, dozens of expositions from the companion work, MekDeut, were added. These irregular expositions can be identified by their clear exhibition of Yishmaelian characteristics, as also by their presence in only a few textual versions, at times in a different place in each manuscript and interrupting the basic exposition. Some are even explicitly labeled as *tosefta* (addition) in the commentaries of Rabbenu Hillel and other Rishonim. Finkelstein indicated these additions by small print.[511] Epstein devoted a special discussion to them, disagreeing with Finkelstein over the origin of some expositions in SifDeut as unoriginal marginal annotations.[512] To date, with the discovery of additional Geniza fragments and Yemenite manuscripts, we can see that these additions made their way from the marginal annotations only to the Ashkenazic manuscripts of SifDeut, but are absent in the Oriental versions.[513]

---

[507] See their description and characterization in Kahana, *Prolegomena*; above, the description of SifNum.

[508] In his first introduction, Finkelstein states that, in his opinion, ms Berlin is the second most important textual version, and at the end of the book, where ms Vat is truncated, he preferred it (this assessment is probably at the base of his strange decision to allocate the letter א to ms Berlin, and ב to ms Oxf). But see my comments on the special nature of ms Berlin, for better or worse, in *Prolegomena*, 12-23.

[509] See the detailed discussion, Kahana, *Manuscripts*, 100-107. After the publication of the book, five additional Geniza fragments of SifDeut were discovered: (1) JTS ENA 957.3 (see Danzig, *Catalogue*, 10), that belongs to Codex 6; (2-4) JTS ENA NS 82.1; T-S AS 93.121; T-S AS 93.184 that belong to Codex 8; (5) JTS ENA 2673.35, that belongs to Codex 18 (cf Danzig, *Catalogue*, Introduction, 58). Transcriptions of all the fragments see Kahana, *Genizah Fragments*, 227-337.

[510] See Kahana, 'Pages', 172f.

[511] See his discussion of this phenomenon in his article: 'Prolegomena', 26-36 (= Finkelstein, *Sifra*, vol 5, 76*-86*).

[512] See Epstein, *Studies*, vol 2, 903-906; see also Epstein's independent discussion, *Prolegomena*, 711-723, that he conducted without reference to the edition by Finkelstein.

[513] See Kahana, 'Yemenite Midrashim', 35.

Regarding the unique nature of SifDeut, Finkelstein observed that it still contains a significant number of early halakhot that follow the view of Beit Shammai, as well as earlier remains from the Second Temple period, possibly even from the period of the prophets.[514] An exacting study of Finkelstein's arguments teaches that many are fallacious; SifDeut does not contain more early halakhot than the other Halakhic Midrashim.[515] An overview of opinions concerning the redactors of SifDeut was offered by Epstein.[516] His own comments on the work were mentioned above, in the section on SifNum.[517]

MEKHILTA DEUTERONOMY

Mekhilta Deuteronomy (MekDeut) is a Yishmaelian Midrash[518] whose exact scope has not been determined since its greater part is not extant. One of the Geniza fragments indicates that its first unit ended with Deut 1:30 and the second one began with Deut 3:23, as does SifDeut.[519] This might indicate that its other sections, as well, run basically parallel to those of SifDeut. In four Geniza fragments, MekDeut is divided into *parashiyyot*,[520] each of which includes an average of four to five verses.[521] In a later fragment that originated in Yemen the work is divided into verses (סליק פסוקא, 'end of verse'),[522] but this

---

[514] See above, 'Early Halakha'.

[515] See, e.g., Finkelstein, 'Hashpaat Beit Shammai' (= Finkelstein, *Sifra*, vol 5, 49-60), in which he concluded that 'the unattributed passages that express the views of Shammai and his school attest that the ancient Sifrei that R. Akiva used for his undertaking was mainly from the school of Shammai' (53). This conclusion is based on only four halakhot in which, according to Finkelstein, SifDeut definitely maintains the views of Beit Shammai; five 'doubtful' halakhot; and other five anonymous halakhot of R. Eliezer who was a pupil of Beit Shammai in SifDeut. The problem, however, is that this is a trivial number of halakhot, in comparison with the thousands of halakhot in SifDeut, one that does not justify Finkelstein's sweeping conclusion. Moreover, a large portion of the halakhot on which Finkelstein based his reasoning were also accepted by rabbis postdating Beit Shammai, and they do not teach of a clear link between SifDeut and Beit Shammai, or to any specifically early halakha.

[516] Epstein, *Prolegomena*, 703-710.

[517] For recent studies of SifDeut, see, esp., Finkelstein, 'Baraita de-beit din shel lishkat ha-gazit', in idem, *Sifra*, vol 5, 61-85; idem, 'An Old Baraita'; Basser, *Midrashic Interpretations*; Fraade, *Tradition*; idem, 'Sifre Deuteronomy'; idem, 'Turn to Commentary'; Hammer, 'Section 38'; idem, 'Rabbinic Response'; Gottlieb, 'Language Understanding'. See also the translation into German of SifDeut: Bietenhard and Ljungman, *Midrash*, that includes many references to parallel material in the Patristic literature.

[518] For a summary of the material concerning the names of this Midrash used by the Rishonim, see Kahana, 'Citations', 20f.

[519] See Kahana, 'New Fragments', 495f.

[520] See *ib.*, 489.

[521] The thirty verses of Deut 1:1-30 are divided into six *parashiyyot* (= *parashiyyot* 1-6; parasha 7 begins with Deut 3:23), and the thirty-two verses in Deut 11:29-12:28 are divided into eight *parashiyyot* (= *parashiyyot* 23-30; parasha 31 begins with Deut 12:29).

[522] See Kahana, 'Pages', 166.

division is probably not original but influenced by the common division of SifDeut prevalent in Yemen.[523]

Hoffmann was the first scholar to methodically demonstrate that R. David ha-Adani used MekDeut in his composition of Midrash ha-Gadol,[524] and, following this premise, also began to reconstruct the former.[525] Schechter then published four Geniza leaves of MekDeut *parshat* Reei that he discovered in Oxford and Cambridge.[526] On the basis of these leaves and of a reexamination of Midrash ha-Gadol, Hoffmann began a second reconstruction of MekDeut in his *Midrash Tannaim* which was published in two volumes (Berlin 1908-1909).

In this edition, used by scholars to the present day, Hoffmann used one font for all passages from Midrash ha-Gadol that markedly differ from SifDeut, reserving a second font for those that resemble it but whose identification as MekDeut he regarded as doubtful. Several times, however, the edition interchanges these fonts,[527] a fact of which the reader must be cognizant.

There are many drawbacks to the edition. As is shown by the Geniza fragments, large parts of MekDeut are not quoted in Midrash ha-Gadol, and the parts that are, were sometimes reworked by Adani or corrupted by the copyist of the one manuscript of Midrash ha-Gadol Hoffmann possessed.[528] He also included expositions that the author of Midrash ha-Gadol had undoubtedly copied from SifDeut, the Bavli, Mishnat R. Eliezer, Mishne Tora of Maimonides, and other sources.[529] Hoffmann generally voices his doubts concerning the authenticity of such passages, but the reader must scrutinize each passage with this problem in mind.

Several additional passages from MekDeut have come to light after the publication of *Midrash Tannaim*. Schechter published a Geniza fragment consisting of two leaves from *parshat* reei.[530] Later on the present author identified an additional two fragments of two leaves each from Devarim-Vaethanan and Haazinu-Vezot haberakhah, along with a lengthy quotation from Ekev and

---

[523] See above, n490.

[524] See Hoffmann, 'Über eine Mechilta'.

[525] See Hoffmann, 'Likutei Mekhilta'; and the addenda, 'Likutei batar likutei'.

[526] Schechter, 'Geniza Fragments'; idem, 'Mechilta to Deuteronomy'.

[527] On p1-24, 63-180, large type = a passage different from SifDeut, small type = a passage similar to it. On p24-62, 180-252, large type = a passage similar to SifDeut, small type = a passage different from it.

[528] Selected textual variants from another MidrGad manuscript are listed at the end of the edition (253-257), but many more variants are to be added to this list; see below.

[529] See Epstein, *Prolegomena*, 632f; Melamed, *Introduction*, 219-222; Kahana, 'New Fragments', 495.

[530] 'Mekhilta Devarim'. The signature of this passage was not mentioned by Schechter, and all my efforts to locate it were fruitless (cf Kahana, *Manuscripts*, 110 n7).

Haazinu in an early collection in the Geniza.[531] The second fragment Schechter published from the Cambridge Geniza collection was republished in a more meticulous way by Epstein,[532] and new editions of Midrash ha-Gadol on Deuteronomy have been published based on several manuscripts.[533] These publications, along with additional manuscripts of Midrash ha-Gadol, enable us to correct many of the corruptions that entered *Midrash Tannaim*. A considerable number of expositions from MekDeut were inserted in the Ashkenazic versions of SifDeut;[534] others are preserved in medieval quotations discovered in recent years.[535] It would seem, however, that the circulation of MekDeut was already quite limited in the Middle Ages.[536] Even the Rishonim who made use of rare midrashim such as MekRSbY and SifZNum no longer possessed the book.[537]

The primary passages from MekDeut discovered to the present contain only some five percent of the work, a fact that severely hinders its research. The most detailed description of MekDeut and its Yishmaelian character was

---

[531] See Kahana, 'New Fragments'; idem, 'Pages'; idem, 'Citations'. For an additional treatment of several of the details of the expositions, see Lerner, 'Novel Explanation'; Fox, 'Difficult Reading'; Basser, 'Kahana's Article'; Kahana, 'Notes to the Mekhilta'; Kister, 'Metamorphoses', 190-199.

[532] See Epstein, *Studies*, vol 2, 125-140. Schechter's copying of the first fragment, as well, is flawed by deletions and corruptions. See, e.g., the omission of the important passage that includes the teaching by R. Yonatan, 'I vow that I will never [be] outside the Land of Israel,' on which Epstein already briefly commented (*Prolegomena*, 639). For the implications of this teaching for the study of MekDeut, see Kahana, 'Importance of Dwelling'. For new transcriptions of all the Fragments see Kahana, *Genizah Fragments*, 338-357.

[533] The first edition of MidrGad on Deuteronomy, based on four manuscripts, was published by M.Z. Hasidah in serial form, until Ki tetse, in *Ha-Segulla*, nos. 1-78. He was followed by S. Fisch's edition of MidrGad on Deuteronomy, based on manuscripts (Jerusalem 1973), but this edition suffers from numerous flaws, both in the text itself, and in the textual variants sections and the glosses. See Lerner, 'Notes on the Editing', 114-116; Kahana, 'New Fragments', 493-494; idem, 'Pages', 168-172.

[534] See above, the description of SifDeut, n511-513. The best version of the quotations is preserved in ms Vat 32 of SifDeut. See, e.g., Kahana, 'Importance of Dwelling', 502-508, for a reconstruction of a passage from MekDeut, based on the combining of a citation that entered SifDeut with sentences that were omitted during the copying by Schechter of the Oxf Geniza fragment that he published.

[535] A relatively large number of quotations from the aggadic passages of MekDeut came to light in ms Cincinnati 2026. See Kahana, 'Pages', 173. It also transpired that R. Tobias ben Eliezer used the text of MekDeut for the portions of Haazinu and Vezot haberakha in his Midrash Lekah Tov; see Kahana, 'Pages', 175f. At the time, Epstein had commented on the many quotations from MekDeut in ms Musery 46; see his article, 'Mechilta and Sifre', 102, 112. Unfortunately, all my requests to check the manuscript, that apparently is held by the family in Paris, were rejected.

[536] As regards the distribution of MekDeut in an earlier period, it, or its expositions, were most likely available to the redactor of LevR (see Kahana, 'New Fragments', 499), the redactor of Semahot (that is attributed to R. Hiyya), and R. Elazar ben Kallir (see Kahana, 'Citations', 35-38). In a later period, Ps-Yon, as well, seemingly made use of this Midrash (see Henshke, 'Pseudo-Jonatan', 206-210).

[537] The question of whether Maimonides possessed MekDeut, or whether he merely made use of the passages that entered into his copy of SifDeut, also requires further study.

composed by Hoffmann after he completed *Midrash Tannaim*.[538] Epstein engaged in a concise discussion of MekDeut following the new edition of one of its passages.[539] It should be mentioned that the halakhic material in the three fragments published by Schechter is notable for its lengthy and detailed expositions. The aggadic material of MekDeut also is characterized by a certain lengthiness in comparison to the parallel material in SifDeut. The aggadic expositions in MekDeut are often superior in language, style, and content to the parallels in SifDeut, where the latter may suffer from discontinuity in style, vagueness and poor logic in the expositions, and a number of corruptions shared by all the manuscripts.[540] Some of the differences between MekDeut and SifDeut apparently result from the varying worldviews of their redactors.[541]

SIFREI ZUTA DEUTERONOMY

From Sifrei Zuta Deuteronomy (SifZDeut) only citations have been found, no primary manuscripts. The main source for its reconstruction is the commentary by the Karaite sage Yeshua ben Yehuda on Deuteronomy that quotes passages from it with relative accuracy.[542] Other citations of a more paraphrastic nature are included in Sefer Pitron Tora which was published by Urbach,[543] and possibly also in Midrash Hadash published by Mann.[544] The name Sifrei Zuta Deuteronomy, which is not documented in the literature of the Rishonim, was proposed in light of its close similarity to SifZNum. The proximity between both works is patently expressed in the singular terminology and shared quotations, as also in their vocabulary and the names of sages cited, their Mishna version which consistently differs from the extant Mishna, and their unique halakhot.[545]

About 130 short citations from SifZDeut have been found to the present; they expound verses from the portions of Devarim, Vaethanan, Ekev, Reei, Ki tetse, and Ki tavo. The aggadic quotations from the portion of *Devarim*, chap. 1, basically resemble their parallels in SifDeut and MekDeut, but evince a distinct and independent style as well as characteristic terms and expressions typical of what may be termed the Akivan 'subschool of Sifrei Zuta'. Like-

---

[538] See his introduction to *Midrash Tannaim*, and in greater detail, his summational article, 'Zur Einleitung in den Midrasch Tannaim'.

[539] See Epstein, *Studies*, vol 2, 125-128; cf idem, *Prolegomena*, 631-633.

[540] See in detail, Kahana, 'New Fragments', 496-507; idem, 'Citations', 24-31; idem, 'Pages', 176-186. Cf the general characterization of the aggadic material in Halakhic Midrashim, above, 'Aggada'.

[541] See, e.g., the outline of the differing attitude by the redactors of these Midrashim to the non-Jewish peoples, Kahana, 'Pages', 180-185; 200f.

[542] For the discovery of the Midrash, see Kahana, 'New Tannaic Midrash'.

[543] Urbach, *Sefer Pitron Tora*; the facsimile edition of the manuscript was published in Jerusalem in 1995.

[544] *Midrash Hadash* was published in Mann, *The Bible as Read*, vol 2.

[545] See, e.g., Kahana, 'Searching Examination'.

wise, the expositions concerned with halakhic issues utilize Akivan terminology and methodology characteristic of Sifrei Zuta.[546]

Selected Bibliography

General Introductions

The *Einleitung* by D. Hoffmann constituted a breakthrough in the modern study of Halakhic Midrashim. A general work on the Halakhic Midrashim that disagrees with several of Hoffmann's fundamental conclusions is *Untersuchungen* by Albeck, who summarized his main deductions, with addenda and updates, in *Introduction*, 79-143. Epstein, *Prolegomena*, 501-746, developed Hoffmann's approach, and provided a detailed treatment of each of the Halakhic Midrashim. A quite detailed summary of Epstein's book, supplemented by additions relating particularly to the Halakhic Midrashim cited by Amoraim, is provided by Melamed, *Introduction*, 161-317, and a concise summation of research into the Halakhic Midrashim that includes an extensive bibliographic survey of monographs written in the field is found in Strack and Stemberger, *Einleitung*.[547]

Reference Works

Detailed data relating to the textual versions of the Halakhic Midrashim, including the joining together of isolated fragments into codices, are to be found in Kahana, *Manuscripts*. An accurate transcription of the all the fragments of the Halakhic Midrashim (apart from Sifra) is included in Kahana, *Genizah Fragments*, as part of the Friedberg Genizah Project. An orderly explanation of the terminology of the Halakhic Midrashim is provided by Bacher, *Exegetische Terminologie*.

Concordances of the four complete Halakhic Midrashim were compiled by Kosovsky, *Concordantiae*.[548] A concordance of the critical editions of the Halakhic Midrashim excluding SifZDeut is provided in the CD-ROM of the Bar-Ilan Responsa Project. A concordance of the best manuscripts of the Halakhic Midrashim (that does not include SifZDeut and the passages in Mek-RSbY, SifZNum, and MekDeut reconstructed in accordance with *Midrash ha-Gadol*) is included in the CD-ROM of the Hebrew Language Historical Dictionary Project of the Academy of the Hebrew language in Jerusalem.

---

[546] For a detailed treatment of the above, see Kahana, *Sifre Zuta*.

[547] ET: *Introduction to the Talmud and Midrash*; Spanish: *Introdución a la literatura talmudica y midrasica*; French: *Introduction au Talmud et au Midrash*.

[548] MekRY, following the printed version (not, as would be expected, based on the version of one of the critical editions), Jerusalem 1965, 4 vols; Sifra, based on ed Weiss, Jerusalem 1967, 4 vols.; SifNum and SifDeut, following the Horovitz and Finkelstein editions, Jerusalem 1971, 5 vols.

Chapter Two

Aggadic Midrash

Marc Hirshman

Introduction

Before defining and outlining the development of rabbinic midrash and aggada, it is essential to bear in mind some key aspects of the regnant rabbinic culture. The first aspect is the rabbis' self-perception of being heirs to an oral tradition which stemmed from Sinai.[1] This claim, coupled with an insistence on transmitting this tradition orally,[2] left little or no room for written creativity.[3] Written works were limited to the twenty-four books of the *Kitvei ha-kodesh* – holy writings which comprise our Hebrew Bible. Thus, in stark contrast to the variegated genres of Second Temple literature and of contemporary Greco-Roman literature, rabbinic 'literature' is marked by the two basic forms of *midrash* and *mishna*, with their subsequent development in the Palestinian and Babylonian Talmudim.

---

[1] Safrai, 'Oral Tora', 42-50.
[2] *Ib.* 45-50. More recently see Jaffee, *Tora in the Mouth* and now Sussman's exhaustive essay, 'Tora she-beal pe'.
[3] The stunning exception is Megillat Taanit, now available in a new edition by V. Noam. Concerning written works of aggada see below.

Another aspect of rabbinic culture, possibly a corollary to its oral nature, is its proclivity to anthologies, as opposed to works of individual authors.[4] Neither in the Talmud nor in the midrash, and I would argue not even in the Mishna, are we given the reflections of a single author.[5] Rather, we have a collection of views, generally differing or opposed, attributed to various sages, named and unnamed.

Aggadic midrash was shaped by these same forces. The rabbis collected their comments on scripture, their anecdotes, maxims, and theological reflections and cast them in the framework of scriptural commentary, even though it is clear that some of this material originated in other contexts. Rabbinic non-legal creativity is presented to us for the most part under the rubric of scriptural exegesis. It has been noted by modern scholarship that rabbinic aggadic creativity is self conscious about displaying its attachment to Scripture. A leading contemporary scholar of midrash has epitomized the dual trademark of rabbinic story-telling as scriptural exegesis and highly polished literary and linguistic stylization.[6] Second Temple Palestinian literature generally did not emphasize the scriptural difficulties or peculiarities that spawned its interpretations or legends.[7] Rabbinic midrash of the classical period (1th-5th cent. CE) is outspoken, and thrives on presenting its 'new' interpretations as intimately connected to the words and syntactical peculiarities of Scripture. In aggadic midrash, the rabbis chose to speak through Scripture, rather than giving independent free standing formulations of their thoughts, as they did in the Mishna.[8]

It is remarkable that in spite of the rabbinic insistence on oral transmission and of anticipated opposition to written texts of aggada, we find prominent rabbis who favoured studying from such texts. The most important Palestinian Amora, R. Yohanan (died c. 279) espoused the opinion: 'It is an established covenant (ברית כרותה) that one who learns aggada from a book, will not soon forget' (yShab 5:1 9a). It has been proposed to interpret this statement as referring to studying aggada 'from the book', meaning while reading the Tora itself.[9] This is an unlikely interpretation, especially since we find R. Yohanan depicted, albeit in the Babylonian Talmud, as 'carrying a book of aggada' (bBer 23a) and 'reading from books of aggada' (bGit 60a). Not only do we have reports that books of aggada circulated in Amoraic times, but we even have testimony as to the contents of one of these books. We can savour this testimony as it comes from someone who vigorously opposed the writing of

---

[4] See Fraade, *From Tradition*, 17f; Hirshman, 'The Greek Fathers'; and most recently Stern, 'Anthological Imagination' Bregman, 'Midrash Rabbah'.

[5] A partial exception can be made for Seder Olam, see below ch. 12.

[6] Fraenkel, *Darkhei ha-aggada*, 469.

[7] Kugel, *Potiphar's House*, 247-264 and the same author's introduction to Kugel, *Traditions*.

[8] De Vries, *Mehkarim*, 296.

[9] A position adopted by Zunz and later Fraenkel, *Darkhei ha-aggada*, 28 and 573 n105 while the latter rebuts Albeck's questioning of that position.

aggada. In one of the classical sources for rabbinic opposition to written sources, we read this comment of R. Joshua b. Levi (3rd cent. CE):[10]

> This aggada – one who writes it has no portion (in the world to come); one who expounds it is scorched; and one who listens to it has no reward. I, in all my days, have never looked in a book of aggada, except once I looked and I found written in it:
>
>> "175 sections (*parshiot*) in the Tora where it is written 'speak', 'saying', and 'command' correspond to the years of our father Abraham as it is written: 'You have taken gifts of men' (Ps 68:19) and it is written 'the man a great among giants' (Josh 14:16); 147 songs written in the Psalms correspond to the years of our father Jacob, teaching us that all the praises with which Israel praises the Holy One blessed be He correspond to the years of Jacob, as it says, 'You are holy, seated on the praises of Israel' (Ps 42:4); 123 times that Israel responds *halleluja* corresponds to the years of Aaron: 'Praise the Lord, praise God in His holiness' (בקדשו, Ps 150:1) – (read:) in (relation to) his holy one, 'to Aaron, the holy one of the Lord' (Ps 106:16)."
>
> Even so, I trembled all night. (yShab 16:1, 15c)

Though this warning lends itself to different interpretations, the most cogent one renders it as inveighing against the use of written aggadic texts, rather than a wholesale attack on aggada in general. The opening statement is construed as follows: 'This aggada – one who writes it... one who expounds it (from a book!)... one who listens to it (being expounded from a book)...' Be that as it may, R. Joshua b. Levi's reaction to his single encounter with a written work of aggada is also perplexing. Was it simply guilt at having read such a work that led to his terrifying night? Or does this seemingly innocuous homily conceal a mystery or encoded message that stirred him? This enigmatic anecdote is immediately followed by another Amora's invective against the writing of aggada.

We have then, by way of introduction, seen that aggada enjoyed a place apart, at least in the view of some of the Palestinian Amoraim. As opposed to the legal discussions, some ancient authorities held that not only might aggada be written down, but that it was preferable to study it from a book. This view was not shared by all and encountered stiff opposition by some.

The Terms 'Midrash' and 'Aggada'

Though the nominal form מדרש appears twice in Scripture (2Chr 13:22; 24:27), its meaning in these late passages seems to be other than its prevalent meaning in rabbinic literature. In Chronicles, מדרש would appear to be something like a

---

[10] On the entire passage see Lieberman, *Yerushalmi Kiphshuto*, 194.

book of history.[11] This is interesting because the Hebrew root דרש is, as has been noted, the functional equivalent of the Greek 'historia', both meaning to investigate.[12]

Yet, the verb דרש quite clearly begins to take on the meaning of 'investigation of Scripture' in the later books of the Bible, when appearing with the nouns Tora or *mitswa* as its object. Many have noted the shift from searching or inquiring after God (Gen 25:22) to searching God's Tora (Ezra 7:10),[13] reflecting a dramatic change in religious consciousness.[14] Within a few centuries, we find the Qumran community pitting their דורש התורה against the דורשי חלקות. By focussing on this and other usages of דרש in the Qumran writings, as also on Ben Sira's famous though evidently textually unsupportable invitation to 'dwell in his Beit Midrash' (Sir 51:23),[15] it becomes abundantly clear that by the second century BCE investigation of Scripture had achieved pride of place in at least some of the varieties of Second Temple Judaism.

So too, Philo's famous description of the Therapeutae accords well with this trend. Though constantly involved in study and contemplation (Vit. cont. 25-29) the high point of the 'sect's' (αἱρέσεως) festive gathering is when 'the President of the company... discusses some question (ζητεῖ) arising in the Holy Scriptures or solves (ἐπιλύεται) one that has been propounded by someone else' (Vit. cont. 75).[16] Philo also mentions the fact the Therapeutae ware in possession of written works of 'men of old... who left many memorials of the form used in allegorical interpretation and these they take as a kind of archetype and imitate the method...' (Vit. cont. 29). It is noteworthy that Philo's description of the Therapeutae's methods of study bears a striking resemblance to his own oeuvre. Indeed, according to S. Daniel-Nataf, the theory that Philo was himself one of the Therapeutae is quite likely on very solid ground.[17]

In rabbinic literature, from Tannaic times and on, the root דרש conveys the meaning of investigating or searching scripture,[18] generally, but by no means always, in order to find a new meaning.[19]

The origin of the word הגדה, *haggada*, and of its aramaicized form אגדה, *aggada*, was treated at length by W. Bacher in an essay at the close of the 19th

---

[11] See I. Heinemann, art. 'מדרש'; Japhet, *Ideology*, 429; Meir, *Ha-sippur*, 16f. Compare Fraenkel, *Darkhei ha-aggada*, 11.

[12] Urbach, 'History and Halakha'.

[13] Hurvitz, *Transition Period*, 130-136.

[14] Gertner, 'Terms', 3 n4 (cited by Hurvitz *ib.* 131); idem, 'Masorah', 249.

[15] See Kister, 'The Interpretation of Ben Sira', 304 n2.

[16] See Kamesar's treatment of *zetemata* or *quaestiones* literature in his fine study, *Jerome*.

[17] Daniel-Nataf, *Philo of Alexandria*, 178.

[18] See Gertner, 'Terms', 26. His assertion that דרש had the meaning of preaching already in Tannaic times is not borne out by the evidence, though it is seconded by Meir, *Hasippur*, 14 but the two examples she adduces are better understood in their usual sense, especially the phrase דרש ב-.

[19] Albeck, 'Einleitung und Register', 26; Fraenkel, *Darkhei ha-aggada*, 11. Some midrashic activity was expended on reinforcing the accepted meaning of scripture.

century.[20] He reviews numerous theories and then suggests that the term came from the common phrase מגיד הכתוב, 'Scripture teaches'. He concludes that 'early expositors investigated exegetically (דרש) whatever the Scripture contained beyond the simple meaning... the outcome of their investigations... is called haggada, deductions'.[21] As attractive as this suggestion is, it does not do justice to the fact that מגיד and מגיד הכתוב are usually used to introduce legal exegeses, as Bacher himself noted.

It is clear that 'haggada' was considered a separate branch of study. In a famous passage, the Tosefta treats procedural issues of the Sanhedrin, as to which kinds of questions or study are given precedence (tSan 7:7). It asserts that practical questions precede theoretical ones, halakha takes precedence over midrash, midrash over 'haggada', and *kal va-homer* over midrash and *gezera shava*. This passage provides the key for the proper reading of the oft-mentioned lists of fields of study, *midrash, halakhot, ve-haggadot* (mNed 4:3).[22] Each is a distinct discipline and the list is not to be understood *midrash halakhot* and *midrash haggadot*. If 'haggada' was not midrash, what was it?

One might follow Zunz's lead that 'haggada' was anything that was spoken, as opposed to שמועה, *shemua*: 'tradition' heard or received.[23] The latter was reserved for legal traditions while the former covered non-legal matters. The early formulaic pair, however, as we saw above is halakha and 'haggada', not *shemua* and *aggada* (the latter found in the Babylonian Talmud albeit sometimes in *baraitot*). It is well to note that as opposed to דרש, we have yet to find a similar usage of 'haggada' in Second Temple times prior to Tannaic literature.

It will be instructive to focus on three or four Tannaic passages which hold the clue to the origins of the word 'haggada'. The first is the most crucial, but also the most opaque: 'Five things R. Akiba would interpret as a kind of haggada (דורשן כמין הגדה): In five things the father endows (זוכה) the son...' (tEd 1:14). This formulation is illuminated by two other very similar statements: 'Five things R. Yohanan b. Zakkai would say as a kind of *homer* (אומרן כמין חומר)' (tBK 7:3);[24] and, ' ...Three things which R. Yishmael would interpret as a kind of parable' (דורש בתורה כמין משל, MekRY nezikin 6, p270). It seems clear, by this comparison, that at least in R. Akiva's statement 'haggada' is a way of treating Scripture, analogous to *mashal* and *homer* in the dicta of Rabban Yohanan and R. Yishmael. In the ensuing discussion, and in the parallel (mEd 2:9), R. Akiva tries to prove that God counts generations rather than

[20] W. Bacher, 'The Origin of the Word Haggada (Agada)', *JQR* 4 (1892) 406-429.

[21] *Ib.* 418.

[22] The Mishna contrasts these three fields of study with the study of Bible (Mikra). On the list itself see Zunz-Albeck, *Derashot*, ch. 3 n18 and Finkelstein, 'Midrash, halachot we-aggadot'. Most recently see Shapira, *Beit Hamidrash*, 279-290.

[23] Zunz-Albeck, *Derashot*, ch. 4 and n1. Zunz probably was following Rav Hai Gaon's contrasting of these two terms as indicated by Albeck *ib.*

[24] Compare Lieberman, *Tosefta Ki-Fshutah*, vol 9, 65.

individual years of a person's life. Other topics are discussed in the Tosefta passage, but unfortunately, it remains unclear what exactly of R. Akiva's interpretation constituted כמין הגדה.

Another two passages are much clearer and will give us a handle on the word 'haggada'. In the first, R. Joshua (b. Hananya) asks his students what was 'new' in the academy. After deferential pleasantries are exchanged, he asks them: 'Where was the haggada?' They reply: '(At) "Assemble the People"' (Deut 31:12). He then inquires 'What did he interpret in it (דרש בה)?' This would imply that 'haggada' was a recitation of Scripture.[25] This seems also to be the meaning of the phrase, when applied to the recitation of verses by the priest, as described in the Sifre 'he says before her words of haggada, things that happened in the early scriptures, like "that which wise men tell, and was not denied by the fathers" (Job 15:18)'.[26]

It would appear then that the original meaning of the term 'haggada' was *recitation of scripture*,[27] often with the intent of making a specific point.

The next stage of the word's development is to be found when 'haggada' has become a branch of study, closely related to theology or even mysticism. Support for this usage comes from the very important passage from the Sifre, where we meet the דורשי הגדות, 'expounders of haggada', for the first time. There we read:

> '...And holding fast to Him', (Deut 11:22) But is it possible for a person to ascend to heaven and to cleave to fire? For has it not been said: 'For the Lord your God is a consuming fire' (Deut 4:24)... Rather, attach yourself to the sages and their disciples... The expounders of haggadot say: if you desire to know Him who spoke and the world came into being, study haggada for thereby you will come to know Him who spoke and the world came into being and cleave to his ways.[28]

It appears that the דורשי הגדות debated the first opinion, that held that ascent to heaven was impossible and substituted for it cleaving to sages. The expounders, on the other hand, emphasized study of 'haggada' as the way of knowing God's ways and of cleaving to God. It is instructive that the passages in the classical Amoraic midrashim wherein a particular rabbi is called a בעל אגדה, *baal aggada*, revolve around mystical or theosophical issues.[29]

---

[25] tSot 7:9 (p193). Lieberman and Epstein debated whether this story purportedly took place on the Sabbath or not; see Lieberman, *Tosefta Ki-Fshutah*, vol 8, 680.

[26] A verse applied elsewhere (tBer 4:18) to the story of Judah and Tamar.

[27] This is similar to the recitation one made when bringing the first fruits at Deut 26:3. See Lieberman, *Hellenism*, 140 n11. M. Kahana reminded me that part of that recitation are the words הגדתי היום, which is translated in LXX, ἀναγγέλλω. Compare also the midrashic term להודיע (mAv 5:1) which in the Bible introduces a classic example of inner-biblical exegesis (Deut 8:3; Fishbane, *Biblical Interpretation*, 326-328) and is likewise translated ἀναγγέλλω.

[28] Translation is based on Fraade, *Tradition*, 92 with some changes.

[29] See Hirshman, 'Place of Aggada, 3 (article submitted in 1995). Recently Lifshitz, 'Aggada and its place, 29 (Hebr) has carried this evidence to the claim that 'aggada then is *torat ha-sod*' i.e. the

Finally, from Tannaic times *haggada* was seen as persuasive and entertaining: it 'pulls at the heart of a person' (MekRY wayassa 5, p171). This recurrent view is expressed through a punning on the Aramaic root נגד which means 'to draw' or 'to pull'. The Tannaic characterization of 'haggada' as being *persuasive* brings the term very close to classical 'rhetoric', a Greek word that means much the same as the Hebrew 'haggada'.[30]

By way of summary, we may say that 'haggada' was used by the Tannaim and the Amoraim to describe both subject matter and a manner of study. In Medieval times, *aggada* was used as a name for collections alongside of the terms we commonly employ today 'midrash' or 'aggadic midrash'. So, for example, a list of books in the Geniza speaks of 'Aggadeta de-Wayikra' and 'Aggadeta de-Shir ha-Shirim'.[31]

In our own terminology, we shall henceforth use the accepted Aramaic form 'aggada', except when translating from the Hebrew, when we shall retain the transcription 'haggada'. Moreover we shall speak of 'aggadic midrash' – as distinct from the halakhic midrash type discussed in the previous chapter – to indicate the subject matter at hand.

Midrash, Aggada, and Halakha

As was evident from our survey of the term aggada, the contents of this branch of rabbinic study varied widely. Generally, scholarship and tradition alike have found it expedient to define aggada as a catch-all term for those parts of rabbinic literature which do not relate strictly to law, i.e. halakha. I think we can now be more precise. Aggada, as it is used in Tannaic and Amoraic sources from the land of Israel, is always related to Scripture, though not necessarily exegetical. As such, it differs only slightly, if at all, from midrash which treated non-legal issues. So, by way of example, R. Yuda b. Pazzi says: 'It is an aggadic tradition that Serach (the daughter of Asher) was chained to the grindstone when she went down to Egypt' (PesRK vayehi 7, p129). R. Shmuel b. Nahman, by virtue of his being a well known 'master of haggada' (בעל הגדה), is asked 'whence was the light created?' His whispered response was: 'God wrapped himself in light like a garment, and his glory shone until the ends of the earth' (GenR 3,5 p20).[32] R. Shmuel is immediately asked why he was so secretive when there is an explicit verse to that effect in Ps 104:2.

---

hidden or mystical teachings. This is surely overstated. Some aggada is that but that is an inappropriate and inexact definition. The essay is rich in bibliography but not nearly nuanced enough in its treatment of the various aspects of aggada, including the proposed etymology.

[30] On the central place rhetoric occupied in Christianity of the period see Cameron, *Christianity*, ch. 1.

[31] See Margulies, 'Mavo', xxviii; Lerner, *Aggadat Ruth*, pt 1, 19. It might very well be that this usage has its roots in the tradition relating to R. Hiyya who asserts that 'I passed my eyes over the entire book of Psalms Aggada' (yKil 9, 32a).

[32] On this source see Aptowitzer, 'Zur Kosmologie der Agada'.

We will not pursue his reason, but will note that queries about creation and natural phenomena were an integral part of aggada, the assumption being, that the answers were somehow found in Scripture. Finally, there is a wonderful story where the people of Simonia probe the expertise of Levi b. Sisi and say: 'Perhaps he is a master (lit. son) of aggada (בר אגדה)? – They asked him verses' (GenR 81,2 p970).

It is instructive that the rabbis collect most of their religious reflections in the Tannaic period within the rubric of comments on or around the Bible. This contrasts with their effort in legal matters to develop a collection independent of Scripture. The Mishna and Tosefta do contain a few representative examples of how the rabbis went about composing a 'Mishna' on aggada. I refer to the Tractate of Avot,[33] the 10th chapter of Sanhedrin and large sections of Tosefta Sota.

The spirit of the aggadic enterprise may be summed up in ben Bag Bag's dictum in Avot 5:22, 'Turn it and turn it again, for all is in it...' There is no antecedent for the 'it', but the presumption is that the reference is to Tora. This accords well with what we saw above, that the rabbis searched Scripture for answers to all sorts of questions. Yet, it was exactly this inexhaustibility and versatility which led R. Zeira to deride 'those of aggada' as 'books' or 'practitioners of enchantment'.[34] Even after another attempt to persuade him of the validity of aggadic interpretation, R. Zeira remains unconvinced. He concludes, in a fine play on ben Bag Bag's statement, 'It (aggada) turns and it turns but you hear nothing from it. Yirmia, my son, stick to your questions regarding the law of forked poles'.[35]

We are well served if we place R. Zeira's critique of aggada within the context of similar critiques of what were perceived to be exegetical extravagances, in halakha and aggada alike. When R. Yishmael could not tolerate R. Eliezer's legal interpretation of a verse in Leviticus, he blurted out: 'Rabbi, behold, you tell the verse to keep quiet until you have interpreted it.' This piqued R. Eliezer, a well known conservative, who replied in kind: 'Yishmael, you are a Mountain Palm' (i.e. which bears no fruit).[36] In fact, the same objection to an explanation that has 'circumvented (עוקפת) the verse' is raised in both an halakhic and an aggadic context.[37]

---

[33] On the editing of Avot see Tropper, *Wisdom*, 17-47.

[34] yMaas 3:4, 51a. Our versions read ספרי קוסמי which would mean 'books of witchcraft' or 'divination' (I have translated tentatively 'enchantment' because it might allude also to the power or attraction aggada held over the people); but some suggest reading ספרי hence 'teachers' of witchcraft, see Sokoloff, *Dictionary of Jewish Palestinian Aramaic*, 386.

[35] Yerushalmi *ib.* The phrase 'to turn and turn again' is originally a commercial term; see Lieberman, *Yerushalmi Nezikin*, 116. There is then no 'profit' in aggada. On the difficult word דוקני, 'forked poles', see Sokoloff, *Dictionary of Jewish Palestinian Aramaic*, 142.

[36] See the chapter by M. Kahana preceding in this volume; Epstein, *Prolegomena*, 522.

[37] yKid 1:2, 59d; LevR 32,1 (p735); see also SifDeut 1 (p6f).

The rabbinic venture to locate both law and lore within the biblical framework, whether exegetically or by loose association, called forth a reaction from within and from without, which questioned the validity of the interpretive methods. Yet, the Bible became the universe of discourse and instruction for almost every imaginable topic, through the agency of Aggadic midrash.

Aggadic Midrash as Creative Exegesis

It was, then, the decision of rabbinic scholars and later editors to use the Bible as a framework or encyclopedia for all their musings. We see this first in the aggadic sections of the Tannaic midrashim, the so-called Halakhic Midrashim. Eventually, this same function was filled by the talmudic editors, who collected relevant rabbinic reflections around the Mishna or around *baraitot*.

It is, however, important to note that the relationship between rabbinic non-legal creativity and the Bible goes far beyond any editorial decision. It is quite evident, from our earliest Tannaic writings, that the rabbis attempted to weave their theological and ethical thoughts into the Bible in a manner and to an extent that was unprecedented in Second Temple times. The heart of rabbinic midrash is the interplay between the biblical text and the rabbinic glosses and musings over the text. Parables and stories, no less than brief exegetical comments, almost always serve an exegetical function and are not fully understood without recourse to the biblical text. In this sense, midrash differs from the Roman practice of touching on various and diverse subjects in the course of the *enarratio* on Virgil, for example.[38] For the rabbis, the Bible is not only the framework for treating other subjects. The rabbis developed a way of reading Scripture whereby the very words and syntax of the Bible were cajoled into saying, by playful exegesis, some of the most serious thoughts which they entertained. One can not and should not try to separate out the exegetical element of midrash from the resultant ideas or ideologies.

It is worthwhile now to survey some examples of aggadic midrash in order to evince the extent to which the exegetical function occupied rabbinic creativity. This preoccupation with finding assorted possible meanings of biblical words and phrases sometime results in heightened appreciation of what might be construed as the 'original' meaning within Scripture. On other occasions, probably the lion's share of aggadic midrash, the Bible is interpreted in a way far from what one would consider a possible 'contextual' meaning of the particular word or phrase. In this latter sense aggadic midrash has aptly been characterized as the converse of paraphrase. If a paraphrase is saying the same thing in other words, midrash is saying something else with the same words.[39]

---

[38] On the term *enarratio* see Hammond-Scullard, *Oxford Classical Dictionary*, 371.
[39] I owe this formulation to Beeri Zimmerman.

GLOSSING TECHNIQUES

Let us begin with a series of short glosses:

> 'Abraham took the wood for the burnt offering and put it on his son Isaac' (Gen 22:6) – as one who bears his cross on his shoulder. (GenR 56,3 p598)

> 'And the two of them walked on together' (Gen 22:6) – this to bind and this to be bound, this to slaughter and this to be slaughtered. (GenR 56,6 p598)

> 'He (Jacob) went, and got them and brought them to his mother' (27:4) – coerced, broken and sobbing. (GenR 65,9 p727)

These are three fine representatives of the midrash's effort to set the mood and the tone of the biblical reading with the aid of the briefest of glosses. Often these glosses are in Aramaic and can be viewed as snippets of Targum. We find, though, similar glosses, which either reinterpret the biblical story or sum up the 'moral' of the verse.

> 'By your sword (על חרבך) shall you live' (Gen 27:40) – R. Levi said: sheathe (Aram. על) your sword and you shall live (GenR 67,7 p762)

> 'Thereupon Abraham bowed low to the people of the land' (Gen 23:7) – from here that we are grateful for glad tidings. (GenR 58,6 p625)

> 'The God of my father has been with me (עמדי, imadi; Gen 31:5)' – [read] amadi, my pillar,[40] my support' (GenR 74,3 p859).

Whereas R. Levi magnificently subverted the original meaning of the verse by reading על as the Aramaic 'to enter', our last example concretized the meaning of the verse by changing 'with me' into 'my pillar'.

We should pay special attention to another kind of short gloss which is one of the more prevalent forms of midrash, especially in its more expanded form. This is זהוי, zihui (from זה, lit. 'this'), a technique of the rabbis to 'identify' a word, place or person in Bible with a degree of specificity that the Bible has not conveyed. I shall bring two examples of this ubiquitous rabbinic method:

> 'He struck his hip at the socket' (Gen 32:26) – he struck the righteous who in the future would stand from him, this is the generation of Destruction (i.e. the Hadrianic persecution). (GenR 77,3 p914)

> 'A fugitive came' (Gen 14:13) – R. Shimon b. Lakish in the name of bar Kappara: that is Og... (GenR 41,8 p413).

More complex forms of midrash include the use of additional verses, stories and parables to highlight some feature of a biblical verse. God's question to Adam, 'Where are you?' (איכה, ayekha, Gen 3:9) is repointed by the midrash to read eikha, 'Alas, how' (i.e., the beginning of Lamentations). Striking parallels

---

[40] Simply re-pointing the word, changing the *hirik* to a *patah*.

116

are then drawn between God's lament over Israel's expulsion and God's early lament over Adam's expulsion (GenR 19,9 p178f).

The fragrant smell of Jacob's borrowed clothes is an occasion to tell two stories of Jewish traitors in Greco-Roman times. One of these recounts a Jew's complicity with the Romans, to the extent that he is duped into entering the Temple and removing the Menorah. Both stories end with the penitence of the traitors, probably based on the word play *begadav / bogdav*, 'clothes' – 'traitors'. Need we point out that Jacob's clothes themselves were a form of treachery? Indeed, one may read the biblical story as Jacob's entering to remove something which did not rightly belong to him. We can only emphasize the complexity of the hermeneutic issues facing the student of midrash in a case like this (GenR 65,22 p740).

In a deservedly famous parable, R. Shimon b. Yohai compares Cain's murder of Abel with two gladiators who fight in the presence of the King (GenR 22,9 p216). When the one is near death, he turns an accusing finger at the king who did not intervene. Can we ignore the fact that this trenchant reading of the biblical story is attributed to one who witnessed the disastrous and bloody Bar-Kochba revolt?

PETIHTA

Another well studied but still elusive midrashic form is the *petihta* or proem. The basic thrust of this form is the interpretation of a verse by reference to a second remote verse. More often than not, a verse from the Ketuvim is employed to epitomize or provide a caption for a verse from the Tora. This juxtapositioning can be executed in a few lines, but no less frequent are highly developed petihtot which can span pages. In the latter, the verse from Ketuvim is usually interpreted in sundry ways until the link is finally made to the verse from the Tora lectional reading (*seder*) of the day. Some have viewed this leisurely rehearsal of interpretations to Ketuvim as a way of arousing the curiosity of the listening audience. This approach assumes that at some stage these highly developed literary creations, were once presented in some oral form to a listening audience. This is an important consideration when dealing with Leviticus Rabba and Pesikta de-Rav Kahana, where the extended literary petihta is pervasive. Finally, we have another kind of proem which opens with a simple halakhic question – introduced with the words ילמדנו רבינו, *ye-lammedenu Rabbenu*, 'Teach us our master' – and eventually wends its way down to the lectionary reading. Though this type predominates in the later Tanhuma/ Yelammedenu Midrashim, to which it lent its name, it can be traced to earlier rabbinic literature.

We can use the following excerpts from an extended petihta in Leviticus Rabba 23 as an illustration of the literary petihta, which spans some twelve pages in Margulies' critical edition (p523-535):

"You should not do as they do in Egypt... and you should not do as they do in the land of Canaan" (Lev. 18,3):
R. Yitzhak opened (פתח): "As a Lily among the thorns" (Cant 2,2);
R. Yitzhak explained (פתר) the verse as referring to Rebecca...;
R. Elazar explained the verse regarding those who left Egypt... just as a lily is difficult to pick, so Israel in Egypt were difficult to redeem...;
R. Yehuda b. R. Simon explained the verse regarding Israel before Sinai...

Each of these explanations is developed at length and is followed by three other identifications of the lily among the thorns: pious deeds, the present generation, and finally, tomorrow's redemption. The entire creation culminates in Moses exhortation to Israel to continue being a lily among the thorns in Canaan as they had been in Egypt. Thus we have come full circle back to our opening verse.

This brief illustration shows on the one hand the epitomizing or captioning of a verse from Tora ('do not do as the Egyptians') with another verse from Ketuvim ('as a lily'). Yet, it is a fully developed and, in this case, somewhat artificial form which has been expanded to house diverse topics under one roof, from the ancient to the contemporary. Often, the juxtaposition of two verses produces startling results. Isaac's request of Esau to bring him venison so that he may bless him is introduced by a verse from the Tora, an unusual literary move.

> R. Yitzhak opened: "Do not take a bribe for a bribe blinds clear vision" (Exod 23:8). – What if one who took a bribe from someone who owed him, his eyes were dimmed; how much more so (if one takes) from someone who does not owe him: "When Isaac was old and his eyes were too dim to see" (Gen 27:1). (GenR 65,7 p716).

POLYSEMY

We have treated a number of the methods of aggada, including various kinds of glosses, parables, stories, identification, and petihta. The next feature of aggadic midrash which demands our attention is what has been called its 'ideological policy of polysemy'.[41] We do have on record, in a number of places in the midrash, the attempt of a single sage to offer multiple aggadic interpretations of a single verse. This ethos is captured beautifully by R. Hanin's preface to his interpretation of Gen 20:13, 'Would that we will expound this verse three ways (אפין) and we shall do it justice' (GenR 52,11 p550). In what we may call an allegorical 'identification', the midrash credits R. Hama b. Hanina with interpreting Gen 29:2-3 in six different ways (שיטין). What holds true for the individual sages, is even more pertinent regarding the

---

[41] Stern, *Midrash and Theory*, 23; Most recently, see A. Yadin's discussion in Scripture as Logos: *Rabbi Ishmael*, 69-79.

midrashic collections. If the trademark of rabbinic aggada is pinpointing new meanings in the biblical text, the hallmark of the aggadic collections is the diverse and often conflicting exegeses brought side by side.

It is characteristic of aggadic midrash to bring more than one opinion on topics of import, as well as on topics which do not seem to be as significant. These opinions sometimes complement one another, but often the two opinions are quite in opposition. Thus, Beit Shammai and Beit Hillel debate whether the heavens were created first or the earth. When Noah is described by the Tora as pious 'in his generation', two sages debate whether this is said to relativize his attainment or to aggrandize his achievement (just imagine how pious he would have been had he lived in Abraham's time). Was Abraham's circumcision by natural means or supernatural? Is prayer or possibly repentance more efficacious in effacing sin? All of these issues are subjected to differing views, usually bolstered by exegetical support.

Though diverse opinions are ubiquitous in the midrash, actual debate and dialogue over differing opinions is far less frequent. Yet, from Tannaic through Amoraic times we do have vestiges of documented discourse and debate in aggadic matters. R. Akiva and the sages differed over whether one's life span was pre-ordained or whether it could be increased by one's righteousness. This debate is found in the Tosefta (tEd 1:14) and what ensues is a duel over scriptural interpretation, each side drawing on verses to combat the other's view.

There is a precious glimpse into R. Tarfon's method of tutoring his students in aggadic exegesis, raising questions and parrying his student's scriptural interpretations (tBer 4:16). R. Tarfon raises a question: 'Why did Judah merit Royalty?' The students answer and bring a prooftext, which is refuted by their teacher – they deferentially reply ילמדנו רבינו, 'Teach us our master' – and he proceeds to demonstrate a winning exegesis.[42] This fine insight into biblical instruction, which reportedly takes place on Shabbat afternoon after Mincha, should take its rightful place in our attempts to reconstruct the place of Bible study in the rabbinic academy.

Finally, in Genesis Rabba alone we find over 30 places where rabbis question another rabbi's exegesis. Often these debates center around the attempt to generate a general rule of aggadic exegesis.[43] So, for example, we find the following extended discussions in one chapter of Genesis Rabba (GenR 41,3 p399-407).

> ... This midrash came up in our hands from the diaspora. Everywhere it says in
> Scripture: "It was in the day," there was trouble. Said R. Shmuel bar Nahman:

---

[42] I have followed Lieberman's interpretation for this difficult passage in tBer 4:16, *ad loc.* and *Tosefta Ki-Fshutah*, vol 1 p68f. The passage attests to the antiquity of the *yelammedenu* form, as Lieberman pointed out the interface of halakha and aggada, typical of that genre in its later development in the Tanhuma-Yelammedenu Midrash and in the Sheiltot.

[43] See Hirshman *ib.* (above n29) 190-208, and n11 there with reference to Meir, 'Responding or Asking'.

there are five... R. Shimon in the name of R. Yohanan: everywhere it says in Scripture: "And it was," functions as trouble or joy; if trouble, unparalleled, if joy, unparalleled. R. Shmuel bar Nahman came and made a distinction: everywhere it says *wa-yehi* – trouble; *we-haya* – joy...

R. Shmuel is then battered by anonymous questions (posed in the plural) which show exceptions to his rule, all of which are rebutted, though a whimsical atmosphere pervades his responses.

RELIGIOUS POLEMICS AND THE VALUE OF AGGADA

In the last paragraphs I have tried to show that aggadic midrash shares in common with rabbinic legal literature the same trait of debate and differing opinions. We can not avoid engaging the question of the seriousness of these debates in aggadic midrash. One searches for hard evidence upon which to respond to this question with little success. Yet, there is, I think, ample grounds for calling into question the Gaonic view of aggada as rabbinic experimentation, which carried with it a 'take it or leave it' attitude.

It is important to emphasize that aggada from its inception was a potpourri of the fabulous, the subtle, the outrageous and the sublime all rolled into one. This was so almost by definition, since the aggadic midrash became the main receptacle for Jewish creativity around the Bible which was then filtered through rabbinic editing. So, popular tales, mystical speculation and running exegesis all found their way side by side in the collections known as aggadic midrash. No wonder then that this literature was a prime target for sectarians, who held different views of rabbinic Judaism.

There is a delightful story in the Babylonian Talmud (bAZ 4a) of how the Babylonian Rav Safra was given a clerical exemption from taxes by the 'heretics' or 'sectarians' (מינאי), on the basis of a recommendation by the well known Palestinian R. Abbahu. Yet, when the sectarians tested Rav Safra on scripture they found him to be wanting. R. Abbahu quickly defended his recommendation explaining that Rav Safra's expertise was in Mishna, not in Bible. When R. Abbahu was asked by the sectarians, why is it that you (pl.) do know? He said to them, 'We who are used to being around you take it upon ourselves to examine the verses of scripture.'[44]

The story accurately portrays the Caesarian Rabbi Abbahu's expertise in countering the heretics. The verse in question was probably a pivotal one for rabbinic exegetes in the charged atmosphere of religious polemics: 'You only have I known of all the families of the earth, therefore I will visit upon you all your iniquities' (Amos 3:2). I do not think it wise to see in this story support for the view that Babylonians did not study Bible. We actually have an explicit reference to the fact that there were Babylonian teachers, such as Rav Pappa, who studied (מעייני) aggada (bShab 89a). We have moreover the technical

---

[44] bAZ 4a ms JTSA, reads ומעיינין בקראי.

Aramaic phrase, 'to arrange aggada', which appears in the Babylonian Talmud and indicates an orderly recitation of aggada in the presence of Babylonian teachers.[45] Much more likely it is that Rav Safra avoided an encounter over scripture with the heretics with whom he had little experience.

The Christians, from the New Testament and on (cf Tit 1:14), derided the aggadot as 'Jewish fables', though many prominent Church fathers drew on Jewish aggadic traditions to sustain their own exegetical work. The heart of the Christian claim was that the key to interpreting the Old Testament was to be found in the New Testament. The Apologists of the second century CE attacked the 'blasphemous' and coarsely anthropomorphic exegesis of the rabbis. Both Christian and rabbinic sources of the time present themselves as being in dialogue with one another over the interpretation of Scripture. This dialogue continues in the third and fourth centuries, with the added phenomenon of prominent Church Fathers consulting Jewish teachers and aggadic works, to gain insight into Scripture. This scholarly deference was accompanied, however, by recurrent maligning of the Jews who refused to concede what the Christians held to be the main point of the entire Bible, the announcement of their Messiah.[46]

It is no wonder then that rabbinic Jews of the Middle ages chose to understate the importance or validity of aggada in the face of Karaitic schism and Christian (and Islamic?) attacks on the aggada. When one adds to this the growing medieval integration of philosophy into the rabbinic world view, one sees further reason for discomfort with a literature which seemed to be unabashedly anthropomorphic and anthropopaic. I would suggest, then, that aggadic midrash became a second class citizen primarily in medieval times, much after the close of the classical midrash and the Talmud. Though the Midrashim and Talmudim have traces of resistance to aggada, I have tried to show that the same resistance is true of some of the Halachic Midrashim. It is also not surprising that in the Talmud we find some rabbis, though few and far between, who disparage the aggada, while in aggadic sections we find the superlatives attached to the study of aggada. It is quite clear that many, if not all, of the prominent rabbis engaged in halakha as well as aggada. For some of these rabbis, aggada was also the focus of their mystical efforts, which some of them certainly held to be their most serious and important endeavour.[47]

We should not, however, underestimate the entertainment aspect of aggada. The aggada prides itself on its magnetism, on its ability to tug at the hearts of the listeners. According to the Talmud, Jews flocked to hear a good preacher, which raised the ire of the snubbed teachers of halakha. We have a midrashic

---

[45] Fraenkel, *Darkhei ha-Aggada*, has collected the four instances in his chapter 'Midrash and Aggada', 35-38 and footnotes. The close connection between the tern מסדר אגדתא and its many halakhic parallels (מסדר מתניתיה) and others should be given more credence rather than less.

[46] See Hirshman, *Rivalry of Genius*.

[47] Cf דבר גדול מעשה מרכבה, bSuk 28a.

account of R. Akiba's ability to bring his audience to tears over a biblical tragedy (GenR 33,5 p310), and another account of his rousing them from their slumber by a most startling aggadic exegesis (GenR 58,3 p621).[48]

It would seem then that our midrashic collections are an amalgam of serious scholarly speculation and popular teaching, refracted through the rabbinic editor(s). We have not, as yet, developed criteria for distinguishing between the different levels of aggada. Indeed, even more elementary questions have not found their definitive answers.

Are some of the fantastic rabbinic interpretations to be taken literally or figuratively? Did the rabbis believe that Adam had been a creature of gigantic proportions and that this stature was to be restored in Messianic times? Or, was this metaphoric play, as Maimonides would suggest in his Guide of the Perplexed? It has been claimed that, although one can find overlap between some Philonic themes and the midrash, philosophical terminology is conspicuously absent from rabbinic literature. Did those of the rabbis who were Greek speakers, like R. Abbahu, consciously refrain from the pursuit of philosophy? Were the rabbis, as one scholar would have it,[49] less philosophically advanced in their conception of God than the contemporary middle and Neo-Platonic philosophers? These very important questions await renewed and exhaustive study.

I have tried to advance the position that aggadic midrash was, in its day, the main avenue of rabbinic reflection and speculation. At the same time, aggadic midrash served a popular function. One would have to agree with Yitzhak Heinemann's view of the serious ends but playful means employed by the aggada. Yet even Heinemann's *magnum opus* leaves us dazzled by the variety of the aggada and in a quandary over the way we should understand the mythical language of the rabbis.

The Social Setting of Aggadic Midrash

We do have testimony within rabbinic literature and also from Patristic sources that elementary Jewish education revolved around Scripture, and that a good deal of Scripture was memorized in one's youth. Beyond this elementary education, there was the lectionary reading of Tora four times a week. In the Land of Israel, the Sabbath reading comprised a small selection of at least 21 verses (*seder*), accompanied by their Aramaic translation and followed by the weekly selection from the Prophets. It is fair to say though that beyond the most elementary levels of education, we notice opposition among some rabbis

---

[48] See Lieberman, *Greek in Jewish Palestine*, 161. S. Krauss cited a testimony from Jerome as to the raucous nature of Jewish preaching, see Hirshman, 'The Preacher and his Public', 111. The text has been challenged as not pertaining to Jewish preaching by Stemberger, 'Hieronymus und die Juden seiner Zeit', 361-362 as cited in agreement by Newman, *Jerome and the Jews*, 45 and n81.

[49] Stroumsa, 'Form(s) of God', 270.

to Bible study. For some it was clearly seen as peripheral at best, when compared to the more important study of Mishna and Talmud. Thus R. Shimon b. Yohai is quoted as saying: 'One who studies Mikra, it is an attribute but not an attribute; one who studies Mishna is an attribute for which one gets recompense; one who studies Talmud, there is no greater attribute that this'.[50]

It seems likely that both economic and intellectual exigencies allowed only the select to continue beyond the initial stages of education. This is reflected in a passage which describes 1000 students who enter the study of Mikra, of whom 100 continue on to Mishna and only ten who advance to Talmud.[51] Beyond the synagogue setting and elementary education, it is not uncommon to find scholars asking one another the meaning of a certain verse. However, it is most unusual to find, in Palestinian sources, scholars who are portrayed as sitting and studying a selection of the Bible. One of the few examples of this is Rabbi Yehuda ha-Nasi's study of Lamentations on Shabbat afternoon which was the eve of the fast of ninth of Av.[52] It is not out of the question that when the Yerushalmi uses the term 'labouring in Tora' (לעי באורייתא), the meaning is study of Bible, since אורייתא often means specifically the Bible,[53] but this is far from certain.

We do find, though, that the Babylonian Talmud knows of a person whose task was to assemble or arrange (מסדר אגדתא)[54] the aggada before the presiding sage. According to the Bavli, this was the case both in Babylonia and the Land of Israel.[55] Yet, we have no explicit reference in Palestinian sources to this practice, and the single attribution in the Bavli mentioned above remains the only shred of evidence, hardly unimpeachable, that such was the case in the Land of Israel also.

Another fine example of advanced teachers discussing aggada is reported concerning R. Ami and R. Assi, the great 'judges of the land of Israel'. Again we rely on traditions brought in the Bavli, for the most part, purportedly reflecting conversations in the Land of Israel. This tradition runs as follows:

> R. Ami and R. Assi sat in the hall[56] of R. Yitshak Nappaha. One master said, let the master say a halakha (שמעתא). The other master said, let the master say an aggada (אגדתא). He began to say aggada and the one did not let him; he began to say halakha and the other did not let him. He said to them: I will tell you a parable, to what is this comparable to a man with two wives, one young and one old. The young one plucks his white hairs and the old one plucks his black ones

[50] yShab 16:1, 15c.
[51] LevR 2,1 p35.
[52] yShab 16:1, 15c.
[53] yShab 7:2, 9b; yNed 6:8, 40a.
[54] The root סדר carries the sense of assembling, see H. Yalon, *Studies in the Hebrew Language*, Jerusalem 1971, 419-423 (Hebr), who cites also S. Lieberman.
[55] E.g. bEr 21b; bBer 10a.
[56] ms: אקילעא or tent, cf Albeck, *Introduction*, 253.

– he ends up bald from both sides. This being the case I will say something which will satisfy both of you... (bBK 60b)

This burlesque parable is itself embedded in an extended treatment of damages caused by fire, in which halakha and aggada alternate with a consummate ending where a Palestinian aggada – David's heroes bringing him water from Bethlehem – is refashioned to contain strong legal content.

We do have an excellent example, preserved in Palestinan sources, of rabbis sitting and discussing a problem related to the verse 'These are the generations of Yishmael ben Avraham' (Gen 25:12):

> A story: R. Hama b. Ukva and the rabbis were sitting and deliberating (מתקשיי):
> Why did Scripture see fit to recount the geneaology of the wicked here? R. Levi
> passed by. They said, here comes the master of the tradition (שמעתתא!), let's ask
> him. (GenR 62,5 p676f)

This same scenario is found in a legal context with the very same technical terms.[57] This formulaic equating of the deliberation in a purely aggadic question to one of a legal nature lends credence to the view that the rabbis engaged in systematic discussion of aggada, similar to that of halakha.[58]

One of the earliest and most revealing examples of instruction in aggada is found in the Tosefta Berakhot (4:16) mentioned above. Interestingly, that long repartee takes place 'in the shade of the dovecot on Shabbat after *Minha*'. Now, we know that much rabbinic instruction took place in informal settings, from the fields to the marketplaces.[59] Yet, it might not be coincidental that our solid evidence for instruction in aggada revolves around Shabbat and especially Shabbat afternoon.[60] I think it a likely conjecture that Shabbat was the day when a broader community assembled and naturally more aggada was treated. This was certainly the case in the Babylonian 'Pirka'[61] and was likely also the main opportunity for rabbinic teaching of aggada.

We remain, unfortunately, without a clear view of how the aggadic curriculum was structured in the academic setting of Roman Palestine. We are quite certain, however, of the enormous popularity that aggada enjoyed, to which we now turn.

The Attractiveness of Aggada and its Popularity

The recurrent playful association of aggada with the Aramaic root נגד (to pull or attract) in Tannaic and Amoraic literature is an indication of the perceived attractiveness of aggada to the population at large. This is borne out also by the

---

[57] PesRK Rosh ha-shana p345 exactly and in yRH 7:1, 59a with slight variations.
[58] See my article (above n29) 190-208 on GenR 12 and 30, chapters which bear the imprint of study in the *beit midrash*.
[59] See Büchler, 'Learning and Teaching'.
[60] tSot 7:9, R. Tarfon; yHag 2:1, 77b, R. Meir.
[61] Gafni, *Jews of Babylonia*, 205-213.

stories of the large crowds attracted by the aggadic preacher and the latter's advantage over the teacher of halakha. We do know, by way of comparison, the power of the Christian medieval preachers over their audiences, as depicted so beautifully by Huizinga in the opening chapter of *The Waning of the Middle Ages*. It is important to point out that the enchantment of aggada is described in rabbinic literature as widespread, appealing to diverse audiences, rabbis and laymen, women and children. This contrasts sharply with the medieval Jewish perception which saw aggada as intended mainly to winning over the hearts of the women and the uneducated, as reflected in Rashi's comments on bShab 30b.

It is abundantly clear that the rabbis were not only conscious of this appeal, but saw it as their duty to fashion the most attractive sermons possible. On the verse 'Sweetness drops from your lips, O bride' (Cant 4:11), there is a series of comments on the responsibility of the one who teaches Tora in public to make his words pleasing to the audience. The series culminates with Resh Lakish (c. 250 CE) who says: 'Anyone who says words of Tora and they are not pleasing to the listeners as a bride is pleasing to her husband under the bridal canopy, it is preferable that he had not said them' (CantR 4,11).

Prominent rabbis directed their students to the premier teachers and traditions of aggada: 'Any time you find the words of R. Eliezer the son of R. Yosi the Galilean in aggada, make your ear a funnel'.[62] Two very famous sources for the popularity of aggada reveal interesting information:

> R. Hanina was leaning on R. Hiyya bar Ba in Sepphoris and he saw everyone running. He said to him, Why are these people running? He said, R. Yohanan is preaching in R. Benaya's *beit midrash* and everyone is running to hear him. He said, Blessed is the Merciful who has shown me (my) fruits in my lifetime, I explained to him all the aggada except for Proverbs and Kohelet.[63]

This first source reveals the extensive instruction in aggada R. Yohanan had received from the elderly R. Hanina, and the great popularity R. Yohanan enjoyed in Sepphoris. Most enlightening is the fact that within the confines of the story, R. Hama assumes R. Yohanan is teaching aggada! This, I think, supports our conjecture above, that the heart of rabbinic popular instruction was aggada.

Finally, the classic story of the rivalry between the teaching of aggada and the teaching of halakha is captured in the people's snubbing of R. Hiyya bar Abba's lecture in halakha and attending in its stead R. Abbahu's aggadic disquisition (bSot 40a). The damage caused to these sages' relationship was irreparable.

It seems apparent that at least in Babylonian sources the study of aggada was considered less strenous. Thus, when R. Zera told his student R. Yirmiya

---

[62] bHul 89a, cf yKid 1:10, 61d.
[63] yBM 2,11. See Hirshman, 'The Preacher', 112.

that he was feeling faint and was not up to handling a legal discussion, the student plied his teacher for instruction in aggada, to which R. Zera acceded. This accords well with the characterization of the teaching of aggada with 'smiling faces'.[64]

Aggadic Midrash – Precursors, Allies and Competitors

An enormous amount of fruitful and enlightening research has been devoted to tracing the beginnings of aggadic midrash to interpretive traditions within the Bible itself.

L. Zunz opened his pioneering and massive study of aggada with a chapter on what he considered early aggadic trends in the Books of Chronicles. In a way, Zunz was following the view expressed in the midrash itself, that 'Chronicles was given only to be reinterpreted' (לא ניתנה דברי הימים אלא להידרש). In the latter half of the 20th century, extensive research was carried out on what has been called 'inner-biblical exegesis'. The contention was that parts of the Bible reinterpret other parts in a very deliberate fashion. This of course is granted by all scholars.

The questions still being debated are: (1) to what extent is this phenomenon really similar to later aggadic exegesis, which though doing some of the same reinterpreting does it from a more outspoken and conscious interpretive posture? (2) can we locate aggadic inner-biblical exegesis only in the later books of the Bible, like Chronicles, or does the phenomenon already surface in the earlier books also?

Zakovitch and Shinan attempted to prove that the salient characteristics of aggada, as depicted by I. Heinemann in his great *Darkhei ha-aggada*, are to be found in all strata of biblical literature and continue on into post-biblical literature. Solving contradictions, juxtapositions, name derivations and other characteristics are claimed to be present in biblical, post-biblical and rabbinic literature. Thus, in their view, aggadic midrash begins in biblical times. This bold view has its merits, but I think, needs modification for two reasons. The first is that the examples they adduce for the earliest strata of biblical literature are on the whole less compelling than those brought from the later biblical works. Secondly, and most important, the fact that the rabbis worked almost exclusively within an exegetical framework distinguishes their work from the early biblical interpretation. The exegetical mentality begins to take hold in the Second Temple biblical works, gains strength in Qumran and Philo and reaches its crescendo in rabbinic times.

This is not to gainsay the extensive exegesis in Qumran and Philo, but rather to emphasize the exclusivity of creative exegesis as the rabbis' way of expressing themselves. Though inner-biblical exegesis is an indispensable tool

---

[64] This characterization is found in a relatively late addition to the PesRK, Bahodesh.

126

for understanding the Bible, so ably demonstrated by M. Fishbane, it remains, I think, a precursor of rabbinic aggada, yet not the same phenomenon.

The extent and riches of Jewish literature of the Second Temple period are only now coming into sharp focus. The Apocrypha, Pseudepigrapha, Qumranic and Hellenistic Jewish writings, all precede rabbinic literature and hold important clues to the development of rabbinic aggadic midrash, as do the early Greek and Aramaic translations of the Bible. They are, along with those sections of the Bible itself of the late second temple period, the link between the Hebrew Bible and its reinterpretation in rabbinic times. Without describing this literature, which has been done at length in earlier volumes of this series, we will try to discuss the selected issues which will bring rabbinic midrash into bold relief.

J. Kugel has persuasively argued for the exegetical roots of many of the motifs found in second temple retelling of the biblical story, such as the Book of Jubilees and the Testament of Levi. Yet, it is clear that their authors, even if they were drawing on a fund of biblical exegeses, as Kugel contends, were not interested in preserving the verbal link between their retold narrative and the original biblical story. This of course differs markedly from classical rabbinic midrash, which tenaciously clung to the original text and expressly infiltrated its creative exegesis into the words of the Bible.[65]

What is striking in this rabbinic insistence on playing off the words of scripture, is their retention of the words while abandoning completely the syntactical logic of the sentence or even the basic meaning of the words.[66] Each word was hollowed out and often refilled with meanings having little or no relation to the range of meanings it normally held. The six Hebrew letters of first word of the Bible, בראשית, 'in the beginning', are divided into two little words, ברא and שית, meaning 'He created six'. We have come a long way from motifs generated by exegetical difficulties, as posited by Kugel, nor is this akin to Louis Ginzberg's folklore model. This rabbinic free-wheeling, innovative and bold refashioning and 're-filling' of the biblical vocabulary is quite different from its Second Temple counterparts.[67] Though rabbinic literature shares many motifs with Second Temple Apocrypha and Pseudepigrapha, the creative exegetical thrust of rabbinic midrash distinguishes it in a very profound way.

There is more in common with the pesher form in Qumran, wherein Scripture is read as forecasting a contemporary event. But for the Qumran community, this was the dominant exegetical posture, whereas this is far less the case in rabbinic midrash. The rabbis can and do interpret the biblical 'Edom' to represent contemporary Rome, or a biblical well to represent the Sanhedrin. But this is by no means the most prevalent form of midrash. A great deal of midrash is devoted to a persistent interlacing of various parts of scripture,

---

[65] See Fraade, 'Looking for Narrative Midrash at Qumran'.

[66] I. Heinemann, *Darkhei ha-aggada* called this 'abandonment of logos'.

[67] Comparison might possibly be made with Philonic etymologies.

relating them intertextually one to the other. In this sense, rabbinic midrash ranges freely from the contemporary to the 'purely' exegetical, the various sorts of exegesis arranged side by side by the compilers.[68]

Comparison with Philo, especially with his Questions and Answers on Genesis and Exodus, is of special interest. It is important to take note of the fact that Philo's biblical commentaries divide out, as has been noted, into topical commentaries, that is allegorical essays around a biblical selection, and his running format of 'Questions and Answers'. This in some way anticipates the two formats of rabbinic midrash: exegetical (Genesis Rabba) and homiletical (Leviticus Rabba). It is striking, though, that in his Questions and Answers, Philo has chosen to offer multiple answers on various levels to the questions raised in the text. It is Philo's consistent differentiation and consciousness of differing levels of interpretation which sets him wholly apart from the rabbis. The rabbis, in the midrashic collections, do not give clear expression to graded approaches to the text, unless we view *maase merkava* and *maase bereshit* (mystical exegesis) in this light. But, since a formal enunciation of levels of interpretation is absent in ancient rabbinic literature, I think that it is more appropriate to assume that the rabbis operated without the same clearly worked out levels interpretation, as did Philo. Nevertheless it is well to remember that both Philo and the rabbis share the basic posture that each verse or part of a verse can and should have multiple interpretations.

The oldest translation of the Bible, into Greek, was well known to some of the rabbis, and there were enthusiastic admirers of it. Some of them used Greek word play to create new exegeses of the Hebrew scripture. In the following example, the reference is to the Hebrew word הֵן (*hen*), 'indeed', in Isa 40:15: 'What is *hen*? Greek language *hen* is one!' (i.e., ἕν, thus in GenR 99,7 p1279). So too the Hebrew word אפס (*efes*) 'but', in Jdg 4:9 is taken by R. Reuven to be Greek ἀφες (*afes*), 'release' (spelled הפס, GenR 40,4 p384). These common words were interpreted via the Greek and certainly such was the case with more difficult words.[69]

As opposed to the works canvassed until now, the Aramaic targum was created in the same circles as rabbinic midrash. That is to say, that targum was an integral part of the rabbis' view of Bible, and the Mishna requires that public reading of the Tora be accompanied by targum. As we noted above, short, targum-like statements are in evidence in a work like Genesis Rabba. In spite of some deprecative remarks about *meturgemanim*, it seems best to see the Targum – certainly the Aramaic and the Greek Aquilas – as faithful allies of rabbinic midrash. As the midrash incorporated bits of targum into its work,

---

[68] Scholars of Second Temple times are divided over the degree of continuity and affinity between the diverse Qumqanic exegetical literature and rabbinic midrash. See Fraade (above n64) and his references to Mandel, 'Midrashic Exegesis'; Kister, 'Common Heritage'.

[69] The crux at Genesis 49:5, מכרותיכם (*mecheiroteihem*) of Simon and Levi is taken by R. Yohanan to be לשון יוני, 'Greek': מכירין, cf μάχαιραι, 'swords' (GenR 49,7 p1278). See I. Heinemann, *Darkhei ha-aggada*, 111ff.

so the targum epitomized some midrashic insights in its more expansive passages.

Finally, a word should be said about the growing alternative explanations of the Bible by the Christians and the Gnostics. The early Christians utilized the typological tools, previously employed by the Qumran community. The hermeneutical key to understanding the Bible was to understand it a 'forecasting the coming of Jesus'. Allegorical reinterpretation of the Bible begins in the Pauline letters and accelerates in Justin's mid second century works. By the mid-second century Gnostics are composing highly mythological interpretations of the Old Testament, seeing the God of creation as the evil and jealous Demiurge. Up until this time, Jewish exegesis had to contend mainly with general pagan critique of the Bible. From the second century CE and on, the midrash had to be responsive to pagan attacks on the Jewish and Christian Bibles, while at the same time combating 'new' interpretations of their Bible by Gnostics and Christians. The midrash is replete with stories of dialogue with pagans, heretics and Christians. It is clear then, that at the very least the midrash is sensitive to attempts to usurp its own interpretation of the Bible and replace it by others. In light of this, it is all the more remarkable that the midrash allowed diverse opinions and even debate over aggadic points of view. As opposed to Second Temple literature, midrash is devoted to presenting varying and sometimes opposing points of view.

Summary

It is fair to say that although the aggadic midrash had its roots in biblical and post-biblical literature, as creative exegesis which encompassed the entire spectrum of religious thought, the rabbinic brand of aggadic midrash is unprecedented, at least in the Jewish world. The rabbis chose to speak through the words of Tora, new ideas and old, sometimes echoing the biblical message, sometimes completely subverting it. Yet, there was an allegiance to the written word of Scripture as being the best medium for presenting their own thoughts.

This framework stretched to encompass motifs inherited from Second Temple times, as well as popular stories and maxims. It seems likely to me, that the elementary education of the Jewish child prepared them for this imaginative reshaping of the biblical message. The people and most of the rabbis were enthralled by the ability of the *darshan* to rearrange a verse or a word in a flash of brilliance and locate in the Tora a new idea. The verses of Scripture became encyclopaedia entries for a wide array of knowledge and reflection.

The Palestinian midrashic collections were shunted to a secondary position in medieval times, as was the Palestinian Talmud itself. When the printing press came into the service of Jewish literature in the 15th century, apparently no midrashic works were considered important enough to reproduce at first. The midrashic collection had been eclipsed by the aggada in the Babylonian Talmud and the aggada contained in Rashi's commentary on the Bible. Yet the

16th century saw a renaissance of midrashic studies. After important contributions by Azariah de Rossi, and two centuries later by Elijah, the son of the Wilna Gaon, it was Zunz who in his magnificent *Vorträge* (1832) restored to aggadic midrash the lustre it had once enjoyed in the ancient Land of Israel.

Appendix:
The Babylonian Talmud and Aggadic Midrash

The place of aggada and Bible study in Babylonia is a subject which demands further study. Though this topic is seemingly tangential to the history of aggadic midrash in the Land of Israel, the truth is that it has serious impact on our study of aggadic midrash. The first fact to be noted is that provenance of all of the collections of aggadic midrash through the Amoraic period is the Land of Israel. In Babylonia, we have no knowledge of collections of aggada which were structured around the Bible and there is no surviving evidence of their composing independent aggadic works. Though as mentioned above, there is ample evidence for a disciplined, sustained and orderly study of the Bible and midrash. But in its final form the aggadic legacy was amalgamated into the framework of the Babylonians' comments on the Mishna – the Talmud. It is for this reason that the Bavli contains much more aggadic material than the Talmud of Israel. Fully one-third of the Babylonian Talmud is aggada, whereas the ratio in the Yerushalmi is one to six, aggada to law.

When one assembles all the aggadot attributed to Babylonian authors, one finds a dearth of material, which contrasts sharply with the productivity of Palestinian rabbis. Yet, we often find Palestinian aggadic material reshaped and reformulated by the Babylonian Talmud. At least one great authority, Zecharia Frankel, was of the opinion that it was in the Babylonian Talmud's reworking that aggada reached the height of its literary achievement.

As has been noted above, it is in Babylonia that we hear of a specialist who would arrange the aggada before an eminent teacher. Moreover, it is well documented that public lectures in Babylonia contained a fair amount of aggadic material. We also find Abaye, the great mid-fourth century Babylonian, being upbraided by his peripatetic countryman Rav Dimi, for his lack of prowess in aggada (bSan 100a). Much scholarly effort has been devoted to analysing the ways in which the Babylonian Talmud appropriated and reshaped Palestinian sources. There is no longer any doubt that the Bavli has taken license with its Palestinian sources and allowed itself great latitude in recasting the Aggadot. Yet, it is simplistic to discount all the aggadot attributed to Palestinian rabbis in the Babylonian Talmud as reflecting only the Babylonian editors, even when they are no longer traceable to their Palestinian sources. Much of the aggada imported into the BT, can be relied upon as reflecting to some extent its Israel origins, though one is less sure of the veracity of the attribution to a certain individual or of the exact formulation. Certainly the more one finds Persian loan words and manifestly Babylonian realia, one is on more solid ground in viewing the aggada as having undergone serious if not definitive reworking in Babylonia.

A good example of the interdependence of the Palestinian aggadic midrash and that of the Palestinian traditions brought in the Babylonian Talmud is to be found in a curious statement by R. Shimon b. Lakish in Leviticus Rabba. R. Shimon is of the opinion that Yael succeeded in maintaining her propriety while luring Sisra to his death. R. Shimon claims that the word שמיכה (blanket) is never used in the Bible as the name of an object, rather it should be understood here as a *notarikon*, שמי כה, 'my name is here – my name testifies that that wicked person never touched her' (LevR 23,10 p542). R. Shimon's adamant stand comes into full light, when held up against R. Yohanan's view on the same issue which is recorded in bYev 103a. R. Yohanan, who was R. Shimon's teacher and friend, held that Yael had been violated many times on that day by the wicked Sisra. We have then a debate between teacher and friend over a sensitive and important issue. M. Margulies, in his fine edition of Wayikra Rabba, alerts the reader to this debate which from our perspective fully exemplifies the need to cautiously and judiciously integrate the aggada from the Palestinian midrashic collection with that of the Babylonian Talmud, which is attributed to Palestinian rabbis.

The inherent and intimate relation of halakha and aggada, of law and legend, of *nomos* and narrative, receives its most sensitive and explicit elaboration in the scores of pericopes that intertwine legal and aggadic discourse. Sometimes the aggada comes to bolster a legal position that might be perceived to need buttressing, e.g. where the aggada elaborates why the assemblies of the idol are to be shunned.[70] On other times the aggada seems to to give voice to a suppressed opinion. Zunz saw the aggada as the rightful heir of the biblical prophetic voice. Aggadic midrash in the Babylonian Talmud both tempered and strengthened the legal voice.

Select Bibliography

It is remarkable that the two great classics on aggadic midrash, Zunz, *Vorträge* (1832/92) and Y. Heinemann, *Darkhei ha-aggada* (1949) have never been translated into English. Zunz is available in the Hebrew translation edited by Ch. Albeck and enhanced by his invaluable notes and comments: *Ha-derashot be-Yisrael* (1954). J. Fraenkel, after his pioneering studies of the literary forms of Aggada that Heinemann had deliberately not treated in his study (stories, parables, apothegms), published a magisterial two volume summary of his own studies, *Darkhei ha-midrash veha-aggada*, including a wide ranging reformulation and re-presentation of Heinemann's work on aggada in the first section. M. Fishbane's classic *Biblical Interpretation in Ancient Israel* is a

---

[70] See bAZ 18b.

masterful presentation of the inner biblical exegesis that adumbrated the aggadic midrash.

The new two volume reprint of L. Ginzberg's magnificent *Legends of the Jews* (1909-1928) remains the finest collection and analysis of Biblical aggada. Ginzberg re-tells the biblical story according to the aggada and appends copious and exhaustive notes. Ginzberg, as the title indicates, approached the aggada from a folkloristic perspective. J. Fraenkel devoted his two volumes mentioned above to refuting that view and placing the aggada firmly within the rabbinic academy. J. Kugel, *Traditions in the Bible* advances Ginzberg's work, adding newly discovered sources, while emphasizing that many of the second Temple legends arose in order to resolve exegetical difficulties in the Bible. Kugel's work was also influenced by J. Heineman's engaging *Aggadot vetoldotehen* (1974), tracing aggadic motifs in second Temple, rabbinic and medieval works. Work of a similar nature, with special attention to the Targum literature was carried out by G. Vermes in two separate works, *Scripture and Tradition in Judaism: Haggadic Studies*, followed by *Post Biblical Jewish Studies*. A. Shinan devoted a number of books to the Targum and Aggada. The meticulous tracing of aggadic motifs has been carried on vigorously by M. Kister in numerous articles.

Path-breaking work on the terminology of the aggada and the collected aggada of the sages was done in the late nineteenth and early twentieth century by W. Bacher in his *Exegetische Terminologie* and his multi-volume work on the aggada of the Tannaim and the Palestinian and Babylonian Amoraim (1903-1913), all of which was eventually translated into Hebrew. The study of terminology can be supplemented with Ch. Albeck, 'Einleitung'.

Monographs have been devoted to various literary forms in the aggada including W.S. Towner's study of enumeration lists; A. Goldberg, J. Heinemann, R. Sarason on the Petihta; D. Stern on the Parable. Exhaustive and illuminating works have been written on *midrash darshani,* the exegetical story, beginning with O. Meir, J. Fraenkel and most recently J. Levinson. The most popular and researched aspect of aggada remains the stories of the sages. Fraenkel's foundational work has been continued forward by many, including J. Rubenstein.

Folkloristic aspects of Aggada have been explored by Eli Yassif and G. Hasan Rokem. Much new and good work has been done on the literary theory of midrash by D. Boyarin, D. Stern and J. Levinson. A rich harvest of comparative studies of Jewish and Christian exegesis can be found in monographs by N. de Lange, H. Newman, M. Hirshman, B. Visotzky, E. Kessler and most recently A. Kamesar, 'Church Fathers and Midrash'.

Individual recent monographs of note are H. Mack on Job and K. Hedner Zetterholm on Laban: *A Portrait of a Villain.*

J. Goldin, *The Song at the Sea* remains the most felicitous extended demonstration of reading aggadic midrash.

Chapter Three

The Works of Aggadic Midrash and the Esther Midrashim

Myron B. Lerner

I. State of the Art: The Study of Midrashic Literature

Ever since the publication of Leopold Zunz's monumental *Gottesdienstliche Vorträge* in 1832, midrashic literature has been dominated by this *magnum opus* of the doyen of Jewish Studies during the nineteenth century.[1] So overbearing was this work – the very first important contribution of the new *Wissenschaft des Judentums* to the scholarly enquiry into ancient Hebrew literature – that, to this very day, it has remained the standard work in the field.

Many of the conclusions of Zunz have become accepted axioms in the research of the Aggadic Midrashim. Even in the middle of the twentieth century, after decades of intensive publication, research and discovery in midrashic literature, Zunz's monumental edifice stood erect in the garb of the new Hebrew translation, which included the additions and corrections of Ch. Albeck, updating and rectifying the original material to that period. The second half of the twentieth century did not change matters very much and the summaries and entries dealing with midrashic literature in the *Encyclopaedia Judaica* and in such works as *Introduction to the Talmud and Midrash* of G. Stemberger, with all its modifications and improvements, are still structured on the foundations of Zunz, relying upon it (and on Albeck's updating) for most of their conclusions.

The traditional approach advanced by Zunz and his followers was to deal with the major collections of midrash according of the dates of origin of the individual works and of the various compilations. The printed editions of the Aggadic Midrashim were usually compared with one another as to mutual usage and dependence and in relation to other works of the talmudic-midrashic corpus, and a date of composition was proposed. Very little attention was paid

---

[1] A second edition containing the corrections of the author, edited by Brüll, was published posthumously in 1892.

to the different manuscripts[2] or to the smaller works and various fragments, as well as to the evidence of all collectanea.[3]

Concerning the smaller works, dozens of these were collected from manuscripts and inaccessible early printed editions by Adolf Jellinek in the latter half of the nineteenth century.[4] It seems, however, that the discovery of the Cairo Geniza towards the end of that century actually encouraged scholars to publish short selections and individual folios, without hardly making any effort to integrate or synthesize the scattered material. This trend, initiated by S.A. Wertheimer,[5] was vigorously continued by A. Marmorstein,[6] L. Ginzberg,[7] J. Mann[8] and Z.M. Rabinovitz.[9]

As far as the Halakhic Midrashim were concerned, the intuition and the foresight of I. Levy,[10] who stressed the importance of textual evidence preserved in various collectanea, especially the Yemenite Midrash ha-Gadol, encouraged scholars (D.Z. Hoffmann and H.Sh. Horovitz) to engage in the more or less accurate restoration of three Halakhic Midrashim, during the first two decades of the twentieth century.[11] These reconstructions were also aided by the initial finds from the Cairo Geniza. Additional folios from the Geniza which became known only later on and published separately by scholars in various journals, as well as an improved edition of Mekhilta de-R. Shimon b. Yohai, served to strengthen and reinforce the building previously constructed by the early scholars. It goes without saying that the reconstruction of the lost Halakhic Midrashim, including the recent remarkable discovery and collected fragments of Sifrei Zuta Deut by M. Kahana (above ch. 1), has enabled a proper evaluation of their contents and their relationship to the standard works of this discipline and to talmudic literature in general.

---

[2] Compared to his major works in early Hebrew poetry (see Schorr, *Payyetanim u-Piyyutim*, 143), Zunz's systematic consultation of midrashic manuscripts is most limited, see the incomplete list of mss in the appendix, 497f. Cf Bibliographies below, p187f, 193f.

[3] In this respect, Albeck's contribution is of utmost importance. However, as a result of his strict adherence to the format of Zunz's text, many of his discussions are somewhat disconnected and some of them are buried in the footnotes.

[4] Jellinek, *Bet ha-Midrasch*.

[5] Wertheimer, *Batei Midrashot* and subsequent publications.

[6] Marmorstein, *Midrash haserot vi-yeterot*, as well as various fragments of GenR, MidrPs *et al.* See the Bibliography of his works in his *Studies*, XVIII.

[7] Ginzberg, *Ginze Schechter*.

[8] Mann, *The Bible*; idem, 'Midrashic Geniza Fragments'. Mann is a notable exception to this trend as he has made earnest efforts to integrate various fragments, see *The Bible* 1, 10-31; 53-68; 2, 167-211. However, since the division into sedarim is crucial for Mann, most of the material is, nevertheless, disjointed, cf *ib.* 1, 87-91 with 1, 53-68. There is also no concentrated effort to summarize and delineate the nature and the structure of the selections from the Geniza midrash to the Pentateuch in *The Bible* 2 (most likely due to the premature death of this fine scholar).

[9] Rabinowitz, *Ginzé Midrash*.

[10] Cf Sussman, 'Schechter the Scholar', 225-230.

[11] MekRSbY; SifZ Num; MidrTann Deut, see the contribution of Kahana, above ch. 1.

However, as intimated above, this has not been the case in the realm of the Aggadic Midrashim. It is most surprising that, aside from the individual efforts of Solomon Buber, who attempted the reconstruction of three lost Midrashim – Midrash Avkir; Midrash Espha; Midrash Deuteronomy Zuta – simply on the basis of citations in Yalkut Shimoni, during the last decades of the nineteenth century,[12] no other successful scholarly endeavour in this sphere has been undertaken during the twentieth century.[13]

One of the pitfalls that lies at the feet of the reconstruction of the lost Aggadic Midrashim is the fact that the exact number of Midrashim is totally unknown. In contrast with other parts of rabbinic literature – Mishna, Tosefta, the Talmuds *et al.* – whose components are readily known and available, the elements that made up the corpus of Aggadic Midrashim were apparently never convened under one roof nor were they ever officially tabulated. It is quite clear that the circulation of these works was sporadic and incidental and that there was probably no single collection of all of them in one location at any one time. In no case do we hear of an overall framework incorporating all the aggadic compilations and it is safe to assume that no such official corpus or 'canon' ever existed. Coupled with the fact that numerous aggadic works have been lost through the passage of time and have thus fallen into oblivion, the task of engaging in their reconstruction is a most formidable one indeed.

However, this endeavour is not as hopeless as it appears offhand. What is actually needed is a concentration of all extant material relating to a specific 'department' of midrashic creativity. By departments we are not referring to the accepted categories of the major collections: 'Midrash Rabba', 'Midrash Tanhuma' etc., which, as we shall see, are actually the hybrid compilations of copyists and early printers. On the contrary, the departmental approach strives to concentrate on a particular biblical book or on some other area developed by the aggadic masters.[14] This means a careful perusal of all printed material, all available manuscripts and Geniza fragments, and all extant collectanea and related texts in the specific department, and their complete integration. Such concentration will enable, on the one hand, a partial reconstruction of lost

---

[12] Buber, *Likkutim mi-Midrash Avkir* (1883); idem, *Likkutim mi-Midrash Elle ha-Devarim Zutta* (1885); idem, 'Midrash Espha' (1886). *Vid.* also the appendices to R. Abraham b. Elijah, *Rav Pealim*, 133-153.

[13] The efforts of Marmorstein, 'Midrash 'Avkir', 119-139 to identify certain Geniza fragments as deriving from Midrash Avkir are most futile. Note, however, the most recent contribution of Geulah (Master's thesis) which, in spite of the progress made, is based solely on citations from medieval sources.

[14] E.g. the Pesikta cycle, i.e., those works dealing with the special sabbaths and the Jewish holidays. Kern-Ulmer, 'Midrashim for Hanukkah' is a welcome step in this direction. However, she has concentrated her efforts on the two Pesikta Midrashim and seriously neglected the so-called 'minor midrashim'; her survey of the latter is limited to a single page. Moreover, this 'survey' fails to take into account the generic origin of most of the minor Hanukka Midrashim, see Lerner, 'Collected Exempla', 868f.

works, and on the other, a proper appreciation of the individual compositions and the interaction – if any – between them.

In the second half of this chapter, an attempt will be made to utilize such a fresh approach in order to focus attention on one small corner, albeit, probably the most complicated one of all, in the vast corpus of midrashic literature: the Midrashim to the Scroll of Esther. This survey of the original midrashic compositions[15] has been augmented by an inspection of all relevant material: midrashic homilies; yalkutim and collectanea which collect material from various sources; and last but not least, in order to effect complete coverage of the field, cognate works which contain an unusually large concentration of midrashic material to the Book of Esther.

Only after a searching analysis of all the above will it be possible to approach a reconstruction of the non-extant works and to obtain a proper understanding and anatomy of the extant texts themselves. It will become apparent that there is no small measure of influence and interaction between non-extant midrashic compositions and existing works, which scholars had no way of perceiving, according to the present state of these texts.

The reconstruction of lost midrashic works which is based on (a) existing manuscripts and manuscript remains (mainly from the Cairo Geniza); (b) relatively long citations in the yalkutim and various collectanea; (c) relatively brief citations in rabbinic literature; (d) inspection of all commentaries on the specific biblical book, especially unpublished manuscripts; (e) listings in various medieval indices of verses;[16] and (f) selections that have been incorporated into existing midrashic works, is not an impossible task.

In addition, such a process involves no small amount of sleuthing and experimenting. However, these should not serve us a hindrance to the proposed scheme, and bar us from making the attempt. The concentration of manuscripts from various libraries in microfilm collections and the recent progress made in the cataloguing of Geniza materials should lend added impetus and momentum to the endeavour. Simply stated, on the threshold of the twenty-first century, the time is ripe for a new approach and a new agenda for the critical investigation of the Aggadic Midrashim.

---

[15] Note well that the present discussion does not include works of an apocryphal nature such as the Aramaic version of the Dream of Mordechai and the Prayer of Esther or the various Aramaic Targumim to Esther, even though the latter definitely exhibit aggadic and midrashic traits, cf below, n222. See Feliks, 'Ha-Targumim'; Grossfeld, 'Haggada'.

[16] In the present framework it was not possible to include items (d) and (e) in the discussion. Incidentally, the researching of biblical commentaries to Esther has been greatly facilitated by the annotated bibliography of Walfish, *Esther*, 308-329 and Katzenellenbogen, *Megillat Esther*.

TYPES OF AGGADIC MIDRASH AND THE STANDARD CORPUS

The Aggadic Midrashim,[17] which are mainly devoted to the non-legal portions of Scripture, are traditionally classified according to their functional approach, and allegedly represent two distinct genres: exegetical and homiletical.[18]

Much like the Halakhic Midrashim of the Tannaim, the Exegetical Midrashim, such as Genesis Rabba, Ruth Rabba and Midrash Samuel, often present a systematic running interpretation of the biblical text, which devotes careful attention to each sentence, phrase and in many instances even to each individual word. On the other hand, Homiletic Midrashim, such as Leviticus Rabba, Midrash Tanhuma and Pesikta de-Rav Kahana, ordinarily focus on a central idea or leitmotif, usually in the wake of a specific scriptural verse from the Writings (*Ketuvim*) or the Prophets (*Neviim*), while their exegetic scope is quite limited. This sort of presentation is effected through the use of the so-called *petiha* (literally: opening), the unique rhetorical-literary proem formula utilized by the sages, supposedly as an 'introduction' to their exposition of scripture. However, in all probability, in many instances, the *petiha* form may very well represent the body of the homily itself.[19]

Nevertheless, it is extremely difficult to present a clear-cut division of the Aggadic Midrashim according to the above mentioned criteria. Even those Midrashim mentioned above which have been classified as 'exegetic', contain varying numbers of homiletical *petihot* at the beginning of important sections. The Homiletical Midrashim are mainly represented by the so-called Tanhuma-Yelammedenu family of Midrashim, which also includes such variegated works as: Exodus Rabba 15-end; Numbers Rabba (excluding Naso 13-14) and Deuteronomy Rabba. In the Tanhuma-Yelammedenu Midrashim, the proems are usually prefaced by a simple rhetorical halakhic question introduced by the formula ילמדנו רבינו, 'Our master, teach us'. In spite of the fact that the Homiletical Midrashim are ordinarily a collection of homilies, with merely a smattering of exegetical material, it is interesting to note that the latter half of Tanhuma Bemidbar, a Homiletical Midrash *par excellence*, was found to contain a series of systematic exegetical comments to various sections of Numbers.[20]

In summation, the traditional division of the Aggadic Midrashim into exegetical and homiletical compositions does not really do justice to the true nature of these works, since in many instances they combine both modes of midrashic exposition.

---

[17] As in previous chapters, the word 'midrash' is written in lower case when the genre or a single unit is meant, but in upper case when a definite edited work, extant or not.

[18] Strack-Stemberger, *Introduction*, 240. This division has recently been questioned by Abr. Goldberg, 'Beayot arikha', 130, 151.

[19] Heinemann, 'The Proem', 104-110. Cf Hirshman, above ch. 2.

[20] Schlüter, 'Auslegungsmidrasch', 73; Schlüter, 'Midrash parshani', 44 has called attention to an exegetical midrash found in Tanhuma Shelah-Balak. However, her detailed analysis is limited to pericope Hukat, cf *infra* n50, n121.

The standard corpus of extant Exegetical and Homiletical Midrashim consists of some thirty-five major works, according to the following breakdown:

Midrash Rabba, Pentateuch + Deuteronomy Rabba, ed Lieberman – 6
Midrash Tanhuma + Tanhuma Buber (Gen-Exod) – 7
Midrash Rabba, Five Scrolls – 5
Midrash Zuta, Five Scrolls – 4 [21]
Additional Midrashic works to Esther[22] and Canticles[23] – 4
Midrashim to Samuel, Psalms and Proverbs – 3
Pesiktot: de-Rav Kahana; Rabbati – 2
Aggadat Bereshit; Pirkei de-R. Eliezer – 2
Ethical Tracts: Seder Eliyahu; Mishnat R. Eliezer – 2

Surprisingly enough, this presentation of midrashic literature differs radically from previous surveys, which have been heavily influenced by the above-mentioned basic distinction between Exegetical and Homiletical Midrashim.[24]

The above skeletal listing should be augmented and complemented by numerous midrashic and aggadic compositions as well as by an unknown number of fragmentary works – many of them stemming from the Cairo Geniza – some of whose physical remains or extant quotations have been published by scholars.[25] Taken together, the complete total of major and minor midrashic and aggadic works, whole and fragmentary, well exceeds the number of one hundred and fifty.[26]

As far as the major midrashic works enumerated above are concerned, it is quite clear that the intensive preoccupation with the exegesis of biblical scripture, whether from an exegetical or homiletical orientation, forms the common denominator shared by all these variegated works. It thus goes without saying that most of the above-mentioned midrashic compositions ordinarily deal with aggadic interpretation, usually of a specific book of the Bible, according to the order of the biblical text. However, even those individual works which form exceptions to this rule,[27] are actually based on the exegesis of salient biblical passages, usually following a well-planned scheme, and should thus not be

---

[21] ms Parma-De Rossi 541, which served as the basis for Buber's edition of Midrash Zutta, does not contain a minor midrash to Esther. There is every reason to assume that the original collection did contain such a midrash, vid. infra 'Midrash Zuta' (p168); 'Midrash Abba Gurion' (p191).

[22] Midrash Abba Gurion; Midrash Panim Aherot I-II, see below.

[23] Midrash Shir ha-Shirim, ed Grünhut.

[24] Strack-Stemberger, Introduction, 240; 276-314. On a serious shortcoming in Stemberger's classification, see below n84; also above n18 and 'Further Reading' below.

[25] Examples of lost midrashic works to Esther are dealt with in detail in the second part of this chapter.

[26] Cf Eisenstein, Otsar Midrashim; Kasher-Mandelbaum, Sarei ha-Elef, 22-62 and index, passim.

[27] E.g. the Pesiktot, Pirkei de-R. Eliezer and the Ethical Tracts.

considered to be random or haphazard compositions, by any means or circumstances.[28]

The Land of Israel in the Roman Period served as the cradle of midrashic literature. This is evident from the ubiquitous mention of the teachings of the Palestinian sages and their immediate milieu in all these works, including numerous exempla which greatly contribute to the biography of these sages,[29] as well as the prolific usage of Palestinian Aramaic, especially in the earlier Midrashim, which also evince an extremely close relationship with the aggadic sections of the Yerushalmi (see below). Even though certain scholars have postulated that individual midrashic works are of Babylonian or even European vintage (see below), the general consensus is, nevertheless, that practically all of these works are to be assigned to the Land of Israel.[30]

The Palestinian origin of the Midrashim to the Pentateuch is fully attested to by the usage of the 'triennial cycle', wherein the reading of the Pentateuch was concluded once every three to three and a half years.[31] The implications of this system are that each individual pericope of the Pentateuch included far less material than the alternate Babylonian one-year division. Suffice it to say that the opening sections of the pericopes ordinarily contain numerous proems, which, in many cases, represent the major division of that particular Midrash *per se*. This observation is extremely important for a correct appreciation of the original structure of these Midrashim, as the printed editions ordinarily feature a division based on the universally accepted practice of completing the reading of the Pentateuch during the course of a one year period according to the Babylonian tradition.

THE TANNAIC PERIOD

It is commonly accepted that the Aggadic Midrashim are a product of the Amoraic period, although their final redaction is usually postulated somewhat later on in the post-talmudic era, *viz.* from the fifth century onward. However, this does not preclude the existence of Aggadic Midrashim during the Tannaic period. It is evident that the Tannaic sages engaged in aggadic exegesis. Large segments of this material have been amply edited in entire sections of the Halakhic Midrashim of the Tannaim,[32] as well as in certain parts of the To-

---

[28] Note that the literary structure of Seder Eliyahu is most enigmatic and *prima facie* defies a logical presentation of the midrashic material. One receives the impression that the author has preserved his ethical teachings in the form of a continuous monologue based on what may be termed: 'a midrashic stream of consciousness'.

[29] Concerning LevR, see the impressive summary of Margulies, 'Mavo', XXVII-XXXI.

[30] One notable exception seems to be NumR, see below: 'On European Soil'.

[31] See Mann, *The Bible* 1-2 and Prolegomenon of B.Z. Wacholder, *ib.* vol 1, LII-LXVII. The liturgical poetry of the early Palestinian paytanim, R. Yannai and R. Elazar ha-Killir, is also based on this cycle.

[32] See above, Kahana, ch. 1.

sefta,[33] which actually contain a host of aggadic teachings deriving from the mishnaic period. Seder Olam is also generally considered to be of Tannaic origin.[34] However, owing to the fact that this work is not structured according to exegetical criteria, it is somewhat difficult to classify it under the rubric 'midrash', according to the classical sense of the term employed above.[35]

Moreover, direct allusions to specific works of supposed Tannaic origin are actually extant in talmudic literature. A bath house incident which towards the end of the Tannaic period took place between R. Yishmael be-R. Yossi and R. Hiyya describes the latter's failure to respect his peer due to an engrossed concentration in the oral study of 'the aggadic interpretation of 'the entire Book of Psalms' (כל ספר תילים אגדה).[36] R. Yaakov bar Aha, a Palestinian Amora of the third generation (c. 300 CE), reports that he found some laws dealing with gentiles (בני נוח) in a certain 'book of aggada from the academy' (ספר אגדתא דבי רב),[37] which apparently alludes to a written tract (see below). It is interesting to note that most of these very same laws appear in Genesis Rabba to Gen 9:6[38] and so this aggadic book, whose title (ספר ... דבי רב) is reminiscent of Tannaic midrash,[39] should be readily identified as a Midrash to the book of Genesis.[40] Most recently, the late Aharon Mirsky has attempted to reconstruct a Tannaic Midrash to Genesis, which was probably one of the precursors of Genesis Rabba, based on the Tannaic stratum of that midrashic composition.[41]

Moreover, it is entirely possible that some Tannaic Midrashim have remained more or less intact in their original form, although the scholarly world, in general, has yet to awaken to this most illuminating reality. A case in point is Midrash Canticles Zuta to the entire Scroll of Canticles, whose first editor, S. Schechter, assigned it to the tenth century![42] Ch. Albeck, who seems to have concurred with this opinion, claiming that the Midrash is collected from other (non-extant) sources, also noted the fact that Canticles Zuta does not contain opening proems and that from chapter two on, it adduces extremely short explanations. In his estimation, these phenomena represent later-day develop-

---

[33] Higger has collected the relevant material in *Aggadot Ha-Tannaim*. Note that an unusually large quantity of midrashic material is concentrated in Tosefta Sota.

[34] See Milikowsky, 'Seder Olam' in this volume.

[35] The claims of Finkelstein, 'Oldest Midrash'; 'Pre-Maccabean Documents', concerning the hoary antiquity of the midrashic explanations to Deut 26:5-8 in the Passover Haggada (pre-Maccabean!), may be readily dismissed. In all likelihood, these explanations are basically post-talmudic, see: Rovner, 'Early Witnesses'.

[36] yKil 9, 32b (175); bKid 33a. Cf also Hirshman, *supra*.

[37] bSan 57b.

[38] GenR 34,14 (p325). In this source the teachings are attributed to the first generation Amora, R. Hanina.

[39] Compare with the expression שאר ספרי דבי רב which apparently alludes to the Tannaic Midrashim, *vid*. bBB 124b, RaSHbaM *s.v.* בשאר ספרי דבי רב.

[40] Note well that R. Yaacov b. Aha's quotation includes the teaching of R. Yishmael, one of the leading figures of the Tannaic Period.

[41] Mirsky, *Midrash Tannaim*. Cf *ibid*, 97f.

[42] Schechter, 'Postscript', 101.

ments.[43] However, it appears that the case is just the opposite. The two characteristics enumerated by Albeck are actually indicative of Tannaic midrash which abounds in short exegetical commentary and does not yet employ the homiletic proem. Furthermore, the exclusive mention of sages of the Tannaic period[44] and the inclusion of several authentic historical traditions dating from Second Temple and Tannaic times[45] also seem to indicate that Canticles Zuta is of much earlier vintage than postulated by most previous scholars.[46] Suffice it to say that the possibility of Tannaic origin must be seriously considered and cannot be automatically ruled out.

Another midrashic composition which might possibly be of Tannaic origin is Midrash Hallel which treats Psalms 113-118.[47] Unfortunately, this Midrash, which has remained extant in a single manuscript and includes the teaching of numerous Tannaim and some very original parables, has been almost completely neglected in scholarly research. Note well that in the only scholarly study of this Midrash to date,[48] the author has even proposed a medieval *terminus post quem*.[49]

It is logical to assume that intensive study and inquiry into the provenance of these and other Midrashim[50] may very well lead to conclusions which point towards an extremely early date of composition, *viz.* the Tannaic period, and a final editing process no later than the third century CE, which represents a significant departure from what has been heretofore postulated by most scholars.

THE AMORAIC PERIOD

However, it is readily apparent that the material contained in most of the Midrashim stems from the Amoraic period, which, compared to previous eras, most decidedly witnessed a tremendous upsurge of aggadic activity. This phenomenon is by no means incidental and actually reflects the trend towards

[43] Zunz-Albeck, *Derashot*, 129.

[44] This conclusion is seemingly contradicted by mention of the Babylonian sage, Rav Nahman in CantZ 2:12, 31 ll. 887-888. However, in the Leningrad Geniza fragment published by Rabinovitz, *Ginzé Midrash*, 267 l. 6, the reading is 'R. Nehemiah'!

[45] E.g. CantZ 8:14, 47 ll. 1390-1396 (cf Lieberman, *Greek*, 179-184); 2:14, 31-32 ll. 904-910 (cf idem, *Tosefta Ki-Fshutah*. 8, 738); 3:8, 34, ll. 975-976; Schechter, 'Notes to Canticles Zutta', 77.

[46] See, however, Scholem, *Jewish Gnosticism*, 56 and Rabinovitz, *Ginzé Midrash*, 252 end, who argue for the early origin of CantZ. Incidentally, the conclusions of the latter are based on research conducted by the present writer, see Hirshman, *Rivalry*, 148 n13.

[47] Ed Jellinek, *BHM*, 5, 87-110 is based on a unicum (ms Münich 222). The 'Traklin' edition mentioned by Lacks, *infra* is nothing more than a doctored version of the Jellinek text. An improved edition based on the original manuscript has recently been published by Deshe-Halevi, *Yalkut Midrashim* 3, 1-39.

[48] Lacks, 'Midrash Hallel'.

[49] Lacks *ib*. 197 ('at the end of the twelfth or beginning of the thirteenth century').

[50] One can thus not rule out the possibility that the exegetical midrash to four pericopes in the book of Numbers (above n20; below n121) is of Tannaic origin.

intensified aggadic preaching, as inferred by the following homilies to Canticles 2:5:

> R. Yitshak said: In the past, the Tora was held in general esteem and the participants [in the Sabbath lectures] were interested in hearing teaching from Mishnah and Talmud. But *nowadays*, the Tora is not held in popular esteem, and they seek to hear instruction in Scripture and in aggadic [homily].

> R. Levi said: In the past, people had enough money to make ends meet, and a person desired to hear teaching in mishna, halakha and talmud, but *nowadays*, when money is hard to get, and especially since they are sick from the subjugation,[51] all they ask to hear is instruction in the benedictions and words of comfort.[52]

R. Yitshak (b. Nappaha) and R. Levi were Palestinian Amoraim of the second and the third generations, *viz.* the latter half of the third century, whose homilies give expression to the fact that people were unable to concentrate during ordinary study sessions devoted to the halakhic teachings of the rabbis held on Sabbaths and holidays, due to a general decline in Tora acumen and to most severe economic problems. As a result, the lectures dealing with the aggadic interpretation of the Bible which were replete with words of wisdom, parables and popular stories, took precedence over the more complicated and less attractive halakhic teachings and thus came to comprise the main agenda of the Sabbath discourses held in the local synagogues and study houses[53] of the Land of Israel during the third and fourth centuries.

It is also logical to assume that the numerous polemics of the Jewish Christians and various heretic groups against the Palestinian Amoraim also served to enhance the volume of aggadic interpretations and the preoccupation of the Palestinian sages in this literary venue.[54]

As intimated by the above sources, it becomes very likely that the popularity of these aggadic sermons led to the development of an amazingly large number of midrashic homilies during the course of the third century. Such an upsurge of aggadic material obviously influenced the field as a whole and was most likely responsible for the following three phenomena.

Specialization in Aggadic Midrash

It is interesting to note that practically all of the sages of the Tannaic period engaged in the exposition and interpretation of salient topics within the realms

---

[51] An apparent allusion to the exorbitant tax levies of the Roman Empire, *vid.* Krauss, *Paras ve-Romi*, 260.

[52] CantR 2:5:1. 'Words of comfort' apparently refer to the aggadic homilies which usually concluded with high hopes for better times during the Messianic age, vid. Stein, 'Peroratio'.

[53] The propagation of aggadic teachings in the *bet midrash* (= academy) as opposed to the synagogue, has been strongly advocated by Fraenkel, *Darkhei ha-aggada*, 17-34.

[54] A propos the Christian-Jewish debate on biblical themes, *vid.* Urbach, *World*, 514-560.

of *both* halakha and aggada. Such great halakhic luminaries as R. Eliezer, R. Akiva, R. Shimon b. Yohai, R. Meir, and R. Yehuda the Prince, whose important halakhic teachings pervade the Mishna and the Tosefta, were also scholars in their own right in the field of midrashic and aggadic interpretation. The only apparent major exception to this rule seems to have been the third generation Tanna, R. Eleazer ha-Modai (of Modiin), whose extant halakhic teachings are actually nil, while his prowess in the aggadic interpretation of Scripture and his midrashic teachings were widely recognized.[55]

On the other hand, the Amoraic period in the Land of Israel witnessed the appearance of numerous talmudic authorities who seemingly chose aggadic interpretation as their almost exclusive field of activity. Among these we may enumerate: R. Shmuel b. Nahman; R. Levi; R. Helbo; R. Berekhya, to name a few, as well as the anonymous 'Rabbanan de-aggadeta',[56] which may very well indicate the existence of a special class of scholars who specialized in aggadic exposition.

We would like to suggest that the enormous popularity accorded the aggadic sermons and discourses by the masses eventually encouraged many of the rabbis to devote all their efforts and expertise to the field of aggadic interpretation.

Circulation of Aggadic Material in Written Form

Even though aggadic midrash was part and parcel of Oral Tora, and as such had to be transmitted exclusively in oral form, one may assume that the immense proliferation of aggadic discourses and the abundance of midrashic material during the third century actually prompted the sages to rescind the all-inclusive ban on writing and actually permit written versions of aggadic texts. The various rabbis could obviously no longer keep track of the voluminous material that increased after each and every Sabbath by leaps and bounds as a result of the numerous sermons voiced throughout the Land of Israel by way of oral transmission, and so it was felt necessary to have these homilies and interpretations collected in written tracts, which were most likely the forerunners of the extant Aggadic Midrashim (see below).

Aggadic literature was therefore committed to writing at a relatively early stage and thus represents the first branch of Oral Literature to undergo this process.[57] Recognition of this reality, which has heretofore not been considered by scholars, is a most crucial factor towards a proper understanding of the essence of text transmission in midrashic literature. Scholars have traditionally focused on oral transmission as the major reason for the wide discrepancies in

---

[55] Cf the expression: עדיין אנו צריכין למודעי, e.g. bShab 55b, 'We are still in need of the interpretation of [R. Elazar of] Modiin', which attests to his virtuosity in the field of aggadic interpretation.

[56] yMaasr 1, 48d; yYev 4, 5c (cf however, RuthR 2:20, 74); yMaas 3, 51a.

[57] *Pace* Safrai, 'Oral Tora', 72-75. Cf most recently, Sussmann, 'Tora she-beal pe', 293-295.

144

manuscripts of various aggadic texts. However, it now becomes evident that it is imperative to place greater stress on transmission via the written – and not only the oral – tradition.[58]

That this was actually the case may be seen from the usage of a written aggadic tract (ספרא דאגדתא) by the second generation Palestinian Amoraim, R. Yohanan and Resh Lakish,[59] and by later Amoraim as well.[60] To be sure, aggadic tracts were actually committed to writing at an even earlier date, but these endeavours failed to receive rabbinic sanction. This seems to be the background for the unusually harsh pronouncements uttered by R. Joshua b. Levi, a Palestinian Amora of the first generation, against all those who engaged in the writing and even in the study of (written) aggadic tracts.[61] This is also the background for R. Joshua's deep fears of Heavenly punishment in the wake of his innocent browsing into the contents of one of these unauthorized copies, since, in his days, this practice was still outlawed. In this context, it is significant to note the conduct of R. Hiyya bar Abba, an important disciple of R. Yohanan. In spite of the pioneering efforts of his masters, R. Hiyya b. Abba zealously attempted to reinforce the ban, only to be most severely punished by the Almighty for his actions.[62] It is thus quite evident that any effort to reverse the dispensation of R. Yohanan and Resh Lakish was doomed to failure.

Note well that the interdict against writing down material relating to other fields of Oral Tora, notably halakha, continued to be in effect until Gaonic times and that the above-mentioned dispensation of R. Yohanan and Resh Lakish to permit the writing-down of oral material was limited to the Aggadic Midrashim alone.

The Embryonic Stage of the Extant Aggadic Midrashim (250-400)

It is quite logical to assume that the greatly expanded number of aggadic homilies that were orally preached and expounded in the Palestinian synagogues and study houses during the third and fourth centuries CE, coupled with the permit to transmit them in written form, contributed immensely to the propagation of the midrashic endeavour. The formation of the earliest aggadic treatises of the Amoraim, whose contents are clearly based on the exposition and on the ideas of the Amoraic sermonizers, may thus be better understood. A careful perusal of the more important Amoraic midrashic compositions paying special attention to the names of the sages quoted indicates that their contents are fundamentally the products of the third and fourth centuries. It is thus quite logical to assume that the initial collection of the material and its integration

---

[58] Note the recent findings of Mandel, *Lamentations Rabbati*, 160-178; idem, Transmission.
[59] bGit 60a.
[60] R. Yaakov b. Aha (n37 above). Rav Nahman and Rava (bBer 23b).
[61] yShab 16, 15c; Lieberman, *Ha-Yerushalmi Kiphshuto*, 194.
[62] yShab *ib.*

into a literary format began at that time. However, even though the oral sermons served as source material for the midrashic compilations, one may very
well postulate that the transcription of the oral material into written form was
not an automatic process. On the contrary, the editors of the written texts most
probably felt themselves free to abridge, delete, add, combine and transfer the
material from one locus to another. Suffice it to say that, in spite of their oral
origin, the homilies and midrashic interpretations of the Tannaim and the
Amoraim seem to have been transmitted in written form at a relatively early
age, which belies their oral nature.

Even so, this does not mean that the earliest Midrashim were a *fait accom-
pli* at the end of the Amoraic period in the Land of Israel. Even though the
final decades of the fourth century (370-400) are ordinarily considered to be
the *terminus ad quem* for the Talmud Yerushalmi, it is generally assumed that
the earliest Aggadic Midrashim of the Amoraic period reached their final
completion only somewhat later on. This would allow for an ongoing editorial
process which assembled the texts, consolidated them and gave them their
final form during the ensuing decades and even somewhat later.

In spite of the fact that no real textual evidence for the existence of pre-400
midrashic texts seems to have remained extant, there seem to be some cogent
proofs for such a reality. Scholars have long noted the close affinity between
numerous parallels from early aggadic literature and the Yerushalmi. The
natural inclination of some has been to postulate the reliance of the later
Midrashim (fifth century onwards) on the relatively earlier Yerushalmi (fourth
century),[63] while others have adopted a different approach, *viz.* both the
Yerushalmi and the Aggadic Midrashim derived material from a certain non-
extant aggadic work, which was actually the fore-runner of that particular
Aggadic Midrash.[64]

However, one recent study has shown that certain textual readings in the
Yerushalmi are actually secondary to those in a midrashic homily preserved in
Pesikta de-Rav Kahana, parashat Ekha.[65] Even though the final redaction of the
Pesikta is postulated in the interim period (see below), it appears that the
Yerushalmi utilized this particular midrashic passage, which was already for-
mulated at a very early stage. This would seem to indicate that one could con-
ceivably discern the embryonic form of certain aggadic homilies by virtue of a
close analysis of the Yerushalmi and its parallels in the early Aggadic
Midrashim.

Taken together, the above-mentioned three phenomena, which are actually
closely connected with one another, appear to be the direct outcome of the

---

[63] Zunz, *Vorträge*, 185f, notes f; aa; Albeck, 'Einleitung', 66-73 (with reservations); Milikowsky,
'Source Criticism', 361.
[64] Margulies, 'Mavo', XVII-XXII; XXXIII; Lerner, *Book of Ruth*, Introduction, 119-131.
[65] Lerner, 'Lexicon and Lectiones', 363-369.

upsurge in aggadic preaching which transpired from the middle of the third century onward.

DATING THE EXTANT MIDRASHIM

The dating of the individual texts has become a major preoccupation of scholars in the field of midrashic literature. Needless to say, the clarification of this point in regard to each and every Midrash is a *sine qua non* for all those interested in using them in various contexts and of prime interest to historians, philologists, theologians *et al*. Pioneering work in this field was done by Leopold Zunz in his *Vorträge*. Even though subsequent scholarship has modified his conclusions somewhat, there is no escaping the fact that Zunz's original scheme of things has actually remained more or less steadfast.

However, dating the various works of midrashic literature is by no means a simple task. Are we to concentrate on linguistic phenomena or on literary phenomena? S. Lieberman has demonstrated the untrustworthy nature of certain 'Babylonian' expressions from the Bavli in midrashic texts as a method for determining their relatively late redaction.[66] The same may be said for the tendency among nineteenth century scholars to fix a relatively late date for those Midrashim which are first quoted by later medieval rabbis, *viz.*, from the thirteenth century onward.[67]

The pitfalls involved in the dating of the various Midrashim have been amply demonstrated by the case of Canticles Zuta cited above. Among the midrashic works dealt with by Zunz, special attention should be focused on Seder Eliyahu Rabba. An allusion to 'more than 700 years' that have transpired since the fourth millennium (= 240 CE) in chapter two[68] prompted Zunz to assign the composition of the work to a Babylonian rabbi c. 974 CE.[69] Nevertheless, almost one dozen scholars of the nineteenth and twentieth century contested these conclusions and have consequently offered multiple conflicting solutions to the date and the provenance of this enigmatic aggadic work.[70]

The usage of parallels (see below) as an important methodological tool in comparing midrashic texts to one another in order to determine their relative antiquity has been generally accepted. Nevertheless, the conclusions evolving from such comparisons are, at times, of a subjective nature and thus open to debate. Suffice it to say that only through painstaking analysis of each and every detail can an exact relationship be established between two (or more) parallel texts.[71] It is also important to determine whether textual variants are the

---

[66] Lieberman, *Midrash rabbah: Deuteronomy*, Introduction, XXII.

[67] *Ib*. Cf Zunz, *Vorträge*, 396 n52.

[68] Ed Friedmann, 7 top.

[69] Zunz, *Vorträge*, 119; cf Braude-Kapstein, *Tanna debe Eliyyahu*, 52 n1.

[70] For a listing of these studies, see Zunz-Albeck, *Derashot*, 292 n130f; Braude-Kapstein, *Tanna debe Eliyyahu*, Introduction, 5-9; Brand, *Seder*, 615-617.

[71] Vid. Milikowsky, 'Seder Olam and the Tosefta', 246; Lerner, 'Lexicon and Lectiones', 369.

result of deliberate editorial embellishment or just run of the mill scribal activity.

In the ensuing paragraphs, an attempt will be made to trace the various phases in the development of the midrashic endeavour and focus on some of the more important Midrashim within this framework. However, before embarking on this more or less historical survey, it is important to focus on the above-mentioned phenomenon of parallel texts, one of the crucial factors involved in assessing the relative timetable of the various Midrashim.

Parallels[72]

An important and interesting phenomenon of talmudic literature in general and of midrashic literature in particular is the existence of numerous parallel passages, most of them of considerable length, which have been diffused among all branches of rabbinic literature. These parallels, which do not ordinarily represent rote borrowings, serve as important tools for gauging the development and propagation of the passages in various literary works and enable a proper appreciation of the innate relationship of one source to another. They are thus most crucial in deciding the symbiotic relationships of the various midrashic and talmudic works to one another.

Even those internal, more or less, rote parallels, utilized by the redactor of a particular midrashic work and termed by Ch. Albeck as העברה, 'transfer',[73] are of prime importance in dealing with the literary composition of that particular work.

A list of parallels is thus *de rigueur* in the preparation of critical editions of midrashic texts. It is interesting to note that beginning with the Warsaw 1867 edition of Rav Henokh Zundel (Ets Yosef), even the traditional publishers of Midrash Rabba became aware of the importance of such an apparatus, which has actually proved most beneficial towards a proper study of the various Midrashim.

However, the listing of parallels is by no means an automatic procedure. It is the editor's responsibility to organize the list in such a manner that the most exact and almost identical parallels are listed first, whereas those which are much more remote will appear towards the end of the list. Unfortunately, such a procedure has not been always followed by the editors of critical editions and much less so by the editors of the various midrashic collectanea and yalkutim. The latter tend to lump together long lists of parallels, usually copied from previous lists, without hitting the nail on the head. To be sure, the compiler of the yalkut normally derived his material from a single major source and specification of this source is ordinarily all that is necessary.[74]

---

[72] *Vid.* Safrai, 'Oral Tora', 80f.

[73] Albeck, 'Einleitung', 2-11.

[74] Note the important study of Hyman, *Sources*, 1f.

Yefe Einayim, authored by R. Arye Leib Yellin and found at the very end of numerous tractates of the Vilna-Romm edition of the Babylonian Talmud, is a most important study aid for the location of parallel sources. Rabbi Yellin ingeniously listed the numerous parallels to the teachings of the Bavli found in the Yerushalmi and in the various Midrashim, as well as in other branches of talmudic literature.

The Earliest Midrashim (400-600)

It is generally agreed that the earliest extant work of aggadic midrash is Genesis Rabba. Zunz, the pioneering scholar of midrashic literature, opined that this work, which is basically written in classical Palestinian Aramaic, was composed during the sixth century.[75] However, Albeck has adduced cogent proofs for even an earlier date: 425-500 CE.[76]

Zunz listed Leviticus Rabba and Lamentations Rabba as the next two important developments in the composition of midrashic literature, assigning them to the middle and to the latter half of the seventh century respectively.[77] However, here too, this view has been somewhat modified by modern scholarship which actually places both of these Midrashim in the sixth century.[78]

Margulies has even proposed a somewhat earlier date for Leviticus Rabba: the middle of the fifth century, arguing that the work was actually contemporary with Genesis Rabba.[79] However, this claim should be dismissed since the proofs offered for assigning such an early date for Leviticus Rabba are inconclusive, whereas those that show that it borrowed from Genesis Rabba rest on solid ground. Margulies likewise argued that Pesikta de-Rav Kahana, a collection of homilies arranged according to the special Sabbath readings and the yearly cycle, was a contemporary of Leviticus Rabba and should be assigned to this period.[80] However, while this may be true for the *piskaot* dealing with the special readings from the prophets before and after the Ninth of Av *et al.*,[81] the *piskaot* identical with Leviticus Rabba are, nevertheless, of later vintage (see below).

This traditional summary of the earliest Midrashim should now be augmented by some additional findings. Midrash Ruth Rabba has been found to contain classical proems combined with brief exegetical comments on most of the scroll of Ruth, as well as original Palestinian Aramaic, and the present author therefore tends to view the basic stratum of this Midrash as a product of

---

[75] Zunz, *Vorträge*, 186.
[76] Albeck, 'Einleitung', 94-96.
[77] Zunz, *Vorträge*, 191, 193.
[78] Zunz-Albeck, *Derashot*, 342 n90; Albeck, 'Vayikra Rabba', 42; Mandel, *Lamentations Rabbati*, 14.
[79] Margulies, 'Mavo', XXXI-XXXIII.
[80] *Ib*. XIII.
[81] Ed Mandelbaum, 225-331.

the fifth century.[82] In his analysis, the author has also uncovered the traces of no less than three earlier redactions which preceded the extant version of Ruth Rabba.[83]

The first part of Midrash Esther Rabba (see below) as well as numerous segments of Midrash Samuel, have also been shown to evince the same early characteristics of Genesis Rabba and so they too should be included as specimens of early Amoraic midrash.[84]

The same could probably be said for Midrash Yelammedanu, for all intents and purposes the precursor of Midrash Tanhuma. In spite of the fact that this midrashic composition has not remained extant, its originality is evinced by numerous quotations in medieval literature and some select Geniza fragments. M. Bregman has recently demonstrated the unique literary components and fine qualities of just such a remnant (T-S C 1.46). This fragment was found to contain some most unique homilies of Midrash Yelammedenu to Exod 7:8-9, which excel in a sophisticated series of flashbacks to the story of the burning bush and the commission of Moses, in picturesque language, rich parables, Greek and Latin loanwords accurately transcribed, as well as considerable use of Galilean Aramaic. Taken all together, it may be assumed that the long-lost Midrash Yelammedenu was a contemporary of the above-mentioned classical Midrashim.[85] One may, therefore, postulate that the earliest phase of this Midrash, as evinced by the Geniza fragment, was already formulated no later then the sixth century.

It is important to note that later versions of this family – Tanhuma, Tanhuma Buber and Exodus Rabba – have completely revised and rearranged the basic material of these homilies.[86] Evidence pointing towards the early usage of Yelammedenu homilies to Exodus presently found in Tanhuma Exodus, has been adduced by Z.M. Rabinovitz, by virtue of the liturgical poetry (*piyyut*) of R. Yannai, the renowned *paytan* of the sixth century.[87]

The Interim Period (600-700)

Among those works written in the style of the classical Midrashim, but, nevertheless, coming somewhat later on, one may enumerate Pesikta de-Rav Kahana and Canticles Rabba.

Even though Pesikta de-Rav Kahana definitely contains large portions of early midrash (see above), it has incorporated five complete *piskaot* which

---

[82] Lerner, *Book of Ruth*, Introduction, 173.

[83] *Ib*. 170.

[84] Zunz-Albeck, *Derashot*, 413 n84. The placement of MidrSam among medieval compilations (Strack-Stemberger, *Introduction*, 357) is a serious blunder; note that in the original Strack, *Introduction*, 223, MidrSam is correctly listed under 'Other Expositional Midrashim'.

[85] Bregman, *Tanhuma-Yelammedenu*, 163-165; *pace* Geula, *Study*, 250.

[86] *Ib*. 166-188.

[87] Rabinovitz, *Halakha and Aggada*, 190f, 193.

appear to have been borrowed verbatim from Leviticus Rabba.[88] A careful study of these texts evinces the inferior quality of the Pesikta version which appears to have been formulated and edited during a subsequent era.[89] In a similar vein, Canticles Rabba exhibits usage of Leviticus Rabba[90] and so should be placed in a somewhat later period than the former. One should also note that Canticles Rabba does not contain classical style proems, the five proems appended to the beginning of this Midrash being either anonymous or pseudoepigraphic and their closing formula differing immensely from the norm of classical midrash.[91]

It is also quite possible that numerous segments of the Tanhuma-type midrash have already received their final form during this era. The ordinary Tanhuma homily seems to lack the originality and polish of the Yelammedenu, which presumably served as its major source. Even though most scholars tend to assign the Tanhuma Midrashim to a later period, it is, nevertheless, plausible to assume that many individual Tanhuma homilies, and possible some entire or partial works, were a product of the seventh century or even somewhat earlier.[92]

Later Midrashic Works (700-900)

The characteristics of later midrashic compositions have been summarized by J. Elbaum:[93]

1. Definite signs of usage of the classical Amoraic Midrashim (e.g. Genesis Rabba) and the reworking of their contents;

2. Possible usage of the Babylonian Talmud;

3. The disappearance of 'early' linguistic phenomena and the transition to a purely Hebrew mode of expression;

4. A synthesis between the exegetical and the homiletical methods of midrash or an organization of the material according to large formats (subject matter or organizational patterns);

5. Rhetorical expressions and extended speech;

6. Differing perspectives in the mention of the names of sages: on the one hand, a tendency to employ anonymity in the quotation of midrashic teachings (i.e., by eliminating the names), and on the other, the addition of various titles and epithets to the names of certain rabbis;[94]

---

[88] Margulies, 'Mavo', XIII n17.
[89] Milikowsky, 'Vayyiqra Rabba Chapter 28`; idem, 'Vayyiqra Rabba Chapter 30'.
[90] Margulies, 'Mavo', XXIII n64.
[91] Kadari, *Redaction*, 157-168.
[92] Bregman, *Tanhuma-Yelammedenu*, 180-184, 188.
[93] Elbaum, 'Character'.
[94] *Vid.* Zunz, *Vorträge*, 330-333. The phenomenon of spurious tradents is dealt with *infra*.

7. Style and content which are similar to the format of medieval Bible commentary.

Elbaum's summary relates to three major works of the midrashic corpus, which are generally considered to be products of the eight and ninth centuries: Midrash Tanhuma; Seder Eliyahu[95] and Pirkei de-R. Eliezer. Additional works which seem to fit the above-mentioned categories include Ecclesiastes Rabba;[96] Midrash Mishlei to Proverbs and Mishnat R. Eliezer, seemingly a Midrash to Prov 31:10-31 but in actuality, a collection of chapters devoted to various aspects of positive and negative moral and ethical behaviour and to the concept of 'holiness'. However, as intimated above, this conclusion does not really do justice to various segments of Tanhuma literature, which are most likely of even earlier vintage and should therefore be assigned to the interim period.

Two additional criteria not dealt with by Elbaum need to be mentioned. The first is the phenomenon of pseudoepigraphic tradents. Although most of the names of the rabbinic tradents quoted in midrashic literature are generally taken on face value and considered to be reliable, there are, nevertheless, certain midrashic works in which no authenticity whatsoever can be vouched for the names of the rabbis cited, and so these traditions must actually be considered pseudoepigraphic.

The most prominent of these works is Midrash Mishlei, an exegetic Midrash expounding a sizeable part of the Book of Proverbs. Even though numerous exegetical expositions found in this Midrash are quoted in the names of various Tannaic and Amoraic sages – most of them of note – it is generally accepted that no credence is to be attached to the names of the tradents. Generally speaking, these traditions are not ordinarily supported by parallels found in the earlier works of midrashic literature.[97] This is evident from several interesting argumentative discussions in Midrash Mishlei, wherein R. Eliezer purportedly addressed certain exegetical questions to his 'master', R. Joshua.[98] To be sure, both of these authorities were the leading sages of the second generation of Tannaim after the destruction of the Second Temple and they often conversed and debated with one another in both halakhic and aggadic context, but there is no evidence whatsoever to show that R. Eliezer was a disciple of R. Joshua. Moreover, the above-mentioned exegetical discussions which supposedly took place between the two are completely unknown in Tannaic sources, or, for that matter, in any other work of talmudic literature.[99]

Pirkei de-R. Eliezer, which is devoted to a retelling of the Bible from the creation till the wanderings of the Israelites in the desert, including some

---

[95] Concerning the dating of these two works, *vid. supra* at n70 and n92.

[96] *Vid.* Kipperwasser, *Midrashim*, 274-276.

[97] Visotzky, *Midrash Mishle*, Introduction, 67f.

[98] Ed Buber, Introduction, 15. The phenomenon itself has been dealt with by Bregman, 'Pseudepigraphy'.

[99] See the excellent summary of Bacher, *Tannaiten* 1, 153-155.

lengthy asides dealing with the prophet Jonah and the Scroll of Esther,[100] is an additional midrashic work following this unreliable approach. Not only is this work fictitiously attributed to the above mentioned Tanna, R. Eliezer b. Hyrkanos, but many – if not all – of the names of the rabbis mentioned there appear to be of a fictitious nature.[101] Additional later Midrashim apparently adopted a similar approach to the names of rabbinical tradents, and one must be constantly aware of this problem when dealing with these works.

The second phenomenon not dealt with by Elbaum is the anti-Karaite polemics. The Karaite schism begun by Anan b. David during the latter half of the eight century evoked various forms of response from the leaders of rabbinic Judaism and it was only natural that anti-Karaite polemics would find their way into contemporary midrashic literature. Surprisingly enough, however, this phenomenon is not too widespread and there is only sporadic evidence for such occurrences in midrashic works dating from the eight to the tenth centuries. Bacher *et al.* have argued that certain halakhic passages in Seder Eliyahu as well as those stressing the importance of Mishna study, instead of concentrating exclusively on the Bible, reflect the author's staunch opposition to Karaism.[102] However, this conclusion has been challenged by some scholars, or simply ignored by others.[103] J.N. Epstein and M. Zucker have focused on a relatively large number of anti-Karaite polemics in Mishnat R. Eliezer,[104] whereas individual attacks are found in Midrash Tanhuma,[105] and possibly in Midrash Mishlei[106] and Pesikta Rabbati.[107] Needless to say, the presence of polemical material against Karaite beliefs and practices in a particular midrash most likely attests to a ninth century or even later origin. However, the somewhat surprising paucity of such material in supposed later midrashic works raises some serious doubts as to the date which scholars have attributed to these works.

On European Soil: The Close of the Midrashic Endeavour (1000-1200)

As stated above, the Land of Israel served as the cradle of midrashic literature throughout the ages, *viz.* until the close of the Gaonic period (1040 CE). However, this did not prevent scholars from proposing alternate origins for specific Midrashim. Zunz, A. Epstein and S.K. Mirsky[108] suggested that Midrash Tan-

---

[100] PRE chs 10, 49-50. Note also chapters 6-8 which are entirely devoted to astronomy and intercalation.

[101] *Pace* Zunz, *Vorträge*, 290. However, cf *ibid.* 286 notes c-d; 288 note c.

[102] Bacher, 'Anti-Karaisches'; Oppenheim, 'Maamar'; Zucker, *Targum*, 116; 205-219.

[103] *Vid.* Gartner, 'Why Did the Geonim', 32 n80.

[104] Epstein, 'Mishnat R. Eliezer', 15; Zucker, 'Baayat 32 middot', 33-35.

[105] Tanh Noah 1. Cf Zunz, *Vorträge*, 247 note d; ed Buber, vol 1, 27 n6.

[106] *Vid.* Visotzky, *Midrash Mishle*, 46-54; idem, *Midrash Proverbs*, 4-7; 10.

[107] *Vid.* Marmorstein, 'Piska zum Wochenfest', 50-52.

[108] Zunz, *Vorträge*, 248; A. Epstein, *Mi-kadmoniot*, 60; Mirsky, 'Midrash Tanhuma', 114-119.

huma – or at least its printed version which contains numerous additions, e.g., from Sefer ha-Sheiltot,[109] a collection of halakhic and aggadic discourses on the weekly reading composed in Babylonia at the beginning of the Gaonic period – was also the product of Babylonian Jewry, whereas Zunz claimed that the supposed mention of two rivers in southern Italy indicates that the Tanhuma was indeed composed in that area.[110] Zunz also concluded that the major segment of Midrash Psalms (1-118, see below), was redacted in southern Italy, partly due to the supposed mention of a specific local area (Apulia) in that midrash.[111] Furthermore, scholars have suggested European origins for Seder Eliyahu and Pesikta Rabbati, as well.[112]

However, the claims that the above-mentioned midrashic works were composed in Italy have failed to take into account the existence of literary activity in eighth-ninth century Palestine. The claims have been refuted by Jacob Mann who seven decades ago concluded unequivocally: 'The whole theory of attributing to Italy is now antiquated and has to be discarded.'[113]

The same could be said for the alleged Babylonian origin of Midrash Tanhuma. Notwithstanding the fact that the printed edition of the Tanhuma evinces direct Babylonian influence via the eighth century Babylonian Sheiltot de-Rav Ahai, it is quite apparent that the overwhelming majority of the various components of Tanhuma literature are actually of much earlier vintage, which most likely indicates a Palestinian origin.

There is no denying the likelihood that at least one prominent branch of Tanhuma literature – the so-called 'printed version' – did undergo a certain editorial process on Babylonian soil. However, it appears that this process was a very superficial one, involving the incorporation of material from various sources, and probably one short anti-Karaitic addition (see above). On the other hand, the main body of the Tanhuma does not seem to have undergone significant changes[114] during the course of time.[115]

In spite of all that, there is ample evidence for midrashic activity on European soil. R. Moshe ha-Darshan of Narbonne (Provence), the eleventh century predecessor of Rashi, is known to have composed various midrashic interpretations and homilies, many of them extant in an anthological work entitled Bereshit Rabbati.

---

[109] Zunz, *Vorträge*, 245 note f.; Mirsky, 'Midrash Tanhuma', 111 n47.

[110] Zunz *ib.* 248.

[111] *Ib.* 280.

[112] Braude-Kapstein, *Tanna Debe Eliyyahu*, Introduction, 10; Zunz, *ib.*, 286; Levi, 'Bari'.

[113] Mann, 'Midrashic Genizah Fragments', 305. Mann's sweeping denial is applicable to other supposed European midrashic origins (Greece, Byzantium etc.) as well, *vid.* Elitzur, *Pesikta Rabbati*, 269f; cf the recent claims of Geula, *Study*, 250 (Thebes).

[114] Note the close correlation between the printed version of Tanhuma Lev-Deut and ed Buber.

[115] Aside from the transition between the ancient Yelammedenu homilies and the more modern Tanhuma, see above.

The first part of Numbers Rabba (1-14), especially par. 13-14 (Naso) which contains a host of allegorical explanations to Num 8 (the sacrifices of the princes of the twelve tribes), has recently been shown by H. Mack to be a product of the homiletical activity of Provençal rabbis during the tenth-eleventh centuries which received its final form in mid twelfth century Provence.[116] The scope and nature of these midrashic allegories are unique by all means and standards and most likely represent the culmination of the midrashic process within its medieval setting. It is also most likely that most of the second part of Esther Rabba (par. 6-10, see below), which contains three rather lengthy selections from Sefer Yosippon, a pseudo-historical work written in tenth century Italy, underwent its final redaction on European soil.

The so-called 'Spanish version' of Deuteronomy Rabba was also completed in medieval Europe and most likely represents the efforts of Spanish[117] scribes to complete an apparently defective copy of the regular (the so-called 'printed') edition of that Midrash. However, during the course of this process, which took place between the twelfth and the fifteenth centuries, stress seems to have been placed on the inclusion or exclusion of large sections of material, rather than on a literary editing of the textual readings of individual passages.[118]

In all likelihood, the final editing process of Numbers Rabba and Esther Rabba took place no later than the twelfth century and these two works seemingly represent the final efforts of the midrashic endeavour *per se*. However, there does not seem to have been any formal announcement to this effect, as no official canon or tabulation exists for this branch of the Oral Tora.

IN THE WAKE OF THE EDITING PROCESS

Hybridization

It is interesting to note that during the course of the editing process, many Midrashim actually wove material from other midrashic works into their fabric. This activity most likely transpired during the final stages of the editing process or somewhat afterward. Such 'foreign' elements are usually easily identifiable by their source and terminology.

Following is an initial list of such phenomena:

> (1) *Exodus Rabba*: Whereas ExodR sections 1-14 is an Exegetical Midrash to Exod 1-10, the latter part – sections 15-52, dealing with Exod 12-40 – represents a Homiletical Midrash stemming from the Tanhuma-Yelammedenu family.

---

[116] Mack, *Prolegomena*, 191-193; idem, 'Numbers Rabba', 99-105.
[117] Basing himself on flimsy evidence, Yahalom, 'R. Moshe ha-Darshan', 146f has endeavoured to show that this Midrash was completed in Provence.
[118] *Vid.* Lerner, 'New Light' [1], 139-141.

(2) *Numbers Rabba*: As mentioned above, the first part of NumR, Bemidbar – Naso 1-14, is itself compiled from various midrashic works, including a Homiletical Midrash of the Tanhuma-Yelammedenu family and a Midrash based on the teachings and exegesis of R. Moses ha-Darshan *et al.*, especially the section dealing with the sacrifices offered by the tribal Princes at the consecration of the Tabernacle (Num 8). However, the second part (Be-haalotkha – Masaei) has been copied almost verbatim from Tanh. The original composition of NumR might possibly be attested by ms München 97, 2, which contains Part I exclusively. Part II was most likely added on to manuscripts of Part I in order to facilitate the acceptance of NumR into the Midrash Rabba collection which was ostensibly designated as a Midrash covering all the pericopes of the Pentateuch.[119]

(3) *Deuteronmy Rabba*: The so-called 'Spanish' version of DeutR is actually a combination of unknown Yelammedenu homilies and selections from the standard version of Tanh, which have been grafted upon the central segment of this Midrash which stems from the regular (Ashkenazi) version (see above).

(4) *Esther Rabba:* As shown below, the extant version of EsthR is basically a very early classical Midrash (par. 1-5 *et al.*) upon which much later midrashic material has been grafted (par. 6-10).

(5) *Canticles Rabba* and *Pesikta Rabbati*: In the Germanic manuscript tradition, CantR was appended to PesR, as evinced by ms Parma 1240 and many of the sources cited in YalShim.[120]

(6) *Midrash Tanhuma*: Lengthy selections from Tanh Shelah-Balak evince the presence of extensive exegetical material in this otherwise homiletical midrash. These may have very well derived from a non-extant exegetical midrash, possibly of Tannaic (?) origin.[121]

(7) *Tanhuma – Printed Version*: This version is replete with numerous additions from external sources, already found in all the manuscripts, including: a) Tanh Noah 3, a paean to the Oral Law, probably deriving from Midrash Ruah ha-Kodesh; b) Large sections of Tanh Bo, Beshalah and Yitro which have been copied almost verbatim from MekRY;[122] c) Large selections from the Babylonian Sheiltot de-Rav Ahai, which have been interpolated into Tanh Genesis, Mishpatim, Hukat, *et al.* (see above).

All of the phenomena described above are attested to by many, and sometimes by all, of the extant manuscripts and it may be assumed that some of them

---

[119] The earliest quotations from the second part of NumR indicate that this unification transpired no later than the beginning of the thirteenth century. Mack, 'Numbers Rabba', 94-97; Yahalom, 'R. Moshe Ha-Darshan', 138.

[120] Goldstein, 'Midrash Canticles Rabba'.

[121] See above n20, n50. Note the following corrections and additions to the list compiled by Schlüter, 'Midrash parshani': Num 13:16-[17], 23; 16:1-32 [2 and 19 are lacking]; 20:7-23 [9, 13, 16, 19-21 are lacking]; 21:1, 4-7, 17-35 [22, 24 and 33 are lacking]; [22:2-7, 9, 12-19, 24-41; 23:1-10, 14-19, 21-25].

[122] *Vid.* Zunz, *Vorträge*, 243 note a.

transpired at a relatively early period. The desire to supply or replenish those sections thought to be lacking in material seems to have been the main impetus for this activity.

Since the manuscript evidence for such works as Numbers Rabba, Deuteronomy Rabba *et al.* definitely shows that the process of hybridization continued throughout the medieval period, one may raise the question as to whether these activities should be considered as a later development of the redactional process or are they to be looked upon as post-redactional, mainly reflecting the activities of scribes?

Incomplete Midrashim?

In spite of the supreme efforts of editors, scribes, and printers to integrate the various midrashic compositions, there are, nevertheless, certain works which appear to be in an unfinished state. Note the following examples:

(1) *Ecclesiastes Zutta*: This early midrashic interpretation of Ecclesiastes (6th-7th centuries) comes to an abrupt end at 9:18, followed by an epilogue: the anecdote dealing with R. Jonathan and the spiteful Samaritan.[123] Suffice it to say that the absence of midrashic explanations to chap. 10-12 remains an enigma.[124]

(2) *Midrash Tehillim* (Psalms): See below, section Later Additions and Insertions.

(3) *Pirkei de-R. Eliezer*:[125] Beginning with chapter 14, the infrastructure of PRE is based on the 'Ten descents made by the Holy One blessed be He upon the earth' and from chapter 27 onwards, various biblical events are related to the benedictions of the weekday Amida prayer. However, only eight descents and only eight benedictions are dealt with, which seemingly attest to the present incomplete condition ot this work.[126]

(4) *Midrash Mishlei* (Proverbs): Nineteenth century scholars who noticed the large gaps in the middle of this seemingly running-commentary exegetical work to Proverbs, attributed those lacunae to the *textus receptus*. However, a recent study[127] has shown that most of these gaps reflect the editorial artistry of the redactor who merely desired to alleviate his task by the unique process of skip-

---

[123] Kipperwasser, *Midrashim* 1, 88-89; 2, 79. Omitted by Buber.

[124] Note that the relatively late parallel EcclR does indeed contain a Midrash to the missing chapters. However, it remains to be seen whether this material derives from the ancient *Vorlage*, or whether it represents later additions designed to complete the obvious lacuna.

[125] The regular printed editions of this work (e.g. Warsaw 1852, 128b) end abruptly in the middle of an explanation in chap. 54 and should be complemented by Wertheimer, 'Last Chapter', 242f; ed Higger, *Horev* 10, 252 and Nahum, *Mi-Yetzirot*, 176.

[126] Treitel, 'Edei ha-Nusah', 6-12 has shown that no extant evidence exists for the supposedly missing chapters of this work and alludes to the possibility that the final editor himself was well aware of the fact that his midrashic endeavor was indeed incomplete, even to the point of apologizing for same.

[127] Lerner, 'Midrash Mishle', 462-470.

ping to a similar verse in another chapter, which enabled him to limit the number of verses covered by his exegesis.[128]

In summation, one may safely assume that the overwhelming majority of those works comprising the midrashic genre described above, have been transmitted in full format, although there are still certain individual works – *viz.* Ecclesiastes Zuta and Pirkei de-R. Eliezer – which are, nonetheless, 'incomplete'.[129]

LATER DEVELOPMENTS

From the thirteenth century onwards, the main thrust of midrashic and aggadic activity was geared towards the adaptation of extant teachings as well as the collection and the practical and handy rearrangement of the numerous sources and to the dissemination of this vast corpus of edifying material, rather than towards creative and innovative endeavours.

Homilies

The decline of the midrashic endeavour, which in its prime had encouraged the creation of original explanations and homilies to the biblical texts, brought with it a renewal and reworking of the older materials. In many instances, the homilies were prefaced by elaborate orative opening formulae (*acclamatio*) such as, יתברך שמו של מלך מלכי המלכים הקדוש ברוך הוא, 'Blessed be the name of the King of Kings, the Holy One, may He be blessed', which are still extant in some of the texts.[130] Many of them also contain appropriate elevated concluding formulae (*peroratio*), sure signs of oral delivery.[131] In some early medieval synagogues, one of the rabbis or a recognized preacher would read appropriate passages from a classical midrashic text and expound them as fulfilment of the *derasha* (public lecture), ordinarily held on the Sabbath.[132]

Holiday lectures seem to have been much more elaborate. Extant minor midrashic works composed for the holidays evince a process of adopting material from earlier sources and moulding them into a coherent whole, dealing with the major themes of the day.[133]

---

[128] It now apparent that the unusually large lacuna between 2:13-4:22 (67 verses), is actually the result of a defective text which has been partially restored by virtue of a Geniza fragment (T-S F 15.1), *vid.* Lerner *ib.* 470-478, 483-488.

[129] Cf also Aggadat Bereshit, whose homilies terminate at Gen 49:1.

[130] E.g. Tanh Hukat 1, ed Buber, 97-100 = NumR 18:22 (Korah!); Mann, *Midrashim* 1, 33f. On this device, *vid.* Zunz, *Vorträge*, 246 note a; Mann, *ib.* 32; Lieberman, *Midrash rabbah: Deuteronomy*, Introduction, XXIIf.

[131] This device is quite frequent in the earlier Midrashim, see Stein, 'Peroratio'; Goldberg, 'Peroratio'. Cf above n52.

[132] Cf the comic episode in Megillat Ahimaaz, 18.

[133] E.g. PesRK Appendix 2, 452-459; Pesikta Hadeta, *Bet ha-Midrasch* 6, 36-70, esp 53, 65; Midr Panim Aherot 1, 45-49.

Most certainly, an organized collection and proper analysis of this literary genre would greatly benefit an appreciation of Jewish preaching during the early Middle Ages, a subject heretofore greatly neglected. Such an undertaking could also conceivably uncover earlier origins of this genre.

Compilations and Collectanea: Yalkutim and Indices (1100-1500)

The gradual termination of midrashic activity during the twelfth century apparently prompted the need for various works designed to assist the rabbi, the student and the layman in their search for appropriate material. To be sure, hundreds of years of ongoing activity in the field of aggadic midrash, which had produced scores of midrashic works, coupled with the vast number of aggadic interpretations in talmudic literature *per se*, rendered it almost impossible to master this field. The situation was further aggravated by the lack of a complete collection of the texts (*i.e.* manuscripts) in the medieval study houses.

As a result, the effort to collect the enormous amount of material in an orderly fashion became most urgent. The initiative for such projects seems to have arisen almost simultaneously with rabbinic scholars in various Jewish communities west and east, who because of the lack of communication between them, had no knowledge of similar ventures, some of which were already in progress at the very same time. However, these obvious duplications should by no means be considered to be wasted efforts since the individual compilers did not all use the same sources nor the same methodology in their collectanea. Moreover, their efforts reflect different manuscript traditions that were located in different communities, and these factors alone leave room for diversification which is certainly a boon to modern scholarship.

There are about twenty extant yalkutim from the medieval period, most of them from Yemen. However, the practical value of most of the Yemenite collections, aside from the monumental Midrash ha-Gadol (see below), remains to be shown.[134]

The earliest compilation representing this genre seems to be Sefer Pitron Tora, which has been identified as a work authored by Rav Hai b. Nahshon Gaon of Sura, who was active at the end of the ninth century (885-896).[135] This work eventually enjoyed a relatively wide circulation as the yalkut of Persian Jewry.[136] Pitron Tora combines both midrashic material and exegetical interpretations of the Bible. Since the latter is mainly directed at Karaite interpretation and doctrine,[137] it may be assumed that the desire to engage in a counter-attack

---

[134] For a concise survey of the various yalkutim, *vid.* Lerner, 'Notes', 109-110; 'Notes: Corrections', 143.
[135] Allony, 'Midrash Ha-Tora'; cf Kahana, *Sifre Zuta*, 30 n3.
[136] Cf ed Urbach, Introduction, 11-13.
[137] Cf *ib.* 30f.

against Karaite teachings served as the impetus for the composition of this yalkut, which was formulated during an age when midrashic creativity was still flourishing. We would like to suggest that the Gaonic author did not wish to engage in open polemics with the Karaites and so he couched his exegetical criticisms within the framework of selections from various Midrashim, an arrangement which most likely encouraged people to consult this work. Pitron Tora thus served as the early forerunner for a group of yalkutim that combine both midrashic and biblical interpretation, which include: Lekah Tov (R. Tobias b. Eliezer); Sekhel Tov (R. Menahem b. Solomon); Midrash ha-Tora (R. Shmuel b. Nissim), *et al.*

Yalkut Shimoni, compiled by R. Shimon ha-Darshan ('the preacher') of Frankfurt, appears to be the earliest compendium devoted completely to a collection of both midrashic and talmudic sources. This collection, apparently dating from the middle of the thirteenth century, represents the most important member of this genre since it covers the entire Bible from beginning to end in a most comprehensive fashion. Moreover, Yalkut Shimoni also provides identification for almost all of the specific sources quoted throughout this voluminous collection, including quotes from several non-extant midrashic works.[138]

Additional compilations which specify their sources, but whose scope is far more limited then that of Yalkut Shimoni are the thirteenth century Yalkut ha-Mekhiri, compiled by R. Makhir b. Abba Mari[139] and Yalkut Talmud Tora, the fourteenth century (as yet unpublished) collection of R. Jacob Sakily.[140]

Among the numerous yalkutim composed in Yemen, Midrash ha-Gadol, compiled by R. David b. Amram ha-Adani in the middle of the fourteenth century takes precedence. Midrash ha-Gadol has preserved material from several important Halakhic and Aggadic Midrashim which have fallen into oblivion, while the text of previously known sources that are included is usually of a superb quality.[141]

Medieval indices of biblical passages, while not containing actual quotations from the Midrashim *per se*, represent yet an additional aid for the study of various midrashic works. Such lists as Mafteah ha-Derashot,[142] partially published by Rabbi J.L.H. Maimon and falsely attributed to Maimonides, as well as Beit Zevul, compiled by R. Eliezer Crescas,[143] are pertinent examples.

---

[138] The recently discovered index of sources in the YalShim sheds new light on the contents and the composition of this work, vid. Geula, 'Riddle'.

[139] *Vid.* the bibliographical summary of Strack-Stemberger, *Introduction*, 353; Lerner, 'New Light' [1], 129f.

[140] A typewritten copy of the manuscripts of this yalkut is now available on a CD Rom issued by 'Otzar ha-Hokhma'. Pericope Bemidbar has recently been published by Deshe-Ha-Levi, *Yalkut Midrashim* 3, Appendix.

[141] Ratzaby, *Teshuvot*, 15; Lerner, 'Notes', 110-118; Tobi, *Midrash Ha-Gadol*. Part 2 of Tobi's thesis includes indices to most of the identified sources of MidrGad and are thus an indispensable research tool.

[142] Maimon, 'Sefer Mafteah' based on ms Oxf-Bodl 2242. See also ms Vat 98.

[143] Gaster, 'Eliezer Crescas'.

Such lists which were designed as reference works whose task is to direct the rabbi and the student to pertinent material, also provide important information concerning the content and internal division of numerous components of midrashic literature.

MANUSCRIPTS

Important evidence for the text and the contents of the various Midrashim is available from extant manuscript copies of these works. However, as might be expected, due to numerous persecutions and book burnings, manuscript preservation has been most haphazard.

The major Midrashim to the first four Books of the Pentateuch have been relatively fortunate, since each of them has remained extant in approximately 7-10 complete manuscripts. However, there is only one single manuscript copy of the printed version of DeutR and the same is true for Pesikta Rabbati, Seder Eliyahu and Midrash Samuel. Ruth Rabba and Esther Rabba, as well as parts of the Midrash Zutta collection, have also not fared too well with only two existing manuscripts from beginning to end. Pirkei de-R. Eliezer, however, one of the later Midrashim, is found in approximately fifty manuscripts, a fact which evidently attests to the popularity and widespread circulation of this work.[144]

The quality of the manuscripts is an entirely different matter. Most of the extant codices are relatively late copies, dating from the thirteenth century onwards. These leave a lot to be desired, since their preservation of early linguistic traditions and the proper textual reading is usually quite faulty. The only totally reliable manuscript of a midrashic text is ms Vatican 30 of Genesis Rabba, and this too only in regard to the material covered by the first and third scribes, who fortunately copied the bulk of this codex.[145] Coming a far second is the British Library manuscript of Genesis Rabba and Leviticus Rabba.[146] Among the later Midrashim, ms Vatican 44, as well as the recent discovery of two very large St. Petersburg fragments, which include approximately 90% of Midrash Mishlei, seem to reflect a relatively reliable text of this Midrash to Proverbs,[147] which has been assigned to the Gaonic period.

Consequently, the uncovering of early-dated fragments from the Cairo Geniza is most certainly an important contribution to the study of the original form and contents of the classical Midrashim. However, in all fairness, it should be stressed that these finds are, on the whole, few and far between.

---

[144] Treitel, 'Edei Ha-Nusah'. It is important to note that more than half of these are copies of printed editions and extant manuscripts and so as far as textual analysis is concerned, they are of no value whatsoever (*ib.* 20-28). Cf Barth, 'Medieval Manuscript'.

[145] Sokoloff, 'The Hebrew', 35-42; Barth, *Analysis*, 27-60 has postulated the work of 4-6 scribes!

[146] Described by Albeck, 'Einleitung', 105-107; Margulies, 'Mavo', XXXIV.

[147] Visotzky, *Midrash Mishle*, 91-93. The St. Petersburg fragments II A 274; II A 543 are almost completely identical with the Vatican text.

Several manuscripts have become contaminated through the activities of energetic scribes. Contesting the claims of M. Sokoloff,[148] M. Kahana has focused attention on ms Vatican 60 of Genesis Rabba, a relatively early codex, which has, nevertheless, grafted on to the fabric of this text to Genesis unusually lengthy selections from parallel selections in other midrashic works.[149] The same could be said for ms Munich 117 of Leviticus Rabba, which in spite of the opinion voiced by some top-rate scholars, is really of inferior quality, due to its practice of implanting parallels from other sources including the Babylonian Talmud, in place of the original readings of Leviticus Rabba.[150]

A case in point is the story of the encounter between Elisha b. Abuya and R. Meir in EcclR 7:8. The version of this story in the *editio princeps* is identical with the parallel in RuthR 6:7(4). However, a perusal of the manuscripts of Ecclesiastes Rabba evinces an entirely different recension of the story.[151] The obvious solution for this phenomenon seems to lie in the scribal practice of deleting lengthy selections which appear in parallel – though by no means identical – versions in other midrashic or talmudic works, while referring the reader to the latter sources.[152] In the case of the Elisha – Meir incident, the manuscript of Ecclesiastes Rabba utilized by R. Astruc of Toulon, the publisher of the *editio princeps*, most likely contained only a short reference to the above-mentioned story in Ruth Rabba, and he obviously copied it word by word from his printing of that source. Interestingly enough, the scribe of ms Oxf-Bodl 164 of Ruth Rabba[153] deleted almost all of this episode by a simple cross-reference to Ecclesiastes Rabba.

It is thus quite clear that in their desire to present a 'complete' text, many copyists of manuscripts containing cross-references to parallel material automatically consulted the parallel texts alluded to by the previous scribe and copied these sources verbatim, without realizing that they were engaging in the process of 'grafting' alternate 'foreign' versions onto the main body of indigenous midrashic texts.

A proper appreciation of these processes enables a suitable refutation to the argument voiced by Peter Schäfer some two decades ago.[154] According to Schäfer, the existence of differing manuscript versions of a certain text could constitute the existence of salient autonomous works identified by the same title (e.g. 'Bereshit Rabba') but stemming from different redactors. He argues

---

[148] Sokoloff, *Geniza Fragments* 1, 212-266.

[149] Kahana, 'Genesis Rabba'.

[150] Lerner, *Perush Kadum*, 24f n33; Milikowsky, 'Vayyiqra Rabba Chapter 28', 22 n14; cf idem, 'Vayyiqra Rabba Chapter 30', 272.

[151] Lerner, 'Beginnings', 17 n26.

[152] The technical term utilized by the scribes for this practice is גר״ש, which has been explained by Lieberman, *Studies*, 210-213: 'shortened-truncated'. See also Rabinovitz, *Ginzàe Midrash*, 199 ll. 14f, 200 n178; 235 n21; Kahana, 'Genesis Rabba', 53f.

[153] Ed Lerner, *Book of Ruth*, 165 l. 78.

[154] Schäfer, 'Research'.

that if this is indeed the case, then we really cannot speak of a definite work identified by a specific name, since this name is merely 'an ideal or fictitious entity'.[155]

It appears that Schäfer has based his argument on the seemingly wide discrepancies between ms Vatican 60 and ms London-British Library *et al.* of Genesis Rabba, which were first demonstrated by M. Sokoloff in his doctoral dissertation on the Geniza fragments of Genesis Rabba, even though Schäfer himself failed to allude to that work in his article.[156] Suffice it to say that the above-mentioned discussion of medieval scribal practices and the study of M. Kahana, which is specifically devoted to the transplanting of various external sources on the text of ms Vatican 60, completely negate the thesis advanced by Schäfer,[157] which he obviously based on the unique readings of that manuscript. In spite of the response of Schäfer,[158] one may fully concur with the conclusions of Ch. Milikowsky, *viz.* that 'the redactional identity [of Genesis Rabba] is clear-cut' and that this Midrash was originally composed in a single *Urtext*, although the ability to reconstruct the original text has been hampered by certain external factors.[159]

LATER ADDITIONS AND INSERTIONS

The fluidity of the medieval textual tradition relating to the Aggadic Midrashim also enabled the copyists to add on new material to the manuscripts that they were copying. These were adopted from various midrashic works of similar content but could also include biblical commentaries and various collectanea.

Following is a list of some pertinent examples of this phenomenon:

> (1) *Genesis Rabba*: In most manuscripts of this *magnum opus* of midrashic literature, the final chapters have incorporated some extremely lengthy selections from Tanh and Midrash Ruah ha-Kodesh *et al.*, especially in the section dealing with the Blessings of Jacob, which have replaced the original text of GenR.[160] However, the *bona fide* text of GenR has remained extant in the *editio princeps*

---

[155] *Ib.* 146f.

[156] I suspect that in the original draft of p146 n38, Schäfer referred to Sokoloff's dissertation, *Geniza Fragments* (1971), since the latter's conclusions regarding ms Vat 60 seemingly support his thesis that, even though they bear the same title, each of the Vatican mss should be considered a separate work. However, with the appearance of Sokoloff's *Kit'e Bereshit Rabba*, he apparently replaced the original citation with a reference to the newly published work (1982), which is based on Part I of the Dissertation only and thus has no bearing whatsoever on ms Vat 60! Note the criticism of Milikowsky, 'Status Quaestionis', 203-206, explicitly dismissing the supposed evidence from ms Vat 60.

[157] Kahana, 'Genesis Rabba', esp 59 n128.

[158] Schäfer, 'Once Again'. In his rejoinder, Schäfer was unaware of the fallacy mentioned *supra* n156.

[159] Milikowsky, 'Status Quaestionis'; idem, 'Formation', 551-560.

[160] E.g. ed Theodor-Albeck, par. 91,5 (p1118-1126); 93,9-12 (p1158-1171); 95-96 (p1185-1230).

and in ms Vat 30.[161] It is thus quite obvious that the major manuscript tradition of GenR descends from a defective manuscript whose end was lacking[162] and so the scribes decided to rectify this situation by collecting material from other midrashic works relating to pericope Vayehi.

(2) *Leviticus Rabba*: Several selections from SER have been appended to some manuscript versions and the *editio princeps* of the concluding sections to the first three pericopes of LevR.[163]

(3) *Deuteronomy Rabba*: A version of Midrash Petirat Moshe has been appended to the printed (Ashkenazic) version of DeutR 11,4 as is evident from a comparison with mss Parma 1240 and Paris 1408.19 which do not contain this section.[164]

(4) *Pesikta de-Rav Kahana*: Some of the manuscripts of this work contain rather lengthy additions. Many of these been collected and edited by B. Mandelbaum in the text and in the Appendices to his edition.[165] However there are also additional homilies, especially to the *piskaot* for Shuva, Ahare mot, Sukkot and Shemini atseret stemming from foreign sources, which have been relegated to the critical apparatus.[166]

(5) *Midrash Tanhuma*: Many of the manuscripts of Tanh, which have been surveyed in extreme detail by S. Buber in the Introduction to his edition of that work, were found to contain large segments of extraneous material from other midrashic works as well as various biblical commentaries.[167] To complicate matters even further, R. Ezra of Fano, the scholarly printer of the Mantua 1563 edition, attempted to 'complete' the text of the *editio princeps* by adding on supplementary material from two manuscripts. In truth, the publisher was most cautious and did indeed do his best to identify the supplementary material. However, it is quite clear that these additions derive from alternate versions of Tanhuma literature, and do not really belong to the printed edition.[168]

---

[161] *Ib.* par. 95-100 (p1231-1296).

[162] This is further corroborated by ms Vat 60 which concludes at the end of par. 94 (p1179) and the scribe even added an appropriate comment to the effect that no further material was forthcoming.

[163] Ed. Margulies 32-34; 46-54; 72-75.

[164] Bregman, 'Edei Nusah', 51f.

[165] Additions are sometimes identified by smaller print (e.g. piskaot Zakhor, 35-36; Sos asis, 330-331; Bayom hashemini, 418-421). However, an extremely lengthy selection (piska Bahodesh 12-25, 213-224), deriving from Tanh Yitro ed Buber, 7-17 (73-80), is nonetheless printed in regular type.

[166] 350 l. 5; 368 l. 8; 400 l. 2; 401 l. 7 = 402 l. 4; 415 l. 10; 416 l. 10; 431 l. 9; 433 l. 10. Some of these apparently derive from homilies, see above.

[167] Concerning early foreign additions to the so-called 'printed' edition of Midrash Tanhuma, as evinced by all extant manuscripts, see above: 'Hybridization'.

[168] The additions to the Mantua printing have been summarized by Buber in his Introduction, 165-180. It remains to be seen whether this material, or parts of it, derive from the long-lost Midrash Yelammedenu.

(6) *Canticles Rabba*: Zunz already noted the peculiar addition of a personal nature in CantR 1.2.2 as well as other short glosses,[169] while M. Hirshman has recently commented on certain eleventh century additions from the pen of R. Eliyahu be-R. Menahem, which also reflect his annual pilgrimage to Jerusalem (see below).[170]

(7) *Ecclesiastes Rabba*: M. Hirshman has also focused upon various eleventh century marginal additions of a rather personal nature to the text of EcclR. These deal with the annual pilgrimage of R. Elijah be-R. Menahem to the Mt. of Olives in Jerusalem *et. al.* and were eventually inserted into the main body of the text of EcclR, as evinced by ms JTS MIC 5529.2.[171]

(8) *Lamentations Zuta*: Selections from PesRK dealing with the *haftarot* for the three Sabbaths of Affliction (דפורענותא 'ג) have been appended to Ashkenazic manuscripts of Midrash Ekha Zuta.[172]

(9) *Midrash Abba Guryon*: ms Parma 563 of this short Midrash to Esther contains several glosses from an unknown parallel Midrash entitled 'a different midrash' (see below), whereas the copyist of ms London 343 has incorporated citations from the commentary of R. Elazar of Worms into the text of the Midrash.[173]

(10) *Midrash Tehillim*: The manuscripts and the *editio princeps* (Constantinople 1512) of this Midrash to Psalms ordinarily terminate at Ps 118.[174] Supplementary material designed to replenish the missing segment (Ps 119-150) was published a few years later (Salonika 1515) and was eventually incorporated into the second printing (Venice 1546).[175]

(11) *Pirkei de-R. Eliezer*: The first two chapters of this work relating to the initial stages of the Tora education of R. Eliezer ben Hyrkanos, adopted from ARN version B, are clearly a later addition.[176]

(12) *Midrash Proverbs*: A short edition of Midrash Eshet Hayil, which identifies each verse in Prov 31:10-31 with a particular biblical heroine is found in almost all manuscript versions of Midrash Mishlei, cf ed Buber, 110-112. However, from a literary analysis of the components of this section of Midrash Mishlei, as well as the evidence presented by the early version preserved in ms

---

[169] Zunz, *Vorträge*, 275 note h.
[170] Hirshman, 'Priest's Gate', 221f; idem, 'R. Elijah'. Cf Mack, 'Sermon'.
[171] Hirshman, 'Priest's Gate'.
[172] ms Parma 563 (= Buber, *Midrasch Suta*, 74-78, par. 29-42); ms Darmstadt 25, 1 (par. 29-35).
[173] Buber, *Sifrei de-Aggadeta*, Introduction, II-III.
[174] Two of the mss utilized by Buber contain midrash to Ps 119:1 (*ibid.* 488-491), whereas the additional material in ms Vat 81 (Ps 119-150), dated 1598, is entirely based on YalShim, cf idem, Introduction, 84.
[175] This material derives from external sources which include an additional Midrash to Psalms (see Mann, 'Midrashic Fragments', 307f) and excerpts from YalShim (Ps 122-137), bearing no relation whatsoever to ms Vat 81 (cf previous n).
[176] Lerner, 'Studies', 49; Treitel, 'Edei ha-Nusah', 16-18.

Vat. 44, it is quite clear that Midrash Eshet Hayil is a later addition.[177] Furthermore, an inspection of the critical apparatus in ed Visotzky reveals an unusually large quantity of lengthy additions to the text found in almost all of the major extant manuscripts.[178]

(13) *Mishnat R. Eliezer*: The copyist of ms A has inserted the text of Tanh Noah 3 into the middle of parasha 13, most likely in order to stress the importance of Tora study.[179]

It goes without saying that some of the scribal practices described above border somewhat on the process of hybridization in the redaction of certain Midrashim, which has been previously discussed. In certain cases, it is rather difficult to decide whether we are dealing with particular individual scribal insertions or with the redactional process *per se*.

MIDRASHIC COLLECTIONS

The formation of the major midrashic corpora to the Pentateuch and to the Five Scrolls was not an instant reality. This situation is understandable in view of the different editors and/or authors as well as the enormous differences in the internal literary composition and structure of the various individual works. Evidence presented by a possibly pre-twelfth century book list from the Geniza[180] indicates that, in Oriental communities, each midrashic composition to a book of the Pentateuch was written in a separate manuscript and that in the library represented in the book list, the collection of Midrashim to the five books of the Pentateuch was more or less an arbitrary option.[181] However, it is quite clear that the formational development of the collection which was eventually entitled 'Midrash Rabba' definitely transpired during the period of handwritten manuscript copies, generations before the advent of printing. Following is a discussion of the most prominent midrashic collections.

---

[177] Visotzky, *Midrash Mishle*, Appendix, 197; Levine-Katz, *Eshet Hayil*, 54-89; 92-95; Lerner, 'Eshet Hayil', 265f n4-5.

[178] E.g. ed Visotzky 3 l. 23 (= EcclR 7,23); 45 l. 41; 67 l. 19 (= Midrash of the Ten Martyrs, Recension 3); 77 l. 8f (= bBB 10a) 107 l. 41 (= PesRK 6,2); 113 l. 43 (= bBB 10a; PesRK 2.5); 140 l. 52; 160 l. 36; 162 l. 56; 170 l. 21; 180 l. 3 (= NumR 13,3); 182 l. 18; 185 l. 34; 186 l. 50; 187 l. 59.

[179] 257-260 (not included in the Table of Contents, 5). An additional lengthy addition deriving from the opening section of Tanh (Bereshit 1) has been interpolated just before this parasha, 235-239, obviously for the same reason.

[180] Mandel, *Lamentations Rabbati* 1, 59f.

[181] Lerner, 'Studies', 45-48 and Appendix 2, par. 5. Note also the composition of ms Roma-Angelica 61: Tanh Gen and Exod; NumR and DeutR (Spanish version). Since this ms is relatively late (15th century), it is logical to assume that such an unusual combination is a conflation of the remains of two midrashic collections: Midrash Tanhuma and Midrash Rabba. Cf also Mack, *Prolegomena*, 253.

Midrash Rabba: Pentateuch

Genesis Rabba and Leviticus Rabba represent the original core and basic works of the Midrash Rabba collection to the Pentateuch. This conclusion is evinced by ms London BL 340 (Add. 27,169), which contains early copies of both works and appears to have been copied from a pre-1000 CE *Vorlage*.[182] These two Midrashim, together with the printed 'Ashkenazic' version of Deuteronomy Rabba are quite prominent in Yalkut Shimoni, a compendium most likely dating from the middle of the thirteenth century (see above). The author-compiler of this Yalkut does not seem to have had any knowledge whatsoever of Exodus Rabba and Numbers Rabba. The earliest evidence for the inclusion of Numbers Rabba in the Midrash Rabba corpus dates from the latter half of the thirteenth century.[183] No such manuscript evidence is available for Exodus Rabba although citations from this work under that name by Spanish authors could possibly indicate that Exodus Rabba was already recognized as part of the 'Rabba' collection as early as the first half of the thirteenth century.[184]

All extant complete manuscripts of the Midrash Rabba collection are of North African and Spanish provenance[185] and date no earlier than the latter half of the fifteenth century.[186] Consequently, they contain the Spanish version of Deuternomy Rabba and it is of course logical to assume that Ashkenazic copies of this collection contained the Ashkenazic or 'printed' version, which is extant in ms Parma 1240 and the *editio princeps*.

In essence, from a pure literary standpoint, Deuteronomy Rabba, wherein halakhic questions and answers precede each pericope, is intrinsically part of the Tanhuma – Yelammedenu tradition,[187] but probably due to its length, this Midrash has, nevertheless, been appended to the Midrash Rabba collection.

Midrash Rabba: Five Scrolls

The collection of 'Midrash Rabba' to the Five Scrolls is a relatively late development. It should, be stressed that the only member of this midrashic collection to bear the indigenous title 'Rabba' is Midrash Lamentations Rabba and that this work too is ordinarily termed: Midrash Ekha Rabbati (not Rabba), while most of the other works are ordinarily identified by medieval rabbis

---

[182] Margulies, 'Mavo', XXXIV.

[183] This is quite evident from the Commentary of R. Isaac b. Yedaia to Midrash Rabba, *vid.* Saperstein, *Decoding*, 22; Mack, *Prolegomena*, 287-290. Cf above at n199.

[184] Shinan, *Shemot Rabba*, Introduction, 22.

[185] *Ib.* 24-26.

[186] Concerning the supposed thirteenth century origin of the fragmentary remains of ms Jerusalem 8° 554 (Milikowsky, 'Vayyiqra Rabba Chapter 28', 22 n16) see now idem, 'Vayyiqra Rabba Chapter 30', 272 n15.

[187] Zunz-Albeck, *Derashot*, 122f; Bregman, 'Edei Nusah', 51-52; idem, *Tanhuma-Yelammedenu*, 49f.

employing such generic titles as: Midrash Ruth, Midrash Esther (Ahasuerus) *et al.* It should also be noted that the mid-thirteenth century Yalkut Shimoni obviously did not possess a copy of Esther Rabba, utilized Ecclesiastes Zutta instead of Eccliastes Rabba, and did not possess an independent copy of Canticles Rabba, which circulated in medieval Ashkenaz as part of Pesikta Rabbati (see above). Ms Oxford 164, written in 1513, just a short while before the editio princeps (1514?),[188] actually represents the earliest manuscript evidence for the complete collection of Midrashim to the Five Scrolls.

It is interesting to note that in the first two printed editions, the original 'non-Rabba' appellations for these Midrashim prevail and, on the title page, the collection itself is simply dubbed: 'Midrash hamesh Megillot'. Only with the Venice printings of 1545 and 1566, which incorporated the two major midrashic collections – to the Pentateuch and to the Five Scrolls – into a single printing, was the latter collection of Midrashim identified (on the title page only), as belonging to the collection of 'Rabbot' (מדרש חמש מגלות מהרבות). Subsequent printings applied the Rabba title to each midrashic works of this collection.

Midrash Zuta

S. Buber published an additional collection of Midrashim of minor proportions to the Five Scrolls (excluding Esther) according to ms Parma 541, which dates from the thirteenth century, and named it Midrash Zuta. Here too, the Midrash to Lamentations is the only work to bear this title indigenously, as this Midrash is ordinarily referred to by medieval authors quoting from it as 'Ekha Zuti' (not Zuta).[189] Nevertheless, the title chosen by Buber seems to be most appropriate since these midrashic works are indeed much shorter than those included in the more quantitative Midrash Rabba collection. On the surface, it appears that the Zuta collection to the Five Scrolls preceded the Rabba set.[190]

The lack of a short midrashic composition to the Scroll of Esther in the Parma manuscript of minor Midrashim to the Five Scrolls supposedly presents somewhat of a problem as to the integrity of such a collection. Even so, it may be assumed that one of the numerous midrashic works to Esther – perhaps the relatively popular Midrash Abba Guryon (see below) – originally formed part

---

[188] Lerner, 'Editio princeps', 293f.

[189] Lerner, *Perush kadum*, Introduction, 46 n34-36. The reading זוטא cited by Buber, Introduction, XVII, par. 14 is a correction, cf Lerner, *ib.*; Horowitz, *Bet Eked*, 29; Maimon (Fishman), 'Sefer Mafteah', V and passim. Note 'Shir ha-Shirim Zuta' in a book-list from the Geniza (Allony, *Library*, 401 l. 8), which most likely alludes to CantZ (see notes *ib.*).

[190] The longest work of the Zuta collection is the incomplete EcclZ (cf above, 'Incomplete Midrashim?'), which is a far cry from the proportions of the full-fledged EcclR.

of the Midrash Zuta collection, although there is no extant evidence to support this view.[191]

Midrash Tanhuma

The earliest manuscript collection of Midrashim to the Pentateuch bearing the title 'Tanhuma' seems to be ms Rome-Vatican 34, which contains a copy of Tanhuma Buber, named after its editor, the indefatigable S. Buber.[192] This version represents an alternate collection of homilies stemming from 'Tanhuma' literature, which is typified by the ordinary printed edition for which far more many manuscripts have remained extant. In the version published by Buber, the Midrash to Genesis and Exodus is on the main much different from the printed version and actually represents an almost completely different recension of Midrash Tanhuma to the first two books of the Pentateuch.[193] This is not surprising owing to the fact that an alternate parallel collection of the Tanhuma family, known as Midrash Yelammedenu, was also in circulation during the early medieval period.[194] Suffice it to say that much confusion exists between these two works.

Indeed, R. Nathan b. Yehiel's quotations from Yelammedenu Exodus-Teruma in his talmudic dictionary (the *Aruch*), are all found in Tanhuma Exodus.[195] However, this does not necessarily lead to the assumption that the manuscript published by Buber contains the original Yelammedenu.[196] On the contrary, it is evident that the editor of the *Aruch* did not possess a copy of the Yelammedenu to Exodus and so he utilized the Tanhuma which he (or the manuscript itself) obviously termed 'Yelammedenu'.

---

[191] It is interesting to note that while the compiler of YalShim (mid thirteenth century) quoted from all of the minor Midrashim to the Five Scrolls, his usage of the Rabba collection is limited to Ruth and Lam exclusively (concerning CantR see above, 'Hybridization').

[192] See the short description of Buber, Introduction, 146-148; Bregman, *Tanhuma-Yelammedenu*, 40f. Owing to its preservation of original readings and early phenomena, this ms should have served as the Vorlage for Buber's edition, *vid.* Bregman, *ib.*

[193] This is evident from the popular edition by J. Weinfeld, Eshkol Publishers Jerusalem, which includes an appendix containing all supplementary material from TanhB (Gen-Exod, 120pp.; Lev-Deut, 22pp.; the latter are overwhelmingly extrinsic additions from other mss).

[194] For a summary of the Tanhuma-Yelammedenu problem, see Herr, 'Tanhuma', 794-796; Bregman, *Tanhuma-Yelammedenua*, 8-13. Midrash Yelammedenu apparently became obsolete in Europe during the 13th century, cf Lerner, 'New Light' [2], 427. But see n168 above.

[195] This is evident from the table prepared by Buber, *Tanhuma*, Introduction, 201f; Kohut, *Aruch completum*, 9, Indices, 115-118. Note that two quotations from par. Mishpatim derive from the Mantua additions (already cited by R. Ezra of Fano in his Preface) and the same could be said for the citations from par. Pekudei.

[196] As noted above, the artistic homily to Exod 7:8-9, which has remained extant in ms T-S C 1.46, evidently derives from the original Midrash Yelammedenu to Exodus. To be sure, this unique version has very little in common with the watered-down versions found in later texts of Tanhuma literature.

Since the title 'Midrash Tanhuma' refers to a specific literary genre – i.e. homilies introduced by simple halakhic questions and answers – one would have assumed that a collection bearing this title would be more or less of a homogeneous nature. Surprisingly enough, Tanhuma Deuteronomy, which lacks the question and answer format throughout, is, nevertheless, included under this rubric. As mentioned above, the midrashic work going by the name Deuteronomy Rabba is actually a Midrash stemming from the Tanhuma family to Deut.

Ms Roma Angelica 61, which includes Tanhuma Genesis-Exodus as well as Numbers Rabba and the Spanish recension of Deuteronomy Rabba, could conceivably be adduced as evidence for same. To be sure, the Spanish recension is probably much more indigenous to the Tanhuma family than the prevalent Tanhuma Deuteronomy (see above). However, it is most unlikely that ms Angelica, which is of Italian provenance, represents an alternate collection of the Tanhuma Midrashim.[197]

PRINTED EDITIONS AND COMMENTARIES

Midrash Rabba to the Pentateuch, published in Constantinople 1512, was the first midrashic work to appear in print. This was followed very soon after by a long list of Midrashim and shorter aggadic tracts, practically all of them published in that Turkish port on the western shore of the Bosporus, in what seems to be a pre-meditated scheme and master plan for the publication of major and minor midrashic compositions, during the first quarter of the sixteenth century.[198]

The Constantinople endeavour actually set the midrashic agenda for more than the next three hundred years, and was only supplanted by the countless efforts of S. Buber, who issued copious editions of numerous unpublished Midrashim as well as new versions of some printed texts from manuscript, during the second half of the nineteenth century.

However, the early Constantinople printings of the Midrash leave a lot to be desired. The publishers did not make special efforts to obtain the best manuscripts available, nor do they seem to have been too careful with their finished product. Numerous additions which include explanations, comments and texts adopted from other midrashic works, were appended to the manuscript *Grundtext*. As a result many of the printed texts are in a sad state of affairs. Subsequent printings only heightened this situation, as new mistakes and unwarranted printers' corrections and deletions were added to the printed texts.

Some of the midrashic texts are even notoriously incomplete. A case in point is Exodus Rabba par. 39. The same could be said for the printed edition

---

[197] Cf above n181.
[198] Lerner, 'Editio Princeps', 295f.

170

of the first parasha of Numbers Rabba, which has actually deleted an unusually large segment of this midrashic work.[199]

Most of the commentaries dealing with midrashic literature are, as might be expected, devoted to the major Midrashim found in the Midrash Rabba collections. The earliest commentaries derive from the Rhineland communities of twelfth century Ashkenaz and may be attributed to the programmatic agenda of the Ashkenazic piety movement (חסידי אשכנז), which adopted a study program designed to encompass the entire realm of rabbinic literature, instead of limiting themselves to the Babylonian Talmud.[200]

Some of these Ashkenazic commentaries which deal with Genesis Rabba and Leviticus Rabba have been published, while others still remain in manuscript. Since the name of the author or authors is unknown, and since they were found to contain words and expressions in old French, they have been falsely attributed to Rashi.[201] Even though these commentaries are occasionally helpful towards an understanding of the Midrash, they are, on the whole, quite simplistic and somewhat imaginitive.[202] A recently published commentary to Lamentations Rabba authored by R. Elazar of Worms (ms Oxf-Bodl 2644) appears to be much more systematic in its approach.[203]

Spanish commentaries to the Midrash dating from the medieval period bear a sharp tendency towards purely allegorical interpretation, thus rendering them irrelevant for one who wishes to engage in the simple interpretation of a midrashic text. These include the unpublished work of the thirteenth century R. Isaac b. Yedaiah and that of the more well-known early fourteenth century philosopher, R. Yedaiah ha-Penini of Beziers, of which very little has been published.[204]

A significant contribution to the study of the Midrashim was authored by R. Meir b. Samuel b. Benveniste. In this work, Ot Emet, Saloniki 1565, which deals with all the major midrashic works published until that time, he included the comments of a predecessor, R. Yehuda Gedalya, who was most precocious in collecting exact readings from manuscripts of midrashic works, which, till this very day, serve as an important study aid towards a proper appreciation of the text and its interpretation. R. Meir also included his own short notes, which unfortunately do not contain any manuscript readings. He is also the author of a companion work, an extensive commentary to the major midrashic works, which is still in manuscript (ms Moscow-Ginzberg 112). The extremely short

---

[199] Published by E.E. Ha-Levi in his edition of Midrash Rabba, 14-22 and Mack, *Prolegomena*, 315-318.

[200] Sussman, 'Mesoret-limmud', 14.

[201] Lerner, *Perush kadum*, Introduction, 52-55.

[202] *Ib.* 24-30.

[203] *Ib.* 55. See : Sifrei ha-R"E Mi-Garmaiza, 2, section 5.

[204] See Saperstein, *Decoding*; Buber, *Erläuterungen*; Benayahu, 'R. Samuel', 457; Katzman, 'Beur ha-haggadot'.

commentary of R. Naftali Herz of Lemberg (Cracow 1569) is thus the second commentary on the entire Midrash Rabba collection to appear in print.[205]

At about that very same time, R. Samuel Yaffe Ashkenazi, a renowned sixteenth century Turkish rabbi of Ashkenazic extraction, was engaged in the compilation of an extensive commentary to the entire Midrash Rabba and Midrash Samuel. A condensed version of those parts of this voluminous commentary which appeared in print is found in some printed editions of Midrash Rabba. However, R. Samuel's commentaries to Numbers, Deuteronomy and Ecclesiastes are only available in manuscript.[206] In addition to being an effort to understand the correct reading and the simple meaning of the midrash, the approach of R. Samuel Yaffe is also of an ethical-philosophic vein.[207]

Other important commentaries composed during this period include Imre Yosher, the commentary of Don Vidal Zarfati of Fez and Matnot Kehuna of R. Issachar Katz-Berman. The latter is an extremely valuable contribution since the author often consulted manuscripts and was well aware of the difficulties involved in his quest for the simple interpretation of the midrashic text.

Additional commentaries of import are mainly those of the nineteenth century Lithuanian rabbinical scholars: (1) R. David Luria; (2) R. Samuel Straschun and (3) R. Wolf Einhorn, whose commentaries accompany the Vilna edition of Midrash Rabba.[208]

The commentaries of R. Henokh Zundel b. Joseph, Ets Yosef and Anaf Yosef, are eclectic and do not represent an original contribution. An elaborate and extensive sixteen volume commentary to the entire Midrash Rabba, entitled Tiferet Zion, by R. Yitshak Zeev Yadler, should also be noted.

Recent attempts to compose a commentary on Midrash Rabba, viz. the works of E.E. Ha-Levi; M.A. Mirkin; Ha-Midrash ha-Mevoar; as well as Canticles Rabba edited by S. Dunsky, are of a popular nature and are ordinarily based on the interpretations of previous commentators.[209]

CRITICAL EDITIONS AND SCHOLARLY COMMENTARIES

In spite of the tremendous energies invested by Buber during the course of his auspicious program to publish midrashic texts based on manuscripts, his endeavours do not bear the hallmark of scientific critical editions. Buber frequently emended the texts that he published and, in many instances, these were simply based on his own personal instinct, without even calling attention to the

---

[205] Early commentaries to Midrash Rabba are discussed by Benayahu, ib. appendix 4, 457-460.
[206] Parts of this commentary to Eccl from ms Paris 151 have been recently published by Y. Hershkowitz, 'Perush'.
[207] Benayahu, 'R. Samuel', 430-437, 444-448.
[208] Cf Fraenkel, Darkhei ha-aggada, 533-539.
[209] The commentary of Halevi, Midrash Rabba is an exception to this rule. The author has utilized manuscript materials (cf above, n199) and occasionally engages in philological enquiries into the meaning of various Greek loanwords.

fact that he had altered the readings. He was also somewhat careless in the transcriptions of the manuscripts, which were usually based on the works of various copyists employed by him.[210] In all due respect to his important contributions, Buber's work has to be redone.[211]

Genesis Rabba was the first midrashic work to be subjected to a genuine critical edition. J. Theodor initiated this monumental and impressive project in 1903, but it was to be concluded only some thirty years later by Ch. Albeck. Upon assuming the task of editor, Albeck became aware of the fact that a fatal mistake had been committed in the selection of the *Grundtext* for the edition: the superb ms Vatican 30 of Genesis Rabba had been superseded by the relatively inferior London codex. Nevertheless, he continued to utilize the London manuscript as the underlying text.[212]

The commentary appended to the Theodor-Albeck edition of Genesis Rabba is, on the one hand, overloaded by numerous quotations from parallel sources and, on the other, frequently insufficient for a proper understanding of the midrashic text. By contrast, the commentary of S. Lieberman to his edition of the Spanish version of Deuteronomy Rabba is quite adequate, although there is no critical apparatus, due to the conditions prevailing at the time (World War II).

The middle of the twentieth century witnessed important editions of Leviticus Rabba (M. Margulies) and Pesikta de-Rav Kahana (B. Mandelbaum), which also included variants from a number of Geniza fragments and a full transcription of the then-known fragments (Leviticus Rabba). A. Shinan has contributed an edition of Exodus Rabba I. (par. 1-14; par. 15ff., in progress), while B.L. Visotzky's critical edition of Midrash Proverbs, which contains an unusual amount of variants, unfortunately does not include the detailed 'Introduction' from his doctorate.

Doctoral dissertations during the past four decades have produced critical editions of Ruth Rabba (M.B. Lerner); Ecclesiastes Rabba par. 1-4 (M. Hirshman); par. 5-7 (R. Kipperwasser) and Lamentations Rabba par. 3 (P. Mandel). Projects are also underway for critical editions of the remaining Midrashim to the Five Scrolls; Esther Rabba (J. Tabory, A. Atzmon, see below) and Canticles Rabba (H. & R. Steller; L. Girón).[213] Among the minor Midrashim, one may note the synoptic edition of Ecclesiastes Zutta (R. Kipperwasser) and the planned edition of Ruth Zuta (M.B. Lerner). Other critical editions nearing completion include: Midrash Samuel (T. Lifshitz) and Aggadat Bereshit (M. Nehorai). Hopefully, the next decade will witness the successful completion and publication of all these projects and thus provide full

---

[210] See the critique of Schechter, 'Midrasch Suta', 181; Elboim, *Aba Gurion*, 17f.

[211] Lieberman, *Studies*, 45; Visotsky, 'Critical Editions', 155f.

[212] Albeck, 'Einleitung', 107f; Rosenthal, 'Leshonot sofrim'; Kutscher, *Studies*, 11-41. Theodor apparently arrived at this conclusion shortly before his death, see Barth, *Analysis*, 3-7.

[213] See Steller – Steller, 'Preliminary Remarks'; Girón, 'Preliminary Description'.

access to all the testimonia of the above-mentioned classical Midrashim, as well as a full understanding of their text, based on scientific standards.

The most recent developments in the field evince the preparation of synoptic editions of midrashic texts. Rivka Ulmer has issued a 'transcriptive' edition of Pesikta Rabbati by presenting the manuscripts in parallel columns.[214] The preparation of linear synoptic editions of Genesis Rabba and Leviticus Rabba has been undertaken by Ch. Milikowsky.[215]

In spite of the fact that such editions greatly facilitate the consultation of the various manuscripts, their feasibility is highly questioned. Ulmer's edition of Pesikta Rabbati encompasses some 1,300 pages in three volumes. As far as the publication of linear synoptic editions is concerned, there does not seem to be a single organization or publisher in the trade who would be willing to underwrite or undertake such projects, even with the assistance of generous subvention. In all probability, the retrieval of material from projects of this type will have to be limited to the realm of electronic software.[216]

AGENDA FOR THE FUTURE AND FURTHER READING

As intimated above, critical editions of all the classical works of midrashic literature have long been overdue. The preparation of such editions, based on all available manuscript material, is thus a *desideratum* which should be granted immediate encouragement and support from all institutional bodies.

Attention should also be focused on the smaller works of midrashic and aggadic literature, which greatly outnumber the classical texts. While most of this material has been published in the collections of A. Jellinek, H.M. Horowitz and S.A. Wertheimer, the uncovering of new manuscripts and new perspectives is a reminder that much remains to be done in an organized, systematic fashion.[217] Undoubtedly, the study of those minor midrashic works, which contain numerous alternate versions treating with a specific common theme, would be greatly enhanced by the 'departmental' approach described in this chapter.

The recent publications of I. Deshe Ha-Levi (*Yalkut midrashim* 1-3), are an attempt to encompass all parallel versions of specific minor Midrashim, including material from manuscript. However, the author lacks the necessary scholarly training for such an endeavour and so in spite of the progress made in collecting various versions and his significant commentary and notes, his

---

[214] See the critique of Milikowsky, 'Editing'.

[215] Note also the above-mentioned synoptic edition of Kipperwasser to EcclZ and several parashiyyot of EcclR as well as the unpublished synoptic edition of Abba Gurion (B. Elboim) and Pirkei de-R. Eliezer (E. Treitel).

[216] Milikowsky's edition of LevR is currently available on the internet: http://www.biu.ac.il/JS/midrash/VR.

[217] A recent step in this direction is Kadari, 'Teshuvat Yona Ha-Navi'.

presentation and analyses of the texts may not be considered definitive by any standard.

Another area that has been completely neglected in the study of the Aggadic Midrashim is the reconstruction of the long-lost works of this literature (see below). In truth, we do not really know how many works of this type are involved and what their scope was. The publication of sporadic individual finds from the Geniza has only heightened the disparity and confusion in this field. It is now high time to undertake a detailed survey of the non-extant works, their physical remains and quotations found in medieval literature, as well as their relationship – if any – to existing works. Only after an exhausting search for all available material will it be possible to engage in the systematic reconstruction of these works.

Finally, it is important to stress the need for a completely new approach to the study of midrashic literature. Various Midrashim dealing with the same biblical book or theme supposedly have very much in common and deserve to be treated together. We have thus defined such treatment as 'departmental analysis'. This is all the more important for the lost works and unidentified fragments of this literature, whose provenance and origin could best be determined against their general and specific common background.

P. Schäfer has shown the validity for such an approach in his synoptic editions of Hekhalot literature and the Midrash devoted to the 'Ten Martyrs' (מדרש עשרה הרוגי מלכות), although he did not attempt to delineate the original works and their merits. Such an approach would also greatly enhance the proper appreciation of such homogeneous midrashic genres as the numerous compositions to the Decalogue (מדרש עשרת הדברות)[218] and the so-far untold number of midrashic works relating to the Scroll of Esther. The accompanying sub-chapter represents an attempt to demonstrate this novel departmental approach in relation to the latter theme.

Further Reading. Entries devoted to most of the midrashic works dealt with above are available in the *Encyclopaedia Judaica*, see appropriate individual titles in the Index. An impressive survey of the various Midrashim including pertinent scholarly research (until 1995) is provided by Strack-Stemberger, 233-359. Note, however, that the editor was completely unaware of Lamentations Zuta and Mishnat R. Eliezer, and also erred in his classification of Midrash Samuel (see above n84). Important methodology for the study and dating of the classical Midrashim is found in the introductions of Albeck, Margulies and Lerner to their editions of Midrash Rabba texts.

Definitive studies devoted to various individual works of midrashic literature (e.g. Sokoloff, *Geniza Fragments of Genesis Rabba*; Mandel, *Midrash Lamentations Rabbati*; Treitel, 'Edei ha-nusah') contain detailed information

---

[218] Cf Lerner, 'Al ha-Midrashim', 217f, 228-236; idem, 'Collected Exempla', 869-891; Shapira, *Midrash*.

concerning available manuscript sources for each individual Midrash, while Bregman, *Tanhuma-Yelammedenu Literature* provides an excellent survey of the literary traditions of the ramified Tanhuma family. The present writer is currently engaged in the preparation of a concise survey of the major manuscripts relating to the midrashic works dealt with herein.

A special issue of *Te'uda* is devoted to basic studies in many of the midrashic works dealt with above, see Friedman – Lerner, *Studies*.

The merits of the synoptic presentation of manuscripts has been ably demonstrated by Milikowsky in a series of articles: 'Editing'; 'Vayyiqra Rabba'; 'Vayyiqra Rabba Chapter 28'; 'Vayyiqra Rabba Chapter 30'; 'Original Text'.

II. A Sample: Midrashim to the Scroll of Esther

The biblical story of Mordechai, Esther, Haman and King Ahasuerus is the subject of an unusually prolific output of midrashic compositions. This influx is most likely due to the practice of holding public discourses dealing with the exposition of the Esther Scroll and the miraculous salvation of the Jewish people portrayed therein, as part of the celebration of the Purim holiday,[219] especially if the 14th of Adar fell on the Sabbath.[220]

A characteristic feature of most of the midrashic expositions of the Book of Esther is the inclusion of what may be termed 'anti-Semitic' outbursts and diatribes against Jewish religion and custom. The midrashic authors portrayed the anti-Jewish sedition of Haman alluded to in Esth 3:8 as viscious references to Sabbath and holiday observance, the dietary laws, separation from the Gentiles *et al.*, much in the spirit of the Histories of Tacitus.[221] In the 'Letter of Haman', frequently found in the Midrashim to Esth 3:9-14,[222] the whole gamut of biblical history was deliberately distorted in order to present the Jewish people as the symbol of cruelty and exploitation of the weak. Jewish leaders, especially Moses, were portrayed as sorcerers and wicked manipulators who engaged in various sorts of ugly acts in all their dealings with non-Jews.

---

[219] See R. Nissim Gerondi to Alfasi, Megilla 4. The exegesis of the Scroll of Esther is specifically mentioned in yMeg 1:1, 70a.

[220] Such a possibility existed during the talmudic era, cf mMeg 1:1; bMeg 4a; Maimonides, Hil. Meg. 1:13 and Lehem Mishne *ib*. Horowitz, *Sammlung*, 48 suggests that Purim discourses were also held on the sabbath (Zakhor) preceding the Purim holiday. This notion is not far-fetched; Sofrim 14:16, 269-270 records the custom of dividing the reading of the Scroll of Esther (1-5; 6-10), between the first two Saturday nights of Adar.

[221] Stern, *Greek and Latin Authors* 2, 25-27; 37-43.

[222] E.g. EsthR 7:12-13; PA II 3:8, 68; PA I (2) 3:12, 47 and cf below, 'Overview', list of topoi, see p225, no. 5. See the thorough treatment of Herr, 'Anti-Semitism', 149 ff, esp 158 top. Note also the diatribe against the removal of the unleavened bread before Passover appended by Buber to PA II 3:8, 68 according to YalShim 1054:19 and compare with Tg Sheni 3:8, 47.

Owing to the large number of works, both in print and in manuscript, that deal with the midrashic exegesis of Esther, it appeared necessary to divide the material into the following categories: 1. Midrashim; 2. homilies; 3. collections; 4. related texts; each of these would ordinarily be subdivided into 'complete works' and, 'fragmentary and partial works'. The ensuing discussion will concentrate on the first category only, discussing 'Complete Midrashim to Esther' and 'Fragmentary and Partial Esther Midrashim'. A comprehensive list of midrashic works on Esther is provided at the end of the chapter (henceforth referred to as 'List, no. 1', etc.) while bibliographies are offered *en suite*.

COMPLETE MIDRASHIM TO ESTHER

1. Midrash Esther Rabba (= EsthR)

Name. The exact name of this midrash is most uncertain. In ms Oxford, the *editio princeps* and in the citations in Yalkut ha-Mekhiri, it is titled 'Midrash Ahashverosh', a name apparently deriving from the opening verse of Esther.[223] Alternative titles include numerous variations: 'Midrash Megilla' (ms Vienna and R. Josef Bonfils, 1, 161); 'Midrash Esther' (ms Vatican) or simply 'Megillat Esther' (ms Cambridge). The titles adduced by early rabbinic authorities such as 'Haggada de-Megilla', 'Haggada shel Megillat Esther' and 'Megillat Esther Rabbati' are most likely indicative of the Ancient Midrash to Esther.[224]

In any event, the present title, Esther Rabba, is unknown in the early sources and most likely derives from the inclusion of this work as part of the Midrash Rabba corpus in the printings subsequent to the edition of Venice 1545. Likewise, the epithet 'Midrash Rabbati de-Ahashverosh' was apparently coined by R. Shlomo Alkabez in his commentary to Esther, Menot ha-Levi.[225]

Internal Division. EsthR is the largest extant midrash to the Scroll of Esther. In its present form, it is divided into ten *parashiyyot* (= sections) corresponding (in number only) to the ten chapters of the biblical book. However, this is a relatively late development initiated by the printers of the Warsaw 1867 edition of Midrash Rabba which contains the commentaries of R. Hanokh Zundel of Bialystock (*Ets Yosef; Anaf Yosef*).[226]

---

[223] See Tabory, 'Division', 191; Lerner, 'Editio Princeps', 292 par. 9; 300 n30. Note also the headings in YalShim *ed princ*. The title 'Aggadat Ahashverosh', which is obviously an earlier tradition (cf Lerner, 'The Aggadic *Midrashim*', 1055-1056), is found in the colophon of ms Vat 291 (Tabory *ib.*).

[224] See below, 'The Ancient Midrash to Esther', esp p204 n358.

[225] Fraenkel, 'Notizen'; Buber, *Sifrei de-Aggadeta*, Preface, VI-VIII n12. Zunz-Albeck, *Derashot*, 145; 441 n38 was misled by this epithet, *vid*. Buber, *ib.* VII (noted by Albeck *ib.*). Cf however, the Novellae of Nahmanides to bAZ 33b and see below n359. Note well that the medieval rabbis are most likely referring to the Ancient Midrash (see above) and not to EsthR, cf below n367.

[226] Tabory, 'Division', 192. Even though R. Hanokh Zundel made certain innovations in the format and the internal division of the Midrash, the subdivision of the chapters is purely the work of the

As a matter of fact, the evidence corroborated by all the manuscripts and by the *editio princeps* attests to a division of six sections (parashiyyot). In the 1867 edition and in most of those following, the extremely lengthy sixth parasha was simply divided into five separate units, the last four having been based on the opening verses of Esther 3-6.

The original sixfold division apparently reflects the Massoretic piskaot (sectional divisions) of the biblical book of Esther, with the exception of section two (Esth 1:4), whose opening passage was mistakenly understood as a proem and so copyists viewed it as the beginning of a new section.[227]

The internal division of the parashiyyot of EsthR into individual paragraphs first appeared in the 1829 edition of R. Hanokh Zundel and was adopted by the publishers of the popular Vilna edition of Midrash Rabba (1878; 1887 and following).[228] A comparison of both printings also enables a logical explanation for the lack of an internal division in the unusually lengthy section of 7:13-18.[229]

Proems. Like all classical Midrashim, EsthR is replete with proems. The relatively large number of proems to Esther is readily understandable in the light of the importance attached to the reading of this scroll in the synagogue service, as stressed by J. Fraenkel.[230]

The opening verse is marked by seven proems, although the petiha of Samuel (Proem 4) is most likely an interpolation based on bMeg 11a, since it lacks the stereotypic refrain bemoaning the reign of King Ahasuerus, which is found in all the other proems.[231] A rather lengthy homily dealing with the first two words of the scroll 'and it came to pass in the days' (...ויהי בימי) could possibly represent an original proem in inverted from.[232] Additional proems, which are instrumental for the division into parashiyyot, not all of them complying with

---

publisher or his proofreader, cf the *ed. princ.* of Anaf Yosef and Ets Yosef to EsthR (Vilna & Grodno 1829) and R. Hanokh Zundel's statement published at the head of the Warsaw 1867 edition.

[227] Tabory *ib*. 198-203.

[228] Note that another popular edition, in a much smaller format (Warsaw 1874; Lublin 1898) contains no internal division whatsoever.

[229] It is apparent that in the first half of parasha 7, the Vilna publisher improved upon the division of his Warsaw 1867 predecessor (cf Tabory, 'Division', 194), which resulted in a discrepancy of four numbers (7:14-17). However, beginning with paragraph 18, which is practically indistinguishable (13a l. 14), the numeration of the Vilna edition in followed until the end of the parasha. The absence of no. 9 in the internal division of parasha 1 (3d) can also be corrected by the Warsaw 1867 printing (l. 5 from the end, preceding: R. Levi).

[230] Fraenkel, *Darkhei ha-Aggada*, 447; 680 n122.

[231] Note that ms Cambridge 495, fol. 75a and ms Firkowitz II A 272 contain the homily of R. Levi (= bBB 88b-89a) immediately following the proem of Shmuel. However, this addition should not be explained as an effort to complete this proem but rather as a marginal addition to the homily of Rav (Proems 1-3) on Deut 28:68, which was misplaced by the copyist.

[232] Cf Lerner, *Book of Ruth* 1, 48-50. Note that in mss Vat 96 and 290:11 the first part of this homily actually serves as an introductory proem.

accepted terminology and structure – especially those from section six onwards – are found preceding Esth 1:9 (= EsthR 3:1-8);[233] 2:1 (= 5:1);[234] 2:5 (=
6:1); 3:1 (= 7:1-3); 3:2 (= 7:6)[235] and at the conclusion of the midrash (=
10:15).[236] Altogether, EsthR contains nineteen proems.[237]

Problems of Composition. As mentioned above, EsthR is by far and large the
most voluminous and the most comprehensive of the extant Midrashim to
Esther. Chapters one and three of the biblical book are treated in most excessive detail, while altogether, roughly more then half of the 160 or so verses of
the Book of Esther are dealt with or mentioned. However, the sequence of the
authentic Midrash seems to terminate at EsthR 8:5, 13d (= Esth 4:7), which
barely represents 40% of the biblical text.

Scholars have long noticed the irregular composition of Esther Rabba;
parashiyyot 1-5,[238] which include approximately 50% of the Midrash, deal
exclusively with no more then 26 verses – less then 20%! – of the biblical
book (Esth 1:1-2:4). While these are written in the style of classical exegetical
midrash and relate to almost each and every verse of the above sections, parashiyyot 6-10, which supposedly cover the remaining 80% plus of the biblical
text, are written mainly in the style of historical – aggadic – imaginative discourse. In these parashiyyot, the actual exegetical elaboration of the biblical
text is most sporadic, especially, from Esth 4:8 ff.

Zunz was the first to call attention to some very late elements in the last
section of EsthR,[239] especially to several passages which appear to have been
copied verbatim from the pseudo-historical chronicle, Yosippon,[240] a work
dating from 953 CE.[241] However, not until the updated version of Zunz's *Vorträge* by Albeck, was EsthR treated to a serious scientific inquiry. Albeck's
searching analysis of this midrash led him to the novel conclusion that EsthR is
actually a fusion of an earlier and a later Midrash, the latter half containing the
additions alluded to by Zunz.

---

[233] Note well that parasha 3 is preceded by no less than six proems.

[234] Since this proem does not deal directly with Esth 2:1, one may assume that it has been borrowed
from LevR 12:1 p243-256.

[235] This proem gives the impression of being a 'circular proem', see below n393. Among the three
proems preceding parasha 7, proem 2, whose opening formula is unusual, is definitely a later
addition, see below, 'Midrash Panim Aherot'. Cf also Tabory, 'Proems', 10.

[236] Fully discussed below, section 'The Finale'.

[237] *Pace* Bacher, *Proömien*, 55, 60, 72, 73, 78, 86, 87, 113 (altogether 16 proems); Herr, 'Esther
Rabbah', 915.

[238] Previous research on the subject evolves around sections 1-6. For various reasons, we have
eliminated parasha 6 from the present discussion.

[239] Zunz, *Vorträge*, 276 and notes d-e (= *Derashot*, 402 n13-14).

[240] Mordechai's dream (8:5) and prayer (8:7); Esther's prayer (8:7) and her unannounced appearance
before King Ahasuerus (9:1), cf ed Flusser, 49-53, who failed to note the citations in EsthR. Note
also the Geniza fragments of Yossippon in TS 10K 16.20 2v and TS C 2.206, cf Hopkins, *Miscellany*, 109.

[241] Ed Flusser vol 2 (Introduction), 83-84. This revelation was, of course, unknown to Zunz.

179

Albeck set the general perimeter of the early Midrash at the end of section 6, and that of the later Midrash at sections 7-10. In addition, his keen eyes carefully delineated the exact contents of the early Midrash, which in his estimation also included small segments of sections 7-10. Albeck used an elimination process whereby he deleted all sections contiguous with Pirkei de-R. Eliezer, a latter-day midrashic composition,[242] as well as those exhibiting the verbose narrative-historical style of later generations.[243] In his estimation, most of the original Midrash from Esth 3:1 ff. was discarded for one reason or other and its early Amoraic exegetical explanations were actually replaced by a completely different type of midrashic exposition, reflecting the tastes of later generations, with the new material greatly overwhelming the old. Albeck also noted the fact that the citations of early rabbinic authorities in the Middle Ages quoting from EsthR and relating to sections 1-6 are found in the text of this Midrash, whereas those citation dealing with verses in parashiyyot 7-10 are not found in the extant version.[244] He tried to bolster his conclusion by drawing upon the parallel material in Midrash Abba Gurion which, according to his view, proves that this Midrash, which made very little use of material found in EsthR 1-6, copied from a Midrash to Esther, which resembled the extant EsthR to sections 7-10.[245]

In his succinct and painstaking summary of the views of Albeck on the distinction between sections 1-6 and 7-10, Herr differentiated between two separate Midrashim: 'Esther Rabba 1' and 'Esther Rabba 2'.[246] However, Herr did not put sufficient emphasis on the fact that EsthR 2, is, in reality, a continuation of EsthR 1 and contains numerous selections from the early Midrash. As a result, later scholars who relied on this summary were actually misled.[247]

Ignorance of Albeck's research has thus had a fatal result on the scholarly inquiry into EsthR. J. Neusner, who has published no less than four different studies on the classical Midrashim to the five Scrolls,[248] knows only of an 'Esther Rabbah I' containing *six* sections. Nowheres in these literary enquiries does he attempt to delineate the difference or draw a distinction between the two components of EsthR. Suffice it to say that by relying on secondary literature[249] Neusner has actually distorted the true nature of EsthR 1 as charted by Albeck.

---

[242] *Vid.* Zunz-Albeck, *Derashot*, 134-140.

[243] *Ib.* 405 n35. This note demands a most careful reading, see below.

[244] However, this is not so in the case of Rav Nissim Gaon who quotes a homily from EsthR 7:10 in his Megillat Setarim, see below, 'The Ancient Midrash to Esther', n358.

[245] This assertion has proved incorrect, cf below, 'Midrash Abba Gurion'.

[246] Herr, 'Esther Rabba', 916.

[247] E.g., Stemberger, *Introduction*, 319; Tabory, 'Division', 194 and English summary, XIX; idem, 'Esther Rabbah', 236.

[248] Neusner, *Esther Rabbah*; idem, *Midrashic Compilations*; idem, *Judaism Behind the Texts*; idem, *Components*.

[249] *Cf* Neusner, *Esther Rabbah*, Preface, XI-XII; idem, *Judaism Behind the Texts*, 180 n3.

J. Tabory[250] has recently adduced statistics – the ratio between the scope and length of the midrashic text to that of the biblical text – in order to justify Albeck's theory concerning the division of Midrash EsthR into two separate Midrashim. However, this theory is entirely dependent on the conclusions of Albeck, which are now in need of revision.

Re-Evaluating the Components. The division of EsthR proposed by Albeck marks an important step in the scholarly enquiry of this Midrash, but is, nevertheless, in need of a more sophisticated approach. This new methodology, which has greatly profited from a survey of all pertinent midrashic material to the Scroll of Esther, upholds many of the conclusions of Albeck[251] and actually represents a modification of his theory.

Albeck's division of EsthR into two different entities is basically correct, with one major reservation: instead of an Early (sections 1-6) and a Late Midrash (sections 7-10), it would be more advisable to speak of: 1. an Ancient Midrash (sections 1-5 and very limited selections from sections 6-10), and 2. Additions to the Ancient Midrash (most of the material in sections 6-10). Note that this modified division is actually supported by the traditional division of EsthR into six sections. That is to say that the various additions already commence with the sixth section and not with the seventh, as proposed by Albeck.

Another important observation in this sphere is the intensive exegesis, or at least systematic mention, of each and every biblical verse in the first five parashiyyot of EsthR, whereas, beginning with parasha 6, numerous omissions may be noted.[252]

One may thus assume that the material indigenous to section 6 (= 6-10) was originally more or less within the confines and the natural contours of the previous sections, but due to the innumerable lengthy additions, this section more than tripled itself. In the ensuing discussion, an attempt will be made to distinguish between these two components of EsthR and to map out their contents, as clearly as possible.

The Ancient Midrash

Proems: most of the introductory proems: 1-3; 5-11 (?).[253]
Sections 1-5:   almost all the material contained in these pericopes.[254]

---

[250] 'Division', 192-196.

[251] Although he was not aware of it at the time, Albeck's theory is actually confirmed by the example he cited from MidrSam (see *Derashot*, 406f n37). The homily to Esth 8:15 in MidrSam 27:4, 128 is found verbatim in the 'Midrash Yerushalmi' (= Ancient Midrash) to Megillat Esther, a Geniza fragment published by Wertheimer already in 1903, which escaped the attention of Albeck, cf below, 'The Ancient Midrash to Esther', near n373.

[252] There is no midrash to Esth 2:8-10; 13-14; 18-19; 22, *pace* Herr, 'Esther Rabbah', 915; Stemberger, *Introduction*, 318.

[253] Note, however, that the first folio of Yalkut Esther from the Geniza (below, List, no. 25) contains only Proems 5, 10 and 11 (first half), whereas AbGur 1-2 is limited to Proems 9 (second half) and 10.

Section 6:   paragraphs 1; 2; 4-5; 7-14.
Section 7:   paragraphs 4; 7-10; 12; 20-25.
Section 8:   paragraphs 1-5 (till the end of 13d); 6; 7, l. 6.
Section 9:   paragraphs 2, ll. 43-45 (?), 14b end - 14c beg.; 4.
Section 10:   paragraphs 1, ll. 3-5; 2, ll. 2-3;[255] 4; 5; 9, ll. 7-9;[256] 13-22;
                10, ll. 4-5; 11, ll. 1-5; 13-15.

The Midrash delineated as a result of this listing is composed in the style of the ancient Palestinian Midrashim to the Pentateuch (GenR and LevR). It contains proems composed in the style of the classical petiha, which usually conclude with the first verse of the biblical pericope as well as exegetical comments, most of them brief and to the point, to the words and phrases of the biblical text. The teachings of the Babylonian rabbis are introduced by the generic cognomen רבנן דתמן, 'our Masters from over there',[257] a usage common to the Yerushalmi[258] and the earliest Aggadic Midrashim.[259]

Although written mainly in Hebrew, the contents of EsthR have strong Aramaic leanings, especially as far as short explanations and various expressions, terminology and exempla are concerned.

It is interesting to note that the unusual comprehensive treatment accorded the Esther Scroll in the first five sections supposedly relates solely to verses dealing with what might be termed as of 'non-Jewish' content: Ahasuerus; his court; his banquets; the Vashti incident et al. However, the Jewish element is not at all played down in these sections, and the rabbis found ample opportunities to manipulate numerous Jewish motifs into this seemingly secular description: Ahasuerus and the rebuilding of the Holy Temple (1:1); the allegorical significance of the six steps to the throne of Solomon; the throne in captivity (1:12); 'the last day as the first day' (2:3-4); Jewish participation in the feasts (2:5); the utensils of the Temple (2:11); a comparison between the Jewish feasts and the obscenities of the Persian feasts (3:14); the Jewish 'wise men' (4:1); the sacrificial nature of the 'seven princes' who 'saw the king's face'

---

[254] There are, of course, possibilities of later additions, e.g., 1:16 which might possibly derive from ARN b 48 end (132), vid. Epstein, Mavo, 50; note, however, Kister, Avot de-Rabbi Nathan, 139 n115. Concerning the three lines at the beginning of parasha 2, see Tabory, 'Division', 198ff.

[255] Cf, however, EcclR. 5:2, 14b (bot.).

[256] This is the only halakhic item dealing with Purim in EsthR, or, for that matter, in all the other Midrashim, aside from the Ancient Midrash, cf below n372. Note that the invective against Zeresh, which is missing from the extant version of yMeg 3, 74b, is preserved in EsthR. However, such an invective was present in the Yerushalmi texts of the medieval period, cf Ratner, Ahawath Zion, Megilla, 77.

[257] 1:2; 8:3, 4 (in opposition to the teachings of local Palestinian rabbis: רבנן דהכא), vid. Bacher, Rabbanan, 92 n2-3; 9:2, 14b end. Cf Also תמן אמרין, which obviously alludes to a Babylonian tradition: 8:7; 10:4, l. 13, vid. Buber, Sifrei de-Aggadeta, Preface, III n5.

[258] Bacher, Tradition, 502f.

[259] E.g., GenR 37,3 (p346); 39,13 (p378); 49,2 (p501) [= 64,4, p704]; 56,11 (p611); 98,3 (p1252). LevR: 23,11 (p542, with רבנן דהכא); LamR: 3:12 (p127); 3:42 (p137, idem).

(4:2-3); Persian law and Jewish law (4:6); Vashti and the building of the Temple (5:2); Gentile-Jewish relations (5:3).

Even though, technically speaking, the Ancient Midrash actually continues until the end of EsthR,[260] as mentioned above, the systematic exegesis of Esther seemingly terminates with the exposition of Esth 4:7 in EsthR 8:4. This observation seems to closely coincide with the evidence provided by mss Oxf-Bodl 155 (= PA I(2)) and Leningrad-Antonin 302 which contain excerpts from the Ancient Midrash until Esth 4:4.[261]

The relationship of the early material in EsthR to other works of the talmudic-midrashic corpus – Bavli, Yerushalmi, Genesis Rabba,[262] et al. – demands clarification and conscientious research and cannot rely on the terse remarks of Zunz claiming that EsthR utilized the early Palestinian works.[263]

Later Additions. It is readily evident that the newly added selections found in the second half of EsthR greatly outweigh the original material of the Ancient Midrash which, for some unknown reason, has actually dwindled out. These later additions derive from a wide range of sources and it would be best to treat them in detail, according to the following summary:

(a) Extant Works

1. Yosippon: see above, n240.
2. Pirkei de-Rabbi Eliezer: 7:5; 8:7;[264] 9:2, 14c; 9: 7-11; 10:1, ll. 1-3; 5-11;[265] 10:8; 10:9, ll. 1-2; 3; 5; 6; 9-10; 12-13; 10:10 ll. 4-5; 10:12.
3. Panim Aherot II: 7:2 ll. 1:7; 7-11, 12a, l. 26; 10:5, 15a, ll. 4-6; 10:6, ll. 2-3;[266] 10:7, l. 2.
4. Bavli: 7:18, 13b, ll. 16-17; 10:2, l. 1; 10:6, l. 1;[267] 10:7, ll. 1-2.[268]
5. Midrash Tanhuma: 6:6 (= Tanh Beshalah 28);
   10-11, ll. 5-7 (= Tanh Toldot 5).

---

[260] The last exegetical comment to Esther seems to be EsthR 10:10 which relates to Esth 9:2.

[261] See below, List, nos. 4, 24.

[262] There are numerous parallels with GenR: EsthR 1:2 = GenR 37,3 (p345f); 1:8 = 58,3 (p621); 1:12, 3a = 13,12 (p121); 3:4, 6d = 65,17 (p729f); 3:14 = 36,7 (p340); 4:1 = 72,5 (p842); 5:2 = 44,5 (p428). Additional parallels to the latter part of EsthR are listed below, 'Later Additions'. Cf n270 below.

[263] Zunz, *Vorträge*, 276 (= *Derashot*, 128). Surprisingly enough, Zunz mentions LevR and not GenR, see previous note. For parallels with LevR, cf EsthR 2:2 = LevR 19,5 (p429f); 3:6 = 3,6 (p69); 5:1 = 12,1 (p243-256); 7:23 = 27,11 (p645f); 10:4-5 = 28,6 (p662-667; also: PseRK 8,3, p145); 10:9, ll. 15-21 = 28,4 (p658; also: PesRK 8,2, p140f).

[264] Albeck, *Derashot*, 405 n35 was prone to include this selection, which clearly derives from PRE (ch. 50, p188 ll. 45-53), in the Ancient Midrash. Cf, however, below p205 no. 11 (Midr Ps).

[265] Cf Gaster, *Chronicles*, chap. 83, 250 par. 7.

[266] For l. 1 cf next entry, Bavli.

[267] This explanation is also found in PA II 6:12 (p76) and in AbGur 6:12 (p41).

[268] There does not seem to be any basis for the claim advanced by Rabinovitz (*Ginzé Midrash*, 158 n27, cf *ib.* 157 n18), *viz.* that EsthR parasha 10 is a later composition and derives from the Babylonian Talmud.

(b) Non-Extant Works

6. Panim Aherot V: 6:2, ll. 1-6; 11-16; 17-20; 6:3, 10b, last line; 7:1 (?).[269]
7. A Narrative Midrash to Esther: 7:11; 7: 13-19; 9:2, ll. 1-43; 9:3.

(c) Unclear Status

8. Genesis Rabba (?): 6:3 (= 30:8, 273-275); 9:2, 14c, ll. 1-7 (= 56:1, 595; 91:7, 1129-1130); 9:3 (= 15:2, 171; 86:6, 1084); 10:3 (= 34:10, 320; 67:8, 763).[270]
9. Panim Aherot II: 7:2, ll. 8-9; 7:3.[271]

From the preceding list it is quite apparent that the editor of the extant version of EsthR sections 6-10 was, in essence, a compiler who added an unusually large quantity of midrashic material from numerous sources to the existing skeletal framework of the Ancient Midrash. However, there are instances wherein the various sources have been integrated into the warp and weave of the Midrash and a closer examination of these processes will most likely reveal additional material culled from other sources and will also enable a proper appreciation of the compiler's editorial techniques. In any event, it is important to stress that, in several instances, sections 6-10 of EsthR evince a conglomeration of variegated sources, thus forming a virtual patchwork.[272] In contrast with the Ancient Midrash which quotes the opinions of Babylonian rabbis as deriving from 'Our Masters over there',[273] the editor of the 'Additions' incorporated anonymous short excerpts from the Babylonian Talmud.

On the other hand, the major source used by the editor was, by far and large, one of the narrative Midrashim to the Esther Scroll.[274] This source provided him with massive sections of material which he adopted *en bloc*. Among the more prominent selections we may enumerate the following: (a) the lots, 7:11; (b) dealings between Ahasuerus and Haman concerning the destruction of the Jews, 7:13; (c) the letter of Haman, 7:13; (d) the evil plot of Haman and the intervention of Elijah and the Patriarchs, 7:18; (e) the advice of Zeresh, 9:2.

---

[269] This identification is uncertain. According to the version in YalShim 1053:52, this is a circular proem which is characteristic of PA V, and might have been borrowed from that source. According to Albeck, *Derashot*, 405 n35 this proem derives from the Ancient Midrash, whereas Tabory, 'Division', 194f has demonstrated its late origin.

[270] Since it is apparent that the editor of the Ancient Midrash utilized much material also found in GenR (cf *supra*, n262), it is entirely possible that the parallels in section 6-10 are also part of the Ancient Midrash and not later additions; This is indeed the opinion of Albeck *ib*. Nevertheless, the unique version of a homily to Esth 5:1 cited by R. Jacob Sikily in Yalkut Talmud Tora seemingly negates the version of GenR = EsthR 9:2, 28a ll. 1-7. Note also 6:2, ll. 7-10 which gives the impression of being a misplaced interpolation ('and his name was Mordechai' before 'a man of Judah'). See also below n361.

[271] See the opinions of Albeck *ib*. and Tabory, 'Division', 194f.

[272] See, e.g., 6:1-3; 7:1-6; 8:5-7; 9:1-3; 10:1-3; 6-12.

[273] Above near n257.

[274] Most likely, the Aggadic-Narrative Midrash, see below.

It is, of course, necessary to clarify the nature of these sources and their exact relationship to the narrative Midrashim, but this can be accomplished only, after the latter have been reconstructed. Chances are that the above material derives from the 'Aggadic-Narrative Midrash',[275] but this conclusion requires further investigation.

On the other hand, these massive selections also evince certain editorial embellishments[276] which most likely reflect upon the editorial prowess of the compiler, and these too demand a closer inquiry.

Editorial Lapses. During the course of compiling his material, the final editor of EsthR seems to have been somewhat lax, as a few apparent lapses are readily evident. In 6:3 it is stated that the explanation of the anonymous 'Rabbanan' will follow the teaching of R. Levi, yet no such explanation is presented.[277] An editorial inconsistency is also evident in the exegesis of Esth 4:4 which is repeated twice during the course of the Midrash.[278]

Some lapses are also evident in the first part of EsthR and it is logical to assume that these too are the responsibility of the final editor. Tabory has commented on the obvious absence of a statement in one of the opening proems, which is found in AbGur,[279] while M. Margulies[280] has noted an apparent deletion in 2:2. Basing himself on the text preserved in Midrash AbGur 3:1, 21, Tabory has also noted that the opinions of R. Nehemia and Rabbanan are lacking in EsthR 4:4.[281]

The Finale. The closing section of EsthR (10:12-15) represents a special feature unique with this Midrash, which is not ordinarily found in other midrashic works. This section is, in essence, a 'grand finale' incorporating several homilies designed to serve as an epilogue to EsthR

The first of these is the homily of R. Pinhas, who has elaborated upon the monarchial prowess of Mordechai and whose conclusion stresses that Mordechai was 'a man of peace and a striver for peace' (10:12). This homily has

---

[275] See below, List, no. 9.

[276] See, e.g. 7:11, 12a l. 26; 7:18, end.

[277] Cf GenR 30,8 (p275 ll. 4-10). In this homily, Mordechai is described as the 'wet nurse' of Esther, by virtue of his mammary glands. Could this be the reason for its non-inclusion in the final redaction of the midrash? On the other hand, it is possible to assume that this passage was deleted due to the activity of puritan scribes.

[278] Cf 7:3 (end), 13b and 8:3. Note that the explanation of the Babylonian rabbis (רבנן דתמן = Rav, *vid.* bMeg 15a) gives the appearance of a general consensus in the anonymous aggadic narrative, even though it is the subject of a controversy in EsthR 8:3.

[279] Tabory, 'Some Problems', 150-152.

[280] LevR 19,5 (p429f). Note that the 'missing' text is extant in Yalkut Esther from the Geniza (below, List, no. 25).

[281] See his cogent argument in Tabory, 'Proems', 18.

been borrowed verbatim from Pirkei de-R. Eliezer, where it also serves as the finale for the Esther Midrash in chapters 49-50.[282]

The ensuing homily of R. Berekhia (10:13) is designed to show that the Almighty already inscribed the redemption of Israel during the epoch of Mordechai and Esther in the verses of Lev 25:47-49. Following is an anonymous homily (10:13, 30c) which reveals that the elements of the Purim story are to be found in Exod 17:14 and Gen 49:27.

This homily is followed by the well-known exemplum wherein R. Hiyya and R. Shimon b. Halafta (10:14) compare the salvation from the evil decrees of Haman to the various phases in the appearance of the morning star (*aurora*). It is interesting to note that this exemplum actually appears in the Geniza fragment of the Ancient Midrash to Esth 8:16.[283]

The grand finale to the entire Midrash is a proem based on Ps 66:3 expressing utter excitement over the grace of Divine justice wherein 'those about to be murdered kill their killers, those about to be hanged hang their hangers' etc. (10:15). The homilist then draws up a list of positive virtues of the Almighty which were presented to mankind in abundance and these are enumerated in piyyutic style,[284] whereas the ninth[285] and final virtue is 'peace'.

It is on this positive message of 'peace' – undoubtedly the most popular and widespread slogan of the ancient rabbis which also served as the closing theme for most prayer rituals and public discourses[286] – that this homily and the Midrash *per se* are finally brought to their dramatic climax.[287]

In essence, aside from the homily of R. Pinhas which undoubtedly derives from Pirkei de-R. Eliezer, the subsequent homilies of this grand finale to EsthR give the impression of being original compositions which most likely derive from the Ancient Midrash.

Date of Composition. The Ancient Midrash which is mainly concentrated in EsthR sections 1-5 resembles the early Exegetical Midrashim – *e.g.* GenR and RuthR - and should therefore be reckoned as one of the earlier Aggadic Midrashim. Albeck[288] has demonstrated the use of this Midrash by Midrash

---

[282] A more complete version of this text is found in the editio princeps (Venice 1544), see ed Horowitz, 184. See also below n287.

[283] See below, 'The Ancient Midrash to Esther'. A list of parallels for this exemplum is furnished by Wertheimer, *Batei Midrashot* 1, 341. However, EsthR is not mentioned there.

[284] Vid. Mirsky, *Reshit ha-piyyut*, 23f.

[285] According to R. David Luria in his Commentary to EsthR, n11, this homily originally included ten virtues, and RaDa"L even attempted to suggest the missing item. However, all the manuscripts, the editio princeps as well as the citations in YalMekh (Isa 54:13, 201-202; Ps 31-35, 202; 119:84, 229 et al.) uphold the version of the printed text.

[286] LevR 9,9 (p194f) and *ib.* n3. Re. the use of שלום in synagogue inscriptions and epitaphs, *vid.* Feist, 'Shalom'.

[287] Note well that the above-mentioned homily of R. Pinhas (10:12) which serves as the conclusion of PRE ch. 50 also concludes with the message of peace.

[288] Zunz-Albeck, *Derashot*, 405f n37-38.

Samuel; Midrash Psalms (Tehillim) and Qohelet Rabba. One may thus concur with the conclusion of Herr[289] that the Ancient Midrash to Esther was composed in the Land of Israel not later than the beginning of the sixth century CE.

As to the additions, Zunz was the first scholar to note the relatively late date of EsthR, sections 6-10. However, his important comment, *viz.* 'some of the items in it (= parasha 6, *i.e.* in the original division of EsthR, see above), may possibly belong to the eleventh century', was obviously misplaced by N. Brüll, the editor of the second edition, who appended it to the discussion dealing with Ruth Rabba [sic!].[290] Zunz's conclusion is essentially correct, since the tenth century would be a bit too early for a compiler to utilize large selections from Yossipon, itself a product of the middle of that century. This would place the final redaction of the unified Midrash, known today as 'Esther Rabba', within the medieval period, possible as late as the twelfth-thirteenth centuries[291] on European soil, as indicated by the editor's use of Yosippon.

Diffusion and Influence. Owing to its late date of composition, EsthR seems to have exerted a most limited influence over Jewish literature of the medieval period. Early rabbinic authorities, such as Rashi[292] and Tosafot, do not quote from this Midrash. What is more, even the compilers of compendia to the Scroll of Esther, R. Tobias b. Eliezer (Lekah Tov) and R. Shimon ha-Darshan (Yalkut Shimoni), as well as the Yemenite Aggadat Esther, did not make use of it in their comprehensive collections of midrashic teachings. As a matter of fact, it is most difficult to pinpoint any of the early medieval rabbis who utilized EsthR in their writings.[293] The proposed late date of composition also raises serious doubts concerning the influence of EsthR over AbGur, a work that is considered in many respects to be an adaptation and shortened version of EsthR; see below Section 2 on that Midrash.

Bibliography. Midrash EsthR is extant in only one complete manuscript of relatively late vintage: ms Oxf-Bodl 164 (written: 1513). A second manuscript, ms Vatican 291:13, already consulted by Zunz in *Vorträge*, 331 n11, contain a large lacuna, from the end of parasha 3 till the first part of parasha 6, see Tabory, *Division*, 194. The whereabouts of an additional codex, ms Vienna 26,

---

[289] Herr, 'Esther Rabbah', 915.

[290] Cf Lerner, *Book of Ruth* 1, 172.

[291] Zunz's statement, *Vorträge*, 276, *viz.* 'this Midrash has been regularly quoted during the past 700 years', would seem to place its redaction during the twelfth century. However, this form of reasoning is somewhat difficult since Nahmanides, the thirteenth century rabbi whom Zunz probably had in mind, most likely quoted his material from the Ancient Midrash and not from EsthR, cf above, n225 and below near n367.

[292] *Pace* Melamed, *Bible Commentators* 1, 376, vid. S. Buber, *Sifrei de-Aggadeta*, Preface IV.

[293] This subject demands a separate study. Concerning Nahmanides, see above, n225 and n291. On Rabbenu Bahya, see below, n361. The excerpts in the homily of R. Joshua ibn Shueib, a disciple of R. Solomon ibn Adret (first half of the fourteenth century), Derashot to Tetsave, ed Metzger, 166 probably derive from the Ancient Midrash.

formerly in the possession of Abraham Epstein are unknown since WW II, see catalogue Schwarz, 12.

In addition, there are three partial manuscripts: ms Cambridge Add. 495 [SCR 235] (until the end of parasha 5); the second part of mss Vatican 96 and 290:11 [fols. 7-18] (= 6:2 – 7:24) which are actually adaptations of material from EsthR, see List, no. 22 [additional excerpts from EsthR are also found in the first part of this manuscript] and ms St. Petersburg-Firkowitz II A 272 (until 5:3), severely damaged and incorrectly bound, which is probably a Geniza fragment, cf Kahane, 'Ginzei Midrash', 60. Concerning the Manchester and the Cambridge Geniza fragments see below p202. On other Geniza fragments purportedly deriving from Est. R. see List, nos. 9 and 25, below.

Shorter excerpts are found in ms Paris 149 (Arles 1291), *vid.* Mack, *Prolegomena*, 245 n2 (= part of EsthR 3:4); ms Sassoon 756, fols. 179-180 (= 7:13, 13a-b), dating from the eighteenth century, see S.D. Sassoon, *Ohel Dawid*, 471b and ms Frankfurt am Main 211. II (= 7:13-18), dating from 1561.

Several improved readings of the Venice 1545 printing are offered by R. Meir b. Samuel Benveniste in his valuable collection of notes to the Midrashim, *Ot Emet*, 101a-103a.

The *editio princeps* of EsthR is evinced by the Constantinople printing, probably dating from 1514, cf Lerner, 'Editio Princeps', 289-294 who has shown that the Pesaro printing of 1519 is based on the Constantinople edition.

To date there is no critical edition of EsthR, although J. Tabory is currently engaged in the preparation of same. Tabory has edited selected texts of EsthR according to manuscripts and the *editio princeps* in his articles: 'Division', 198-199 (2:1) and 'Proems', 8-9 (7:1-3). Tabory's student, A. Atzmon, *Esther Rabbah II* has laid the groundwork for a critical edition of the 'Late Midrash'.

General Surveys of the Midrash have been written by the following scholars: Zunz-Albeck, *Derashot*, 128-130, 402f, 405f; Weiss, *Dor dor*, 242; Buber, *Sifra de-Aggadeta*, Preface, III n5; Herr, 'Esther Rabbah', 915-916; Tabory, 'Esther Rabbah', 236. The Palestinian origin of EsthR has been emphasized by Horowitz, *Sammlung*, 51. Tabory, 'Division', 191-203 has dealt with some basic problems concerning the internal division of the Midrash.

Scholarly research on EsthR is mainly found in additional studies by Tabory, 'Problem'; 'Words of the Wise'; 'Proems'. On the first and the last of the Introductory Proems, see Segal, 'The *Petihta*', 178-183. In his article, 'Esther Rabba', Rabinowitz offers a prosaic commentary to the latter half of parasha 6. Segal, *Babylonian Midrash*, *passim* offers numerous comments, explanations and comparisons between the talmudic Midrash in Tractate Megilla and EsthR, see his introductory remarks *ib.* 1, 22. D. Noy explains certain humorous aspects of the Midrash in *Yesodot humor*. Sperber, 'Etymological Studies', 63-65 has dealt with a loanword in 1:12, 4a, according to manuscript readings. Segal, 'Human Anger', 248 elaborates upon the theme of anger in EsthR 3:15 and in other Midrashim.

EsthR has been translated into German by Wünsche, *Bibliotheca Rabbinica* 9, accompanied by the copious notes of Fürst, 75-102; par. 2:5-13 has been translated by Stemberger, *Midrasch*, 123-132 (including notes) and most recently by Börner-Klein and Hollender, *Midraschim*, 153-266. It has been translated into English by M. Simon, *Midrash Rabbah*, IX and by Neusner, *Esther Rabbah* 1, who has limited his analytical translation to the first six sections of the Midrash. A Yiddish translation with accompanying notes by Dunsky is also available.

In addition to his translation, J. Neusner has published three additional studies, which deal with the literary structure and the 'message' of EsthR, in the following works: *Midrashic Compilations* 2; *Judaism Behind the Texts* 4, 71-86; *Components* II.

The various commentaries to EsthR will be dealt with elsewhere.

2. *Midrash Abba Gurion (AbGur)*

Name. The appellation Abba Gurion is based on the opening passage of this Midrash which quotes several Aramaic statements attributed to the Tanna Abba Gurion of Saidon.[294] It is interesting to note that in the Cambridge Geniza fragment (TS C 1.48), the teachings of Abba Gurion are preceded by a quote from the opening verse of Esther, its exegesis 'woe in the days of Ahasuerus' (ווי בימי אחשוירוש) and, possibly, the passage from Job 34:30, found in the parallel proem (9) in EsthR, which is most likely the source for the teachings of Abba Gurion herein (see below).

In his Commentary to 1 Kings 10:19, Rashi[295] apparently alluded to this Midrash by the title *Aggadat Megillat Esther*, whereas the rubric in the Oxford manuscript is: *Aggadeta de-Megilta*. The copyist of the Hamburg manuscript obviously had no title available and simply stated that he was going to copy 'a Midrash from Megilla (= Esther)'. The earliest usage of the peculiar title *Abba Gurion* is apparently found in the thirteenth century compendium of R. Shimon of Frankfurt, *Yalkut Shimoni* who, quoted from this Midrash profusely.

Division, Scope and Contents. No division of AbGur is evident in the manuscripts, and the section headings which are nothing more than the division of the biblical Book of Esther into chapters, represent the additions of the editor, Solomon Buber.

---

[294] Note well that in numerous mss (incl. ms Hamburg 37, see below) the exact title is *Abba Uryan* or *Uryon* (אורײן or אורין, of EsthR proem 9), see Elboim, *Aba Grurion*, 11. This may indicate that the present title is actually a misnomer! It is not clear whether Tsaidan (צײדן) refers to the seaport city, Sidon (צידון) or to the village Beth Saida, located on the banks of Lake Genneseret, *vid.* Klein, *Sefer ha-yishuv*, 120.

[295] On Rashi's usage of AbGur cf his commentary to Judg 5:8 (= 3:9, 27) and the commentary to bMeg 15b, s.v. נדדו עליונים, an oral communication from his teacher (= 6:1, 38).

Actually, there is no need for an internal division since AbGur is devoid of proems, with the exception of the two opening proems, at the very beginning of the Midrash, which have their almost exact parallel in EsthR

AbGur provides midrashic explanations to some 52 verses of Esther, most of those in chapters one and three, whereas the material from chapter four onwards is somewhat sporadic The Midrash actually concludes at the end of Chapter six[296] and only a single homily dealing with the tree prepared by Haman for the execution of Mordechai appears at the end of Chapter seven (7:10, 41-42).

Among the more lengthy selections, the following may be enumerated: the throne of Solomon (2-7); the casting of the lots (24-26); the absurdities of Jewish religious practices (26-27); dealings between Haman and Ahasuerus (27-29); the letter of Haman (29-31);[297] Haman's evil plot, the heavenly decree and the dramatic events in heaven and on earth (32-34); Nebuchadnezer and Hananiah, Mishael and Azariah (34-35); Haman and Zeresh (36-37); Haman confronts Mordechai and his disciples (32; 37-38); Haman and Mordechai (40-41); the trees volunteer to serve as Haman's gallows (41-42).

In the closing note to AbGur, the homilist expresses the popular theme of the Purim celebration that just as the Almighty punished Haman (and his sons) for his wicked deeds and conspiracies, so will He thwart 'the evil plots of our enemies'[298] and bring 'peace upon Israel'.

This is the concluding message of AbGur as attested by a Geniza fragment. However, the Casanata manuscript published by Buber as well as ms Vatican 470 conclude with the talmudic homily of R. Joshua b. Levi praising 'the low in spirit'.[299] Needless to say, this homily has nothing to do with the Esther Midrash, and was apparently appended to AbGur as an additional closing formula that was utilized by preachers to conclude their discourses with a note of encouragement to the lowly.[300]

Midrash Abba Gurion and Midrash Esther Rabba. Even though it is a much shorter compilation to the Esther Scroll, the contents of AbGur are quite similar to EsthR and properly evaluated, these two Midrashim should be classified as works of unusual similarity and numerous parallels. Nineteenth century

---

[296] However, some of the manuscripts contain additional material, vid. ed Buber, 41 n1 (ms Cambridge) and ms Firkowitz I 246 (and in the additional folio therein).

[297] Note the Aramaic version, 31-32 (from ms British Library).

[298] This idea, which received its initial impetus in the traditional Al ha-Nissim prayer, reverberates throughout many midrashic works relating to the Esther Scroll, cf the endings of Pesikta Hadeta, 58; PA V, 82; PA I (1) 49 (top); EsthR 7:3; AbGur 3:1, 21; 7:10, 42 n7 (end).

[299] bSot 5b; bSan 43b.

[300] This is readily evident from an Oxford Geniza fragment of novel Sheiltot published by Epstein, *Studies* 2, 495 l. 31. Note that Epstein was unaware of this phenomenon and attempted to link this homily to the contents of the Sheilta. See also Pesikta Hadeta, 52f; Sefer ve-Hizhir 1, 139, 231; 2, 39.

scholars (Jellinek, Gräz, Horowitz and Buber) tended to view AbGur as the earlier of the two works and claimed that EsthR built upon the foundations of the former. However, a far more sober approach is presented by Brüll, Albeck and Tabory who have offered ample proof to justify the late origin of AbGur and its dependence upon EsthR

Even so, AbGur is not to be treated lightly. The *Vorlage* of EsthR utilized by the former contained an earlier version of the text than the extant version (= The Ancient Midrash, see List, no. 4) and as shown by Tabory, it is possible to restore original passages that are somehow missing in EsthR, according to the textual version of AbGur, which has preserved them intact.

It is interesting to note that Midrash AbGur enjoyed immense popularity and almost like the principle of Gresham's law, pushed EsthR to the sidelines. This is evident from the numerous extant manuscripts and Geniza fragments of AbGur as well as from the quotations of this work in the various compendia such as Lekah Tov and Yalkut Shimoni.

In Buber's edition of Midrash Zutta to the Five Scrolls, based on ms Parma 541, there is no Midrash to the Book of Esther. Owing to the immense popularity of AbGur and its abridged format, we would venture to say that, in all probability, AbGur was considered to be the 'minor Midrash' to this biblical scroll.

Novel Versions? The so-called 'Novel Version of Midrash Abba Gurion' published by Z.M. Rabinovitz[301] really has very little to do with AbGur, and is based on a completely mistaken identity (see below p202); ms St. Petersburg-Antonin 302 was found to contain material from the Ancient Midrash, which was clearly one of the sources of Midrash AbGur. On the other hand, a non-published parchment Geniza fragment in the library of the Jewish Theological Seminary, New York, may possibly contain an introduction to AbGur which is not found in any other copy of this Midrash. On the face of it, this fragment, which is most difficult to decipher, consists of (a) the opening section of Ab-Gur until the middle of King Solomon's throne (= 1:1-21, 1-4) and (b) the dealings between Haman and Ahasuerus (= 3:9, 27-29).[302]

The first part of this fragment is actually a paean to the Almighty, expressing the gratitude of the Jewish people for their salvation and the need to praise the Lord, through the usage of such biblical passages as: Ps 22:23, 25; Isa 43:11 and Ezek 9:9. Special focus should be placed on the inclusion of an exegesis of Ps 26:44, which is similar to the teachings of the baraita quoted in conjunction with the exegesis (opening proem?) of Samuel to the Esther scroll, in bMeg 11a and to a quotation of all eight verses of Ps 124,[303] whose first verse serves as the opening proem of Rav Nahman b. Yitshak in bMeg 11a.

---

[301] *Ginzé Midrash*, 161-170.
[302] Folio 6b is completely illegible.
[303] To the best of our knowledge, a quotation of this scope is unprecedented in midrashic literature.

One may thus ask whether this most verbose text is an original introduction to AbGur deleted somehow from all other copies of this Midrash, or merely a lengthy addition of later vintage? Suffice it to say that the influence exerted by the Babylonian tradition over this 'Introduction' and the lack of such 'Introductions' in midrashic literature in general, apparently allude to the latter conclusion.

Sources and Date. As mentioned above the original version of EsthR in the form of the Ancient Midrash served as the major source for Midrash AbGur whose compiler borrowed from it freely in his exegetical comments to Esth 1-3.

A preliminary examination of the novel material in AbGur Chapter 1, 11-17, for which no parallel is found in EsthR, has shown that practically all of these homilies and explanations derive from Midrash Panim Aherot II.[304] However, the lengthy detailed description of the 'throne of King Solomon' and its captivity at the beginning of the Midrash (1:2, 4-8), which does have a close parallel in PA II (1:2, 57-58), was not taken from the former. On the contrary, the PA II parallel not only differs in structure and content but actually contains an additional explanation based on the text of AbGur.[305] It is this writer's conjecture that the extensive section devoted to the Solomon throne in Midrash Abba Gurion, as well as some other lengthy passages,[306] derive from other midrashic works to the Scroll of Esther that are no longer extant.

In this respect it is important to note that AbGur evidently made use of an entire homily of the 'ruah ha-Kodesh Midrash' (PA V), cf pp. 34-35 with the Geniza fragment containing material from that Midrash (ms Oxf-Bodl 2851, ff. 43-44), see below, List, no. 27.

In summation, it is now apparent that Midrash AbGur does not represent an original Midrash. On the contrary, the editor seems to have had access to several different Midrashim to the Scroll of Esther and he borrowed from them freely. While his short exegetical comments generally derive from the Ancient Midrash (= EsthR) and from Panim Aherot II, the lengthier selections based on aggadic narrative are most likely taken from such lost aggadic works as Panim Aherot V, Midrash Aher *et al.* Notwithstanding the eclectic nature of Midrash AbGur, the editor certainly deserves a few words of approbation for his literary contribution. In spite of the fact that it is logical to assume that all the material of this Midrash derives from other sources, he has combined the various ele-

---

[304] Cf AbGur 1:8, 11-12 = Panim Aherot II, 59; 1:9, 12-13 = 59 end; 1:10, 13 = 60; 1:11, 14-15 = 1:10, 60; 1:13, 15 = 1:10, 60; 1:14, 16-17 = 61. The only material unaccounted for is 14 l. 5, a short explanation to 1:10 containing seven words.

[305] Cf PA II., 57 ll. 32f, with AbGur 1:2, 3-4, and the remarks of Buber n24. Buber's emendation is corroborated by the Geniza fragment published by Rabinovitz, *Ginzé Midrash*, 175 ll. 22-24.

[306] E.g., 3:7-9, 24-29; 3:12, 29-31; 4:1, 32-33; 5:14, 36-38. Note that the parallels in EsthR to these lengthy selections derive from the 'Additions' to the Ancient Midrash, *supra* p183f; cf the thesis of Albeck, *Derashot*, 424.

ments and fused them together into a unified whole. Compared to the lapses and editorial bungling prevalent in EsthR (see above), AbGur excels as a work of artistic craftsmanship.

In lieu of the fact that Rashi, who flourished in the eleventh century, seems to have utilized Midrash AbGur, it seems most likely that this Midrash is a product of no later then the tenth century. This could also explain the relative popularity enjoyed by AbGur; the extant version of Midrash EsthR is definitely of much later vintage.

Bibliography. Midrash Abba Gurion was first published in 1853 by Jellinek as the opening selection of his collection of minor Midrashim, *Bet ha-midrasch*, 1, 1-18, see the review by Gräz, 347-350. Jellinek's selection of ms Hamburg 37:8 leaves much to be desired as the scribe of this manuscript not only deleted lengthy passages and made numerous copying errors, but also added material from bMegilla. On the text of this edition see Elboim, *Aba Gurion*, 12-16. Several short notes to the text, mainly comparisons with the parallels, are found in the Introduction, XXVIII-XXIX. Corrections to the text are offered by Buber, *Tanhuma*, Introduction, 142 n3.

Buber issued an improved edition of AbGur in 1886 as the first part of his *Sifrei de-Aggadeta*, 1-42, which was based on ms Casanata 63:4 (I 14) with variants from five additional manuscripts: Parma 563:5; Oxf-Bodl 155:2 (Michael 577, written 1470) [mss Parma and Oppenheim (see below) are already mentioned by Zunz, *Vorträge*, 291 n. e]; British Library 343 (Add. 15,402); Cambridge, SCR 64 (Mm. 6. 26. 2) and ms London Beth-Din 6:5. On this last manuscript, see Jellinek, 'Berichte', 243-244. Buber chose the Casanata codex as his *Grundtext* and commented on the readings of the other manuscripts, quotations in Yalkut Shimoni and parallels in EsthR *et al.* in his copious notes and commentary, which actually inundate the text of the Midrash; see the critique of Brüll in his review, 149-151. In spite of the progress made, Buber failed to base his edition on the best available manuscript and so, due to its corrupt state, his basic text also leaves much to be desired. Numbering the individual verses would have considerably facilitated the usage of this edition.

Additional manuscripts, not utilized by Buber, include: Vatican 470:2; Paris 1467 = Warsaw 260:4, ff. 19a-26a (= Vienna Jewish Community, 34) incomplete, from 1:2-4:4; Oxf-Bodl 1755:3 (Opp. 128), ff. 153-159; Paris 174:5, ff. 97v-119r and St. Petersburg- Firkowitz I 246 (dated: 1454, see Kahana, 'Ginzei Midrash', 61). The last folio of an additional manuscript has been appended to the Firkowitz codex. Also: Paris 250 (118-119 margins); Budapest Kaufman A291:45. All the above are amply summarized by Elboim, *Aba Gurion*, 21-29, who has also provided a most detailed stemmatic analysis.

Several excerpts from AbGur are evident in mss Vatican 96 and 290:11, fols. 5r-7r. Two pages in Italian script, removed from a binding, containing the end of the Midrash are in the private collection of Manfred Lehmann, see Lehmann 'Nethanel b. Yeshaya' 355 n127.

The material in Sefer ha-Zikhronot of R. Elazar b. Asher, chap. LXXXII (= ed Yassif, 274-277), does not stem from AbGur 4, as proposed by Schwarzbaum, 'Prolegomenon', 84, but rather from Midrash Aher, see below Section 8.

Versions of the text dealing with the 'throne of Solomon', 2-8, some of them containing additions and variants, are found in: *Bet ha-Midrasch*, 2, 83-85, (from *Kolbo* 119); Gaster, *Exempla of the Rabbis*, no. 115, 78-79; R. Azriel, *Commentary on Aggadoth*, 123-124; ms Cam Add. 506.4 (SCR 338); mss Oxf-Bodl 913 [Opp. 738] and 2797 [Heb. d. 11], 90b-91a (= *Sefer ha-Zikhronot* 8:14, ed Yassif, 279-281, two versions, cf below n411); Midrash Ha-Beur 1, 546f. Unknown novel versions are evinced by the Commentary of R. Elazar of Worms, 13-14, and by the Aramaic compendium, *vid.* Kasher-Klein, 'New Fragments', 99, ll. 6-13. Note well: Ginzberg, *Legends* 6, 452f.

The Geniza fragment from the Taylor-Schechter collection, Cambridge, identified as 'concerning King Solomon's throne' (Brody, *Hand-list*, 140: NS 254.96), bears no relationship whatsoever to this genre.

See also the notes of Ginzberg, *Legends* 3: 157-160; 5: 296-297; 453-454, n13; Gaster, *Exempla*, English section, 209; Schwarzbaum, 'Prolegomenon', 84f. Note also Rabinovitz, *Ginzé Midrash*, 172-176; Buber, AggEsth 1:2, 8-9. The numerous versions of the 'throne of Solomon' deserve special treatment as to the origin and development of this genre.

Geniza fragments of AbGur include: (1) TS C 1. 48, three pages from the beginning of the Midrash, including the introductory verse from Esth 1:1 and its short exegesis, until 2:7 (= ed Buber, 1-18); the text includes an addition to 1:14. Folio 1r contains writing in a later hand, also probably related to AbGur; the closing line seems to be taken from 5:14, 37., cf with the description of Rabinovitz, *Ginzé Midrash*, 161-162; (2) JTS-Adler ENA 3724. 5-6, cf with the identification of the present writer in Danzig, *Catalogue*, 225. This fragment contains the novel introduction to the Midrash (described above); (3) TS C 2.89, from 3:4 – 3:7 (= 22-24); (4) JTS-Adler ENA 2933.20, 3:12 (= 30-31); (5) TS 20.84b, 5:14 – end (= 38-42). The above-mentioned Firkowitz manuscript (I 246) which is complete and the additional folio appended to it were also most likely taken from the Geniza. The single folio in the British Library, ms OR 5559 A, fol. 39 has very much in common with AbGur 4:1, 33-34 but, nevertheless, derives from an entirely different Midrash, cf below, Section 9, 'Aggadic-Narrative Midrash'.

In lieu of the abundant material now available, as well as the obvious faults of ed Buber, a modern critical edition of AbGur is certainly a desideratum. A detailed study on the sources of AbGur and its exact relationship to the other Midrashim to Esther would also be welcome. B. Elboim has compiled a synoptic edition and plans his dissertation on same.

Important information concerning AbGur is found in Buber, Preface I-V and in Zunz-Albeck, *Derashot*, 141, 423. Linguistic comments on the text, especially on the loan words, are offered by Gräz and Brüll in their respective reviews. Tabory, 'Problems', 150-152 and idem, 'Proems' has demonstrated the importance of AbGur to the textual study of EsthR. Numerous comparisons and explanations are provided by Segal, *Babylonian Midrash, passim.* Noy, 'Yud-bet ha-Mazzalot' discusses the signs of the Zodiac (3, 25-26).

The German translation of Wünsche, *Lehrhallen* 2, 95-138, is based on the defective Hamburg ms published by Jellinek whereas the recent translation of Börner-Klein and Hollender, *Midraschim*, 23-64 is based on the Buber version. The English translation of the more complete version of the 'throne of Solomon' from ms Oxford 2797 is found in Gaster, *Jerahmeel*, LXXXIV, 251-253.

3. Midrash 'Panim Aherot' II (= PA II)

Name. The epithet פנים אחרות, *i.e.* 'a different version' (lit. 'different face'), has no bearing whatsoever on the title of certain midrashic compositions to the Esther Scroll and was never meant to serve that purpose. It is obvious that after copying Midrash Abba Gurion, the scribe of the original codex of the manuscript tradition preserved in ms Oxf-Bodl 155 encountered numerous midrashic works to the Book of Esther. Since he had no knowledge of their specific titles, he referred to them generally as 'Panim Aherot', i.e., an additional version of the midrashic exegesis of Esther, non-identical with Abba Gurion.[307] The generic reference[308] was utilized by Buber who published these texts under the dubious title: 'Midrash Panim Aherim'.[309]

However, Buber failed to list all the appearances of the generic reference found in the Oxford manuscript in his edition of these texts (*Sifrei de-Aggadeta*).[310] In the ensuing discussion of the various complete and fragmentary Midrashim to Esther, we shall frequently call attention to the term Panim Aherot (= PA), which apparently indicates the existence of some additional unknown midrashic works to the Esther Scroll. In order to distinguish between the various segments, the appropriate folios of the Oxford manuscript will also be noted. Unfortunately, none of the various midrashic selections in the manuscript can be identified by name and so they will be referred to by consecutive

[307] An exact parallel to this phenomenon is evinced by ms Parma 541, 174v; immediately following a copy of 'Midrash Ruth' (= RuthR), the scribe introduced his copy of Ruth Zuta with the heading: מגלת רות בישובה בפנים אחרות.

[308] The word *panim* is used by the sources to indicate different interpretations of a single text, cf ySan 4:2, 22a; CantR 2:4; LevR 26,2 (p589); PesR 12 (53a). The expression *panim aherim* (or *panim aherot*, see next n.) is not found in the ancient sources and is clearly of medieval vintage, *vid.*, e.g., Rashi to Gen 49:11, 12, 15, 96-97; Deut 32-43, 44; Eccl 4:12; YalShim Num 736:6, 213 l. 92.; R. Abraham b. David (RAVa"D), Commentary to Sifra Shemini 45a, par. 29; Epstein, *Mavo*, 1. Cf Geula, *Study*, 240 n72.

[309] In spite of the fact that the headings of the Oxford manuscript read throughout פנים אחרות (cf, Mack, 'Mediaval Midrash', 112), Buber tenaciously altered them to read: פנים אחרים. A similar case is noted in his description of Ruth Zuta, Introd. to Midrash Zuta, XIV, cf n307 above.

[310] This has now been corrected by the present author in Bet Arie, *Supplement*, 20-21.

numbers added to the appelation 'Panim Aherot', according to their appearance in the manuscript after Panim Aherot II: thus 'PA III'; 'PA IV', etc.

Text. In Buber's edition, this Midrash is printed on p53-77 (= fol. 123b-130a of ms Oxf-Bodl 155). A small segment of PA II – the Midrash to Esth 2:5-6, 62-63 – which appears as the external framework of 'Midrash Aher – ms Hamburg' (List, no. 23), was first published by A. Jellinek.

The text of PA II evinces several lacunae due to the activity of the scribe who deleted those passages which supposedly duplicate the material of Midrash Abba Gurion, already copied by him. In three instances, he abruptly curtailed his copy with the short note 'etc. as above' (וכו' כדלעיל).[311] These deletions are most unfortunate as other texts indicate that the deleted material was not always identical with the AbGur text.[312] Buber also took the initiative of inserting certain midrashic homilies from Yalkut Shimoni into the text of his edition, assuming that they belonged to PA II,[313] even though the scribe of the Oxford manuscript had not made any announcement whatsoever concerning such deletions. Needless to say, these texts should be approached with caution, since there are some citations in Yalkut Shimoni to Esther whose source has not been definitely identified[314] and these may very well derive from one of the lost midrashic treatises to this biblical scroll.

The Geniza fragments of PA II also attest to the fact that the unique version of ms Oxford 155 is actually incomplete in certain places.

Numerous excerpts from PA II, preceded by the generic appellation 'midrash',[315] appear in Yalkut Shimoni while the Yemenite yalkut, Aggadat Esther, which does not cite its sources, quotes from this Midrash profusely.[316] Massive usage of PA II is also evinced by the commentary of R. Avigdor Cohen-Zedek, who frequently refers to it as 'Pirkin (Perakim) de-R. Eliezer',[317] but many of his citations are anonymous.[318] The commentary ascribed to R.

[311] 1:2, 57, l. 11; 1:8, 59; 3:1, 66 (cf *ib.* n105). These lacunae have been completed by Buber, who utilized YalShim.

[312] Note: Rabinovitz, *Ginzé Midrash*, 174-176; YalShim Esth 1048:17; 1053:49.

[313] 2:10, 64; 3:6, 67; 3:8, 68; 6:1, 74. See his relevant notes *ib.*

[314] See below near n450 and List, no. 16.

[315] Here too, this is an indication that R. Shimon of Frankfurt, the compiler of the YalShim, did have any knowledge of a specific name for this midrash. A complete summary of the sources is offered by Hyman, *Sources* 2, 581.

[316] See the discussion of Tobi, *Midrash ha-Gadol* 1, 310-313 and the list of sources, *ib.* 2, 265. Note, however, that some of this material actually derives from the homily of R. Shmuel, see below, List, nos. 12 and 21.

[317] Usage of this strange title for PA II possibly intimates that R. Avigdor's copy of this Midrash was bound together with PRE. Note that he also cites the latter work, cf e.g., ed Leitner, 1:10, 22-23; 1:14, 25; 2:5, 28.

[318] E.g., ed Leitner, 3:9, 38-39; 3:15, 39; 4:4, 41; 4:16, 42; 5:1, 44-45 *et al.*

Elazar of Worms also made extensive anonymous usage of PA II.[319] The homily of R. Shmuel, which is one of the sources of Aggadat Esther, actually utilized PA II as the mainstay of his homily.[320]

R. Shlomo Alkabez made copious secondary usage of PA II via Yalkut Shimoni.[321] However, he evidently had access to a manuscript of this Midrash since, in at least one instance, he adduces a quote not found in the Yalkut.[322]

Parts of the text of Midrash PA II were translated into Aramaic by an unknown anthologist who incorporated material from various midrashic works into an Aramaic compilation of sources to the Scroll of Esther, together with material from the two Targums to Esther. Kasher and Klein, who have published six folios from this unknown compilation according to various fragments in the Taylor-Schechter Collection, Cambridge,[323] have rightfully stressed the parallels in PA II, chapters 5-6.[324] Moreover, the Aramaic version is actually of utmost importance as it contributes readings and explanations to the Hebrew text as well as positive support for Buber's interpolation of a problematic text from Yalkut Shimoni into PA II.[325]

Structure and Division. Midrash PA II is an explanatory Midrash to the narrative section of the Book of Esther and covers chapters 1-7.

The opening section is preceded by a short anonymous proem containing the introductory formula זהו שאמר הכתוב, 'This is what Scripture said', in abbreviated form זש"ה. This proem depicts the battle between Mordechai and Haman over the rebuilding of the Holy Temple. It resembles EsthR, Introductory Proem 5, and seems to be modelled after it. Note that this proem too concludes with the stereotypic refrain bemoaning the reign of King Ahasuerus. Another lengthy anonymous proem with the same introductory formula precedes the second verse of Esther (56-58). Additional anonymous proems, all preceded by זש"ה, are found at the beginning of 2:5; 3:1 and 6:1, passages which represent the crucial turning points of the Esther narrative in the Bible, as demonstrated by Tannaic halakha.[326] The sum total of proems in Midrash PA II is, therefore, five.[327]

---

[319] Cf ed Konyevsky, 2:5, 24; 2:9, 27; 2:16, 29; 3:1, 33; 3:11, 42 *et al.* Limited usage is also found in the (original?) commentary of R. Elazar of Worms (entitled: Shaare Bina), cf ed Lehmann, 2:19, 21 and Introduction, 17 (bottom).

[320] See below, near n342.

[321] See the list compiled by Buber in his Preface to *Sifrei de-Aggadeta*, VI-VIII.

[322] R. Shlomo Alkabez, Menot ha-Levi to Esth 5:13, 155a. Curiously enough, the origin of this selection is attributed to 'a (different) midrash', (מדרש אחר), cf below, p214-218.

[323] Kasher – Klein, 'New Fragments'. See below, List, no. 27.

[324] PA II 5:10, 72 = 92; 6:1, 74 = 94, 95; ib. 75-76 = 96.

[325] Cf PA II 6:1, 74 (= YalShim 1057:10) and Kasher – Klein, 'New Fragments', 95, ll. 11-12.

[326] tMeg 2:9 (p350). Cf mMeg 2:3; yMeg 2, 73b; bMeg 19a. *Vid.* Offer, 'Sidre', 158.

[327] *Pace* Bacher, *Proömien*, 113 who listed eight proems, being misled, on the one hand, by the additional Midrashim following PA II and, on the other, by failing to note the proems preceding 2:5, 62 and 6:1, 73.

The anonymous terminology for introducing the proems (זש"ה) as well as the concluding formulae employed in PA II – 'therefore ...' (לפיכך), and, 'that is the reason why [the petiha verse] was said' (לכך... נאמר) – are emblematic of Tanhuma – Yelammedenu literature.[328] However, the combination of opening proems and a consecutive systematic Exegetical Midrash is most uncommon in the Tanhuma type Midrashim.[329] On the contrary, such an arrangement is most indicative of Genesis Rabba and the early Exegetical Midrashim to the Five Scrolls (see above).

In his edition, Buber arbitrarily divided the Midrash into chapters, according to the biblical Book of Esther, but apparently, in order to save space, deleted the heading of chapter 7 at the bottom of p76. Here too, he failed to indicate the numbers of the individual verses in each chapter, a simple procedure which would have greatly facilitated the usage of this text. In all likelihood, the original division of the Midrash reflected the proem passages cited above, which would lead us to the assumption that Midrash PA II was based on a fundamental division of four parashiyyot: 1:1; 2:5; 3:1 and 6:1.

Scope and Contents. The Midrash itself is an explanatory, at times, very short, running commentary[330] to the Purim story and covers roughly 70% of the biblical passages in Esth 1-7, although the Midrash to Chapter seven is limited to three of the ten verses of that chapter.

Among the novel homilies of note in PA II, one may enumerate: (1) the raison d'être for the rule of Ahasuerus (1:2, 56-57); (2) the 'throne of King Solomon' (1:2, 56-58); (3) the events leading up to the marriage Vashti to Ahasuerus (1:13, 60); (4) the genealogy of Mordechai (2:5, 62-63); (5) four momentous salvations that transpired on Passover eve (6:1, 73); (6) The dramatic events of 'that night' (6:1) which led to the downfall of Haman (6:1-7:10, 74-77); (7) Haman's tree (7:9).

Relation to other Midrashic Works to Esther. Albeck viewed PA II as 'an alternate version of AbGur with certain variants, additions and deletions'.[331] The implication of such a perspective, which is completely unfounded, would be that PA II is also a product of the ninth-tenth centuries. Even though several points of contact between the two works are evident (see above, 2. 'Midrash Abba Gurion'), these have been shown to be the result of a borrowing process whereby AbGur incorporated material from PA II. For all intents and purposes, PA II is an independent Midrash containing original homilies and interpretations to the Esther scroll. Any comparison between this Midrash and AbGur,

---

[328] *Vid.* Bacher, *Terminologie* 2, 62, 96, 102; Lerner, 'New Light' [2], 424 n52.

[329] The closest available example of such a midrash seems to be Tanh Korah, Hukkat and Balak, cf Schlüter, 'Auslegungsmidrasch', 71-98; see above p156 and n121.

[330] Note that the midrash to 2:9-10, 64 appears in the middle of the explanation to 2:15.

[331] Zunz-Albeck, *Derashot*, 425.

whose first chapters are actually a shortened version of the Ancient Esther Midrash with certain additions (mainly from PA II!), is unfounded.[332]

No serious study has centred on the relationship of PA II to EsthR,[333] but suffice it to say that even though both relate to the same biblical text, actual points of contact are minimal. Aside from the similarities between the opening proem and EsthR Proem 5 mentioned above, there are several additional parallels in the Midrash to Esth 1:1 and very few others.[334] However, due to various differences, it is not always possible to speak of direct usage and borrowing.[335]

In all likelihood, it is logical to assume that PA II is dependent upon EsthR, i.e. the Ancient Midrash to Esther, as ably shown by Albeck on the basis of an extremely short parallel.[336]

Attribution of Teachings. All of the authorities cited in PA II, with one possible exception,[337] are Amoraim. It is interesting to note that among the twenty-seven names mentioned, R. Levi, the third generation Palestinian Amora, is by far and large the most oft-quoted authority, appearing in no less than fourteen citations throughout the Midrash.[338] R. Yitshak is mentioned three times; two other rabbis, R. Yehuda b. Pazzi and R. Helbo, are mentioned twice each, while the remaining six are given single mention only.[339] PA II also abounds in numerous other teachings which are introduced by the anonymous term 'and there are those who say' (ויש אומרים), as well as a prolific number of alternate explanations (ד"א).[340] The origin of these teachings and explanations deserves special study, especially the possible relationship of the term, 'and there are those who say' to the Aramaic Targum Sheni to Esther.[341]

---

[332] Concerning the 'throne of Solomon' tradition introduced as an alternative explanation (וי"א) in PA II 1:2, 57 end, cf above p195f.

[333] I.e. the Ancient Midrash exclusively. The additions to the Ancient Midrash stemming from PA II have been enumerated above, near n266.

[334] E.g., 2:17, 65 = EsthR 6:11.

[335] It is interesting to note that the petiha verses of Rav and Shmuel in the proems of EsthR (Deut 28:66 and Lev 26:41) have been utilized as closing themes in PA II 1:1, 56 (end), 57. In 1:1, 55 (near n. 4), the tradent is R. Levi and not the rabbis enumerated in EsthR Proems, 11. See also below, near n434ff. Note also the difference between 1:1, 56 (near n. 12) and EsthR 1:2, 3a.

[336] Zunz-Albeck, *Derashot*, 425 relating to PA 1:1, 56 l. 2. Cf also *ib.* l. 3. Albeck's second proof relating to the public discourse of R. Akiva (EsthR 1:8) is not at all convincing.

[337] R. Berekhia in the name of R. Elazar (3:8, 68), cf CantR 7:21 and Bacher, *Tradition*, 103 par. 25.

[338] 1:1, 55; 1:1, 56; 1:8, 59; 2:5, 62; 2:14, 64; 2:15, 64; 2:17, 65; 2:21, 65; 3:1, 66; 6:1, 74; 6:1, 75; 6:1, 76 (twice); 6:12, 76. See below, p222 on R. Levy.

[339] 1:9, 59; 1:16, 61; 2:8, 64 (R. Yitshak); 1:1, 56; 2:14, 64 (R. Yehuda b. Pazzi); 2:17, 65; 6:1, 73 (R. Helbo).

[340] ויש אומרים, 1:1, 56; 1:2, 57; 1:3, 58 (twice); 1:13, 61; 2:1, 61; 2:21, 65 (twice); 2:23, 66 (twice); 5:1, 71; 6:1, 74-75 (twice). ד"א, 1:1, 55-56 (6 times); 1:4, 58 (twice); 2:10, 64 (twice); 2:21, 65 (twice); 3:8, 68; 4:15, 70; 6:1, 73-74 (6 times). Some of these obviously allude to explanations taken from EsthR (i.e. the Ancient Midrash), cf above, n333.

[341] E.g., 1:3, 58; 2:7, 63; 2:21, 65.

Redaction and Date. Basing himself on numerous quotations from PA II in AggEsth prefaced by the introductory formula 'R. Samuel said...' (ר' שמואל אמר), Bacher concluded that this unidentified sage was the editor of PA II.[342] However, it is now apparent that these attributions actually allude to a Purim homily delivered by the unknown R. Samuel, which was mainly based on selections from PA II.[343] It is thus quite clear that he cannot be considered to be the editor or author of PA II, as proposed by Bacher, since his usage of the work was purely secondary.

In a similar vein, attention should be focused on the superscription 'R. Levi said'[344] preceding the anonymous homily (זש"ה) in EsthR 7:2. Since this homily clearly derives from PA II 3:1, 66 one could conceivably draw the conclusion that the final redactor of EsthR considered PA II to be a work edited or compiled by R. Levi.[345] However, notwithstanding the overwhelming number of the teachings and homilies of R. Levi in PA II,[346] such a conclusion is untenable for a number of reasons.[347] Suffice it to say that the editor of EsthR simply transferred the name of R. Levi from the parable of the *galearius* (helmeted soldier) in PA II to the head of the proem,[348] thus creating a most unusual proem heading.[349]

As mentioned above, the terminology employed by the proems of PA II is indicative of Tanhuma-Yelammedenu literature while the exegetical process itself is reminiscent of the classical Exegetical Midrashim. Another point of interest in PA II is the purely Hebrew text with an admixture of some Greek and Latin loan words, among them ὑπατεία,[350] μῖμος,[351] and *disciplina*.[352] It should be stressed that such usage is also indicative of classical midrash and seems to reflect an early development in Tanhuma-Yelammedenu literature.

There are no indications of parallels with the Esther Midrash in Bavli Megilla, although the Hebrew version of an Aramaic adage found in another

---

[342] Bacher, 'Midraschcompilation', 352f.

[343] See below, List, nos. 17 and 13.

[344] This reading is supported by all the mss including Oxf 164; Vat 291 and Vat 96, see Tabory, 'Proems', 8 l. 11. However, YalMekh Ps 92:8, 97, does not contain the name of R. Levi which was arbitrarily inserted by Buber.

[345] Cf also the citations from PRE in MidrGad and AggEsth, Tobi, *Midrash ha-Gadol* 1, 284 n1229.

[346] See above, n338.

[347] E.g. mention of later rabbis (R. Helbo; R. Berekhia).

[348] This reminds one of the construction of artificial proems by the editor of GenR, cf Albeck, 'Einleitung', 15-17. On the parable of the *galearius* see Tabory, 'Proems', 11.

[349] A proem based on the formula 'R. X said, זש"ה ...' apparently does not appear in the sources. Bacher, *Proömien*, 60, 113, seems to have ignored this proem completely.

[350] 6:14, 76, contra Buber n182. The Hebrew reading should be emended accordingly (איפטייון). Concerning the usage of this term which refers to the Roman consuls in midrashic literature, see Lieberman, 'Roman Legal Institutions', 13 n75. Cf Friedman, 'Royal Era'. Note that the plural form in PA II is a unicum.

[351] 1:10, 60 contra Buber n51. *Vid.* Krauss, *Lehnwörter*, 326, *s.v.* מומוס.

[352] 5:9, 72; Krauss, *Lehnwörter*, 209f.

tractate may be noted.[353] An interesting phenomenon is a citation from Megillat Taanit 1 by Mordechai in response to Esther's demand to announce a three day fast during the Passover holiday.[354] The unique version of this quotation is unattested to by any other source and deserves special attention.

All in all, the above-mentioned observations would seem to place PA II in the earliest stratum of Tanhuma literature. Although the basic Midrash represents the teachings of various Palestinian Amoraim, it is apparent that the editor utilized other sources as well, among them EsthR in one of its early formulations. This would seem to indicate that the final reduction of PA II took place between the seventh and the eighth centuries CE.

Bibliography. The small segment of PA II from ms Hamburg 37 was published by Jellinek in *Bet ha-Midrasch* 1, 19, 23-24. The rather late ms Oxf-Bodl (written: 1470), is a unicum and to date, no other manuscript of PA II has been uncovered, with the exception of four folios from a vellum Geniza manuscript, containing additional material. One of these (TS C 2.204), which contains parts of 1:2, 57-58 (the 'throne of Solomon', with additions) and 1:14-2:5, 61-62, has been published by Rabinovitz, *Ginzé Midrash*, 171-178. The other fragment (ms Oxf-Bodl 2860:11), which is part of the same fascicle and as yet unpublished, includes parts of 1:1-2, 56-57 and 2:7-10, 63-64.

Very little research has been conducted on PA II. For one reason or other, the summary of Herr does not appear in *EJ* 16, 1515, even though it is alluded to therein. There is still room for a major in-depth study of this Midrash, its cohesion and its *Weltanschauung* as well as its relationship to the other Midrashim to Esther and to midrashic and talmudic literature in general. Buber's Preface to *Sifrei de-Aggadeta*, V-VIII does not deal with the Midrash *per se*. In his recension of *Sifrei de-Aggadeta*, 151-153, Brüll merely commented on some textual readings and loan-words. Albeck, *Derashot*, 424f has offered a few terse remarks on the relationship between PA II and the other complete Midrashim to Esther, but his conclusions are unacceptable, see above. A step in the right direction has been taken by Segal, *Babylonian Midrash, passim*, offering numerous parallels and explanations

Midrash PA II has been translated into German by Börner-Klein and Hollender, *Midraschim*, 83-142. The translation of Wuensche (Stemberger, *Introduction*, 321) is limited to the narrow confines of the Hamburg manuscript published by Jellinek, *Lehrhallen* 2, 139f. See also Börner-Klein and Hollender *ib*. 144, 151f.

---

[353] Cf 7:9, 77 (near n185) to bShab 31b.
[354] 4:16, 71. Cf ed Lichtenstein, 318 which does not offer any comment on this unique version; see now Noam, *Megillat Ta'anit*, 385.

FRAGMENTARY AND PARTIAL ESTHER MIDRASHIM

In addition to the three more or less full length Midrashim to Esther described above, there seem to be numerous other midrashic compositions to this biblical scroll which have not survived the passage of time. These have reached us in a most fragmentary fashion, but thanks to the work of propitious scribes, various collectanea, and last but not least, the fragments from the Cairo Geniza, it has become possible to trace the sources and the original literary provenance of much of this material.

4. The Ancient Midrash to Esther

The Geniza Remains. The existence of an ancient Midrash to the Esther scroll has been known ever since the publication of a Geniza fragment, consisting of one folio, by S.A. Wertheimer in 1903. Rabbi Wertheimer gave his publication the title: 'A Yerushalmi Midrash to the Scroll of Esther', since he found this text to be based on 'the language and the style of the Yerushalmi aggada'.

Some seventy-five years later, Z.M. Rabinovitz published an additional folio, deriving from what he described as 'an ancient unknown midrash to Esther 6:11-7:8', found in a Cambridge Geniza fragment, while suggesting that it might belong to the same midrashic work evinced by the fragment previously published by Wertheimer. This hypothesis is now proof positive, owing to the fact that both folios are actually part of the same manuscript. Two small fragments from this very same manuscript have also been located in the Jacques Mosseri Geniza collection.

Components. Following is a survey of the various components for a proposed reconstruction of this lost Midrash:

(1) Midrash EsthR: Most of the opening proems and most of parashiyyot 1-5 which cover Esth 1:1-2:4, cf above, Section 1. 'Midrash Esther Rabba'.

(2) ms Manchester, Rylands B2374: a fragment of Introductory Proems 1-3.

(3) ms Cambridge TS F 2(2). 66:[355] from Proem 11, 2b, l. 26-1:4, 3b, l. 4.

(4) Nahmanides to bYev 76b: A short quotation from 'Haggada shel Megillat Esther' to Esth 1:13 (= EsthR 4:1).

(5) ms St. Petersburg-Antonin 302: Four (five?) folios, partially published by Z.M. Rabinovitz under the misnomer: 'A Novel Edition of Midrash Abba Gurion', see above p191 and List, no. 24. This manuscript contains the Midrash from Esth 2:7 to 4:4.[356] Another deleted and partial copy of this work, containing the Midrash from 3:4 to 4:4 found in ms Oxf-Bodl, fol. 122v-123v, was published by Buber in *Sifrei de-Aggadeta*, 49-51 as 'Midrash Panim Aherim I'

---

[355] In a private communication, Dr. Edna Engel has dated this fragment to c. 900 CE.
[356] Note the novel material to Esth 2:9, 11; 14; 18; 3:14 in Rabinovitz, 'Novel Edition'.

(= PA I(2)). Several selections from PA I(2) are also included in YalShim Esther.[357]

(6) Rav Nissim Gaon, Megillat Setarim, ed Kafih, 394: a short citation relating to Esth 3:6 (= EsthR 7:10), quoted from 'Haggada de-Megilla'.[358]

(7) YalShim Esth 1094:12: the casting of lots by Haman according to the days of the week and the months, see p223 no. 2; p225.

(8) Tosafot to bAZ 33b s.v. כסי: a short selection from the sedition of Haman (3:8) dealing with utensils touched by Gentiles, quoted from 'Midrash Esther'.[359]

(9) ms Vienna-Reiner H 145: fragments of two folios, containing the Midrash to Esth 3:8-13.[360] Even though some of the material is known from parallels in other works, there are, nevertheless, novel midrashic formulations as well as unknown explanations to 'and their laws are different to those of every people' (3:8) and to 'the satraps' and 'the governors' (3:12).

(10) Midrash EsthR: Selected passages from 8:4-10:15 (end), which cover Esth 4:5-9:2, cf above, Section 1: 'Midrash Esther Rabba'.

(11) MidrPs 22:5; 24; 27: Short homilies to Esth 4:13-5:2, see List, no. 30.

(12) R. Yaakov b. Hananel Sekili, Yalkut Talmud Tora: Gen., ms Sasson 783, 375: A short explanation to 'now it came to pass on the third day' (5:1a) taken from 'Midrash Esther'.[361]

(13) R. Natan b. Yehiel, Arukh, s.v. זייטוס : a short excerpt of the Midrash to Esth 5:1b dealing with the rare word קונעתו, quoted from 'Midrash Megillat Esther'.[362]

(14) ms TS C2.184: one folio containing the Midrash from Esth 6:10 to 7:8, published by Z.M. Rabinovitz.

---

[357] These are listed in Hyman, *Sources* 2, 580 (end) – 581 (top).

[358] This title is consistent with the midrashic titles in Megillat Sefarim, cf Abramson, *Rav Nissim Gaon*, 187 and add the present citation to his list, cf Lerner, 'The Aggadic *Midrashim*', 1056 n5. Incidentally, this citation from EsthR chap. 7 refutes the claim of Albeck, *Derashot*, 130 and 405 n36, cf above, n244.

[359] Some medieval rabbis in Spain and Provence quote this source from Megillat Esther Rabbati, cf Nahmanides, Meiri, Rav Nissim (Commentary on Alfasi) to bAZ 33b and R. Shlomo b. Adret in Torat ha-Bayyit 5:6, whereas R. Yom Tov b. Avraham of Sevilla to bAZ 33b, 148, quotes it from Haggadat Ahashverosh, cf Albeck, *Derashot*, 405 n36 and above, n225. Cf, also, the Commentaries of R. Aaron ha-Levi; R. Yosef ibn Haviva and R. Samson of Sens to bAZ 33b.

[360] In Allony-Loewinger, *List*, 14 no. 107, this fragment has been identified as 'Midrash Esther' while in Catalogue Schwarz-Loewinger-Roth, *Handschriften*, 63 no. 47 as 'Bruchstück von Ester Rabba (?)'.

[361] Catalogue Sassoon, *Ohel Dawid*, 643 par. 11. This homily also appears in Kad ha-Kemah of R. Bahya b. Asher, s.v. Purim, 336 (top); in n53, the editor refers to EsthR but fails to notice the differences. Cf also GenR 91,7 (p1129) and above, n270.

[362] Contra Buber, *Sifrei de-Aggadeta*, Preface, III n5.

(15) ms Mosseri VIII. 440.2: a small fragment containing the Midrash to Esth 7:8-9, which is a direct continuation of the previous folio.

(16) ms JTS R. 1912.1: a single folio containing the heading of parasha 5, which includes the Midrash to 8:15-17, 16 (in that order), published by S.A. Wertheimer. The two comparatively lengthy selections which precede this heading (the martyrdom of Yehuda b. Nekosa and his son and the scriptural portions that must be recited in the original Hebrew) apparently relate to 8:8[363] and to 8:9 respectively.

(17) ms Mosseri VIII, 440.1: a small fragment containing remnants of the homily found in LevR 28:4 (657f) whose final segment appears in EsthR 10:9, relating to Esth 8:1.[364]

(18) ExodR 41:2: the copyist of a manuscript which was apparently used by the printer of the Venice edition of ExodR[365] deleted the exemplum of Abun 'the Deceiver' by referring to 'Megillat Esther in the Midrash'. It is postulated that this exemplum appeared at the very end of the Midrash, in conjunction with Esth 10:3.[366]

Name, Division and Scope. In spite of the fragmentary nature of the Ancient Midrash, it is still possible to draw several important conclusions concerning its name, division et.al.

The two earliest authorities to quote from this Midrash – Rav Nissim Gaon (d. 1050) and Nahmanides (d. 1267) – both use the term 'Haggada' as the title of the Ancient Midrash.[367] As we have shown elsewhere,[368] the earliest titles of the Midrashim ordinarily included the term Haggada and so it is logical to assume that the original title of the Ancient Midrash was 'Haggadat Megilla'.[369]

Important information concerning the division of the Ancient Midrash is evident from the fragment published by Rabbi Wertheimer (no. 16). Since parasha 5 commences at Esth 8:15, it would be logical to assume that the four previous parashiyyot consisted of: (1) Esth 1:1; (2) 2:5; (3) 3:1; (4) 6:1.[370]

From the two complete folios it is evident that the Ancient Midrash was a sort of running exegetical commentary to the Book of Esther, covering most of

---

[363] Contra Lieberman, 'Roman Legal Institution', 12.

[364] In Catalogue Mosseri, 261 this fragment has been mistakenly identified as LevR 28,4.

[365] On the additions to GenR in this printing of Midrash Rabba, cf Albeck, 'Einleitung', 130f. Concerning ExodR, cf Shinan, *Shemot Rabba*, Introduction, 27 n120.

[366] This exemplum appears in LevR 5,4 (p113f), cf the commentary of Margulies to l. 4.

[367] Note that in his commentary to bAZ 33b, Nahmanides employed a different title (cf above, n225, n359). It is our assumption that the novel title 'Megillat Esther Rabbati' was influenced by the citation of the Tosafists, cf above, p177.

[368] Lerner, 'The Aggadic *Midrashim*', 1055f.

[369] Tabory, 'Esther Rabbah', 236 lists this title verbatim.

[370] Cf above, 'Midrash Panim Aherot II' and *ib.* n326.

its verses. Only a few in-between passages are not dealt with in the pages of the two published fragments.[371]

The scope of this Midrash is also very edifying. Among the 'complete' Midrashim, only EsthR goes beyond Chapter 7 of the biblical book, and that too in a most limited fashion. The remains of the Ancient Midrash seem to indicate that this Midrash covered the entire Scroll of Esther from beginning to end, including pertinent halakhic discussions.[372]

The finds from the Geniza also fully justify the conclusion of Ch. Albeck concerning the missing portions in the latter part of EsthR.[373]

Parallels in Early Palestinian Literature. An analysis of the midrashic teachings in the pages published by Wertheimer and Rabinovitz, which cover the later chapters of Esther, shows that the Midrash itself is most original and does not seen to have had too much in common with the other extant midrashic works to Esther. However, the St. Petersburg and the Vienna fragments which deal with earlier chapters, do evince certain parallels in EsthR and AbGur. The Ancient Midrash actually bears close affinity with Talmud Yerushalmi, which may readily be seen from the lengthy parallels in the folio published by Wertheimer,[374] as well as with GenR, as may be noted from the Antonin fragment published by Rabinovitz.[375] This close relationship of the Ancient Esther Midrash to early Palestinian literature is further enhanced by its composition in the style of early classical Midrash as far as terminology, loan words from the Greek and interspersing of Aramaic expressions are concerned.[376] The language, style and spelling are archaic and pristine. The Midrash has preserved numerous original midrashic explanations to the Esther scroll as well as rare idioms and expressions from the midrashic locution of the rabbis, some of them unknown from any other source.[377]

It is important to stress that the terminology and the traits of the Geniza material from the Ancient Midrash may be readily identified with the early stratum of Midrash EsthR which we have also termed 'The Ancient Midrash'. Moreover, it is important to note the appearance of the teachings of the Babylonian rabbis in the guise of 'the sages over there' (רבנן דתמן), which are sometimes pitted against the teachings of the local Palestinian rabbis, in the guise of

---

[371] 7:1-3; 8:10-14. Then again, the situation in chap. 8 is rather uncertain. It is quite possible that the missing passages are due to the manipulations of the editor (or of a scribe?).

[372] Note, especially, the halakhic items which are ordinarily not found in the midrashim to Esther. EsthR 10:9, ll. 7-9 is a notable exception, cf above, n256.

[373] See also above, n251. Cf, however, above, near n244 and n358.

[374] See Wertheimer, *Batei Midrashot* 1, 340 n6-10; 341 n13-16; 342 n20-26.

[375] See Rabinovitz, *Ginzé Midrash*, 166 n43; 168 n65, n67. Cf to the fragment from the Ancient Midrash, *ib.* 159 n42.

[376] *Vid.* Rabinovitz *ib.* 156 par 5-7; Wertheimer, *Batei Midrashot* 1, notes 3-4, 13, 16, 18. Note also the Aramaic term ודכותה.

[377] Rabinovitz *ib.* 156 ff.

'the sages over here' (רבנן דהכא). These teachings which are adduced in the Geniza fragments of the Ancient Midrash form a common denominator with those in the ancient portions of EsthR[378]

An Unknown Historical Incident. As mentioned above, the Wertheimer fragment contains an account of evil decrees against the Jewish people and the martyrdom of Yehuda b. Nekosa.[379] It is important to note that there is apparently no other allusion to this seemingly authentic story in any other work of talmudic or midrashic literature. Most unfortunately, the extant fragment contains only part of this somewhat enigmatic historical tradition, whose background has become the subject of scholarly debate and speculation.

Date. The Ancient Midrash thus gives every indication that it is one of the earliest midrashic compositions deriving from the Amoraic period. From the findings presented above, it is evident that it is on a par with GenR, whose redaction took place during the fifth century, and which is generally considered to be the earliest of the Amoraic Midrashim. The same could probably be said for the Ancient Midrash which, to our great chagrin, has survived in a most fragmentary fashion.

Bibliography. The Geniza fragment published by Rabbi Wertheimer first appeared in his *Leket Midrashim*, 2b-4a. It has been reprinted with some corrections in his collected series of midrashic texts edited by his son, *Batei Midrashot* 1, 340-343; Introduction, 318, which is the version referred to herein. The original Geniza fragment is now located in the library of the Jewish Theological Seminary, New York under the class mark: R. 1912.1, see the description in Danzig, *Catalogue*, 38; a photographic facsimile of the verso is presented in plate 10.

The Cambridge fragment (TS C 2.184) was published by Rabinovitz in *Ginzé Midrash*, 155-160 and a facsimile of the verso (in negative) appears opposite p303. The selections from ms Antonin 302 were also published by Rabinovitz *ib.* 163-170; see also additional comments 305f.

For the scholarly debate on the unique tradition dealing with the martyrdom of Yehuda b. Nekosa and his son, see Lieberman, 'Roman Legal Institutions', 11-13; idem, 'Persecution', 237-239; Baer, 'Israel', 38f n130, 237. An inspection of the original manuscript reveals that most of the emendations

---

[378] *Vid.* Rabinovitz *ib.* 158 ll. 13-14 (to Esth 6:12); 160 ll. 21-22 (to 7:12); Wertheimer, *Batei Midrashot* 1, 342 (from yMeg); *supra*, n256. Note also AbGur 2:7,18 which derives from the Ancient Midrash, cf Rabinovitz *ib.* 163 ll. 1-2 (to Esth 2:7).

[379] This is the name of an important sage during the epoch of R. Yehuda the Prince, i.e. the end of the Tannaic period (c. 200-230 CE), cf Hyman, *Toldoth*, 566. However, there is no way of definitely establishing this identity, cf Lieberman, 'Roman Legal Institutions', 69 n76; Baer, 'Israel, the Christian Church', 38 n130; Lieberman, 'Persecution', 238. On the theological debates of R. Yehudah b. Nekosa with the (Christian?) heretics and their aftermath, see EcclR 1:8:4, 4b.

proposed by Lieberman are irrelevant. A detailed study of this incident is being prepared by the present writer.

Numerous references and explanations to the fragments published by Rabinovitz are provided by Segal, *Babylonian Midrash*, e.g., vol 2, 248 n33; vol 3, 91 n252; 97-98 n301; 308-309.

5. Midrash Panim Aherot III (=PA III)

Uncovering the Midrash. Immediately following Midrash PA II, ms Oxf-Bodl 155, fol. 130r-131r adduces a series of homilies and explanations to Esth 2:5, introduced by the heading: פנים אחרות. It is thus clear that these homilies, which elaborate on the theme of 'a man of Judah named Mordechai in Shushan the edifice' derive from yet an additional unnamed Esther Midrash. Further proof for this contention may be brought from the fact that the final explanation[380] is similar to PA II, 62 but, nevertheless, differs from it considerably both in language and in the name of the tradent.

Even though Buber noted the above-mentioned heading,[381] he nevertheless, published these homilies on p78f as if they were a part of PA II and not a completely separate midrashic work.[382] This is probably due to the 'Other Midrash to the Scroll of Esther' (ms Hamburg 37) published previously by A. Jellinek, wherein these homilies appear integrated together with the homilies of PA II to Esth 2:5.[383] Albeck carefully referred to this unit as well as to the ensuing sets of homilies as 'various extracts', but this designation also belies their real nature as representatives of additional midrashic compositions to the Scroll of Esther. In any event, it is important to note that heretofore, most scholarly quotations from these homilies and their continuations have been mistakenly attributed to PA II.

An additional series of homilies in the Oxford manuscript (fol. 131r-131v), which forms a direct continuation to the above, was published by Buber on p79-81. This segment is introduced by the heading 'a different pericope' (פרשה אחרת)[384] and contains four (three of them rather lengthy) homilies to Esth 3:1 ('After these things did King Ahasuerus promote Haman, the son of Hammedatha ...').[385] It is logical to assume that this additional series of homilies is

---

[380] 79, near n198.

[381] See his comment, 78 n187.

[382] This is very clearly evident from the identical page headings and the consecutive sequence of the footnotes.

[383] Note that some of these homilies are also found in Yalkut Shimoni and it appears that R. Shimon ha-Darshan's copy of PA II already included these additions.

[384] Buber failed to mention this heading.

[385] Note that ed Buber, 80 gives the impression that the third homily, is followed by a homily to Esth 6:1 ff. However, the verses from Esth 6 are all part of that homily and Buber mistakenly printed them as paragraph headings, which also misled Börner-Klein and Hollender, *Midraschim*, 137.

also part of PA III. Following Wünsche, Börner-Klein and Hollender recognized the individuality of this section and granted it the title: 'Mordechai Midrasch, PAB II'.

Contents. In the homilies to Esth 2:5 – all of them anonymous – the rabbis concentrated on the expression 'the man of Judah' (איש יהודי) as an appellation for Mordechai, who, nevertheless, stemmed from the tribe of Benjamin. These homiletical explanations extol (1) Judah's devotion to Benjamin; (2) David's compassion for Shimi, the Benjaminite; (3) Mordechai's abstention from eating Gentile dishes (יהודי, 'observant Jew'); and (4) stress the idea that just as the redemption from the decrees of Haman was implemented by 'a man of Judah', so too will the future redemption be achieved by 'a man of Judah'.

The novel ideas in the homilies to 3:1 include: The Almighty purposely withholding punishment from the wicked in order to fully publicize their iniquity, and Mordechai's Benjaminite ancestry as a reason for not bowing down before Haman.

Division, Terminology and Scope. As noted above,[386] pericopes 2:5 and 3:1 reflect the classic division of the biblical Book of Esther, and it may thus be assumed that PA III was a Midrash which concentrated its homilies on the initial verses of the pericopes. The terminology employed in these selections includes the familiar proem introductory formula 'This is what Scripture said' (זש"ה) and some other examples of expressions common in Tanhuma-Yelammmedenu literature.[387]

PA III does not seen to have been a too lengthy Midrash as the actual number of pericopes to Esther is quite limited. Most of the missing material probably related to Esth 1:1 and 6:1.

Additional Components? On the basis of the above data on terminology and pericopes it is possible to suggest some additional segments from this long lost Midrash, which have remained extant in midrashic literature:

(1) Mss Vatican 96 and 290:11, ff. 2b-3a; 4a; 5a. This manuscript which bears the mistaken Latin title, 'Midras Homelia R. Thanchuma in Esther', actually contains some Tanhuma type proems to Esth 1:1, see List, no. 22.
(2) Aggadat Esther, 60, ll. 9-13 (near n8): A homily to Esth 6:1 commencing with the expression מה כתיב למעלה מן העניין, 'What is written before our verse?'

Nature. In summation, it may assumed that PA III was an additional Midrash of the Tanhuma-Yelammedenu type which focused attention on the opening

---

[386] 'Midrash Panim Aherot II' and *ib.* n326.
[387] Especially the closing formulae: 'for that reason is it written / said' (לכך נאמר \ אמר); 'to fulfil what is written' (לקיים מה שנאמר).

verses of the pericopes. This Midrash apparently did not serve as a running commentary to the Esther story, as did its counterpart, PA II. In spite of their being more or less members of the same family of Midrashim, the extant material does not provide any evidence of interaction between both works.

Bibliography. The homilies to Esth 2:5 from PA III were first published by Jellinek, *Beit ha-Midrasch* 1, 19-21; 22-23. The short comment of Albeck concerning this text is found in Zunz-Albeck, *Derashot*, 425. The only other textual evidence for these homilies et al. is four excerpts in Yalkut Shimoni, *vid.* Hyman, *Sources* 2, Indices, 581b (to 40a and 41a). The material published by Buber has been translated into German by Boerner-Klein and Hollender, *Midraschim*, 130-139, l. 2; see *ib.*, 83.

6. Midrash Panim Aherot IV (= PA IV?)

The ensuing selection in ms Oxf-Bodl 155, fol. 131v is a short extract of four lines under the heading Panim Aherot. This excerpt, which is introduced by the formula תנו רבנן, ordinarily used for quoting a baraita in the Bavli, relates to the lots drawn by Haman in Esth 3:7. Buber did not publish this short homily as part of PA II, nor did he allude to it in his Introduction or in his notes.

At first glance, this source seems to derive from EsthR 7:11, 11d. However, upon closer scrutiny, it becomes apparent that there are numerous differences in language and style between both sources. In spite of the similar contents, it is not at all certain that this short excerpt, which is abruptly curtailed by the note: 'etc. as above' (כו' כדלעיל) supposedly referring to the scribe's copy of Midrash AbGur, the first Midrashic work to Esther in this manuscript,[388] actually derives from EsthR. Moreover, in lieu of the abundant material in EsthR which the scribe of ms Oxf-Bodl 155 could have certainly utilized in his compendium of Midrashim to Esther, one would venture to conclude with almost complete certainty that EsthR is not the source of this short excerpt. It is thus entirely possible that we are dealing here with an additional unknown midrashic compilation to the Esther scroll known to the scribe, to which we have allotted the title PA IV.

To complicate matters even further, attention should be paid to yet another very close parallel to the four line excerpt, which appears in the Purim homily (= PA I (1)) 3:7, 46. The possibility presents itself that the scribe of the Oxford manuscript was actually referring to the latter source and not to AbGur. In any event, attention should be focused on the fact that by copying the four line excerpt, the scribe of ms Oxf-Bodl 155 was saying, in effect, that this excerpt and its parallel in the Purim homily mentioned above – which according to our hypothesis, derives from Midrash Aher (see below) – are not one and the same! On the other hand, such a limited extract might indicate that we are

---

[388] Cf AbGur 3:7, 24. Note also the additional parallel in PAI (1), 46, see below.

herein dealing with an additional copy of one of the above-mentioned Midrashim, in which the scribe noted a significant variant to the first day of the lots in the Midrash to Esth 3:7, and not to an additional midrashic work.

Nothing more is known about this midrashic composition. In lieu of such scant material, there does not seem to be much hope of ever retrieving other sections of this work, nor of relating it to the other known fragmentary Midrashim, which were not included in the collection assembled by the first copyist of the scribal tradition preserved in the Oxford manuscript.[389]

7. Midrash Panim Aherot V (= PA V, Midrash Ruah ha-Kodesh)

Uncovering the Midrash. Immediately following the above-mentioned four line homily, ms Oxf-Bodl 155, fol. 131v-132v, continues to adduce yet another selection introduced by the heading, 'Panim Aherot'. Buber, who did not heed this heading nor mention it in his notes, printed the new selection as if it was the direct continuation of the preceding one (PA III) on p81f.

Like the first part of PA III, this new selection, which we have termed PA V, also contains a homily and several explanations to Esth 2:5. Here too, most of the material appears verbatim in the Hamburg manuscript published by Jellinek,[390] wherein the homily and the explanations have been integrated into the framework of the homilies deriving from PA II and PA III on this very same verse. It is most probable that this arrangement also misled Buber to consider this selection a part of PA II. As mentioned above, Albeck described these additional homilies as 'various extracts'.

Basic Terminology and Structure. Nevertheless, the integrity of this selection as an independent Midrash can be readily established. The opening homily employs a unique formula which identifies it as a special genre of Aggadic Midrash: ...זהו שנאמר ברוח הקודש על ידי, 'This is what was said through the Holy Spirit by...', followed by the name of the author of the biblical work[391] quoted in the petiha. In the wake of this formula, these midrashic works should be entitled the 'Ruah ha-Kodesh Midrashim'.[392]

A usual feature of this genre is the inclusion of a circular proem[393] based on the opening verse and the use of a rhetorical question preceded by the formula: כנגד מי אמר המקרא הזה?, 'In regards to whom did he recite the verse?' This unique composition concludes with the repetition of the opening verse, intro-

---

[389] Cf below, p212-219.

[390] Excluding the third explanation to איש יהודי (Buber, n210) as well as the last three lines of the text.

[391] *Viz.* the prophet (or king) to whom the rabbis attributed the authorship of the biblical book, e.g.: Isaiah – The Book of Isaiah; Jeremiah – The Book of Jeremiah and Lamentations; David – The Book of Psalms; Solomon – Proverbs, Canticles and Ecclesiastes, etc.

[392] Cf Mann, *The Bible*, Hebr. section, 1, 44ff; Bregman, 'Circular Proems', 40; Lerner, 'Notes on the Editing', 115 n21; Elizur, *Pesiqta Rabbati*, 54-57.

[393] On this literary device, *vid.* Bregman, 'Circular Proems'; Fox, 'Circular Proem'.

duced by the formula: לכך נאמר, 'For this reason it has been said...'. Needless to say, this formula is followed here in full and the circular proem commences and concludes with Ps 18:19.

A special feature of this proem is the inclusion of an anecdote describing a theological debate between R. Meir and an unnamed Roman prefect (*hegemon*),[394] concerning the plight of the Jewish people among the Gentile nations. This is a unique episode which does not have any parallel in other works of traditional literature.[395]

The homily to Esth 2:5 is followed by a series of three explanations equalizing Mordechai with Moses and with Abraham and portraying him as one who professed the unity of God in the world. All of these have very close parallels in EsthR 6:2, 10a-b, a fact unnoticed by Buber. Close study of these parallels has shown that they were utilized by the final redactor of EsthR as part of the additional material appended to the latter half of that Midrash, cf above.

Additional Material. Further textual material deriving from PA V is evinced by an Oxford Geniza fragment which incorporates various homilies from AbGur and PA V. This fragment contains all the exegetic explanations to PA V 2:5 (= Buber, 82) as well as large segments from an additional opening proem, ostensibly to 6:1, but in reality to 3:1 ff.[396] This proem is also phrased in Ruah ha-Kodesh terminology. A large segment of this homily is found in AbGur 4:1, 34-35 which evidently had ready access to its contents. It is interesting to note that the compiler of AbGur actually utilized all the contents of this homily as evinced by the Oxford fragment, including the 'letter of Haman',[397] and simply deleted the opening Ruah ha-Kodesh formula. Fortunately, the closing section of this proem has been preserved intact in Aggadat Esther 3:9, 33 (preceding n42).

Novel Homilies. Among the additional novel homilies of PA V, we may enumerate the following: (1) the merit of the wife of Shimi b. Gera; (2) the exaltation of the power of the Almighty in taking revenge from Haman and His exaltation in the future Redemption; (3) the Gentile nations subjugating the Jews and aiming at annihilating them; (4) the martyrdom of Hannania, Mishael and Azarya and their fears of the fires of Hell; (5) God as the redeemer of the

---

[394] Cf Herr, 'Dialogues', 125, 128-129.

[395] It is logical to assume that this source relates to a rabbi of the third or fourth/centuries and not to the fourth generation Tanna, R. Meir, cf Urbach, *Sages*, 545. The repudiation of the Jewish people by the Almighty does not seem to have been on the agenda of the theological debates dating from the Tannaic period, cf Herr *ib.* 142f, 146.

[396] This may be readily seen from the Yemenite compendium AggEsth to 3:9, 32-33 l. 12, which adduces the entire proem. Note well that the 'letter of Haman' is lacking there.

[397] AbGur 3:12, l. 2, 29-30, l. 12. On the other hand, there is still some possibility that the 'letter' is not an integral part of this proem, cf AggEsth 3:9, 32-33; 3:14, 36-38; cf above, n396.

Jewish nation in answer to the claim of Haman that 'they do not have a re-deemer'.

Scope. It is thus quite evident that even though the Ruah ha-Kodesh Midrash to Esther (PA V) seems to have been of limited scope, concentrating mainly on the classical verse divisions (sedarim) of the biblical Book of Esther, the tex-tual remains of two of these homilies (to 2:5 and 3:1 ff.) have shown that they are, nevertheless, of relatively lengthy proportions and that one of them, ap-parently covered several segments of the Purim narrative.

Date. Midrash Abba Gurion, which incorporated a large amount of homiletical material from PA V, is apparently a product of no later than the tenth century (see above, 2. 'Midrash Abba Gurion'). This would seem to indicate that the Ruah ha-Kodesh Midrash itself was completed no later than the ninth century. However, a more definite conclusion awaits the discovery of additional mate-rial from this long-lost midrashic work.

Bibliography. The homily and explanations from PA V were first published by Jellinek in *Bet ha-Midrasch* 1, 21-23. Some extracts from the text are found in Yalkut Shimoni, vid. Hyman, *Sources* 2, Indices, 581b (to 40 [correct: 42] b; 42b).

Remnants of this text containing some variants, as well as a host of novel material to 3:1 ff. are found in a Geniza fragment: ms Oxf-Bodl 2851 (e. 77), fol. 43v-44. For the short comment of Albeck, see Zunz-Albeck, *Derashot*, 425. Jellinek's text has been translated into German by Wünsche, *Lehrhallen* 2, 143-147 and by Börner-Klein and Hollender, *Midraschim*, 139-142.

The theological debates between Roman dignitaries and Jewish sages have been studied by Herr, 'Dialogues', 127-150, although the debate between R. Meir and the prefect is dealt with incidentally (145 n115).

8. Midrash Aher

The Evidence of ms Parma 563. The existence of yet another Midrash to Esther, which a copyist dubbed מדרש אחר,[398] literally: 'a different Midrash' to Esther, was first noted by Horowitz in his description of Midrash AbGur ms Parma 563, during the course of his survey of the Midrashim to Esther.[399] Midrash Aher is mentioned as the source for certain glosses excerpted from some other unknown midrashic work to Esther, which the scribe of ms Parma interpolated into his manuscript of Midrash AbGur, during the course of copy-ing the latter Midrash. In any event, the appelation 'Midrash Aher' attests to

---

[398] This Midrash is not to be confused with the selection in ms Hamburg 37:8, fol. 124 published by Jellinek in *Bet ha-Midrasch* 1, 19-24, which is also entitled: Midrash Aher.

[399] Horowitz, *Sammlung*, 50. See also Buber, Preface to *Sifrei de-Aggadeta*, III.

the fact that the scribe had no knowledge whatsoever of the name of this Midrash; note that there is no appreciable difference between Panim Aherot and Midrash Aher.

An inspection of the Parma manuscript has yielded only three such glosses, two to AbGur 3:7, 24 (75b-76a) and a third to 4:1, 32 (78b), whose contribution to the text is rather unclear. Buber published the first gloss which deals with the arguments of the fifth day of creation against Haman's plans to liquidate the Jews on that day, in his notes, although this gloss is also in need of clarification.[400]

The second gloss, which deals with the burning of Haman and his sons in Gehenna, is most elucidating, since this tradition is found verbatim in the Purim homily which Buber published under the title Panim Aherot, Version A (= PA I (1)), 46.[401] It is thus apparent that the Midrash termed 'Midrash Aher' served as one of the sources for this homily. Given this information, it is logical to assume that other novel selections of the Purim homily also derive from this same unknown Midrash.

The Evidence of Sefer ha-Zikhronot. If the above assumption is correct, it will enable the reconstruction of an unusually large segment of Midrash Aher – a supposedly long lost Midrash – from Esth 3:12 until 6:10. Even though the text of the Purim homily published by Buber contains numerous scribal deletions,[402] the full undeleted version is readily available in Sefer ha-Zikhronot of R. Elazar b. Asher the Levite, 'The Chronicles of Jerahmeel', ms Oxf-Bodl 2797, ff. 87-90, ed Yassif, 271-279, as well in an additional manuscript in the Cambridge University Library. It is thus possible to identify the midrashic material in these sources as the text of Midrash Aher.[403] Incidentally, the existence of the Cambridge manuscript, which is almost identical with the text of Sefer Ha-Zikhronot, suggest that the author drew his material from a similar excerpted text and not from the Midrash *per se*. The almost identical captions in both sources seem to bolster this conclusion.

An inspection of this material reveals an unusually large amount of parallels with AbGur, which seemingly relied on it as one of its sources.[404] In fact, the only novel material in the extant remains of Midrash Aher is the unique

---

[400] AbGur 3:7, 24 n72. Note that Buber corrected the text of the gloss (ממדרש אחר) to read: ובמדרש אחר. The original version seemingly alludes to the previous material (ignored by Buber!) which actually contains a different version.

[401] See below, List, no. 11.

[402] Concerning the systematic deletion of duplicate material in the scribal tradition of ms Oxf-Bodl 155, cf above p197f.

[403] Note that the compiler of Sefer ha-Zikhronot ed Yassif, 279 specifically states that 'the material from the "letter of Haman" until here [= the end of the selection] derives from a Midrash'. Gaster's translation of this statement, p251, is somewhat misleading.

[404] E.g. AbGur 4:1, 32-34 l. 2. Note, however, that very similar parallels are also evinced by the Aggadic-Narrative Midrash, cf below, and note AggEsth 4:1, 38-40.

version of the 'letter of Haman' (LXXXI, 241-242, ed Yassif, 271-274), which was partially copied by the scribe of ms Oxf-Bodl 155 within the framework of the Purim homily (*Sifrei de-Aggadeta*, 47), and the short prayer of Mordechai (LXXXII, 5, 247, ed Yassif 276, ll. 6-8).[405]

The 'Letter of Haman'.[406] In the imaginary epistle attributed to Haman, which was supposedly sent out to 'all the kingdoms of the earth', Haman announces his plans for the total annihilation of the Jewish people. The version of this epistle in Midrash Aher is cloaked in one of the most vicious anti-Jewish tirades of all time, comparing the Jewish nation to the 'great eagle',[407] which through the use of various tactics and manipulations, actually threatens to effect complete domination and wreak havoc on the entire civilized world. This description of the Jewish people somewhat approximates the infamous 'Protocols of the Elders of Zion' and may rightly be considered to be one of its precursors. The letter itself, whose complete version is found in the Oxford manuscript of Sefer ha-Zikhronot, is coached in picturesque language and contains unique dramatic effects.

Midrash Aher and the Other Midrashim to Esther. From the scribal glosses in ms Parma 563 and from the Esther Midrash which serves as the backbone of the Purim homily, it is apparent that the text of Midrash Aher formed such a close parallel to AbGur that the scribe who copied them one after another could indeed eliminate most of the material in the second work, due to what might be termed as 'mass duplication'. It is thus not surprising that, owing to the immense popularity of AbGur, and due to the unusual similarity between both works, Midrash Aher fell into almost complete oblivion, to the point of not even one single extant manuscript.

Midrash Aher also seems to have had a great deal in common with yet another lost Midrash: the Aggadic-Narrative Midrash which has survived in two Geniza fragments and in some lengthy citations in Aggadat Esther, see below, 'An Aggadic-Narrative Midrash'. Both of these midrashic works parallel each other to such an extent that it is extremely difficult to distinguish between them.

The rediscovery of Midrash Aher also enables the identification of the sources of several lengthy selections and parallels in various medieval com-

---

[405] This prayer appears in the section deleted by the copyist who obviously alluded to his copy of AbGur (כדלעיל), see PA I (1), 47. This is a reference to AbGur 4:1, 32-34 l. 2; 5:14, 37 l. 2; 38 l. 7 and the copyist may have not noticed it. It is also found in MegEsth 4:1, 70 which probably, borrowed if from Midrash Aher. On the other hand, a comparison with parallel accounts in the Aggadic-Narrative Midrash and YalShim 1057:4-5 seemingly infers that Mordechai's prayer is an interpolation.

[406] For the anti-Semitic aspects see also 'Further Reading' at the end of the chapter.

[407] Ezek 17 probably served as an antecedent for this parable.

pendia such as Yalkut Shimoni to Esther[408] and Midrash Megillat Esther.[409] It is also quite possible that some of the variant readings and additions evinced by ms Parma 563, which were recorded by Buber in his notes, also stem from Midrash Aher, even though there is no additional mention of this Midrash in the manuscript. Further research will have to compare the readings of this manuscript with the text of Sefer ha-Zikhronot in order to arrive at a more definite conclusion.[410]

Scope. From the evidence presented by the glosses in the Parma manuscript and the lengthy excerpt in Sefer ha-Zikhronot, it appears that Midrash Aher dealt mainly with the Purim saga *per se*, beginning with the appearance of Haman in Esth 3:1 and concluding with his execution at the end of Esth 7. Neither the Purim homily (PA I (1)) nor the anthology of R. Elazar b. Asher the Levite or the Cambridge manuscript, evince any midrashic material to the first two chapters of the Esther Scroll, apart from the 'throne of Solomon', which does not seem to have derived from this lost Midrash .[411]

New Areas of Research. Undoubtedly, the uncovering of large selections from Midrash Aher and the Aggadic-Narrative Midrash (see below) opens new vistas of research into the literary history of the Midrashim to the Scroll of Esther. Fundamental questions surrounding the original provenance of the numerous extraordinary lengthy parallels in EsthR, AbGur, Midrash Aher *et al.*, will require new areas of investigation into the make-up and the mechanism of each of these midrashic works. Hopefully, this projected research will also lead to a proper appreciation of EsthR 2.

Suffice it to say for the time being that preliminary study has demonstrated a very close inter-relationship and inter-dependence between Midrash Aher and some of the lengthy parallels in the final sections of EsthR and AbGur.

Bibliography. The lengthy passages from Midrash Aher in Sefer ha-Zikhronot, compiled by R. Elazar b. Asher ha-Levi, are found in ms Oxf-Bodl 2797 [Heb. d. 11], 87r-90v. A scholarly Hebrew edition of this material is available in

---

[408] YalkShim Esther 1056: 2-5, 7-8. In his efforts to attribute these citations to EsthR and AbGur, Hyman, *Sources* 2, 473 divided them in a most awkward fashion.

[409] E.g. MegEsth 4:1, 70; 6:13, 73. It also remains to be seen whether the Purim homily entitled Pesikta Hadeta is dependent on Midrash Aher for its material.

[410] Cf e.g., AbGur 6:3, 39 n7 with Sefer ha-Zikhronot, 278f end (Mordechai's dream).

[411] Note that the material to Esth 1:1 in PA I(1), 45 is from the Talmud (bMeg 11a). A very much deleted version of the 'throne of Solomon' midrash, introduced by the term אמרו חכמים, 'The Sages said', is found in PA I (1) 1:2, 45. Note that the Sefer ha-Zikhronot text (ed Yassif 279-281) contains two versions, a very short one with some lacunae and a relatively lengthy version, both of them *following* the selections from Midrash Aher. This would seem to indicate that they derive from some other source(s).

Yassif's ed of Sefer ha-Zikhronot, 271-279. An additional manuscript containing identical contents is ms Cambridge Add. 2661 (SCR 874), fol. 34b-40b.

The English translation of Gaster, *Jerahmeel*, chapters 81-83, 241-251 has been available for over one hundred years. See also the notes of Schwarzbaum, 'Prolegomenon', 83, who was unaware of the fact that this text is actually an original Midrash and should not to be classified as PA I (1). Large sections of Midrash Aher have been incorporated into the Purim homily (PA I (1)) published by Buber in *Sifrei de-Aggadeta*, 46-48.

An additional copy of the apocryphal 'letter of Haman' is found in ms Oxf-Bodl 1755 [Opp. 128], fol. 159. These should be compared with other examples of this genre: ms Parma 924, published by Perreau, 'Rundschreiben', 46f; AbGur 3:12, 29-32, including the Aramic version in the British Library; EsthR 7:13, 12c-d; AggEsth 3:14, 36-38, cf Buber, n61; Horowitz, *Sammlung*, MegEsth 68f and n93 *ib.*; Schwarzbaum, 'Prolegomenon', 83; Ginzberg, *Legends* 4, 408-412; 5, 466 n115. See also the list of topoi below, 'Overview', no. 5.

9. An Aggadic-Narrative Midrash

A Geniza Fragment in the British Library. A single folio from the Geniza in the British Library (OR 5559A, fol. 39) contains a detailed description of the legendary behind-the-scenes scenario that transpired in the heavenly sphere after the severe sins of the Jewish people during the epoch of Ahasuerus; their participation in the non-kosher feast and accompanying debauchery, which according to the Midrash were perpetrated by Haman and Ahasuerus, gave vent to the malicious sedition and blasphemy of Satan, who juistifiably demanded that the Almighty annihilate the entire Jewish Nation.

The author of the unpublished hand-list of manuscripts in the British Library described this Geniza fragment as 'a midrashic commentary on Esther 7:18 [sic],[412] substantially agreeing with Midrash Rabba'. However, even though there are many points of agreement with EsthR 7:18, there are also many discrepancies between the two sources, especially from the point where Mordechai, upon hearing of the heavenly decree against the Jewish people, rents his garments.

Additional lengthy parallels to this fragment are evinced by AbGur 4:1, 33-34, l. 2;[413] YalShim Esther 1057: 4-5; 7 and Midrash Aher, which has been preserved in Sefer ha-Zikhronot of R. Elazar b. Asher, the Levite.[414]

---

[412] The cataloguer of the hand-list mistakenly listed the number of the parasha in EsthR instead of the biblical reference, which should read: 3:9.

[413] The continuation of this homily in AbGur, 35 l. 3ff is an adaptation from PA V, cf above following n306.

[414] Ed Yassif 275 l. 11 - 276 l. 15. Cf above, Section 8.

All these parallels deal with the same material and are of similar content. In addition, the language of each individual text is extremely close to the parallel versions. On the other hand, numerous differences in style and content should not be obscured. One is thus rather uncertain whether the British Library fragment, whose contents more or less approximate those of the above-mentioned parallels and whose language is quite similar, represents a variant version of one of the other texts or, alternatively, does it derive from an independent midrashic source?

The Evidence of Aggadat Esther. The answer to this question is provided by an almost exact parallel to the Geniza fragment in several lengthy selections of the Yemenite yalkut to the Scroll of Esther, the so-called 'Aggadat Esther' published over 100 years ago by Buber. Indeed, such an identification enables the partial reconstruction of an additional missing Midrash to Esther. The AggEsth version has divided the material between two different verses and thus includes the beginning and the end of both lengthy selections (4:1, 38-40, l. 14; 4:17, 45-46), which are lacking in the Geniza fragment.

Since the above-mentioned midrashic elaborations in AggEsth abound in lengthy heroic-dramatic descriptions of the Purim saga, we have entitled them: 'An Aggadic-Narrative Midrash', which alludes to the extended and verbose style of this text.

Identifying Additional Selections. In the wake of the completed version of the British Library fragment in AggEsth 4:17, 45-46 it is possible to identify an additional selection from this Midrash in yet another Geniza fragment. As already noted, ms Oxf-Bodl 2851 (e. 77), fol. 43-44 is an anthology which derived material from various Midrashim to the Scroll of Esther, including two rather lengthy homilies from PA V.[415] However, the first 16 lines of fol. 43r are apparently part of the Aggadic-Narrative Midrash dealt with herein, as they form a relatively close parallel to AggEsth 4:17, 46, ll. 5-14. This selection highlights the fasting and the pious supplications of the young disciples of Mordechai which were aimed at cancelling the evil decrees and evoke the positive response of the Almighty.

It is thus probable to assume that additional lengthy unidentified selections of AggEsth also stem from this very same Aggadic-Narrative Midrash, whose only direct remnants are found in the British Library fragment. Likewise, it may be assumed that the lengthy section dealing with the debate between Ahasuerus and Haman over the feasibility of destroying the Jewish nation, which precedes the above-mentioned selections in AggEsth, as well as an additional lengthy midrashic source dealing with the deliberations over the

---

[415] See above, 'Midrash Panim Aherot V'.

217

selection of a tree for the execution of Haman following them, also belong to the Aggadic-Narrative Midrash.[416]

It is thus apparent that the Yemenite compiler of AggEsth possessed a copy of the Aggadic-Narrative Midrash and drew upon it freely. This generosity enables the restoration of large chunks of material and the subsequent restoration of this long-lost Midrash.

Scope and Parallels. From the extant remains in AggEsth, it appears that, similar to Midrash Aher, the Aggadic-Narrative Midrash encompassed the epic portions of the Purim story, from the advent of Haman until his execution. As in the case of Midrash Aher, the fact that this heretofore unknown Midrash composed in the style of the aggadic narrative shares so much joint material with other Midrashim to the Esther Scroll, invites new areas of investigation as to the original provenance of these aggadic teachings and their course of development in the various Midrashim to the Scroll of Esther: EsthR; AbGur and Midrash Aher, as well as several lengthy excerpts extant in Yalkut Shimoni,[417] et al.[418]

10. A Short Midrash (?)

In his treatise, 'Rav Pealim', a digest of information concerning the various Midrashim, based on traditional sources, R. Abraham b. Elijah of Vilna enumerated 'the short Midrash' to Esther quoted in Menot ha-Levi, the Commentary of R. Shlomo Alkabez to Esther, which was first published in Venice 1585.[419]

In truth, Alkabez does not seen to have possessed a copy of such a Midrash since his quotations relating to same are specifically recorded as deriving from 'an appendix copied by R. Judah b. Shoshan immediately following the latter's Commentary' to Esther. Note the following midrashic interpretations:

> Esth 1:11, the erotic intentions of Vashti in her nude appearance before the king 'with the crown royal' (1:9, 37a).[420]

> Esth 7:4, Esther's declaration to Ahasuerus that she is the great grandchild of King Saul (7:5, 170b).

---

[416] *Vid.* AggEsth 3:9, 33 (near n42) to 34 l. 14; 6:1, 60 ll. 13-61.

[417] Cf e.g. YalShim Esther 1059:5, ll. 56-60 (note that contra Hyman, this is the correct division and the beginning of a new paragraph) with AggEsth 6:1, 60 ll. 5-8.

[418] Additional parallels are evinced by Aggadat Esther and Pesikta Hadeta.

[419] R. Abraham b. Elijah, *Rav Pealim*, 103. Note that in the example adduced by him (near n420), no 'short Midrash' whatsoever is mentioned. However, the additional quotations from Menot ha-Levi to Esth 7 cited below do mention 'a short Midrash'.

[420] This Midrash is attributed to the 'Commentary of R. Yehudah b. Shoshan', without mention of the 'appendix' or the 'short Midrash', see previous note.

218

Esth 7:5, in response to Esther's unspecified accusation (against Haman), the king asks, 'who is he and where does he live?' (7:5, 171b).

Esth 7:7, the king, confronted by angels of destruction resembling humans, who reveal the pernicious instructions that they have received from the sons of Haman, becomes furious over the outrage (7:7, 172a).

An examination of these sources proves that they are not found in any of the extant Midrashim to Esther. Since the fourth quotation relates to the same passage as the material from the Ancient Midrash published by Z.M. Rabinovitz,[421] but is nevertheless, of differing content, we may assume that the citations of R. Judah b. Shoshan do not derive from that Midrash, and should most likely be attributed to some other unknown midrashic work.

OVERVIEW: DESCRIPTION OF THE ESTHER MIDRASHIM

In previous sections of this sub-chapter, we have dealt with no less than ten different midrashic works to the Scroll of Esther – a surprisingly rich harvest in comparison with previous scholarly discourse on the matter. Even though only three of the above-mentioned ten midrashic works have reached us intact, there is sufficient evidence to postulate the existence of most of the others, usually from more than one direction. This does not mean that future research may not be able to subtract from this number by proving that one or more of these works should actually be combined with one of the other heretofore unknown Midrashim, especially in the case of PA IV, whose scanty remains do not allow any linkage whatsoever with the other works. On the other hand, there is no guarantee that these ten midrashic works actually represent the sum total of Midrashim on Esther. There is every possibility that the compiler of Aggadat Esther possessed yet an additional Midrash which he utilized in the composition of his yalkut.[422]

Understandably, the various Midrashim usually differ in character and in complexion, especially in their relationship to the biblical text. Following is a brief summary of the works (with their numbers) according to their literary leanings:[423]

Exegetical: EsthR (1), Ancient Midrash (4); Short Midrash (10)

Homiletical: EsthR, proems (1); PA II, Proems (3); PA III (5); PA V (7)

Narrative: EsthR, Later Additions (1b); AbGur, parts (2); PA IV ? (6); Midrash Aher (8); Aggadic-Narrative Midrash (9).

---

[421] Rabinovitz, *Ginzé Midrash*, 157.

[422] Note the series of novel texts to Esth 5 introduced by the introductory formula אמרו חכמים etc. interspersed in AggEsth 5:2, 52f; 5:9, 55; 5:11, 56 (near n69); 5:14, 57f.

[423] The numbers in parentheses refer to the various sections.

A most conspicuous factor of this list is the fact that just as in the case of the Midrashim to the Pentateuch, here too the midrashic corpus includes a wide variety of literary works: classical exegetical, in the style of GenR (1a; 3; 4; 10); homiletical, in the style of Midrash Tanhuma, although lacking the 'Yelammedenu Rabbenu' halakhic questions and answers (5); homiletical in the style of the Ruah Ha-Kodesh genre (7); and narrative, reflecting the epic style of PRE (8; 9).

An interesting aspect is the scope of these works in terms of coverage of the Book of Esther. Aside from the Ancient Midrash (4) and the core of this Midrash preserved in the first part of EsthR, most of the other midrashic compositions have limited themselves to expounding the dramatic events that transpired in the Kingdom of Persia from Ahasuerus` access to the throne, until the execution of Haman (Esth 7:10).[424] This is also evident from the list of the various topoi (below, p223f). It is thus logical to assume that most of the editors of the Midrashim to Esther viewed their literary task as an exposition of the Purim story itself, while stressing the miraculous salvation of the Jewish people from the evil decree of Haman. They therefore made very little effort to engage in the systematic exegesis of the Esther Scroll from beginning to end, including items of halakha and ritual which appear in the later chapters. Note well that some of the more important yalkutim[425] and compendia have generally adopted the latter approach.

Another intriguing facet is the fact that many of these works borrowed freely from one another. During the course of our survey, it became readily apparent that, in numerous loci, the contents of some of these works are most unoriginal. Midrash Abba Gurion is a composite work which derived its material from the Ancient Midrash, from PA II, from PA V, et al.[426] The same could be said for the late Additions to Esther Rabba 6-10, which even appear to have utilized a wider array of sources.[427] It is interesting to note that there are hardly any appreciable differences between several lengthy segments of Midrash Aher (8) and the Aggadic-Narrative Midrash (9). We may safely conclude that many of the Midrashim as delineated and described here for the first time give the impression of actually having borrowed from one another. However, only after a critical reconstruction of these lost texts will it be possible to assess their exact inter-relationship. Suffice it to say that, in certain cases, such borrowing and influence seem to have reached rather large proportions.

Another safe hypothesis concerns the disappearance of texts. We would like to suggest that the very fact that so many works resembled each other

---

[424] Some of the Midrashim apparently glanced over the first two chapters of Esther and concentrated their interpretations on the events that transpired from the advent of Haman onwards, cf Midrash Aher (List, no. 8) and the Aggadic- Narrative Midrash (List, no. 9).

[425] E.g. Lekah Tov; Yalkut Shimoni and Aggadat Esther.

[426] This is obviously the reason for the inconsistent literary nature of this work, which is an uneven combination of exegetical and homiletical midrash, cf above p192f.

[427] Cf above, p183f.

quite closely accelerated the disappearance of many texts, since large segments of the material had been incorporated into the more popular Midrashim. The inclusion of lengthy narratives in EsthR and AbGur most likely weakened the initiative of scribes to copy the original works, and of printers to engage in their publication, and so they fell by the wayside.

It appears that this process began at a relatively early date. We have already noted the efforts of the scribe of ms Oxf-Bodl 155, fol. 121ff to copy numerous midrashic works to Esther. This copyist was most scrupulous in his choice of material since he deleted relatively lengthy segments whenever they gave the impression of duplicating the contents of the initial text in this manuscript – Midrash Abba Gurion – which he supposedly copied in full.[428] However, in spite of the fact that the Bodleian manuscript is a product of the late fifteenth century (1470), it is now apparent that the deletion process began hundreds of years earlier. Note well that there is evidence for this phenomenon in a manuscript utilized by R. Shimon ha-Darshan, the compiler of Yalkut Shimoni,[429] which probably dates from the twelfth century.[430] It is therefore safe to assume that the tradition preserved in the Oxford codex[431] is of much earlier vintage and that the disappearance and dilution of some of the original Midrashim to Esther already transpired during the twelfth century.

The proliferation of numerous minor aggadic compilations to the Book of Esther in the form of Midrashim, homilies, and collectanea was most likely an additional factor that contributed to this process. Once the outstanding homilies and exegetical comments were absorbed into the more popular works, it was probably felt that the original works had become more or less irrelevant. This assumption is amply illustrated by the Yemenite Aggadat Esther. Even though the compiler utilized numerous midrashic works in the composition of his yalkut, none of these has survived among the literary remains of Yemenite Jewry. To be sure, the only extant midrashic work to the Scroll of Esther in Yemenite script is indeed Aggadat Esther, notwithstanding other indigenous Yemenite compilations, viz. Midrash ha-Hefets (List, no. 18), Midrash Ha-Beur and Leket Midrash (List, no. 19).

In spite of the fact that most of these midrashic works ordinarily would have possessed an individuality and an identification of their own, including literary structure, terminology, context, etc., there is no escaping the fact that

---

[428] A comparison of the end of chs. 6 and 7 of AbGur with the additional material found in ms St. Petersburg-Firkowitz I 246 seems to indicate that the final passages of this Midrash have been somewhat shortened.

[429] See the list of Hyman, *Sources* 2, 581b and cf above, n383 and p210, bibliography.

[430] Both Zunz and Albeck place the Yalkut Shimoni during the thirteenth century (*Derashot*, 148, 445 n67) and so it may be assumed that the manuscript of PA II with the additions from PA III and PA V, utilized by R. Shimon ha-Darshan, dated at least from the twelfth century.

[431] This scribal tradition is evidently the base for the selection entitled 'Midrash Aher' in ms Hamburg 37 (= *Bet ha-Midrasch* 1, 19-23), which has obviously been re-arranged and edited according to the sequence of the verses, see below, List, no. 23.

only one of them, by far the most popular work to the Esther scroll, came to be identified by a specific title: Midrash Abba Gurion. This resulted in the anomalous situation whereby a purely eclectic work has received permanent status and a positive identity, while the names and the literary traditions of the more original midrashic compositions have remained obscure.

In view of such an unusually large harvest of literary works, an essential issue that must be addressed is the basic concept and *raison d'être* for each individual midrashic composition. One receives the impression that most of the editors of the works nurtured certain individual ideas and concepts which they attempted to incorporate into their literary endeavours.[432] However, positive results in this area will have to await further progress in the reconstruction of the various lost works. It is to be expected that the eventual reconstruction of the sporadic remains of the missing Midrashim will enable modern scholarship to cope with the formidable task of clarifying and defining the outlook of each individual work.[433]

An additional corollary to the panoramic study of the various Midrashim to Esther conducted above involves the pivotal role played by R. Levi in the aggadic interpretation of the Scroll of Esther. We have already noted the unusually large number of explanations attributed to this Palestinian Amoraic sage of the third generation in PA II.[434] This list should now be augmented with numerous additional aggadic teachings of R. Levi in EsthR,[435] the Babylonian Talmud[436] and in other sources as well.[437] Moreover, it should also be noted that Tracate Sofrim even credits R. Levi as the author of the homily which supports the basic halakhic ruling that the Scroll of Esther is to be read both on the night

---

[432] The recent efforts of Neusner (e.g., *Judaism behind the Texts*, 71) to delineate certain messages developed by the editor of each of the aggadic midrashim are worthy of emulation. Unfortunately, Neusner did not include any of the minor parallel Midrashim to the same biblical book on his agenda. See also the following note.

[433] Among the items to be investigated, one might include: (a) The reasons for Haman's evil decree against the Jewish people; (b) The relative roles and the leadership of Mordechai and Esther; (c) The attitude to the minor characters of the Scroll: Memukhan; Hatakh and Harbona.

[434] See above, 'Midrash Panim Aherot' II, esp n338. Cf Bacher, *Amoraim* 2, 356-359; 390 who listed only 18 sources. Incidentally, the lengthy section concerning the sedition of Haman (cf also the Hebrew translation, 61-65) does not belong to the teaching of R. Levi, but rather to R. Shimon b. Lakish. Bacher was obviously misled by the abbreviation in EsthR (ר"ל), cf PA I(1), 46 (= Midrash Aher); AggEsth 3:9, 33 (= Aggadic–Narrative Midrash ?).

[435] EsthR Proems 3; 5; 7. 1:1; 3; 5; (6); 9. 2:1; 7. 3:(4); 11. 4:10. (5:1; 3). 6:3; 7; 13; 14. 7:2; 8; 22; 24. Those sources which do not bear any direct relationship to the exegesis of the Esther Scroll have been placed in parentheses.

[436] bMeg 10b (= The very beginning of the aggadic Esther Midrash in bMeg chap. 1); 11a; 12b; 15b.

[437] E.g. Ancient Midrash (= Rabinovitz, *Ginzé Midrash*), 157, l. 7; 163, ll. 3, 10; 167, l. 15; 168; l. 20; 169, l. 30. PA II (2) (= ms St. Petersburg-Antonin 302): 3:4, 49; 3:8, 50; 3:12, 50 (twice); 3:14, 50. See also the following novel loci in AbGur: 1:10, 13-14. 2:15, 18. 3:6, 23; 3:8, 27. Note also Midrash Aher (= Sefer ha-Zikhronot, 275 (top); Gaster, *Jerahmeel* 82:2, 245) and cf to parallels (e.g., AbGur 4:1, 32).

and on the day of Purim.[438] Such a proliferation of expositional comments and homilies attributed to R. Levi apparently indicates that this Palestinian sage was most diligent in the interpretation and the elaboration of the teachings of the Book of Esther.[439] It is logical to assume that each year, during the course of the Purim holiday and before, R. Levi would electrify the masses who thronged to hear his original aggadic discourses and novel interpretations.[440]

The comprehensive survey has also underscored several basic themes and concepts common to many of the Midrashim involved. It is apparent that aside from the regular task of explaining the Scroll of Esther via the systematic or partial exegesis of the Purim story by virtue of a close study of the individual passages, numerous stock topics, herein referred to as 'topoi', have come to be accepted as standard literary devices of the Esther Midrashim. One may thus postulate that groups of students and laymen feverishly anticipated the public and the private Purim lectures of the rabbis and the homilists wherin they presented their novel approach and presentation of the various topoi. As a result, each author, redactor, preacher, or compiler made extensive efforts to include these tactical literary embellishments in his oral and written endeavours.

Following is a list of the more popular topoi, according to the order of events in the Esther Scroll, which have been interpolated in the various Midrashim:

1. The 'throne of Solomon' (1:1): EsthR 1:12, 3d-4b; AbGur 1:1, 2-8; PA II 1:1, 56-58; Midrash Aher: Sefer ha-Zikhronot 8:14 (2 versions); Kasher – Klein, Aramaic Compendium, 99. See also above, Bibliography p193f.

2. The casting of the lots 'from day to day and from month to month' (3:7): EsthR 7:11, 11d-12b; AbGur 3:7, 24-26; PA II 3:7, 67-68;[441] PA IV; PA I(1), 46 (= Midrash Aher); AggEsth 3:7, 29-32 (= Aggadic-Narrative Midrash ?). See also Ginzberg, *Legends* 4, 399-402; 6, 464f n108-110.

3. Anti-semitism and the Jews: 'And their laws are diverse from those of every people' (3:8), EsthR 7:12, 12b; AbGur 3:8, 26; PA II 3:8, 68;[442] Ancient Midrash (ms Vienna-Reiner H 145); bMeg 13b. See also Further Reading, p228f.

4. The dealings between Ahasuerus and Haman (3:9): EsthR 7:13, 12c; AbGur 3:9, 27-29; PA II 3:9, 68-69; Midrash Aher (PA I(1), 46); AggEsth 3:9, 33 (= Aggadic-Narrative Midrash ?).

---

[438] Sofrim 14:15, 268-269. In the talmudic sources (yMeg 2, 73b; bMeg 4a), this teaching is attributed to other Amoraim.

[439] A noteworthy, example of this tendency is evident in LevR 28,6 (p662) and parallels.

[440] On the prowess of R. Levi as a preacher and a homilist, vid. ySan 2, 20b; GenR 98,11 (p1261f); PesRK 23,12 (p345f); CantR 1:1 (end).

[441] Note that Buber added this topos to his edition of PA II from Yalkut Shimoni. There is thus some possibility that it derives from some other midrash, see below, near n450.

[442] Note the additional misplaced criticism concerning the Passover holiday which Buber added to PA II, 68, end of paragraph 3 according to Yalkut Shimoni; cf above n222.

5. The 'letter of Haman' (3:12-14):[443] EsthR 7:13, 12c-d; AbGur 3:12, 29-32; PA II 3:12, 69; PA V (ms Oxford 2851, fol. 44); Midrash Aher, Sefer ha-Zikhronot 12 (= PA I(1), 47). See also above, Bibliography p215f.

6. The evil plot of Haman; the Heavenly decree; the intervention of Elijah; the Patriarchs and Moses; Mordechai rents his clothes: EsthR 7:18, 13a-b; AbGur 4:1, 32-34; Midrash Aher (Sefer ha-Zikhronot, 13); Aggadic-Narrative Midrash (= AggEsth 4:1, 38-40, l. 14).

7. The reactions of Mordechai and his young students: EsthR 9:4, 14c; AbGur 4:1, 32, 34; 5:14, 37-38; PA II 6:10, 75; Midrash Aher (Sefer ha-Zikhronot, 13); Aggadic-Narrative Midrash (= AggEsth 4:17, 45-46).

8. Haman's consultation concerning the best method to kill Mordechai (5:13): EsthR 9:2, 14b; AbGur 5:14, 36-37; PA II 5:9, 72; AggEsth 5:14, 58.

9. Selecting the tree of Haman (5:14): EsthR 9:2, 14b; AbGur 7:10, 41-42; PA II 7:9, 77; Midrash Aher (Sefer ha-Zikhronot, 13); AggEsth 6:1, 60-61 (= Aggadic-Narrative Midrash?); AggEsth 5:14, 58-59; Yalkut Shimoni 1059:5 (= Additions to AbGur 7:10, 42, n. 7; ms Sasoon 756, fol. 185);[444] Aramaic Compendium 7:9, 100f.

Such an extensive selection of topoi found in a large array of parallel sources seemingly invites new areas of investigation into the literary composition of the Esther Midrashim and their teleology. It should also be noted that the midrashic usage of recurring topoi appears to be unique in these Midrashim. Other spheres of midrashic literature do not ordinarily employ such phenomena, or at most do so in a subdued fashion.[445]

An interesting by-product arising from the above-mentioned topoi is related to the literary development of the various Midrashim. A careful follow-up of the appearance of these topoi in the various literary texts could conceivably assist in building models for the proper evaluation of early and later literary developments in aggadic literature. In any event, one receives the impression that the earliest Midrashim, as well as those of an exegetical character, contain relatively fewer topoi, which suggests that they were composed at a relatively early stage of development.[446]

The earliest topos of all seems to be the fragmentary remains of topos no. 3 in the Ancient Midrash, as evinced by the Vienna Geniza fragment from the collection of Archduke Reiner. In the midrash to Esth 3:8, 'and their laws are diverse from those of every people', it is possible to decipher the remains of the expression 'theatres and circuses'. This would seem to indicate that the contents of this topos, which stresses the sedition of Haman against the Jewish people, concentrated on the basic differences between Jews and Gentiles as

---

[443] In the Purim homily in ms Vienna 26:4, fol. 4b (quoted in Catalogue Schwarz, 12), this letter is attributed to Ahasuerus.

[444] Cf above n429.

[445] Cf below n447.

[446] This would justifiably include the Aramaic Targumim and the early piyyut as well.

emphasized in classical midrash by the words of Naomi to Ruth: 'My daughter, it is not the practice of Israel to attend either theatres or circuses, but rather synagogues and houses of study'.[447]

Another topos of early origin is related to Haman's 'casting the lots from day to day and from month to month' (topos no. 2). It serves as the theme of two elaborate piyyutic compositions by R. Elazar be-R. Killir,[448] the renowned paytan, who was active during the first four decades of the seventh century.[449] R. Elazar's piyyut is obviously based on the text found in YalShim 1,054:12,[450] whose exact provenance has not yet been determined. Convinced that the Yalkut text was part of Midrash Panim Aherot II, S. Buber, mistakenly interpolated it into his edition of PA II 3:7, 67-68. If this were indeed the case, it would antedate the redaction of PA II to the sixth century and equate it more or less with the Ancient Midrash. However, in all likelihood, the 'casting of the lots' homily probably derives from the Ancient Midrash itself and its utilization by the seventh century paytan is thus readily understandable. In any event the piyyutic composition of R. Elazar ha-Killir obviously represents the earliest datable evidence for the existence of topoi relating to the Scroll of Esther in ancient Hebrew literature.

COMPREHENSIVE LIST OF MIDRASHIC WORKS ON ESTHER

Midrashim: Complete Works
(1) Midrash Esther Rabba
        Constantinople 1514 (?); Vilna 1887 (see bibliography p187-189)
(2) Midrash Abba Gurion
        S. Buber, *Sifrei de-Aggadeta*, 1-42 (see bibliography p193-195)
(3) Midrash Panim Aherot II (= PA II)
        S. Buber, *Sifrei de-Aggadeta*, 55-97 (see bibliography p201)

Midrashim: Fragmentary and Partial Works
(4) Ancient Midrash to Esther
        Midrash Esther Rabba – Selections
        Assorted citations
        ms Manchester-Rylands B2374
        ms Cambridge TS F2 (2).66
        ms Vienna – Reiner H145

---

[447] RuthR 2:22 (to Ruth 1:16), 76. Incidentally, this selection most likely reflects a topos of the midrashic exegesis to Ruth, cf Ruth Zuta 1:16, 49; bYev 47b; Midrash 'Eshet Hayil' (= Midrash Proverbs, ed Buber), 112.

[448] חוק אל אספרה and אמל ורבך, which are actually two parts of the same composition, see Ha-Kohen, 'Relationship', 47.

[449] *Vid.* Fleischer, 'Qiliri Riddle', 405f.

[450] A careful perusal of the Yalkut text indicates that the compiler apparently used two separate sources for this entry. Cf, however, Ha-Kohen, 'Relationship', 63-69.

Rabinovitz, *Ginzé Midrash*, 155-160.
ms Paris-Mosseri VIII 440. 1-2
S.A. Wertheimer, *Batei Midrashot*, 1, 340-343
(5) Midrash Panim Aherot III (= PA III)
S. Buber, *Sifrei de-Aggadeta*, 78-81
(6) Midrash Panim Aherot IV (= PA IV)
ms Oxf-Bodl 155, fol. 131v.
(7) Midrash Panim Aherot V (= PA V)
S. Buber, *Sifrei de-Aggadeta*, 81-82
ms Oxf-Bodl 2851, ff. 43v-44.
(8) Midrash Aher
Buber, *Sifrei de-Aggadeta*, 46-48 (= PA I (1)), selections
Sefer ha-Zikhronot 8:13-14, ed Yassif 271-279
(9) Aggadic-Narrative Midrash
ms British Library OR 5559A, fol. 39
ms Oxf-Bodl, 2851, fol. 43r
Aggadat Esther, *passim*
(10) Short Midrash
R. Shlomo Alkabez, *Menot ha-Levi*, Venice 1585, *passim*

Homilies: Complete Works
(11) Panim Aherot I (1) (= PA I (1)): An Elaborate Purim Homily
Buber, *Sifrei de-Aggadeta*, 45-49.
(12) Pesikta Hadeta for Purim
Bet ha-Midrasch 6, 53-58

Homilies: Fragmentary and Partial Works
(13) Excerpts from the homily of R. Samuel to the Esther Scroll
Aggadat Esther, *passim*
(14) ms Vienna 26:4, ff. 1r-8r
Cat. Schwarz, 12, no. 26

Compilations: Complete Works
(15) Midrash Lekah Tov
Buber, *Sifrei de-Aggadeta*, 83-112
(16) Yalkut Shimoni
Yalkut Shimoni II, Sections 1044-1059
(17) Aggadat Esther
ed Buber, Krakau 1897; Vilna 1925
ed S.Yitshak Ha-Levi, Benei Berak 1994
Midrash Ha-Beur, ed Qafih, 1, 545-566 (selections)
(18) Midrash ha-Hefets
Nahum, 'Midrash Megillat Esther'

(19) Leket Midrash al Esther
  Qafih, *Hamesh Megillot*, 325-326
(20) Midrash Megilla
  Gaster, 'Oldest Version', 167-178
(21) Midrash Megillat Esther
  Horowitz, *Sammlung* 1, 56-75

Compilations: Fragmentary and Partial Works
(22) Haggada de-Megillat Esther (A. Atzmon)
  mss Vatican Ebr. 96 and 290:11
(23) Another Midrash to the Scroll of Esther
  Beit ha-Midrash 1, 19-24 (= ms Hamburg 37:8)
(24) A Midrash Anthology from the Geniza
  ms TS CI.48
  ms St. Petersburg-Antonin 302
  Buber, *Sifrei de-Aggadeta*, 49-51
(25) Yalkut Esther from the Geniza
  mss TS: NS 259.93; NS 88.24; CI.66; FI (2).67; C2.65; FI (2).24;
  NS 258.43
(26) Selections from Midrash Panim Aherot V and the Aggadic-Narrative
  Midrash
  ms Oxf-Bodl 2851, ff. 43-44
(27) An Aramaic Compilation from the Geniza
  Kasher – Klein, 'New Fragments'

The Esther Midrash in Related Texts
(28) The Babylonian Talmud
  bMeg 10b-17a
(29) Pirkei de R. Eliezer
  Chapters 49-50, ed Horowitz, 179-180; 187-188; 183-184;
  ed. Warsaw 1852, 117a-123a
(30) Midrash Tehillim
  Psalm 22, ed Buber, 180-197

POSTSCRIPT AND FURTHER READING

We can categorize the items in the preceding list according the following breakdown: (a) ten (or more?) full-fledged Midrashim; (b) four separate homiletic sermons, which were obviously addressed to various congregations; (c) thirteen different collectanea (yalkutim) that have accumulated material from numerous midrashic works and from the first chapter of Tractate Megilla in the Babylonian Talmud; (d) three cognate works from talmudic-midrashic literature which contain a relatively high concentration of midrashic material to the Esther Scroll. Altogether, thirty distinct and separate corpora which have concentrated their efforts towards the midrashic exegesis of the Book of Esther and the events surrounding the Purim holiday. Compared to the other four biblical Scrolls, the number of extensive Midrashim and cognate sources to Esther is overwhelming; a preliminary survey evinces that none of the other scrolls comes even close to this number.

It remains to be seen whether the Scroll of Esther can maintain its supremacy over other areas of midrashic literature as well. Only after the completion of an exhaustive inquiry and study of all midrashic works relating to each of the Five Books of the Pentateuch, especially to Genesis and to Deuteronomy, which also seem to have been the subject of numerous midrashic treatises, compilations and compendia, will it be possible to illuminate this subject.

In spite of the huge number of midrashic compilations to Esther, the actual variety is not very great. Understandably, most of the teachings in the oral homilies and in the various compendia are repetitive of other works and represent secondary sources. We have also seen that many of the Midrashim themselves also duplicate one another very often, especially in the lengthier passages and in the 'topoi'.

However, this does not seem to be the case as far as the 'Ancient Midrash' is concerned. From the initial parashiyyot of Esther Rabba and from the scanty remains of the 'Ancient Midrash' *per se*, it is quite evident that this opus contained numerous interpretations and exegetical comments of an original nature, most of which have not been incorporated into other works. It is most difficult to fathom the reasons which guided the later editor(s) of Esther Rabba in his (their) decision to delete and replace most of the original material of the 'Ancient Midrash', which is actually one of the earliest compositions of midrashic literature.[451]

Even though one receives the impression that almost all of the available sources for the reconstruction of the Midrashim to Esther have been exploited, there, is still a sliver of hope that additional material from the 'Ancient Midrash', a true gem of midrashic literature, as well as from some of the other non-extant works, will eventually turn up.

Further Reading. A survey of various midrashic works on Esther was first conducted by Horowitz, *Sammlung*, 47-53. See also Fishman, *Hagim*, 131-135. Albeck's notes and updating of Zunz, *Vorträge* are of utmost importance: Zunz-Albeck, *Ha-Derashot* 129f, 150, 402-406, 423-425, 447. The discussion of midrashic works dealing with the Esther Scroll by Baum-Sheridan, *Esther-dichtungen*, 29-50 is based on secondary sources and lumps together works from various disciplines in a most disjointed fashion. On the other hand, the recent two volume project of Boerner-Klein and Hollender, *Rabbinische Kommentar* represents the most comprehensive summary of the Esther

---

[451] Cf the theory of Fraenkel, *Midrash and Agadah* 3, 825, which is not substantiated by the significant remains of the Ancient Midrash in the second half of EsthR, see above, p183.

Midrashim to date, see *ib.* II, 13-21. This publication, whose second volume bears the title: *Die Midraschim zu Ester*, represents an impressive systematic collection of aggadic material relating to Esther in translation and encompasses minor Midrashim, collectanea, and cognate material, thus approaching the agenda of study proposed herein.

Kasher, *Torah Shelemah*: *Esther* has conveniently arranged the midrashic expositions of the sources according to the biblical verses. The implications of the aggadic and midrashic sources for the rabbinic retelling of the Esther saga have been ably summarized by Ginzberg, *Legends* 4, 365-448; 6, 451-481, who also enlarges on many of the above mentioned topoi. On the other hand, the studies of Katzenellenbogen, *Buch Esther* and Davidson, 'Megillat Esther' are superficial.

The anti-Semitic aspects of the sedition of Haman in the extant Midrashim and the Targums to Esther have been summarized by Herr, 'Antisemitism', 151-159; 'Persecution', 88-90; Segal, 'The Same' 2, 114-133 and Berman, 'Aggadah'. Segal, 'The Same', 164f has asserted that certain Purim homilies are to be found in Genesis Rabba.

Chapter Four

Seder Olam

Chaim Milikowsky

Short Description

Seder Olam is an exegetically-based chronography focussing on the biblical period, which is attributed to the second century Tannaic sage, R. Yose. The literal translation of סדר עולם is the 'ordering of the world'; presumably *olam* here has a temporal connotation. The work has been preserved in some twenty manuscripts and was first printed in Mantua, 1513.[1] In comparison with other parts of rabbinic literature it has some exceptional literary features which merit a separate investigation.

The use of the name *Seder Olam Rabba* is still very rare during the Middle Ages; however, because of the influence of the *editio princeps* (wherein it is so named at its conclusion), this name came into general usage during the modern period. Nonetheless, since it is called *Seder Olam* in the Babylonian Talmud as well as in the vast majority of medieval citations, it is that name which we shall use. *Seder Olam Zuta*, also included in the 1513 edition, is a completely unrelated work.[2]

The first sentence of Seder Olam already tells us of its essential concerns: 'From Adam until the Flood there passed one thousand six hundred and fifty-

---

[1] The edition was reprinted, with minor changes, several dozen times since. On further editions see bibliography.

[2] *Seder Olam Zuta*, a much shorter work – approximately one sixth the size of *Seder Olam* – is entirely chronological, with no exegetical element. The format of the book is that of a chronicle. The first part, a little more than half the book, deals with the biblical period until the Babylonian exile, and the second part relates the thirty-nine generations of exilarchs in Babylon, all stemming from Jehoiachin, the exiled king of Judah. Its apparent purpose was to authenticate the Davidic descent of the exilarchs.

six years.' This is not a self-contained history; the work can only be used as an adjunct to the Bible, and knowledge of the latter is assumed. Using the events of the Bible as its base, it concerns itself with chronological questions and deals with dates and ages.

The following is only a very small sampling of the numerous issues touched upon in this work: the number of years from the Flood until the Dispersion, the age of Isaac at the time of the Binding, the age of Jacob when he arrived at Laban's house, the number of years the Children of Israel remained in Egypt, the number of years they were subjugated, the day of the week they left Egypt, the day of the month Jericho fell, the number of years Rehoboam observed the Tora, the year of Ahaziah's reign that Elijah ascended to heaven, and the year of Jehoiakim's reign in which Nebuchadnezzar ascended to the throne. In addition, Seder Olam devotes a great deal of effort to synchronizing the regnal lists of the kingdoms of Judah and Israel and to resolving the contradictions between the biblical books of Kings and Chronicles.

Until the middle of the thirtieth and last chapter, Seder Olam deals with the biblical period, beginning with Adam and ending with the rise and fall of Alexander the Great as portrayed in Daniel 10:3-4. At this point, the author or editor injects, prophecy stopped and leadership passed to the elders and wise men. For the author/editor, this marks the end of an era, and also the end of his chronological concerns. As a sort of appendix, he adds several statements concerning the Second Temple period, consisting altogether of some twenty lines. Most interesting of these are two chronological overviews of the Second Temple period. Thus there is a clear disproportion between the biblical period and the post-biblical period: twenty-nine and a half chapters versus some twenty lines. This suggests we are dealing with later additions to the original chronography which focused solely on the biblical period.

It is not the only passage which can be identified quite easily as an editorial addition to Seder Olam. Chapters twenty and twenty-one list the various prophets and prophetesses who prophesied to Israel and to the nations of the world, occasionally mentioning prophets who are unnamed in the biblical narrative. The subject matter of these two chapters, as well as the fact that they break the chronological continuity between chapters nineteen and twenty-two, make it all but conclusive that this is an independent tradition-unit inserted into Seder Olam by an editor or redactor.

Another large section which breaks the continuity of Seder Olam is the second half of chapter three and all of chapter four. First, a list of four events which lasted or will last twelve months is cited. Thereupon follows an extended discussion of the punishment of various types of sinners in *gehenna*, and the following chapter, the fourth, is devoted to a chronology of the Flood, which according to the chronological framework of Seder Olam belongs in chapter one, not in chapter four.

Language

The language of Seder Olam is Mishnaic Hebrew, that dialect of Hebrew which was used in the composition of the Mishna, Tosefta, and the halakhic midrashim. The only exceptions are biblical verses, of course, and two short epigrammatic statements in Aramaic. Without entering into a detailed analysis of its language, it is sufficient to point out that the syntax, morphology, and orthography of Seder Olam are those of Mishnaic Hebrew.[3]

There is, however, one exceptional element in the language of Seder Olam: the use of the *vav*-conversive to transfer an imperfect verbal form into the perfect tense. This form, so common in Biblical Hebrew but just about unknown in rabbinic Hebrew (and already in general disuse in Late Biblical Hebrew), occurs several times in Seder Olam. This is probably due to an intentional attempt by Seder Olam to biblicize its language, in accordance with its many biblical citations. A related phenomenon is the occasional practice – extremely rare in rabbinic literature though quite common in non-rabbinic Jewish literature of late antiquity[4] – of amalgamating biblical phraseology and exegetic expansion into one sentence, which cannot be separated into its component parts without comparing it to the biblical text.

The vocabulary of Seder Olam shows some peculiarities as well. There is repeated use of certain words in a unique sense, and of phrases which are otherwise unknown in rabbinic literature. These usages have important ramifications, as we shall see, for the question of the formation of Seder Olam.

Authorship

It is immediately apparent that Seder Olam belongs to rabbinic literature. First of all, as noted above, it is written in Mishnaic Hebrew. Furthermore, Tannaic sages are cited by name nineteen times, and finally, close to one hundred passages in Seder Olam are paralleled by similar passages in such works as Mishna, Tosefta, Halakhic Midrashim, and Talmud. Since the Hebrew of Seder Olam is free of any Aramaic admixture, and portrays no signs of syntactical and morphological deterioration, as in post-rabbinic midrash collections, the obvious conclusion is that this work belongs to the Tannaic stratum. When one adds the fact that only Tannaim are cited, and that the parallels in rabbinic literature are generally either located in Tannaic texts or, in the Talmud, cited

---

[3] There is extensive use of the copula and the participial form of the verb, and very limited use of the imperfect. With regard to morphology two points are indicative: the *hitpa'el* has changed to *nitpa'el*, and the third person feminine singular of third radical weak verbs end in *tav*, without the additional *heh* as in the Biblical Hebrew form. Orthography is very much dependent upon individual manuscripts, but there is a general tendency to use the *mater lectionis* more often, the loss of the radical *aleph*, and an occasional interchange of *sin* with *samekh*.

[4] For example, the Damascus Covenant, the Temple Scroll, Jubilees.

with headings announcing a baraita (e.g. *tanya*), the evidence is conclusive.[5] Furthermore, it has been shown that the editor of Tosefta Sota used Seder Olam as one of his sources.[6]

However, the classification of Seder Olam as a rabbinic text has led to mistaken perceptions of its formation. As is well known, when speaking of rabbinic literature, it is improper to refer to an 'author'. Thus, R. Yehuda the Prince was not the author of the Mishna but its compiler-redactor. Hundreds of sources were used in its compilation, and these sources were originally formulated by many different people during the centuries preceding the redaction of the Mishna. The same is true, with varying degrees of similarity and with the only exceptions stemming from the post-amoraic period, for all works generally included in the rabbinic corpus. It is not true, however, for Seder Olam.

The unique style and vocabulary of Seder Olam suggest that many different sections of this work were authored by one hand. Even more indicative are the cross-references between different sections and the impossibility of understanding some passages without referring to other passages not found in their immediate context.[7]

It is further noteworthy that Seder Olam cites the chronological data concerning the kings of Judah and Israel even when it adds absolutely nothing to the information found in the Bible. Only if we recognize that a specific goal underlies this work, i.e. the establishment of a chronological continuum from Adam until the end of the biblical period, can we understand the inclusion of these passages. Of course, while doing so the author dealt with many chronological issues not specifically tied to this goal. Though Seder Olam does not generally sum up the number of years between different points in history, it provides the basic data with which these calculations can be performed.

It cannot therefore be maintained that Seder Olam was pieced together by simply collecting various unrelated chronological traditions, thereby creating a sort of chronological commentary on the Bible. On the contrary, it has at its core a single unified work which was authored by one person or, at the most, by a small group of persons. This is not to say that this unified work is identical to the Seder Olam we have today. As noted earlier, Seder Olam contains a

---

[5] The short paragraph found in Strack, *Introduction*, 225 (essentially the same in the seventh German edition prepared by Stemberger, 297), which states that Seder Olam 'was probably compiled in early Amoraic times, but subsequently enlarged or revised', is based on Ratner's introduction (especially 52-56, 132-138). This is not supported by the evidence. As is explained below, the evidence indicates that the composition of the work must have occurred before the fourth Tannaic generation, major editorial activity occurred during that generation, and some minor editorial revisions took place during the last (fifth) Tannaic generation or in the beginning of the Amoraic period. The presence of interpolations within specific manuscript traditions is of course irrelevant to the questions of redaction and editing with which we are dealing.

[6] Milikowsky, '*Seder Olam* and the Tosefta'.

[7] See, e.g., the passage discussed *ib.* 247-251.

number of passages which were added during the process of redaction and are clearly not part of the original chronography.

The Attribution to R. Yose

All of these conclusions concerning Seder Olam have been derived from the study of the text itself. We shall now turn to a tradition concerning Seder Olam preserved in the Babylonian Talmud. Twice, the third century Palestinian Amora R. Yohanan is cited as saying, 'Who taught Seder Olam? R. Yose.'[8] Since internal criteria, as well as the analysis of the parallel passages in other rabbinic texts, support the hypothesis that Seder Olam is a Tannaic work, there is nothing concerning the text we know as Seder Olam which would conflict with R. Yohanan's statement. It can further be shown that this talmudic attribution will help us understand several salient aspects of this text.

First we must establish the meaning of the term 'taught' (*tanna*) in the question 'Who taught Seder Olam?' Clearly, it refers to some sort of author's or editor's activity having to do with the work as a whole and not to the attribution of various isolated passages within the work. From the same usage regarding other rabbinic works – R. Shimon of Mitspe 'taught' Mishna Tamid and R. Eliezer b. Yaakov 'taught' Mishna Middot[9] – and from Seder Olam itself, the following conclusions can be drawn. The person who is said to have 'taught' the work in question was not the author of the work; his role was more that of a transmitter who edited (revised?) the text and added his own comments to it. He 'taught' the text in the academy and his students continued the process of transmission, adding the 'teacher's' name to those passages he had added to the text.[10]

Earlier we noted that nineteen times, Tannaic sages are cited by name in Seder Olam. Of these, nine are attributed to R. Yose and ten to various other sages. Obviously, this testifies to some sort of fundamental input from R. Yose in the final formation of Seder Olam. None of the statements, including those attributed to R. Yose, belong to the basic chronological stratum; in other words, if all were removed, the flow of the central text would not be interrupted. In addition to this quantitative distinction, there is a qualitative difference between the statements of R. Yose and those of the other sages. Several of R. Yose's statements refer to an immediately previous chronological statement and comment upon it; none of the latter do this.

Evidently, R. Yose's role was one of a transmitter and glossator. This may explain why R. Yose is cited in Seder Olam even though it is considered his work, and why he is cited so many more times than any other Sage. It was he

---

[8] bYev 82b; bNid 46b.
[9] bYom 14b, 16a.
[10] A very different understanding of the talmudic phrase attributing Seder Olam to R. Yose underlies the comments of Albeck, *Mavo*, 229.

who 'taught' Seder Olam to his students, and added his own comments to the text. A later editor, when re-editing the chronography transmitted by R. Yose, must have affixed R. Yose's name to those comments which the latter had added to the text.

We conclude, therefore, that there existed a chronography antecedent to R. Yose, but it was R. Yose who gave it its form and shape as we know it today. It would be futile to speculate what exactly was R. Yose's contribution (apart from those statements specifically attributed to him); perhaps those passages which stylistically diverge from the main part of the text were his additions. The editorial process did not entirely conclude with R. Yose, although only a handful of passages were added after his time. Unfortunately, we have no way of determining who affixed R. Yose's name to his additions, who added these last few passages, or when the editorial process finally came to an end.

Bibliography

As stated above, the first edition of Seder Olam was printed in Mantua, 1513. The second edition, Constantinople 1517, is not based upon this edition and thus has independent value for the study of the text. Three editions utilizing manuscript material were published during the years 1895-1903. Neubauer, *Chronicles* 2, 26-67 published the text according to an eighteenth century edition, making limited use of several manuscripts. Ratner, *Seder Olam Rabba*, used even later editions for his text, made extensive use of the two manuscripts to which he had access, and authored a detailed commentary to the entire text. Marx, *Seder Olam*, edited the first ten chapters, using a sixteenth century manuscript for his base text and including in his critical apparatus variants from six other manuscripts plus several Geniza fragments, and published a German translation of these chapters with notes. For a number of reasons none of these editions are satisfactory; see Milikowsky, *Seder Olam*, 86-90. A new critical edition, based upon ten manuscripts plus thirteen Geniza fragments, two of which include more than half of Seder Olam, was prepared by Milikowsky, *ib.*, 209-448. This edition, which also includes an introduction and commentary, is presently in press at the Israel Academy of Sciences and Humanities.

The Latin commentary of J. Meyer, *Seder Olam Rabba*, Amsterdam 1699 was the first commentary to Seder Olam ever published. Next were the annotations of R. Yaakov Emden, *Seder Olam Rabba*, Hamburg 1757 and of Elijah the Gaon of Wilna, *Seder Olam Rabba*, Shklov 1800. In addition, there exist the commentaries and annotations of Zundel, *Ets Yosef, Anaf Yosef* and *Yad Yosef* in the edition of the work, Wilna 1845; M.Y. Weinstock, *Seder Olam* 1-3, Jerusalem 1956-65; Y.M. Leiner, *Meir Ayin* to *Seder Olam Rabba*, Warsaw 1904; M.D. Yerushalmi, *Seder Olam Rabba*, Jerusalem 1955; none of which have any pretensions to critical analysis. As stated, Ratner's edition includes an extensive commentary and that of Marx's short notes.

In addition to his text and commentary, Ratner, *Mavo* published an introduction with a mass of valuable material. However, its critical judgments cannot be accepted; cf. Albeck in Zunz-Albeck, *Ha-derashot*, 268.

Though innumerable books and articles have touched upon various passages in Seder Olam, there has been a noticeable lack of critical studies dealing with the work as a whole. During the eighty years which elapsed between the dissertations of Marx and Milikowsky, only two such articles appeared. The attempt by Gaster, 'Demetrius and Seder Olam,' to show that the Hellenistic chronographer Demetrius and Seder Olam share exegetical traditions is marred by unsubstantiated speculations and an unfortunate misreading of Seder Olam. Milikowsky, '*Seder Olam* and the Tosefta', argued that the book we know as Seder Olam was already used by the editor of Tosefta Sota. Idem, '*Seder Olam* and Jewish Chronography', analyses Seder Olam within the contexts of Jewish chronography and biblical exegesis, and tentatively suggests that Seder Olam may be, at its core, a pre-rabbinic work.

Appendix:
The Scroll of Antiochos and the Scroll of Fasts

(by *Zeev Safrai*)

This appendix deals with two works found in the margins of classic rabbinic literature and originating beyond its temporal limits. They seem to reflect popular narrative traditions that had been embedded in local liturgical customs from the Amoraic period onwards.

THE SCROLL OF ANTIOCHOS, מגילת אנטיוכוס, is a brief description of Hasmonean events leading up to the festival of Hanukka. Modern scholars at once recognized the Scroll to be a later adaptation of events described in the Books of Maccabees. It is a melange of facts and names presented in a chronologically incorrect framework based on Seder Olam, but in an independent formulation. As a result of the inaccuracies, the Scroll was neglected by historians.[11]

There are two main versions, which split into numerous secondary versions. The primary version is in Aramaic, the other is its Hebrew translation. The translation is sometimes exact, sometimes freer, and is strongly influenced by biblical Hebrew, obviously reflecting the wish to imitate biblical language.

The Scroll is found in ancient Jewish prayer books, mainly those that reflect the Sephardi and Yemenite versions. The prayer books contain the Hebrew version, but various manuscripts preserve the original Aramaic. The circulation in prayer books caused the existence of hundreds of versions in the manuscripts and in early printed editions. Gaster published a first critical edition based on five manuscripts, Kadari another, mainly on the basis of the Berlin-Tübingen 12/8 version.[12] Recently, additional manuscripts have been published in Aramaic and in Hebrew.[13]

The earliest possible mention of the Scroll is in Sefer Halakhot Gedolot, written by Rav Yehudai Gaon in ninth century Babylonia. He refers to two works called 'Megillat Taanit', one of which must be the text we know under that name and the other is either the Books of Maccabees or the Scroll of An-

---

[11] With the exception of Kasher, 'Hareka hahistori'. A bibliography is offered by Rapeld, 'Megillat Antiochus'. See also Nemoy, *The Scroll of Antiochus.*

[12] Gaster, *Studies and Texts*, vol 1, 174; vol 3, 33-43; Kadari, 'The Aramaic Megillat Antiochus';

[13] The first edition of the Aramaic was published by Filipovsky, *Mivhar ha-pninim* (1851), from British Museum ms Harl no. 5686, see Yoel, 'Editio Princeps'; another by Toropower, *Kevod ha-Levanon* (1863) p21, from a ms in Leipzig. See Kasher, 'Hareka hahistori'; Fried, 'Nusah ivri hadash'; Fried, 'Al Megillat Antiochos'; Haberman, *Hadashim*, 75-83. See also Jellinek, *Beit ha-midrash* 1, 142-146; Wertheimer, *Batei midrashot*, 309-330; Hirschfeld, *Arabic Chresthomathy*, 1-6.

tiochos. There is clearer evidence in Rav Saadia Gaon's Sefer ha-Galui (tenth century).[14] He mentions our Scroll, asserts that it was written in Aramaic, as was the Book of Daniel, and attributes its composition to Hasmonean times. He says the Scroll was divided into verses and written with cantillation marks, as though it were Scripture, though he did not think that correct. He had the work translated into Arabic.

Linguistic analysis of the Aramaic version indicates that the Scroll dates from some time between the sixth and eighth centuries.[15] The upper limit is about a century before Rav Saadia Gaon, or possibly before Rav Yehudai Gaon. The Aramaic is Babylonian for the most part, with various influences from the Palestinian Aramaic of the Midrashim.

Interestingly, the Scroll appears in some Tora manuscripts, and furthermore in prayer books, mainly versions of the Yemenite Takhlal (תכלאל) that present it with an Arabic translation, apparently based on that of Saadia. It was not considered part of Scripture, as it usually lacks cantillation marks and has a separate colophon. Later Yemenite prayer books give the Hebrew as source, along with Aramaic and Arabic translations. No commentaries were apparently written, which also shows that the Scroll was not considered part of Scripture. In the literature of the Rishonim there is evidence that some congregations read the Scroll as part of the prayer service.[16] Other prayer books rule that, 'It is customary to read the Scroll of Antiochos at the Minha service (on Shabbat) after Kaddish.'[17] This would point to the custom of reading the Haftara during Minha, but the place of the reading rather indicates that it was considered an addition to the prayer service. In other prayer books, it was ruled that the custom was to read the Scroll after the Tora reading on the Shabbat of Hanukka.[18] There is no mention of the custom in prayers of Palestinian provenance.

As to contents, the Scroll combines two different stories, one of which describes the killing of the Greek military leader, and the other tells of a series of wars against the Greeks and the purification of the Temple. In some versions, there is also a third plot involving the *jus primae noctis* and a Hasmonean princess who urged her brothers to preserve her honour.

Overall, the story adheres to 1 Maccabees, with clear deviations. According to the Scroll, Judah was killed in battle, and the campaign was further conducted by Matityahu. This is in sharp contrast to the story in 1 Maccabees, which attributes the leadership to Judah, who took over from his father who had died. The Scroll begins with a long story about how Matityahu killed the

---

[14] Harkavi, *Ha-sarid veha-palit*, 205-209.

[15] Cf Kadari, 'Be-eizo Aramit'. Kadari noticed the similarity to the language of Onkelos, assuming that this Targum was written in the first century CE. Today it is clear that the Babylonian Aramaic of Onkelos is later than the fourth century.

[16] R. Yeshaya di Trani (16th cent.), Tosafot to tSuk 44b.

[17] That is in the Mahzor following the custom of Kappa and Karsov, see Fried, 'Al Megillat Antiochos'.

[18] Usually Sephardi, but also Yemenite prayer books, see Fried *ib*.

Greek military leader, a story that has no source in 1 Maccabees. The Scroll does contain traces of a number of stories from 1 Maccabees, but these adaptations are not faithful to the source.

The Scroll was apparently written in a period when the stories of the Hasmoneans had already become a vague legend, and when Aramaic had become an artificial language. The author's geographical milieu is Babylonia-Syria. His plot resembles 2 Maccabees in that the events end with the victory of Nicanor. However, he probably did not use 2 Maccabees but summarized some oral narrative version. The strange sentence, מכבי קטיל תקיפן, 'Maccabee killed the strong,' possibly is a vestige of the author's use of a foreign language that he did not know well. At the time, 1 Maccabees was probably familiar only in its Greek version, and the author and those around him could not make direct use of it. This evidence confirms the possibility that the text is of Babylonian or Syrian provenance.

The author also freely interwove midrashic passages from the Talmud and the Halakhic Midrashim in his story. 1 Maccabees is noteworthy for its 'secular' tendency. The military victory is the fortuitous result of the efforts of the heroes, and God's help is of secondary importance to the plot. The author of the Scroll knew how to adapt the story in the spirit of the prevailing religious viewpoint, placing the Shekhina center stage.

The Scroll illustrates how in its days the events of Hanukka were understood. The criticism of the Hasmoneans found in rabbinic literature has disappeared; all that remains is admiration for the heroes of the past and gratitude for God's intervention. Historical details are blurred, and the stories of the past are integrated into a variegated popular tradition that functions within the prevailing halakhic framework.

THE SCROLL OF FASTS, מגילת הצומות, is even more obscure. It consists of a list of 22-26 days decreed as fast days because of tragedies which occurred on them. Some of these are days on which biblical figures died while others relate to the passing of sages such as R. Akiva or R. Hanina b. Teradion. The list also includes such catastrophic events as the translation of the Tora into Greek or earthquakes.

There are two versions: a Babylonian and a Palestinian one. The Babylonian version first appears in a number of Gaonic works such as Sefer Halakhot Gedolot and the Siddur of Rav Amram Gaon,[19] but it is not contained in the

---

[19] A selection of the places of appearance: Sefer Halakhot Gedolot, ed Hildesheimer, 396-398; Siddur Rav Amram Gaon, Hilkhot Taanit 49; Sefer Ha-Eshkol, vol 2, 9; Shibbolei Ha-Leket 378; Kolbo 63; Tur Shulhan Arukh, Orah Hayyim, 580; Mahzor Vitry 271; Siddur Rashi 541; Midrash Ha-Hefetz ms British Museum 363 (p246) and additional mss of this work; R. Eliezer b. Yoel Ha-Levi, 879 and numerous piyyutim. The list also appears in mss and citations of Megillat Taanit (Vat. 229-5; 285-9; Sasson 368-14; 262; London, British Museum 1056-49 et al.). See also Tseda la-derekh 1:8, p247; Maor Enayim 67, ed Mantua p130. Shnei Luhot Ha-Berit (Tractate Taanit, ed

Siddur of Rav Saadia Gaon, and it is possible that some of the Babylonian Geonim were not familiar with it. The Palestinian version appears in four formats discovered in the Cairo Geniza and in various other manuscripts.[20]

There are many differences between the Babylonian and the Palestinian list, both in the events and in their dates. Only the Palestinian list mentions the earthquakes which occurred in the Land of Israel in 363 and 747.[21] It also has a fast day apparently meant to commemorate the deaths of Pappos and Lulianos, leaders of the revolt under Trajan (115-117), or possibly, the attempt to rebuild the Temple under Julian the Apostate,[22] and it mentions the day of passing of one Shmuel b. Tuviah, who is as yet unidentified.

It would appear that both the Babylonian and the Palestinian versions are late adaptations of a list deriving most likely from the Amoraic period. The custom of updating such lists in view of contemporary events is known from similar works from the Middle Ages.

Some of the dates of commemoration have biblical or rabbinic parallels: the days of passing of Aaron and his sons, of Moses, and of Joshua.[23] However, the custom of observing these as fast days is unknown in talmudic literature. It rather belongs to the cult of saints which began in the late Second Temple period and continued through the period of Mishna and Talmud. Some of the fasts are even fixed on Rosh Hodesh (New Moon) when, according to the halakha, it is forbidden to fast at all. The list then probably originated in popular circles who fostered the cult of saints without the support of the sages and, perhaps, against their wishes. Some of these popular traditions managed to be incorporated into late Byzantine halakhic works, although their observance was probably never mandatory.[24]

Jerusalem 1959, p121) lists the differences in the versions of the Tur, Kolbo, and Halakhot Gedolot. Most of the printed versions no longer differentiate between these versions.

[20] Marmorstein, 'Kiddush Yerahim', 232; Fleischer, 'Haduta-Hadutahu-Chedweta', 92-96; Margulies, *Hilkhot Erets Yisrael*, 141f; *He-Halutz* 13 (1889) 107 – an Italian ms uniquely similar to the Palestinian version, but containing Babylonian elements, see Fleischer, 'Compositions'.

[21] Margulies, 'A New Document'.

[22] On this matter see Brock, 'A Letter'. See also Geiger, 'Gallos Rebellion'. It is not clear whether Jewish settlement during that time suffered injury in the wake of the Gallos Rebellion or in the wake of the earthquake. See Geiger ib. 202-208. It would appear that the fast day on 18 Iyyar mentioned only in the Palestinian version refers to the earthquake of 362/363.

[23] See for example RuthR petihta 2; EcclR 7,4; MidrShmuel 23; bShab 105b.

[24] As mentioned above: Siddur Rav Amram Gaon; Sefer halakhot gedolot (only ed Hildesheimer; already the Tur is aware that the list appears in Sefer Halakhot Gedolot) but not in Siddur Rav Saadia Gaon. Nor does it appear in Maimonides or Sefer Ha-Manhig. Some works were familiar with the list but somewhat cautious as to its obligatory nature. See, for example, Magen Avraham on Shulhan Arukh, Orah Hayyim 580 and Beth Yofef, *ad loc*. See also Sefer Ha-Eshkol 2, p9; Shibbolei Ha-Leket 278 and other Rishonim. Various works comment on the list for manifold purposes. See Urbach, *Arugat ha-bosem*, 309f.

Chapter Five

The Targums as Part of
Rabbinic Literature

Zeev Safrai

Introduction

The Targums are a part of the literature of the sages whose purpose is to translate and explain the Hebrew Scriptures into Aramaic. Unlike the translations of the Bible into Greek, these Aramaic translations were especially intended for the Palestinian Jewish communities. This makes them of great importance for our understanding of the attitudes to the Tora in the Land of Israel during the period of Mishna and Talmud. Supposing that this is true also of the earlier period and that light is shed on the circumstances of the New Testament, many non-Jewish scholars have been paying more attention to the Targums than to any other branch of rabbinic literature. The purpose of the present chapter is to describe the Targums in view of their being an integral part of the literature of the sages. An earlier chapter in this series dealt with them while focussing on yet another aspect, their relationship to the scriptural text.[1]

After the following sections dealing with introductory matters, we shall discuss each of the extant Targums; bibliography will be given along the line.[2] A general bibliography is found in Grossfeld, *Bibliography*. Other study instruments are the concordances by Brederek, *Konkordanz* and de Moor and Houtman, *Bilingual Concordance*.

TERMINOLOGY

The phrase *targum* (תרגום) derives from the root r.g.m, meaning 'to read aloud' in Akkadian. The form מְתָרגם, *meturgam*, appears once in the Bible (Ezra 4:7) and apparently means 'translated'. In Amoraic parlance the word *targum* has various meanings:

(1) an explanation of a Tannaic saying (*memra*), sometimes by way of a translation into Aramaic,[3] but also as a direct explanation;

(2) a *derasha* or homiletic explanation on any matter[4] – in most instances a midrashic explanation on a verse which may have been part of the translation or 'targum' of the reading of the Tora; in one instance, however, a verse from the Psalms was commented on, which was certainly not read aloud in the synagogue;

(3) a translation, particularly during the reading of the Tora. This is the meaning we shall mostly deal with below.

The official associated with the 'targum' was called the (מ)תורגמן), *(me)turge-man*. That phrase also has various meanings: (1) the person who recites targum during the reading of the Tora; (2) the sage who calls out aloud and explains the words more softly spoken by the teacher during a public lecture or class,

[1] Alexander, 'Jewish Aramaic Translations'.
[2] Apart from the references in other footnotes see the following general studies: Alexander, 'The Targumim and the Rabbinic Rules'; Anderson, 'The Interpretation of Genesis 1:1'; Beattie and McNamara, *The Aramaic Bible*; Bowker, *Targums*; Chilton, *Targumic Approaches*; Clarke, 'The Bible and Translation'; Flesher, 'Mapping the Synoptic Palestinian Targums'; idem, 'The Targu-mim'; idem, *Targum Studies*; idem, *Targum and Scripture*; Fraade, 'Rabbinic Views on the Practice of Targum'; Gooding, 'On The Use of the LXX'; Goshen-Gottstein, 'Targum-Studies'; Hayward, 'Major Aspects of Targumic Studies'; Heinemann, 'The Targum of Ex. 22:4'; idem, 'Early Halakhah'; M. Kasher, *Torah Shelemah*, vol. 35; R. Kasher, 'A New Targum'; idem, 'Beliefs of Synagogue *Meturgemanim*'; Klein, 'Additional Targum Manuscripts'; idem, *Targumic Manuscripts*; Le Deaut, 'The Targumim'; Levine, 'The Targum'; McNamara, 'Targumic Stud-ies'; idem, 'Aramaic Translations'; Melamed, *Bible Commentators*; Z. Safrai, 'Origins of Read-ing'; Shinan, 'Live translation'; idem, 'The "Palestinian" Targums'; idem, 'Targumic Additions'; idem, 'Aramaic Targum as a Mirror'; idem, 'Aggadah of the Palestinian Targums'; Syren, 'Isaiah-Targum'.
[3] E.g. bSan 104b; ySuk 5, 55b; yShek 5, 48c.
[4] yBik 3, 65d; MidrPs 19:2; ySan 2, 20d; GenR 80,l (p950) and its parallel in MidrGad Genesis 34:1 – *derash*.

244

and who is also called by the Aramaic term אמורא, *amora*. Occasionally the meturgeman translates even in matters not connected to teaching or Tora reading. This, however, is for the most part a rather secondary meaning.[5]

The phrase 'targum' usually refers to a 'creative' translation from one language into another. It appears in this sense in the following tradition: 'Whence (what biblical verse serves to justify the) targum? Rav Zeira in the name of Hananel (said): "And they read in the book of the Tora of the Lord" (Neh 8:8) – this implies the Bible; "...clearly, [and they gave the sense]" (*ib.*) – this is the targum' (yMeg 4, 74d and parallel sources).

Originally 'targum' implied translation into any language. Eventually, however, it came to mean specifically translation into Aramaic, as Aramaic translations became the most popular: 'They were written (in) *targum* or in any language' (bShab 115a). The phrase also occasionally took on the meaning of any short passage written in Aramaic (bShab 43b). In most cases, however, a particular and definite work written in Aramaic is intended. It is in this sense that we shall use the term here, capitalised 'Targum' when it refers to our written documents, and lower case 'targum' when it concerns the genre, the act, or particular instances of translating or rendering into Aramaic.

ORIGINS

In the period of Mishna and Talmud it was customary to translate the portion read out in the synagogue on the Sabbath morning into Aramaic – or in other words, to have it accompanied by targum. The origins of this custom, however, are far from clear. The tradition from Yerushalmi Megilla just quoted might indicate that the sages were of the opinion that the custom originated together with the ceremonial reading out of the Tora. However, the parallel in Genesis Rabba (36,8 p342) refers to a translation into Greek, not into Aramaic. The biblical verse cited in the tradition, then, has nothing to do with the custom of targum in the synagogue. Moreover, this talmudic tradition may certainly not be viewed as a historical tradition.

There are a number of early traditions regarding the public reading of the Tora, such as that undertaken by the High Priest, or during the course of the appearances of Jesus in Galilean synagogues or of Paul in the Diaspora.[6] These traditions refer to the actual reading of the Tora, the reading of the portion from the prophets (*haftara*) and even to a sermon. The targum, however, is not mentioned. There are no halakhot dealing with the synagogal custom of targum before the Usha period (140-180 CE). mShab 15:1 (and parallel sources), while referring to translations of Scripture, seems to mean actual written translations of various biblical selections and thus, although it probably predates the

---

[5] As, for example, mMak 1:9; Neof, PsYon, FrgTg, and Onk on Gen 42:23; Tg 2Chr 32:31.
[6] E.g. mSot 7:7; mYom 7:1; Luke 4:17-20; Matt 13:54; Acts 13:15, 'reading of Law and Prophets'. See also Perrot, 'Reading of the Bible', 149-159.

Usha period, is of no value in terms of dating the liturgical function of targum. Likewise, the custom of writing the Tora 'in any language' (mMeg 1:8) does not pertain to the liturgical use of targum in the synagogue. In the opinion of the present author, there are no sources which would allow us to date the custom before the Usha period, or at best before the late Yavne period (100-135 CE).[7]

The accepted practice was to read a section of the Tora, to 'translate' (*le-targem*) and then to read the selection a second time: 'Twice Scripture and once targum' (mBer 8:1). We possess a number of references to this type of targum. Thus in mMeg 4:5, 'He that reads in the Tora... may not read to the meturgeman more than one verse at a time, or three in the case of the reading from the prophets (*haftara*).' Thus, the targum was recited after every verse in the case of the Tora, and after every three verses in the case of the *haftara*.[8]

The author of Tractate Sofrim (18:5) stated that the targum was recited after the completion of the *seder*, namely at the end of a section when a new person would be called to the reading of the Tora. There were those, however, who claimed that this source relates to a derasha and not to the reading of the Tora. Certain Babylonian Geonim felt that the targum should be recited after every three verses, as the Mishna stated in the case of the reading from the Prophets.[9] This would appear to be a compromise between the tradition of the Mishna and that of Tractate Sofrim.

The role of the meturgeman was more or less defined, and he was even considered to be semi-professional.[10] The reading of the Tora, however, was done by the worshippers called up for that particular purpose. The sages were very particular in preventing the reader from serving as his own 'translator'. Likewise they were insistent that the translation was to be done by only one person. Only with regard to the reading of the *megilla* (Esther scroll) on Purim the sages were more lenient and allowed the targum to be recited by two translators, just as the reading of the Tora may be divided among two readers (tMeg 4[3]:20, p227). In spite of all this, it seems that at times the reader did also serve as translator. Perhaps this was the case if there were no other qualified people to do so.

---

[7] In a baraita in both Bavli and Yerushalmi it is stated that Queen Helena made a tablet upon which was written the Tora chapter of the 'suspected wife' together with its targum (ySot 2, 18a and parallels). However, this biblical selection was read to the woman in whatever language she understood and, thus, the meaning of 'targum' in that case is not the same as the one we are dealing with. A Second Temple mention of targum would seem to appear in tSuk 2:10, but the particular citation does not appear in the parallels in ySuk 3, 54a; bSuk 41b. From the discussion in the Yerushalmi it is clear that its author possessed a Tosefta version that did not contain the cited passage.

[8] See S. Safrai, 'Education', 966f.

[9] See Lewin, *Otsar Ha-Geonim*, V, 41. There were also other customs.

[10] There were nevertheless small settlements without an official meturgeman.

R. Yehuda (140-180) was of the opinion that the person referred to as the reader was also capable of serving as translator (bKid 49a). R. Shmuel b. Yitshak, however, reprimanded a bridegroom who read the Tora and also served as his own translator (yMeg 4, 74d). The sage stated that 'just as the Tora at Sinai was handed down through an intermediary (Moses), so we should act in the same manner and hand it down through an intermediary.' This was the basic underlying principle behind the role of the meturgeman (and of the *amora* in the case of *derashot*). The sage requires an intermediary between himself and the congregation or community.

The translator must fulfil his function with proper respect (yMeg 4, 74d), just as the *hazan* (prayer leader) must. However, unlike the *hazan* he may be a minor (mMeg 4:6). The sages stipulated that the recitation of the targum should be on the same level of importance as the reading of the Tora and therefore required that it be done in the same intonation (bBer 45a). The targum was for the most part connected to the reading of the Tora, although strictly speaking it was not necessary in order to fulfil the obligation of the reading of the Tora. As we have also seen, there was at times a targum of the reading of the Prophets. Less attention, however, was paid to this targum.

There was also a 'targum on the *megilla* (scroll)' and it would seem that the scroll of Esther is meant (tMeg 4[3]:20). Tractate Sofrim 18:4 mentions a targum of Lamentations which was read on the ninth of Av. There is no other evidence relating to the reciting of a targum at public occasions of the reading of the Tora, such as the reading of the Tora during the week.[11] The Mishna and Tosefta also contain a list of biblical selections which should not be translated since they were considered to be insulting to the biblical Patriarchs, or for various other reasons. We shall deal with this phenomenon below.[12] Likewise, it seems that there was no targum during the reading of the Tora on public fast days (yMeg 4, 74d). This was the case perhaps since the ritual of these days was quite ancient and may have even predated the concept of targum.

PURPOSE AND STATUS

The purpose of targum was twofold: translation and explanation. Translation was necessary because many worshippers no longer understood Hebrew. This may have been the result of a drop in the status of Hebrew at this time. As Y. Kutscher has shown, the transference of the Jewish population center from

---

[11] Some mss. of bMeg 21a mention a Targum of the Hallel (Psalms 113-118, important in the festival liturgy). In the ninth century we hear of the custom to translate a selection of Isaiah used in the synagogue liturgy; the source of which is not clear. The Gaon Rav Natronai (ninth cent.) thought that it derived from the practice to read every day a selection from the Prophets and to read a Targum of them. See Lewin (n9 above). Targum was also common in derashot and in lessons, whether by way of derasha or simply for the purpose of a translation; see GenR 50,3 (p520); and cf bYom 20b for a Targum recited in the middle of a lecture by a/the meturgeman.

[12] mMeg 4:9-10; tMeg 4(3):31-37.

Judaea to Galilee in the wake of the Bar-Kokhba revolt resulted in the strengthening of the status of Aramaic which was a much more widespread language in the Galilee than in Judaea.[13] It should be remembered that the first evidence of Targum during the liturgical reading of the Tora dates from this period. The element of explanation is most likely related to the desire of the sages to further promulgate the study and understanding of the Tora. This was facilitated by targum which combines elements of the written Tora and the oral teaching of the sages.

The sources state that the purpose of targum was to explain the Tora to the public at large which did not know enough Hebrew. Thus Sofrim 18:5 states: '...And he translates in order that the rest of the people may understand, as well as women and children.' It should be remembered that this was basically the purpose of the derasha. Thus it would seem that both the derasha and the targum derive from the desire of the sages to make the Tora more widespread among the people as well as connecting it to the oral teaching tradition. The imagery seen above comparing the meturgeman with the intermediary role of Moses in the giving of the law is in keeping with this concept. This is also apparent in the teaching of Sofrim that, 'If there was on the Sabbath a meturgeman or an expounder of a derasha, then one may read only three verses of the *haftara* of the prophets... and one need not worry about the requirement of twenty-one verses.'[14] If there was targum or a derasha on the Sabbath, it was allowed to shorten the required number of verses read in the *haftara*. Both of these institutions, the targum and the derasha were seen to some extent as substitutes for the *haftara*.

The targumic ideal of the sages was: 'He who translates a verse in its literal sense lies, while he who adds to the translation mocks' (tMeg 4[3]:41). This stresses the essence of targum as a commentary, while at the same time trying to avoid extended and exaggerated derashot. As we shall see, the contemporaneous reports about the actual practice of the ancient targum confirm this aim.

The connection between targum and derasha is evident also from the form of the extant Targums. At times the beginning of a Targum on a certain matter will contain extended derashot without any attempt at literal translation. This is very often the case at the beginning of a reading portion of the Tora. These targumic derashot are similar in format to the *petihta* ('proem') which was an accepted format of the public derasha. Certain of these *petihta*-type Targums contain number motifs such as: ten songs, twelve miracles, four keys, four nights (Neof, PsYon, FrgTg on Exod 12:12); four groups (Neof, PsYon, FrgTg on Exod 14:13-14), and three angels (Neof, PsYon and FrgTg on Gen. 18:1). There also appear set formulae of the *petihta* such as: 'God of the universe, may his name be extolled' (FrgTg on Gen. 35:9). Another such formula is:

---

[13] See Kutscher, *Studies*, 43-95. It is still not clear as to what extent the general public actually knew Hebrew. Kutscher's conclusions may be somewhat exaggerated.

[14] Sofrim 18:5. This represents a summary of the discussion in yMeg 4, 75a.

'Blessed be the name of The Master of the universe who teaches us His ways' (PsYon Deut 34:6).[15] The opening formula, 'My people, house (or, children) of Israel', appears numerous times in the Targums and is even quoted as a Targum in the Palestinian Talmud (yBer 5, 9c and parallels).

Thus, it is clear that targum is also explanation and commentary. We have seen above that the justification for this approach was connected to the biblical phrase, 'clearly, [and they gave the sense]', and therefore the sages said, 'the words are expounded plainly' (PsYon and FrgTg Deut 27:8). The targum, then, was addressed to the general public and this, as we shall see, affected its nature.

Thus the targum occupied, as it were, a middle position between the written Tora and the oral teachings of the sages. This situation is reflected in number of halakhot relating to the nature and form of the public targum. Thus, as we have seen, there were written Targums, but these could not be used during the reading of the Tora: 'R. Shmuel be-R. Yitshak went into a synagogue and saw the reader recite the targum from a written book. He said to him: This is forbidden to you: things which were imparted orally are to be presented orally; things which were imparted in writing are to be read from the writing' (yMeg 4, 74d). R. Shmuel is referring to a well-known halakha to the effect that oral teaching should not be written (bGit 60b; bTem 14b). It is interesting to note that this law refers to the proscription against writing halakhot, while R. Shmuel actually forbids the *liturgical* use of a written text, or in our case of a Targum. bShab 115a, mentioning written Targum, records differences of opinion regarding their sanctity. In so doing, this halakha stresses the important status of the Targums: they may not be as holy as the written Tora, but they possess a higher level of sanctity than the oral tradition itself.

The targum was included in the curriculum of the ancient academy already before the Usha period. Thus it is mentioned in the course of study of R. Akiva, and in other contexts.[16] The most clear-cut tradition is the permission granted teachers of Tora and targum to collect a fee for their efforts, a privilege denied instructors of the oral tradition. The reason for this permission is undoubtedly the fact that the teacher (*sofer*) became a professional who devoted his full time efforts to his teaching endeavors. Mentioning targum together with the Bible shows how important it was in the teaching curriculum.[17]

---

[15] For the opening phrase 'Lord [In de tekst: God] of the Universe' (*Elohei ha-olam*), see SER 16(17) p88; 18 p89, 100; 22(20) p121. Occurrences of the opening formula in Aramaic בריך שמיה, 'Blessed be His name' have been collected by Liebreich, 'The Benedictory Formula'. The Aramaic phrase, 'Blessed art Thou, God, Who exists forever' (FrgTg ms Paris on Gen 16:13) and 'Blessed art Thou, God, Sustainer of All Worlds' (FrgTg ms Vat on Gen 16:13)' also belongs to this category. The entire matter of opening formulae requires further discussion.

[16] ARN b 28 (p58); Sofrim 16:6 (289). Cf, however, ARN a 14 (p58); bBB 134a ; bSuk 28a; ARN b 12 (p29). Cf however idem ARN a 6 (p29). See also SifD 161 (p211f) and parallels.

[17] yNed 4, 38d. The word *targum* is missing in the Mishna and in the Babylonian sources. Perhaps the custom in Babylonia was different. It would seem likely that the intent is to a translation (into

LITERARY FIXATION AND ANTIQUITY OF THE MATERIAL

In this area it is necessary to distinguish between two questions: (1) When did targum become a standard literary process? (2) When did the literary fixation of the Targums take place? While the answer to the first question is to be found in talmudic literature, the answer to the second one must be searched from the texts of the Targums themselves.

Did the sages possess a fixed version of targum? As indicated above, the custom of Targum in the synagogue began in the Usha period. Targum in general, however, was known before then. The first concrete reference to a written targumic work dates from the end of the Second Temple period:

> It happened that Abba Halafta went to Rabban Gamliel be-Rebbi (96-115 CE) at Tiberias and found him sitting by his table... with in his hand the book of Job in *targum* (i.e. in Aramaic), from which he was reading. R. Halafta said to him: I remember your grandfather, Rabban Gamliel the Elder (20-50), who was standing on the steps leading up to the Temple Mount, and the book of Job in *targum* was brought to him. He turned to the builder and said: place it under the building stone. Likewise he (Rabban Gamliel of Yavne) commanded and had it set aside. (tShab 13(14):2, p128)

The nature of the sages' opposition is not clear. Did they oppose elements contained in the Targum which they feared might lead to apostasy? Were they simply opposed to the writing (or even the formulation) of targum? Or were they opposed to the concept of targum which by its nature was not meant to be read in public? Such was certainly the case regarding the Targum of Job. It is clear, however, that for whatever reasons the sages may have opposed this particular Targum, they were not successful in suppressing it. Thus, even though Rabban Gamliel the Elder tried to suppress it, it appeared again during the time of his grandson, as we have seen. Rabban Gamliel the Younger may also have tried to suppress it, but the work is mentioned again in Tractate Sofrim (appendix II, Higger p377). A Targum of Job has also been found in the caves of the Judean Desert which we shall discuss below. It should be remembered that the book of Job is an extremely difficult work and this may have instigated the various translations.

Talmudic tradition differentiates between targum on the Tora and that on Prophets and Hagiographa. Targum on the Tora was given, as it were, to Moses on Mt. Sinai (yMeg 4, 74d). This tradition is undoubtedly connected to the idea current at that time that the entire oral Tora was given to Moses on Mt. Sinai and this certainly can not be understood, therefore, as a historical tradition. On the targum on the Prophets, the Bavli states: 'The Targum on the

Hebrew) of the Book of Daniel which was written partly in Aramaic. A number of verses in Daniel, in addition to the difficulty in interpreting them, served as the basis for certain eschatological calculations and projections.

Prophets was authored by Yonatan b. Uzziel who received it from Haggai, Zechariah and Malachi... He also wished to reveal the Targum on the Hagiographa but a heavenly voice came forth and prevented him (from such)...' (bMeg 3a). This Targum was thought to hint at the eschatological arrival of the Messiah and, therefore, was not permitted to be publicized.[18]

Yonatan b. Uzziel was a student of Hillel (first century), but his Targum is, as it were, brought in the name of prophets from the post-exilic period. In addition to a Targum to the *haftarot* (portions of the Prophets read after the reading of the Tora), we also hear of entire Targums on Isaiah and Jeremiah (Sofrim appendix II, Higger p377). The ascription of Targums to Moses or to Yonatan b. Uziel would appear to be legendary. It also seems clear that the Babylonian Amoraim possessed a Targum on the Tora and the Prophets, but were not familiar with a Targum on the Hagiographa. Apart from the 'festal scrolls', the Hagiographa were not read in the synagogue and therefore, a Targum on this part of Holy Scripture would by nature have been formulated at a later date. A Targum on Esther, which was read as a 'scroll' in the synagogue, is mentioned in tMeg 4[3]:20; Sofrim 18:4 mentions a Targum on Lamentations.

An interesting tradition is found in bKiddushin 49a. The *sugya* brings a Tannaic source stating that if someone proposes as a condition for betrothal that he be a 'reader' – 'if he should read three verses of the Tora in the synagogue then the betrothal is valid; R. Yehuda says: (it is not valid) until he reads three verses *and translates* them.' The continuation of the *sugya*, though, raises a number of questions regarding the opinion of R. Yehuda. How can one translate by himself of his own accord? Did not R. Yehuda (c. 140-180) himself state (tMeg 4[3]:41): 'He who translates a verse in a literal manner is a liar, and he who adds to it is a blasphemer.' The Talmud answers that R. Yehuda is referring to 'their targum'. Thus it would appear that at the time when the *sugya* was formulated in Babylonia, there were fixed versions of targum and no one would think of independently translating or creating a new rendering, while R. Yehuda's statement refers to a period before the final redaction of the targum.

Talmudic literature contains explicit instructions regarding the manner in which particular verses of the Bible were to be translated.[19] This would seem to

---

[18] bMeg 3a. Traditions regarding Targum and fragments of established Targumim are found in additional sources. See e.g. GenR 79,7 (p946-948) *et al.*

[19] Cf mMeg 4:9, re Lev. 18:21, the forbidden Targum follows the opinion of R. Yishmael, yMeg 4, 75c; yBer 5, 9c. In both cases the forbidden Targum appears in PsYon. Instructions regarding the Targum of Gen 29:17 appear in an Amoraic statement in GenR 70,16 (p815) and parallels; see below. On a number of traditions regarding the list of verses not to be included in the Targum see Alexander, 'Rabbinic Lists'; Vermes, *Scripture and tradition*, 215f and McNamara, *The New Testament*, 45 ff. See also yMeg 4, 74d for two additional examples of Targumim. The halakha there requires that they be translated literally, even if this results in a deviation from the plain

imply once again that a final and standardized version of targum had not yet been formulated. However, such instructions also seem to imply the beginning of the process of targumic redaction. Rabbinic literature also contains quotes from the targum to particular verses from Tora, Prophets and Hagiographa.[20] It is impossible to prove from these citations that there was a set and established version; they may simply represent local versions of targum which each were common or accepted in a different region. Moreover, nowhere in talmudic literature is targum ever used as a source of authority in a halakhic argument or for that matter in an aggadic discussion with a moral or religious significance.[21] It is brought only as an illustration somewhat tangential to the discussion at hand. If there were a set version of the targum, it would seem likely that it would have been used as a proof or counter-proof in numerous halakhic discourses. The fact that targum was not used in this sense most likely proves that there was no set version in the talmudic period.

Nevertheless, targumic traditions and targumic ways of dealing with certain issues did exist, and we shall discuss these at greater length below. There were also written translation of the Tora, or of parts of it, in several different languages. These books were considered to be part of the literature of oral Tora, as we have already seen. Targums on Job and Leviticus have been found in the caves of the Judaean Desert. It should be remembered, however, that the members of the Dead Sea Sect were also wont to write down their own version of oral teaching and the Pharisaic distinction between 'written and oral Tora' was not accepted among them.

Much scholarly effort has been expended on trying to date targumic literature, but the endeavour largely seems to have remained fruitless. It would seem that the problem is methodological and the various opinions are based upon different approaches. We shall deal with certain aspects of the problem in the course of our discussion of the particular Targums. For the moment we shall restrict our remarks to a brief summary of the various opinions from a general methodological standpoint.[22] The various types of proofs brought by scholars can be presented in the following categories:

---

meaning of the text. These Targumim might be forbidden because of their sectarian origin, see Alexander, 'rabbinic lists'.

[20] E.g. bShab 10b; bShab 28b; bMK 26a; bNed 38a; GenR 61,5 (p663); NumR 13,3.

[21] If the Targum is actually brought in for support, it is not considered an argument against the opposite opinion. Support from a Targum is considered only an additional possibility, not as an early tradition such as a Tannaic source or even an Amoraic tradition; cf bKid 72a; bMK 26a.

[22] The literature on this matter is vast. For the purposes of convenience we have tried to limit the bibliography on this point to the bare minimum. It is possible to point out two different approaches, one which seeks an early date for the literary formulation of the Targum (first-second cent. CE), the other seeking a later date for these phenomena (fourth-fifth cent. CE or possibly even later). For the major studies on the subject see Geiger, *Urschrift*; Kahle, *Masoreten*; Black, *Aramaic Approach*; Heinemann, 'Early Halakhah'; McNamara, *New Testament*. For a summary see York, 'Targum'.

(a) *Targumic citations in Amoraic literature*. Talmudic literature includes dozens of targumic citations. Some are found in our Targums while others are not. The similar or identical citations may be simply coincidence, or they may be the result of the influence of talmudic and midrashic literature on the extant Targums. It is important to note that in the Babylonian Talmud the Targums on the Prophets are usually cited in the form 'as Rav Yosef translated' (*ki demetargem rav Yosef*), and are almost always found in the extant Targums. However, here it is still possible to claim that the Talmud influenced the formation of the Targum and not the opposite.

(b) *Early material*. It is clear that the Targums often preserve references to early aggadic and halakhic material (see, for instance, Ps-Yonatan on Deut 33:11). However, early material is also found in rabbinic works that were composed much later,[23] and it is quite difficult to date a work based on this method.

(c) *'Early' halakha*. The Targums and particularly Neofiti and Ps-Yonatan contain early halakhot which were expounded during the course of many generations.[24] They also contain minority opinions which were not accepted in the halakha.[25] There are also translations which were explicitly forbidden according to both Tannaic and Amoraic literature.[26] Certain scholars claim that this serves as proof that the Targums were formulated before the legal decision

---

[23] A good example is PdRE which was composed in the 7th-8th cent. CE, but contains material parallel to traditions in the Apocrypha not later than first cent. CE. Moreover, the supposed early nature of material in the Targum requires examination in the case of each and every instance.

[24] E.g. Ps-Yon Deut 26:12. The stem תלה (hang) is always translated as 'crucify', although this is not in keeping with the accepted halakha. See the Targumim on Deut 21:23; 2Sam 18:10; Ruth 1:17; and see below. However, this rendering appears in both Targumim on Esth 7:10, which are certainly both late and Jewish; likewise, in the late midrash Aggadat Esther 7:19 and in other late Midrashim (like Megillat Antiochos). It would therefore appear that the authors of the targum did not always distinguish between 'hanging' and 'crucifying', and this proof then is not conclusive. Another example often discussed is the Geniza FrgTg and Neof on Exod 22:4, which in the prevailing halakha relates to damages wrought by an animal (mBK 2:1-3), but differently in the Targumim. The example was cited by Kahle and discussed by many others. Teicher, 'A Sixth Century Fragment', 125-129 attempted to show that the supposed non-normative interpretation was simply a copyists' error; similarly Schelbert, 'Exodus 22,4', but it appears also in Neofiti and thus the claim cannot be correct, see Heinemann, 'Early Halakhah'. However, it is important to remember that the opinion expressed in this problematic targum is the simple meaning and is actually stated in MekRSbY on Exod 22:5 (p198). Thus, it should not be considered as a non-normative targum, but rather as expressing a halakhic minority opinion. This example, then, belongs to the category discussed in the next note. Another noted example of this motif is PsYon Exod 22:6, 9, see further below.

[25] Thus a number of verses are translated in accordance with the halakhic opinion of Bet Shammai, even though their tradition was factually rejected by the Tannaic period. See e.g. PsYon Lev 23:42; mSuk 1:1 and parallels. At times the Targum does not follow the 'official' halakhic opinion, while it turns out to reflect actual practice in Palestine (though not necessarily 'official'). See e.g. PsYon Deut 25:7; cf tYev 12:9. See Margulies, *Hilkhot Erets-Yisrael*, 27. For forbidden Targumim see n19 above.

[26] See n19.

forbidding certain renderings of particular verses. It is possible to claim, however, that the Targumim were not considered to be 'authoritative' literature and, in fact, contain a popular strain at times in opposition to established rabbinic thought.[27] This discussion among scholars is connected with the problem of the nature and purpose of targum. We shall deal further with this problem below. In any event, it should be noted that early halakha is also found in late midrash collections, although less frequent than in Ps-Yonatan.

(d) *Late material*. No doubt there is also a degree of late material found in the Targums (mainly Ps-Yonatan) such as the mentioning of the names of the wife and family of Mohammad (Gen 21:21) or the mentioning of the city of Constantinople (Num 24:19) which was founded in the fourth century.[28] It is doubtful, however, that these few traditions can serve as a method for dating the Targum. This is especially true since sometimes these references are missing in part of the manuscripts.[29] Moreover, we shall also see below that many of these late references stem from 'additions' (*toseftot*) which for the most part are rather late and can hardly be considered an integral part of the Targum. However, the absence of late material in a particular Targum can not be considered as proof of its early date. Such 'late material' is in any event difficult to pinpoint. Moreover, similar late material is also missing from the late midrash collections at times and this is usually more a matter of format and style than a matter of chronology. Thus, for example, the last 'evil kingdom' is usually Esau-Rome and not Islam even in such a late midrash collection as Midrash on Psalms.

(e) *Proto-Christian material*. It is claimed that many targumic renderings contain early eschatological traditions which in the course of time turned into Christian ideas. Thus, for example, the targumic tradition that the Messiah will be born in Bethlehem[30] was used by some to claim that the Targums were composed before Christianity became widespread, since the authors of the individual Targums would not espouse such ideas once they became accepted in Christianity. This claim is difficult to make since similar motifs are also found in later midrashic material, which by all accounts was written after the advent of Christianity. Moreover, we have no proof that the sages actually sought to suppress such motifs. At best, these motifs in targumic literature may

---

[27] For a clear expression of this claim see Albeck, 'Apocryphal Halakha', and Bamberger, 'Halakhic Elements'. This claim is based on the perspective that the Targum was a semi-popular work whose text remained in a fluid state until the middle Ages. Accordingly, the meturgeman also occupied a rather low place in the rabbinic hierarchy. Our discussion presupposes these views. The opposite trend seeks to see the Targum as belonging to authoritative literature and, thus, any elements which contradict accepted halakhic practice are considered to be early. Cf Kahle 203; Geiger, 113-126; Black 50-53.

[28] PsYon Gen 21:21. On the citing of the Byzantine city Sycomazon (Šūq Mâzon) see Neof Num 34:4; FrgTg Num 34:15 and perhaps Yon Sam 22:32. See Levey, 'The Date of Targum Jonathan to the Prophets'; Shinan, *Aggadah*, 193-198.

[29] E.g. the mentioning of Constantinopolis in Tg Ps 110:75; PsYon Num 24:24.

[30] E.g. Yon Mich 5:1. However, this belief also appears in a late aggada, see yBer 2, 5a.

imply that the material itself might be early, but it certainly is of no value in dating the targumic corpus in general (see sections b and c above).

(f) *Greek and Latin expressions.* This element probably tells more about *where* the Targums were edited than about *when* they were composed.[31]

(g) *Early geographic material.* Certain scholars are of the opinion that the Targums, and particularly Neofiti, contain early geographic material.[32] At most, however, this implies that certain individual traditions are early. Moreover, the Targums do not seem to contain material which relates to historical and geographical situations which pre-date the third-fourth centuries CE, and if they do contain such material, such particular situations also existed during the later centuries. On the other hand, however, even if the Targums contain traditions which seem to relate to late Byzantine geography, they can hardly be dated to this time on the basis of such considerations, as we have stated above in analogous circumstances.

(h) *Liguistics and philology.* These fields could serve as important tools in dating but they are difficult to use and a sound methodology of dating based on them has not yet been established. Moreover, insofar as the Targums consist of dynamic material, certain late linguistic developments may be visible. However, the attribution of Targum Onkelos to Babylonia was made basically on this linguistic consideration; we shall discuss this further below. Recently, and based for the most part on the work of Kutscher, it has become clear that the Aramaic of the Targums is early and is grounded in the reality of the first-second centuries CE in Palestine. Onkelos was edited in Babylonia, while the rest of the Targums were apparently edited in Palestine; the import of the 'additions' in this context shall be discussed below. It remains doubtful, however, whether such linguistic considerations can help to solve the problem of dating the Targums, since the editor of the Targum may be using archaic language or traditions, and such archaisms might never have been written down or editorially formulated yet have been in existence for a long period. The targum did, however, merit a degree of sanctity and was not arbitrarily changed.[33]

(i) *Dependence on early literary formulations.* The only way to determine the date of the Targums is to examine their dependence on established literary works. This method is by no means easy and there have been few studies in the field. Thus, there have been scholars who claimed that the author of Pesher

---

[31] See for example Komlosh, *The Bible in the Light of the Aramaic Translations,* 252-256.

[32] See Díez-Macho, *Neofiti,* vol 1, 1ff. One of his examples is the translation of the children of Hagar by the phrase 'Saracens'. The phrase represents Arab tribes which, according to Albright, were found until the second century. However, a similar identification is cited by Jerome, Ep. 5:129. The tribe is also mentioned in rabbinic literature. We discussed Sycomazon in n28 above. The matter requires further study.

[33] On an archaic Targum which was not understood by those who used it see above n24. On the language of the Targum see below n74.

Habakkuk found in the Judaean Desert made use of TgYonatan on Habakkuk.[34] At best, however, we can state that both works made use of the same source. This method can be used only regarding certain parts of the Targum since it remains yet to be proved that there existed an internal unity in the individual Targums. Thus, for example, it would appear that Ps-Yonatan on Exod 12:24 is dependent on Mekhilta de-R. Yishmael. This dependence is expressed not only by the fact that all of the *derashot* found in the Targum appear also in the Mekhilta, but by the fact that the Targum also presents opposing ideas which for the most part are expressed only in the Mekhilta (apart, of course from the Targum).[35] However, this conclusion is correct only for the particular passage of Ps-Yonatan and does not hold for the Targum in general. It is possible that Ps-Yonatan on Chronicles and possibly on Proverbs are dependent on *sugyot* in the Babylonian Talmud.[36]

(j) *The biblical text of the Targum.* The question whether part of the Targums had a different biblical text has been examined elsewhere in this series.[37] It would appear, however, that this matter is of little relevance for the question of dating the Targum.

As should be clear by now, there are no clear-cut indications regarding the dating of most of the Targums. All in all, the evidence we have cited for the relatively late date of the custom of reading the Targum in the synagogue, as well as the fact that most of our Targums are not cited in the Babylonian or Palestinian Talmud, would seem to indicate that the Targums were not really formulated before the third-fourth centuries CE. The dating of the Targums is, as we have seen, a matter of much controversy, and the conclusion stated here is that of the present author.[38]

Apart from the various extant Targums we possess dozens of targumic fragments referred to as *toseftot*, 'additions'. These fragments are for the most part characterized by their homiletic nature and, in fact, are really independent targumic derashot which have been added to the extant Targums. Some of these additions have been included in the standard version of the Targums on the Tora and the Prophets. Proof of this is the fact that some of the targumic derashot referred to elsewhere as 'additions' are fully integrated in the extant

---

[34] Wieder, 'Habakkuk Scroll'; Brownlee, 'Habakkuk Midrash'. The conclusions may not be correct, but the methodology is sound.

[35] See PsYon Exod 12:2; 13:9; 15:25 (twice); 16:22; 17:5; 17:9, 12, 13, 14, 16; 21:16. In all of these instances PsYon uses the arrangement and format of the Mekhilta, except for the last example where there is a parallel arrangement in tBK 2:10. In two examples the derasha appears in a corrupted form because the Targum presented it in a condensed format, and here the dependence on Mekhilta is even more clearcut: see PsYon Exod 17:5, 14; in FrgTg only one derasha of this type appears (Exod 15:25); they are all missing in Neofiti. It should be pointed out though that PsYon on Exod 15 and 19 is late and is more or less in the form of an addition.

[36] See below on these Targumim.

[37] See Alexander, 'Jewish Aramaic Translations'.

[38] For a summary of opinions on the matter see York. For the citing of these Targumim see McNamara, *New Testament* and Shinan, *Aggadah*.

Targums.[39] Thus R. Meir of Troyes (thirteenth cent.) informs those dealing with Targums how to integrate 'additions' into the Targum on certain verses of Exod 14-15.[40] Part of these derashot are actually found in Neofiti, Ps-Yonatan and the Fragmentary Targum on these verses. It would appear that a similar process took place in other sections of our Targums, even though we have no proof of this process. The 'additions' have their own literary style which we shall discuss below. However in order to uncover these 'additions' it is not sufficient simply to use literary tools, and further textual evidence should also be examined. Textual variants in the manuscripts and the appearance of the same midrash in the Targum on different verses may indicate the presence of an 'addition'.

It would appear, then, that the Targums were not edited at one go, but developed over a long period of time, in different regions and through many 'authors'. In the course of this process certain derashot became popular and were accepted by all meturgemanim. The Targums which have survived represent then the common targumic tradition. Other traditions were deposited in the 'additions' or went lost.

TYPES AND CONTENT

A basic distinction can be made between targums that purport to give a literal rendering (*peshat*) and those that gives a homiletical exposition (*derash*), often expanding and adding material. As to the relation to the biblical text one can go further and distinguish seven, increasingly expansive types or levels of targum.

(a) *Strictly literal.* Such a targum renders the biblical verse in a literal and exact manner. This is the case, for instance, in Onkelos on Num 1:1, or the targum of Lev 14:52 found in bNid 31b and in Onkelos, Ps-Yonatan and Neofiti *ad loc.* Hundreds of such translations are found in the Targums.

(b) *Loosely literal.* This type still sticks to the biblical verse, but changes it somewhat in order to fit the Aramaic to the Hebrew, to explain a phrase, or to attain to a more simple syntax of the sentence. We shall cite examples in our discussion of Onkelos.

---

[39] This phrase is often found in the title of various targumic passages in both the printed versions and manuscripts. Some fragments have been printed as addenda to FragTg (Ginsburger) or as alternate reading in Sperber's edition of TgYon on Prophets. Many are still hidden in early manuscripts and printed editions, see below n110. On additions integrated into our texts see the Targumim on Exod 15. See also Díez-Macho, 'Deux nouveaux fragments'; Kasher, *Targumic Toseftot.* There are more publications on the matter, but this is not the place to discuss them.

[40] See e.g. Weiss, *Siddur Troyes,* 3-23; *Siddur Rashi,* ed Buber 1913, 223; *Responsa of the Maharam of Rothenberg* (ed Parma) 59. See Komlosh, 'A Fragment'. Rav Hai Gaon states that on special occasions many people would compose and recite Targum and it seems likely that they were not repeating one another, but presented different targumic variations. See Lewin, *Otsar ha-Gaonim,* Megilla, p37.

(c) *Switching words*. The targum will at times replace a particular word found in the biblical text with a different one and by the choice of the replacement hint at a manner of explanation, an idea or a midrash. Thus, for instance, the phrase in Exod 12:15, 'And it shall be eaten in one house', is translated in Onkelos and in Neofiti as, 'it shall be eaten in one group' (*havura*). The Targums here refer to the halakha that the paschal sacrifice is to be eaten in groups.

(d) *Adding words*. The targum by this manner seeks to hint at a midrash. Thus on Exod 12:21, 'Draw out and take you', Ps-Yonatan translates: 'Pull away your hands from the folly of Egypt', and thus refers to a well-known midrash (e.g. MekRY pisha 11, p36). In this particular case the Targum expands succinctly on the commandment.

(e) *Adding sentences*. The targum at times will add a complete sentence or an independent phrase. Thus, for example, at Exod 12:11, 'And thus shall you eat it', Ps-Yonatan adds: '"And thus" – this is the halakha; "shall you eat it" – this time but not in all perpetuity.' A breakdown of this stage reveals the use of two prior levels of targumic *derash*. The first addition represents level (a) while the second represents level (c). The ability to weave the *derash* into the targum was of great importance for targumic authors, but they were not always successful in their attempts.[41]

(f) *Inserting midrashim*. In this type, the translation element is quite unimportant and the bulk of the Targum is midrash, and, at times, consists of complete midrashim. These, however, are not regular midrashim. Normally, a midrash will not make use of biblical verses in the course of its exposition, but it might bring formal quotes introduced by such phrases as 'as it is written', 'it says', etc. In the case of these targumim, though, we find a running story paraphrasing the biblical narrative and adding midrashic motifs.

(g) *Additions*. These passages concern set, complete midashim completely similar to those found all across rabbinic literature, sometimes even beginning with the phrase 'as it is written'.[42] Many such additions are found at the beginning of a topic or a *parasha* with a function resembling that of the *petihta* in midrashic literature.[43] All of the 'additions' belong to this type, but for the moment not all of the targumic derashot which seem to fit the category can be defined as 'additions'.

---

[41] A number of examples have been collected by Shinan, *Aggadah*, 171f.

[42] The following is the list of additions to FrgTg, serving as an illustration for the other Targumim: Gen 15:1; 18:1; 28:1; 30:22; 35:9; 44:18; Exod 12:1 (with a clear reference to a verse just as in a regular midrash); 13:1; 15:1; 22:1; Num 12:1 (with a reference to a verse); 15:1; 21:5; Deut 1:1; 25:17; 32:1 (citing a verse); 32:3; 33:1. Most of them appear also in Neof and only a few in PsYon.

[43] On the petihta see ch. 2 in this volume. A classic petihta is found in Neof and FrgTg on Gen 35:9. The unique part of this derasha is the beginning.

All of the extant Targums contain one or more of the levels described above. The number of combined levels decides on the character of a given Targum, and we shall demonstrate this in our description below.

If it is clear by now that the characteristics of the Targums are not identical, certainly neither is their content. There are, however, certain common elements regarding content which we shall now try to point out. The material in the Targums fits within the larger framework of the oral tradition of the rabbis. Many of the motifs in the Targums have parallels in talmudic literature, whether in whole or in part. Some of the more prominent motifs, such as love and the fear of God (especially by Targum Yonatan); the study of Tora; the sanctity of the Land of Israel; observance of the commandments; and the belief in the coming of the Messiah, are based upon accepted ideas in rabbinic thought and literature. Even the technique of the derasha is often found in such parallels in the midrashic works. At times the actual renderings appear in such parallels, although obviously with less frequency than in the Targum as such. Characteristic of the Targums is the open use of incidental references to other verses and their Targum. This is reminiscent of rabbinic derashot and the use of biblical verses there.

It is difficult to know how the various halakhot, derashot and additions were chosen. Various scholars have sought to solve this problem based on theological conceptions or reactions to specific sects, but no sufficient answer has been found for all instances. However, from the start of scholarship on this literature, two prominent tendencies were observed. First is the elimination of anthropomorphisms. The Targums sought to remove any phrase or idea which might be interpreted towards the personification of God. Thus, for instance, the biblical phrase 'the mouth of God' will usually be translated as 'the decree of God', or the 'decree of the word of God'.[44] Rabbinic literature also sought to tone down anthropomorphisms, but there are strains in rabbinic literature, usually more simplistic in nature or of a more popular bent, which did not refrain from describing God in a human manner. This was usually the case regarding early rabbinic mysticism. A second tendency is to defend the honour of the Patriarchs. This trend is recurrent in those few talmudic *sugyot* dealing with the methodology of targum.[45] It appears also in general in rabbinic litera-

---

[44] Even so, certain phrases connected with this matter have at times actually been translated and incorporated into the Targum. See e.g. Onk Gen 1:27; 5:1; Deut 33:27; Exod 33:18. Much material on this matter has been collected by Komlosh and Melamed, see n62 below.

[45] mMeg 4:9; bMeg 25b, etc. On this rule in the Targum see e.g. Onk Gen 27:3; 27:35; Num 12:1; PsYon Gen 35:22 *et al.* GenR contains instructions of R. Yohanan how a particular verse (Gen 29:17) should be translated in order to avoid deprecating Leah. FrgTg translates in the manner theoretically forbidden; in the parallel to this tradition in TanhB Wa-yetse 20 the Targum of another verse is forbidden for the same reasons. This forbidden Targum appears in PsYon *ad loc.* Neof and Onk translate in accordance with the instructions of R. Yohanan.

ture, but at times the rabbis were also willing to find fault with the Patriarchs if they sinned, in accordance with the plain meaning of Scripture.[46]

Both of these ideas are prominent in and characteristic of all Targums. Other such motifs common in all targumic literature have hardly been examined. In fact, it should be remembered that the Targums are not independent works, but rather eclectic collections of halakhic and aggadic traditions, and, therefore, attempting to uncover a common thread of content may be somewhat of a superfluous task. Thus, targumic eschatology is not really different from rabbinic eschatology in general, as we have already stated above. It is hard to accept the claim that there was a 'targumic aggada' that was created by the meturgemanim.[47] The ties between the Targums and the midrash collections are so clear that it is impossible to talk about the independent work of the meturgemanim. At most, it is possible to discuss the methodologies employed in creating their individual anthologies.

The authors of the Targums appear to have been particularly fond of prayers, and the frequency of prayers in targumic literature is much higher than in rabbinic literature in general. Targumic literature, however, does not represent an innovation in ideas regarding prayer during this period. The high frequency of prayers in targumic literature is probably explained by the fact that the Targums were associated with the synagogue liturgy.

Certain scholars have rightly pointed out the high incidence of popular traditions in Ps-Yonatan such as the stress on miracles and magic (Gen 3:6; 6:4; 11:28; Num 31:8). Ps-Yonatan also has many 'fantastic traditions' and often cites the names of angels. This 'popular' trend, however, is characteristic only of Ps-Yonatan. Such traditions are, for the most part, found in such late midrashic works as Pirkei de-R. Eliezer, but parallel traditions are usually also found in non-rabbinic literature, indicating, once again, the popular nature of such targumic motifs and their possible acceptance outside the established rabbinic circles.[48]

The popular nature of the Targums is evident both in the approach of the Targums to anthropomorphisms, to the honour of the Patriarchs, and to the use of decent language. However, the Targums were not meant just for the general population. As we have seen, the Targum has both clear and veiled references to midrashim and to other biblical verses and passages, and the authors of the Targum thus assumed a general awareness of rabbinic texts and traditions. Thus Ps-Yonatan mentions a woman by the name of *Pelaytit*. Only someone familiar with the midrash identifying this woman as the wife of Lot would understand the Targum on this verse. In this particular case we are familiar with the entire tradition from the late Midrash Pirkei de-R. Eliezer, ch. 25. As we mentioned above, this trend is found for the most part in Ps-Yonatan, but it

---

[46] Onk to Gen 35:22; Yon 2 Sam 11:4.
[47] Shinan, *Aggadah*.
[48] Shinan, *Embroidered Targum*, 164-167.

exists also in Neofiti and in Fragmentary Targum.[49] Further tendencies in the exegetical-homiletical sphere that may be mentioned in this context are: the removal of abstract terminology; the completion of 'deficient' parallelisms; the avoidance of rhetorical questions; and the giving of simple renderings of flowery expressions or parables.

The targumic ideal is expressed in the words of R. Yehuda we have quoted earlier: 'He who translates a verse literally is a liar; he who adds to the translation is a blasphemer.'[50] It would seem that R. Yehuda was of the opinion that it is necessary to express the meaning of the verse even if that requires somewhat of a deviation from a literal translation. However, at the same time new ideas should not be introduced into the translation. The first part of R. Yehuda's statement was quite strictly observed, but the second part was understood in a more liberal manner and thus many of the ideas contained in rabbinic tradition became more or less the accepted meaning of Scripture. This, of course, should not be surprising since it corresponded with the supposed relationship between the written Tora and oral teaching, and the study of 'Scripture' integrated the clarifications and homiletic explanations of the sages as an organic whole of Tora.[51] Likewise, similar targumic passages are included in midrashic literature.

The sages as well held the view that the targum is to be regarded as an organic part of rabbinic literature, similar in characteristics to the derasha. Only in this manner can we understand the 'liberty' with which the authors of the Targum treated the biblical text. By contrast, the Septuagint is essentially a translation that only hints at matters of theology and the like and, for he most part, attempts to produce a literal rendering of the text.

Targumic literature was, however, largely intended for the common public and was not greatly valued by the sages; in fact, they often looked down upon the meturgeman.[52] Targum was not considered part of the official rabbinic curriculum[53], i.e., the establishing and explaining of halakha and, therefore, even intoxicated persons could engage in the study of targum.[54] Talmudic literature has little to say about praising targum[55] and when talmudic traditions cite a learned literate person they refer to the sage or to the scribe (and

---

[49] PsYon Gen 18:21; 21:11. The phenomenon is most frequent in this Targum, but also found elsewhere, e.g. FrgTg Gen 15:2; 16:5; 31:12; as well as Onk and Neof on this verse.

[50] tMeg 4(3):41; bMeg 49a.

[51] See above p248.

[52] KohR 7,9; 9,12 and parallels. This may refer to an Amora who was a meturgeman. On the negative attitude to the meturgeman one can learn more from the traditions cited below.

[53] But it was part of the curriculum at school, see n16 above.

[54] Sifra Shemini 1,9. In MidrGad Lev 10:11 the version is reversed and Targum is included within the realm of instruction.

[55] The source in SifDeut 161 (p212) is rather unusual and the Targum does not appear in all the versions.

teacher), but never to the meturgeman. This of course indicates the level of prestige of the meturgeman, at least as far as the sages were concerned.

There is no sufficient proof for the assertion that the meturgemanim created of their own accord and whims new teachings and derashot. The choice of the targumic motif, however, be it halakha or aggada, was made by them. This results, at times, in the presentation of a targumic motif which was a minority opinion and which may, therefore have no parallels in the talmudic literature which we possess.[56]

The most common forms were the literal targum and the homiletic targum sticking to the biblical text (levels a-c); both types were usually created by the meturgemanim under the influence of rabbinic derashot. In addition, there was a large pool of developed midrashim that were directly dependent on rabbinic teachings and motifs, and that the meturgemanim inserted at the appropriate passages (levels d-g). In this respect there was a great deal of leeway and development that lasted until the appearance of printed Targum versions. The clear-cut proof of this process is not only the existence of the additions as such, but the internal contradictions within the Targum itself and the not always successful combination of literal and a homiletic targum on one particular verse.[57] Moreover, when the Targum quotes a verse, the quote often appears in Hebrew or in a somewhat different translation than the one which we have.[58]

In summary, it is possible to state that the targum by its very nature was rather fluid, and was never really edited to the level that was required. The targum, though, was not intended only for popular circles. Proof of this is the fact that it often contains references to midrashim or to rabbinic teachings which would be unintelligible to a reader or to an audience totally uninitiated in such teachings. In such cases, the translators obviously assumed that the audience had at least a minimal background, acquired at a school or by listening to derashot on the Sabbath.

---

[56] It should be remembered that at times a minority opinion may have been the accepted halakha in the area from which the Targum derived, or an ancient hasidic custom accepted in general practice. See the example cited in n24.

[57] These contradictions consist e.g. in the fact that the same phrase is translated differently, or derashot are cited which contradict derashot cited earlier on in the same verse. See e.g. PsYon Gen 37:32 as against 38:36; Gen 46:17 as against 49:21; see Vermes, *Scripture and Tradition*, 75ff; Lewin, 'Some Characteristics'. In addition one can cite the inclusion of two contradictory derashot on the same verse, see examples cited above n34. This characteristic is most particular to PsYon. On internal contradictions see e.g. PsYon Gen 11:8; 50:13; FrgTg Gen 3:72. These phenomena are also sometimes the result of copyists' errors.

[58] E.g. Neof and FrgTg Gen 35:9; Neof, PsYon and FrgTg Gen 40:18; and many other examples in different Targumim, esp Tg Est and Tg Song.

Description of Extant Targums

THE TARGUM OF LEVITICUS FROM QUMRAN

A short and rather fragmentary selection of a Targum of Leviticus was found on ripped parchment in the caves of the Judaean Desert and has been dated to the first century BCE – first century CE. An edition of the text was published in De Vaux, *Qumrân grotte 4*, vol 2, 86-89.

The fragment is too short to provide a clear-cut indication of the nature of this Targum, which undoubtedly came from the Dead Sea Sect. Its language is different from that of the other Targums and the points of similarity are fewer than is the case regarding such similarities between the other Targums. It is an almost literal translation, although it is important to remember that the other Targums do not contain derashot on these verses in Leviticus or on similar ones. It is too early, therefore, to determine the nature of this Targum. The fact that a Targum was discovered in the library of the Dead Sea sects is interesting. Unfortunately, this can teach us little regarding possible Pharisaic prototypes since the Dead Sea sect had a rather large literature of the type which the Parisees did not permit to be written down. As we have already stated, the sect members did not always distinguish between the written Tora and oral tradition; the Temple Scroll, for instance, represents a combination of the two.

THE TARGUM OF JOB FROM QUMRAN

A number of fragments of a Targum of Job, forming a rather large section of the book, have been found in the caves of the Judaean Desert and have been dated to the second century BCE.The Targum is for the most part literal, except for a few changes and additions which do not really constitute 'additions' or midrashim. There are mistakes in the manuscript, some of which are undoubtedly the fault of the copyist. There is no apparent connection between this Targum and the traditional Targum of Job.[59]

Editions were published by Van der Ploeg and Van der Woude, *Le Targum de Job*, and Sokoloff, *The Targum to Job*.

TARGUM ONKELOS ON THE TORA

The source of the name is in a tradition in bMeg 3a which states that the proselyte Onkelos translated the Tora 'according to (lit. from the mouth of) R. Eliezer and R. Joshua' (80-120 CE). However, this refers to the Greek translation, since the parallel in yMeg 1, 71c refers to Aquilas, explicitly mentioning a translation into Greek. In fact, there are a number of quotations from such a 'translation' ascribed to Aquilas in our literature and it is clear that the source

---

[59] See Weiss, 'Ha-Targum'; Van der Woude, *Targum Job*; Sokoloff, *Targum Job*; Mangan, 'Some Observations'.

of the translation is Greek. During the Middle Ages, Onkelos became the official Aramaic Targum and the Gaon Sar Shalom (ninth century) explains that 'as the Targum which we possess, but the other Targums do not have the same implicit holiness as Targum Onkelos'.[60] The Targum is already cited by name in the earliest midrash collections of the Middle Ages and it is clear that Onkelos was composed no later than by the end of the Amoraic period.[61]

Onkelos is essentially a literal Targum. The number of midrashim or halakhot hinted at is rather small, at least compared to the other Targums. Most of the translations are literal and the exceptions can usually be understood in light of the text. Thus, the Targum tries to aid the reader by occasionally changing grammatical conjunctions, vocabulary, and biblical verbal forms, or by adding words missing in the biblical text. Sometimes it changes the biblical plural into the singular and the reverse, or it rewrites poetic, flowery or abstract sentences in 'everyday' language.[62] Onkelos seems to have undergone a much more exact editorial process than the other Targums and very often the same word will be used for a specific term in the biblical text. While as stated there are few deviations from the plain meaning of the text, there are some which cannot be explained simply as a matter of a dependence on a different biblical text. Most of these changes or deviations reflect the desire of the author to include rabbinic motifs. Onkelos is also quite consistent in attempting to remove all anthropomorphic biblical references to God and in upholding the honor of the Patriarchs (see above). There are a few anthropomorphisms which were not changed (Num 11:29), but this seems to be the exception to the rule.

The author usually prefers the plain meaning of the biblical text even if at times it contradicts halakhot or well-known aggadot.[63] Even so, there are times when the Targum deviates from the plain sense in order to solve certain exegetical difficulties,[64] and especially to hint at a well-known halakha or aggada. This is the case, for instance, regarding the change of 'house' into 'group' discussed above, or regarding the verse in Exod 20:7, 'Thou shalt not take the name of the Lord thy God in vain (lashav) ...he that take His name in vain (leshav)...' The first Hebrew expression lashav is translated with the verb

---

[60] Lewin, *Otsar Ha-Geonim*, vol 5, 29. We should not conclude, however, that the Geonim of Babylonia were not familiar with other Targumim, see below.

[61] Generally PRE 38 is cited as proof, but the attribution to Onk is missing in the mss cited in Higger's edition. Scholars do not cite the reference to Onkelos in NumR 89,54, a reference that appears both in the printed ed. and in ms Paris 150. This part of the Midrash is considered to be rather late.

[62] For changes of grammatical mood, vocabulary and verbs see: Exod 26:29; 35:34; Num 24:4. Addition of words: Exod 3:8; 13:5; Gen 25:20. Changes from singular to plural: Gen 24:60; Exod 16:4. Re-writing of flowery sentences: Gen 25:28; Exod 1:8. The literature on these matters is extensive, see Melamed, *Bible Commentators*; Komlosh, *The Bible*; and for a summary of relevant bibliography, Kadari, '*Targum Onkelos* Today'.

[63] E.g. Exod 12:6, contra to mPes 5:1; Exod 21:6 contra to MekRY Nezikin 2; Exod 21: 24 contra to mBK 8:1 and more..

[64] E.g. Gen 30:20; 36:24; 32:1; 41:35.

'make nought', the second with 'to lie'. This was the accepted halakhic explanation.[65] Onkelos also refers at times to well-known aggadot. Thus on the verse in Num 24:17, 'There shall step forth a star out of Jacob', Onkelos translates: 'A king shall rise forth from Jacob.' This motif appears both in the New Testament and in early and late midrashim.[66] In fact, most of the derashot in Onkelos have parallels in rabbinic literature.

Much scholarly effort has been expended on trying to determine exactly when Onkelos is hinting at a halakha or aggada. It would seem that there is no key to this problem. The *derash* in Onkelos basically sticks to the biblical text (levels a-b above). This Targum does not contain halakhot in conflict with the prevailing halakha, and the particular forms of Targum forbidden according to talmudic traditions do not appear in Onkelos. In both content and form, Onkelos serves as a good example of the adage cited above that, 'He who translates a verse literally is a liar. He who adds is a blasphemer.'

Geographic names are usually cited as they appear in Hebrew in the Bible or in an Aramaic form of such. At times the names are translated into Aramaic. Only rarely does the Targum attempt a simple identification[67] or an aggadic one.[68] Among the attempts at identifications in Onkelos are a large number of sites in the Transjordan and the Negev. It is not quite clear why this is so.

The Aramaic of Onkelos is Babylonian and, therefore, it would seem that the Targum was edited in Babylonia at the same time as the Babylonian Talmud, or perhaps sometime afterward. There are scholars, however, who claim that Onkelos is a Palestinian Targum, but even they must admit that it then underwent some kind of editing in Babylonia and was influenced by Babylonian Aramaic.

Starting from 1482 it became customary to print Onkelos alongside the text of the Tora in most printed editions and traditional commentaries in Hebrew, in the wake of many Tora manuscripts.

Important critical studies were published by Barnstein, *The Targum of Onkelos to Genesis*; Aberbach and Grossfeld, *Targum Onqelos to Genesis*.[69] Critical editions based on a number of manuscripts were published by Berliner, *Targum Onkelos*; Sperber, *The Bible in Aramaic* 1: *Onkelos*. Translations into

---

[65] This is the explanation of mBM 3 and parallels. An extensive discussion on this matter is found in E.Z. Melamed, *Bible Commentators*, 120-352; Komlosh, *The Bible*, 156-207. For examples of the changing of the Targum according to the halakha see Gen 9:6; Exod 21:19; 21:30; Lev 15:21. For examples of the changing of the Targum based on an aggada see Deut 1:1; 7:10 (two cases of derashot on levels c or d above). There are, however, also small additions (level d, c) such as Gen 32:11; Exod 15:16; Deut 33:6.

[66] E.g. yTaan 4, 68d in the name of R. Akiva; or the end of the late midrash Va-Yisau according to most mss.

[67] Gen 14:7, and likewise in the Genesis Apocryphon; Deut 3:4, 14.

[68] Num 21:18f; Deut 1:1; 3:25. On this type of derasha see below, the chapter on Geography.

[69] See also Churgin, 'The Halakhah'; Flesher, 'Is *Targum Onqelos*'; Heinemann, 'Rabbinic Relations'; Rappel, *Targum Onkelos*; Vermes, 'Haggadah'.

English were prepared by Drazin, *Targum Onkelos*, and, in the series *The Aramaic Bible*, by Grossfeld, *Targum Onqelos*.

TARGUM PSEUDO-YONATAN ON THE TORA

In the manuscripts, the Targum is called *Targum Yerushalmi* and is also cited in them in abbreviated form as 'TY'. As a result of the Babylonian tradition about the Targum of Yonatan b. Uziel, the abbreviation was thought to mean 'Targum Yonatan', even though that tradition did not refer to a Targum on the Tora. The Targum is mentioned by name only from the twelfth-thirteenth centuries on. This fact, however, does not help in the dating of the Targum. At best it aids in understanding when it became widespread. Even so, all the issues regarding the initial publication of the Targum and its distribution are far from clear and many methodological problems remain regarding these issues.[70]

Ps-Yonatan is in many respects the opposite of Onkelos. We saw that Onkelos is for the most part a literal translation. Over fifty per cent of Ps-Yonatan, however, represents *derash*. The literal translations of Ps-Yonatan are, however, very similar to Onkelos, although the editing process of Ps-Yonatan seems to have been less systematic that that of Onkelos. Ps-Yonatan is also less consistent in its translations. Thus, for instance, the combination 'turtle-doves and pigeons' is once translated in Ps-Yonatan as '*large* turtle-doves or two baby pigeons' (Lev 14:22), at other times as 'turtle-doves or two baby pigeons' (Lev 19:14; 15:29, etc.). There are also contradictions in the Targum regarding certain ideas expressed, and the frequency of derashot differs from chapter to chapter. As we stated above, it is unlikely that the Targum was composed by one author, nor did it undergo a rigorous editing process.[71] However, generally the principle was observed that regardless of the amount of midrashic material incorporated into the translation of a verse, the verse was not to be left without some sort of word by word translation, although this need not be a literal translation.

As stated above, many 'additions' (*Toseftaot*) were appended to this Targum. Some were included in the standard printed versions, while others appear only in the manuscripts of this Targum. Certain chapters which were of great liturgical importance, such as Gen 49, Exod 12, or Exod 19, also contained a large number of 'additions'. Geographic names are treated in this Targum in a manner similar to that of Onkelos, although there are more identifications and in general there is more midrashic material on place names than in Onkelos. This is true, as we saw, in all spheres of comparison between the two Targums.

---

[70] In spite of the comments of the Gaon (n60), it would seem that the Geonim were familiar with some sort of Palestinian Targum, although they considered be less holy. This is not the place for discussion on the matter.

[71] See examples cited above n24.

A large number of sites identified or discussed are, as in the case of Onkelos, in the Transjordan.

Most of the homiletic motifs and exegeses in Ps-Yonatan have parallels in midrashic or halakhic literature. The Targum does contain, however, many deviations from the prevailing halakha. Many of the directives discussed in talmudic literature regarding the methodology of Targum are not carried out in Ps-Yonatan.[72] The contrary seems to be true. The Mishna in Meg 4:9 forbids a particular translation which is actually found in Ps-Yonatan on Lev 18:21. There are other cases of such deviations from rabbinic directives regarding Targum. As stated above, many of the derashot in Ps-Yonatan are not in keeping with normative practice. Many scholars have cited as an example Exod 22:6[7] and 9[10], 'If a man delivers to his neighbour...' The accepted halakhic explanation is that the first verse relates to an unpaid bailey and the second to a paid bailey. However, in most of the manuscripts of Ps-Yonatan, both verses are explained, 'without wages does he watch', i.e., an unpaid bailey. This example is quite important because it shows a case of the Targum dealing with a matter discussed in halakhic literature, being familiar with the particulars of most of the matters discussed there, but deviating from normative practice regarding one key crucial detail. There are more such examples in Ps-Yonatan. In other cases, as we have seen above, the Targum preserves halakhot which were disregarded by the sages. Such phenomena occur also in Neofiti and the Fragmentary Targum, but they are most frequent in Ps-Yonatan.

This Targum contains early derashot such as the one mentioning Yohanan the High Priest (first cent. BCE). It also contains, however, late derashot such as that on Gen 21:21 which mention Aisha, the wife of Mohammed, and Fatima, his daughter by his earlier wife.[73] The traditions supposedly aiding in the dating of this Targum have been collected and studied in scholarly literature, but it is still not clear to what extent they can actually be used in dating the Targum.

The Aramaic of Ps-Yonatan is Palestinian and does not contain the particular language or style of Babylonian halakha.[74] The Targum also reflects to a great extent the *realia* and lifestyle of Palestine and, therefore, it would seem that the correct name of the Targum, 'Yerushalmi', was appropriate. In general, it is possible to state that this Targum particularly exemplifies a 'popular' Targum style and the influence of the sages and their academies on it was minimal compared to the other Targums.[75]

---

[72] Above n24.

[73] See Alexander, 'Jewish Aramaic Translations'.

[74] On the language of PsYon see Tal, 'Dialects' and Kutscher, *Studies*. There are of course parallels in the Bavli to material cited in this Targum, but no clear indication of the use of a complete Babylonian *sugya*. It is interesting to note that PsYon Num 33:36; 34:3f as well as Neof and FrgTg Num 34:4 are based on an incorrect understanding, or at the very least on an associative *derasha* of mSuk 3:1.

[75] Cf the studies by Hayward, 'Date', and 'Pirqe de Rabbi Eliezer'.

This Targum is also often published alongside the standard printed versions of the Tora and traditional commentaries. Ginsburger, *Pseudo-Jonathan* is a classical edition; the most recent standard edition, with a concordance, is Clarke *et al.*, *Targum Pseudo-Jonathan*. Translations were published by Clarke-Magder and Maher, *Targum Pseudo-Jonathan*, in the series *The Aramaic Bible*.

THE FRAGMENTARY TARGUM YERUSHALMI ON THE TORA

The name of this Targum was chosen as a result of the similarities between this Targum and the homiletic sections of PsYonatan (Yerushalmi). This Targum, which must be distinguished from the Palestinian targum fragments from the Geniza (below p270), consists of a collection of targumic passages on various verses of the Tora. Today it is generally accepted that these fragments were taken from a complete Targum. The collator chose to present this particular collection because of its homiletic nature (were these perhaps all the derashot from the source Targum?). The derashot represent types e-g from our list above. It also contains, however, Targum on parts of biblical verses or on individual words.[76] Certain biblical chapters appear *in toto* in this Targum and it would appear that these chapters attracted a large amount of midrashic comment or were of liturgical importance.[77] These selections are likely to be of value in determining the nature of the complete Targum from which the Frg Targum was derived.

Some scholars are of the opinion that the Frg Targum was derived from Ps-Yonatan or from Neofiti.[78] A close examination, however, reveals that neither served as the source for Frg Targum, although the prototype for this Targum undoubtedly derived from the same targumic family.[79] It should be pointed out that the material from the Frg Targum is more similar to Neofiti than to Ps-Yonatan. As we shall see, however, ultimately all these Targums derive from the same family.

The Frg Targum contains many 'additions' and often there is no direct commentary on the verse itself within the complex of Aggadic exposition. The Targum also contains 'additions' composed in the format of a derasha.

The Frg Targum generally appears in the the printed editions of Tora and commentaries alongside or together with Ps-Yonatan. Ginsburger, *Fragmententhargum* has published an edition based on a manuscript with a limited

---

[76] FrgTg has a relatively smaller number of halakhic derashot than the other Targumim.

[77] The following chapters were of special importance: Gen 1, creation; Exod 14-15, the song of the crossing of the Red Sea which was read on the seventh day of Passover and a chapter on which many piyyutim or additions were composed; Exod 19-20, the Ten Commandments; Num 21, the prophecy of Bileam.

[78] Díez-Macho, *Neophyiti* 1, 128ff.

[79] See below.

number of variant readings. A further critical edition based on two manuscripts has been published by Klein, *The Fragment-Targums*.

TARGUM NEOFITI

The Neofiti manuscript was a lost part of targumic literature until its rediscovery in the 1950's by A. Díez-Macho.[80] His discovery aroused tremendous scholarly interest and certain scholars anticipated important breakthroughs not only vis-a-vis targumic literature, but regarding talmudic literature in general.

Neofiti occupies basically a middle position between Onkelos and Ps-Yonatan regarding form, style and content. For the most part it is a literal translation, although it does contain a good many derashot. However, not only does it contain fewer than Ps-Yonatan, the derashot in Neofiti are also far less complex than those in Ps-Yonatan. Neofiti follows the talmudic guidelines regarding Targum, and the halakha contained in it is closer to accepted halakha than that in Ps-Yonatan.[81] The literal translations are often similar to Onkelos. The major difference, though, is the sloppiness of the editor or of the copyist who often skipped words or parts of verses, e.g. Dt 21:19. In this particular case it would seem to be the fault of the copyist. Other instances show clearly, however, that the author was at fault and simply skipped parts of verses.

The *derash* in Neofiti is similar in content, style and format to the derasha in Ps-Yonatan. As stated above, though, Neofiti has fewer derashot. It does, however, contain some derashot not included in Ps-Yonatan. Neofiti is influenced by both the halakha and the Aggada of the rabbis. Thus we read in Dt 21:4, '...a rough valley which may neither be plowed nor sown.' The Hebrew phraseology is somewhat ambiguous and allows for the imperfect verbal forms to be understood in the past tense – 'a field which was not plowed in the past' – or in the future, to the effect that after the ceremony the field shall lie fallow. The Targum states: 'it was not plowed' (i.e. in he past) 'but it shall not be sown', i.e. in the future. In fact, this is how the halakha understood the verse (mSot 9:5; SifDeut 207: 242 and parallels). Neofiti is connected then to the world of the sages, but it also contains certain non-normative halakhot. This phenomenon is connected with the discussion on the date of Neofiti.

Díez-Macho concluded that the Targum is rather early (first-second cent. CE) because it contains a number of halakhot in opposition to prevailing halakha, as well as phrases and ideas prevalent in the Second Temple period and derashot similar to early Christian homilies. It is hard to imagine, in his opinion, that the Jews would use such derashot after Christianity became a widespread religion. We have discussed other contentions of Díez-Macho above, and it is not clear to what extent they can help us date the Targum. In our opinion, there is no proof that the Targum is earlier than the fourth century

---

[80] Díez-Macho, *Targum Neophyti*.
[81] See Bamberger, 'Halakhic Elements'; Bernstein, 'The Halakhah'.

CE.[82] On the other hand, Neofiti does not contain the late motifs found in Ps-Yonatan. Marginal notes and comments have been added to Neofiti which seem to have been taken from an additional and, indeed, different targumic text. It is possible that they derive from a different Targum of the same family, since they are generally homiletic in nature and are reminiscent of the relationship of the Frg Targum to Ps-Yonatan.

The critical edition was published by Díez-Macho, *Neophyti 1*. Grossfeld, *Targum Neofiti* offers a volume of commentary on the Genesis part. Five volumes of translations were published by McNamara, in part together with Hayward, *Targum Neofiti 1*, in the series *The Aramaic Bible* that is edited by McNamara.

LOST TARGUMS

Medieval Jewish literature, particularly the *Aruch* of R. Natan of Rome and Bereshit Zuta of R. Samuel b. Nissim, hint at additional targumic works. In addition to Onkelos, nine other Targums are mentioned.[83] Medieval Jewish literature also contains dozens of targumic citations which are different from the extant Targums, in addition to the 'Additions' which were taken from Targums which also went lost. No real attempt has been made as yet at a systematic analysis of these citations.

GENIZA TARGUM FRAGMENTS

Special mention should be made of the Geniza fragments published by Kahle.[84] These fragments could actually be included in the above category of lost Targums. It concerns a collection of fragments from various manuscripts and belonging to the type of Palestinian Targum. For the most part they are translating literally, but some contain a good deal of derasha. It is not clear whether every fragment represents a complete Targum which has been lost. It is possible that some of the fragments derive from fragmentary collections.

The fragments were first published by Kahle, *Masoreten*, and subsequently by Klein, *Genizah Manuscripts*, and 'New Fragments'.

TARGUM YONATAN ON THE PROPHETS

The name of this Targum derives from the aggada in bMeg 3a stating that Yonatan b. Uziel translated the Prophets. As we saw above, there is no histori-

---

[82] Komlosh, *The Bible*, 50-56; York, 'The Targum', 49-62.
[83] Many of the Targum fragments cited in the Middle Ages have been collected by Goshen-Gottstein, *Shekiin*; Cohen, *Midrash Bereshit Zuta*; Neuhausen, 'Targumic Citations'; McNamara, *The New Testament*, 59ff.
[84] Kahle, *Masoreten*; Klein, 'Nine Fragments'. See Alexander, 'Translations', 220.

cal basis to this tradition and there is no connection between the Targum of the Prophets and the historical personality mentioned it the tradition. Certain medieval sages called it 'Targum Rav Yosef' because of the Targums associated with this sage, who is mentioned in the Babylonian tradition we referred to. It would seem that the original name of this Targum was also Targum Yerushalmi (abbreviated as 'TY') and only by mistake was it attributed to Yonatan or Rav Yosef.

The status of Yonatan on the Prophets is similar to that of Onkelos on the Tora. Yonatan on the Prophets became rather widespread and was accepted as the official Targum on this part of the Scriptures. It is similar in most respects to Onkelos and for the most part provides a good and exact rendering of the simple meaning of the Prophets. Relatively speaking, however, it does contain a greater number of derashot than Onkelos. The derashot basically correspond to halakhic or aggadic motifs in rabbinic literature.

Generally the *derash* fits in well with the simple exegesis of the text, although this is not always the case. The Targum is for the most part consistent, and this would seem to prove its uniform nature. Thus, for example, many proverbs are only translated on the basis of their moral, such as in the case of 1 Kgs 12:10, 'My little finger is thicker than my father's loins.' The Targum translates: 'My weakened state is stronger than the youthful strength of my father.' However, there are also internal contradictions. Thus, verses and phrases which may be identical but appear in different verses are not always translated identically. This is also the case in the Targums on the Tora.[85]

Yonatan on the Prophets is the only Targum on the Prophets to have survived. Medieval literature hints at other such Targums. There are also many targumic additions to the Prophets which we shall discuss below.

The date of this Targum is less evident. There appear a number of late phrases,[86] but even if these are an integral part of the text, they could also be late additions. Moreover, until it has been conclusively proven that the work is uniform, it is impossible to use individual phrases as a means of dating the whole work.

As most other Targums, the language of TgYonatan on the Prophets is essentially early Palestinian Aramaic, and those Babylonian elements in it are usually later 'additions' (see below).[87]

The standard printed editions of the Prophets with classical commentaries usually include this Targum. Sperber has published a critical edition based on a number of Yemenite manuscripts (*The Bible in Aramaic 2, The Former Prophets* and 3, *The Latter Prophets*). Some of the 'additions' (*Toseftaot*) are

---

[85] See Churgin, *The Targum to the Prophets*; Levy, 'Date of Targum Jonathan'.

[86] Levy, 'Date' essentially makes use of a Muslem phrase found in the Aramaic translation in Yon 2 Sam 22:32 ('There is no God but the Lord'). However, this is almost a verbatim translation of the biblical text. Moreover, it is impossible to know whether the phrase ultimately derives from the Hebrew or the Aramaic from the pre-Islamic period. For other opinions of early Targum see n32.

[87] For an important discussion on the language of the Targum see Tal, *Language*.

included in this edition, while others are found only in the various manuscripts.[88] In the series *The Aramaic Bible*, translations of Yonatan on the Former Prophets, Isaiah, Jeremiah, and Ezekiel were prepared by Chilton, Harrington and Saldarini, Hayward, and Levey. Another translation is the one by Cathcart and Gordon, *The Targum of the Minor Prophets*.[89]

THE TARGUM ON THE HAGIOGRAPHA

The Targum on the Hagiographa does not concern a unitary work. In fact we are dealing here with a number of different works:

(a) *Targum on Psalms and on Job.* Both of these are similar in their form and content to Tg Yonatan. However, since both Psalms and Job are difficult works and since their language is rather poetic, the author of these particular Targums had to add and expand his comments in order to explain the simple meaning of the biblical text. Very often this Targum will add the moral to a proverb cited in the Bible or complete a missing parallelism. It is possible to state that these Targums contain a greater number of complete and developed midrashim (levels b, c, d-g) in proportion to the more simple midrashim of Tg Yonatan on the Prophets or Neofiti.[90] The relationship of these Targums to those of the Tora or the Prophets is not clear, and it is impossible to prove whether the Targum on the Hagiographa in general used any of the extant Targums. This is the case even though many phrases, verses and even chapters found in Psalms, for instance, appear in other biblical works, which would favour such borrowings.[91]

The language of these Targums is for the most part Palestinian, although there appear a fair number of Babylonian words and artificial elements. It is difficult to date these. The Targum Psalms does mention, e.g., Constantinople,[92] but it is impossible to date such a complex work on the basis of a single expression. Moreover, those very words which might indicate a late dating are not usually found in the manuscript tradition and would appear to be additions. We have discussed this phenomenon before and it reflects the often fluid state of the Targum texts. Targum Job mentions the Sons of Ishmael a number of times, in both marginal glossae and in the text itself,[93] and this might hint, therefore, at a final editing of the work after the Moslem conquest of Palestine

---

[88] See above n83.

[89] See further the studies by Churgin, *Targum Jonathan*; Gordon, 'Targum as Midrash'; Izchaky, *The Halacha*; Smolar, *Studies in Targum Jonathan*; Stenning, *The Targum of Isaiah*; Wieder, *Studies*.

[90] Churgin, *Targum of the Hagiographa*.

[91] Ps 86:8 // Exod 15:11; Ps 118:4 // Deut 32:36 *et al.*

[92] Ps 108:1.

[93] E.g. Job 4:11; 12:6; 15:20.

(637-640). It is also possible that the Targum made use in its editing of a *sugya* of the Babylonian Talmud.[94]

The Targum of Job contains a number of verses with two and sometimes three versions of targum. Some of these are of a semi-aggadic nature. This could reflect the existence of a number of Job Targums in the past. It should be repeated, though, that the Targum has noting to do with the Qumran Job Targum discussed above.

This Targum appears in the traditional printed editions of the Hagiographa and is included in Sperber's edition, *The Bible in Aramaic* 4a: *The Hagiographa*. Further editions are Techen, *Das Targum zu den Psalmen*; Díez Macho, *Targum de Salmos*; and Stec, *The Text of the Targum of Job*. Translations of the Targum on Job and Proverbs are found in vol 15 of *The Aramaic Bible* by Mangan, Healey, and Knobel.[95]

(b) *Targum on Proverbs*. This Targum is quite unusual since its language is rather similar to the Syriac language and is essentially a simple Targum dependent on the biblical text. In fact it is rather close to the Syriac version of Proverbs (Peshitta). There were even scholars who claimed that Targum on Proverbs is simply a variation of the Syriac translation.[96] Even if this conclusion is somewhat exaggerated, it is clear that both translations ultimately derive from the same family, which is Syriac in origin. It is likely that this Targum was edited in Babylonia, or to be exact at Nisibis, where there was close contact between the Academy and the *ulphina*, the Syriac-speaking Christian academies. The Targum is printed in the standard editions of the Hagiographa and commentaries and appears in Sperber's edition. For translation see previous paragraph.

(c) *Targum on Chronicles*. This Targum, unlike the others, was not widespread and was first printed in the early modern period (1680-1683). The language of the Targum is Palestinian, but it has a number of Babylonian words. It is essentially a literal translation, although like the others it does contain *aggadot*. However, the *aggada* is not always successfully woven into the Targum and sometimes it completely overshadows the translation, which may even be entirely pushed aside. This Targum has few developed midrashim and those included emphasize usually names of persons or places.[97] It not only contains Babylonian phrases, but appears to be familiar with complete *sugyot* from the Bavli.[98] This would seem to indicate that the work was edited rather

---

[94] Job 33:20; bYom 83a.
[95] Cf the review article by Stec, 'Recent English Translation'.
[96] Churgin, *Targum of the Hagiographa*.
[97] Especially in 1 Chr 2-4.
[98] I have found the following examples of dependence on *sugyot* in the Bavli: 1Chr 20:2 – bAZ 44a; 1Chr 21:15 – bBer 62b; 1Chr 29:11 – bBer 58a; and possibly also 1Chr 11:18. Some of these cases also contain an additional pilpulistic type derasha – could these be derashot of the post-talmudic Babylonian sages? An explicitly Babylonian phrase is *Resh metivta*, 'head of the academy', 1Chr 11:11. This institution did not exist in Palestine.

late in Babylonia, or at the very least under the influence of the Bavli. Many of the aggadot in this Targum have parallels in rabbinic literature, but sometimes its aggadic motif is more developed. It could be that this embellishment represents the independent contribution of the editor. It is more likely, however, that it reflects aggadic motifs developed by the late Babylonian sages. This would be of extreme importance, since this phenomenon is not known from other literature.

Targum on Chronicles is printed only in some of the standard editions of the Hagiographa with classical commentaries. It is included, though, in Sperber's edition. An edition of the Vatican ms Codex Urbinas 1 was published by Le Déaut and Robert, *Targum des Chroniques*.

TARGUMS ON THE FIVE MEGILLOT

The Targum on the Five Megillot is already mentioned in talmudic literature (see above p251). This is most likely the result of the fact that they were read in the synagogue in conjunction with the various *megillot* read during particular festivals. However, those Targums mentioned in talmudic literature are not the ones which we possess today.

The Targum on Lamentations, Ruth and Ecclesiastes are not uniform works and it would seem that each represents an individual work. They are all similar in nature, however, to Tg Yonatan on the Prophets. Certain scholars were of the opinion that the Targum on Ruth was sectarian or very early,[99] but these contentions were based on claims discussed above that have been shown to be unfounded.[100]

The Targum on Esther is really composed of two Targums referred to as Targum Rishon (First) and Targum Sheni (Second). The Targums on Esther and on Song of Songs are really on the border between targum and midrash. The Targum on Song of Songs does maintain some of the characteristics of targum, although in a somewhat unclear form. Targum Rishon on Esther is more aggadic than the one on the Song of Songs. Targum Sheni, though, is for all sakes and purposes a midrash. Its only targumic elements are the Aramaic language and its division into chapters and verses. All of these Targums do not strictly stick to the aim of translating the biblical text and contain a large amount of independent midrashim (levels d and especially g).[101]

---

[99] A somewhat scientific edition was put out by Neuhausen, 'Targum Megillat Ruth'.
[100] Churgin, *Targum Ketuvim*. See further the studies by Alexander, 'Textual Tradition'; idem, 'Textual Criticism'; idem, 'Tradition and Originality'; Beattie, 'Towards Dating the Targum of Ruth'; Churgin, 'Targum Ekha'; idem, 'Targum Shir ha-Shirim'; Crane, *The Targums*; Diez Merino, 'El Targum de Ester'; idem, 'Targum al Cantar de los Cantares'; idem, 'Targum de Rut'.
[101] The Babylonian Geonim mention additional Targumim of the Book of Esther.

The Targum on Song of Songs contains markedly Babylonian terminology.[102] It would seem to be, then, post-fourth century CE. However, in spite of the wealth of homiletical material, there is only one suspect instance in which the Targum might depend on a Babylonian *sugya*,[103] and the bulk of the material is Palestinian. This Targum has a basic framework of trying to describe the history of Israel in a chronological manner. There are deviations from this framework, but the very attempt is quite unusual and worthy of mention.[104] In spite of its late date, it contains many halakhot which were not accepted, but these seem to be mistakes or imprecise translations.[105]

This late Targum, then, seems to be an excellent illustration of the fluid state of the Targum text, of its popular nature and of its ties with the atmosphere of popular derashot given in the synagogue.[106]

The Targum on Esther is also rather late, although the argument of its dependence on the Babylonian Talmud is rather questionable. In any event, it would appear that both Targums on Esther were composed in Palestine after the completion of the Palestinian Talmud, and that neither were meant to serve as Targum in the sense which we have been discussing so far. It is also unlikely that either of these Targums served liturgical purposes in the synagogue.[107] The sages produced much aggadic material on Esther and the Song of Songs and that would appear to be the reason why these somewhat unusual Targums were composed.

The Targums on the Megillot are usually printed in the standard versions of the Tora with classical commentaries, as an appendix to the particular book of the Tora which corresponds to the time of the year in which the individual *megillot* are read in the synagogue. Some of the *megillot* have been published in scientific editions and all appear in Sperber's edition.

The following editions have been published: Grossfeld, *The Targum to the Five Megilloth*; idem, *First Targum to Esther*; Van der Heide, *Yemenite Tradition*; Levine, *The Targum to the Five Megillot*; idem, *The Aramaic Version of Ruth*; ...*of Jonah*; ...*of Lamentations*; ...*of Qohelet*; E.A. Melamed, 'Targum Megillath Ruth'; R.H. Melamed, 'Targum to Canticles', and *The Targum to*

---

[102] E.g. the phrase *Resh metivta*, TgSong 4:4; 7:3; 8:13 (see above n98). Likewise, Ishmael is mentioned as a nation (1:7). Scholarship, however, is somewhat divided regarding this.

[103] Tg Song 1:2; bShab 88b; Tg Song 2:6 is apparently connected to and based upon a section of PsYon Exod 12:37. This part of PsYon is apparently an addition incorporated into the Targum (see below). It also has much material in common with other Targumim such as PsYon on Exod and Num (Churgin, *Targum Ketuvim*, 118-129). However, the use of such material and the extent of the use is not uniform. This is another indication of the fluid nature of the targumic text.

[104] Ch 1-2: The exodus and sojourn in the wilderness; ch 3: Tabernacle, entering the Land and the Temple of Solomon; ch 4: the monarchy; ch 5: destruction of First Temple and Babylonian Exile; ch 6: Second Temple period; ch 7: teachings praising the sages, Daniel and his fellows; ch 8: the Redemption and the Messiah.

[105] Song 6:6. Melamed, 'Targum Song of Songs' has collected a number of exceptions to the rule.

[106] See above.

[107] Churgin, *Targum Ketuvim*, 188-235.

Canticles. Translations were published in the series *The Aramaic Bible* by Alexander (Canticles); Beattie and McIvor (Ruth); Grossfeld (Esther); and Mangan, Healey, and Knobel (Qohelet).

THE TOSEFTOT

In the course of our discussion we have mentioned *Toseftot*, 'additions', a number of times, especially as proof of the fluid state of the Targum. As we have mentioned, there are such additions to Ps-Yonatan, Frg Targum on the Tora, and the Targum on Prophets and the Hagiographa.[108] A typical 'addition' consists of a developed targumic-midrashic fragment and does not contain a translation of the biblical passages being discussed. It may relate to one verse or on a longer biblical passage. The additions are also found in manuscripts of the Targum, some appearing in many while others may appear in only a few manuscripts of one targumic source. Sometimes they are actually incorporated into the Targum, but other times they are cited in the middle or at the end of a targumic selection under the heading 'addition'. It is important to remember that what may clearly be an addition to one selection may appear in another targumic passage as an integral part of the Targum. Most of the additions are found in selections of liturgical importance such as the beginning of the *haftara*, in accordance with Palestinian or Babylonian custom,[109] or in those targumic sections of the Tora which played a role in the liturgy. Only occasionally are there additions whose role or connection to the synagogue liturgy is not clear.

It is likely that some of the more developed midrashim in the Targum were original additions which were included at an early date and are not basically, then, an integral part of the Targum. There is more than enough proof for this claim regarding the material that has been examined.[110] It is also clear that not all such passages have been discovered, nor has there been a systematic study of Targum manuscripts to examine this phenomenon. Most of the additions are Palestinian, although some, going by language and style, are clearly Babylonian. The 'addition', then, represents the efforts of the local authors and editors who added material at will to establish targum. Scholars who seek to define

---

[108] Epstein; Kasher; Komlosh, 'Manuscripts'; Kasher, 'The Targumic "Additions"' ; Grelot, 'Une Tosephta'.

[109] This does not serve as a clear-cut indication as to the Babylonian origin of such an 'addition'. There were communities in Palestine which followed 'Babylonian' custom, at least in the late Amoraic period.

[110] A number of additions were collected by Ginsburger and Klein in their edition of FrgTg. We have not found additions to Onk Bereshit Rabbati of Rabbi Samuel b. Nissim contains a number of targumic additions. See his commentary on Gen 13:7 (addition found in Neof, PsYon and FrgTg with minor changes); Gen 15:1 (addition found in Neof, PsYon and FrgTg with minor changes); Gen 44:18 (addition not in extant Targumim).

targum as being an authoritative literature and as having a fixed established text will have great difficulty in explaining these 'intractable' additions.

Editions were published by Kasher, *Targumic Toseftot to the Prophets* and Díez Merino, 'Tosefta targumica a Genesis y Exodo'. See also Bernstein, 'A New Manuscript', and Díez Macho, 'Nuevos Fragmentos'.

RELATIONSHIPS BETWEEN THE EXTANT TARGUMS ON THE TORA

Since there are three Targums on the Tora and additional targumic fragments, it might reasonably be asked what the relationship between these various documents was. Many studies have been devoted to this matter within the last few years and this seems to have become one of the major focal points of targumic studies. Geiger and Kahle were among the first scholars to contribute important studies on this matter. Within recent years Vermes, Díez-Macho and Kuiper have dealt with this issue.[111]

At first glance, there would seem to be great similarity between the Targums. (1) Many of the literal translations are similar even though a verse could be translated or explained in a variety of manners. (2) Literary characteristics are similar, such as the manner of including the *derash* in the explanation of the verse and the manner in which the plain meaning is then understood. (3) All of the Targums exhibit such similar tendencies as refraining from the use of anthropomorphisms or protecting the status of the Patriarchs. (4) Many derashot are repeated in different Targums, even though at times in a slightly revised or changed form and at times even on different verses. (5) Very often the same biblical verses merit detailed treatment in the Targums, although the details themselves may be different. It would seem then that the Targums derive from a common source or a similar branch of that source. However, for that very reason the differences between the Targums are very important.

All of the above refers to the Palestinian Targums. The connection between these Targums and Onkelos, for instance, is rather weak and Kuiper is of the opinion that there is really no connection whatsoever between these Targumim and Onkelos. Any similarities that may exist, according to this, are the work of copyists. However, it is generally accepted in scholarship that somewhat of a literary connection and perhaps even dependence existed between Onkelos and the other Targums. This, of course, results in the question of determining which Targum is earlier.

Earliest scholarship claimed that Onkelos was the first Targum and that it was used by Ps-Yonatan who expanded upon it and added midrashim.[112] This theory, however, is not accepted today.[113] At best it is possible to state that Ps-

---

[111] See Kuiper, *The Pseudo Jonathan Targum*, 17-34 on the state of research. See also Kaddari, '*Targum Onkelos* Today', 352 ff.

[112] E.g. Bassfreund, 'Das Fragmenten-Targum'.

[113] Thus Díez-Macho and Vermes.

Yonatan was somewhat influenced by Onkelos, but certainly not in its formative state, but during the early Middle Ages in Babylonia. During this time Onkelos became the most important and 'official' Targum and the interest it raised also favoured the interest in other Targums. Detailed study of Onkelos and of Ps-Yonatan has shown that there are certain sections of Onkelos which can be understood only in light of Ps-Yonatan,[114] and that Onkelos also refers to Ps-Yonatan and at times condenses motifs taken from it (Vermes *et al.*). Geiger even claimed that Onkelos was nothing more than a poor imitation of the Palestinian Targums.

This situation is open to several explanations: (1) Onkelos used and depended upon Ps-Yonatan; (2) Onkelos and Ps-Yonatan used an earlier source, the prototype of Palestinian Targums; (3) the extant Onkelos is a shorter version of the original one which must have contained midrashic material; (4) Onkelos condensed and hinted at midrashim, and these are found only by chance in Ps-Yonatan. In light of our discussion above, it would seem to the present author that we must accept the second opinion,[115] i.e., that both Onkelos and Ps-Yonatan used an early Palestinian proto-type, maybe oral tradition.

Regarding the connection of Neofiti to other Targums, scholars have been of the opinion that Neofiti served as the basis for Ps-Yonatan and Frg Targum. On the other hand, it has also been shown that Neofiti condenses midrashim which are found *in toto* in Ps-Yonatan.[116] It would appear that the basic connection between the Targums is clear. What is not clear is their common source. All of the Targums apparently derive from the oral targumic tradition of Amoraic Palestine. It is doubtful whether at this formative period there existed written Targums. Rather there must have been a live tradition based on a similar or common source. This live tradition underwent change, development and additions on a local basis. Neofiti may be closest to this development since it lacks many of the late characteristics found in Ps-Yonatan or in Frg. Targum. However, this Targum also contains 'additions' and it is, therefore, difficult to accept the view that it represents the earliest Targum and best example of pure targumic tradition.

It should be mentioned that the similarity between Frg Targum, Neofiti, and the Geniza fragments is remarkable. These Targums represent, then, a definite group of texts deriving from an earlier prototype which was different than Ps-Yonatan. However, since the question here revolves around hypothetical proto-types, it is difficult to be more specific regarding the relationship between the various Targums.

---

[114] Tur-Sinai, 'On the Understanding' adduced much evidence, but for some reason this important article did not arouse much scholarly interest.

[115] Thus for example, McNamara, *New Testament*, 257.

[116] Reider, 'On Targum Yerushalmi'.

Section Two
Liturgy, Poetry, Mysticism

Chapter Six

Prayers and Berakhot

Joseph Tabory

Introduction

THE BACKGROUND

Rabbinic literature includes much material about prayers and blessings (*berakhot*). Most of this material consists of instructions for their correct performance but the literature also contains a significant amount of full texts and assorted phrases such as those that are found in the later prayer books. Although one may argue that prayers and blessings were a popular phenomenon which the sages were trying to control but which had grown out of the various traditions shared by the people, the degree of control achieved is sufficient for this to be considered a branch of rabbinic literature.

The phrase 'prayers and berakhot' might be thought pleonastic but the two words are meant to describe different types of communication with God. Prayers are thought to be supplicatory or precatory, while berakhot, ordinarily translated as blessings, are thought to be expressions of praise of God. However, for reasons discussed below, the definitions of these two terms are not precise nor do they provide us with a complete, or even adequate, classification of the nature of communication with God in Jewish law and ritual. Therefore we prefer the more general term 'liturgy' which we shall further define and classify.

We shall use the term 'liturgy' to describe the direct connection between God and humanity. Although the main desideratum of a God fearing person is to fulfil the commandments of God, both those of moral content and those which are called ritual commandments, liturgy (while it may not be a commandment) is a central theme of religion because it stresses the direct connection between humans and God. We may distinguish between two directions for this communication. God speaks to humanity, and human beings speak to God. The first direction, God communicating with human beings, is accomplished by two methods – either through His prophets or through His word. The first method, communication through prophets, is not considered liturgy. However, the second method, as exemplified in the public reading of the Tora, is included in the category of liturgy and is part of Jewish liturgy from its earliest times until today. The second direction, man communicating with God, is also accomplished by two methods – sacrifice and prayer. The Tora does not demand prayer but rather emphasizes sacrifices, from the animal kingdom and/or from the vegetable kingdom, as the major and most direct connection between man and God. The Tora does present some requirements of oral communication with God, which we shall discuss below, but this is of very limited importance. The worship of God by sacrifices, according to the Tora, is the main feature of liturgy. However, since the cessation of sacrifice with the destruction of the Second Temple, the main aspect of liturgy is prayer, verbalized and vocalized communication of human beings to God.

The Tora does prescribe a few cases in which one is required to talk to God. One case is those statements of recognition and thanks which accompany the bringing of the first fruits and the tithes to the priests (Deut 26:1-15). Neither of these statements is spontaneous but, rather, the Tora prescribes precise formulas which are to be recited at these ceremonies. Indeed, the sages ruled that in some of the cases that one of the statements in these formulas did not reflect the reality of the situation, the person could not bring the first fruits at all, while in other cases he would omit the entire formula – even though only one clause was not relevant The formula could not be amended (mBik 1:1-4).

In several other cases, the Tora requires one to talk to God without prescribing a specific text. The most notable example of this is when one is required to bring a sacrifice as an atonement for sin. It is not sufficient to bring the sacrifice; one must also confess the sin for which the sacrifice is being brought. However, the Tora does not prescribe a formula for this confession. Presumably, a spontaneous statement was expected which was meant to fit the circumstances of the individual sinner. Similar to this is the commandment 'When you have eaten your fill, give thanks to the Lord your God for the good land which He has given you' (Deut 8:10), which was understood by the rabbis to be a positive commandment to recite Grace after meals, although no specific text is prescribed.[1]

The two types of prayer appearing in these cases, the fixed formula and the spontaneous prayer, represent a basic problem in the history of liturgy which underlies many, if not most, liturgical developments. On the one hand, spontaneous prayer would seem to be the best method of communication. Spontaneous prayer represents a true communication with God. It is only in spontaneous prayer that one can say what is on one's mind and achieve the feeling that one has told God exactly what one feels. On the other hand, a demand for spontaneous prayer presents two major problems. A practical problem is that people often feel that they do not have the talent to speak properly to God and they either copy prayers used by others or ask others to compose prayers for them as, indeed, the disciples of Jesus asked him 'teach us to pray' (Luke 11:1). A theological problem involved in spontaneous prayer is that people who pray spontaneously may use phrases that others may consider heretical or the prayers may make requests that others think inappropriate. Although fixed prayers may solve these problems, they present other theological problems. They may become empty ritual without any inner significance or they may take on aspects of a magical formula which can be effective only if recited precisely as formulated.

If we turn to the Bible in its totality, examining the reality of the biblical world, we find a great deal of prayer but these are spontaneous prayers, spoken to God in unique times of sorrow or joy. The importance of these prayers for the understanding of prayer in later times is twofold.

The first aspect of biblical prayer which is important for the history of prayer are the genres of prayer found in the Bible. The Bible presents us with what were considered, in later times, as the main genres of prayer: (1) supplicatory prayers; (2) prayers of thanks (and praise) for particular help and salvation; (3) praise of God as worship, not associated with any particular event; and, finally, (4) arguments with God about the way that He runs the world. The first two genres continue in rabbinic literature as prayers and blessings; the third is generally, in rabbinic law, the singing of the *Hallel* (a selection of psalms meant to be sung at various occasions; mostly on festivals); while the fourth, although reported and recognized in rabbinic literature, is outside

---

[1] Josephus portrays the Essenes as praying both before and after meals (*War* 2.8.5; 2:131).

the patterns of rabbinic legislation. This article focuses on the first two types of prayer.

The second aspect is the pattern of the individual supplicatory prayer. In many biblical prayers we find the structure common to later prayer: the prayer opens addressing God, with a varying number of His attributes; the prayer continues with an expression of the bonum desired from God; the prayer closes with an explanation, occasionally in argumentative form, of the reason that God should fulfill the request.[2]

BERAKHOT

Although there are similarities between rabbinic patterns of prayer and biblical patterns, there is a distinct difference as to the precise textual formula used for prayer. One of the most important aspects in the history of Jewish prayer is the development of a formula or pattern for prayer known as ברכה, berakha, 'blessing', which is found in rabbinic literature. The main feature of the berakha pattern is that the phrase ברוך אתה יי, 'Blessed art Thou, Lord,'[3] appears either as the opening phrase of the blessing or as the closing phrase or in both positions. This justifies the term berakha for this pattern. We must distinguish here between the use of the term berakha as a signifier for the content of an utterance and its use as a signifier for the pattern of an utterance. The pattern of berakha, originally used only for expressions of thanksgiving, was adopted by the rabbis as the official pattern of all prayer, including supplicatory prayer. This, in turn, meant that supplicatory prayer must always be preceded by an expression of praise. As a result of this, many supplicatory prayers came to be known as berakhot, even though their main function is pleading rather than blessing.

There are three basic patterns for the berakha. A blessing which opens and closes with 'blessed' was termed a 'long' blessing.[4] Enveloping the body of the berakha with the declaration that God is blessed[5] fits well with the require-

---

[2] Greenberg, 'Patterns of Prayers'. A similar pattern has been found in Greek prayers, except that the argument follows the invocation – before the request itself. See Pullyen, *Prayer*, 132. For a more detailed discussion of prayer patterns in the Bible see Greenberg, *Biblical Prose*.

[3] Rabbinic sources seemed to have required the use of the tetragrammaton in blessing formulas (see tBer 6:20, p39) and this should be either transliterated, as a personal name, or translated as 'God'. However, reading אדני (Lord) for the Tetragrammaton is an early practice, already used in the Septuagint, which became common in rabbinic practice. For this reason, the usual translation of the blessing formula uses 'Lord'.

[4] Although the source for this term is mBer 1:4, its explanation in the context of the Mishna is not totally clear. The explanation adopted above is that of Maimonides. For others see Ta-Shma, *Early Ashkenazic Prayer*, 84-90.

[5] The word ברוך may be understood as the wish that one may be blessed, or as a statement that one is blessed (see Brown – Driver – Briggs, *s.v.*). Later Jewish theologians explained the statement as meaning that God is the source of all blessings.

ment, which we shall discuss below, that prayer should open with praise of God and conclude with His praise.

A blessing which closed with praise of God but did not begin with his praise was termed a 'short' blessing. This pattern was considered by the Amoraim as somewhat anomalous and they noted that it usually appeared in a series of connected blessings, in which the first blessing of the series followed the long pattern, opening and closing with praise of God. The short version may then be explained as a secondary pattern of the long form, eliminating the opening 'blessed' since it so closely followed the closing 'blessed' of the prior berakha. However, this pattern does also appear in berakhot which do not follow a closing blessing and many attempts have been made to explain this anomaly.

There is also a third pattern, which has only the opening phrase. This is usually a very short text, such as ברוך אתה יי בורא פרי הגפן, 'Blessed art Thou, O God, creator of the fruit of the vine'. It is likely that the reason that this berakha does not close with praise of God is that it would seem somewhat redundant to require such a closing so close to the opening phrase. However, there is evidence that the body of some of the blessings of this type was eventually expanded and closing phrases were added. People who expanded the simple phrase 'who has created the fruit of the vine' by additional appellations, perhaps even including a request of God to bless the fruit of the vine and so on, were required to add a closing phrase which served two purposes. On the one hand, it provided a conclusion with the praise of God – which was now widely separated from the opening phrase.[6] On the other hand, it provided an opportunity to sum up the main theme of the blessing by adding an appropriate appellation of God.

The syntax of the opening phrase has been a subject of much discussion. The standard formula is ברוך אתה יי אשר..., 'Blessed art thou, O God, who has...[done something or other]'. This phrase begins addressing God in second person and then seems to change to third person. The change in person seems syntactically difficult, especially in light of the fact that the phrase 'blessed is God who...' appears numerous times in the Bible and consistently refers to God in the third person. The 'thou' approach appears in two biblical passages but they are consistent in using the second person throughout the prayer (Ps 119:12, 1Chr 29:10). Both patterns appears in the berakhot of the Dead Sea Scrolls but they are both internally consistent: they are either in second person or in third person, with no mixture of the two.

There are three basic approaches to the solution of this problem. One denies the existence of a problem, maintaining that this type of syntax is not uncommon, referring to biblical verses such as Isa 54:1.[7] A second approach is

---

[6] See Tabory, *Passover Ritual*, 313 n20.
[7] A literal translation is: 'Sing, O barren one, who did not bear', with a transition from vocative (2nd person) to 3rd person. Standard English translations, such as the modern JPS translation, read

proposed by medieval Jewish theologians who state that the familiarity of second person breeds awe which causes the prayer to distance oneself by the use of third person. Both of these approaches have been rejected by J. Heinemann who thinks that the correct solution is historical.

Heinemann, basing himself on suggestions by Spanier and Audet, suggests that a form-critical analysis of the opening and closing phrases shows that they were originally two separate types. The opening phrase followed the biblical pattern of referring to God in third person while the closing phrase was an innovation of Second Temple times,[8] referring to God in second person. This new pattern was meant to stress the intimate relationship of the prayer to God. Eventually, the influence of the new pattern caused the addition of 'You' to the older pattern, without influencing the basic pattern of this formula, which remained in the third person.[9]

The formula of the blessing was further enhanced by adding the appellation 'our God, King of the world' immediately after the opening declaration. This addition, stressing the kingship of God, is assumed to be a protest against other claims of kingship in the ancient world.[10]

Blessings are the backbone of rabbinic prayer texts. Official prayer had to bear the formulaic stamp of a blessing. This enabled the sages both to exert control over prayer and to allow free and spontaneous prayers. The sages decreed which blessings were required and, to a great extent, how they were to be formulated. Later rulings were strict about keeping to the rules and not uttering unnecessary blessings. However, if a prayer did not use the berakha formula, it was not included in rabbinic legislation and people were free to pray as they wished.

Many rituals were built out of a series of blessings, not always directly connected to each other. The most notable prayer of this type is the Amida which we shall discuss below. Among the rituals consisting of series of blessings we may mention here the Grace after meals and the series of wedding blessings, which shall also be discussed below. Many rituals, whether consisting of a single blessing or of multiple blessings, were conducted over a cup of wine, lending a festive atmosphere to the ritual and adding another blessing, the blessing over the wine.

'O barren one, you who bore no child!', which reflects the meaning of the sentence but does not reflect the syntax of the Hebrew.

[8] Although the question of whether it was necessary to say 'You' in the blessing formula was argued by third century Amoraim (yBer 9:1, 12d), the evidence from Qumran shows that this pattern existed in Second Temple times.

[9] Heinemann, *Prayer*, 77-103.

[10] The precise reason for this was a subject of scholarly discussion. For a list of the articles see Tabory, *Jewish Prayer and the Yearly Cycle*, 94f. For the last word on this subject see Heinemann, *Prayer*, 93-95.

Second Temple Liturgies

As far as patterns are concerned, prayer in the Second Temple period follow the biblical patterns. Spontaneous prayers which are said to have been offered in this period are amply documented in the Apocrypha, the Pseudepigrapha, Qumranic writings, Gospels and Epistles, and rabbinic literature. A categorization of prayers which are first documented in the Amoraic period but probably originated much earlier has been proposed by Joseph Heinemann. He defines two categories based on their contents and form-patterns. One is prayers of 'law-court' origin. The essence of these prayers is an argument with God, much like that of a lawyer in a court, claiming that justice, or mercy, require God to grant the request of the prayer. This follows a biblical tradition as Abraham's argument with God about the salvation of the people of Sodom is one of the earliest examples of this type of prayer.[11]

A second classification proposed by Heinemann is the prayer of the study hall or *beit midrash*. The *Sitz im Leben* of this type of prayer was a Tora study session, or sermon, which began and/or ended with a prayer to God. This prayer included, generally, an expression of thanks to God for the giving of the Tora. One of the most unique aspects of these prayers is that they address the people in second person and refer to God in third person. Additional aspects of this type of prayer are the use of epithets, such as 'the Holy One (Blessed be He)', rather than the name of God; the use of the vernacular (Aramaic) and ending the prayer with a call to the community to reply 'Amen'. Most of the features which typify this pattern appear in the Tora, although the *Sitz im Leben* was different. Most of the berakha formulations in the Bible reflect the first aspect of this pattern. They take the form: '...Thank God who has done this for you'. Precatory prayers in the Bible also frequently use this pattern as, for example, 'May God give you of the dew of heaven and the fat of the earth' (Gen 27:28) or 'And may *El Shaddai* dispose the man to mercy toward you' (Gen 43:14). Especially noteworthy in this context is the priestly blessing (Num 6:24-27) which follows this pattern. Nevertheless, the combination of all these aspects is what Heinemann considers to constitute prayers of the study hall.

All the prayers we have discussed until now are voluntary and spontaneous, apart from several specific prayers mentioned in the Tora. In rabbinic literature we first find that regular, obligatory prayer has becomes a major feature of Jewish religious life. We find both public liturgies and private prayer which are obligatory and whose nature was regulated in rabbinic literature.[12] This chapter will focus on such these liturgies and try to show how they appear in

---

[11] Heinemann, *Prayer*. For a more recent discussion of this type of prayer in Jewish tradition throughout the ages see Laytner, *Arguing with God*. The book has a comprehensive bibliography on this subject.

[12] See Heinemann, *Prayer*, chapter 7.

the earliest sources and how they developed in the period that is our time frame here.

Although there is no doubt about the centrality of the Temple in the life of Second Temple Judaism, there was no known attempt to make it serve as a house of public prayer. Solomon is reported to have requested of God that it serve as the focus of private prayer, and we have extensive evidence about the relationship of private prayer to the Temple. We find people coming to the Temple to offer their prayers or, when unable to come, synchronizing their prayers with the time of the sacrifices – especially the time of the incense offering. Nevertheless, the Temple never became a place of public prayer. It is well known that it was described, by a modern scholar, as a Sanctuary of silence.[13] The only sounds heard within the sacrificial court were the songs sung by the Levites at the time of the wine libation (mTam).[14] R. Yonatan, an Amora, explained that wine and song go together for the joy induced by wine brings about song (bAr 11a and parallels). According to an appendix to the Mishna, there were seven songs, taken from the book of Psalms, repeated in a weekly cycle. A document from Qumran maintains that there was a yearly cycle, with a different, unidentified, Psalm for each day of the year.[15] The Hallel was also sung on certain occasions.

PUBLIC LITURGIES

Public liturgies known to us in the Second Temple period focussed on readings from the Bible, especially the Tora. The earliest known example is the reading from the Bible by Ezra (Neh 8). The ceremony is presented in bare detail. Ezra read from ספר תורת משה, 'the book of the Law of Moses', and this reading was preceded by a blessing: 'Ezra blessed the Lord, the great God, and all the people answered, "Amen, Amen", with hands upraised' (Neh 8:2, 6). The exact identity of the biblical passage read is unknown. The importance of determining which passage was read is because the nature of the passage qualifies the nature of the reading: Did they read passages which emphasized the covenantal relationship between God and His people or did they read passages which contained laws which were to be studied and obeyed? Events subsequent to the reading imply that they read a passage from the Tora which dealt with the approaching Sukkot festival.

Less is known of the blessing which introduced the reading. Rabbinic literature identified this as the blessing prescribed by later literature for intro-

---

[13] Knohl, *Sanctuary of Silence*. Knohl uses a phrase which first appeared in Yechezkel Kaufmann's *History of the Israelite Faith* (Hebrew).

[14] The daily songs are hinted at in Qumran (see Fleischer, 'Beginnings', 419).

[15] It is of interest to note that this difference between Qumran and rabbinic tradition finds a parallel in daily prayers. The daily prayer found in Qumran, Prayer of the Luminaries, gives a different prayer for each day of the week, in a weekly cycle, while the rabbinic daily prayer, as discussed below, is identical for every day of the week.

ducing the reading of the Tora, but it is possible that this may have been just a generic praise of God.[16]

The liturgy of Ezra appears in the Bible as a one-time affair, although it may have been repeated under special circumstances. Another liturgy which was held only occasionally was the liturgy for fast days, described in the tractate Taanit. The details of this liturgy, as given in the Mishna, are so intertwined with the details of post-Temple liturgy that it is difficult to decide what parts of this liturgy are actually from the time of the Temple. For this reason, we shall postpone presenting and discussing it until later.

The Mishna gives us details of two liturgies which were conducted during Second Temple times at regular times.[17] These are the Yom Kippur rite, held annually in the Temple, and the *hakhel* (הקהל) ceremony, held once in seven years as prescribed by the Tora (Deut 31:10–13). Although detailed descriptions of these rituals are first found in the Mishna, finally redacted only at the turn of the second century CE, an acceptable working hypothesis is that the details of these descriptions are not anachronistic, unless there is a particular reason to suspect them.

On Yom Kippur, the High Priest read the Tora publicly during a break in the sacrificial rite (mYom 7:1).[18] The *hakhel* ceremony consisted of a public reading of the Tora by the king. This was connected to the Sukkot festival although its precise point in time has been the subject of much discussion.[19] The readings from the Tora, in both cases, were selections appropriate to the occasion. It is noteworthy that the Yom Kippur reading consisted of the laws of the Yom Kippur sacrifice and the *hakhel* reading, while much lengthier and including varied texts, also including the passage which prescribed the *hakhel* ritual. Each reading was followed by seven blessings whose motifs were described in the Mishna as: (1) Tora; (2) the [ritual] service [עבודה, *avoda*]; (3) forgiveness of sins [on Yom Kippur; at the *hakhel* ceremony a specific blessing associated with that day, whose content is not detailed, was substituted]; (4) the Temple; (5) the people of Israel; (6) the priests; (7) prayer (mSot 7:8–9).[20] This ritual is slightly different than that of Ezra for here the blessings follow the reading rather than precede it. It is also more developed as we have seven blessing rather than the one of Ezra. However, we still do not know whether the blessings were statements of thanks or pleading. Some of the motifs may easily be explained in both manners. Thus, for example, the blessing of Tora may be an expression of thanks for giving the Tora to the Jews or it

---

[16] See Hammer, 'What Did They Bless?'.

[17] For a fuller discussion of these liturgies see Tabory, 'Precursors of the Amida'.

[18] The High Priest also recited a spontaneous prayer while he was in the Holy of Holies (mYom). The content of this prayer would have varied according to the personality of the High Priest. For a discussion of the suggestions offered in rabbinic literature and in liturgical poetry as to the content of this prayer see Tabory, 'Prayer of the High Priest'.

[19] For the most recent discussion see Henschke, 'When is the Time of *Hakhel*?'

[20] A slightly different list appears in the parallel discussion of this ritual in mYom 7:1.

may be a request, as found in later liturgy, that God help the Jews learn and understand the Tora. Other motifs are more easily explained as requests. We may assume that the blessings of the ritual and of prayer were actually requests to accept the ritual and to hearken to the prayers, but it is not impossible to imagine that they were expressions of thanks for prescribing a ritual which creates a relationship with God and for His listening to one's prayer.

SECOND TEMPLE SHEMA

A third liturgy of this basic form is the one which was later known as the reading of Shema. This liturgy is described in the Mishna in the context of the description of the sacrificial ritual (mTam 4:3–5:1), in a passage which is considered one of the most important for the history of rabbinic prayer. According to the Mishna, the priests interrupted the sacrificial ritual and retired to the Chamber of Hewn Stone in order to read the Shema. As in the liturgies described above, here too, the central part of the liturgy was the reading of biblical passages, four in number: (1) the Ten Commandments; (2) 'Hear, O Israel', Deut 6:4-9; (3) 'If, then, you obey the commandments', Deut 11:13-21; (4) 'The Lord said to Moses as follows', Num 15:37-41. The reading of these verses was accompanied by a number of blessings, in a fashion similar to that of other liturgies mentioned above. However, before we present an analysis of this liturgy, we should consider the time at which it was held.

The Mishna rules that the Shema should be read twice a day: somewhat before sunrise and at sunset, although it could be read for some time after these hours (mBer 1:1-2). However, the slaughtering of the daily offering began at sunrise (mTam), and the gathering of the priests for this liturgy must have taken place a considerable time after sunrise. There is no report of the priests gathering for a second reading of the Shema in the evening. However, this does not have much significance as the Mishna does not give us any description of the evening ritual in the Temple. We may assume that the Mishna thought of the evening sacrifice as just a repetition of the morning ritual. Nevertheless, there is no direct rabbinical evidence of a diurnal liturgy during the Second Temple. The most accurate conclusion to be drawn from this is, perhaps, the randomness of rabbinic historical evidence – as there is other evidence for a diurnal liturgy, morning and evening, from other Second Temple sources.

The very precise statement found in the Letter of Aristeas that God commands that '..."On going to bed and rising" men should meditate on the ordinances of God' (Arist 160) seems to clearly imply an obligation to recite some passages from the Tora twice a day. Philo reports that the Therapeutae pray twice a day, in the morning and the evening, and the precatory nature of their prayer is very clear (VitCont 27, 89). Josephus also mentions a diurnal liturgy (Ant 4:212) but it is very possible that he is thinking of some type of thanksgiving prayer rather than reciting biblical passages.[21] Diurnal prayers, with clear instructions that they were to be said at sunrise and in the evening, were found at Qumran (Daily Prayers; 4Q503). A daily prayer was also found at Qumran (Words of the Luminaries; 4Q504), but there is no indication of what time in the day this was supposed to be said.[22] Besides the direct evidence of these prayers, probably non-sectarian, certain evidence has been interpreted to mean that the Qumran sectarians prayed regularly between three to six times in each twenty-four hour period, although later scholarship favours the diurnal pattern even among the sectarians.[23]

We may now turn to the description of this liturgy as it appears in the Mishna. We are told that the priests entered the Chamber of Hewed Stone 'to read the Shema' (mTam 4:2). Judging by this appellation, one would say that the Shema was the main focus of the liturgy. However, even if we ignore the surrounding blessings and consider them as ancillary, the liturgy does not begin with the Shema passage but with the reading of the Ten Commandments. This gives us the remarkable result that the Ten Commandments passage is, conceptually, in a secondary position, even though it is the first passage read. For this reason, and others, the mishnaic title of the four biblical readings, 'Shema', may be considered anachronistic, derived from a later period in which the Decalogue had already disappeared from the daily reading. Nevertheless, there is a significant body of evidence which shows that the Decalogue and the Shema were coupled together and they may be considered cotexts.[24] This theory can not, of course, denigrate the theological importance of the verses of the Shema reading in first century Judaism. Jesus states that the first, or most important, commandment is 'And thou shalt love the Lord thy God with all thy heart, and with all thy soul, and with all thy mind, and with all thy strength' (Mark 12:30; Luke 10:27; Matt 22:37). However, the emphasis is on the second verse of the Shema reading and only Mark prefaces it with the first verse ('Hear, O Israel...').

Furthermore, the inclusion of the passage which begins, 'The Lord said to Moses as follows' (Num 15:37-41), in this liturgy is somewhat suspect and may also be anachronistic. The main content of the passage is the commandment to put fringes on garments. Although it does mention that the fringes will remind one of all the commandments of God, this is not its main thrust. Nor is its concluding with God's reminder that He was the One who redeemed the Jews from Egypt. The Mishna implies that the main reason for including it in the Shema liturgy is it discusses the commandment of fringes which was considered a daily obligation (mBer 2:2). The Palestinian liturgy of the Tannaic

---

[21] Naeh and Shemesh, 'Manna Story'.

[22] It has been suggested that 4Q408 is also a daily prayer. See: Annette Steudel, '4Q408'; Falk, 'Other Evidence for Daily Prayer'.

[23] See Chazon, 'When Did They Pray?. For a list of apocryphal evidences for diurnal prayer see Fleischer, 'Beginnings', 418 n49.

[24] Kimelman, 'Shema' Liturgy', esp 68-80.

and Amoraic period included the passage only in the morning Shema and not in the evening, because the commandment of fringes was not considered obligatory in the evening.[25] This is, of course, no reason for assuming that the passage was not included in the Shema during the Second Temple period. For a better understanding of this issue, we are lead, in turn, to consider the reason for the twice daily, or diurnal, reading of the Shema.

Two possible reasons have been suggested for the daily reading of the Shema. One is that it is considered a daily renewal of the covenant between God and his people or, as phrased by the rabbis, an acceptance of the kingdom of God (mBer 2:2). This purpose would be well served by the reading of the Ten Commandments, the opening verse of the Shema: a declaration of belief in the one God and the following chapter. The other reason is that this reading was ordained in order to fulfill what was understood as the biblical commandment to study the Tora 'on going to bed and rising'. These two purposes are well exemplified in a passage found in the Rule of the Community, 1QS 10:10, 'At the onset of day and night I shall enter the covenant of God, and when evening and morning depart I shall repeat his precepts'.[26] It is not far-fetched to presume that the passages selected for the fulfilment of this obligation were those passages which actually mention it (i.e. Deut 6 and 11),[27] especially since the Septuagint has a preamble to the Shema which reads, 'And these are the ordinances and the judgments which the Lord commanded the children of Israel in the wilderness, when they had gone forth from the land of Egypt.'[28] Of course, the daily reading of the Ten Commandments is well suited for both objectives. They were the statements made by God at Mount Sinai when He declared His covenant with the Jewish people, and reading them is a repetition and renewal of this experience. They were also eminently suited as a daily recapitulation of the Tora, especially when we consider the position of Philo that all the commandments of the Tora are subsumed under the Ten. Significant evidence links the Ten Commandments with the first chapter of the Shema, including the Nash papyrus and phylacteries found in Qumran.[29] Neither of these two reasons justify the inclusion of Num 15:37-41 in this liturgy and it may have been added at a later period. In this case, its inclusion as part of the rite in Temple times may be anachronistic.[30]

---

[25] See Albeck, *Shisha sidrei Mishna* to mBer 2:2.

[26] García Martínez and Tigchelaar, *Dead Sea Scrolls* (translation).

[27] See Tabory, 'Precursors of the Amida', 247.

[28] Some have suggested that this addition in the Septuagint is not a preamble to the Shema but rather a peroration for the prior passages. However, the presence of this passage before the Shema in the Nash papyrus shows that, in early antiquity, it was considered an introduction to the Shema.

[29] Yadin, 'Tefillin'.

[30] Philo's discussion of the Shema is thought to be further evidence that the chapter of *tsitsit* was not included in the Shema liturgy (Cohen, *Philo Judaeus*, 167–176). Hoenig, 'Tefillat ha-Kohanim' has surmised that the third chapter was not read, as the first two chapters, but was recited from memory. His theory is based on the fact that the first two chapters appear in close conjunction, in that order, in Deuteronomy while the third chapter is found earlier, in the book of

The reading prescribed by the Mishna was accompanied by blessings, much in the nature of the other readings which we have presented. However, unlike those other readings which had blessings recited either before or after the reading, this one had blessings both before and after it. It was introduced by a single blessing whose content is not described and about which we can conjecture as we did about the blessing of Ezra, and it was followed by three blessings. The first of these is described by its opening phrase, 'it is true', and it is presumed that this blessing was actually an affirmation of the reading, an acceptance of the charges and duties arising from the passages read. Thus this text, counted as a blessing, is actually another form of 'amen'. The affirmation gave the reading the nature of a covenantal renewal. The following two blessings are for the ritual (*avoda*) and the priestly blessing. On Shabbat they added an additional blessing for the priestly course which ended its weekly service on that day.

The Mishna tells us that the biblical passages of the Shema liturgy were preceded by two blessings and followed by two blessings in the morning and three blessings in the evening (mBer 1:4). R. Simon points out, in the name of R. Shmuel bar Nahman, that there was actually a type of symmetry between the morning and evening rituals (yBer 1:4, 3c). As we have mentioned above, in the Land of Israel they read only the first two chapters of the Shema in the evening so that both morning and evening prayers totaled seven units each.

The Mishna seems to take for granted the knowledge of the contents of these blessings, as it does not add any information which would enable us to identify them. The first two are identified in the Talmuds either by significant words from the text or by a general description of the motif of the blessing. The first blessing is referred to in both Talmuds as 'creator of luminaries' which is the traditional closing phrase of this blessing. From the Bavli we learn also that the parallel evening blessing closed with 'who brings the evening' (bBer 12a). The Bavli (11b) also refers to this blessing as 'creator of light, and former of darkness', which is the opening phrase of this blessing and is taken from a verse in Isaiah (45:7). The second blessing, referred to by the Yerushalmi as a blessing for the Tora, is referred to in the Bavli by its opening words: either 'great love' or 'eternal love' (11b-12a). Both Talmuds assume that this blessing was identical with the one blessing recited by the priests in the Shema liturgy mentioned above, explaining that the first blessing, which refers to the creation of the luminaries, could not be said by the priests as their Shema was recited before sunrise.[31]

Numbers. It is worth noting that Moshe Weinfeld, in his comprehensive *Decalogue*, mentions only Num 15:39-40 in a totally non-related context.

[31] There is an anomaly here as the priestly Shema was apparently read much later in the day but this is not relevant to our discussion.

The blessing following the Shema is referred to by the Mishna, in another context, as אמת ויציב (*Emet ve-yatsiv*), 'True and established',[32] which is an affirmation of the Shema. R. Yehuda, a third generation Tanna, ruled that one may not interrupt between the third passage of Shema and *Emet ve-yatsiv*, giving this blessing the status of a chapter of the Shema itself (mBer 2:1). The Yerushalmi implies that the blessing in the evening was identical with that of the morning (yBer 1:1, 2d) but an Amora attributed to Rav the statement that in the evening one must rather say אמת ואמונה (*Emet ve-emuna*), 'True and firm' (bBer 12a).

The final blessing is referred to in the Bavli (4a, 9a-b) as השכיבנו, *Hash-kivenu*, 'Lay us down (to sleep)'. This is clearly a bedtime prayer and its origins are to be found in the reading of the Shema just before going to sleep.[33] This understanding is clearly evidenced by the statement of R. Zera that one should omit the blessing in the event that the reading of Shema had been delayed until close to morning (bBer 9a).

The three liturgies described by the Mishna as taking place in the Temple precincts were not actually Temple liturgies and had no connection with the sacrificial ritual. They were not held in the Temple court where the sacrifices were offered but rather in the Women's Court. In the cases of the readings on Yom Kippur and during the *hakhel* ceremony, the presence of multitudes of people required a larger space for these activities and the multitudes were not allowed into the Temple court anyway. The Shema reading was conducted in the Chamber of Hewn Stone which was considered of lesser holiness than the Temple court, and it was here that the Sanhedrin, composed of non-priests, met to conduct its sessions. Since, however, there is no authentic evidence of the reading of Shema by non-priests or of its being read outside the Temple,[34] it has been argued that this liturgy was originally a priestly, Temple liturgy which was later adopted by the general population.

OTHER LITURGIES

The Mishna reports of yet a fourth liturgy based on a reading from the Tora, which had a more direct connection with the Temple. This is the liturgy known as מעמדות, *maamadot*. One of its important aspects is that, although it was obligatory, it was not incumbent on every Jew. A select group conducted the rite daily (except for Shabbat!), rotating weekly in a semi-annual cycle. This group was considered representative of the community of Israel. Here we have clearly the principle of the sacrificial ritual that surrogates conduct a ritual for

---

[32] Translation according to Hoffman, *My People's Prayer Book*. Jastrow, *Dictionary s.v.* יציב translates: 'true and irrefutable'.

[33] See Gilat, *Studies*, 287-289.

[34] Scholars have pointed to Arist 160 as evidence for the twice daily recitation of the Shema in Second Temple times (Kimelman, 'Shema' Liturgy', 70 n212).

the whole community. The only information given us about the time of this rite is that it was usually conducted four times a day which does not parallel the times of sacrifice. We also know that the heart of the ritual was the reading of the passage from Genesis dealing with the creation of that day and that it included the priestly blessing (mTaan 4). No other blessings are known to have been associated with this reading although, if we consider the rite as analogous to those described above, there would have been some other blessing accompanying it. It has been suggested that one of the non-sectarian liturgies for which no *Sitz im Leben* exists may have been part of the *maamadot* liturgy. The implication of rabbinic literature is that the *maamadot* ritual was founded as an adjunct to the sacrificial ritual. However, critical analysis of the sources suggests that it may have its origins in a desire to create a substitute for the sacrificial ritual.[35]

Finally, in the context of prayer in the Second Temple period, we may turn to the weekly reading of the Tora as a setting for liturgy. The weekly reading is well documented as a reading which was not just ceremonial but served as a basis for the study of the law. The extent of this reading is unknown, nor is it known whether the Bible was read in a continuous fashion, completing the cycle in between one to three and a half years (as evidenced in later rabbinical practice),[36] or whether passages were selected on an ad hoc basis. There is evidence that the reading of the Tora was followed by a reading from the prophets and that, as far as the prophets were concerned, there was no fixed reading. There is no extant evidence for any liturgical ritual associated with it. Nevertheless, there is some likelihood that blessings were recited either before the reading or after the Tora, or possibly in both occasions.[37] It is possible that the reading of the prophets was also preceded and/or followed by blessings. This likelihood is based both on an analogy to the other readings described above, although they were ceremonial readings rather than readings for purposes of study, and on retrojection of later rabbinical practice.

The earliest reference to an obligatory prayer of a semi-fixed nature is found in a report attributed to the Houses of Hillel and Shammai, who were active in the last century before the destruction of the Temple and whose activity continued some years after it. The Tosefta reports that there was a difference of opinion between the Houses about the order of blessings when a festival fell on Sabbath. The House of Hillel required seven blessings, six whose

---

[35] For a fuller discussion of this ritual see Tabory, 'Ma'amadot'. Fleischer, 'Beginnings', 415 lists the Therapeutae (as described by Philo), the Essenes (as described by Josephus, Wars) and the Qumran separatists (= Essenes?) as groups who practice regular, public prayer during the existence of the Second Temple. The factor common to all these groups is that they had no access to the temple – either for geographical reasons (Therapeutae) or for ideological reasons (Essenes / Qumran).

[36] For a revision of the accepted history of the reading cycles see Fleischer, 'Annual and Triennial Reading'.

[37] Fleischer, 'Beginnings', 412.

nature is not specified and are assumed to be similar (if not identical) with those which appear in standard Jewish prayerbooks, and a seventh whose motif was the sanctity of the Sabbath and the festival. The House of Shammai ruled that the sanctity of Sabbath and festival should each have a separate blessing, for a total of eight (tRH 2:17, p320 // Ber 3:13, p15). The Tosefta also reports that the House of Hillel reminded their opponents, the elders of Shammai, that they had all been together when Honi Junior recited seven blessings. The elders of Shammai argued that case was exceptional due to extenuating circumstances.[38] The story gives us the flavour of what seems to be an historical incident, presumably taking place some time in the century before the destruction of the Temple. Indeed, if not for the accompanying story, one might argue that the disagreement is somewhat anachronistic and that the actual disagreement between the Houses referred to the blessing of the sanctity of the day which accompanied the reading of the Tora: The House of Shammai maintaining that two separate blessings should be said when a festival fell on Shabbat, while the House of Hillel maintained that both days be incorporated in one blessing. The accompanying story, while not totally ruling out hyper critical theories,[39] makes them more difficult to be accepted.

There is no other evidence in rabbinic literature of a required public liturgy at regular times during the Second Temple period. It is worthwhile noting that R. Yohanan b. Zakkai, considered one of the great reformers of Judaism who did so much to adjust religious practice with the reality of the destruction of the Temple, made no changes or innovations in the field of liturgy.

Post-70 Liturgies

THE SHEMA

Although the daily reading of the Shema, at least once a day, was apparently customary already in the Second Temple period, we know very little about its performance and structure. Post-destruction sources give us significant material about this but we can only conjecture how much of it was practiced before the destruction. The main feature preserved in the Mishna is that the Shema was a fully developed liturgy, preceded by two blessings and followed by blessings, with a third blessing added in the evening. Although this complex is perceived as a unit, scholarly investigation shows that it is really a conglomeration of blessings which are not all directly connected to the Shema reading. In fact, the Shema reading itself is not really a coherent unit. The first two passages are conceptually connected: the first is an expression of the acceptance of God's kingdom while the second is an expression of the acceptance of

---

[38] Fleischer, 'Beginnings', 425, in spite of his tendency to deny the existence of any general obligation to pray during the existence of the Temple, seems to grant this point.
[39] See Ben-Shalom, *School of Shammai*, 233-235.

the rule of His law (mBer 1:2). The third passage refers to a specific commandment, the commandment of fringes, and was said only in the morning since this commandment is obligatory only during the day. This passage which, as we have already noted, may not have been part of the rite in the Second Temple period, was clearly part of the rite in post-destruction times.

The blessings enveloping the Shema are also not a cohesive unit. The first blessing of this complex refers to God as the creator of nature, specifically the sun, moon and stars which signify the change of the day. Thus, the closing formula of this blessing in the morning refers to God as the creator of lights while its parallel in the evening praises Him as the bringer of evening. According to talmudic tradition, the morning blessing was not said by the priests as part of their Shema liturgy since they recited this liturgy long after the day had begun.

The second blessing refers to God's love of Israel, shown especially by His giving them the Tora. This has been understood by the sages as being a blessing of thanks to God for giving the Tora, a statement both appropriate and necessary before the reading of passages from the Tora. This blessing contributes to the understanding of the purpose of the twice daily reading of the Shema as a way of fulfillment of the biblical command to study Tora on arising in the morning and before going to sleep.

The blessing following the reading of the Shema is actually a two-partite blessing. The first part is an affirmation of the Shema, opening with *Emet ve-yatsiv* in the morning and *Emet ve-emuna* in the evening. This reflects the understanding of the Shema as a renewal of the covenant. The motif of the second part of this blessing is an expression of thanks for the redemption of the Jews from Egypt. There is evidence that this second part was added to the Shema liturgy some time after the destruction of the Temple (mBer 1:5).[40]

In the evening, the Shema liturgy concludes with a final blessing. This blessing, also, has nothing to do with the Shema passages. The blessing opens with *Hashkivenu* and is a petition to God for protection during the night, a bedtime prayer.

THE AMIDA

Introduction

The institution of an obligatory daily prayer of fixed pattern is attributed to R. Gamliel, who became the head of the academy of Yavne and the spiritual leader of rabbinic Judaism some years after the destruction of the Temple – after the retirement of R. Yohanan b. Zakkai. The attribution of this revolutionary idea to R. Gamliel is based on his statement in mBer 4:3 that everyone is required to pray eighteen blessings every day. A contemporary, R. Eliezer,

---

[40] See Albeck, *Shisha sidrei Mishna* to mBer 2:2.

seems to have rejected the idea of obligatory prayer (4:4).[41] However, another contemporary, R. Joshua, agreed with the basic idea of eighteen blessings but maintained that the obligation is limited to an 'abstract'[42] (מעין) of the eighteen (4:3). A generation later, R. Akiva gave a compromise ruling: 'If one is fluent in prayer, he recites a prayer of eighteen. And if not, an abstract of eighteen'.[43] These eighteen blessings became the basic unit of prayer and the term 'prayer' (תפילה, *tefilla*) became a technical term for the prayer.[44] To prevent ambiguity, we shall use a later term, עמידה, *Amida*,[45] to refer to the prayer. The term Amida means 'standing', and it emphasizes one aspect, i.e., that it was the only prayer one was required to recite in a standing position.[46] The Bavli adds that Shimon ha-Pakuli[47] arranged the eighteen blessings under the guidance and supervision of R. Gamliel (bBer 28b // bMeg 17b).

R. Gamliel found it necessary to emend the work of Shimon ha-Pakuli. The Bavli adds that R. Gamliel asked for a volunteer to 'order' a blessing against sectarians (*minim*) and Shmuel the Younger accomplished this task (bBer 28b).[48] Exactly what Shmuel did is not clear. A minimalist approach is that he modified an original blessing about the downfall of the wicked in order to include specific mention of a particular group. Most scholars think that he did add a blessing but it is likely that the theme existed in the Amida of Shimon ha-Pakuli and that Samuel the Younger gave it greater emphasis by creating a separate blessing for it.

A further point on which scholars have disagreed is whether this blessing was to be added to the earlier eighteen, creating a prayer of nineteen blessings, or whether some other blessings were coalesced into one in order to maintain the number of eighteen. We know that somewhat later evidence shows that there were two separate traditions: the Babylonian tradition consisted of nine-

---

[41] Cf Zahavy, *Mishnaic Law*, 59.

[42] The translation is that of Zahavy *ib.* 57.

[43] Zahavy *ib.*

[44] Jastrow, *Dictionary*, 1686f, *s.v.* The use of the number of blessings in a rite as a technical term for the rite appears also in the term 'three blessings' for Grace after meals and 'seven blessings' as a term for the marriage ritual (see below).

[45] This term for this prayer first appears in Gaonic times (Sofrim 16:9, p295; Responsa Shaarei Teshuva, 347). The term appears in Amoraic literature in the more generic sense of prayer (yBer, 4:1, 7a). The use of this term is preferable to the more common term *shmone esre* (eighteen blessings), as the number of blessings in this prayer range from seven to nineteen.

[46] For the sources of this requirement and its significance see Ehrlich, *Non-Verbal Language*, 17-30.

[47] This individual is otherwise unknown. For a discussion of his epithet see Bickermann, 'Civic Prayer', 290 n3.

[48] It is, perhaps, somewhat remarkable that the original vesion did not contain a plea for the downfall of the wicked. This is a common theme in Psalms, although we find also an approach which calls for the repentance of the wicked (see Jacobs, 'Praying for the Downfall'). The identity of these heretics, Christians or others, has been the subject of much discussion. Flusser, 'Some of the Precepts' maintained that it was originally directed against the Essenes. For balanced surveys see Van der Horst, 'Birkat ha-minim'; Horbury, *Jews and Christians*, 19-61.

teen blessings while the Palestinian tradition consisted of eighteen. The difference between them is that the Babylonian tradition has a blessing for the kingdom of David and another for the rebuilding of Jerusalem while the Palestinian tradition includes both motifs in one blessing which ends 'Blessed art Thou, o Lord, God of David and builder of Jerusalem'. Elbogen has suggested that the Babylonians split this blessing into two, creating a nineteenth blessing, in order to honour the Exilarch, who was of the House of David. However, the fact that the Palestinian version concludes with two motives, the only blessing to do so, seems to imply that this originally involved two separate blessings which were combined into one blessing in the Land of Israel, probably to retain the total number of eighteen blessings.[49]

Structure

Although R. Gamliel ordained a prayer of eighteen blessings, Tannaic sources do not give us even a basic list of these. The Mishna does give a list of nine blessings recited on Rosh Hashana (mRH 4:5). Each blessing is referred to by a code word reflecting its main motif. They are: (1) ancestors, or forefathers; (2) [God's] powers; (3) sanctification of God's Name, which on Rosh Hashana includes the mention of his Kingdom; (4) the sanctity of the day; (5) memories; (6) *shofarot*; (7) Service [of God]; (8) acknowledgement of gratitude; (9) the priestly blessing.

The blessings listed here form a pattern which is the basis of every Amida. The first three and final three blessings create a standard framework which envelopes one or more blessings which are specific to the day. The framework has been described in a Tannaic midrash as being similar to the rhetoric pattern used by an advocate before the king. He opens with effusive praise of the king, continues with his request, and concludes with further praise of the king. The prayer structure has the same pattern: it opens with praise of God, presents the needs of Israel, and concludes with grateful acknowledgement (Sifre Deut 343, p394f). The analogy is not absolute for the conclusion of the prayer is not an expression of further praise but rather of thanks. Modern students might consider the structure of prayer as similar to that of a letter to the authorities. After the invocation with its proper titles and addresses, the letter continues with the request to be made, and concludes with gratitude for the attention paid and, perhaps, an expression implying the confidence of the writer that the request will be granted.

In spite of the apparent simplicity of the framework, it does present a number of problems. The opening praises are divided into three discrete blessings for no apparent reason. On the one hand, the call to God as being the 'God of

---

[49] Some scholars have argued that the original set of blessings numbered only seventeen and it was the addition of the blessing against the heretics that created the total of eighteen (Cf Ginzberg, *Commentary*, vol 3, 28. See also Erlich, 'Ancient Version'.

the forefathers' concludes with His appellation as specifically 'the shield of Abraham'. On the other, in a litany found in Ben Sira, which has great affinity to the Amida as we shall see further on, we find the following (Ben Sira 51:x-xii [found only in the Hebrew text; between 12–13 of the Greek]):

Give thanks unto the Shield of Abraham,	For His mercy endureth forever
Give thanks unto the Rock of Isaac,	For His mercy endureth forever
Give thanks unto the Mighty one of Jacob,	For His mercy endureth forever

It would seem that the first blessing should either have concluded with 'God of the forefathers' or, if it was deemed fit to close with Abraham, there should have been separate blessings for each of the forefathers. Indeed, Babylonian sages suggested that the reason for the preference of Abraham in the conclusion of the blessing is due to the verse 'And you shall be a blessing' (Gen 12:2; bPes 116b).[50]

The second blessing presents a problem of content. It is called 'powers' and it praises God by mentioning His powers. However, the types of powers are not clearly defined. The Geniza has preserved two traditions of the text of this blessing. The one which has survived as the standard version includes the powers of God who quickens mortals, provides sustenance, supports the fallen, and redeems the suffering. In many manuscripts of this version we find also that God heals the sick and, in a few of them, that he supports the poor and raises people who are bowed down.[51] The gist of the blessing seems to be praise of God for His daily support, and even the phrase מחיה מתים (quickens mortals) may refer to when a person gets up in the morning, arising from the sleep of the dead. However, the other version lacks these clauses and the emphasis is clearly on the eschatological resurrection. If this is to be considered the main theme of the blessing, it is to be understood more as a statement of belief in the future resurrection than a praise of God based on human experience.[52]

The third blessing has yet other problems. It praises God and His name as holy but it also includes an angelic prayer (kedusha). This is connected with other problems and we must delay its discussion.

In spite of the problems involved in the first three blessings, they do have a common factor of praising God. Although the final three ones are also sup-

---

[50] Cf Van der Horst, 'Greek Synagogue Prayers'. The author finds a parallel to this blessing in the Apostolic Constitutions, a prayer which is a complete entity to itself and focuses on the God of Abraham. The sacrificial ritual in the Temple also began with a memento of the God of Abraham. According to Matitya b. Shmuel, the person in charge would ask if the sky was lit up until Hebron (mYom 3:2). The reference to Hebron was to invoke the merit of the forefathers (yYom 3:1, 40b). Although all the forefathers were buried in Hebron, it was Abraham whose name was especially connected to it.

[51] See Luger, Weekday Amida.

[52] Cf Flusser, 'Second Blessing'. Flusser found a parallel to expressions in the Babylonian form of this blessing in a document found in Qumran. He maintained that the earlier form of this blessing did not stress the eschatological quickening of the dead.

posed to contain this factor, a closer examination shows that the structure of section they constitute is problematic. Only the middle blessing of the three, which opens with 'we gratefully acknowledge', fits clearly into the pattern of praise of God. As we have noted above, this section is more acknowledgement than praise, but that makes it even more appropriate to serve as the conclusion of the Amida.

The first of the three final blessings is called עבודה (*avoda*), 'service', and a blessing of this name appears in Temple times, both in the series of blessings recited by the priests after the reading of the Shema and in the one recited by the king and the High Priest at the end of their prescribed readings from the Tora. Here again the Geniza fragments of the Amida present us with two main traditions. This is one of the rarer cases in which the difference between the two traditions extends to the closing formula. One tradition concludes with, 'Blessed are You, God, for you alone do we serve with awe.' This formula is unique among the blessings of the Amida in that it is not an attribute of God but rather an expression of fealty or even a request. The other tradition ends with, 'Blessed are You, God, who returns his presence to Zion.' The motif common to both traditions is a request that God return to Jerusalem so that the Jews may worship Him there. It has been surmised that the first tradition represents the form that was used while the Temple existed and that this blessing was then either an expression of thanks to God for ordaining the Temple service or a request that He accept it. After the destruction, the blessing was modified and its conclusion was replaced, by some, with a request for the restoration of the Temple.[53] The second tradition is the one which has survived until today and it includes a prayer for the restoration of the sacrificial ritual with the a request that God accept this ritual and the prayers of the Jews. Although the history of the blessing is somewhat contorted, it is hard to see how it could have been considered as the first in a series of blessings expressing praise of God.

We may now turn to the blessing which concludes the Amida, referred to in the Mishna as 'the priestly blessing'. This blessing, at least since the time of the Geonim, is composed of two units. One unit consists of the formulaic blessing (Num 6:24-27) with which the priests were required to bless the people. This blessing of the people is recited only by priests (*kohanim*) and only in public prayer when there is a sufficient quorum (*minyan*). The second unit is an ordinary blessing which has two themes: a request for peace, which is the theme of the concluding phrase of the priestly blessing, and a request for God's blessing. This unit is always part of the Amida, whether said in private or publicly, whether there are priests present or not. It is not clear whether this blessing was originally ordained in these two parts or was one of them the original requirement which was later supplemented by the other. We should

---

[53] Erlich, 'Earliest Versions'. See Luger, *Weekday Amida*, pp. 173-183 for earlier literature on this subject.

note that the only term for this blessing found in early sources is 'the priestly blessing', a term which refers specifically to the blessing prescribe in Numbers. Although the Tora does not state specifically when the priests were supposed to do this, it has been generally assumed that it was part of the sacrificial ritual.[54]

We have already noted that this blessing appeared in Temple times in non-sacrificial contexts: as part of the *maamadot* ritual and at closure of the Shema liturgy. Based on the fact that the Tora stresses that the role of the priests in this blessing is secondary – it is a blessing of God and the priests are not acting independently but as His representatives – it has been suggested that the blessing is meant to serve as an acknowledgement by God of the ritual and a signal of His acceptance of it.[55] This, of course, justifies its use as a closing ceremony of prayer. However, the rabbis were very strict with this blessing and insisted that it could only be recited by priests. The insistence was so great that a passage in the Mishna stating that the priestly blessing may not be read or translated (mMeg 4:10) has been explained to mean that these sentences could not be even be read as part of the Tora reading.[56] Thus, in the individual recital of the Amida the priestly blessing was neither appropriate nor possible.[57] It was replaced by a blessing whose main theme is a request for peace – the concluding phrase of the priestly blessing – and a request for God's blessing. This is somewhat anomalous for a last blessing, as it negates the idea of closing the requests with praise of God. It is possible that the request for peace was thought to be similar to saying goodbye to God at the end of the prayer,[58] but, considering the early term for the blessing, explanation seems somewhat less likely.

The Middle Blessings

Within the framework outlined in the above are sandwiched the middle blessings, of variable number. We have already mentioned that the daily prayer consists of twelve (Land of Israel) or thirteen (Babylon) requests. On Shabbat

---

[54] Cassuto, 'Birkat Kohanim'. He considers the theme of peace as the main idea of this blessing, comparing it to the custom of saying goodbye with an expression of peace.

[55] See Tabory, 'Priestly Blessing'. I would add here that, although the priests blessed the people just before the meat of the sacrifice was brought to the altar, this was immediately after the incense offering. The incense offering was the preferred time of private prayer and thus, here also, the priestly blessing follows prayer.

[56] See Henshke, 'What Should be Omitted'.

[57] In the Gaonic period we first find evidence of the recital of these verses by the precentor according to the Babylonian custom, but this was listed as a point of disagreement between Babylonian and Palestinian Jews, who forbade the recital of these verses by a precentor who was not a priest; Margulies, *Hilluqim*, 145f. Margulies refers to another interpretation in his notes.

[58] Cf Ehrlich, 'Significance'. The author uses anthropological theory in maintaining that all three blessings are part of a farewell ritual. For a further discussion of ways of saying goodbye in talmudic custom see Ehrlich, *Shefa Tal*, 13–26.

and festivals only one blessing appears, making a total of seven, and its theme is not a request but rather an expression of gratitude over the sanctity of the day. On Rosh Hashana an additional three blessings are added to the seven but one of them coalesces with one of the standard blessings for a total of nine. On fast days six blessings were part of the ritual of the day and they were merged with regular Amida for a total of twenty-four blessings. There is a scholarly consensus that most of these additional blessings had an independent existence before the institution of the Amida.[59] Before we address this issue, we will present an analysis of the middle blessings of the daily rite.

The middle blessings of the daily rite are all petitionary. Their motifs, as they appear in the Babylonian rite, are: (1) Knowledge; (2) Repentance; (3) Forgiveness; (4) Redemption; (5) Healing; (6) Sustenance;[60] (7) Ingathering of the exiles; (8) Justice; (9) Heretics; (10) Righteous, (11) Jerusalem, (12) David, (13) Prayer. As we mentioned above, in the Palestinian rite Jerusalem and David are combined in one blessing.

The reason for the order of these blessings is a subject of discussion in both Talmuds. R. Joshua b. Levi pointed out the rational sequence of the blessings: knowledge brings repentance, which is followed by forgiveness and redemption. After the spiritual needs are taken care of, one prays for health and wealth. Once the individuals needs are fulfilled, a second series of requests begins and this one portrays the needs of the nation.[61] The series begins with a request for the return of the people to its land, which is followed by reestablishing the legal system, which punishes the heretics and rewards the righteous. Then Jerusalem is rebuilt and the house of David rules over it. Alhough the prayer is for a messianic redemption, the messiah is the final stage of the redemption rather than the one who brings the redemption.[62] Finally, one prays that the prayer be accepted (yBer 2:4, 4d-5a).

The Bavli, in an anonymous statement (bMeg 17b-18a), prefers biblical analogies to explain the order of the blessings. The most cogent parallel is to Psalm 103:3-4, 'He forgives all your sins, heals all your diseases; He redeems your life from the Pit' – which matches blessings 3-5 with a change in the order.[63] This parallel helps explain an anomaly in the list of blessings. Although the first series clearly reflects individual needs, it includes a request for

---

[59] For the fast days see Levine, *Communal Fasts*, 55f.

[60] Although this blessing is referred to in talmudic literature as the 'blessing of the years', I prefer 'sustenance' which gives a clearer idea of its meaning.

[61] The earliest clear statement that the central blessings of the Amida consist of two series: one of private needs and a second for the nation's needs, appears in the work of David Abudirham (13th c.).

[62] This has been pointed out by Kimelman, 'Messiah of the Amida'.

[63] See also Mirsky, 'Sources of Prayer', 24. Mirsky finds other linguistic connections between the Amida and this psalm, many of them based on the wording of blessing rather than on their themes. Since the dating of the words themselves is problematic, I have not included these connections here.

redemption which was understood, at least by the time of the Amoraim, to be a request for the redemption of Israel. Based on the biblical parallel, it seems that this request was originally thought to be a request for the individual's release from suffering, perhaps referring to pain which comes before healing.

Scholars, however, have tended to think that the order of blessings reflects an attempt to impress a pattern on a collection of earlier liturgical material. They are lead to this conclusion by the existence of apparent anomalies in the order – which can best be explained by the idea that the blessings are not a new creation but an anthology of earlier material.[64] One of the most important sources for this theory is a litany from Ben Sira which we have referred to above. The litany reads (Sir 51:i-xvi, Hebrew text):

Give thanks unto God, for He is good	For His mercy endureth forever
Give thanks unto the God of praises,	For His mercy endureth forever
Give thanks unto Him that keepeth Israel,	For His mercy endureth forever
Give thanks unto Him that formeth all,	For His mercy endureth forever
Give thanks unto the Redeemer of Israel,	For His mercy endureth forever
Give thanks unto Him that gathereth the outcasts of Israel,	For His mercy endureth forever
Give thanks unto Him that buildeth His city and His sanctuary,	For His mercy endureth forever
Give thanks unto Him that maketh a horn to sprout for the house of David,	For His mercy endureth forever
Give thanks unto Him that choseth the sons of Zadok to be priest,	For His mercy endureth forever
Give thanks unto the Shield of Abraham,	For His mercy endureth forever
Give thanks unto the Rock of Isaac,	For His mercy endureth forever
Give thanks unto the Mighty one of Jacob,	For His mercy endureth forever
Give thanks unto Him that hath chosen Zion,	For His mercy endureth forever
Give thanks unto the King of king of kings,	For His mercy endureth forever
And he hath lifted up the horn for his people,	for the glory of all His faithful ones
For the children of Israel, the people close to Him	Hallelujah.

The similarity between this passage and the motifs of the second series of blessings in the Amida is too close to be coincidental. Since the passage appears in Ben Sira, written several hundred years before R. Gamliel, the assumption is that it either reflects a series of requests which was common at that time or that it served as a source and influenced the pattern of the Amida. Other scholars have rejected this conclusion, noting that the litany found in Ben Sira is not found in the Greek text. It exists only in the Hebrew text found in the Cairo Geniza. Thus, this litany may be based on the Amida rather than

---

[64] On the anthological nature of prayer see Tabory, 'The Prayer Book (Siddur)'.

having influenced its composition.[65] However, the mention of the sons of Zadok as priests implies that the litany is of Second Temple origin.

Perhaps a more apposite passage from Ben Sira (33:13) is the following:

> Gather all the tribes of Jacob,
> that they may receive their inheritance as in the days of old.
> Compassionate the people that is called by Thy name, Israel,
> whom Thou didst surname firstborn.
> Compassionate Thy holy city, Jerusalem,
> the place of Thy dwelling.
> Fill Sion with Thy majesty,
> And Thy Temple with Thy glory.
> Give testimony to the first of Thy works,
> and establish the vision spoken in Thy name.
> Give reward to them that wait for Thee,
> that Thy prophets may be proved trustworthy.
> Thou wilt heark the prayer of Thy servants,
> according to Thy good favour towards Thy people:
> That all the ends of the earth may know that Thou art the eternal God.[66]

This text includes requests for ingathering of the exiles, rebuilding of Jerusalem, and rewarding the righteous, and concludes with a request for the acceptance of the prayer.

Perhaps even more significant is a prayer found in 2 Macc 1:23-51.

> [23]And the priests offered prayer, while the sacrifice was being consumed, – priests and all, Jonathan leading and the rest saying it after him, as did Nehemiah. [24]The following was the prayer:
> O Lord, Lord God, the creator of all things,
> who art terrible and strong and righteous and merciful,
> [25]who alone art King and gracious,
> who alone suppliest every need,
> who alone art righteous and almighty and eternal,
> thou that savest Israel out of all evil,
> who madest the fathers thine elect, and didst sanctify them:
> [26]accept this sacrifice for all thy people Israel,
> guard thine own Portion, and consecrate it.
> [27]Gather together our dispersion,
> set at liberty them that are in bondage among the heathen,
> look upon them that are despised and abhorred,
> and let the heathen know that thou art our God.
> [28]Torment them that oppress us and in arrogancy shamefully treat us.
> [29]Plant thy people in thy holy place, even as Moses said.
> [30]Then the priests sang the hymns.[67]

---

[65] The most thorough discussion of this issue is still Marmorstein, 'Jesus Sirach'. For the history of scholarship on this subject see Mirsky, 'Sources of Prayer'.
[66] Charles, *AOT* 1, 441f.

Although this passage has not yet been discussed as a precedent for the Amida, its similarities to the Amida are striking. It is a petitionary prayer which opens with an invocation of God, noting that He has chosen the fathers of the people and made them elect. The invocation stresses the powers of God, praising Him who suppliest every need. The only feature of the opening blessings of the Amida which is missing here is specific reference to God as Holy, although He is mentioned here as sanctifying the fathers. The petitionary part of the prayer includes an appeal for acceptance of the sacrifice, taking this opportunity to petition also for ingathering of the exiles, redemption of the elect and punishment of the wicked. Finally, the rite concluded with hymns, presumably of praise, sung by the Levites.

These passages, and other texts, support the theory that the middle blessings are themselves anthologies of groups of blessings or requests, prayed, perhaps, by individuals. The first group was a series of petitions for personal health and wealth, while the second group consists of petitions for the welfare of that people and its relationship to God.[68] Shimon ha-Pakuli could have used these blocks of blessings in constructing the Amida but limited his editorial changes and rearrangements, creating a number of anomalies. Perhaps the most glaring anomaly is the double request for the reception of prayer – the last of the twelve/thirteen and the first of the last three.

Although we have no early evidence for a full text of the Amida, both Talmuds have preserved an abbreviated form. First generation Amoraim, Rav and Shmuel, offered distinct definitions of the abstract of the Amida advocated by R. Joshua. According to Rav, the abstract was actually a shortened version of each blessing, thus retaining the total of eighteen/nineteen blessings of the Amida. However, Shmuel stated that the idea of the abstract was to compress all the twelve/thirteen blessings into one blessing, creating an Amida of seven blessings. The Babylonian text, as reported by Shmuel, is the following:

> Give us discernment, O Lord, to know Your ways,
> and circumcise our heart to fear You,
> and forgive us
> so that we may be redeemed,
> and keep us far from our sufferings,
> and fatten us in the pastures of Thy land,
> and gather our dispersions from the four corners of the earth,
> and let them who err from Thy prescriptions be punished,
> and lift up Thy hand against the wicked,
> and let the righteous rejoice in the building of Thy city
> and the establishment of the temple
> and in the exalting of the horn of David Thy servant

---

[67] *Ib.* 133.

[68] Bickerman, 'Civic Prayer' has called this a Civic Prayer for Jerusalem. Note that Josephus has posited a reverse order. In his Ag. Ap. 2.23 he states that 'prayers for the welfare of the community must take precedence of those for ourselves' (see Fleischer, 'Beginnings', 416f).

and the preparation of a light for the son of Jesse Thy Messiah;
before we call mayest You answer.
Blessed are You, O Lord, Who hearkenest to prayer. (bBer 29a)

The Yerushalmi gives us a somewhat different text which is also meant to satisfy the requirement of Shmuel:

Give us discernment,
accept our repentance,
forgive us,
redeem us,
heal our maladies,
bless our years,
for You gather the scattered
and it is for You to judge those who stray,
and You shall put your hand on the wicked
and all those who rely on You will rejoice in the building of your city
and in the rededication of Your temple[69]
for You answer us before we call as it is said,
'Before they call I will answer; while they are yet speaking I will hear'.[70]
Blessed are You, Who hearkenest to prayer. (yBer 4:3, 8a)

Comparison of the two texts reveals some interesting things about how the Amida was understood in their times. Both texts begin with 'Give us discernment' (הבינגו), an opening term which does not exist in the extant full texts of the Amida, and they both have identical concluding blessings. This shows that the common tradition focused on the opening and closing elements, while allowing variation in the body of the text.[71] The most blatant difference between the two is the mention of the kingdom of David in the Babylonian text, which is lacking in the Yerushalmi. We have already mentioned that this was one of the characteristic differences between the two traditions. Both texts also attempt to mold the separate themes of the various blessings into one syntactical unit – with various degrees of success. Both change the blessing of the righteous, which in the complete texts is a general request for God to bless them, into a specific request that they be privileged to rejoice in the redemption. The reason for this is, apparently, to create, as much as possible, one unified request out of slightly disparate themes. The Babylonian text has succeeded in doing this also to other requests, specifying that the prayer requests

---

[69] In the only complete ms of the Yerushalmi, the Leiden ms, the words 'and in the sprout of Your servant David' have been added by a later glossator (see *Talmud Yerushalmi According to Ms. Or. 4720*, 38). These words have been added to conform to the Babylonian tradition.

[70] *The Holy Bible : English Standard Version*. 2001 (Isa 65:24). Wheaton: Standard Bible Society.

[71] However, a Geniza text of the *havinenu*, which basically follows the pattern of this text in the Yerushalmi, begins 'give us knowledge' (חונינו דעה) rather than the havinenu common to the Bavli and Yerushalmi. See Margulies, *Hilkhot Erets Ysrael*, 144.

forgiveness so that he may be redeemed, while the Palestinian version connects the requests asyndetically.[72]

A Fixed Text?

Although no full text of the Amida earlier than the ninth century has survived, if there ever was one, some current expressions or phrases are found in the Talmud. The opening blessing invokes God as 'the great God, the mighty, and the awful' (based on Deut 10:17). A story preserved in both Talmuds tells us of one who recited the prayer in the presence of a first generation Amora and added several epithets such as, '...the Glorious, the Strong, the Honourable...' The sage rebuked, ironically asking whether the supplicant had exhausted the appropriate epithets. According to this sage, only the phrase taken from Deuteronomy was sanctioned for this prayer (bBer 33b; yBer 9:1, 12d). From this story we learn, on the one hand, that the text was not absolutely fixed, as the prayer assumed that he was entitled to add words to the text, while on the other, the rabbis decreed exact wording of the text, at least in certain cases. An interesting difference between the two reports is that, according to the Bavli, the Amora waited for the man to finish before complaining, while the Yerushalmi reports that the sages silenced him immediately. The implication is that in Babylonia they were more tolerant about deviations from the normal pattern.

Information about the wording of the Amida from talmudic and midrashic literature is sparse. We know that the first blessing concluded with 'shield of Abraham' and that the third blessing ended, 'the holy Lord'. This information is mentioned in the context of a statement that during the days between Rosh Hashana and Yom Kippur, the ending should be changed to 'the holy King'. In a similar context we find that the concluding formula of the blessing of 'justice' was, normally, 'He who loves righteousness and justice' – which was to be changed during those days into 'the King of justice'.[73]

In several other blessings there were differences between the Yerushalmi and the Bavli. The blessing of 'worship' concluded, according to the Yerushalmi, with, 'for You alone we shall worship with awe', while its Babylonian counterpart ended 'who returns his presence to Zion'. The difference may reflect chronology rather than geography. We have noticed that the theme of 'worship' appeared as a blessing in the Second Temple period. It has been suggested that the Palestinian tradition retained the ancient form of the conclusion, while the Babylonian tradition reflects a change made after the destruc-

---

[72] A similar situation is found in Papyrus Egerton 5, which contains what has been suggested to be an abstract of the Amida. See Van der Horst, 'Papyrus Egerton 5'.

[73] An analysis of the text shows that it is very likely that there was an earlier version of this concluding formula 'The Lord of justice'. See Tabory, 'Ancient Version'.

tion of the Temple.[74] Another difference is found in the concluding blessing of the Amida which ended 'who makes peace', according to the Yerushalmi, while the Babylonians said, 'who blesses his people, Israel, with peace'.

The earliest texts of the complete Amida stem from Gaonic times. The two well known prayer books of R. Amram Gaon and R. Saadia Gaon preserve full texts of the Amida as it was said in their times – according to the Babylonian tradition. Geniza texts from the same period present us with many variants, and most of the blessings of the Amida present at least two variant traditions, at times even three, with a plethora of different readings within each main tradition.[75] There is evidence for the presumption that the differences in the textual traditions reflect differences between the texts common in the Land of Israel and those common among Babylonian Jewry.

The lack of evidence about the early text of the Amida, coupled with the fact that the post-talmudic period presents us with a variety of texts, has lead scholars to wonder if an official text was promulgated and, if so, when this was done. Many have concluded that there never was an official text of the Amida. The most recent proponent of this theory, Joseph Heinemann, has suggested that the standardization of the text was accomplished in stages. R. Gamliel took prayer patterns and popular customs that existed before his time, even before the destruction of the Temple, expanded and refined them, and made them obligatory on all Israel.[76] He was not the beginner of the process but the first to impose a pattern on what had, until then, been various collections of blessings of a spontaneous nature and to impose this prayer as a normative obligation. However, R. Gamliel only imposed a pattern, i.e. the number of blessings and their order – not a definitive text. Even in this he was not totally successful as the number of blessings differed between the Land of Israel and Babylon. The next stage was the standardization of the concluding formulas and, perhaps, even the opening phrases. This took place in the Amoraic period, and here again differences exist between the versions of the two main Jewish centers. The final stage, a tendency to standardize the body of the blessing, began only in Gaonic times and it has not yet been successfully completed.[77]

Heinemann's theory was the dominant until the end of the twentieth century, when it was challenged by Ezra Fleischer. Fleischer maintained that R. Gamliel ordained a complete text of the prayer. However, in order to explain the plurality of versions found in post-talmudic times, he added that there was opposition to R. Gamliel and that his version was not universally ac-

---

[74] See Uri Erlich, 'Earliest Versions'.

[75] A large number of the manuscripts have been collated and analyzed by Luger, *Weekday Amida.*

[76] Some mss of the Talmud report, in the name of R. Yohanan, that prayers and blessings had been instituted in the time of Ezra. The talmudic resolution of this contradiction is that they had been forgotten, fallen into desuetude, and R. Gamliel reinstituted them. See Schepansky, *Takkanot,* 232.

[77] Heinemann, *Prayer,* ch. 2. Heinemann lists a number of phrases and motifs which various Amoraim have declared as essential to the proper fulfillment of the obligatory prayer.

cepted. We shall discuss below the nature of the Amida but, in the context of the question of a text, it is necessary to point out a few other considerations.

The positions represented by Heinemann and Fleischer, whether there was a fixed text or not, reflect different assumptions about mass culture in rabbinic times and the nature of the Amida. Heinemann presumes that people were capable of creating a spontaneous text following the pattern ordained by R. Gamliel. This understanding is based, in part, on the theory that prayer patterns had developed during the Second Temple period. Thus, people were already used to these patterns and could improvise prayers following the structure of R. Gamliel. Indeed, it has been suggested that the invitation to Shimon ha-Pakuli to 'order' the eighteen blessings before R. Gamliel was just to show that even people who had no reputation as scholars could do so. However, there is evidence that many people did not consider themselves capable of praying on their own. They asked others to pray for them or to tell them how to pray.[78]

On the other hand, there are two major impediments to accepting Fleischer's theory. The first is based on observations about the pre-70 era; the second on post-talmudic evidence. As far as the first is concerned, it is hard to deny the affinity between the Amida and motifs found in Second Temple literature, such as Ben Sira and Maccabees. At times, we find even more exact linguistic parallels. This seems to support Heinemann's theory about a gradual development. Fleischer suggests that the parallels are due to the fact that the people who created the Amida in the time of R. Gamliel were aware of earlier literary works and used them in creating the text of the Amida. We would stress that Fleischer states that Shimon ha-Pakuli and his collaborators were even aware of apocryphal literature.[79]

The second impediment is based on the plurality of versions found in the post-talmudic era. If there was a fixed text, how did these come into existence? Fleischer's response is two-pronged. On the one hand, all texts transmitted in the rabbinic period show variant readings and thus we would rather be surprised if there were no variants. This reasoning does seem to justify the existence of minor variants but the differences are too great to be dismissed as variants in transmission. The other prong of Fleischer's response is much more powerful. We find that R. Gamliel's colleagues disagreed with him about the

---

[78] Fleischer has tried to separate his contention that the prayer was fixed from the question of written texts in rabbinic times. He argues that the text of the Amida must have been taught in schools. However, he adds, 'there is no doubt that prayer texts were distributed in written form and there is no halakhic prohibition of this' ('Beginnings', 435 n96). He argues that the prohibition found in the Tosefta against writing blessings (tShab 13:4, p96), which appears also in both Talmuds (see apparatus, *loc. cit.*), is actually against the writing of amulets rather than against prayer texts. However, Sussmann, 'Oral Tora – Literally Understood', 376f has amassed considerable evidence which shows that the interdiction was against writing prayer texts. On the other hand, such an interdiction shows that people did do so, as emphasized in the story which appears in the Tosefta. This implies that there was a text. Cf Ginzburg, *Gaonica* 1, 119f who argues that it was not permissible to pray from a text even in Gaonic times.

[79] Fleischer, 'Beginnings', p433.

eighteen blessings, a disagreement which Fleischer thinks focusses on the text of the eighteen rather than on the basic principle. Thus, the variant readings reflect the acceptance of their approach that the eighteen blessings should be improvised, perhaps spontaneously. It is not clear how they would expect people to be able to compose prayers in this manner, but perhaps there was some compromise in which people who could not do so would use texts composed by others. Fleischer agrees that there is no evidence that the extant texts are direct descendants of R. Gamliel's text, nor is there any way that the early text can be reconstructed.

The question of a fixed text is not crucial to an important part of Fleischer's theory, i.e., that no fixed series of blessings or prayer pattern existed before the destruction of the Temple. Even if R. Gamliel created a new obligation without any precedents, it is possible that he did not create a word-for-word text. However, the existence of a fixed text is essential for another part of Fleischer's theory. He maintains that 'the Amida was not meant to be a prayer in the common meaning of the term, but rather a ritual of collective worship'.[80] The Amida was meant to be a substitute for sacrifice and, as such, it followed the rules of sacrifice, leaving no room for individual improvisation. Ironically, the evidence seems to show that even if there was an original text – it has not survived in a recognizable manner. R. Gamliel's innovation was only partially accepted and the Amida was considered personal prayer. There is further irony in that, eventually, the Amida did come to be considered as a rigid entity and a surrogate for sacrifice, which left little or no room for improvisation. However, this is a later development which is outside the scope of this paper.

Embolisms

Another feature concerns the structure of the text of the Amida. On certain occasions, additional passages were inserted into existing blessings, by way of complement. There is reason to distinguish between these types of insertions, or embolisms, and the type of prayers which joins together two originally separate sets of blessings. Of the latter nature are the prayers of Rosh Hashana, which combine the three blessings of the day with the standard festival Amida of seven blessings, as well as prayers for fast days which combine the six petitions of the fast days with the standard Amida.

The earliest mention of an insertion in the Amida is found in the Mishna which lists three additions to the Amida. During the appropriate season, the power of God who gives rain is mentioned in the blessing of the quickening of the dead, and a request for rain is inserted in the petition for sustenance; furthermore a *havdala*, a declaration of the distinction between the holy Sabbath and the weekdays, is added to the petition for knowledge when the Amida is said at the outgoing of Shabbat (mBer 5:2). The Mishna preserves disagree-

---

[80] Fleischer, 'Response'. 381f.

ments about the exact date for adding the passages about rain, but it is clear that they are said only during the winter, in the rainy season which extended from shortly after Sukkot to sometime in the month of Nissan (mTaan 1:1-2). Although the exact dates were the subject of Tannaic disagreement, most agreed that they were based on the climate of the Land of Israel and left no room for other local considerations. This is exemplified by a story about the community of Nineveh who wished to pray for rain in the months which were the dry season in the Land of Israel, because in their locality this was the rainy season. Permission to do this was refused by R. Yehuda the Prince, arguing that one could not change the order of prayer ordained by the sages (bTaan 14b; cf yTaan 1:1, 63d).[81] Babylonian authorities did rule that, since the climatic conditions in Babylon were very different, the request for rain should begin some six to eight weeks later than in the Land of Israel (yTaan *ib.*; bTaan 10a). Although this seems to follow the reputed ruling of R. Yehuda, the fact is that rain was insignificant in Mesopotamia and irrigated agriculture was possible only in areas remote from Jewish settlement.[82] It would seem that the request for rain was based on a sense of identification with the Palestinian Jews, though the opening date for this request was based on local conditions. The importance of the mention of rain, an issue of presumably minor importance in Mesopotamia, is emphasized by the ruling of R. Hanina, an Amora of the transitional period, that if the mention of rain was omitted during the rainy season or the request for rain was included in the dry season, the whole Amida was be invalidated and had to be repeated (yBer 5:2, 9b; bTaan 3b).[83]

Two Tannaim disagreed about the place of the *havdala* in the Amida. R. Eliezer agreed that it is to be inserted into an existing blessing but he thought that it should be added to the penultimate blessing of thanksgiving. It would seem that the nature of the *havdala* would be affected by the locus of its inclusion. If it was included in the petition for knowledge, it would probably petition God for the wisdom to enable one to distinguish between the sacred and the secular, between Shabbat and weekdays. However, if it were included in the penultimate blessing of thanksgiving it would be more in the nature of thanksgiving rather than petition. R. Akiva ruled that it should not be subordinate to another blessing but should rather be said as a separate blessing – im-

---

[81] The Bavli argues that R. Yehuda, a Tanna of the post Bar-Kokhva era, who maintained, in another case, that local conditions and changing times should be taken into consideration, would have disagreed with R. Yehuda the Prince (bTaan 14b; cf yBer 1:1, 63d). If this were true, it would permit us to trace a historical development from flexibility to rigidity.

[82] Mean annual rainfall in the lowlands ranges from about 4 to 7 inches (100 to 180 millimetres); about 90 percent of this rainfall occurs between November and April ('Iraq', in *Encyclopaedia Britannica*, 2003).

[83] Although it was considered inappropriate to mention the power of God as bringer of rain in the dry season, it was always considered proper to mention his power as the resurrector of the dead for this was always desirable.

mediately following the third of the opening blessings of the Amida (mBer 5:2).

Further insertions are mentioned in other texts. The Tosefta mentions that on biblical festivals one should mention the sanctity of the day in the blessing of 'service', while on other special days, Hanukka and Purim, mention of the day's events should be inserted into the thanksgiving blessing (tBer 3:10). The Tosefta distinguishes between the two types of occasions by referring to the biblical festivals as 'days on which the additional sacrifice is offered', rather than calling them days of biblical origin. It is reasonable to assume that the days were defined by this term because it served to explain why this mention was inserted in the blessing of 'service' which, as we have mentioned before, dealt mostly with the sacrificial ritual. Nevertheless, R. Eliezer thought that the mention of the sanctity of the biblical day should be rather inserted into the blessing of thanksgiving. He was consistent in his approach that all insertions referring to specific dates in the calendar be included in the penultimate blessing. We may assume that, in spite of his attitude that the Amida should be a spontaneous prayer, he considered the pattern so important that he relegated all insertions which did not relate directly to the nature of any specific blessing to the penultimate blessing. We have already noted that this penultimate petition served as a closing of the Amida.

Here too, the disagreement about the placing of the blessing would seem to reflect a disagreement about its nature. If it was inserted in a petitionary blessing, it must have had some petitionary content – such as a request to restore the Temple worship. If it was included in the thanksgiving blessing, it must have been worded as an expression of thanks for the day.[84] However, it is noteworthy that the earliest texts of the insertion for Hanukka and Purim, which all agreed should be inserted in the thanksgiving blessing, ended with a petition that God perform miracles for His children as He had done for them in earlier times. This petition was rejected by later tradition on the grounds that such a request was out of place in the blessing of thanksgiving.[85]

Although the addition of references to rain and of the *havdala* are mentioned in one breath in the Mishna, there is an important conceptual difference. The disagreement about the placing of the *havdala* and of other references to special days shows that the main idea was to refer to the day – whether in a petitionary formula or in a formula of thanksgiving. This is further exemplified by a later ruling that if one had forgotten to mention the day one did not have to repeat the Amida, since the day would be mentioned either in a later Amida or in some other ritual (bBer 30b).

These embolisms shed some additional light on the nature of the Amida. Even though it had a rigid pattern, and perhaps even a rigid text, it was meant

---

[84] Cf Gilat, *R. Eliezer ben Hyrcanos*, 87f, suggesting R. Eliezer's opinion reflects the pre-destruction halakha.

[85] See Tabory, *Jewish Festivals*, 361f, 387.

to reflect the significance of the day on which it was said. Although the Tannaim disagreed about how this significance was to be incorporated into the Amida, they all agreed that its text was not rigid and mechanical but demanded an awareness of the time and occasion on which it was being said. On the other hand, even such additions to the prayer seem not to have been improvised but were rather subjects of direction and control.

A further type of insertion in the Amida was meant to meet the needs of the individual. According to a report preserved in both Talmuds, the Tannaic contemporaries of R. Gamliel, R. Eliezer and R. Joshua, felt that the Amida did not serve as a prayer for personal needs. They thought that one should request his personal needs either before prayer or after it, both calling upon biblical precedent.[86] The importance of the disagreement is that it shows that the text of the Amida was sufficiently rigid for early Tannaim to think one could not add to it.

However, Nahum the Mede (second half of the first century CE) ruled that one could add prayer for individual needs in the blessing, 'He who hears prayer', the closing benediction of the petitionary section.[87] The ruling was accepted by unidentified sages who rejected the opinions of R. Eliezer and R. Joshua (bAZ 7b; cf yBer 4:4, 8b). The blessing, 'He who hears prayer', was considered an appropriate place for other additions to the Amida. Individuals who were fasting should add a section about the fast and its purpose to this blessing. It was even ruled that one who had forgotten to request rain in its appropriate place could do so in this blessing, obviating the need to repeat the Amida.

A change in the nature of the Amida is reflected in a ruling of Rav. He modified the ruling about adding prayer to the final blessing of the petitionary section, permitting one to expand on each blessing of the Amida to include personal requests, although the additions must comply with the general nature of the benediction. Thus, for instance, one could pray for a particular sick person at the end of the blessing which refers to God as healer of the ill. If one had a particular request for economic help, this could be added to the petition for sustenance.

Performance

Unlike many other prayer rituals, the Amida is accompanied by a set of rules which regulate its performance. Analysis of these helps us understand what was the actual concept of the prayer.

---

[86] Cf Gilat, *R. Eliezer ben Hyrcanos*, 84–86.
[87] As Nahum the Mede's main period of activity was before the destruction, it is likely that he was not referring to the final blessing of the Amida but rather stating that any individual could pray to God, using the formulat 'He who hears prayer'.

The frequency of prayer, as related to the frequency of sacrifice, is problematic. There is variegated evidence of daily prayer rituals during the Second Temple period. It is presumed that the Shema was recited twice a day, morning and evening, although our only direct evidence for its being recited a second time during the evening stems from somewhat later times. Daniel is said to have prayed three times a day (Dan 6:11) and this pattern is also found in the book of Psalms 'Evening, morning, and noon, I complain and moan, and He hears my voice' (55:18). The only obligatory liturgical ritual, the *maamadot*, was conducted four times a day: morning, noon, afternoon and close to sunset (mTaanit).[88] However, if prayer was to be considered a surrogate for sacrifice, one would expect to find an obligation to pray no more than twice a day, once in the morning and once in the evening, parallel to the twice a day tamid sacrifice. There was no need or place for a prayer during the night as the Temple doors were closed at sunset and no sacrifices were offered during the night. Indeed, Amoraic sources tell us that R. Gamliel's insistence that the night prayer was obligatory was the source of a major disagreement with his colleagues which brought about his deposition from his post (yBer 4:1, 7b // yTaan 4:1, 67d; bBer 27b-28a).[89] R. Gamliel's opponents carried the day and the evening prayer was considered optional. However, the fact that the time of the evening prayer was defined in a very vague way enabled Amoraim to connect it with the burning of the sacrificial meat on the altar, which was continued throughout the night if it had not been completed during the day (bBer 26b).[90]

Although the regular pattern for prayer is two or three times a day, on biblical festivals there was another prayer, known as מוסף, *mussaf* or 'additional prayer'. Thus, these days had actually four prayer times during the day. Yom Kippur and other fast days also had a special evening prayer known as נעילה, *neila* or 'closing', which raised the total to five prayers during the day. Both these prayers were associated with the sacrificial ritual. The extra prayer was considered to be a parallel to the additional sacrifice offered on festivals or as a surrogate for it. However, we have already noted that a service conducted four times a day was a feature of the *maamadot*, which was conducted only on days on which no additional sacrifice was offered. The descriptions of the *maamadot* call this prayer a 'noon prayer' rather than an additional prayer. On the other hand, we have already noted that a liturgy for Shabbat and festivals seems to have existed before R. Gamliel ordered a thrice-daily ritual. It may be

---

[88] For a fuller discussion of times of prayer see Chazon, 'When Did They Pray?'

[89] For a discussion of this issue see Shapira, 'Deposition'.

[90] tBer 3:1 (p11), which also relates the times of the morning and evening prayers to the times of sacrifices, adds nothing about the night sacrifice, except for quoting opinions which ruled that the night prayer should be said at the time that the gates [of the Temple] were locked. The Yerushalmi also quotes the opinion that the daily prayers were linked to the time of the sacrifices but it adds the Rabbis could not find any parallel to the evening prayer and they left this rubric blank (tBer 4:1, 7b).

that the 'additional' prayer was actually the original prayer to which was added the thrice daily ritual of R. Gamliel. It is noteworthy that the time of this prayer is designated as 'all day' (mBer 4:1). The Talmud quotes a disagreement about the time of the additional prayer. According to one opinion, it may be said all day, just as the additional offering could be offered all day. R. Yehuda said that it could be said only until the seventh hour, because that was the last hour in which the additional offering could be brought (bBer 26b). Rabbinic law forbade bringing the additional offering before the morning *tamid* (daily sacrifice) had been sacrificed nor could it be brought after the evening sacrifice. Therefore, if the additional prayer was actually related to the additional sacrifice, it would seem more reasonable to define its time in terms of the *tamid* sacrifices. The fact that its time is 'all day' seems to justify the theory that the prayer on Shabbat and festivals was originally the only prayer said during the day.[91]

The *neila* prayer was also connected to the Temple ritual, even though no connection could be found between it and any actual sacrifice. The *neila* prayer was to take place at the hour of the closing of the doors of the Temple.

Neither do the actual hours determined for prayer reflect a clear relationship to the Temple sacrifices. The Mishna does not define the morning hour at which prayer may begin (mBer 4:1) although the morning *tamid*, if slaughtered before sunrise, was invalidated (mYom 3:1). The rabbis did define the end of the time in which the prayer could be recited, although there is a disagreement about this. The Mishna permitted reciting the morning prayer until noon while R. Yehuda limited its recital to the first third of the day (mBer loc. cit.). R. Yehuda's statement finds a corollary in sacrifice as R. Yehuda b. Baba, a generation before R. Yehuda, testified that the morning sacrifice could be offered until the end of the first third of the day (mEd 6:1).

An important aspect of the Amida is that it appears in a double form: as a daily prayer it is required of each individual, and it must also be recited in a community of at least ten people with one of the quorum reciting the prayer out loud.

The requirement of the individual is found in unattributed statements in the Mishna that every Jew, including women and children (mBer 3:3), is required to recite the Amida three times a day (mBer 4:1-3). Although this may seem obvious, we must remember that the only obligatory service or worship of God until the destruction of the Temple was the sacrificial ritual in the Temple – which was conducted by priests on behalf of the people of Israel. The *maamadot* ritual seems to have been of a similar nature, with a group of people representing the nation. As we shall see below, even the Amida, in certain cases, was understood to be a representative action which was of benefit even to those who did not participate in it.

---

[91] Cf Elbogen, *Jewish Liturgy*, 97-99.

The ruling that everybody is obligated to recite the Amida is of great significance for understanding the difference between this obligatory prayer and Temple worship. R. Joshua b. Levi (first half of the third century CE) maintains that the prayers were instituted as parallels to the sacrificial ritual (yBer 4:1 7b; cf bBer 26b), implying that prayer was meant to be either a form of worship which was held at the same time as the sacrifices or a form of worship which was meant to take the place of sacrifice. However, the ruling of the Mishna that everybody must pray contrasts with the sacrificial ritual whose performance is limited to the priestly class. Indeed, the Mishna seems to stress that the prayer ritual is not similar to the sacrificial ritual, ruling that a person who wishes to wear white clothing or pray barefoot, thus emulating the priest in the Temple, may not serve as an emissary at all (mMeg 4:8).[92]

Recitiation by the Sheliah Tsibbur

Rabbinic literature refers to the leader of prayer as שליח צבור, *sheliach tsibbur*. Although this term is generally translated 'precentor', this does not reflect the reality of the situation. A precentor is one who directs the service; the leader is actually (and literally) the 'emissary of the community', calling upon God in the name of the community. As far as we know, the prayer service has always been of a double nature: first the individuals recited the prayer silently; then the emissary of the community recited the prayer in the name of the community. This double aspect of prayer is a source of confusion and it is unclear whether the original institution was actually private prayer, with the repetition meant only for those who were unable to recite the prayer on their own, or the original institution was the communal prayer of the emissary, with various reasons given for the seemingly unnecessary silent prayer which preceded it. Among the reasons given for this silent prayer was the necessity of giving the emissary a chance to rehearse the prayer or to give those who wished to say the prayer on their own – a chance to do so.

A significant disagreement preserved in the Mishna illustrates the problem of the dual nature of the Amida. R. Elazar b. Azarya states that the mussaf prayer should only be recited in a חבר עיר (*hever ir*, mBer 4:7) a term whose meaning is not precisely known but implies some sort of urban organization.[93] The implication of this statement is that this prayer, at least, was indeed a parallel to sacrifice which was offered by a group representing all the individuals, including those who were not actually present. Indeed, people who were not associated with any *hever ir* would not say this prayer at all. The

---

[93] Many of the sources mention the *hever ir* as an organization in charge of charity. A connection with liturgy seems to be mentioned also in connection with the blowing of the shofar (bRH 34b) and, possibly, with the priestly blessing (tMeg 3:29, p362). For a discussion of this institution see Levine, *Rabbinic Class*, 105 n105; Safrai, *Jewish Community*, 74f.

sages disagreed, maintaining that this prayer was incumbent upon everyone but we do not know whether the sages required an individual who was present at the prayer of the *hever ir* to recite this prayer himself. R. Elazar b. Azarya's statement was modified by R. Yehuda, who reported that R. Elazar b. Azarya had only meant to say that an individual who resided in a place where there was a *hever ir* was not required to say this prayer, implying that others, who could not rely on the *hever ir*, would be required to say the prayer themselves (mBer 4:7). An early Babylonian Amora accepted the ruling of R. Yehuda and the first generation Babylonian Amora, Shmuel, is said to have remarked that he only once prayed the mussaf prayer privately, when the presence of government troops in the city prevented gathering for the public prayer (bBer 30b).

The dichotomy of public and personal prayer is exemplified by a custom which arose among the sages. Although the communal prayer was meant to be recited by the *sheliah tsibbur*, while others just listened to him as he represented them, some sages recited the penultimate blessing (*Modim* – which, as we have already noted, is the functional end of the Amida) by themselves. They did not use a standard text but each one had his own version for this blessing, a number of which have been preserved in the Talmuds (yBer 1:5, 3d; bSot 40a).[94]

There are two significant additions to the Amida when recited by the *sheliah tsibbur*. The first of these is the expansion of the third blessing to include the verses recited by the angels who praise God, as portrayed in the visions of Isaiah and Ezekiel. These verses, the *Trishagion* recited by the seraphim (Isaiah) and the phrase, 'Blessed is the Presence of the Lord, in His place', recited by the wheeled angels (Ezek 3:12), are complemented by a third verse expressing the kingdom of God, which is the contribution of the children of Israel to the heavenly choir. The whole unit is known as קדושה, *kedusha*. The idea of praying as the angels, or with the angels, is not very common in Jewish liturgy, although it does appear in two other places in the daily liturgy. Praying with the angels is well developed in Qumranic prayer and in Hekhalot literature and many scholars have suggested that these have influenced the development of the rabbinic *kedusha*.

The second addition is the recital of the priestly blessing by priests. This is only done when there are priests (*kohanim*) present. According to the Bavli, it is not recited in the afternoon prayer since this was usually said after people had drank wine as part of their afternoon meal. Since priests should not recite this blessing while under the influence of alcohol, the rabbis ruled that it should be skipped in the afternoon.

---

[94] Cf Ginzburg, *Commentary* 1, 185f.

THE COMPOSITE LITURGY

Although the Amida was an independent prayer, and it is still so in the case of mussaf and *minha* (afternoon prayer), its morning occurrence was joined together with the Shema liturgy. This was accomplished simply by reciting it immediately after the reading of the Shema. In Amoraic times the connection between these two liturgies was enhanced by the declaration that one should not make any break between the blessing of redemption (the final blessing of the Shema) and prayer (bBer 4b; yBer 1:1, 2d). The relationship between the evening Shema and the Amida (for those who said it) was a point of disagreement. Some ruled that also in the evening the Amida should be recited immediately after the Shema, possibly based on a desire to create an evening service parallel to the morning service. Others ruled that the Shema should be said after the evening Amida, apparently considering the Shema a bedtime prayer.

The morning ritual was further expanded by including a series of passages from the Psalms recited before the Shema. These passages, known collectively as פסוקי דזימרה (verses of praise), are not mentioned in Tannaic literature. The earliest reference to this unit is just a mention of its name in the Bavli. Nevertheless, Weinfeld claimed to have found a similar idea in Qumranic literature.[95]

BLESSINGS ON AWAKENING

Awakening in the morning is accompanied by thanks to God for having survived the dangers of the night. Both Talmuds record that the first thing to do when one awakens is praise God who either 'quickens the dead' (yBer 4:2, 4d) or 'returns the soul to lifeless bodies' (bBer 60b). A blessing for intelligence is to be said upon hearing the cock crow, the ancient equivalent of an alarm clock (yBer 9:1, 13c; bBer 60b). The Bavli follows these blessings with a series of blessings, later known as 'blessings for activity', which are to be recited in the morning as an expression of thanks to God for restoring one's bodily functions. Thus, when one opens one's eyes, one should praise God 'who opens the eyes of the blind'. When one gets dressed, one should praise God who 'dresses the naked'. There is a fixed list of these blessings in the Bavli (bBer 60b), totalling some eighteen blessings, and later tradition did not permit any additions to the list. Although they are not mentioned in the Yerushalmi, prayer books written according to the Palestinian tradition some centuries after its formation included these blessings and even more than those listed in the Bavli.[96] We might include, in this category, relieving oneself as another occasion for a blessing, praising God for the proper function of the complex mechanisms of the body (yBer 9:6, 13b; bBer 60b). However, this blessing is not only said in the morning but any time during the day after bodily functions.

---

[95] Weinfeld, 'Morning Prayers'.
[96] Mann, 'Genizah Fragments'.

BLESSINGS OF SELF-IDENTITY

Some time after the fall of Betar we find R. Yehuda stating that one is to recite three blessings daily, thanking God for not having been created a non-Jew, nor a boor, nor a woman (tBer 6:18, p38). In Amoraic Babylon, thanks for not being a boor was replaced with thanks for not being a slave (bMen 43b-44a). Parallels to these blessings are found in Greek and Christian sources.[97]

BLESSINGS OVER FOOD

Besides the two major liturgies, the Shema and the Amida, we find in early rabbinic literature a requirement that one recite a number of blessings during the day. These blessings are, in the main, statements of thanks for various experiences during the day which the believer recognizes as gifts of God.

The tractate Berakhot devotes its second half to the laws pertaining to these blessings. This section, which opens with blessings recited before eating food, follows immediately upon the chapters dealing with the laws of Shema and the Amida. Presumably, the editor of the Mishna was following one of his usual methods of organizing the material in chronological order – after one prays, one eats.

The sages ruled that one could not eat anything without blessing God, stating that one who did not do so was actually 'embezzling' from God's creation (tBer 4:1, p18).[98] The details of the laws of these blessings give us an insight into the psychology and methodology of rabbinic prayer. The sages gave rules and texts for every type of foodstuff. Some of these are general, such as the blessing of God as 'Creator of the fruit of the tree' for all types of fruit, while others are very specific, such as 'Creator of the fruit of the vine' for wine and 'Bringer forth of bread from the earth' for bread. Some sages disagreed about exact formulations. R. Yehuda declared that the proper blessing for vegetables is, 'Who makes the earth fruitful by His word' (tBer 4:4, p19). On the other hand, R. Meir argued for a freer form of blessing, stating that even if one had blessed 'He who created this bread, how beautiful it is' he had fulfilled the obligation of blessing (ib.). R. Yehuda expressed the more stringent view forcefully 'Anyone who deviated from the rabbinic form of blessing has not fulfilled his obligation' (ib. 4:5). Although R. Yehuda's opinion was followed, we find that the first generation Amora Rav recognized a blessing which did not follow the rabbinic formula. This blessing, reported to have been uttered in Aramaic by a simple shepherd, was: 'Blessed is the Merciful One, owner of this bread' (bBer 40b). There was also a generic blessing,

---

[97] For a detailed history of these blessings and their parallels in ancient sources see Tabory, 'Benedictions of Self-Identity'.

[98] Cf Bokser, 'Ma'al and Blessings'.

thanking God by whose word all was created, which could serve, in a pinch, for almost any other blessing (mBer 6:2).

The Mishna continues with a discussion of the laws pertaining to Grace after meals. Although the blessing before food was always required, the Grace after meals was contingent upon the type of food eaten and its quantity. Nevertheless, the sages considered the Grace after meals as being of greater importance than the blessings before food. The former was considered to be of biblical origin, based on the verse 'When you have eaten your fill, give thanks to the Lord your God for the good land which He has given you' (Deut 8:10; yBer 1:1, 2a). The thrust of the verse (and its context) is a command to be thankful for the Land. Although the rabbis understood this to be a command to bless God for the food – after it had been consumed, the basic meaning of the verse is reflected in the opinion of R. Gamliel that one is required to recite the full Grace after eating any of the seven kinds of produce which was considered the pride of the Land of Israel (tBer 4:15, p21f; cf mBer 6:5). Other sages accepted the principle that the seven kinds of produce had special significance but they ruled that a shortened form of the Grace, an abstract of the full liturgy, was sufficient (mBer 6:5). Other foods required no blessing at all after them (cf tBer 4:7, p19) although later practice decreed a short blessing after any type of food (bBer 37a; cf yBer 6:1, 10b).

While the blessing before food is a short, simple one, the Grace after meals is a full-blown liturgy consisting of four blessings. The motif of the first blessing is praise of God who sustains the world; the second, thanks God for the gift of the land of Israel; the third, a prayer for the rebuilding of Jerusalem; and the fourth is a general praise of God 'who is good and does good'.

The basic Grace liturgy is expanded when the Grace is said after a meal at which at least three people participated. In that case, the Grace opens with an invitational rite in which one of the participants invites the others to join him in praise of God. Although this invitation is called a berakha in rabbinic literature, it does not follow the rabbinic formula for a blessing. Heinemann has suggested that the origin of this invitation is to be found in the ceremonial meals held by members of the *havurot* (Pharisaic 'associations'), instituted before the crystallization of the rabbinic blessing formula.[99] The Grace after meals was also enhanced by texts inserted within it on various days of importance in the Jewish calendar, such as Sabbath and festivals, Hanukka and Purim.

Although Grace after meals consists of four blessings, in rabbinic literature it is consistently referred to as 'three [blessings]'. The simplest way to explain this is to assume that one of the four is a later addition to the rite. We find two approaches to the resolution of this problem. The first approach is based on rabbinic tradition which reports that the fourth blessing, 'who is good and does good', was added after the dead of Betar had been properly buried (c. 135 CE)

---

[99] Heinemann, 'Birkath Ha'zimmun'.

– as an expression of thanks to God that this had finally been done. The idea that this blessing is a later addition is supported by the fact that does not fit the pattern of the preceding blessings. The second and third blessings of the Grace have the appropriate form for blessings which appear in a series: they are long blessings with no formal opening but ending with the formulaic. The fourth blessing is a short text, opening with a blessing of God and without the closing formula. Although the internal evidence can not be denied, the dating of this blessing is not so simple. There is considerable evidence that this blessing was included in the Grace before the rebellion and, if indeed it was tacked on to an earlier liturgy of three blessings, the date of this event can not be determined.[100]

Another approach to the solution of this problem is that the first blessing was originally part of the invitation ritual and was not considered part of the basic Grace.[101] A ramification of this approach is that the content of the first blessing after the invitation is an expression of thanks for the Land of Israel, which is more appropriate to the biblical source of this blessing (see above).

OCCASIONAL BLESSINGS

The final chapter of tractate Berakhot is devoted to occasional blessings, blessings which seem meant to remind one that behind everything is the power and providence of God. Thus, for instance, when one sees unusual sites, such as the sea, mountains or rivers, one is to praise God 'who makes the work of creation', and when one becomes aware of the power of nature, by seeing lightning or hearing thunder, one praises God whose 'power fills the world' (mBer 9:1). Additional occasions which require one to praise God are listed in the Tosefta (tBer 6:2-6, p33f) and further expansions of these lists are found in the Talmud.[102]

The Mishna also requires one to praise God on more personal occasions: such as when buying new household items or when receiving important information – whether good or bad. For good news one praises God 'who is good and does good', while for bad news one praises Him 'who is the true judge' (mBer 9:2-3).

A special category of occasional blessings is the blessing on the occasion of fulfilling a commandment. Although not even hinted at in the Mishna, the Tosefta declares that one is required to recite a blessing upon the fulfilment of any commandment (tBer 6:9, p36). The earliest mention of this obligation includes a formula for this blessing. The quotations begins with the closing formula of the blessing, 'who has sanctified us by his commandments and

---

[100] For a suggested resolution of this problem see Büchler, 'History of the Blessing'; Albeck, 'Vierte Eulogie'. The abstract of the three also includes this blessing, see Elizur, 'Abstract of Three'.

[101] Shemesh, 'Grace after Meals'.

[102] Flusser has suggested that the antecedents of one of these blessings, 'who has given of his wisdom to human beings', is found in early Christian sources: Flusser, 'Lost Jewish Benediction'.

commanded us to [do a particular commandment]'. It is presumed that this blessing began with the same opening formula used for all other blessings. Later sources preserved a disagreement about whether the blessing should conclude with the phrase 'commanded us to [do a particular commandment]' or with the phrase 'commanded us about [a particular commandment]'. Rules were formulated about when each type of conclusion should be used (bPes 7a-b). The main importance of this question for the scholar is the insight it gives us into the rabbinic desire to have strictly formulated blessing with no diversity possible.

Some commandments require two blessings. Besides the required blessing when fulfilling a commandment, one was expected to recite a blessing when making an object required for fulfilling a commandment, such as a *sukka* or phylacteries. In this case, one should praise God 'who has kept us alive and sustained us till this time' (tBer 6:9-11, p36). This latter blessing, known as שהחינו (*sheheheyanu*), became a standard expression of particular joy at reaching a milestone in time.

LITURGIES OF SPECIAL DAYS

Festive days, specifically those mentioned in Num 29 as requiring sacrifices additional to the daily sacrifice (Sabbath, New Moon days, the three pilgrimage holidays, the festivals of Tishri), were marked by an additional Amida, known, as observed before, as mussaf. Later theology maintained that this additional prayer was instituted in memory of the additional sacrifice offered in the Temple on Sabbath and festivals. However, critical analysis of the sources suggests that a liturgy on these days was customary before R. Gamliel ordered daily prayers. It is thus possible that this liturgy, performed on Sabbaths and festivals, represents the earliest public liturgy.

The Amida on these days, both the additional one and the one which was part of the regular daily liturgy, was notably different from the Amida on regular week days. We have already noted that the festivals not mentioned in the Tora were marked by an addition without further modification of the prayer. However, on the special days listed above, the regular Amida was modified by the elimination of the middle 12 or 13 blessings, to be replaced by one blessing expressing the significance of the day (*kedushat hayom*). This created an Amida which consisted of only seven blessings. Talmudic sages differ as to the reason for the elimination of the heart of the daily Amida. One theory is that it is not proper to offer petitionary prayer on Sabbath and festivals, while another opinion is that these blessings were eliminated to shorten the service, which could be very long on these days. Scholarly conjecture is that the festival Amida served as a pattern for the weekday Amida, exchanging the single blessing of the holiday for the lengthy series of supplications. It is noteworthy that the New Moon day had both types of Amida. The regular eighteen/nineteen blessing Amida was said in the morning, enhanced by a section about the day which was included in the blessing about acceptance of worship. The additional Amida was then recited, consisting of seven blessings.

There was one notable exception to the seven blessing Amida. On the first of Tishri, the Jewish New Year, three blessings associated with the sounding of the shofar on that day were incorporated into the Amida. Although this would seem to give us a total of ten blessings, there was a consensus that one of the three blessings should be combined with one of the seven standard festival blessings, creating a total of nine. Scholars who were active in the second century CE disagreed about the way that one of the blessings of the *shofar* should be meshed with one of the blessings of the Amida, supporting the scholarly theory that the *shofar* liturgy existed, originally, as an independent liturgy which was later incorporated into the Amida.[103]

LIFE CYCLE LITURGIES

The first ritual of the life cycle, for male Jews, is circumcision. The ritual is accompanied by a short liturgy. According to tBer 6:12f, the circumciser and the father of the child both recite the blessing for commandments. The priest praises God who commanded the circumcision itself while the father of the child praised God who commanded him to bring his son within the covenant of Abraham (*ib.*). A third blessing was recited, probably by yet a third person, which consisted of praise for God who had marked the Jews with the sign of the circumcision (*ib.*). Later sources report that the spectators would wish the father that he may be privileged to raise his child to Tora and to his marriage (KohR 3,2). It has been suggested that this blessing emphasizes circumcision as a sign of salvation as part of an argument with Christianity about these issues.[104]

The next ritual in the cycle of life, the redemption of a first born male, is not represented by any liturgy in the early sources. The earliest source, a report of an event in which R. Simlai (2nd generation, Land of Israel) participated, tells us only that the father made a blessing for the fulfilment of the commandment and that there was a discussion about who should say the *sheheheyanu* blessing (bPes 121b). Later sources present us with a more developed liturgy for this rite.[105]

The literature of the sages gives us no evidence of any rite or liturgy connected with coming of age. An early midrash tells us that the father of a child who comes of age should say, 'blessed is He who has freed me from the responsibility for this one' (GenR 63,10 p693). It is not clear whether this was meant to be an aphorism or the prescription of a formal blessing.[106]

---

[103] See Tabory, 'Place of the "Malkhuyot" Blessing'.
[104] Hoffman, 'Rituals of Birth'.
[105] *Ib.*
[106] See Blank, 'Jewish Rites'.

One of the most imposing liturgical texts in talmudic literature is connected with the marriage ceremony. The ceremony is actually composed of two separate rites. The first is considered a betrothal ceremony and it is marked by a blessing which bears the nature of those blessings recited upon fulfilling a commandment. It is unusual for this type of blessing as it is a long one, opening and closing with the *barukh* formula. It is first mentioned in the Bavli (bKet 7b) in the name of R. Yehuda, a second generation Babylonian Amora. The wedding ceremony itself is celebrated by a series of seven blessings, which includes a blessing over wine.[107]

The final stage of the life cycle is death. Although a person upon his death bed was expected to repent, early sources do not present any fixed liturgy. The confession was much like the biblical confession which accompanied sacrifice – a free composition. Fixed liturgy focussed on the mourners. The blessing for bad news ('the true judge') was also prescribed for a person who heard of the death of a loved one. There was a blessing known as ברכת רחבה (*birkat rahava*), said in the public square after the funeral, which is today unidentifiable. We know that there was an addition to the Grace after meals said in the home of the morners, but this custom has also disappeared and we can not identify it with any certainty.[108]

Appropriate to this section is a blessing recorded in the Tosefta for one who is in a cemetery. One should say, 'Blessed is He who knows your number, He will judge in the future, He will raise you in future in justice. Blessed is He who faithful in His word, quickener of the dead' (tBer 6:6, p34). This blessing returns us to the biblical pattern of blessings. It does not speak to God but rather to the dead, about God. However, it also shows later, perhaps rabbinic, influence in that it is a 'long' blessing, opening and closing with praise of God.[109]

---

[107] For a more detailed analysis see Hoffman, 'Jewish Wedding Ceremony'.

[108] For a more detailed description see Hoffman, 'Rites of Death'.

[109] This blessing is expanded in both Talmuds (bBer 58b; yBer 9:2, 13d) but neither source gives a version which includes the 'thou' formula. In later tradition, this blessing takes the regular form, beginning with 'thou' and creating the incongruity of saying 'blessed art Thou, O God, who... will raise you [from the dead]!'

Select Bibliography

Tabory, *Jewish Prayer* offers a comprehensive bibliography of articles on Jewish prayer published before 1990.

Heinemann, *Prayer in the Talmud* is the English translation of a work based on the author's doctoral dissertation. It was seminal in introducing form-critical methods into the study of Jewish prayer. It presents a study of prayer based on analysis of the prayer texts themselves, rather than on what tradition said about them. Tabory, 'Precursors of the Amida' is a critical, comprehensive survey of Jewish liturgy during the Second Temple period. Falk, *Daily, Sabbath, and Festival Prayers* collects and analyses the prayers found in the Dead Sea Scrolls. It serves as an important source for comparison with rabbinic prayer. Tabory, 'Ma'amadot', is a critical, detailed study of what is known about the liturgy of the *maamad* and includes a suggestion for the origin of this type of liturgy.

Ehrlich, *Nonverbal Language* is a translation of the author's work in Hebrew based on his dissertation. It is a pioneering work on the meaning of the gestures prescribed for prayer (standing, bowing, etc.) for the understanding of the meaning of prayer. Luger, *Weekday Amida*. Based on the author's dissertation, this work provides us with the largest collection of Geniza mss of the Amida, organized as a critical edition of the Amida. It thus presents us with a great number of texts of the earliest version known to us.

Elbogen, *Jewish Liturgy* is the standard work on Jewish prayer, published in 1913, republished in a somewhat updated volume in Hebrew in 1972, and translated into English some twenty years later. Levine, *Ancient Synagogue* offers a critical survey of all aspects of the synagogue, including what was done inside it. Reiff, *Judaism and Hebrew Prayer* is very concise overview of Jewish liturgical history from its earliest times until modernity.

Chapter Seven

The Passover Haggada

Joseph Tabory

The Passover Haggada is the text that is read during the *seder*, the celebration of the Paschal meal. Like prayers and blessings, the Haggada is a text composed for use at home by everybody, scholars and non-scholars. In this sense, it is unlike most of rabbinic literature which was composed by scholars for scholars. Nevertheless, it belongs within the category of rabbinic literature because the formulation of the text was strongly influenced by the rabbis, although they granted the reader of the text a certain amount of flexibility in adjusting it to his own taste and concerns.

For a true understanding of the nature of the Haggada it is, perhaps, best to think of it Haggada as the script of a play, which often includes not only the words said but also the instructions for the performance of the drama. Rabbinic literature contains precise details of the way that the ritual is to be performed, while giving mainly rubrics for the text itself. Modern scholarship has pointed out the resemblance of this performance to the way a symposium was conducted in late antiquity and has even found parallels in the way that the ritual of the *seder* and the ritual of the symposium developed and changed their nature.[1] This article will focus on the text and its development.

The Pre-Mishnaic Haggada

The antiquity of the text that we have today has intrigued scholarship for many generations. It is accurate to say that we have no evidence for any text used prior to the first century before the destruction of the Second Temple. From what we know of patriarchal societies, it is hard to imagine that the meal in which the family sacrifice was consumed was not accompanied by some verbal

---

[1] See Tabory, 'Towards a History'. Cf Brumberg-Kraus, 'Not by Bread Alone'.

elaboration on either the history of the celebration or its significance. This is especially true since the Tora mandates, on several occasions, the explanation of *mitsvot* as part of children's education. One of the more significant passages in this context is: 'And when your children ask you, "What do you mean by this rite?" you shall say, "It is the passover sacrifice to the Lord, because He passed over the houses of the Israelites in Egypt when He smote the Egyptians, but saved our houses"' (Exod 12:26f). However, what form this took is pure speculation.[2]

Apocryphal and Hellenistic literature provide us with some incidental details about the celebration of the Paschal meal in Second Temple times, but the earliest comprehensive description of the Paschal meal, the deeds and the acts, is found in the tenth chapter of Mishna Pesahim, finally redacted by R. Yehuda the Prince at the beginning of the third century CE. Scholars are divided on the value of this description for understanding how the meal was conducted during the Second Temple period. Most agree that some of it does represent practice during the Second Temple, but there is disagreement about the details.

The Haggada According to the Mishna

The mishnaic description of the Paschal ritual tells us that there were three types of texts recited during the evening. We shall list these in the order of their appearance during the evening:

> (1) a set of texts about the food eaten during the evening and explanations of their significance;
> (2) a 'midrash' based on the recapitulation of Jewish history from the times of the forefathers until the entry into the Land of Israel given in Deut 26:5-10;
> (3) songs of praise which included, at least, Ps 113 and, according to the House of Hillel, also Ps 114.

Besides these texts, the mishnaic description refers to blessings which were not unique to the Passover evening: (a) sanctification of the day over a cup of wine at the beginning of the evening; (b) Grace after Meals at the close of the evening and various blessings over foods eaten and commandments performed which were of standard nature.

As far as the antiquity of the three types of passages is concerned: the first is connected with the name of Rabban Gamliel, who flourished in the years after the destruction of the Temple; the second can not be dated at all; and the third includes a disagreement between the Houses of Hillel and Shammai, whose main period of activity is the century before the destruction of the Temple. Our discussion will follow the verifiable antiquity of these passages, beginning with the last element, the songs of praise. We shall then turn to the

---

[2] Cf Hauptman, 'How Old is the Haggadah', 9.

texts about food, and we shall close our discussion with the anonymous midrash whose date can not be determined, even though it may be the earliest of them all.

The Songs or Hallel

Let us begin with the Houses of Hillel and Shammai. The Mishna (mPes 10:6) tells us that a Psalm beginning 'Halleluja' was sung or recited during the evening ceremony, the Passover *seder*. The Houses seem to agree that this refers to Ps 113 which indeed begins: 'Halleluja: O servants of the Lord, give praise; praise the name of the Lord.' However, while the House of Shammai said that only this Psalm was read, the House of Hillel claimed that they read also Ps 114 which began: 'When Israel went forth from Egypt, the house of Jacob from a people of strange speech...'

The Mishna does not give us sufficient information to determine whether this Psalm was said before eating the Paschal meal or afterwards. The Tosefta reports of a dialogue between the Houses which implies that the Shammaites did not reject the reading of Psalm 114 but thought that it should be postponed until after the meal. The reason for this is that this Psalm refers to the Exodus, which had not yet taken place at the original Paschal meal. The Hillelites held that the postponement was pointless since the Exodus did not take place immediately after the meal but only in the morning.

Whether this dialogue is authentic[3] or represents later thought, it reflects a fundamental difference in the understanding of the Paschal meal. The idea that Ps 114 could not be read before the meal because the Jews had not yet been redeemed assumes that the meal is not a celebration of the Exodus but rather a re-enactment of the first Paschal meal. The appropriateness of Ps 113 as part of the re-enactment was explained in later midrashim. This Psalm refers to the Jews as the servants of God, implying that they are no longer servants of Pharaoh. The Jews felt their freedom from Pharaoh at the first Paschal meal, even though the actual Exodus did not take place until morning.

The reading of the Psalm(s) was followed by a blessing which dealt with the redemption and which is generally assumed to be connected with the reading of Psalm(s).[4] R. Tarfon thought that the blessing was a short one,[5] praising God for redeeming the Jews and their ancestors from Egypt. R. Akiva thought that it should be a long blessing, including a prayer that the participants would be privileged to partake of the Paschal meal in the future, in a restored Temple. Scholars have argued that R. Tarfon's version was the older one, prevalent before the destruction, while R. Akiva's was a revised version, reflecting messianic hopes after the destruction.

---

[3] For a general discussion of this problem see Weiss, 'Authenticity'.
[4] See Tabory, previous chapter in this volume.
[5] *Ib.*

This earliest evidence of the Passover eve ritual is consistent with what we know about this evening from non-rabbinic sources. The Book of Jubilees refers to the Jews as follows: 'And all Israel was eating the flesh of the Paschal lamb, and drinking the wine, and was lauding and blessing, and giving thanks to the Lord God of their fathers. and was ready to go forth from under the yoke of Egypt, and from the evil bondage' (Jub 49:6). A similar reference is found in the Wisdom of Solomon where the Jews while participating in the Egyptian Paschal meal are portrayed as, 'Singing the while the fathers' songs of praise' (Wis 18:9).[6] Philo reports that the content of the evening is 'prayers and hymns' (μετ' εὐχῶν τε καὶ ὕμνων, Spec. leg. 2:148), but we have no idea of what type of prayers he was thinking. Both Matthew (26:30) and Mark (14:26) notice that Jesus' last supper concluded with a hymn but its nature is unknown.

The Texts Connected with the Food

We may now turn to the first block of text, the prescribed discussions about the special foods eaten during the evening. After a general question, asking 'How is this night different from all the other nights', three points of difference are singled out in specific questions to be asked: 'The participants dip twice during the evening; they eat only unleavened bread and they eat only roasted meat' (Pes 10:4).[7] The significance of this text has been obscured as the original question about roasted meat was eliminated from the text actually recited during the *seder* in later centuries and two others were added (see below). Based on the original text, scholars have pointed out that these items deal with the three foods required to be eaten at the Paschal meal: *maror*, which was dipped; *matsa*; and the roasted lamb. Once this has been established, one can see a clear relationship between this text and what may be called the Haggada of Rabban Gamliel. The Mishna reports:

> Rabban Gamliel said: Whoever did not say these three things on Passover did not fulfill his obligation:
> פסח (*pesah*, Paschal lamb) – because the Omnipresent skipped over the houses of our ancestors in Egypt.
> מרורים (*merorim*, bitter herbs)[8] – because the Egyptians embittered the lives of our ancestors in Egypt.
> מצה (*matsa*, unleavened bread) – because they were redeemed.[9]

---

[6] The translation is that of Samuel Holmes in Charles, *Apocrypha of the Old Testament*, vol 1, 564f.

[7] The order of these points follow the best mss. See Tabory, *Passover Ritual*, 260-262.

[8] *Merorim* is the generic term for all bitter herbs that may be used at the seder. The term *maror* originally referred to one of these herbs, but in later times, it replaced the *merorim* as a generic term.

[9] The translation follows Bokser, *Origins of the Seder*, 30. Traditional Haggadas have a different explanation for the use of matsa at the seder: because the dough did not manage to rise before God

Rabban Gamliel stressed that it was not enough to point out these differences – their significance had to be explained. The custom of explaining the significance of foods eaten during the meal has parallels in the genre of sympotic literature of antiquity, literature describing in detail meals and the discussions held during them and after them. However, scholars have pointed out that there may be a connection between Rabban Gamliel's explanations of the significance of these foods and the explanations of the significance of the bread and wine consumed at the last supper, whether it was a Paschal meal or not. Indeed, some scholars have thought that Rabban Gamliel's stress on the proper meaning of these foods was meant in opposition to Christian explanations of the bread and wine used in their rituals.[10] It is possible, of course, that early Christian practice picked up on an existing Jewish tradition of explaining the significance of foods, a tradition which was fluid enough to permit Christian re-interpretation. In this case, Rabban Gamliel's statement would have been meant to put an end to this fluidity and establish the one 'correct' explanation.

The dating of Rabban Gamliel's statement is of importance in considering his relationship to Christian ritual. It is generally assumed that Rabban Gamliel is the one who flourished somewhat after the destruction of the Second Temple. This would support the idea, suggested by several scholars, that his emphasis on the proper significance of the unleavened bread eaten at the meal is part of a polemic against Christological interpretations of the bread. It has even been suggested that the emphasis on the eating of bitter herbs as a remembrance of the bitterness of the slavery in Egypt is meant as a polemic against interpretations focussing on these herbs as a remembrance of the bitterness of Jesus' passion.[11] In any case, if Rabban Gamliel's statement is actually a response to the question about dipping at the *seder*, this would support the post-destruction dating as the separate dipping of bitter herbs before the meal seems to be a feature of the *seder* which was added some time after the destruction.

The Midrash

We may now turn to the remaining text mentioned in the Mishna, the midrash based on the Deuteronomic recapitulation of Jewish history (Deut 26:5-10) recited by one who brought his first fruits to the Temple. Regarding the recitation of the midrash, the Mishna gives the specific instruction that one 'starts with shame and ends with praise, and expounds from "My father was a fugi-

---

appeared to redeem the Jews. Naomi Cohen found a parallel to this in the writings of Philo (*Philo Judaeus*, 308f). For a discussion of the rabbinic sources see J. Tabory, *Passover Ritual*, pp. 51-53.

[10] For the most recent discussion of this issue, with references to earlier literature, see Yuval, 'Easter and Passover', 106f. He expanded his ideas in a Hebrew volume entitled *'Two Nations in Your Womb'*.

[11] Yuval *ib*. However, the earliest evidence for a connection between the bitter herbs and the suffering of Jesus seems to be found in Aphrahat, who flourished some 250 years after Rabban Gamliel.

tive Aramean" (Deut 26:5), until he concludes the portion' (mPes 10:4).[12] All three clauses of this sentence have been the subject of vast amounts of scholarly discussion. For purposes of clarity, we shall deal with them in reverse order.

We shall first deal with the interpretation of the closing phrase of the instruction, 'until he concludes the portion'. The phrase can not be taken literally, for the portion closes with the verse, 'Wherefore I now bring the first fruits of the soil which You, O Lord, have given me' (Deut 26:10). This is obviously irrelevant and inappropriate for the *seder* evening and is not part of the *seder* nor could it ever have been. The scholarly discussion revolves around the penultimate verse: 'He brought us to this place and gave us this land, a land flowing with milk and honey' (26:9). This verse does not appear in the rabbinic tradition as part of the Haggada. However, it would have been appropriate for the people who ate the Paschal lamb in Jerusalem, especially when taking into account to the rabbinic midrash that 'this place' refers to the Temple (SifDeut 301, p319). Therefore, it has been suggested that this last verse was originally part of the Haggada, accepting this reading as customary in Second Temple times, and was eliminated after the destruction, or perhaps even earlier, by people who conducted a Paschal meal outside of Jerusalem and the Land of Israel.

Now let us turn to an understanding of the correct translation of the opening biblical verse. The translation cited above, 'My father was a fugitive Aramean', is the modern JPS translation, reading the Hebrew, ארמי אבד אבי, as *Arami oved avi*. Rabbinic tradition reads the verse differently: *Arami ibbed avi*, 'An Aramean [sc. Laban] tried to destroy my father'. Medieval and modern commentators have tended to accept the modern translation as the correct meaning of the verse. In addition, modern scholars have shown that this explanation was also known in antiquity, and it became necessary to explain why the rabbis interpreted the passage differently.[13] It is possible that the issue is related to the preceding one. While the Temple existed, people who included the penultimate verse of the portion in their Haggada understood the passage as presenting a radical change in status. The people had started out as wandering nomads, and now they stand in their permanent home, the land given to them by God. This interpretation fits in well with the Mishna's description of the text as 'beginning with disgrace and ending with praise'. After the destruction of the Temple and the elimination of the penultimate verse, the portion now closed with the salvation from Egyptian oppression (Deut 26:8). Perhaps

---

[12] For the influence of this direction on Christian thought see Ferguson, 'The Disgrace and the Glory'.

[13] Tigay, *Commentary*, 243 has suggested that the rabbis found it difficult to think of their ancestors as Arameans.

this was the reason that the first verse was reinterpreted to deal with oppression rather than with landlessness.[14]

Although the Mishna demands the exposition of the biblical portion, it does not give any details about the nature of the exposition. We have three midrashim on this chapter: one found in Sifrei Deuteronomy (301, p318); a second one is found in the traditional Haggadas; a third is found in Geniza Haggadas.[15] Although the version in Sifrei Deuteronomy might be thought of as the earliest of the three, its great similarity to the version found in the traditional versions has suggested to scholars that it is an interpolation from the Haggada. Be that as it may, the similarity between the two eliminates the necessity to deal separately with the version in Sifrei.

The two versions found in the Haggadas apparently reflect differences between the Babylonian version found in the traditional Haggadas, and the Palestinian version as found in the Geniza Haggadas. The identification of the Geniza version as Palestinian is based, mainly, on two factors, one negative and one positive. The negative factor is that a *responsum* of the Babylonian Gaon Rav Natronai (853–858) vehemently rejects the type of Haggada which is found in the Geniza, going so far as calling any one who uses it as being an apostate.[16] This would seem to show that this text was not prevalent in Babylonia. The positive factor is the fact that some of the halakhic instructions about blessings over food follow the Palestinian tradition as known to us from the Yerushalmi.[17] We may assume that elements common to both traditions reflect practice before Amoraic times, when the division between the Land of Israel and Babylonia became so pronounced.

The Palestinian version of the midrash has very little midrashic material. In fact, it consists only of a few midrashic explanations of the opening verse and an expansion of the closing verse. There are only two comments which are common to both traditions. The first is the opening comment that the meaning of the biblical passage is that Laban tried to destroy Jacob. The second is an expansion of the verse 'and he went down to Egypt', explaining that Jacob did not do so by choice but was forced to do so by the word of God.

There is one other comment which seems to be common to both traditions, i.e., the midrashic expansion to the verse, 'The Lord freed us from Egypt by a mighty hand, by an outstretched arm and awesome power, and by signs and portents' (Deut 26:8). The midrash took this to be a hint to the ten plagues. The first three terms ('mighty hand, outstretched arm, awesome power') would

---

[14] For the possibility that the reinterpretation was influenced by Christian typology see Yuval, 'Easter and Passover', 111-113.

[15] One of the most complete texts of a Geniza Haggada has been published by Fleischer, 'Early Siddur'.

[16] For a further discussion of this see Hoffman, *Canonization*, 7-23. He points out that the polemical tone of Natronai is due to the controversy with the Karaites.

[17] A fuller discussion of the Byzantine Haggada by me will appear in a volume to be published by Yad Ben Zvi.

refer to six plagues, as each term consists of two words; and the final two terms ('signs and portents') refer to four plagues as each of the two terms appears in plural form. Although this explanation appears in both traditions, in the Babylonian tradition it follows another, less fanciful, explanation to the verse and it is preceded by the words 'another explanation' (דבר אחר). Thus, this may be an addition to the Babylonian tradition and an example of the influence of the Palestinian tradition on that of Babylonia.[18] The traditional Haggada, in turn, enhanced this explanation by adding an expanded numerical midrash counting the plagues, an explanation which was yet considered by Rav Saadya, in the tenth century, as a permissible option but not necessary.[19]

The midrash of the traditional Haggada has been shown to be of two distinct patterns. The most common pattern does not really expound the biblical passages but just quotes biblical prooftexts which show the basis for the Deuteronomic passage.[20] Thus, for instance, the verse stating that the Jews went to Egypt 'with meagre numbers' (Deut 26:5) is substantiated by quoting another verse: 'Your ancestors went down to Egypt seventy persons in all; and now the Lord your God has made you as numerous as the stars of heaven' (Deut 10:22). The prooftext is introduced by, 'as it is said', and there is no further explanation. This pattern of what might be called 'primitive midrash', does not appear in the Palestinian version. It has been suggested that it is actually a later version of the midrash.[21]

The other pattern follows more traditional midrash and adds explanations to the biblical text. An example is a text that we have mentioned above, "'And he went down into Egypt" (Deut 26:5) – compelled by the [Divine] word'. This is a remarkable example as there is nothing in the verse which mandates this interpretation, which therefore cries out for a proof text.[22] Another example is the opening passage of the midrash which is also explanatory, without any prooftext at all. However, this example does not follow the regular method of first quoting the verse and then giving the explanation but reverses it, first quoting the explanation and bringing the biblical verse as a quasi prooftext for the explanation.

Many of the expositions are conflations of the two methods. Thus we read: "'...And sojourned there' (Deut. 26:5) – this teaches that Jacob our father did not go down to settle but to sojourn there, as it is said: "For to sojourn in the land are we come; for thy servants have no pasture for their flocks; for the famine is sore in the land of Canaan: now therefore, we pray thee, let thy servants dwell in the land of Goshen" (Gen 47:4).' The first part of this text, "this teaches that Jacob our father did not go down to settle but to sojourn there", is

---

[18] For examples of mutual influence see Rovner, 'Early Passover Haggadah'.

[19] *Siddur R. Saadja Gaon*, 243.

[20] See Henshke, '*Midrash*'. He argues that this was the original part of the midrash.

[21] Rovner, 'New Version'.

[22] See Kasher, *Hagadah Shelemah*, 34.

an example of traditional midrash which expounds the passage. Nothing further is needed here. The second part, 'as it is said: "For to sojourn in the land are we come ... let thy servants dwell in the land of Goshen"', is of the first pattern, quoting a proof text which doesn't really add anything to the exposition.

We have one example of a parallel between the Babylonian and the Palestinian version which demonstrates clearly the issue of conflated midrash. The Babylonian text reads: '"...And the Lord brought us forth out of Egypt' (Deut 26:8) – not by an angel, not by a seraph, nor by a messenger, but the Holy One, blessed be He, in His own glory and He alone, as it says: "On that night I will go through the land of Egypt and strike down every first-born in the land of Egypt, both man and beast; and I will mete out punishments to all the gods of Egypt, I the Lord" (Exod 12:12).' The Palestinian version lacks the proof text, ending with 'He alone'. We can not be sure, however, what the comparison implies. On the one hand, we might think that the original version was an ordinary midrash as it appears in the Palestinian version, and the Babylonian version added a prooftext to make it conform to the other midrashim. On the other hand, it is also possible that the Palestinian version eliminated the proof text.

Once again, the passage has been discussed as a component of the Jewish-Christian polemic in its stressing that Moses was not the redeemer, 'thereby refuting the view that Moses is an archetype of Jesus'.[23] It is notworthy, however, that the polemic, if it really exists, is much stronger in the Babylonian version, where anti-Christian polemic would seem much less relevant, than in the Palestinian version, the home of such polemic as existed.

Later Developments

Changes to the traditional Haggada are documented in Amoraic times. In the Yerushalmi, Rav is quoted as saying that one should recapitulate Jewish history as Joshua had done, beginning with, 'In olden times, your forefathers – Terah, father of Abraham and father of Nahor – lived beyond the Euphrates and worshiped other gods' (Josh 24:2; yPes 10:5, 37d). The passage suggested by Rav appears in both versions of the Haggada.

Rav's suggestion appears in the Bavli in another context. Here it appears as a disagreement with Shmuel over the definition of the mishnaic rubric for the Haggada that one 'starts with shame'. Apparently, the editor of the passage felt that this demand was not fulfilled by expounding the above mentioned Deuteronomic verses but thought that it was reading the passage from Joshua as Rav suggested. However, Shmuel suggested to use another Deuteronomic passage: 'We were slaves to Pharaoh in Egypt' (Deut 6:21). This passage is actually

---

[23] Yuval, 110. Cf P. Winter, 'ΟΥ ΔΙΑ ΧΕΙΡ ΠΡΕΣΒΕΩΣ'; Goldin, 'Not by Means of an Angel'.

prescribed by the Tora as the beginning of a lesson to children who ask about the significance of the commandments. It is interesting to note that it also concludes with the gift of the Land of Israel to the children of Israel. Samuel's suggestion was accepted in the traditional Haggada but it does not appear in the Palestinian Haggada as documented in the Geniza material.

Most of the remaining material in the traditional Haggada can not be dated. The evening ritual opens with an inaugural blessing for the day (*kiddush*), recited over a cup of wine. This is not specific to the Haggada and was customary on all Sabbaths and festivals. The kiddush is followed by dipping of vegetables in a liquid, usually salt water or vinegar. This custom, although not common in most Sabbath and festival meals, is still habitual at modern, festive occasions, although the foods dipped and the sauces may be different.

The Haggada itself opens with an Aramaic presentation of the matsa used at the *seder* as the bread of affliction eaten by the Jews in Egypt, adding an invitation to one and all to participate in the meal. It is almost impossible to date this passage. On the one hand, attempts have been made to show a parallel to this statement in Philo[24] while, on the other hand, it has been suggest that this is an anti-Christian polemic.[25] However, the fact that it does not appear in Palestinian versions of the Haggada suggests that it is late material and of Babylonian origin. The conclusion of the passage, expressing the hope that the participants will yet be free men and will return to the Land of Israel, also argues for a Diaspora provenance.

These Aramaic declarations are followed immediately by the questions prescribed by the Mishna. However, with the passage of time, the number of questions rose from three to four and their content has changed. Changing customs about dipping before the meal caused various changes in the text of this question. When due to these changes the connection between the dipping and the bitter herbs became unrecognizable, an additional question was added which related directly to the bitter herbs, making a total of four questions. In later times, when it was no longer customary to eat roast meat on Passover eve, the question relating to it was replaced by a question about the custom of eating while reclining, rather than eating while sitting upright.

The story of the Exodus begins with the passage suggested by Shmuel, followed by the one proposed by Rav, concluding with the midrash prescribed by the Mishna. Between the passage of Samuel and that of Rav we find two interpolations, but only in the traditional version. The first interpolation is similar to many passages in sympotic literature. It tells of sages who were discussing the story of the Exodus throughout the night until their students came and told them that it was time to recite the morning Shema. Rather than do so, the story tells us that the sages began a discussion *about* reading the Shema, discussing whether there was an obligation to do so in the evening.

[24] Cohen, *Philo Judaeus*, 306.
[25] Yuval, 'Easter and Passover', 105f.

The second part of the story is taken out of context and it is only its inclusion here, following the first part, which gives it its sympotic nature.

The second interpolation is also a composite passage, presenting us with four different types of children and explaining how one should relate to each type.[26] There is no clear reason for including the two interpolations at this point. However, they may be understood as a justification for continuing with different versions of the Exodus, as the sages did and as necessary for the different types of family members.

The midrash is followed by a litany of thanksgiving to God for all the benefits he bestowed upon His people, beginning with the Exodus and concluding with the building of the Temple. The list of benefits appears twice, first as a litany in which every phrase ends with the response *dayyenu* (it would have been sufficient) and the second time as prose. Eric Werner was the first to call attention to the similarity of this list of benefits to the list of benefits given by God to the Jews in the Christian *Improperia* or Reproaches.[27] Werner, convinced of the antiquity of the Haggada, thought that the Reproaches were modeled on the Haggada. Yuval has argued that the relationship should be reversed: *dayyenu* is a response to the Reproaches.[28] The similarity is striking but the fact that the earliest documentation for *dayyenu* is from Gaonic times, and then it is referred to as optional, makes one wonder whether there can be any relationship between it and Christian liturgy.

The litany is followed immediately by Rabban Gamliel's explanations of the foods which were required to be eaten. This, in turn, is followed by the singing of the Psalms mentioned in the Mishna. This part of the Haggada is concluded with a final blessing about the redemption from Egypt whose text and history has been discussed above.

This first part of the Haggada is followed by the meal and the after dinner singing which has become part of the ritual. However, a discussion of those matters is beyond the scope of this paper.

[26] See Francis, 'Baraita of the Four Sons'.
[27] Werner, 'Melito of Sardis'.
[28] Yuval, 'Easter and Passover', 104f.

Selected Bibliography

Tabory, 'Towards a History of the Paschal Meal' summarizes the main ideas presented in idem, *The Passover Ritual throughout the Generations*. This Hebrew work focusses on the history of the ritual from Second Temple times until the modern era.

Yuval, 'Easter and Passover as Early Jewish Christian Dialogue' tries to show that much of the Passover Haggada is a Jewish response to Christian theology about the Passover. Yuval has expanded his presentation and included additional issues in a Hebrew volume entitled *'Two Nations in Your Womb'*. For a critique of his theories see Leonhard, 'Die Pesachhaggada als Spiegel religiöser Konflikte'.

Hoffman, *The Canonization of the Synagogue Service*, deals with developments in the Gaonic period (seventh to eleventh century), arguing that it was in this period that the earlier fluidity of the text was hardened into a precise ritual.

Rovner, 'A New Version of the Eres Israel Haggadah Liturgy' is one of the latest publications of a Haggada from the Geniza, which enables us to recognize the alternate form of the Haggada as it was read in the seder in the Land of Israel. For a more general overview see Leonhard, 'Die älteste Haggada'.

Chapter Eight

Megillat Taanit – The Scroll of Fasting

Vered Noam

Introduction

Talmudic scholars have on occasion wondered at the lack of historiography and historical awareness in the literature of the sages. Many have concluded that our rabbis were indifferent to the events of their day as well as to the rest of the post-biblical Jewish history. These scholars have argued that the rabbis had viewed their own purpose as limited solely to their work in the fields of halakha and exegesis.[1] In this light, it is surprising to discover that a document of a semi-historical character is the first to have been produced by our early sages, and that they regarded this document with respect and granted it special status. This Document is Megillat Taanit.

MegTaan originated among the sages of the Second Temple era and is the earliest known Pharisaic document to have survived. The Scroll is essentially a list of about thirty-five dates drawn up in Aramaic and arranged in calendar order. Its goal, as stated in its opening sentence, is to keep the Jews from fasting on 'days on which miracles had been performed for Israel'.[2] On days commemorating especially important events, in the opinion of the compiler of the Scroll, it was forbidden not only to fast, but even to eulogize the deceased. The dates listed are, in the main, those of joyous events of various kinds that befell the Jewish people during the Second Temple era. The Scroll is aimed at preserving their memory and turning them into minor festive days.

---

[1] See e.g. Herr, 'Conception of History'.
[2] See yTaan 2:13, 66a [= yMeg 1:6, 70c] (Neusner Translation p204; all Yerushalmi translations are from Neusner, *The Talmud of the Land of Israel*, with adaptations where necessary).

MegTaan does not belong to the genre of historical writing, but rather to the halakhic genre, as may be concluded from a number of its characteristics: (a) its purpose, as declared by its initial sentence, is halakhic: to prohibit fasting and eulogizing on certain dates of the year; (b) the historical events commemorated on these dates are hinted at in the Scroll only in brief, little or no relevant detail being provided; (c) events are listed in the Scroll in calendar order, rather than chronologically. Nonetheless, the Scroll reflects a paradoxical relationship between an overt halakhic aim and a covert historical goal. Whereas the historical events mentioned in the Scroll are adduced only for a halakhic purpose, the prohibition of fasting exists only in order to preserve the memory of those very same historical events!

It may thus be said that MegTaan does, in fact, reflect an interest the early sages showed in the history of the Jewish nation in the Second Temple period, and the religious significance they accorded to this history. The redactors of the Scroll singled out about 35 events they deemed worthy of being fixed in the Jewish calendar. These events had transpired during a period of c. 500 years, from the days of Ezra and Nehemiah to the times, at least, of Caligula. However, the means they adopted to shape the collective memory were, typically, not those of historiography, but rather those of halakhic authority.[3] This feature, namely the ambition to shape some kind of historical awareness, alongside the abstention from historiography, has important ramifications for our understanding of the sages' outlook and self-image, in the generation of the creation of the Scroll, as in subsequent generations that maintained it and delivered it to their successors.

It must be noted that the commonly employed name of this compilation, lit. 'Scroll of Fasting', is misleading. It concerns not a list of fast days, but a list of days of rejoicing on which it was *not* allowed to fast. The original name of this list may well have been merely מגילה, 'Scroll', in which case only later was the word תענית, 'fasting', added to it.[4]

An explanatory commentary in Hebrew was later added to the Scroll, known in scholarly literature as the 'Scholion'. Its intention is to identify and elaborate on the events intimated in the Scroll. Thus it adds stories, legends

---

[3] See Yerushalmi, *Zakhor*, 5-26.

[4] The mss reflecting the Palestinian version of the Mishna (Kaufman, Parma, Cambridge-36) as well as the first printed version of the text in Naples, all read in mTaan 2:8 'Any day whereof it is written in the Scroll...' (cited, as all Mishna passages, from Danby, *Mishnah*, adapted where necessary), and not 'Any day whereof it is written in the Scroll of Fasting...', as in the other printed versions of the Mishna (for this mishna see *infra*). The name Megilla, rather than Megillat Taanit, is also to be found in other sources. Grätz, *Geschichte*, 559 n1 viewed it as an abbreviated form. On the assumption that the original name of the document was indeed Megilla, and that it had degenerated into Megillat Taanit at a later stage, see already Dalman, *Dialektproben*, 2; Cassel, *Messianische Stellen*, 71; Ratner, 'Notes on Megillat Taanit', 501; Zeitlin, *Megillat Taanit as a Source*, 4; Lichtenstein, 'Fastenrolle', 258; Urbach, *The Halakha*, 248 n43. But see also: Bar Ilan, 'Character and Origin', 114 n4.

and homilies of various types, relating directly or indirectly to those dates. The Scholion has been transmitted in two versions.

Text,[5] Translation, Structure

1. (אתחיל מגלת תענית בסד)
2. אלין יומיא דלא לאתענאה בהון ומקצתהון דלא למספד בהון
3. מן רש ירחא דניסן עד תמניא ביה[6] איתוקם תמידא דלא למספד
4. מן תמניה ביה ועד סוף מועדא איתקין חגא[7] דלא למספד
5. בשבעה לאייר חנכת שור ירוש' ודלא למספד
6. בארבעה עשר ביה פסחא זעירא ודלא למיספד
7. בעשרים ותלתא ביה נפקו בני חקרא[8] מן ירושלם
8. [בעשרים ושבעה ביה איתנטילת כלילא מירושלם ומיהודה דלא למספד][9]
9. בארבעה עשר לסיון אחידת מגדל [שר][10]
10. בחמשת עשר ביה ובשיתא עשר ביה גלו אנשי בית שאן ובקעתא
11. בעשרים וחמש ביה [נטלו][11] דימוסנאי מן ירוש'
12. בארבעה[12] בתמוז עדא ספר גזרתא
13. בחמשה עשר באב זמן אעי כהניא ודלא למספד בהון[13]
14. בעשרים וארבעה ביה תבנא לדיננא
15. בארבעה באלול חנכת שור ירוש' ודלא למספד
16. בשבעה עשר ביה נפקו רומאי מן ירוש'[14]
17. בעשרין ותרין ביה תבו[15] לקטלא משמדיא
18. בתלתא בתשרי אתנטלת[16] אדכרתא מן שטרא

---

[5] The text herein is that of ms Parma de Rossi 117 [hereunder: ms Parma]. Where necessary, I have made slight corrections to the wording of the ms. Significant additions have been inserted in parentheses, and their nature has been explained in the footnotes. No technical details have been adduced here, such as superscript or subscript letters and so on. In the footnotes a number of prominent textual parallels have been noted from other mss. For complete details, see: Noam, *Megillat Ta`anit*.

[6] ביה [מן] yTaan 2:13, 66a [= yMeg 1:6, 70c]: 'On the first day of the month of Nisan'. According to this wording, the festivity lasted a single day, not eight days as in the extant version.

[7] חגא איתקין] In ms Oxf-Bodl Michael 388 [hereunder: ms Oxf] and in the mss of the Hybrid Version (see *infra*; henceforth HV), and also in bTaan 17b; bMen 65a, in almost all the versions of the text: איתותב חגא דשבועיא (The Festival of Shavuot was restored). According to this version, the event is the 'restoration' of the festival of Shavuot (Pentecost) and not the establishment of an unknown festival.

[8] חקרא בני] This phrase is distorted in ms Oxf: הקראים ביה, 'Karaites'.

[9] This date is missing in ms Parma, but appears in ms Oxf and HV.

[10] שר] This is what it should be, but it is distorted in the mss of the Scroll as צור, צר, For the variants and the identification of the site with Straton's Tower – Caesarea see Noam, *Megillat Ta'anit*, 193-195.

[11] Distorted in ms Parma. For the textual variants see Noam, *Megillat Ta`anit*, 44.

[12] בארבע] In ms Oxf: בעשרה. In the sources of the HV: בארבעה עשר.

[13] בהון] Missing in ms Oxf.

[14] ירוש' - נפקו] In ms Oxf: איתנטילו ביה חומאי ביהודאי מיהודה ומירושלם

[15] תבו] In ms Oxf and in HV: תבנא.

[16] אתנטלת] In ms Oxf: איתבטילת.

19. בעשרים ותלתא למרחשון סתור סורגיא מן עזרתא
20. בעשרים וחמשה ביה אחידת שומרון שורא
21. בעשרים ושבעה ביה תבת סולתא למיסק למדבחא
22. בתלתא בכסלו אתנטלו[17] סמואתא מן דרתא
23. בשבעה בו [יומא טבא][18]
24. בעשרים ואחד בו יום הר גריזים
25. בעשרים וחמשה בו חנכת יומין תמניא[19] ודלא למספד
26. בעשרים ותמניא לטבת יתיבת כנשתא על דינא
27. בתרין בשבט יום טוב ודלא למספד[20]
28. בעשרין ותרין ביה בטילת עבידתא דאמיר סנאה לאיתאה להיכלא ולא למספד
29. בעשרים ותמניה ביה נטל אנטיוכוס מן ירוש'
30. בתמניה ובתשעה לאדר יום תרועת מטרא
31. [בתרין עשר ביה יום טורײנוס][21]
32. בתלת עשר ביה ניקנור
33. בארבעה עשר ביה ובחמשת עשר ביה יומי פוריא אנון ולא למספד
34. בשיתת עשר ביה שריאו למבני שור ירוש' ולא למספד
35. בשבעה עשר ביה קמו עממיה על פליטת ספריה במדינת כלבוס בבית זבדי והוה פורקין
36. בעשרים ביה צמו עמא[22] על מטרא ונחת להון
37. בעשרים ותמניה ביה אתת בשורתא טבא ליהודאי דלא יעידון מן אוריתא[23] ולא למספד
38. להן אנש דאיתי עלוהי אסיר בצלו[24]

1. (I shall begin Megillat Taanit with Heaven's help).
2. These are the days on which one is not to fast and on some of which one is not to eulogize.
3. From the beginning of the month of Nisan until the eighth of it[25] the daily sacrifice was settled – one is not to eulogize.
4. From the eighth of it [Nisan] until the conclusion of the festival the holiday was fixed[26] – one is not to eulogize.
5. On the seventh of Iyyar – the dedication of the wall of Jerusalem, one is not to eulogize.

[17] אתנטלו] ms Oxf: עדו.
[18] יומא טבא] Missing in ms Parma but found in ms Oxf and HV.
[19] חנכת יומין תמניא] In ms Oxf: ימי חנוכה.
[20] ודלא למספד] Missing in ms Oxf.
[21] This date is missing in both mss Parma and Oxford; it is found in the HV and is mentioned in both Talmuds. In the Yerushalmi the reading is: יום טיריון.
[22] עמא] Missing in ms Oxf.
[23] דלא-אוריתא] Missing in ms Oxf.
[24] להן-בצלו] Missing in ms Oxf. Appears in the HV and is cited in both Talmuds.
[25] According to the wording in the Yerushalmi, this occurrence was on the first day of Nissan only. See n6 supra.
[26] According to a variant reading: 'The festival of Shavuot was restored'. See n7 supra.

6. On the fourteenth of it [Iyyar] – the Little Passover, and one in not to eulogize.
7. On the twenty-third of it, the men of the Akra [the fortress] left Jerusalem.
8. [On the twenty-seventh of it, the coronation tax was removed from Jerusalem and from Judea, and one is not to eulogize.]
9. On the fourteenth of Sivan, Sher Tower [= Straton's Tower,[27] later Caesarea] was captured.
10. On the fifteenth of it and on the sixteenth of it, the people of Beth Shean and the Valley went into exile.
11. On the twenty-fifth of it the 'Demosnaei' [= tax collectors[28]] left Jerusalem.
12. On the fourth of Tammuz, the book of decrees was removed.
13. On the fifteenth of Av [falls the] time for the wood of the Priests, and one is not to eulogize (on them).
14. On the twenty-fourth of it we returned to our law.
15. On the fourth of Elul, the dedication of the wall of Jerusalem, and one is not to eulogize.
16. On the seventeenth of it, the Romans left Jerusalem.
17. On the twenty-second of it, they[29] began again to kill the apostates.
18. On the third of Tishri the mention was removed[30] from the documents.
19. On the twenty-third of Marheshvan the *soreg* (latticed partition) was torn down from the [Temple's] courtyard.
20. On the twenty-fifth of it Samaria was captured – the wall.
21. On the twenty-seventh of it, the fine flour was once again offered up on the altar.
22. On the third of Kislev the banners of the Roman Emperor[31] were removed from the courtyard.
23. On the seventh of it [a festival].
24. On the twenty-first of it – the day of Mount Gerizim.
25. On the twenty-fifth of it – Hanukka of eight days,[32] and one is not to eulogize.
26. On the twenty-eighth of Tevet the 'Kenishta'[33] took its seat for judgment.
27. On the second of Shevat a festival and one is not to eulogize.[34]
28. On the twenty-second of it, the (pagan) cult which the enemy ordered to bring into the Temple was cancelled, and one is not to eulogize.
29. On the twenty-eighth of it, Antiochus left Jerusalem.
30. On the eighth and ninth of Adar – the day of the rain blast.
31. [On the twelfth of it – the day of Turianus[35].]
32. On the thirteenth of it – [the day of] Nicanor.

---

[27] Στράτωνος πύργος, see Josephus, Ant 13:324-335.

[28] Probably from the word δημοσιῶναι, tax collectors.

[29] They] According to ms Oxf and the HV: חבנא = in first person. See *supra* n15.

[30] Was removed]. According to ms Oxf and the Bavli: 'was nullified'. See n16, *supra*.

[31] In the Aramaic original סממאות. Probably from the word σημαῖαι, 'standards'. See Josephus, War 2:169-174.

[32] Hanukka of eight days] or 'the days of Hanukka'. See *supra*, n19.

[33] 'Kenishta' – Knesset, Sanhedrin.

[34] one is not to eulogize] See n20, *supra*.

[35] Turianus] See n21 *supra*.

33. On the fourteenth of it and the fifteenth of it – these are the days of Purim, and one is not to eulogize.
34. On the sixteenth of it, they began to build the wall of Jerusalem, and one is not to eulogize.
35. On the seventeenth of it the gentiles rose up against the remnant of the scribes in the city of Chalcis[36] in the House of Zabdi, and a salvation occurred.
36. On the twentieth of it the people[37] fasted for rain, and it [rain] fell on them.
37. On the twenty-eighth of it good tidings arrived for the Jews that they need not deviate from the Tora,[38] and one is not to eulogize.
38. Except for a person who has [previously] taken a fast-vow [who has taken it upon himself in prayer?].[39]

The list has a halakhic heading, stating 'These are the days on which one is not to fast'. It also closes with a halakhic utterance, restricting the validity of the prohibition on fasting and allowing only a person who already 'has taken a fast-vow' to fast on those days. A baraita cited in the Talmud alongside these words explains them in the following manner:[40]

> An individual who accepted upon himself [to fast] every Monday and Thursday (and Monday) of the entire year and holidays recorded in MegTaan occurred on them: If his vow preceded our decree, his vow will nullify our decree, and if our decree preceded his vow, our decree will nullify his vow.

According to this ancient commentary, the Scroll states that 'its decree', as the prohibition on fasting in the Scroll is called in this source, applies from the day on which the Scroll was made public on, but not retroactively.[41]

The main part of the Scroll is a list made up of short sentences, each of which includes a date and an event that occurred on it. The list follows the calendar, rather than the chronological order of events mentioned. It breaks down into months according to the biblical calendar, from Nisan to Adar. The first date in each month mentions the name of the month; those that follow use the notation ביה, 'in it'. The various events are referred to in the Scroll by means of mere hints, characterized by extreme brevity. The time, circum-

---

[36] Chalcis] This name has become distorted in the mss of the Scroll. See Noam, *Megillat Ta'anit*, 48. This is the correct reading, and it appears in this way in the Yerushalmi.

[37] The people] see n22, *supra*.

[38] Need not deviate from the Tora] see n23 *supra*.

[39] The meaning of the word בצלו is disputed: 'by vow' or 'in prayer'. This entire sentence is obscure and difficult to understand. The sages of the Talmud already questioned its spelling and meaning. See bTaan 12a, as well as the commentaries of Rosenthal, 'Words Sorting', esp 36-43 and Schremer, 'Concluding Passage'. Further opinions were adduced by Schremer *ib.* 413-414 and n9; see also Noam, *Megillat Ta'anit*, 337 n42.

[40] bTaan 12a. This baraita can be found, with certain textual changes, in both Scholia (see Noam, *Megillat Ta'anit*, 130, and below).

[41] A number of medieval commentators suggested another interpretation, more remote from the simple meaning of this baraita. See Noam, *Megillat Ta'anit*, 337f.

stances and protagonists of those events are not explicit, and consequently many of them have remained obscure.

Historical Events Mentioned

Many scholars who have studied the Scroll, starting with Heinrich Grätz,[42] classified the festive days in accordance with the periods of the historical events that gave rise to them. The descriptions of these days are, however, laconic and obscure, and the nature of about half of the events hinted at, is uncertain. Each scholar established identifications following his own preferences, resulting in great differences of opinion. An attempt shall be made here to classify the events listed in the Scroll in as objective a manner as possible, separately discussing festive days which can be identified with certainty and those which are doubtful, in accordance with the various hypotheses prevalent in the scholarly literature.[43]

The events the Scroll puts on the calendar took place, in the main, during the Second Temple period. Among those identifiable with certainty, nine relate to the Hasmonean era down to the times of Alexander Yannai, and another four or five with probability. Only a few events precede the Maccabean insurrection, while a very few belong to the Roman period. Almost half of the events cannot be identified with any degree of certainty.

Events identifiable with certainty are: the Hasmonean dedication of the Temple (25 Kislev, 1. 25); the victory over Nicanor (13 Adar, 1. 32); Antiochus' departure from Jerusalem[44] (28 Shvat, 1. 29); capture of the Jerusalem Akra (23 Iyyar, 1. 7); a date linked with a new dating formula used in documents from the Hasmonean period[45] (3 Tishri, 1. 18); the conquest of Samaria (25 Marheshvan, 1. 20); the conquest of Beth-Shean (15-16 Sivan, 1. 10); the destruction of the Gerizim Temple in the days of John Hyrcanus (21 Kislev, 1. 24); the capture of the 'Sher Tower' – Straton's Tower – in the days of Alexander Yannai (14 Sivan, 1. 9).

It is probable that at least one of the three dates of the building of the wall of Jerusalem (7 Iyyar, 4 Elul and 16 Adar; ll. 5, 15 and 34) commemorates the completion of a Hasmonean wall. Likewise, it would seem that at least one of

---

[42] The first comprehensive study of MegTaan was made by Grätz, *Geschichte*, 559-577, as an appendix to the third volume of his great work. This served as the jumping-off point for all those who followed him. Grätz was the one who informed the world of the nature of the distinction between the Scroll and its Scholion, and also coined the term, 'Scholion', for this commentary. He was the first to interpret the events referred to in the Scroll independently of the explanations proposed in the Scholion.

[43] For a detailed discussion of the identification of all dates to be listed *infra*, see Noam, *Megillat Ta'anit*, 163-315, 'The Meaning of the Moadim'.

[44] Scholars argue whether the Antiochus mentioned was Antiochus Epiphanes or Antiochus Eupator. In either case, the relevant period was doubtlessly the early Hasmonean era.

[45] The precise nature of the event is unclear. Yet this obscurity does not cast doubt upon its accepted belonging to the Hasmonean period.

the dates of 27 Iyyar and 25 Sivan (ll. 8, 11), dealing with the cancellation of taxes, refers to one of the cases known from the Hasmonean period,[46] in which a burden of taxation was lifted from the shoulders of the Jews.

The nature of the event hinted at on 23 Marheshvan (l. 19) is obscure. Yet the wording of the Scroll at this point, together with the language of the relevant explanation in the Scholion, points to the Hasmonean period. The mysterious 'Salvation' that occurred in Lebanon (17 Adar, l. 35) has been ascribed by several scholars (following the Scholion) to the days of Alexander Yannai, while others see it as relating to the war waged by Yonatan the Hasmonean. In either case, it, too, belongs to the period of the Hasmonean kingdom.

Only two dates from the entire list belong clearly to the Roman period: the voiding of the 'idolatry in the Temple' decree in the days of the Emperor Caligula (22 Shevat, l. 28), and the mysterious departure of the Romans from Jerusalem on 17 Elul (l. 16). Whatever event this may be referring to, it seems that it, just like the first, occurred before the destruction of the Temple.

Besides these, the Scroll commemorates two biblical festive days (14 Iyyar and Purim, ll. 6, 33) and another which reflects an ancient custom of bringing wood to the Temple, the precise inception of which is difficult to define (15 Av, l. 13). It is possible that yet another date, one of three dates relating to the construction of the Jerusalem wall (7 Iyyar, 4 Elul or 16 Adar), is early, referring to the days of Nehemiah.

Between fourteen and seventeen dates in the Scroll are unclear and uncertain: 1-8 Nissan (l. 3); 8 Nissan to the end of the festival (l. 4); 4/10 Tammuz (l. 12); 24 Av (l. 14); 22 Elul (l. 17); 27 Marheshvan (l. 21); 3 Kislev (l. 22); 7 Kislev (l. 23); 28 Tevet (l. 26); 2 Shvat (l. 27); 8-9 Adar (l. 28); 12 Adar (l. 31); 20 Adar (l. 36); and 28 Adar (l. 37).[47]

The Scholion explains six of these dates as denoting the victory of the sages over the Sadducees or the Boethusians: 1-8 Nissan; 8 Nissan until the end of the festival; 4/10 Tammuz; 24 Av; 27 Marheshvan; and 28 Tevet. These commentaries of the Scholion have been studied thoroughly in the scholarly literature dealing with the Second Temple period, especially in the framework of the historical debate concerning the nature of the 'sects' of Second Temple Judaism. Some scholars rejected *a priori* all the anti-Sadducean commentaries on the dates adduced in the Scroll,[48] while others accepted them.[49] Those who

---

[46] A minority opinion links the date 27 Iyyar with the banishing of idolatry, rather than with an exemption from taxation. Yet even according to this opinion, the event occurred at the onset of the Hasmonean period.

[47] The only ones listed here are those whose historical period is entirely unknown. Doubts concerning details of the events exist also in the cases listed above. To this list of 'doubtful' cases one may add the three dates of the construction of the wall noted *supra*. One of these may refer to the days of Nehemiah, one or two of them – to the Hasmonean Period, and one might actually commemorate the third wall begun by Agrippas and completed at the onset of the Great Revolt.

[48] See, e.g., Zeitlin, 'Nennt Megillat Taanit'; Wellhausen, *Pharisäer und Sadducäer*, 56-63; Moore, *Judaism*, vol 1, 160; vol 3, 27, 46; Efron, *Studies*, 167-171.

basically accept the Scholion's exegesis of these six dates, link the Pharisaic victories hinted at in the Scroll with the days of Queen Shelomtsion (Salome Alexandra, early first cent. BCE) or even earlier. Others reject the identification with Pharisaic victories over the Sadduccees and tend to explain the Scroll's intimations[50] as the renewal of the sacrifices in the Temple or the removal of gentile rule following the Hasmonean victories. One way or the other, these dates belong to the Hasmonean period.

Of the other doubtful dates four have been linked, according to a few scholarly opinions, with the Roman Era. 1. One of the two dates defined in the Scroll as 'a festive day' without further explanation (7 Kislev, 2 Shevat – ll. 23, 27) is explained in the Scholion as commemorating the death of Herod.[51] 2. The סמואתא expelled from the courtyard on 3 Kislev (l. 22) have been identified by many scholars with the Roman *signa*, banners, and the date has generally been explained as the removal of the banners of the Emperor Tiberius from Jerusalem. 3. The date 12 Adar (l. 31), according to its wording in the Babylonian Talmud: Turyanus day, and the tale that appears there as an explanation, has been linked by scholars to the period of the Emperor Trajan. 4. The 'good tidings' of 28 Adar (l. 37) have been ascribed by some, in accordance with one of the two versions of the Scholion and its parallel in the Bavli, to the abrogation of Hadrian's decrees.

In summation, MegTaan fixes for commemorative purposes a long series of Hasmonean victories, together with several early dates and a few isolated later ones. The later events are from the seven decades between the death of Herod and the destruction of the Temple. Two dates may cautiously be interpreted as relating to events from the second century CE and, if so, may have been added at a later stage. It would seem that many of the semi-festive dates listed in MegTaan were already well-established when the Scroll was redacted, during the decades immediately preceding the destruction of the Temple (see below). This is certainly true of the biblical dates, the date of the Wood Sacrifice and a number of Hasmonean dates (the fixation of Hanukka and Nicanor Day and the commemoration of the capture of the Akra appear explicitly in Maccabees I). The opinion held by many that the compiler combined well-known ancient dates with later ones fixed by him and his 'faction'[52] therefore seems reasonable. One cannot be sure whether he was responsible for the precise halakhic wording whereby it was 'decreed' forbidden to eulogize or to fast, thus transforming a mere anthology of historical events from popular

---

[49] See, e.g. Lichtenstein, 'Fastenrolle'; Mantel, 'Megilat Ta'anit'; Herr, 'Who Were the Boethusians?' esp 7-9.

[50] The settling of the issue of the daily sacrifice, the fixing of a festive day, the removal of the book of decrees, the return to the law, the restoration of the fine flour to the altar, the convening of the 'Kenishta' to judge.

[51] The Scholion to 7 Kislev. Many scholars, however, ascribe this explanation to the other date – 2 Shevat.

[52] bShab 13b, see below.

tradition into a halakhic document.[53] Alternatively, the prohibition of fasting on these occasions may have been transmitted while embedded in the custom of earlier generations, the final redactor being merely an available scribe. It may be noted in passing that the term גזירה, 'decree', used in the Scroll in connection with the prohibition to fast,[54] is typical of anonymous, institutional halakha of the earliest Tannaim.[55]

Date and Origin

Both internal features and external indications testify to the time when Meg-Taan was compiled. Its antiquity is demonstrated by the very authority of its composers to impose 'decrees' of fast prohibition overriding vows. The picture we get of the multiplicity of fasts[56] and vows[57] is characteristic of Second Temple Jewish society in the Land of Israel. Furthermore, the Aramaic dialect in which the Scroll is written matches that of contemporary Intermediate Aramaic. The latest event which can be identified with certainty[58] (22 Shevat, 1. 28) relates to Caligula's plot to introduce an idol into the Temple and the abrogation of his decree upon the timely murder of the Emperor. These events took place in the years 39-41 CE, and the Scroll must have been written after that date. However, it is difficult to assume that the initiative to promote events such as provisional Jewish victories over the Romans (see 17 Elul, 1. 16) to actual festive days was taken after the destruction of the Temple, when the bitter result of the insurrection against the Romans became obvious. These considerations limit the period during which MegTaan was compiled to the last thirty years prior to the destruction of the Temple, i.e., between 41 and 70 CE. Such internal conclusions are compatible with the testimony of a baraita in bShab 13b: 'The Rabbis taught: Who wrote Megillat Taanit? They said: Hanania ben Hizkia and his faction, who cherished (the memory of) the troubles.' The baraita was adduced in the Talmud because Hanania ben Hizkia was mentioned in the Mishna (mShab 1:4) discussed there: '...These are among the halakhot which the Sages enjoined in the upper room of Hanania ben Hizkia ben Garon when they went up to visit him. They voted, and Beit Shammai outnumbered Beit Hillel; eighteen things did they decree on that day.'[59] Further on in the Babylonian sugya we read:

---

[53] See, e.g., the opinion of Urbach, *The Halakha*, 44, 248.

[54] See *supra*, 'Text, Translation, Structure'.

[55] For the antiquity of the term גזירה 'decree', its meaning and relevant literature see Urbach, *The Halakha*, 11, 15f, 55-57, 239 n1, 254 n59.

[56] See Margulies, 'Moadim ve-tsomot'; Grintz, *Sefer Yehudith*, 132; Alon, 'The halacha', 189f; Alon, 'Le-yishuva shel baraita ahat'; Gilat, 'On Fasting', 3-7 [= Gilat, *Studies*, 110-114]

[57] See S. Lieberman, *Greek*, 115 ff.

[58] For events which possibly belong to the second century CE, see above, 'Historical Events Mentioned'. Nevertheless, these identifications are doubtful, see *ib*.

[59] Danby, *Mishnah*, 100.

> Rav Yehuda said in the name of Rav: Indeed, that man is to be remembered favourably, Hanania ben Hizkia is his name, because if not for him, the Book of Ezekiel would have been concealed because its words contradicted the words of the Tora. What did he do? They brought up to him three hundred barrels of oil and he sat in an upper chamber and expounded them.[60]

The legendary figure of the sage who 'wrote Megillat Taanit' combines three extraordinary features: in his upper room, Beit Shammai outnumbered Beit Hillel; he struggled over the preservation of Ezekiel; and he headed a 'faction' that tried to fix a commemoration of miracles because of its predilection for 'troubles', i.e., for the salvation that follows them. One version of the Scholion repeats the tradition about the composition of the Scroll with a minor change: 'The faction of R. Eliezer [sic] ben Hanina ben Hizkiahu from Goron: they wrote down Megillat Taanit because they were not used to troubles and there were no troubles which befell them...' A number of Tannaic traditions mention the name of Elazar ben Hanina ben Hizkia.[61] It would seem from these traditions that the son of Hanania ben Hizkia lived at the time of the Temple,[62] that he too was close to Beit Shammai,[63] and that an attempt to resolve textual questions in the Book of Ezekiel[64] was attributed to him as well.

A fascinating historical hypothesis about this person and his work was proposed by Grätz.[65] He identified Elazar ben Hanania, the disciple of Beit Shammai and the alleged compiler of MegTaan, with Eleazar son of Ananias the priest, the *strategos* of the Temple and leader of the zealots mentioned by Josephus – indeed the man to interrupt the sacrifice for the Emperor at the outbreak of the insurrection.[66] According to Grätz, a zealous-patriotic trend from the insurrectionist camp, the men of Beit Shammai, was an undercurrent of the composition of the Scroll. These people desired to perpetuate and magnify past Hasmonean victories in order to stir up the national insurrectionist spirit in the present. To these historical glorious victories they added temporary achievements made at the onset of the Revolt against the Romans, for which they determined days of commemoration as well. According to this theory, the precise time of compilation of the Scroll is to be restricted to the years of the Great Revolt against the Romans, the very last years the Temple stood.[67]

[60] Cf bHag 13b and bMen 45a.
[61] See the discussion by Grätz, *Geschichte*, 819 n1.
[62] Semahot 6:11, p135.
[63] See MekRY, Ba-hodesh 7 (p229). Compare the words of Shammai, MekRSbY 20:8 (p148); bBetsa 16a; PesR 23 (115b).
[64] SifDeut 294 (p313).
[65] Grätz, *Geschichte*, 805-813.
[66] Josephus, War 2:408.
[67] The proponents and opponents of this theory are listed by Ben-Shalom, *The School of Shammai*, 252f and n7-9. See also Epstein, 'Sifrei Zuttah Parashat Parah', 52f [= Epstein, *Studies*, 147f]; idem, *Prolegomena*, 513; Lieberman, *Greek*, 182-184. Ben Shalom ib. 252-272 and Hengel, *Zealots*, 203 accept Grätz's theory almost word for word and state that MegTaan and the 'eighteen

Grätz's theory combines internal and external testimony into an impressive historical picture. Yet one should remember that the political trend Grätz associated both with the controversy between Beit Shammai and Beit Hillel and with the compilation of MegTaan is a construct based upon a hypothesis. The combination of Josephus' Eleazar son of Ananias with the legendary attribution of MegTaan to the Tanna Elazar ben Hanania is tempting but far from depicting historical facts. Thus there is no compelling need to assume the existence of a political background for the composition of MegTaan.

Bearing in mind all of this we might conclude that the combined internal and external data indicates that the Scroll was written sometime during the three decades preceding the fall of the Temple. It may have originated in circles close to Beit Shammai, and it is possible that the motivation behind its writing was a zealous, nationalistic doctrine, though there is no unambiguous evidence for this hypothesis.

The Scholion and its Two Versions

From ancient times an explanatory tradition dubbed the 'Scholion' has been appended to the Scroll. In its extant form the language of this document combines Mishnaic Hebrew spotted with ancient terms, with infelicitous, incorrect phrases and influences from Babylonian Aramaic. Large sections of the Scholion contain parallels to the Talmud and to other Tannaitic and Amoraic literature, but nearly half of it is unknown from any other source. Scholars differed as to the degree of literary and historical authenticity to be ascribed to this unique testimony to the Temple period, just as they differed as to its nature in general. Some have viewed it as an anthology of very early traditions edited either at the conclusion of the mishnaic period or during that of the Talmud, while others have suggested that it is nothing but a late mixture of isolated quotations and independently phrased passages, compiled in the later Middle Ages.[68] However, many of these scholars have studied the traditions of the Scholion in light of a prior reconstruction as to the sectarian struggle during the Second Temple period and the nature of the spiritual movements prevalent in those days.[69] Moreover, a renewed examination of the manuscripts has revealed that many historical conclusions were based on philologically uncertain grounds.

The printed version of the Scholion which was at first available for scholarly research is, in fact, a late medieval composition which combined and

---

things' decrees 'were perpetrated by Zealots who had an important role in the development of the events which led in the end to the outbreak of the Great Revolt'; see Hengel *ib.* 93, 154, 235-236, 264, etc. It is possible that the explanation of one of the dates in the Scroll confirms this theory to some extent, see Noam, 'The Seventeenth of Elul'.

[68] For a bibliographical review of the advocates of the various opinions see Noam, 'Scholion', 56f n11.

[69] See *ib.* 57f and footnotes.

mixed two separate and, on occasion, mutually contradictory commentaries of MegTaan. The contradictions contained in this hybrid work and the secondary processing it underwent at the hands of its redactors has misled scholars and concealed from them the content and nature of the original documents.[70] It actually appears that there was not a single Scholion, but two separate editions of a commentary to the Scroll which are preserved in their purest state in one single late manuscript each, apart from additional Geniza fragments. I have dubbed these two editions 'Scholion O' and 'Scholion P', after the Oxford and Parma manuscripts which preserve them.

In about half their length, the two editions lack even a single point of contact, handing down completely different basic reasons for the same festive dates. For an example let us cite the explanation of the festive date of 24 Av. The Scroll itself defines this date as follows: בעשרים וארבעה ביה תבנא לדיננא, 'On the twenty-fourth of it [Av] we returned to our law.' The two Scholia explain:

> The Sadducees used to judge on the basis of their own laws, saying: A daughter inherits with the daughter of a son. Rabban Yohanan ben Zakkai said to them: On what grounds do you say so? But they could bring no proof from the Tora...The day on which they (the sages) overcame them (the Saducees), they designated as a festive day. (Scholion P)

> During the kingdom of the Greeks judgment was rendered according to gentile law, and when the kingdom of the Hasmonean House got the upper hand, they went back to render judgment according to the law of Israel. (Scholion O)

Scholion O explains the festive day as a return from 'gentile law' to 'Jewish law' during the period of Greek ascendancy, while Scholion P relates the date to an internal legal dispute: the disagreement between Pharisees and Sadducees over problems of daughters inheriting. As mentioned above, in about half their length the two Scholia hand down a different reason for the festival. A comparison of the two Scholia with regard to the other half of their explanations shows common features ranging from two quite different texts to similar content handed down in slightly different wording. Sometimes a single nuclear tradition is common to both scholia, but this tradition is then phrased in two different versions, regarding either the actual event or various particulars associated with it. Each redaction is also characterized by distinct terms for identical concepts. The date of 4 Tammuz can serve as an example. The event mentioned is: באארבעה בתמוז עדא ספר גזרתא, the book of decrees was removed. The explanation given in the Scholia is as follows:

> Because thus there was written and kept [i.e. publicized] by the Sadducees a book of decrees: These are to be burned, these are to be slain (and) these are to be strangled. And should someone say to them: How [is it learned] that this one is liable to stoning and this one is liable to burning? – they were unable to bring proof from the Tora, only that a book of decrees was written and kept by them

---

[70] On the misleading nature of Lichtenstein's critical edition see *infra*, 'Editions'.

[i.e. publicized]. The day they [the sages] annulled it [the book] they designated as a festive day. (Scholion P)

For the Boethusians used to write down halakhot in a book, and a person would ask and they would show him in the book. The sages said to them: But does it not state: 'According to [lit. "following the mouth of"] these things I have drawn up a Covenant with you and with Israel;'[71] 'According to [lit. "following the mouth of"] the Tora that they teach you etc.'[72] – this teaches that we may not inscribe [halakhot] in a book [but rather divulge them by word of mouth]. A different matter [= Another explanation]: ['A book of] decrees': The Boethusians used to say: '[An] eye for [an] eye, [a] tooth for [a] tooth'[73] – if [one] knocked his fellow's tooth, his tooth shall be knocked; if one blinded his fellow's eye, his own eye should be blinded, and both shall be equal; 'And they shall spread out the garment before the elders of the town'[74] – the actual garment; 'And she shall spit in his face'[75]: that she should actually spit in his face. The sages said to them, Has it not been already said: 'The Tora and the commandment which I have written to teach them'[76], and it is written: 'And now, write down this song for yourselves and teach it to the children of Israel, put it in their mouth'[77] – 'and teach it': this refers to the written Tora; 'put it in their mouth': these are the halakhot [= the Oral Tora]. (Scholion O)[78]

In this case, there is a single infrastructure underlying the two explanations. The abolition of the 'Book of Decrees' is interpreted in both, unexpectedly, as a victory over the rivals of the Pharisees. But from this point on, the two versions are decidedly different. Scholion P deals, as always, specifically with the Sadducees. It attributes to them a 'book' in which the various death penalties enforced by the courts were inscribed, as the Sadducees 'did not know how to bring proof' for them from the Tora. In this explanation there is no trace of any complaint made by sages against the dissident sect. No mention is made of the prohibition to write down halakhot in a book, nor of a literal interpretation of biblical verses. Even the term בייתוסין, 'Boethusians', does not appear in it, nor anywhere else in Scholion P. However, Scholion O describes two specific disputes with the Boethusians. In this version there is no mention of Sadducees, court-enforced death penalties, or adducing proofs from the Tora. Scholion O itself integrates two clearly distinct traditions, the second one being introduced by the phrase דבר אחר, 'a different matter' or 'another explanation'. The first tradition focuses on the dispute between 'the sages' and the Boethusians on the inscribing of halakhot in a book, while the other lists disagreements over the interpretation of three biblical phrases. The Boethusians

---

[71] Exod 34:27.
[72] Deut 17:11.
[73] Exod 21:24; Lev 24:20.
[74] Deut 22:17.
[75] Deut 25:9.
[76] Exod 24:12.
[77] Deut 31:19.
[78] For a detailed treatment of these traditions see Noam, 'From Philology to History'.

believe these phrases should be understood literally, while the sages reply that there is no 'biblical verse' without accompanying 'halakhot'. While the allegation levelled against the Sadducees in Scholion P is that they were unable to adduce proof from the Tora, in Scholion O the Boethusians are accused of adhering to a literal interpretation of the biblical verses.

Generally, there is a relative distance between the traditions of Scholion O and the parallel traditions brought in the Babylonian Talmud, while in certain points it is more similar to Genesis Rabba,[79] the Yerushalmi,[80] and the teaching of a Palestinian Amora.[81] This gives one the impression of a Palestinian origin for these traditions, as opposed to a more 'Babylonian' origin of Scholion P. This impression is reinforced by the history of its transmission: Scholion O was transferred along the Italian-Ashkenazi route, common to Palestinian traditions, while Scholion P was known in medieval Spain, heir to the Babylonian tradition.

As to the value of the Scholion's evidence, research has shown that some rare, authentic units of literary and historical significance are integrated into both redactions of the Scholion. They each contain historical facts unparalleled in Tannaic literature.[82] Some of these are confirmed by external sources such as Maccabees, Josephus, and Philo, or Qumran writings. At the same time, we find both in O and in P complete units which are nothing but faint, artificial inventions. In many cases it is clear that the compilers were not using any authentic tradition, but merely paraphrased the language of the Scroll or settled for a shallow, evasive wording.[83] Sometimes a fixed literary formula appears in the comments on a number of different festive dates.[84] In both Scholia the language of quotations from the Mishna shows signs of editing. On occasion, certain inner erosion has taken place in one of the compositions, causing vari-

---

[79] See Noam, *Megillat Ta`anit*, 202-205.

[80] See Noam, 'The Seventeenth of Elul', 438.

[81] See Noam, 'From Textual Criticism', 23f.

[82] See Noam *ib.* and the cross-references there.

[83] See, e.g., Scholion P for 14 Sivan, 15-16 Sivan, 3 Kislev, Purim, 17 Adar; Scholion O for 23 Marheshvan and 3 Kislev.

[84] Thus did Scholion P interpret the three dates of the building of the wall (7 Iyyar, 4 Elul, 16 Adar) with the following formula: מפני שבאו גוים וסתרו מחומתה, יום שהתחילו לבנותו עשאוהו יום טוב, 'Because the gentiles came and distroyed from its wall; the day they began to build it, they designated as a festive day.' Wherever the redactor of Scholion P encountered in the Scroll references to hostile elements leaving Jerusalem (23 Iyyar, 17 Elul, 28 Shevat) he attached to it the obscure description: מפני שהיו מצירים להם, ולא יכלו לצאת ולבא מפניהם אלא בלילה, יום שיצאו משם עשאוהו יום טוב, 'Because they were troubling them and they could not exit and enter because of them, but at night; the day they left, they designated as a festive day.' Similarly, the compiler of Scholion O made the following non-obligatory statement on three separate occasions (7 Kislev, 2 Shevat and, similarly, 15-16 Sivan): ששמחה לפני המקום במות רשעים, 'Since there is happiness before the Lord when the wicked ones die.'

ous dates or details in their explanations to merge with one another.[85] On top of all this there are, at least in the extant Oxford and Parma manuscripts, omissions, fragmentation, and serious transmission errors. After generations of debate on the reliability of the Scholia, it seems that one may sum up by saying that neither Scholion O nor Scholion P is a uniform text. Both include vague supplements, difficult spots, and errors. But alongside this reservation, one would do well to recall that a considerable part of the material in both versions represents a small but highly consequential section of ancient traditions of the sages. With regard to their literary and historical value, these sections are not inferior to rabbinic literature as a whole, and should be judged as an integral part of it. This ancient source, however, has suffered two types of damage during its final redaction and transmission: foreign materials have been inserted into it, while its entirety has been adversely affected by a thin layer of errata and omissions.

It appears reasonable to assume that mss O and P reflect two independent attempts at assembling tradition units to constitute a continuous commentary on the Scroll. It seems that the two redactors drew on sources that differed in time and possibly also in location. These collections of sources included historical baraitot as well as aggadic and halakhic homilies. Most of these existed *per se*, without any connection with MegTaan. Only a few were especially composed to explain or comment on a particular date in the Scroll.[86] In some cases the association of a date in the Scroll with a particular event was commonly known, and so it was passed down to both redactors. On occasion they relied on two variations of a single theme. In other cases, an authentic source reached one of the redactors, but not his colleague. It seems that several of the dates lacked explanations or explanatory traditions, as far as both redactors were concerned. So they, or their successors, made up for the deficiencies in an artificial manner, loosely attaching the subject of the date with suitable aggadic or halakhic homilies, developing and expanding the language of the Scroll into an 'explanation', or using vague wording of their own invention.

It seems likely that Scholion O, Scholion P, and the version of the Scholion that is partially adduced in the Bavli, are only three coincidental representatives out of a larger group of aggadic anthologies that were appended to Meg-Taan during the talmudic period. These anthologies, like all orally transmitted traditions and especially aggada, may have been rather incoherent at the outset, both by content and editing. They may have been open to penetration of various aggadic materials over the generations. It is also likely that they were originally incomplete, with various dates being unexplained. One of them had

---

[85] See, e.g., the way Scholion O for 15-16 Sivan uses the explanation of the previous date (14 Sivan), the penetration of elements from the explanation for 21 Kislev into the explanation for 22 Shevat in Scholion P, and the identical motives in the sectarian explanations of Scholion P.

[86] This may be so with the explanation of Scholion O for 14 Sivan; the two explanations for 8-9 Adar, and the Hebrew baraita כל שנדרו קודם לגזרתנו, 'Each person whose vow is previous to our decree', attached to the sentence concluding the Scroll.

the good fortune to be partially quoted in the Bavli, with which it was transmitted and preserved, to be studied again and again by the Bavli adepts. If this text originally contained defects and lacunae, these were rapidly glossed over by the talmudic copyists and experts. However, the non-talmudic commentaries on MegTaan continued their independent and dynamic existence until they reached a final form. When MegTaan went into practical disuse, interest in the dates it mentions waned. The interest in the non-talmudic commentaries aroused only marginal interest, leaving them at the mercy of chance error. Many of their original units were truncated and their language lost more and more of its clarity. Two of these compilations, Scholions O and P, then reached us by chance, both being familiar to us almost solely from the final stage in their transmission: the two unique but defective and erroneous late medieval manuscripts.

All other mss of MegTaan and its commentary, including the printed version, are representative of the artificial combining and processing of the O and P editions carried out in the Middle Ages and reflecting the influence of the Bavli as well. I have named this version the 'Hybrid Version'. The hybridization process was sometimes effected by the simple joining of the O and P versions sequentially.[87] At other times the compiler showed a preference for the wording of one of the two versions, while integrating into it expressions or short phrases taken from the other.[88] There are also instances where one of the basic versions has been inserted between sections of the other: the beginning and the end reflecting O, with the middle section representing P.[89] This is the case, for example, with the aforementioned comment on 24 Av.[90] The explanation referring to the date as that of an external victory (O) – 'During the kingdom of the Greeks, judgment was rendered according to gentile law' – was carelessly joined to its explanation as an internal dispute (P): '...Because the Sadducees used to say...'[91]

When was this coarse compilation created? There are some clues which may reveal its provenance. First to cite the Hybrid Version are two medieval compositions: a tenth century compilation based on the Jerusalem Talmud, known as 'Ha-Yerushalmi ha-Ashkenazy' and created in the vicinity of Italy; and the eleventh century *paytan* R. Menahem be-R. Makhir, who was a transmitter of Italian traditions from Italy to Germany and used the Hybrid version in a poem written for Hanukka.[92] A mention of Karaites which entered the Hybrid Version from a copy of Scholion O demonstrates that it could not predate the eighth or ninth century. It would thus seem that the Hybrid Version originated between the ninth and the tenth centuries somewhere in the Mediter-

---

[87] For details and examples see Noam, 'Scholion', 68-74 and n95.
[88] Details and examples *ib.* 75-77 and n99.
[89] *Ib.* 77-79 and n100.
[90] See above p351.
[91] See Noam, *Megillat Ta'anit*, 86f, 223-225.
[92] For these citations see Noam, 'Two Testimonies'.

ranean basin, where similar anthologies and compilations were common at this period.

The Scroll's Status in Rabbinic Literature

All of rabbinic literature was delivered orally, not only according to its own testimony but also as appears from the phrasing of its rulings, its dialectics and its terminology. The sages and teachers are named תנאים, oral transmitters, and אמוראים, speakers.[93] Yet, this literature consistently refers to our Scroll as a 'written' work. In other words, MegTaan was the only written work used by the Sages, besides the Holy Scriptures. Rashi expressed this as follows: 'All other mishnayot and baraitot were not written down, for it was forbidden to write them down, yet this one was indeed written as a memorial…, therefore this one was called a *megilla*, as it was written in a book scroll.'[94] The extraordinary character of MegTaan is evident not solely from its unusual description as a 'scroll',[95] but also from the terminology adopted by the rabbis who cite the Scroll using the root k.t.v: 'Who *wrote* Megillat Taanit?';[96] 'Festive days *written* in the Scroll';[97] 'These days which are *written* in Megillat Taanit';[98] 'Everything *written* in the Scroll';[99] etc. The sages of the Talmud viewed MegTaan as an unambiguous example of a ruling 'written and deposited' and unassailable by doubt.[100] The phrase used by the Talmud to describe MegTaan, כתיבא ומנחא, 'written and deposited', is an expression of Second Temple period origin meaning 'determined in writing', or 'made public and known to all'.[101]

The halakhic authority assumed by MegTaan is overwhelming. The strict Tora prohibition against violation of an oath[102] is set aside, as we have noted, in favour of the rabbinical prohibition in the Scroll, for if anyone has vowed to

---

[93] See Sussman, 'Oral Tora Literally'.
[94] Rashi's commentary on bShab 13b *s.v.* מגילת תענית. See also Rashi to bEr 62b *s.v.* כגון מגילת תענית.
[95] Recognised as early as Grätz, *Geschichte*.
[96] bShab 13b; see above for the discussion of this baraita.
[97] tTaan 2:4; see also bTaan 10b top.
[98] bRH 19b, and cf bTaan 12a and the Scholion on the last sentence in MegTaan, ופגעו בו ימים טובים הכתובים במגילת תענית, 'And he was encountered by festive days which are *written* in Megillat Taanit.'
[99] mTaan 2:8. See the commentary attributed to Rashi to bTaan 15b *s.v.* שאין משלימין: '…And that which is said: All that is written in Megillat Taanit – as if it was the Bible;' and *ib.* 12a *s.v.* בצלו, 'That which is said 'that it is written' is because Megillat Taanit was written alone.'
[100] bEr 62b.
[101] See Lieberman, *Hellenism*, 86.; Urbach, 'The Derasha as a Basis', 181 [= Urbach, *World of the Sages*, 65]; Rosenthal, 'The Teacher', 8; Kister, 'Notes', 134f; Kister, 'Additions', 44-48; Friedman, 'Publication of a Book'.
[102] See Num 30:3. For an oath overriding the performance of a Tora commandment see mNed 2:2. For the attitude of the sages and of the masses towards the severity of an oath see Lieberman, *Greek*, 115-143; Epstein, *Prolegomenas*, 376-378. For the oath as an institution during the Second Temple period see Benovitz, 'Prohibitive Vow'.

fast on one of the dates listed in the Scroll, his vow is nullified![103] Moreover, the Mishna teaches us that those who decreed the prohibitions against fasting contained in MegTaan also issued additional restrictions to strengthen them. mTaan 2:8[104] states it as follows:

> Any day whereof it is written in Megillat Taanit: 'one is not to eulogize', it is [also] forbidden to eulogize [the day] before; but it is permitted the following day; R. Yose says: It is forbidden both the day before and the following day. [where it is written] 'one is not to fast', it is permitted [to fast on the day] before and the following day; R. Yose says: it is forbidden [to fast the day] before but permitted the following [day].

From this mishna we learn that a public fast must be decreed not only on the days listed in MegTaan,[105] but also on the adjoining days; which ones, is disputed between the first anonymus opinion and R Yose.

Tannaic literature quotes and discusses MegTaan from the generation of Yavne onwards.[106] Hence we may conclude that it was already widely known towards the end of the Second Temple period. From the direct or indirect halakhic discussions of the Tannaim about the Scroll, the impression is gained that the rules promulgated in it were considered valid after the destruction of the Temple as well. Nevertheless, changes did take place in its status on two levels. The applicability of its fasting prohibition was restricted, and its potential expansion was barred. In the Yavne period, Rabban Gamliel rejected the Scroll's prohibition of fasting on Hanukka and Purim (and it is likely that this applied to the other dates listed in the Scroll as well) in the case of a series of fasts which was already under way.[107] After Rabban Gamliel's decease, R. Eliezer and R. Joshua attempted to 'lessen the effect of his ruling' and to strengthen the position of the dates of the Scroll, but to no avail.[108] Another reduction in the status of MegTaan is revealed in a surprising comment from his son, Raban Shimon ben Gamliel at bShab 13b:

> The Rabbis taught: Who wrote Megillat Taanit? They said: Hanania ben Hizkia and his faction, who cherished (the memory of) the troubles. Said Rabban Shimon ben Gamliel: We, too, cherish the troubles, but what can we do? For if we were to come and write, we would not manage [to do so]. Another explanation: a fool is never hurt. Another explanation: the flesh of a dead person does not feel the scalpel.

We may observe that in the generation of Rabban Shimon ben Gamliel, during the Usha period, no miracles and no new dates were added to the Scroll, whether because the 'troubles' – and the subsequent miracles – were too nu-

---

[103] See *supra*, 'Text, Translation, Structure'.
[104] Danby, *Mishnah*, 197 (adapted).
[105] See also mTaan 2:10; tTaan 2:4; bTaan 10a.
[106] See tTaan 2:4-5; R. Joshua's statement in the baraita, bHul 129b.
[107] mTaan 2:10.
[108] tTaan 2:5 and parallels.

merous ('we do not manage'), or because Rabban Gamliel's generation lacked the sensitivity required to identify miracles, like 'the dead' or 'a fool' who do not feel pain.

The comment by Rabban Shimon ben Gamliel shows that he defined the Scroll as a chapter already sealed. It also reflects an attitude of distant respect for MegTaan. When added to our above discussion of mTaan 2:8, this teaches us that the Scroll was well known to the generation of R. Akiva's disciples and that they accepted its halakhic rulings as valid.[109] Some sages even adduced the Scroll as an authority for more remote halakhic issues.[110]

As to Amoraic literature, the opening and the conclusion of MegTaan are quoted in the Bavli, in addition to eleven of the dates it lists. The Yerushalmi adduces the opening as well as the conclusion, together with seven dates. The Bavli also sports a commentary on the dates of the Scroll, a kind of 'Scholion', as it were, referring to eleven of the twelve passages to which we have an explanatory commentary.[111] In most of these cases, the explanation is not presented as a separate commentary, but rather as a direct continuation of the Scroll itself, subject to the first introductory phrase of each date. Thus, for example, the discussion in bShab 21b cites the date of 25 Kislev, Hanukka, as follows:

> (1) What is Hanukka?
> (2) [For it is taught]:
> (3) On the twenty-fifth of Kislev <commence> the days of Hanukka, eight [are] they, on which one may not eulogize [and may not fast].[112]
> (4) For when the Greeks entered the Temple, they defiled all the oils in Temple and when the Hasmonean dynasty prevailed against and defeated them, they made search and found only one crouse of oil which lay with the seal of the High Priest, but which contained sufficient [quantity] only for one day's kindling; yet a miracle was wrought therewith and they kindled [the candelabrum] from it for eight days The following year they designated and appointed them [the days] a Festival with [the recital of] Hallel and thanksgiving.

After (1), the talmudic introductory question, follows unit (2), the introductory phrase, then (3), the quotation from MegTaan, and (4) the explanation, a kind of talmudic scholion which is presented directly following the words of the Scroll without any distinguishing sign.[113]

---

[109] Though from a baraita adduced in bRH 19b we learn that R. Yose is of the opinion that the entire Scroll was invalidated at the time of the destruction of the Temple. Yet this baraita itself, worded as it is in the Tosefta and in the Yerushalmi, undoubtedly focusses on the days of the wood sacrifice alone, rather than on the dates appearing in the entire Scroll. See Tabory, 'When was the Scroll of Fasts Abrogated?'; Noam, *Megillat Ta'anit*, 349f, 355-359.

[110] See e. g. the statement by R. Joshua in the baraita, bHul 129b.

[111] For the opening paragraph of the Scroll neither of the Scholia available to us has any explanation either.

[112] ודלא להתענאה בהון – a mistaken addition not appearing in the mss.

[113] For more details see: Noam, 'Miracle'.

The explanations of the dates of the Scroll adduced in the Bavli clearly resemble more closely the explanations of Scholion P than those of Scholion O. But despite the similarity, Scholion P is not dependent upon our Talmud, for two thirds of it do not appear in the Talmud at all, including authentic, reliable sections. Moreover, Scholion P does not reflect two certain explanations appended to two dates of the Scroll in the Talmud. For these dates Scholion P has other explanations. Scholion O lacks four explanations appearing in the Talmud; in three of these cases, Scholion O bears different and even contradictory explanations. In six other cases, where the contents of Scholion O generally resemble those of the Talmud, they appear in a different version. Thus, neither of the two Scholion redactions available to us is the one that served the Babylonian Talmud, while, on the other hand, neither Scholion O nor Scholion P was familiar with the Talmud's explanations, nor did they make use of them. My study has brought me to the conclusion that the versions O and P are independent parallels – one more similar and the other less so – of the version adduced in the Talmud.

In most cases, the Bavli cites the contents of the Scroll using introductory phrases used for a baraita: תנינא, תני רבנן, תנו, תניא, 'We learned', 'Our rabbis taught', 'It is taught', and so on. However, in a number of extraordinary instances, the Scroll is quoted *without subsequent explanation* after the introductory phrase כתיב, 'It is written', normally employed when citing biblical verses. This reflects the distinction the redactors of the Bavli made between quotations from the 'written and deposited' Scroll itself, and quotations followed by a commentary. In the first case, expressions of reading a written (usually biblical!) text are used. In the second case, the commentary accompanied to the Scroll passage appears to have been recited orally, and thus required an introductory phrase characteristic of Tannaitic quotations.

In the Yerushalmi, only the dates of the Scroll are adduced, without any commentary.[114] Contrary to the introductory formula כתוב, 'It is written', used for biblical quotations by the Tannaim and to some extent by the Bavli as well, the Talmud Yerushalmi always makes use of phrases introducing Tannaic tradition: תנינן, תני, 'We learn', 'It is taught', etc.

Ten *sugyot* in the Bavli deal with MegTaan from various angles and for different purposes; two do so more extensively,[115] the others only briefly.[116]

---

[114] Only with regard to Nicanor day (yTaan 2:13, 66a – yMeg 1:6, 70c) does the Yerushalmi adduce the event involving Nicanor. However, this story does not appear together with the wording of the festive day cited from the Megilla, but rather as a responsum to a separate question: what is Nicanor day? Thus we have no evidence that the Yerushalmi was ever familiar with a continuous scholion.

[115] bRH 18b-19b; bTaan 17b-18b.

[116] See bShab 21b; bEr 62b; bYom 69a; bMeg 5b, 6a; bTaan 12a; bBB 115b-116a; bSan 91a; bMen 65a-b; yTaan 3:10, 66d; yNed 8:1, 40d.

There is also a single, broad discussion in the Yerushalmi (with the addition of two short fragments).[117]

Though the halakhic validity of the Scroll was debated in the Amoraic era (see below), its importance and reputation were in no way diminished. The Amoraic discussions concerned the halakhic status of the Scroll and that of the days preceding and following the dates therein.[118] Both in the Land of Israel and in Babylonia attention was paid to the text of the Scroll as well: R. Hiyya and R. Shimon be-Rabbi debated matters pertaining to its spelling and interpretation.[119] Explanations were also given in both Talmuds for what seemed to be an excess of Scroll dates where the prohibition of fasting might have been derived from some other source.[120]

The central position of the Scroll in the awareness of those generations appears especially from discussions which mention it casually. In bEr 62b, R. Yaakov bar Abba challenges Abaye: '[A halakhic question] such as [halakhic matters concerning] Megillat Taanit, which is written and deposited, may [a disciple] render a legal decision in the vicinity of his teacher?' From this one may deduce that in the generation of Abaye the Scroll was a single written book, and that in addition it was commonplace and of a compulsory nature.[121] The language of the Scroll and even that of its explanatory commentary served as halakhic evidence even in remote matters.[122] Thus, for example, the Talmud in Tractate Yoma used the commentary of one of the Scrolls dates in a peculiar way. This commentary cites the legend of the meeting between the High Priest and Alexander the Great in Antipatris. It is adduced in the Talmud only in order to prove that it is permitted to go out of Jerusalem with priestly garments.[123] A fourth generation Palestinian sage voiced his opinion of the aim of the Scroll: not merely to prohibit fasting and eulogizing, but rather to count the days on which miracles had been performed for Israel.[124] Indeed, there are cases where the talmudic discourses show an interest in the historical nature of the events and try to explain their significance. The aforementioned citation of the Scroll paragraph and its commentary in Tractate Shabbat is quoted there in order to explain, 'What is Hanukka?' In similar fashion the *sugya* in Tractate Taanit asks, prior to the citation of the Scroll with its scholion: 'What is Nicanor?' and, 'What is Trajan?'[125]

Calls for the halakhic invalidation of MegTaan started to be heard, both in Palestine and in Babylonia, during the first generations of the talmudic sages.

---

[117] yTaan 2:13 and the parallel discussions.

[118] See bTaan 17b-18b; bMeg 5b; yTaan (previous note).

[119] bTaan 12a.

[120] Supra, n103f.

[121] See Rashi bTaan 12a *s.v.* מהו לאורויי תלמיד במקום רבו.

[122] See e.g. bTaan 12a.

[123] bYom 69a.

[124] yTaan 2:13, 66a [= yMeg 1:6, 70c].

[125] bTaan 18b.

360

For the entire talmudic period, the halakhic validity of the Scroll was open to debate in both centres.[126] It was only decided, apparently, in the post-Amoraic period to invalidate it entirely, except for Hanukka and Purim. From Tractate Sofrim we learn that in Palestine the Fast of Esther was postponed until after Purim, 'because of Nicanor and his colleagues'.[127] This may indicate that Nicanor's Day, and perhaps additional dates, were still observed in Palestine in the Gaonic Period.

Editions

MegTaan and its Scholion were first printed in Mantua in 1514, and many published editions appeared afterwards based on this edition.[128] Scholars relied at first on the printed text only, which was actually the misleading Hybrid Version. Towards the end of the nineteenth century, it was reported that manuscripts of the Scroll and of the Scholion had been found, but these were not made public, except in the form of lists of occasional textual variants.[129] In 1895 Adolf Neubauer published a first try at a critical edition of the Scroll and the Scholion,[130] but this first venture was of minimal value.[131]

The texts of the mss of the Scroll and the Scholion were first published in full in the critical edition of Scroll and Scholion by Hans Lichtenstein in 1932. He displayed the text in two separate sections, one of the Scroll and the other of the Scholion, in the format of an eclectic inner text with a critical apparatus, together with a list of talmudic parallel sources and a list of medieval quotations of the text. He also listed the numerous printed editions, added an historical introduction for each date, and reviewed the research literature that had been published until his day. However, this edition, which was intended to supplant the earlier printed versions, provided scholars with a 'reconstructed' eclectic text, no less misleading than its printed predecessors. In his inner text,

---

[126] See bRH18b-19b; yTaan 2:13, 66a and its parallels; yNed 8:1, 40d. For a discussion see: Noam, *Megillat Ta'anit*, 355-359; Tabory, 'When was the Scroll of Fasts Abrogated?'; Schremer, 'Concluding passage'.

[127] Sofrim 17, 3.

[128] A list of the printed editions up until the beginning of the twentieth century appears in: Lichtenstein, 'Fastenrolle', 260-263.

[129] In 1864 N. Coronel, *Commentarios quinque*, v-viii reported of a manuscript containing a large collection of works, including MegTaan. The ms, eventually known as ms Vienna, was transferred to S.Z. Halberstamm and afterwards to Avraham Epstein, and was described in detail by Marx, 'Sammelhandschrift'. In 1875 Joel Müller offered a list of differences between the text of the ms and that of the first Mantua printed edition: Müller, 'Der Text der Fastenrolle'. In 1897 Moshe Schwab mentioned the existence of additional mss in the libraries of Parma and Oxford, without reviewing their texts: Schwab, 'Meghillath Taanith'. Three years later Schwab published comments in the name of Alexander Marx, in which he listed also a few textual variants between the mss: Schwab (A. Marx), 'Quelques notes'.

[130] See Neubauer, *Mediaeval Jewish Chronicles*, 2-25.

[131] The inner text is an inconsistent combination, whose continuity and sources are sometimes difficult to identify. The textual variants are defective.

Lichtenstein mixed the two fundamentally different basic versions – O and P – and to this he added the Hybrid Version which he considered a Scholion representation of equal value. His critical apparatus is also defective and does not facilitate the separate reconstruction of each manuscript.[132] The damage caused by the new patchy composition which had come into being in Lichtenstein's edition was greater than the damage caused by its printed predecessors, since it enjoyed the authority of a critical edition and was therefore accepted by scholars who based their historical research upon it, without any re-examination of its component parts.

A new edition of the Scroll and its Scholion was published by the present writer in 2003.[133] The Scroll is edited on the basis of ms Parma, with a critical apparatus that includes the variants in ms Oxford and in the mss of the Hybrid version, together with the variants found in the quotations of the Scroll in the two Talmuds and the variants stemming from medieval quotations. The edition of the Scholion presents synoptically the texts of both Scholia, according to mss Oxford and Parma respectively. Alongside them, one manuscript of the Hybrid Version is displayed, noting in the critical apparatus the textual variants occurring in other mss of this hybrid text. A study of the historical background of the events indicated in the Scroll and in the Scholion is also included, as well as the history of the formulation and transmission of these compositions.

Selected Bibliography

Editions: Lichtenstein, 'Fastenrolle'; Neubauer, *Seder ha-Hakhamim*; Noam, *Megillat Ta'anit*; Fitzmyer and Harrington, *Manual*, 184-187, 248-250.

Studies: Bar-Ilan, 'Character and Origin'; Bickermann, 'Notes'; Brann, 'Entstehung'; Derenbourg, *Essai*; Eshel, 'Megillat Ta'anit'; Grätz, *Geschichte*; Lauterbach, 'Meghillat Taanit'; Lichtenstein, 'Fastenrolle'; Lurie, *Megillath Ta'anith*; Mantel, 'The Megilat Ta'anit and the Sects'; Müller, 'Der Text der Fastenrolle'; Noam, 'From Philology to History'; Noam, *Megillat Ta'anit*; idem, 'Miracle'; idem, 'Scholion'; idem, 'Two Testimonies'; Ratner, 'On the Antiquities of the Jews'; Ratner, 'Notes'; Schmilg, *Über Entstehung*; Schremer, 'Concluding Passage'; Schwab, 'Meghillath Taanith'; Tabory, 'When was the Scroll of Fasts Abrogated?'; Wellhausen, *Die Pharisäer und die Sadducäer*; Zeitlin, *Megillat Taanit as a Source*; Zeitlin, 'Nennt Megillat Taanit?'

---

[132] For details see Noam, 'Scholion', 92 and n155.
[133] Noam, *Megillat Ta'anit*.

Chapter Nine

Piyyut

Ezra Fleischer

Post-biblical liturgical poetry in Hebrew is known as פיוט, *piyyut*, and the poet producing it as a פיטן, *paytan* (sometimes *poytan*), from Greek ποιητής.[1] Dating the beginnings of piyyut remains difficult. Former scholars, puzzled by the fact that no mention of it is apparently to be found in the Talmudic corpus, placed it rather late (seventh-eighth centuries).[2] But modern research, based mainly on Geniza finds,[3] nowadays agree that if strictly defined – as mature poetry deliberately intended for use in public prayer – its emergence cannot be put later than the end of the fourth century. In a broader sense, taking in more or less poetic formulations of some benedictions or prayers, it may be dated somewhat earlier.

Pre-Paytanic Poetry

Poetry was not in fact lacking in the Talmudic period. Several sections of the Mishna, especially those describing Temple ceremonies, are written in a lofty and rhythmic style. Moreover, the Talmud contains here and there sections which demonstrate poetic activity throughout the times of the Tannaim and the Amoraim, and which also point to the function of this poetry.[4] Incidental frag-

---

[1] See below n5. For a broad overview and a tentative list of paytanim (compiled by Avraham David) see Fleischer, 'Piyyut'.

[2] For a customary approach see Elbogen, *Jewish Liturgy*, 210-271 and bibliography there. This chapter was updated (until about 1970) by J. Schirmann.

[3] On the Cairo Geniza see e.g. Reif, *A Jewish Archive*. See particularly (though without regard to piyyut) Goitein's introduction to his monumental book, *Mediterranean Society* 1, 1-28. For the impact of the Geniza findings on the study of paytanic poetry see Fleischer, 'Terumat ha-Geniza'.

[4] For selected texts of this kind see the anthology by Brody and Wiener, *Mivhar*, 3-15. For an analysis of these texts and their relationship to the prosody of Piyyut see Mirsky, 'Ha-shira'.

ments of epithalamia, dirges, private prayers and even riddles occur in Talmud and early Midrash. Even the technical terms piyyut and paytan appear.[5] All these texts allow us to state with certainty that Jewish congregational life in the period of the Mishna and Talmud was in no way devoid of poetic expression. How much poetry was composed or written, we cannot say, but there was more than the few fragments which actually appear in Talmudic literature. This literature naturally makes reference only to those elements which were relevant, directly or indirectly, to the House of Study; poetry was outside its scope.

The poetic fragments which have been handed down to us in the Talmud are essentially secular in nature.[6] Their links with regular worship are either few or indirect. Even those brief prayers, which appear in the Talmud in the name of various Tannaim and Amoraim are personal, non-obligatory prayers, which never aspired to acceptance as part of congregational worship. From this it is clear that the poetry of the period had no function in public prayers. But since the halakha allowed freedom in the wording of the statutory prayers, it is highly presumable that some of the standard benedictions meant to be performed in the public prayer, especially on festive occasions, were re-formulated in a poetical style, comparable to that of contemporary (secular) poetry. Several 'versified' benedictions of this sort have reached us. To judge from their language and prosody, they appear to be very old, and some of them, although not mentioned in the Talmud, may have actually been composed in the Talmudic period. Such apparently pre-paytanic fragments intended for liturgical use have been uncovered in literary material found in archaeological excavations in the ancient Levant.[7] Furthermore, some litanies of the *hoshana* and *selihot* types (on which see below) seem to belong stylistically to this early stage of Hebrew poetry, as it gradually drew close to the liturgy.[8]

To the list of probably pre-paytanic texts one might also add several passages of Aramaic poetry, often remarkable for their beauty and dramatic character, which are mostly known from the Palestinian Targumim. These passages were doubtlessly recited by the *meturgemanim*, the official translators, during the morning service on Sabbaths and holidays, and served as a poetical illumination of central verses from the festive readings.[9] Of all the texts mentioned so far, these are the most complete and developed with regards to form and content. Some are remarkable for their popular character and for their daring, unusual phrasing.

[5] PesRK 27,1 (p. 404), R. Lazar be-R. Shimon was a דורשן פוייטן וקרוב ותני קרי; CantR 1,7 and KohR 1,13: הדין פרייטנא כד הוה עביד אלפאביתין זמנין חשל ליה וזמנין מחסר ליה.
[6] See Joseph Yahalom elsewhere in this volume.
[7] Among the locations are Dura Europos in Syria, and Fayum and Oxyrhynchus in Egypt. For an evaluation of these fragments see Schirmann, 'Hebrew Liturgical Poetry'.
[8] See Heinemann, *Prayer*, 139-155. However, Heinemann's view on the antiquity of these texts is far fetched.
[9] See Yahalom-Sokoloff, *Jewish Palestinian Aramaic Poetry*; Kasher, *Targumic Toseftot*.

The above-mentioned fragments, despite their small number and some-times problematic nature, allow us to posit a theory of pre-paytanic poetry. Somewhere in the third century CE, a silent but significant revolution must have occurred in Hebrew poetry. Until then, it had endeavoured to emulate the biblical way of making poetry, but now it relinquished the high ideals associ-ated with that form and adopted new means of expression. It readily used later and more colloquial strata of Hebrew. The hallmarks of biblical poetry, such as *parallelismus membrorum* and the frequent use of the consecutive *vav*, disap-peared. Typical to this new kind of poetry is also its prosody. Most of the extant compositions follow a pure stress metre system. This is essentially a continuation of the metrics found in the Bible, but unlike it, is not a function of the *parallelismus membrorum* but an independent prosodic factor. The lines, generally short, present a fixed number of heavily accented words (two or three, rarely four), at times disregarding prepositions, conjunctions, numerals, construct cases, and mono-syllabic words. In the targumic poems, as well as in some versified benedictions, we meet the first use of a more complicated me-tre, consisting of a long verse divided into four feet of two stressed words each. This is called the מרובע, *meruba* or fourfold line; it was destined to be-come a major form of early piyyut.

The revolution of Hebrew poetry as described here is doubtlessly part of the radical change which occurred in the social framework of the period. Po-etry ceased to be the art of kings, prophets and sages and to speak solely to the learned. Professional singers, mourners and *meturgemanim* now sought to reach and serve common people and indeed all elements of society. Hebrew poetry was liberated from the burden of biblical prosody and style and set out on new paths.

The Rise of Piyyut

Strictly speaking, piyyut is not a continuation of the various kinds of poetry which preceded it. It may be that from a chronological standpoint, the bound-ary between pre-paytanic poetry and piyyut is not clear and there is some degree of overlap. Yet piyyut represents a new start, if not from the point of view of its poetics, then certainly with regard to its function.

There is no consensus among scholars as to the factors which led to the rise of paytanut.[10] In the view of medieval Hebrew authors, piyyut did not seem a natural part of Jewish liturgy, but was supposed to have been invented as a subterfuge to elude religious persecutions, such as decrees against Tora study and public prayers, which theoretically Jewish communities suffered under Byzantine (or Persian) rule. Others considered it a substitute for the sermon which at the period under discussion was in decline in the Land of Israel. In more or less modified form, these explanations regarding the emergence of

---

[10] For an extensive survey of opinions see Fleischer, *Hebrew Liturgical Poetry*, 51ff.

paytanic poetry recur among modern scholars as well. However, the discovery of a vast amount of piyyutim in the Cairo Geniza revealed the tremendous wide-spread nature of early paytanut. Actually, the bulk of classic piyyut was created in Byzantine Palestine and by the time of the Arab conquest (mid seventh century) its classic period was close to its end. The theory that it resulted from oppressive measures proved inadequate. So too, the hermeneutic character of piyyut and of the sermon is utterly different. Even though the emergence of piyyut coincided with the decline of the sermon, there is no certain link between the two phenomena.

Today it is no longer doubted that the rise of paytanic verse was an immanent development of public worship in early Palestinian communities.[11] Here indeed lies the essential difference between pre-paytanic poetry and piyyut. Whereas earlier poetry largely remained outside the synagogue and was only incidentally related to public prayers, piyyut was created precisely in order to offer a poetic alternative for the wording of public synagogue service, especially on Sabbath and holidays. As is well known, the obligatory parts of Jewish worship consist of berakhot which conclude with a eulogy (*hatima*). These texts were fixed in set forms at a very early stage,[12] and when performed in public, they were recited twice, once by the worshippers and another by the precentor (*shaliah tsibbur*). At a certain stage, this unvarying repetition of the prayers became tedious. Thus, in order to introduce change, the precentors began to move away from the fixed wording of the prayer and to replace it with new formulations richer in content, style and form, and frequently changing. Paytanic verse, then, was meant to provide a substitute for the fixed liturgy in the precentors' repetition of the prayer. Actually, the paytan formulated a new wording for the body of each of the berakhot, leaving untouched only the hatima or occasional biblical verses found in the original (prose) wording of the prayers. These 'liturgical stations' served as the bare framework of the paytanic composition; they were also the (only) meeting points between the versified prayers chanted by the precentor and the fixed prayer maintained by the congregation.[13]

The development of paytanut should not be considered as a process occurring simultaneously in all Palestinian communities. It may have originated first in important communities with a large number of learned members, and these communities in turn may have served as examples for others. Paytanut probably first was adopted mainly for worship on major holidays, then for ordinary Sabbaths and finally, in some communities, as part of the daily worship. This caused the demand for piyyutim to increase rapidly, and expanded production

---

[11] See Fleischer, 'Liturgical Function'.
[12] See Fleischer, 'On the Beginnings'.
[13] In fact, some fragments of the regular prayer survived in the versified prayers in liturgical practice, just before or after the versified sections themselves. See Fleischer, *Hebrew Liturgical Poetry*, 55ff.

led in turn to ever-greater acceptance, until finally paytanic prayer became the dominant practice in most Palestinian communities. From Palestine it spread to the Diaspora, first to communities under Palestinian influence and gradually to other communities as well.

Paytanut is quite clearly a product of the Land of Israel, not unlike aggada, and it reflects an attitude towards prayer peculiar to the Palestinian communities.[14] Babylonian sages had a reserved attitude to paytanut, ranging from passive resistance to outright hostility.[15] This doubtlessly stemmed from a different attitude to prayer in general on their part. The teaching of the Babylonian sages and of the early Geonim shows a deep respect for the accepted wording of the statutory prayers. Thus they had difficulty in accepting the main genres of piyyut which displaced the fixed text in the precentor's repetition. Nevertheless, the Babylonian sages were generally sympathetic to peripheral genres of piyyut whose recitation did not disturb the revered fixity of the prayers.[16]

Genres and Contents

A correct understanding of the liturgical function of piyyut gives insight into the diversity of its various genres. The versified alternative to the main prayer (the Amida) in its various modes is the genre called *kerova*. Thus a *kerova* for week days is called *kerovat shemone-esre* after the eighteen benedictions of the daily Amida; the one meant to replace the Sabbath Amida (of seven benedictions) is called a *shivata*,[17] while the one replacing the Amida of seven benedictions including a *kedusha*[18] is called *kedushta*.[19] A versified set of the benedictions said before and after the Shema in the morning service is called *yotser*,[20] and a corresponding one for the evening, *maariv*. Similarly, a piyyut versifying the benedictions of the Grace after Meals is entitled *birkat mazon*, or, as often in the Geniza texts, simply *berakha*. Specific benedictions are expanded in *kerovot* for special days of the religious calendar by one or by many piyyutim particular for these days. Thus we find the sixth section of

---

[14] The classical genres of paytanic poetry are shaped according to the Erets Israel rite of prayer and reflect Palestinian liturgical customs. The Talmudic literature alluded to in early Piyyutim is prominently Palestinian as well. Even the language of piyyut reveals characteristical traits of Palestinian Hebrew.

[15] See Ginzberg,'Yahas Hakhmei Erets Yisrael'; Beeri, 'Early Stages'.

[16] This concerns *hoshanot* for Succoth, *selihot* for days of fasting and repentance, *kinot* for the Ninth of Av, *sidrei avoda* for the Day of Atonement, and so forth. For these genres of piyyut see below.

[17] On this genre see Elizur, *Mahzorei Shivatot*.

[18] *Kedusha* (similar to the Christian *sanctus*) is a festive insertion in the third benediction, based on Is. 6:3 and Ez. 3:12. See above chapter 6.

[19] The ancient Palestinian practice of saying the *kedusha* in the Amidot differed from the later practice which followed the Babylonian. See Fleischer, 'Diffusion'. The *kedushta* is the most revered and wide spread genre of classic piyyut.

[20] For a detailed monograph on this genre see Fleischer, *The emergence*.

kerovot for fast days containing *selihot*, and the fourteenth for the Ninth of Av containing *kinot*. *Kedushtaot* for the *musaf* prayer on New Year contain the so-called *tekiot* in honour of the blowing of the *shofar*, and those for the *musaf* service on the Day of Atonement have *sidrei avoda* describing the sacrificial service of the high Priest on Yom Kippur in the Temple. *Shivatot* for the first day of Pesah and Shemini Atseret are expanded upon in their second section with series of poems asking for dew or rain. Special poetic insertions occur also in the *kerovot* for Purim, mainly in the twelfth benediction.[21] The only kind of early piyyut which does not fit into the framework of the regular prayers is the genre of *hoshanot* (chants for the ritual processions on the Festival of Sukkot); these apparently stem from ancient, pre-paytanic traditions (see above). The rest of the known kinds of piyyut, such as those intended for home or private religious ceremonies (circumcisions, weddings, funerals, festive meals etc.) or those meant to express individual religious feeling, are of later provenience, and do not belong to the classic piyyut.[22]

Versified prayer was not meant for worship by the individual. It was intended to serve the precentor who prayed in the name of the congregation and at their behest. Thus the piyyut solely expresses the concerns of the community and, in broader terms, of the entire Jewish people. Almost always, the paytan relates to the metaphysical sphere beyond time and space where God and the people of Israel meet face to face in their complex and intricate relationships. In consequence, the paytan intentionally and consistently eliminates his own personality from his poetry, and almost as deliberately he also distances himself from the specific problems of the congregation in whose name his versified prayer is offered. Some famous exceptions notwithstanding, there is hardly any real historical reference to contemporary events in classical piyyut. The search for the historical background of classical piyyut is almost always fruitless and 'discoveries' are most often deceptive.

In view of its liturgical function, we might expect to find in piyyut the same subjects as those dealt with in regular prose prayers. No doubt, its contents initially were largely in the sphere of prayers and supplications. But as more and more was produced, the standard subjects might have become tiresome. It should be remembered that these subjects were fully covered in the regular wording of the prayers as uttered by the worshippers; their repetition in verse by the precentor was as such superfluous. Thus at a fairly early stage the paytanim began to move away from the subject matter of the prayers and to relate to other subjects. This process did not affect all genres of piyyut to the same degree. Those intended for days of fasting and repentance remained more or less faithful to those topics. But those for Sabbaths and Festivals did not.

---

[21] For details see Fleischer, *Hebrew Liturgical Poetry*, 137-261. See also Weinberger, *Jewish Hymnography*, 49-67.

[22] On the *zemirot* for shabbat meals and the *bakashot* meant for personal devotion, see Fleischer *ib.*, 395ff., 471ff.

The *yotserot* and *kerovot* began to deal with matters proper to the respective Festivals, explaining their sources and significance and sometimes discussing the laws and customs pertaining to them. Thus, the piyyut became more and more highbrow in content, a phenomenon less strange than it may appear, considering the fact that Jewish liturgy always reserved a central place for study. Nevertheless, piyyut did not become didactic; it only grew more and more learned. The quantity of halakhic and aggadic material alluded to in the works of the great paytanim is indeed often astonishing. Appreciating of it requires an all but absolute knowledge of the Talmudic literature. Amazingly enough, the erudition did not exert any real influence on the vocabulary of the paytanim. The authors 'translated' the aggadic and halakhic material into paytanic Hebrew without leaving any trace of its sources. Obvious quotations from the Talmud or the Midrashim are very rare in classical piyyut: even in the expressly homiletic passages, the special paytanic Hebrew is never abandoned.[23]

With the paytanic custom to compose complete sets of piyyutim for each Sabbath it also became accepted to integrate their contents with the reading of the weekly biblical portion, not always an easy task when this portion did not lend itself to poetry. Many *kedushtaot* and *yotserot* for regular Sabbaths show a remarkable balance between erudition and prayer and hymn. Some of these compositions are reminiscent of the Syrian *memra* or the Byzantine *kontakion*, though this Christian religious poetry has a different function and location in the liturgy.[24]

Special sets of piyyutim, *kerovot* and *yotserot*, were composed to celebrate in public prayer and in such familiar events as circumcision, marriage and mourning. These subjects were fitted into the regular course of paytanic poetry by means of generalization and often allegorization. In some early Palestinian communities, most likely in towns populated by priestly families, it was customary to dedicate the Shabbat *kerovot* to the memory of the priestly order that would have served in the Temple during the given week. Special piyyutim were also dedicated to the rare concurrence of different liturgical events.

An especially complicated problem is the relationship of paytanut to ancient Jewish mysticism as represented in the Hekhalot literature. As mentioned above, the *kedushta,* the oldest and most central genre of piyyut, was meant to embellish Amida prayers in which a *kedusha* is said. The *kedusha* is also known to be central to most of the extant poetical fragments from the Hekhalot literature. But the link between the ecstatic Hekhalot poetry and the poetics of the *kedushtaot* is very slight indeed. Only in isolated cases does one find hints of authentic mysticism in classical piyyut. The poetry of paytanut is 'orthodox' by nature and has a marked aversion to esoteric topics. Its community function

---

[23] On the use of some rhetorical devices characteristic of aggada in early Piyyut see Mirsky, 'Le-Mahtsavtan'.

[24] See Schirmann, 'Hebrew Liturgical Poetry'.

called for moderation on this subject as well. Only the Central-European schools of piyyut, which developed at a time when basic elements of mysticism were already absorbed into official Jewish thought, allowed themselves a little more freedom in this regard.

Patterns and Structural Ornaments

In the beginning, paytanic poetry did not create new forms. Since production was still small and irregular, it was content to follow the usual forms of contemporary secular poetry. There was no use of rhyme, and the stress counting metre was not over-precise. A natural preference developed for the complex *meruba*, but other, simpler metrical patterns are also found.[25] The wider production of piyyut proper both demanded and provided a more organised and sophisticated structure. The acrostic, arranging lines or stanzas so that their first letters form an alphabetic sequence, was adopted by paytanic poetry at its very inception as an almost absolute rule. The use of it became highly perfected during this period: we find paytanim making equally adroit use of straight, reverse, combined, doubled, tripled, quadrupled and other kind of acrostics. The phenomenon is found in Syriac, Byzantine Greek and Latin poetry as well, but nowhere did it become so widespread as here. The acrostical signature of the poet was still unknown at the early period of piyyut.[26]

From this point on, the formal development of piyyut went more and more its own ways. The paytanim make frequent use of *shirshur*, the technique of placing the last word of each line or section at the beginning of the next. There is also quite frequent use of the *petiha mikrait* in which the words of a biblical verse or the first phrases of consecutive biblical verses relevant to the subject of the piyyut are placed at the beginning of each line or section. Very often, the paytanim try their hand at the device of *millot keva*, placing a particular word in a chosen, fixed place in each line. This word (or phrase), generally alluding to the essence of the liturgical event celebrated, thus regulates the development of the piyyut throughout.

As the products of this creative activity grew and spread, the various kinds of structural ornament also became increasingly perfected.[27] It was the discovery of rhyme, however, that gave a jump-start to piyyut (c. 500). Rhyme as an ornament in piyyut at first appears only sporadically; its absolute domination did not come about at a single stroke. Yet, the transition was swift, as opposed to Latin poetry, for example, and virtually total. Paytanic rhyme is to be under-

---

[25] On the metrics of pre-classical and classical piyyut see Fleischer, 'Metric System'.

[26] It is found at that time in the work of Ephraem the Syrian as well as in some early Samaritan poetry.

[27] On structural ornaments see further Fleischer, *Hebrew Liturgical Poetry*, 70-83.

stood as an independent creation of Hebrew poetry; from the start its character and rules are unparalleled in other poetry.[28]

It is rhyme which ushers in the classic period of paytanic poetry, enabling the text to be shaped in strophic units, which differing from fragment to fragment may determine the character of the larger composition. The structural ornaments which had come down from the earlier period attain their full expression in the rhymed stanza. No longer are they used occasionally and one by one, but appear as characteristic components of particular types or units of piyyut; when used in combination they sometimes attain a high degree of architectural sophistication.[29]

With the rise of rhyme, the paytanim also began to sign their names, mostly after completing the alphabetic acrostics, using the first letters of the lines or strophes of their poems. At first these acrostical signatures contained only the name of the paytan himself; later, patronymics and other designations also appear.[30]

Classical piyyut is for the most part strophic in structure. The occurrence of mono-rhymed fragments is rather rare. The size of the strophes varies widely, but the overall poem always maintains an absolute symmetry of its stanzas, even if these are of an extremely complex structure. The strophe of the classical piyyut has only one rhyme; the occurrence of poems presenting a fixed rhyme (i.e. word) at the end of the last line of each stanza (a common feature in later, and especially in Spanish piyyut), is extremely rare in the classical period.[31]

A new phenomenon in the development of classical piyyut is the appearance, within the main body of the poetic text, of short intermezzos meant to function as refrains or choral responses. This innovation without doubt corresponds to a somewhat later reform in the manner of chanting the poetic texts at worship, and it resulted in some new or reshaped types of piyyut.[32]

Among all these formal aspects, it is only the metrical aspect of piyyut which remained in its primary state. Although it flourished in a cultural milieu (Greek, Latin and Syriac) with rich, precise systems of metre, both syllabic and quantitative, Hebrew liturgical poetry remained faithful to its early pure stress metre.[33] As stated, this derived from the secular poetry of the preceding period,

---

[28] On rhyme systems in Piyyut see Hrushovski, 'Major Systems', esp. 738-742; idem, 'Prosody'. On the emergence of rhyme in piyyut see Fleischer, 'Behinot'; idem, 'Early Hebrew Liturgical Poetry', 76-80; Yahalom, *Poetry and Society*, 137-172.

[29] The genres of Piyyut are shaped in stereotyped, often highly complex forms. For details see Fleischer, *Hebrew Liturgical Poetry*, 137-261.

[30] E.g. the designation כהן or לוי. Some poets mention their occupation (חזן) or place of birth or residence. Fairly early, words of encouragement appear such as חזק, יחי, later also יזכה (i.e. לחי העולם הבא) etc.

[31] There is no hard evidence on the existence of these structures before Elazar b. Killir (see below); see Fleischer, 'Girdle-Like Strophic Patterns'.

[32] See Fleischer, 'Choral Elements'.

[33] See Fleischer, 'Early Hebrew Liturgical Poetry', 80ff.

as a distant and slightly petrified echo of biblical verse. It did not reach any degree of perfection in rhymed piyyut. On the contrary, with the transition to rhymed verse, traditional metrics seem to have been applied more loosely. Particularly in the less important genres, it is often difficult to find any clear trace of them. However, there is also evidence of a complete formalisation of the system. In some compositions, the stress-based metre loses its flexibility, and the line, instead of counting only significant words, presents a fixed number of words regardless of their importance.

Language and Style

The language of piyyut is mixed. From pre-paytanic poetry it inherited not only a link to the Bible, but one to post-biblical Hebrew as well. However, like all ancient poetry and perhaps more so, paytanut sought to turn an elegant phrase and adopt an unusual expression. Poetry's new position in the liturgy once again bestowed upon it an increasingly elitist and intellectual character. The initial search for unusual means of expression was cautious. The text was embellished here and there with lexical innovations, but remained clear and understandable. With the transition to the rhymed stage the emphasis shifts and a potent, highly organized but hermetic beauty becomes the goal. The classic paytan avoids as far as possible common words. He looks for *hapax legomena* and puzzling, brilliant or surprising formulations. He recasts usual roots in unusual morphological forms, and imparts words with new grammatical status: nouns, adjectives, prepositions and conjunctions are transformed into verbs and vice versa.[34] The poet's language naturally became obscure in this process. Yet at this stage, as only so often in the history of poetry, obscurity was not considered a flaw, rather the opposite. Piyyut at its best was the domain of learned men who delighted in its powerful phrasing and enigmatic language.[35]

One of the typical paytanic stylistic means to be mentioned in this context is the frequent use of *kinnuyim,* i.e. emblematic designations for recurring notions, such as God, Israel, the Tora, biblical heroes and events, etc. Together they form a rich and complex network of alternative expressions, sometimes conventional but very often fresh and inventive, denoting concepts frequently dealt with in piyyut.[36] Another important attribute of paytanic style is the *shibbuts,* i.e. the frequent embedding of biblical phrases in the paytanic text. The Bible, known by heart by most of the more learned worshipers, served as the common framework within which the paytan met his public. Early on, this led him to use biblical phrases as a natural stylistic ornament. The biblical wording hidden in the verbal embroidery of the piyyut confronted the listener with a

---

[34] On the language of Piyyut see Yahalom, *Poetic Language.* See also Zunz, *Synagogale Poesie,* 372-437; Zulay, 'Leshon ha-paytanim'; id., 'Iyunei lashon'; id., *Ha-askola ha-paytanit,* 14-40.
[35] See Elizur, 'The Enigmatic Nature'.
[36] See Fleischer, *Hebrew Liturgical Poetry,* 104-107.

pleasant surprise in meeting an old acquaintance. The biblical verse with its original connotations also enriched its new context with secondary meanings. It also displayed, time and again, the virtuosity of the paytan; not only in the way he succeeded in expressing his ideas in revered, ancient phrases, but also in the manner in which he skilfully concealed the borrowed material in the wording of his poem.

Nevertheless, piyyut is not rhetorical poetry. Apart from the peculiar language – the foremost pursuit of classical paytanic aesthetics – as seen also from the *kinnuyim,* the *shibbuts,* and some common figures of style without which no poetry can exist, paytanut does not stylistically show off. It displays little passion and even less ecstasy. Neither does it seek to impress by means of concretization; its vocabulary is poor in decorative epithets, in adjectives and adverbs. The descriptive language of the paytan is usually rather thin. The exceptions found in some *selihot* and *kinot* confirm, as usual, the general rule. Paytanic poetry is sober and balanced; its aesthetics rely on its unique, terse and powerful style, on its sophisticated, highly refined structure and its stupendous erudition.

The Early Paytanim

As early piyyutim are all anonymous, the names of the first paytanim remain unknown to us.[37] The first poet to be known by name is Yose ben Yose, a half-legendary figure whose name is connected with about twelve extant piyyutim some of which are very long and complex.[38] He still belongs to the period of pre-classical, unrhymed piyyut, and he may well be its last representative. He never signed any of his piyyutim, but they are ascribed to him in ancient, reliable sources. The classic period of piyyut is represented by a group of authors writing rhymed poems signed with their names in acrostics. The first, and foremost, seems to be Yannai (c. 500) a poet of rare stature. Major fragments of his compositions, reflecting the triennial Tora cycle of Palestine, were preserved in the Cairo Geniza.[39] Two slightly less important paytanim, Hadutahu[40] and Shimon ha-Kohen ben Megas,[41] apparently flourished in the generation immediately following. Scholars agree that these three paytanim were active in Palestine before the Arab conquest (638). Yosef ben Nisan mi-Sheve Kiry-

---

[37] For an impressive anthology of early paytanic poetry collected from Geniza manuscripts see Spiegel, *The Fathers.*

[38] See Mirsky, *Piyyutei Yose ben Yose.*

[39] Yannai's poems were published by Zulay, *Piyyutei Yannai.* This excellent edition was followed by scattered publication of some more fragments. For a comprehensive edition, in two volumes, of Yannai's extant works, see Rabinovitz, *The Liturgical Poems.*

[40] See Kahle, *Masoreten;* Zulay, 'Le-toledot ha-piyyut', 128-137; Fleischer, 'Haduta'. Hadutahu is known by his series of 24 Kedushtaot celebrating the 24 priestly orders. Fragments of this series, published by Kahle and supplemented by Zulay, are known from a very old Geniza manuscript.

[41] See Yahalom, *Piyyutei Shimon bar Megas.*

ataim (Naveh in Trans-Jordan)[42] and Joshua ha-Kohen probably still also lived under Byzantine rule.[43] The most important of the ancient paytanim is Elazar ben Killir (c. 570-c. 640), a great poet who gave piyyut its classic form. His creative output was enormous and extremely varied.[44] All later paytanim are indebted to him. The classic period of paytanut draws to a close with the very important compositions of Pinhas ha-Kohen ben Yakov who came from Kafra, a suburb of Tiberias, and lived at the end of the eighth century.[45]

The history of piyyut did not end with its most brilliant period. On the contrary, it spread to all known Jewish communities. In the post-classical period of eastern piyyut (ninth–eleventh centuries) the number of writers reaches several hundred, composing tens of thousands of poems. The genres of piyyut, their diction and content, continued to develop in accordance with new circumstances, practices of worship and aesthetic priorities. The creative activity of the two European schools of piyyut[46] as well as that of the other centres, in North Africa, the Land of Israel, Turkey and Yemen continued for hundreds of years and died out only on the threshold of the modern era of Hebrew literature.

[42] See Zulay, 'Le-toledot ha-piyyut' 175-186; Fleischer, *The Yozer*, 711-729.
[43] See Zulay, *ib.* 155ff. Two of his larger Piyyutim were published by Fleischer, 'Havdala shiva-tot'; see bibliography there. See also Spiegel, *The Fathers*, 211-223.
[44] There is as yet no complete edition of Killiri's work. For partial editions see Elizur, *Kedushtaot*; idem, *Kedusha va-shir*; id. *Be-toda va-Shir*; Spiegel, *The Fathers*, 97-210.
[45] For a comprehensive edition of his extant work see Elizur, *Piyyutei Rabbi Pinhas*.
[46] The Italian school emerged in the ninth century and spread to central and southeastern Europe. The famous Spanish school arose in the middle of the tenth century and later included the North African and oriental areas. Its impressive artistic achievements changed the face of Hebrew liturgical poetry with regard to form and content.

Chapter Ten

'Syriac for Dirges, Hebrew for Speech' – Ancient Jewish Poetry in Aramaic and Hebrew

Joseph Yahalom

It is not always justified to barricade oneself behind fortified lines in areas that should be viewed as open, connected with one another, and complementary. This is true of the distinction that is made between literary and documentary material from the early medieval manuscripts preserved in the Cairo Geniza. The Jews of that society wrote highly personal letters and preserved them like the apple of their eye, until they ultimately found their way into the welter of documents in the Geniza, and Jews from that very society often wrote horribly conventional poetry, which the community also preserved for some reason. Furthermore, the absolute distinction between the formal aspect and the thematic aspect, which often fails to receive true attention, is problematic, especially in the private area of poems of mourning and eulogy and of the personal hymns of reproach, which are, on the one hand, so private, and on the other hand, thoroughly universal and even intended for public performance. In this sense, the domain of grief and mourning permits us to observe Jewish society in critical hours of trial, and also to examine its special dispensations according to typical social and literary norms.

The Types of Eulogy and the Functions of the Languages

Aramaic was spoken in the East for more than a thousand years until Arabic supplanted it toward the end of the first millennium of the common era.[1] Until then, it maintained interesting coexistence with the Hellenistic languages of

---

[1] Hoyland, 'Language and Identity'.

culture. In fact, a permanent division of function was created between it and the foreign languages of culture: Greek and Latin. From the style prescription of R. Yonatan of Beit Govrin (yMeg 1:11, 71b) one may learn about the different languages that were in use in the Land of Israel during late antiquity, each of which was meant for a different purpose in life and literature. Presumably Aramaic was the spoken language closest to everyday language. Since in times of grief and distress, a person has only his or her mother tongue, the stylistic prescription culminated with the declaration: סורסי לאיליייא, 'Syrian is for dirges' – that is to say, nothing is as fitting for dirges and lamenting as Aramaic, the language of eulogy.[2] The first item in the style prescription is Greek: the language of poetry and belles lettres: לעז לזמר, 'Foreign speech is for song' – where לעז, as often, means 'Greek'. Second to it is Latin, the language of the ruling authorities and of the bureaucracy. At that time Hebrew had already been relegated to a minor position. The poetical eulogy in Aramaic was indeed a widespread literary genre, not only in late antiquity, when the spoken language was Aramaic, but even afterward, when Arabic was the spoken language. Eulogy poems in Aramaic from the Land of Israel during the first Muslim period (634-1099) have indeed been found in the Cairo Geniza. However, alongside them, Hebrew eulogy poems are also found, especially from the Arab period.

The matter of eulogies was undoubtedly extremely current for the court poets in the Arab-Jewish cultural realm. In the mid-tenth century Menahem ben Saruk tells that, upon the death of his patron's mother, the bereaved son, the vizier Hasdai ben Shaprut, rushed to him in the middle of the night, to have him write eulogies for the days of mourning, and he already found him writing on his own initiative. Afterward, too, when his father died, he wrote the eulogies that were recited every day during the days of mourning.[3] The need to supply the congregation's appetite for new poetical works was great, especially on the occasion of events in private life. One of the most pressing events for cantors and poets was the death of leaders and magnates, for whom eulogies had to be written on minimal notice. The poet had to supply appropriate scripts for the days of mourning. The religious functionaries of the communities also used to draw upon, among other things, an available repertoire of works prepared for similar lugubrious occasions. The great Jewish centre in affluent Cairo had an especially great need for eulogies. This emerges, among other things, from the continuous correspondence among poets and cantors, which is preserved among the documents of the Geniza.

Being in difficulty, the cantor from Cairo, R. Meir ben Yakhin, turned to Alexandria, a cosmopolitan city with connections, for help in obtaining fresh material. The correspondence from the early thirteenth century reflects his distress in marvellous fashion. The correspondent in Alexandria, who made an

---

[2] Lieberman, *Mehkarim be-torat Erets-Yisrael*, 58.
[3] Schirmann, *Ha-shira ha-Ivrit* 1, 23f.

effort to respond to Rabbi Meir's request, sent him thirty eulogies. However this did not meet the expectations that had been pinned on him in Cairo. The poet, under duress, quickly informed his correspondent that all of those eulogies were well known, and there was nothing new in them. In an answer to the letter the correspondent in Alexandria protests indignantly that this could not be, for at least some of the eulogies were novel, and they had been composed for people who had recently died.[4] The pressure upon him was apparently unbearable, for in an earlier letter, he had expressed himself quite explicitly: 'Would you be so good, in requesting from your servant a hymn or lament or penitential prayer, to write down the incipits, and I will write them quickly and send them to you... But if you ask for something anonymous, I am puzzled: what can I write? My enthusiasm for writing cools off.'[5]

It appears that in making frequent use of existing eulogies, the poets would adapt existing texts and construct variable compounds according to them, on demand. Of the thirty eulogies sent to Cairo, the truly new material was apparently minimal. However, the addressee in Alexandria was also right. He was merely a quick scribe and a busy school teacher, and he could not enter the thick of things and examine the texts that came his way with respect to their originality. Ultimately, both the literary material and the accompanying documentary material were sent to the Geniza, and from our point of view everything is new and significant.

The eulogies that were still written in the authentic Palestinian Aramaic are especially interesting. The Geniza was in the synagogue of the Palestinian community, where Aramaic was used for eulogies. According to their headings, the various Aramaic eulogies found in the corpus of Jewish Palestinian Aramaic poetry were each intended for different class groups. There were eulogies for women, for priests, or for children, and the like. To exemplify the absolute power of death, they presented famous figures of people from the same class to the mourners, people whom death did not spare. A common image in eulogies for priests is that of Aaron the Priest who, by means of the incense pan that he held in his hand, halted death (Num 17:13). However, he himself was ultimately hunted down like a fish with the fishing rod held in the hand of the Angel of Death: צדיה מלאך מותה / כנונה בחכתה, 'The Angel of Death hunted him/ like a fish with a fishing rod.'[6] The image taken from the realm of fishermen and water is used in another eulogy. In it the soul reproaches the body, after the partnership between them has been dissolved, that it has made

---

[4] Strauss-Ashtor, *Toldot ha-Yehudim* 3, 101-105; also Goitein, 'Kitvei Geniza', 70. In the document is written אלקינות, and Goitein understood this as 'dirges for the Ninth of Av.' However, the heading appears to mean personal lamentations (eulogies). The admonition hymn (a form of penitential prayer) is called מרת״יה (dirge) in Arabic. S. Abramson has written about the poems of the al-Ammaani family, see his 'Selihot R. Yaakov', 165f.

[5] Goitein, *Sidrei hinukh*, 102; Frenkel, *Kehilat Yehudei Alexandria*, appendix 'Documents', doc. 71, p255-257.

[6] *Shirat benei maarava* 52,36.

the soul into a shipwreck, whereas it had been stable[7] and flying like a bird: צניעה הויני וטיסה כעופה / את הוא דעבדת יתי מטרפה כאלפה, 'I was stable and flying like a bird/ you are the one who rocked me like a ship' (Shirat benei maarava 57, 36-37). The eulogy cited in the Babylonian Talmud in the name of Bar Kipok, as ordered by Rav Ashi (bMK 25b) uses three images from the same realm and all constructed in the form of an a fortiori argument: if death had dominion over a great righteous man, how much the more so over simple people like ourselves:

בארזים נפלה שלהבת	Lightning has struck the cedar
מה יעשו אזובי הקיר	what will the moss on the wall do? (Job 1:16; 1 Kgs 5:13).
לויתן בחכה הועלה	He has caught Leviathan on his fishing rod
מה יעשו דגי רקק	what will tiny fish do? (Hab 1:15; Job 40:25).
בנחל שוטף נפלה חרבה	Drought has struck a running stream
מה יעשו מי גבים	what will pond-water do? (Exod 14:21; Jer 14:3).

In similar fashion, with regard to the image and the rhetoric, the mourning women are approached by Jesus, who is being brought out to be crucified, according to Luke 23:31. He laments and says that if this has happened to a moist tree, it will happen even the more so to a dry one: 'For if they do these things in a green tree, what shall be done in the dry?' Certainly, however, this may be merely the beginning of a broader eulogistic formula, such as the one presented in the Babylonian Talmud in the name of Bar Kipok, which, not by coincidence, begins with similes of plants, fire, and water.

Images of water and moisture naturally belong to the Galilee and the landscapes of the Sea of Galilee, and the realm of fishing is also that of the first Christians who were active in the Land of Israel. When these images were transmitted in Hebrew and transferred to the urban environment of Babylonia, they were sharply criticized. According to Rav Avin, indeed it is inconceivable to depict the death of righteous people with images of fishing rods, water, and fire: חס וחלילה דחכה ושלהבת בצדיקי אמינא, 'Perish the thought that we should say fishing rod and flame about righteous men' (bMK 25b) – as though it were possible to describe the death of a righteous man as a simple accident. Beyond the content and the image, language, too, most certainly played an important role. The local iconography, describing the death of a priest with images of a fishing rod and in Galilean Aramaic, which used idiomatic expressions for this purpose, was not suitable for the atmosphere and mentality of a Babylonian House of Study, and it is possible that the expressions were no longer understood correctly.

The distinction between Hebrew and Aramaic is also significant in the realm of literary genres. Personal laments in Hebrew were written in the con-

---

[7] Leslau, Comparative Dictionary of Ge'ez, 559: ṣan'a = firm. I was made aware of this meaning of the root צנ"ע, according to the Ethiopian by Prof. M. Kister, to whom I am grateful for other ideas that found their way into this article.

text of intensification of sorrow and grief. Here they used to proclaim out loud: תלמיד חכם שמת מי מביא לנו חליפתו, מי מביא לנו תמורתו?!, 'A sage who has died, who will bring us a replacement, who will bring us someone in his stead?' (yBer 2:7, 5c). The formulaic eulogy poems that contain acknowledgment of divine justice mainly use the Aramaic phrase: הצדיקו דינכון, 'Justify your decree' (Shirat benei maarava 64,9). Here they seek to restore the mourners to the circle of life and creativity and they emphasize to them that such things have already happened in the world. Acknowledgments of divine justice in Aramaic generally contain sermons to those in attendance, telling them to repent for their deeds while they are still young:

תתובה עביד	Repent
עד דאת ברשותך	so long as you are in your own power.
שפר עובדך	Improve your actions
ביומי טליותך	in the days of your youth. (Shirat benei maarava 61,2-3)

At the conclusion of these public poems there is also an appeal to those in attendance and a promise that for their act of charity in attending the funeral and for the words of consolation that they uttered, they will be rewarded (the conclusions of poems 56, 58, 61, 64, 65).

The ceremonies of acknowledging divine justice were accompanied by headings that defined them by name: aftara (Shirat benei maarava 51-54, 56, 59-61) and once again within one of the poems, at the conclusion:אמרין אפטרתא, 'They say aftarata' (ib. 61). This term refers to words that the mourners said to those attending them at the end of the ceremony, when they dismissed them and told them to go. The purpose of the aftara was to dismiss, to cause the mourners to dismiss those attending them, and thus as it were to console them by telling them to go home in peace (bMK 21b). The cantor, who directed the ceremony, would give the mourners the sign to perform it. This man is even mentioned by name in wills from the Geniza in connection with burial expenses.[8] The cantor would therefore address the mourners and encourage them: and you our bereaved brethren, come and receive words of consolation from our brothers and turn to your brothers (those attending the funeral) and tell them to go in peace (Shirat benei maarava 65). The role of the mourners in sending the people home at the end of the ceremony symbolizes the acceptance of consolation and transposes them from the status of consoled to that of consolers, who share in the fate of the general community. The aftara thus leads the mourners in the rite of transition, after their separation from the community; they depart from the world of death and the dead and return to the bosom of society and life and reintegrate into them.[9]

The words of reproach and acknowledgment of divine justice were phrased in useful formulae, with a form that is repeated with variations corresponding

[8] Goitein, 'Tsavaaot mi-Mitsrayim', 111-113.
[9] Mandel, 'Veha-hai yiten el libo'.

379

to the status of the departed, whether they were young or old, men or women, a priest or an ordinary Jew, and so on. These texts were worded according to the age, class, and gender of the deceased, and they were intended for repeated use when the occasion demanded it. Originality and creativity did not play a real role here. The status of personal laments was different. Here the mourner was expected to say unique things according to the particular status of the deceased and according to the attitude of the society toward him. The use of worn out images from the realm of acknowledging divine justice was not well regarded in that of the personal eulogy, however penetration and transfer from one genre to another were certainly inevitable. Therefore, it appears that we can also understand Rav Ashi's severity toward two eulogists, both Bar Kipok and Bar Avin, for saying things from the area of acknowledging divine justice when he wanted to hear a personal lament (bMK 25b).

We may now return to the distress of the cantor from Cairo, though he lived several centuries afterward. From his point of view, the treasury of eulogy clichés had been exhausted, and he needed new material and fresh imagery. Instead of that, perhaps, the scribe from Alexandria supplied him with materials that were included in 'The Collected Eulogies for the Head of the Yeshiva of the Land of Israel and Other Defunct People', copied before the Crusader conquest.[10] The person eulogized is not mentioned here by name but rather with an abbreviation, the letters מ"פ or simply a פ'. The lament was attended for מרן פלן ('Mr. so and so') from a family of Tora scholars (מגזע הוגים במארכת ימים, 'From the stem of thinkers on the [book that] lengthens of days [the Tora]'). Among his other virtues, he was one of those who took part in declaring a leap year (וסוד עיבורים בחכמה מעבר, 'And privy to the secrets of the calender, with wisdom he intercalates a month'), which is something that could be said about many of the leaders of the Palestinian academy. A series of alternative formulations were provided for the lamenting cantor, each mentioning one of the large centres of Jewish settlement in the Land of Israel before the crusades, allowing the author of the lament to choose the appropriate one for the deceased: שמועה קשה באה מרקת, 'Grave news came from Tiberias'; שמועה רעה באה מירושלים, 'Grave news came from Jerusalem,' and so on.[11] The fact that this is not an authentic poem but rather a collection of material from which the eulogist could choose according to his needs is supported by the unorganized state of the texts, which are not arranged according to the demands of the symmetrical pattern customary in ancient Hebrew poetry in general and in eulogy poems in particular.

[10] Elitsur, 'Le-korot ha-Geonut'.
[11] Cohen, 'Ketaim hadashim', 451, 457.

The Triple Meter

The triple meter was apparently one of the distinguishing marks of the eulogy style and for the expression of sorrow among both Jews and gentiles. Thus, for example, the Babylonian Talmud (bMeg 6a) presents a lament for R. Zeira, which was given in Tiberias in the fourth century. The preacher mentions the two important stations in the life of the deceased, the Land of Israel and Babylonia, devoting a short hemistich to each of them. The man was born in Babylonia and grew up in the Land of Israel, now he is laid to rest in Tiberias, which weeps for his death in the third and final hemistich. Each of these places receives an epithet of its own in the poem. Babylonia is biblical Shinar (Gen 10:10), the Land of Israel is 'ארץ חפץ' (the land of desire), for everyone desires its honour, and for that reason it is called ארץ צבי, 'the desirous land', Dan 11:16. In Aramaic צבי means 'desire' or 'request'; and Tiberias is Rakkath, mentioned in the heritage of the tribe of Naphtali (Josh 19:35). Hence, the preacher begins:

אֶרֶץ שִׁנְעָר הָרָה וְיָלְדָה	The land of Shinar conceived and gave birth
אֶרֶץ צְבִי גִידְּלָה שַׁעֲשׁוּעֶיהָ	The precious land raised her delights
אוֹי נָא לָהּ אָמְרָה רַקַּת כִּי אָבְדָה	Woe has Rakkath said, for she has lost
(כְּלִי חֶמְדָּתָהּ)	(the vessel of her desire).

We find a literary eulogy for Moses in similar style, attributed to one of the great Samaritan sages, Marka (the Aramaic form of Marcus). The words were apparently written in the fourth century: גדול הוא העץ שניטע במצרים / ונקלע למדבר / ונקטע בהר נבו, 'Great is the tree that was planted in Egypt/ that found itself in the desert/ and was cut down at Mount Nebo.'[12] Moses, the tree that was planted in Egypt, managed to stay alive even for forty years in the desert, but it was cut off at Mount Nebo. S. Lieberman has already noted that such a style was very common in ancient eulogies. He presents an example from lines engraved on the tombstone of a famous woman in Greece, Lais:

> The one to whom Irus gave birth
> and Corinth raised her
> Now lies on the famous plains of Thessaly.[13]

Hymns of admonition were also written in the triple meter from their beginning. These are a form of penitential prayer that moved rather freely in the world of the synagogue during the holidays of Tishri, the month of repentance and mercy. In these poems, the sinner addresses himself and encourages himself to turn from his evil ways. To demonstrate the depth of the sin and the punishment, in these poems there is often a description of the person's last hour and of the debate between the body and the soul before the celestial court. One ancient remonstrance poem is recited on the Day of Atonement: אנוש מה

[12] Ben-Hayim, *Tivat Marka*, 332.
[13] *Deipnos* XIII, 589b. Lieberman, *Yevanit ve-Yavnut*, 51.

יזכה... בלחים אם תבער האש מה בחציר יבש, 'Of what is man worthy... if fire burns moist things, what will be with dry straw?'[14] In the ninth verse, beginning with *tet*, the anonymous poet states that man is miserable:

טָמֵא מִשְׂאֹרוֹ	Impure in his leavening
וּמְטַמֵּא בְּעוֹדוֹ	and made impure in his life
וּמְטַמֵּא בְּמוֹתוֹ	and making impure in his death.

The poetical device used here is anaphora. The first word of each hemistich is a different form of the verb, relating to three critical stages in a person's life. It begins with birth in sin. According to the midrash in Avot de-R. Natan: 'Since the first drop that a man casts into a woman is the evil impulse, when the baby is lying in its cradle... it wants to kill you, so that it can pluck from you by its hair' (ARN a16, 32a-b : the expression is 'from it by its hair,' meaning: he is already bad then, and he tries to pull your hair). That, then, applies to birth: impure from its leavening, the leavening of the dough is the evil impulse.[15] In the second stage, throughout his life, a person is liable to contract impurity by contact with anything impure, and thus he himself may become impure. However, worst of all, upon his death, he becomes the ultimate source of impurity. Those, then, are the three stages in a person's life, according to the hymn, which is not a eulogy, though it is similar. The triple meter is also used for pessimistic rabbinical teachings.

A pithy and pessimistic proverb used to be said by R. Meir when he finished reading the Book of Job, as reported by the Babylonian Talmud (bBer 16b):

סוֹף אָדָם לְמָוֶת	The end for a person is death
וְסוֹף בְּהֵמָה לִשְׁחִיטָה	the end for a beast is slaughtering
וְהַכּוֹל לְמִיתָה עוֹמְדִין	and all for death are destined.

The conclusive character of the third hemistich is expressed both in the intentional change in the word order, for the prepositional phrase, 'for death', does not conclude the hemistich, as in the preceding ones, and in the conclusive and summary character of the word 'all'. It appears that the pattern, with its three hemistichs, was well absorbed in a particularly short version, which was included in half of a set of paired lines in the early 'Order of Worship' (part of the High Holiday service), אספר גדולות ('I shall tell great things'):

הִיא לְעֶצֶב	She is to sadness
וְהוּא לְיָגֵעַ	and he is to weariness
וְהַכֹּל לְדָקָב	and everything to putrefaction.[16]

Following her sin, Eve was doomed to giving birth in great pain (Gen 3:16), and Adam was doomed to eat his bread after hard labour (Gen 3:19). The

---

[14] Goldschmidt, *Mahzor*, 117f.

[15] Abramson, 'Midrash milim', 122-125.

[16] Mirsky, *Piyutei Yosei ben Yosei*, 204.

entire world is transitory. The symmetrical and relaxed structure is based on pairs – 'man and beast,' 'he and she' – which the poets break by adding a third hemistich, interrupting the paired symmetry and creating a sensitive cyclical system over which man, as it were, has no control: she and he, but all... A similar phenomenon can be seen in various verses of the well known remonstrance, אנוש מה יזכה, 'Of what is man worthy', verse 12:

לַיְלָה לֹא יִשְׁכַּב	At night he will not lie down
יוֹמָם לֹא יָנַח	in daytime he will not rest
עַד יֵרָדַם בַּקֶּבֶר	until he sleeps in the grave.

The sleep of the grave is of course metaphorical, and it rounds out the dual symmetry of day and night in fantastic fashion: there, as it were, and there alone, in the darkness of the grave, will a person find the desired sleep, after he has not succeeded in lying down or resting. A similar expression is found in another admonition, איום ונורא צום העשור, 'Dreadful and horrible, the fast of the tenth', which is used in the Italian rite on the Day of Atonement and was found in an early Geniza fragment.[17]

Various concluding hemistichs direct the gaze to the mysteries of the divinity. Thus, for example, in the verse for the letter *tsade*: צַקְתָּנוּ כְחוֹמֶר / וְנִשְׁבַּרְנוּ כְּחֶרֶשׂ / וּלְךָ יְכוֹלֶת לְחַדֵּשׁ, 'You cast us like clay/ we are broken like pottery/ and You have the ability to renew.' In the ancient remonstrance, אתה מבין שרעפי לב, 'You understand the heart's devices', every third hemistich ends regularly with the declaration: ואתה חי לבדך, 'And You alone live'. Thus, for example, the letter *dalet* reads: דְּמְיוֹנוֹ כְנֵבֶל / נִשְׁבָּר כְּמוֹ חֶרֶשׂ / וְאַתָּה חַי לְבַדֶּךָ, 'His image is like a pitcher/ he breaks like pottery/ and You alone live.' Then, in the letter *he*, we read: הָיָה הַיּוֹם / וּמָחָר אֵינֶנּוּ / וְאַתָּה חַי לְבַדֶּךָ, 'He was today/ and tomorrow he will not be/ and You alone live.'[18] All our illustrations derive from ancient poems belonging to the pre-history of rhyme in the synagogue.

Also in parting words that were recited in Tiberias at the end of the third and the beginning of the fourth centuries, we find similar phenomena in style and wording. The beginning of the text is reused, not coincidentally, on a tombstone from southern Italy, dating from the eighth or ninth century. In the Talmud (bBer 17a) parting words are spoken in the second person: you will see your world in your lifetime, etc. However, the dirge engraved on the tombstone refers to the deceased in the third person:

עוֹלָמוֹ רָאָה בְּחַיָּיו	He saw his world in his life
אַחֲרִיתוֹ לְחַיֵּי עוֹלָם	his end is eternal life
תִּקְוָתוֹ לְדוֹר דּוֹרִים	his hope is for generations.[19]

---

[17] *Mahzor le-khol ha-shana kefi minhag Italiani*, Livorno 1856, vol 2, p149f; Ormann, *Sündenbekenntnis*, 24-27.

[18] Goldschmidt, *Mahzor*, 298-299. For the admonition אנוש מה יזכה, see p118.

[19] Colafemmina, 'Hebrew Inscriptions'.

In the first two of its hemistichs, this world and the world to come are juxta-posed to one another, but the final hemistich goes out to the world of eternity.

The Dispute Between Body and Soul

One of the common pairs in this pattern is that of body and soul, spirit and matter, which are confront with the pair of the lame and the blind. The com-parison between the pair of spirit and matter and the pair of lame and blind apparently derives from the Hindu philosophical tradition of Samkhya. Ac-cording to this philosophical tradition, a creation comes into the world from the bond between the two. They are abandoned in the forest of ignorance, from which the spirit can break out only with the help of matter. In this situation, the spirit is compared to a lame person, who can see but not move about, and matter is compared to a blind person, who can move about and act in the world, but who cannot see.[20] This comparison passed from India into the Jew-ish tradition through a Persian intermediary. As evidence for this move, schol-ars point to the transition of the arena of events from the Indian forest to the Persian orchard.[21]

In the Indian source, Purusa (the spiritual) is masculine. For the sake of meditation, it wishes to look at Prakriti (the bodily, which is feminine), and to move by means of it. In order for him to observe Prakriti contact takes place between them, like the contact between the lame person and the blind man, and in this way the world is created. One day a lame man and the blind man went on a journey, and when robbers attacked their caravan, they were left to their fate by their companions, and they wandered in the forest. They met and formed a covenant in order to see and walk. The blind man bore the lame man on his shoulders, and, since the lame man could see while perched on the blind man's shoulders, the blind man took the right path together with his burden. In that manner, like the lame man, Purusha is able to see, but he is unable to act, whereas Parakriti is capable of action, like the blind man, but he is unable to see. Just as the lame man and his blind bearer will separate the moment they reach their destination, so, too, Parakriti, after she has attained the liberation of Purusha, will distance herself from all action, whereas Purusha, after seeing Parakriti, will seclude himself. Upon attaining their goals, they will therefore part from one another. Just as a child is born from the contact between man and woman, so, too, as a result of the contact between Parakriti and Purusha, the world is born.[22]

---

[20] Larson, *Classical Samkhya*, 266.
[21] Stemberger, 'Auferstehungslehe', 250f.
[22] *Sānkhyā Kārikā* 21, with the interpretation of Gaudapāda. I am grateful to A. Cherniak of Tel Aviv University for translating this story for me.

The sages used the parable of the lame and blind partners to clarify the moral issue of how the spiritual partner could possibly sin. They created an allegory on the phrase, 'Horse and its rider He threw into the sea' (Exod 15:1):

> The Holy One, blessed be He, brought a horse and its rider and placed them in judgment. He said to the horse: Why did you run after my children? It said to Him: An Egyptian made me run against my will... And He said to the Egyptian: Why did you run after my children? He said to Him: The horse made me run against my will. As it is said, 'For the horse of Pharaoh went in with his chariots and with his horsemen into the sea' (Exod 15:19), and the Holy One, blessed be He, brought the horse and its rider [and judged them together].[23]

Here the comparison to the body and the soul comes in. The Holy One, blessed be He, judges them together after death, even though each of the two argues its ignorance, because of its inability to act independently.

The entire move arises following the query of the philosopher emperor, Marcus Aurelius (161-180), a Stoic who devoted considerable attention to ethical issues. He wondered about the body's responsibility for sin, seeing that it is ruled by its rider, the spirit. Our Jewish sources pin the solution to the problem on a sophisticated parable that was recited by the Jewish Nasi (R. Yehuda) in a controversy with the philosopher king: just as the sin is shared by the body and the soul, so, too, must be the punishment: 'Just as you ask me about an impure body, so you should ask me about the soul, which is pure.'[24] Why is the soul punished?

R. Yehuda demonstrates his approach in a parable about a king's orchard and its two watchmen, one lame and other blind. Neither of them, by himself, can reach the fruit, but in cooperation, they lay waste to the orchard. When the king comes, each claims to be innocent. The king who judges them mounts one upon the other and proclaims: this is what you did and how you ate. From the parable, R. Yehuda goes on to its lesson: the Holy One, blessed be He, brings the soul and places it in the body and judges both of them together.[25] Here is the parable as it appears in the Babylonian Talmud (San 91a):

> The body can plead: The soul has sinned, [the proof being] that from the day it left me I lie like a dumb stone in the grave [powerless to do aught]. Whilst the soul can say: The body has sinned, [the proof being] that from the day I departed from it I fly about in the air like a bird [and commit no sin].' He replied, 'I will tell thee a parable. To what may this be compared? To a human king who owned a beautiful orchard which contained splendid figs. Now, he appointed two watchmen therein, one lame and the other blind. [One day] the lame man said to the blind, 'I see beautiful figs in the orchard. Come and take me upon thy shoulder, that we may procure and eat them.' So the lame bestrode the

---

[23] MekSbY p76; also MekRY shira 2, p125. The completion of the parable according to manuscripts in Rabinowitz, *Ginzei Midrash*, 9.

[24] Wallach, 'Colloquy'.

[25] Milikowski, 'Gehinnom', 322f.

blind, procured and ate them. Some time after, the owner of the orchard came and inquired of them, 'Where are those beautiful figs?' The lame man replied, 'Have I then feet to walk with?' The blind man replied, 'Have I then eyes to see with?' What did he do? He placed the lame upon the blind and judged them together. So will the Holy One, blessed be He, bring the soul, [re]place it in the body, and judge them together. (Soncino Translation)

On various occasions, when it was necessary to voice reproaches to the community, to subdue the individual and his urges, use was made of the parable of the body and the soul. This is what we seen in an early text on the acknowledgment of divine justice, which has been preserved in the original Palestinian Aramaic. The words are meant for the ears of those who accompany the body to burial. They unwillingly overhear, as it were, the debate between the body and soul of the deceased. The sharp words are quoted directly as the accusations that the body and soul hurl at one another, the former being masculine and the latter feminine, which is the opposite of the genders in the Indian original. She says, among other things: I was stable and would fly like a bird/ and you made me a wreck like a ship. And he, for his part, accuses her: you are the one who aroused me and weakened me/ indeed, now that I have given up my soul, I am without power to speak/ without discourse and without ornament, is that not sufficient? However, she abuses the body thoroughly and answers him: You are the one who did everything bad/ beneath soil your corpse is crushed/ enclosed and given over to a prison. The last word is given to God Himself, and He warns both of them that on the Judgment Day they will stand trial together (*Shirat benei maarava* 57). Interestingly, in both instances, the blame falls on the masculine element, whether it is the spirit or the body.

Aside from the acknowledgment of divine justice, no hymns are more appropriate for presenting the dispute between body and spirit than the admonitions of the Day of Atonement. Hymns of this type are meant to arouse people to repent, and the mutual recriminations that emerge, as it were, from the person himself, are meant to attain this goal. The body and the soul level these recriminations against one another according to what is reported by the poet, the emissary of the community, a reliable observer from the side. The recriminations are especially stylized and generally presented only in the third person. The congregation joins in with a refrain of supplication: What is the soul for me? What is the body for me? For in any event they are all Yours:

הַנְּשָׁמָה לָךְ	The soul is Yours
וְהַגּוּף שֶׁלָּךְ	The body is Your deed
חוּסָה עַל עֲמָלָךְ	Have mercy on Your work.

– only the congregation addresses the Supreme Addressee. Of course the Aramaic language and the direct formulations of acknowledgment of divine justice are entirely different in character from the Hebrew formulations of admonition.

'Awesome and Dreadful the Fast of the Tenth'

One of the earliest hymns of the unrhymed kind is the admonition, איום ונורא צום העשור, 'Awesome and Dreadful the Fast of the Tenth'. The triple meter of the admonition is used in order to put man in the place he deserves:

עֶצֶם לְרִיקָבוֹן	Bone to decomposition
וּבָשָׂר לְתוֹלַעַת	and flesh to the worm
וְהַגּוּף לְרִימָּה	and the body to maggots' (l. 46).

This is said immediately after the fixed refrain with which the worshipers address God, and which we just heard: 'The soul is Yours/ The body is Your deed/ Have mercy on Your work.' This refrain, which introduces a new dimension of supplication, the triple rhythm, appears after every bloc of three triple-metered lines, all beginning with the same letter (of course, the blocs are in alphabetical order). The masterful climax in the admonition is the dispute between the body and the soul before the Judge of All. The arguments are ordered in apparently endless cycles of dispute, and the triple meter is fitting for them. The triple meter naturally invites a continuation, and thus the dispute rolls on. There are thirty-three triple lines, each with its own speaker and its own letter of the alphabet. The permanent refrain appears between every block of three lines: 'The soul is Yours/ The body is Your deed/ Have mercy on Your work.'

The first bloc of three lines brings us into the atmosphere of the Days of Awe. The juridical discussion begins in the second bloc, that of the letter *bet*. God summons the accused: the soul from heaven and the body from the earth. In the interrogation, God asks no more than a single little question: who has sinned against me? In response, an argument ensues between the body and the soul. The body is always masculine in gender and is called בשר (flesh) or גולם (lump). The נפש (soul) or נשמה (spirit) is always of the feminine gender. The entire dispute consists of two rounds. The body begins by accusing the soul, and she responds. He describes himself as blind. The soul misled him, and he concludes the first round with proof of his innocence:

גַּם בְּעוֹפְפָה מֶנִּי	She flew away from me, too
הֻשְׁלַכְתִּי לְרִימָּה	I was thrown to maggots/
כְּמוֹ אֶבֶן דּוּמָם	mute like a stone.

The soul claims that she is pure and pristine by virtue of her creation, and her dwelling in the body is like a saint and a sinner sharing a house. The sinner feeds her with what it has stolen, but she never achieves satisfaction, which is spiritual: ולא מילאני, 'And he did not fill me' (a quote from Eccl 6:7, 'All the labour of man is for his mouth, and yet the soul is not filled'). Since the soul mentions that matter, the body begins the following round with malicious thoughts about the spirit, which guided him in his actions:

הִרְהוּר הַלֵּב	Thoughts of the heart
וּמַרְאִית הָעַיִן	and the look of the eye
וְהָעָרַת יֵצֶר	and waking of lust.
הוּסְעָה מֶנִּי	Taken away from me
לֹא תֹאַד וְלֹא שִׂיחַ	no appearance and no discourse
וְלֹא עָוֹון לִי	no sin to me.[26]

It appears that the sense of morality and justice cannot agree to such a leave-taking. The body, as it were, has cleared itself and proved the great wickedness of the partner, who flies away and leaves. Therefore, she receives the right to the last word, but in the process she is entrapped and punished. In her answer, which concludes the second round and the entire discussion, tempers flare, and for the first time the soul addresses the body directly (in the second person), no longer speaking to the Judge (in the third person):

וְהַנֶּפֶשׁ חֹּאמַר	And the soul says
אֵיךְ תַּרְשִׁיעֵינִי	how can you declare me guilty
לְמַעַן תִּיצַדַּק	to justify yourself.
וְאַתָּה נִיכְסַפְתָּה	And you desire
לְבָצַע מַעֲשָׁקוֹת	to commit oppressions
גִּיוְוִיךְ לְמַלֹּאות	to fill your body.

Material needs are those of the body alone, and the lofty soul has no part in them. Here it would appear that the body's arguments are refuted, and that he has nothing to answer, but then God intervenes and mocks both of the disputants. He restores the body and the soul to their earlier partnership on Judgment Day, forcing both to be silent, for it is their cooperation that gave rise to the sin. The dispute ends with the marvellous parable, presented in the poem in the poet's voice:

חֲשׁוּבִים הֵם כְּצֶמֶד	They are regarded as a pair
כְּחִיגֵּר וְשׁוֹמָא	like the lame and the blind
שׁוֹמְרֵי בִּשְׂדֵה מֶלֶךְ	guards in the king's field.
חוּבְּלוּ פֵּירוֹת	The fruit was damaged
עַל יַד שְׁנֵיהֶם	by both of them
וְכִיחֲשׁוּ לְהוֹדוֹת	and they refused to confess.
חָשׁ מֶלֶךְ לְהוֹדִיעַ	The king rushed to announce
כַּחֲשָׁם בַּמִּשְׁפָּט	their blame in trial
וְהִירְכִּיבָם וְדָנָם	and put them together and judged them.
הַנְּשָׁמָה לָךְ	The soul is Yours
וְהַגּוּף שֶׁלָּךְ	The body is Your deed
חוּסָה עַל עֲמָלָךְ	Have mercy on Your work.

This is the parable of the pair of handicapped guards who were posted in an orchard full of fresh fruit. Their handicaps prevent each of them from enjoying the fruit on his own, but their presence is sufficient to chase away thieves of

---

[26] Spiegel, *Avot hapiyut*, 387-424 ('The Battle of the Organs'), esp 392 n19.

various sorts, including birds. Very cleverly, they join together and plunder the fruit. Now we remember the image contained in the body's first argument, that the soul was an obstacle for him, like the obstacle placed before a blind person. He is blind, the blind guard of the parable. The lame soul cannot reach the fruit because of her handicap, but she has vision and thought and especially urges that are her undoing. The lame guard is therefore the one who plans the criminal act, but the blind guard is the one who commits it, because he brings the lame one up to the treetops. In the end, 'They are regarded as a pair,' and just as both of them benefit from the deed together, a shared punishment is appropriate for them. This is a particular view of the sages, and it is expressed in most perfect form in the pattern of the ancient poems of admonition; in disputes between male and female, the pure female (soul, spirit) ultimately has the upper hand. In philosophical thought, it was earthly matter, again female, that had the upper hand, and her unique voice accordingly concluded the round of debates as well.

Further Development in Medieval Spain

The poets of Spain, who perfected this genre and its structure, introduced original refrains of their own in the admonitions. They also refreshed the triple rhythm by completing the third hemistich with a biblical verse cited word for word. The verse lent its power to the entire poetical line and also determined its rhyme. The classical distance between the words of sinners as they appear in the Bible from the midrashic dispute between the body and the soul created a striking and particular parodic effect. In a new and original way, it also broke the symmetry of the paired distichs that begin each line. Thus, for example, Shlomo ibn Gabirol places the words of Eve against the serpent, 'The serpent beguiled me and I did eat' (Gen 3:13), in the mouth of the soul, who argues that she cannot bear and support the deceitful body:

נִלְאֵיתִי מְאֹד כַּלְכֵּל	I am very weary of supporting
כִּי הַגּוּף הַנּוֹכֵל	for the deceitful body
הִשִּׁיאַנִי וָאוֹכֵל. [27]	beguiled me, and I ate. [27]

Similarly, Yehuda Halevi places Adam's words against Eve, 'she gave me of the tree' (Gen 3:12) in the mouth of the body, who complains that the soul gave him a staff of wrath from the branches of the tree:

שַׂמְתִּיהָ לִי לְיוֹעֵץ	I made her an advisor
וְהִנֵּה שֵׁבֶט רוֹעֵץ	and behold a stumbling-block staff
נָתְנָה לִי מִן הָעֵץ. [28]	she gave me of the tree. [28]

---

[27] Yarden, *Shirei ha-kodesh*, vol 1, p33 l. 12.
[28] Fleischer, 'Shirim', 80 ll. 31-32.

389

The scene of the dispute between the body and the soul is common to all of the early admonitions. The order of the dispute is also fixed. The body begins, in the guise of a guilty party that feels an urgent need to protect itself, and the soul regularly concludes by bringing the dispute to a climax and levelling justified accusations against the body. The verdict is usually delivered after hearing the soul's arguments, as she accuses the body and clears herself. Only God, as it were, can counter her arguments.

An interesting variant in the order of disputants takes place in a Sephardic admonition. The poetry of Spain is rich in ideas and innovations and did not neglect the genre of the admonition. The greatest poets and thinkers contributed the fruit of their pens to this genre, including Shlomo ibn Gabirol and Yehuda Halevi, as we have seen, and many others. Here the soul begins the dispute and the body regularly concludes it, for according to their views, the gravest accusations were his, since the soul bore responsibility. As Yehuda Halevi expresses it:

מֵאִתָּהּ הַדַּעַת	From her is consciousness
הִיא רוֹאָה וְשׁוֹמַעַת	she sees and hears
וְאָנֹכִי תוֹלַעַת	and I am a worm (Ps 22:7).[29]

The stage of transition between the traditional poetry of the Orient and the poetry of Spain is fascinating. Among the first religious poets in Spain was Yosef ibn Abitur. Like the poets who followed him, he, too, concludes the dispute with the arguments of the body. Nevertheless, because of the tradition, which still obligated him, he also begins with the body. Indeed, Abitur pays a heavy price for this, for he is forced to break the rules of symmetry of full rounds of dispute: body soul, body soul, body soul. He must add a final stanza for the body. The body of course argues in its defense: indeed, I committed crimes, but she twisted my path.[30] Here we see the influence of philosophy, as it struggled with the rules of this genre, which had been formed five hundred years earlier in the Land of Israel. Having the body begin the dispute is one of the traditional signs of the genre, but the poet who lived at the turn of the eleventh century already felt that the most severe arguments, which demand divine intervention, are those of the body, and therefore it must be the last of the disputants, who necessitates the judge's intervention to bring the argument to a close. It appears that the dichotomy between the body and the soul grew stronger in the philosophical doctrines that reached the Jews of the Iberian peninsula from Greek philosophy by means of Arabic. The total negation of matter, which is distant from celestial spirituality, grew stronger. Hence, according to these views, it is impossible to place the responsibility upon the body. From now on, the responsibility falls upon the soul, according to a late

---

[29] *Ib.* ll. 27-28.
[30] Schirmann, *Shirim hadashim*, 154f.

390

version of the philosophical system of Antoninus, and therefore the order of the dispute must change.

The pre-hymnal processes of the genre are also fascinating. Divine intervention and levelling the accusation equally upon the two rival camps is peculiar to the hymns of admonition and to the disputes between body and soul alone. In the earliest models of Akkadian and Sumerian poems of debate, the dispute takes places in wisdom style between typical mythological pairs such as heaven and earth or also between fowl and the female fish, and the like. The representative of the gods appears at the end of the drama, resolving the complications unequivocally and regularly determining in favour of one of the parties.[31] The ethical discussion in which responsibility ultimately falls equally upon the two disputants is quite different. In Hebrew literature this genre had an extremely long life, and until the thirteenth century poems were written in Spain in the genre of admonitions, which included disputes between the body and the soul.[32] We find that at the same time a particularly long literary continuum had been created, lasting four thousand years from the beginning of the literature of dispute until its waning. The genre made quite a long journey between its distant origins in Mesopotamia and its final applications in the western extreme of the known world of that time.

---

[31] Klein – Shifra, *Ba-yamim ha-rehokim ha-hem*, 583-600.
[32] Schirmann, *Hashira halvrit* 2, 285-290. Cf the comment by E. Fleischer in Schirmann, *Toldot hashira halvrit*, 433 n27.

Chapter Eleven

Mystical Texts

Michael D. Swartz

Along with the Talmuds, Midrashim, and liturgy, Hebrew literature in late antiquity includes a body of esoteric texts that describe visionary experiences and magical rituals. Since the nineteenth century, scholars have argued that in the rabbinic period small circles of Jews cultivated a type of visionary mysticism that involved the cultivation of visions of the heavens and of ecstatic journeys through the seven 'palaces' (היכלות, *hekhalot*) or layers of the celestial world to the throne-room of God, where he is seated on his 'chariot-throne' (מרכבה, *merkava*).[1] The evidence for this phenomenon exists primarily in manuscripts from early medieval Europe and the Cairo Geniza in what is known as Hekhalot literature, as well as short passages in rabbinic literature. This essay will concern these texts and what can be learned from them about mysticism in rabbinic Judaism and related cultural phenomena.

---

[1] When used as literary terms, 'Hekhalot' and 'Merkava' will be capitalised in the following, but not when denoting the heavenly 'palaces' and 'chariot-throne'.

The Idea of Merkava Mysticism

Visions of God are described in several places in the Hebrew Bible.[2] Visions of God seated on His divine throne appear in Isaiah chapter 6, Ezekiel chapters 1-3, and Daniel chapter 7. The term מרכבה, literally meaning 'chariot', does not appear in the Massoretic text of the Hebrew Bible when describing the throne of God. However, the term is used in 1 Chron 28:18 to designate the structure formed by the cherubs that frame the Ark of the Covenant in Solomon's temple. In Ben Sira 49:8 the throne of Ezekiel's vision is called the *merkava*: 'Ezekiel saw a vision, and described the different (creatures) of the chariot' (תבנית המרכבה). Visions of the divine throne appear in Biblical and post-biblical literature, from Isaiah 6 and Ezekiel 1-3 to the 'tours of heaven' in apocalyptic texts such as the Books of Enoch and 4 Ezra. However, in these literatures journeys to heaven are not undertaken actively by the human traveller; rather they occur at God's initiative. It is only with Hekhalot literature that human beings are described as initiating travels through the heavens to the throne of God.

Early scholars of rabbinic Judaism and Jewish history characterized Hekhalot literature as mystical.[3] Heinrich Graetz, who saw the sages as ancient rationalists, argued that the Hekhalot literature was a marginal post-talmudic phenomenon, the result of the influence of Islam in the early Middle Ages.[4] Although a few portions of Hekhalot texts were published, mostly in anthologies of 'minor Midrashim',[5] the literature received little attention from scholars for decades.

It was Gershom Scholem who brought this literature into the foreground as an important episode in the history of Jewish mysticism and rabbinic Judaism, when he dedicated Chapter 2 of his *Major Trends in Jewish Mysticism* to the subject of 'Merkabah mysticism and Jewish Gnosticism'.[6] In this chapter, and in his subsequent book *Jewish Gnosticism, Merkabah Mysticism, and Talmudic Tradition*,[7] Scholem presented a compelling, coherent portrait of a mystical discipline that extended back to the early days of the rabbinic period. Hekhalot literature, Scholem argued, reflected a mystical system centered on the cultivation of elaborate visions of heaven. The Merkava mystics, in ecstatic trances, saw themselves ascending to heaven, fighting off powerful angels, and finally reaching God's throne-room, where they would behold him in acutely anthropomorphic form. In order to reach this state of ecstasy, they fasted, secluded themselves, and sang extravagant, numinous hymns, which may have func-

---

[2] For a useful survey of biblical and rabbinic attitudes to visions of God see Wolfson, *Speculum*, 13-51.

[3] The most important early studies are Bloch, 'יורדי מרכבה'; and Graetz, 'Mystische Literatur'.

[4] On Graetz's conception of Merkava mysticism approach see Biale, *Gershom Scholem*, 19-25.

[5] Jellinek, *Bet Ha-Midrash*; Wertheimer, *Bate Midrashot*.

[6] Scholem, *Major Trends*, 40-79.

[7] Scholem, *Jewish Gnosticism*.

tioned as a kind of mantra. Furthermore, Scholem argued, this form of mysticism as depicted in Hekhalot literature is the very practice alluded to in talmudic warnings against spreading esoteric teachings about the book of Ezekiel in mHag 2:1 and its talmudic commentaries.[8] Hekhalot literature, therefore, according to Scholem, dates back to the early rabbinic period (third-to-fourth centuries if not earlier), and can be used to illuminate several obscure passages in talmudic literature. Scholem also characterized the phenomenon as a 'Jewish concomitant to Gnosticsm', reflecting a theology in which a high, spiritual God makes Himself manifest as an embodied, accessible being, which initiates endowed with esoteric gnosis can approach after an agonistic struggle.[9]

In the past two decades, this characterization of Merkava mysticism has been called into question. Scholars, beginning with Ephraim Urbach and most prominently David J. Halperin, have questioned whether rabbinic passages alleged to be related to Merkava mysticism are in fact part of the same phenomenon.[10] Others, notably Martha Himmelfarb, ask whether this literature is in fact evidence for an ecstatic practice.[11] Moreover, Halperin and Peter Schäfer ask whether the ascent literature in the Hekhalot corpus is as central to understanding it as Scholem argued.[12]

In order to understand the terms of this debate, we should consider what it might mean to characterize Hekhalot literature as mystical.[13] Early twentieth century theorists of religion such as Evelyn Underhill and William James defined mysticism primarily in terms of an individual experience that occurs suddenly and passively.[14] They also saw mysticism as a phenomenon that transcends specific religious traditions. In contrast, Gershom Scholem understood mysticism to be inseparable from the tradition in which it was formed. As he stated, 'There is no mysticism as such, there is only the mysticism of a particular religious system.'[15] He went on to define mysticism primarily as a way of closing a perceived abyss between God and humanity created by revelation and religious institutions. For Scholem, then, mysticism must be placed in historical context, even though individual experience plays an essential part. After Scholem, other theorists, especially Steven Katz, questioned whether the experience itself was not something constructed by the cultural environment of the mystic.[16] More recently, Elliot Wolfson has sought to understand mysticism

---

[8] Scholem, *Major Trends*, 52f; *idem*, *Jewish Gnosticism*, 14-19, where he relates the phenomenon to Paul's testimony in 2 Cor 12:2-4.

[9] Scholem, *Major Trends*, 73-75. Cf. Alexander, 'Comparing'.

[10] Urbach, 'Ha-mesoret'; Halperin, *Merkabah*.

[11] Himmelfarb, *Ascent to Heaven*; *idem*, 'Heavenly Ascent'.

[12] Halperin, *Faces of the Chariot*; Schäfer, *Hidden and Manifest God*; idem, 'Aim and Purpose'.

[13] On the concepts of mysticism and mystical experience and how they have been applied with regard to rabbinic Judaism and its milieu, see further Swartz, *Scholastic Magic*, 15-18; and Schäfer, 'Merkavah Mysticism and Magic'.

[14] Underhill, *Mysticism*.

[15] Scholem, *Major Trends*, 5f.

[16] See Katz, *Mysticism and Philosophical Analysis* and *Mysticism and Religious Traditions*.

as a hermeneutical process, thereby calling into question the presumption of a gap between raw experience and cultural interpretation.[17]

In the case of Hekhalot literature, the designation of the phenomenon as mysticism rests on the premise that the authors of the Hekhalot texts cultivated ecstatic visions of the heavens, which they then described in the literature, attributing their own experiences to Rabbis Akiva and Yishmael. Scholem related the phenomenon to a passage in a responsum by the post-talmudic authority, Rav Hai Gaon (939-1038 CE), who described a procedure for seeing the merkava that involves fasting, laying one's head between one's knees, and whispering prayers to the ground. In this way, says the Gaon, 'you can glimpse inside it and its chambers as one who sees with his eyes the seven hekhalot.'[18] However, the literature itself presents obstacles to this characterization. For one thing, there are few indications that the authors conceived of the ascent exclusively as an internal process. Unlike those mystics who report mystical experiences as alterations of consciousness or visions undertaken by the soul, the authors of the Hekhalot texts seem to have believed that Rabbis Akiva and Yishmael actually ascended to heaven. The pseudepigraphic and composite nature of this literature also bears on the question of whether it yields decisive evidence for individual mystical experience. Moreover, David Halperin has shown that Rav Hai Gaon was interpreting a ritual that appears in for assuring success in the New Year and therefore his responsum does not yield evidence for a practice of ecstatic vision of the merkava.[19]

The Merkava and Rabbinic Literature

In this chapter, the term 'Merkava mysticism' will refer to the cultivation of an ecstatic state in which the individual believes himself to have a vision of the heavens, supernatural beings, and the image of God. Using these criteria, scholars have debated for centuries whether rabbinic literature is aware of a mystical practice of cultivating visions of ascent to heaven and whether the central shapers of rabbinic literature engaged in such a practice. The chief texts that have figured in this debate are a series of cryptic laws and stories in tractate Hagiga that seem to portray discourse on the first chapter of Ezekiel as a dangerous, esoteric discipline. Those who hold that the early sages were aware of or participated in Merkava mysticism see these restrictions as warning the general population against such a practice. Others argue that the early rabbinic evidence does not support such a conclusion.

---

[17] Wolfson, *Speculum*.
[18] Scholem, *Major Trends*, 49, citing Lewin, *Otsar ha-Geonim* 4 (Hagiga), 14.
[19] Halperin, 'New Edition', 550, citing Schäfer, *Synopse* §424 in Hekhalot Zutarti. Hai may have been relying on oral reports rather than the written text in the Hekhalot corpus.

THE MISHNA

mHag 2:1 restricts the expounding of certain biblical texts to a small number of students:

> Forbidden sexual relations (*arayot*, Lev 18 and 20) may not be expounded among (*be-*) three, nor the work of creation (*maase bereshit*, cf Gen 1) among two, nor the Merkava by one, unless he is wise and understands on his own.

This mishna does not hold to the main themes of the tractate; it is apparently building on the tractate's discussion of the scanty scriptural basis for rabbinic law in mHag 1:8. There are several difficulties in interpreting this brief passage. One question is whether the numbers refer to a maximum or minimum number of participants. As we will see, the Tosefta interprets them to mean that one may expound the *arayot* to two or one, and creation to one only. David Halperin argues, however, that the third restriction, that on expounding the Merkava, may refer not to expounding before one student (which would mean ליחיד, 'to one'), but studying it on one's own (taking ביחיד, 'in one's [own presence]' literally).[20]

mHag 4:10 prohibits certain biblical texts from being recited or translated in the synagogue publicly. These include scandalous stories of the ancestors, such as Gen 34:22 and Gen 38, as well as the episode of the Golden Calf. The text specifies, 'The Merkava is not used as a *haftara*' (supplementary lectionary reading). Once again, no justification is given for the prohibition. Considering the context does not yield significant clues, unless we consider that all the other biblical texts portray Israel in a disgraceful light.

TOSEFTA

The Tosefta passage corresponding to this Mishna, tHag 2:1-6, is more explicit on several details and includes some intriguing additions. This cluster of baraitot was also incorporated, with changes and expansions, into the commentary to the Mishna in the Palestinian and Babylonian Talmuds. The Tosefta specifies that these restrictions refer to a maximum number of participants:

> Forbidden sexual relations may not be expounded among three, but they may be expounded among two; nor the work of creation among two, but it may be expounded with one; nor the Merkava by one, unless he is wise and understands on his own.

The rulings in this baraita become increasingly restrictive. The Tosefta thus makes it clear that the Mishna is structured so as to denote increasing levels of secrecy.[21] However, here, as in the Mishna, no reason is given for the restrictions. In its elaboration of the laws concerning the expounding of Maase Mer-

[20] Halperin, *Merkabah*, 29-31.
[21] Halperin, *Merkabah*, 36.

kava, the Tosefta also adds stories concerning the subject. In the first, Rabban Yohanan ben Zakkai asks R. Elazar ben Arakh to recite a passage (*perek*) of Maase Merkava. He does so, at which point his teacher praises him as one who is able to 'understand and expound on the glory of his Father in heaven'. This phrase makes it clear that the subject of Maase Merkava concerns the description of the divine presence, known as *kavod* or glory. However, the story does not indicate how this knowledge is arrived at. Yohanan then goes on to praise Elazar as one who 'expounds well and upholds well' (נאה דורש ונאה מקיים). This cryptic phrase is not explained.

The Tosefta (tHag 2:2) goes on to provide a 'chain of tradition' listing a succession of sages who studied with (literally, 'lectured before') teachers since Yohanan ben Zakkai:

> R. Yose ben Yehuda says: R. Joshua lectured before Rabban Yohanan ben Zakkai, R. Akiva lectured before R. Joshua, Hanina ben Kinai lectured before R. Akiva.

The story then establishes that the tradition of expounding the Merkava was passed down through a line of sages central to the mishnaic tradition. The mention of R. Akiva apparently occasions a story about Akiva and three colleagues. This story has played a pivotal role in the debate over whether the early Sages engaged in Merkava mysticism:

> Four entered the *pardes*: Ben Azzai, Ben Zoma, *Aher*, and R. Akiva. One glimpsed and died, one glimpsed and went mad,[22] one glimpsed and cut the shoots. And one went up safely and went down safely. Ben Azai glimpsed and died. About him scripture says: 'Precious in the eyes of the Lord is the death of His faithful ones' (Ps 116:15). Ben Zoma glimpsed and went mad. About him scripture says: 'If you find honey, eat only what you need, [lest you be sated with it and vomit it]' (Prov 25:16). Elisha glimpsed and cut the shoots. About him scripture says: 'Do not let your mouth cause your body to sin' (Eccl 5:5). R. Akiva went up safely and went down safely. About him scripture says: 'Draw me after you, let us run; [the king has brought me to his chambers]' (Cant 1:4).[23]

From the early centuries of the rabbinic period to the present day this enigmatic story has served as a kind of *tabula rasa* for our understanding of mystical and visionary dimensions of rabbinic civilization. It has served as evidence that the early sages engaged in philosophical experimentation, methods of biblical hermeneutics, and mystical practice.[24] In recent decades this story and its parallels in talmudic and cognate literatures has been the subject of several scholarly studies.[25] One of the suppositions of these studies has been that if we can decipher this story, we can determine if the early sages were also mystics.

---

[22] Literally, 'was afflicted'.

[23] tHag 2:3.

[24] On interpretations of this passage in the Middle Ages see Idel, 'PaRDeS'.

[25] See for example Davila, 'The *Hodayot* Hymnist'; and Morray-Jones, *Transparent Illusion*.

However, the story provides only a few details. The word *pardes* (פרדס), an early loanword from Persian, means 'orchard'. Each of the figures in the story is familiar from other rabbinic texts. R. Akiva was one of the founders of the mishnaic tradition and a heroic figure in rabbinic legends.[26] His colleagues Ben Azzai and Ben Zoma are the source of numerous teachings and stories. *Aher*, as we see from the subsequent expansion of the brief statement at the beginning, is a term meaning 'the other one', for Elisha ben Abuya, who was notorious in rabbinic literature for having been a prominent rabbi who became a heretic.[27] However, the story itself yields little about its context and meaning. We are not told whether the pardes is a physical place, a metaphor of some sort, or a term for a spiritual state or supernatural location. Nor are we told what it is that the sages 'glimpsed' or why they met with tragic fates.

Subsequent rabbinic traditions do not clarify these questions. The Yerushalmi (yHag 2, 77b) interprets the phrase 'cut the shoots' to mean that Elisha ben Abuya 'killed masters of Tora'. The Tosefta and the Yerushalmi also relate a story whereby Ben Zoma's speculation about the nature of creation (*maase bereshit*) drives him to madness and death.[28] The Tosefta follows the pardes story with a parable likening it to a king's orchard with a raised platform built over it; one is allowed to peek, but not to feast one's eyes on it. This parable may be alluding to the fact that R. Akiva is not listed as having 'glimpsed', but simply entered safely and departed safely. A second parable likens the matter to a road flanked by two paths, one of fire and one of snow, so that one must one must walk in the middle. The only thing these stories indicate is that the pardes, whether a real place or a metaphor for a kind of activity, is fraught with danger. At the same time, the story does not discourage the reader entirely from entering it. The story implies that if one is somehow like R. Akiva, entry to the pardes is possible.

The parables in the Tosefta and the stories in the Yerushalmi constitute the earliest commentaries to the passage. However, they do not support one particular interpretation. The parable of the king's orchard might lead the reader to think of the pardes as a real, if supernatural, place, perhaps the precincts of the Divine presence. However, the story of Ben Zoma's madness might support the interpretation of the pardes as a metaphor for exegetical speculation on the secrets of creation and cosmology. It should also be pointed out that the two notions are not mutually exclusive. Exegetical conclusions can serve as a basis for a mystical practice; conversely, mystical traditions often develop contemplative techniques of scriptural interpretation.[29] All told, however, the early interpretations of the pardes episode do not lead us to firm conclusions

[26] The subtitle of Louis Finkelstein's 1936 biography, *Akiba, Scholar, Saint and Martyr*, summarizes how Akiva was known in talmudic tradition.
[27] On legends of Elisha ben Abuya, see Goshen-Gottstein, *The Sinner and the Amnesiac*; cf Liebes, *Hatato shel Elisha*.
[28] tHag 2:6; yHag 2:1, 77a.
[29] On this point, see especially Wolfson, *Speculum*.

about visionary activity among the early sages. Indeed, the divergent streams of interpretation suggest that the meaning of the passage was lost even to the editors of the Tosefta.

David J. Halperin has succeeded in calling into question whether the phenomenon to which modern scholars refer as 'Merkava mysticism' is what the Tannaim meant by 'expounding the Merkava'. His and other studies have also cast doubt on whether the pardes episode refers to a practice of mystical ascent.[30] However, this does not exhaust the significance of these enigmatic texts. Taken together, they seem to indicate that there is something dangerous and mysterious about discourse on the Merkava. tHag 2:1-6 clearly warns the reader that there is something that could drive one to insanity, heresy, or death. At the same time, R. Akiva's success at entering and departing safely indicates to the reader that approaching the pardes is possible.

Whatever their original meaning, these passages played a significant role in the textual traditions that subsequently developed around the divine throne and human ascent. One passage in Hekhalot literature in particular has been singled out for its intriguing relationship to interpretations of the pardes story. In bHag 14b, after quoting the pardes story, the Talmud relates:

> R. Akiva said to them, When you arrive at the pure marble stones, do not say, 'water, water', as it is said, 'He who speaks untruth shall not stand before my eyes' (Ps 101:7).

A passage in the Hekhalot text known as Hekhalot Zutarti describes a moment when the traveller is invited to enter the sixth palace, whereupon it seems to him as if millions of waves of water are raining down on him. But those waves of water are an illusion and it is only the marble plates with which the palace was tessellated.[31] Scholem argued that this passage preserved the original meaning of R. Akiva's warning in the Bavli's version of the story, and that the term pardes stands for Paradise or the inner chambers of heaven. Whether or not Scholem's argument applies to the Tosefta's version of the pardes episode, it does raise the possibility that the ascent tradition was known to the editors of the Bavli before the sixth century CE.

Despite these possible connections between Merkava mysticism and the rabbinic canon, Hekhalot literature does not take talmudic traditions about the Merkava as their central literary or historiographic model. For example, R. Akiva, the hero of the pardes episode, does figure prominently in some texts, especially Maase Merkava. However, R. Yishmael is more commonly the protagonist of ascent and conjuration narratives in Hekhalot literature. He does not feature in the talmudic passages explicitly dealing with the Merkava.

---

[30] Cf. Morray-Jones, *Transparent Illusion*, which seeks to prove the relevance of the Merkava tradition for the original meaning of the pardes story.

[31] The text from Hekhalot Zutarti appears in Schäfer, *Synopse*, §408. The passage was also cited in connection with the pardes story by Hai Gaon (Lewin, *Otsar ha-Geonim* 4:14); and by Hananel ben Hushiel's commentary to bHag 14b.

Rather, the clue to the prominence of R. Yishmael in Hekhalot literature may
lie in bBer 7a, where R. Yishmael is portrayed (anachronistically) as a priest
having a vision of God in the Temple.[32] Having established that Hekhalot
literature reflects a literary and religious phenomenon distinct from rabbinic
Judaism if related to it, we now turn to the Hekhalot texts themselves.

Hekhalot Literature

The Hekhalot texts exist primarily in manuscripts from medieval Germany and
Southern Europe.[33] The most important manuscripts were compiled and transmitted by the Ḥasidei Ashkenaz, the Jewish pietiests of the Rhineland of the
eleventh-thirteenth centuries and their successors.[34] There are also several
fragments of Hekhalot manuscripts in the Cairo Geniza.[35]

In Scholem's initial publications on Hekhalot literature, he set forth what
he considered to be the principal texts.[36] He gave those texts titles such as
Hekhalot Rabbati ('The Greater [book of the] Palaces'), Hekhalot Zutarti ('The
Lesser [Book of the] Palaces'), Maase Merkava ('The Work of the Chariot'),
and so on, based on Hai Gaon's *responsum* as well as other citations in early
medieval literature.[37] Since then it has been customary to divide the literature
into several textual units bearing these titles.[38] However, the research of Peter
Schäfer for his monumental edition of Hekhalot literature has shown that the
manuscripts yield a far more complex picture of how this literature took
shape.[39] Schäfer showed that manuscripts vary greatly in the way the literature
is distributed. Several paragraphs may appear in one order in one manuscript,
and in a radically different order in another. Moreover, whole sections of a text
may be absent in a given manuscript or manuscript family. This led Schäfer to
the conclusion that the assumption that all manuscripts derive ultimately from
one *Urtext* is mistaken. It means that Hekhalot literature consists not of well

---

[32] On the figure of R. Yishmael as a hero of Hekhalot literature, see Abusch, 'Rabbi Yishmael's
Miraculous Conception'; cf Elior, *Three Temples.*

[33] For a comprehensive list of manuscripts, see Schäfer, 'Handschriften'.

[34] Of the seven major manuscripts published in the *Synopse*, three are Ashkenazic (Oxf 1531, NY
8128, and Munich 40; the Oxford and New York manuscripts, two of the most important, come
from the circles of Hasidei Ashkenaz); one, Dropsie 436, is a fifteenth century Sephardic manuscript; one, Vat 228 is a Greek or Byzantine manuscript from the fourteenth or fifteenth century;
and two, Budapest 238 (fifteenth century) and Munich 22 (1550) are Italian. See Schäfer, *Synopse*,
ix-x.

[35] The first major Geniza manuscript of Hekhalot literature (TS K1.95.C) was published by Gruenwald, 'Ketaim hadashim'; see also idem, 'Tikkunim ve-hearot'. The manuscript was then
published by Schäfer in *Geniza-Fragmente*, 97-109 as G8.

[36] Scholem, *Major Trends*, 45f; and the more complete list in *Jewish Gnosticism*, 5-8.

[37] On the case of Maase Merkava see n71 below.

[38] See, for example, Schäfer's *Hidden and Manifest God*, which, while making a forceful argument
against seeing these texts as unitary documents, necessarily uses these titles for organizing its
survey of the literature.

[39] Peter Schäfer, 'Tradition and Redaction'.

defined texts the beginning and end of which can be delineated, but of smaller textual units that were combined by scribes in different ways, depending on the material they had and their own interests. Schäfer published the most important European manuscripts in his *Synopse zur Hekhalot-Literatur,* in which manuscripts appeared in parallel columns, allowing each to stand by itself.[40] He coined the term macroform for a larger unit, identifying it as a combination of smaller textual units corresponding to what Scholem had designated as Hekhalot Rabbati, Hekhalot Zutarti, and so on.

Schäfer's *Synopse* remains the definitive edition of the major Hekhalot texts. His subsequent publication of Geniza fragments of Hekhalot literature not only made some of the earliest manuscripts available, but served to advance the argument that this literature is highly fluid; in the Geniza fragments textual units appear in radically different order from those in the European manuscripts, thus supporting the argument that Hekhalot texts did not originate in a single version.

The implications of this critical research for the study of early Jewish mysticism are profound. These findings show that a Hekhalot text cannot be treated as a cohesive document written by a single author, but must be seen as a composite, made up of several traditions combined in different ways at different times. Schäfer argued that this was also true of rabbinic literature in general, although this argument has been debated.[41] Such Rabbinic compositions as the Tanhuma-Yelammedenu complex, the Mekhilta, and Avot de-R. Natan, appear in multiple versions with significant variants; it has been argued that these texts constitute examples of this phenomenon.[42] Equally significant are the implications of these findings for Merkava mysticism as a phenomenon. If these are composite texts, they cannot be taken as records of an individual's personal experience, but must be seen as the product of a process of accretion of literary expressions by many people over a span of time.

This textual state, while precluding a description of Merkava mysticism as a single phenomenon, does offer many opportunities for anyone who wants to understand its historical and cultural background. Because these smaller passages ('microforms') are separable units that can be combined in many ways, they open up the possibility that the prior history of the texts can be recovered. Moreover, the nature of the literature shifts the focus of study from these larger macroforms to the intermediate units, which reveal the interests and dynamics of their authors and redactors more clearly. Thus some of the most promising recent studies of Hekhalot literature are those that work intertextually, comparing texts within macroforms and paying close attention to form-critical and

[40] Schäfer, *Synopse.* All references to Hekhalot literature will be cited according to the paragraph numbers in the *Synopse* unless otherwise specified.
[41] Schäfer, 'Research into Rabbinic Literature;' cf Milikowsky, 'Status Quaestionis'. Cf also the views of Kahana, chap. 1, and Lerner, chap. 3 in this volume.
[42] On the Tanhuma see Bregman, *Sifrut Tanḥuma-Yelamdenu;* on the Mekhilta, see Nelson, *Textuality and Talmud Torah.* For Avot de-R. Natan see Kister, *Studies.*

literary questions.[43] Studies of individual texts have found that macroforms exhibit varying degrees of cohesion and that in some cases the redactional history of a text can be determined. This finding has implications for the dating of the texts as well. It is sometimes customary to identify a single element or motif of a text and date the entire text based on that element. But because the Hekhalot texts cannot be said to have originated in a single place and time, the best attempts to date them cannot rely on this method. Rather, it is more productive to identify smaller units and date the process by which the resulting recensions took shape. Based on these criteria, certain elements of the Hekhalot corpus, such as the hymns and some magical elements, are considered by many scholars to have originated in the Land of Israel of the Amoraic period (third to fifth centuries CE); it has been suggested that other elements, such as some of the ascent narratives, evolved in the early post-talmudic period (sixth to eighth centuries CE), in the Land of Israel and Babylonia.[44] Other estimations place the later stages of redaction in the early middle ages (ninth to tenth centuries CE).[45]

With these considerations in mind, this survey of Hekhalot literature will proceed with a description of some of the major texts (macroforms), especially those that have a recognizable overall character. This description will at the same time pay attention to the discrete genres and phenomena within the literature, especially the ascent texts and conjuration texts. It will begin with texts or portions of texts that depict ascents to heaven or visions of the divine presence. Then texts concerning the conjuration of angelic beings and similar rituals will be described.

Ascent and Visionary Texts

HEKHALOT RABBATI

Hekhalot Rabbati is perhaps the most influential of the Hekhalot texts. Its narrative of ascent has served as the paradigm for how Merkava mysticism has been described at least since the nineteenth century.[46] It includes several unique elements, including a historical narrative adapted from the Apocalypse of the Ten Martrys,[47] an unusual vocabulary, and a distinctive style of hymnology. Not all section of this textual complex are found in all manuscripts, but several

---

[43] Two recent examples are Lesses, *Ritual Practices*; Boustan, *From Martyr to Mystic*.

[44] See for example, Swartz, *Mystical Prayer* and Cohen, *Shi'ur Qomah*.

[45] Schäfer, *Hidden and Manifest God*; cf Boustan, *From Martyr to Mystic*.

[46] A good preliminary description of Hekhalot Rabbati is Smith, 'Observations'.

[47] Schäfer, *Synopse*, §§107-121. The story of the Ten Martrys has a long and complex history in Hebrew literature of late antiquity and the Middle Ages. For the principal text see Reeg, *Geschichte von den Zehn Märtyrern*. On the relationship between the Ten Martyrs' tradition and the version in Hekhalot Rabbati, and pseudepigraphic and apocalyptic narratives in Hekhalot in general, see Boustan, *From Martyr to Mystic*.

larger units do stand out.[48] For the purposes of this description, the ascent narrative and hymns will be emphasized. The *Sar-Tora* section will be dealt with separately.

One unusual feature of the text is that the journey to the merkava is called ירידה, *yerida* or 'descent'. No definitive explanation has been found for this terminology; it is possible, as Scholem suggests, that the term *yrd* is influenced by the term ירד לפני התיבה, lit. 'descending before the ark', used of someone who goes to lead prayers in the synagogue.[49] It is also possible, as Elliot Wolfson, as suggested, that the term refers only to the last stage of the ascent, whereby the traveller enters the throne-room itself after having ascended through six hekhalot.[50] At any rate, the terminology is most common in Hekhalot Rabbati and other text modeled after it, such as the ascent text found in the Geniza entitled 'Hotam ha-Merkava'.[51]

The main ascent section of Hekhalot Rabbati is a continuous narrative from §198 to §277 as published in Schäfer's *Synopse*. The section begins with an introduction in which R. Yishmael, the narrator of the text, tells that when R. Nehunia ben ha-Kana heard that Rome was planning to destroy the sages, he gathered a company of rabbis together to 'reveal the nature (*midda*) of the secret of the world'.[52] This is most likely an allusion to the Apocalypse of the Ten Martrys, a widely disseminated narrative tradition about ten second-century sages put to death by the emperor Hadrian, a version of which appears elsewhere in Hekhalot Rabbati.[53] R. Nehunia then likens the technique to having a ladder in one's house, on which anyone can go up and down. This is valid, he says, for 'anyone who is pure and innocent of idolatry, sexual sin, bloodshed, libel, desecration of the divine name, and causeless hatred, and observes every positive and negative commandment'.[54] At this, R. Yishmael reports, he despaired that there was no one on earth so virtuous. In response, R. Nehunia instructs him to gather their colleagues so that he can reveal the secrets of creation that will allow anyone to make the journey.

The rest of the ascent section[55] consists of the instructions, presumably given by R. Nehunia, for ascending to heaven and 'descending' to the merkava. There are at least two sets of instructions, the second set interrupted by

---

[48] For an analysis of the distribution of textual units in Hekhalot Rabbati, see Schäfer, '*Hekhalot Rabbati*,' i; and idem, *Übersetzung* 2, xiv-xxxvi.

[49] Scholem, *Major Trends*; cf Stroumsa, 'Mystical Descents'.

[50] Wolfson, *Yeridah la-Merkava*. For a survey of the evidence, see Kuyt, *'Descent' to the Chariot*.

[51] See n35 above.

[52] Schäfer, *Synopse*, §198.

[53] Schäfer, *Synopse*, §§107-121. This passage also reflects a motif found frequently in Jewish literature that a crisis forced the sages or a given author to write down what had been an esoteric tradition handed down exclusively by oral transmission; a similar explanation is offered for the writing down of the Babylonian Talmud by the tenthcentury authority Rav Sherira Gaon; see Strack and Stemberger, *Introduction*, 192-194.

[54] Schäfer, *Synopse*, §§199-200.

[55] Schäfer, *Synopse*, §§202-258.

several excurses and interpolations. The first set of instructions (§§204-218) describes the ascent through the hekhalot, culminating in a detailed description of the seventh hekhal. The second set (§§219-248) lists briefly the instructions for passing through the first hekhal through the fifth and proceeds to detailed descriptions of the sixth and seventh hekhalot, especially the process of 'descent' at the final stage. These instructions are interrupted for two stories in which R. Nehunia clarifies a cryptic detail.

In the first ascent narrative, R. Nehunia explains the cosmology of the hekhalot:

> R. Yishmael said: Thus said R. Nehunia ben ha-Kana: יי י תותרוסאי, God of Is-
> rael[56] dwells in seven hekhalot, a chamber inside a chamber, and at the gate of
> each hekhal there are eight guards of the doorway at the right side of the lintel.[57]

The descriptions that follow list in detail the names of the guardians of each gate and frightening angels, celestial horses, and rivers of fire at the seventh hekhal. Following a litany praising God as king, a testimony assures the reader that God awaits the יורדי מרכבה, 'those who descend to the merkava', as much as He anticipates the redemption that is reserved for Israel:

> When will those who descend to the merkava see the redemption on high?
> When will he hear the tidings of salvation?[58] When will he see what no eye has
> seen? When will he ascend and tell the seed of Abraham?[59]

This passage states explicitly that God desires the visit of the travellers to the merkava to the divine court. However, the traveller encounters severe and frightening obstacles. At the gate to each palace stand fearsome angelic guards who are waiting to attack anyone who is not properly qualified to enter. The narrative emphasizes the the awe and terror that grips the traveller as he confronts the angels or witnesses the rivers of fire or vast chambers of the divine realm. The secret to success is to possess elaborate divine names, often known as 'seals', which the traveller presents to the angelic guard, and to have esoteric knowledge of the heavenly topography and the names and characteristics of specific angels. If he presents these names successfully, the traveller is reassured that he has been expected and will be honoured by the heavenly hosts.

A passage from the second ascent narrative in Hekhalot Rabbati illustrates this dynamic of fear and acceptance. The passage depicts the moment when a man who wishes to travel to the merkava arrives at the gate of the seventh hekhal. He is met by the angel Anafiel, who opens the gate for him. However, when the *hayyot*, the holy creatures described in Ezek 1:5-12, cast their five hundred and twelve eyes on him,

---

[56] This name seems to be derived from the Greek *tetra*, 'four,' as in the Tetragrammaton. On magical names in Hekhalot literature, see Scholem, *Jewish Gnosticism*, 75-83.

[57] Schäfer, *Synopse*, §206.

[58] Hebr, קץ ישועה.

[59] Schäfer, *Synopse*, §218.

He trembles, quakes, recoils, panics, and falls back fainting. But the angel
Anafiel and the sixty-three guards of the seventh palace assist him and say, 'Do
not fear, son of the beloved seed! Enter and see the King in his beauty. Your
eyes will see, you will not be slaughtered, and you will not be burned!'[60]

The passage portrays the tension between the terror felt by the traveller when
confronted with the angels and God's desire to receive him to the divine
throne-room. This tension recalls in a way the paradox of the pardes narrative
as well; the story warns of the danger but still holds out the possibility that
under the right circumstances the rewards of the journey can be acquired.
Where this passage differs is in its depiction of the emotions of fear and hope
that beset the individual who experiences the journey.

Hekhalot Rabbati is also distinguished by several sets of hymns written in
unusual poetic styles. Hymns are set into the main ascent narratives;[61] others
are independent collections that are framed only by a brief introduction such as
the question that begins one section of Hekhalot Rabbati: 'What are the different songs (הפרש שירות) that a person sings when he descends to the merkava?'[62]
One unit, which begins Hekhalot Rabbati in most manuscripts, describes the
wonders available to the travellers to the merkava:

> It is a wonder beyond any (גדולה מכולם)
> that he may look into the what human beings do
> even in their innermost chambers,
> whether good deeds or foul deeds.
> If a man is a thief he will know it;
> if he is an adulterer he will know it.[63]

This section is interesting because it serves as an introduction to Hekhalot
Rabbati as a whole, but it does not deal directly with the theme of ascent.
Rather it seems to be advertising the practical benefits of practicing the ascent
techniques and rituals described in the body of the text.

Most hymns, however, deal with the praise of God, the appearance of the
angels, and the dynamics of the ascent. Many of these hymns culminate in the
recitation of the Kedusha, the angelic liturgical declaration of God's holiness
in Isa 6:3. Some of these hymns are characterized by a profusion of synonyms
in series; sometimes these are adjectives describing God or the angels and
sometimes they are verbs for praise. Thus, once the traveller has arrived at the
seventh hekhal, the text breaks into a litany of adjectives for God as king:
'Righteous king, faithful king, gentle king, humble king, compassionate king,

---

[60] Schäfer, Synopse, §248.
[61] For example, Schäfer, Synopse §249 and §§252-257.
[62] Identifiable collections appear in Schäfer, Synopse, §§81-92 (the גדולה hymns described below);
94-106 (Kedusha hymns); §§152-196 (another set of Kedusha hymns); §§252-258; and §§269-
277, a set of hymns that includes the acrostic litany Ha-aderet ve-ha-emuna, which also appears in
the liturgical rites of many communities.
[63] Schäfer, Synopse, §83.

holy king, pure king,' and so on.[64] Likewise, when he stands before the throne he recites 'a song that the throne of glory sings every day: psalm, song, music, blessing, praise, exultation, acclamation, thanks, thanksgiving, triumphant praise, melody…'[65] This repetitious style seems to have influenced at least one version of the *Kedusha de-yotser* in the Babylonian liturgy, which describes the praise of angels in similarly profuse language.

Other hymns are written in distinctive styles, maintaining an unusual rhythm, syntax, and set of themes. One type of hymn used extensively in separate sections of Hekhalot Rabbati follows a complex pattern and contains allusions to the travellers to the merkava and the journey itself. These culminate in the recitation of the liturgical Kedusha, the doxology sung by the angels in Isa 6:3. One such hymn addresses the angels directly:[66]

> You who annul the decree, who dissolve the oath,
> who repel wrath, who turn back jealousy,
> who recount love, who array authority
> before the magnificent splendor of the wondrous hekhal,
> why is it that you sing praises, and at times you rejoice?
> Why is it and you are fearful, and at times you recoil?
> They said, 'When the wheels of the divine glory darken,
> we stand in great dread,
> but when the radiance of the Shekhina[67] gives light,
> we are happy, very happy,'
> as it is said, 'Holy, Holy, Holy is the Lord of Hosts,
> the fullness of the earth is his glory' (Isa 6:3).

This composition presupposes that the speaker of the hymn is in heaven witnessing the angelic liturgy and is engaging in a dialogue with the angels. This fits the general scheme of Hekhalot Rabbati in which the individual ascends to heaven. However, the hymn does concern an idea that does not figure in Hekhalot narrative, that the wheels (אפנים) of the divine throne sometimes darken and sometimes give light.[68] This may be an indication that the hymns come from another source, perhaps within the same circles that produced the ascent narrative. In another the angels that bear the wheels of the merkava sing to the merkava itself:

---

[64] Schäfer, *Synopse*, §249.

[65] Schäfer, *Synopse*, §251.

[66] Schäfer, *Synopse* §158, according to ms Munich 22. This translation has drawn from Morton Smith's in Scholem, *Jewish Gnosticism*, 22.

[67] The Divine Presence. In ms Oxf 1531 the word מרכבה is inserted above the line.

[68] One important manuscript tradition (Munich 22 and Budapest 238) does not mention the merkava by name, although it does mention the hekhal. However, other hymns in this section do mention the merkava.

Rejoice, rejoice supernal dwelling!
Shout, shout for joy, precious vessel!
Made marvellously and a marvel.[69]

Scholem showed that this passage is related to a poetic fragment found in the Bavli, Genesis Rabba, and other sources.[70] In this passage the kine that drew the Ark of the Covenant are said to address it directly in song, in the same way the angels sing to the merkava. It cannot be proven that one parallel is derived from the other, but the affinity does attest to the degree to which Hekhalot hymnology was immersed in the poetic environment of late antiquity.

MAASE MERKAVA

Maase Merkava is the name given by Gershom Scholem to a text in the Hekhalot corpus that emphasizes the prayers to be recited to achieve a vision of the divine throne or to conjure the Sar-Tora.[71] Excerpts from the text were first published by Alexander Altmann and a more complete version was published by Scholem.[72] The text appears in Schäfer's *Synopse* (§§544-596). The text contains four sections, dealing with two themes. The theme of Sections I (§§544-59), III (§§579-591) and IV (§§592-596) is how Rabbis Akiva and Yishmael used prayer to see God and the heavenly array.[73] Section II (§§560-570) concerns the conjuration of the angel of Tora (Sar-Tora).[74]

The narrative, in which R. Yishmael quizzes R. Akiva concerning the prayers that he recited in order to gaze at the merkava, is not the detailed, descriptive ascent narrative of Hekhalot Rabbati, but more of a framework for the prayers that form the bulk of the work. These prayers are described by R. Akiva as the vehicles for his vision, as well as the instruments that protect him from harm in the divine presence. Thus in §544 R. Yishmael asks R. Akiva the prayer of praise that that one recites when one ascends to the merkava. Soon afterward R. Akiva attests, 'I said a prayer for mercy, and because of it I was saved' (§547). In a few passages R. Akiva lists such images as the chariots of fire, the flames that go forth from them, and the distance between the celestial rivers. However, this scheme does not form the structure for the work as a

---

[69] Schäfer, *Synopse*, §94, translated by Morton Smith, in Scholem, *Jewish Gnosticism*, 26.

[70] Scholem, *Jewish Gnosticism*, 24-26. The passage appears in bAZ 24b, GenR 54 (p581f) and parallels.

[71] The text was given this name on the basis of a quotation from Elazar of Worms' work, Sodei razaya; see *Jewish Gnosticism*, 76, 101. However the passage quoted by Elazar seems to have circulated independently of the rest of the text and therefore it is doubtful that this was the early title of the text.

[72] Altmann, 'Shirei Kedushah'; Scholem, *Jewish Gnosticism*, 101-117. For analyses of the text, see Swartz, *Mystical Prayer*, and Janowitz, *Poetics of Ascent*.

[73] In sections I and IV R. Akiva describes his visions before R. Yishmael; in section III R. Yishmael describes his experiences before his teacher R. Nehunia, who gives him advice and teaches him additional prayers.

[74] In one manuscript, ms NY 8128, an Aramaic ritual text has been inserted.

whole. In almost all other cases, the dialogue between Rabbis Yishmael and Akiva serves to introduce an extensive prayer or set of liturgical phrases. In fact one passage in which the chariots (merkavot) of fire are described at each hekhal, the enumeration is accompanied by a listing of the doxologies that the merkavot sing to God at each hekhal.[75]

The prayers themselves have a distinctly liturgical quality. Most of them end with a liturgical blessing (berakha or *hatima*) such as, 'Blessed are You, Sage of Secrets' or, 'Blessed are You, magnificent in the chambers of greatness.' Moreover, they bear strong similarities to the earliest forms of liturgical poetry (piyyut) as found in poetic fragments from the Talmuds and the rabbinic liturgy. This style is characterized by a consistent but not strict rhythm, usually of three or four feet, synonymous parallelism, and the use of novel construct pairs. A version of the prayer for Rosh Hashana known as *Alenu leshabeah*, 'It is [incumbent] upon us,' appears in Maase Merkava (§551); in this case, however, it is cast in the first person plural and introduced as the prayer that R. Akiva recited upon seeing the angels of Glory facing the divine throne.[76]

These compositions usually hold to a fairly well-defined structure, which sets out a kind of rhetorical argument about the worshipper. They begin with a vocative address directly to God, often in the form of a liturgical berakha. The body of the prayer then begins with a statement regarding God's creation of heaven and earth:

> In glory You spoke and the world came into being;
> With the breath of Your lips You established the firmament;
> And Your great name is pure and exalted
> Over all those above, and those below. [77]

The first two lines exhibit a parallel structure; God's act of creation of the world is placed in parallel to his creation of the firmament. In the next two lines as well, the poet insists that God's name is exalted both over angels ('those above') and human beings ('those below'). This point is reinforced two lines down in the same composition:

> Angels stand in heaven,
> And the righteous are sure in their remembrance of You,
> And Your name hovers over them all.[78]

The prayer thus emphasizes the parity of angels and human beings, especially in their right to praise God. At a certain point in the middle of the prayers, elaborate divine names or mysterious phrases are inserted. These names and

---

[75] Schäfer, *Synopse*, §554.

[76] On this prayer and its history see Swartz, '*Alay le-shabbeah*'. Relationships between Hekhalot literature and the liturgical tradition are also examined in Bar-Ilan, *Sitre teflila*.

[77] Schäfer, *Synopse*, §587.

[78] *Ib.*

phrases break the rhythm and structure of the prayers and seem to have been included in order to reinforce the power of the prayer, especially in an esoteric or magical context. Near the end of the prayer the angels are said to praise God for the reasons given before: 'Therefore, the Mighty Ones of Heaven give praise before You.'[79] At times the worshipper declares that he himself will praise God:

> Therefore, we shall call Your name,
> We will bless Your might;
> We will lift up and present acclamation before Your Throne.[80]

The prayers conclude with a blessing. Some of these are blessings found in the statutory Jewish liturgy, such as 'Blessed are You, Lord, the holy God,'[81] which is the third blessing of the statutory Amida and the blessing concluding the Kedusha. Others are specific to the Merkava tradition, such as 'Blessed are You, Lord, the Holy One in the Merkava, Rider of the Cherubim.'[82]

Taken together, these prayers constitute an argument concerning the relationships between angels, human beings, and God. God, who created both heaven and earth, also rules over both angels and human beings. Therefore, both have an equal right to participate in the praise of God. This theme can be traced to one of the sources of Merkava mysticism: The corresponding prayer of angels and human beings. This idea is reflected in the statutory Kedusha and in such earlier documents as the angelic liturgy (Songs of the Sabbath Sacrifice) from Qumran.[83] It is expressed in the rabbinic Kedusha for the morning service in this way:

> We sanctify Your name on earth,
> As they sanctify it in the heavenly heights
> As it is written by Your prophet:
> 'And they called to one another, saying:
> Holy, Holy, Holy is the Lord of Hosts!
> His presence fills all the earth!'

The premise behind the Kedusha, and behind the prayers in Maase Merkava, is that the angels are conducting a liturgy in heaven while the human community praises God on earth. The prayers in Maase Merkava go further in their assertion that both liturgies are equally valid. However, these prayers do not explicitly mention an ascent to heaven, unlike many of the hymns in Hekhalot Rabbati. The context of an actual ascent to heaven and vision of the celestial topography was added by the narrative, probably in a later stage in the evolu-

---

[79] Ib. §589.
[80] Ib. §596.
[81] Ib. §594.
[82] Ib. §588.
[83] On the angelic liturgy, see Newsom, *Songs of the Sabbath Sacrifice*; on the Dead Sea Scrolls and Merkava mysticism see Swartz, 'Dead Sea Scrolls'.

tion of the text. Likewise, although the prayers do mention the name of God, the elaborate divine names in the prayers are most likely later additions designed to lend the prayers the potency claimed for them in the narrative, by which they are vehicles for divine vision and protection. Maase Merkvah thus attests to a strand of Merkava mysticism in which a liturgical corpus of prayers praising of God in correspondence with the angels was then adapted into a framework in which those prayers were seen as the instruments that could effect ascent.

3 ENOCH

'Sefer Hekhalot' (The Book of the Palaces), also known as 3 Enoch, is a late fusion of Hekhalot and apocalyptic narrative traditions. Although this text also presupposes a scheme of seven hekhalot, the bulk of the text concerns Enoch's narrative of how he ascended to heaven, and, having resisted the challenge of angelic guards of the divine presence, was transformed into Metatron, the archangel who stands at God's right hand. This text was first published in 1928 by the biblical scholar Hugo Odeberg, who ascribed to it great antiquity and was apparently unaware of its identity as a Hekhalot text.[84] It was then published in the *Synopse*.[85] A comprehensive study of the text is Philip Alexander's introduction to his translation in the Charlesworth translation of the Pseudepigrapha.[86]

This complex text is remarkable for a number of reasons. One important reason is its relationship to the pseudepigraphical Enoch traditions of the SecondTemple period. Although it stands clearly in the Hekhalot tradition, the text centers around the figure of Enoch, who does not figure prominently in any other Hekhalot text. Furthermore, as Jonas Greenfield, Philip Alexander, and others have shown, the text incorporates several elements of Enoch myths and other motifs known only from Second Temple pseudepigrapha.[87] Another striking feature is the emphasis on angelology, especially the figure of Metatron. Metatron is an archangelic persona found elsewhere in Hekhalot literature, as well as in ancient Jewish magic. Metatron figures in several magical texts including the Aramaic incantation bowls of sixth-century Jewish Babylonia and a magical amulet text from the Cairo Geniza, where he is represented as 'The High Priest, chief of priests...who is head of all the camps'.[88]

---

[84] Odeberg, *3 Enoch*; on Odeberg's edition and 3 Enoch in general see Jonas Greenfield's valuable 'Prolegomenon' to the second edition; see also n86 below.

[85] Schäfer, *Synopse*, §§1-80 in ms Vat 228 (= §§866-936 ms Munich 40).

[86] Alexander, '3 (Hebrew Apocalypse of) Enoch'. See also *idem*, 'Historical Setting' and '3 Enoch and the Talmud'.

[87] For a summary of these, see Arbel, 'Seal of Resemblance'; on 3 Enoch and the Enochic literature see also Orlov, 'Celestial Choirmaster'.

[88] ms TS K1.168, published in Schiffman and Swartz, *Incantation Texts*, 143-159.

The text begins with a first-person narrative by R. Yishmael, who describes an ascent to the merkava. To affect this ascent, R. Yishmael prays for safety form Katspiel, the angel of divine wrath. In answer to his prayer, he is met by Metatron, who takes him by the hand to the seventh hekhal where he witnesses the heavenly Kedusha. When he arrives, however, Metatron is challenged by the other angels, who ask, 'From what people is he and what is his nature?' Metatron answers that he is from the tribe of Levi and a priest. This episode serves to introduce the extended narrative that describes Enoch's transformation into Metatron. The introduction also signals a shift in the Enochic myths that brings the text into the realm of early Jewish mysticism. In this introduction, Metatron serves as a mentor for R. Yishmael; having been human, his ascent is meant to serve as a signal that R. Yishmael (and by extension any human traveller to the merkava) not only deserves to ascend to the heavenly realm, but that his ascent is desired by God.

Metatron's status as the former human hero Enoch and his elevation to a place alongside the divine throne are both occasions for expressing ambivalence.[89] On the one hand, since Enoch is a human who has dared to enter the precincts of heaven, he arouses suspicion among the other angels. His elevated status as a divine assistant, or Lesser YHWH (*YHWH katan*), as he is called, is also not taken at face value. Building on talmudic legends about Elisha ben Abuya having declared that there are 'two powers in heaven', as well as the pardes narrative, a story in the text tells how Elisha mistook Metatron's status for that of God himself and worshipped him as a second deity. As a result, Elisha was therefore punished and Metatron was demoted and his stature diminished.

The transformation of Enoch into Metatron is described very graphically. It encompasses a physical transformation, a bestowal of seventy divine names on Metatron by God, and his acquisition of vast powers of knowledge and wisdom. Together with this description of his transformation are extensive cosmological traditions. Elliot Wolfson, analyzing the dynamics of the final stages of 'descent' in Hekhalot Rabbati, argues that a crucial element in Merkava mysticism is the traveller's transformation into an angelic being.[90] He sees 3 Enoch as an important testimony to this element: 'It thus makes perfect sense that at some stage in the literary development of Hekhalot mysticism a book such as *3 Enoch* would have been composed, in which Enoch, the prototype of the Merkava mystic, is transformed into Metatron, the very angel who occupies a throne alongside that of God.'[91]

---

[89] On this ambivalence see Arbel, 'Seal of Resemblance'.

[90] This transformation is particularly evident in the Hotam ha-Merkava text from the Geniza, in which the traveller is told by the angel Ozhayah that he will be seated on a throne in the seventh Hekhal. See Schäfer, *Geniza-Fragmente*, text G8, on which see n35 above.

[91] Wolfson, *Speculum*, 83.

SHIUR KOMA

Although the sages rarely shied away from anthropomorphic depictions of God, the Hekhalot tradition represents a particularly strong example of anthropomorphic theology in ancient Judaism.[92] One hymn in Hekhalot Rabbati describes God as 'Exalted by rows of crowns' and goes on to say that 'abysses flame from His beauty, and skies flame from his body'.[93] Extravagant numbers and enormous dimensions for the heavens and its inhabitants are also part of the literature; thus Maase Merkava measures the gargantuan distances between the celestial bridges, rivers, and the merkava itself (§559).

The 'Shiur Koma' (Measurement of the Body) consists of enumerations of the dimensions of the body of God. Each part of the divine body is given a specific measurement, given in *parsangs* (Persian miles), as well as an esoteric name. Thus the left ankle of the Creator is named 'תרקם and measures 190,000,000 *parsangs* tall', and so on.[94] The text explains that one of the divine *parsangs* equals 1,640,000,025,000 terrestrial *parsangs*. Because of the detail, and over all, the numerical specificity of this description of the divine body, the Shiur Koma was criticised on theological and cultural grounds in the Middle Ages and even into the modern period.[95] The text was first published by S. Musajoff in an anthology of Hekhalot texts entitled *Merkava Shelema*; it appears in several places in the *Synopse*, but was also edited comprehensively by Martin S. Cohen, who also wrote an extensive monograph on the text.[96] It may be that the Shiur Koma is not a single text but a genre that took shape in several forms over time.[97]

The purpose of the text has been debated. Joseph Dan argued that the numbers given in the text for the divine body are so outlandish that the text must be expressing the opposite – the impossibility of limiting the form of God to finite dimensions.[98] Howard Jackson, however, has shown that the Shiur Koma can be placed within a long tradition in the ancient Near East of ascribing enormous size to gods and supernatural beings.[99] Martin Cohen has argued that the text, which contains several hymns, was written for the purpose of liturgical recitation.

---

[92] For a survey of scholarship on rabbinic anthropomorphism see Jackson, 'The Origins and Development,' 376.

[93] Schäfer, *Synopse*, §253. Cf Scholem, *Major Trends*, 59.

[94] Cohen, *Shi'ur Qomah*, 30f.

[95] On criticisms of the *Shi'ur Qomah* see Jackson, 'Origins and Development', 373-377.

[96] Cohen, *Shi'ur Qomah*.

[97] Cohen also argued that one early manuscript, British Library ms 10675 (Gaster 187), was a witness to the *Urtext* of the work, an argument that has been called into question by Herrmann, 'Text und Fiktion'.

[98] Dan, 'Concept of Knowledge'.

[99] Jackson, 'Origins and Development'.

OTHER VISIONARY TEXTS

Other macroforms in the Hekhalot corpus are more like loosely edited anthologies of discrete traditions than cohesive narratives or collections. Hekhalot Zutarti[100] contains some unusual passages in Palestinian Aramaic, a debate about whether the deity can be seen at all,[101] and few poetic fragments describing the powers of the visionary. Merkava Rabba[102] likewise is a title that does not designate a coherent body of material but a series of unrelated materials including a Sar-Tora text, a recension of the Shiur Koma, and adaptation of the pardes story, and some brief ritual texts.

Among the Geniza fragments, one of the most interesting is a unique narrative text entitled 'Hotam ha-Merkava' (Seal of the Merkava). It has also been called the 'Ozhaya fragment'.[103] In this text, the angel Ozhaya instructs the reader about the procedure for ascent and entrance to the seventh hekhal. From the themes and vocabulary of the text, it is evident that the author was acquainted with the Hekhalot Rabbati tradition. The main narrator of the text is R. Yishmael, who reports his conversations with an angel named Ozhaya regarding how to travel to the merkava and obtain the secrets of wisdom. That angel instructs the rabbi, who writes down the angel's instructions and receives several other aids to the journey from him: a scroll, a 'seal', and a 'path'. He describes the dangers of the journey in frightening detail, warns him about how to avoid them, and tells him his reward: he will be seated in the divine throne-room along with other visitors. Among several interesting features of the text is the glorification of an unnamed Babylonian sage, a scion of the 'house of the Master in Babylonia', for whom a special divine name has been reserved since creation. Another unusual detail is the text's instruction to the traveller to dig his fingernails into the 'ground of the firmament' of the sixth hekhal and plug up his orifices so that his breath does not escape. This is probably an indication that the mystical circle responsible for this text did not distinguish sharply between body and soul.

Contemporary scholars have not resolved the question of whether the ascent texts in Hekhalot literature constitute evidence for the ecstatic cultivation of visions. Scholem and those who accept his interpretation argue that they are the results of visionary experiences.[104] Others, such as Martha Himmelfarb, argue that 'the Hekahlot literature should be understood not as rites to be en-

---

[100] Schäfer, *Synopse* §§335-74 and §§407-26.

[101] *Ib.* §350. It is possible that this debate was inserted by a medieval editor, perhaps from the circles of Hasidei Ashkenaz. See Wolfson, *Speculum*, 96.

[102] Schäfer, *Synopse* §§655-708.

[103] MS TS K1.95.C (= G8 in Schäfer, *Geniza-Fragmente*). On this fragment, see n35 above. The Hotam ha-Merkava section of the fragment was translated in part by Halperin, *Faces of the Chariot*, 368f and Himmelfarb, 'Heavenly Ascent'; and in full by Swartz, 'Seal of the Merkava'.

[104] For arguments in favour of this position, see Gruenwald, *Apocalyptic* and *Apocalyptism to Gnosticism*.

acted but as stories to be repeated.'[105] Schäfer stresses the liturgical and magical aspects, suggesting that the authors believed that recitation of the hymns and divine names contained within them would effect participation in the heavenly liturgy.[106] While the internal states of mind that engendered these texts in their present form are most likely irrecoverable, it may be most productive to analyze this literature as myth and ritual, uncovering the cultural and social factors that contributed to its creation.

Conjurations and other Rituals

Although the ascent and visionary texts in the Hekhalot corpus have received the most attention from modern scholars, they do not constitute the only major sector of the corpus. Along with the visionary texts are texts that tell of rituals for the acquisition of practical and spiritual powers on earth, such as wisdom and skill in learning Tora and good fortune. Some of these texts are narratives of how famous sages became great scholars through the conjuration of an angel of Tora or wisdom; some are instructions for rituals for conjuring angels and similar purposes; and some are magical texts that are virtually indistinguishable from other magical handbooks from late antiquity and the early Middle Ages.[107]

Several macroforms in the Hekhalot corpus, including Hekhalot Rabbati and Maase Merkava, contain extensive texts about the conjuration of the 'Prince of the Tora' or Sar-Tora. Most of the texts are framed as narratives in which the hero, usually R. Yishmael, receives information about how to adjure the Sar-Tora. Usually his teacher is R. Nehunia. The instructions are then given. The narrative continues with a testimony to the success of the procedure, which is often said to make even the weakest student into a great Rabbi.[108] One Sar-Tora narrative in Hekhalot Rabbati is an extensive poetic apocalypse. Although the story is narrated by R. Yishmael in the name of R. Akiva and R. Eliezer the Great, it takes place in the setting described in the book of Haggai. The elders charged to supervise the rebuilding of the Temple complain that they cannot carry out the construction and engage in the study of Tora at the same time. God then engages in a poetic dialogue with Israel in which He announces that He will reveal the 'secret of Tora',[109] which will guarantee that no fool or simpleton will be found among the people and that

---

[105] Himmelfarb, *Ascent to Heaven*, 109. For the full argument see Himmelfarb, 'Heavenly Ascent'.
[106] Schäfer, 'Aim and Purpose'.
[107] For a survey of magic in late antiquity, see Swartz, 'Jewish Magic;' for its relevance for Hekhalot literature see Schäfer, 'Merkava Mysticism and Magic' and *idem*, 'Jewish Magic Literature'.
[108] This is the basic outline of the Chapter of R. Nehunia complex, which is found in several versions in Hekhalot Rabbati at §§278-80 and §§307-14, Merkava Rabbah at §675-85 and Maase Merkava at §§560-70. For detailed analysis see Swartz, *Scholastic Magic*, 62-92.
[109] Schäfer, *Synopse*, §297.

riches and wealth will accumulate for them.[110] Zerubbabel then specifies the names of the Sar-Tora. R. Yishmael then gives the instructions for the Sar-Tora ritual and tells a story testifies to the success of the ritual.

The Sar-Tora tradition is significant for a number of reasons. It is important for the history of rabbinic Judaism and its milieu as an example of the importance of memorization and the scholastic ethic in the wider Jewish culture of late antiquity. Magical traditions in Jewish and Greco-Roman cultures include recipes for the acquisition of memory, often through the ingestion of special substances or the aid of a supernatural intermediary. It is also important as evidence for ritual in Hekhalot literature. Scholem and others had held that the ascent to the merkava was preceded by rituals of preparation, in which the practitioner undergoes a procedure of fasting, ablution, social isolation and prayer. This, in his view, prepared the mystic for a state of trance. However, in the Hekhalot corpus such rituals appear not in the ascent texts, but in the Sar-Tora materials and related texts. Therefore, anyone who studies ritual in Merkava mysticism must analyze rituals in which the individual prepares not for ascent to heaven, but for bringing a heavenly being down to earth.

Analysis of these rituals yields some striking patterns. The main concern of the ritual is the removal of all traces of impurity and other forms of contamination. A typical passage instructs the practitioner to...

> ...fast continuously for forty days, eat bread that he makes with his own hands, drink water that he fills with his hands, and not eat meat, drink wine, and not taste any kind of vegetable. If an emission occurs he must go back to the beginning of the procedure.[111]

Two aspects of this ritual that stand out are social isolation and the avoidance of all kinds of impurity. By eating bread that he makes with his own hands, the practitioner not only avoids contact with others, but all possibility that the bread may be contaminated with menstrual impurity (*nidda*). Seminal emission also invalidates the procedure. The avoidance of vegetables may be a precaution against bodily odors. The ritual is designed to ensure a supererogatory degree of purity, beyond that required by the halakha. This is because angelic beings will only tolerate the presence of the purest of human beings. That angels are repulsed by the smell of humans is shown by a passage in which Metatron, who used to be the human Enoch, approaches and the angels complain about the smell of this being 'born of woman' rising up to them.[112] This concern with ritual purity as a prerequisite for being in the presence of supernatural beings is not absent from the ascent texts. In Hekhalot Rabbati, R. Nehunia is brought down from his ascent to heaven by his students, who con-

---

[110] *Ib.* §§289-90
[111] *Ib.* §684.
[112] *Ib.* §§147-49 and §§315-17. On this passage see Swartz, *Scholastic Magic*, 167.

taminate him with a marginal degree of menstrual impurity.[113] As Saul Lieberman points out, this degree of impurity would be permitted on earth, but not according to the heavenly court.[114] This is an indication that at least some of the authors of the ascent texts saw purity as a prerequisite for ascent.

Scholem saw the Sar-Tora tradition as evidence of a late stage in the evolution of Merkava mysticism, in which genuine mystical experience had ceased to be part of the tradition and it had degenerated into 'mere magic.'[115] On the other hand, David Halperin considered the Sar-Tora tradition to be the 'centre' of the Hekhalot corpus.[116] In his view, lower-class Jews (which he identified with the *ammei ha-arets*) built on popular midrashic and targumic interpretations of the ascent of Moses to receive the Tora and constructed stories of how R. Yishmael and others acquired supernatural skills in Tora through the agency of the Sar-Tora. Halperin argued that the ascent traditions grew out of the Sar-Tora tradition and not the other way around. As Schäfer points out, this argument reverses Scholem's and like his assigns priority to one strand in the literature, when it is more likely that the two strands developed independently of each other.[117] Nonetheless, the Sar-Tora tradition yields interesting evidence of attitudes to rabbinic authority, halakha and Tora in the cultural milieu of early Jewish mysticism.

Sefer Yetsira

In bSanh 65b and 67b, it is said that Rav Hanina and Rav Oshaya occupied themselves with the "book of formation" (*sefer yetsira*, bSanh 65b) or "laws of formation" (*hilkhot yetsira*, bSanh 67b) on the eve of the Sabbath and by means of it made a three-year-old calf and ate it. However, the brief story contains no further details about what this book or corpus of laws might be. In the tenth century a brief and mysterious text known as the 'Sefer Yetsira' began to appear. During the early Middle Ages, this text had become the subject of several commentaries and studies by Jewish scientists, philosophers and mystics.[118] Eventually Sefer Yetsira provided key inspiration and terminology for the Kabbalistic tradition, which adopted the text's term *sefirot* as well as many of its main concepts. The text exists in three main recensions, one of

---

[113] Schäfer, *Synopse*, §§225-28. On this complex passage see Scholem *Jewish Gnosticism*, 9-13; Schiffman, 'Recall of R. Nehunia'; Lieberman, 'Knowledge of *Halakha*'; and Schlüter, 'Erzählhlung'.

[114] Lieberman, 'Knowledge of *Halakha*;' cf also Schlüter, 'Erzählung'.

[115] On this argument see Schäfer, 'Merkavah Mysticism and Magic;' cf Alexander, 'Response'.

[116] Halperin, *Faces of the Chariot*, 376-87.

[117] Schäfer, *Hidden and Manifest God*, 151f.

[118] For a survery of the history of Sefer Yetsira and its reception, as well as a selection of the vast bibliography on the subject, see Dan, 'Three Phases.'

which was redacted by Saadia Gaon; the so-called shorter recension is usually thought to reflect the earlier form of the text.[119]

Sefer Yetsira concerns the process by which God formed the universe out of ten mathematical entities, known as *sefirot belima*. The term employs the neologism *sefira*, from the root *spr* "to count," to mean number. The term *belima* comes from Job 26:7 and could mean 'closed' (that is, 'ineffable'), 'unpronounceable', or 'basis'. The text goes on to speak of three (or four) primordial elements, 'twenty-two elemental letters' and 'thirty-two paths of wisdom' as components of creation. The text is then taken up with metaphysical, mathematical, and linguistic permutations of these components.

The question of the origin and history of Sefer Yetsira has confounded scholars from the Middle Ages to modern times. Although tradition ascribes the text to the patriarch Abraham, the text is striking for the relative paucity of specifically Jewish references, especially in the shorter recension. Aside from a few terms for God and scattered biblical allusions,[120] the text seems to bear several affinities to the Neo-Pythagorean and Hermetic forms of spirituality that flourished in the Hellenistic world, while it does not resemble Hebrew texts of the rabbinic period.[121] Scholars have also noticed similarities to texts written in Arabic in the eighth and ninth centuries during a revival of Greek esoteric cosmological ideas.[122] As a result, scholars have suggested widely divergent dates for the text, ranging from the first century[123] to the second or third centuries,[124] to the early Muslim era.[125]

Does Sefer Yetsira belong in the category of early Jewish mystical texts? The text bears little resemblance to the Hekhalot literature; it does not concern a journey to divine throne or the conjuration of angels, nor does it speculate on the topography of the heavens. However, unlike the Hekhalot texts, Sefer Yetsira does offer an explicit indication of how it is to serve as a source of meditation:

> Understand with wisdom, and be wise with understanding. Test them and investigate them, and get the matter clearly worked out and restore the Creator to his place.[126]

---

[119] For a comprehensive edition and the best account of the redactional state of the text see Hayman, *Sefer Yeṣira*. Important previous editions and publications of manuscripts include Gruenwald, 'Preliminary Critical Edition'; Weinstock, 'Le-Virur ha-Nusah'; and Allony, 'Sefer Yesira.'
[120] For example the word *belima* mentioned above, and a brief citation of Ezek 1:14 in §5 (Hayman, *Sefer Yesira*, 72).
[121] On Hellenistic influence see Pines, 'Points of Similarity.'
[122] See especially Wasserstrom, 'Sefer Yesira and Early Islam'.
[123] Liebes, *Torat ha-Yetsira*.
[124] Hayman, 'Temple at the Center of the Universe'
[125] For a summary of the arguments for this dating as well as further evidence, see Wasserstrom, 'Sefer Yeṣira and Early Islam'.
[126] §4 (Hayman, *Sefer Yeṣira*, 60f). Hayman's translation is adapted here.

The meditation described here seems to be the cognitive contemplation of the relationships between the letters and numbers spelled out in the texts, which will lead to a proper understanding of creation, or even the restoration of God's rulership.[127] If the dating of Sefer Yetsira is ever determined with greater certainty, we may be able to place it into the early history of Jewish mysticism. Nonetheless, its influence on medieval Jewish mystical and philosophical thought is undoubted.

Early Jewish Mystical Texts in Context

Hekhalot literature encompasses many literary forms and phenomena. It includes strange tales of vision and danger, rituals for achieving both spiritual and practical goals, sublime poetry, and unique cosmological schemes. Is this literature evidence for visionary mysticism within the central circles of the rabbinic elite? If not, what does it tell us about the practice of Judaism in late antiquity?

It has been shown that rabbinic texts regarding discourse on the Merkava cannot be taken unambiguously as evidence for the presence of Merkava mysticism within the early rabbinic movement. At the same time, the Hekhalot texts themselves are related to rabbinic literature in complex ways. It must be understood that this body of literature is not unified and may reflect several times and social settings. Nonetheless, some generalizations can be made about the major texts. The heroes of the Hekhalot texts were rabbis; the authors generally make it clear that Rabbis Yishmael, Akiva and Nehunia ben ha-Kana were participants in the ascent and Sar-Tora practices and taught it to all who are privileged to receive its secrets, including the reader. Many of the hymns and poems in the literature are consistent with the poetic forms of the early rabbinic period, and may have influenced the statutory rabbinic literature in some ways. Many features of the anthropomorphic theology and layered ouranology of the literature are consistent with rabbinic Judaism. In the case of the Sar-Tora tradition, the very premise of the literature – that the highest goal of the Jew is to become a great scholar of Tora – is a value central to the rabbinic ethos.

At the same time, there are elements in this literature that diverge significantly from the mainstream of the rabbinic canon. While the concept of a God enthroned on the merkava is inextricably a part of rabbinic theology, the idea of seven hekhalot guarded by angels is not.[128] Likewise, while the ethos of the learning of Tora is central to rabbinic values, memory is cultivated in talmudic

---

[127] Cf. Hayman, 'Temple'. On the idea in Rabbinic literature that human thought can affect the nature of God's sovereignty, see Moshe Idel, *Kabbalah* 156-166.

[128] Rabbinic cosmology does speak of layers of heaven, especially in GenR; on rabbinic cosmological traditions and their more esoteric expression in such texts as Seder Rabba de-Bereshit see Schäfer, 'In Heaven as it is in Hell'.

literature not by magical conjurations but by laborious study.[129] Although rabbis are the heroes of the stories, many aspects of the literature betray priestly concerns. For example, R. Yishmael is known in the texts for his priestly descent. The Temple is also the setting for one of the most important ascent texts, the vision of R. Nehunia in Hekhalot Rabbati, as well as one of the most extensive Sar-Tora texts, the poetic Sar-Tora narrative in Hekhalot Rabbati. In addition, some of the purity rituals and liturgical texts go well beyond the halakha, prescribing avoidance of people, clothes, and foods that are permitted according to talmudic law.

This characteristic of Hekhalot literature has led some historians to ask whether its origins can be found in social groups outside the rabbinic estate. Halperin identified the authors with the lower classes, *ammei ha-arets*.[130] The presence of such elements as reverence for the priesthood and interest in the Temple have led Rachel Elior to argue that the primary forces behind the Hekhalot literature were circles of priests going back to the Second Temple era.[131] The extra-rabbinic influences and other factors may indicate that the authors of this literature may be found not among the rabbinic elite or the lower classes, but in circles of secondary elites, who drew upon rabbinic values and popular religious traditions alike.[132] Whatever the origins of this remarkable literature, it is important not only for the history of Jewish mysticism, but to the history of Judaism in late antiquity as well.

[129] See Swartz, *Scholastic Magic* 33-43. The rabbis do at times prescribe special foods or diets to improve memory; see *ib*. 41-43.

[130] Halperin, *Faces of the Chariot*. On this argument cf Schäfer, *Hidden and Manifest God*, 157-159 and Swartz, *Scholastic Magic*, 12.

[131] Elior, *The Three Temples*.

[132] For this argument regarding the authors of the Sar-Tora literature, see Swartz, *Scholastic Magic*; for secondary elites as the social location of magic, see Idel, 'On Judaism, Jewish mysticism, and magic'. Recently Davila, *Descenders to the Chariot*, has argued that the Hekhalot tradition is the product of a class of shamanistic practitioners.

Section Three
Contracts, Inscriptions, Ancient Science

Chapter Twelve

Contracts: Rabbinic Literature and Ancient Jewish Documents

Mordechai A. Friedman

Contracts Appearing in Rabbinic Literature

Hillel the Elder expounded the text of the marriage contract. In Alexandria someone would betroth a woman; and someone else would come and snatch her (and marry her). When such a case appeared before the sages, they intended to rule that the children were bastards. Hillel the elder told them (the children), 'Produce your mothers' marriage contracts.' They did, and they were found to contain the following text: 'When you enter my home, you will become my wife, according to the law of Moses and the Jews.' Accordingly, it was ruled that the children were not bastards.[1]

This story purports to be of the oldest strata of the Tannaic literature. While dealing specifically with the marriage contract, it illustrates several of the

---

[1] tKet 4:9 (p68) and parallels, with slight variations. See Friedman, *Jewish Marriage* 2, 496 (index); cf the sources and discussion by Katzoff in Gulak, *Legal Documents*, 55 n26; idem, 'Philo'.

points, which we shall consider in the following paragraphs that concern legal documents in general. The כתובה, *ketubba* or 'marriage contract', was introduced in Jewish practice in the (late) Second Temple period and represents a significant change in halakha. The text of the contract was not uniform; at least that in use in Alexandria implicitly differed from that with which Hillel and the sages were familiar in the Land of Israel. Important documents were retained by the next generation; thus the children were able to produce their mothers' marriage contracts. The sages recognized the text of the document as a valid source for deciding questions of law of such primary significance as legitimacy. The passage's introductory line attributes this decision not to a literal reading of the text but to its exposition.

The Bible refers to only two legal documents, the bill of divorce (Deut 24:1, 3; Isa 50:1; Jer 3:8) and the deed of purchase for a field (Jer 32:10-14, 16), while the former alone is prescribed by law and required for effectiveness of the act itself.[2] Their is no clear indication of the text of either, although some scholars have taken Hos 2:4 ('For she is not my wife, and I am not her husband') as a divorce formula.[3] Other contracts may have been in use (note the growing number of *bullae* found), but this is a matter of speculation. As to the Apocrypha, the book of Tobit mentions a deed of loan (5:3, 9:2 [long version], 5) and a marriage contract (7:14).[4]

By the Persian period, as evidenced by the book of Tobit, by other literary sources and by manuscript finds discussed below, legal documents played a more central role. When we come to the talmudic evidence, we find clear testimony of their importance both to the sages and the common people. In the Mishna and related works, two tractates are named for specific documents: Ketubbot and Gittin, but this is only partial indication of the significance of legal documents, especially for family law. An impressive number of different types of written contracts are mentioned and discussed in talmudic literature. The literary sources are complemented by extant ancient Jewish documents, discussed in the second part of the chapter.

TERMINOLOGY

Before we note some of the talmudic contracts and the role associated with them, some remarks are in order concerning terminology. Talmudic Hebrew and Aramaic do not have one specific term for 'written contract' but rather a number of words that denote contracts, documents in general or other writings.

---

[2] So understood by the talmudic sages; see bGit 85b (and sources and discussion in Friedman, *Jewish Marriage* 1, 125); on the deed of purchase as a document of evidence for that transaction, see bKid 26a.

[3] See Friedman, 'Israel's Response', 199.

[4] On the marriage contract in Tobit, see Katzoff in Gulak, *Legal Documents*, 56f n31.

שטר, sh^etar, from Akkadian shataru,[5] the most common word for 'document', is coupled with other words to designate most specific kinds of contracts, e.g., שטר אירוסין 'betrothal deed'. When not defined, sh^etar either refers to 'document' in general or to a bill of loan.[6]

גט, get, from Akkadian gittu, 'document',[7] appears in some Tannaic sources as a general term for document (e.g., mGit 1:5).[8] Sometimes it occurs with a modifier; גט חוב is a 'bill of loan', גט שחרור 'deed of emancipation'. The most common pair, גט אשה, literally 'a woman's document', denotes the bill of divorce. In the formulary from that deed, cited in the name of R. Yehuda in mGit 9:3, some texts refer to it as גט פטורין, 'bill of divorce', others (ms K) by the synonymous גט גרושין. The Masada divorce document (P. Mur. 19) has the equivalent, and another document from the Judean Desert refers to the bill of divorce by the pleonastic גט שבוקין ותרכ[ין] (XHev/Se 13). גט without any modifier in the sense of the divorce deed is commonplace, as in the name of the tractate, 'Gittin'. L. Finkelstein identified one instance of גט without a modifier that connotes a deed of betrothal (ARN a2, p11), but the text may be corrupt.[9]

ספר, sefer, most common for 'book', is the biblical term for document; it is used regularly in Elephantine (see below) for various deeds.[10] In rabbinic literature it occurs in two passages: ספר כתובה, 'marriage contract' (lit., 'deed of delayed mohar payment'; see below) in mYev 15:3 (and parallels) and ספר תירוכין 'bill of divorce' in mGit 9:3 (ms K). Its subsequent disuse supports the authenticity of these two mishnas as old formulations. Internal and external evidence can be adduced for this. The participants in the dialogue reported in the first are the early Tannaic Schools of Shammai and Hillel, and the second, part of the formulary of the bill of divorce transmitted in the name of R. Yehuda, was not introduced by that mid second century sage but predates him, as has now been proven by the appearance of the same phrase in the writ of divorce issued in Masada found in the Judean Desert.

אגרת, iggeret, familiar in the sense of 'letter', is used for 'document' in the Aramaic dockets on some Neo-Assyrian deeds, written from the ninth century BCE on.[11] One of the synonyms used for 'bill of divorce' in the formulary

---

[5] See Kaufman, Akkadian Influences, 101.

[6] The same process has occurred with the Greek χάρτης, which refers primarily to the material, on which a document was written, then to the document itself, then, in Palestinian talmudic sources especially to the bill of debt. See Sperber, Dictionary, 193ff.

[7] See CAD 'G', 112 ff; Kaufman, Akkadian Influences, 52.

[8] Cf Rosenthal, 'Inscription', 369f.

[9] Finkelstein, Mabo, 128; Kister, Studies, 48 adduces additional manuscript evidence for this. Perhaps in an earlier version a transmitter introduced the word גט here, instead of כתובה as found in the parallels, because he understood פטר in the continuation, in the sense of divorce, rather than dismiss, reject. In a latter development, פטר was understood to denote acquit, which may have caused a further revision and created a text, in which גט seems to be used for deed of betrothal. In his edition, Schechter already noted that the manuscripts to this passage are hopelessly corrupt.

[10] See Muffs, Studies, 207 and Kaufman, Akkadian Influences, 29.

[11] Muffs ib. 187; Kaufman ib. 48; cf Rabinowitz, Studies, 12-3.

transmitted by R. Yehuda in mGit 9:3 (ms K) is איגרת שיבוקין.[12] It also appears in mGit 6:5 ('if one says: write an איגרת, *iggeret*, and give it to my wife'). Elsewhere in mishnaic Hebrew *iggeret* is used for certain court-issued documents. As noted by S. Lieberman, in the Yerushalmi, *iggeret* usually means 'a secular document'.[13]

כתב, *k̄etav*, 'writ', is used in Palestinian literature from the talmudic and post-talmudic periods as a general term for 'document', often combined with specific modifiers, e.g., כתב קידושין, 'betrothal deed'.

כתובה, *ketubba*, is used in mishnaic Hebrew for the delayed *mohar* payment or, less regularly, for the dowry, written in the marriage contract and sometimes for the marriage contract itself. In a few places, as a secondary development, it is used as a general term for 'document'.[14] The expression כתובת חתנים for marriage contract seem to be a stage in this direction.[15] Similarly, כתובת אשה, literally 'a woman's *ketubba*', may be patterned afterגט אשה.

זכו, *z̄ekhu* is used in the Bavli for a 'document conveying or attesting to rights'.[16]

SOME TALMUDIC CONTRACTS

The following is a list of legal documents mentioned in the talmudic literature, with the terms used for them in rabbinic sources and a few brief comments. Often multiple terms refer to the same document, but at times they may denote subtle variations in the deed itself. For the sake of convenience the contracts are here divided into those related to family matters and those connected with business affairs, although the division is not always clear.

---

[12] The three terms for the divorce deed in that mishna are each found in different Targums of Deut 24:1. See Kasher, *Torah Shelemah* vol 24, 22ff.

[13] Lieberman, *Hellenism*, 109. Faur, 'Term', who ignores the talmudic use of *iggeret* for 'document', challenges Lieberman's interpretation. His challenge is without foundation in my opinion, but this is not the place for a detailed critique. I cite one example. On p22, he quotes Lieberman, *Tosefta Ki-Fshutah* 1, 32, who wrote: '"Fixed" does not mean that one must change the liturgical text every day'. Faur seems to have understood this to mean that changing the liturgical text every day was prohibited. Lieberman clearly intended the opposite: the prohibition of praying with a fixed liturgical text does not require one to alter it daily. Even infrequent variations are adequate to assure that prayer not be like reading an *iggeret*.

[14] yYev 15:3, 14d (and parallel), 'PN expounded the *ketubba*' refers first to the marriage contract then (by extension?) to deeds for lease, receipt (but see Lieberman, *Tosefta Ki-Fshutah* 6, 248) and loan. In yKet 4:12, 29b, אין אדם מזכה אלא בכתובה 'one does not transfer rights except by a כתובה', it immediately follows *ketubba* in the sense of marriage contract, and the word may be an error for בכתב. For the parallel of כתובה in one text of 'Maasim li-vne Erets Yisrael' to כתב in another, see Friedman, *Jewish Marriage* 2, 191.

[15] bGit 88a; for חתנים for 'marriage' cf the phrase ברכת חתנים 'marriage blessing'.

[16] See Friedman, *Jewish Marriage* 2, 162f. While this usage has not been identified in Palestinian Jewish Aramaic, one might speculate that it is reflected in the elusive adage כל בר נש ובר נש זכוותיה גו קופתיה 'every man has his *zekhu*(s) in his basket' in yKid. 1:7, 61b (and parallel).

Family-Related Contracts

Deeds of betrothal and marriage are sometimes referred to as a general category, שטרי ארוסים ונשואים (mBB 10:4, ms K), כתב נישואין ... כתב קידושין (yGit 4:4, 45d). Deeds of betrothal (also called קידושי נשים, mMK 3:3) served primarily as the contract whose transfer affected the formal act of betrothal (see below), but it is probable that they frequently included various stipulations and undertakings of the parties.[17] The כתב \ שטר נשואין, 'marriage deed', is likely to refer to the *ketubba*, the marriage contract, or some other document written before or at the wedding.

The marriage contract is called שטר \ ספר (כתובה) in Hebrew and Aramaic. In Palestinian rabbinic literature from the Amoraic period it is often designated by various forms of Greek φερνή in halakhic and aggadic contexts and of γαμικόν or γάμος in aggadic passages. The use of φερνή (in halakhic discussions), lit., 'dowry', is to be understood against the background of the marriage contract or, more specifically, the delayed marriage settlement written in it, as a late development in Jewish law, which reflects some degree of Greek influence.[18] During the talmudic period, the ketubba was written at the betrothal in some localities and at the wedding in others.[19] The שטר פסיקתא, *pesiqta*, 'allocation document', is mentioned four times in late passages of the Bavli. In bKet 102a its essential contents are identified as 'How much will you give for your son? How much will you give for your daughter?'[20]

Bill of divorce, גט (see above on the terms used for 'document'). The Palestinian Amora R. Yohanan cites the Greek ריפודין (Latin *repudium*), 'deed of unilateral dissolution of a marriage', but only in reference to divorce among gentiles.[21] In connection with the bill of divorce, mention should also be made of the חליצה and מיאון deeds, neither of which was required for the respective efficacy of the levirate release ceremony (Deut 25:5-10) or the annulment of the marriage of a child bride whose marriage was arranged after she had been orphaned from her father but was written to serve as proof of her marriageability.[22]

A last will is referred to exclusively by the Greek דייתיקי, διαθήκη, in Tannaic and Palestinian Amoraic sources. As noted by R. Yaron, the use of the Greek is 'prima facie evidence that the institution is new to Jewish law ...taken over together with its name from a foreign system'.[23] In the Bavli we

---

[17] See Friedman, *Jewish Marriage* 1, 194.

[18] See Friedman, *Jewish Marriage* 1, 76-79; idem, 'Marriage and the Family'; Sperber, *Dictionary*, 161-163, 207f; Katzoff, 'Review', 334f.

[19] See Friedman, *Jewish Marriage* 1, 194f; cf, e.g., bKid 50b and bBK 17b.

[20] For a recent discussion of the פסקתא, see Lifshitz, *Asmakhta*.

[21] GenR 18:5, p166 (ms Vat 60); see Katzoff, 'Review,' 330f.

[22] See tYev 12:15, 13:1 (p44f) and Lieberman, *Tosefta Ki-Fshutah* 6, 146ff.

[23] Yaron, *Gifts*, 19. But see below n24.

also find פקדתא.[24] And in bSan 91a (as quoted by the *Arukh*), לגטון (λεγᾶτον, *legatum*): אב שכתב לגטון לבנ[י]ו, 'a father who wrote a bequest to his children'.[25]

Emancipation of slaves (שחרור). The manumission deed, which seems to have been introduced formally in the second century CE as a means to formalize the emancipation process,[26] is likened often to a bill of divorce, and many of the formulae and regulations of the latter are applied to the former.

Business-Related Contracts

Sale, Hebrew מכר, *mekher* (מקח וממכר) or Greek אוני (ὠνή, literally, 'purchase') in Tannaic and Palestinian Amoraic sources, Aramaic זבינא (and אשקלתא) in the Bavli. As the bill of sale dates back to the biblical period, the use of Greek אוני in talmudic literature is noteworthy, and may reflect the frequency with which Jews wrote this deed in Greek and, registered it in the official archives, as suggested by S. Lieberman.[27] On the basis of linguistic considerations, R. Katzoff suggests that the Greek term entered Hebrew during the first three centuries BCE.[28] An apparent misinterpretation of *one* for the sale of a slave in an Amoraic passage in the Bavli is discussed below.

Sale in trust, a fiduciary transfer of property, in which the buyer holds the property in trust and agrees to return it under certain conditions, Greek פיסטיס, πίστις, or Hebrew אמנה. These appear to have been two separate deeds, but, if so, the difference between them is unknown. A woman about to marry would issue such a document, if she wanted to prevent her property from falling into her husband's hands (שטר מברחת).[29]

Loan, promissory note, usually called חוב (שטר), or just שטר (כרטיס / קרטיס, from Greek χάρτης, in the Yerushalmi); הלואה or אודיתא in the Bavli.

Receipt, Hebrew שובר; in Babylonian Aramaic תברא and in the Greek of the Yerushalmi אומולוגייה (ὁμολογία – also אפוכי, ἀποχή, in midrashic literature).

---

[24] In his formulary, R. Hai Gaon distinguishes between the דייתיקי and the פקדתא.

[25] The quote in Sperber, *Dictionary*, 104 is to be corrected.

[26] See Urbach, *World of Sages*, 207ff.

[27] Lieberman, *Tosefta Ki-Fshutah* 10, 343 refers to the use of the term in connection with the registration of the document, and the same logically applies to its language. H. Cotton has explained that Jews wrote documents from the Judean Desert in Greek because they often registered them in public archives; see *DJD* 27, 153f, 207, 254.

[28] Katzoff, 'Dictionary', 203. The examples of אוני listed in Sperber, *Dictionary*, 34 should probably be translated 'his bill of sale' (in yBM 1:8, 8a, אונו may be an error for אונו). Katzoff, 'Dictionary', 198 discounts the significance of the variants in spelling for the supposed survival of dialectical forms.

[29] See Sperber, *Dictionary*, 145f and literature cited there plus Lieberman, *Tosefta Ki-Fshutah* 10, 344. There is no reason to place tKet 9:2 (p86) in a separate category of 'trust'; besides yKet 2:3, 26b and its parallel in bKet 19b, the Hebrew and Greek are mentioned together as separate documents in bGit 19b and BB 154b. πίστις is used in Greek documents from the Judean Desert in the sense of *bona fide*; see Lewis, *Documents*, 18.

The sages debated whether or not a debtor could demand that a receipt be written on payment of his debt or merely return of the original bill of debt.[30]

Additional business deeds: lease, tenancy (אריסות); rental (שכירות, חכירה); contractor's agreement (קבלה); deposit or mortgage (משכנתא/משכון; הפותיקי – ὑποθήκη, שעבוד); deposit (מפקיד בשטר); gift (מתנה), partnership (כיס); order of payment (דיוקני[31]); mutual agreements (קומפרומיסין, κομπρόμισον, *compromissum*).[32]

Contracts are mentioned with great frequency, variety and detail in talmudic literature, not only in theoretical discussions but in passages which depict daily life. Bunches of personal documents were kept together in rolls and bundles, preserved for safekeeping and held from one generation to the next. 'You are holding ten bags filled with documents for me' (tShev 5:11; see below concerning Babatha's archive); 'We did not find among our father's documents that this contract was collected' (mShev 7:7). When walking through the market, one would hear scribes training their students to write documents (mGit 3:1).

This proliferation of documents, in sharp contrast with the biblical evidence, is to be seen as the result of a number of interacting forces. The increase of literacy, while certainly a contributing factor, should not be overemphasized, as most contracts during the talmudic period (and later) were written by scribes rather than the parties, and illiteracy was still widespread, cf mGit 8:8, 'If a scribe wrote a bill of divorce for the man [to give to his wife] and a receipt for the woman [to give to her husband] and mistakenly gave the bill of divorce to the woman and the receipt to the man, and they exchanged...'[33]

More significant is likely to be the transformation in the Hellenistic period of Jewish society from one whose economy was based almost exclusively on agriculture to one in which commerce played an increasingly dominant role. Furthermore, from the Babylonian exile on there was a significant increase in contacts with non-Jewish societies in whose common law written contracts played a central role. We have already noted the use of Akkadian terms for 'document'.

CONTRACTS AS A SOURCE OF HALAKHA

Discussions of the sources of halakha have paid little attention to the role played by that branch of a customary legal tradition associated with documents in antiquity. Many contracts revolutionized biblical legal practice. The introduction of some was recognized as the result of specific enactments, a striking

---

[30] For the original meaning and *Sitz im Leben* of the terms שובר and תברה, literally, break, see Naveh and Shaked, 'Knot'.

[31] Greek etymology uncertain; see Sperber, *Dictionary*, 83f; cf Katzoff, 'Review', 335.

[32] See Sperber, *Dictionary*, 171f and the two meanings given there.

[33] For a discussion of literacy in the biblical period, see Haran, 'Literacy'; for its increase in the post-biblical period see Bar-Ilan, 'Polemics', 204ff.

example in the late Second Temple period being the ketubba.[34] Other contracts had became such an integral part of the legal system that by late Tannaic times it was possible to imagine that they were (implicitly) defined in the Bible itself.

This is illustrated by the old law at the beginning of tractate Kiddushin that rules that betrothal can be effected by either transfer of a symbolic sum of money, or a document, or by intercourse. It is fairly clear that biblical law required the payment of bride money (*mohar*) for the betrothal to be valid, and there is no basis to assume that it could be contracted exclusively by a written document, which would state, for example, 'Your daughter is betrothed to me' (bKid 9a), or, for that matter, that such a document was known at all. A baraita cites a formalistic midrash, concerning the juxtaposition of divorce – which requires a writ – and marriage in Deut 24:2, as the supposed biblical source for the betrothal deed,[35] but such a derivation is manifestly an attempt to recon-struct a proof text for an accepted legal usage whose origins were no longer remembered. In the absence of any tradition of an enactment, it seems best to assume that the betrothal writ evolved as part of the customary law in which it was intuitively viewed as an effective way to formalize the change in the par-ties' status, after the *mohar* had become a delayed payment. The Mishna might not reflect any practice, as such, of performing the betrothal by writ without a symbolic payment of bride money,[36] just as there seems to have been no such custom for betrothal by intercourse only, but rather the theoretical decision by the ancient sages that these methods be considered valid ways to contract the betrothal. In the case of the writ this would attest the importance that deeds had achieved in the legal system in general.

The Tannaim refer to the texts of contracts as לשון הדיוט, literally 'layman's language' (tKet 4:9 and parallels). This phrase is used elsewhere (tBB 11:13) for the language of the common man and was so understood by R. Hai Gaon and talmudic commentators. In connection with contracts it defines the docu-ments written according to customary law and formulated by scribal practice (so Rashi, bBM 104a: '...Which common people were accustomed to write, not according to the enactment of the sages').[37] New light on the concept of 'lay-men's language' is shed by modern research which has identified formulae found in deeds quoted in the talmudic literature with those in ancient contracts

---

[34] See Friedman, 'Marriage and the Family'.

[35] SifDeut 268 (p287f); yKid 1:1, 58b; bKid 5a.

[36] PesRK Anokhi 3 (p305) and parallels has been mistakenly cited by Meir, 'Wedding', 21 as a case of a parable in which the betrothal was effected by writ.

[37] The translation of הדיוט depends on the context. In ySan 7:16, 25d, לשון הדיוט, in contrast with לשון הקודש, means a foreign language. In Sifra 2,1,1 (ed Finkelstein 2, 13) the speech heard from God (הקודש) is contrasted with the speech (i.e., oral lesson; Naeh, 'Structure', 70, imprecisely refers here to 'text') heard by one human from another (הדיוט מהדיוט). For Hai Gaon, see the sources in Friedman, *Jewish Marriage* 1, 3 n6 and his father's responsum edited by Abramson, *Ba-Merkazim*, 131f, where לשון הדיוט is contrasted with Ben Sira.

written elsewhere in the ancient Near East. In some cases, the correspondence is literal and involves use of the same terms in Aramaic. An example concerning the defension clause, quoted in bBM 15a in a fourth century CE passage, is cited below in association with fourth century BCE deeds from Samaria. Another example is noted here in the continuation.

Literal correspondence is often difficult to demonstrate, but the contents of many stipulations leave little doubt as to their ancient Near Eastern antecedents. This presumption is particularly clear where their provisions counter biblical law (as understood by the sages) or rabbinic law. The sages, for example, taught that when a married woman died, her husband was her sole heir.[38] This rule caused no particular problems when the wife left sons from her husband who, after his death, would inherit her possessions together with the rest of his estate. But society considered it to be inequitable when, because of a man's multiple marriages, either simultaneous or consecutive, most of one wife's property was eventually inherited by his sons from another woman or if a wife died childless. Elsewhere in the ancient Near East, a woman's blood relatives inherited her property. Two clauses, introduced in the marriage contract in different periods, respectively made adjustments that conform to the Near Eastern practice. The first, בנין דכרין, deals specifically with the wife's ketubba money and was already considered obligatory (see below) in mKet 4:10: 'Male children whom you will have by me shall inherit your ketubba money beyond their share with their brothers.'[39] Here an exact parallel to the opening words of the clause have been found in a second century BCE Edomite marriage document: בנין דכרין זי יהוון לי מנה.[40] The second clause appears in a fourth century passage in the Yerushalmi (yKet 9:1, 33a; yBB 8:6, 16b) and is referred to as a custom observed by some ('those who write'): אין מיתת דלא בנין יהא מדלה חזר לבית אביה, 'If she dies without children, her possessions will return to her father's house.'[41]

Modern scholars have addressed the complex questions associated with the relationship of the formularies of talmudic contracts with those customary in surrounding societies. Among those who have made important contributions in this area mention should be made of A. Gulak, J.J. Rabinowitz and R. Yaron. Besides comparisons with Greek and Demotic papyri from Egypt, recent scholarship has studied similarities with contracts in the ancient Near East in Akkadian and Aramaic. Comparable formulations are attested in several cultures. Where Aramaic formulae almost identical with talmudic ones are found earlier elsewhere in the ancient Near East, it is reasonable to assume that these

[38] There is, of course, no basis for the oft-repeated assertion that this was biblical law as such. It was evidently an ancient tradition, which talmudic rabbis associated with the Bible by midrash. But even they debated whether the rule had biblical or rabbinic authority (see Friedman, *Jewish Marriage* 1, 391f n2).
[39] Discussed in Friedman, *Jewish Marriage* 1, 379ff.
[40] See Eshel and Kloner, 'Ostracon'.
[41] Discussed in Friedman, *Jewish Marriage* 1, 391ff.; idem, 'Relationship'.

may be direct antecedents of the latter. But more often than not it is still unclear whether there was a direct borrowing from one culture to the other. Similarities in formulation could be the result of comparable conditions or common
legal traditions shared by the peoples of the ancient Near East and their
scribes. Much work remains to be done in this fascinating area, and the complexity of traditions, contacts and mutual influences preclude simple solutions.
In any event, comparative studies between the talmudic formularies and those
of Israel's neighbors are mutually rewarding for students of both literatures
and cultures.[42]

The study of contemporary non-Jewish documents has even assisted in
ascertaining the correct reading of talmudic texts. On the basis of the Greek
דייתיקי διαθήκη, 'will', Yaron has suggested that in the phrase associated by
the sages with the name of that deed, דא תהא לי לעמוד ולהיות (tBB 8:10, p158,
and parallels) the last word should be read לחיות, with ח rather than ה: 'May
(writing) this (will) portend that I recover and live.'[43]

Another example, speculative by nature, is offered here. The sale of a slave
does not require a bill of sale. In tAZ 3:16 (p464, and parallels) Rabban
Shimon b. Gamliel rules that if a Jew sold his slave to a non-Jew and wrote
him his אוני (ὠνή, bill of sale), this was equivalent to a deed of emancipation.
In bGit 43b and parallels in bGit 85b and bKid 6b, Rav Sheshet (alternatively,
Rav Ashi and Rav Huna) explains 'his אוני' in this *baraita*: לכשתברח ממנו/ממני
אין לי עסק בך, 'When you flee from him/me, I will have no business with (=
claim against) you.'[44] This makes no sense as an explanation of the Greek אוני
in context, and as it stands (and was understood by later sources) refers to a
deed written by the slave owner to the slave, a situation whose rationale is
obscure. I suggest that the passage was altered at an early stage of transmission
and that it originally contained or was based on the text of a clause from the
bill of sale, in which it was stated that should the slave flee from the buyer, he
would have no claim against the seller.[45] Just such a clause is found in the

---

[42] The several relevant studies include Gulak, *Legal Documents*; Rabinowitz, *Jewish Law*; and
Yaron, *Gifts*. Among scholars who have dealt with ancient Mesopotamian formularies and their
relationship to talmudic contracts mention should be made of Y. Muffs (*Studies*), J.C. Greenfield
(e.g., 'Babylonian-Aramaic Relations') and A. Skaist (e.g., 'Background', on the validation formula הכל שריר וקים – on which see also the material discussed in Friedman *Jewish Marriage* 1,
473ff). Also cf Falk, 'Neo-Babylonian' and other studies.

[43] Yaron, *Gifts*, 22ff.; cf Lieberman, *Tosefta Ki-Fshutah* 6, introduction, 18; 10, p427f.

[44] For the variants, H. Porush's edition of bGit, vol 2, 204 and the Lieberman Institute of Talmudic
Research-JTS CD-ROM were consulted (according to the latter, ms Vat 140 reads בו in bGit 43b;
but Shamma Friedman checked the photograph for me and ascertained that the reading of the last
letter is uncertain).

[45] Were we to assume that in the talmudic text תברח rather than 2nd pers. masc. was 3rd pers. fem.,
referring to a female slave, and that this was a statement of the buyer to the seller, no emendation
whatsoever would be required: 'If she flees from me, I will have no business with (= claim
against) you.' As noted above, אוני literally means 'purchase', not sale. But there is no transparent
reason to assume that the formula would refer specifically to a female slave.

Syriac bill of sale for a female slave from Dura-Europos, dated 243 CE (P. Dura 28), a document whose importance for the research of talmudic and medieval Jewish formularies was recognized by J.A. Goldstein. In ll. 17-18, we read the following condition: *d'n ḟrq lh 'mt' hd' mn ywmn' wlhl mn gdh dtyrw zbwn'*, 'If this female slave runs away, from today onward it will be from the (bad) fortune of Tiro, the buyer.'[46]

As custom was a recognized source of halakha, it need not surprise us that the sages were prepared to base rulings on the contracts that people were accustomed to use. The texts of these documents thus became a source for halakhic decisions. Many examples both from the Tannaic and Amoraic periods can be cited. At times the reliance on a contract is explicit. An obvious example involving an actual case is that of Hillel the elder, cited at the beginning of this chapter, who told the Alexandrians to produce their mothers' marriage contracts, or R. Mana who instructed the relatives of a woman who objected to his decision that she should be divorced with half of her ketubba payment, 'Bring the marriage contract, and we will read it' (yKet 7:7, 31c).

In several instances the sages derived general rules from the interpretation of contract formulae, the direct quotes of which are introduced by the phrase 'for so he writes'. A number of explicit cases in which Tannaim derived legal principles from interpreting different contracts (and one implicit one) were collected and appear in the Tosefta and Talmuds, where the process is given a technical term: 'expounding a layman's language', דרש לשון הדיוט, or מדרש כתובה.[47] Besides Hillel the Elder, the House of Shammai, R. Meir, R. Yehuda, R. Joshua b. Korha, R. Yose and R. Elazar b. Azaria are identified as having engaged in this kind of midrash. The reference to an implicit case is to the mishna (Ket 4:6) concerning R. Elazar b. Azaria. Though it states that his rule is based on a midrash, the relevant clauses of the ketubba are alluded to by a Hebrew paraphrase only.[48] An anonymous passage in bKet 81a identifies מדרש כתובה as a method employed by the House of Shammai. But it seems to have been practiced by all the sages, or at least none is cited as opposing it; and the Yerushalmi equates Hillel the Elder's exposition of the Alexandrians' marriage contracts with the House of Hillel.[49]

---

[46] See Goldstein, 'Syriac Bill', 2 (text), 6 (translation), 13f (comment). Instead of 'from the (bad) fortune', Goldstein paraphrases: 'at the risk' (see his discussion on p12f of בגדה in l. 15, which in my opinion was an error, influenced by the appearance of מן גדה in l. 18). Gulak, *Legal Documents*, 133-139 discusses the responsibility of the seller for the fleeing slave in Roman law and Greek papyri, and suggests that because of the dissimilar approach to the rights of the fleeing slave in Jewish law, such a clause was absent in the talmudic formulary.

[47] tKet 4:(8)9ff; yYev 15:3, 14d; yKet 4:8, 28d; bBM 104a. 'For so he writes' expositions not included in this collection may postdate it: tBM 5:11; 9:13; also cf an Amoraic passage in bBM 15a.

[48] Cf Friedman, *Jewish Marriage* 1, 374-377.

[49] yYev 15:3, 14d; yKet 4:8, 28d. Cf Tosafot Ket 53a, *s.v.* שאין. Cf bBB 138b: ר' עקיבה היא דדייק לישנא יתירא, 'It is R. Akiva who analyzes the extra language.'

As with midrash in general, the relationship of interpretations to the simple meaning of the text were likely to vary considerably with מדרש לשון הדיוט. It could be used to clarify the intention behind an ambiguous statement, as in a case concerning a will, where the sages ruled that this method was *not* to be employed: 'If one says, "Emancipate my slave Tavi" and there were two Tavis, we do not interpret a layman's language and say that he favored this one and did not favor that one, rather both are emancipated.'[50] Not all of the rules explicitly based on the analysis of contract formulae appear to correspond to the original intention of the writers. This can be illustrated by R. Elazar b. Azaria's curious rule that support of daughters is obligatory only after their father's death, derived by him from interpreting the juxtaposition of theבנן נוקבן clause, concerning daughters' support, with בנין דכרין. The latter takes effect after the father's death, but it is evident from extant ancient marriage contracts and other sources that בנן נוקבן had not been intended to be restricted in this fashion.[51] Such a degree of free exposition is reminiscent of certain midrashim applied by the sages to the text of the Tora. An Amora, in fact, cited the Tannaim's willingness to freely interpret contracts as precedent for his contemporaries' license to interpret the Tora in a non-literal sense. 'Rav Hisda said...: They engaged in *midrash ketubba*, should we not engage in *midrash Tora*?!' (bYev 117a).

In some sources rulings are based on phrases from documents without explicit attribution. One indication that a document is being referred to is the appearance of an Aramaic word or phrase in the middle of a Hebrew context. tBM 11:25-26 (p126), for example, includes the following: 'The bakers may make a רגיעה (guild agreement) among themselves. The ass-drivers may say, "If anyone's ass dies, we shall supply him with another." If it died through negligence (בבוסיא), they need not supply him with an ass; without negligence (דלא בבוסיא), they must supply him.' The Aramaic words for 'through negligence' and 'without negligence' probably allude to the text of a document consisting of a guild agreement (a type of partnership) between the ass-drivers.[52] Since the sages frequently paraphrased the text of contracts in Hebrew, it may be difficult to ascertain when reference is made to a contract. The identification of the text of R. Elazar b. Azaria's midrash, referred to above, as ketubba clauses, has caused some confusion in the scholarly literature.

The example of betrothal by deed illustrates how the sages applied midrash to justify certain widespread practices relating to contracts. But some provisions manifestly conflicted with legal theory and, in certain cases, with rules understood to be rooted in the Tora; and these did not easily lend themselves to harmonization. Second century sources reflect how the sages addressed this issue. At times restrictions were placed on the effectiveness of provisions. The

---

[50] tBB 11:13 (p170), see Lieberman, *Tosefta Ki-Fshutah* 10, 463f.
[51] See Friedman, *Jewish Marriage* 1, 356ff.
[52] Cf tBM 5:11-12 (p89); Lieberman, *Tosefta Ki-Fshutah* 9, 212 (n9), 323.

בנין דכרין rule was limited to cases where the father's estate was at least one dinar larger than the combined value of the wives' ketubba money (mKet 10:2), so that through division of the excess among all the sons, the biblical law of inheritance could be fulfilled, or, as explained by R. Abun (yKet 10:2, 33d): 'When you cannot fulfill their words and the words of the Tora, you cancel their words and fulfill the words of the Tora.'

The anonymous Tanna whose opinion is brought in mBB 8:5 invalidated a will in which a testator assigned his inheritance to a third party instead of his daughter, for example, 'because he has made a stipulation which counters what is written in the Tora,' but R. Yohanan b. Beroka considered it valid as long as the assignee was in the line of inheritance. In mKet 9:1 a husband's written waiver of his rights to inherit his wife's property is upheld by the anonymous Tanna but invalidated by Rabban Shimon b. Gamliel, 'because he has made a stipulation which counters what is written in the Tora, and any condition which one makes that counters what is written in the Tora is invalid.' In bBM 94a R. Meir is identified as holding the latter rule. R. Yehuda, contrariwise, accepted the principle of freedom of contract in monetary matters and affirmed the efficacy of such stipulations; and his opinion won acceptance by later sages.[53] So, for example, in the case of the clause concerning inheritance of the childless woman cited above, R. Yose ruled that 'this is a monetary stipulation, and it is binding'.[54]

As the writing of certain contracts and their formulae achieved wider acceptance among the people, the sages attached greater weight to them. Eventually, in the absence of evidence to the contrary, they assumed that the parties agreed to certain clauses and the provisions embodied in them, even when not written. In other words, these clauses lost their constitutive force and became part of the corpus of obligatory law. Several of the stipulations of the ketubba listed in mKet 4:7ff were accordingly recognized as 'court stipulations/ enactments', binding even when not written. In some cases the sages disagreed whether or not the provisions of a clause took effect when not written. R. Meir and the anonymous sages disputed whether the courts would enforce collection of a bill of debt that had been found, which lacked a clause pledging the borrower's property as security (mBM 1:6). According to the Amora Shmuel, the sages ruled that it would be collected because they believed that the omission of the pledging clause was merely a scribal error (bBM 14a).[55]

The relationship between scribes and sages was one of mutual give and take. The former preserved ancient formulae, which developed in the common law and were paralleled by provisions elsewhere in the ancient Near East. The

---

[53] For sources, references to scholarly literature, and a discussion as to what monetary matters include, see Friedman, *Jewish Marriage* 1, 320.

[54] yKet 9:1, 33a and parallel; see Friedman, *ib.*, 1, 394ff.

[55] The latter principle, with which R. Yehuda is identified by the anonymous *sugya* in bKet 51a (or its converse, that according to R. Meir held the omission is not a scribal error), apparently is not found in the Yerushalmi.

latter adopted and interpreted these and based many halakhot on them. Scribes, furthermore, were attached to the courts, and the sages realized that at times the scribes were better acquainted with procedures for writing documents than they were (bSan 29b). But the formularies were also directly influenced by the legal theories of the sages. Many examples of emendations of the texts of documents by the sages are found in the Talmud. To mention only three, R. Natan and R. Yehuda the Prince debated the text of the בנין דכרין clause to be fixed in the Mishna (yKet 4:12, 29a and parallels); Rabban Shimon b. Gamliel instructed how to write a bill of sale that would be irreversible even if only part of the price was paid (bBM 77b); and Rabban Gamliel the Elder fixed the formula for writing the names in a bill of divorce (mGit 4:2).

Discussions of points of law in talmudic literature often revolve around contracts. These frequently concern the effectiveness of various formulae and begin 'if one wrote...' So in tBB 7:17 (p156), concerning the deed for a gift in contemplation of death, 'If one wrote "an inheritance" below and "a gift" above ... his words are valid.' אמר, 'said' is often used for 'wrote', as in the parallel to this tosefta in mBB 8:5, 'If he said, "as an inheritance"...' The Bavli (Ket 102b) notes the correspondence of 'write' and 'say' but unconvincingly suggests that the former is used in place of the latter, instead of the opposite.[56] Where 'say' is not paralleled in other sources by 'write', its identification as introducing a contract formula may by somewhat elusive, especially when the particular wording of the text under discussion is not familiar. For example, mGit 4:6, 'if one sells his slave abroad, he is emancipated', is explained by a baraita in yGit 4:6, 46a: 'I, So-and-so sell my slave to So-and-so the Antiochian, ...who is in Lod, he is not emancipated.' In the parallel in bGit 44b, 'If one said, "I have sold So-and-so my slave ...to an Antiochian, who lives in Lod," he is not emancipated.' In the talmudic period, it was common to identify the places of origin and residence of the parties to a contract, and here the text of the deed of emancipation is interpreted by the sages in deciding the law.[57]

The numerous relationships between halakhic material in the Talmud and the provisions of contracts rooted in custom and scribal tradition that can be identified by explicit and implicit references lead us to speculate that such connections existed where no allusion can be found as well. Much of civil law as well as the obligations associated with marriage may correspond to the practices formulated by the people in their documents. We give here two examples. In the first, later sages identified the correspondence in the Talmud; in the second, it has been suggested by modern research. Shmuel (first generation Amora) ruled that a creditor collects from the appreciation of mortgaged prop-

---

[56] For several examples of 'say' = 'write', see Friedman, *Jewish Marriage* 1, 112; add, e.g., tGit 5:12 (p268): 'whether he "said" orally or "said" in a deed'. Cf Lieberman, *Tosefta Ki-Fshutah* 8, 868.

[57] See Friedman, 'Linguistic Chronology', 61f.

erty that the debtor had sold to a third party, and Rabba (third generation) adduced proof for this from the wording of the defension clause found in sale contracts. Consequently, R. Hiyya bar Abin concluded that the creditor may not attach the appreciation of property of which the debtor had made a gift, since the defension clause is not written in a deed for a gift, and Rabba concurred (bBM 15a).[58] Elsewhere Shmuel ruled that a widow lost her right to support from her late husband's estate as soon as she agreed to a proposal of remarriage (bKet 54a). This is probably based on an interpretation of a ketubba clause according to a variant preserved only in the Erfurt ms of the Tosefta (Ed 1:6) (and paralleled in extant fragmentary ketubbot from the Geniza): 'When you consent to marry, you shall collect your ketubba money.'[59]

CONTRACTS IN THE AGGADA

Mention must also be made of the relationship of contracts to aggada, a subject that merits a separate investigation. The role played by legal documents in the Jewish community or in the non-Jewish society in which the sages lived was fully reflected in their aggadic teaching as well. Contemporary practices were attributed to biblical figures. Abraham's servant took 'all of his master's bounty with him' when he was sent to find a wife for Isaac (Gen 24:10); 'this means a דייתיקי (will)' (GenR 59,11; p637). When Rebecca sent Jacob to take two choice kids to prepare for Isaac's blessing, she was not commissioning a theft from her husband's flock, since Isaac had written in her marriage contract that he would give her as an additional payment a daily gift of two kids (GenR 65,14; p725). David's soldiers wrote bills of divorce to their wives before going into battle (bKet 9b). The wording of biblical verses was reminiscent of contract formulae. 'Esther was taken to King Ahasuerus, in his royal palace, in the tenth month, which is the month of Tevet, in the seventh year of his reign' (Esth 2:16) purportedly alludes to the dating formula used in Esther's ketubba. The midrash adds that Esther was the only woman to be granted a marriage contract by Ahasuerus; his other wives were married and divorced without any deed. This comment seems to reflect the realities known from Greek papyri and other classical sources. Marriage deeds were written for upper-class women only. Roman law did not require bills of divorce until 439 CE; before that date their issuance presumably depended on social status.[60]

The tablets of the Decalogue were taken to be the deed with which God betrothed Israel. According to Rabban Yohanan b. Zakkai, this explains why the second tablets were written by Moses, while God merely signed them – at

---

[58] The preference for reading Rabba (see *Dikduke Sofrim*), rather than Rava, is proven by the exchange with the former sage's contemporary R. Hiyya b. Abin.

[59] See Friedman, *Jewish Marriage* 1, 432ff.

[60] For the sources and embellishments of these themes in midrashic literature, see Friedman, 'Royal Era'.

the top (!), as a groom signs a marriage contract: 'I'.[61] Other sages took the first word of the Decalogue אנכי as an acronym for a formula similar to that used by scribes in signing their documents: אנא נפשי כתבת יהבת 'I myself wrote and gave it' or for a formula that validates God's signature.[62] Yet others identified the tablets as Israel's deed of manumission from slavery.[63]

FORM AND LANGUAGE

In a few instances, some examples of which have been cited above, the sages gave precise instructions for writing contract formulae; and for the *get* the Talmud contains directions for spelling words and even for the proper length of certain letters (bGit 85b). But these are the exception. Extant documents written hundreds of years after the talmudic period still exhibit an amazing degree of variation in formulation, and this applies to all contracts, even the bill of divorce (see below). Clarity of content was essential; form usually was not.

Contract formulae are most often cited in the Talmud in Aramaic, even in the Mishna, in Hebrew context. Aramaic was used for official purposes and was the lingua franca of the ancient Near East. Most extant Jewish documents from the talmudic period and later are in Aramaic, and these serve as important sources for the study of this language as spoken in the talmudic period.[64] When Tannaim cited from contracts in Hebrew they probably paraphrased from the original Aramaic formulae,[65] but the question is complicated by the Hebrew language documents from the Bar-Kokhba period found in the Judean Desert, discussed below. The sages lived in a multilingual society, and they could not ignore the reality that people wrote contracts in other languages as well. Documents written in Greek or even in five different languages were held to be valid (mGit 9:8; tBB 11:11, p169),[66] and Persian documents are mentioned in the Bavli (e.g., Git 19b). The extant Judean Desert documents shed new light on these sources. The sages even discussed the efficacy of particular formulae written in Greek: 'Rabban Shimon b. Gamliel says, If one writes דיותימין in Greek, it is a valid gift' (i.e., διεθέμην, tBB 9:14, p162).[67] The clearest expression that the content of a contract is all important and not its exact form or

---

[61] tBK 7:4, p29; see Friedman, 'Second Tablets'.

[62] See Friedman, *Jewish Marriage* 1, 489-492; idem, 'Handwriting'.

[63] mAvot 6:2, see Lieberman, *Tosefta Ki-Fshutah* 10, 423 n11.

[64] See Friedman, *Jewish Marriage* 1, 48ff and literature cited there.

[65] *Ib.*, 1, 431ff.

[66] Different texts of tGit 7:11 (p274) are divided as to whether or not the bill of divorce is valid if written in mulitple languages; see Lieberman, *Tosefta Ki-Fshutah* 8, 910.

[67] See Gulak, '*Diethemen*'; Sperber, *Dictionary*, 81f; Lieberman in *Yerushalmi Neziqin*, 219; idem, *Tosefta Ki-Fshutah* 10, 441. 'In Greek' appears to be the editorial comment of the transmitter rather than of Rabban Shimon b. Gamliel.

language is the rule that affirms the validity of a document issued in a gentile court, including, with certain qualifications, a bill of divorce (mGit 1:5).[68]

Extant Ancient Jewish Contracts and Rabbinic Literature

Quotes from many contracts appear in the talmudic literature. Most of these were collected in the 1920's and studied, in conjunction with extant Jewish contracts known at the time, by A. Gulak.[69] In no case do the talmudic sources cite the full formula of the document. Since significant portions of talmudic law (and lore) are explicitly or implicitly associated with contracts and their provisions, the study of ancient documents from Palestine and the surrounding countries discovered in the past generations is particularly important. They make it possible to fill many lacunae concerning contracts in the talmudic literature and illustrate how these deeds functioned in real-life situations. Furthermore, they reveal interesting points of contact with other cultures, some of which illuminate the talmudic passages as well. Conversely, the Talmud provides the background for understanding many fragmentary and obscure clauses in the extant deeds. Five separate finds, from the pre-talmudic, talmudic and post-talmudic periods are particularly relevant for our purposes.[70]

ELEPHANTINE PAPYRI

Some thirty Aramaic contracts from the fifth century BCE Jewish community of Elephantine in Upper Egypt have been found. Most of these come from two archives: the woman Mibtahiah's, with dated documents from 471-410 BCE, and the temple servitor Ananiah's, from 451-402 BCE; they were published in 1923 and 1953. The contracts include: gifts of property, acknowledgement of ownership of property or goods or of dowry rights, marriage contracts, grants of property rights, division of rights to slaves, sales of houses or parts thereof, loans, emancipation of slaves, exchange of shares, and acknowledgement of a child as son.

The relevance of the Elephantine contracts to the talmudic material is questionable for two reasons: they precede by several centuries the earliest datable traditions which were incorporated in talmudic literature; and they emanate from a community upon which foreign, non-Jewish culture exerted remarkable influences, evident, *inter alia*, by apparently syncretistic elements in its religious cult. The contracts are invaluable for the study of various aspects of the

---

[68] See Lieberman, *Tosefta Ki-Fshutah* 8, 788; *ib.* 10, 423; cf Friedman, 'On the New Fragment'.
[69] Gulak, *Otzar ha-Shetarot* (1926).
[70] Note must also be made of the many Greek deeds from Egypt written for Jews (published in CPJ).

society and culture of the Elephantine community.[71] But it is not clear to what extent their formulation and content reflect an independent variant of Jewish law and scribal custom originating in Palestine, or that of the community's non-Jewish ambience.[72]

This and related questions have been debated since the earliest publications of Aramaic papyri from Elephantine in the first decade of the twentieth century. While I believe that the contracts are to be seen more as a link in the chain of Near Eastern common law than of Jewish tradition, that matter need not concern us here. Suffice it to say that even if there is no vertical relationship between the Elephantine documents and the talmudic ones, there are numerous similarities in the contents and formulation of these two corpuses which are mutually illuminating.

The marriage contracts from Elephantine, for example, contain an interesting clause, which deals with the consequences of divorce, associated with the word שנאה, 'hatred', initiated by the wife or the husband. A similar stipulation is referred to some seven centuries later in the Yerushalmi ('Those who write: "If he hates", "if she hates"'). Compare the text of a quote from the protasis of such a clause cited there from an actual marriage contract, 'If this So-and-so (fem) hates this So-and-so, her husband, and does not desire his partnership...', with that of one of the Elephantine contracts (Kraeling 7): 'If J hates her husband A and says to him, "I hate you; I will not be your wife"...' Such a divorce clause, dependent on the tradition of the Yerushalmi, is found later in the Geniza documents (see below).[73]

SAMARIA PAPYRI

Eighteen large fragments or groups of fragments of Aramaic papyri from 375-335 BCE, written in Samaria, were found in 1962 in a cave in Wadi al-Daliya. Ten have been described as slave conveyances, others as manumission, real estate transactions, loans, settlements of broken contracts including divorce and loan agreements. As of this writing, only two documents (Nos. 1 and 2), deeds of sale for slaves, have been published.[74] The formulation and language of these papyri resemble the Elephantine material, and some of the same ques-

---

[71] For the texts, see Porten and Yardeni, *Textbook*, and for the society in general, Porten, *Archives*.

[72] See, inter alia, Muffs, *Studies*, and Yaron, *Introduction*, passim.

[73] yKet 5:10, 30b and yBB 8:9, 16c; yKet 7:7, 31c. The complex questions of relationship between formulae with certain similarities, yet distinct one from another in wording and details of provisions, that appear, for example, in Elephantine, the Talmud and Geniza texts, must be considered with utmost caution through a critical analysis of the specific sources and their historical and social background. Otherwise, one may tend to harmonize diverse materials, as is the case with Gottlieb, 'Succession' concerning the provisions, written in marriage contracts, for the estate of a childless wife.

[74] See Cross, 'Discovery'; idem, 'The Papyri'; idem, 'Samaria Papyrus 1' (the description of the content of the papyri varies somewhat in these publications); Gropp, 'Wadi Daliyeh Documents'; idem, 'Samaria Papyri'.

tions concerning relevance to the talmudic contracts raised in reference to those deeds apply to them. Nevertheless, definite points of contact with the talmudic formularies can be adduced. An outstanding example is the defension clause, which has a long history of comparable terms in ancient Near Eastern documents and has been the object of much scholarly scrutiny. In the Samaria papyri, the seller promises that if the purchaser's rights to his newly acquired possessions are challenged, *'qym 'mrq 'ntn lk*, which may be translated approximately: 'I shall make (it) stand, pay (for)/ cleanse (it) and give (it) to you'. In talmudic literature the defension clause is quoted only in bBM 15a in a fourth century CE passage: ואוקים... אנא איקום ואשפי ואדכי ואמרק זביני אילין [ואיקום] קדמך, which may be rendered: 'I shall rise up/ make good, cleanse/ pay for (with three synonymous terms) this sale ...and make (it) stand before you.'[75]

JUDEAN DESERT DOCUMENTS

Most significant for their legal formularies as well as for their historical and social background are the documents from the Judean Desert. These exciting recent discoveries open new vistas for the study of contracts and their relationship to the Talmud. Some of the papyri date from the first century CE, approximately from the period of the first revolt against Rome. Most come from the early second century, from the years preceding and coinciding with the second revolt. Several dozens of documents, including numerous small fragments, have been discovered in the Judean Desert since the 1950's, most at two sites: Wadi Murabbaat and the 'Cave of the Letters' at Nahal Hever. There is also a group of texts supposedly from Nahal Seelim. The provenance of some texts is not known for sure. The Murabbaat documents were published in 1961. The texts from the Cave of Letters were described in 1962, shortly after their discovery by an expedition led by Y. Yadin. In recent years, a proliferation of publications have made available the editions of these documents and numerous researches devoted to them.[76]

The largest single collection, from the Cave of Letters, is the archive of the Jewish woman Babatha, which includes thirty-six documents pertaining to her affairs and those of members of her family. These were found in a leather pouch, wrapped in sacking and tied together with twisted ropes. Within the

[75] See Cross, 'Samaria Papyrus 1', 13f, 16; Kutscher, 'Terms'; Yaron, 'Defension Clauses'; idem, 'Murabbaat Documents', 168f; Friedman, *Jewish Marriage* 1, 80f (on מרק), 342f (for קום ב- in medieval Aramaic sources from the Geniza in the sense of 'make good', 'fulfill an obligation'; also cf Arabic *aqām*, 'pay'); *DJD* 27, 49f, and literature cited there; Gropp, 'Wadi Daliyeh Documents', 34f.

[76] See *DJD* 2; Lewis, *Documents*; Yardeni, *Nahal Seelim*; *DJD* 27; Yardeni, *Textbook*; Yadin et al., *Documents*. Bibliography for earlier publications is cited in these studies. For a survey of these collections and how the papyri are cited, see Cotton, 'Documentary Texts'; for a wider survey of the papyri in the Roman Near East, see Cotton, Cockle and Millar, 'Papyrology'. See now Katzoff and Schaps, *Law*.

441

pouch, documents relating one to another were folded and tied in bundles (two, five or six documents in each batch), while some particularly important personal contracts, such as Babatha's own ketubba (P. Yadin 10), were wrapped individually. Both the manner in which Babatha kept her documents and their discovery remind one of mBM 1:8, 'If one found documents in a satchel or bag, or a roll of documents or a bundle of documents, he should return them. How many count as a bundle of documents? Three tied up together.'[77]

The Judean Desert documents include deeds of sale for real estate, leases and the distribution of leased property, acknowledgements of debts, marriage contracts, a bill of divorce, a deed for a gift of property, and a number of texts that deal with various matters, such as guardianship and mortgage. Most of the texts are rather fragmentary and in scripts that are difficult to decipher. They are nevertheless treasure troves of information for the student of talmudic literature and the history of the (first and) early second century Jewish community in the Land of Israel.

The documents are written in Aramaic, Hebrew and Greek. Babatha's archive includes several Nabatean documents, which relate to properties in the area formerly controlled by the Nabateans. These texts are written in Nabatean-Aramaic, a dialect of Aramaic, the *lingua franca*, rather than the Arabic which the Nabateans spoke – though there are Arabic loan words in the documents. They too contain legal formulae known from talmudic sources and other Jewish Documents.[78] Many of the Greek documents concern property in Provincia Arabia (the Zoar area). The differentiation between the documents written in Hebrew and those in Aramaic is a question of some interest. The Bar-Kokhba letters imply that Hebrew remained in colloquial use during this period, a finding of some significance for the study of the language of the Mishna. As to the contracts, some bills of sale and documents relating to the leasing of property are written in Hebrew. All of these seem to come from the Bar-Kokhba period, and Yadin has suggested that the use of Hebrew may have resulted from an official nationalistic policy of Bar-Kokhba.[79]

Greek-language contracts were written not only for transactions involving non-Jews but also for the exclusive use of Jews, and Jewish scribes wrote these instruments. This should not be dismissed as evidence of assimilation and may

---

[77] See Yadin, 'Expedition D', 235f; idem, *Bar-Kokhba*, 222ff, where photographs of the pouch and wrapped documents are provided.

[78] Cf, e.g., Greenfield, 'Legal Terminology', 67ff.

[79] See Yadin, 'Expedition D', 238 ff.; Yadin, *Bar-Kokhba*, 234; Greenfield, 'Languages', 150-152; Naveh, *Sherd and Papyrus*, 23-25, 98; Cotton, 'Languages', 225. Official policy: Yadin, *Bar-Kokhba*, 181. Some scholars have speculated that the purported transfer from the (Aramaic) marriage formula 'according to the law of Moses and the Jews' found in the Yerushalmi and, for example, in Babatha's *ketubba*, to the familiar (Hebrew) 'according to laws of Moses and Israel' might be explained by religious or political developments. As argued by Friedman, *Jewish Marriage* 1, 166 the appearance of the '...and the Jews' formula in the Palestinian-type marriage contracts written through the eleventh century, found in the Geniza, suggests that the variation might originally reflect linguistic or dialectical preferences.

have been done in order to register the documents in public archives or enforce them in a Greek-speaking court.[80] Some of the Greek-language contracts, the parties to which were Jews, contain significant elements known primarily from Jewish legal sources; an example from the marriage contracts will be discussed below. Other documents bear little resemblance to Jewish legal traditions or the formularies known from Jewish documents and seem to be fundamentally Greek in form and legal content. But these too may reflect practices evidenced in talmudic sources.

The relationship between the Judean Desert documents in general and those written in Greek in particular to talmudic tradition is a fascinating but elusive subject of research. Prima facie we cannot be certain to what extent individuals who wrote these documents or were party to them were concerned with having them accord with Jewish law.[81] The difficulties in research transcend the inherent limitations in deciphering and translating the fragmentary papyri. Even when parallels with Jewish literary sources can be identified, we often cannot be certain whether the parties understood these formulae or practices to be Jewish in nature, as they might have been shared with the non-Jewish milieu, in which the parties lived and to which they were conforming.

The nascent state of Tannaic law at the time complicates the situation. Most of the sages with whom legal traditions are associated were active in the years following the writing of the Judean Desert texts, and many more years passed before their rulings were crystallized and accepted as binding law. Furthermore, we know the Tannaic traditions only after they underwent an extended period of transmission, editing and interpretation. These processes sometimes altered the form or meaning of the Tannaic traditions. The critical analysis of these sources involves difficulties of its own, which in comparative studies have not been consistently addressed. The complex relationship of scribes and sages, already noted above, must be considered as well.

The Ketubbot

The Judean Desert marriage contracts contain a plethora of formulae whose critical comparison with talmudic traditions should prove mutually illuminating and rewarding. Their research also illustrates some of the methodological problems cited above. A relatively large number of papyri in this category have been preserved. These include three Aramaic ketubbot and a fragment

---

[80] See H. Cotton in *DJD* 27, 153f, 207, 254; idem, 'Languages', 227-231; idem, 'Rabbis and Documents', 169f.

[81] See, e.g., Cotton in *DJD* 27, 153-157, 274.

that seems to come from a fourth.[82] Five Greek-language marriage contracts written for Jews have also been published.

The ketubba is of pivotal importance for Jewish law, and in recent years these papyri have elicited many studies. The recently published ketubba of Babatha (P. Yadin 10) is a particularly rich source for comparative studies with the Talmud.[83] Here we briefly address a few of the issues raised by the relationship between the Greek-language marriage contracts and the Aramaic ketubbot and the extent to which the first category was compatible with Jewish instruments. I agree with those scholars who have rejected as gratuitous A. Wasserstein's suggestion that a Greek-language marriage contract implies that the same couple had a separate Aramaic ketubba, which has not been preserved.[84]

Salome Komaïs's marriage contract (P. Yadin 37 = XHev/Se 65), from Mahoza, 131 CE, had been described before publication as a 'Jewish *ketubbah* ... written in Greek'. In the first edition, the resemblance to the ketubba assumed smaller proportions: essentially, the structure, as demonstrated by the reference to the action of the groom in taking the bride. The formula in question – 'Yeshua son of Menahem, domiciled in ... acknowledged of his own free will (?) that he has taken Salome ...' – is only partially preserved, and while parallels in Palestinian-style ketubbot are found, it is hardly inherently Jewish.[85] 'In all probability' Jewish custom was supposedly reflected in the statement that the bridal pair was to live together 'as also before this time'. The reality reflected by this phrase and its purported Jewish character are not self-evident and have aroused much speculation.[86]

---

[82] The fourth is P. XHev/Se/ 11, ed Yardeni, *Nahal Se'elim*, 61-63; *DJD* 27, 57-59. As A. Yardeni noted, the fragmentarily preserved inner text of three lines of this double document (which, other than a few letters from the outer text, is all that is extant) is too short to have comprised the complete text of a ketubba. For the inner text consisting only of a brief, even one sentence summary, see Lieberman, *Tosefta Ki-Fshutah* 10, 452; Goldstein, 'Syriac Bill', 1-f, 7; Lewis, *Documents*, 9 and the literature cited in these studies. In l. 3, [ל]ואנה מקב could be part of the groom's acceptance clause of the obligations in the contract; see Friedman, *Marriage* 1, 481f; P. Mur. 21, ll. 17-8, according to Yardeni's reading in Yadin *et al.*, *Documents*, 140.

[83] For the publication, see Yadin *et al.*, *Documents*, 118-141. On talmudic parallels see esp Friedman, 'Babatha's *Ketubba*'.

[84] See Wasserstein, 'Marriage Contract', 120f; Lewis, 'World', 39f; Cotton, 'Rabbis and Documents', 177.

[85] See Cotton's criticism in *DJD* 27, 225f.

[86] See Lewis, Katzoff and Greenfield, 'P. Yadin 18', 230 (there P. Yadin 37 is referred to as a 'Jewish *ketubbah* ... written in Greek'); Lewis, *Documents*, 130. I call attention to the similarity of the phrase in question to 'as his wife, as in former days' in a *ketubba* written in Ramle 1051 CE (ms Cambridge TS 16.123, ed Friedman, *Jewish Marriage* 2, 155-165), written for a couple that had been divorced and was remarrying (P. Mur. 115 is also for a remarriage and does not have such a formula). According to Ilan, 'Cohabitation', 250f the Greek in P. Yadin 37 would have been worded otherwise, had a remarriage been intended. Cf Cotton, 'Rabbis and Documents', 178f.

T. Ilan, for one, discounted the possibility that the couple had previously been married according to Jewish law without a marriage contract. Quoting bBK 89a, 'Said R. Meir, "A man may not keep his wife even one hour, without a ketubba",' Ilan deduced that marriage without a written marriage contract 'certainly negates the main gist of Jewish *ketubbah* legislation'.[87] Whatever 'Jewish ketubba legislation' might denote, the fact that an early second-century couple might have behaved contrary to 'the main gist' of those laws is of questionable significance. If we assume that those people were in fact concerned with the halakhic propriety of their marriage, what would have prevented them from following what may have been defined (later) as a minority rule?[88]

R. Meir's purported rule cannot be a taken to be a basic principle of Jewish marriage without further examination, however. It is not cited as a baraita in the late, anonymous *sugya* in bBK 89a (and 89b) but is introduced by the formula: ...'מני ר' מאיר היא דאמ, 'Who (= whose opinion) is it? It is R. Meir, who said...' This formula is used in the Bavli to indicate that the words that follow are not the sage's verbatim statement but that they can be deduced from something else, which he had said. Furthermore, it is not clear whether the word ketubba in this dictum means 'marriage contract' or 'delayed *mohar* payment', its usual meaning in mishnaic Hebrew and so used in bBK 89a (and 89b). Contrariwise, in bKet 67a, when the family of certain Amoraim lost the wife's ketubba – which here obviously refers to the writ – they asked the fourth century sage Rav Yosef whether it was necessary to write a new deed. He responded: 'This is the opinion of R. Meir. But the sages say, "A man retains his wife for two or three years without a ketubba."'[89] As they stand, these sources date centuries after P. Yadin 37 (= XHev/Se 65) and support a majority ruling that one is permitted to live with his wife for several years without a marriage contract. The early third century sage Rav and later Amoraim explicitly speak of 'a place where they do not write a ketubba (deed)'.[90]

H. Cotton has explained the background of this papyrus as a transfer from an unwritten marriage to a written one, a practice known from Greek papyri from Egypt. This very well may have been the case, but it need not exclude the

---

[87] Ilan, 'Cohabitation', 254. She also cites an aggadic passage from bGit 57a, the relevance of whose testimony to an early second century practice is questionable for a number of reasons. J. Neusner's assertion quoted on p249 that 'It is beyond the Mishnah's imagination for a man and woman to live together without the benefit of ...a marriage contract', etc., is not based on any explicit source.

[88] Cotton, 'Rabbis and Documents', 178 correctly rejects the notion that at the time there existed a coherent and operative system of Jewish law, which had become normative. But she assumes that R. Meir's ruling was an essential part of that soon-to-be-adopted 'system'.

[89] It is immaterial for our purposes that in the continuation of the talmudic discussion, in bKet 67b, Abaye, Rav Yosef's student, ruled that the law should be according to R. Meir. That discussion explicitly concerns a lost marriage contract, but there is no reason not to apply the purported opinion of the sages to a newly wed couple as well. Concerning the formulae 'who is it? ...who said' and 'this is the opinion of ....', see Halivni, *Sources, Baba Kama*, 180-183.

[90] yKet 9:9, 33c; bKet and parallels. These statements do not refer to a specific place.

possibility of a Jewish practice as well. Whether or not P. Yadin 37 (= XHev/Se 65) fulfilled the essential requirements of a ketubba does not prejudice the issue of whether the marriage, when originally contracted, had been believed to accord with Jewish custom.[91]

While P. Yadin 18 and 37 (= XHev/Se 65) appear prima facie to be essentially Greek documents in form and content,[92] the three other Greek-language marriage contracts, P. Mur. 115 and 116 and XHev/Se 69, also contain versions of important elements of the ketubba, viz., the 'court stipulations' listed in mKet 4:10-12.[93] Whatever their ultimate origin may have been, these clauses are known primarily from Jewish sources. The order and wording of the clauses demonstrate much variation both in these three papyri and in the three Aramaic ketubbot. Though this can be seen as demonstrating the fluid nature of Jewish law during this period,[94] the lack of uniformity in the papyri should not be overemphasized. The sages established what in these stipulations was legally binding but did not necessarily require the use of a uniform text. Individual scribes retained for centuries a remarkable degree of independence from the rabbinic academies. Considerable variations in writing the same stipulations appear in the tenth and eleventh century CE ketubbot written according to the Palestinian custom preserved in the Geniza.

The monies written in the Aramaic ketubbot and in the Greek marriage contracts, the distinction between the deeds in these two categories, and the relationship between them and talmudic sources, are of special interest, as this matter is basic to the institution of the ketubba.[95] Tannaic sources identify the ketubba debt as payable to the wife after she is divorced or widowed and as an institution that developed from and replaced the biblical *mohar*, paid by the groom at betrothal. The ketubba debt was the most essential element of the deed, which eventually was designated by the same term. The debt's centrality to the marriage institution is epitomized in R. Meir's dictum: 'Whoever assigns less than 200 (*zuz*) for a virgin and 100 for widow – this is fornication' (mKet 5:1). By the mid second century CE, when R. Meir was active, those

---

[91] See Cotton in *DJD* 27, 227-229; idem, 'Women and Law', 138: 'Perhaps the most striking evidence of the remarkable degree of assimilation ... unwritten marriage,' etc.; idem, 'Rabbis and Documents', 177: 'We can perhaps take this argument one step further and question the assumption that a written marriage contract was a *sine qua non* for the conclusion of marriage between Jews'.

[92] There are, however, several elements in P. Yadin 18 that might reflect Jewish practice and formulae. A number of these are mentioned in other notes here. See Lewis, Katzoff and Greenfield, 'P. Yadin 18', 236-247; Wasserstein, 'Marriage Contract', 108-130; Katzoff, 'Rejoinder'; idem, 'Hellenistic Marriage Contracts', 40f; Lewis, 'World', 36-41.

[93] The statements that P. Mur. 115 and 116 'basically reflect the Aramaic Jewish *ketubba* formula', in Friedman, *Marriage* 1, 8 and (with slight differences) 368, are hereby superseded. Cotton, 'Cancelled Marriage Contract' 85 correctly noted my error (but I had not written that the contracts in question were 'a Greek translation', etc.).

[94] See Cotton, 'Rabbis and Documents', 172, 175-177.

[95] See Cotton's discussion in *DJD* 27, 266-268; Cotton, 'Rabbis and Documents', 174f.

figures appear to have been fairly well established as standards; priestly and distinguished families insisted on doubling the payment.[96] R. Meir's disqualification of any marriage that involved smaller sums was not universally accepted, however. His contemporary R. Yehuda (mKet 5:1) upheld the standard in theory but prescribed a legal device for circumventing it: the wife could write a fictitious receipt for half of the money or for any other figure.[97] His contemporary R. Yose permitted marriages in which smaller figures than the standards were agreed upon, even without the use of a legal device (bKet 66b). We can assume that these two Tannaim were reacting to popular custom. Not everyone assigned the minimum sums, and society accepted the legitimacy of such marriages.

Giving a dowry, that is, the money, outfit and furnishings or other property provided by the bride's family, was a prevalent custom during the Tannaic period. The sages instructed men to provide their daughters with dowries and employed various methods to encourage the bride's family to be generous in doing so. Unlike the ketubba money, however, no one suggested that the marriage would be illicit, were the bride not endowed.[98]

The relationship between these two marital-divorce payments requires further elucidation. The term ketubba is ambiguous. In Mishnaic Hebrew, besides the usual meaning of the husband's delayed payment, it sometimes denotes the dowry.[99] According to Tannaic sources, the process by which the *mohar* was transferred from an immediate payment to a fictitious one and became a debt involved certain use of these funds as dowry money. It has been suggested that the entire transition be explained by society's preference of marriage by dowry to marriage by *mohar*.[100] Moreover, once the principle of the delayed ketubba payment was established, it would appear to be inconsequential if the money, which the groom promised to pay the bride at the dissolution of the marriage, was the very property that her family had provided as dowry. The ketubba was binding even if the groom had no funds at all at the time of the wedding.

With this we turn to a brief summary of the payments referred to in the Judean Desert marriage contracts. The Aramaic ketubbot make no explicit mention of dowry but rather speak of ketubba money, which, as we have seen could be taken to refer to dowry as well. In Babatha's ketubba, her husband

---

[96] For a reconstruction of how the various practices for increasing the standard developed during this period, see Friedman, 'Babatha's *Ketubba*', 58-60.

[97] For any other figure, see yKet 5:1, 29d. In the continuation there: 'These are the words of R. Meir and R. Yehuda, but the sages say, 'One may marry a woman and stipulate that he not provide her with food and clothing. Moreover, (he may stipulate) that she provide him with food and clothing and enable him to study Torah.' The contrast with R. Meir's and R. Yehuda's opinions implies that according to the sages, no ketubba debt was necessary.

[98] See the sources and discussion in Friedman, *Jewish Marriage* 1, 288-291.

[99] See the sources and discussion in Friedman, *Jewish Marriage* 1, 293, 310f, 383.

[100] See Friedman, 'Marriage and the Family', 62.

undertook a debt of 400 *zuz*, the same sum which according to the Tannaim was demanded for (virgin) brides by distinguished families.[101] Of the five Greek-language marriage contracts, four preserve text that deals with the dowry, the husband's acknowledgement of receipt and his liability for future payment.[102] In P. Mur. 115, a remarriage, the dowry was valued at 200 drachmas. The dowry in P. Yadin 18 was evaluated at 200 denarii, to which the husband added his own debt of 300. In the Aramaic subscription to this document, the groom acknowledged the debt of 500 denarii, all of which was called *pherne*, the Greek term for dowry, which as we have seen denotes ketubba in the Yerushalmi. It is worthwhile to note here R. Katzoff's thought-provoking suggestion that P. Yadin 18 be associated with the practice described in mKet 6:3, which can be translated approximately: 'If she pledges to bring him 1,000 dinars, he counters it with a pledge of 1,500.'[103] Salome Komaïs's marriage contract (P. Yadin 37 = XHev/Se 65) registers her dowry evaluated at 96 denarii. The dowry in XHev/Se 69 was evaluated at 500 denarii.

These documents attest early second century Palestinian Jewish marital practices. It is likely that the Jewish and non-Jewish populations shared many of the customs associated with the marriage payments. Some have clear parallels in Jewish sources. A comparison with the Tannaic traditions surveyed above indicates that as far as these payments were concerned, none of the contracts, including the one that fixed the dowry at 96 denarii, need have been considered contrary to contemporary Jewish law or practice.

The Aramaic ketubbot contain a formula that affirms that the groom is taking the bride to be his wife 'according to the law of Moses and the Jews' (P. Yadin 10 and Mur. 20).[104] This or some other variant of the more familiar formula 'according to the law of Moses and Israel' is commonplace in ketub-

---

[101] The ketubba money is mentioned in P. Mur. 21, l. 13; P. Yadin 10, ll. 5, 6, 8, 9, 11, 16. The text of P. Mur. 20, l. 11, mentions the '*ketu[bba]*' money; for the reading see Friedman, *Jewish Marriage* 1, 429. On the figure of 400 *zuz* in Babatha's ketubba and its relation to talmudic sources, see Friedman, 'Babatha's Ketubba', 57-60.

[102] P. Mur. 116 is too fragmentary.

[103] Hebrew: פסקה להכניס לו אלף דינר והוא פוסק כנגדן חמשה עשר מנה; the above translation differs slightly from Katzoff's. In Lewis, Katzoff and Greenfield, 'P. Yadin 18', 242 n35 Katzoff identified difficulties in this interpretation of a separate, counter pledge of 1,500 by groom (for a total of 2,500; also see Katzoff, 'Hellenistic Marriage Contracts', 40). He referred to his interpretation, with reservations, as 'the Mishnah requires'. It would be more precise to say that 'a statement in the mishna requires'. As Wasserstein, 'Marriage Contract', 114, noted, this statement is followed in mKet 6:4 by Rabban Shimon b. Gamliel's view: 'All is according to local custom'. The latter does not disprove, however, that mKet 6:3 attests a mid-second century practice. Wasserstein's objections (p113) on the basis of Maimonides' ruling and Albeck's comment are at best irrelevant on methodological grounds. Katzoff alluded to the contextual problems in the mishna. In my opinion, the mishna might be a composite of different sources; the Bavli notes the redundancy between mKet 6:3 and 4. They also use different terminology: mKet 6:3 פוסק (so in the best mss; but some have כותב), mKet 6:4 נעשת.

[104] P. Mur. 21 is too lacunal here.

bot throughout the ages.[105] It is missing, however, in all of the Greek-language marriage contracts from the Judean Desert.[106] Its absence has been taken as singular proof of the non-Jewish nature of these documents.[107] This assertion appears to be based on a certain misconception concerning the significance of the formula in Jewish law and practice. Not only is the formula not required by any halakha; its use in the ketubba is far from universal. An examination of the first twenty ketubbot written according to Palestinian custom during the tenth and eleventh centuries and preserved in the Geniza demonstrates that this formula or its equivalent is definitely or presumably absent in eight cases.[108]

Various Legal Aspects

Several of the Greek-language documents have subscriptions in Aramaic (or Nabatean-Aramaic), in which the main contents of the document are summarized and the parties acknowledge their acceptance of it.[109] Differences notwithstanding, the practice of writing such a subscription is comparable to one to which a passage in the Tosefta may be referring (tBB 11:4, p168): 'What is its קיום? "I, So-and-so, have borrowed from So-and-so..."'[110] S. Lieberman explained that here *qiyyum* means 'substance', as in Christian Palestinian Aramaic.[111] Shortly following this the Tosefta reads (11:8, p168f): 'A document may be translated from Hebrew to Greek or from Greek to Hebrew, and a קיום בית דין is made for it' – thus ms Vienna and the first printed edition. Since *qiyyum* is mostly used for 'confirmation', the text seems to mean: '...and we make a court confirmation for it' (for the accuracy of the translation).[112] But in ms Erfurt the words *bet din*, 'court', are missing. The special use of *qiyyum* in the preceding passage (11:4) as explained by Lieberman and the contemporary

---

[105] See Friedman, *Jewish Marriage* 1, 162-167; Katzoff, 'Marriage Formulas'; Kister, '*Ke-Dat*'.

[106] In P. Yadin 18, l. 39, the bride is given 'for the partnership of marriage according to the laws (*nomos*)', and in l. 51, the groom undertakes to provide for her and her children 'according to Greek custom'. See the discussions on these formulae in Lewis, Katzoff and Greenfield, 'P. Yadin 18', 238, 241f; Wasserstein, 'Marriage Contract', 108f, 113; Katzoff, 'Rejoinder', 174-176; idem, 'Hellenistic Marriage Contracts', 40; Lewis, 'World', 38f; *DJD* 27, 273f. For the imprecise 'according to the *nomos*' in l. 39, cf mGit 6:5, 'perform for her the *nīmōs*'. If you prefer you can substitute the Hebrew נימוס where this formula is considered ineffective for ordering a bill of divorce (cf Friedman, *Jewish Marriage* 1, 475).

[107] *DJD* 27, 273. Also see Cotton, 'Rabbis and Documents', 174: 'The crucial formula "that you will be my wife according to the law of Moses and the Jews" is absent from all of them'; idem, 'Women and Law', 135: 'Above all they lack the well-known formula,' etc.

[108] Friedman, *Jewish Marriage* 2, nos. 1, 7, 9, 10, 14-16, 18, 20.

[109] See Lewis, *Documents*, 135-149.

[110] The continuation, 'and So-and-so borrowed from him', may be an alternate formula, in the third person; cf the beginning of tBB 11:4.

[111] Lieberman, *Tosefta Ki-Fshutah* 10, 456.

[112] So explained by Lieberman, *Tosefta Ki-Fshutah* 10, 457. Cotton, 'Rabbis and Documents', 170 translates the words ועושין לו קיום בית דין, 'and make it valid', a usage which, to the best of my knowledge, is not attested.

practice of the Judean Desert documents suggest that we might render this: 'we make an abstract of it' (in the other language). On the other hand, the Tosefta may be here referring to the practice of rendering Jewish documents in Greek, while retaining essential elements of the Jewish formulary, as is the case with some of the Greek-language marriage contracts cited above.[113]

Both similarities and differences between these contracts and talmudic formulations and traditions are instructive. A few additional examples are noted here. The Bavli mentions the אודיתא, *odita*, document for 'acknowledgement' of a debt, in Amoraic sources dating only from the fourth century. This could lead one to conclude that such formulations originated in Babylonia during that period. However, two IOU's from the Judean Desert open with the formula איתודי (*itode*) 'he received the acknowledgement'.[114]

The bill of divorce issued at Masada (P. Mur. 19) is of special significance for the history of the *get*. Its formulation is remarkably similar to that cited in the Mishna and employed in later periods and thus proves the degree of conservatism which guided the scribes throughout the ages in writing the *get*.[115] The text contains unique formulations, and even subtle differences warrant careful comparison with talmudic sources. The opening formula illustrates this. The sages taught that it was necessary to write a date in the bill of divorce. According to the Tanna Abba Shaul[116] this requirement would be fulfilled '...even were there written in it, "I have divorced you today".'[117] Such a formula, with 'today' (היום), has not been noted in later preserved bills of divorce.[118] Abba Shaul's rule would be considered entirely hypothetical,[119] were it not for the fact that after the regular date formula the operative portion of the Masada deed begins this way (in Aramaic): 'I ... today (יומא דנה), of my own

---

[113] As suggested by Lehmann, 'Studies', 71.

[114] bBB 149a and San 29b-30a. See Yadin, Greenfield, Yardeni and Levine, *Documents*, 60; Broshi and Qimron, 'Debt'; *DJD* 27, 121; Segal, 'IOU'; Naveh, *Sherd and Papyrus*, 87-89. Also cf a formulary for a bill of divorce from Tiberias, dated 938/9 CE and one from 'Hilkhot Reu', in Margulies, *Hilkhot Erets Yisrael*, 120 and a marriage contract from Damascus, 956 CE, ed Friedman, *Jewish Marriage*, 2, 198, with the *mode* formula in Aramaic; Goldstein, 'Syriac Bill', 9f.

[115] *DJD* 2, 104ff (re-edited in *Inscriptions Reveal*, 200f; Naveh, *Sherd and Papyrus*, 89-91; Yardeni, *Textbook*). See Yaron, 'Gerushin'. For the date, Yaron *ib.*, 335f; cf Yadin, *Bar-Kokhba*, 188f.

[116] On the period of his activity, see Lerner, 'Enquiries', 104ff.

[117] tGit 7:6 (p273), see Lieberman, *Tosefta Ki-Fshutah* 8, 903f.

[118] It is to be distinguished from the (truncated?) 'from this day and evermore' in bGit 85b, which in the traditional bill of divorce appears towards the end of the document, in a different context ('no one will challenge you in my name, from this day and evermore'); the scholarly literature for this expression is cited in Friedman, *Jewish Marriage* 2, 330; cf Rivlin, *Inheritance*, 160ff. Lehmann, 'Studies', 63 associates the two phrases and consequently adduces unwarranted evidence for his dating of P. Mur. 19.

[119] Gulak, *Otzar*, 70 did not include it in talmudic citations from the *get*. As to Albeck's comment in his *Shisha Sidre Mishna*, Nashim, 266f, see Friedman, 'Shenei ketaim', 24 n5.

free will, divorce you.'[120] It can be assumed that Abba Shaul was familiar with this wording and saw it as meeting the minimum requirement for a date, even should a bill of divorce be produced without the standard formula.[121]

Abba Shaul's text, citations of the bill of divorce in Amoraic passages in the Talmud, and later preserved deeds of divorce express the operative formula with verbs in the perfect form, as do other kinds of documents from the Judean Desert. In the Masada *get*, contrariwise, the present participle is used.[122] The two forms may reflect an insignificant variation of different scribal traditions or the like. On the other hand, hypothetically, the perfect form may have been an intentional revision. The present participle is used in Mishnaic Hebrew for the future tense.[123] What may have originally functioned as a special formulation for the *get*, conveying its constitutive force – 'I hereby divorce you today' – could have been misunderstand as 'I shall divorce you today'. This would be construed as a statement of intention only, thus invalidating the divorce itself. The perfect form may have been substituted to avoid this difficulty. It seems that the transition to perfect form verbs was a gradual one, however, since two mishnayot and a baraita, while all dealing with somewhat hypothetical situations, cite the formula of the *get* with present participle verbs.[124] Perhaps the two forms were used interchangeably until the Amoraim opted for the perfect.[125]

The bill of divorce as well as many of the other documents from the Judean Desert are 'double deeds' or 'tied deeds', to use the talmudic terminology. This ancient, widespread practice, known elsewhere in the Near East, protected

---

[120] The 'today' formula appears – after the date – in the opening operative clause of other Judean Desert documents. In a formulary for a bill of divorce from Jerusalem 872/3 CE, TS NS 308.25, ed Margulies, *Hilkhot Erets Yisrael*, 121 ll. 9f, 'today I have divorced you' has been transferred to the middle of the deed. Dr. Yehezkel David has called my attention to a similar formula in TS J 3.31 and also to that of a Babylonian incantation text for exorcising a demon (Montgomery, *Incantation Texts*, no. 18) which begins: 'Today of all days, years and generations, I ... have divorced you.'

[121] Another analogy is worth noting. Tucker, 'Israelite Contracts', 44f suggests that in a number of biblical passages *ha-yōm* might have had technical implications in the legal process and compares the 'date' formula in Akkadian legal texts from Ras Shamra, where documents begin with the phrase *ištu ūmi annīm*, '(dating) from today', without any precise designation of the date. It stands to reason that Abba Shaul was more familiar with the formula in the Judean Desert documents.

[122] The difference is noted by Yaron, 'Gerushin', 337.

[123] See Friedman, *Jewish Marriage* 1, 259 n81, and literature cited there; Sharvit, 'Tenses', 112f; cf GenR 50,9 (p525); bNed 16a; bBK 69a.

[124] mGit 9:5, 'If five men wrote collectively in a bill of divorce, "So-and-so divorces So-and-so and So-and-so, So-and-so," etc.' On the possibility that this refers to a historical situation, such as when a number of men were detained in a distant place and wanted to divorce their wives collectively, see Friedman, 'Important *Ma'ase*', 201f; mGit 3:1, 'If one heard the scribes dictating: Mr. So-and-so divorces So-and-so from such and such a place', etc.; yGit 2:3, 44b: 'R. Zeira said, "Bina bar Shela taught: Even if he writes 'I So-and-so divorce my wife', it is valid"' (a version of Abba Shaul's tradition?). tBB 9:14 (p. 162) recognizes the effectiveness of the present participle in a declaration of emancipation.

[125] Cf the text 'enacted' by Rava (?) in bGit 85b. The Amoraim in bGit 87a paraphrase mGit 9:5 with the perfect, while in yGit 9:7, 50b and yShev 5:5 36b, the present participle is retained.

a document from being tampered with, yet left a text exposed for easy reference. The גט מקושר is mentioned several times in Tannaic literature. But later generations were unfamiliar with its origin. A late passage in the Bavli understood *get* in this phrase not as 'deed' in general but rather 'bill of divorce' and suggested that this procedure had been enacted by the sages in a locality where there were many priests, as an obstacle to capricious divorces.[126]

In contrast with the correspondence of the Masada deed with talmudic literature, decades before the publication of another papyrus (as XHev/Se 13), J. Milik cited from it a brief passage and characterized the document as a bill of divorce issued by a woman to her husband. This sensational find already aroused skepticism on the basis of the few words that had been quoted: הוי <הוא> לך גט שבקין ותרכ[ין]. The recently edited text bears little similarity with the known *get* formula. It presents problems in decipherment, restoration, translation and interpretation. It has elicited several studies, which variously have suggested that it is a bill of divorce issued by the wife, her receipt of marriage payment, her waver of claims that also states that she had divorced her husband, or that he had divorced her. I consider the last interpretation most likely, and evidence for the wife's right to issue a *get* is yet to be found.[127]

Having mentioned the dating formula in one of the documents, we draw attention here to the practice in several Greek and Aramaic papyri from the Judean Desert to designate the year (also) according to the Roman consulate, using the Greek term ὑπατεία. This practice was evidently so common among Palestinian Jews that the Greek word entered talmudic literature in the sense of any royal era, and the early post-talmudic legal work, Maʿasim livne Erets Yisrael, ruled that: 'A deed issued without an ὑπατεία ... is invalid.'[128]

---

[126] bBB 160b. See Rosenthal, 'Inscription', 370 n142. For a description of the execution of a tied deed, see Yadin, *Bar-Kokhba*, 329ff; cf Lieberman, *Tosefta Ki-Fshutah* 8, 899f; Lewis, *Documents*, 6-10; *DJD* 27, 11, 141; Goldstein, 'Syriac Deed', 1, 14f. Koffmahn, *Doppelurkunden* is devoted to the double deeds from the Judean Desert. P. Yadin in Yadin, Broshi, Qimron, 'Kefar Baru', has the upper text in Aramaic and the lower, exposed text, only (parts of) a few words of which are intact, in Hebrew.

[127] See Milik in *DJD* 2, 108; Friedman, *Jewish Marriage* 1, 319 n26; Yardeni and Greenfield, 'Receipt'; Yardeni, *Nahal Se'elim*, 54-60; *DJD* 27, 65-70; Ilan, 'Notes'; idem, 'Response'; Cotton and Qimron, 'Renunciation'; Fitzmyer, 'So-Called Divorce Text'; Schremer, 'Divorce'; idem, 'Question'. I follow Schremer in translating the line in question: '[You (m) said:] This is from me to you (f) a bill of divorce and release'. For the requirement that the husband make such a statement when delivering the *get*, see yGit 9:1, 50b and parallels and the sources and discussion in Friedman, '*Shenei ketaim*', 32-36; David, 'Divorce', 295f. For לך as fem., see Fitzmyer, 'So-Called Divorce Text', 18*. The papyrus lends itself to multiple interpretations. To the extent that more than one is consistent with the language, the burden of proof falls on whoever interprets the text as a radical break with other sources.

[128] On the legal ruling and other relevant sources, see Neuman, 'Ha-Maasim', 66f, 75f. The use of the term in talmudic sources is discussed in Friedman, 'Royal Era'; see *ib.*, 207f, references to the Judean Desert documents and related studies, to which reference should now be added to *DJD* 27, 146-149.

According to the Mishna, a lien is attached to all of a man's property for payment of his wife's ketubba debt (mKet 7:7). In order to protect himself from subsequent claims, when one purchased property from a married man, he insisted that the seller's wife renounce her rights to it (mKet 10:6). This practice is attested in bills of sale from the Judean Desert, where the wife also cosigned the deed, a procedure known from the Yerushalmi. The waiver uses the same formula found in the Mishna.[129]

P. Yadin 7, the gift deed that Babatha's father Shimon wrote for his wife Miriam in 120 CE, contains many interesting parallels with talmudic literature. As a provision to the property, which he gave his wife, he stipulated that should their daughter Babatha be widowed, she would be granted a residence. It was hers for the duration of her widowhood, and she was not permitted to bring a new husband to live there.[130] This parallels tKet 11:7 (p94): 'If one says: Give a widow's residence to my daughter, they do not give it to her, unless she undertakes to dwell in it; and the heirs can constrain her that she not rent it to another. Consequently, if she dies, they inherit her (it).' One of the Tosefta's commentators intuitively interpreted the law as denying the daughter's rights, were she to remarry, as explicitly stated in P. Yadin 7.[131] The wording in the papyrus כל יומין די תהוא ארמלה, lit., 'all the days that she is a widow', is an exact parallel of mKet 4:11, the ketubba clause in which the husband promises that his wife will be provided with a residence and other rights כל יומי מיגד ארמלותיך, lit., 'all the days of the duration of your widowhood'. Why would a man find it necessary to provide a 'widow's residence' for his daughter, since she was to be provided one from her husband's estate according to that ketubba clause? The most obvious place where such a gift was necessary was in Judea, where in contrast to Galilee, the widow's rights terminated the moment her husband's heirs paid her the ketubba money.[132] Needless to say, the Judean version of the stipulation appears in Babatha's marriage contract (P. Yadin 10).

Differences between these contracts and talmudic literature can be equally instructive. This can be illustrated by the practice for the 'signature' of illiterates. In the Judean Desert documents and in contemporary non-Jewish texts, the parties to the contract affixed their own signatures; talmudic sources refer to a similar practice. When they were unable to write, someone else signed for them, using such a formula: 'A son of B (testified) to himself (על נפשה), C son

---

[129] Milik, 'Deux Documents', 265; *DJD* 2, 145 (no. 30); *DJD* 27, 34-37, 123-128, with references to earlier literature. Cosigning: yGit 5:6, 47b. For an example of the significance of the Judean Desert documents for the economic situation of Jewish Palestine, see Lieberman, *Texts and Studies*, 208f.

[130] See Yadin, Greenfield, Yardeni and Levine, *Documents*, 82-86, upper text ll. 24f, lower ll. 65-69, discussion, p105.

[131] The commentary of Ḥasde David is summarized and rejected by Lieberman, *Tosefta Ki-Fshutah* 6, 368.

[132] For the stipulation providing for the widow, see Friedman, *Jewish Marriage* 1, 427-443.

of D wrote upon his instructions.'[133] The talmudic sages, contrariwise, taught that if a witness does not know how to write, he must trace the letters of his name with his own hand. It is likely that they were familiar with the former practice (which, as proven by Geniza documents, persisted through the eleventh century), and rejected its validity.[134]

These documents provide invaluable information also on non-legal matters. Several of the contracts relate directly to Bar-Kokhba's administration, and letters from his hand have been found as well. The importance of this material for the study of one of the most pivotal periods in the historical consciousness of the Jewish people cannot be overestimated. Furthermore, the Babatha papyri accord a rare insight into the affairs of a colourful, twice married, wealthy woman, whose second husband also had another wife.[135] No study of the talmudic family will be complete without a careful analysis of her archive.[136] Students of Hebrew and Aramaic during the talmudic period have been provided with primary sources of lexicographical, morphological and syntactical importance which, inter alia, illuminate the language of talmudic literature.[137]

PAPYRI FROM BYZANTINE EGYPT

Some one hundred and fifty Egyptian papyri written in Hebrew characters during the Byzantine and early Islamic period have been identified recently in libraries around the world by Colette Sirat and published in facsimile editions with brief descriptions. These texts include pieces of approximately twelve Aramaic Jewish documents from the Byzantine period. Most are so fragmentary and effaced that they can only with difficulty be identified as documents. In some cases this identity is uncertain, while with many the type of deed cannot be ascertained.[138]

One fortunate exception, while still incomplete, comprises most of the text of a large ketubba from Antinoopolis, dated 417 CE. Portions of the entire length of this handsomely written document, running 32 lines, are preserved. Its edition, prepared by a team of scholars, was published in 1986. This ketubba, the only preserved dated document in Hebrew characters from the

---

[133] For the sources and a discussion of this and other formulae, with reference to previous literature, see Yadin, Greenfield, Yardeni and Levine, *Documents*, 11-13. For the factitive use of the verb כתב discussed there cf Zucker, *Saadya*, 424; Friedman, 'He Writes'; *DJD* 27, 172f.

[134] bGit 9b and parallels. See the discussion in Friedman, *Jewish Marriage* 1, 485-487. For additional discussions on the relationship of the Judean Desert documents to talmudic literature, see *ib.* 2, 498, 504 (index) and the literature cited in the preceding notes.

[135] Scholars disagree whether he was married to the two simultaneously or consecutively. See Katzoff, 'Polygamy'.

[136] Many of these issues are referred to with analysis in Cotton, 'Women and Law'.

[137] See the survey in Yadin, *Bar-Kokhba*. For the language of these documents, cf Kutscher, *Hebrew and Aramaic Studies*, Hebrew section 36ff et passim; Greenfield, 'Languages', 150-152; Yadin *et al.*, *Documents*, 14-32.

[138] Sirat, *Papyrus*.

Byzantine period which has been identified, is contemporary with the completion of the Yerushalmi and bridges the chronological gap between the Judean Desert marriage contracts and those found in the Cairo Geniza. It illustrates an amalgam of Jewish tradition and non-Jewish influence in a Diaspora community.

The basic text is written in the 'Official-Galilean' Aramaic dialect used in Jewish documents from Palestine and is by and large consistent with the formulary of later Palestinian-style marriage contracts known from the Geniza. But two sections are in Greek written in Hebrew characters: the first portion of a double dating formula, according to the consul – the second portion follows the Jewish calendar – and the names of the items which comprise the bride's dowry. The latter usually are in Judeo-Arabic in Egyptian ketubbot written a few centuries later and found in the Cairo Geniza. The Jewish dating formula is a good example of contact with Palestinian tradition preserved in literary sources. Midrash Tanhuma cites the ketubba date as, 'In such and such Sabbatical cycle, in such and such year, in such and such month, so many days therein'. While some of the ketubbot from the Geniza count the year in the Sabbatical cycle, the Antinoopolis document is the only one known to preserve the formula in the same descending order. Thus it provides unique testimony to a fifth century Palestinian practice preserved in a late midrash compilation.[139] The bride undertakes to honour and serve her husband בדכו 'in purity', a formula typical of the Palestinian-style ketubbot found in the Geniza.[140] Contrariwise, instead of the regular debt undertaken in the Jewish marriage contract by the groom, to be collected only when the marriage were dissolved, in this papyrus he presents the bride with a gift called by the Greek הדנה (ἔδνα). And as found in some non-Jewish marriage contracts from Egypt, the groom promises that his property stands surety for his obligation to feed and clothe his wife.[141]

The other documents, despite their extreme fragmentariness and effacement, are still of interest. Five of them appear to be pieces of marriage contracts. A betrothal document between תאומסי (Thomas?) and מטרונה (Matrona) mentions a betrothal ring, עזקה דקדושה , apparently evaluated at three dinars.[142] Performing the betrothal with a ring, so familiar today, is not explicitly men-

---

[139] For sources and discussion, see Friedman, 'Royal Era'.

[140] See Friedman, *Jewish Marriage*, 187f; idem, 'Relationship', 148-152. In the Geniza *ketubbot* the parallel phrase is בדכיו ובנקיו. This phrase also appears in magical texts preserved in the Geniza, e.g., TS K 1.74, ed Schäfer and Shaked, *Magische Texte* 2, 119.

[141] Sirat *et al.*, *Ketouba*. On the 'Official Aramaic' of the document, see Friedman, *Jewish Marriage* 1, 48ff.

[142] Berlin, Staatliche Museen P 8497; Sirat, *Papyrus*, 111 and pl. 46 (the identification of the document as a betrothal deed was made by M.A. Friedman). The words appear one under the other, and the continuation is broken (there is an א after עזקה). But they seem to belong together and may be written this way as part of the list of items that are evaluated (compare, for example, how the dowry items are listed in Friedman, *Jewish Marriage* 2, 7f).

tioned in talmudic literature. Among Jews in the early post-talmudic period, it was recognized as a peculiarly Palestinian, rather than Babylonian, custom. The same phrase, עזקה דקדושה, appears, with minor variations, in the Geniza documents from the eleventh century. Its use in the Byzantine papyrus attests the custom several hundred years earlier.[143]

Even small scraps of papyrus merit attention. One, minute piece contains only a few letters from two lines in Aramaic. The second one clearly reads סימפונה, the *symphon* (σύμφων).[144] This Greek word appears a number of times in Tannaic and Palestinian Amoraic sources for a condition added to a document or written within a contract.[145] The Yerushalmi brings the text of a conditional betrothal agreement called סימפון: 'I, A son of B, betroth you, C daughter of D, on the condition that I give you such and such a sum and take you as my wife by such and such a day; and if such and such a day arrives and I have not married you, you will owe me nothing.' The *symphon* betrothal undoubtedly alleviated many problems, such as in the case of the Alexandrians brought before Hillel the Elder, cited above.[146] As for the condition added to a document, we read, for example, in tBM 1:13 (p64): 'A *symphon* ... which is not signed by witnesses, if produced by a trustee, is valid, (even if written) below the conclusion of the document (viz. the effected party's signature).' The Babylonian sages did not always understand the Greek *symphon* as 'condition' and sometimes took it to mean 'receipt'.[147] In bBM 21a the text of this baraita appears with a variant: '... produced by a trustee or produced below,' etc. As clarified by the comment which follows in the Talmud, this presumably means that a receipt added below the signatures on a bill of loan is valid if produced by the creditor, since he would not disqualify his IOU had it not been paid. The text of the baraita was probably emended because of the Babylonian interpretation of *symphon*.[148] No documentary evidence for *symphon* in Jewish contracts

---

[143] See the sources and discussion in Friedman, *Jewish Marriage* 1, 207-210; idem, 'Contribution', 280. Cf Kasher, *Torah Shelemah* vol 6, 1524. Kasher's attempt to attribute betrothal by ring to Babylonia rather than Palestine counters the bulk of literary evidence to which the Geniza documents and this papyrus from Egypt (written in Palestinian Aramaic) are to be added. The story in the Palestinian Midrash PesRK Wayehi 6 (p180f), in which the king's daughters who had celebrated their weddings in private in their father's absence proved publicly that they were married by producing their husbands' signet rings (חותם, see Friedman, *ib.* 1, 209 n53), might reflect the same practice.

[144] Vienna, Österr. Nationalbibl., Papyrus H 58 (see Sirat, *Papyrus*, 99 pl. 17).

[145] See Sperber, *Dictionary*, 119.

[146] yKid 3:2, 63d and parallels. See Gulak, 'Simfon' and cf Friedman, *Jewish Marriage* 1, 196.

[147] See Lieberman in *Yerushalmi Neziqin*, 132f.

[148] Similarly, yBM 1:8, 8a, 'R. Yirmeyahu said in the name of Rav: A *symphon* which is produced by the creditor in the creditor's handwriting is invalid', etc., appears revised in bBM 20b: '...even though written in his handwriting,' etc. The end of the Yerushalmi passage seems to follow the Babylonian interpretation, however. See Gulak, 'Symphon,' 127 n5 and Lieberman's criticism in *Yerushalmi Neziqin*, 132. For an alternate interpretation of the Tosefta passage, see Lieberman, *Tosefta Ki-Fshutah* 9, 149. For a similar confusion on the meaning of *symphon* in the Bavli in reference to betrothal, see bKet 57b and Halivni, *Sources and Traditions Nashim*, 200 ff.

has been identified other than this papyrus, and we are left to imagine the contents of its text.

CAIRO GENIZA DOCUMENTS

The next major find of Jewish manuscripts including legal documents is the Cairo Geniza, whose contents were discovered and removed to libraries around the world in the late nineteenth century.[149] A few documents from the ninth century have been preserved in the Geniza, many from the tenth; and as of the eleventh century an abundance of documents were preserved there. The Geniza remained in use through the nineteenth century; but those documents dating from the so-called classical period of Geniza study, that is, through the thirteenth century, are especially relevant for our purposes. Most contracts were written in Egypt and the Land of Israel; many originated in other countries, from India to Spain. These date four, five or more centuries after the conclusion of the talmudic period. But due to the conservatism of the scribes, the enormous quantity of fragments, and the social realities which they reflect, they are of considerable importance for talmudic studies.

Many formulae and terms that date from the talmudic period were still used by the scribes in the Middle Ages. The Geniza documents illustrate this repeatedly. Certain formulae alluded to in the talmudic literature or quoted in part there are preserved in entirety in the Geniza texts. Thus yKet 7:7, 31c quotes from a fourth century CE marriage contract a divorce clause, whose antecedent from Elephantine has already been noted above: 'If this So-and-so (fem.) hates this So-and-so, her husband, and does not desire his partnership, she will take one half of her ketubba money.' This source cites only that portion of the clause essential for the legal issue being considered. The text of the complete clause, with variants, has recently been identified among the tenth and eleventh century Palestinian ketubbot preserved in the Geniza.[150]

The Palestinian-style marriage contracts, some seventy of which have been identified and studied, illuminate a tradition for writing the ketubba separate from the Babylonian one preserved in the writings of the Geonim and the practice of later Jewish communities.[151] This type of ketubba contains elements that appear to convey to the document the form of a mutual contract between bride and groom. It manifests points of contact not only with the Palestinian talmudic literature but with its ancient, independent scribal traditions. The marriage contracts from the Judean Desert from the early second century, for example, preface the stipulations concerning obligations to take effect after the death of husband or wife with a protasis such as 'If So-and-so, the groom, goes

---

[149] For a description of the Geniza, its discovery and contents, see Goitein, *Mediterranean Society* 1, 1 ff.

[150] See Friedman, *Jewish Marriage* 1, 312-346, and above at n73.

[151] *Ib.* 1, 3 ff.

to his eternal home before So-and-so, his wife,' etc. No mention of such clauses is found in talmudic literature, but they appear in the marriage contracts written according to Palestinian custom during the tenth and eleventh centuries preserved in the Cairo Geniza.[152] Some unique formulae in these ketubbot might reflect traditions known from the Greco-Roman world but not preserved elsewhere in Jewish documents or literature. According to one of the standard versions of these marriage contracts, for example, the bride is taken 'as wife and the mother of children'.[153] In Greek marriage formulae the bride was given or taken 'to produce lawful children', and the phrase 'for the purpose of begetting children' was common in Roman marriage contracts.[154]

If the Geniza texts allow the reconstruction of ancient formulae in the case of documents such as the marriage contract, specimens of which have been preserved from the talmudic period and numerous quotations of which are found in the literature, then one can assume that much stands to be gained from the research of types of deeds not preserved from the talmudic period and rarely quoted in its literature. The case of the ketubba is somewhat special in this respect, because of its central function and its unique retention of the ancient Palestinian formulations which essentially disappeared after the eleventh century. A thorough study by J. Rivlin on the wills preserved in the Geniza has uncovered much material relevant to the study of the Talmud.[155] Y. David has researched in detail the bills of divorce from the Geniza and their relationship to talmudic literature.[156] A. Ashur has written an illuminating study on engagement deeds.[157] Interesting adaptations of rabbinic contract traditions are found in the Karaite marriage contracts studied by J. Olszowy-Schlanger.[158] Studies on other categories of Geniza documents will undoubtedly produce valuable results as well.

It is important to compare these documents with formularies that also have been preserved in the Geniza. M. Margulies edited ancient formularies from the Land of Israel;[159] S. Assaf, who edited many deeds from the Geniza, pub-

---

[152] *Ib.* 1, 360 ff.

[153] *Ib.* 1, 159f.

[154] See Katzoff, 'Marriage Formulas', 230-232 (the last line in the note on p232 on the absence of such a phrase in the formulary surrounding Jewish marriage is to be emended accordingly).

[155] Rivlin, *Inheritance.*

[156] David, 'Formulae'; idem, 'Divorce'. A few of the Palestinian bills of divorce preserved in the Geniza contain a formula, whereby the issuer assures his divorcée that after she marries someone else, he will not try to void the divorce. This is foreshadowed in Egyptian divorce deeds from 230-100 BCE and parallels talmudic tradition. See Friedman, 'Remarriage', 198. Note that according to Josephus, Ant. 15.7.10 (15:259), 'not even a divorced woman may marry again on her own initiative unless her former husband consents.'

[157] Ashur, 'Engagement'.

[158] Olszowy-Schlanger, *Karaite Marriage Documents.* On the relationship of these documents to rabbinic tradition, see also Friedman, 'Relationship'.

[159] Margaliot, *Hilkhot Erets Yisrael*, 17ff and 118ff.

lished R. Hai Gaon's formulary;[160] and M. Ben-Sasson has recently edited many fragments of R. Saadiah's formulary.[161] Anonymous formularies are also of much interest, as demonstrated by Rivlin's recent publication of texts written in Lucena, Spain, in the early eleventh century.[162]

Most of the Geniza documents are fragmentary, but the fantastic number of contracts – a realistic estimate would place them in the thousands – is itself of great significance. This broad database enables the student to reconstruct complete formulae and note many local variations. There is no comparison for such a wealth of sources. The major limitation to studying the other document finds described above is the dependence on few, fragmentary items. Unlike those earlier contracts, the deeds from the Geniza, furthermore, reflect a stage of legal development consistent with the fully crystallized talmudic halakha.

Sometimes, singular items in the Geniza documents and even one word can be of interest. A deed of release written in 995 CE, apparently in Damascus, concludes, in Hebrew, by stating that it was issued to serve 'as a deed of rights and of proof and as *asphaleia*'. The last word is Greek, in a contract written some three and a half centuries after Greek ceased to be used in this geographical area. Apparently the term means the same as in one of the Greek documents from Babatha's archive: a '(document of) security'. The word appears, three times, in one of the Bar-Kokhba letters and once in talmudic literature, in DeutR 7,1. No other occurrences have been found in Hebrew sources. The Geniza text from Damascus serves as a further example of the great tenacity with which scribes preserved legal terminology.[163]

The legal documents preserved in the Geniza demonstrate more clearly than those from any other source the degree of variation allowed in these formularies. We are often able to identify the circumstances under which a new stipulation was introduced and trace its gradual acceptance until it became standard practice, processes which can be assumed to mirror parallel events in talmudic times. Despite the adherence to formularies, many of the contracts reflect the particular conditions of the place and time as well as the circumstances of the individual parties. These documents, together with other Geniza texts, such as court records and letters, serve as a faithful source for studying social realities. S.D. Goitein in his monumental five-volume study, *A Mediterranean Society*, completed a fascinating reconstruction of the society of the Geniza Jews based on a survey of thousands of documents. The Jews represented by the Geniza documents belonged to communities that had existed

---

[160] Assaf, 'Formulary of Hai Gaon', to which additional manuscripts can now be added (cf Groner, 'Works', 31-33; the item on p31 [from TS Misc. 28.8] should be read אכרזתא rather than אבדזתא).

[161] Ben-Sasson, 'Fragments' (M. Ben-Sasson and R. Brody are preparing for publication a new edition of the formulary that includes additional fragments).

[162] Rivlin, *Bills*.

[163] See Friedman, 'Linguistic Chronology', 67f. The Greek document: Polotsky, 'Three Documents', 49, comment 7; see now Lewis, *Documents*, 59-61, and for the Bar Kokhba letter Yadin *et al.*, *Documents*, 308, 310.

continuously since antiquity, and they escaped many of the upheavals, which were the lot of their coreligionists elsewhere in the Diaspora. They can be assumed to have faithfully preserved patterns of life, many of which bear comparison to those of their talmudic antecedents. Each phenomenon must be examined separately to appraise the varying degrees of continuity and adaptation to the Islamic ambience.[164] Even the most stereotyped contracts, viz. bills of divorce, depict social realities, such as the frequency of divorce and remarriage, especially when these deeds are studied together with other documents, many of which deal with the same parties. Rich documentation has for the first time enabled a study of a traditional polygamous Jewish society.[165] Systematic research of other social and religious phenomena also can be expected to produce results to be reckoned with when studying the society of the Jews who lived in the Land of Israel and Babylonia during the talmudic period.[166]

[164] See, e.g., Friedman, 'Marriage as an Institution', 37ff.

[165] Friedman, *Polygyny*.

[166] Interesting contracts and other relevant material are to be found in Gil, *Foundations*; idem, *Palestine*; idem, *Ishmael*. – This chapter was submitted in 1989. References to some but not all relevant studies published since then have been added. The late Prof. J.C. Greenfield read the original manuscript and made many valuable suggestions. Research for the final version was assisted by the Joseph and Ceil Mazer Chair in Jewish Culture in Muslim Lands and Cairo Geniza Studies, Tel-Aviv University.

Chapter Thirteen

Jewish Inscriptions and Their Use

Jonathan J. Price and Haggai Misgav

Sources and Limitations

Jewish inscriptions, defined as texts written or commissioned by Jews, comprise a tiny subset of the many hundreds of thousands of inscriptions surviving from Graeco-Roman antiquity in Greek, Latin and other languages. Despite 150 years of scholarship on Jewish epigraphy, no firm criteria have been developed – or are likely to be developed – to distinguish Jewish inscriptions from others. Conventionally an inscription is marked as 'Jewish', or at least suspected to be so, if it contains one or more of the following signifiers: Hebrew or Aramaic (discounting magical tablets); typically Jewish symbols (menora, lulav, etc.); mention of typically Jewish institutions (e.g., *proseuche*); use of typically Jewish terminology (*Ioudaios*, *theos hypsistos*), formulae (*shalom al Yisrael*) or titles (*rabbi*, *archisynagogos*, etc.); typically Jewish names; location in an identifiably Jewish site, such as a Jewish cemetery or a synagogue.[1] A single criterion is usually not in itself sufficient evidence for the Jewishness of the author or commemorand of a text, so that there are inevitably some texts in the standard corpora which are not in fact Jewish (it is often especially difficult to distinguish between Jewish and early Christian epitaphs). Conversely, many inscriptions which were written by and/or commemorate Jews are not identifiable as Jewish because they lack identifying characteristics, which should not however be interpreted as the author's lack of interest in Judaism or detachment from personal Jewish identity; quite the opposite may

---

[1] The most detailed discussion is Ameling in IJO I, 8-21; compare the prefaces to the other volumes in that series, IJO I, v, and IJO III, v; V. Tcherikover in CPJ I, xvii; Noy and Horbury in JIGRE, x-xi. There have been some surveys of Jewish inscriptions and their use for the historian, e.g., Kant, 'Jewish Inscriptions', and Williams, 'The Contribution of Jewish Inscriptions'. It is not the purpose here to give another such summary, but to highlight methodological and interpretive problems, with the focus on material from the Land of Israel.

have been the case. Thus the absolute true number of surviving 'Jewish inscriptions' can never be known. It follows that, without those inscriptions put up by fully self-identifying Jews but containing no mark of Jewishness, the use of Jewish epigraphy to study such questions as cultural and social assimilation is *a priori* defective and misleading.

Another factor skewing the sample is the high destruction rate of Jewish inscriptions. This is of course true for almost all types of inscriptions from antiquity, but it is even more restricting in the case of Jewish texts, given the Jews' dispersion over the huge, far-flung tracts of the Rome empire and beyond the Euphrates and their relatively small numbers in most regions: the loss of a synagogue or a Jewish cemetery, which could have been the only way of identifying the existence of a Jewish community, is proportionally a greater loss than that of a pagan temple or a set of Roman epitaphs. The places where the Jewish population was most concentrated generally suffered the worst episodes of destruction, especially the Land of Israel, where repeated conquests had particularly harsh effects, and Egypt. This, combined with heavy looting of known sites, has resulted in incalculable epigraphic losses. Even a relatively large and apparently coherent body of material, such as the approximately 300 ossuaries from burial caves around Jerusalem dating to the period between the reign of King Herod and the Bar-Kochba Revolt, may not be statistically meaningful, for during the same 150-year period, hundreds of thousands of people lived and died in the city, and moreover ossuaries represent a smaller, economically more privileged class. Some sites which have yielded no inscriptions probably did have them – archaeologists arrived too late.[2] Moreover, most funerary inscriptions in the Land of Israel come from burial caves, where they were preserved: open burial grounds also existed, but their number and location have been all but effaced by subsequent activity such as building, destruction, agriculture.

With these provisos in mind, we may survey the surviving material. Based on standard criteria, approximately 4000 Jewish inscriptions, dating from the end of the fourth century BCE to the sixth or seventh century CE (from Alexander to Muhammad), have been identified. The types and stylistic range of Jewish epigraphy are more limited than the epigraphy of the era: the vast majority of Jewish inscriptions come from burial grounds – witness the large corpora from the necropoleis in Rome, Beth Shearim and Jaffa – and the second-biggest group is synagogual texts, although Jews did inscribe other kinds of texts and wrote on other media, such as ostraca and amulets. Monumental inscriptions, such as those few found in the excavations around the Temple Mount, are exceedingly rare. Roman epigraphy, too, is heavily weighted to-

---

[2] For a recent example, see the report on the Roman-period burial caves around the Sumaqa on the Carmel, Dar, *Sumaqa*, 108-17; some of these caves had carved reliefs on the outside; but their interiors were so badly looted and damaged that it was sometimes difficult even to reconstruct their internal design.

wards funerary inscriptions, but there is more variety in types and settings than one finds in Jewish epigraphy.

The publication of the Jewish texts in separate corpora was at first haphazard and generally poor, but has recently seen vast improvement. The 'Jewish Inscriptions Project' at Cambridge University produced three fine volumes containing the inscriptions from Rome, the rest of Western Europe and Egypt, together with an index of the Jewish inscriptions from Cyrene.[3] Y. Le Bohec published the other texts from North Africa (although this now stands in need of updating).[4] Three additional volumes of excellent quality have just emerged under the series title *Inscriptiones Judaicae Orientis*, covering all texts from Asia Minor, Syria and Cyprus and Eastern Europe. Once the *Corpus Inscriptionum Iudaeae/ Palaestinae* is finished,[5] covering the richest area of Jewish inscriptions, only the distant peripheries of the Graeco-Roman world, e.g. Arabia and parts of present-day Jordan, will not have seen the re-edition and re-publication of Jewish inscriptions.[6] Thus all the old, woefully inadequate scholarly *instrumenta* – above all, Frey's highly defective *Corpus Inscriptionum Iudaicarum* – will soon be almost completely replaced. Only the next generation, however, is likely to see all Jewish inscriptions available on more flexible electronic media, which will allow instant updating and correction, the two plagues of even the newest epigraphic corpora in standard book form.

Comparing the different volumes of Jewish inscriptions reveals regional differences in the style and content, reflecting to a large degree the different epigraphic cultures of the different languages and immediate environment in which the inscriptions were found. Jews adopted and adapted the languages and cultural institutions of the places where they lived. It would be difficult to identify any single unifying element in all known 'Jewish inscriptions', even though, despite the recently popular concept of 'varieties of Judaism' in antiquity, Jews in disparate places had an obvious religious and emotional bond with each other. These points will be elaborated below.

Since the present volume is devoted to the literature of the sages, the remainder of this survey will give special attention to the connections between inscriptions and rabbinic Judaism, with the focus on the Land of Israel, where the sages lived.

Historical Information on Jewish Inscriptions

Inscriptions can be used by the cautious historian in a variety of ways. First, and easiest, inscriptions can confirm, often dramatically, information known

---

[3] Egypt: JIGRE, containing the index to the Cyrenaica corpus by Lüderitz, *Corpus.* W. Europe and Rome: JIWE I-II.

[4] Le Bohec, 'Inscriptions juives'.

[5] See the announcement in *ZPE* 127 (1999) 307ff.

[6] Some material can be found in the recent volumes in the series, *Inscriptions grecques et latines de la Syrie*, in periodic bulletins in the journal *Syria*, as well in the publication of individual sites.

from literary sources. This is the case when tombs of known historical figures are found. For example, the inscription identifying an ossuary as belonging to Yehohana, granddaughter of the high priest Theophilus,[7] mentioning a high priest known from Josephus (Ant. 18:123; 19:297); but the text adds no new information aside from the names of the high priest's otherwise unknown son and granddaughter. Similarly if a bi-lingual ossuary inscription found near the Akeldama convent in Jerusalem, reading:

'Αρίστων	Ariston
אריסטון אפמי[	Ariston of Apamaea
יהודה הגיור	Yehuda the proselyte

did indeed contain the bones of Ariston of Apamaea mentioned in the Mishna (mHal 4:11), then we learn that this person, who brought first fruits from Apamaea, was buried in Jerusalem, but aside from family relations conjectured from other ossuary inscriptions from the same site, no more secure information is forthcoming (presumably 'Yehuda the proselyte' is not Ariston but someone else whose bones were buried with Ariston's).[8] In both of these cases, the people mentioned, and their historical importance, are identified by literary evidence.

A more difficult case is another ossuary inscription from the Mount of Olives, which has been known from more than 100 years and is today housed in the British Museum:[9]

ὀστᾶ τῶν τοῦ Νεικά-	The bones (of the sons?) of Nica-
νορος 'Αλεξανδρέως	nor of Alexandria,
ποιήσαντος τὰς θύρας	who made the gates.
נקנר אלקסא	Nicanor the Alexandrian.

This Nicanor is most likely to be identified with the Nicanor of Alexandria who according to a rabbinic tradition was aided by a miracle in bringing his eponymous bronze 'Gate of Nicanor' to Jerusalem (mMid 1:4; 2:3, 6; tYom 2:3-4; bYom 38a). But the text of the inscription is difficult and ambiguous. The first two words, if parsed correctly, read 'the bones of those [i.e., children] of Nicanor', in other words, not of Nicanor himself, although the Hebrew text seems to indicate that the ossuary belongs to Nicanor himself. To bring the Greek in line with the Hebrew it has been suggested to omit the word τῶν, to read the first two words as one, i.e., ὀστάτ[ο]ν, 'ossuary', or to read the last line as the name of the father Nicanor's two sons, 'Nicanor and Alexas'. Fi-

---

[7] Barag-Flusser, 'Ossuary of Yehohanah'; Rahmani, *Catalogue*, no. 871. Similarly the family tomb of the high priest Caiaphas *may* have been found, but the identification is disputed, see Reich, 'Ossuary Inscriptions', and Puech, 'A-t-on redecouvert'.

[8] Ilan, 'The Ossuary and Sarcophagus Inscriptions', 66; Ilan has suggested that Ariston was a convert and that Yehudah was his new Hebrew name.

[9] CII1256; *SEG* VIII, 200; JIGRE 153. See discussion and full bibliography in Boffo, *Iscrizioni*, 343-8.

nally, the last line, which is usually taken to mean 'Nicanor of Alexandria', can also be interpreted 'Nicanor (son of) Alexas'. The interpretation of the obscure language in each part of the inscription determines the quantity and kind of extra information which is added to the literary sources, but the connection of this Nicanor with the Temple doors would probably not be acceptable without the base in literary evidence.

As a last example of connecting an inscription to a literary text, we may cite the famous Temple warning inscription:[10]

μηθένα ἀλλογενῆ εἰσπο-	No foreigner is to en-
ρεύεσθαι ἐντὸς τοῦ πε-	ter within the forecourt and
ρὶ τὸ ἱερὸν τρυφάκτου καὶ	the balustrade around the
περιβόλου. ὃς δ' ἂν λη-	sanctuary. Whoever is caught
φθῇ ἑαυτῷ αἴτιος ἐσ-	will have himself to blame
ται διὰ τὸ ἐξακόλου-	for his death which
θειν θάνατου	will follow.

Here the literary source which mentions the existence of the inscription – Josephus – is rather terse and is not only fleshed out but even corrected by the actual text. In Ant. 15:417 Josephus merely mentions the existence of one inscription prohibiting entry by a foreigner (ἀλλοεθνής) into the inner court, and death penalty for infraction; in the earlier and fuller account in War 5:194 (cf 6:124), he states that there were several inscriptions in Greek and Latin – which explains why in addition to the full text now in Istanbul there were found in addition slabs of another identical Greek text – forbidding the foreigner (ἀλλόφυλος) to advance beyond the outer court into the 'holy area' (τὸ ἅγιον) on pain of death, because of the Jewish law of purification. The actual stone from the Temple Mount not only helps us control Josephus' language – both the terms for 'foreigner' and 'holy place' are different[11] – but also reveals a surprising colloquialism[12] used for the threatened death penalty. Here the literary and epigraphic texts complement each other in more equal measure, but the main historical debate raised by the inscription, namely the Jews' jurisdictional authority in capital cases involving local, parochial and ritual issues in first-century Judaea, is not improved or sharpened by the inscription; on the contrary, the wording of the inscription has opened up more interpretive possibilities than Josephus' text allowed.

Conversely, the inscription sheds some light on Josephus' working methods. No doubt he saw the inscription many times in the course of his service as a priest in the Temple, yet he does not quote the text exactly: he was working

[10] CII 1400, OGIS II 598, *SEG* VIII 169, *SEG* XX 477; Bickerman, 'The Warning Inscriptions'; Segal, 'The Penalty'; further bibliography in Boffo, *Iscrizioni*, 283-4, and in Bieberstein-Bloedhorn, *Jerusalem*,1723.1319-1320.

[11] See Bickerman's discussion, 'The Warning Inscriptions'.

[12] Segal, 'The Penalty', suggests that the phrase ἑαυτῷ αἴτιος ἔσται is equivalent to מתחייב בנפשו.

from memory, and conveyed only the most important features of the content, using his preferred expressions for 'foreigner'. Further, in his Jewish War he added an interpretation, connecting the prohibition to the laws of ritual purity, although no mention of this is made on the stone. Thus even in this case, in which the epigraphical text is in some ways fuller than the literary parallel, the literary text is required to confirm and refine the historical setting of the inscription.

So much for the problems associated with the intersection of epigraphical and literary texts. For most Jewish inscriptions – and as noted above, the great majority are epitaphs and the second-largest group is synagogue inscriptions – literature can provide not the immediate setting or identification of persons mentioned, but only the general context. Yet inscriptions are indispensable when they supply information which is otherwise unknown. Jewish epitaphs have vastly enriched the Jewish onomasticon of the period.[13] Epitaphs also provide valuable evidence about the Jews' social and community life; many titles and professions (especially the more modest ones) held by Jews are known solely or primarily from inscriptions; although for reasons which will become clear below, the inscriptions from the Land of Israel are much poorer in biographical detail than elsewhere.[14]

More substantial cases can be cited. The existence of a certain synagogue in Jerusalem in the first century CE, founded probably by a Diaspora Jew named Theodotos and provided with guest facilities, would not have been known if not for a unique inscription.[15] There are of course references in the New Testament and rabbinic literature to synagogues in the city before the destruction of the Temple in 70 CE,[16] but no indisputable evidence existed of any until the discovery of this important stone, which not only testifies to the existence of the synagogue but also gives some indication as to the administration of the structure and the activities which took place inside. Another example of new and valuable information provided by inscriptions alone is the (probable) existence of a Jewish community from Egypt, established in Jaffa and burying their dead there from the second or third centuries CE through the fifth.[17] This fact fits well into a known historical context: the persecution of the Jews in Egypt from the second century CE on and the near-destruction of the community there.

Much information about daily life can be found on ostraca, which are especially plentiful from the area of Syria-Palestine and yield different kinds of information from that to be found in inscriptions on stone and mosaic. People

---

[13] Note the first volume in a valuable project: Ilan, *Lexicon of Jewish Names*.

[14] For an exemplary study relying on epigraphic evidence see Rutgers, *The Jews*, and for the use of historical information on epitaphs see also Van der Horst, *Ancient Jewish Epitaphs*, esp. 85ff.

[15] CII 1404; see bibliography of extensive discussion of this stone in Boffo, *Iscrizioni*, 274ff. and Bieberstein-Bloedhorn, *Jerusalem*, 1724.1309.

[16] See now the discussion in Levine, *Jerusalem*, 394-8.

[17] Price, 'Five Inscriptions'.

wrote everything on shards: private lists, letters, legal documents, magical texts. Especially interesting are the legal documents, usually written on papyrus or inscribed on shards.[18] Not only the existence of such legal documents but also their validity is confirmed in rabbinic sources. For example, the Mishna allows a writ of divorce to be written 'on anything' (mGit 2:3:על הכול כותבין); the Tosefta specifically mentions the validity of a marriage contract written on a shard of pottery (tKid 1:1-2:כתב על חרס ונתן לה... הרי זו מקודשת); and the Babylonian Talmud adds the same stipulation regarding the sale of a field (bKid 26a).[19] The most common use of ostraca, however, was for everyday needs: short letters and notes, as in the collection from Idumaea datng to the late Persian or early Hellenistic period;[20] and notes and private lists from the Hellenistic period, dated, when dates were absent in the texts themselves, only by palaeographical criteria since they were acquired on the antiquities market and thus lacked any archaeological context.[21]

Inscribed shards from other periods are found in many places in the Land of Israel. A selective inventory will represent the nature and variety of these texts:

- a marriage deed from Maresha, from the 2nd century BCE, dated by both its archaeological context and a date in the text;[22]
- an ostracon from Murabaat containing two legal texts, dated palaeographically to the beginning of the first century BCE. Closely related to this ostracon is a document from Qumran, a formula of gift, whose interpretation is controversial;[23]
- a large group of ostraca from Masada, dated archaeologically to the first century BCE and containing lists of names and letters, and other types of documents;[24]
- a small group of ostraca, as yet unpublished, from the recent excavations at Qumran, containing names, contents of jars and lists.[25]

Most of these texts on ostraca – especially lists, notes, writing exercises – are of a private nature and were written for the immediate needs of the present or near future: they were not composed for anyone else, much less posterity, and therefore provide a relatively intimate glimpse into the daily lives of people who lived in that era. From this point of view, the letters on shard, wood or papyrus are somewhat different since they were written for at least one other

---

[18] DJD II; Sirat, *Les Papyrus*; DJD XVII; Yadin, *Documents*, 35-276.

[19] See also DJD II, no. 72; Misgav, 'Jewish Courts', n. 16.

[20] Eph'al-Naveh, *Aramaic Ostraca*; Lemaire, *Nouvelles inscriptions*.

[21] Yardeni, 'New Jewish Aramaic Ostraca'.

[22] Eshel-Kloner, 'An Aramaic Ostracon'.

[23] Cross-Eshel, 'An Ostracon from Khirbet Qumran'; Yardeni, 'A Draft of a Deed'.

[24] Yadin-Naveh, *Masada* I.

[25] Forthcoming in *Judea and Samaria Publications*, under the auspices of the Israel Antiquities Authority.

pair of eyes (although usually not, again, for future generations). Thus in documents of that sort one can learn about modes of communication on an everyday basis. Even the letters on papyrus from Bar-Kokhba to his subordinates, found in the Judaean Desert, lack the formal tone which might be expected in any administrative communications between a 'president' and his functionaries. These private documents from the Judaean Desert, studied together with the similar material from Byzantine Egypt which was perhaps written by Jews from the Land of Israel,[26] containing different formulae and ways of writing, are crucial pieces in the picture of the continuity of Hebrew culture through the generations.

Epigraphic Cultures: Content and Language

Despite the recurring refrain in professional and popular literature, no inscription can be expected to 'speak for itself'. Interpretation of a text begins even with the most basic literary element, its language.

In the Land of Israel and the entire Near East, Jewish inscriptions are in Greek, Aramaic and Hebrew; Jews writing in Latin are found only in the Roman West and North Africa.[27] But there are regional variations: although Greek is almost everywhere preponderant, it is the minority language in the Jerusalem ossuaries (dating mostly to the first century CE or earlier), and synagogue inscriptions from the interior of the Land of Israel are more likely to contain Aramaic and Hebrew and have less Greek than those from the coast and more cosmopolitan areas. These patterns correspond generally to what has been reconstructed as the distribution of spoken languages in the Land of Israel (and in fact the whole Roman Empire).[28] Here again, methodological rigor must be exercised when using epigraphical remains to draw language maps, for the meaning of the distribution of languages in inscriptions in intensely multi-cultural areas like the Land of Israel in the Roman period is not self-evident.

The language of an epitaph, for example, does not perforce reflect the native or preferred language of the deceased. The text was first of all not necessarily composed – much less written – by the deceased or even a family member; it is not usually known (barring the rare explicit indication in the text) what part the inscriber, if not a family member, had in the wording. Even if the deceased dictated his or her own epitaph, the choice of language could reflect not the native tongue but the intended audience of the inscriber. It can even be an ostentatious demonstration, such as Greek verse epitaphs at Beth Shearim,

---

[26] Mishor, 'A Hebrew Letter'.

[27] There are exceptions. Note for example the two rare ossuary inscriptions in Latin, one found in Jerusalem and the other probably from there, Rahmani, *Catalogue*, nos. 202 and 497; and the curious one from there inscribed in Palmyrene, *ib.* no 579. None is thought to have belonged to a local Jew.

[28] Barr, 'Hebrew, Aramaic and Greek'; Rabin, 'Hebrew and Aramaic'; Mussies, 'Greek'; extensive earlier bibliography in Schürer II, 20-8; see most recently Millard, *Reading and Writing*.

or a feeling of obligation – a Hebrew phrase which may or may not have been understood by the inscriber and/or deceased. A similar although more limited caution applies to the donors and artisans who identify themselves in synagogue inscriptions, not to mention the extent to which they reflect the languages spoken in their communities. To cite an obvious example, the presence of a phrase like שלום or שלום על ישראל on Greek epitaphs does not necessarily reveal any knowledge of Hebrew: even in the Land of Israel, this phrase is often inexpertly carved.[29]

A particularly instructive example is the epitaph of 'Nicanor who made the gates', quoted above. Assuming that the historical identification is correct, this is the epitaph of an important Egyptian Jew who brought bronze doors to the Temple in Jerusalem, and then died and was buried there. As we see from Horbury and Noy's corpus,[30] all Jewish inscriptions from Egypt are purely Greek in Nicanor's time, aside from the occasional שלום, and following Alexandrian practice, Nicanor would not have had his name written in Jewish script if he had been buried in Egypt; thus the last line is a reflection of the place where he was buried, Jerusalem. The introduction of Hebrew, even if in this case the meaning is obscure to us, was demanded by the epigraphic convention of the place. This impression is further strengthened by the fascinating phenomenon of Hebrew words appearing in Greek transliteration in Jewish texts from the Land of Israel – such as σαλώμ (for שלום, peace) or ουρουν (for עורון, blindness, in a curse).[31] Such texts were composed or inscribed by people who did not read Hebrew fluently but knew important Hebrew words and, for authenticity's sake, in the spirit of the place, felt compelled to use the Hebrew word, albeit in Greek transliteration rather than translation.

Another factor limiting the conclusions to be drawn from the languages of Jewish inscriptions is chronological. Languages spoken in any given area, especially one which underwent so many momentous changes as the Roman Near East, are sensitive to historical vicissitudes, and one must pay close attention to the time and circumstance of epigraphic documents. Surviving Jewish inscriptions from the Roman period, excepting several hundred epitaphs from first-century CE Jerusalem, mostly date to the third century and later. The reasons for this are probably circumstantial, but in the final analysis, unclear. The chronological distribution could represent a genuine historical phenomenon, that is, it should not be ruled out that Jews started producing greater and greater numbers of inscriptions – epitaphs and synagogue texts – from the third century onward. If this were the case, then the Jewish 'epigraphic habit' began

---

[29] Cf e.g. the varied expertise in Hebrew carving on the epitaphs from Jaffa, CII 903, 920, 922, 930, 933, 934, 93, 943, 948, 951, 956 (some illustrations in Clermont-Ganneau's original publications, cited by Frey; new photos in a forthcoming monograph on the Ustinov collection in Oslo by J.J. Price and H.M. Cotton).

[30] JIGRE.

[31] See Schwabe-Lifshitz, *Beth Shearim* II, nos. 21, 25, 28, 72, 91; Rahmani, *Catalogue*, no. 559, and in general, 13 n16.

to grow when the Roman epigraphic habit, according to MacMullen who coined phrase, declined.[32] In this regard it should be noted that only a minority of the hundreds of ossuaries from the first century bear inscriptions (although accompanying inscribed plaques are easily lost or destroyed), and there is not a single tombstone from the cemetery at Qumran, which contained more than 1000 graves, and the same goes for the burial ground at Wadi Ghweir. By contrast, the open cemeteries at nearby Zoar, which is from a much later period, and Leontopolis in Egypt, have provided rich deposits of inscriptions – although at Leontopolis, inscriptions identified solely by find-site cannot be identified invariably as Jewish. But it is just as likely that the evidentiary phenomenon does not point to a real one. As noted above, Jewish inscriptions, especially in the Land of Israel, suffered a high rate of destruction. Most are preserved in burial caves, but there were also open burial grounds, which were more likely to be destroyed, even disappear. The number of lost burial sites, with their epigraphic treasures, is incalculable.

Furthermore, inscribed synagogue floors preserve only the latest level, and most synagogue inscriptions come from the third or fourth century CE or later. While there is no reason to suspect the loss of abundant first-second century synagogue inscriptions, especially given the rather bare examples at Gamala and Masada, the first-century Theodotus synagogue inscription from Jerusalem could not have been unique,[33] and the traces of previous mosaic floors in the Hammath Tiberias synagogue[34] and others cause one to wonder about buried or destroyed inscriptions. What was the practice in preserving or destroying inscriptions containing the names of previous donors, or even a reference to God, in an earlier level when a synagogue floor was entirely redesigned and re-laid? These are questions without unequivocal answers.

Since MacMullen's article on the 'epigraphic habit' was published in 1982,[35] the term has taken on an additional meaning, that is, it has come to include the use of formulae, language, and other matters of epigraphic style and content, rather than mere frequency. And indeed, the Jewish inscriptions from the Land of Israel form one of the best bodies of evidence to observe the fact that languages in inscriptions contribute significantly to form and content. This has partly to do with the intended audience of each language, but also with more deeply ingrained practices associated with language. These differ-

---

[32] MacMullen, 'Epigraphic Habit', who showed that the numbers of Roman inscriptions increased through the first and second centuries CE until tailing off, often steeply, in the third; his student Meyer, 'Explaining the Epigraphic Habit', links the phenomenon to the prestige associated with Roman citizenship, which was severely diminished by Caracalla's universal citizenship decree of 212.

[33] Challenges to the conventional first-century dating have been unsuccessful, see bibliography listed above, n15.

[34] See Dothan, *Hammath Tiberias*.

[35] Above, n32.

ences are most visible in the languages of Jewish epigraphy in the Land of Israel.

First and most obvious, dating formulae: each language has its own conventions, emblematic of the culture in which the language is dominant. A dramatic illustration occurs in a rare bi-lingual Jewish inscription from Zoar:[36]

Μνημῖον Μουσίου	The grave of Mousios / Son of
Μάρσου πλησθέντος	Marsas, who, having completed
ἒ<τ>ους <ἀπο>θανόν-	the year x of his life, died
τος ἒτ(ους) σνγ´	in the year 253
εὐμοιρίτῳ	Let him fare well!

הודה נפשה דמוסיס בר מרסה דמית בשתה	This is the grave of Mousios son of Marsa who died in year
תליתה דשבועה בירח כסלו בעסרין ושבעה	three of the Sabbatical cycle, in the month of Kislev, on the
יומין ביה היא שנת רצ שנין	twenty seventh day of it, which is the year 290
לחרבן בית מקדשה	after the destruction of the Temple

This inscription has three different dating systems. The Greek portion uses the date of the founding of the province of Arabia (22 March, 106 CE), whereas the Aramaic portion uses the Sabbatical Year cycle and the year of the Destruction of the Temple. Both systems coincide to produce the year 358 CE, if the Destruction year started on 1 Tishri of 69 CE (i.e., the first day of the Jewish year in which the month of Av in the Julian year 70 CE fell).

The important point here is that each language had its own conventions. It should be noted that the Christian tombstones in Greek from Zoar reveal yet another method, the indiction system, perhaps in parallel to the cyclical Sabbatical Years.[37] By contrast, the legal documents on papyri from the Judaean desert use three different Roman dating systems (provincial year, consular year, emperor's regnal year), regardless of language. Legal documents, however, have their own requirements and formulaic habits, and are intended for use in very specific judicial contexts, not necessarily exclusively Jewish; other documents on papyrus were intended for limited use in private and everyday contexts. In epigraphy, the audience is usually different and more general. In fact, dates appear less frequently in Semitic Jewish burial inscriptions overall, as a quick glance at the evidence from the ossuaries and from the large corpus of epitaphs from Beth Shearim makes immediately evident; the precision of the double-dating system of the Aramaic Zoar inscriptions is unusual in Jewish epigraphy.

---

[36] Cotton-Price, 'Bilingual Tombstone'; Naveh, 'Two Tombstones'. For the dating system see Stern, *Calendar and Community*; Misgav, 'Two Jewish Tombstones'.

[37] Canova, *Iscrizioni*.

The distinct epigraphic conventions in different languages is most pronounced in synagogue inscriptions, which are different from pagan and Christian dedicatory inscriptions in many respects. Foremost is the fact that very few have a date, and the dates which are mentioned are quite late in the ancient period, from the sixth century CE, such as the synagogue inscription at Kefar Nevuraya: '494 according to the era of the Destruction', or 564 CE.[38] These are texts which are most commonly written in mosaic, less frequently engraved in stone. Normally the dedicatory texts are peripheral in the main artistic scheme of a synagogue floor, that is, they are written in the borders and frames. Only in the floors at Ein Gedi and Rehov[39] do the texts, in Aramaic and Hebrew-plus-Aramaic, occupy the main part of the mosaic, and each records provisions directly connected to the regulation of the life of the community. The Rehov mosaic, most strikingly, preserves agricultural laws in almost direct quotation of the Palestinian Talmud as we have it today.[40] The laying of the mosaic floor was actually preceded by inscriptions painted in fresco on the pillars of the building and containing a shorter version of the halakhic regulations. In addition, there is a great dedication inscription with a list of unique names, another one mentioning Torah study, an enigmatic calendar list, and other inscriptions, totalling eight altogether.[41]

Yet the cultural baggage carried by different languages in inscriptions goes way beyond different dating systems. Let us examine the connection between epigraphic habit and language in synagogue inscriptions from the Land of The Land of srael, which not only has the highest density of synagogues and inscriptions, but is also the only place of significant 'epigraphic density' (to coin a phrase), i.e. it is the only confined geographical location in the ancient world where it is meaningful to talk about synagogue inscriptions as a group. It is also the only place where the synagogue inscriptions in Aramaic/Hebrew outnumber those in Greek.

Generally speaking, the Greek synagogue inscriptions follow the expected pattern of Greek dedications from the region and elsewhere, reflecting a Graeco-Roman euergetistic ethic.[42] They exhibit the same self-advertisement, pride in community, dedication formulae and even concern with details of the contribution, which are familiar from the vast numbers of Graeco-Roman euer-

---

[38] Naveh, *On Stone and Mosaic*, no. 13.

[39] Naveh, *On Stone and Mosaic*, nos. 70, 49.

[40] Cf. *Literature of the Sages, First Part*, 408 and photograph opposite p379. For discussion see Sussman, 'Halakhic Inscription', 'Additional Notes', 'Boundaries', 'Inscription'; and Lieberman, 'Halakhic Inscription'.

[41] To be published by H. Misgav under the auspices of the Israel Antiquities Authority.

[42] It is true that the heyday of Graeco-Roman euergetism in pagan contexts was over by the time the synagogue inscriptions were produced, but euergetistic epigraphy continued nevertheless in pagan contexts and was continued on a large scale by Christian benefactors. See Baumann, *Spätantike Stifter*; Quass, *Honoratiorenschicht*; also Gauthier, *Les cités grecques*. In general for what follows, see Roth-Gerson, *Greek Inscriptions*, 147-162.

euergetistic texts. The synagogue texts also fall into the four categories known to epigraphers of Greece and Rome: donor, artisan, votary and building dedication/dating.[43] And the Greek ones, as mentioned, although often rather concise, follow typical patterns of wording and content. For example, the simple, prosaic and entirely unexceptional donor inscription at Caesarea:[44]

Βηρύλλος ἀρχισ(υνάγωγος)	Beryllos, *archisynagogos*
καὶ φροντιστὴς	and *phrontistes*,
υὸς ᾽Ιούτου ἐποί-	son of Iou(s)tos,
ησε τὴν ψηφο-	donated the mosaic pavement
θεσίαν τοῦ τρι-	of the triclinium at
κλινίου τῷ ἰδίῳ/	his own cost

Here all the expected elements from Greek epigraphy are present: the name of the donor, his patronym, his titles, details of the donation and the assurance that his benefaction came from his own funds; often the amount donated is also specified.

The Jewish dedications in Greek adopted formulae from the Hellenistic epigraphic culture. A good example is the formula *hyper soterias*, which appears in synagogues in Israel and the Diaspora.[45] It was a common formula in pagan dedicatory inscriptions, in which the expressed wish is for the the well-being of the ruler(s), and it was adopted in Christian epigraphy as well, although there it has clear eschatological meaning, which it does not necessarily have in Jewish texts. Thus even the late instances of *hyper soterias* in synagogues, such as at Ashkelon, should be considered as imitative of Greek euergetistic practice, not a direct borrowing from Christianity. The *hyper soterias* inscription in the synagogue at Beth Shean – Scythopolis was put up by a man from Cyzicus who may have brought this particular habit with him, for in Asia there are quite a few inscriptions, Jewish and pagan, bearing this formula and related ones like ὑπὲρ ὑγίας.[46] In fact, in the Diaspora, Jews even followed the custom of inscribing wishes for the health of the emperor, such as at Ostia, Egypt and Pannonia,[47] but this practice, with one possible exception at Qazion,[48] was not followed in the Land of Israel. The important point here is that this common Greek formula, whether applied to Jewish benefactors or Gentile rulers, was adopted by the Jews when they inscribed dedications in Greek; it has no equivalent in Hebrew and Aramaic inscriptions. Equally important is the fact that the formula *hyper soterias*, which was a widespread

---

[43] This represents a different typology from that devised by Yahalom, 'Synagogue Inscriptions', but he was looking at the inscriptions with a different purpose.

[44] Lehmann-Holum, *The Greek and Latin Inscriptions*, 93 no. 79.

[45] See Roth-Gerson, *Greek Inscriptions*, nos. 2, 3, 7, 8, 23, 28, 30; Lifshitz, *Donateurs*, nos. 39, 41-46, 51, 55, 56, 62, 91.

[46] For the Jewish examples, see the index in IJO II, s.v.

[47] JIWE, no. 13; JIGRE, 13, 22, 24, 25, 28, 117; IJO I, Pan3 and Pan5.

[48] Roth-Gerson, *Greek Inscriptions*, no. 30.

phenomenon throughout the Roman East, was adopted widely in Syria-Palestine, but other formulae with more localized dispersion among the Jews, such as *pronoia* found in Asia Minor, were not.

Jews likewise adapted votary formulae – that is, inscriptions indicating fulfilment of a vow – from pagan inscriptions to their own needs. An example is in the elaborate synagogue floor from Hammath Tiberias, in which there is a checkerboard group of nine Greek texts by donors who contributed to the synagogue's construction 'in fulfillment of a vow' (εὐχόμενος) – formulaic expressions which could have appeared in any pagan context, with the addition of the name of the God to whom the vow was made; God's name is of course not mentioned in the synagogue floor, because it was understood and is rarely mentioned in Greek Jewish inscriptions in the Land of Israel. In any case He could not be named directly. Similarly with the dating formulae in Greek synagogue inscriptions: except for the Jewish titles, there is nothing to distinguish them from their pagan counterparts, as illustrated by the relatively elaborate building inscription on what is believed to be a lintel to a synagogue at Sepphoris.[49]

In sum, the Greek synagogue inscriptions from the Land of Israel – and *a fortiori* throughout the Jewish world of antiquity – do not exhibit unusual forms or 'epigraphic habits', but elements which were common in dedicatory inscriptions in that language. That said, it should be noted that some elements are missing from the inscriptions from the Holy Land which appear on synagogue texts from the Diaspora. As noted above, the names of pagan rulers never, or almost never, appear on Jewish inscriptions, and except for *instrumenta* like weights, dating formulae are much rarer in synagogue inscriptions in the Land of Israel than in the Diaspora.[50]

Finally, although difficult to quantify, it should be noted that while the Greek dedicatory inscriptions reveal no formulaic deviations, the self-congratulation in Jewish inscriptions from the region is somewhat less elaborate than in non-Jewish euergetistic inscriptions.[51] Donor inscriptions in the Land of Israel, in both Greek and Aramaic, are usually phrased in the third person, something which has caused some perplexity: Naveh's explanation is that synagogue officials wrote the texts for others and naturally adopted the third person, whereas Lapin suggests that the third-person dedications were written by the dedicatees themselves and reflect a 'communal rhetoric', which is reasonable and corresponds with the evidence from the synagogue pavements that the construction was more of a community effort than other public buildings in

---

[49] Roth-Gerson, *Greek Inscriptions*, no. 24.

[50] This is something which Hayim Lapin, in an important article, 'Palestinian Inscriptions', explained as reflecting the lack of hierarchical organization within the synagogue, but this explanation is open to question.

[51] Rajak makes this point regarding Diaspora inscriptions in their larger surroundings, cf. *Jewish Dialogue*, 373-91.

Graeco-Roman cities. Indeed, it is as if the community itself is speaking.[52] Not only the third-person dedications but overall the relative modesty of synagogue donor inscriptions reflects a community ideal and ethic. Donors did not receive crowns or conspicuous honours, but public recognition for their benefaction. There is probably also some residual influence from Aramaic epigraphic habits to be detected (see below). Regionality is once again important: the understated nature of synagogue inscriptions from the Land of Israel is less noticeable in synagogue inscriptions elsewhere, as the ostentatious inscription from Stobi testifies, not to mention the more elaborate forms and style of synagogue inscriptions from Asia Minor.

When we turn to the Aramaic-Hebrew synagogue inscriptions from the Land of Israel, which represent the majority from the region, we find ourselves – once again – in a different world. Generally speaking, they are found in less urbanized or less cosmopolitan settings – Ein Gedi, Jericho, Rehov – and the few exceptions to this, such as Hammath Tiberias and Sepphoris, are found in predominantly Jewish cities. The Aramaic texts have patterns of their own. The most typical formula is דכיר לטב 'may he be remembered for the good', exactly as in the Greek μνησθῇ εἰς ἀγαθόν – indeed the Greek is probably an imitation of the Semitic formula. As noted above, this third-person formulation draws attention away from the individual and stresses his contribution to the community at large. It is true that Aramaic inscriptions can sometimes imitate Greek epigraphic patterns. For an example, see the dedication found at Na'aran:

דכיר לטב פינחס כהנה יוסטה דיהב	May he be remembered for the good, Pinchas the priest, son of Iouste, who donated
טימי פסיפסה	the cost of the mosaic
מן דידה ומרושת<ה>	from his own resources and property (?)

It can practically be translated back into Greek.[53] But neither case – Greek texts imitating patterns typical of Aramaic, and *vice versa* – should be over-interpreted: a certain degree of cross-cultural imitation is natural, and by and large languages maintain their own epigraphic habits.

The distinctiveness of Aramaic dedicatory inscriptions goes further than peculiar formulae. In the Hebrew-Aramaic dedications, the personal details of the donors and artists are not only minimized but often omitted altogether, in contrast with Greek dedicatory inscriptions which not only invariably record the names of benefactors but often add personal details, such as profession and title. Yet aside from the occasional *kohen*, practically the only title mentioned

---

[52] A point made by G. Foerster, 'Synagogue Inscriptions', and by S. Schwartz, *Imperialism*, 283.

[53] Naveh, *On Stone and Mosaic*, no. 58. Similarly, some Aramaic inscriptions imitate local Aramaic epigraphic patterns, such as the apt comparison to Hatrean texts from the first-third centuries CE suggested by Foerster, 'Synagogue Inscriptions'.

in Hebrew-Aramaic inscriptions in Iudaea-Palaestina is 'rav' (with variations), without further elaboration (on 'rabbi' see below).[54] The omission of patronyms in dedications is much more likely to occur in Greek than in Hebrew or Aramaic. In the more Hellenized regions outside the Land of Israel, the epigraphic habit of Aramaic more resembled that of the Greek. One need only cite the elaborate inscriptions from Dura Europos, prominently exhibiting the names and titles of the heads of the community as well as dating formulae.[55]

The difference between Greek and Aramaic epigraphic cultures, dependent not only on language but also on region, can be seen in two features of some Semitic texts (mostly those furthest from cosmopolitan centers) which directly contradict both the practice and spirit of Graeco-Roman euergetism. The donors remain anonymous and the specific nature of their contributions remains obscured, although the sums contributed are often mentioned; and the reward for their benefaction is not conceived as immediate or even actualized in present society: it will be given by God. The second feature follows from the first: if the donors are anonymous, the immediate reward of social respect and honour is of course not forthcoming. These are two epigraphic practices which are practically inconceivable for someone writing in Greek, because of its grating disharmony with one of the most central ethics in Hellenistic culture: honour as a publicly recognized virtue.

An astonishing example of an anonymous Aramaic donor inscription, well illustrating the community ethic lying behind the individual anonymity, can be found in the famous synagogue pavement at Jericho:

> May they be remembered for the good, and may their memory be for the good: the entire holy congregation, the old along with the young (or: the great along with the small), whom the Lord of the universe aided and who contributed to and made the mosaic. May He who knows their names and (the names) of their sons and of all the members of their households inscribe them in the Book of Life [together with] the righteous. May all Israel be united. Shal[om Amen].[56]

Here, apparently, the community took the decision to put down one inscription for all donors, 'old and the young'.[57] But usually the decision to remain anonymous was an individual one, as illustrated most remarkably by the artisan who chose not to publicize himself at Beth Shean: 'May he be remembered for the good: the artisan who made this work'.[58]

Another instructive case of an individual decision to remain anonymous is that of Hammath-Gader, where the names of several benefactors, along with information about family relationships and amounts of contributions, are

---

[54] The inscription from Susia, with the title הכהן מכובד, honorable, is exceptional, see Naveh, *On Stone and Mosaic*, no. 75.

[55] See Naveh, *On Stone and Mosaic*, nos. 88-104.

[56] Naveh, *On Stone and Mosaic*, no. 69.

[57] Cf. the similar text from Chusipha, on the Carmel, Naveh, *On Stone and* Mosaic, no. 39.

[58] Naveh, *On Stone and Mosaic*, no. 47.

spelled out in detail. In one inscription, however, we find a combination of public disclosure and anonymity. After a *dekir letav* formula mentioning a certain *kyrios* Leontis and *kyria* Kalanik(e), we read:

> ... and may a certain righteous (?) woman be remembered for the good, who gave one *dinar* for the benefit of the synagogue; may the Lord of the universe give his blessing to her (good) deeds, amen, amen, sela shalom.[59]

Thus the decision to mention one's name or not was a personal one. It cannot be the case that the anonymous donors gave less and therefore did not earn the privilege of public recognition, because it takes as much effort and material to spell out in mosaic tiles their anonymous mention as their actual names. But this choice was possible, and regular, in Aramaic – which, again, is not an infallible marker of the native language of the donor.

Now it is true, as both T. Rajak and S. Schwartz have pointed out, that the community most likely knew who the anonymous donors were. But there was nothing consequently disingenuous about their anonymity, for the public memory weakens with each generation, and the purpose of the trouble and expense involved in inscribing in mosaic and stone is that the record be as permanent as possible, as a memorial for all time, or at least to future generations which the donor will perforce not know. Thus the Aramaic anonymous dedications represent a different ethic from Graeco-Roman euergetism, an ethic associated intimately with the language of the inscription.[60] The exceptions to this in Greek are rare. For example, the brief text at Beth Shean, 'A contribution from those whose names the Lord knows, may He preserve them eternally,'[61] should be considered a direct imitation of the Aramaic epigraphic habit, and in fact, there is at Beth Shean an anonymous donor inscription in Aramaic: 'May they be remembered for the good, the sons of the holy community who contribute to the repair and upkeep of this holy place; may they have a blessing, amen ...'.[62] In both these dedications, the Greek and the Aramaic, the dedication hides not the name of one individual, as so often in anonymous dedications, but is written on behalf of the entire community.[63]

By contrast, Greek and Aramaic inscriptions found side-by-side in the same synagogue reveal the different epigraphic habits of each language. It is true that synagogue inscriptions have to be read in their immediate archaeological and artistic context – i.e., the inscriptions were part of the *program* of the synagogue floors – but the actual forms and content of the texts came not

---

[59] Naveh, *On Stone and Mosaic*, no. 34.

[60] It is necessary to note the place which the idea of abstention from public acclaim and reputation, *doxa*, holds in Stoic thought, see Rajak, *Jewish Dialogue*, 375; but this leaves barely an imprint in Graeco-Roman epigraphy, and it is reasonable to assume that the Jewish epigraphical practice of anonymity comes from within the Jewish community.

[61] Roth-Gerson, *Greek Inscriptions*, no. 9.

[62] Naveh, *On Stone and Mosaic*, no. 46.

[63] As at Caesarea as well, see Roth-Gerson, *Greek Inscriptions*, no. 25.

from artistic but epigraphic traditions. In the language of modern scholarship, not different 'Judaisms' are reflected in the different social and religious ethics suggested by the different forms of dedication and commemoration, but different epigraphic cultures.

The point can best be brought home by a fascinating example. In the east aisle of the artistically and epigraphically elaborate synagogue mosaic at Hammath Tiberias, two inscriptions were placed side by side:[64]

Σευῆρος θρεπτὸς τῶν λαμπρο-	Severos the *threptos* of the most illustrious
τάτων πατριαρχῶν ἐτελίωσεν	patriarchs completed (this work); a blessing
εὐλογία αὐτῷ κὲ ᾽Ιούλλῳ τῷ προνοητ[ῇ]	upon him and also upon Ioullos the *parnas*
יהי שלמה כל מן דעבד מצותה בהדן	May there be (a blessing of) peace upon everyone
אתרה קדישה ודעתיד מעבד מצותה	who has performed an act of charity (benefaction)
תהי לה ברכתה אמן אמן סלה ולי אמן	in this holy place, and who will in the future perform acts of charity. May there be a blessing upon him. Amen, amen, sela. And also upon me, Amen.

We shall pass over the many fascinating issues raised by the two texts, above all, who were the 'patriarchs' mentioned in the Greek – to which we shall come back below. We shall now focus on the different content and modes of expression in the two adjacent texts. The Greek text informs us that Severos, who is mentioned in another inscription in the same pavement, single-handedly 'finished the work'; whether the entire pavement, or just that section, is unclear. Equally unclear is the reason why Severos decided to include Ioullos, whose name is likewise recorded elsewhere, in the final blessing, although the wording and syntax of the dedication suggest that Ioullos did not actually contribute to the completion of the work to the same degree as Severos, if at all. In any case, if Severos exercised his privilege of publicizing his completion of part of the pavement in the appropriate place, then it is reasonable to suppose that the Aramaic text, which appears in an identical box underneath the Greek and was laid out at the same time, records the same act. That is, it concerns not a different benefaction but the same one: the Greek and the Aramaic were meant to be read together. If this is the correct interpretation, and if the final two words in the Aramaic inscription do in fact mean 'and *upon me*,

[64] Roth-Gerson, *Greek Inscriptions*, no. 18; Naveh, *On Stone and Mosaic*, no. 26.

Amen',[65] then we see that not only different donors in the same pavement, but the same person in the same pavement, expressed himself in dramatically different ways in Greek and in Aramaic –in this case Severos would have circumvented the inevitable result of anonymity by identifying himself in the Greek half of the dedication.

The differences between Greek and Hebrew-Aramaic inscriptions are repeated, *mutatis mutandis*, in epitaphs. Just as Greek dedicatory texts contain more personal details about donors and craftsmen than do the Hebrew-Aramaic ones, so too in epitaphs the subject's personality and achievements are generally advertised more prominently in Greek, and Semitic texts may even downplay the person's importance in this life. Greek epitaphs in the Land of Israel, and even more so those in the Diaspora, resemble funerary epigraphic practice in their environment, including, aside from the name of the deceased, other names and nicknames, details of his/ her life, blessings, curses on disturbers of the grave, even thoughts about death. In the Land of Israel, Beth Shearim, where a large number of Diaspora Jews are buried, contains the largest number of examples of 'fuller' epitaphs, including even Greek mythological references.

Jewish epitaphs in Hebrew and Aramaic are different. Ossuary inscriptions are notoriously brief. A practical reason could be argued: the inscriptions were generally used only for identification purposes in family burials. But other types of Semitic epitaphs are characterized by the same brevity: usually spare information beyond the name, and in later periods, dates of death and very short blessings.[66] Other epigraphic aspects were dynamic, but the brevity remained. Standard additions were made for practical reasons, to prove ownership of the grave, or to indicate the date for the annual visit by relatives. Epigraphy is a poor source for expressions of religious beliefs by the Jews in antiquity, but this is truer in Semitic languages than in Greek. Semitic epitaphs contain very few theological expressions, and almost no clue regarding belief in the afterlife, as opposed to the numerous indications in Greek.[67] It is true that tombs of Jews in Hejra are similar to Nabatean tombs with their explicit statements of ownership, but they are distinguished by the absence of curses or mention of local deities. (e.g., CII 1356). The difference in the amount of data felt necessary in each language can be seen clearly in the Nicanor

---

[65] See Naveh *ad loc.* for discussion of difficulties.

[66] The epigram on an ossuary from Jerusalem, לא סכל אנש למעלה ולא אלעזר ושפירא ('nobody succeeded to prevent his entry [to the next world], even not Eleazar and Shafira did'), is unique, see Naveh, 'Burial Inscription'. Noteworthy is the enigmatic elegy from the first-century 'Yason tomb': Avigad, 'Aramaic Inscriptions from Jason's Tomb'; and note also the unclear formula וי לה שלום ברת יהוחנן from Issawiyeh (CII 1245); an ossuary from Shuafat has a Palmyran inscription, with the word חבל (pity), CII 1222, cf Puech, 'Ossuaires et inscriptions'.

[67] Exceptions are rare, see e.g. the unusual eight-line Hebrew text from Beth Shearim including the phrase [צדיקים עם עמידתן], Avigad, *Beth Shearim* III, 241-243, no. 15; and phrases such as יתעורר לקול משמיע שלום from Zoar, albeit from a later period, Naveh, 'Seven New Epitaphs'.

inscription quoted above. It mentions in Greek Nicanor's accomplishment for which he wished to be remembered, but in Hebrew records only his name and origin. Aside from the ubiquitous שלום on Jewish epitaphs, there is practically no blessing or other formula in the Hebrew-Aramaic inscriptions to match the widespread blessings or wishes in Greek texts such as θάρσει, οὐδεὶς ἀθάνατος and ἐν εἰρήνῃ ... (*shalom* cannot be considered a shortened form of this).[68]

Relation to Rabbinic Judaism

The rabbis of the Mishna and Talmud knew of the practice of setting up inscriptions. A *baraita* teaches that the righteous do not need epitaphs since their good deeds are their memorial (yShek 2:7, 47a; GenR 82,10, p988 in the apparatus), implicitly acknowledging that most people do require or desire epitaphs. Certain prohibitions against reading inscriptions on Shabbat are recorded, although the subject there is not inscriptions set up by Jews.[69] There is, finally, the intriguing possibility that an inscription is actually quoted in the Yerushalmi. An inscription set up at a fair at Tyre during the visit there by the emperor Diocletian recorded the dedication of the fair to his brother Heraclius for eight days, and thus served as the basis for prohibiting purchase of goods there for that period (yAZ 1:4, 39d). The text of the inscription is quoted in Aramaic. Whether this inscription is genuine,[70] and if so whether the Aramaic is a translation of a Greek or Latin original, or was part of a bi-lingual or trilingual text, are questions which do not affect the use of this passage as evidence of the rabbis' notice of, and even use of, inscriptions. But these notices are exceptional rather than exemplary in the surviving rabbinic corpus: they are but a few drops in a vast sea. The reason for this relative absence is not self-evident. Do inscriptions gain so little notice from the rabbis because they were considered unimportant, or on the contrary potentially dangerous? Or could it be that the process of editing and ultimate survival has biased the sample?

However this may be settled, it is safe to say that the content and style of Jewish epigraphic texts developed with little if any influence from the sages of the Mishna and Talmud. The rabbis of the Mishna did not, for example, establish formulae for burial inscriptions or for dedications in synagogues. But this should cause no surprise given that, from the evidence of the Judaean Desert finds, the rabbinic formulae for legal documents, e.g. marriage contracts and divorce decrees, had apparently not yet solidified by the second century CE,

---

[68] See in general Park, *Conceptions of Afterlife*.

[69] tShab 17:1, 8; and see the curious provision for keeping accounts written on a wall, tShab 17:5f; bShab 149a; our gratitude to Moshe Benovitz for helping us find these passages.

[70] As J. Greenfield thought it was, see his paper in *Al Kanfei Yonah*, 449-452.

and even if they had, they were certainly not imposed upon, or adopted by a majority of, Jews in the area at that time.[71]

Even with the methodological cautions outlined above, it is clear that the current corpus of Jewish inscriptions – both those from the Land of Israel and those of the Diaspora – reflect a different world from the one of the rabbis.

There is, first of all, the vexed question of whether any talmudic rabbis are mentioned in inscriptions. Shaye Cohen, in a much-quoted article,[72] argued that none of the 'epigraphical rabbis' can be securely identified with a talmudic sage. Subsequent argument and discovery have done little to change this essential conclusion, but there are still a few cases in which the connection is attractive, like Eliezer ha-Kappar,[73] who despite the fact that the inscription mentioning him is from the Golan is indeed one of the best candidates for a talmudic 'epigraphical rabbi', given the mention of his *bet midrash*. Also debatable are the names R. Joshua ben Levi (Beth Shearim) and Yudan the son of R. Tryphon (Jaffa).[74] Cohen's point was not that none of the 'epigraphical rabbis' could be talmudic sages with similar or identical names, but that none are necessarily so, because of the lack of corroborating data; in any case, there is general agreement that the large majority of the 'rabbis' in inscriptions are definitely not talmudic sages. And as Cohen points out, most rabbis mentioned in synagogue inscriptions (not just in Israel) are donors, not holders of authority. The only 'rabbi' known to have been an *archisynagogos* is from Phrygia, his epitaph in *Greek*, with a standard *shalom*-blessing in Hebrew on the end, found in Israel (CII 1414).

Even if the name of a talmudic sage in an inscription could be definitely confirmed as such, that need not affect the interpretation of the title 'rabbi', which was fluid and varied in other inscriptions. The appearance of 'rabbi' on inscriptions does reinforce the general impression that the title had a wide semantic range and could be used merely as a title of honour, not any official position or authority, until quite late in antiquity. What is interesting, however, is that the great majority of the rabbi inscriptions come from the land of Israel, where there is a significant paucity of other titles in comparison to the proliferation of titles throughout the Diaspora, both internal to the Jewish community and in the Roman administration. Some of the titles found on inscriptions in the Land of Israel were imported, such as the *archisynagogus* from Asia Minor whose epitaph was found in Jerusalem[75] or the one from Phoenicia

---

[71] See for example Cotton, 'The Rabbis and the Documents' and 'Die Papyrusdokumente'.

[72] Cohen, 'Epigraphical Rabbis', and see now Miller, '"Epigraphical" Rabbis', esp 39ff.

[73] Naveh, *On Stone and Mosaic*, no. 6.

[74] See Cohen, 'Epigraphical Rabbis', for discussion and references, and on R. Joshua see now Rosenfeld, 'Rabbi Joshua'. Also from the Golan is a sarcophagus bearing the name Rabbi Abun and his son Shimon, see N. Cohen, 'R. Abun'.

[75] IJO II, no. 184.

buried at Beth Shearim,[76] both of whom obviously served in their countries of origin and not in the Land of Israel.

Moreover, the title 'rabbi' is fairly late. Just as the earliest sages, like Hillel and Shammai, were called only by their names, and the historical traditions refer to other scholars of the Second Temple period only by their names,[77] so epigraphical attestation of 'rabbis', too, dates from a later period, roughly the fourth century and onwards.[78] This concerns not only the epitaphs from Beth Shearim and Jaffa, but also synagogue inscriptions in Greek and Aramaic, and in amulets. The title 'rav' appears only hundreds of years after the destruction of the temple, and was of Babylonian origin. The sages of the Yerushalmi are called 'rabbi', while their Babylonian colleagues are called 'rav', until the end of the Gaonic period (cf below ch. 19). The title 'rabbi' is also usually not modified by an adjective indicating that the bearer of the title is distinguished, 'exalted', 'shining', etc. In addition to 'rabbi' we find the occasional 'priest' or 'high priest', 'scribe' and even *saba* (= grandfather), which is, according to Sukenik, a title like 'elder', member of the elders council.[79] Thus the inscriptions, when combined with the documents from the Judaean Desert, provide a picture of the late appearance and gradual spread of the title 'rabbi' in Israel, although the relation between these rising epigraphical rabbis and the rabbinic establishment in the Mishna and Talmuds still requires clarification.

Finally, regarding the connection between the sages of Israel and the Diaspora, we note that no patriarch appears by name on an inscription, though the office is mentioned in a few tantalizing texts. The Greek inscription from Hammat Tiberias quoted above calls Severus a *threptos* of 'the illustrious patriarchs', which probably does refer to the Palestinian patriarchs, who were resident in Tiberias when the floor was laid. But neither of the two Diaspora inscriptions mentioning the patriarch or patriarchs indisputably refers to the *Nasi*. The grand third-century inscription from Stobi in Macedonia stipulates a large fine to be paid 'to the patriarch' if the provisions in the inscriptions are violated, and an epitaph from Catania, precisely dated to 383 CE, appeals to the reader *per honores patriarcarum* not to open the tomb.[80] The former, as has been suggested, could refer to a local official, and in any case, being unique and consequently of questionable relevance as evidence of a larger phenome-

---

[76] Schwabe-Lifshitz, *Beth Shearim* II, no. 221.

[77] Cf bShab 15a. The Mishna mentions 'two judges of robbery that were in Jerusalem, Hannan and Admon' (mKet 13:1).

[78] In Hammat Gader a 'Rav Tanhum' is mentioned, and Sukenik suggested that a *Yod* was omitted, but 'rav' could have been the title of a Syrian Jew, as most of the visitors of this site were; alternatively it could have been a Babylonian title. An ossuary, published in 1913 and reading 'Rav Hanna' (CII 1218), seems to be a mistake, see Misgav, 'Nomenclature': according to the drawing of the ossuary it has to be read תחנה.

[79] Rahmani, *Catalogue*, no. 12; Sukenik, 'Coffins and Inscriptions'. It should be noted that the Bar Kochba letters contain the title *nasi* (Bar Kokhba himself) and 'parnas' (Mur. 42), and one Rabbi appears, the unknown Rabbi *Btnyh*.

[80] IJO I, Mac1; JIWE I, 145, both recording extensive bibliography.

non, does not go far in illuminating the formal relationship between the Patriarch and Diaspora communities; the latter could very well refer to biblical patriarchs, and is of as much use in understanding the patriarchal office.

One obvious area of consultation with the Palestinian sages would be in determining calendrical issues,[81] but there is little help in this important question forthcoming from inscriptions. For this complex subject of the contacts between the sages and Jewish communities in the Diaspora, the literary sources are more plentiful; epigraphy offers little new or unique material, and always poses problems of interpretation. But at least the phenomenon of Beth Shearim illustrates, probably, the influence and reputation of at least one rabbi, Yehuda the Prince, the codifier of the Mishna. The presence of his grave there (although, despite a popular identification of one burial cave as his, for no other reason than its rich ornamentation, his grave has not been definitely located) is the standard explanation not only for the size of the necropolis but especially for the impressive geographical diversity of the Jews buried there. The geographical diversity of the graves at Beth Shearim, where Greek predominates, reflects a similar diversity in epigraphic practices found there: Jews brought not only their languages but the cultural habits attached to them.[82]

[81] IJO II, 36.

[82] Although it must be noted that the most elaborate Greek epitaph, replete with mythological language, seems to be of a local, see Schwabe-Lifshitz, *Beth Shearim* II, no. 127 with commentary *ad loc.*

Chapter Fourteen

Medical Interest in
Ancient Rabbinic Literature

Samuel S. Kottek

It has been often emphasized that extant ancient Hebrew or Jewish literature contains no specifically medical texts, in contrast to some other ancient civilizations.[1] However, it is well-known that the Palestinian and Babylonian Talmuds are interspersed with statements of medico-historical interest; the classical work of Julius Preuss from 1911 gives sufficient proof of their importance. In four introductory sections of this paper, we shall review some of these, as also some where medical instruments are mentioned. The next four sections review some extant texts of medical interest from rabbinic literature and from writings closely associated with it. We shall not refer here to similar passages that are scattered over the range of Jewish works of the Second Temple period and that we have analysed elsewhere, such as the Qumran texts,[2] the Pseudepigrapha,[3] or the works of Josephus,[4] but we shall study one passage in Ben Sira.

---

[1] The 'Book of Medicines', Sefer Refuot, mentioned in bBer 10b, which was allegedly hidden away by King Hezekiah (8th cent. BCE), has not been documented by any other historical source.
[2] Cf Kottek, 'The Essenes'.
[3] Cf Kottek, 'Magic and Healing'.
[4] Cf Kottek, *Medicine and Hygiene*.

Passages of Medical Interest

Several methodological problems render the task of the medical historian rather difficult when it comes to rabbinic literature. In the first place, some statements are so brief, fragmentary and/or unclear that they remain obscure. Then, a precise dating of these statements is merely conjectural. Even when we are told who was the author, the latter does not always indicate his source, and when he does, this does not necessarily mean that the earlier authority was the primary source of the statement, given the fact that it concerns in an oral tradition. Furthermore, the talmudic sages were basically discussing halakhic matters, and medical notions were, just as astronomical ones or questions related to the calendar, nothing more than incidental and informative. Moreover, 'scientific' and popular medicine were closely intertwined, not without some analogy to Pliny's medical notes that can be found in his Natural History, books 20-32. Another introductory paragraph will illustrate this.

The Gaonic writings, especially those of Saadia and Hai, also contain some medical references. It has long been believed that no medical Jewish literature existed before the ninth or tenth centuries (Donnolo, Yitshak Yisraeli).[5] Thanks to the work of Venetianer, Muntner and others, we now know that the Babylonian physician Asaf the Jew, who lived in the sixth or seventh century, has left us a medical treatise often cited in medieval manuscripts. Although his very existence has been questioned by certain authors,[6] there is some evidence that he was not just a mythical figure, although it is probable that his teachings were recorded by his pupils and not by himself. ספר אסף, 'The Book of Asaf', is a real piece of medical literature, with an introduction of historical interest. The author traces the filiation from Hippocrates, Dioscorides, and Galen and cites sources from India, Syria, Macedonia and Egypt.[7] This clearly shows that Asaf lived before the time when Arabic medicine played any significant role. The work then deals with anatomy, physiology, pathology and therapy. It ends with the famous Oath, which is a valuable document on early Jewish medical ethics and will retain our attention below.

As for the talmudic texts of medical interest, it is much more difficult to find statements of some length that form a real body of literary interest. It mostly concerns short notations, more or less in accordance with the knowledge of the surrounding civilizations. We shall present three texts, one taken from the Mishna, the treatment of a rabid dog's bite; one taken from the Babylonian Talmud dealing with the description of hemophilia, featuring one of the really original medical statements of the Talmud; and a third text from Avot de-R. Natan, describing the famous microcosm-macrocosm analogy. The latter

---

[5] Shabbetai Donnolo (tenth cent.), see my paper, 'Šabbetay Donnolo'; Yitshak Yisraeli (ninth-tenth cent.), Jewish physician in Kairawan, whose works were taught in medieval universities.
[6] Cf Rappoport, introduction to *Sefer Otsar Hokhma*.
[7] Regarding this introduction to *Sefer Asaf*, cf Jellinek, *Bet ha-Midrasch*, vol 3, 155.

two texts are linked by the personality of R. Natan. Finally, we shall study the Oath of Asaf we mentioned and a passage from Ben Sira illuminating it.

The Status of Medicine

This important topic can only be briefly delineated within the framework of the present study. The sages interpret the verse in Exod 21:19 as permission given to the physicians to heal: 'If the man (hurt in a fight) rises again and walks abroad with his staff, he that struck him shall be clear; only he shall pay for the loss of his time, and shall have him thoroughly healed.' It is reported that physicians were sometimes consulted by the sages and quite a number of the latter displayed at least an interest, if not a training, in medicine. It is also stated[8] that a scholar should not dwell in a city where there is neither a physician nor a barber-surgeon.

An often cited midrashic passage illustrates the fact that, although the Lord is the supreme healer, man is granted permission to heal:[9]

> R. Yishmael and R. Akiva were walking through the streets of Jerusalem in the company of a peasant. A sick man approached them and asked for medical advice, which they readily provided. The peasant objected: 'Are you not dealing with a matter that is not your business? The Lord afflicted that man with illness, and you try to heal him!' But they answered: 'What are you doing yourself? The Lord has created the earth and the plants, however you are compelled to plow, to till, to fertilize and weed if you wish it to yield produce. Is it not written: "As for man, his days are like grass."[10] This may be expanded as follows: the body is like a tree (or grass), the medication is the fertilizer, and the physician is the tiller of the earth.'

A physician who involuntarily injures his patient will not be sanctioned if he was licensed to practice by the court, 'because of the regulation of the world'.[11] For social reasons (the world's regulation), an exception is made to the general rule on involuntary injuries, in order that there be found physicians to cure. It has been stressed[12] that the 'license' given by the court is one very early example of such official control of the profession. However, the assertion of Preuss that this רופא-אומן (*rofe-umman*) was a town-physician[13] cannot be accepted as certain. He appears together with the priest, the court-official and the special case of the embryotomist, i.e., the man who dismembers an embryo in the womb to save the life of the mother: he will not be sanctioned if he involuntarily caused damage to the woman. These three characters: the court-official, the

---

[8] bSan 17b.
[9] Midrash Shmuel 4, ed Venice 1546, fol. 52a.
[10] Ps 103:15.
[11] מפני תיקון העולם, tGit 3:13.
[12] Leibowitz, 'Problem'.
[13] 'Ein approbierter Gemeindearzt' (Preuss, *Medizin*, 22).

rofe-umman and the embryotomist, are met with again in tMak 2:5. Should they involuntarily cause the death of the patient or the mother, they must flee to a 'town of refuge' – as involuntary murderers.[14]

Such deontological rules are particularly interesting when compared to other ancient civilizations. The Codex Hammurabi rules that the hand of the physician who has harmed his patient should be cut off, but it is not said whether or not the deed was committed voluntarily. On the other hand, the Greek and Roman physicians were free of any castigation, even in case of the patient's death.

Popular Medicine

Speaking of medicine in talmudic lore, we must comment briefly on the theme of popular medicine, in which there can be found quite a number of recipes collected from different sources over many centuries. The Babylonian environment provides a self-evident explanation of the appeal of incantations and amulets, and the sages were wise enough to be permissive towards any practice that did not endanger the faith. During the Tannaitic period, by contrast, it was stated that 'whoever utters an incantation over a bodily ailment (using biblical verses) will have no share in the world-to-come.'[15] But the later Amoraim openly permitted amulets מן המומחים, i.e., from those who have proved at least three times effective. This is summarised in the talmudic adage:עולם כמנהגו נוהג, i.e., 'The world goes its own way', and the following passage illustrates it:[16]

> Zonin (Zenon?) said to R. Akiva: we both know that idolatry has no efficiency whatsoever. On the other hand, we see people going (to the shrine of idolatry) as they are broken and coming back mended.[17] How can such a thing happen? R. Akiva answered: I shall answer with a parable. It resembles the case of a true and honest man who was living in the city; all the citizens used to borrow money from him against pledges without any witness. Only one man always did it with testimonial proof. But once he forgot and pawned an object without witness. Said the wife of the pawn-broker: This is the occasion to pay him back (for his lack of trust). But he answered: Shall we lose our confidence because this man behaved badly? – Such is the case with suffering:[18] When it is inflicted on someone, it is decided beforehand what day it will initiate its course, what day and what hour it will end, through what man and through what medication. Now imagine that (our sick man) decides, on the very day that his ailment was due to leave him, to go to the House of Idolatry. Say the diseases: Strictly

[14] The rule applied only as long as there was a Temple in Jerusalem with a High Priest.
[15] bSan 90a.
[16] bAZ 55a.
[17] Literally, 'bound up', i.e., healed.
[18] 'Suffering', i.e., diseases.

speaking[19] we should not leave, and then they add: Shall we violate our oath because this stupid man has acted in this unduly manner?

To put it briefly, there is nothing in common between the theological and cosmic values of disease and trial, and the hazardous practices of idolatry and magic. The sages were prepared to permit any therapeutic procedure, whatever its origin, placing the safeguarding of human life as the highest standard. However, three limitations were agreed upon: to refrain from murder, idolatry and prohibited sexual acts.

Medical Instruments

Medical instruments are referred to in the Talmud among the utensils susceptible to impurity – i.e., they belong to the tools available to Jews.[20] The following merely represents a selection from the extant data on medical instruments and technology in talmudic times. Thus we hear of a metal medicine box, apparently a kind of traveller's box, called טני, close to the biblical טנא (*tene'*, Deut 26:2). A so-called 'tower' (מגדל) for the use of physicians is also mentioned. It is interpreted as a wooden closet or cupboard (ארמריום, *armarium*, cf French *armoire*) for instruments. The 'blood-letter's pin', מסמר הגרע, is also recorded. We are told about an instrument used for trepanation (מקדח), and two kinds of scalpels: the larger סכין (knife) and the more common איזמל used *inter alia* for circumcision. Another case containing drugs and called נרתק or נרתיק (*nartiq*) appears in a short story that we present here:[21]

> One individual once stole the *nartiq* of a physician. Just as he came out, his son was injured, so he came back to the physician and asked him to heal his son. The physician answered: go and bring back my *nartiq*, as there are several kinds of drugs inside, and I shall heal your son.

This medicine chest is so named from the Greek νάρθηξ.[22] In Latin, it appears as *narthecium*, a case for drugs or perfumes.[23] Most of these terms are of Semitic origin, such as טני, מגדל, מקדח, סכין. Others are derived from the Greek: *nartiq*; *ismel* (from σμίλη).

---

[19] Meaning: according to the Law, this man being guilty should not be relieved of his ailments.

[20] mKel 12:3.

[21] yBer 5:2 (9b).

[22] Νάρθηξ is the Greek name for the ferula plant and its wood, of which the wooden case named נרתיק or נרתיקא was most probably originally made.

[23] *Narthecium*: see for instance Cicero, De Finibus 2.22 or Martialis 14.78.

The Mishna: Treatment of the Bite of a Rabid Dog

If someone has been bitten by a mad dog, then he should not be treated by the ingestion of its liver appendage (חצר הכבד).[24] R. Mattia b. Heresh opines that this is permitted. The same Mattia b. Heresh said: If someone has pains in his throat, it is permitted to pour medicine in his mouth on the Sabbath, as there is in this case a condition that possibly threatens life;[25] any such condition is suspending the laws of the Sabbath. (mYom 8:6)

The prohibition against using the חצר הכבד of the rabid dog as a medicine is not motivated by the fact that the dog is an unclean animal. The Mishna says just before the passage cited above: 'If someone is stricken with בולימיה (boulimia), he may be given even forbidden foods, until his eyes light up.'[26] The discussion between the editor of the Mishna and R. Mattia b. Heresh is only about the therapeutic value of the treatment. R. Mattia lived in Rome[27] and probably relied on authors such as Pliny (Nat. hist. 29:32), but even 'scientific' authors such as Dioscorides and Galen[28] recommended the treatment. R. Yehuda the Prince, however, the editor of the Mishna, witnessed how this nostrum was given to a Germanic slave that had been bitten – and failed to cure him.[29]

It is of course nonsense to consider such therapy as an equivalent to modern antitoxic serum-therapy, as has been contended at the end of the nineteenth century when this kind of cure was brand-new. It was rather based on the theory of sympathies[30] or on the principle dating back from ancient Greek sources: Similia similibus.[31]

The Babylonian Talmud: A Case of Hemophilia

(A woman) who has (had) her first son circumcised and he died, her second (son) and he died – the third (son) will not be circumcised: words of Rabbi (Yehuda the Prince). Rabban Shimon ben Gamliel said: the third she should

---

[24] The 'liver appendage' corresponds to the biblical יותרת הכבד. The term חצר is of Syrian origin and is equal to the Hebrew אצבע (הכבד), as in mTam 4:3. This appendage or 'finger' is generally considered as featuring the lobus caudatus of the liver, but there are diverse opinions.

[25] A condition that possibly threatens life (ספק נפשות), means that even when life is not now in danger, but the disease may spread or develop into a dangerous condition, the laws of the Sabbath are suspended (פיקוח נפש).

[26] βουλιμία is a disease characterised by a constant, insatiable hunger. The lighting up of the eyes means that the sick person regains his senses, and comes back to consciousness.

[27] R. Mattia b. Heresh lived in the second century CE. He headed a talmudic academy in Rome.

[28] Dioscorides (440-490 CE), Materia medica 2:49. Galen: De simplic. medic. temper. ac facult., 11:10 (Kühn vol 12, 335).

[29] yYom 8:5, 45b. R. Yehuda thought nobody can say he was bitten by a rabid dog and live (i.e., be cured).

[30] A theory that has persisted in folk medicine, and is transcultural. Another custom was to take a hair of the mad dog to heal the bite.

[31] Similia similibus curantur, 'like cures like', is the chief principle of homeopathy; it has however a long history, having been mentioned already in the Hippocratic corpus.

circumcise, the fourth not... Said Rabbi Hiyya bar Abba, said Rabbi Yohanan: it happened that there were four sisters at Sepphoris. The first had (her son) circumcised and he died. The second (did the same) and he died. The third (also) and he died. The fourth came before Rabban Shimon ben Gamliel. He said to her: do not circumcise (him). But (it is objected) he would perhaps have said the same to the third if she would have come to him! What could then be the meaning of Rabbi Hiyya bar Abba's statement ? Perhaps he wanted to teach us that there is also a possibility of *hazaka*[32] with sisters and not only if it appears 3 times with the same mother. Said Rabba, if you state that there is a hazakah with sisters, then no man should marry a woman coming from a family of epileptics or of lepers.[33] (bYev 64b)

We shall not delve into the details of this matter; what is evidently meant is the influence of heredity on the disease now known as hemophilia. Several lines later on the same page of the Talmud, the case of circumcision is presented: 'There are families where the blood is thin (i.e., who bleed profusely) and families where the blood is tied up (i.e., they bleed little when wounded).'

Another case related to circumcision and to the distribution of blood in the body appears in bShab 134a:[34]

Said Rabbi Natan: Once I travelled to the sea-district[35] and a woman came before me who had circumcised her first son and he died, the second (son) the same, the third she brought before me. I saw that he was red and said to her: wait till his blood will get swallowed [or: absorbed] into him. So she waited till his blood was absorbed, and had him circumcised and he lived. They called him Natan-the-Babylonian after my name.

Yet another case follows in which a child was pale (ירוק, green)[36] and R. Natan 'saw no blood of the covenant';[37] the mother was advised to wait till 'the blood would fall into him' and the child lived. The first case apparently presented a danger of bleeding; the second, a danger of anemia and feebleness.

Firstly, let us make some brief comments on the protagonists of these two statements. 'Rabbi' (Yehuda the Prince), of the fifth generation of Tannaim, was the main compiler of the Mishna. R. Natan 'the Babylonian' was a con-

---

[32] חזקה is a legal principle according to which an actual condition is considered established and immutable, until evidence of a change is produced.

[33] Epilepsy and leprosy were often considered heriditary in antiquity. It should moreover be clear that the צרעת of the Bible was certainly not (only) leprosy and that in later times the term remained indefinite and equivocal.

[34] See also bHul 47b. The same text (with minor changes) may be found in tShab 15:8.

[35] The Yerushalmi reads that R. Natan travelled to Caesarea in Cappadocia. This town was the capital, also called Mazaga, where an important Jewish community existed since the first century CE. Political links are documented since Hasmonean times between Cappadocia and Judaea.

[36] One should be very cautious in the translation of ירוק. In modern Hebrew it means 'green', but in ancient times it was also used for 'yellow' (cf chlorosis). In our case, the newborn was anemic, not jaundiced.

[37] Thus, circumcision would be dangerous, and furthermore inadequate, as covenant blood is required.

temporary of the above mentioned (c. 165-200). R. Yohanan (ha-Nappah) died in 279. He was born in Sepphoris, where he later headed the talmudic academy. He founded the academy of Tiberias. He is twice called 'approved physician' (רופא מומחה),[38] although this does not necessarily mean that he practised medicine. R. Hiyya bar Abba, who was a pupil of R. Yohanan, lived in the third century, in Babylonia and Palestine.[39] R. Shimon b. Gamliel II lived and flourished in Usha (140-170). Although his son R. Yehuda the Prince began to lead the academy of Beth Shearim when Shimon b. Gamliel abandoned his leadership at Usha, the eleventh century commentator Rashi curiously remarks that R. Yohanan could possibly have witnessed the case if it had happened at the end of R. Shimon's life. This seems hardly possible, knowing that R. Yohanan was born around 180.

The text cited above has the usual characteristics of talmudic discussions: short and concise statements, disagreement between two Tannaim, followed by an illustration by Amoraim, who present a brief case-history. The first case occurred in Sepphoris, a town in western Galilee where R. Yohanan was born and lived and where he could personally know members of the family that was stricken by hemophilia.

The remarkable comment appearing later on in the text, to the effect that there are families where the blood is 'thin', lends to this description an unusual air of clinical and epidemiological accuracy. Hemophilia is a disease transmitted by women but affecting only their male offspring. The disease was nowhere mentioned throughout antiquity and the Middle Ages and its hereditary transmission was recognized only in the early nineteenth century.[40]

Our second fragment, from the tractate Shabbat and involving the Tanna R. Natan, has a very lively and congenial styling: 'Once I travelled ...and my name was given to the child'. The terms red (אדום) and pale (ירוק) could describe a plethoric new-born and an anemic one, possibly as a consequence of what is called a maternal-foetal, resp. a foeto-maternal transfusion. Here, the hereditary aspect is less evident, as these symptoms have nothing to do with hemophilia. But again, the power of observation of the sages should be stressed, as should their unanimous decision to break the law as soon as a life is in danger.

A final comment on this passage involves the interesting information that Rabbi Yehuda the Prince and R. Natan the Babylonian were near contemporaries of Galen, the famous physician of Pergamon and founding father of medieval medical science, who initiated his practice in Rome in 164.

---

[38] See bAZ 28a, where the same title is given to Rabbi Abbahu as well.
[39] We are told (bBer 5b) that when R. Hiyya bar Abba was ill, his teacher and colleague R. Yohanan came to visit him and reached him a helping hand, and 'brought him up'.
[40] The paper of J.C. Otto (1774-1844) on hemophilia appeared in *Med. Repository*, N.Y., 1803, VI: 1-4.

The Minor Talmudic Tractates:
The Macrocosm-Microcosm Analogy

The following story involves the Tanna R. Yossi ha-Gelili, one of the great scholars of Yavne who lived at the beginning of the second century. He was a 'master of aggada' and performed miracles such as successful prayers for rain.

> Said Rabbi Yossi ha-Gelili: everything that God has created on earth he (also) created in man... and he formed in man everything he created in his world. He created forests in the world and created forests in man – these are man's hair. He created evil beasts in the world and evil beasts in man – these are man's entrails.[41] He created fissures in the world and fissures in man: these are man's ears. He created scents[42] in the world and scents in man – these are man's nostrils. Sun in the world, sun in man – this is man's light [or rather: forehead]. Stagnant waters in the world, stagnant waters in man – this is the nasal rheum of man. Salt waters in the world, salt waters in man – these are man's tears.[43] Streams in the world, and streams in man – urine.[44] (ARN a31, 46a-b)

More details follow of the analogy between microcosm and macrocosm, and a schematic overview may be given:

walls	– lips	mashing-mills	– spleen
doors	– teeth	pits	– navel
firmaments	– tongue	running waters	– urine[45]
sweet waters	– spittle	life	– blood
jaws (stars)	– cheeks	trees	– bones
towers	– neck	hills	– buttocks
masts	– arms	pestle + mortar	– joints
pegs	– fingers	horses	– legs
king	– head[46]	angel of death	– heels
counsellors	– kidneys	mountains	– standing man
mill-stones	– stomach	and valleys	– and fallen man

We do not intend to present a detailed account of the topic of microcosm and macrocosm in Jewish tradition.[47] The man-to-world analogy was a favourite

---

[41] Other (more accurate) version: 'vermin' or 'worms', see below at n49.

[42] Other version: 'wind', see below at n51.

[43] Other version: 'urine'.

[44] Other version: 'tears'.

[45] Other version:'blood'.

[46] Other version: 'heart'. This seems more accurate, although there was a long-lasted quarrel whether the seat of the soul (hence, the 'king') was in the heart or in the brain.

[47] This theme was particularly developed during the Middle Ages by such Jewish authors as Joseph Ibn-Zaddik (a contemporary of Maimonides), Bahya ibn Paquda, Ibn Gabirol, and prior to all of these, by Saadya Gaon. In ancient Jewish writings, the topic is also treated in MidrGad Exod 26:30, also in Midrash Tadshe 2 and Tanh Pikude 2. In these midrashic sources, the analogy is drawn between the world (cosmos), the tabernacle, and man. Philo also develops this theme in several of his works.

topic throughout antiquity, even from before the time of Aristotle, through the Hermetic, Gnostic, Neo-Platonic, Orphic and Stoic schools, and cultivated also by the Arabic Brethren of Sincerity, by Al-Kindi and, probably under his influence, by the Jewish physician Yitshak Yisraeli who was mentioned above.

The language used in this text is taken from Scripture in part, and in particular from the anthropomorphic descriptions in the Song of Songs and Ecclesiastes (ch. 12). Other terms of comparison are taken from homiletic commentaries which also appear in the Talmud and/or the midrash. Some analogies are based on ancient physiological ideas (spleen – mashing mills; stomach – millstones...), some others on alliterative analogies.[48]

Several philological problems could be raised with regard to our text, owing to its different versions. For example, as to the 'evil beasts' in man and in the world, for the more correct reading 'entrails'[49] the printed editions usually have 'vermin'. The reason is probably an error of the copyists, whereby the original כנים, which can also be termed כנימות (vermin), was distorted into בני מעים (entrails, intestines).[50] These 'evil beasts' (vermin) are in the hair (just preceding) and the general order of the analogy (de capite ad calcem) excludes the entrails from this location. A similar error of copyists exists between the word 'wind' (רוח) and 'scent' (ריח), the latter being more plausible.[51]

The fifth analogy reads: 'Sun in the world, sun in man, this is man's light (or forehead).' This opinion is apparently based on a commentary on Eccl 12:2 in the Babylonian Talmud which states: '"Until the sun and the light become dark" – these are the forehead and the nostrils (nose)' (bShab 151b). Rashi ad loc. explains: the forehead is glossy and therefore shines more than any other part of the face.

The same text also provides an explanation for the analogy between stars and cheeks. Not only the sun and light, but also the moon and stars become darkened. The Talmud explains: 'The moon is the soul; the stars are the cheeks.' According to Rashi on Eccl 12:2 this refers to the upper part of the cheeks, פומ"ליש, 'pommelles' – or in modern French: 'pommettes' – which also 'shine'.

The philosophical interpretation of the microcosm-macrocosm analogy is ambivalent. It can be seen as an attempt to view the whole creation as directed towards man, who was created last. It is, in fact, an effort to achieve unity, to reconcile man and nature. Thinking in analogies has always been a temptation of the human spirit, although this has not always been fruitful. Self-knowledge does not necessarily lead to knowledge of the whole world, though it should certainly precede it. As regards the influence of man's behaviour on the cos-

---

[48] Cf עצים – עצמות (etsim, trees – atsamot, bones); עגבות – גבעות (gevaot, hills – agavot, buttocks).
[49] Cf n41 above.
[50] Specialists well acquainted with the decipherment of manuscripts will not find this distortion too far-fetched.
[51] Cf n42 above.

mos, the same R. Yossi ha-Gelili said: 'A gathering of wicked people is bad for themselves and bad for the world; a gathering of the righteous is an enjoyment for themselves and for the world as well' (bSan 72b).

Two Extra-Rabbinic Texts Pertaining to Medical Ethics

Let us now turn to the 'Oath of Asaf':[52]

> This is the oath that was sworn by the disciples of Asaf son of Berakhyahu and Yohanan son of Zavda in these words:
>
> ...Do not follow the writs of the magicians, do not seek the help of idolatry for healing purposes...
>
> And now, put your confidence in the Eternal your God, Lord of truth, Living God, who kills and revives, smites and heals... He induces the growth of medicinal plants and in his great mercy places in the heart of the sages intelligence to heal... Remember Him at any time, pay him respect in truth, righteousness and straightforwardness, so that you succeed in all your undertakings and you will be offered His help to achieve successful work... Do not be led by haughty spirits and carry high your eyes and heart ...but keep His decrees and commandments and walk in His ways, in order to find grace in His eyes, be pure, faithful and righteous.

We have chosen this fragment featuring ethical and theological exhortations; not the paraphrase of the Hippocratic Oath which also appears in the same text, even twice. Before we attempt any further explanations, let us quote a closely similar passage from another famous but much earlier text, the Wisdom of Ben Sira or Ecclesiasticus:

> Honour the Physician before the time you need him,
>> he too is part of (the work of) God.
> From God he gets his wisdom
>> and he gets presents from the king.
> The physician's learning uplifts his head,
>> he stands erect before dignitaries. (...)
> My son, when diseased, do not grudge,
>> pray to God that He heal you. (...)
> Also to the physician provide a place (at your side),
>> there he should stay, he too is requisite:
> Some times success comes through his hands
>> As he also will pray the Lord. (...)
> He is a sinner before his Maker
>> whoever behaves haughtily in front of the physician. (Sir 38:1-15)

The Oath of Asaf was composed for physicians in Babylonia in the sixth or seventh century CE, whereas Ben Sira wrote for the average Jewish or rather Hebrew reader by the early second century BCE. Both texts insist on the ne-

---

[52] My translation. Full translation of Asaf's Oath: Friedenwald, *The Jews and Medicine*, 22f.

cessity of both the sick and the physician to pray to the Lord and Healer; both also stress the fact that God endows the physician with skill and wisdom and is the creator of medicinal plants. The style of the two texts, however, differs greatly. The Oath of Asaf is a formal exhortation, employing the plural, full of biblical reminiscences or slightly altered quotations. It is interesting to note that there is no talmudic reference or even mishnaic citation. It has nothing of the conciseness of the Hippocratic Oath, but is, on the contrary, a fine example of redundant oriental style.[53] On the other hand, the text of Ben Sira is a piece of unrhymed poetry in the style of the biblical Proverbs. Well balanced, the second part of the verse explains, completes or opposes the first half. Just as in Proverbs, the author addresses the reader directly, calling him 'my son'. The wording is biblical, being particularly close to that of Proverbs, Psalms and Job.[54] Many of Ben Sira's maxims have been used later on. For instance, the first verse quoted in our fragment: 'Honour the physician...' can be found, only slightly altered, in the Palestinian Talmud and various midrash collections.[55]

The significance of these two texts is worth noting. Ben Sira, though extra-canonical, is cited several times in the Talmud. Its attitude towards medicine and physicians stands in strong contrast to that of most prophetic and hagio-graphic texts. The latter usually exhorted kings and dignitaries not to rely on physicians, but rather pray to the Lord. Ben Sira, on the contrary, considers it sinful to despise the physician.

It should be noted that Asaf warns young physicians against the dangers of haughtiness, whereas Ben Sira apparently justifies a certain degree of pride and a high social status, owing to the knowledge of the physician, who is hon-oured by the King himself. A dissuasion from using magic cures or idolatry does not appear in this chapter of Ben Sira, but it is briefly referred to in an-other chapter[56] of the work. Both Asaf and Ben Sira, however, ultimately arrive at the same conclusion. The physician should be aware of the fact that he is but an intermediate agent of the Lord, his basic ethical exhortation throughout the centuries being a call for humility.

---

[53] On the Oath of Asaf see also Friedenwald *ib.*; Melzer, *Asaph*; Pines, 'Oath'; Lieber, 'Covenant'.
[54] On Ben Sira's Wisdom see e.g. Segal, *Sefer Ben Sira*; Kahana, *Ha-sefarim ha-hitsoniim*; Skehan – Di Lella, *Wisdom of Ben Sira*.
[55] yTaan 3:6, 66d; ExodR 20,1; Tanh Mikets 10; Alpha-beta de Ben-Sira s.v. *alef*. The 'Alphabeth of Ben Sira', existing in several versions, is a much later work of satirical and folkloric content, probably written in the Gaonic period.
[56] Sir 34:5, 'Magic, divination and dreams are mere vanity...'

Chapter Fifteen

Geography and Cosmography in Talmudic Literature

Zeev Safrai

The ancient Greeks and Romans pursued the study of geography and maintained a literature devoted to this discipline. Strabo, Pliny, Pausanias, Ptolemy and others devoted works or studies to this field. The sages of ancient Palestine were not so inclined. The Greco-Roman geographer was also wont to travel the world in order to get to know it, but in talmudic literature we do not find this phenomenon.

Nevertheless, the literature of the sages contains many passages reflective of a comparatble interest in geography, especially concerning the Land of Israel, that are worthy of study. The geographic traditions of the sages are not only helpful for understanding the geography of their own times, but also of the biblical period. They often preserve names and traditions from the biblical world which did not survive in other types of sources and thus span a chronological gap between that world and our times. To that extent, studying the traditions of the sages is relevant for ancient historical geography.

The Byzantine period saw the development of a new type of geographic literature: pilgrims' literature. This literature is basically a journey into the past, while mentioning holy sites of both the past and the present.[1] The relationship of the sages to holy sites was somewhat mixed. Jewish law dictates a blessing to be recited at the site of a miracle,[2] while there are different opinions

---

[1] For example, Wilkinson, *Egeria's Travels*; idem, *Jerusalem Pilgrims*; Notley and Safrai, *Onomasticon*.

[2] mBer 9:1. This halakha may well explain the discussions regarding the identification of sites mentioned in the Bible.

regarding the sanctity of holy graves.[3] In any event, there does not seem to have developed a Jewish pilgrim literature or guides to the 'holy sites' during the Mishna and Talmud periods. In fact, our sources do not indicate a very developed independent pursuit of geography for its own sake on the part of the sages.

Rabbinic Literature as a Source for Geography

We possess hundreds of geographic statements in rabbinic literature, but most appear embedded in traditions devoted to various realms of law or legend. An exception may be the rabbinic interest in 'cosmography' – a discipline located somewhere between the fields of geography and natural sciences. Even this subject, however, did not merit more independent treatment than that found in some rabbinic attempts at a description of the universe. Most of our geographic material, therefore, must be culled from various non-geographic tradition units. We can divide these into direct geographical statements, made either in the course of a narrative, or in a halakhic discussion, or in an aggadic discourse, and into statements made by way of commenting on the Bible, or midrash. The second type is a little more complicated and will be discussed in the following section.

In the first place, there is geographical information may be contained in narrative reports. Talmudic literature contains hundreds of traditions regarding various events of an assorted nature. These often contain information regarding the site of the event and other important details. Thus, for instance, a tradition describes sages travelling from Achzib to Acco who on their journey met a non-Jew who lived in one of the *burgi* in the area. The location of the events described may be of secondary importance for the purposes of the tradition, but in any event, it provides us with important information regarding this region, the forms of settlement in it and its inhabitants. Traditions such as this appear very often in talmudic literature and serve as sources of great importance in our understanding of the historical geography of Roman Palestine.[4] It should be added, however, that although most sources in talmudic literature are generally trustworthy, each source should of course be examined individually and carefully.[5]

In the second place, we find geographical information in halakhic discussions. The sages often explain a halakhic principle with the aid of geographic material. Thus, in a discussion of the laws of interest the sages mention 'Kefar Hanania and its environs' and, 'Kefar Sihin and its environs' as having many

---

[3] There are many traditions on this issue. See, for example, bSot 34b, bTaan 16a. Cf yTaan 1, 65a. The New Testament relates that Jesus expressed opposition to the cult of holy sites. See Luke 1:47; Matt 23:29. See Taylor, *Christians and the Holy Places*.
[4] tPes 1:15. Most sources of this type were collected by Klein, *Sefer Ha-Yishuv*.
[5] Klein, *On the History*.

ceramic workshops.[6] The principles involved could certainly have been explained in an understandable abstract manner. The geographic examples, however, provide a more tangible and concrete framework for the understanding of the issue at hand. This method is in keeping with the general 'causal' method of explanation in talmudic literature.[7] Of particular importance are the border sites mentioned in the description of the halakhic boundaries of the Land of Israel. There are a number of commandments which apply only to the Land of Israel. Halakhic boundaries were usually equivalent to the extent of Jewish settlement. Many sources deal with the halakhic status of various settlements or regions. These sources are usually extremely important in tracing demographic developments in the Land of Israel. Thus, as we have just stated, the source which systematically describes the halakhic boundaries of the Land of Israel is of paramount importance for the understanding of the demography of the Land of Israel and the extent of Jewish settlement. Similar sources are, likewise, of similar importance.[8] Halakhic sources are more exact by nature, since observance depends on the exactitude of description. This is also the case with the geographic information they contain, and it is also less liable to error in the course of transmission. There are, however, exceptions which must be examined carefully before their geographic information can be utilized.

In the third place, geographic information appears in aggadic and moralistic literature. Thus, in describing the damage caused when the Torah is not studied for one day, a tradition relates a parable of two people who travel from Tiberias to Sepphoris and meet at Mashkanah. Indeed, Khirbet Meskene is exactly halfway between the two cities mentioned and remains of the ancient road station have perhaps even been found there.[9] As was the case in the halakhic traditions, this information is generally trustworthy, provided there are no copyists' errors or errors in transmission. However, aggadic traditions do at times engage in exaggeration, and this may of course influence some of the geographic material.

Geographical Traditions in Midrash

When commenting on the Bible, the sages dealt also with the geographic passages contained in it, explaining geographic idioms and providing identifications for sites mentioned. These midrashim differ from the material discussed so far since in this case the geographic information becomes the purpose of the rabbinic teaching and no longer is simply tangential to halakhic or aggadic

---

[6] tBM 6:3 and parallel sources.
[7] See S. Safrai, 'Halakha', 163-168.
[8] See, for example, Büchler, 'Der Patriarch R. Jehuda'; Hildesheimer, *Beiträge*; Klein, 'Grenzverzeichnis'; Sussmann, 'Halakhic Inscription'; Sussmann, 'Baraita of the Boundaries'; Z. Safrai, 'Marginal Notes'. See also mMS 5:2; tAZ 6(7):8; bGit 40a.
[9] yBer 9, 14d; bShab 26a; bSuk 45a

motifs. Identifications of this sort are quite prevalent in the Targumim. We can discern various types of midrash containing geographical information.

First to be mentioned is simple midrash, i.e., midrash that seeks to explain the plain meaning of the geographic information in the Bible. Thus the many traditions on the olive oil in the portion of the tribe of Asher are based on knowledge of the region. Likewise, the biblical phrase 'couching down between the sheepfolds' regarding the territory of Issachar was taken by the sages to apply to the two plains in this territory: the plain of Exaloth and the plain of Jezreel.[10] This explanation may not reflect the real meaning of the phrase, but it certainly is in keeping with the geographic reality of the region and it is likely that the author of the tradition thought that it was the 'simple' explanation of the verse.

In like manner, the sages identified settlements mentioned in the Bible. The simple identifications are usually based on a phonetic similarity between the name of the settlement in the Bible and the contemporary talmudic name. In most regions of the Land of Israel, there was a continuity of settlement from biblical times to the period of Mishna and Talmud, and similar languages were spoken by the inhabitants of thee regions. The biblical name was, therefore, often preserved or some similar form to it existed. Thus a whole series of sites listed in the territory of Naphtali were identified (Josh 19:33): Heleph – Heleph; Elon – Eilin; Bezaanannim – Agenia d'Qadesh (based on a translation of the name); Adami – Damin; Yabneel – Kefar Iamma; Lakum – Lukim.[11] Such identifications were often based on the switching of similar letters in the Hebrew alphabet such as aleph and he. This phenomenon is quite prevalent in all of Midrashic literature and at times is even justified from a philological or phonetic standpoint.[12]

Phonetic similarity is accepted even today as the major tool in the identification of sites, although it is clear to modern scholars that additional factors must be taken into consideration.[13] In particular, it is necessary to pinpoint the region in question and to determine the relationship of the site in question to neighbouring settlements. The sages, however, seemed to have a rather limited regional and spatial approach.[14] Thus, for instance, Kinneret in the territory of Naphtali was identified with a site with a similar name near Beth Shean, even

---

[10] GenR 98(99), (p1263). Z. Safrai, 'Geographical Midrashim'; idem, Boundaries and Administration, 178-194.

[11] yMeg 1, 70a; yShev 9, 38d and many additional identifications.

[12] Aharoni, Land of the Bible, 115-118; Kampffmeyer, 'Alte Namen im heutigen Palastina und Syrien'. The rules of transcription must be examined anew in light of modern research, as e.g., Rainey, 'Toponymics' has already done.

[13] Aharoni ib. 124-129. The dependence on simple phonetic identification has lead to many errors. A discussion of this phenomenon is beyond the scope of this study.

[14] Thus, for example, when the sages sought an identification for Tiberias, they knew that it was to be found in the biblical sites near the Sea of Galilee. See yMeg 1, 70a; bMeg 5b-6a. See also Z. Safrai, 'Geographical Midrashim', 85f.

though this place was quite distant from the territory of Naphtali.[15] In all fairness to the sages though, such mistakes are characteristic of historical geography until modern times, and are found in Eusebius, or Christian pilgrim literature, or for that matter in scholarly literature before the twentieth century.[16] These derashot are, as we have stated, extremely important for the study of the historical geography of the period of Mishna and Talmud. Their value for the study of the biblical period is much more limited.

A second type to be mentioned is homiletic midrash. Here, the author makes the verse and the geographical content in it dependent on the particular idea that he is trying to impart. Thus, for instance, the third century sage R. Yohanan states that 'Adam' and 'Zarethan' mentioned in Josh 3:16 regarding the waters of the Jordan were twelve miles apart. This is not based on the actual distance between these two settlements, but rather on the derash that the size of the camp of the Children of Israel was twelve miles. The distance between the two cities mentioned above was accommodated to this legend.[17] Other 'identifications' were made in a similar manner. The plain meaning of a geographical text in the Bible was often ignored and identifications were made based on derash, legend or allusions to events or places that were not included in the original intent of the verse. It should be stressed that these derashot do not indicate a lack of knowledge regarding the geography of the Land of Israel, but rather an accepted literary motif.

A third type is midrash that contains factual information, either based on historical tradition, on contemporary reality, or on etymology. The Yerushalmi contains a list of identifications of settlements in the Transjordan, some of which are based on phonetic similarity, a method which we have already discussed, but two are quite strange. Succoth is identified with Tarelah and Zaphon with Amathu,[18] undoubtedly on the basis of some ancient tradition

---

[15] GenR 33,7 (p309). See GenR 98(99),15 (p1267). This appears together with derashot identifying it with Gennesaret. See GenR ib.; yMeg 1, 70a; bMeg 6a. Even so it appears that there were settlements near Beth Shean called Kinneret and Arav. The mistake of the sages was identifying them with the sites mentioned in the Bible. The mistake undoubtedly was the result of their lack of a regional and spatial approach.

[16] See Notley and Safrai, Onomasticon, xxxiii-xxxvi; Aharoni, Land of the Bible, 94-117.

[17] tSot 8:3; bSot 34a; see there for additional examples. PesRK, Ki Tisa (p30f); bYom 22b. In this case the author of the derash had difficulty with the simple meaning. but the solution offered is more of a homiletical nature. Thus, the place name Hadrach was explained as being sharp (חד) to Israel and soft (רך) to the nations. See SifDeut 1 (p7); PesRK, Roni akara 7 (p317) and parallels. There are many other examples. See Safrai, 'Geographical Midrashim', 81f. To this type of derasha it is necessary to add the associative translations often found in the Targumim. Thus 'Zin' in the Negev is translated as 'Thorn-Palms of the Iron Mount' (PsYon Num 33:36; Neof Num 34:3-4; FrgPTg Num 34:4). This is an associative translation based on the Mishna which states that 'Thorn-Palms of the Iron Mount' are valid as lulavim (palm branches) used on the Sukkot festival. These branches did indeed come from the Iron Mount in the Peraea (mSuk 3:1). Likewise, the translations of Ps-Yonatan and Neophyti to the section dealing with the boundaries of the Land of Israel are perhaps based on the Baraita of the Boundaries of the Land of Israel (see n7 above).

[18] yShev 9, 38d.

possessed by the sages. Today it is clear that at least one of these identifications is not correct. Succoth is not to be identified with Tarelah (Deir Alla) but with a nearby Tell.

The midrash may also be based on contemporary reality. The sages state, for example, that Shilo was an enclave of the territory of Joseph within the territory of Benjamin. It is clear, however, that Shilo was within the geographic territory of Joseph. The author of the teaching, however, was faced with the problem of identifying a Jewish settlement in an area which by his time had become identified with the Samaritans.[19] In a similar manner, the city of Caesarea was 'identified' with the Philistine settlement Ekron whose correct location was not known by the sages.[20]

Finally, there is etymological midrash which explains a geographical name from its philological connotation or geographic nature. Thus, Tsippori (Sepphoris) lies on the top of a mountain like a bird (צפור, bird)[21] and indeed, Tsippori is located on the top of a steep hill. Of course, there are also purely homiletic etymologies such as the Desert of Shur which is explained by the desire of Israel to make there many lines (from שורה, line: ExodR 24) or Tseltsah by 'shade' (צל) as clear (צח) as the light of day (Midrash Shmuel 14). The etymologies, even the simple ones, present a problem. It is impossible to know whether the etymology occasioned the name to be given or, conversely, was intended to explain an existing name. In any event, simple etymologies are often an aid in the identifying of sites[22] or describing them, although most often the etymology is anachronistic. Etymologic midrash often is based on the switching of related letters of the alphabet, as we have observed also with the simple midrash.

The Geography of the Land of Israel According to the Sages

Talmudic literature deals with the geography of the Land of Israel on two levels. The first deals with the contemporary geography of the sages, while the second examines the geography of Land of Israel during the biblical period. This second sphere might be described as the historical geography of the biblical period. As we have seen above, the sages did not always draw a fine line

[19] yMeg 1, 72d; bZev 118b. This is likewise assumed by Epiphanius, De XII Gemmis 5.12. See Safrai, 'Boundaries', 183f.
[20] bMeg 6a. This is also found in Jerome's translation of the Onomasticon of Eusebius p12, line 23 on the entry Ekron; Notley and Safrai, Onomasticon 1, 22f. There are many other such examples.
[21] bMeg 6a. For additional etymologies see bSot 48b; bTem 16a. See also Ezek 48:2-5, MidrTann Deut 32:12 (p197); MekRY shira 10 (p149).
[22] For a collection of these derashot see Harduf, Biblical Proper Names; idem, Exegesis of Biblical Proper Names. The collection is extensive, but the use of the material is quite unsophisticated. An example of this type of derasha is that the name Jordan derives from the fact that one of the sources of the Jordan is the Dan. See bBekh 55a and parallels.

between these two spheres, and in all fairness, they were perhaps not even aware of the two categories. Just as the sages could describe Moses in terms of a contemporary sage, they could identify biblical sites in light of contemporary geography. Thus, some of the material which purports to deal with earlier periods probably deals with the contemporary geography of the sages.

Although the sages occasionally evince a tendency towards exaggeration and their descriptions may be schematic due to the requirements of literary aggadic forms, they also exhibit an excellent knowledge, and their traditions are the best source for the geography of the Land of Israel in the Roman-Byzantine period.

Talmudic literature has preserved the names of hundreds of ancient settlements and numerous traditions on the various regions of the Land of Israel, the crops grown in each region and the demographic developments there. There are also traditions regarding the economic structure of cities and villages and the relationship between the various levels and types of settlement. The expertise of the sages has served as the framework for many modern works of scholarship and the research into the geographic traditions of the sages continues to produce fruitful results today.[23]

The geographic traditions of the sages rarely contain gross errors or such fantastic legends as found at times in the works of Josephus[24] or more often in the pilgrim literature of the Byzantine period or the Middle Ages. The sages do not tell such tales of rivers that do not flow on the Sabbath, or of asphalt in the Dead Sea which can be cut only by menstrual blood. Nor did they present many schematic descriptions of the geography of the Land of Israel. An exception might be the tradition that the future portions of the tribes would be a rectangle which measured 'length by width 25,000 reeds, which are 75 miles'.[25] And this teaching is actually dependent on the biblical account in Ezek 48:2, 6, 7.

The expertise of the sages, however, was mostly limited to the Land of Israel west of the Jordan. Their knowledge of the lands east of the Jordan was quite limited and there are only a few traditions which relate to this area. Moreover, some of their information in these traditions is not correct. The description of the Peraea in the baraita which describes the halakhic boundaries of the Land of Israel is schematic and dependent on biblical verses.[26] Likewise, the rabbinic division of the Peraea (yShev 9, 38d) is dependent on the biblical selection of Numbers 32 and on the description of the lighting of

---

[23] See e.g. Avi-Yonah, *Holy Land*; Klein, *Eretz Yehudah*; idem, *Galilee*; J. Schwartz, *Jewish Settlement*.

[24] Shahar, *Josephus Geographicus*. Cf the aggada that the source of the Jordan is the pool of *Phiale*, War 3:510f. The legend of the Sambation River appears only in late Midrashim such as NumR 16,25 or in medieval Midrashim. It does, however, appear in PsYon to Exod 34:10.

[25] MidrTann Deut 32:12 (p197), MekRY, Shira 10 (p149). Ezek 48:2-5 is the source of this schematic approach.

[26] Sussmann, 'Baraita', 233-238.

torches to indicate the new moon in this region (tRH 2:2). This is the case even though these texts deal so to say with actual halakhic instructions.[27] It is also the most likely reason for the great number of identification of sites in the Aramaic translations of the Bible (simple identifications, some of which are incorrect) dealing with the Peraea. The translators sought to identify those sites which were not generally familiar to their readers.[28] This manner of identifying sites based on earlier biblical references is more characteristic of the Middle Ages when the geography of the Bible was better known than contemporary geography and every quote from Holy Scriptures was considered to possess an eternal actuality? It should be remembered that Christian and Jewish authors wrote geographies of the 'Holy Land'. One of the purposes of these works was to explain the Holy Writ.[29] The lack of rabbinic knowledge regarding the Peraea was probably the result of the destruction of Jewish settlement there after the Bar- Kokhba revolt.[30]

The Bavli is less familiar with the geography of the Land of Israel. Although this Talmud does at times evince detailed knowledge of geography and attendant factors, it tends to err more often. This higher degree of error undoubtedly stems from a lack of knowledge in certain spheres. Thus the Bavli relates that the distance from Tiberias to Migdal was only a mile, while the actual distance was closer to four miles as is stated in the Yerushalmi.[31] The Bavli also states that the boundaries of Jewish settlement during the Second Temple period were the same, or perhaps even smaller than those of the Land of Israel during the First Temple period.[32] The Bavli was also under the impression that one could traverse the distance between the Land of Israel and the Euphrates in three days' time. Both of these incorrect assertions appear in discussions relating to the application of various laws and not in legend or aggada. It is difficult to know if this phenomenon is indicative of the Amoraic period in Babylonia, or at least of part of the Amoraim there, or whether it simply reflects the later editors of this literature. In any event, important geographic traditions were preserved in the Bavli, although, as we have seen now, there is an incidence of mistakes and questionable geographic traditions. However, these types of mistakes in the Bavli are not limited to geography, history and related fields also suffer in this aspect, and this seems to be a result of the

---

[27] Z. Safrai, 'Bar-Kochva Revolt'.

[28] Translations of names and identifications appear, for the most part, regarding areas outside of the Land of Israel. This issue has yet to be studied.

[29] For this type of writing see Dillon, *Pilgrims*.

[30] On the Jewish settlement east of Jordan and its history see Sagiv, *Jewish Settlement*.

[31] yPes 3, 30a; bPes 46a.

[32] bBM 28a. Extremely strange is the comment that there were two cities called Jerusalem. Even the traditional commentators considered this to be unusual. See bAr 32a-b, and Rashi and Meiri *ad loc*. See also bPes 93b. In the last two examples the deviation from the real geography may result from the requirements of the Talmudic discussion. This is not the case in the last example since it is this deviation which causes the difficulties.

willingness of the Bavli to sacrifice realism for the sake of internal dialectics. We are unable to estimate how familiar they were with Babylonian geography.

The knowledge of the sages, including the Palestinian ones, regarding all aspects of the biblical period was quite limited. Thus, for instance, the rabbinic list of walled cities in the Land of Israel from the days of the sages (mAr 9:6; Sifra Behar 4,1) and not the biblical period.

The sages probably did possess some real traditions regarding the biblical period, but these can hardly serve as a basis for the study of that period. The facts that they do preserve in this sphere do, however, often serve as a chronological bridge of sorts between the biblical period and modern times.

World Geography and Cosmography

If the sages did not deal with the geography of the Land of Israel as a separate discipline, it is understandable that they did not do so vis-a-vis world geography. Even so, through logical deliberation and study, the sages often were able to arrive at correct geographical conclusions. Thus, for example, talmudic literature contains laws regarding land use[33] and ecology,[34] issues which were also important in the Roman world. The sages intuitively often understood models which were developed only at the end of the nineteenth century. Thus the sages exhibit a basic understanding of the model developed by von Thünen regarding the zoning of land usage and the importance of proximity to an urban centre.[35] This model was also familiar in an elementary form to the ancient Romans.[36] They were also aware of aspects of physical geography, such as water cycles in nature[37] and the various climates in the Land of Israel and the world.

The sages did not often elaborate on the regions outside of the Land of Israel. They did have knowledge on other countries. The sages also travelled throughout the Jewish Diaspora, and there were social and economic ties between the Palestinian Jews and those in the Diaspora. Even so, few descriptions of foreign lands have remained in talmudic literature. This does not include Babylonia, the largest Jewish Diaspora during the Talmud period. The Jews there also established local academies and it is understandable, therefore, that both the Palestinian sages and, especially, those of Babylonia transmitted numerous traditions about many aspects of Babylonian life and geography.[38] Thus, for example, the sages describe the extent of Jewish settlement in Baby-

---

[33] E.g. Sifra Behar 6,4. For a basic collection of sources on ecology see Kotler, *Human Ecology.*

[34] E.g. bBer 46a. Von Thünen, *Isolated State.*

[35] Varro 1.16; Columella, De re rustica 1.22 *et al.*

[36] GenR 4,5 (p28f) and the discussion there 12,1 (p119-121). See also GenR 12,1 (p119-120) as against bTaan 8b. It goes without saying that many of the opinions of the sages on these matters are unacceptable today. See, for example, GenR 13,17 (p126); yBer 9, 14a; mAZ 3:3; ExodR 5,9.

[37] Oppenheimer, *Babylonia Judaica.*

[38] SifDeut 38-40 (p73-84); bTaan 24b.

Ionia. The description itself is realistic enough, although it is based on aggadic identifications of sites mentioned in the Bible.[39] A few traditions do refer to Egypt and compare conditions there to those in the Land of Israel.[35] Some additional sources deal with Italy, but it is easy to see that the sages were not overly familiar with that country.[40]

The structure of the world was of great importance for the sages. As we have stated, however, they did not devote independent works to this field, unlike their Greek and Roman counterparts, but there are fairly large collections of baraitot and sayings dealing with the form of the world and the history of creation. The study of the form and shape of the world was considered an important means of understanding the Divine nature, together with Merkava mysticism and creation. The sages placed strictures and limitations on the last two because of the importance and sensitivity of the issues involved.[41]

There was no uniform Jewish cosmogony. It is possible, though, to isolate a number of factors or motifs common to the talmudic outlook on cosmography. Two basic categories can be discerned: mythological cosmography and realistic cosmography.

Mythological cosmography was popular in Greek geographic research in the fifth-fourth centuries BCE. It was characterized by a schematic approach and by a geographic approach to the gods in the sense that Oceanus was thought to encompass the world, or that Atlas held it on his shoulders. This mythic-geographic framework served as the basis for rabbinic cosmography. The sages also state, for instance, that Oceanus surrounds the world,[42] the earth is similar to a plate or platter and the heavens are like the cover to this plate[43] and that the world floats upon the waters and the earth floats upon the sea like a boat.[44] The mythological basis for these midrashim is in a synthesis of Greek mythology, ancient eastern mythology (Canaanite?) or ancient Israelite epic poetry which is similar to this mythology. All of this is then placed within a framework of Jewish thought and morality. Thus the midrashim cited above are based on Greek mythology. Other midrashim state that the earth floats on the waters of the abyss. This is an eastern motif since the 'abyss' (*tehom*) is really the name of the Canaanite goddess Tiamat. Likewise, the midrash that the 'Leviathan, the slant serpent which resides in the middle waters and holds

---

[39] bKid 72a and parallels
[40] Scott, *Geography*.
[41] mHag 2:1; tHag. 2:1; yHag 2, 87a; bHag 11b-12a. For a collection of sources see yHag *ib.* and bHag 11b-16a. See also late Midrashim such as Midrash Maase Bereshit, Midrash Konen and Midrash Neelam. These works deal with the cosmographical elements of creation ('Maase Bereshit') and the Merkava ('Maase Merkava'). The sages had various definitions for the exact meaning of the phrase 'Maase Bereshit', see yHag *ib.*
[42] E.g. yAZ 3, 42c; PRE 3; DEZ 9; GenR 23,7 (p228f); Midrash Konen; bEr 22b; bBer 17a; bShab 25b; MidrGad Gen 1:9 (p30); MidrGad Gen 1:6 (p26). See also Krauss, *Lehnwörter, s.v.* Oceanus.
[43] E.g. GenR 4,5 (p28f); GenR 3,10 (p119f). NumR 13,16; EsthR 1,7; MidrPs 93:5 (p415) *et al.*
[44] E.g. MidrPs 93:5 (p415); PRE 5; Midrash Neelam *et al.*

the middle foundation of the earth between his two fins,[45] is based on early Israelite myth, as Cassuto has shown.[46]

The mythological tradition regarding the pillars which hold up the world illustrates the incorporating of the mythological into Jewish thought: 'It rests on one pillar, and its name is "Righteous", for it is said, "But Righteous is the foundation of the world".'[47] Here the mythological material is used for an expressed Jewish purpose. The specific Jewish element of this cosmography is represented by the combination of various mythologies with Jewish thought and morality

As we have seen above, most rabbinic traditions on cosmography were influenced by Greek mythology. By the third century BCE, however, Greek geography had begun a process of de-mythologization and geographic study began to take on a more realistic approach.[48] This development is hardly reflected in talmudic literature. There are, though, a few examples of the more sophisticated approach to geography. Thus a tradition states that the 'length of the world was five hundred years, its width five hundred years and its thickness five hundred years. Some say it is round and that the ocean returns to the world like a vault.[49] Another tradition establishes that the world is a third settlement, a third water, and a third desert.[50] The only tradition about the circumference of the earth which does not represent a number chosen simply at random is the tradition of 6000 *parsa* (35,000 km).[51] According to Aratus of Soli (third century BCE) the circumference of the earth was 78,000 stadia. Marinus of Tyre (first century CE) claimed it was 91,000 stadia.[52]

The sages also tried to determine the number of different peoples or nations in the world. Their conclusions, however, were somewhat strange. The accepted number of seventy nations is schematic. The two hundred and fifty eparchies or the hundred states (*medinot*)[53] may not be schematic, but they are certainly not realistic. The same can be said for the tradition that the world

---

[45] bBava Batra 74b; PRE 9; Midrash Konen; Seder Rabba de-Bereshit 17 *et al.* The combination of Canaanite mythology with Greek mythology is exemplified by the description of the revolt of Oceanus, a Greek mythological figure identified with Rahab or Tehom who are Canaanite deities. See ExodR 21,2 *et al.*

[46] Cassuto, 'Israelite Epic'. Cassuto showed that the Bible contains veiled references to Canaanite mythology. Some of these motifs were then formulated in the Bible or in Talmudic literature in a way acceptable in Jewish thought, cf Smythe, *Babylonian Influence*.

[47] bHag 12b; MidrPs 136,5 (p520); Seder Rabba de-Bereshit 17; Midrash Konen. For a similar moralistic and theological approach see ExodR 2,13.

[48] Harley and Woodward, *History of Cartography*; Dilke, *Maps*.

[49] Seder Rabba de-Bereshit 17. Cf PRE 23; bBB 25a; Midrash Konen.

[50] Midrash Konen. Cf PRE 24.

[51] bPes 94b; yAZ 3, 42c; NumR 13,16.

[52] Dilke, *Mathematics*.

[53] EsthR 1,5; PRE 36.

contains a hundred and four states, ninety-nine islands, seventy-two languages and sixteen types of script.[54]

In sum, the sages may not have been conversant in Greek geography, but they were well acquainted with the geography of the Land of Israel and of Babylonia and their traditions and teachings on these two countries may well serve the scholar of ancient geography.

---

[54] MidrGad Gen 10:32 (p196).

Chapter Sixteen

Biology in Rabbinic Literature: Fact and Folklore

Abraham Ofir Shemesh

The literature of the sages contains extremely interesting material regarding many aspects of human and animal biology. The sages drew their knowledge of biology and nature from three primary sources of information: firstly, observations and experiments on vegetation and animal behaviour, with the aim of exploring laws relating to various areas of halakha;[1] secondly, common knowledge and rumours in the scholar's locality, originating from travellers, nomads and sailors who, in their travels in the ancient East, learned of unfamiliar and sometimes legendary creatures and phenomena;[2] and thirdly, the writings on botany, zoology and medicine by Greek and Roman authors such as Aristotle (384-322 BCE), Theophrastus (370-287 BCE), Pliny the Elder, (23-

---

[1] The Amora Rav notes that his knowledge on animal defects is based on his own unmediated experience: 'I grew up with a herdsman for 18 years to know which imperfection is permanent and which is temporary' (bSan 5b). Cf also observations on ants, their nutrition and social life (Yal-Shim Proverbs, Warsaw 1878 no. 938); remarks by Rabban Shimon ben Gamliel on the matter of the distribution and ecology of plants (tShev 7:11, p197); and experiments conducted by the sages on pomegranates and capers to understand their anatomical structure and development (bBer 36b).

[2] For example, Babylonian sailors assisted in interpreting the term שמן קיק mentioned in mShab 2:1 as a combustible material produced from the fat of a bird named קיק. On additional information originating from sailors, see bShab 90a; bBB 73a.

79 CE) Dioscorides (c. mid-first century CE), Galen (130-200 CE) and others, on science and nature.[3]

While non-Jewish authors wrote books specifically on nature-related topics, the sages expressed their opinions on these topics in the framework of their religious-halakhic discussions. Consequently, reference to animals in the mishnaic and talmudic literature is random. While certain tractates deal extensively with biological topics, others address such topics in a limited manner – all according to the subject matter. A prominent example of an extensive treatment of nature-related topics is Tractate Bekhorot, which addresses animal physiology and veterinary medicine.

The information in rabbinic literature takes up a rather broad range of topics relating to animals, including the use made of them and their function in rituals and beliefs. The fields of biology that touch upon the animal world are: genetics, embryology, zoology and ecology. A review of rabbinic literature on these issues indicates that the information was of two kinds: factual information based on experimentation and observation, and data gleaned from popular traditions and folklore with no base in reality, but grounded in the beliefs or mythologies of various nations. The factual information also frequently suffered from inaccuracies because thinkers and scholars of the ancient world lacked systematic scientific methods to define and analyze the laws of nature and natural phenomena. Furthermore, several sages attributed legendary knowledge with the status of factual information; consequently, in such cases it is difficult to discern with certainty whether the source of information is reality-based or imaginary.

The first section of this paper deals with two general areas of biology that are related to the animal world – reproduction and embryology. This section will focus primarily on the sages' reality-based information in these areas relating to animals and humans. In the second section of the paper, we discuss several of the major animals mentioned in rabbinic literature. The information on these animals was influenced both by the world of classical Greek and Roman science and by ancient popular traditions and folklore.

General Biology

REPRODUCTION

Although the sages generally recognized the fact that living creatures originated from other living creatures, they believed that several creatures, such as lice, develop from the inanimate (see below). The sages also grasped that the

---

[3] The influence of the Greeks and Romans on the sages' knowledge of biology was investigated in a rather limited area. See, for example, Lieberman, *Hellenism*, 180-193 and Feliks, *Nature and Land*, 20f.

creation of an organism is a natural process, which cannot be imitated by man.[4] The central approach of the sages was that a specimen of an organism is identical to its parents.[5] However, it was also conventional to believe that new hybrid creatures could evolve. For example, according to several sources, a dangerous animal known as the *arvad* (ערוד) or *horor* (חורור) was the result of the mating process between a snake and an uromastyx.[6]

The sages defined rules regarding the types of offspring born from various classes of animals: 'In any species which has its male balls outside [the female] gives birth [to its young]. But where the male balls are inside, [the female] lays eggs.'[7] Further on in the discussion on this issue, a slightly different opinion is presented: 'Whoever has its male genitalia outside – gives birth, but whoever has its male genitalia inside – lays eggs.'

The reproductive organs of oviparous birds are internal, however, and several mammals such as elephants or procaviidae, whose testicles are concealed inside the body adjacent to the kidney, also have internal reproductive organs, and nonetheless are viviparous. Consequently, although these determinations have some grounds in reality, they do not account for all animals, due to the limited tools and information available to the early sages in studying modes of reproduction.

Mishnaic and talmudic sages also linked the time of birth of animals during the day to their time of mating and conceiving. 'Whatsoever copulates in the daytime, gives birth in the daytime. Whatsoever copulates in the night, gives birth in the night. Whatsoever copulates in the day and night, gives birth both in the day and in the night. "Whatsoever copulates in the daytime gives birth in the daytime" – for instance, a cock. "Whatsoever copulates in the night, gives birth in the night" – for instance, a bat. "Whatsoever copulates in the day and night time, gives birth both in the day and in the night" – for instance, man and all beings resembling him.'[8] This also appears to be an example of unsubstantiated observations that are difficult to confirm. Evidently, the sages believed that bats mate and give birth in the night because they are nocturnal, while during the day, they are difficult to track since they remain hidden in caves. In contrast, cocks mate during the day. Laying eggs is also a biological process dependent on daylight, although there is no biological connection between both processes.

---

[4] Compare ARN a12 (27a).

[5] This fact is noted in various contexts, for example: bNid 31a and SifDeut 306 (p332): 'Perhaps you sowed seeds in it but nothing grew, or perhaps you sowed seeds of wheat but barley grew.'

[6] bHul 127a; GenR 82,14. 24 (p995) – *Horor*; in the Wilna edition 1878, 82,15 – *arvad*.

[7] bBekh 8a. Cf also tBekh 1:11, where a new rule was presented regarding the manner of reproduction of marine animals: 'The dolphin gives birth and raises [its young] as a human; the impure fish spawns; the pure fish lays eggs.'

[8] bBekh 8a.

EMBRYOLOGY

Compared to the Bible, the Talmud and the Midrashim offer a rich repository of information on embryonic development, a fact which apparently attests to the increased knowledge in this field during the period of the Tannaim and Amoraim. Although familiar with the opinions of Greek and Roman scholars in this field, the sages sometimes departed from or expanded on these texts, on the basis of their own personal experience. In any case, this field also reflects a juxtaposition of correct observations and legendary perceptions.

In early times, the birth of male children was preferred to female children, due to ethnic, cultural and economic reasons. As a result, rabbinic literature contains various recommended interventions to determine the sex of the new-born, as early as at intercourse. According to one opinion, if the man reaches orgasm (מזריע) first, the child will be a female, while if the woman does, it will be a boy. However, if they reach orgasm simultaneously, the sex of the foetus is determined only forty days later.[9]

Roughly speaking, the sages adopted Aristotle's opinion on the passive role played by woman in creating the infant, i.e., in providing the raw materials (=blood) in which the man's sperm performs its function.[10] They also accepted the fact that the embryo appears to be a crude mass of cells.[11] However, in complete contradiction to the Greek view, the sages adopted a view that was correct according to knowledge at that time, i.e., the embryo is a live organism from the moment of conception.[12] Thus, they significantly anticipated their Greek contemporaries, who extensively debated when a foetus is considered a live creature.[13] Furthermore, in contrast to Greek scholars who perceived the woman exclusively as an incubator and source of nutrition for the foetus, while the man was perceived as conferring the foetus' attributes, the sages of Israel argued that both parents are equal partners in creating the newborn, although they thought they each had a separate role in the development of different organs.[14] The division they proposed in their writings has, however, no basis in light of the modern genetic knowledge that both parents bestow attributes, which, if dominant rather than recessive, are expressed in the phenotype.

Some of the early scholars, including Aristotle[15] and Pliny,[16] viewed the heart as the point of origin for foetal development. Galen, in contrast, believed

---

[9] See bBekh 60a; bNid 25b; cf bNid 31a-b. According to another view, males will be the product of additional intercourse.

[10] LevR 14,9 (p314).

[11] *Ib.* 14, 8. (p312-314)

[12] GenR 34,8. 21 (p321).

[13] See for example, Plutarch, De placitis philosophorum (LCL) 5.15. His volume contains an enormous amount of information of the early scholars.

[14] See yKil 8:3 (31c).

[15] De Generatione (LCL) 2.78. Aristotle's essay is a systematic text on the creation and development of the foetus.

[16] Naturalis Historia (LCL) 11.69.

that foetal development begins from the liver; next the heart develops, and finally the brain.[17] On their part, the sages, consistent with the position of Alkemion of Kroton, a physician and philosopher active in southern Italy (c. 500 BCE), claimed that the foetus was formed first from the head.[18] The sages also knew that the foetus is fed exclusively through the navel,[19] and is initially 'skin and flesh,' i.e., soft tissues, while the skeleton is the product of subsequent development.[20] The sages distinguished several stages in foetal development: until forty days, the foetus is likened to water only;[21] after forty days it is known as a foetus;[22] after three months, the woman's pregnancy becomes visible[23] and finally, the woman goes into labour and the foetus is born.[24]

Although the sages categorized the creation of infants together with 'things hidden from man's sight',[25] some sources provide descriptions of the foetus in the womb, including the state of his organs, his position,[26] his floating in amniotic fluid,[27] and his motions within the womb during the pregnancy.[28] We assume that the sages' descriptions were grounded in observations of foetuses during Caesarean sections, or in surgical procedures designed to open the womb and extract the foetus of women who died in childbirth.[29] These descriptions contain legendary motifs, but also some surprisingly accurate details, such as those pertaining to the foetus' position or its nourishment through the navel. In any case, it is clear that the observations were not systematic.

Rabbinic Zoology and Early Classic Influences

As we noted, the information on animals in Mishna and Talmud drew on early Greek and Roman scientific literature as well as on popular folklore. Myths, legends and parables constituted a dominant component in the folkloristic literature of early nations. Various animals featured prominently in this field of

---

[17] Formatus Foetus (LCL) 5.292.

[18] bYom 85a; bSot 45b; LevR 14,8 (p312); Tanh Pikude 3 (p452f).

[19] CantR (Vilna ed) 7 a [3]: 'An infant, when living in its mother's intestines, only lives through its navel.'

[20] GenR 14,5 (p129); LevR 14,9 (p316).

[21] bYev 69b.

[22] We note that the sages and Rabbi Yishmael disagreed is the gestation period of foetuses is equal in males and females. See yNid 3:5 (50b). On the opinions of the early scholars in the matter the creation of female and male, also see Preuss, *Medizin* (ET) 389 – 391.

[23] bNid 8b.

[24] bAr 7a.

[25] EcclR (Vilna) 11,1,5

[26] See bNid 25a and corresponding passages in yNid 3:2 (50d); LevR 14,8 (p312-314) where the sages described the appearance and position of the foetus. See also bNid 30b.

[27] The amniotic sac and placenta were well known to the sages and they may have learned of these from their wives or midwives. See LevR 14,3 (p304); yNid 3:2 (50d).

[28] bNid 31a.

[29] See tNid 4:17 on a unique surgical procedure on pregnant women, which produced a wealth of medical knowledge.

literary and cultural activity, generally originating from local geography,[30] and were used to express ethnic and religious ideas and conceptions.[31] In the following, we shall examine conceptions, beliefs, legends and myths concerning several animals and their behaviour, as reflected in the writings of the sages.

WILD MAN-LIKE CREATURES (אדני שדה)

In Mishna Kilayim 8:5, the Tannaim are divided on the question whether wild, man-like creatures called אדני השדה (literally: 'masters of the field') were considered human, with the result that their death generates the highest level of impurity, causing what is known as טומאת אהל ('impurity of the tent'), or whether such creatures are considered an animal: 'Wild man-like creatures are deemed as belonging to the category of animal. Rabbi Yose said: [When dead] they [or part of their corpses] communicate uncleanness [to men and to objects susceptible thereto, which are [under the same roof].' The Sifra debates the status of these wild man-like creatures in the context of dietary laws[32] and believes that the creature is considered impure and is forbidden for eating.

On the identity of the אדני השדה (also appearing as אבני השדה), the Yerushalmi presents a tradition (in that version, אדני השדה), which describes the creature as a human being of the mountains which receives nourishment through its navel and which dies if its navel is disconnected (yKil 8:4, 31c). Modern research literature offers two main approaches to the identity of the אדני השדה. According to the folklore scholar R. Patai, the source before us is a legend reflecting early beliefs of 'vegetable-animals', i.e. beliefs of the existence of creatures who are animals connected to and sustained by the earth, similar to plants.'[33] According to a second approach, the rumours regarding the existence of אדני השדה originated from belief in legendary animals. The zoologist M. Dor proposed that אדני השדה should be identified as a type of ape – a chimpanzee or gorilla; ordinary monkeys mentioned in rabbinical literature in

[30] On the geography of animal myths and legends in culture and literature, see Krappe, *Science of Folklore*, 250.

[31] As folklore scholars have shown, animals appear in legends, fables and popular stories in various motifs such as friends or enemies of man, animals with demonic traits, human-like or para-normal features. See Leoni, *Folklore and Wisdom*, 11-23; Noy, *Jewish Animal Tale*; idem, *Folk Stories*, 102-133; Yassif, *Hebrew Folk Story*, 298f. On animal fables in Jewish literature see Ausubel, *Treasury*, 621-627.

[32] Sifra Shemini 4,6,5 (51d). Another medieval tradition based on this verse identifies אדני השדה as an animal used to produce means of witchcraft. On this point, see the gloss of Rabbi Ovadia of Bartenura on mKil 8:5.

[33] Patai, *Man and Land*, 220-226. Among the examples of this are the belief in fruit-birds that was common in Europe or the Mediterranean belief of Autumn Mandrake (Mandragora autumnalis) whose shape was man-like and was therefore believed to positively affect fertility. On fruit-birds, see Löw, *Flora* 4, 347-349, and extensively in Shemesh, 'Attitude of the Halacha'. On legends which grew around the Autumn Mandrake, see e.g. Josephus, War 7.6.3 (7:185), and extensively in Dafni, *Autumn Mandrake*, 21; Preuss, *Medizin* (ET), 462.

various contexts have been identified as Macaca or Langoor (Presbytis monkeys).[34] However, the suggestion of its identification as the orang-utan (Pongo pygmaseus), whose name in Malay and in Indonesian literally means 'the man of the forest', appears to be more relevant despite its failure to meet the criterion of a positive identification. It may be assumed that the sages of the talmudic period heard legends of such creatures, and they deliberated on their halakhic implications, despite the fact that it is safe to assume that few people had apes in their possession and therefore, this was a rare halakhic problem. If the creature was an orang-utan, rumours of the existence of a 'man of the forest' may be assumed to have reached the Near East through caravans or ships bringing goods or perfumes from the tropical areas of South East Asia. The orang-utan, whose indigenous name literally means 'man of the woods', is common in the Indonesian islands of Borneo and Sumatra.

LICE, FLEAS AND WORMS

From time immemorial, various pests caused harm to man, his property, his farm animals, and his agricultural fields. This topic has been addressed by various scientists and historians[35] and, in the present study, we focus on aspects of the early 'scientific' conceptions mentioned in rabbinic literature regarding the reproduction of lice, fleas and worms. Both the Bible and rabbinic literature describe the offensiveness of lice.[36] One way to overcome the problems of lice on a person's body or hair, was to search for and kill them.[37] The question of whether killing lice is permitted on the Sabbath was debated in the Talmud Bavli. The Tanna R. Eliezer determined: 'He who kills a louse on the Sabbath – it is as though he killed a camel on the Sabbath.' In contrast, other sages believed that killing lice was permitted because they do not reproduce by mating, but rather develop from perspiration and dirt. Although the Talmud attempts to challenge this ruling, because, after all, lice lay eggs, it accepts the opinion of the sages and distinguished between fleas (probably *pulex irritans*), the killing of which is prohibited because they mate to reproduce, and lice which may be killed. In fact, the sages thus expressed an approach that was conventionally accepted among Greek scientists including Aristotle.[38]

The view of the spontaneous generation of lice and their lack of sexual reproduction appears in several sources throughout the Bavli. One passage states: 'Gossip comes from peddlers, and lice from rags.'[39] In other words, lice naturally reproduce from rags. Another passage (in Aramaic) maintains:

[34] Dor, *Animal Life*, 87.

[35] See for example, Bodenheimer, *Animal Life* 1, 121-123; Nevo, *Pests in agricultural crops*.

[36] Exod 8:12-14; Ps 105:31; ARN a 19 (35b); bNid 20b.

[37] Cf bShab 12a; bHag 5a.

[38] 'Insects such as lice, fleas and bugs – all these are the result of copulation generate what are called nits, and from these nothing is produced' (Hist. anim. 5.51).

[39] bBer 51b and Rashi *ib.*

'White lice: If one launders his garment and does not wait eight days before putting it on, the lice are produced...'[40] It is almost certain that the white vermin mentioned by the sages was the light-coloured human body louse, *pediculus humanus*.[41] Lice that are parasites on humans (body, hair and pubic hair) reproduce by mating, and therefore, the sages' determination on this issue is inconsistent with our own knowledge. Apparently, the question of whether lice do or do not mate, stems from the fact that the sages' observations were insufficient to confirm the facts of nature. Clearly, there was an objective difficulty to observe the reproductive behaviour of lice, due to their small size and the fact that they are generally found in hidden places.

Worms were treated similarly by the sages since they permitted fruit, foodstuffs and certain beverages to be consumed even if they contain worms.[42] However, only in recent centuries, with the development of the scientific method and tools for observations of tiny creatures, did scientists prove that worms do not multiply in a process of spontaneous generation, but reproduce from eggs laid in the fruit or food by flying insects.[43]

A WATER MOUSE AND A MOUSE HALF FLESH, HALF EARTH

On the topic of purity and impurity, one mishna describes a mouse whose body is half flesh and half earth: 'A mouse which is half flesh and half earth, if a man touches the flesh – he is unclean; if he touches the earth – he is clean.'[44] The Sifra discusses the impurity of mice more extensively[45] and refers to three types of mice: a land mouse, a water mouse[46] and a mouse that is half flesh and half earth. The existence of this astonishing mouse whose body is divided into two, has been described in the texts of Roman and Greek scholars. The sages, having learned of this extraordinary creature, deliberated on its halakhic status regarding impurity.[47]

In his essay *Naturalis Historia*, Pliny the Elder (23-79 CE) offers support for the existence of the creature in the context of the frequent floods in the

---

[40] bPes 112b.

[41] On types of lice and their impact see Kosta, *Insects Against Man*, 111-114.

[42] bHul 67a-b.

[43] Cf the maxim of the great French scientist, Louis Pasteur (1822-1895): 'Vivo e vivo.'

[44] Cf the sugya bHul 127a.

[45] Sifra Shemini 5,4-6 (51a-51b)

[46] Mice do not live in or near the water, and therefore it is difficult to know which animal this is. The Sifra passage (above) on a mouse which lives on land but enters water may refer to Blernnius sp. which lives on the Mediterranean shores of the Land of Israel in areas of high and low tides. Oppian also notes this fish-like attribute (Halieutica 1.155).

[47] See for example, Ovid (LCL) Metam. 1.423-438; Pomponius Mela, Chorographia, (Leipzig 1880) vol 1, 9.3.52 See Romer, *Pomponius*, 52, p49. Similar evidence of this creature in Egypt was mentioned by Maimonides in the Middle Ages, in his commentary on mHul 9:6, where he reports that many people claim having seen this type of mouse.

Egyptian Nile area.[48] The description in rabbinic literature is similar: 'Go forth into the field and see a mouse, which today is part flesh and part dust, and yet tomorrow will develop and become all flesh; and you should not say, 'That takes a long time, go up to the mountains where you will see but one snail, and by tomorrow, the rain has descended and [the mountain] is covered with snails' (bSan 91a). Surely this phenomenon has no basis in reality. It may stem from incorrect observations of other animals such as toads or snails that dig into the earth during dry periods, and come out of the earth when rain falls or during flooding. In this way, when buried, they may appear as creatures that are half-earth, and when they emerge from the earth, they appear as ordinary creatures of flesh.

SIRENS

Sirens, or mermaids (in Greek: Σειρήν), appear in Greek and Roman mythology as magical singers of the sea, who have the head of a woman and the body of a bird, or who are half-woman, half-bird.[49] In European folklore, sirens were frequently equated with marine nymphs, half-woman half-fish.[50]

Influenced by the Greeks, these sirens also penetrated into the sages' houses of learning. Sirens were mentioned in the debates of the Tannaim in the context of dietary laws permitting their consumption, as well as in laws of purity and impurity. The Sifra interpreted the following verse as applicable to sirens: 'But anything in the seas or in the streams that has no fins or scales, among all swarming things of the water and among all the other living creatures that are in the water – they are an abomination for you' (Lev 11:10).[51] According to the Sifra, this verse implies that there are creatures of the sea, such as the sirens, that have a soul and are forbidden for consumption; but although they are half-human, they do not cause impurity as a human corpse does.

---

[48] 'But creditability is given to all these statements by the flooding of the Nile, with a marvel that surpasses them all: This is that, when the river withdraws its covering, water-mice are found with the work of generative water and earth uncompleted – they are already alive in a part of their body, but the most recently formed part of their structure is still of the earth' (Nat. hist. 9.84).

[49] On sirens in ancient myths, see an extensive discussion in Brunel, *Companion*, 1040-1043. We add that sirens appear in Christian traditions as an eternal symbol of seduction. See Shorey, 'Sirens'; Barkai – Shiller, 'Symbols'.

[50] It is possible that the origin of the figure of the siren is the Dugong dugon hemprichi – a vegetarian marine mammal with a distaff-like body, which lived along the shores of the Indian Ocean. Since ancient times, there have been legends on marriages between men and Dugong. On the source of legends and their biological origin, see Bodenheimer, *Animal Life* 1, 82; Dor, *Animal Life*, 59.

[51] Sifra Shemini 3,7 (49d).

SALAMANDERS

The sages were similarly influenced by Roman and Greek writings of a mythical creature known as the salamander (σαλαμάνδρα). Greek scholars of nature described the salamander as a wingless lizard or a dog-lizard that either spits fire or is ringed by flames.[52] In the world of the sages, the salamander was described as a creature formed in ovens whose fire is incessant and prolonged.[53] According to their beliefs, the creation by fire granted the salamander a special ability: application of its blood on the skin may prevent burns in case of a fire.

The salamander in talmudic literature is conventionally identified as *Salamandra salamandra*. This black reptile's skin is studded with yellow-orange patches, and is found in almost all of Europe, and the area ranging from south-western Africa to Israel. Apparently the creature's colour combination was the foundation of the belief of the salamander's origin in ovens, a belief which is of course groundless. Salamanders are found adjacent to watering holes and, in contrast to the legends, this reptile prefers the cold, and is primarily active in winter evenings and nights.

HYENAS

Hyenas were surrounded by mythical legends and traditions in the time of the sages. These legends describe hyenas as a 'demonic,' unpredictable and dangerous animal. There is no doubt that the animal should be identified as the *Hyaena hyaena syriaca*, found in Israel and Babylonia.[54] The hyena's devilish image has no grounds in reality, but stems from common folk beliefs of the area. Such beliefs were apparently related to the fact that hyenas feed off carcasses of animals and humans, tend to hide in dark caves, and are active at night.

Early echoes of these myths appear in the Mishna and Talmud and apparently had an effect on early rulings on halakhic issues.[55] Other legends and midrashim indicate some changes in the hyena's image. The Yerushalmi states that a hyena can change its sex ('male hyenas become female').[56] Although this

[52] On legends and beliefs regarding salamanders, see Cooper, *Animals,* 196.
[53] See Sifra Shemini 5,7 (52a); bHag 27a; bSan 63b; Tanh Vayeshev 3 (p149).
[54] On types of hyenas in the Land of Israel and elsewhere, see Nowak, *Walker's Mammals,* 1177-1183; Ruuk, 'Feeding and Social Behavior'; MacDonald, 'Observations'.
[55] Thus, for example, in tort laws in yBK 1:5 (2c) it was determined that the male hyena can be as dangerous as a lion. However as far as it is known, the hyena is not dangerous to man. We note that under the influence of the classic sources, both Jewish and non-Jewish, the negative attitude to hyenas passed to the world of beliefs of the Middle Ages and modern times. See extensively Shemesh, 'Striped Hyaena'.
[56] yShab 1:3 (3b). Some believe that the source of this belief is the appearance of the large female clitoris, which is similar to the male sexual organ. However, this is true only for the spotted African Hyena which distribution reaches Egypt (Dor, *Animal Life*, 66).

tradition does not point to the hyena's dangerous nature, it most certainly hints to its mysterious and unpredictable nature.[57] Another source by the sages adds that a male hyena may change into other animals and therefore appears in rabbinical literature under three different names: ברדלס, נפרזא and אפא, besides the common name צבוע:

> The male hyena (צבוע) after seven years turns into a bat (עטלף), the bat after seven years turn into an *arpad* (ערפד), the *arpad* after seven years turns into a *kimosh* (קימוש), the *kimosh* after seven years turns into a *hoah* (חוח), the *hoah* after seven years turns into a demon (שד); the spine of a man after seven years turns into a snake (נחש). (bBK 16a)

As noted by M. Dor, it is difficult to identify the animals in this talmudic passage with certainty, and it may refer to mythical animals.[58] According to the passage, the hyena ultimately turns into a devil, undoubtedly a creature arousing fear in the ancient world, which alludes to the hyena's potential to cause harm and develop a 'devilish' behaviour.

Another passage describes the hyena's colour in exaggeration: 'R.Huna, on behalf of Rav Matna, said that the hyena, from one drop of white sperm, has 365 kinds of hues, as the number of days of the solar year.'[59] R. Huna's intention was that the hyena was formed, as were the other creatures, from the male's white sperm, but at the end of the process, the hyena appears to have many colours. Nonetheless, a hyena's fur is not as colourful as described and its fur is generally yellow and black. L. Ginzburg, the scholar of Jewish law and lore, noted that in another talmudic source (bBer 6b), the beauty of its hues was likened to another legendary bird called the *kerum* (כרום).[60] This source also apparently was designed to reflect the hyena's status as an extraordinary and legendary animal.

---

[57] The sexual change of the hyena was previously described in pagan and Christian sources. Pliny, for example, wrote: 'The hyena is popularly believed to be bi-sexual and to become male and female in alternate years.' The female bearing offspring without a male; but this is denied by Aristotle (Nat. hist. 8.105). Although Pliny referred to Aristotle, he did not accept his belief in the hyena's ability to change sex, as we can see from another passage where Pliny expresses his opinion without qualification, see Nat. hist. 28.92, and compare Ovid, Metam. 15.409 who presented a similar view.

[58] Dor, *Animal Life*, 259. For a discussion on the identification of these creatures, see Ginzberg, *Legends* 5, 58.

[59] GenR 7,4 (p52f).

[60] Pliny described a similar creature (Naturalis Historia, X, 67). See also Ginzberg, *Legends* 5, 58 n190.

Chapter Seventeen

The Sages and the Occult

Yuval Harari

Sources and Method

In recent decades nothing short of a revolution has taken place in the way we understand ancient Jewish magic and its place within the broad spectrum of Jewish culture in Palestine and Babylonia, in the Mishnah and the Talmud period. Two principal factors can be pointed out: (1) a growing stream of publications of primary sources from Late Antiquity and the early Middle Ages – amulets, incantation bowls, and magic recipes from Babylonia and Palestine and the surrounding region – that has basically relegated rabbinic literature into a secondary resource for the clarification of the essence of ancient Jewish magic culture;[1] (2) a re-examination of the rabbinic discourse on

---

[1] The study of amulets stemming from the region of Palestine has especially benefited from the publication of two books: Naveh – Shaked, *Amulets*; *Magic Spells*. In these works also a few dozen Babylonian magic bowls were published. Additional corpora of Jewish incantation bowls may be found in the following: Montgomery, *Aramaic Incantation Texts* (and p49f n1); Segal, *Catalogue*; Levene, *Corpus*. Dozens of additional bowls were published by C.H. Gordon, S. Shaked and others. Alongside these findings there are also the demonological findings from Qumran (below, n92), and a number of Jewish magical gems and papyrus fragments from Egypt, that despite their publication have not received the requisite attention (I thank Gideon Bohak for

magic that has increasingly been based on methodology found in the fields of the social sciences, cultural studies, gender studies, and comparative religion. This has replaced the traditional scholarship that sought to subordinate the discourse as a whole to one factor within it: the halakha, and to examine it in light of the halakha, alone. The nullification of the essential dichotomy between religion and magic in Jewish studies, part of a more general trend in the study of religion in recent decades, and replacing it with an approach that sees them as parallel and complementary ritual power systems has brought about an important change. It has diverted the focus of discussion about the rabbis' attitude towards magic and magicians (and especially sorceresses) from the ideological to the social. Here, the main concern is the rabbis' aspiration to acquire a monopoly over knowledge and power and the removal of competition – ideological, ritual, and societal, by labeling such competitors as illegitimate.[2]

These two fundamental changes often play a key role in additional fields of research of what can be called the rabbinic occult discourse: demonology, divination, dreams and astrology. An understanding of Jewish demonology, for instance, enhanced by the magical demonological findings, calls for a reexamination of the demonological stories interspersed throughout talmudic literature. The focus is now diverted from the demonological phenomenon revealed within them to the nature and the purpose of its rabbinic utilization. The same is the case with divination, dreams and astrology. The study of the rabbinic 'discourse of the occult' in recent decades is characterized by an approach that rejects its subordination to the religious-moral-ideological message as the one and only key to its explication. It renounces the plain innercultural distinctions between sorcery and miracle, divination and prophecy, sorcerers and rabbis (and likewise, 'forbidden' and 'fitting', 'them' and 'us') that are apparently to be assumed. Instead, it calls upon us to see it as the multivocular expression of a rabbinic elite, whose social aspirations were no less important than its spiritual ones. This discourse must, therefore, be understood, not only as a varied and on occasion contradictory expression of beliefs and actions in these subjects among the rabbis, but also, and sometimes, princi-

---

this information). There is widespread agreement among scholars that the magic material that is documented in the Cairo Geniza from the beginning of the second millennium is to be seen as a direct continuation of the palestinian magic. A clear connection between them has been demonstrated in the past. Most of the magical material from the Geniza that has been published, to date, was published in Schäfer – Shaked, *Magische Texte*. Additional fragments were published in Schiffman – Swartz, *Incantation Texts*, and in the above mentioned books by Naveh – Shaked. Three magical compositions that originate in late antiquity have been published: Sefer ha-Razim, the Sword of Moses, and The Havdala of R. Akiva. See Margulies, *Sepher Ha-Razim*; Harari, *The Sword of Moses*; Scholem, 'Havdalah'. For a comprehensive survey of the magical material from Palestine and the surrounding region see: Harari, *Early Jewish Magic*, ch. 4.
[2] For a comprehensive survey of the shift in scholarship concerning the attitude to magic in rabbinic literature see Harari, *Early Jewish Magic*, ch. 2.

pally, as an expression of their own aspirations to achieve a monopoly over knowledge, power, and authority.[3]

Sorcery

The Jews of late antique Palestine and Babylonia believed in the power of magic and used it for their benefit,[4] as is evidenced by the products of ancient Jewish magical activity: amulets and magic bowls. The magic recipe books inform us that this activity was founded on a clear and comprehensive world outlook, and formulated as a systematic strategy. This was organized and put into writing by educated professionals well versed in the Bible as well as in rabbinic, mystical, and other traditions. These traditions filled a number of objectives. Firstly, they served as the basis for the very notion that humans might possess metaphysical power. They also justified the manipulation of this power – by virtue of the heavenly source of the knowledge and the Divine patronage over its use.[5] These traditions could also, on occasion, participate in its systematic execution, such as through the sympathetic use of scriptural verse, portions of the prayers, and historiolas from various Jewish sources. The ancient Jewish sorcery literature indicates that magic functioned in all fields of life,[6] in the hands of professional sorcerers, and perhaps even as self-service practices, and this with two fundamental conditions: (a) expertise in the relevant knowledge concerning angels and demons, including their names, location, function, and principally the adjuration language by which they are compelled to obey the sorcerer and the ritual framework whereby it is to be carried out; (b) self-preparation rituals for the efficient use of this knowledge. It would seem, therefore, that in late antiquity magic was at home in Jewish culture, a complementary ritual practice, perhaps even an alternative to the canonical religious practice endorsed by the rabbis, for the improvement of the human condition and the magic discourse of the rabbis themselves needs to be examined in this light.

---

[3] The nature of this article and limitations of space do not allow for detailed historical, geographical, or genre-related discussion on the phenomena that will be examined below. Issues of manuscript variants will also largely remain outside the discussion and are mentioned only where they impact on the conclusions.

[4] The use of the terms 'magic' and 'sorcery' is not based on a dictionary definition but on a broad phenomenological description of the culture that is documented in the ancient Jewish magical texts. On the choice of the texts on the basis of a linguistic definition of an adjuration text and the family resemblance between magic and religion see Harari, 'What is a Magical Text?'

[5] This is particularly prominent in the Sword of Moses, see Harari, *The Sword of Moses*, 54-73. Sefer ha-Razim ascribes the revelation of magic to Noah (and in other versions, to Adam) and even connects the construction of the ark to this knowledge. See Margulies, *Sepher ha-Razim*, 65f.

[6] See Harari, 'If You Wish to Kill'; idem, 'Love Charms'; idem, 'Power and Money'; idem, 'Opening of the Heart; *Early Jewish Magic* (diss.), 113-226.

ACCEPTING THE THEORY BUT REJECTING THE PRACTICE

The rabbis' opposition to magic, in principle, is explicit. They continued the resolute biblical inclination to reject sorcery as a foreign cultural indicator and fix a harsh sanction: 'You shall not suffer the sorcerer to live' (Exod 22:17).[7] The Mishna expresses the judgement that 'harlotry and sorcery have destroyed everything' (mSot 9:3). From the legal perspective the punishment for sorcery is execution by stoning (mSan 7:4). At the same time, sorcery is not precisely defined. There is only the rule that as opposed to trickery sorcery is a real act, that is, it entails a real change of reality. As such, the legal punishment for the two differs. One who practices sorcery is guilty, but practicing trickery, the mere pretence of sorcery, is an act of deception and thereby exempt from punishment (mSan 7:11). In the Talmud this exemption is restricted in the course of a discussion on a broad array of activities that are connected with the ritual power and the illusion of its existence. Abaye asserts:

> The laws of sorcery may be compared to the laws of the Sabbath, they possess (the category of death) 'by stoning', and they have (the category of) 'exempt (from punishment) but (the act is) prohibited', (and the category of) 'permitted *a priori*': one who commits an act – (is punished) 'by stoning'; one who tricks – is 'exempt but (the act is) prohibited'; (the category of) 'permitted *a priori*' as in the case of Rav Hanina and Rav Oshaya. Every Sabbath eve they occupied themselves with the laws concerning the Creation and a three-year old heifer was created for them and they consumed it.[8]

This distinction between sorcery and trickery bears testimony to the rabbis' recognition of the power of the sorcerer to carry out tangible actions in the world. It is, in fact, precisely this, and not the deception of an illusory feat, that they categorized as a sin and prohibited. Furthermore, the fact that the examples of deception offered here and elsewhere connect it mainly to gentiles confirms the trend towards presenting *their* sorcery as unreal, a mere conjuring trick, and so to negate from them any true metaphysical power. The eyewitness testimony of one Yannai, concerning 'a heretic who would take a bundle and toss it up into the air and it would descend and become a calf', ultimately a story about uncovering a fraud, is of particular relevance (ySan 7:19, 25d). Similar testimony of R. Hinena son of R. Hananya concerning such a 'creation' concludes with his father's statement: 'If you have eaten from it – that is a proof [that a real act has been carried out], and if not – it is a deception' (*ib.*). Now the difference between sorcery, deception, and the sacred study of the rabbis that produced a calf, which they did, indeed, consume, is absolutely

---

[7] The Bible is not, of course, devoid of explicit magical traditions. However, these traditions, when applied to its heroes, are removed from the category of 'sorcery', just as a 'man of God', a prophet, or a seer is not viewed as a 'diviner'. On divination and sorcery in the Bible there exists an extensive literature. See recently Jeffers, *Magic and Divination*; Cryer, *Divination*; idem, 'Magic'. For a comprehensive bibliographical survey see Harari, 'Opening of the Heart', 307f n11.
[8] bSan 67b.

clear. Since Tora study is the ritual that brought the creature into existence, and since it is rabbis who performed it, not only is the act not sorcery (and certainly doesn't fall into the category of deception as in the 'creations' of the gentiles), but it is 'permitted *a priori*'. It is, in fact, even desirable as a demonstration of the ritual power deriving from the religious norm to which the rabbis are committed.

Recognition of the manipulative magical human power for both beneficial and maleficent purposes is widespread in many halakhic and aggadic traditions. One could mention, for instance, traditions that recognize the power of those who utter charms in order to cause rain,[9] and the impact of sympathetic acts for the fertility of trees.[10] A particular example is the magical recipes for healing that are based on the pronouncement of a charm[11] and the testimony for the use of written amulets and those using 'roots'.[12] With regard to the latter, mention should be made of the discussion of the kinds of amulets that may be carried on the Sabbath for medicinal purposes. Here we find a category known as 'amulets prepared by an expert'. This refers to an amulet whose efficacy, or perhaps the credibility of the one who wrote the amulet, has been demonstrated at least thrice.[13] Within this topic we discover testimony for the use of therapeutic objects such as a locust egg, a fox tooth, a nail from one who has been crucified, which R. Meir permits to be carried on the Sabbath 'on account of their healing', and the rabbis prohibit even on weekdays on account of the prohibition to follow in the 'ways of the Amorites' (mShab 6:10). We also learn of traditions Abaye received from his nursemaid regarding the therapeutic practices of 'knots': 'Abaye said: My mother told me: three cause the sickness to cease, five heal it, seven work even against sorcery' (bShab 66b).

Even as the details of the actual practice in this last source are uncertain, it indicates that sickness, especially of the most severe kind, was perceived as the

---

[9] bTaan 8a. The explanation attributed to Rashi *ad loc.*, whereby 'those who whisper charms – for they do not recite their prayers in a whisper' is to be rejected. Cf further below n34.

[10] b Shab 67a; yShev 4:4, 35b. See further, Harari, 'Power and Money', 27f.

[11] bShab 66b-67a; bGit 68b-69b. In my view, the incorporation of a charm in an act of healing is the basis for its inclusion in magical healing. Many of the recipes mentioned in these sources are not as such and can be seen as non-magical 'popular medicine'. Concerning the Babylonian foundations of these recipes see Geller, 'Akkadian Medicine'; idem, 'Akkadian Vademecum'. Alongside these practices there also existed 'scientific' medicine in antiquity, based on the school of Hippocrates and later Galen. All of these methods made not infrequent use of astrological principles.

[12] For a detailed discussion on amulets in rabbinic literature see Blau, *Zauberwesen*, 86-96. Cf also Urbach, *The Sages*, 130-132; Trachtenberg, *Magic and Superstition*, 132-152.

[13] mShab 6:2; tShab 4:5, 9f; bShab 53a. The talmudic sages were divided on the question of whether the record of efficacy referred to the writer or the amulet. See bShab 61a. Concerning the empirical foundations of the pragmatic approach of the rabbis to magical practices for medicinal purposes, which is evident in this discussion, see Veltri, *Magie und Halakha*, 221-282, 286-293; idem, 'Influence of Greek Wisdom'; idem, 'Other Physicians'.

result of harmful sorcery.[14] A similar notion lies behind the snake's response to the rabbis' surprise at the potency of its harm: 'If a snake bites without a charm' (yPea 1:1, 16a; cf Eccl 10:11). Its response, linking the snake's deadly power to its role as a harmful agent in the service of the charmer, is a part of the world that also produced the 'rabbis' snake' (חיויא דרבנן). The 'rabbis' snake' is a snake dispatched by the rabbis against transgressors who turn to heretics for help, and its bite 'has no remedy at all'.[15] An additional source that is presumably connected is the statement that 'whosoever is modest in the convenience is saved from three things: snakes, scorpions and *meziqin*. And there are those who say: even his dreams are at ease with him' (bBer 62a). The theory that this refers to exposure to the evil injury of harmful magical agents finds support in the explicit comments of Ben Azzai there: 'touch yourself and sit down, but do not sit down and touch yourself for whosoever sits down and touches himself, even one who practices sorcery in Aspamia will affect him'.

These traditions form part of a more extensive series of testimonies concerning the rabbis' profound recognition of the potency of harmful sorcery.[16] Its most pronounced expression may be found in the many traditions on the power of cursing by means of evoking of the Divine name, which is, in turn, part of a more comprehensive notion of the executive potential in God's name.[17] Even though the rabbis prohibited cursing by means of evoking God's name[18] its menacing potential remained a constant fear. According to a number of midrashim Moses slew the Egyptian taskmaster in this way.[19] In the Yerushalmi its use is attributed to the priests of the Second Temple 'who would kill each other through sorcery' (yYom 1:1). The Bavli evokes it often within the context of the ritual power possessed by the rabbis. Other traditions, however, suggest that its power was available even to common people and to gentiles.[20] The extent to which it inspired awe is evidenced in the stories concerning those who are cursed. These stories describe how they deliberately attempt to pre-empt the true harmful effects of the curse by fulfilling it, word for word, in a harmless manner so as not to be harmed by the actual curse. In these stories, however, their efforts were to no avail and ultimately the curses were fulfilled also in accordance with the original intention (bGit 35a, bBB 153a).

---

[14] Cf Harari, 'If You Wish to Kill'; concerning knots see *ibid*, 133f. See, too, the knot garment from the Judean Desert, Yadin, *The Finds from the Bar-Kokhba Period*, 256-258 and plate 89.

[15] bShab 110a, bAZ 27b, yShev 9:1, 38d.

[16] Cf Blau, *Zauberwesen*, 49-54.

[17] See Urbach, *The Sages*, 124-134; Blau, *Zauberwesen*, 117-146; Trachtenberg, *Jewish Magic*, 78-103.

[18] mSan 7:4, 8; mShavu 4:13; mYev 2:5; tMak 5:10.

[19] LevR 32,4, p745. Cf ExodR 1,29; PRE 48. The subject is treated in detail in Harari, 'Moses'. In MidrPs 36,8 we find the following explanation: 'What is the weapon of war? It is the Tetragrammaton. They would go to war, and not fight and their enemies would fall [before them].'

[20] On the rabbis' curse see, for example: bBer 56a; bSan 90b; bMak 11a. For the curse of a commoner and a gentile see: bBK 93a; yYom 3:7, 40d; EcclR 3,11.

Belief in sorcery's aggressive potential was not limited to 'women and common people' or 'provincial commoners'. It penetrated the rabbinic conversation in general, and in particular the halakhic sphere, in areas that we have mentioned above and others such as compulsion, the disturbing of sexual relations, and averting a verdict through sorcery.[21] All of this points to the rabbis' profound recognition of its power. One must, therefore, reject the view that considers the basis for the rabbis' struggle with sorcery and sorcerers in their denial, in principle, of sorcery's very efficacy on account of the tension between it and a belief in Divine omnipotence.[22] Statements such as, '"There is none other besides Him" (Deut 4:35) – even in the matter of sorcery' (bSan 67b), or, 'R. Natan said: The Holy One, blessed be He said: Were all the magicians of the world to gather together and try to change morning into evening they would not succeed' (Tanh Korah 6, Buber 44a), must, then, be understood not as negating the very possibility of sorcery but as determining its limits within the cosmos over which God commands sole responsibility.[23] At the same time sorcery implied a degree of human audacity, the forceful intrusion into God's exclusive, that apparently narrowed His unlimited realm of activity. This perception of sorcery, that R. Yohanan articulated with his statement 'Why are they called *keshafim* [sorceries]? Because they contradict/limit the Heavenly *familia*',[24] attributed to it the want of blessing in the world and specifically the unhappy state of the Jewish people.[25] At the same time, in view of the mass of testimonies to the ritual power of the rabbis, in itself, and in particular within the context of their struggle with sorcerers and sorcery, it is not possible to confine the rabbis' objections to sorcery to the realm of ideology, alone. As we shall see, social considerations played a decisive role in shaping the rabbis' hostile attitude to sorcery.

---

[21] On Jewish erotic magic in antiquity see Harari, 'Love Charms'. On sorcery for changing a legal verdict see Harari, *Jewish Magic* (diss.), 202. On these practices in the Hellenistic world see Gager, *Curse Tablets*, 116-150. In the Tosefta we find the following statement: 'When the number of whisperers in court increased, wrath came upon the world and the Shekhina departed from Israel' (tSot 14:3). It may have been for this very reason that R. Yohanan held that the members of the Sanhedrin should be 'masters of sorcery' (see below).

[22] Urbach, *The Sages*, 97.

[23] This is, indeed the way the authors of the Jewish magical writings understood their activity. It was portrayed as an expression of the explicit will of God to transmit to man the knowledge and the accompanying power to subordinate the angels to serve him. See Harari, *The Sword of Moses*, 67-73.

[24] bSan 67b. The Hebrew root כחש has a double significance here. It has both the meaning to 'contradict' and to 'limit'. The former refers to the spiritual significance of the act of sorcery, and the latter, to its practical aspect.

[25] mSot 4:5, 9:13; tSot 14:3. This approach might also lay behind Rabban Yohanan b. Zakkai's response to his disciples, as cited in PesRK 4,7, p74. His disciples are surprised when, for the benefit of a gentile, he compares the red heifer purity ritual to the exorcism of an evil spirit. His response: 'It is not the dead that defiles, nor is it the water that purifies, but the decree of the Holy One, blessed be He', denies the religious ritual itself any performative power, and presents it as the technical execution of the Divine decree.

'WAYS OF THE AMORITES'

Although we do not possess a broad and comprehensive essential definition of sorcery as a practice, as understood by the rabbis (and it is doubtful whether they possessed such a definition at all) the category 'ways of the Amorites' (literally: ways of the Amorite – דרכי האמורי), common in their writings, offers the possibility for a partial clarification of activity in this field and the basis for opposition to it. The 'ways of the Amorites' signifies activity prohibited on account of the scriptural prohibition 'and do not go according to their laws' (Lev 18:3). Hence, it is due to the desire to differentiate the People of Israel from the surrounding nations. In Deuteronomy 18:10-14, the injunction not to imitate the gentile nations is explicitly related to divination and sorcery practices. These practices are therefore portrayed as the most typical characteristics of the foreign surrounding culture.[26] For this, the rabbis pointedly singled out the term, 'ways of the Amorites'. This category is mentioned in the Mishna as a basis for the prohibition of acts of a magical-apotropaic nature such as carrying a locust egg, a fox's tooth, or a nail from someone who has been crucified (mShab 6: 10) or the ritual use of an animal placenta (mHul 4:7). The Tosefta makes dual use of this category: The categorization of ritual (and other) acts as prohibited and the consent for acts that would appear to fall under this category but, in fact, do not (tShab 6-7, tShev 1:10). The rabbinic discussions of ritual practices that may or may not fall under the category of the 'ways of the Amorites'[27] indicate their identification with the gentiles. This notion fits well with the tendency observed extensively in recent decades whereby sorcery is perceived as the ritual used to achieve power that is carried out by the 'other'.[28] It would appear, then, that dubbing ritual practices as the 'ways of the Amorites', meaning that they are prohibited because they are foreign, reflects an attempt by the rabbis to uproot foreign potent forms of worship in favour of the canonical Jewish form of worship of the type that they, themselves, have fashioned, but which also has power. This is alongside their attempts to 'convert' and symbolically re-fashion similar customs, which they were, apparently powerless to uproot.[29] The trouble is that in all the discussions on the 'ways of

---

[26] Cf further Lev 20:23; Exod 23:24. Concerning the Amorites' sorcery cf 2 Bar 60:1. Cf further, Harari, 'Opening of the Heart', 309f n19.

[27] See mShab 6:10; mHul 4:7; tShab 6-7 (Lieberman, 22-29); tShev, 1:10 (Lieberman, 168); yShab 6:10, 8c; bShab 67a-b; bSot 49b; bBK 83a; 91b; bSan 52b; bAZ 11a; bHul 77a-b; Semahot 8:1. For discussion of these sources see Lieberman, *Tosefta Ki-Fshutah*, vol 3, 79-105; vol 2, 492; Lieberman, *Greek*, 101f; Avishur, 'Ways of the Amorite'; Veltri, *Magie und Halakha*, 93-220; idem, 'Other Physicians'; Seidel, 'Charming Criminals'.

[28] E.g., Petterson, 'Magic-Religion'; Braavig, 'Magic'. Concerning the Hellenistic-Roman and early Christian context see, for instance, Philips, 'Sociology of Religious Knowledge'; Liebeschuetz, *Continuity and Change*, 126-139; Segal, 'Hellenistic Magic'; Gager, *Curse Tablets*, 24-25; Brown, 'Sorcery, Demons and the Rise of Christianity'; Aune, 'Magic in Early Christianity'; Nock, 'Paul and the Magus'.

[29] See Lieberman, *Greek*, 102f.

the Amorites' we find no systematic discussion or model for establishing the *type* of actions falling under this category but only the application of this category as a marker to label certain acts.[30] Rather than informing us about the common essence of the practice it indicates, and defining it, these sources only bear witness to the hostile attitude of the rabbis to the ritual power of the 'other' and to the rhetorical-halakhic means employed to delegitimize it.

In this light a ruling by Abaye and Rava, offering a utilitarian approach, is of particular interest: 'All that which is related to health is not deemed as the ways of the Amorites' (bShab 67a). Such an empirical pragmatic approach, which was also reflected in the ruling that permits carrying an 'amulet prepared by an expert' on the Sabbath, was not accepted by all. R. Akiva opposed the use of charms for healing.[31] R. Yishmael and R. Joshua b. Levi drew the limits to its use when they preferred the death of their dear-ones to their recovery through the use of the name of Jesus.[32] These cases, while reflecting the ideological struggle with Christian culture, express more than anything the rabbis' fear of the penetration of Jewish society by its agents of ritual power. The gap between the view held by Abaye and Rava and that of R. Yishmael and R. Joshua b. Levi, apart from their different geographical-historical realities, reflects well the gap between the rabbis' degree of tolerance towards foreign practices, on the one hand, and agents of foreign power, on the other. As we shall see, regarding the latter, the rabbis took a consistently hostile and uncompromising view.

RABBIS, WOMEN, AND HERETICAL SORCERERS

Many of the sages are depicted in rabbinic literature as agents of ritual power. It is they, and not others, who are the fitting and legitimate agents of this power that, almost by definition, dose not derive from sorcery but rather from their own spiritual life-style. It is the result of their perpetual ritual contact with God, to the point of identification with Him through the internalization of His words – the Tora.[33] The rabbis' metaphysical power is clearly visible in the stories that describe their far-reaching powers. They are able, for instance, to curse; to cause rain or to control it as they desire;[34] to grow gourds and gather

---

[30] It is possible that more systematic discussions existed in the non-extant chapter of the Amorites (פרק אמוראי) that is mentioned in bShab 67a.

[31] mSan 10:1. On the magical use of the scriptural verse cited there (Exod 15:26) in ancient Jewish magic see Naveh-Shaked, *Magic Spells*, 23. The Mishnaic evidence allows for a date that is considerably earlier than the magical sources, themselves.

[32] tHul 2:22; yAZ 2:2, 40df; yShab 14:4, 14d.

[33] On the ritual of being a rabbi and its consequences within the context of ritual power see Neusner, 'Phenomenon'; idem, 'Phenomenon II'; Blau, *Zauberwesen*, 54-61; Gruenwald, 'Ha-ketav, ha-mikhtav'; Garb, *Manifestations of Power*, 28-46.

[34] For the sources on Honi the Circle-drawer, see mTaan 3:8; bTaan 23a; yTaan 3:10f, 66df. And cf further bYom 53b; bTaan 24b; and see Harari, 'Power and Money', 23f.

them by means of speech (bSan 68a); to fill a valley with golden dinars (MidrPs 92,8, Buber, 204a, Exod R. 52:3); to have control over the sea (ySan 7:11); to kill a snake by mere contact (bBer 33a); to kill with words or with a stare;[35] or to send a snake whose bite knows no remedy (see above); to raise corpses from the earth (yShev 9:1, 38d) or to revive the dead (bMeg 7b); to divine; to contend with demons and to overcome sorceresses and sorcerers. The climax is in attributing to sages the capacity to create. In this context we should observe, alongside the story of the three year old heifer that was created by the sages through their studies (see above) Rava's words: 'If the righteous so desired, they could create a world', and the juxtaposed story of the *golem* that he created and sent to R. Zera.[36]

From the standpoint of this study, it makes no difference whether one attains influence in reality through study, prayer, and Divine succour, or whether through incantation and the aid of an angel or a demon. All of these are ritual means and agents of metaphysical power that help someone in this world. From the inner-cultural perspective of the sages who saw themselves as God's representatives in this world, and whose social authority they also sought to affirm by means of metaphysical proofs such as these, the difference was tremendous. Since 'magic', 'sorcerer' and 'sorceries' (כשפים כשוף, מכשף,) were rhetorical terms that served for unfavorable labeling of the 'other' and of the forbidden, the rabbis were automatically removed from this designation. There was no question about the derivation of their powers, which originated in normative righteousness and closeness to God.[37] This was manifest in such statements as the following: 'I rule over man, who rules over me? – the right-eous man' (bMK 16b); 'you decree below; and the Holy One, blessed be He fulfills your words above' (bTaan 23a), or 'the Holy One, blessed be He annuls His decree on account of the decree of the righteous man' (yTaan 3:12, 67a). From here, as a lively expression of the norms of the sanctified life which they had fashioned and sought to bequeath to their communities, the rabbis wrestled with other agents of ritual power – the 'sorcerers' as they describe them – above all women and heretics. It was apparently this struggle that brought about the dispensation to study and teach sorcery (bShab 75a) and even the notion that those who sit in the Sanhedrin should be 'masters of sorcery' (בעלי כשפים).[38]

---

[35] yTaan 3:10f, 66d; bBer 58a; bShab 34a; bBB 75a; PesRK 18,5, p298, and many more. See, too, Ulmer, *Evil Eye*, 83-104.

[36] bSan 65b. See Idel, *Golem*, 27-43.

[37] In this way the rabbis were the successors of Moses not only in the sense of being leaders but as following along his miraculous and magical path. On this side to the image of Moses see Harari, 'Moses'. On Moses as controlling God – 'He decrees over the Holy One, Blessed be He, and He fulfils, and he raises Him up... and makes Him sit down' – see DeutR 2,3.

[38] bMen 65a; bSan 17a, and see Rashi's commentary there.

A link between women and sorcery is suggested in Babylonian sources.[39] This is a later development of a direction manifest in the words of Hillel in the Mishnaic tractate, Avot, (2:7): 'One who increases women increases sorcery'. Linking sorcery with fornication and both with the obliteration of blessing in the world (mSot 9:13) portrays sorcery as spiritual complement to the physical mode of female licentiousness.[40] The expressions of this tendency are varied: 'Most sorcery is with women'; 'most women engage in sorcery'; 'The daughters of Israel offer up incense to sorcery'; 'sorcery is widespread among The daughters of Israel'; 'the most acceptable of women is a sorceress', and so on.[41] One tradition attributes sorcery to old women, in particular,[42] while others speak, in general terms, of women who 'dabble in sorcery' or are witches (כשפניות), and consider all women suspect of sorcery.[43] The picture is completed by stories of female sorcery in which women function as characters that participate in the concrete and familiar reality, yet at the same time, being almost always anonymous, they represent any woman, and the entire female collective.[44] In practice, almost all talmudic traditions that are concerned with the practical execution of sorcery attribute the activity to women. Nevertheless, one need not see this as an expression of historical reality in which sorcery *was* the explicit domain of women, but rather as an expression of a different socio-patriarchal reality, whereby men in general, and rabbis in particular, attempted to cope with the intimidating power of women through symbolizing it as mystical-metaphysical power and categorizing it as illegitimate – sorcery. The term 'witch', identified in the Talmud with females and with each and every woman, more than being instructive regarding the ritual behaviour of women, reflects anxiety over the power of the 'other' in masculine society

---

[39] A basis for this view is already to be found in the biblical ruling 'you shall not suffer a *sorceress* to live', which uses the feminine form whilst the matter relates to a concrete accusation of sorcery. Ascribing sorcery to women is also common in the apocryphal literature. See, below, n40. On this topic, and the rabbis' attitude to women as sorceresses see further Bar-Ilan, 'Witches'; Fishbane, 'Most Women'; Ilan, *Jewish Women*, 221-225.

[40] Harlotry and sorcery were placed together already in the Bible. See, for example, 2 Kgs, 9:21-22; Nah 3:4. 1 Enoch 6-8 links sorcery to the female act of making themselves up (symbolizing seduction and licentiousness) and the two together with the hybrid coupling of the fallen angels and the women they took for themselves. An additional apocryphal tradition attributes to the women, themselves, lustful for licentiousness and harlotry the seduction of the fallen angels by means of sorcery (Test Reub 5). On the linkage between women, sorcery, and lust in the Greco-Roman compositions see Baroja, *World of the Witches*, 31-34.

[41] See, following the order of the citations, MekhSbY Mishpatim, p209; bSan 67a; bBer 53a; bEr 64b; yKid 4:11, 66b; Soferim 15:7.

[42] bSan 100b. On the misogynous tendency in the talmudic citations from Ben-Sira of which this citation is one expression, see Ilan, 'Ben-Sira's Attitude'.

[43] bPes 110a; 111a; bYom 83b; yYom 8:5, 45b.

[44] bGit 35a; 45a; bShab 81b; bSan 67b; bBB 153a; bPes 110b; ySan 7:19, 25d. If indeed Yohani bat Retivi, mentioned in bSot 22a is a sorceress she was then the only one mentioned by name. See below, n45.

with the rabbis at the centre, and the effort to remove this power beyond the acceptable social order.

The most outstanding expressions of this anxiety are found in the traditions that connect sorcery with women over whom society had little control. Elderly women and inn-keepers, who cohabit the public – male – space, and perhaps also widows,[45] fall into this category, and traditions concerned with the struggle with organized sorceresses, that too, are linked with the un-supervised existence of women in the public space. Anxiety about organized female sorcery, led, according to one source by 'the leader of witches' (bSan 110a), was considerable. Its very mention in the sources is accompanied by instructions on how to overcome these women (bSan 110a-b, bPes 110a), or stories that describe moments of triumph over them. The best known, and indeed most developed of such stories describes a combat between Shimon b. Shetah and 80 sorceresses in a cave in Ashkelon and ends with the hanging of them all on the same day.[46] The focus is a description of the struggle between two opposing camps: on one side we have men, rabbis, cunning, knowledge and physical power; on the other, women, sorcery, and licentiousness. Shimon b. Shetah overcomes the sorceresses by appearing to cooperate with them, yet his deeds are nothing less than male heroic craftiness against the female power of sorcery. To this end, he manipulates two essential components of female sorcery (or, to be more precise, its popular image), that the story divulges: (a) its licentious nature, expressed not only in their gathering together in the cave, but in the objective of their sorcery that they choose to display before him – food and drink for the celebration, and their desire for the men that he brings with him into the cave; (b) the earthy sub-terrestrial source of their magical power (in

---

[45] This, if indeed Rashi is accurate in his comment regarding Yohani bat Retivi, whereby she would, as a midwife, close the wombs of women in labour through sorcery and release them later under the guise of prayer and piety (Rashi on bSot 22a). We must however remember that the talmud preserves no information about this widow, whose name it does, indeed, discredit, and yet the common tendency to attribute to the Talmud itself Rashi's commentary has, it would appear, no basis. This would appear to be an illustrative example of the gender-determined manner by which males observed, from the outside, the activity surrounding the exclusively female occasion of birth, in which they were denied the possibility to participate, yet heard much about, and were indeed full participants in all that concerned the often-tragic results. The attribution of harmful sorcery to the midwife, the one whose power, tied to exclusive control over knowledge, unseats the males and leave them powerless and helpless outside the life-forming event, makes a profound statement concerning the anxiety of the power of women that is based on the very dependence of male society on women for its very existence. A close expression of this hostile notion of female power is found in the attribution of the 'demonic' harm linked to the birth pains and the death of the mother and child in the birth process to Lilith, a *female* demon. In both instances the male consciousness links the mysterious power of life-giving within the female to another kind of mysterious female power which is destructive, magical and demonic, and thereby increases, to the extent of becoming life-threatening, the very existence of uncontrolled and unrestricted female power.

[46] ySan 6:9, 23c; yHag 2:2, 77df. See Amir, 'Shimeon ben Shatah'; Ilan, 'Witch-hunt'; Yassif, *Hebrew Folktale*, 156-158.

contradistinction to the celestial source of the rabbis' power and wisdom), that can be separated from them by means of their physical severance from the ground. The physical might of a 'unit' of disciplined men lead by a wise leader, overcomes, as is to be expected, the magical unruly licentiousness of the women gathered in the cave, and eradicates them.

An additional important aspect in the stories of the struggle between rabbis and sorcerers is the superiority of the Jewish holy rabbi over the heretical sorcerer.[47] Alongside the tendency referred to above to depict foreign sorcery as a mere deception, two dispute stories deserve special note, that appear in the Yerushalmi (San 7:19, 25d) and feature R. Joshua and his companions, R. Eliezer, R. Akiva, and Rabban Gamliel. In the two narratives, the principle whereby the rabbi is unable to annul the harmful sorcery of the other, directs the plot beyond the battle against sorcery, itself, in which R. Joshua reveals impressive ingenuity in bringing about the submission of the sorcerer, the 'other'. In one, set in Rome, R. Joshua overcomes a local sorceress and compels her to annul her acts of sorcery that damaged the potency of their Jewish host. In the other, that takes place in the bathhouse of Tiberias, he compels a heretic that put a spell on him and his companions, to release them by means of counter-magic.[48] Afterwards, when the latter boasted his ability to split the sea and walk between the waves in imitation of Moses, R. Joshua decreed over the prince of the sea, and it swallowed him up. Decree and guile are bound together in this story to destroy and remove those whose arrogance overruns the limit, and with great peril even succeed (!) in using the power as Moses. This is achieved by those who saw themselves as the sole legitimate heirs of Moses in both knowledge and deed.

Demons and the Evil Eye

As with sorcery, so the textual evidence associated with demons and the evil eye is so extensive, that one must re-evaluate rabbinic texts in this light. This results in an interesting picture concerning rabbinic demonology, and in particular, concerning the rabbinic use of the demonological theme in their stories.[49] The Jewish magical amulets, bowls and recipes from antiquity reveal the notion that identified calamities in general, and sickness, in particular, with demonic affliction. The evil eye appears often in them amongst the agents of metaphysical harm from which the users seek to distance themselves. For Jews and others in antiquity, demons were a part of reality: hidden beings and elu-

---

[47] See now Bohak, 'Magical Means'.

[48] Regarding the phrase 'he said what he said' as indicating the ritual activity of both the heretic and R. Joshua see Sperber, *Magic and Folklore*, 60-66. For a similar parallel see bShab 81b (=bHul 105b).

[49] For an excellent summary of the rabbinic sources on this topic see H.L. Strack and P. Billerbeck, 'Dämonologie'; and see further, Blau, *Zauberwesen*; Yassif, *Hebrew Folktale*, 144-156; Gafni, 'Babylonian Rabbinic Culture'.

sive, that might change form as they so desired, and, especially, they possessed a tremendous potential to inflict damage. As we find reflected in the magical literature, man's attitude towards demons and the evil eye was clear-cut. It strove to restrict them to beyond the living space of the one seeking protection, the members of his household and farmstead and sought protection from them. It aimed to remove them from this boundary or even from a person's very body in the case in which life's circumstances indicated that they had already penetrated and were engaged in their harmful activity there.[50] rabbinic literature completes this picture and expands it on the one hand, and is illustrative with regard to the didactic-propagandistic use made of it by the rabbis, on the other.

'EVIL EYE' AND 'THE EVIL EYE'

Many rabbinic sources refer to 'an evil eye' (עין רעה) or to 'the Evil Eye' (עין הרע). Though seemingly synonymous these terms have a different meaning.[51] The sages use them in the sense of both feelings of jealousy, animosity, or depreciation towards the other,[52] and injury inflicted upon a person that derives from these feelings and is based on the act of gazing upon him. It is the second meaning that is important for the current discussion. Expressions of the notion of the harmful power of the evil eye, usually manifest bodily harm to the victim, and occasionally even resulting in death, appear within the context of both aggada and halakha. Of particular notice are midrashim in which the jealousy on the part of biblical characters is intensified up to bringing them to cause the evil eye to enter their opponent (GenR 45:5, p453; 84:10, p1013; DeutR 1,25). Although rabbinic literature indicates that the influence of the evil stare penetrates the body of a person and dwells in it, it does not explicitly admit to the notion of the demonic personification of the power of the human evil stare, such as the spirit of *maskorita* (רוחא מסקוריתא) found in the incantation literature.[53]

Similar to this, and also found in both magic literature and rabbinic literature, is the harm caused by the gaze of evil superhuman beings.[54] This may be what lies behind the term 'the evil eye' (עין הרע), not only as interpreted in a human context, but as the gaze of metaphysical evil – 'the eye *of* the evil' – the

---

[50] For the study of demonology in Jewish magical literature see above, n1. The scholarship on Jewish demonology and the demonology of the earlier surrounding cultures is considerable. See, now, Eshel, *Belief in Demons*, and the extensive bibliography brought there; and see below, n80.

[51] For discussion on the evil eye see: Ulmer, *Evil Eye*; Blau, *Zauberwesen*, 152-156; Cohen, *Everyman's Talmud*, 270-274; Ford, '"Ninety-Nine', and 'Additions and Corrections'.

[52] Evil eye also designates stinginess (for example, mTer 4:3) and similarly, the term עין צרה (a 'narrow eye'). This contrasts with the positive עין טובה ('a good eye') or עין יפה ('a nice eye').

[53] See Naveh-Shaked, *Magic Spells*, A26/14-15, and see *ib.*, 64f for the meaning of סקר in magical texts. Cf further idem, *Amulets*, A1/16-17.

[54] See, for example, Naveh-Shaked, *Magic Spells*, A23.

name of which, for fear, may not leave one's lips. Such evil might be the Angel of Death or a demon called 'Ketev Meriri'. Regarding the latter we have an
explicit statement: 'Ketev Meriri is made of many peels, many hairs, and many
eyes... and one eye is fixed in its heart and whoever sees it will never have life,
whether man or beast. And whoever it sees will collapse and die.'[55] As for the
former, described in the Bavli as totally covered with eyes (bAZ 20b), it would
appear that its evil eye is documented in traditions that tie it with the sin of the
Golden Calf and the shattering of the tablets of the Law.[56] Apparently, this is
the same eye from which Abraham delivered Isaac after his binding.[57]

The evil eye has the potential to affect everything.[58] For this reason: 'blessing is only to be found in a matter that is hidden from the eye', since in such
circumstances, 'the eye has no control over it' (bTaan 8b).[59] The vast majority
of traditions associate it with sickness and death, as documented in amulets
and magic bowls.[60] Rav attributed to it 99 out of every 100 deaths (bBM 107b;
yShab 14:3, 14c). As in the case of demons, harm caused by the evil eye is
mostly described in terms of penetration, possession, and control over a person, which can occur to both an individual (yShab 14:3, 14c) or to a number of
people (bSan 93a; ySan 1:2, 18c). For this reason the rabbis determined, 'one
must beware of the evil eye' (bBB 118a) and urged people not to awaken it.[61]
For one who feared the harmful powers of his own eye they recommended that
he 'look at the opening of his left nostril' in order to avoid it entering another
person (bBer 55b).

All are exposed to the harm of the evil eye with the exception of the seed of
Joseph who, like Joseph himself, are immune from it.[62] Protective measures
were therefore essential. The rabbis mention, in this context, the use of amulets[63] and apotropaic magical measures. One such measure involved creating a
circle with one's limbs, and reciting: 'I, so-and-so, the son of so-and-so, I am
of the seed of Joseph, over whom the evil eye has no power' (bBer 55b). If,
despite this one was nevertheless harmed and required healing, the rabbis
permitted it, even on the Sabbath: 'One may whisper a charm over the eye and
over the snake and over the scorpion and remove the eye on the Sabbath, but

[55] NumR 12:3. Cf LamR 1,3 (Buber, 32a); MidrPs 91,3 (Buber, 199ab).
[56] bShab 89a; NumR 12,4; ExodR 41,7; Tanh Ki tisa 13 (Buber, 56bf).
[57] GenR 56,11, p611. On Satan's involvement in the binding of Isaac see further bSan 89b; PesR
40, p170b. Cf Jub 17:15-18:13.
[58] See, for example, its damage to property (bPes 26a; GenR 58,7, p627) and to marriage (NumR
12,4).
[59] For this reason the eye has no control over fish (bBB 118b).
[60] For example, Naveh-Shaked, *Magic Spells*, A19.
[61] bPes 26b. Cf further bBer 10a; bBB 118a; bBM 107a, and Rashi *ad loc*. See, too, the traditions
about activity carried out by the Patriarchs Abraham and Jacob (GenR 56,11, p611; 91,6, p1121)
and Joshua (bBB 70a).
[62] bBB 118a; bBer 20a; 55b, bBM 84a.
[63] ExodR 12,4. For an amulet to heal from the evil eye see Naveh-Shaked, *Amulets*, A2. Cf, too, the
eyes mentioned in the healing amulet, *ib.*, A1.

one may not whisper a charm relating to demons.'[64] We see that a distinction was maintained between sickness related to the evil eye and demonic sickness. It would seem that, at least within the circles where this distinction was formulated, the evil eye was not perceived as a part of the demonic inventory but rather as a collateral phenomenon.

DEMONS AND EVIL SPIRITS

Demons, harmful beings, or evil spirits (as they are often described) were an important part of Jewish cosmology in antiquity.[65] Yet, as opposed to the other metaphysical beings, God, the angels and the dead, their place was in *this* world alongside human beings. Our knowledge about them, deriving mostly from the Bavli, has been transmitted by the rabbis in three principle forms: general comments relating to them, instructions on how to protect oneself from them, and anecdotes about them. The following survey follows this order.

The rabbis offered two answers concerning evidence for the existence of demons in the world, one explicit: God created them (mAv 5:6); and the other, alluded to in various fragments of tradition whereby they derive from the hybrid mating between Adam, the first man, and a demoness, called 'the First Eve', who was created before Eve, 'the mother of all life', and was then abandoned (bEr 18b; GenR 17,7, p158; 22,7, p213f). Later tradition identified this demoness as Lilith.[66] The rabbis portrayed them as falling between man and angel: possessing wings, swiftness, and hidden knowledge commensurate with angels, but who also eat, drink, reproduce and die as human beings (bHag 16a). They believed they were considerably more numerous than human beings, and attributed to them failure, catastrophies, sickness and death, and held that were they visible people could not confront them (bBer 6a).

Here and there we hear descriptions of their physical appearance.[67] Their legs are 'as the legs of a cock' (bBer 6a). Lilith is winged and has disheveled hair.[68] As for Ketev Meriri, mentioned above, 'its head is like a calf, and a horn protrudes from its forehead... it is made with many peels, much hair, and many

---

[64] tShab 7:23. This is the version of ms Erfurt (Zuckermandel p119). But cf the reading in ms Vienna (Lieberman p28f), and see yShab 14:3, 14c; bSan 101a.

[65] Demons possessed many appellations that were on occasion generic names indicating the subgroups within the broad category 'demons'. See Strack – Billerbeck, 'Dämonologie'. The most important amongst them, such as Ashmedai, Ketev, Lilith, Agrat bat Mahalat are called by their individual names. On the various groups of demons in magical sources see Montgomery, *Incantation Texts*, 67-94; Shaked, 'Jews, Christians', 72-80.

[66] See Yassif, *Tales of Ben Sira*, 63-71, 231-234; Krebs, 'Lilith', 147ff; Stern-Mirsky, *Rabbinic Fantasies*, 183f. On the biblical and Mesopotamian background to Lilith see Krebs, *ib.* 141-147; Hurwitz, *Lilith*, 19-66; Hutter, 'Lilith'. On Lilith in the demonology of the magic bowls see Fauth, 'Lilits und Astarten'; Lesses, 'Exe(o)rcising Power', 354-359.

[67] On the iconographic images of demons on the babylonian magic bowls see Hunter, 'Who are the Demons'; 'Typology of the Incantation Bowls'; 'Technical Tables'.

[68] bEr 100b, bNid 24b, NumR 12,3, Cf Lesses, 'Exe(o)rcising Power'; Levene, 'Heal O' Israel'.

eyes... and one eye is fixed in its heart'. They are capable of changing their form[69] and adopting the shape of a man (bMeg 3a), a seductress (yShab 1:3, 3b), or a monster with seven heads (bKid 29b). They are generally totally hidden from view and are only visible to a person when he is alone (and then the harm they inflict is severe) or sometimes also when in a pair.[70]

The incantations written in magic bowls indicate that no time or place is immune from the harmful beings, and this also emerges from rabbinic literature. As a rule, the night is their domain, but there also exists the possibility of a daytime attack.[71] There are demons of shade and *shabririm* of the day (bGit 69a) for whom the daytime is preferable. Ketev Meriri was said to rule over midday.[72] Certain days and seasons are particularly perilous. *Agrat bat Mahalat* and her host are active on the Sabbath eve and on Wednesday evenings (bPes 112b). All of these harmful beings 'are certainly present' from the first of the month of Tamuz until the sixteenth of the same (bPes 111b), while Ketev Meriri is active from the seventeenth of Tamuz until the ninth of Ab.[73] Also, they are not limited by space. Some fly through the air and strike as an arrow (NumR 12,3) whilst others are based on the ground. The latter might be found anywhere: in bodies of water,[74] along paths (DEZ hayotse 18, Higger, 319f), on the roads and alleyways of the cities, on the roofs of the houses and in rooms, on, or underneath the bed, in food, drinking water, and even in the crumbs on the floor.[75] Shady places are particularly dangerous, and there were those who avoided them altogether.[76] They were not absent from even the holiest of places. One tradition states they were present at Mount Sinai when the Tora was given (NumR 12,3), another that they might even be in the House of Study (bKid 29b). And yet a third tradition asserts that from the moment the Sanctuary was set up and the Divine Presence dwelled below 'the harmful beings were annihilated from the world' (DeutR 12,3).

Demons are mentioned in the rabbinic literature as large and small, as individuals and as groups, as male and female. They are divided into generic groups on the basis of their place and time of activity. They include humble and noble types, and even those who ride horses (bPes 112b-113a). Ashmedai is their sovereign, yet he is not described as leading their activity in the

---

[69] bYom 75a. Cf in the magical literature: Naveh-Shaked, *Magic Spells*, B25.

[70] bBer 43b, however cf bPes 111b where *Ketev Meriri* appears to Abaye who is accompanying Rav Papa and Rav Huna.

[71] Demons at night: bBer 5a; 6a; bMeg 3a; bShab 151b; bKid 29b; bGit 69a; ExodR 12,3. Demons during the daytime: bHul 105b; bKid 29b; bPes 111b; LamR 1,3 (Buber, 32ab).

[72] bPes 111b; NumR 12,3; LamR 1,3 (Buber, 32ab); MidrPs 91,3 (Buber, 199ab).

[73] ExodR *ib.*; LamR *ib.*; MidrPs *ib.*

[74] bPes 112a; LevR 24,3, p553ff; Tanh Kedoshim 9 (Buber, 39a); MidrPs 20,7 (Buber, 88b).

[75] bPes 111b-113a; bBer 6a; bShab 151b.

[76] bPes 111b. *Ketev Meriri* was active in the narrow margin 'between shade and sun' (ExodR 12,3; LamR 1,3, Buber, 32ab; MidrPs 91,3, Buber, 199ab). The shade spirits (טולין) appear in magical sources. See Naveh-Shaked, *Amulets*, 270; idem, *Magic Spells*, 268.

world.[77] Agrat bat Mahalat, on the other hand, stands at the head of a 'chariot' of harmful beings[78] – 180,000 destroying angels, and each and every one of them 'has permission to wreak destruction independently' (bPes 112b). Lilith and Ketev Meriri, also mentioned by name, were apparently perceived as especially powerful and dangerous.

According to rabbinic traditions, harmful beings function both individually and as a group. They might initiate an attack without provocation or cause.[79] On occasion they might act in response to some human action. They might be provoked by remaining within their domain while alone, (beyond the city limits, in a toilet, under shade), or at the hour of their activity (at night), drinking water in which they reside, and a variety of activities such as drinking an even number of cups, or relieving oneself (bPes 110a-111b). Occasionally they wait for the right moment when a person carries out an act exposing oneself to their harm, and then they envelop him (bBer 51a).

The malicious harm of demons and evil spirits is described in rabbinic literature, parallel to what is known in great detail from the anti-demonic magic literature, as penetration of the body of a living being and dwelling therein, bringing about sickness and death.[80] Demonic possession may occur in human beings, animals, and inanimate objects, and its presence is contagious. Shmuel, one of the main spokesmen in medical matters in the Bavli, and the rabbi who asserted that the majority of cases of death are the result of a spirit,[81] attributed to an evil spirit, 'the spirit of restlessness' (תזזית), the behaviour of a mad dog (rabies) whose bite, as is known, spreads the death that resides in it.[82] For the same reason the rabbis warned against the consumption of food or drink placed underneath the bed ('and even when covered with an iron vessel') or drinking water left uncovered on Wednesday and the Sabbath eve, or of the use of a knife made of the peel of reed canes, for fear of infection with the evil spirit that dwells in them by inhaling it or even contact with it.[83] An attack

---

[77] bPes 110a; bGit 68a. On the Persian source of Ashmedai, first mentioned in Jewish sources in the Book of Tobit, see Hutter, 'Asmodeus'; Pines, 'Wrath and Creatures of Wrath'. On Persian demons in Babylonian Jewish magic see, further, Shaked, 'Bagdana'.

[78] ExodR 12,3. The term 'chariot' is widespread in the ancient Jewish mystical literature to indicate the horde of angels beneath the Throne of Honour. See above ch. 12.

[79] bKid 29b; bHul 105b; bPes 112b.

[80] An exception to this rule is the tradition, brought in yShab 1:3, 3b, relates the harm to the moral aspect. In Qumran literature, too, the demons are perceived as instigators. See Alexander, 'Wrestling'; idem, 'Demonology'. The scholarly literature on possession and the expulsion of demons in late antiquity is extensive. See, for instance, Eshel, *Belief in Demons*; Twelftree, *Jesus the Exorcist*; Kotansky, 'Greek Exorcistic Amulets'.

[81] bBM 107b. The word רוח is presumably used here to mean an evil spirit and not 'wind'. Cf, there, also R. Hanina's view that links death to coldness.

[82] bYom 83b; yYom 8:5, 44b. Cf further GenR 12,9, p107.

[83] bPes 112a; yShab 8:6, 11c. The 'law of contact' is one of the two laws that Frazer proposed to account for the notion of the impact of magic on those who use it (the second principle is the 'law of similarity'). See Frazer, *Golden Bough*, vol 1, 52-54, and the extensive discussion there, 214-

initiated by the demons brought about possession and this was expressed, as we noted, by various illnesses. The spirit of צליחתא, *Tsalihta*, also known as פלגא, *Palga*, was identified as a migraine (bGit 68b). The spirit of קצרין, *Katsarin*, was identified as asthma, and perhaps also with epilepsy (bBekh 44b). קורדייקוס, *Kardiakos*, mentioned in the Mishna with the sense of delirium, was considered later as a demon whose harm was linked with drinking new wine.[84] The harm of the 'spirit of restlessness' was connected with the loss of self-control and disorderly behaviour.[85] שברירי, *Shabriri*, of day and night were identified with blindness.[86] It is possible that אשתא, *Eshata* (fever) was not only perceived as a fever that spreads throughout the body, but also as an evil spirit that inflamed it, as is found in many Jewish magical amulets.[87] This may also be the meaning of the ברוקתי, *Barokti*, cataract (bGit 69b). This is the 'male and female *Barakata*', mentioned in magic bowls as demons.[88] Likewise, we find mentioned *simata*, a skin disease, for which one must recite an incantation, in the second person singular, that it should not multiply (bShab 67a). כודא, *Kuda*, known from other sources as harmful to women in confinement,[89] שיבתא, *Shivta*, apparently perceived as attacking infants and killing them,[90] and the spirit of צרדא, *Tsereda*, that attacks at the hour of the banquet are also mentioned (bHul 105b).

The daunting reality of living one's life alongside demons resulted in diverse means of defense against them. The most important documents relating to this are, of course, the apotropaic amulets and bowls and the related magical recipes. The information in rabbinic literature fits in well with the world view reflected in these texts. First of all, the very existence of the rabbinic discourse on demons contributed to the ability to protect oneself against them, as it made them perceivable, predictable, and better understood. The clarification of their forms, nomenclature, favourite dwelling places, times of activity, and circumstances of harm they cause equipped one with the means to address the danger and to make active efforts in order to cope and to minimize the harm. In addition, the rabbis offered specific instructions on how to repel demons. The principle of active practices for protection against demons and their expulsion is the use of performative verbal formulae, in oral or written form.[91] Among

---

255. For an examination of these principles in rabbinic thought see, now, Bar-Ilan, 'Between Magic and Religion'.

[84] mGit 7:1 (and cf bGit 70b); bGit 67b. The Greek origin of the word *kardiakos*, at any rate, indicates harm to the heart or the stomach, perhaps as an indication of melancholy. See Krauss, *Lehnwörter*, 519; Preuss, *Medicine*, 178f, 320f.

[85] PesRK 10,3, p164; 4,7, p74 and parallels. Cf GenR 12,9, p107.

[86] bGit 69a. And see Sokoloff, *Dictionary, Babylonian*, 1106.

[87] bShab 66b-67a, and see Naveh – Shaked, *Magic Spells*, 36f.

[88] *Ib.*, B25.

[89] bAZ 29a, and see Sokoloff, *Dictionary, Babylonian*, 555.

[90] bYom 77b, bHul 107b, and see Kohut, *Aruch*, vol 8, 24.

[91] On the performative language within the context of Jewish magic see Harari, 'How to Do Things'.

these are certain canonical formulae: (a) Ps 3 and 91, known as 'the Song of Injuries' (bShev 15b; cf yEr 10:12, 26c). Ps 91 has a long anti-demonic history,[92] and according to the Midrash, it was even used by Moses for this purpose when he ascended Mount Sinai (NumR 12:31; MidrPs 91,1, Buber, 198b); (b) bedtime recital of the Shema, concerning which R. Yitshak said: 'The *mazikin* (demons) stay away from whosoever recites the bedtime Shema' (bBer 5a). In addition to these, amulets and various charms were used, whose formulae were transmitted, in order to expel demons and to provide protection from them.[93] A seal and chain, with the Tetragrammaton engraved upon it, are mentioned amongst the means of controlling the demons in the story of Solomon and Ashmedai,[94] whereas the story of R. Yosi of Tsitur and the demon of the well teaches of the belief in the power of iron to expel, and perhaps even to kill them.[95]

Alongside such technical and the practical information concerning demons, attention should also be paid to the manner in which the sages made use of the demon motif in their stories for their own social and didactic purposes. The pertinent primary magical sources have for their sole objective the absolute separation between man and demons through the performance of protective rites. The relationship between humans and demons tends to be different in the rabbinic demon stories – stories of rabbis in which demons have a secondary role. Here, a variety of relationships between demons and human beings is outlined, while the underlying notion is the inclusion of demons within the unitary ethical system that is governed by God in the world and has the rabbis for its spokesmen and representatives. In consequence, the demons are subject to the legal or charismatic power of the rabbis.[96]

As to protection against demons, the sages have an advantage. First and foremost, Tora study provides them with a permanent immunity (NumR 12,3).

---

[92] See Nitzan, 'Hymns from Qumran' (and see the notes to this article, Ta-Shema, 'Notes'; Baumgarten, 'Qumran Songs'); Nitzan, *Qumran Prayer*, 206-265. On the notion of demons at Qumran and the means of protecting oneself from them see Alexander, 'Wrestling'; idem, 'Demonology', and recently, Eshel, *Belief in Demons*, 295-320.

[93] bShab 67a; bGit 69a; bPes 111b. In light of the identification of the illness with demonic possession, it would appear that even the entire discussion about amulets for healing, and in particular that which addresses the subject of amulets prepared by an expert, where epilepsy is mentioned, should be viewed as an expression of anti-demonic practice, even if this is not mentioned explicitly.

[94] bGit 68a-b. The story is founded on ancient traditions relating to Solomon's control over demons. A well-developed expression of this is the apocryphal work known as the Testament of Solomon. See Charlesworth, *Pseudepigrapha* 1, 935-987; Duling, 'Solomon'. For research on the talmudic story see Yassif, *Hebrew Folktale*, 87-89, n19-20. On the use of a magical seal – a ring with a root buried under its seal – for the expulsion of demons see Josephus, Ant. 8.2.5 (8:46-49).

[95] LevR 24,3, p553ff; Tanh Kodashim 9, (Buber, 39a). In the parallel in MidrPs 20,7 (Buber, 88b), there is no mention of beating with an iron tool but only with sticks in order to aid the friendly Name to kill the one that is causing harm. Also the other traditions conclude with seeing blood on the water surface, however there is no explicit mention of the killing of the demon.

[96] For discussion of demonic stories in rabbinic literature see Yassif, *Hebrew Folktale*, 144-156.

As a consequence, they are exempt from the bedtime recitation of the Shema.[97] This is articulated in traditions such as the one about Abaye who saw Ketev Meriri approaching a group of rabbis and protected them by placing Rav Papa in front as a human shield; or the one that links magical knowledge to rabbinic study and asserts that only one who is a true rabbinic scholar possesses the knowledge necessary for the writing of effective amulets to expel demons (bPes 111b). However, the rabbis' advantage did not end with protection against demons; some even succeeded in overcoming them. Thus R. Hanina ben Dosa and Abaye are mentioned as having dictated to Agrat bat Mahalat and her cohorts limits concerning time and place for their demonic activities. They were confined to Sabbath and Wednesday evenings, and to the alleyways on the outskirts of the inhabited areas.[98] Others expressed their power in the struggle against demons and the harm they do. One tradition states that the prayer of the rabbis helped to heal R. Bebai b. Abba who had sought to gaze at them (bBer 6a). Another links the miracle of protection from an especially violent demon residing in Abaye's House of Study with the personality and sword of the prayer of R. Aha b. Yaakov (bKid 29b). A third tradition relates how a demon was summoned to judgement and Mar b. Rav Ashi's verdict against him, thereby 'taming' the demon and bringing him under the rabbinic social-ethical framework (bHul 105b). Finally, we are witness to the expansion of the network of relations between the rabbis and the demons to the extent of cooperation between the two.[99]

Alongside the technical magical practices of the expulsion of demons through amulets and charms, the sages, then, place their very own ethical-religious model as an efficient means not just of protection against demons but even for controlling and manipulating them. This was not done in the usual way of magic practice by means of incantations,[100] but in the normative rabbinic method of the miracle.

---

[97] bBer 4a. Abaye's objection, there, and the connection that is drawn further on between the bedtime recitation of the Shema and protection from *mezikin* indicate that the discussion is focused on the advantage of the protection of scholars from the demons.

[98] bPes 112b-113a. On this tradition in the Babylonian magic bowls see Shaked, 'Form and Purpose'.

[99] Cf information transmitted by 'Yosef the demon', יוסף שידא, bPes 110a; R. Yosi of Tsitur and the friendly demon of the well, above n95; and the help offered by the demon Ben Tamalion to R. Shimon b. Yohai by entering the body of the Caesar's daughter, bMeila 17a-b. This is not historical reality, nor a parody of the expulsion of demons by Christians (cf Jabez, *Toledot Yisrael*, vol 6, 318-320; Bar-Ilan, 'Exorcism', 23f; Yassif, *Hebrew Folktale*, 154f), but hagiography, meaning the use of miracle stories to propagate for the values represented by the holy man.

[100] See Harari, *Jewish Magic* (diss.), 156f.

Divination

Divination is a generic term for practices aimed at attaining information not through regular means of study.[101] Thus, also the knowledge acquired by means of divination is not regular knowledge but hidden knowledge, and divination agents are the ones with exclusive access to it. Such means and agents were widespread in the cultures of Mesopotamia and the eastern Mediterranean in Antiquity as part of a common culture of divination that encompassed local variations. This culture acquired a place of honour in the system of knowledge in the societies concerned, including that of the Jews.[102] Social institutions were not indifferent to the advantage of power associated with knowledge, in particular the secret knowledge that was the domain of divination agents. Just as the agents of occult power were divided into the permitted and the forbidden, so, too, were the agents of occult knowledge, and here, too, the distinction was based as much on social affiliation as on the actual practices.[103]

Divination is based on the premise that all that occurs in the world in past, present and future, within this world or beyond it, and in every dimension of reality, exists and is available as potential knowledge for humans to attain. In the Hellenistic world the methods of divination were categorized according to two main groups: inductive divination based on signs and symbols, and intuitive divination based on special psychic powers.[104] Both are documented in the rabbinic literature. The first group includes various phenomena perceived and interpreted as signs, as well as astral signs and dreams. The second group consists of divination by such that by their very nature are agents of hidden knowledge: rabbis, children, and the insane. To these one should add the בעלי אוב, *baalei ov*, mediums or necromancers who are called after the *ov* practice; those who consult with the dead (דורשים אל המתים); ידעונים, *yidonim*, 'wizards'; and those who consult with demons and angels.

Even though the rabbis prohibited divination, it is unlikely that they succeeded in containing it and certainly they did not eliminate it. The real situation is revealed in the words of Ahava b. R. Zera: 'Whoever does not divine is brought into an enclosure where even the ministering angels are not able to

---

[101] For a general survey and for the categories of divination see Zuesse, 'Divination'.

[102] For comprehensive bibliography on divination in these cultures see Harari, 'Opening of the Heart', 306-308 n10-11.

[103] On the social contexts of divination in the Roman world see for example MacMullen, *Enemies*, 128-162.

[104] This division, the foundations of which are already to be found in the works of Plato (Phaedrus, 244c-d, cf Timaeus, 71e-72b), was formulated in a systematic fashion by Cicero. See Marcus Tullius Cicero, *De divinatione*, LCL, London 1923, esp. 1.6, pp. 234-235. It is also accepted today in the modern study of ancient divination. See Harari, 'Opening of the Heart', 304 n3. Recently, Zuesse, 'Divination' has proposed an alternative typology of divination.

enter' (bNed 32a; cf yShab 6:10, 8d). If such was the reward for those who did not divine, surely they were few and far between.[105]

MEDIATORS

The Bible recognizes and mentions a few practices and mediators of divination, including: 'anyone who practices divination, a soothsayer, an augur, a sorcerer, a charmer, a necromancer, a wizard, or one who consults the dead'.[106] However, it rejects them as 'abominations of the gentiles' in favour of the legitimate form of the acquisition of occult knowledge – prophecy.[107] The rabbis, too, adopted this model. They saw in the biblical prophets (headed by Moses) the primary mediators of secret knowledge that was brought down to earth at God's command, and accordingly they associated the cessation of prophecy through the Holy Spirit with the disappearance of prophets.[108] At the same time, they, too, recognized a broad range of alternative means and of mediators of knowledge, both for divulging the words of God and for attaining essential day-to-day knowledge. The vast majority of the mediators (together with their means of divination) were rejected by them as illegitimate, for reasons that tie together, as with the case of sorcery, ideological and political considerations. However, all were judged to be effective. Some of them, such as astrologers, necromancers, wizards, and dream interpreters were professionals.[109] Some were laypeople trained in popular folk divination practices, mostly of the kind that was prohibited. Others, children, fools, and sages, were mediators of knowledge by their very nature.

As to the rabbis, this is no surprise. As with their metaphysical power, their proficiency in the occult, too, was portrayed as the result of their special proximity to God and their inherent holiness due to their being imbued with Tora.[110] An explicit reflection of this tendency may be found in the following statements, the context of which is a discussion on matters of prophecy (דברי נבואות), i.e. secret knowledge: 'R. Avdimi from Haifa said: Since the day when the Temple was destroyed prophecy has been taken away from the prophets and given over to the sages [...] Amemar said: and a sage is preferable to a prophet' (bBB 12a). Wisdom, bound to Tora study, is therefore an alternative

---

[105] For general surveys on divination and the rabbis see Jöel, *Aberglaube*, vol 1, 89f; Cohen, *Everyman's Talmud*, 274-297; Rabinowitz, 'Divination, in the Talmud'.

[106] Deut 18:10f: קוסם קסמים מעונן ומנחש ומכשף וחבר חבר ושאל אוב וידעוני ודרש אל המתים.

[107] Alongside the legitimate prophets of God, for whom the content of their tidings testifies to its Divine origin and truth (Deut 13:2-6), mention should also be made of the *urim* and *tummim* and the revelation dream as means of divination that were not entirely rejected. See below.

[108] See Urbach, 'Matai paska ha-nevua?', in idem, *World of the Sages*, 9-20; Yavin, 'Conclusion of Prophecy'.

[109] On astrologers and dream interpreters see below. *Baalei ov*: mSan 7:7; tSan 10:6; bSan 65b; bKer 3b; bBer 59a. *Yidonim*: mSan 7:7, tSan 10:6; bSan 65a; ySan 7:13, 25c. See further below.

[110] Cf Urbach, *The Sages* 2, 948f n20.

virtue to prophecy with regard to all that is related to revealing God's will to man in this world.[111] This may be connected to the many traditions regarding the echo of the word of God that had been explicitly conveyed to the prophets, the 'Divine voice' (בת קול) received and 'used' by rabbis.[112] The messages transmitted were varied. The 'Divine voice' served as a means to reveal God's judgement on various matters. For instance, it revealed His view on the value of the translation of the Prophets composed by Yonatan ben Uziel; the suicide of Hanna the mother of seven sons; and the study of the Heavenly Chariot (Merkava) by rabbis. The 'Divine voice' appeared in halakhic debates (but was not accepted as grounds for determining the halakha),[113] offered expressions of sorrow over the destruction of the Temple and the plight of the exile, heralded tidings concerning the nation's future, revealed the use made by angels of the secret declaration 'we shall do and we shall hear', and announced the special holiness of certain rabbis and their place in the world to come. In addition, it served as a vehicle for clearcut 'earthly' matters, whether national – the proclamation of military defeats or victories and the annulment of evil decrees – or personal, relating to matchmaking and property.[114] In any event, the 'Divine voice' in the sense discussed here would appear of its own accord, as a matter of course or on account of the sanctity of the people associated with its message. It was not summoned through any ceremony or performative verbal formula.[115]

---

[111] This would appear to be the meaning of 'prophecy' here. Another aspect of it – seeing a hidden reality – is discussed further along in the talmudic *sugya* (see below). At any rate, one should emphasize that the rabbis' attitude towards prophecy and the question of the relationship between prophet and sage is far more complex than the statement made by Avdimi and Amemar. See Urbach, *ib.*; idem, 'Halakha u-nevua', in idem, *World of the Sages*, 21-49; idem, 'Prophet and Sage in the Jewish Heritage', in: idem, *Collected Writings*, 393-403.

[112] bSot 48b; yShab 6:10, 8d. *Bat kol* is discussed here in the limited and common context of spontaneous Divine speech that is revealed (in the rabbinic sources: 'that comes out'). Such Divine revelation is also attributed to biblical figures in rabbinic literature. See Urbach, 'Halakha u-nevua', 26f. More broadly speaking, the term *bat qol* designates divination by means of human speech whose source is unknown. The reference to *use* (שמוש) within this context (bMeg 32b) alludes to an active role in attaining the human *bat kol* (yShab 6:10). In light of the explicit references to the use of the *bat kol* that belongs to the latter category (*ib.*, mYev 16:6) it would appear that we should see all the references to the use of the *bat kol* and acting in accordance with it within *this* context and not in the context that we shall discuss below. See Lieberman, *Hellenism*, 194-199; Urbach, *ib.*, 23f.

[113] bBM 59ab. Cf R. Joshua's statement: 'We do not take *bat kol* into account' (אין משגיחין בבת קול), bBer 52a; bYev 14a; bHul 44a.

[114] See the sources gathered by the following: Urbach, *ib.*, 23-27; Margaliot, *Sheelot u-teshuvot*, 27-35.

[115] The צפיה, visioning, or כוונה, *kavana* through the Holy Spirit differ a little from this and refer to the ability to know the occult as the result of the sages' special sanctity. See, for example, tPes 2:15; ySot 1:4, 16d; yAZ 1:9, 40a; GenR 95, p1232 (ms Vat); LevR 9,9, p192; 37,3, p862. Vision through the Holy Spirit is also attributed to biblical figures. See, for example, Kalla R 3,15; yHor 3:7, 48b; ySan 6:3, 23b; GenR 93,12, p1170; NumR 19,3. On the 'use' of the Holy Spirit, see GenR 37,7, p349.

An additional means of knowledge available to the sages was revelation by a heavenly being, Elijah or an angel. In both cases, sages do not summon these mediators of knowledge by the force of some ritual, but they reveal themselves of their own accord. At least in one event, however, we learn of a ceremonial initiative to encourage such revelation. After Elijah ceased to reveal himself to R. Joshua b. Levi, '...[R. Joshua] fasted a number of times and he was revealed to him'.[116] In most stories, Elijah assumes some human figure when revealing himself to the rabbis, meeting them along the road, or even appearing to them on a regular basis. In most cases he directs them in theory and practice concerning the Divine will. On occasion he reveals to them hidden knowledge on occurrences in this world and the beyond, and various other matters.[117]

Traditions relating to angelic revelation are closely tied to the idea basic to early Jewish mystical literature that contact with angels produces knowledge of great value, and yet there is little of this reflected rabbinic literature.[118] We do find it in connection to Moses' ascent to receive the Tora and his struggle with the angels who ultimately bestowed upon him 'gifts of words', i.e., names with which to control them.[119] Another version expands greatly on the theme of Moses' journey to the throne of Honour, along which he encounters 'an angel, Galizur, standing and declaring: this year the wheat crop will prosper and wine will be cheaper' (PesR 20, p97b). A similar source of knowledge is available to the rabbis, as seen in the tradition attributing to Rabban Yohanan b. Zakkai the study of 'the conversation of the ministering angels' (bSuk 28a; bBB 134a). In the cases of R. Yohanan b. Dahabai's pronouncements about the connection between sexual transgressions and birth defects (bNed 20a), issuing from his angelic knowledge, and of the three warnings R. Yishmael b. Elisha received from 'Suriel, the angel of the Presence' (bBer 20b), it appears to concern concrete information. At the same time, rabbinic literature informs us of the wariness of the sages to depend upon angelic knowledge. Such is probably a well thought out response to the proliferation of knowledge traditions in general, and in particular, practices that involve the adjuration of angels (the Prince of the Presence, the Prince of the Tora), that were popular among contemporary magical-mystical circles.[120]

[116] yTer 8:10, 46b. I do not wish to assert that R. Joshua compelled Elijah to reveal himself to him through the fast. The fast, prompted by the handing over of Ulla to the Gentile authorities, paved the way for the revelation and did not, in itself, awaken it. At the same time, it is not possible to ignore the connection between it and the attainment of the revelation. For more on R. Joshua b. Levi and Elijah see Schwarzbaum, Roots and Landscapes, 33-44.

[117] See for example bShab 33b; bBM 59b; PesRK 18,5, p298f. See further the many traditions on this topic: Margalioth, Sheelot u-teshuvot, 36-39; Gross, Otsar ha-aggada 1, 63-65.

[118] The most outstanding expression of this is in the opening of Hekhalot Rabbati. See Schäfer, Synopse, §§ 81-92.

[119] bShab 88b-89a. See Harari, 'Moses'.

[120] From the extensive literature on this subject see: Swartz, in this volume; idem, Scholastic Magic; Lesses, Ritual Practices. Cf further the angelic affirmation of knowledge based on expounding the mystery of the Chariot (bHag 14b).

A number of sages employed more concrete methods for divining. Shmuel 'inquired by means of a book' (בדיק בספרא), i.e., bibliomancy, bHul 95b); R. Yohanan divined by means of a scriptural verses recited by children (*ib.*); and Hanina b. Dosa used prayer (mBer 5:5; bBer 34b). Finally, there were those who employed a 'sign' (סימן), which in the eyes of the rabbis differed categorically and qualitatively from divination (bHul 95b, and see below).

Fools and children were also associated with prophecy. R. Yohanan declared: 'Since the day when the Temple was destroyed, prophecy was removed from the prophets and handed over to fools and children' (bBB 12b). His words were to be understood literally, as is seen from three adjacent sources. One is the statement of R. Avdimi of Haifa cited above. A second concerns Mar bar Rav Ashi, who sustained his rise to leadership in the academy of Mata Mehasia in accordance with the declaration of a street fool. The third relates to Rav Hisda's daughter, who naively predicted her marriage to both Rami bar Hama and Rava. Children were viewed in the ancient world as especially effective agents of divination.[121] From the Talmud we learn how they were used as living books – a form of oral bibliomancy – with the sages and others listing to an incidental scriptural verse pronounced by a child or even asking it, 'Recite for me your scriptural verses' and deriving straight answers to the issue at hand.[122]

The rabbis speak little of the divinatory power of fools. It might stem from the very lack of intelligence of fools, that is supposed to make them a suitable receptacle for secret knowledge. Alternatively, they might be seen as possessed, and thereby expressing verbally what the indwelling demon chose to convey.[123] It is also possible that their propensity towards frequenting cemeteries (tTer 1:3) and their contact with the dead gave them their knowledge. According to this last approach, fools were human intermediaries to knowledge that originated with unnatural agents: demons and the deceased.

According to the Bavli, demons, like archangels, 'know what is to be in the future' (bHag 16a). Although their knowledge was limited to what they heard 'behind the curtain' (and not in the presence of God), it was desired and sought after. Study of 'the conversations of demons' was attributed to Rabban Yohanan b. Zakkai (bSuk 28a; bBB 134a). If Rashi is correct in explaining that the debate on the question of whether 'one may make requests concerning matters related to demons on the Sabbath' (bSan 101a), relates to the act of consulting with demons (in order to locate a lost item), then the Talmud pro-

---

[121] Lieberman, *Hellenism*, 195-198; Johnston, 'Charming Children'; Brashear, 'Greek Magical Papyri', 3503 and n511.
[122] For the first possibility see yShab 6:10, 8c. On the use of the phrase 'recite for me your scriptural verses' see: bHag 15a-b; bGit 56a; 68a, bHul 95b; EsthR 7,13. According to one of the traditions Caesar Nero used this practice (bGit 56a). Another tradition relates that Elisha b. Avuya inquired from thirteen children in this way in the hope of getting the satisfactory answer to his question (bHag 15a).
[123] Cf the demon possession in Luke 4:31-37.

vides testimony to the act of initiating their use as agents of knowledge. As we have noted, demonically derived information is incorporated into a talmudic discussion as if it were the opinion of the rabbis, themselves. This is the case with Joseph the Demon, who discusses the harm caused by demons in the context of 'drinking in pairs' (bPes 110a).

The deceased, too, are perceived as being mediators of hidden knowledge, which was attained by their souls departing from their graves and listening in on conversations 'behind the curtain' (bBer 18b; ARN a3, Schechter, 8af). Not only did the rabbis see them as mediators of knowledge, but this view was common to the ancient world, in general, and to the culture of Jewish magic, in particular.[124] According to one tradition the period when it was possible to summon them was limited to the twelve months from the time of their death (bShab 152b-153a). Knowledge might be acquired from the dead either through a revelation in the course of a dream,[125] or by means of necromancy, or through consulting them in a cemetery. However, whereas consulting them was apparently available to all who tried, necromancy necessitated professional intermediacy. The methods of the *ov* and consulting the dead will be discussed below. Here, we shall bring two stories of notable socio-theological context. The first is the story of Onkelos b. Kalonymus, the nephew of Titus, who on the eve of his conversion to Judaism called up the spirits of Titus, Bileam, and Jesus (bGit 56b-57a). At his question, they convey authoritative information concerning the favour awaiting Israel in Heaven and the punishments affecting its enemies, and they support Onkelos in his intention to convert. For this reason, the story is integrated into the conversation of the House of Study and it does not elicit surprise. This is a good example of the way in which the *ov* divination entered this conversation as a legitimate source of knowledge, so long as it was able to support its didactic objectives. The other story concerns a dispute between R. Katina and an osteo-necromancer (אובא טמיא) regarding an earthquake, which the latter explained in terms of the tears of God that drip into the sea on account of Israel's sufferings in exile (bBer 59a). R. Katina's concluding remarks are particularly revealing. He confesses that his antagonist was right, however 'the reason he did not admit this to him (that is, in public), was to prevent others from being lead astray by him'. The struggle over authority and social power that accrue from professional divination is admitted here with urgency and candor.

As we have mentioned, angels were also perceived of as potential superhuman mediators of divination. Their revelation to the rabbis has been discussed above. Here, I wish to mention one further matter – the mention of 'princes of oil and princes of eggs' from whom it was permitted to consult,

---

[124] See Harari, 'Opening of the Heart', 335f.
[125] For example, bShab 152b; bMK 28a; and see below.

only that they falsify.[126] If our hypothesis is correct that 'princes' (שרים) are angels, in the usual sense of this term in rabbinic literature (and the Hekhalot and Merkava literature) and not demons (as Rashi explains there), then the Talmud allows us a partial view of the magical praxis related to the act of consulting them.

Finally, mention should also be made of the tradition whereby 'the conversation of the hills and valleys, trees and grass, wild and domesticated animals' serve as a source of information for one skilled in the appropriate art of interpretation.[127] An example of this is the story about Ilish, where 'a certain man who understood the language of birds' interpreted the calls of the crow and the dove as beckoning him to flee his captivity (bGit 45a).

PRACTICES

Many and varied divination practices are described in rabbinic literature. As we have mentioned, some methods, such as the 'Divine voice', a revelation by Elijah, or a vision through the Holy Spirit, were associated with the sanctity of the person who received the divination. These were perceived as a faint echo of prophecy and were an acceptable and even desirable means of attaining knowledge of the occult. They were revealed to a person without being sought for (intuitive divination), and rabbis were well trained in them. Others, such as bibliomancy, divining through a child, or consulting the dead, were carried out by rabbis or were explicitly permitted by them, and one may therefore assume that they were considered acceptable. Also, astral divination connected with foreign professional diviners was perceived in many traditions as not being harmful because it was irrelevant to the Jewish people. On the other hand, the practices of the *ov* and the *yidoni*, also performed professionally, were prohibited and declared punishable by stoning.[128] Additional means of divination, almost all of which were the divination of omens, that is, establishing the meaning behind a given event as a sign regarding a matter that affects a person who consults them, were prohibited and perceived as 'the ways of the Amorites'.

Regarding the divination of omens, the rabbis sought to distinguish categorically and qualitatively between two forms: divination, which was forbidden, and signs, that were permitted. The key text in this regard is a story that relates to Rav, who saw in an approaching ferryboat a propitious sign, and his

---

[126] bSan 101a. The precise meaning of the phrase, which in the original, is 'but since they falsify' (אלא מפני שמכזבין) is not clear. Rashi explains as follows: 'For this reason people refrained from consulting them.' Hence, it is permitted to consult them, however since they lie, people refrained from it. According to the reading in the mss and early printings of Alfasi (Rif) and R. Asher (Rosh) the word אלא is lacking and the meaning of the statement is different: since they falsify it is permitted to consult them. See *Dikdukei sofrim*, Sanhedrin, 306 n9.

[127] Soferim 26:7. Cf bSuk 28a; bBB 134a.

[128] mKer 1:1; mSan 7:4, 7; tSan 10:6.

ruling in this connection: 'Any divination that is unlike that of Eliezer, Abraham's servant, or Jonathan, the son of Saul, is not divination.'[129] The governing principle behind this distinction is the temporal relationship between the event and its determination as an omen: establishing in advance that a given event will be interpreted as an omen (as Eliezer and Jonathan acted) is divination, whilst treating it as such *post eventum* is viewed as a sign. This, however, raises a problem, for according to this distinction, the divination of omens by means of a candle, a hen, or shadows, as R. Ami suggests (bHor 12a), or the interpretation of the howling of dogs (bBK 60b) would not be included in the category of signs. In these two cases, the sages attribute significance prior to the actual occurrence, and this is precisely in accordance with the prohibited methods that were categorized as the 'ways of the Amorites'.

The means of divination that are included in the 'ways of the Amorites' are varied. The Tosefta mentions the sparks of a candle, the calls of fowls, a snake falling onto one's bed, consulting by means of a rod, and it elaborates as follows:

> Who is a diviner? One who says: my rod has fallen from my hand, my bread has dropped from my mouth, So-and-so called me from behind, a crow called out to me, a dog barked at me, a snake passed me on the right hand side, and a fox on the left, and a gazelle crossed the path before me, don't start with me for it is the morning, and it is the new moon, and it is after the Sabbath.[130]

Additional sources mention divination through a mole, fowl, fish, and arrows.[131] One may add to these the art of bibliomancy, as mentioned above,[132] and divination by means of scriptural verses. The latter includes both the method that uses children and the method whereby the verse appears of its own accord. Concerning the second form, R. Yohanan states the following: 'One who wakes up and a verse drops from his mouth – this is a minor prophecy' (bBer 55b). In all of the above visual, audible and verbal omens serve as a basis for the study of the occult. Additional practices allowed a more direct

---

[129] bHul 95b. See Rashi *ad loc.* Cf Gen 24:12-14, 1 Sam 14:8-11. See Keller, 'Nihush ve-Siman', 50-58.

[130] tShab 7:13. In the parallels in SifDeut Shofetim 171 (p219), and bSan 65b-66a the word שהרי is lacking and the examples that follow are not connected to the phrase אל תתחיל בי. Cf Lieberman, *Tosefta ki-fshuta* 3, 97, and cf Rashi *ad loc.* For discussion on these divination practices see Lieberman *ib.* 79-105; Avishur, 'Ways of the Amorite'; Veltri, *Magie und Halakha*, 93-220. R. Akiva adds to this also the soothsayers (מעוננים) that divine the appropriate time for an act (tShab 7:14). See the parallels in the Sifrei and the Bavli *ib.*, and the discussion by Lieberman, *ib.* 97-99. Rabban Yohanan b. Zakkai's study of the 'seasons' is probably also connected to this (bSuk 28a; bBB 134a). Blau, *Zauberwesen*, 46 at any rate, linked the matter to astrology.

[131] For the first three see bSan 66a. Cf the version in the Sifra, Kedoshim 6 (Weiss, 90ab), and below. See further Harari, 'Opening of the Heart', 310f n26-28. On divination by means of archery see bGit 56a. Cf Ezek 21:26-27. See Greenberg, 'Nebuchadnezzar'.

[132] bHul 95b. Bibliomancy was also common in the Hellenistic world, also through the Homeric epic. See Brashear, 'Greek Magical Papyri', 3503 and n511; Alexander, 'Bavli Berakhot', 233.

method through summoning the metaphysical agents of knowledge: the deceased, angels, and demons.

Consulting the dead, *ov* necromancy, and apparently also the practice of the *yidoni* that is mentioned together with them in the Bible (Deut 18:11; Lev 19:31, 2 Chr 33:6) and in rabbinic literature, are the common designations in our sources for necromantic practices, even though the sources are not unanimous concerning their precise nature.[133] The practice of the *ov* and the *yidoni* were apparently carried out by professionals and through a variety of methods. A number of sources note that the *baal ov*'s speech was not through his own mouth but from 'between his joints and arms' or 'from his armpits'.[134] We learn from the Babylonian Talmud that a dead person 'rises and sits between the joints and speaks' (bSan 65b). In this context the sources also seek to distinguish between two kinds of necromancers – those who conjure up using a membrum (המעלה בזכורו) and those who use a skull (הנשאל בגולגולת) – while addressing the subject of their efficacy on the Sabbath.[135] R. Yasa's opinion, brought in the Yerushalmi, that the *baal ov* 'offers incense to the demons' (ySan 7:13, 25c), partially illuminates the ritual context of the *ov* praxis, or at least, the way it was perceived by the sages. Other sources mention the *baal ov*'s act of knocking his arms together (bSan 65a; bKer 3b). The *yidoni*, on the other hand, speaks through his mouth, and according to a number of sources, by means of a bone that he placed in it.[136] Pseudo-Yonatan on Lev 19:31 translates the word *yidoni* as 'consulter of the *yedoa* bone'. The version in the Bavli harmonizes the explanations: 'The *yidoni* is one who places the bone of a *yedoa* in his mouth' and adds, 'and he speaks of himself' (bSan 65b). Perhaps, in this way the Talmud connects the practice of the *yidoni* with the practice of automatic speech.[137]

The Tosefta and the Yerushalmi mention consulting the dead as an analogy to or sometimes as being identical with the practices of *ov* cited in the Bavli; it is the practice of conjuring up the dead by means of the membrum or the skull.[138] In the Bavli, on the other hand, it is connected to the location of the dead and is described as a practice based on fasting and on spending the night among the tombs of the dead: 'And the one who consults the dead – this is one

---

[133] On necromancy in the ancient world, including the bible, see Harari, 'Opening of the Heart', 332 n137-138.

[134] For the first possibility see tSan 10:6; and for the second, see mSan 7:7; Sifra Kedoshim 11 (Weiss, 93b); ySan 7:13, 25c.

[135] ySan 7:13, 25c. On the practice of conjuring up by means of the membrum cf Targum Ps.Jonathan, Lev 19:31. Jewish magical use of skulls is testified by five adjuration skulls known today. See Levene, 'Calvariae Magicae'.

[136] mSan 7:7; ySan 7:13, 25c; tSan 10:6.

[137] For the later rabbinic interpretations on the sages' allusions regarding the *ov* and *yidoni* practices see *Talmudic Encyclopedia*, vol 1, 244-249; vol 22, 20-26.

[138] tSan 10:7; ySan 7:13, 25c. The Yerushalmi adds an additional distinction within this context: the status relationship between the בעל אוב and the deceased whom he seeks to conjure up, here a common person and a king.

who starves himself and goes and spends the night in a cemetery so that a spirit of impurity may rest upon him' (bSan 65b; cf bHag 3b). A 'spirit of impurity' in this context is the spirit of divination of 'one who adheres to impurity' (Sif-Deut 173:12 p220). With respect to source and legitimacy it is the counterpart of the 'holy spirit' through which prophets and rabbis gained illuminations and visions.[139] This may also be the origin of the identification of fools as mediators of divination: sleeping among graves is one of the signs of a fool (tTer 1:3), and at least one passage (yTer 1:1, 40b) connects it to offering incense to demons, mediators of knowledge who also reside in cemeteries. Either way, a number of stories teach that consulting the dead in the sense of seeking their help for some form of knowledge was not perceived as negative and forbidden in itself. The story of a pious man (*hasid*) who 'went and slept the night in a cemetery' seems to testify explicitly to the possibility of seeking the help of the dead in order to know the future and is devoid of criticism of the practice. This man 'heard two spirits conversing with one another...', based his farming method on their words and succeeded where all others failed, and then returned to sleep there twice in order to make more gains on the basis of their conversation (bBer 18b). Similarly, one can mention stories that relate to Zeiri and Shmuel who entered a cemetery to consult with certain deceased in particular, Zeiri's inn-keeper and Shmuel's father, in order to find out the location of money that had been deposited with them (*ib.*).[140] These sources indicate that the sages authorized the cemetery as a meeting place of those who are alive with the deceased. It would therefore seem that rather than condemning contact with the dead for the sake of learning occult knowledge, it was the professional mediation to this aim and the accompanying ritual practices that they rejected.[141]

As mentioned, both angels and demons were perceived as mediators of knowledge that could be summoned and consulted. If Rashi is correct in combining the following two sentences into one unit – 'It is permitted to consult princes of oil and princes of eggs, except that they falsify. One may whisper a charm over oil that is in a vessel, but one may not whisper a charm over oil

---

[119] To 'starve oneself' is a derogatory expression aimed at distinguishing between the ritual abstention from eating with the aim of attaining the spirit of impurity in the cemetery and the fast, which is the normative abstention from eating for acquiring the spirit of holiness, or attaining a sacred revelation. Cf, for example, the story of R. Joshua above (near n116). Rashi suggests that the entire matter is aimed at attaining the help of the demon of the kind that resides in the cemetery, for a magical activity (apparently on the basis of that which is written in yTer 1:1, 40b; cf ySan 7:13, 25c). However, it would not appear to agree with the explicit statement 'in order that a spirit of impurity come upon him'.

[140] See also the story about Rav who went to a cemetery and 'did what he did' and thus learned about the cause of death of people (bBM 107b). Blau and Trachtenberg understood the matter as a case of divination (Blau, *Zauberwesen*, 53; Trachtenberg, *Jewish Magic*, 222). The Bavli, at any rate, does not indicate explicitly speech with the dead and there is no need to explain the case in this way.

[141] Cf Blau, *Zauberwesen*, 53.

that is in the hand, therefore, we anoint with oil that is in the hand and we do not anoint with oil that is in a vessel' (bSan 101a and Rashi *ad loc.*) – then the second sentence teaches us of the practice of the divination of oil that is in a bowl that is associated with charms. Despite the great uncertainty in understanding this matter, it might be possible to connect this to testimonies from both Hellenistic and Jewish magical sources and to explain it as divination by means of the shiny stains of oil or eggs.[142] Those sources indicate that this kind of divination was often carried out by children who were instructed to examine the shiny surface or liquid and to try and identify in them the image of a god or a demon (and in this case, a prince, that is, an angel), and to cause it to speak, following the instructions of the sorcerer.[143] And yet, the Talmud might be hinting at a different kind of oil divination such as the method documented, for instance, in Sefer ha-Razim.[144] Rashi, at any rate, explained the entire passage as having to do with consulting demons. The practice is not explicitly mentioned in our sources but is alluded to, it would seem, in the discussion whether 'one may consult demons on the Sabbath' (bSan 101a, and cf Rashi *ad loc.*) and in any case remains obscure.

Dreams and Interpretation

In many cultures of the ancient world, dreams were seen as a source of knowledge superior to the knowledge acquired while awake. As a rule, not only was the dream considered a refined inner expression of the remains of the day, but also, primarily, a message transmitted to a person from a metaphysical reality in that special time of existence between being and non-being.[145] There were two sides to the content of the dream: message (explicit) and symbol (enigmatic).[146] Also, there were two sides to dream divination: explaining the signs that appeared in the incidental dream, and summoning a solution dream to a pre-set question by ritual means such as incubation and dream request. The biblical attitude to dreams is not uniform and oscillates between accepting

---

[142] Cf Rashi *ib.* For the possibility that the reference is to a charm on the oil for medicinal purposes and not for divination see Harari, 'Opening of the Heart', 316 n48.

[143] See Johnston, 'Charming Children'; Daiches, *Babylonian Oil Magic*; Trachtenberg, *Jewish Magic*, 219-222; Dan, 'Princes of Thumb'; and cf also Schäfer – Shaked, *Magische Texte*, vol 3, 92(2a)/10 ff.

[144] Margulies, *Sepher ha-Razim*, 71.

[145] For extensive bibliography on the notion of the dream in ancient cultures see Harari, 'Opening of the Heart', 337 n161.

[146] For the biblical distinction between the two forms of dream, the revelation and the riddle dream, see Fidler, *Dreams Speak Falsely?*; Gnuse, *Dream Theophany*, 57-118; Jeffers, *Magic and Divination*, 125-139. Artemidorus of Daldis also notes it in his famous book on the interpretation of dreams from the second century CE: Artemidorus, *The Interpretation of Dreams* (Oneirocritica, tr. and com. R.J. White), Torrance 1990, 23f, and see further, Cox-Miller, *Dreams in Late Antiquity*, 77-106.

them as a form of Divine revelation and totally rejecting them.[147] The approach of the rabbis to the question of dreams and their interpretations was also not uniform, and we find three approaches: (1) acceptance of dreams as prophetic messages; (2) linking them to the psychological state of the dreamer and negating their significance as a means of divination; and (3) seeing in them the potential for interpretation that does not *reveal* the buried meaning but rather *determines* the message of the dream and makes this meaning reality.[148]

There is considerable evidence for the notion that a dream is a true message originating in metaphysical reality and which not only indicates the future of the dreamer and the subjects of his dream but is capable of actually bringing about this future.[149] Thus we find: 'A dream is one sixtieth of prophecy.'[150] Rava makes the following remark: 'The Holy One, blessed be He said: even though I have hidden my countenance from them, 'in a dream I shall speak to him'' (bHag 5b, cf Num 12:6). He also requested that the solution to a halakhic problem be revealed to him in a dream (bMen 67a). We also find ritual practices for reversing a bad dream: a dream fast and the reversal of a bad dream,[151] and the statement that one excommunicated in a dream must be released before a *minyan* of men knowledgeable in the halakha (bNed 8a). In addition we learn of the notion that 'when one sleeps his soul leaves him and wanders through the world, and these are the dreams that one sees' (MidrPs 11,6, Buber, 51b). These traditions join a profusion of stories that point to a belief in the reception of true messages through dreams, whether on one's own or through dream agents such as God, angels and demons, as generally responsible for the dream.[152] The 'dream man' (איש החלום) or 'dispenser of dreams' (בעל החלום), Elijah the prophet, and the deceased appear in the dreams as bearers of particular messages.[153] All of them, with the exception of demons (bBer 55b), transmit a reliable and generally explicit message. Occasionally they are

[147] See, for example, Gen 20:6, Num 12:7, and on the other hand Jer 29:8, Zach 10:2, Eccl 5:6.
[148] On the rabbinic perception of dreams and their interpretation see: Lewy, 'Zu dem Traumbuche'; Kristianpoller, *Traum und Traumdeutung*; Alexander, 'Bavli Berakhot'; Kalmin, *Sages, Stories,* 61-80; Afik, *Hazal's Perception of the Dream*; Hasan-Rokem, 'A Dream Amounts to the Sixtieth Part'; idem, *Web of Life,* 88-107; Lieberman, *Hellenism,* 71-78.
[149] Margulies, *Sepher ha-Razim,* 84f; Harari, *The Sword of Moses,* p42 §70, p141 §150.
[150] bBer 57b. Cf GenR 17,5, p156f; 44,17, p 438f.
[151] For a dream fast see bShab 11a; bTaan 12b. For reversing a bad dream see bBer 55b; EcclR 5,4.
[152] bHag 5b; bBer 55b. A distinction must be made between expressions that relate to the source of the dream and stories of revelation through it. God, Himself reveals Himself to the dreamer in many dream stories whose protagonists are biblical. However, as far as I know He does not reveal Himself to rabbis in their sleep. Also angels do not appear as direct dream agents. This is in contrast to the way they are used for a revelation in a dream documented in Jewish magical practice. See Harari, 'Opening of the Heart', 325-331.
[153] On the 'dream man' and the 'dispenser of dreams' see bSan 30a; tMS 5:9; ARN a17 (Schechter, 33b); MidrTann 32,30 (Hofmann, 199). Cf the adjuration of the 'Great Ragshael, the prince of the dream', and the mention of Azriel as an emissary of knowledge in the dream in ancient Jewish mystical writings: Schäfer, *Synopsis,* §§ 501-507, and Lesses, *Ritual Practices,* 325-336. On the prophet Elijah see GenR 83,4, p1000; PesR 22, p111b. On the dead: bShab155b, bMK 28a.

revealed on their own initiative, and at other times, such as in the case of the dead, they respond to a call from the living. There is little evidence for ritual practice of this kind.[154] The Tosefta mentions kissing the coffin of the deceased in order to see him in a dream, and upturning the garment and sitting on a broom in order to receive a dream, all dubbed 'the way of the Amorites' (tShab 6:7). The Bavli alludes to the gentile practice of incubation in a pagan temple for this purpose (b AZ 55a).

In many cases, the dream is revealed to the person without a medium. In this case, the contents might be explicit,[155] or might appear in a symbolic form. This could be textual – a scriptural verse 'read' before the dreamer whilst he is asleep[156]– or visual. Both types of symbols required interpretation to disclose their hidden message. However, while the textual symbol was anchored in the culture of the sages and so by its very nature called for interpreters who were well versed in the Tora, the visual message belonged to the broader, inter-cultural phenomenon of dream symbolism and interpretation.

A long list of dream symbols and their interpretation appears in a sort of professional lexicon in the Bavli (bBer 56b-57b). The material can be divided into two categories. In the first are 'dream midrashim' – interpretations based on connecting the dream symbol to a scriptural verse in order to produce a propitious meaning (see below). In the second category are interpretations that are founded on a broader network of linguistic, cultural, and associative contexts. Many of the dream symbols that appear here have a universal character and include animals, plants, beverages, eggs, metals, colours, the breaking of a vessel, a snake bite, rising and falling, blood-letting, intercourse with forbidden women, nakedness, entering into a forest or a lake, or answering the call of nature. Others are typically Jewish, such as the 'seven species' (of plants), biblical kings and books, sages, prayer, and donning phylacteries. Common to all is a consistent tendency towards an auspicious interpretation. Alongside this technical and professional trend, some traditions deal with systematic dream interpreters and dream interpretation, be they rabbis, heretics, or others. Such traditions illustrate for us both the current methods of dream interpretation, in which economic considerations play a role, and the use the sages made of the motif of dream interpretation in their literature to polemicise against gentiles.[157]

The importance of the category of the 'bad dream' in the dream discourse of the sages, and especially the fear of bad dreams, is a further articulation of the belief of the mantic value of dreams. The detailed list of differences between good and bad dreams that appears in the Bavli (bBer 55a-56b) is a nota-

---

[154] Cf the ritual practices for summoning a dream in ancient Jewish magical literature, Harari, 'Opening of the Heart', 325-331.

[155] For example bHag 14b; yHag 2:2, 77d; LevR 3:5, p66ff.

[156] E.g., bBer 56a; bSan 81b-82a; bHul 133a; bSot 31a. Cf the adjuration for the prince (*sar*) of dreams: 'That you should come to me on this night [...] and speak to me and give me a sign and a miracle or a scriptural verse in my hand'; Schäfer, *Synopsis*, § 505.

[157] bBer 56a; yMS 4:9, 55c; LamR 1,1 (Buber, 26aff).

ble example. A practical manifestation of this aspect is the call to avoid a bad dream through study of the Tora, supplications, rejoicing in the command-ments, or the appropriate behaviour in the toilet.[158] Likewise we find sugges-tions on how to save oneself from the materialization of these dreams by ac-knowledged means such as prayer, charity, repentance, and supplications (ySan 10:2, 28c; bBer 10b), or by ritual means: the dream fast and reversal of the dream. Noteworthy in this context is Shmuel's method in distinguishing between good and bad dreams, declaring the latter null and affirming the for-mer as revelation (bBer 55b). The liberty he took to connect the mantic value of the dream to its content is a partial expression of the drive for total control of conscious thought over the dream, while removing it from the power arena it is implicated in – a shift whose more radical expressions will be considered below.

A total negation of the dream's mantic value, especially in the context of halakhic decision making, is articulated in the oft-occurring rule that 'the words of dreams have no affect'.[159] Another side to this tendency is anchoring the dream in the psychological reality of the dreamer, in the language of the Talmud: 'One only shows a person [in his dream] his own ponderings' (bBer 55b). The story relating to the dreams of Caesar and King Shapur (bBer 56b) reflect the rabbinic process of 'psychologisation' of the dream whereby the dream is no longer an external message but is internally generated by the dreamer. Upon being challenged to predict the sovereigns' dreams, the rabbis describe a disturbing scene. The monarchs, each in turn, ponder over the scene throughout the day, and dream about it at night. At the same time we find the statement that 'there is no dream devoid of vain matter', thus, 'even though a dream is partially fulfilled it is not wholly fulfilled' (bBer 55a; cf bNed 8b). Shmuel, too, as we have seen, adopts a mid-way position between absolute acceptance and rejection of dreams. Likewise, the view of Rava, brought in an adjacent passage, explains the disparity between two scriptural verses: 'In dream I shall speak to him' (Num 12:6) and, 'and dreams speak vanity' (Zach. 10:2) – 'In the former instance, through an angel; in the latter, through a de-mon' (bBer 55b). Similarly, R. Yohanan and others connect the mantic po-tency of the dream to the dream occurrence itself: 'Three kinds of dream are fulfilled: a morning dream; a dream that another has dreamed about oneself; and a dream that is interpreted within a dream. Some add: Also a dream that is repeated' (ib.; GenR 89,5, p1092).

Yet a third approach was to place the authority for the fulfilment of the dream, which according to Shmuel could be only true or false, in the inter-preter. This is expressed in the saying, כל החלומות הולכים אחר הפה, 'All dreams follow the mouth,' meaning that dreams are fulfilled in accordance with their

---

[158] bBer 14a; 60b; bShab 30b; bPes 117a.

[159] דברי חלומות לא מעלין ולא מורידין, bGit 52a; bSan 30a; bHor 13b; tMS 5:9; yMS 4:9, 55b; GenR 68,12, p784. Cf the parallel case of *bat kol* n113.

interpretation.[160] Linking up with the scriptural verse, 'And as he [Joseph] interpreted to us, so it came to pass' (Gen 41:13), this is expressed in a remarkable way in the story related by R. Banaa: 'There were 24 dream interpreters in Jerusalem. Once I had a dream and I went to all of them; their interpretations were different form one another, but they were all fulfilled' (bBer 55b). This approach deprives the content of the dream from all significance as to its fulfilment and turns it into a mere exegetical tool. This has clear social implications. By establishing that 'a dream that is not interpreted is like a letter that has not been read' (ib.), the sages transferred the centre of gravity of the interpretive discourse from the dream symbols to their interpretation, and by implication, to the interpreter. By so doing, they withdrew the power of interpretation from the professional interpreters, experts in the gamut of dream symbolism, and opened up the possibility of focussing on the moral qualities of the interpreter. The interpreter could determine the dreamer's destiny and should be chosen with care. The impact of this notion on the great inherent dangers is expressed in two sources. First, there is the story of Bar Hadaya, to whom Abaye and Rava bring identical dreams for interpretation. Abaye, who pays, consistently receives fortunate interpretations whereas Rava, who withholds payment from Bar Hadaya, only gets ominous interpretations. As a result two series of events occur: a beneficial one for Abaye and a disastrous one for Rava (bBer 56a). The other story tells about 'this woman' whose husband the disciples of R. Eliezer killed, because they thought this was the interpretation of her dream about a broken beam in her house.[161] This is also the basis for rejecting R. Yohanan's ruling, 'One who sees a dream and his soul is distraught should go and have it interpreted before three', in favour of the saying: 'He should reverse it (lit., make it better) before three [people]' (bBer 55b). This preference alludes to the tendency to reject dream interpretation altogether – perhaps even to refrain from telling dreams.

This danger at once reveals the advantage of the potential power that the sages sought to reserve for themselves regarding dream interpretation and its fulfilment. The dream is a wild and anarchical element that bursts forth from beyond reality into the helpless consciousness of the sleeper, undermining his quietude and breaking apart life's order.[162] It was this that the sages sought to curtail by the normative means that made up their spiritual and social world. If, as the adage goes, 'life and death are in the power of the tongue', a dreamer had best choose well from among the interpreters one that will provide a positive interpretation. The list of positive dream interpretations by means of scriptural verses, mentioned above, indicate that this expertise was to be found

---

[160] bBer 55b. Cf yMS 4:9, 55c; GenR 89,8, p1096f.

[161] yMS 4:9, 55c; GenR 89,8, p1095f; LamR 1,1 (Buber, 28a).

[162] See the dream interpretation stories relating to the students of R. Akiva. Their bad dreams prevented them from studying until R. Akiva interpreted them in a positive manner and thereby removed the obstacle. LamR 1,1 (Buber, 27b).

amongst the sages. Thus we may also understand the 'do it yourself interpretation' by means of a good scriptural verse 'before another verse might intervene' – i.e., a bad verse – and thereby lead the dream in its direction, as advocated by R. Joshua b. Levi (bBer 56b). Perhaps one might also understand in this light the 'dream midrashim' that interpret the dream symbols, however difficult, as boding well by tying them to a scriptural verse that conveys a positive message.[163] This method of providing any dream with a positive outcome through scriptural verse represents an exegetical potential that all would aspire to but only few can realize. Trained in the Tora and in the midrashic discourse it entails, those few are the address where to obtain this expertise in the metaphysical domain of dream interpretation that joins knowledge to power in order to determine destiny.

This understanding underlies the polemical use rabbinic literature makes of dream interpretation stories. We can see this in light of the more general tendency to undermine external agents in the domain of spiritual knowledge and power in favour of the sages who sought to acquire a monopoly in this realm. An outstanding example is the dispute story between a Samaritan who pretended to be an interpreter, who always interpreted favourably, and R. Yishmael be-R. Yose, who every time could reveal embarrassing details of transgressions by the dreamers and their relatives by means of symbols from their dreams (LamR 1,1, Buber, 26aff). In this case R. Yishmael's unnerving power was directed against those who dare to turn to foreign dream interpreters who by definition are suspect of charlatanry. In an additional narrative unit about a man whose dreams have already been interpreted favourably by the Samaritan, R. Yishmael even suggests to re-interpret them for a wage so that he 'would not lose out'. Despite this direct threat, the man prefers the Samaritan, and R. Yishmael interprets-fulfils his dreams unfavourably. The polemical message is clear and unambiguous: in the power-struggle over the fulfilment of dreams, the interpretation of the rabbis has the upper hand, and whoever does not turn to them will regret it.

A climax is found in the story in which the Samaritan invents a dream in order to ridicule 'this Jewish elder', as he derisively calls him, and R. Yishmael who accepts to interpret it.[164] His response is impressive. 'This is no dream,' he determines, 'and even so you shall not leave empty-handed.' The unfavourable interpretation of the fake dream is indeed fulfilled, and at the same time the power of the rabbis to sever the bounds of the power of creation

---

[163] bBer 56b-57a. Even if some of the interpretations in this list in tractate Berakhot are parallel to such that are found in Babylonian or Hellenistic lists, its methodological uniqueness is remarkable. On this interpretative lexicon and its connections with Artimidorus' *Oneirocritica* see Lewy, 'Traumbuche'' Alexander, 'Bavli Berakhot'; Lieberman, *Hellenism*, 71-78.

[164] yMS 4:9, 55c. The traditions of R. Yishmael's interpretation appear in the Yerushalmi independently of the polemical context in which they appear in LamR. The didactic, menacing message is transmitted here too, and only the climax – the struggle with a Cuthean – features within the polemical context.

is established before the reader.[165] This power, which earlier had been attached to the metaphysical potential of the dream, is now completely detached from it and is presented as an immanent quality of the sage. The clear distinction between dream and reality which is the basis for every interpretative methodology of dream symbolism, and which had already been blurred by the notion that 'a dream follows its interpretation', is here totally obliterated in the face of the rabbi's power to govern reality and fashion it as he desires. In this manner, it would seem, the chaotic and disturbing power of the dream over the dreamer's consciousness is completely domesticated within the walls of the House of Study.

Astrology

In the ancient cultures of Mesopotamia, Egypt, and the Hellenistic world, astrology – the belief in the inner-worldly influence of the heavenly elements and the wish to observe these for the purpose of learning about the future – was a popular and central method of divination.[166] The Jews, who came into successive contact with these cultures, were well acquainted with this method but variously reacted to it. The Bible alludes to astrology and rejects it as foreign to Israelite belief.[167] Apocryphal literature is ambivalent, rejecting some aspects and accepting others: its origins are indeed heavenly, but it is a part of the corruptive knowledge that was brought down to the world by the fallen angels. The Jewish Hellenistic authors Artapanus and Pseudo-Eupolemos offer a different approach, taking pride in the fact that Abraham taught astrology even to the sages of Egypt, which was considered to be the cradle of this wisdom. Similarly, Philo and Josephus explained symbols of the Temple service in light of it. The practical manifestation of astral divination is attested in fragments of scrolls found in Qumran and it is possible that its impact may even be discerned in contemporaneous Jewish politics in the Land of Israel.[168]

---

[165] On the rabbis' power of creation see, for example, Gruenwald, 'Ha-ketav'; Idel, *Golem*, 63-72; Neusner, 'The Phenomenon'.

[166] For a good recent survey of ancient astrology see: Barton, *Ancient Astrology*. Comprehensive studies in this field in the Graeco-Roman world include: Bouché-Leclercq, *L'Astrologie*; Cramer, *Astrology*; Cumont, *Astrology*; Gundel and Gundel, *Astrologumena*. For a limited selection of studies on astrology in Egypt and Mesopotamia see: Oppenheim, 'Divination'; Rochberg-Halton, *Aspects*; idem, 'Babylonian Horoscopes'; Parker, 'Egyptian Astronomy, esp. 723ff; von Beckerath, 'Astronomie und Astrologie'; von Stuckrad, *Frömmigkeit und Wissenschaft*.

[167] E.g., Isa 47:13f, and the mention of the Chaldean / Babylonian seers, among the Babylonian sages in Dan 2:5, 10; 4:4, 7; 5:7, 11. And see Ness, *Astrology and Judaism*, 87-105; Catelli, 'Astrology', and see below n172.

[168] The principal apocryphal works on this subject are the Book of Shem, the Epistle to Rehoboam, the Testament of Solomon, 1 and 2 Enoch, Jubilees, and the Sibylline Oracles. For a survey of the astrology in these works, Jewish-Hellenistic, and Qumran literature see von Stuckrad, *Das Ringen um die Astrologie*, 160-222; idem, 'Jewish and Christian Astrology'; Ness, *Astrology*, 169ff; Charlesworth, 'Jewish Interest in Astrology'. On horoscopes and additional astrological texts in Qumran see: Wise, *Thunder in Gimini*, 13-50; Greenfield – Sokoloff, 'Astrological Text'; Albani,

Textual and archaeological sources bear witness to the place of astrology in Jewish culture in the period following the destruction of the Temple. The sorcery manual from the second quarter of the first millennium, Sefer ha-Razim, reveals the place of astrology in Jewish magic.[169] The Palestinian synagogue mosaic floors from the fifth-sixth centuries that are decorated with the image of the sun god Helios (Sol) on his chariot in the centre of the Zodiac, document the penetration of astral motifs in Jewish places of worship.[170] The evocation of such motifs in sermons and piyyutim evidences their entrance into the actual conversation that took place there.[171]

The sages, too, were familiar with the astrological world view, with the divination it implied – in their language, אצטגנינות, itstagninut – and with the professionals who engaged in the field: איסטרולוגין, istrologin, or כלדיים, 'Chaldeans'.[172] This familiarity is affirmed by the numerous Babylonian and Palestinian traditions that deal with the matter, whether recognizing astral fate and the possibility to divine it, or whether rejecting them.[173] The uniqueness of astrology as divination (both in itself and in the context of other related domains such as sorcery and healing) is in the structured and systematic complexity of the astral data that the astrologer is required to master and interpret. Extensive astronomical and mathematical knowledge was an essential precondition for engaging in astral divination. Hence, it comes as no surprise that few were the sages whose words display true astrological knowledge. Furthermore, astrology was, by its very essence, tainted with paganism. The sun, the moon, the planets and stars, and the movements of the Zodiac were all

'Horoscopes in Qumran Scrolls'. On the topic of astrology for the interpretation of the symbols of ritual and in Jewish politics in Palestine in the Hellenistic period see von Stuckrad, ib.

[169] See Margulies, Sepher ha-Razim; Ness, Astrology, 206-217; Charlesworth, 'Jewish Interest', 936f.

[170] The scholarly literature on this topic is considerable. See Goodenough, Jewish Symbols, vol 4, 3-62; vol 8, 167-177, 195-218; vol 12, 40-48; Urbach, 'The Rabbinical Laws'; Foerster, 'Zodiac'; Stern, 'Figurative Art and Halakhah'; Mack, 'Unique Character'; Levine, Judaism and Hellenism, 149-160; Smith, 'Helios in Palestine'; Ness, Astrology, 218ff.

[171] See PesR 20, p95aff; 27, p133b; Yahalom, Poetry and Society, 20-24.

[172] The Palestinian sources make use of Greek transcription, אסטרולוגין, אסטרולוגוס and other variations of this word to designate divination through the stars (e.g. yShab 6:10, 8d; yAZ 2:2, 41a; GenR 1:4, p7; ExodR 1,18; 1,21; NumR 19,3; EcclR 1,1). In the Bavli 'Chaldeans' is common for those who divine the future (for example, bBer 64a; bShab 119a; 156b; bPes 113b). The basis for the designation lies in the identification of divination with the Chasdean tribe, well-known for their divining skills, and are mentioned as such (chaldaioi) in Graeco-Roman literature within the context of astrological divination (but also in the context of wisdom, especially mathematics and sorcery). See Dickie, Magic and Magicians, 110-112. It is almost certain that the Chaldeans mentioned in the Talmud are astrologers (Sokoloff, Dictionary, Babylonian, 581), however this is not stated explicitly. 'Chaldean' (כלדאי) also appears in the magic bowls. See Naveh-Shaked, Amulets, B13.

[173] On astrology in rabbinic literature see now: von Stuckrad, Das Ringen um die Astrologie, 431-511. See further: Wächter, 'Astrologie und Schicksalsglaube'; Charlesworth, 'Jewish Interest', 930-932; Neusner, History of the Jews, vol 4, 330-334; idem, 'Rabbi and Magus'; Urbach, The Sages, 276-278; Lieberman, Greek, 97-100; Gafni, Jews of Babylonia, 165-167.

perceived as individual metaphysical powers or as being governed by them. Thus, astral fatalism, problematic in itself for the rabbinic world-view in which one's moral freedom is fundamental to one's divinely determined fate, diverged from the mere principle of predetermination underlying the entire system of divination in its being subject to the belief in the existence of these powers that control reality. It was not, therefore, for naught that the rabbis rejected the examination of the stars by asserting that it contradicted the injunction, 'You shall be whole with the Lord, your God' (Deut 18:13; bPes 113b), and even linked it to the biblical commandment, 'You shall not divine'.[174] *Itstagninut* (astral divination) was perceived as gentile wisdom, associated in particular with Egyptian magicians.[175] In spite of all that, recognition of astral fate and outright familiarity with astrology is documented in rabbinic literature both in direct statements and in narratives. At the same time, as we observed, traditions on the study and knowledge of astrology and astronomy by sages are rare. First to be noted is the talmudic statement that, 'It is one's duty to calculate the cycles and planetary courses' (bShab 75a). The comment provided there removes the discipline of astronomy from its pagan associations: 'He who knows how to calculate the cycles and planetary courses, but does not calculate them, of him Scripture says: "But they regard not the work of the Lord, neither have they considered the operation of his hands" (Isa 5:12).'[176] Additional traditions associate certain sages with astronomy and astrology. Shmuel is said to testify concerning himself: 'The paths of heavens are clearer to me than the paths of Nehardea, with the exception of the comet star, about which I know not what it is' (bBer 58b). Elsewhere, however, he makes an absolute distinction between rabbinic and astrological knowledge and establishes a hierarchy between them:

> What is the meaning of the verse, 'It is not in heaven' (Deut 30:12)? Shmuel said: the Tora is not to be found with astrologers whose profession is with heaven. They said to Shmuel: But, behold, you are an astrologer and an expert in the Tora. He said to them: I would only peer at astrology when I was free from the Tora. (DeutR Nitsavim 6, Lieberman, 118f)

It is possible that also the knowledge of 'cycles' that is listed among the wisdom that R. Yohanan b. Zakkai acquired is related to this matter.[177]

---

[174] Sifra Kedoshim 6,2 (Weiss 90ab. Cf Lev 19:26). Cf, further, bSan 66a ms Munich (*Dikdukei sofrim* Sanhedrin, 187).

[175] E.g., bSan 95a; 101b; bSot 12b; 13b; 15b; bShab 75a; GenR 63,2, p679; ExodR 1,21; PRE 44; Tanh Vayakhel 5 (Buber, 61b).

[176] Cf further bShab 75a: 'And it is forbidden to converse with one who can calculate the seasons and planetary courses but does not do so'. Rashi (*ib.*) connects this 'calculation' to divination. The aspiration to uproot the pagan element from the astral system finds clear expression in the law 'One who sees the sun at its turning point, the moon in its power, the planets in their orbits, and the sign of the zodiac in their orderly progress, recites: blessed be He who has wrought the work of creation' (bBer 59b. Cf LevR 23,8, p536f).

[177] bSuk 28a; bBB 134a. See Blau, *Zauberwesen*, p. 46.

As against these general statements, traditions about R. Joshua b. Levi attribute him with concrete astrological knowledge. In one place it is said that he attributed sickness to the influence of the moon (bGit 70a). Elsewhere, horoscopal knowledge is summoned from his notebook relating to the influence of the particular day of the week on which one was born and the star governing one's character (bShab 156a). The statement is explained by connecting a person's character with the character of the respective day of creation, and together this is an illustrative case of the assimilation of astrological elements into Jewish culture.[178] Other rabbis, too, made similar statements. There is a tradition in the name of R. Efes concerning the durations of the stellar orbits in the sky, and another by R. Meir and R. Yoshiya on the ominous nature of eclipses.[179] These general comments were later complemented with details regarding the significance of the eclipse as related to the position of the sun in the sky, and the meaning of irregular appearances of the sun.[180]

Alongside these traditions concerning expertise in actual astral knowledge, many others fundamentally acknowledge the influence of the stars on the world. Here are some of the more remarkable ones. R. Simon and others state: 'There is not a single herb that does not have its own star in the sky that strikes it and tells it, Grow!' (GenR 10,6, p78f). Also, we find this comparison: 'Just as the stars rule from one end of the world to the other, so, too, Israel' (DeutR 1,14). Similarly, there is the statement that combines *mazal* (planetary influence), sorcery, and healing: 'Man, who has *mazal*, is helped by it [the amulet]; an animal, that has no *mazal*, is not' (bShab 53b; cf bBK 2b). We also find the mention of the *mazal* that accompanies man and influences his lot and even his halakhic thinking.[181] Finally, there is Rav Papa's recommendation not to attend court together with a gentile during the month of Av because then a Jew's *mazal* is bad, but rather during the month of Adar when his *mazal* is positive (bTaan 29b). Likewise there are a number of midrashic stories and tales of sages that are based on the recognition of astral divination and related fatalism. In one of these, Abraham saw 'Isaac's *mazal* among the stars, for Abraham was an astrologer of the *mazalot*, ...for he prophesied that he and Isaac would return in peace from the altar' (Midrash Zuta on Canticles 1,1, Buber, 4). Another concerns Rav Yosef's refusal to accept the leadership of the academy of Pumbedita on account of a prophecy by Chaldeans that he would only rule for two years and his fear, that proved justified, that he would die two years after

---

[178] Cf Lieberman, *Greek*, 97-100.

[179] GenR 10:4, p76; tSuk 2:6; MekhRY Bo 1, p7. Cf, however, the perception of the eclipse as the result of moral eclipse in the world in tSuk 2:6; bSuk 29a.

[180] bSuk 29a. Epiphanius, Panarion 16.2.2 claims that the rabbis were interested in astrology (ed K. Holl, Leipzig 1915, 211). However, when one takes into consideration the tendency of the church fathers to oppose astrology, and the polemic involved, one must treat his assertion with suspicion. On the attitude of the Church Fathers to astrology see Barton, *Astrology*, 64-85; Flint, *Rise of Magic*, 92-101.

[181] bYev 64b; bShab 146a; bMeg 3a; bBB 12a.

the commencement of his leadership (bBer 64a).[182] Particular attention derserve two sayings that somewhat defiantly express an explicit and total belief in astral fate. R. Hanina's stated: '*Mazal* determines wisdom, *mazal* determines wealth, and Israel does have *mazal*' (bShab 156a). This blatantly contradicts the opinion that we shall examine below, i.e., that 'Israel has no *mazal*'. And Rava said: 'Life, children, and sustenance are not determined by merit, but by *mazal*' (bMK 28a). Here, astral fate is seen as overriding Divine reward and punishment based on a persons' deeds.

There is a collision here between astrological fatalism and the principle of free choice as the basis for man's destiny, and this is what motivated the sages towards the solution proposed in the saying: 'Israel has no *mazal*'. This is no denial of astral influence in the world, but rather Israel' exclusion from its governance as the chosen people of God, who created the stars. While the gentiles are subject to the influence of stars and planets and therefore have a reason to validate astral fate and astrological divination, Israel has its Father in heaven and His Tora, and as a result can count on Divine omnipotence, free choice, and individual providence.[183] R. Yohanan derived this from the scriptural verse: 'Do not adopt the ways of the nations or take alarm at the heavenly signs, alarmed though the nations may be at them' (Jer 10:2), concluding: '*They* shall be alarmed but not *Israel*' (bShab 156a; cf bSuk 29a). Rav, following earlier traditions, derived the matter from the call to Abraham to go *outside* and count the stars: 'Whence do we learn that Israel has no *mazal*? As it is said: "And He took him outside" (Gen 15:5) ...[Abraham] said before Him: Master of the World! I observed my astrological devotion (*itstagninut*) and I am unworthy of giving birth to a child. He said to him: Depart from your astrological devotion, for Israel has no *mazal*.' (bShab 156a; = bNed 32a). Abraham was therefore originally an astrologer. In fact, 'great astrological devotion was in his heart' (bYom 28b), and he enjoyed great fame, 'such that all the kings of the east and west would rise early to greet him at his gate' (bBB 16b). According to R. Elazar ha-Modai he was blessed with the '*itstagninus* that he possessed... such that all would come before him' (or according to another ver-

---

[182] See further bSan 95a; bTaan 25a; bShab 119a; 156b. However, see, too, the interpretation of the story in bShab 119a of 'Joseph who honours the Sabbath' who seeks to distinguish between the gentile's fate – that is foretold in the stars – and Joseph's fate, determined by free will and reward (Fraenkel, *Iyunim*, 16-18). The story of R. Nahman b. Yitshak (bShab 156b) is indeed brought to support the argument that 'Israel has no *mazal*' (see below), however, behind it lies the notion that the astral fate is the suppressed default position that also accompanies 'Israel' and bursts forth at the moment when it relinquishes its 'fear of heaven'. 'Israel' here is not the seed of Abraham that is automatically free of the astrological fate but the God-fearers among them. Cf further bYev 21b.

[183] The deliberation between free will and astral fatalism was common beyond the Jewish world. On the church fathers' struggle with astrology for this very reason see Barton, *Astrology*, 64-85. See there a parallel to the notion that 'Israel has no mazal', whereby baptism releases the Christian from astral fate (p76 and n47). For a similar notion amongst the hellenistic mystery cults see Bram, 'Fate and Freedom'. Cf further the words of Firmicus Meternus that the Caesar has no astral determination, Barton *ib.* 65f.

sion, all the kings of the east would rise early to greet him at his gate).[184] His election by God, therefore, delivered him from the astral destiny of one who was not only subjected to it, but also expert in its mysteries. One set of formative knowledge was therefore replaced by another, fear of the stars with fear of God; one form of authority with another: "'And he lead him outside" ...The rabbis say: You are a prophet and not an astrologer.'[185] However, it was not Abraham alone who was brought outside, but his entire seed. The election of Israel meant their release from the arbitrariness of astral destiny through the power of the Tora and its commandments. This principle is indeed clearly demonstrated in a few stories that deal with the victory of the power of moral merit over fate, even to the degree of saving life from predetermined death (bShab 156b; yShab 6:10, 8d).

The sages do not, therefore, dissociate themselves from the astrological outlook with all that it entails in the realm of theory and practice. Rather, they limit it, extracting from it those who have the priviledge to fall under the direct providence of God, the Creator of all stars and planets, through his word and his harbingers, and therefore the priviledge of moral choice.[186] If Israel will subjugate themselves to the Tora and the commandments (in the format determined by the sages) then they shall succeed in 'going outside' like Abraham, and release themselves from the rule and fear of stars and planets.

Further Reading

Magic and Demonology. Avishur, 'The ways of the Amorite'; Bar-Ilan, 'Between Magic and Religion'; Blau, *Das Altjüdische Zauberwesen*; Bohak,

---

[184] bBB 16b; tKid 5:17. Lieberman is of the opinion that the word איסתגנינוס cited in the Tosefta is not the word for astrology, as apparently in the Bavli, there, but means a precious stone, the Greek word for which has become corrupted (Lieberman, *Tosefta Ki-Fshutah* 8, 985f). His suggestion, however, which he offers with some hesitation, is difficult. It is true, indeed, that the traditions on removing Abraham from astrology are not easily reconciled with the verse exposition that appears there – 'And Abraham was old, and well stricken in age, and the Lord had blessed Abraham in all things' (Gen 24:1), meaning that he had been blessed with astrological wisdom. However, they do fit the view of Artapanus and Ps-Eupolemos concerning Abraham's outstanding astrological knowledge, as also the tradition that relates to Abraham's astrological knowledge about Isaac's fate (above), and another, late one that tells about the astrological gifts that Abraham gave the offspring of his concubines (Midrash Sekhel Tov, Gen 25:6).

[185] GenR 44:12, p432ff. Cf further *ib.*, the midrash that describes God taking Abraham above the heavenly firmament and the resultant freedom he acquires from fear of the stars. Cf NumR 2,12; DeutR 1:14, Lieberman, 12; and see further GenR 44:10, p432. The hierarchical relationship between astrological knowledge and its agents and the normative 'prophetic' counterpart, with its own agents, derives, of course, from here. See EcclR 1,14.

[186] A clear expression of the relationship between God and the planets is in the following: 'That he showed him [God to Abraham] all the planets that encompass the Divine Presence... The Holy One, blessed be He said to him: Just as the planets encompass me and My honour is in the middle, so your children shall multiply and encamp with their many banners and my Divine Presence will be in the middle' (DeutR 1:16, Lieberman, 16).

'Magical Means'; Fishbane, 'Most Women'; Green, 'Palestinian Holy Men'; Harari, 'Moses, the Sword'; Lesses, 'Exe(o)rcising Power'; Neusner, 'Phenomenon I'; idem, 'Rabbi and Magus'; Seidel, 'Release Us'; Strack, – Billerbeck, 'Zur altjüdischen Dämonologie'; Trachtenberg, *Jewish Magic*; Veltri, *Magie und Halakha*; Ulmer, *Evil Eye*; Urbach, *Sages* 1, 97-134; Yassif, *Hebrew Folktale* 1, 144-165.

Divination, Dream interpretation and Astrology. Alexander, 'Bavli Berakhot'; Alexander, 'A Sixtieth Part of Prophecy'; Hasan-Rokem, *Web of Life*, 88-107; Kalmin, *Sages, Stories*, 61-80; Keller, 'Nihush ve-siman'; Kristianpoller, *Traum und Traumdeutung*; Mack, H., 'Unique Character'; Niehof, 'A Dream'; Stuckrad, von, 'Jewish and Christian Astrology'; Wächter, 'Astrologie und Schicksalsglaube'.

Section Four
The Languages of Rabbinic Literature

Chapter Eighteen

Mishnaic Hebrew:
An Introductory Survey

Moshe Bar-Asher

Mishnaic Hebrew and Rabbinic Literature

1. Mishnaic Hebrew – henceforth MH, as distinct from biblical Hebrew or BH – is the language of the Tannaim and Amoraim in Palestine and Babylonia.[1] The Hebrew name for the language of these writings is לשון חכמים, *leshon hakhamim*, meaning: 'the language of the sages'. Literature in MH covers a period of about 450 years, roughly between 70 and 500 CE. The literature of the Tannaim – which includes the Mishna, the Tosefta, the Halakhic Midrashim and Seder Olam Rabba – was redacted between 70 and 250 CE approximately. The literature of the Amoraim was formed over a period from the end of the third century down to about 500 CE. In Palestine, the work of the Amoraim includes the Jerusalem Talmud and the ancient Aggadic Midrashim, such as the Genesis Rabba, Leviticus Rabba, and Pesikta de-R. Kahana; in Babylonia, the work of the Amoraim is represented by the Babylonian Talmud.

2. Most Tannaic texts were redacted in roughly the period 200–250 CE, when Rabbi Yehuda the Prince completed his compilation of the Mishna. However, research has shown that the Mishna contains a great deal of material contemporary with the destruction of the Second Temple in 70 CE. Most of this material consists of texts describing the ceremonies performed while the Temple still stood.[2] Thus the offering of first fruits (mBik 3) is described almost wholly in the present tense, by one who had been present at this ceremony.

3. Research has further shown that Hebrew was spoken in Palestine until roughly 200 CE. The view is generally accepted that the Hebrew preserved in Tannaic literature reflects living speech current in various regions of Palestine.[3] The literature of the Amoraim, however, was formed in an environment where, in all probability, Aramaic rather than Hebrew was spoken. The dialect then current in Palestine is now termed Galilean Aramaic, or Jewish Palestinian Aramaic,[4] while the dialect current in Babylonia is termed Babylonian Aramaic. It is well known that certain portions of the literature of the Amoraim, both in Palestine and in Babylonia, are written in Aramaic, or on occasion in a mixture of Hebrew and Aramaic.

4. The language reflected in the texts of rabbinic literature is equally known to us through external evidence, such as the Copper Scroll from Qum-

---

[1] This article was translated into English by my learned friend Dr. Michael Weitzman who passed away in spring 1998 in London.

[2] Epstein, *Prolegomena*, 21-58.

[3] There is little doubt that Hebrew continued to be spoken here and there in Palestine at the time of the Amoraim, several generations after the close of the Mishna. See Kutscher, 'Some Problems', 57-60, and the Oxford papyrus mentioned in §4 below.

[4] It is very likely that in Galilee, during the period of the Amoraim, the Jews spoke Aramaic only (except that Greek too was spoken in such cities as Tiberias and Beth-Shean). For this dialect see Sokoloff, *Dictionary, Palestinian Aramaic*. Some of their major literary works, however, continued to be produced in Hebrew (cf Kutscher *ib.*).

ran,[5] the letters of Simon Bar-Koseba (Bar Kokhba) discovered in the Judean desert and dating from about 130–140 CE,[6] further inscriptions discovered in synagogues elsewhere,[7] and more recent letters, like that found in an Oxford papyrus dating from about 500 CE.[8] All these documents attest Hebrew as a spoken language, used in daily life, and not merely as a language of scholarship confined to the learned.

The Origin of Mishnaic Hebrew

5. Down to 200 BCE, that is to say before the Hasmonean period, the literary language was BH, even in the late books of the Bible, such as Ezra-Nehemiah, Chronicles and Esther. Literary works from before and after the exile, despite their grammatical and lexical differences, share an impressive array of common features. Most of the Qumran writings, composed (or copied) between 200 BCE and 100 CE, likewise exhibit a biblical style, despite the presence of certain special features, some of which re-appear in MH.[9] MH did not become

---

[5] The consensus of scholarly opinion would date it around the middle of the first century CE.

[6] Kutscher *Studies* (Hebr section, pp. 66-67) surveys briefly the features which MH shares with the Hebrew letters of Bar-Koseba. Examples are אַתֶּן (*'atten*, as second person masculine plural pronoun) and אֵלּוּ (*'ēllū*, plural demonstrative). Compare the important observations of Yalon *Introduction*, 204-208, in his chapter on spoken Hebrew.

[7] This corpus is analysed in detail by Joseph Naveh, *On Stone and Mosaic*. See for example the inscription of Kfar-Baram (19f): יהי שלום במקום הזה ובכל מקומות ישראל, יוסה הלוי בן לוי עשה השקוף הזה, תבא ברכה במע[ש[ש]יו של[ו]ם – 'May there be peace in this place, and in every place in Israel. Yose the Levite son of Levi made this lintel. May blessing come upon his works. Farewell.' This text presents at least two features that point clearly to MH. The first is יוסה (*yōsē*), a name characteristic of the rabbinic period, and very probably an abbreviated form of יוֹסֵף (*yōsēf*). The spelling of the final vowel with *he* rather than the usual *yod* is peculiar to Palestine. The second feature is the form for 'lintel'. While biblical Hebrew (e.g. at Exod 12:7, 22, 23) uses מַשְׁקוֹף (*mašqōf*), the inscription instead has שְׁקוֹף, which is typical of the Mishna, as at mNeg 12:4 (in both manuscripts and printed editions). It is true that H.J. Kosovsky's concordance to the Mishna shows seven occurrences of משקוף. However, this concordance is based on printed editions, and in six of these passages the best mss (Parma-B, K) have שקוף. The six passages are as follows: (a) אין בינה לבין השקוף (mOh 10:10, 'between it and the lintel there was not...'); (b) והיא נוגעת בשקוף (mOh 10:7, 'it would. touch the lintel'); (c) and (d) מכנגד השקוף (mOh 10:7, 'opposite the lintel'); (e) and (f) מודבק לשקוף, נוגע בשקוף (mOh 12:8 [10], '[if it] cleaved to the lintel. [if one] touched the lintel').The editions, however, systematically show the biblical form משקוף. There is only one place in the Mishna where the true reading appears to be משקוף, namely וטען הזאה באגודת אזוב על המשקוף ועל המזוזות (mPes 9:5, 'this required sprinkling with a bunch of hyssop on the lintel and the sideposts'). This is however a clear reference to the biblical prescription: ולקחו מן הדם ונתנו על שתי המזוזות ועל המשקוף (Exod 12:7, 'they shall take of the blood and put it on the two side-posts and on the lintel,' ועל המשקוף). See further §§13-15 and n33 below.

[8] Cf Mishor, 'New Edition'. A few examples from this document are לעזר בן יוסה (1.4, 'Le'azar son of Yose'); מפני שבאת לכן (1.7, 'since you came here'); בערב השבת (1.16, 'on the eve of the Sabbath'). This document tends to confirm the hypothesis that Hebrew continued to be used in daily life in some corner of the Land of Israel during and even beyond the period of the Amoraim (see n4 above).

[9] See e.g. Ben-Hayyim, 'Massoret'; Yalon, *Studies* (p29f, 32f, etc.).

a *literary language*, as stated above, until the end of the first century CE. What exactly is its origin?

6. Most scholars agree that MH originates in the language spoken in various regions of Palestine throughout the period of the Second Temple.[10] Some even believe that it reflects a Hebrew dialect of the era of the first Temple. It is true that certain characteristics of the language of the Mishna already appear here and there in the Bible, proving that they then existed in a living dialect, some centuries before their appearance in MH. For example, the word ביזיון (*bizzāyōn*), meaning 'outrage' or 'contempt', is a typically mishnaic term, as in the following examples: לו רצה הכהן לנהוג ביזיון בעצמו אין שומעין (tSan 4:1) ('If a priest wished to behave without respect for himself, one does not listen to him'). שלא לנהוג ביזיון בקדשים (yShab 9, 13a) ('so as not to treat holy things with contempt'). This word appears for the first time in Esth 1:18, וכדי ביזיון וקצף, 'whence (will come) contempt and anger'.

A second example: it is well known that MH uses the form *pā'ōl* as a *nomen agentis*, e.g. סרוק (*sārōq*), 'wool-comber' (mKel 26:5);[11] טחון (*tāḥōn*) 'miller' (Makhshirin III 5).[12] This form is typical of MH, setting it apart from BH. Yet we find the first traces of this form in the book of Jeremiah, written more than 700 years before the close of the Mishna.[13] There we find the words בחון (*bāḥōn*) (Jer 6:27) 'watcher', עשוק (*āšōq*) (Jer 22:3) 'oppressor', צרוף (*sārōf*; Jer 6:29) 'metal-founder', בגודה (*bāgōdā*; Jer 3:7, 10) 'traitress'. Likewise it seems that the word חלומותיכם (*ḥ*a*lōmōtēkem*, Jer 27:9; 29:8) should not be derived from *ḥ*a*lōm* and rendered 'your dreams', but rather understood as 'your dreamers', from *ḥālōm*, 'dreamer'.[14]

---

[10] See Lifschitz, 'Ha-dikduk', 40; Bar-Asher, 'Study of Mishnaic Hebrew Grammar', 6, §4 (and literature there cited).

[11] עור הַסָּרוֹק (ms K), 'the hide of the comber', i.e. 'the hide worn by the wool-comber'.

[12] The text in fact has הַמּוֹלִיךְ חיטים לַטָּחוֹן, 'one who carries the wheat to the miller' (for grinding). The reading לַטָּחוֹן (la-ṭāḥōn) is found in two excellent manuscripts: Parma-B and Antonin. In K and the editions, however, the word (לטחון) has been vocalised (*li-ṭḥōn*) 'to grind', as an infinitive from the *Qal* conjugation. Likewise, in another passage of the Mishna, namely mDem 3:4, the printed editions show three successive occurrences of the form טוחן (*ṭōḥēn*), i.e. the present participle of the same conjugation in use as a noun: המוליך חיטין לטוחן כותי או לטוחן עם הארץ, לטוחן נכרי... ('one who brings wheat to a Samaritan miller, or an ignorant miller, or a gentile miller...'). The manuscripts, however, K and Parma-A, as well as 10 others, have instead three successive occurrences of the type *pa'ōl*: טָחוֹן (*ṭāḥōn*). Cf Segal, *Dikduk*, 75, 94.

[13] Cf Segal, 'Ḥālōm', 154-156; Bar-Asher, 'Rare Forms', 135-137; Bar-Asher, 'Historical Unity, 93f.

[14] The vocalisation חֲלוֹמֹתֵיכָם (*ḥalōmōtēkem*) might have been expected. Indeed, the Massoretic vocalisation חֲלֹמֹתֵיכֶם (*ḥ*a*lōmōtēkem*) may well intend the plural of חֲלוֹם (*ḥ*a*lōm*) rather than חָלוֹם (*ḥālōm*). However, the context shows that dreamers (and not their dreams) are meant, as the ancient versions recognised (cf the excellent analysis in Segal, 'Ḥālōm', 154f). Furthermore, the vocalisation (*ḥ*a*lōmōtēkem*) need not in fact indicate that *ḥ*a*lōm* was confused with *ḥālōm* at all. This reading may rather reflect dissimilation of vowel quantity *ḥālōmōtēkem* > *ḥ*a*lōmōtēkem*), to avoid too many long vowels in succession. This phenomenon can be observed in the Bible in relation to other words. Thus the feminine plural of צִידוֹנִי (*sīdōnī*) is צֵדְנִיּוֹת (*sēdnīyyōt*) rather than

Cases of this sort may be found in the biblical texts from the end of the First Temple period onwards, but especially in the post-exilic period. They attest the existence of a Hebrew dialect which was gaining currency towards the end of the biblical period but was to become a written language only after several centuries. It was in fact to become the *written language* of the Tannaim, i.e. mishnaic Hebrew.

Biblical Hebrew and Mishnaic Hebrew

COMMON AND CONTRASTING FEATURES

7. On comparing the grammar and vocabulary of MH with those of BH, one discovers numerous features common to the two eras (and literary corpuses) of the language. A few scholars go so far as to consider the grammar of BH and MH identical, particularly as regards morphology.[15] However, there are undeniable differences between the two periods.[16] Here let us note the following phenomena:

(a) Certain features of BH have disappeared in MH. For example, the modal forms of *yaf'ul*, such as the cohortative (אשׁירה, *āšīrāh*, 'Let me sing'; אקומה, *'āqūmāh*, 'Let me arise'; נגילה, *nāgīlā*, 'let us rejoice!') are common in BH but completely absent in MH. Similarly, the shortened *yaf'ul* (or jussive, e.g. יקם, *yāqēm*, 'may he fulfil'; תאמן, *ta"mēn*, 'have faith'), current in BH, has disappeared almost completely from MH.

(b) Certain features typical of MH are wholly or almost absent from BH. One example is the type *pa'lān / po'lān*, used for nouns indicating occupation or quality, such as גזלן, *gazlān / gozlān* ('thief'); סרבן, *sarvān / sorvān* ('rebel').[17] Another feature of MH, never found in the Bible, is the type *nitpa'el*, with *nun* (alongside *mitpa'el*, with *mem*), for the present participle of the intensive-reflexive conjugation.[18]

(c) Other features too are rare in BH but exceedingly frequent in MH. Thus there are hardly 30 occurrences of -*in* as the plural ending in the Bible; examples are מלין, *millīn*, 'words' (Job XII 11 and twelve further occurrences, as against מלים, *millīm* in ten passages) and צידונין ('Sidonians', 1 Kgs 11:33). Such cases are probably Aramaisms, limited to a few texts. However, the phenomenon becomes very common in MH. Its widening currency should be

---

ṣēdōniyyōt; the proximity of the other long vowels has caused syncope of the long vowel /ō/ in the second syllable.

[15] This question is the subject of Ben-Hayyim, 'Historical Unity'.

[16] Thus the position of Bar-Asher, 'Historical Unity', as against that of Ben-Hayyim *ib.*

[17] The only example of this pattern in BH is רַחֲמָנִיּוֹת (Lam 4:10), 'clement' (pl. fem.).

[18] See Bar-Asher, 'Rare Forms', 128-135.

attributed not to Aramaic influence but rather to a phonological law connected to the treatment of the consonants *m/n* at the end of a word.[19]

The differences between BH and MH are particularly obvious in the domain of vocabulary. We need only cite one example, the word *ṣibbūr*. In the Bible, its meaning is 'heap', as in שימו אותם שני צְבֻּרִים פתח השער (2 Kgs 10:8) – 'Put them in two heaps at the entrance of the Gate'. This sense is likewise found in MH, e.g.: שני ציבורי זיתים וחרובים – 'two heaps of olives and carobs' (mPea 6:4). The principal and far commoner meaning of the word, however, is 'community', as in the following examples: אל תפרוש מן הציבור (mAv 2:4) – 'do not separate from the community'; העוסק בצרכי ציבור כעוסק בדברי תורה (yBer 5, 8d) – 'He that occupies himself with the needs of the community has as much merit as he that occupies himself with Tora'.

DIACHRONIC DIFFERENCES

8. The differences between BH and MH can be attributed in large measure to the chronological gap between them. The linguistic situation of MH reflects a stage subsequent to that of BH. For example, the reflexive-passive form of the new intensive conjugation is expressed by *hitpa'al / hitpa'el* in the Bible, but by *nitpa'al* in MH. Linguistic analysis shows that the mishnaic form results from a development due to the analogy of the reflexive form of the simple action, *nif'al*, whence initial *nun* has been borrowed.

9. In the semantic domain, we may cite the word מְזוּזָה, *m'zūzā*. In the Bible this indicates one of the two doorposts, which stand to the left and right of the threshold and support the lintel. Examples are: (a) והגישו אדניו אל האלהים והגישו אל הדלת או אל המזוזה (Exod 21:6), 'His master shall bring him before the tribunal, and take him near the leaf or post of the door'. (b) ולקחו מן הדם ונתנו על שתי המזוזות ועל המשקוף (Exod 12:7), 'They shall take the blood and put it on the two doorposts and the lintel'.

In the Mishna, however, *m'zūzā* indicates the little parchment scroll upon which two extracts of Deuteronomy (6:4-9 and 11:13-21) were copied, and which is fixed upon the right-hand doorpost in a Jewish house. For example: אין כותבין ספרים תפילין ומזוזות במועד (mMK 3:4) 'one does not copy scrolls (of the Tora) or (verses of) phylacteries or *m'zūzōt* on (the intermediate days of) a festival'.

In this case too it is clear that the sense of the word in MH results from later evolution of the language: metonymy leads from a general sense to a specific sense, connected with the Jewish way of life as determined by rabbinic law in the time of the Mishna.

---

[19] See Bar-Asher, 'Historical Unity', 84 n44, and references there cited. A fuller discussion of the examples mentioned in this paragraph will be found *ib.* 77-86.

Dialectal Differences

10. However, diachronic explanations do not suffice to explain all the differences between the two states of the language. In fact on close scrutiny one can find cases where MH actually shows a more ancient form than BH. Consider for example the proto-Semitic word *laylay*, 'night'. This appears in the Bible in three forms: (1) *layla*, (2) *layil*, (3) *lēl*. The first of these forms shows the reduction of the second diphthong *ay* > *ā*.[20] The two other forms, *layil* and *lēl*, are due to haplology. That is to say, one of the two diphthongs *ay* has dropped out: *laylay* > *layil* / *lēl*. Now in MH we find a fourth example: *lēlē*, in the construct state of the singular. For example: לילה ויום כְּלֵילֵי שבת ויומו (mNid 4:4) 'a night and a day, like the night and the day of the Sabbath'. The context shows clearly that לֵילֵי is a singular, not a plural.[21] This form derives from *laylay* and has undergone in both syllables the normal monophongisation *ay* > *ē*. Remarkably, it is in MH, the later stage of the language, that we find the form which most resembles the original quadriconsonantal form *l.y.l.y.*, *laylay*.

Let us take a further example. In BH, the nearer demonstrative ('this') in the singular is זֶ (masc. *ze*) / זאת (fem. *zōt*). In MH, however, the two corresponding forms are זֶה, *ze*, and זו, *zō*.[22] Comparative grammar shows that the form זו, parallel to Aramaic דָּא,[23] is the older. By contrast, זאת is a secondary form, *zōt*: the ending *-t* has been added to mark the feminine more transparently.[24]

---

[20] The diphthong *ay* is usually reduced in Hebrew to *ē*, e.g. בַּיִת (*bayit* / *bait*) > בֵּית (*bēt*). Sometimes, however, it is reduced to *ī*, as in דַיִש (*dayiš* / *daiš*) > דִּישׁו (*dīšo*, Deut 25:4). Occasionally it is reduced to *ā* (*â*), as in עֵינָם ('*ēnām* / '*ênâm*, Josh 34:34), which is simply a development of עֵינַיִם ('*ēnayim*, e.g. Gen 38:14). (However, *laylā* can be explained as *layl* + *ā* [indicating adverb: *laylā* - 'at night'] which became a noun).

[21] The Mishna speaks of a period of 24 hours (לילה ויום 'a night and a day'), and takes as an example לילי שבת ויומו, i.e. the duration of the night and day of the Sabbath.

[22] The demonstrative *zō* is hardly ever found in the Bible, while *zōt* hardly ever appears in rabbinic literature. For further details, see Bar-Asher, 'Historical Unity', 90f, with notes 67-68.

[23] The Arabic cognate, as is well known, is *hādā*, which is however used for the masculine only.

[24] Evidently one could hardly maintain that *all* the linguistic forms which appear in a more ancient state in MH than in BH go back to dialect variants. This caveat applies particularly to matters of vocabulary. For example, חתך ('cut, slice') is confined in the Bible to the figurative sense 'decide', 'decree' as in שָׁבֻעִים שִׁבְעִים נֶחְתַּךְ עַל עַמְּךָ (Dan 9:24, 'Seventy weeks are decreed upon thy people'). Yet the concrete sense, which must have been primary, first appears in MH. One occurrence is חתך את הראש, חתך את הכרעים, חתך את הידים (mTam 4:2, 'he cut off the head, he cut off the shanks, he cut off the fore-legs'). Another occurrence is at mBets 4:4, ואין חותכין את הפתילה לשנים 'nor may one sever a wick into two'). Another word whose primary sense appears in MH rather than BH is זֶרֶת. In BH it indicates a unit of measurement: זרת ארכו וזרת רחבו (Exod 28:16; 39:9, 'its length was one span, its breadth was one span'). In MH, by contrast, זרת indicates the little finger (perhaps from זערת), as at bMen 11a, which gives the different terms for the five fingers: זו זרת, זו קמיצה, זו אמה, זו אצבע, זו גודל. In these two cases (cited by Lifschitz, 'Ha-dikduk', 40 n27), the concrete sense first appears in MH, while BH has the figurative sense alone. From the semantic viewpoint, MH evidently reflects the older state. One may suppose, however, that the mishnaic usage already existed in the biblical period but happens not to be attested in the Bible.

11. How can one explain the fact that MH sometimes presents a more ancient form than BH for the same word? It is not enough simply to posit two successive states of the language. We have rather to think of two simultaneous but distinct states, reflecting two different dialects. In other words, MH is the continuation not of BH itself but of a related dialect. There is no other way to explain how the later form of Hebrew (i.e. MH), which one would have expected to show in every area a general development from the earlier form (i.e. BH), in fact exhibits at certain points a more archaic state.[25]

DIFFERENCES OF TRADITION

12. Quite apart from this question of historical and dialectal differences, there is one further point in which MH diverges from BH. This further difference is in the traditions by which BH and MH have come down to us. Let us recall that in Hebrew, as in other Semitic languages, not all the elements of the word are transcribed. Thus the form דבר (*d.b.r.*) may be read *dāvār* ('word, thing'), *dever* ('pestilence'), *dibbēr* ('he spoke'), *dabbēr* ('speak!'), *dubbar* ('it was spoken of'), etc. In itself, a certain written word, or grapheme, may be interpreted in various ways. Only a wholly vocalised text can give a complete image of the word. Without full vocalisation, even the full context of a written word may leave us in doubt as to the precise form. An example is the vocalisation of חרש at Gen 4:22, in the phrase לוטש כל חרש נחשת וברזל, (*lōtēš kol*) *hrš* (*nᵉḥošet ū-barzel*). The Tiberian Massora has חֹרֵשׁ, *ḥōreš*, while the Babylonian has חָרָשׁ, *ḥaraš*. This is one of the cases where we have two divergent traditions, giving equally credible readings – even though in purely historical terms one form alone could have been intended by the author.[26]

The fact that the script does not record every element in pronunciation has important implications in many areas of the history of Hebrew, not least as regards the differences between BH and MH. For example, the name הלל occurs both in the Bible (Judg 12:13, 15) and in the Mishna (e.g. mShev 10:3). Today the name is read in both cases הִלֵּל (*hillēl*); however, certain manuscripts of the Mishna give הֶלֵּל (*hellēl*). Some researchers have tried to explain this divergence in diachronic terms: in an unstressed closed syllable, the vowel [*i*] changed in MH to [*e*]: *hillēl* > *hellēl*.[27] However, a very different explanation is possible. The difference between *hillēl* and *hellēl* is not diachronic, but reflects a difference in the traditions of the reading of this name. One tradition, at-

---

[25] Compare further Kutscher, 'Present State', 30 n5; Bar-Asher, 'Historical Unity', 89-93.

[26] See Yeivin, 'Hebrew Language', 1163. Yeivin lists at length many differences between the Tiberian and Babylonian traditions of the biblical text. Most of these differences concern the vocalisation, though many concern the consonantal text itself. Examples are the Tiberian שָׁבַר (*šābar*) against Babylonian שִׁבֵּר (*šibbēr*) at 1 Kgs 13:28; or Tiberian לָקְקוּ (*lāqᵉqū*) against Babylonian לִקְקוּ (*liqqᵉqū*) at 1 Kgs 21:19. Further discussion of the differences between the two traditions in individual passages would lie beyond the scope of the present work.

[27] This is the thesis that Kutscher, *Studies*, Hebr section, 135-166 sets out to prove.

tached to a certain place (a dialect or school), read *hillēl*; the other, reflecting a different school or dialect, read *hellēl*; but those who pronounce *hillēl* do so consistently both in the Bible and in the Mishna, and those who pronounce *hellēl* are equally consistent. Now we have solid evidence for either readings both in the Bible[28] and in the mishnaic language.[29] We have no compelling argument to show which is the older of the two forms. The form for which we have the oldest attestation is in fact *hellēl*. The Septuagint gives, in its text of Judges, the reading Ελληλ,[30] identical with *hellēl*. However, we cannot conclude that the form *hillēl* is the younger, on the ground that the sources attesting it are later than the Septuagint.[31] We can only accept that we have here two traditions with different readings for the same word. This example is far more unique.[32]

THE LITERARY INFLUENCE OF BIBLICAL HEBREW

13. The points raised above show how complex and delicate is the distinction between BH and MH. We now turn to another aspect of the problem, namely that MH is not only later than BH but inferior in prestige. The biblical text enjoyed such authority that its influence could not be escaped. This influence is apparent both in the redaction of rabbinic literature and in its transmission, through the Middle Ages down to the present. Let us consider two examples:

14. To signify 'further' or (of time) 'onward', BH uses הלאה, while MH uses להלן or מכאן ואילך. However, there is one mishnaic passage where the word הלאה occurs twice: נדרים (...). כשרין מיום שלושים והלאה (...) חטאות הציבור ועולותיהן (...). ונדבות הבכור והמעשר והפסח כשרים מיום השמיני והלאה ואף ביום השמיני (mPar 1:4) 'The sin-offerings and burnt-offerings of the community (...) are valid from the thirtieth day onward. (...) Vows and freewill offerings, the first-born, the tithe,

---

[28] The reading הִלֵּל (*hillēl*) is attested by the Tiberian vocalisation (as shown in the example from Judges cited above) and also by the Babylonian vocalisation (see Yeivin, *Hebrew Language*, 963). The reading הֵלֵּל (*hellēl*) is attested by the Septuagint, which reads Ελληλ.

[29] As to MH, we find הֵלֵּל in Italian mss such as K, as noted in Kutscher, *Studies*, Hebr section, 84f, 150. The same form appears in ms Parma-A (cf Haneman, *Morphology*, 2) and of the Paris ms, as well as other works of Italian origin (see Bar-Asher, *Tradition*, 11, 64, 92). On the other hand, we find הִלֵּל in ms Parma-B (see Bar-Asher, 'Introduction', 171, 183) and in the Babylonian vocalisation of the Mishna (cf Yeivin, *Hebrew Language*, 963). One should perhaps emphasise that we have no case of a manuscript of the Bible and a manuscript of the Mishna both copied and vocalised by a single scribe.

[30] See n28 above.

[31] The evidence for vowels in the text of the Septuagint pre-dates all the vocalisation systems applied to the Hebrew text of the Bible and the Mishna. However, the vowels shown by those systems reproduce a linguistic situation far earlier than the date of the invention of those systems. Thus the Massoretic system of vocalising the Bible is no earlier than the seventh century CE, and the corresponding system for the Mishna is later still. The vowels that those systems present, however, reproduce the linguistic situation many centuries earlier, (cf Yalon, *Studies*, 16ff; Kutscher, 'Some Problems', 52f; Kutscher, *Studies*, 73ff).

[32] See further §45 below.

and the Passover sacrifice are valid from the eighth day onward, and also on the eighth day.'

Normal usage would have been מיום שלושים ולהלן (or מיום שלושים ואילך), but instead the word והלאה is used. Evidently whoever formulated this mishna recalled the underlying biblical verse: ומיום השמיני והלאה ירצה לקרבן אשה לה' (Lev 22:27) 'from the eighth day onward, it shall be accepted as a fire-offering to the Lord'. This borrowing is due to the literary influence of the biblical text. It seems authentic and in all probability goes back to the very author of this mishna in tractate Parah.

15. On the other hand, there are changes which must doubtlessly be attributed to later scribes who substituted biblical forms for the original forms of mishnaic language. For example, the nominative first person plural pronoun at the time of the Mishna was *'ānū*, as in הרי אנו מטמאין את כולכם (mTer 8:12) 'we declare you all unclean'. However, in two places the biblical form *"naḥnū* has crept into the printed editions of the Mishna. These places are: (a) לפיכך אנחנו חייבים להודות וכו' (mPes 10:4) 'therefore we are in duty bound to praise.'; (b) אנחנו מעלין על נכסי אבינו (mKet 10:2) 'we add to the value of our father's property'.

The biblical form is the reading given by the Livorno edition and by M.J. Kosovsky's concordance to the Mishna. However, all the major manuscripts (K, Parma-A, Cambridge, Paris), as well as the *editio princeps* (Naples 1492) show, in both passages, the form *'ānū*. It was evidently the later copyists who replaced the mishnaic form *'ānū* by the biblical *"naḥnū*. Such modifications, due to the literary influence of the biblical text on the rabbinic writings as transmitted by copyists, are certainly common,[33] though far less so than was thought in the past.[34]

Unity and Diversity in Mishnaic Hebrew

THE PRECONCEPTION OF UNIFORMITY EXAMINED

16. For a long time there has been a widespread tendency to view MH as utterly homogeneous. The grammar by M.H. Segal, *Dikduk*, is a prime representative of this conception: its many chapters offer examples culled indifferently

---

[33] The example of משקוף, discussed above n7, is relevant here too, since it well illustrates the literary dependence of the Mishna upon the Bible. That dependence affected both the author of the mishnaic passage, at the point of redaction, and the copyists in the Middle Ages. In this particular case, the use of the term משקוף in mPes is authentic, inasmuch as the author of this Mishna had the text of Exodus in mind (12:7, 22, 23). Thus Exod 12:23,ועל שתי המזוזות ועל המשקוף את הדם וראה has influenced the author of the phrase ועל שתי המזוזות והמשקוף על אזוב באגודת הזאה וטען in mPes 9:5. By contrast, the introduction of the word משקוף in place of שקוף in tractate Oholot in six places is probably due to the secondary change by copyists, see n7 above.

[34] Kutscher, *Studies*, Hebr section, 73ff; idem, 'Present State', 39f, argues that cases where MH texts have been conformed to BH are very numerous. Against this see the detailed analysis in Bar-Asher, 'Different Traditions', 27-32.

from the language of the Tannaim and of the Palestinian and Babylonian Amoraim. Thus, when Segal discusses denominative verbs, he cites examples from the Mishna מתריעין (mTaan 2:1): 'one plays the trumpet', from תרועה 'trumpet blast', etc., and from the Babylonian Talmud הנגיב (bEr 53a) 'turn to the south', from נגב 'south'; ידרים 'turn to the south', from דרום 'south', and יצפין 'turn to the north', from צפון 'north' (bBB 25b). Similarly, in his chapter on פ"י verbs (with initial consonant *yod*), he gives ליישן ('to sleep'), which is mishnaic (mBB 2:3); ליגע ('to touch'), which comes from the Yerushalmi (yBer 9:5, 14d); and לינק ('to suck, to nuzzle'), to be found in the Bavli (bPes 112a).

H. Yalon likewise studied together different periods and different literary units. For example, in chapter XXVII (Yalon, *Introduction*, 171-175) he speaks of 'the present participle of the simple form of the ע"ו verbs and of geminate verbs with vowel *ō*'. Yalon takes his examples from Tannaic literature (Mishna and Tosefta), from Genesis Rabba, Leviticus Rabba and other Midrashim, from both Talmuds, and so on.

The above approach treats the language of MH as uniform. Its adherents set out to show the cohesion of the language in its different layers and constituent works. More recent research, by contrast, takes care to distinguish between the different elements and the manifold traditions, and emphasises the differences, in order to obtain a more exact and focussed view of MH. Seven aspects that should be kept in view are presented below.

THE LANGUAGE OF THE TANNAIM AND THE AMORAIM CONTRASTED

17. Although MH presents a measure of unity, two main components can be distinguished: the language of the Tannaim (which may be denoted MH1) and that of the Amoraim (MH2). Within MH2 one must also distinguish between Palestine and Babylonia. This division was proposed and indeed demonstrated by E.Y. Kutscher.[35] For example, האלו/אלו, *ēllū* / *hāēllū* are the plurals demonstrative in the language of the Tannaim, while the Palestinian Amoraim use הללו, *hallālū* / *hallēlū*. The latter form is a combination of two demonstrative elements: *hāl* (*halla*) and *ēlū*, as Segal (*Dikduk*, 50) already showed.

Another example is the first person singular of the future (*yaf'ul*) tense. In the language of the Tannaim and Babylonian Amoraim, the form is *'ep'ōl* (with initial *aleph* as in BH). In the language of the Palestinian Amoraim, however, there are abundant examples to show the form to have been *nif'ōl*, through the influence of Galilean Aramaic. One example may be drawn from Genesis Rabba 29 (p268, ms Rome 4 mss): מעשה בחסיד אחד שיצא שיצא לכרמו וראה עוללה אחת וברך עליה, אמר: כדיי העוללה הזאת שנברך עליה – 'There is a story of a pious man who went out into his vineyard and saw one bunch of grapes. He blessed it, saying: "This bunch is worthy that I should bless it".'

---

[35] See Kutscher, 'Present State', 30 (§4) and 40ff (§32ff).

577

The form שנברך, with *nun*, appears in the best manuscripts, though some correct to שאברך. Similarly one may cite PesRK 5 p80: כל אותו היום היה אברהם יושב ותמה בליבו ואומר: לאיזו מהם נבור, לגיהנם או למלכיות? – 'All that day, Abraham sat and wondered in his heart, saying: Which of them shall I choose, hell or the [heathen] kingdoms?' The verb 'shall I choose' has the form of נבור (*naḇōr*) and not אבור (*'āḇōr*).[36]

A third and final example is provided by the expression כל שהוא, literally 'whatever it be'. In the language of the Tannaim this is used to mean 'a little', as in חגב חי כל שהוא (mShab 10:7): 'a grasshopper that is half alive'. The usage of the Amoraim of Palestine seems identical, as in yBer III, 6d: נתן בתוכו מים כל שהוא – 'he put into it a little water'. However the Babylonian Amoraim express that sense instead through the word משהו (literally 'something'), as in bPes 12a, שתי שעות חסר משהו – 'a little less than two hours'.[37]

18. In the Tannaic period, when MH was a living language spoken in several regions, it was clearly not uniform. It is only natural that different areas should exhibit differences of language. Even though the texts in general show a reasonably homogeneous written language, evidence for the existence of different dialectscan still be traced, both in literary sources and in certain external documents.

For example, the word *šel*, indicating possession (equivalent to English *of*), may be used in two different ways, both attested in various texts. In the letters of Bar-Koseba, it is written as a separate word from the noun that it governs, as in שהיו של הגואין (Letter II),[38] 'that belonged to the gentiles'. In the manuscripts of the Mishna, however, it is always prefixed to the following word: if the letter contains the definite article ה, syncope of the ה takes place, so that we find systematically שֶׁלַּגּוֹיִם instead of של הגוים. See for example mKel 8:7: שלכירה [...] שלתנור 'of the oven... of the double stove.'[39]

Another example involves the root *'.l.m.n* in the *nitpa'al* conjugation, meaning 'be widowed' in MH. In the best manuscripts of the Mishna we find נתאלמנה, *nit'alm'nā(h)* in the third person singular and נתאלמנו, *nit'alm'nū* in the plural (mYev 2:10; mNed 11:10, mMak 1:1 and eight further references).[40] In the editions of the Mishna and the Bavli (and other texts), however, we find the reading נתארמלה, *nit'armelā(h)* (mYev 6:3; 13:4 [twice]; mKet 2:1; 4:2 [twice]; 5:1; mNed 11:9), coming from another root namely *'.r.m.l.* Some consider the latter a Babylonian form, since it is frequent in the Bavli's edi-

---

[36] Further details will be found in Sokoloff, 'The Hebrew', 284-288.
[37] See Breuer, 'Hebrew Dialect', 139f. a study of the linguistic features of the Hebrew of the Babylonian Amoraim.
[38] See Kutscher, *Studies*, Hebr section, 57.
[39] Kutscher *ib.*; Yalon, *Introduction*, 26f (§18), 189-193.
[40] See Bar-Asher, *Tradition*, 33.

tions and in mss of Halakhic Midrashim.[41] However, it is also attested in a Palestinian Hebrew dialect. At Qumran, in a passage of the Damascus Scroll, we find the very similar form התארמלה, *hit'arm^elā(h)*, which is *hitpa'al* of the root *'.r.m.l.*[42]

Our third and last example involves the word מעין, *ma'ayān*, 'spring', which is very frequent in MH (e.g. at mBik 1:6). In SifNum 22 (p26), however, in the story of the shepherd from the south who came to Simon the Just, we find a different pronunciation of this word. Ms Rome 32 reads: והלכתי למלאות מים מן הנעיים ('I went to draw water from the spring'). The form here is *na'ayām*, with metathesis of the consonants *m* and *n*.[43]

These three examples show clearly that various dialects were current in the different regions of Palestine. The literary language of the Mishna (which belongs to a specific place or region within Palestine) may be contrasted with the language of neighbouring places: the letters of Bar-Koseba in the south (של הגואין as against שלגוים); Qumran in the region of the Dead Sea (התארמלה = [נתארמלה] as against נתאלמנה); the shepherd from the south (נעיים as against מעין).

19. In relation to this question of dialectal variants, there is a particular aspect of rabbinic literature which should be considered. J.N. Epstein pointed out that some of the controversies in the Mishna and Tosefta are merely apparent. There are discussions in which the rabbis agree on the substance but disagree on the wording, each following the linguistic usage of his own region or school.[44] Thus we read in one Mishna (mKel 8:9): בור שיש בו שפיתה טמא, ושל עושי זכוכית. כבשן של סידין ושל זגגין ושל יוצרים טהורה – 'A pit in which a fire can be lit is susceptible to uncleanness, as is also the pit of a maker of glass. The furnace of limeburners or of glassmakers or potters, is not susceptible to uncleanness.' In the first sentence, the artisans who work the glass are called עושי זכוכית (literally, 'the makers of glass'); in the second, they are called by the single word זגגין. Similarly, the artisans called חייטין 'tailors' (mShab 1:3; mPes 4:6 etc) are also called תופרי כסות 'those who sew garments' (mKil 9:6).

Another example may be found at mPar 2:5: היו בה שתי שערות שחורות או לבנות בתוך גומא אחת פסולה. רבי יהודה אומר בתוך כוס אחד. – 'If one found on [the red cow] two black or white hairs within one single hole it is invalid. Rabbi Yehuda says: inside one single hollow.' The Yerushalmi explains (yAZ 12, 42a): הן כוסות הן גומות – 'holes and hollows are the same'. The discussion between the first teacher and R. Yehuda thus rests on a simple problem of language. However, we cannot always trace the provenance of a particular dialect form.

---

[41] See Moreshet, *Lexicon*, 105.
[42] See Bar-Asher, *Linguistic Studies*, 185f.
[43] See Epstein, 'Perushei ha-Rivan', 192.
[44] For further details see Epstein, *Prolegomena*, 234-240.

Linguistic Differences within the Mishna

20. Even in a closed Tannaic corpus like the Mishna, the language is not absolutely uniform. Of course the six orders of the Mishna exhibit general homogeneity of language, but some units are marked by particular features. These units, as a rule, depart from the norms of MH in the direction of BH. Some of these peculiarities are discussed below.

a) The most ancient passages, dating from around 70 CE (and therefore contemporary with the destruction of the Second Temple), exhibit grammatical or lexical usages proper to BH. An example is the verb for 'begin'. The usual word in the Mishna is the secondary form *hithīl* as at mPea 7:2, התחיל בו 'he began it'. However, tractate Tamid uses the biblical form *hēḥēl*: החלו מעלין, 'they began bringing up' (mTam 2:2, 3), החלו עולין, 'they began going up'.[45]

Another example is the verb for 'take'. In BH, this is the primary sense of the root *l.q.ḥ*. In MH, however, the meaning of this root has usually shifted to 'buy'. Contrast, for example, לקח את ספר התורה הזה (Deut 31:26)[46] – 'Take this book of the Tora!', with לקח מן הנחתום ככר בפונדיון (mShev 8:4) – 'He brought from the baker a loaf for a *pondiyon*'. To signify 'take', MH uses the root *n.ṭ.l.*, as in נטל ממנה מקל או שרביט (mAZ 3:10): 'he took from it a branch or a twig'. However, we find the biblical usage in an ancient Mishna, from the period of the Second Temple, dealing with the sanctification of the new moon: ואם צודה להן לוקחין בידן מקלות. ואם היתה הדרך רחוקה לוקחין בידן מזונות 'and if any lie in wait for them, they take staves in their hands. and if the journey be long they take food in their hands' (mRH 1:9). In this passage, it is the verb *lōqᵉḥīn* and not *nōṭᵉlīn*[47] which is used twice in the sense 'take'.

b) In general, it is in the realm of the cultus that the language is most conservative and closest to BH. Examples are the phrases והשתחווה ויצא, 'he bowed down and went out' (mBik 3:6), or התנדב, 'he made a freewill offering' (mMen 12:6). These two passages deal with matters linked to the sanctuary, and most of our sources show *hitpa'al* forms (with initial *he*: *hištaḥᵃwa*, *hitnaddab*). These are the biblical forms, rather than the expected mishnaic forms (*nitpa'al*, with initial *nun*), such as appear in mHul 10:4, נתגייר, *nitgayyar*, 'convert to Judaism'; mHal 4:3, נתחייב, *nitḥayyab*, 'be liable'; mEr 7:5, נתמעט, *nitma'at*, 'be reduced'.[48]

c) The mishnaic texts which imitate the style of biblical poetry likewise show particular affinity with BH. The best examples can be found among the exhortations of the tractate Avot, e.g. the use of the jussive form in אל תעש עצמך (mAv 1:8) 'do not make yourself'; אל תאמן בעצמך עד יום מותך (mAv 2:4)

---

[45] Epstein *ib*. 27; Bar-Asher, 'Historical nity', 94-98.

[46] One passage where BH perhaps comes within sight of the sense usual in MH is Gen 19:14 לוקחי בנותיו ('those who took his daughters'). Here the probable reference is Lot's future sons-in-law, who were due to 'take', i.e. 'acquire', his daughters.

[47] See Kutscher, *Words*, 55; Bar-Asher, 'Historical Unity', 96f (§27).

[48] Compare the excellent analysis by Haneman, *Morphology*, 208-211.

'do not believe in yourself until the day of your death'. The forms *'al ta'as* and *'al ta'amēn* are used instead of *'al ta'ase* and *'al ta'amīn*, which would have been the regular future forms in MH. Compare further יהי כבוד חברך חביב עליך כשלך (mAv 2:10):[49] 'Let the honour of your friend be as dear to you as your own', with the form *y'hī* (יְהִי) and not *yihye* (יִהְיֶה), or *y'hē* (יְהֵא), the usual form in MH).

<h2 style="text-align:center">EDITIONS AND MANUSCRIPTS</h2>

21. The works of the Tannaim were edited more than 1700 years ago, and those of the Amoraim more than 1400 years ago. We possess no manuscripts going back to those periods. Most of the extant manuscripts are no more than a thousand years old; very few rabbinic texts survive that were copied before the year 1000.[50] Of these manuscripts, few are complete. Nevertheless, several of these manuscripts have been the subject of research to assess their fidelity to the original language. Most were copied between 1100 and 1400 or thereabouts. The printed editions follow, from the end of the fifteenth century onward. The first edition of the Mishna dates from 1492.[51]

22. Even after the final redaction, the Mishna (and other Tannaic texts) continued to be transmitted orally. Most scholars are agreed that few people possessed written copies. Many centuries were to pass before the Mishna came to be copied in a large number of exemplars, probably around 700. In these circumstances, it was almost inevitable that modifications would be introduced into the text transmitted. This is the reason that even the oldest manuscripts already reflect certain departures from the original language. Research has shown that, overall, most of the manuscripts from before 1250 (and even, to a great extent, those from before 1400) have faithfully preserved the original language. Divergence from that standard is to be found, however, in manuscripts copied from 1400 onwards and even more so in printed editions.[52] The reasons for this situation are beyond the scope of this work. It is sufficient to note that many differences can be found between the manuscripts and the printed editions of the Mishna.

23. Some examples will illustrate the phenomenon. The words קרדום, *kardōm*, 'axe' and קרסול, *qarsōl*, 'peg' appear in those forms in the printed editions, while the manuscripts have *qordōm / qurdōm* and *qorsēl / qursēl*: קוֹרְדּוֹם (mKel 29:3, ms K), קוּרְסֵל (mOh 1:9, mss Parma-B and K). The reason

---

[49] Haneman *ib*. 31-33; Sharvit, *Textual Variants*, 12-14.

[50] See Rosenthal, *Mishna Aboda Zara*, 96ff; Kutscher, 'Present State', 52 (§53).

[51] See Kutscher, *Studies*, Hebr section, 73-107, an outstanding study on the special value of ms K. See also Haneman, *Morphology*, on Parma-A, as well as Bar-Asher's evaluations of the importance of mss Parma-B (1971) and Paris (1980). Compare further Bar-Asher, 'Different Traditions', esp 5f, on various mss.

[52] See Kutscher, *Studies*, Hebr section, 73ff; Bar-Asher, *Tradition*, esp 34, 53-58; idem, 'Vocalisation Errors'; idem, 'Different Traditions', 27ff.

that such forms were eliminated from the printed editions may be their incompatibility with BH.[53] Another example involves the *nitpaʿal* conjugation. This could be used transitively when MH was a living language, as the manuscripts well attest, e.g. גזל ועריות שנפשו של אדם מתאווה להן ומתחמדתן – 'robbery and incest, which a man's soul longs for and desires' (mMak 3:15, ms K). The verbal form is here accompanied by an accusative pronominal suffix: ומתחמדתן is equivalent to ומתחמדת אותן, 'she desires them' (*mitḥammedet* + pronominal suffix). In the editions,[54] however, this form is replaced by the corresponding intensive (*piʿel*) form: ומחמדתן (*meḥammedet* + pronominal suffix), which would be usual for the active sense.[55] Examples of this sort could easily be multiplied.

LINGUISTIC TYPES IN THE MISHNA MANUSCRIPTS

24. Even the oldest manuscripts, which might have been expected to exhibit the language in its original state, do not in fact give the impression of a uniform language. The totality of manuscripts, complete and fragmentary, of Tannaic literature, and of the Mishna in particular, may be classified from the linguistic viewpoint into three groups. A detailed study by the present writer sought to show that these three groups represented three different linguistic traditions (or types). The manuscripts may be divided into a Babylonian branch and a Palestinian branch, of which the latter is subdivided into a western and an eastern type. Each of these represents, to some extent, the different linguistic traditions current in Palestine when Hebrew was still spoken there, i.e. before 200 CE.[56]

25. The distinction between the Palestinian and Babylonian branches is marked by numerous linguistic differences, affecting various aspects of the language. For example, in the Palestinian branch we find the construction of relative ש + third person pronoun present participle, e.g. שהוא שולח, 'who sends', שהיא עושה, 'who (fem.) does', שהן אוכלין, 'who eat'. By contrast, the Babylonian branch uses a shorter construction, namely relative ש + present

---

[53] See Bar-Asher, 'Introduction', 171, 176, and references cited there. One possible explanation is that the process (which here led to the replacement, in certain editions, of *qursēl* by *qarsōl* and of *qordōm* by *qardōm*) is due to the influence of the biblical vocalisation. However, one could equally well suppose that there were traditions of MH in which these (and other) words had been read from the very first in the same forms as are attested in the biblical vocalisation. See §12 above and §46 (especially n126) below.

[54] Even some good mss have lost the reading ומתחמדתן; for example, Parma-A gives ומחמדתן.

[55] Occasionally, even the printed editions preserve the special usage of the *nitpaʿal* with a direct object. In particular, the verb *nitqabbal* provides a number of examples, such as אלמנה...נתקבלה כתובתה (mKet 11:4, 'A widow... she has received her *ketuba*'), or התקבלתי ממך מנה (mKet 5:1, 'I have received from you one *mina*').

[56] The various aspects of this question are examined in Bar-Asher, 'Different Traditions'.

participle: שׁשׁוּלֹח, שׁעוּשָׂה, שׁאוכלין. It can be shown that both constructions go back to the origins of the MH.[57]

26. The Palestinian branch, as mentioned above, may be divided into two types: the Western, represented for the most part by manuscripts of Italian origin, and the Eastern, appearing in manuscripts copied in the Near East. The main differences between these two types are phonetic or morphological. In other words, we find the same words (graphemes) but differently formed or pronounced.[58] For example, the word צפורן, 'nail', is read as צִפֹּרֶן (ṣippōren) in the Western type but as צְפֹֿרֶן (ṣᵉfōren) in the Eastern.[59] Similarly, the plural of the noun אָחוֹת ('aḥōt, 'sister') is אֲחָיוֹת ('aḥyōt) in the Western and אֲחָיוֹת (ahayot) in the Eastern.[60] The present participle of the nifʿal conjugation of ל"י verbs (i.e. verbs having yod as their third radical consonant) is usually of the pattern nifʿe in the western type, with the sole exception of the verb עשׂה (do, make), which shows the pattern nifʿā: neʿesā. By contrast, we find both nifʿā and nifʿe in the eastern type, with a growing preference for the former.[61]

27. In summary, it is clear that the two types (eastern and western) within the Palestinian branch differ in phonetic and morphological matters, while the differences between the Palestinian branch as a whole and the Babylonian branch are not only phonetic and morphological but also concern matters of syntax.

SPECIAL TRADITIONS

28. There are a number of linguistic forms attested in one manuscript alone. Linguistic analysis of these features shows that there is no reason to suspect the authenticity of these uniquely attested forms. Of course, we cannot determine at what date these forms entered the language. Hence, when confronted with such a form, we can hardly determine whether it reflects actual spoken Hebrew or whether it results from a transformation that occured in the course of textual transmission during the Middle Ages. Given the complexity of this question, the most prudent course is simply to note carefully the linguistic facts offered by the manuscripts concerned, until new tools and data are available to help us trace the transmission process. Here are three examples of peculiarities of this sort.

a) The word צָפוֹן (ṣafōn, 'North') appears in that form in all manuscripts, except for one passage in ms Parma-A, where we instead find ṣippūn: לְצִפּוּנָה (mRH 2:6: 'Northwards'). This is identical with the Aramaic form, and also occurs in the Hebrew of the Samaritan Pentateuch (cf Gen 13:14, ṣibbūnā).[62]

---

[57] Ib. 27.
[58] Ib. 21.
[59] Ib. 20.
[60] Ib. 20f.
[61] Bar-Asher, 'L'hébreu mishnique', §§253-259.
[62] See Kutscher, 'Present State', 69.

b) The totality of manuscripts and oral traditions give the plural of אֵבֶר ('ēber, 'limb') as אֵבָרִים ('ēbārīm), nearly always written *plene*: איברים; see for example mShek 7:3. However ms Parma-B stands apart in reading consistently אֲבָרִים (''bārīm), e.g. at mKel 18:9. We may note in passing that H. Yalon (*Introduction*, 30) considered that this form reflected a biblical vocalisation, but this is hardly justified, as the plural of אבר never occurs in the Bible.

c) The word עֶגְלָה ('eglā, 'heifer') is extremely common in MH. When the Mishna has the phrase עגלה ערופה ('the heifer whose neck was broken', cf Deut 21:6), ms K vocalises עֶגְלָה ('eglā), e.g. at mSot 7:2; 9:1, etc. However, when the definite article is prefixed, this manuscript stands alone in reading העגלה (hā-''gālā), as at mSot 9:7; mSan 1:3; mHul 1:6;[63] although there is no obvious reason for such a distinction between the definite and indefinite forms. The remaining manuscripts all agree in הָעֶגְלָה / עֶגְלָה ('eglā / hā-'eglā).

WRITTEN AND ORAL TRADITIONS

29. Those manuscripts which reflect ancient traditions faithful to the original language were written before 1400, and in the main before 1250. Despite the many centuries that have elapsed, they stand far closer than any of the printed editions to the spoken language. Quite apart from the manuscripts, however, the research of the last fifty years has demonstrated the need to consider also the oral traditions preserved by the scholars (early sages) of different countries. H. Yalon was the first to draw attention to the reading traditions of ancient Jewish texts, transmitted orally from master to pupil over the generations.[64] Following Yalon's lead, specialists in MH began to examine closely the manner in which the Mishna is read, within the various Jewish communities, by the oldest sages, steeped in the tradition. It was found that these sages, while perfectly well acquainted with the proper reading of the Bible, preserved in their reading of the Mishna a number of linguistic forms which differed from those of the Bible. The oral traditions recorded in our day, while they attest primarily the situation of the most recent centuries, can be shown on careful scrutiny to have preserved forms that agree perfectly with those transmitted by manuscripts a thousand years old. Such research has as yet concentrated on the traditions of the Yemenite Jews and of other Oriental Jewish communities such as those of Iraq, Syria and North Africa.[65] There is also a growing interest in the Ashkenazic traditions of the Jews in Europe.[66]

30. A few examples must suffice here. The Yemenites, like the Sefaradim, read the form נתפעל with *patah* in the last syllable, i.e. as *nitpa'al*, not *nitpa'el*

---

[63] This point is also discussed in Bar-Asher, *Tradition*, 55 n262.

[64] See for example Yalon, *Introduction*, 11-23; Bar-Asher, 'L'hébreu mishnique', §254.

[65] Compare Morag, *Yemenite Jews*; Shivtiel, 'Massorot' (about the tradition of the Yemenite Jews); Morag, *Baghdadi Community* (those from Baghdad); Katz, *Hebrew Language Tradition* (from Djerba in Tunisia); Maman, 'Reading Tradition' (from Tétouan in Morocco).

[66] See Mishor, 'Ashkenazi Traditions', on the traditions of the Ashkenazi Jews.

(with *ṣerē*).[67] Again, the Yemenites, Sepharadim and Ashkenazim read the pronominal suffix of the second person masculine singular as ךָ- (-*ak*), not ךָ- (-ʿ*ka*); thus *bētak*, 'thy house', *sifrak*, 'thy book', and so on.[68] Another phenomenon, preserved by both the Yemenite and Sefaradi traditions, is to double the *reš* no differently from other consonants, as in עֵרֵב (ʿ*irrēv*, 'he mixed'), אֵרֵס (ʿ*irrēs*, 'betroth'), לְעָרוֹת (*le-ʿarrōt*, 'to pour').[69] A recent study has shown that the same phenomenon is also attested in Ashkenazic tradition. The pronunciations *meʿuravin* (with *u* after the *ʿayin*) and *miṣtarpin* (with *a* after the *tet*), have been rightly interpreted as evidence of the ancient pronunciations *mᵉurraḇīn, mistarrᵉpīn*.[70]

Mishnaic Hebrew and Other Languages

THE SITUATION OF MULTI-LINGUALISM

31. Throughout the Second Temple period and for centuries later, indeed for more than 700 years altogether, Hebrew was in direct contact with other languages. The biblical books of the Second Temple period reflect this multi-lingualism. In the first place we must consider contact with Aramaic, mainly Imperial Aramaic, which leaves traces in the books of Ezra-Nehemiah, Daniel, Esther, and elsewhere. The biblical text even includes continuous passages in Aramaic.[71] In addition, Persian and Greek also intrude to some extent into the later biblical books, and Akkadian too has exerted an influence, no doubt through Aramaic.[72]

Contact with Aramaic continued into the Tannaic period. This contact was however no longer with Imperial Aramaic but with a later form of Aramaic, with its own distinctive dialectal features. Here too Aramaic carried the influence of yet other languages, notably Persian and Akkadian. Furthermore, the language of the Tannaim, and later that of the Amoraim, bears clear marks of growing contact with Greek and of the encounter with Latin.[73] This question will now be treated in detail, with particular emphasis on the contact between MH and other languages.

---

[67] Compare Yalon, *Introduction*, 15-18.

[68] *Ib*.13-15; Kutscher, *Studies*, Hebr section, 91f.

[69] See for example Shivtiel, 'Massorot', 211; Katz, *Hebrew Langage Tradition*, 217.

[70] See Mishor, 'Ashkanazi Traditions', 102.

[71] These are יגר שהדותא (Gen 31:47, 'heap of testimony'), the verse in Aramaic in Jer 10:11 and the Aramaic portions of Ezra and Daniel.

[72] See Tur-Sinai, 'Millim sheulot', 261-264.

[73] The basic materials will be found in Krauss, *Lehnwörter*, though very many details have been corrected by subsequent scholarship, notably in the works of J.N. Epstein on the *Mishna* and *Talmudim* and of S. Lieberman on the Tosefta and Palestinian Talmud.

MISHNAIC HEBREW AND ARAMAIC

32. Whether a situation of bilingualism existed here is much debated. Some maintain that true bilingualism existed throughout Palestine, so that speakers could express themselves equally well in either Hebrew or Aramaic. Others however believe that in certain areas only one of these two languages was spoken, although it would have been exposed to influence from the other.[74]

Contact between Hebrew and Aramaic is well attested in the written language. The extent of the influence of Aramaic upon Hebrew is however the subject of intense debate. For example, some consider the usual form in MH of the second person masculine pronoun, namely אַתְּ ('*at*), to be a borrowing from Aramaic, the original Hebrew pronoun being, אַתָּה ('*atā*).[75] Others, however, regard '*at* as an original Hebrew form.[76] The form '*at* is certainly attested occasionally in the Bible, e.g. ואם ככה אַתְּ עושה לי הרגני נא הרג (Num 11:5) – 'If you will treat me thus, kill me rather, I pray.' However, it does not become established in the written language until we reach MH.

Let us pass to another example. The best mishnaic manuscripts attest a particular verbal form, the *pā'ēl (pē'ēl)*, characterised by long *ā* after the first radical and the absence of doubling of the second, as in מְאַבְּקִים, *m°āḇ°qīm* ('they cover with dust', ms K, mShev 2:7).[77] One scholar tried to find here a conjugation borrowed from Aramaic and parallel to Arabic *fā'ala* (with long *ā*).[78] Another opinion however regards this form as a development within Hebrew: on this view, the form derives from the Hebrew *pi'ēl* conjugation, but with the expected doubling of the second radical replaced by lengthening of the preceding vowel.[79] On this view, *m° 'āḇ°qīm* is a variant of *m° 'abb°qīm*.[80]

However, even those who posit the least Aramaic influence agree that MH adopted certain grammatical, lexical and semantic elements peculiar to Aramaic. An example is the *nittap'al* conjugation, used for פ"י verbs (i.e. verbs whose first radical is *yod*), e.g. *nittōsap* (נְתּוֹסְפוּ, *nittōsepū*, mEr 7:7, 'they were increased'); *nittōqad* (מִתּוֹקֶדֶת, *mittōqedet*, LevR 7,8 (p159, apparatus): '[the fire] is consumed'). This conjugation is generally interpreted as a late development, peculiar to Hebrew, of the Aramaic form *hittap'al* which is common in several Aramaic dialects.[81]

---

[74] The theory was once proposed that MH had never been a living language, but an artificial creation, and that the Jews in the Tannaic period had spoken Aramaic exclusively. This view has now been universally abandoned. See Yalon, *Introduction*, 204-208; and Kutscher, *Studies*, Hebr section, 68f.

[75] Ib. 86; Gluska, *Influences of Aramaic*, 186f.

[76] See Bar-Asher, 'Introduction', 172; Haneman, *Morphology*, 460-465.

[77] See Bar-Asher, *Tradition*, 70 n361.

[78] See Morag, 'Pa'el and Nitpa'el', esp 96.

[79] See Ben-Hayyim, *Oral and Literary Tradition*, vol 5, p82f.

[80] See Bar-Asher, *Tradition*, 125f.

[81] See Yalon, *Introduction*, 127-135.

33. Various Aramaic terms and expressions likewise entered the Hebrew language. One example, (הכבד) חצר (mTam 4:3), which indicates the lobe (of the liver), is a loan from the Aramaic; thus Onkelos translates the Hebrew היותרת על הכבד (Exod 29:13, etc) by חצראה דעל כבדא.

Similarly the word *šibbūqīn*, found in the expression אִגֶּרֶת שִׁבּוּקִין (mGit 9:3, 'bill of divorce') is a Hebrew form, following the pure Hebrew pattern *pi'ūl*,[82] but based on the Aramaic root *š.b.q.* meaning 'forsake'. As a final example, the expression שכב מרע (mPea 3:7; mBB 9:6) 'one that lay sick' is borrowed from Aramaic, in which language we find not only the adjectival שכב מרע but also the verbal expression ישכוב מרע with the verb in the imperfect.[83]

34. Aramaic influence is equally evident in calques, i.e. words that in themselves are Hebrew but derive a new usage or meaning from Aramaic. Such a calque may be either semantic or grammatical.

An example is the verb *'āḥaz*, which in Hebrew means 'grasp, hold', as in שלח ידך ואחוז בזנבו (Exod 4:4, 'put forth your hand and grasp its tail'). The Aramaic cognate *"ḥad* has also the sense: 'close'. The influence of the Aramaic verb causes the Hebrew likewise to bear the sense: 'close'. This already occurs in Nehemiah, a book of the Second Temple period: יגיפו הדלתות ואחזו (Neh 7:3, 'let them close and bolt the doors'). The context leaves no doubt that closing, not grasping, is meant. The same meaning for Hebrew *'āḥaz* recurs in MH, in a midrashic explanation of the name of Ahaz, the wicked king of Judah: למה נקרא שמו אחז, שאחז בתי כנסיות ובתי מדרשות – 'Why was he called Ahaz? Because he closed (*'āḥaz*) the synagogues and houses of study' (LevR 11,7 p230). In this case, the Aramaic meaning has been transferred to the Hebrew cognate, whence a semantic calque.[84]

Let us now consider calques of a grammatical nature. The words *śāde* 'field' and *kōs* 'cup' occur both in the Bible and in the Mishna, but change gender between the two. In the Bible, *kōs* is feminine, as in Lam. IV 21: תעבור כוס 'the cup will pass'. In MH, however, it is masculine e.g. : כוס ראשון (mPes 10:2, 'the first cup'). This change of gender no doubt derives, as a calque, from Aramaic *kās*, which is masculine.[85] Similarly, the word *śāde* is masculine in the Bible, as in ויקם שדה (Gen 23:20, 'the field was assured'), but almost everywhere feminine in MH, e.g. שדה שקצרוה גוים (mPea 2:7, 'a field harvested by gentiles'). In this case likewise it seems that the Aramaic *ḥ"qal*, which is feminine, has influenced the Hebrew.[86]

35. Aramaic has sometimes been the channel whereby Akkadian and Persian forms and terms entered MH. Here again, a few examples will suffice.

---

[82] Many terms related to family life are formed in MH on the pattern of *pi'ūl* in the plural (*pi'ūlīn*). Examples are *qiddūšīn*, 'bethrothal'; *nissū'īn*, 'marriage'; *gērūšīn* (<*girrūšīn*) 'divorce'; and *šibbūqīn*, 'release'.

[83] See Gluska, *Influences of Aramaic*, 1197f.

[84] See Kutscher, *Studies*, Hebr section, 389, 404; Gluska, *Influences of Aramaic*, 139f.

[85] Kutscher *ib.* 404; Gluska, *Influences of Aramaic*, 542-544.

[86] See Kutscher *ib.* 405; Gluska *ib.* 1233-1235.

The first occurence in Hebrew of the word *'asquppā(h)*, meaning 'threshold', is in the Mishna, e.g. היה קורא בספר על האסקופה (mEr 10:3, 'if one was reading a scroll on the threshold'). This evidently goes back to Akkadian *askuppātu*, which had been borrowed and become current in many Aramaic dialects, including those of Palestine.[87] By the medium of Aramaic, which had long been in contact with Akkadian (which it had in fact replaced as the spoken language of Mesopotamia), this word penetrated into Hebrew.

Another example is the word *'etrōg*, 'citron', which likewise appears for the first time in the Mishna: רבי ישמעאל אומר: שלושה הדסים, שתי ערבות, לולב אחד ואתרוג אחד (mSuk 3:4), 'R. Yishmael says: Three [branches of] myrtle, two [branches of] willow, one palm [branch] and one citron.' Research has shown that this term comes from Persian *turung*. It occurs in Aramaic texts of the Tannaic period, such as Targum Onkelos: פירי אילנא אתרוגין לולבין (Lev 23:40) – 'fruits of the tree, citrons, palm-branches'. Another Aramaic source is a letter of Bar-Koseba: וישלחן למחניה לותך לולבין ואתרוגין (Letter 8, line 3: 'and they shall send you at the camp palm-branches and citrons'). This word also occurs in the Palestinian Aramaic dialects of the period of the Amoraim.[88] It therefore seems certain that Aramaic was the channel whereby this word entered MH.[89]

BORROWINGS FROM GREEK AND LATIN

36. Greek and Latin have also penetrated MH,[90] but their influence is essentially limited to vocabulary. Many terms borrowed from one or other of these languages have become naturalised in Hebrew. Having appeared in MH, they remained in use throughout the Middle Ages and still feature in Modern Hebrew. Such words as אֲזֶל (σμίλη) 'chisel, scapel', פולמוס (πόλεμος) 'polemic', פִּנְקָס (πίναξ) 'booklet', קתדרה (καθέδρα) 'platform, pulpit' have been current ever since the mishnaic period. The same applies to words of Latin origin such as לַבְלָר (*libellarius*) 'clerk', סַפְסָל (*subsellium*) 'bench'. It may be noted that in old manuscripts these words appear in a form that stands particularly close to the form in the language of origin. For example, לבלר is vocalised לִבְלָר, with its original vowel [*i*];[91] ספסל has the form סַפְסָל with [*e*], again as in the original language.[92] The difference between Hebrew *pinqās* (פִּנְקָס) and Greek *pinaks* (πίναξ) arose because Hebrew phonetic structure avoids a cluster of consonants at the end of a word. Hence the consonants *ks* (or *qs*) were separated by the vowel *a*. However, the original form is preserved by the

---

[87] Gluska *ib.* 170f.
[88] *Ib.* 187f.
[89] For further material see Tur-Sinai, 'Millim sheulot', 265-278. Compare further Kutscher, *Words*, following the index, 126-136.
[90] This was the subject of Krauss, *Lehnwörter*, See also Albeck, *Introduction*, 203-215.
[91] See Bar-Asher, 'L'hébreu mishnique', 271f.
[92] *Ib.*

manuscripts in the plural פְּנַקְסִיוֹת[93] (mKel 24:7), to be transliterated *pinaqs-āyōt*, not *pinqas-āyōt*. The reason that the original structure is preserved here is that it is compatible with the laws of Hebrew phonology: the combination *qs*, not being at the end of the word, can stand (the *q* ends one syllable, the *s* opens the following one).

37. Lastly it is important to note that nouns and adjectives borrowed from Greek or Latin have sometimes become so well naturalised in Hebrew that they have given rise to verbs of a purely Hebrew pattern, which remain in use to this day.

Thus the term σφόγγος, which in Hebrew became סְפוֹג (*s^ep̄ōg*, 'sponge'), gave rise to several verbal forms. The Qal *sāp̄ag* means 'sponge up, absorb', as at mZev 6:6, וְלֹא סָפְגוּ הַמֶּלַח 'and the salt did not absorb it'. The *Pi'ēl* (intensive) pattern *sippēg* appears in mPar 12:2, יְסַפֵּג 'it absorbs'. We also find the *Nitpa'al* form נְסְתַּפֵּג in Makh 2:1, as well as the nouns *s^ep̄āg* (in the expression מִטְפְּחוֹת הַסְּפָג, mKil 9:3: 'bath-towels') and *sippūg* (mZav 1:4, 'act of drying oneself').

The word κατήγωρ gave rise to the verb *qitrēg*, 'accuse', with metathesis of the consonants *g* and *r*: אֵין הַשָּׂטָן מְקַטְרֵג אֶלָּא בִּשְׁעַת הַסַּכָּנָה (yShab 5:2, 7b): 'Satan accuses only in the hour of danger'.

From the adjective καλός 'good, fine' came the verb *qillēs* 'extol'. Examples occur in לְפִיכָךְ אָנוּ חַיָּיבִין לְהוֹדוֹת וּלְהַלֵּל וּלְקַלֵּס (mPes 10:5, 'therefore we are bound to thank, praise and extol') and in אַשְׁרֵי הַמֶּלֶךְ שֶׁמְּקַלְסִין אוֹתוֹ בְּבֵיתוֹ (bBer 3a: 'happy is the king who is extolled in his own house').

Lastly, Greek βάσις gave rise to the noun בָּסִיס and then to the verb *bissēs*, as in וּמִי בִּסֵּס הָעוֹלָם (CantR 1,9): 'and who laid the foundation of the world?'

Mishnaic Hebrew from Indirect Sources

DIRECT AND INDIRECT SOURCES

38. In linguistics the principle is taken for granted that a dialect or language can only be described on the basis of direct evidence, which may be in either written or (preferably) oral form. This rule is easy enough to apply to the languages of today, given the advanced techniques of recording and preservation now available. It breaks down, however, when one is dealing with languages no longer spoken. Of course the investigator of a language of the past, however ancient it may be, must go back to witnesses that are as close in time as possible to the linguistic information that they transmit. Unfortunately, however, one does not always have access to documents containing all the linguistic data necessary for a complete description of the grammatical and lexical system. This is the case for ancient Hebrew, whether biblical or mishnaic.

---

[91] The vocalisation פְּנַקְסָיוֹת (*pinaqsāyōt*) appears in ms Parma-B. Ms K has the slightly different form פְּנַקְסִיוֹת (*pinaqsīyōt*). Both however preserve the stem *pinaqs* before the plural ending.

39. The study and description of MH, which was spoken about 1800 years ago, encounters a number of difficulties. (Similar difficulties beset the study of biblical Hebrew, where at least 2200 years separate us from the spoken language). Two problems are particularly serious:

a) The virtual absence of contemporary documents from the era when MH was spoken. As stated earlier, a few of our manuscripts date from the end of the first millennuim CE while the majority from the beginning of the second.[94] One of the most ancient Tannaic documents extant is the halakhic inscription discovered in the excavations at Rehov, in the Beth-Shean valley. It probably belonged to the seventh century CE,[95] some centuries after Hebrew ceased to be a living spoken language.

b) The lack of information from the graphic system of Hebrew. That system records the consonants, but even these are not recorded without ambiguity.

The phonemes שׂ and שׁ are not distinguished, nor are such allophones as ב and ב. Vowels are only partially recorded. Thus כפר (when it is to be read כָּפַר, *kāpar*) bears no indication of the vowels; in כיפר (= כִּפֵּר / *kippēr*), only the first vowel is indicated. Hence a single written sequence of letters may stand for a number of different forms: for example, מכתב could be read as any of מִכְתָּב (*miktāb*), מַכְתֵּב (*maktēb*), מְכַתֵּב (*mᵉkattēb*), מְכֻתָּב (*mᵉkuttāb*), and so on. This very word in fact gives rise to divergence among the manuscripts at mKel 13:2, מכתב שניטל הכותב טמא מפני המוחק – 'If a stylus has lost its writing point it is still susceptible to uncleanness because of its eraser.' Mss Parma-A and Parma-B read מַכְתֵּב, while mss K and Paris have מִכְתָּב.[96]

40. The problem of lack of information in the written text of Tannaic literature is partially solved by recourse to vocalised texts. Most of these, however, are later than 1000 CE. This fact prompts one to ask how early the vocalisations themselves can be. We in fact know that these texts were subject to conscious adjustments and involuntary errors in their transmission throughout the Middle Ages.

Of course, when a certain form is attested by several (if not all) of the extant witnesses, and these come from different geographical regions, this form is very likely to be original. It could then be attributed with some confidence to the era when Hebrew was a living language. The word שעה (*šā'ā*, 'hour') provides an example. Many sources attest in the first syllable a stable *qāmeṣ* that remains throughout the declension: שָׁעַת (not שְׁעַת); שָׁעָתִי (not שְׁעָתִי); שָׁעָתוֹ, שָׁעָתָם, and so on. As Yalon showed, the evidence of vocalised manuscripts and oral traditions converges here.[97] It is a fair conclusion that this is an authentic form going back to before 200 CE. The sheer number of witnesses, and their mutual independence, point cogently to this conclusion.

[94] See §21 above.
[95] Cf Sussmann, 'Halakhic Inscription'.
[96] Further details will be found in Bar-Asher, 'Vocalization Errors', 14f.
[97] Compare Yalon, *Introduction*, 117-123.

41. There are a number of indirect sources which enable us to check the antiquity of the information given by the oral and written traditions whereby Tannaic literature has been handed down. The witnesses (written and oral) that transmit those traditions are many centuries later than the spoken language of MH; but when the forms attested by those witnesses are supported by outside documents, this agreement forms a powerful argument in favour of the forms concerned.

There is a variety of sources of indirect evidence: the writings discovered in the Judean desert (including the Qumran manuscripts and the documents from the time of the Bar-Koseba revolt), the Hebrew of the Samaritans, transcriptions of Hebrew words into Greek in the Septuagint, and other transcriptions into Greek and Latin by the church fathers. These sources have the advantage of being independent of the traditional transmission of Jewish literature.

The reason that we need such an outside check on the information presented by the traditional (written and oral) Jewish witnesses lies in the continuing tension between the different languages and dialects in which the various literary corpuses handed down by the Jews have been edited. The language of the Bible, MH and the language of prayer each comprises a more or less separate linguistic system. Furthermore, the Aramaic portions of the Bible, the Targums, the Yerushlami, the Aggadic Midrashim and the Bavli all reflect different Aramaic dialects. In such a vast collection, some corpuses inevitably enjoy greater prestige than others. Hence the suspicion that the language of one corpus may have been assimilated in transmission to the language of a more prestigious corpus.[98] Sources outside the Jewish tradition are not susceptible to this particular problem, and are therefore more objective, as a few brief examples will show:

DOCUMENTS FROM THE JUDEAN DESERT

42. The suffixed preposition forms הֵימֶנּוּ (hēmennū, 'from him'), הֵימֶנָּה (hēmennā, 'from her'), are common in the Mishna according to the Babylonian tradition. However, the Palestinian text of the Mishna[99] prefers the forms מִמֶּנּוּ (mimmennū, 'from him'), מִמֶּנָּה (mimmennā, 'from her').[100] At first sight it would seem that the forms hēmennū, hēmennā originated in Babylonia in the Talmudic era. But this pattern can now be shown to have existed already in Palestine in the second century CE, when Hebrew was still a living spoken language. In the letters and documents discovered in the Judean desert and dated from the beginning of the second century we find such examples as יותר

---

[98] See Kutscher, *Studies*, Hebr section, 73, where, however, the formulation is too categorical. Contrast Bar-Asher, 'Different Traditions', 27-33.

[99] The question of different linguistic types is considered in §§24-27 above.

[100] The material is presented in detail in Bar-Asher, 'Different Traditions', 30-32.

הימנו עוד דינרים ששה עשר – 'more than 16 dinars more than that' (in a document from the 'Cave of Letters').[101]

Again, the preposition *b-* is realised in rabbinic literature in two forms, exemplified by בְּבֵית (*b*'*bēt*) and אַבֵּית ('*abbēt*).[102] The latter pattern is rare in MH,[103] and for a long time its date of origin was not known. The Dead Sea Scrolls now show that it already existed in the second century: יעקב בן יהודה שיושב אבית משכו (Letter 8 of Bar-Koseba, lines 3-4)[104] – 'Yaakov son of Ye-huda, dwelling at Bet-Mashko'. Here אבית (משכו) stands instead of the more familiar בבית (משכו).

There are many more examples[105] that fill out the record of the rabbinic sources. Some of the forms attested in these indirect sources reflect a living Hebrew dialect spoken somewhere in Palestine at the time of, or shortly after, the existence of the Second Temple. The two examples given here seem to reflect dialects from the south of the country.[106]

THE SAMARITAN TRADITION

43. This tradition is known to us primarily through the masterly work of Zeev Ben-Hayyim, who devoted a series of thoroughgoing studies to Hebrew and Aramaic in the Samaritan tradition.[107] Although much of the information has been gathered from the Samaritans in modern times, Ben-Hayyim has used the linguistic texts of the Samaritans[108] to show that most of the features of the Samaritan tradition of today go back to the period when Hebrew was still a spoken language.[109] Hence if any linguistic feature found in our witnesses of MH is also attested in the tradition of the Samaritans, that feature will be espe-cially likely to represent an authentic survival from the era when Hebrew was a spoken language. Two examples will illustrate this:

44. The pronunciation צִפּׁרֶן, *ṣ*'*pōren* (the *p* being realised as a spirant) is representative of the Eastern tradition of MH.[110] The Western tradition instead

---

[101] *Ib.* 31 with n169.

[102] This form evolved in the following way. The original *b*'*bēt* first became *bbēt*, with loss of the initial *shewa*. This created a consonant cluster, consisting of a doubled consonant, at the beginning of the word. Hence a prosthetic vowel was needed, whence '*abbēt*. Compare Yalon, *Studies*, 69; Kutscher, *Studies*, Hebr section, 63; Ben-Hayyim, *Literary and Oral Tradition*, vol 5, 38.

[103] See Epstein, *Mavo*, 1258f.

[104] See Kutscher, *Studies*, Hebr section, 62f.

[105] Compare the remarks in §18 above *hit'arm*'*lā(h)* in the Damascus document.

[106] Compare §§18-19 above.

[107] Ben-Hayyim, *Oral and Literary Tradition*.

[108] The linguistic literature of the Samaritans is the subject of the first two volumes of Ben-Hayyim, *ib.*

[109] Ben-Hayyim's works provide abundant evidence that the transmission of texts by the Samaritans preserves a language that goes back to the time when Hebrew and Aramaic were still spoken languages.

[110] See §26 above; Bar-Asher, 'Introduction', 181, 183; idem, 'Different Traditions', 20.

uses the form צִפּוֹרֶן (ṣippōren),[111] found also in the Bible (in both the Tiberian[112] and Babylonian[113] biblical texts). It is tempting to view the eastern form as a secondary medieval development that arose somewhere in the Eastern Diaspora. However the Samaritan tradition reads sēfērən,[114] and so tends to show that the spirant form of the p is not late at all but was already current when Hebrew was still spoken.[115]

Again, the Mishna attests two prununiations for the name אילת: either אֵילָת ('ēlat), or אַיְלָת ('aylat). The former appears in mss K and Parma-A at mMS 5:2. The latter is supported by various other witnesses in the same passage of mMS[116] and by the adjectival form אַיְלָתִית ('aylātit) in ms K at mMakh 6:3.[117] This name occurs in the Bible at Deut 2:8; 2 Kgs 14:22, and elsewhere. The Tiberian system of vocalisation in these passages gives אֵילָת ('ēlat). The Samaritan Pentateuch, however, where it is available, namely at Deut 2:8, shows mi'ayyâlat (מאילת),[118] i.e. a form with diphthong ay in the first syllable of the name. The Greek transcriptions likewise have Αιλα, Αιλαθ, as already observed by Kutscher.[119]

GREEK AND LATIN TRANSCRIPTIONS

45. Transcriptions into Greek and Latin are a rich additional source for verifying the authenticity of mishnaic forms. Some of the forms shown in these transcriptions differ from those of the Tiberian vocalisation of the Bible and yet agree perfectly with the readings of manuscripts (vocalised or unvocal-

---

[111] Ib., ib.

[112] Compare צִפֹּרֶן (Jer 17:1); צִפָּרְנֶיהָ (Deut 21:12).

[113] See Yeivin, Hebrew Language, 1069.

[114] Compare ṣēferniyya, 'her nails', Deut 21:12, on which see Ben-Hayyim, Literary and Oral Tradition, vol 3a, 134. Ben-Hayyim reconstructed what he thought was a hypothetical Hebrew form צְפֹּרֶן (ṣᵉpōren), corresponding to the Samaritan reading. As it turns out, this form is actually attested in the mss Parma-B and Antonin, and in the Mishnayot with Babylonian and Yemenite vocalisation (see references in n110 above).

[115] The present writer has suggested elsewhere that צְפֹּרֶן could be a development from צִפֹּרֶן (ṣippōren) by haplology. On this view, the consonant p ceased by haplology to be doubled, whereupon the vowel i was reduced to shewa (see Bar-Asher, 'Introduction', 181). There is however an alternative possibility. It may be that both ṣippōren and ṣᵉpōren are derived from an original form such as *ṣipōren. As Ben-Hayyim (ib.) has shown, the cognate word in other Semitic languages does not exhibit gemination of this p. The form may have developed in two different directions: (a) the short vowel i continued to exist in a closed syllable; and (b) ṣᵉpōren, where the first syllable remains open and the vowel i is reduced to shewa. The same double process of development seems to underlie the doublet אִסָּר ('issār) and אֱסָר (ᵉsār), meaning 'vow'. Both forms seem derived from an original * 'isar, which evolved both to 'issar (אִסָּר, Num 30:3) and to ᵉsār (as in וְאֶסָרֶיהָ, Num 5:6).

[116] See Bar-Asher, Tradition, 127.

[117] See Kutscher, Studies, Hebr section, 444f; but Parma-B in the mMakh reads אֵילָתִית, 'ēlātīt.

[118] See Ben-Hayyim, Literary and Oral Tradition, vol 4, 317.

[119] See Kutscher, Studies, Hebr section, 444f. (At Deut 2:8, מאילת, the inseparable preposition מ- 'from' precedes the name. The Tiberian vocalisation is mē- while the Samaritan is mī].

ised) of rabbinic literature. Two instances from the Septuagint have already been cited: Ελληλ, corresponding to הָלֵל,[120] and Αιλα, Αιλαθ corresponding to אֵילַת.[121] Space allows us to cite no more than one out of many possible examples.

46. The word קרסל 'ankle' appears in two parallel passages in the Bible, namely 2 Sam 22:37 and Ps 18:37, in a suffixed form which the Tiberian system vocalises as קַרְסֻלָּי: ('my ankles'). The singular would presumably have been, on the Tiberian vocalisation, *qarsōl* (< *qarsul*). This agrees with the form קַרְסוּלָיו 'his ankles' found in ms K at mBekh 7:6[122] and also in the Babylonian vocalisation of the Mishna.[123] However, we also find the form קורסל at mOh 1:8; these are the consonants in ms K,[124] Parma-B vocalises as קוּרְסַל. Now this form agrees with Origen's transcription in the second column of his Hexapla at Ps 18:37, χορσελαι.[125] Thus Origen's form is identical with the form *qursēl* / *qorsēl* attested in mss Parma-B and K (the first hand). Origen lived at the time of the closure of the Mishna, and his evidence is in effect contemporary with the era when Hebrew was spoken, many centuries before the Mishna manuscripts extant today.[126]

THE LANGUAGE OF LITURGY AND PIYYUT

47. The importance of indirect sources for knowledge of the grammar and lexicon of MH should now be clear. Other types of Jewish sources may be added, such as the language of the liturgy and piyyut, which both contain forms parallel to those of the Mishna. It was shown by Yalon[127] and Kutscher,[128] and more recently by Eldar[129] and Yahalom,[130] that many forms that are characteristic of the language of the Mishna have been incorporated into the language of liturgy and into numerous piyyutim. An example is the *nup̄ 'al* conjugation. This is found in the manuscripts of the Mishna, e.g. at mSot 9:12,[131] נוטל טעם הפירות 'and the taste of fruits has been taken away'. A form

---

[120] See §12 above.
[121] See §44 above.
[122] The last two letters of this word are written over an erasure: קרסול[יו].
[123] See Yeivin, *Hebrew Language*, 987.
[124] These are the consonats written by the scribe, but the vocaliser erased the *vav* and read קַרְסֻל (*qarsūl*).
[125] Cf Kutscher, *Language*, 359.
[126] It is worth emphasising once more that alternations of the type *hēmennū / mimmennū, ṣippōren / sᵉpōren, 'ēlat / 'aylat, qarsōl / qursēl*, need not represent two diachronic stages of a single form, even though Kutscher tended to regard them as such. Instead, one could see two alternative forms that were in simultaneous use, perhaps in different dialects (see §12 above).
[127] See Yalon, *Introduction, passim,* and n131 below.
[128] See Kutscher, 'Present State', 53f.
[129] See notes 132 and 133 below.
[130] See Yahalom, *Poetic Language*, 162-176.
[131] See Yalon, *Introduction*, 152-159.

594

(*nuṭṭal*) from the same conjugation is found in the liturgy. One example occurs within the phrase וְנִטַּל כְּבוֹד מבית חיינו, 'and glory has been removed from the house of our life', from the prayer אתה יצרת recited when the New Moon falls on a Sabbath. Many piyyutim offer further examples of this conjugation.[132] Another example of a pattern in the piyyutim which is very frequent in the manuscripts of the Mishna is the noun of the type *po 'lān / pu 'lān*, as Eldar has shown;[133] examples from the Mishna are בּוֹיְשָׁן, *bōyšān* (= *bayšān*, בַּיְשָׁן or 'shy' at mAv 2:5) and תּוֹרְגְמָן – תּוּרְגְמָן (*torgᵉmān / turgᵉmān*, 'translator', twice in mMeg 4:4). Further examples of this phenomenon are easily multiplied.[134]

Conclusion

48. This survey has attempted to outline the basic issues in research into MH. First, having defined the literature written in this language, we examined its origin and its character in relation to biblical Hebrew (five different aspects of that topic were examined). Second, we considered the question of the homogeneity of MH, under seven different headings. Third, we examined the relationship between MH and other languages. We indicated what light could be shed by indirect sources, and in particular by three of those sources, upon our knowledge of MH; and we also pointed out the kinship between MH and the Hebrew of the liturgy and piyyut.

49. Each of these topics offers ample material for decades of scholarly research. The purpose of the present work is not, of course, to exhaust the field but to open up perspectives for those interested in an area of Jewish scholarship which has recently entered a new phase of expansion, and is attracting – especially in Israel[135] – a new generation of investigators. Careful examination of numerous manuscripts and research into oral traditions[136] are constantly modifying our understanding of this discipline. In this way, research and analysis of problems old and new, both of grammar and of lexicon, have become more rigorous than ever before.[137]

---

[132] See Eldar, *Hebrew Language Tradition*, vol 2, 381-383, and bibliography there cited.

[133] Eldar *ib.*180, 184; etc.

[134] This question of the proximity of MH to liturgical language and to *piyyut* has been the subject of a number of important observations (see notes 127-133), but room remains for a full in-depth analysis.

[135] The number of doctoral dissertations devoted to MH and presented over the last twenty years at Israeli universities (especially the Hebrew University of Jerusalem) runs into double figures.

[136] See Bar-Asher, 'Quelques phénomènes', §§8-21.

[137] For a comprehensive bibliography on Mishnaic Hebrew see Bar-Asher, *Studies*, 429-467.

Chapter Nineteen

The Aramaic of the Talmudic Period

Yohanan Breuer

The Aramaic Vernacular of the Jews

The Hebrew and Aramaic languages are related tongues and resemble one another in many ways. They both belong to the north-western branch of the Semitic Language family. According to the text of the Pentateuch the Hebrews originate in Aram, since Abraham, the ancestor of the Jews, came from there, as did all the Matriarchs.[1] Nevertheless, the Aramaic language was almost

I would like to thank Profs. Moshe Bar-Asher and Steven Fassberg for their comments on an earlier version of this article.
[1] The awareness of this is especially evident in the verse 'And you shall make response before the Lord your God, A wandering Aramean was my father; and he went down into Egypt' (Deut 26:5);

unknown in the Land of Israel during the period of the First Temple. Clear evidence of this is the story of Rabshakeh, which took place not long before the end of this period. Rabshakeh was sent by the King of Assyria to Jerusalem, where he spoke to the besieged inhabitants in the language of Judaea, *Yehudit*, despite the request of the Judaean princes: 'Pray, speak to your servants in the Aramaic language, for we understand it; do not speak to us in the language of Judah within the hearing of the people who are on the wall' (2Kgs 18:26). The significance of this is that only the princes spoke Aramaic, as they came into frequent contact with foreigners, whereas the commoners of Judaea did not understand that tongue.

The knowledge of Aramaic in the Land of Israel spread ever since the return of the Babylonian exiles. This development had two causes: first of all, the Return to Zion was marked by the arrival of a large wave of Babylonian Jews whose main language seems to have been Aramaic. Secondly, the status of the Aramaic language was rising and strengthening throughout the entire region during this period until it became the major language throughout the East. Even in Babylonia, for instance, Akkadian was on the decline and was being replaced by Aramaic. This strengthening of the status of Aramaic in the region took place in the Land of Israel as well, and so the use of Aramaic spread until it became dominant.

Scholars were first of the opinion that after the return of the Babylonian exiles, Hebrew no longer served as a spoken language. Their opinion was that Hebrew retained its status as a holy tongue and was used in prayer and in Tora study, and for this reason the Mishna and contemporary Tannaic literature was composed in Hebrew, while in everyday life Aramaic alone was spoken.[2] Today this opinion is no longer accepted, everyone agreeing that Hebrew speech survived in all walks of life at least until the end of the Tannaic period (beginning of the third century CE).[3] Nonetheless, during this period the status of Aramaic undoubtedly became very strong in comparison with Hebrew. This can be seen first and foremost in the large number of texts written in Aramaic. In all the books of the Bible until the destruction of the First Temple, Aramaic is not to be found except for two words in Genesis (31:47 – uttered by Laban the Aramean) and in a single verse in Jeremiah (10:11 – aimed at the Gentiles). During the Second Temple period, the situation underwent a complete change: lengthy sections in Aramaic appear in the Bible (in Ezra and Daniel) and in the Judaean Desert Scrolls; many Aramaic sentences can be found in Tannaic literature, while in the period of the Amoraim most literature was written in Aramaic. In addition, Aramaic translations of the Bible were compiled during this period. These translations were read in public when excerpts from the Tora

the historical review recited annually with the bringing to the Temple of the first fruits begins with mention of the Aramaic origin of the Hebrews.
[2] See, e.g., Geiger, *Lehr- und Lesebuch*, 1f; Rosenthal, *Aramaistische Forschung*, 106.
[3] See, e.g., Kutscher, *History*, 117f.

were read, and their very existence bears witness to the fact that many Jews were no longer able to understand Hebrew without an accompanying translation.

The Hebrew of this period, Mishnaic Hebrew, too, reflects considerable Aramaic influence. This topic will not be dealt with hereunder, for it is part and parcel of the regular description of Mishnaic Hebrew.[4] It remains only to be noted here that the vernacular during this period, at least in certain areas, reflected this influence to an even greater degree than the contemporary literature. Here are two examples of this: in the Bar Kokhba Letters there appears the sentence, שהפרה שלקח יהוסף בן ארצטון מן יעקב בן יהודה שיושב אבית משכו שהי... שלו מזבנות – '...That the cow that Yehosef son of Ariston took from Yaakov son of Yehuda, who is residing in Beit Mashko, that it (the cow) is his through purchase' (Murabaat 42).[5] זבנות, 'purchase', is the equivalent of זבינות,[6] from the root z.b.n. This root appears nowhere in the Hebrew of the mishnaic sources, and its appearance here in a Hebrew context demonstrates that it had penetrated from the Aramaic into one of the Hebrew dialects spoken in that period. The second example is more instructive, and shows the complexity of the relationships between Hebrew and Aramaic. In the Mekhilta, a Midrash Halakha composed during the Tannaic period, the word תָּכֹסּוּ appearing in the verse איש לפי אכלו תכסו על השה – 'according to what each can eat tākossu the lamb' (Exod 12:4) is interpreted thus: רבי יאשיה אומר, לשון סורסי הוא זה, כאדם שאומר לחבירו כוס לי טלה זה – 'R. Yoshia says: This (tākossu) is a Syriac expression, as e.g. when one says to his neighbour: Slaughter (kos) for me this lamb' (MekRY 3, p12). The Aramaic verb נְכַס 'slaughter' does not appear in Mishnaic Hebrew, and here it is considered Aramaic ('a Syriac expression'). Nevertheless, it appears in a purely Hebrew sentence – כוס לי טלה זה – ascribed to 'one saying to his neighbour'.[7] It may thus be concluded that it was by virtue of the close relationship between the two languages that so free a borrowing of a verb could take place from one language to the other. These two examples show that in the spoken Hebrew there existed a certain degree of 'openness' towards Aramaic, which enabled the Hebrew speaker to borrow a word from Aramaic on occasion and to use it in his natural speech, without considering the question whether it actually belonged to the stock of the Hebrew vocabulary.

It seems, on occasion, that the linguistic awareness of the Tannaim was Aramaic even when they were speaking Hebrew. This is especially noticeable in Bible commentaries. For example:

---

[4] See the article by Moshe Bar-Asher here preceding, §§32-34. And see *ib.* §42 for the passage from the Bar Kokhba letter quoted in the following sentence.

[5] Yardeni, *Textbook*, vol 1 p155; cf translation, vol 2, p64.

[6] See Kutscher, 'Language II', 16.

[7] While the verb is adduced in order to explain the verse, such a sentence could not have been framed without suitable background in the vernacular.

"קח את אהרן ואת בניו אתו", מה תלמוד לומר, והלא בכמה מקומות נאמרות בו במשה לקיחה
בבני אדם, שנאמר "ולקחת את הלוים לי אני ה'", [..] וכי מפשיל היה משה בני אדם לאחריו, אלא
אמר לו הקדוש ברוך הוא, קחם בדברים, שלא יהיה לבם לדבר אחר

"Take Aaron and his sons" (Lev 8:2) – what is the point of this statement? And is it not the case that in a variety of passages, there is reference to Moses' taking other people, for instance, "And you shall take the Levites for me" (Num 3:41)... Now did Moses throw people over his back [and seize them]? The Holy One, blessed be He, said to them: Take them through persuasion, so that their intention should not be for some other matter [than my service]. (Sifra 40d).

The difficulty of the midrash is obscure, for the verb לקח is often used to signify 'taking' people, and the Hebrew sentence, קח את אהרן ואת בניו, does not give rise to any difficulties at all. The difficulty is understandable only on the basis of Aramaic, which has two verbs in place of the Hebrew לקח. The verb נסב is used with objects, and דבר with animals or people, such as, ונסיב שמן וחלב – 'Then he took curds and milk' (Onk Gen 18:8), in contrast to, ודבר ית תרין עולימוהי עמיה – 'And he took two of his young men with him' (Onk Gen 22:3). Since the Hebrew verb לקח parallels Aramaic נסב which is used for objects which one can 'throw over one's back', it became necessary to make it clear that the sentence, קח את אהרן ואת בניו, contains a verb which is not the equivalent of נסב but rather of דבר (d'var), and this is done by means of the similar sounding Hebrew expression קחם בדברים, 'Take them bi-devarim, through words [of persuasion]'.

The coexistence of Hebrew and Aramaic and their similarity to one another resulted in a sense of close connection between them, so that a speaker of Greek could feel that they were a single language. Thus in certain sources Aramaic words are termed 'Hebrew',[8] while on the other hand Philo states that the Tora was written in the language of the 'Chaldeans', i.e., Aramaic.[9] This sense of linguistic similarity was discussed explicitly in the Talmud: 'The Holy One, blessed be He, exiled Israel to Babylonia only because... their language is akin to the language of the Tora' (bPes 87b). Nevertheless, despite the steadily growing use of Aramaic, this language was still considered inferior to Hebrew. Consequently, Hebrew is 'a holy tongue' while Aramaic is merely a 'secular' or a 'popular language', as in: 'One who incites [to idolatry] speaks in the holy language, while one who seduces [to idolatry] speaks in the popular language' (ySan 7, 25d); 'Secular matters may be uttered in the Holy language, whereas sacred matters must not be uttered in secular language' (bShab 40b). In these cases it may well be that reference is made to any foreign language and not specifically to Aramaic, but it seems that even among the foreign languages the status of Aramaic was not very prestigious, Greek and Persian being considered superior to it: 'For Rabbi said: Why use the Syrian language in the land

---

[8] For example: ἡ ἐπιλεγομένη Ἑβραϊστὶ Βηθεσδά, 'which is called in the Hebrew tongue Bethesda' (John 5:2). The name is not Hebrew but rather Aramaic: בית חסדא, 'the house of Hisda'.
[9] τὸ παλαιόν ἐγράφησαν οἱ νόμοι γλώσσῃ Χαλδαϊκῇ, 'In ancient times the laws were written in the Chaldean tongue', Life of Moses 2:26; see Dalman, Grammatik, 1.

of Israel? Either use the holy tongue or Greek! And R. Joseph said: Why use the Syrian language in Babylon? Either use the holy tongue or Persian!' (bSot 49b).

Such principles, however, indicate ambition rather than reality, Aramaic undoubtedly being in practice the dominant language during much of the mishnaic period.

PERIODS AND DIALECTS

Within the larger history of the Aramaic language, the following subdivision is generally accepted at the present time and will serve to structure our discussion:[10]

(a) *Early Aramaic*: up until 700 BCE; this material includes in the main inscriptions found in Syria;

(b) *Imperial* or *Classical Aramaic*: from 700 to 200 BCE This period includes, for example, both Biblical Aramaic and the Aramaic of the Elephantine Documents;

(c) *Middle Aramaic*: from 200 BCE to 200 CE;

(d) *Late Aramaic*: from 200 to 1000 CE;

(e) *Neo-Aramai*c: from 1000 CE to the present day.

Two distinct branches have been identified from the period of Late Aramaic on – Eastern Aramaic and Western Aramaic. Each of these two branches subdivides into three dialects: Jewish Palestinian Aramaic or Galilean Aramaic; Samaritan Aramaic and Christian (Syro-Palestinian) Aramaic belonging to the western branch; while Jewish Babylonian Aramaic or the Aramaic of the Babylonian Talmud, Syriac, and Mandaic belong to the eastern branch.

This paper shall present a survey of Jewish Aramaic after the period of Imperial Aramaic, i.e., the Aramaic used during the time of the Tannaim and Amoraim. In light of the aforesaid subdivision, this language embraces two periods of time and two lands: two periods of time, period (c), which includes Middle Aramaic until the end of the Tannaic period, and period (d), including Late Aramaic of the Amoraic and post-Amoraic periods; two lands, Palestinian Aramaic belonging to the western branch and Babylonian Aramaic belonging to the eastern branch of the language.

SOURCES

Three categories of Aramaic Jewish sources have survived from the periods treated here.

---

[10] See Fitzmyer, *Wandering Aramean*, 60-63. Because of the nature of this paper, I shall not provide a full bibliography for each and every item, especially in topics commonly treated in research literature, but merely references to basic literature.

1. *Halakhic Literature.* The Mishna, the Tosefta and the Halakhic Midrashim were compiled during the Tannaic period. This literature is written in Hebrew, but short Aramaic sentences are scattered through it. During the Amoraic period the Babylonian Talmud and Palestinian Talmud were compiled, as well as some of the Aggadic Midrashim: Genesis Rabba and, later, Leviticus Rabba and Pesikta de-Rav Kahana. During this period the situation changed completely. While in Amoraic literature, too, there is a good deal of Hebrew material, including quotations from Tannaic sources and much material written in Hebrew during this period as well, the usual language of halakhic discussion is Aramaic. An early document written entirely in Aramaic during the period of the Second Temple should be noted: Megillat Taanit.[11] After the Amoraic period several halakhic documents were written, mainly in Babylonia, which included comprehensive works (such as Halakhot Pesukot, Halakhot Gedolot) and many *Responsa* which were sent from the Gaonic academies to various communities in the Diaspora.

2. *The Targumim.* Five types of Jewish Targum or 'translation' of the Pentateuch have survived to the present day: (a) Targum Onkelos;[12] (b) Targum Pseudo-Yonatan;[13] (c) The Fragment Targum;[14] (d) The Fragments of the Palestinian Targum;[15] (e) Targum Neofyti.[16] Only one Targum of the Prophets has reached us, that is known as Targum Yonatan.[17] There are a number of different types of Targum to the Hagiographa, which change from one book to another. All these Targums can be classified by character and language to a number of types. From the standpoint of character, some are literal translations with but few aggadic additions (Onkelos, Neofyti and Yonatan), while others contain lengthy, midrash-like elaborations (Pseudo-Yonatan, the Fragment Targum, and the Fragments of the Palestinian Targum). With regard to their language they divide up into two groups: (1) Onkelos to the Tora and Yonatan to the Prophets, which are to all intents and purposes a single Targum; they were well known in Babylonia, and they are quoted word-for-word in the Babylonian Talmud,[18] whereas in Palestine there is no evidence of them what-

---

[11] Edited by Lichtenstein, 'Fastenrolle'. See V. Noam, art. in this volume with text, translation, and literature.

[12] Edited by Sperber, *Bible in Aramaic*, vol 1.

[13] Edited by Ginsburger, *Pseudo-Jonathan*.

[14] Edited by Klein, *Fragment-Targums*.

[15] Edited by Klein, *Genizah Manuscripts*.

[16] Edited by Diez Macho, *Neophyti 1*.

[17] Edited by Sperber, *Bible in Aramaic*, vol 2.

[18] For instance: "יום תרועה יהיה לכם", ומתרגמינן "יום יבבא יהא לכון" – "'It shall be a day of *teru'a* unto you", and we translate [in Aramaic], 'a day of *yebaba'*" (bRH 33b); "כי יבעל בחור בתולה", ומתרגמינן "ארי כמה דמיתותב עולם עם בתולתא יתיתבון בנייך" – "'For as a man be the husband (*yib'al*) of a maiden, so shall thy sons be as husbands unto thee", and we render [in Aramaic], 'Behold as a young man settles down with a maiden, thy sons shall become settled in the midst of thee'" (bMK 2a). These translations appear word for word in Onk Num 29:1 and Yon Isa 62:5, with slight changes in spelling.

ever; there are also Babylonian traces in their language; (2) the Fragment Targum, the Fragments of the Palestinian Targum and Neofyti, whose language differs from that of the first group, and most of their material belonging has only been discovered during the past century.

Much has been written about the origin and the age of the Targumim. Scholars tended to believe that Onkelos and Yonatan were late targumim that had been composed in Babylonia, while those of the second group were earlier, having been compiled during the period of early Christianity. This belief did not stem from linguistic analysis of any kind, but rather from considerations of content and halakha, which can not be treated here. Modern linguistic analysis has reached the opposite conclusion: Onkelos and Yonatan were compiled during the Tannaic period (first or second centuries CE), while the Targumim of the second group were written in the age of the Amoraim.[19] The other Targumim mentioned above, Pseudo-Yonatan and the Targumim to the Hagiographa, may have an early origin, but they clearly have absorbed later elements and so were undoubtedly edited at some later date. These considerations about dating the Targumim will inform our discussion.

3. *Epigraphic Material.* From the Land of Israel, the Aramaic scrolls discovered at Qumran are especially significant: they date from the period between 100 BCE and 100 CE. Similarly important are the Aramaic Bar Kokhba letters from the middle of the second century CE.[20] This material belongs to the period of Middle Aramaic. Other inscriptions have been discovered in the Land of Israel from the periods of the Tannaim and the Amoraim. From Babylonia, we have much epigraphic material, including incantation texts written in an Aramaic similar to that of the Babylonian Talmud.[21]

Aramaic up to the End of the Tannaic Period

We are dealing here with the period of Middle Aramaic. It was quite similar to the Aramaic of the previous periods of time, yet contains many features heralding Late Aramaic as well.

QUMRAN ARAMAIC

The Qumran documents discovered in recent decades constitute the most important source for the Aramaic of this period.[22] They preserve many early features:

---

[19] Tal, *Language* is devoted to proving the early origin of Yon, and his articles (see infra n40), to proving the late origin of the Targumim of the second group.

[20] Published in Martinez – Tigchelaar – Van der Woude, *Discoveries in the Judaean Desert XXIII.*

[21] Most of the incantation texts have been published in the following books: Montgomery, *Incantation Texts*; Naveh-Shaked, *Magic Spells*; Naveh-Shaked, *Amulets*; Rossel, *Handbook.*

[22] The pioneering article on this topic is Kutscher, 'Language of the "Genesis Apocryphon"'.

(1) In Early Aramaic the relative pronoun is דִי, as in צלמא די הקים נבוכדנצר מלכא – 'The image which King Nebuchadnezzar had set up' (Dan 3:2), and so it is in the Aramaic of this period: ארע מדבר די לא אנש בה – 'The land of wilderness, where there are no people' (TgJob 38:26, col. 31:3-4, p151). In Late Aramaic the pronoun is contracted, and takes the form -דְ : דסלק כְאנש מטבריא לציפורין – 'As a man who goes up from Tiberias to Sepphoris' (yYom 6, 43d).

(2) Early Aramaic has a special form to denote the passive of the verbal theme Qal, i.e., qᵉtīl, as in בה בליליא קְטִיל [23] בלשאצר מלכא כשדיא – 'That very night Belshazzar the Chaldean king was slain' (Dan 5:30). This form has survived in the Aramaic of Qumran: ושביקת אנה אברהם בדילהא ולא קטילת, 'And I, Abram, was spared because of her; I was not killed' (GenAp 20:10, p62). In Late Aramaic this form has disappeared, and its place is taken by the verbal theme 'itpᵉʿēl: לא מֶתְקְטָלָא אֶתְקטֵל יוסף ברי – 'Joseph my son has not been killed' (FrgPTg Gen 37:33, p81).

(3) The first person plural possessive suffix in Early Aramaic is -נָא , as in הרגזו אבהתנא לאלה שמיא – 'Our fathers had angered the God of heaven' (Ezra 5:12), and so also in the Aramaic of Qumran: חלפנא ארענא – 'We crossed (the border of) our land' (GenAp 19:13, p58). In Late Aramaic, however, the final vowel has been dropped, the suffix now being -ן, as in לית מבועין מספק לן – 'Our spring does not supply us' (yDem 1, 22a).

These are examples of ancient features surviving in this period. In contrast, there are many new features resembling Late Aramaic:

(4) The Aramaic verbal theme hafʿēl, like its Hebrew parallel hifʿīl, begins with ה; this is the regular form e.g. in Biblical Aramaic, e.g., והשכחו לדניאל בעא ומתחנן קדם אלהה – 'And they found Daniel making petition and supplication before his God' (Dan 6:12). In the Aramaic of Qumran, an א appears instead of the initial ה, and the verbal theme is 'afʿēl. This is the only form, e.g., in the Genesis Apocryphon, as in ואשכח אנון שרין בבקעת דן – 'And he found them encamped in the valley of Dan' (GenAp 22:7-8, p72); this is so in Late Aramaic as well: ונפק ולא אשכח בר נש – 'And he went out and did not find anyone' (yKil 9, 32b). Similarly, in Early Aramaic the conditional particle begins with ה, i.e., הֵן, as in הן על מלכא טב – 'If it seem good to the king' (Ezra 5:17), but in the Aramaic of Qumran א may appear in place of the ה, as in אן מן חוט עד ערקא דמסאן – 'That I shall not take so much as a thread or a sandalstrap' (GenAp 22:21, p74), and this applies to Late Aramaic as well: אין את עליל את מקלקל את וורדיה – 'If you enter, you will ruin the roses' (yMaas 2, 49d).

(5) In Early Aramaic the masculine demonstrative pronoun is דנה, as in דנה פשר מלתא – 'This is the interpretation of the matter' (Dan 5:26). In the Aramaic of Qumran, the final vowel has been elided and the form דן results: מנך זרעא דן ומנך הריונא דן – 'This seed is from you; from you is this conception' (GenAp

---

[23] The vocalization throughout this article is always taken from the source quoted.

2:15, p52), as it is in Late Aramaic: דֵּין הוא בכורא – 'This is the firstborn' (FrgPTg Gen 48:18, p155).

(6) A prominent late feature in the Aramaic of Qumran is the *plene* spelling of short vowels, which is characteristic of Late Aramaic, such as ואודית תמן קודם אלהא על כול נכסיא וטבתא – 'And I gave thanks there before God for all the flocks and the good things' (GenAp 21:3, p66), as well as the use of א as a *mater lectionis*, such as והואת כתשא לה – 'and it kept afflicting him' (GenAp 20:17, p64). In Early Aramaic all such cases show *defectiva* spelling, e.g.: להנעלה קדמי לכל חכימי בבל – 'That all the wise men of Babylon should be brought before me' (Dan 4:3); והות בטלא – 'And it ceased' (Ezra 4:24).

All these features, when considered together, show that the Aramaic of Qumran represents an interim stage between Imperial Aramaic and Late Aramaic.

A similar type of interim-stage Aramaic is found in the Bar Kokhba letters.[24] For example, in the sentence, די אנחנה צריכין לה – 'Because we need him' (Nahal Hever 56)[25] there appears the early first person plural personal pronoun אנחנא. This pronoun in Late Aramaic is אנן, as in לית אנן ידעין – 'We do not know' (FrgTg Gen 42:13, p63). In addition, we encounter in the previous example the ancient pronoun די, but we also find together with it the later form of this pronoun -ד, as in דכל דאלישע אמר לך עבד לה – '...That all that Elisha says to you, do for him' (Nahal Hever 53).[26]

TARGUMIM

Targum Onkelos and Targum Yonatan belong to the period of Middle Aramaic. The many features which link their language with Qumran Aramaic demonstrate that these Targumim were indeed compiled during this period.[27] For example, in the Aramaic of the Dead Sea Scrolls we find the sentence, עשר שנין שלמא מן יום די נפקתה מן חרן – 'Ten years have elapsed since the time you departed from Haran' (GenAp 22:27-28, p74). The third person plural feminine form of the past tense is denoted by a final *ā* in the word שלמא. Such a formation is common in Targum Onkelos, as in ודחילא חיתא מן קדם ה' ולא עבדא כמא דמליל עמהון מלכא דמצרים – 'But the midwives feared God, and did not do as the king of Egypt commanded them' (Onk Exod 1:17), whereas in Late Palestinian Aramaic the corresponding form is קטלין (*ī* vowel + *n* to close the final vowel), e.g., נפקין תרתין נשין מתמן – 'Two women went out from there' (GenR

---

[24] For a linguistic analysis of these letters see Kutscher, 'Language II'.

[25] Yardeni, *Textbook*, vol 1, 176; translation vol 2, 67.

[26] *Ib.* vol 1, 170; translation vol 2, 67.

[27] For a review of the prominent features in the Aramaic of Onk, see Kaddari, 'Research', 370-374. For the language of Yon, see Tal, *Language*. For the dating of Onk and Yon to the Tannaic era, prior to the 'Palestinian' Targums (FrgTg, the Cairo Geniza FrgPTg, and Neof), see Kutscher, 'Language of the "Genesis Apocryphon"'; Tal *ib.* For a list of the differences between Onk and Galilean Aramaic, see Dalman, *Grammatik*, 44-51.

34,15 p327). Another example: in the sentence just quoted from the Genesis Apocryphon the past tense of the verb in the second person masculine singular form נפקתה is denoted by a suffixed *-tā*, as in Hebrew, and as is the case in Onkelos: מא עבדתא – 'What have you done?' (Onk Gen 4:10). In Late Aramaic the final vowel has dropped, leaving the suffix *-t*, as in מה היא דא דַעֲבָדְתְּ – 'What is this, that you have done?' (FrgPTg Gen 4:10, p9). The following items are two vocabulary examples: the word ארי appears regularly both in Qumran Aramaic and in Targum Onkelos, as in ארי לך ולזרעך אנתננה – 'For I shall give it to you and to your descendants' (GenAp 21:14, p68); וחזת אתתא ארי טב אילנא למיכל – 'And the woman saw that the tree was good for food' (Onk Gen 3:6), yet it does not appear in Late Aramaic. The word לחדא, 'very (much)', is also common in this Aramaic, as in עתרך ונכסיך ישגון לחדא – 'Your wealth and your flocks will increase very much' (GenAp 22:31-32, p74), or, אגרך סגי לחדא – 'Your reward shall be very great' (Onk Gen 15:1), but has vanished from Late Aramaic.

Though the language of Targum Onkelos is basically Palestinian, eastern features also appear. Over a long period of time this Targum was only known in Babylonia, and the extant text has certainly come from there.[28] Scholars have deduced from this that it was compiled in Palestine and that it picked up the eastern features during the transmission process in Babylonia. In contrast, were we to assume it originated in Babylonia, we would be unable to explain its western features. The following example is an eastern feature. In Classical Aramaic the plural form of the active participle in ל"י verbs is *qātayin*, and in Galilean Aramaic, *qātay*, as in הוו בעין עלה להשכחה לדניאל – 'They sought to find a ground for complaint against Daniel' (Dan 6:5); ואתון בעיי מבטלה מצוותא מינן – 'And you want to abolish the commandments from us' (yBer 2, 4c). The original diphthong in these forms broke up in Biblical Aramaic: *ayn > ayin*, while in Galilean Aramaic the final *n* was dropped: *ayn > ay*. In Eastern Aramaic another development took place: the diphthong contracted, *ayn > an*, and the result was the form *qātan* which appears both in the Babylonian Talmud, such as בען במערבא – 'In the West they ask' (bTem 21a), or הנך אינשי דסגן בעלילותא – 'Those people who walk in perversity' (bShab 88b); and in Targum Onkelos: ארי יתה אתון בעַן – 'for that is what you desire' (Onk Exod 10:11), or הלא אחך רעַן – 'Are not your brothers pasturing the flock at Shechem' (Onk Gen 37:13). Nevertheless, as noted above, the language of Targum Onkelos is mainly western in character, and so it undoubtedly originated in Palestine.

THE ARAMAIC IN TANNAIC LITERATURE AND MEGILLAT TAANIT

Though Tannaic literature is written in Hebrew, it does have scattered short passages in Aramaic which are not part of the main halakhic argument: say-

---

[28] For a proposed explanation of how Onk was preserved in Babylonia while disappearing from the land of its origin, Palestine, see Kutscher, 'Language of "Genesis Apocryphon"', 10 n44.

ings, documents, prophecies, proverbs, etc.[29] Thus, for example, the *ketubba*, the marriage contract, a legal document, is in Aramaic: בנין דכרין דיהוו ליכי מינאי, אינון ירתון כסף כתובתיך יתר על חולקיהון דעם אחוהון – 'Male children which thou shalt have by me shall inherit thy ketubba besides the portion which they receive with their brethren' (mKet 4:10). So is the *get*, the writ of divorce: ודין – דיהוי ליכי מינאי ספר תירוכין ואגרת שבוקין וגט פטורין למהך להתנסבא לכל גבר דתצבייין 'Let this be from me thy writ of divorce and letter of dismissal and deed of liberation, that thou mayest marry whatsoever man thou wilt' (mGit 9:3). There are also sayings: בן בג בג אומר: הפוך בה והפוך בה, דכולה בה, ובה תחזי, וסיב ובלה בה, ומינה לא תזוע – 'Ben Bag-Bag said: Turn it and turn it again for everything is in it; and contemplate it and grow grey and old over it and stir not from it' (mAv 5:22).

Though it has never been studied systematically, this Aramaic appears to be similar to that of contemporary sources such as Targum Onkelos, yet seems to have many signs of Late Aramaic.[30] For instance: יוחנן כהן גדול שמע דבר מבית קדש הקדשים: נצחון (מרא) טליא דאזלון לאגחא קרבא באנטכיא – 'Yohanan the High Priest heard a word from the house of the Holy of Holies: The young men who went to fight in Antioch won the battle' (tSot 13:5). The phrase לאגחא קרבא, 'engage in war', in this sentence is characteristic of the Aramaic of Onkelos as well, e.g., האחיכון ייתון לאגחא קרבא – 'Shall your brethren go to the war' (Onk Num 32:6); the later Palestinian Targum Neofyti translates the same verse as האחיכון יעלון לסדרי קרבא (Neof Num 32:6, p297). On the other hand, two features in the sentence heard by the priest are characteristic of Late Aramaic: טליא is a common form in Galilean Aramaic, as in טליא [הו]א בגובא לית – 'The boy is not in the pit' (FrgPTg Gen 37:30, p81), as opposed to עולימא ליתוהי in Onkelos to the very same verse; the past tense form of the third person masculine plural נצחון and אזלון end in *n* as in Galilean Aramaic (the form in Classical Aramaic is קטלו).[31]

The Aramaic of Megillat Taanit, the ancient Scroll of Fasts resembles classical Aramaic and displays very few late features. For example, the passive of the *qal* verb theme still appears in it: אחידת מגדל צור, 'The Tower of Tyre was captured' (MegTaan, Sivan 14, p319). A late feature that does appear in this scroll is the verb theme *'ittaf'al* (the passive of the *haf'ēl* verb theme), as in אתוקם תמידא – 'the *tamid* was established' (MegTaan, Nisan 1-8, p318), which is characteristic of Late Aramaic.

---

[29] For a list of the Aramaic sentences in the Mishna, see Dalman, *Grammatik*, 9f.
[30] See in the meantime Talshir, 'Nature'.
[31] See *infra*, section 'The Targumim as compared with the Talmudim'.

The Aramaic of the Amoraic Period

In this period Aramaic split into two branches, eastern and western.[32] In both, changes occurred from Classical Aramaic, but in the eastern branch this is more noticeable.

GALILEAN ARAMAIC

In the wake of the Bar Kokhba revolt (132-135 CE), Judea was destroyed and the Jewish cultural center moved to the Galilee.[33] This is where the Palestinian Amoraim were active, and so the Aramaic they spoke is known as Galilean Aramaic. This dialect belongs to the western branch of Aramaic. I shall adduce a number of features of Galilean Aramaic that distinguish it both from Classical and from Babylonian Aramaic.

(1) In Classical Aramaic a final *ā* could be marked either with ה or with א. The choice between them was one of grammatical category. For example: רחום בעל טעם ושמשי *ספרא* כתבו *אגרה חדה, על* ירושלם – 'Rehum the commander and Shimshai the scribe wrote a letter against Jerusalem' (Ezra 4:8); the definite noun form was denoted by a final א and thus we have ספרא, whereas the feminine noun form was marked with ה and so: אגרה חדה. In Galilean Aramaic this distinction no longer existed, and a final ה denotes all final *ā* vowels, as in זערה לא שאל בשלמה דרבה – 'The lesser does not greet the greater one' (YFrg, p6), the ה appearing in definite noun forms as well.[34]

(2) While Aramaic, like other Semitic languages, has its first person singular of the future tense beginning with א, in Galilean Aramaic this form begins with *n* under certain circumstances, as in אמר ליה לאחוי, צלי עלי, אמר ליה, מה *נצלי* עלך – 'He asked his brother: Pray for me; he replied: Why should I pray for you?' (GenR 6,5 p44);[35] and it is identical to the first person plural form. This feature may possibly have developed from prefixing אנא to the verb, i.e., אנא נקטול > אקטול.[36]

(3) The *qal* infinitive is *miqtal* in Classical Aramaic; the vowel of the second syllable is *a* even when the forms of the future tense have some other vowel. Thus, for example, the future of *qᵉtal* is *yiqtol*, while the form of the infinitive is *miqtal*, as in וּגבר ארי יִקְטוֹל כל נפשא דאנשא – 'He who kills a man' (Onk Lev 24:17), as contrasted with דלא לְמִקְטַל יתיה כל דישכחניה – 'Lest any who

---

[32] Traces of dialectical differences may appear already in Early Aramaic, see Greenfield, 'Dialects'.

[33] See, e.g., Schwartz, *Settlement*, 42-46.

[34] Kutscher, *Studies*, 16. The difference is only orthographical.

[35] In Freedman-Simon, *Midrash Rabbah*, vol 1, 45 this form is translated, 'Why should we pray', but the context renders the 'I' certain. The form of the imperative in the first sentence is צלי in the 2nd person singular masculine, i.e., the request was that his brother pray for him, and if so then מה נצלי is singular and not plural.

[36] Kutscher, art. 'Aramaic', 272. For other explanations, see Fassberg, *Grammar*, 167.

came upon him should kill him' (Onk Gen 4:15). In Galilean Aramaic the infinitive assimilates to the form of the future tense, thus forming *miqtol*, as in the Palestinian Targum fragments to the same verse: דלא לְמֶקְטוֹל יתה כל דמשכח יתה (FrgPTg Gen 4:15, p9).[37]

(4) In Classical Aramaic the *qal* infinitive opens with *m*: *miqtal*, whereas in the other verb themes the infinitive begins with the theme pattern; the infinitive of the *pa'ēl*, for example, is *qattālā*, as in לְקַיָּמָה קים מלכא וּלְתַקָּפָה אסר – 'That the king should establish an ordinance and enforce an interdict' (Dan 6:8). But in Galilean Aramaic the infinitive form of each theme opens with *m*, and thus the infinitive form of the *pa'ēl* theme is *m^eqattala*, as in ובעית מקיימה הדין קרייא – 'And I wanted to fulfil this verse' (yBer 7, 11b). The prefixed *m* seems to have been transferred from the *qal* to the other verb themes.[38]

(5) The following is a vocabulary example. 'To see' in Aramaic is חזה, as in חלם חזית וידחלנני – 'I had a dream which made me afraid' (Dan 4:2), whereas in Galilean Aramaic it is חמה, as in חמית בחילמי דרקיעא נפל – 'In my dream I saw the sky falling down' (yKil 9, 32b).

These features reflect development in contrast to Early Aramaic, but many features have remained the same. Thus Galilean Aramaic includes a number of ancient words the use of which sheds light on their meaning in the early sources. For example, in the verse, עיניו כיונים על אפיקי מים, רחצות בחלב, ישבות על מלֵאת – 'His eyes are like doves beside springs of water, bathed in milk, sitting on *milleth*' (Song 5:12), the word מלֵאת appears for the first and only time in the biblical text and its meaning is obscure. In Galilean Aramaic, however, it appears in a clear context: אזל למליתה, שמע קלהן דמלוותיה אמרן, בתו שלחכיניי, מליי קולתיך וסוק ליך – 'He went to the מלית and heard the voice of the women water-drawers saying: Daughter of Hakhinai, fill your pitcher and go up' (GenR 35 p1232). Its use here makes it clear that it denotes 'a place of drawing water', which seems to be the meaning in the verse as well.[39]

THE TARGUMIM AS COMPARED WITH THE TALMUDIM

Though most of the features of Galilean Aramaic are shared by all its sources, there are features that enable us to distinguish between the language of the talmudic literature and that of the Targumim (i.e., the Fragment Targum, the Palestinian Targum Fragments and Targum Neofyti). These features do not reflect dialectical differences but rather temporal ones, and they serve to indi-

---

[37] Dalman, *Grammatik*, 279; Tal, 'Forms of the Infinitive', 202f (the *segol* of the מ results from the shift i > e under certain phonetic circumstances). Mishnaic Hebrew shows a similar feature: the biblical infinitive form לָתֵת has been replaced by the form לִתֵן which reflects the form of the future tense יִתֵּן.

[38] Dalman, *Grammatik*, 278; Tal, 'Forms of the Infinitive', 211.

[39] Kutscher, *Studies*, 33.

cate that the Aramaic of the Targumim was earlier than that of the Talmudim.[40]
Let us review three examples.

(1) The closing of final open syllables with *n*. The Aramaic of Qumran already shows traces of this phenomenon, the word תמה 'there' becoming תמן, as in לאתרא די בנית תמן בה מדבחא – 'The place where I (had) built the altar' (GenAp 21:1, p66); but in this dialect the feature still is rare. In Galilean Aramaic, it has become much more common. In the Targumim, it appears only with ל"י verbs. Thus in the verse, וּסְגוֹן מיא וּטְעַנוֹ ית תיבותה – 'And the waters increased and lifted the ark' (FrgPTg Gen 7:17, p21), the word סגון is closed with *n*, as it belongs to the ל"י category, while the strong verb טענו appears without such *n*. In Talmudic Aramaic the feature has spread to all categories. The third person plural of the past tense *qatlu* always appears as *qatlun*, as in אזלון ופשפשון ואשכחון חכינתה – 'They went and searched and found a snake' (yShab 6, 8d); and the second person plural imperative form *qitlu* has become *qitlun*, as in אזלון ואמרין לון צומא רבה הוא – 'Go and tell them, it is the great fast' (yYom 8, 45a); and similarly in additional categories.[41]

(2) The position of the demonstrative pronoun. In Targum Aramaic the demonstrative pronoun generally appears after the noun it refers to, as in דחילמא הדין חלם ביש הוא – 'because this dream is a bad dream' (FrgTg Gen 40:18, p62), while in Talmudic Aramaic it normally appears before its noun, as in לא תילפון מיני הדין עובדה 'do not learn that case from me' (yRH 3, 58d).[42]

(3) The object pronominal suffix. In Classical Aramaic the pronominal object is suffixed to the verb, as in וְהַשְׁלְטֵהּ על כל מדינת בבל – 'And he made him ruler over the whole province of Babylonia' (Dan 2:48). In Targum Aramaic this pronoun is no longer attached to the verb, but rather appears after ית, as in ונסב יתהון ועבר יתהון ית נחלא 'And he took them, and brought them across the river' (FrgPTg Gen 32:24, p67). In Talmudic Aramaic the particle ית is contracted to ת and is attached to the verb, thus forming once again an object pronominal suffix, which is now attached to ת, as in אזל ונסבתון מן תמן – 'He went and took them from there' (yKet 12, 35b). Similarly, רבי שמעון בן לקיש צם תלת מאוון צומין למיחמי רבי חייה רובה ולא חמתיה, 'R. Shimon b. Lakish fasted three hundred fasts in order to see R. Hiyya the Great, but he did not see him' (yKil 9, 32b); the development which took place is *hᵃma yateh > hᵃmateh*.[43]

[40] Kutscher pointed out the existence of differences between the Aramaic of these Targumim and the Galilean Aramaic of the Talmudim, and concluded from this that the Targumim "present a type of Aramaic which is *slightly different* from the Galilean type"; see Kutscher, *Studies*, 4 and n14; 50. Tal demonstrated on the basis of clear evidence that these differences are temporal ones; see Tal, 'Layers'; Tal, 'Studies'; Tal, 'Forms of the Infinitive'. For a grammar of the Cairo Geniza fragments, see Fassberg, *Grammar*.

[41] Tal, 'Layers'.

[42] Tal, 'Studies', 49-51, 54.

[43] Dalman, *Grammatik*, 360; Fassberg, *A Grammar*, 252; Kutscher, 'Language of the Hebrew and Aramaic Letters', 131 n59, 132 n62b.

PSEUDO-YONATAN AND THE TARGUMIM TO THE HAGIOGRAPHA

These Targumim, though they apparently originated in an early period, absorbed late features during the process of transmission and do not reflect a pure Galilean Aramaic. It is possible to distinguish in them traces of the influence of the Babylonian Talmud as well, which in later periods was to be found everywhere, its language influencing the transmission of many texts.[44] Let us take two examples from the Pseudo-Yonatan: וקרא ית עשו בריה רבא בארביסר בניסן – 'He called Esau, his older son, on the fourteenth of Nisan' (PsYon Gen 27:1, p47); ואפילו הכי בריך יהי 'And even so, he will be blessed' (PsYon Gen 27:33, p49) – the forms ארביסר and אפילו הכי are clearly Babylonian and do not appear in Palestinian Aramaic.

BABYLONIAN ARAMAIC

Babylonian Aramaic (BA) belongs to the eastern branch of Aramaic. Following are a number of features rendering it unique amongst Aramaic dialects:

(1) Spelling. Denoting a final *a* with ה is almost non-existent in BA, where א is the regular suffix denoting a feminine noun as well, as in דאיתתא שכיחא בביתא ויהבא ריפתא לעניי 'because a wife stays at home and gives bread to the poor' (bTaan 23b).[45]

(2) Eclipse of emphatic state. The mark of the emphatic state of the noun in Classical Aramaic is a final *a*, such as כתב חֶלְמָא באדין ...חֵזֵה חֵלֶם דָנִיאל – 'Daniel had a dream... then he wrote down the dream' (Dan 7:1); חֵלֶם 'a dream' as compared with חֵלְמָא 'the dream'. In BA the form ending in *a* has become predominant, so that it also denotes an indefinite noun, as in האי מאן דחזא חלמא ולא ידע מאי חזא – 'If one has seen a dream and does not remember what he saw' (bBer 55b), or, יומא חד שקל תרנגולא 'one day he took a cock' (bBer 7a).[46] As a result of the predominance of the final *a*, BA has no way to denote a definite noun form, which means that this category no longer exists in BA. The disappearance of the emphatic state apparently stems from the influence of Akkadian, which has no definite noun form either. Akkadian was the vernacular of Babylonia before Aramaic spread to the area, and for some time both languages were spoken there. BA preserved a number of traces of disappearing Akkadian, including the disappearance of the emphatic state.[47]

(3) Weakening of guttural consonants. The gutturals weakened in Akkadian and, under its influence, in Aramaic as well.[48] For example, in accordance with the rules of phonetic shifts one would expect the Hebrew root חזר, 'return', to have as its Aramaic counterpart the root חדר, as actually appears in Syriac, but

---

[44] For the language of Ps-Yon, see Cook, *Rewriting the Bible*.

[45] Margolis, *Manual*, 3-4.

[46] *Ib.* 62.

[47] For Akkadian influence in Aramaic see Kaufman, *Akkadian Influences*.

[48] Kara, *Babylonian Aramaic*, p57-76; Margolis, *Manual*, 8; Morag, 'Background', 141-144.

this root exists in BA as הדר, as in האי מאן דבעי ניפוק באורחא ובעי דנידע אי הדר
לביתיה 'When one is about to go on a journey and wishes to know whether he
will return home' (bKer 5b). Also, in BA the word הדדי, literally 'one by one',
derives from the word חד 'one', as in ינאי מלכא ומלכתא כריכו ריפתא בהדי הדדי –
'King Jannai and his queen were taking a meal together' (bBer 48a). Furthermore, the word מברא, 'a ferry', in BA is derived from the root עבר, 'cross', as
in רבי זירא כי הוה סליק לא"י לא אשכח מברא למעבר – 'When R. Zera went up to the
Land of Israel he could not find a ferry wherein to cross [the river]' (bKet
112a).

(4) Elision of final consonants. In BA final consonants tend to be elided.[49]
Thus the classical plural suffix in Classical Aramaic is –in, as in ולאלהי כספא
ודהבא... די לא חזין ולא שמעין ולא ידעין שבחת – 'And you have praised the gods of
silver and gold... which do not see or hear or know' (Dan 5:23). In BA, however, the final n was dropped resulting in the morph –i, as in והנך לא ידעי ואזלי
וכתבי ויהבי – 'And those do not know and they go and write [the get] and give
[it to her]' (bGit 33b). Similarly, the final b has been elided from the word תוב,
counterpart of Hebrew שוב, resulting in Babylonian תו, as in ולימא האי פסוקא ותו
לא – 'Let us then say this one verse and no more' (bBer 12b). Also, instead of
the form ניקום, 'let us arise', from the root קום, the form ניקו appears, as in ניקו
מקמיה, דגבר דחיל חטאין הוא – 'Let us arise before him, because he is a sin-fearing
man' (bShab 31b).

(5) Elision of final vowels. In BA the elision of final vowels is widespread
as well.[50] For instance, the first person possessive suffix in Classical Aramaic
is denoted by final –i, as in Hebrew, whereas in BA this vowel tends to drop,
as in ההוא דאמר להו, תלתא לברת ותלתא לברת ותלתא לאיתת – '[Once] a certain [dy-
ing] man said to them: A third [shall be given] to [one] daughter of mine, a
third to [the other] daughter of mine, and a third [of the fruit] to my wife' (bBB
132b). This, too, is the origin of the title of the Babylonian Amoraim: רב, such
as רב פפא, which corresponds to the original Palestinian form רבי.[51]

MORPHOLOGICAL VARIETY IN BABYLONIAN ARAMAIC

A very common feature of BA, though otherwise a rare phenomenon, is the
use of a number of alternate forms in the same role and with the same meaning.

(1) As a result of the elision of the final consonant, the form קאי is usual in
BA instead of קאים, 'he is standing'. Yet the ancient form קאים has not disappeared, and קאים and קאי co-exist without any distinction, as in רבי אלעזר הוה
קאים קמיה דמר שמואל – 'R. Eleazar was once standing before Mar Samuel'

[49] Boyarin, 'Loss of Final Consonants', 103-107; Epstein, Grammar, 18f; Kara ib. 87-92.
[50] Kara ib., 121; Margolis, Manual, 14; Morag, 'On the Background', 144-145.
[51] See Breuer, 'Rabbi'.

(bHul 111b), in contrast to גידל בר מניומי הוה קאי קמיה דרב נחמן 'Giddol bar Ma-nyumi was once standing before Rav Nahman' (bBer 49a).

(2) The classical form of the third person singular feminine of the past tense is *q^{e}talat*. In BA this becomes *q^{e}tala* by elision of the final consonant, and by elision of the final vowel this again becomes *q^{e}tal*, a form identical with the third person singular masculine.[52] In effect BA has three different forms for the third person feminine singular of the past tense: *q^{e}talat*, *q^{e}tala*, *q^{e}tal*. Compare, for example, these three sentences: אזלת הא איתתא ואינסיבא לחנואה – 'This woman went and married a shopkeeper' (bPes 110b, ms Mun 6); אזלא דביתהו דחסא ואינסיבא – 'Hasa's wife went and married' (bYev 121b, ms Mun 141); דההוא גברא דגרשה לדביתהו ואזל אינסיב לחניא – 'A man who divorced his wife and she went and married a shopkeeper' (bPes 110b, ms JTS Rab. 1623). Similarly, we have ההיא איתתא דעלת להההיא ביתה למיפא – 'A certain woman entered a neighbour's house to bake [there bread]' (bBK 83a, ms Flor II-I-7); ההיא איתתא דעלא למיפא בההיא ביתא – 'A certain woman entered a neighbour's house to bake [there bread]' (bBK 48a, ms Flor II-I-7); and שבשתא כיון דעל על – 'Once a mistake entered, it entered' [once a mistake is implanted it cannot be eradicated] (bBB 21a, ms Flor II-I-7).

(3) As already noted, final vowel elision included elision of the vowel denoting the first person possessive suffix, hence ברת = 'my daughter'. Yet this suffix often survives, as in הבו ליה ארבע מאה זוזי לפלניא ולנסיב ברתי – 'Give four hundred *zuz* to So-and-so and let him marry my daughter' (bBetsa 20a, ms Lon 400).

The reason for this variety is difficult to guess. The BA appearing in the Talmud may have developed out of a mixture of several dialects.[53] Some also postulate that the variety stems from a mix of the language being transmitted and the vernacular. In transmitting the talmudic text from one generation to the next, efforts would have been made to preserve the archaic language, as is common when an ancient text is being transmitted, but the changes which had taken place in the spoken language penetrated into the language of the transmitted text, resulting in the morphological mix.[54] Most likely, however, the various alternating forms relate chronologically to one another. The threesome third person feminine singular past tense, for example, results from a clear chronological process, *q^{e}talat* > *q^{e}tala* > *q^{e}tal*. Since the Talmud came into being over a period of at least three hundred years, it appears that the variation in morphological forms records the development which took place during its formulation.[55] This would mean that the Talmud never underwent a unified

---

[52] Kutscher, 'Research', 168-169.

[53] See, e.g., Boyarin, 'Review', 254; Kara, *Babylonian Aramaic*, 70.

[54] Morag, 'Background', 145-147.

[55] See, e.g., Kutscher, 'Research', 167; Morag, 'Some Notes', 75. In the end these forms were all mixed together, and so, it seems, there is no linguistic differentiation between the early and the later strata (see Levias, *Grammar*, 2). Nevertheless, Eljakim Wajsberg, 'Aramaic Dialect' is of the opinion that early Amoraim tend to use early forms.

linguistic editing, and ancient forms were allowed to survive alongside more modern ones.

THE ARAMAIC OF THE GEONIM

The period of the Amoraim was followed by that of the Geonim. The Aramaic of that period has not yet been systematically analyzed. It resembles that of the Bavli, but on occasion differs in a number of basic features. Let us take these two sentences from Gaonic *responsa*: הכין חזינא, דהדא שאלה לא כשאלתא קדמייתא – 'So we have seen that this question is unlike the first question' (Müller, *Lehrer*, 21b); ופקידנא וקרו יתהון קדמנא ועיננא בהון וקמנא על כל מאי דכתיב בהין ופקידנא וכתבו תשובות דילהין לפום דאחזו לנא מן שמיא – 'And we ordered that they read them [the questions] in our presence and we studied them and we investigated all that was written in them and we ordered that they write answers to them according to what we were shown from heaven' (Lewin, *Ginzei kedem*, p1). These sentences contain many forms which differ from the Bavli, such as:

הכין, whereas in the Bavli the final *n* has been elided and the form הכי resulted, as in מאי טעמא עבדת הכי – 'Why did you do [it] like that?' (bBer 18b).

הדא, where the Bavli has the *d* been elided resulting in הא, as in כי הא מילתא – 'Such a thing' (bZev 44a).

קדמייתא: in the Bavli the *d* has assimilated to the *m*, yielding קמייתא, as in גזרתא קמייתא – 'the first decree' (bGit 55b).

קדמנא, לנא: in the Bavli the final vowel has dropped and the forms are קמן and לן, as in כי קא מיבעיא לן רובא דליתיה קמן – 'Our question relates to cases where the majority is not before us [the majority is undefined]' (bHul 11a).[56]

It is not surprising that the Aramaic of the Geonim differs from that of the Talmud, for language is subject to change. Yet it is unexpected that the Aramaic of the Geonim, being later than that of the Talmud, should show such features indicating an early language; the Geonic form הכין is undoubtedly earlier than the talmudic הכי. There is no agreed answer to this question. One could suppose that the Aramaic of the Geonim reflects another dialect which preserved various archaic features, but this seems unlikely since the earliest Geonim lived in the very same places as the Babylonian Amoraim.[57] An answer may be found in the fact that the Talmud and contemporary literature were mainly compiled orally by the Amoraim, and were not written down until a later period of time. Even as the talmudic text was being transcribed, the original wording – an oral text in the vernacular – was preserved. Gaonic literature, on the other hand, was written from the start, and the Gaonic *re-*

---

[56] See, e.g., Levias, *Grammar*, 4. For a summary of this unusual BA (Gaonic Aramaic and the language of the special tractates and of the incantation texts) and for a review of the theories propounded concerning its origins, see Harviainen, 'Diglossia'.

[57] According to Harviainen *ib.* 17-19, this language is that of the rural areas, which tends to preserve ancient features, whereas standard BA is an urban tongue.

sponsa, for example, were written down to be sent to the diaspora, and this is true of other Gaonic literature as well. As is well known, a written language generally preserves classical features, in contrast to a spoken one. It is thus possible that the Aramaic of the Geonim represents the official, more archaic written language, whereas that of the Talmud reflects the spoken, vernacular tongue.

THE LANGUAGE OF PARTICULAR BAVLI TRACTATES

A number of talmudic tractates display an Aramaic different from the usual language of the Talmud and rather resembling that of the Geonim. These tractates are: Nedarim, Nazir, Keritot, Meila, Tamid, and part of Temura.[58] Some examples: הדין אמר: שבועתא דהכי אמר רב; והדין אמר: שבועתא דהכי אמר רב: – 'One said, I swear that Rav taught this, and the other said, I swear that he taught this' (bNed 25b). In standard BA both the *d* and the final *n* of the word הדין were elided, thus facilitating the appearance of the form האי, as in: האי אמר דידי הוא והאי אמר דידי הוא – 'One said, It is mine, and the other said, It is mine' (bBK 117a). Similarly, רבא, יומא *קדמאה* דחליש אמר להון, לא תיגלו לאיניש – 'Whenever Rava fell sick, on the first day he would ask them, do not reveal [it] to any one' (bNed 40a). Instead of קדמאה, standard BA has קמא; and instead of להון, it has להו, as in יומא קמא אמר להו – 'On the first day he said to them' (bGit 68b). Actually, the language of these tractates is not uniform; rather, it contains an incomprehensible mixture of the usual language of the Talmud and that of the Geonim, as in, הא לא קא מיבעיא לי דעללתא כל מילי משמע, *הדא* הוא דאיבעיא לי – 'Of *this* I have no doubt, that עללתא means "everything"; it is of *this* [other thing] that I am doubtful' (bNed 55a). In this sentence both early *hada* and BA *ha* appear. There is no satisfactory solution for the special nature of these tractates. They would seem to have been edited separately from the rest of the Talmud,[59] but where and when, remains a mystery.

PALESTINIAN INSERTS IN THE BAVLI

A special type of Aramaic that appears in the Bavli is that of Palestinian inserts dating from the Amoraic period.[60] Palestinian elements may actually reflect the wording of the original speaker. Let us hear one sentence in the name of the Palestinian Amora R. Yohanan and another introduced by the phrase 'a word was sent from there [Palestine]': א"ר יוחנן, כס דחרשין ולא כס דפושרין – 'R. Yo-

---

[58] See, e.g., Epstein, *Grammar*, 14-16; Levias, *Grammar*, p2-18; Margolis, *Manual*, 2. For a study of the language of Nedarim, see Rybak, *Aramaic Language*.

[59] See Epstein *ib.* 15.

[60] See, e.g., Epstein *ib.* 16. The reference here is to quotations from Amoraic sources, and not to quotations from Tannaic sources, which appear in the Talmud in their original language – whether Hebrew or Aramaic. Of course, whenever the language of the Tannaic source is Aramaic, it will be found to be Palestinian Aramaic.

hanan said: A cupful of witchcraft, not a cupful of tepid water' (bBM 29b, ms Hamburg 165); והיינו דשלחו מתם, יבעו רחמי אתכליא על עלייא, דאלמלא עליא לא מתקיימין אתכליא – 'This is what was meant when word was sent from there [the Land of Israel], Let the clusters pray for the leaves, for were it not for the leaves the clusters could not exist' (bHul 92a, ms Hamburg 169). Three clearly Palestinian features may be distinguished in these quotations.

כָּס: noun determination. In the Bavli, even indetermined nouns usually end in *a*, and the form כָּסָא is to be expected, as in דעבידי אינשי דשתו כסא בצפרא וכסא בפניא – 'It is usual for people to drink one cup in the morning and another in the evening' (bEr 29b).

יבעו רחמי: prefixed *y* in the third person plural of the future tense. In BA the corresponding form opens with *l* as in לבעו רחמי האידנא – 'Let them pray now' (bTaan 24b).

חרשין, as opposed to אתכלייא and עלייא. This preserves the form of Classical Western Aramaic, where the plural of indeterminate nouns is denoted by the suffix –*in* and the plural of determinate nouns is denoted by –*ayya*. In BA neither of these suffixes has survived, both having been replaced by –*ē* which denotes a plural noun, either determinate or indeterminate, as in ואישתפך הנהו זוזי לארעא – 'And the money poured out on the ground' (bNed 25a).

This phenomenon is extremely instructive: despite these sayings having been brought from Palestine and transmitted orally in Babylonia for hundreds of years in a different linguistic environment, and despite them not being collected up in a single place but rather being scattered throughout the Bavli and embedded in a BA environment, they have preserved their original Palestinian grammatical markings.

INCANTATION TEXTS

Additional texts written in BA are the epigraphic material discovered in Babylonia, some of which was certainly composed by Jews. This material includes incantation texts against demons and hostile spirits, and it is especially important because the texts it includes were never treated by copyists. The language of this material is very similar to BA, though it displays ancient features which do not appear in the usual BA.[61] For example: *תוב מומינא ומשבענא וגזרנא ומשמיתנא ומבטילנא ית כל רזי חרשין* – 'Further, I adjure, invoke, decree, ban and annul all mysteries of sorcerers' (Naveh-Shaked, *Magic Spells*, 19:5-6, p124). On the one hand, the forms מומינא, משבענא, etc. are characteristic of BA in which the participle is declined by persons. So משבענא equals אנא משבע, e.g., in the Talmud אנא טרחנא וזרענא ומייתינא – 'I will exert myself, sow it, and bring [you the crop]' (bKid 61a).[62] This feature does not exist in Classical Aramaic or even in Western Aramaic. On the other hand, the forms תוב and ית do not appear in the usual BA, in which תוב has become תו, and the direct object is not

[61] For a grammar of the language of the incantation texts, see Juusola, *Linguistic Peculiarities*.
[62] Margolis, *Manual*, 40.

usual BA, in which חוב has become תו, and the direct object is not marked by the preposition ית, but rather by the preposition -ל, as in אשכחיה רבי יוחנן לינוקיה דריש לקיש – 'R. Yohanan met the young son of Resh Lakish' (bTaan 9a).[63] It is known that ancient phrases preserving early features are common in incantation texts, and so it is not surprising that this Aramaic preserves ancient features.

EASTERN AND WESTERN ARAMAIC

As already stated, Jewish Aramaic of the talmudic era falls into two different categories. The Aramaic of the Bavli belongs to the eastern branch, and most of its features are characteristic also of the other dialects of this branch, while Galilean Aramaic belongs to the western branch, with most of its features resembling those of the other dialects of this branch. For example: as has already been pointed out, in BA the indeterminate form of the noun ends in *a*, too, as in ריש גלותא בנא ביתא – 'The Exilarch once built a house' (bMen 33a). This feature is common to Syriac and Mandaic as well. For example, in the Western Aramaic Targum Neofyti we find, ארום תבנה בית חדת – 'When you build a new house' (Neof Deut 22:8, p185), whereas in the Peshitta, which is written in Eastern Aramaic, the same verse is written as follows: ומא דבנא אנת ביתא חדתא. In contrast, Galilean Aramaic is related to the other dialects of the western branch. For example, as already noted, the infinitive of all the verb themes in Galilean Aramaic begins with *m*, such as בעיין מנחמתיה ולא קביל עלוי מתנחמה – 'They wanted to comfort him, but he refused to be comforted' (yDem 1, 22a); here both the infinitive of the *pa'el* מְנַחְמָתֵיה and that of the *'itpa'al* מִתְנַחָמָה begin with *m*. This is also true of Samaritan Aramaic. For example, in the Samaritan Targum we find וקעמו כל בניו וכל בנאתה למנחמאתה ומעי למתנחמה – 'All his sons and all his daughters rose up to comfort him, but he refused to be comforted' (SamTg Gen 37:35, vol 1 p156). In contrast, in Targum Onkelos, which is written in an earlier form of Aramaic, the same verse reads as follows: וקמו כל בנוהי וכל בנתיה לְנַחָמוּתֵיה וסריב לְקַבָּלָא תנחומין.

Because of the unbroken bond between Babylonia and Palestine, the differences between the branches of Aramaic were familiar to the Amoraim, and in talmudic literature one encounters explicit references to these differences.

(1) In the Palestinian Talmud the following question is raised: איש מהו להתפיש לו נזירות בלשון אשה? – 'As for a man, can he take upon himself the Nazirite's vow in the language of a woman?' (yNaz 2, 51d). If the man used feminine forms and said, הרי אני נזירה, instead of נזיר, is his vow valid or not? The answer to the question is: תמן אמרין: הא נזירה איעבר – 'There [in Babylonia] they say: Behold, a Nazirite (*n'zira*) is passing by [even though it is a man, i.e., *n'zira* can also denote a man].' The Babylonian usage does not stem from a weakening of the gender distinction, but rather from the way the Babylonian

language was interpreted in the Land of Israel. In Babylonia every noun ended in a final *a* and any Nazirite was termed *nᵉzira*. In the Land of Israel, on the other hand, the indeterminate form was preserved as well, and so נזיר was pronounced *nᵉzir* when the intention was not to determine it. A Palestinian Jew, upon hearing that in Babylonia a Nazirite is called *nᵉzira* even when there is no intention to determine the word, will automatically interpret the form as being feminine, and thus he concludes that in Babylonia נזירה denotes the masculine form as well.[64]

(2) The Babylonian Talmud tells of a series of errors stemming from a mutual lack of understanding between speakers of the two dialects:

ההוא בר בבל דסליק לארעא דישראל, נסיב איתתא, [...] אמר לה: זילי אייתי לי תרי בוציני,
אזלת ואייתי ליה תרי שרגי. אמר לה: זילי תברי יתהון על רישא דבבא. הוה יתיב בבא בן בוטא
אבבא וקא דאין דינא, אזלת ותברת יתהון על רישיה. אמר לה: מה הדין דעבדת? אמרה ליה: כך
ציוני בעלי. אמר: את עשית רצון בעליך, המקום יוציא ממך בנים כבבא בן בוטא.

A certain Babylonian went up to the Land of Israel and took a wife [there]... He said to her, 'Go and bring me two *buṣine* [cucumbers].' So she went and brought him two candles. 'Go and break them on the head of the *baba* [door]'. Now Baba b. Buta was sitting on the threshold, engaged in judging in a lawsuit. So she went and broke them on his head. He said to her, 'What is the meaning of this that you have done?' She replied, 'Thus my husband did order me'. 'You have performed your husband's will', he rejoined; 'may the Almighty bring forth from you two sons like Baba b. Buta.' (bNed 66b)

Two dialectical features can be distinguished here: בוצינא in Babylonia meant 'cucumber', as in בוצינא טב מקרא – 'A cucumber is better than a pumpkin' (bSuk 56b), while in Palestine it meant 'candle': איזל אדלק לי בוצינא – 'Go and light a candle for me' (GenR 36,1 p335), and the Babylonian word for 'candle' was שרגא, as in אתא ההוא נכרי אדליק שרגא – 'A Gentile came and lit a candle' (bShab 122b). Furthermore, בבא 'a door' is a very common word in the Bavli but does not exist in Palestinian Aramaic, where the same concept is expressed by the word תרעא; compare אזל רב ששת קם אבבא – 'Rav Shesheth went and stood at the door' (bEr 11b) onאזל וקם ליה על תרעא דמערתא – 'He went and stood at the entrance to the cave' (yHag 2, 78a). In Palestine בבא was merely a proper noun.

(3) The Babylonian Talmud tells of an argument between R. Hiyya, whose origin was from Babylonia and who was a student of R. Yehuda the Prince, and R. Shimon, the son of R. Yehuda the Prince:

אמר ליה רבי חייא לרבי שמעון בר רבי: אלמלי אתה לוי פסול אתה מן הדוכן, משום דעבי קלך.
אתא אמר ליה לאבוה. אמר ליה, זיל אימא ליה, כשאתה מגיע אצל "וחכיתי לה'" - לא נמצאת
מחרף ומגדף?

R. Hiyya said to R. Shimon bar Rabbi: If you were a Levite, you would not be qualified to chant, because your voice is thick. He went and told his father, who said to him: Go and say to him, When you come to the verse, 'And I will

---

[64] Lieberman, 'Tiqqune Yerushalmi 5', 456.

618

wait [*we-ḥikkiti*] for the Lord', will you not be a reviler and blasphemer?' (bMeg. 24b)

One who pronounces *h* instead of *ḥ* will replace 'וחכיתי לה – 'I will wait for the Lord' (Isa 8:17) with 'והכיתי לה 'I will hit the Lord', a clear case of blasphemy. Because of the weakening of the guttural consonants occurring in Babylonia R. Hiyya, a Babylonian, found it difficult to pronounce the *ḥ*, replacing it with *h*.[65] Residents of the Land of Israel, where there were only occasional indications of a weakening of the gutturals,[66] had no difficulty in pronouncing the *ḥ*.

Foreign Language Influence

Aramaic was greatly influenced by the languages spoken in its vicinity. Jewish Aramaic was especially influenced by Hebrew. For example, in Qumran Aramaic there appear the words הריון and עליון with a *ḥōlam* in their final syllable, from which we conclude that they are Hebrew words, for in Aramaic the corresponding vowel would have been *qāmeṣ*, as in the sentence cited earlier:[67] מנך זרעא דן ומנך הריונא דן – 'This seed is from you; from you is this conception' (GenAp 2:15, p52); or, לאל עליון – 'To the Most High God' (GenAp 12:17, p56).[68] In Targums Onkelos and Yonatan use is made of the word ארון, which originates in Hebrew: וסמוהי בארונא במצרים – 'And they put him in a coffin in Egypt' (Onk Gen 50:26); דתמן ארונא דה – '...Where the ark of God was' (TgJob 1 Sam 3:3).[69] In Galilean Aramaic there appear, for example, the Hebrew words מצווה and תהום, as in דר"ש בר אבא מדקדק במצוותא סגין – '...That R. Shimon bar Abba is very exacting in observing commandments' (yBer 2, 4b); or, חפר חמש עשר מאוון דאמין ולא אשכח תהומא – 'He dug 1500 cubits and did not find the lower depth' (ySan 10, 29a). In BA, too, Hebrew influence is very widespread, in words such as הגדה, הלל, קידושין, which were transformed in BA into אגדתא, הלילא, קידושי, e.g., כיון דבעי למימר אגדתא והלילא – 'Since he is to recite the Haggada and Hallel' (bPes 115b); קביל ביך אבוך קידושי – 'Your father accepted *kiddushin* on your behalf' (bKid 12b, ms Oxf Opp. 248). Even Hebrew verbs made their way into Aramaic, such as the verb אֶתְחַל derived from the root *t.ḥ.l*, a secondary root derived in Hebrew from the word תְּחִלָּה, as in אתחולי בפורענותא לא מתחלינן – 'We do not begin with a record of suffering' (bBB 14b).[70]

---

[65] Dalman, *Grammatik*, 58-59.

[66] Kutscher concludes that the guttural consonants in Galilean Aramaic did not weaken to any great extent; see Kutscher, *Studies*, 67-96.

[67] Fitzmyer, *Wandering Aramean*, 26.

[68] For additional comments on Hebrew influence on the Aramaic of the Dead Sea Documents, see Fassberg, 'Hebraisms'.

[69] For Hebrew influence on the language of Yon see Tal, *Language*, 159-175.

[70] For Hebrew influence on Babylonian Aramaic, see Breuer, 'Hebrew Component'.

Aramaic also has an abundance of words from Greek.[71] For example: הוה הדין מסיק ליה *בטימי* והדין מסיק ליה *בטימי* עד דמטא בי"ב דינרין, ונסתיה ההוא חייטא. בעַנתה *דאריסטון* אמר *אפרכוס* לטליא, למה לא אייטיתה נון – 'This one was raising the price and this one was raising the price, until it reached twelve dinars, at which price the tailor bought it. At dinner the governor asked the servant, Why have you not served fish?' (GenR 11,4 p91f). There are three Greek words in this short tale: טימי, 'price', from the Greek τιμή; אריסטון from the Greek ἄριστον, 'meal'; אפרכוס, 'ruler', from the Greek ἔπαρχος. Greek influence was so strong that on occasion entire sayings are quoted as they appear in Greek: פרא בסיליוס או נומוס או גריפיס – Παρὰ βασιλέως ὁ νόμος ἄγραφος, 'On the king the law is not binding' (yRH 1, 57b).[72] Words were borrowed into Aramaic from Latin as well, such as רבי אחא ורבי זעירא הוון מטיילין באיסטרטין – 'R. Aha and R. Zeira were walking the streets' (yShab 6, 8a); איסטרטין is Latin *strata*, 'street'.[73]

Greek and Latin were far less known in Babylonia, and the Greek and Latin words appearing in BA seem to have got there via Hebrew. On the other hand, Persian words are common in BA as a result of Persian rule.[74] For example, איכא חד גברא ביהודאי דקא דיין דינא בלא *הרמנא* דמלכא, שדר עליה *פריסתקא* – 'There is a man among the Jews who passes judgment without the permission of the government; an official was sent to [summon] him' (bBer 58a). There are two Persian words in this sentence: הרמנא which originates from *farmān* 'an order',[75] and פריסתקא from *frēstag*, 'a messenger'.[76]

The Relationship of Late Aramaic to Early Aramaic

As described above, there are many features which clearly indicate the development of Late Aramaic from Early Aramaic. Nevertheless, there are also features which do not seem to fit into the recognized patterns of development, and these features appear to demonstrate that Late Aramaic did not develop directly from the Early Aramaic with which we are familiar. I shall adduce two examples of this, one from Galilean Aramaic and the other from Babylonian Aramaic, both of which are related to a single principle.

---

[71] For a lexicon of Greek and Latin words in talmudic literature, see Krauss, *Lehnwörter* (covering loan words both in Hebrew and Aramaic).

[72] Lieberman, *Greek*, 37f.

[73] The Latin words borrowed into Aramaic were mainly from the military and administrative fields. The relationship of Latin words to Greek ones is about one to a hundred. Many Latin words reached Aramaic via the Greek, but many others arrived directly from Latin. For this see Krauss, *Lehnwörter* 1, 231f.

[74] Macuch, 'Iranian Legal Terminology'; Shaked, 'Iranian Loanwords'; Telegdi, 'Essai'.

[75] Dov Geiger in Krauss, *Additamenta*, 163; Heinrich L. Fleischer in Levy, *Chaldäisches Wörterbuch* 1, 559.

[76] Dov Geiger *ib*. 343; Heinrich L. Fleischer in Levy, *Chaldäisches Wörterbuch* 2, 573.

It is well known that in both Hebrew and Aramaic the diphthong *ay* tends to contract and turn into *ē*. For example, the original diphthong in the word בַּיִת (originally **bayt*) changes in certain cases to *ē*: בֵּית מלכא – 'the king's house' (Ezra 6:4). The reverse phenomenon is non-existent, and the vowel *ē* never becomes *ay*. The assumed original form of the plural demonstrative particle is **'ilay*.[77] In Biblical Aramaic the original diphthong has contracted, and the form of the particle is *'illēn*, as in סרכיא ואחשדרפניא אִלֵּן – 'These presidents and satraps' (Dan 6:7).[78] In the form appearing in Galilean Aramaic, the diphthong reappears: [*ha-'illayn >*] *ha-'ellayin*: גבריא הָאֵלֵּין – 'These men' (FrgPTg Gen 34:21, p71); דביריה הָאֵלֵּין – 'these words' (FrgPTg Deut 5:19, p335).[79] Since it is not feasible to assume a development *'illēn > 'illayin*, Galilean Aramaic seems to have developed from a dialect in which the diphthong did not contract.[80]

Babylonian Aramaic has a similar feature. In the Bible, the form of the possessive third person plural suffix attached to certain nouns is *-ēhōn*, as in עֲלֵיהוֹן – 'on them' (Ezra 5:1) and בְּנֵיהוֹן – 'their sons' (Dan 6:25), as a result of the contraction of the original diphthong (originally **-ayhun*[81]). In BA its form is *-ayhu* (with the elision of the final *n*), as in עלייהו – 'on them' (bBer 36a) and בנייהו – 'their sons' (bBer 17a).[82] Here it is the original diphthong that has been preserved, and so we may conclude that BA developed from a dialect in which the diphthong had not contracted.

Vocalization Traditions

The difficulty in describing Early Aramaic is that the spelling facilitates the drawing of conclusions regarding the consonants and some of the vowels, but not about the overall structure of the language. A full description of the language requires vocalized texts, but these are few and far between. The following are the main sources upon which to base a description of Aramaic in the period under discussion:

---

[77] Bauer-Leander, *Grammatik*, 83.

[78] In the Bible the spelling of the word is sometimes plene: אִלֵּין (as in Dan 2:44), and in these cases the contraction of the diphthong is shown only by the vocalization, but in the case adduced here it is shown by the defectiva spelling as well. Such spelling is also found in the epigraphic material, and this, too, indicates that the diphthong has indeed contracted, as in קשתא וחציא אלן – '(this) bow and these arrows' (The Sefire Inscription, Gibson, *Textbook*, SSI 7:A38, 32).

[79] See Fassberg, *A Grammar*, 58.

[80] Orally from Prof. Moshe Bar-Asher in a seminar on Galilean Aramaic at the Hebrew University in 1984.

[81] Bauer-Leander, *Grammatik*, 80.

[82] The reading *-ayhu* is proved by the spelling with a double yod, which is very widespread both in the printed versions and in the manuscripts, and is confirmed according to the vocalization in Halakhot Pesukot ms Sassoon and according to the tradition of the Yemenite Jews in reading the Talmud; see, e.g., Morag 'Vocalization', 91; Morag, *Babylonian Aramaic*, 114.

- manuscripts and fragments of Targum Onkelos and Targum Yonatan with Babylonian vowel signs;[83]
- some of the Palestinian Targum Fragments testifying to Galilean Aramaic have Tiberian, others Palestinian vocalization:[84]
- main sources for BA are two partially vocalized Gaonic manuscripts: Halachot Pesukot ms Sassoon[85] and Halachot Gedolot ms Paris;[86] to these must be added the Yemenite pronunciation tradition of the Babylonian Talmud, several features of which have been described comprehensively;[87]
- vocalized words scattered through talmudic mss and in Cairo Geniza fragments;[88] also transcriptions of Aramaic words in foreign languages such as in Greek and Latin sources give significant clues on the pronunciation of Aramaic in this period.

These sources are extremely important, for only upon them can we base a full linguistic description. For an example, let us take a detail which can be learned only from the vocalized sources: the pronunciation of the past tense feminine form. The reconstructed original form is *qatalat.[89] In Biblical Aramaic the corresponding form is generally qitlat, as סֶלְקַת – 'came up' (Dan 7:20). From the spelling of this form, there is no telling how it was pronounced in Late Aramaic. According to the vowel signs, we see that in Galilean Aramaic the form is qatlat, as in וקמת וְאָזְלַת... וְלַבְשַׁת לבושי ארמלותה – 'And she started up and went... and put on her widow's garb' (FrgPTg Gen 38:19, p87).[90] In this form the a vowel in the first syllable has been preserved, and so the form is closer to the original form *qatalat than the biblical form is.[91] Another form appears in Targum Onkelos: according to the vocalization, this form is qᵉtalat, as in וַאֲכַלַת וִיהֲבַת – 'She ate, and she also gave [to her husband]' (Onk Gen 3:6).[92] As already noted, this vocalization survives in mss with Babylonian vocalization; it follows that this form was used in Babylonia. The form, too, is extremely interesting, for three reasons. First, it preserves the a in the second syllable;

---

[83] See the editions adduced above n12, 17.

[84] See the edition adduced above n15.

[85] Sefer Halachot Pesuqot by Rav Jehudai Gaon: Codex Sassoon 263, A Facsimile edition, Jerusalem 1971.

[86] Sefer Halachot Gedolot: Codex Paris 1402, A Facsimile edition, Jerusalem 1971.

[87] The verb has been fully described according to this tradition in Morag, Babylonian Aramaic. Other features have been described in other articles by Morag, such as, 'Baylonian Aramaic Tradition'.

[88] For an anthology of vocalized words in Geniza Talmud fragments, see Morag, Vocalized Talmudic Manuscripts. In this book there appears only the list of words, without any linguistic analysis.

[89] Bauer-Leander, Grammatik, 102.

[90] Fassberg, A Grammar, 173.

[91] Kutscher, art. 'Aramaic', 272.

[92] Dalman, Grammatik, 78, 256, 259.

hence it, too, is closer to the original form *qatalat than the biblical form.[93] Second, it seems to indicate that in Babylonia the penultimate syllable was stressed: according to the rules of Aramaic, an (originally short) vowel cannot exist in an unstressed open syllable, and thus the form $q^e talat$, with the vowel of the second syllable surviving, is comprehensible only if the assumption is made that in Babylonia the penultimate syllable was stressed.[94] Third, the form is confirmed by an analysis of the Aramaic of the Bavli: the third person feminine singular form in ל"י verbs in BA is $q^e tay$, as in אתאי ההיא איתתא – 'A woman came' (bShab 55a), or, וסגאי ספינתא – 'And the ship went' (bBB 73b). This form is explicable only in the following manner: *$q^e tayat$ > $q^e taya$ (with elision of final consonant) > $q^e tay$ (with elision of final vowel),[95] and if so, the feminine form is of necessity $q^e talat$. We thus find the Babylonian vocalization of Onkelos coordinated with the Aramaic of the Bavli. It should perhaps be stressed that although this form occurs in Onkelos which was composed in the Tannaic period, it gives us only a foothold on its pronunciation at the time it was transmitted in Babylonia.

The pronunciation of Aramaic words can also be inferred from their transliteration in Greek and Latin sources. Let us review two examples from the New Testament.[96] In all Semitic languages the ב of the word אב is always fricative, as in אָבִי (Gen 19:34), and so, for example, in Syriac the determinate form of the word is אַבָּא ('avā). In the New Testament the word appears in Greek transcription as ἀββὰ ὁ πατήρ, 'Abba, Father' (Mark 14:36); the transcription shows that the b was doubled. The doubling of the b is attested in later sources as well, such as the Cairo Geniza fragments and in Mishnaic Hebrew manuscripts.[97] It seems to be an analogous formation to the doubling of the m in the word אִמָּא.[98] There is nothing revolutionary in this doubling, for it is known from other sources as well, but the New Testament seems to provide the earliest evidence of it. On occasion there occur other forms which are unknown from other sources. For example, the name of the festival פסח appears in the New Testament in its Aramaic form πάσχα (pascha, e.g. Matt 26:2) with a in the first syllable, and so it is in other Greek sources, while in all

---

[93] Whether our conclusion is based on the Galilean form qatlat or on the Babylonian form $q^e talat$, we have further evidence that Late Aramaic does not derive directly from the Early Aramaic we are familiar with (see above, section on 'The Relationship of Late Aramaic to Early Aramaic').

[94] This is the way Dalman, Grammatik, 78 explained this phenomenon. From the writings of Kutscher ('Research', 165; art. 'Aramaic', 286), he appears to have thought that this form was constructed according to the singular form, though in that case the form contradicts the basic rules of Aramaic. It thus seems to me that the form indeed indicates a penultimate stress, as Dalman states. Kutscher himself assumes that in Babylonian Aramaic the stress was on the penultimate syllable, see Kutscher, art. 'Aramaic', 280.

[95] Kutscher, 'Research', 165, 169.

[96] For a list of the Aramaic words appearing in the New Testament, see Kautzsch, Grammatik, 7-12.

[97] For example: אמ' לנו אבא – 'my father said to us' (mEr 6:2, ms K).

[98] Kutscher, Words, 1f.

the first syllable, and so it is in other Greek sources, while in all known Aramaic sources the form of the word is *pisha*.[99]

Conclusion

The above review gives a first impression of the types of Aramaic common in the time of the sages. In this period Aramaic was a spoken language, and many literary works were written. Subsequently, Aramaic ceased to be a vernacular, and only in a very few places has it survived in speech to the present day. Nevertheless, by virtue of its central position in talmudic literature, every scholar of this literature is familiar with it, and so it continued to be known even after it ceased to be a spoken language. In the Middle Ages, it was passively known only from the ancient texts, yet to a limited extent it was also an active tongue, for the writers of Hebrew often integrated Aramaic into their writings. It remains important in Modern Hebrew, which is replete with Aramaic words and expressions that are borrowed from talmudic sources and serve in every day life.[100] The Jews have spoken many languages over the generations, but besides Hebrew, Aramaic has undoubtedly been the most important language of their culture.

Suggestions for Further Reading

For the Dead Sea Scrolls Kutscher, 'The Language of the "Genesis Apocryphon", is still valuable and presents the place of this language within Aramaic dialects. For texts Beyer, *Die aramäischen Texte* is very useful.

Onkelos and Yonatan: Dodi, *The Grammar of Targum Onqelos* Tal, *The Language of the Targum*. The best texts are included in Sperber, *The Bible in Aramaic*.

For the Tannaic period the recommended edition of Megillat Taanit is Noam, *Megillat Ta'anit*.

Galilean Aramaic: A basic grammar is Stevenson, *Grammar of Palestinian Jewish Aramaic*. A comprehensive description according to Geniza fragments is Fassberg, *A Grammar of the Palestinian Targum Fragments*. Kutscher, *Studies in Galilean Aramaic* deals with primary issues in the research of this dialect.

Babylonian Aramaic: Levias, *A Grammar of the Aramaic Idiom*. Two books describe the Yemenite tradition: Kara, *Babylonian Aramaic in the Yemenite Manuscripts* is based on manuscripts, and Morag, *Babylonian Aramaic: The Yemenite Tradition* is based on the oral tradition. Juusola, *Linguistic Pecu-*

---

[99] As in פִּסְחָא הוּא קֳדָם ה' (Onk Exod 12:11), and similarly in Syriac: פֶּצחָא. This form is confirmed also from the *plene* spelling common in talmudic literature, as in אימר פיסחא "the Passover lamb" (yMeg 1, 72b).
[100] For the status of Aramaic in Modern Hebrew see Bar-Asher, 'Place of Aramaic'.

liarities describes the language of the epigraphic material, and M. Morgenstern, *Jewish Babylonian Aramaic in Geonic Responsa* is a description of the Geonic Language.

The most important and up-to-date dictionaries of the last two dialects are Sokoloff, *A Dictionary of Jewish Palestinian Aramaic*; idem, *A Dictionary of Jewish Babylonian Aramaic*.

The best texts of Rabbinic Literature appear in the site of the Academy of the Hebrew Language: http://hebrew-treasures.huji.ac.il/ according to carefully chosen mss.

Chapter Twenty

Rabbinic Knowledge of Greek

Daniel Sperber

That some people in Palestine spoke Greek during the Greco-Roman and Byzantine periods cannot be doubted.[1] Not merely because there are well over a thousand Greek words in rabbinic literature,[2] for this in itself is no clear indication of the knowledge of the spoken language. After all, there are over a thousand Yiddish words – many of Hebrew origin – in German,[3] but no one would suggest that Germans speak Yiddish. The real question is: who spoke Greek and how much?

Levels of Greek

Clearly there was a greater knowledge of the Greek language among the aristocratic[4] literati,[5] the rabbinic and priestly class, and among the monied urban

[1] I have not discussed the place of Latin, which was much less in use. See below n9.
[2] Of course, every dictionary dealing with rabbinic literature must deal with Greek, and to a lesser extent Latin, loanwords. For a survey of the lexical literature in this field, see Brisman, *History and Guide*, 110-114, 214-216. For the most important studies see below, 'Select Bibliography'. Lieberman, *Greek* was given an important critical review by Alon, 'Ha-Yavanit be-Erets Yisrael ha-yehudit', but Lieberman's conclusions have withstood the passage of time and criticism. See also Sevenster, *Do You Know Greek?*, 60.
[3] See Althaus, *Kleines Lexikon*.
[4] Rabban Shimon (son of Rabban Gamliel the Prince) tells us (bSot 49b) that 'There were a thousand young men in my father's house; five hundred of them studied Tora, while the other five hundred studied Greek wisdom.' Lieberman, *Greek*, 1 wrote: 'This is the firsthand evidence that an academy of Greek wisdom existed in Jewish Palestine under the auspices of the Patriarch. It was established in the beginning of the second century [CE] for the purpose of facilitating the relations between the house of the Patriarch and the Roman government.' The same Rabban Shimon tell us (yMeg 1:11, 71c) that there was an examination of which language the Tora could be translated into, and the findings were that it could only be faithfully translated into Greek.
[5] R. Yonatan, third cent. CE, is of the opinion that Greek is suitable for *zemer*, meaning song or poetry (yMeg 1:11, 71b), at which Lieberman, *Greek*, 21 observed: 'Only a man who knew the

dwellers, than among the rural communities.[6] So too, inhabitants of the large, partially Hellenized cities, with centers of Roman administration, like Tiberias and Caesarea, who had greater contact with the Roman army and bureaucracy, would of necessity have required a working knowledge of Greek. Thus, on the one hand, R. Abbahu, who lived in Caesarea (died 309) and had extensive connections with the local administration, must have had a fine command of the Greek language. This is evident from a passage in Genesis Rabba:

> They (gentiles) asked R. Abbahu: From where do you know that a child formed [to be born] after seven months [of pregnancy] can live? He replied to them: From your own [language] I will prove it to you: זיטא איפטא איטא אכטו, *zita epta ita okhto*. (GenR 14,2 p127)

This enigmatic passage has been successfully decoded as follows: ζῇ τὰ ἑπτὰ [μᾶλλον] ἢ τὰ ὀκτώ, meaning: 'Infants of seven months are more likely to survive than those of eight.' This is a very clever wordplay, since ζ = 7 and η = 8.[7] Only one with a considerable degree of linguistic competence could formulate such a clever response. And indeed, this is in no way surprising, since in

---

Greek literary style well could express an opinion on the superior suitability of Greek for the genre of poetry.' R. Abbahu taught in the name of R. Yohanan: 'A man is permitted to teach his daughter Greek, if it serves her as an ornament' – meaning that (thus Lieberman): 'Greek literature only, and not vulgar Greek, could serve as an ornament to young ladies of social standing...' (yPea 1:1, 15c; Lieberman, *Greek*, 24). See also Sevenster, *Do You Know Greek?*, 183f on Greek as a language of trade; *ib.* 186 on its use in the rural areas.

[6] Lieberman, *Greek*, 2 writes: 'Probably even the peasants knew a limited practical every-day vocabulary of Greek...' Thus, for example, many plants have Greek names in rabbinic literature (see Löw's index in Krauss, *Lehnwörter* 2, 626-267), and similarly there are a number of such Greek agricultural terms (*ib.* 636). Note also the Babatha letters from the South, see Lewis, *Documents*.

[7] See Lieberman, *Greek*, 22f with bibliography. Lieberman (*ib.* 22) comments as follows: 'Perhaps they were stimulated by the Haggada stating that all prophets were born after seven months of pregnancy [MidrGad Exod 2:2, p24], and they taunted R. Abbahu by questioning the survival of these children.' I would question this suggestion, in view of the fact that in antiquity seven-month children were regarded as something very special. Thus, in Pseudo-Philo 23:8 (ed and transl. M. Jacobson, Leiden 1996, vol 1, p9) we read: 'I gave him Isaac in the womb of her who bore him and commanded... to restore him quickly and to give him back to me in the seventh month. Therefore, every woman who gives birth in the seventh month, her son will live, because upon him I summoned my glory and revealed the new age'. Jacobson (*ib.* vol 2, p721) refers us to bRH 11a, that Isaac was a seven-month child, and to Van der Horst, *ETL* 54 (1978) 346-360, on seven-month children in ancient literature. Apollo and Dionysus were born in the seventh month; see Lucian, Dial. deor. 9.2; Arnob., Adv. nat. 3.10; Pind., Pyth. argum. 1; Schol. Kallim. h. Del. 251, etc, cited by Cook, *Zeus* 2, 1237. See further Kerenyi, *Dionysus*, 106 n197, referring to Ovid, *Metamorphosis* 3, 308-312; Hyginus, Fabulae 179; Diodorus Siculus 1.234; cf Kerenyi *ib.* 295. See also Dawkins, 'Modern Carnival', 196. Finally, see Cook, *Zeus* 1, 750: Antiochos I of Commagene was a seven-month child. In view of the above, it seems more plausible to suggest that the pagans asked R. Abbahu if the Jews had any rational explanation or tradition relating to the viability of seven-month premature births. See also my article '7...in jüdischen Gesetzen und Gebräuchen', 51f.

Caesarea it would appear that Greek was the predominant language. Thus we read in the Yerushalmi:

> R. Levi bar Haita (fourth cent. CE) went to Caesarea [and] heard them declaiming the Shema אילוניסטין (*Ellenistin* i.e. in Greek). He wanted to stop them. R. Yosa heard [what R. Levi wished to do] and was angered. He stated: So say I: He who does not know to read אשורית (*Ashurit* i.e. in Hebrew), should he not say it (the Shema) at all? Rather, he may fulfil his duty (and say it) in any language he knows. (ySot 7:1, 21b)

From here we learn that in the Hellenized city of Caesarea, there were Jews who recited that main passage in the daily prayer service in Greek.

On the other hand, as Lieberman wrote, in the similarly Hellenized city of Scythopolis (Beth Shean), 'Eusebius informs us that Proconius (around 286 CE) was *a reader and interpreter from Greek into Aramaic...*' Apparently, in the late second century CE it was necessary to render a Greek passage in Aramaic before the people could understand it.'[8]

From the above we may deduce that there was a considerable diversity in the degree of knowledge of Greek, depending on time, place and social class. This having been said, we can still state with a goodly degree of certainty that a large portion of the population in Greco-Roman and Byzantine Palestine knew Greek – and not only Greek, but also Hebrew and Aramaic. So, actually many were trilingual, frequently mixing together these three languages.[9] However, among the three languages Greek often found a very prominent place. Thus, R. Yehuda the Prince says: 'Why speak Syriac [Aramaic] in Palestine? Talk either Hebrew or Greek' (bSot 49b). Likewise, the majority of recorded

---

[8] Lieberman, *Greek*, 2, referring to Mart. Pal., Syriac version, ed Cureton p4. See also Alon's additional remark, 'Ha-Yavanit be-Erets Yisrael he-yehudit', 275.

[9] Lieberman *ib*. By the sixth century CE the degree of Hellenization was so advanced that in the synagogue donated by one Leontis there is a mosaic floor, one of whose panels features scenes from Homer's Odyssey, while a second depicts the god of the Nile together with Nilotic motifs, a series of animals and fish, and also a symbolic representation of Alexandria with its customary Nilometer and between these two panels is Leontis' dedicatory inscription. For the inscription, see *Lifshitz, Donateurs et fondateurs*, 68. On this synagogue, see Levine, *Ancient Synagogue*, 200f. On Beth Shean in general and its archeological remains, see Stern, *New Encyclopedia*, 198-226.

inscriptions in Roman Palestine are in Greek, between 50-60 per cent,[10] although most of them are 'in very poor and vulgar Greek'.[11]

However, there are inscriptions which are written in fine literary Greek, and even in poetic form.[12] Thus, for example, a funerary inscription from Beth Shearim,[13] first half of the second century CE, read as follows:

> I, the son of Leontius, lie dead, Justus, the son of Sappho, who, having plucked the fruit of all wisdom, left the light, my poor parents in endless mourning, and my brothers too, alas, in my Beth Shearim. And having gone to Hades, I, Justus, lie here with many of my own kindred, since mighty fate so willed. Be of good courage, Justus, no one is immortal.[14]

The importance of this inscription lies not only in the fact that it is written in alternating dactylic hexameters and pentameters (disticha), as is used in epigrams, but rather that it constitutes clear proof that 'the Palestinian Jews were not only familiar with the Greek language but also with Greek literature, for the poem is full of Homer's phraseology and diction...'.[15] Note also the names: Justus, Sappho, Leontius, fine Hellenized names, and the fact that Justus has no problem using the terms Ἄδης – Hades, and Μοῖρα – Fate. Indeed, it is of interest to note that around 30 per cent of names found in Palestinian sources

---

[10] See Spolsky, 'Triglossia and Literacy'. His study actually covers much more than the first century; it covers much of the period of the Second Temple and the Roman period. See also the remarks in Sperber, *Dictionary*, 25. See further Black, *Aramaic Approach*, 15ff., 47-49, who concludes that in first century CE Palestine there were four languages in use: 'Greek was the speech of the educated "Hellenized" classes and the medium of the cultural and commercial intercourse between Jew and foreigner; Latin was the language of the army of occupation...; Hebrew, the sacred tongue of Jewish scriptures, continued to provide the lettered Jew with an important means of literary expression and was cultivated as a spoken tongue in the learned coteries of the Rabbis; Aramaic was the language of the people of the land and, together with Hebrew, provided the chief literary medium of the Palestine Jew of the first century' (Sevenster, *Do you know Greek?* 183). This seems to be a fair description for the whole of the Roman period, and the Byzantine period, though the use of Latin among Jews was minimal, and probably even decreased during the Byzantine period. Most Latin loanwords came in rabbinic parlance via the medium of Greek (see Krauss, *Lehnwörter* 2, index 681-684). Latin inscriptions are six times less numerous than Greek (Van der Horst, *Epitaphs*, 34). See, e.g., Krauss, *Lehnwörter* 2, 306 in Löw's corrections, *s.v.* אטרן = οὐετερανοί, and not בטרן or וטרן from Latin *veterani*. Note also –ion (or –in) terminations in Latin words, instead of –ium; e.g., *ib.* 349b, *s.v.* מקטורין, מקטורין for *amictorium*, etc. Cf Daris, *Lessico Latino*. Likewise, only about 10 per cent of names are from Latin, as opposed to around 30 pct. from Greek: Ilan, *Lexicon*, 54.

[11] See Van der Horst, *Epitaphs*, 23. For a discussion of the 'use' of Greek Jewish inscriptions, cf above Jonathan Price and Haggai Misgav, chapter 14.

[12] Van der Horst *ib.* 23.

[13] Schwabe – Lifshitz, *Beth She'arim* 2, 45-51.

[14] Van der Horst, *Epitaphs*, 151.

[15] *Ib.* 151f. He points out that l. 2, where Justus claims to have 'plucked the fruit of all wisdom', πάσης σοφίας, 'seems to indicate not only Jewish wisdom (i.e. Tora study) but also Greek learning...' He also notes (following Schwabe-Lifshitz) that, 'in this one... pentameter concepts from two different worlds meet and are combined'.

between 330 BCE and 200 CE are Greek,[16] and probably if the statistics were extended to include the Byzantine period, the percentage would be greater.

And in yet another funerary inscription (third century CE) from Beth Shearim, of one Kartēría, brought to burial by her daughter Zenobia,[17] in a mixture of dactyles and trochees there is once again much Homeric phraseology and diction.[18]

We have then seen indications of the knowledge of Homer's literature and motifs both in epigraphic sources and mosaic remains. Indeed, the Homeric corpus is directly referred to in rabbinic literature, such as in this first cent. CE report from the Mishna:

> The Sadducees say, 'We cry out against you, O ye Pharisees, for ye say, "The holy scriptures render the hands unclean, [and] the writings of Hamiras do not render the hands unclean".' Rabban Yohanan ben Zakkai said, 'Have we naught against the Pharisees save this? – for lo, they say, "The bones of an ass are clean, and the bones of Yohanan the High Priest are unclean." ...He said to them, 'Even so the Holy Scriptures, as is our love for them so is their uncleanliness; [whereas] the writings of Hamiras (*Homeros*) which are held in no account do not render the hands unclean.'[19]

Furthermore, scattered throughout rabbinic literature there are traces of Homeric phrases and motifs.[20] Thus, in EcclR 9,11 the swiftness of Asahel is described as follows: 'He used to run on the ears of corn and they were not broken', a phrase that occurs verbatim in Homer (Iliad 20:227), where he speaks of the half-divine horses of Erichtonias: 'They would run over the topmost ears of ripened corn and did not break them.'[21] Lieberman summarizes his findings as follows:[22] '...Although rabbinic acquaintance with the Homeric epics cannot be proved, the ensemble of all the abovementioned sources[23] gives

---

[16] See Ilan, *Lexicon*, 55.

[17] Schwabe & Lifshitz *Beth She'arim* 2, no. 183, p76-81; Van der Horst, *Epitaphs*, 152f.

[18] Van der Horst, *Epitaphs*, 153.

[19] mYad 4:6 (translation Danby p784 with slight changes). I have followed ms Parma (mYad 4:6) המירס; cf ms Vienna (tYad 2:19) המורים. See Lieberman, *Hellenism*, 105-111, where he examines all the relevant sources, showing that this term should be understood as referring to the Homeric writings. See further ySan 10:1, 28a; bHul 60b; MidrPs 1,1 Buber p9.

[20] See, for example, what I wrote in my article, 'Studies in Greek and Latin Loanwords', on the word καταῖτυξ.

[21] Lieberman, *Hellenism*, 113f, although he points out that this figure may have reached the rabbis from some orator, or they may have read it in some Jewish apocryphon composed by a Hellenistic Jew. The phrase is also found in Oppian, Cynegetica 1, 230, ed Loeb p29 (third cent. CE), and in a slightly different form in Virgil, Aen. 7, 808 (cf. Macrobius, Saturn. 5.8.4), as noted by Lieberman *ib*.

[22] *Ib*. 114.

[23] *Ib*. 113. He shows that the rabbis mention the Siren by name (Sifra Weiss 49b); Lieberman *ib*. 183), the centaurs (GenR 23:6, p227), etc. See further Sevenster, *Do You Know Greek?* 59, who also doubts any direct knowledge of the Iliad and the Odyssey. See my (somewhat unfair) review of this book in *Leshonenu* 24 (1970) 225-227. However, we should not go as far as did A.A. Halevy, in his various works, who found Homeric and other Greek mythological motifs throughout

the impression that some of the Rabbis who knew Greek most likely did read Homer.'

Legal and Economic Terms

While there may be doubt as to direct rabbinic knowledge of Homeric literature, there is no doubt that they had (some) direct knowledge of Roman legal sources in Greek. Thus, Lieberman[24] has identified in a rabbinic homily by the fourth century Palestinian scholar R. Berekhia, a quotation from a law well known in his time. The rabbi expounded Gen 12:17, 'And God plagued Pharaoh and his house with great plagues', by saying: על דטלמסן למגע בסמא דמטרונ'[25], 'Because he dared touch [seize] the body of a matron [Sarah],' or in Lieberman's reconstruction, ἐτόλμησε ματρώνης σώματος ἅψασθαι. Lieberman compared this with a statement by Valerius Maximus (first cent. CE), who describing the legal status of the Roman matron writes: *in ius uocanti matronam corpus eius attingere non permisserunt*.[26] In Justinian's Novellae 134.9 this reads:

καὶ σωματικαῖς πονaῖς αὐτὸν καθυποβάλλεσθαι... ἐπειδὴ πρόσωπον ἐλεύθερον ὑπὲρ χρέους ἐτόλμησε κατασχεῖν – and corporal punishment shall be inflicted upon him... since he dared seize a free person for debts.

Lieberman continues that though R. Berekhia did not preach in Greek, but rather in a mixture of Greek and Aramaic, he did quote part of a law in its original form, and his audience – presumably in the synagogue during a Sabbath sermon – apparently understood, not only the language, but also the legal allusion, catching the play of words associated with the biblical verse and the law, and Berekhia's innovative interpretation.

Likewise the phrase in yRH 1:3, 57a, in a statement by R. Elazar (ben Pedat, third cent. CE): פרא בסיליוס אונומוס אוגרפוס may be transcribed: παρὰ βασιλέως ὁ νόμος ἄγραφος (or: οὐ γραφός),[27] 'For the king the law is unwritten (or: not written)'. This was a well-known Greek proverb. Again, what is significant here for us was that R. Eleazar in third century Tiberias is quoting *in Greek* a Greek legal proverb, and presumably his audience understood it, and when the rabbis used to give an example of two witnesses, they

---

the aggada. Cf his *Olama shel ha-aggada*, and my cautionary remarks in *The Jewish Review* 28, March 1973, p6.

[24] Lieberman, *Greek*, 39-43, referring to yKet 7 end, 31d. One must read the whole passage to appreciate both Berekhia's and Lieberman's brilliance.

[25] On this word see what I remarked in *Leshonenu* 64 (2002) 345f.

[26] Factorum dictorum memorabilium 2.1.

[27] Lieberman, *Hellenism*, 37f. Sara Mandell, 'Did Saul Lieberman Know Latin or Greek?' rejected Lieberman's interpretation of this passage as violating the norms of Greek. However, Lieberman's explanation makes contextual sense, which hers does not. See Jacobson, 'Did Saul Lieberman Know Greek and Latin?', 22, and Marblestone, 'Lieberman φιλόλογος'.

would talk of Gaius and Lucius (see below note 66), and not merely Reuven and Shimon.

Not only did the sages have a fondness for the use of legal phrases, and their interjection into a Hebrew-Aramaic statement, but apparently the use of such terminology was common among the general populace. Thus in yNed 3:3, 38a, we read in the name of R. Hela (fourth cent. CE) that: 'It is usual for a person (כן אורחא דבר נשא) to say to his fellow: כורוסתי בייה' – read: כריזסתי בייה, which transcribed into Greek reads: χαρίζασθαι βία, meaning, 'I give you perforce'. Would that be the way a person would state to his friend in a deed of gift that he is giving him a present against his will? Here R. Hela was alluding to a very common legal formula in deeds and gifts: ὁμολογῶ χαρίζεσθαί σοι, adding βία,[28] and claiming that this was current phraseology in his circles.

And indeed, it seems as though people, even in the marketplace, would throw in Greek words as part of their jargon. Thus, in LamR to Lam 1:1, we read about a trader haggling over the sale of a large consignment of peppers, and he is asked by a prospective purchaser: מזבן את קטלפטא?, 'Will you sell it κατὰ λεπτά,[29] in small amounts?'[30]

Furthermore, Jews would write, or have scribes write for them legal documents in Greek. Thus, in yBB 10:1, 17c we read:

> A document passed from R. Huna to R. Shammai in which ογδοη- was blurred and -κοντα was clear. R. Huna said to R. Shammai: Go and see which is the lowest number in Greek that -κοντα is combined with. He went out and said: It is τριάκοντα (thirty). When the litigants left R. Huna remarked: That party wanted to gain thirty [by the erasure] and lost twenty.

In other words, the creditor, who was obviously Jewish and who had come to a Jewish court, wanted to get ὀγδοήκοντα (eighty), having apparently erased πεντήκοντα (fifty). But R. Huna awarded him the minimum amount with which the suffix -κοντα could be combined, viz. τριάκοντα (thirty), so that the creditor lost twenty.[31] Lieberman points out that both these sages were of Babylonian origin and immigrated to Palestine, and hence, had not (yet) ac-

---

[28] Lieberman, *Greek*, 44. See, e.g., P. Grenf. II. 68³ (247 CE): ὁμολογῶ χαρίζεσθ[αι] σοὶ χάριτι ἀναφαιρέτῳ καὶ ἀμετανόητῳ... See Moulton & Milligan, *Vocabulary*, 684a *s.v.* χαρίζομαι. On ὁμολογία see Pringsheim, *Law of Sale*, 36, 109f, 395; Walter Jones, *Law and Legal Theory*, 221f; Taubenschlag, *Law of Greco-Roman Egypt*, 293f and index p786a *s.v.* ὁμολογία.

[29] The word appears in papyrological sources with a slightly different meaning. See Liddell – Scott – Jones, *Lexicon*, 898a *s.v.* κατάλεπτον, giving κατάλεπτα as 'petty cash', referring to P. Teb 120.85 (1st cent. BCE), P.Oxy.1729.6.13 (4th cent. CE).

[30] Ed Buber p44 n37; Krauss, *Lehnwörter* 2, 526 *s.v.* קטלפטא.

[31] Pineles, *Darka shel Tora*, 134, was the first correctly to explain this text. So too Jastrow, *Dictionary*, 21, *s.v.* אוגדווייקונטא. Lieberman, *Greek*, 26f, who points to a similar case in a Greek document written in 88 BCE in Persia (E.H. Minns, *Journal of Hellenic Studies* [1915] 28f): δραχμὰς τρία (altered to τεσσαρ) κοντα τειμὴν ἀμπέλου..., on which the editor remarks (p49), 'This is too obvious to be fraudulent'.

quired this foreign language,[32] and therefore had to consult as to the nature of these (to them) foreign terms. Similarly, R. Joshua ben Levi (mid third century CE) was not acquainted with the Greek term διεθέμην, *diethemin*, 'I bequeathed', a term he found in a statement of Rabban Shimon ben Gamliel (tBB 9:14): 'He who writes דיאתימון (i.e. דיאתימין, *diethimin*) in Greek, it is a present' (yBB 8:8, 16c). We have already noted above that Rabban Shimon ben Gamliel knew Greek;[33] it is somewhat more surprising that R. Joshua ben Levi did not understand the term.[34]

The last few examples have come from the area of legal terminology. In this area there is a large concentration of loanwords, around two hundred,[35] perhaps because there were many contacts with the local courts, the *ἀρχή, very frequently referred to in rabbinic literature;[36] they had to meet the ארכי יודיקי: *ἀρχὴ ἰουδικη (from *archi-judix), chief judge;[37] deal with the סקיפטורין: σκέπτωρ, scribe of the court;[38] hire a סניגור: *συνήγωρ, defense attorney,[39] or a קטיגור: *κατήγωρ, prosecutor;[40] register one's אוני, ὠνή or deed of sale,[41] with the אפיקלין: ὀφφικιάλιοι (Lat. *officiales*), officials attending the magistrate,[42] etc.

And quite a number of such words appear both in rabbinic literature and in the New Testament, such as:

> πίστις (Sperber, *Dictionary*, 145-147; cf Danker, *Lexicon*, 818-820);
> διαθήκη (Sperber *ib.* 84-86; Danker *ib.* 228f);
> ὁμολογία (Sperber *ib.* 33; Danker *ib.* 708);
> ὁρκωμόσια (Sperber *ib.* 35, Danker *ib.* 723);
> διάταγμα (Sperber *ib.* 79-81, Danker *ib.* 237).

However, a detailed comparison will show that the meanings are not always identical.

We find a similarly large number of loanwords in areas dealing with bureaucratic administration,[43] with which, unfortunately, people had to have regular recourse. Likewise, with regard to military terminology,[44] presumably

---

[32] Lieberman, *Greek*, 26 n70, referring to yMaas 5:7, 52a; yShab 4, 8a.
[33] A. Gulak, *Tarbiz* 1 (1930) 144f; Lieberman, *Greek*, 26; Sperber, *Dictionary*, 81f.
[34] Moreover, see Lieberman *ib.* n76.
[35] See Sperber, *Dictionary*, and comments in Sperber, *Nautica Talmudica*, 155.
[36] See Sperber, *Dictionary*, 62-65; cf *ib.* 66 *s.v.* ארכיון = ἀρχεῖον, also meaning a court house, office of magistrate.
[37] *Ib.* 65.
[38] *Ib.* 136.
[39] *Ib.* 126-128.
[40] *Ib.* 178-180.
[41] *Ib.* 34. Cf the legal terminology in the chapter on contracts, in this volume.
[42] *Ib.* 60f.
[43] Krauss, *Lehnwörter*, 628-630, Löw's subject indices.
[44] *Ib.* 631f.

because all military affairs were handled by Roman army units garrisoned in Palestine.[45]

Popular Syncretism

What might have been common parlance in those days, readily understood by the audience, and in some cases by the readers, became greatly corrupted over the course of time, due to the faulty transmission of the scribes, since copyists in post Byzantine, i.e. mediaeval Europe, north Africa and other countries, had no knowledge of Greek, and often misread what they were copying. Hence, we sometimes find whole passages in what appears to be Greek embedded in Hebrew texts from the Roman and/or Byzantine period, but which are hopelessly corrupt. Occasionally, by dint or careful research, they can be restored to their original form, and at times are most instructive.

A remarkable example of this phenomenon is that of a five-line passage, clearly in (some kind of) Greek, found in a fifth or even fourth cent. esoteric Hebrew text, belonging to the genre of the Merkava literature entitled Sefer ha-Razim.[46] Because of its importance I shall cite the whole text in its Hebrew transcription, its Greek restoration (according to the editor) and an English translation:[47]

ואחר שתראהו כן תשתחוה ותפול על פניך ארצה והתפלל את התפלה הזאת:

And after you see him, bow down, prostate yourself upon the earth, and pray the following prayer:

אבצבי אנתוליפון היליוס נאטוס אגדור אפיסטוס אקט
קוריפוס איופיסטוס הזפלה טרוכוס אובינוס
קאטאאסיטס קזמונטס סגימוס
פילי פאנטור קירי פומאוס איופוטוס
תיוריונוס אסטראטיוטוס

εὐσεβῶ ἀνατολικόν ῞Ηλιος, ναύτης ἀγαθός, πιστοφύλαξ,
κορυφαῖος εὔπιστος [ὕψιστος], ὅς πάλαι τροχὸν ὄβριμον [οὐράνιον]

---

[45] Interestingly enough, there are also a large number of foreign terms relating to clothing; see ib. 641-643. Could this be in any way connected to the international textile manufacturing facilities and trade in Scythopolis, Tiberias, Usha, etc.? See Heichelheim, *Roman Syria*, 191f.

[46] Margulies, *Sefer ha-Razim*. In his introduction, 23-28, the editor tries to date this text to the third or fourth cent., and the general consensus is between the fourth and fifth cent. CE. He surmises (27) that it was written in Palestine, in a city with a mixed population of Jews and pagans, Christians and Gnostics. The author had perfect command of Hebrew and was educated with knowledge of the Bible but not of talmudic literature. He had access to Alexandrine magical Gnostic material, of which he made generous use. There are, as yet, many points of uncertainty in these conclusions. The book was translated into English by M.A. Morgan, under the title *Sepher ha Razim*, with some improved readings of our passage (p71). See further Shifra Sznol's article, 'Sefer Ha Razim'.

[47] Margulies, *Sefer ha-Razim*, 12, 99; and cf the reading of Sznol ib. 278. The actual details as to which of the readings are more correct is of less importance to us here, than the overall phenomenon of this passage.

καθίτης, κοσμητής [κοσμώντης] ἅγιος,
πολοκράτώρ· πολυπράκτώρ, κύριε, πόμπος εὔφωτος,
τύραννος, ἀστροθητής.

I revere you, Helios, who rises in the east, the good sailor, who keeps faith,
the faithful [most high] leader, who turns the great (or celestial) wheel,
who orders the holiness (of the planets),
who rules over the poles (or who does many things), Lord, radiant leader,
Ruler, who fixes the stars.

The appearance of Helios in the middle of a Jewish, albeit syncretic, text is somewhat surprising, but not overwhelmingly so. For we recall that Helios appears in the center of a zodiacal mosaic floor both in the synagogues of Beth Alpha, Hammath Tiberias, and Sepphoris.[48]

Levine writes, 'Little or no consensus... has been reached with regard to why these signs [of the zodiac] and the figure of Helios were so popular'.[49] Then he offers a variety of possible interpretations, finally making 'an interesting suggestion', that 'the Helios – zodiac motif refers to power of the God of Israel, which will facilitate... redemption'. However, what I found to be most intriguing is the fact that whereas Helios in the synagogue mosaics is mounted upon his *quadriga*-chariot (i.e. drawn by four horses), which is how he is usually portrayed,[50] in the Sefer ha-Razim text he is said to be 'a good sailor' (ναύτης[51] ἀγαθός). It is only in the older (?) Greek sources that one finds him travelling in a golden boat, that was the work of Hephaestus. It would seem, then, that the memory of this less current tradition has survived in the passage.

Yet another shorter passage appears in this same work (on p13, 80). It reads as follows:

ואם בקשתה להתירו השלך מן המים לשמים ג' פעמים
מן הים או מן הנהר אשר אתה עומד עליו ואמור תחת לשונך:
אורודי גריביאל פוטמוס סרגרי טליגוס אספדזופורוס,
התרתי התרתי השקע ושוב לדרכך.
ואמור כן ז' פעמים. וכל דבר עשה בטהרה ותצליח.

---

[48] See Levine's discussion in his *Ancient Synagogue*, 563-596, 572-278, and see index p726a, *s.v.* Helios. See further Goodenough, *Jewish Symbols* 13, index *s.v.* 'Helios', p114f.

[49] Levine *ib.* 576, following Weiss – Netzer, *Promise and Redemption*, 34-39.

[50] He makes his nightly voyage with horses and a chariot, first described in the Homeric hymn on Helios (9.15), and which are described in minute detail by later poets (Ovid, Met. 106; Hygin. Fab.193; Schol. ad Eur. Phoen 3; Pindar, Ol. 7.71). See Smith, *Dictionary* 2, 375b. See further Cook, *Zeus* 1, 200 n6, 226f; index 813a, *s.v.* Helios.

[51] Preferable to Sznol's ναύτος.

Transliterated into Greek, the formula, which we have italicized, reads:

ἀόρατε κύριε βουήλ,[52] ποτ᾽ ἡμᾶς ἄκριε, τελικός ἀσπιδηφόρος.

We translate as follows:

And if you wish to loose[53] him, throw from the water three times towards the heavens,
[or ?] from the sea or from the river over which you stand, and say under your tongue:
Bouel the unseen Lord, he is for us a haven, bearing the perfect shield;
I have loosed, I have loosed, sink down and go your way.
And say it seven times, and every thing do in [a state of] purity, and you will succeed.

There are a number of Greek phrases scattered throughout this text, all related to Greco-Egyptian magical formularies, such as:

כרתים ירטיקון, χάρτης ἱερατικόν, hieratic papyrus;
בזמירנא מלנון, σμυρνόμελαν, a mixture of ink and myrrh used in magic;
פסוכרופורון, ψυχροφόρον, a lead tablet made out of a water-pipe used for amuletic purposes.[54]

Some of these words appear in the directions given to the user-client, such as, 'Take a *psuchrophoron* and write on it the names of the following angels...'[55] They must have been understandable to the reader, be he the 'client' or the magician. The longer texts were, presumably, unintelligible to the general public, but perhaps made some sort of sense to the magician. But, in any case, it is well known that magical formularies respected no borders, and were used even if they could not be understood, as they would serve as *glossolalia.*[56]

Yohanan Levy found fragments of additional Greek phrases in yet another esoteric work from the early rabbinic period (third-fourth cent.) called Hekhalot Rabbati.[57] Here we shall bring just one such example. At the end of chap. 18 l. 6, the charioteers argue about the meaning of the name of the angel Dumiel. One of them asks:

[52] Apollod. 2.5.10; Athenaeus 9.469; Eustath. ad Hom.p. 1632; Smith, *Dictionary* 2, 375b. See further Cook, *Zeus* 1, 358 n3, on the solar barque in Egyptian religion, of which there are few traces in Greek literature and art. However, he refers us to a Apulean Krater from Basilicata, now in the Louvre, which has Helios and Silene in a four-horse chariot, which rises out of a boat(!). This would seem to be a conflation of the two myths.

[53] See Margulies' note to l. 234 *ib.*, that this was Prof. Morton Smith's suggestion, rather than simply transposing the letters to read גבריאל, Gabriel, who figures frequently in magical texts. However, Bouel also is to be found in Preisendanz' PGM 1. p106 l. 972, etc., as Margulies notes there.

[54] Equivalent to Greek ἀπόλυσις, found frequently in magical amulets.

[55] Margulies, *Sefer ha-Razim*, 1-4.

[56] *Ib.* 3.

[57] See discussion in Sperber, *Magic and Folklore*, 81-98. Cf also chap. 11 on 'Mystical Texts' in this volume.

And is his name דומיאל, Dumiel? Is not אביר גהידרייהם his name? ... Said R. Yishmael: So said R. Nehunia ben ha-Kana: Each and every day a heavenly voice calls out from the firmament Aravit and announces and says: In the heavenly court they say thus: טעוס וברמן צהז פורי גש שגעשת [Lord God of Israel]. Call him Dumiel according to my name. And what I say and remain silent, so too Dumiel.

The letters printed in Hebrew look at first sight to be gibberish. But Levy transcribed and decoded the first Greek phrase as follows: אביר גהידרייהם – ἀήρ γῆ ὕδωρ [πῦρ], 'air, earth, water, [fire]'; and the second one: ... טעוס וברמן שגעשת – θεὸς οὐρανῶν ... σιγή ἐστι, 'God of heaven ... is silence.' Dumiel, of course, is the Hebrew for 'The silence of God', or 'The silent God'. However, at the gate of the next firmament the charioteers (in the Merkava) have to call the angel gatekeeper by a Greek name!

Within the framework of this chapter and the constraints of space we cannot hope to cover all aspects of rabbinic Greek, such as the phonology and morphology of Palestinian *koine* and rabbinic dialectology,[58] regional variations between Judea and the Galilee,[59] varying degrees of literacy (alluded to above), different periods of time,[60] and so forth. And when we attempt to assess the degrees of knowledge of Greek on the bases of literary and epigraphic evidence,[61] we must take into account different forms of spelling and orthographic interchanges, influence of Aramaic (and Latin, to a lesser extent) on terminations, syntactical oddities, and straightforward mistakes due to insufficient knowledge of the language.[62] Thus, for example, in Genesis Rabba we read as follows:

'...She shall be called Woman (אישה, *isha*), because she was taken out of Man (איש, *ish*)' (Gen 2:23). From here you learn that the Tora was given in Hebrew. R. Pinhas and R. Hilkia in the name of R. Simon (Lod, late third cent. CE): Just as [the Tora] was given in Hebrew, so too the world was created in Hebrew. Have you ever heard *gini ginia, ita iteta, anthrope anthropia, gavra gavreta*. Rather *ish* and *isha*. Why so? For they are similar-sounding words (לשון נופל על לשון). (GenR 18,23 p164; and parallel 31,8 p281)

איתתא, *iteta* is woman in Aramaic, but there is no masculine form *איתא, *ita*. Likewise *gavra* is the Aramaic for man, but it has no feminine complement *gavreta*. *Gini ginia* in our texts makes little sense. It should have read γυνή, a

---

[58] Levy, *Olamot Nifgashim*, 259-265; *Bet ha-Midrasch*, ed Jellinek, vol 3, 83-108; *Otsar Midrashim*, ed Eisenstein, 111f. There is a great deal of literature on this subject. However, I will mention Morton Smith's study, 'Observations on Hekhalot Rabbati'. See also Bohak, 'Remains of Greek Words'.

[59] I touched upon these issues in my 'Greek and Latin Words', 73f. See also Krauss, *Lehnwörter* 1; this pioneering work now requires radical revision.

[60] See remarks on funerary inscriptions in Jerusalem by Sevenster, *Do you know Greek?*, 143-146.

[61] See Sevenster *ib.* 59-61, 177-180.

[62] Note the very poor Greek in numerous funerary inscriptions from Jaffa and Beth Shearim, Sevenster *ib.* 182.

woman, but there is no γυνος (*gini–ginos*), for *ginia*-γυνια could in any case not be a masculine form. So too, what we would have expected is *anthropós-anthrópia*, but not *anthrópe* (vocative?). Furthermore, *anthropós* can actually mean a woman,[63] just as in Laconian Greek *anthrópó* can be a woman. – But, of course, R. Simon would not be acquainted with the Laconian dialect. So apparently this Lyddan scholar knew some Greek, but in a very imperfect manner.[64]

How Much Greek?

Many years ago, Prof. Saul Lieberman wrote a seminal essay entitled: 'How much Greek in Jewish Palestine?'[65] He reformulated the question in his article as follows: 'How much knowledge of the world which surrounded them did the builders of rabbinic Judaism possess?' His answer was: 'We do not know exactly how much Greek the Rabbis knew.[66] They probably did not read Plato and certainly not the pre-Socratic philosophers.[67] Their main interest was centred in Gentile legal studies[68] and their methods of rhetoric. But the rabbis knew enough Greek to prevent them from telling stories about Greek principles and their civil laws. Jewish opinion on the non-Jewish world was the product of knowledge and not of ignorance, and this knowledge was undoubtedly a great asset.'[69]

We have progressed a great deal in the last forty years since his article appeared. We have a wealth of additional epigraphic and other archeological evidence, new literary texts, and better editions of the old texts, much more comparative material, both papyrological and epigraphic, and fine comprehensive dictionaries and reference works, all of which has led us to realize the extreme complexity of the question. Thus, our answer today remains much as it did forty years ago: 'We do not know *exactly* how much Greek the rabbis

---

[63] See Liddell – Scott – Jones, *Lexicon*, 141b, *s.v.* ἄνθρωπος.

[64] It should be borne in mind that during the 3rd century CE Lod was a predominantly Jewish city, with a relatively small pagan and Christian population. See Rosenfeld, *Lod and its Sages*, 182; Schwartz, *Lod (Lydda)*, 105-108, referring to the Syriac version of Eusebius' De Martyribus Palestinae (c. 308 CE), according to whom Lod was 'teaming with population, of which all the inhabitants were Jews' (ed Cureton 1861, p29, Syriac p27 translation).

[65] Lieberman, *Biblical and Other Studies*, 123-141.

[66] Similarly Sevenster, *Do you know Greek*, 60 writes: 'Just how deep the knowledge of Greek went, is not always clear.'

[67] They seem to have known only of Philo (?) and Oenomos of Gadara (Krauss, *Lehnwörter* 2, 6f, *s.v.* אבנימוס); Lieberman, 'How Much Greek', 129f, where he also notes that 'a general impression of the cynic philosophy was probably conveyed to the Rabbis through personal contact with these esoteric teachers who so much aroused the curiosity of the populace'.

[68] Thus גייס לסקס – Gaius Lucius are fictitious names of witnesses, much as are Reuven and Shimon. See Sperber, *Dictionary*, 73f; Lieberman, *Texts & Studies*, 412.

[69] Lieberman, *Biblical and Other Studies*, 123, 135.

knew', but now our emphasis has shifted to the word 'exactly'. Further research will no doubt refine our state of knowledge.

Select Bibliography

This subject has been discussed a good deal in the scholarly literature. Hower, most of the studies have dealt mainly with the late Second Temple period, and the first century of the common era, although some have also related to the following three or four centuries.

The main studies dealing with the subject are: Fitzmyer, 'Languages of Palestine'; Muussies, 'Greek in Palestine and the Diaspora' (with a fine bibliography, 1060-1064); Rosen, *East and West*, 489-494; Spolsky, 'Triglossia and Literacy'; Barr, 'Hebrew, Aramaic and Greek'; Heszer, *Jewish Literacy*, 227-250 ('Language Usage'); Van der Horst, 'Greek in Jewish Palestine'.

As to Greco-Rabbinic lexicography, the classic pioneering works are: Fürst, *Glossarium Graeco-Hebraeum* and Krauss, *Lehnwörter*. See also my *Dictionary*. An outstanding, though non-systematic, contribution to the field was made by the later Prof. Saul Lieberman, in his many writings, but most especially in his *Greek* and *Hellenism*.

Abbreviations

For ancient Jewish sources, SBL style has largely been used, while omitting the pervasive use of italics. For rabbinic sources, see the following lists. Full references are given in the bibliography.

1. Mishnaic Tractates

Ah	Ahilut (Tosefta)	Mik	Mikwaot
Ar	Arakhin	MK	Moed Katan
Av	Avot	MS	Maaser Sheni
AZ	Avoda Zara	Naz	Nazir
BB	Bava Batra	Ned	Nedarim
Bekh	Bekhorot	Neg	Negaim
Ber	Berakhot	Nid	Nidda
Betsa	Betsa	Oh	Oholot
Bik	Bikkurim	Par	Para
BK	Bava Kamma	Pea	Pea
BM	Bava Metsia	Pes	Pesahim
Dem	Demai	Pis	Pisha (Tosefta)
Ed	Eduyot	RH	Rosh HaShana
Er	Eruvin	San	Sanhedrin
Git	Gittin	Shab	Shabbat
Hag	Hagiga	Shek	Shekalim
Hal	Halla	Shev	Sheviit
Hor	Horayot	Shevu	Shevuot
Hul	Hullin	Sot	Sota
Kel	Kelim	Suk	Sukka
Ker	Keritot	Taan	Taanit
Ket	Ketubbot	Tam	Tamid
Kid	Kiddushin	Tem	Temura
Kil	Kilayim	Ter	Terumot
Kin	Kinnim	Toh	Toharot
Maas	Maasrot	TY	Tevul Yom
Mak	Makkot	Ukts	Uktsin
Makh	Makhshirin	Yad	Yadayim
Meg	Megilla	Yev	Yevamot
Meila	Meila	Yom	Yoma
Men	Menahot	Zav	Zavim
Mid	Middot	Zev	Zevahim

2. Other Sources

AbGur	(Midrash) Abba Gurion	MidrProv	Midrash on Proverbs
AggEsth	Aggadat Esther (List p226, no. 17)	MidrTann	Midrash Tannaim
		Neof	Targum Neofiti (ed Díez-Macho)
ARN a / b	Avot de-R. Natan, version A / B (ed Schechter)	NumR	Numbers Rabba
		Onk	Targum Onkelos
CantR	Canticles Rabba	PanAh	(Midrash) Panim Aherot
CantZ	Canticles Zuta	PesR	Pesikta Rabbati (Friedman)
DER	Derekh Erets Rabba		
DeutR	Deuteronomy Rabba	PesRK	Pesikta de-Rav Kahana (ed Mandelbaum)
DEZ	Derekh Erets Zuta		
EcclR	Ecclesiastes Rabba	PRE	Pirkei de-R. Eliezer
EsthR	Esther Rabba	PsYon	Targum Pseudo-Yonathan (ed Ginsburger)
ExodR	Exodus Rabba		
FrgPTg	Fragments of the Palestinian Targum (Klein, *Genizah Manuscripts*)		
		SamTg	Samaritan Targum
		SER	Seder Eliyahu Rabba
		SEZ	Seder Eliyahu Zuta
FrgTg	Fragmentary Targum	SifDeut	Sifrei Deutronomy
GenAp	Genesis Apocryphon	SifNum	Sifrei Numbers
GenR	Genesis Rabba (ed Theodor-Albeck)	Sifra	Sifra
		SifZDeut	Sifrei Zuta Deuteronomy
Kalla R	Kalla Rabbati	SifZNum	Sifrei Zuta Numbers
KohR	Kohelet Rabba	SOR	Seder Olam Rabba
LevR	Leviticus Rabba (ed Margulies)	SOZ	Seder Olam Zuta
		Tanh	Tanhuma
MegEsth	Midrash Megillat Esther (Horowitz, *Sammlung* 1, 56-75)	TanhB	Tanhuma ed S. Buber
		Tg	Targum
		TgJob	Qumran Job Targum
MegTaan	Megillat Taanit	YalShim	Yalkut Shimoni
MekDeut	Mekhilta Deuteronomy	YalMekh	Yalkut ha-Mekhiri
MekRY	Mekhilta de-R. Yishmael	YFrg	Yerushalmi Fragments from the Genizah (ed Ginzberg)
MekRSbY	Mekhilta de-R. Shimon ben Yohai		
MidrGad	Midrash ha-Gadol	Yon	Targum Yonatan
MidrPs	Midrash Psalms		

3. Manuscripts

ms Antonin	(Mishna) Seder Teharot, Codex Antonin, in Katsh, *Ginze Mishna*, 169-319
ms Cambridge	see Lowe, *The Mishna on which the Palestinian Talmud Rests*
ms Flor	manuscript Florence
ms JTSA	(GenR) manuscript Jewish Theological Seminary of America, ed Abramson
ms K	(Mishna) manuscript Kaufmann (see Beer, *Faksimile-Ausgabe*)

ms Lon	manuscript London
ms Mun	manuscript Munich
ms Oxf	manuscript Oxford
ms Oxf-Bodl	manuscript Oxford-Bodleian
ms. Paris	(Mishna) Codex Paris, B.N. 328-329, facsimile, introd M. Bar-Asher, Jerusalem 1973
ms Parma-A	(Mishna) Codex Parma, De Rossi 138, facsimile, Jeruaslem 1970
ms Parma-B	(Mishna) Codex Parma, De Rossi 497, facsimile, introd M. Bar-Asher, Jerusalem 1971
ms Vat	manuscript Vatican

4. Periodicals, Series, Collections

AASOR	Annual of the American Schools of Oriental Research
ANRW	Aufstieg und Niedergang der römischen Welt (ed H. Temporini – W. Haase)
AOT	Charles, Apocrypha of the Old Testament
AJP	American Journal of Philology
AJS Review	Association for Jewish Studies, Review
BAR	Biblical Archaeology Review
BASOR	Bulletin of the American Society of Oriental Research
BJRL	Bulletin of the John Rylands Library
BSOAS	Bulletin of the School of Oriental and African Studies
CBQ	Catholic Bible Quarterly
CII	Frey, Corpus Inscriptionum Iudaicarum
CPJ	Tcherikover – Fuks, Corpus Papyrorum Judaicorum
CRINT	Compendia rerum judaicarum ad Novum Testamentum
DJD 2	Benoit – Milik – de Vaux, Les grottes de Murabba'at
DJD 27	Cotton – Yardeni, Aramaic, Hebrew and Greek Texts from Nahal Hever
DSD	Dead Sea Discoveries
EJ	Encyclopaedia Judaica (Jerusalem 1971-92)
ETL	Ephemerides Theologicae Lovanienses
FJB	Frankfurter judaistische Beiträge
HTR	Harvard Theological Review
HUCA	Hebrew Union College Annual
IEJ	Israel Exploration Journal
IJO I	Noy – Panayotov – Bloedhorn, Inscriptiones Judaicae Orientis 1: Eastern Europe
IJO II	Ameling, Inscriptiones Judaicae Orientis 2: Kleinasien
IJO III	Noy – Bloedhorn, Inscriptiones Judaicae Orientis 3: Syria and Cyprus
IOSCS	International Organization for Septuagint and Cognate Studies
JAAR	Journal of the American Academy of Religion
JAOS	Journal of the American Oriental Society
JIGRE	Noy – Horbury, Jewish Inscriptions of Graeco-Roman Egypt
JIWE	Noy, Jewish Inscriptions from Western Europe
JJS	Journal of Jewish Studies
JJTP	Journal of Jewish Thought and Philosophy
JNES	Journal of Near Eastern Studies
JRS	Journal of Roman Studies

JRSB	Jahresbericht des Rabbiner-Seminars zu Berlin
JQR	Jewish Quarterly Review
JSJ	Journal for the Study of Judaism in the Persian, Hellenistic and Roman Period
JSP	Journal for the Study of the Pseudepigrapha
JSQ	Jewish Studies Quarterly
JSS	Journal of Semitic Studies
JTS	Journal of Theological Studies
KS	Kirjat Sepher
LOW	Müller, Responsen der Lehrer des Ostens und Westens
MGWJ	Monatsschrift für Geschichte und Wissenschaft des Judentums
nF	neue Folge
NS	New Series
OGIS	Dittenberger, Orientis Graeci Inscriptiones Selectae
PAAJR	Proceedings, American Association for Jewish Research
PIASH	Proceedings of the Israeli Academy of Sciences and Humanities
PSBL	Proceedings of the Society of Biblical Literature
PWCJS	Proceedings, World Congress of Jewish Studies
RB	Revue biblique
REJ	Revue des études juives
RQ	Revue de Qumrân
SBLSP	Society of biblical Literature, Seminar Papers
SCI	Scripta Classica Israelica
ScrHier	Scripta Hierosolymitana
SEG	Supplementum Epigraphicum Graecum
SJOT	Scandinavian Journal of the Old Testament
SSI	Gibson, Textbook of Syrian Semitic Inscriptions
STDJ	Studies on the Texts of the Desert of Judah
TSAJ	Texte und Studien zum antiken Judentum
VT	Vetus Testamentum
VTSup	Supplements to Vetus Testamentum
ZAW	Zeitschrift für die alttestamentliche Wissenschaft
ZDPV	Zeitschrift des deutschen Palästina-Vereins
ZHB	Zeitschrift für hebräische Bibliographie (1900-1921: A. Freiman, H. Brody)
ZPE	Zeitschrift für Papyrologie und Epigraphik

Cumulative Bibliography

The subsection 'Midrashic and Medieval Rabbinic Works' primarily regards chapter 3, listing traditional compilations and commentaries and a number of critical text editions. Full data of the latter are found in the section 'Modern Scholarly Literature', although the boundary between both sections may often look arbitrary. In the last section, entries under one author name are listed alphabetically by the first noun in their title.

Text Editions and Translations

Midrashic and Medieval Rabbinic Works

Aggadat Esther, ed S. Buber, Krakau 1897; Vilna 1925

Bereshit Rabba: see Genesis Rabba

Bereshit Rabbati, Ex libro R. Mosis Haddarshan ed Ch. Albek [Albeck], Jerusalem 1940, repr 1967

The Chronicles of Jerahmeel, transl M. Gaster (see also: Sefer ha-Zikhronot)

Commentary on Avoda Zara, R. Yom-Tov of Seville, ed M. Goldstein, Jerusalem 1978

Commentary on Sifra, R. Abraham b. David, in ed Weiss, Vienna 1860

Commentary on Talmudic Aggadoth, Rabbi Azriel of Gerona, ed I. Tishby, Jerusalem 1982

Derashot al ha-Tora, R. Joshua ibn Shuaib, ed Metzger, Jerusalem 1992

Exodus Rabba, see Shemot Rabba

Genesis Rabba: Theodor – Albeck, *Midrash Bereshit Rabba*

Iosippon (Josephus Gorionides), ed Flusser

Kad ha-Kemah, R. Bahya b. Asher, Collected Writings, ed Chavel, Jerusalem 1970

Leviticus Rabba: Margulies, *Wayyikra Rabbah*

Mahzor Vitry, ed S.H. Horowitz, Jerusalem 1963

Megillat Ahimaaz, R. Ahimaaz b. Paltiel, ed B. Klar, Jerusalem 1945

Megillat Setarim, Rav Nissim Gaon, in Qafih, *Collected Papers* 1, 375-442

Menot ha-Levi, R. Solomon Al-Kabez, Venice 1585; Levov 1911

Midrash Ha-Beur, 1-2, ed J. Qafih, Kiryat Ono 1998

Midrash ha-Hefets, ms Brit. Mus. 363

Midrash Megillat Esther, in Horowitz, *Sammlung Kleiner Midrashim*, 47-50; 56-75

Midrash Mishle, ed S. Buber, Vilna 1893; ed Visotzky, New York 1990

Midrash Psalms, ed S. Buber, 1893

Midrash Rabba, Genesis – Deuteronomy, ed E.E. Ha-Levi, 1-8, Tel-Aviv, 1956-1963

Midrash Samuel, ed S. Buber, Krakau 1897

Midrash Tanhuma, ed S. Buber, Vilna 1885

Midrash Tehillim (Shokher Tov), ed S. Buber, Vilna 1891

Midrash Zuta (Suta), ed S. Buber, Berlin 1894

Midrash Yerushalmi al Megillat Esther, in Wertheimer, *Leket Midrashim*, 2b-4a; idem, *Batei Midrashot* 1, 340-343

Mishnat R. Eliezer, ed H.G. Enelowe, New York 1933

Novellae to the Babylonian Talmud, Nahmanides (R. Moshe b. Nahman), ed M. Hirschler, 1-5, Jerusalem 1970-1995

Ot Emet, R. Meir b. Samuel Benveniste, Salonica 1565

Perush Megillat Esther, Rabbenu Avigdor Cohen Zedek, ed Z. Leitner, Jerusalem 1994

Pesikta de-Rav Kahana, ed Mandelbaum

Pirke de Rabbi Eliezer, A Critical Edition, Codex C.M. Horowitz (Hebrew), Jerusalem 1972

Pirke de Rabbi Eliezer, with the commentary of R. David Luria (RaDa"L), Warsaw 1852

Piyyutei Yose ben Yose, Jerusalem 1977

Raschi über den Pentateuch, ed Berliner, Frankfurt/M 1905

Ruth Rabba, ed M.B. Lerner, in idem, *Book of Ruth*

Seder Olam Rabba, with ann. by Jacob Emden, Hamburg 1757

Seder Rav Amram Gaon, ed D. Goldschmidt, Jerusalem 1971

Sefer Agadeta de-Megilla (= Agadat Esther), ed Sh. Y. Halevi, Jerusalem 1994

Sefer Halakhot Gedolot, ed E. Hildesheimer, Jerusalem 1971-80

Sefer ha-Zikhronot of R. Eleazar b. Asher, ed E. Yassif, Tel Aviv 2001 (see: Chronicles of Jerahmeel)

Sefer Minhagim of the School of Rabbi Meir ben Baruch of Rothenburg, ed I. Elfenbein, New York 1938

Sefer Pitron Torah, ed E.E. Urbach, Jerusalem 1978

Sefer Rav Pealim, R. Abraham b. Elijah, Warsaw 1894

Sefer Raviya, ed D. Dablitski, Bnei Brak 2000 (Hebr)

Sefer Rokeach, R. Eleazar of Worms, Esther – Shir Hashirim – Ruth, ed Rabbi Ch. Konyevsky, Bnei Brak 1985

Sefer ve-Hizhir, ed A. Freimann, 1-2, Warsaw & Leipzig, 1873-1880

Shemot Rabba 1-14, ed Shinan

Siddur R. Saadia Gaon, ed I. Davidson – S. Assaf – B.I. Joel, Jerusalem 1941

Sifrei de-Aggadeta al-Megillat Esther, ed S. Buber, Vilna 1886

Sophnath Pa'neah, R. Joseph Bonfils (Tobh ʾElem), ed D. Herzog, 1-2, Heidelberg 1911-1930

Torat ha-Bayyit, R. Solomon b. Adret, repr Jerusalem 1963

Yalkut ha-Mekhiri: Psalms, ed S. Buber, Berdichev 1900

Yalkut Midrashim, vol 1-3, ed I. Deshe Ha-Levi, Safed 2003-2005

Yalkut Shimoni, R. Shimon ha-Darshan, ed Shiloni-Hyman, 1-9, Jerusalem 1973-1991

Targums: Text

Aberbach, M. and Grossfeld, B., *Targum Onqelos to Genesis: A Critical Analysis Together With An English Translation of the Text*, New York 1982

Barnstein, H., *The Targum of Onkelos to Genesis – A Critical Enquiry, Yemen MSS Compared with that of the European Recension*, London 1896

Bernstein, M. J., 'A New Manuscript of "Tosefta Targum"', *PWCJS* 9:1 (1986) 151-157

Berliner, A., *Targum Onkelos*, 1-2, Berlin 1884

Clarke, E.G. *et al.*, *Targum Pseudo-Jonathan of the Pentateuch: Text and Concordance*, Hoboken 1984

Déaut, R. Le – Robert, J. (eds), *Le Targum des Chroniques*, (Analecta Biblica 51) Rome 1971

Díez Macho, A., *Neophyti 1: Targum Palestinense Ms de la Biblioteca Vaticana* 1-6, Madrid-Barcelona 1968-1979

Díez Macho, A., 'Nuevos Fragmentos de Tosefta targumica', *Sefarad* 16 (1956) 313-324

Díez Macho, A., *Targum de Salmos*, Madrid 1982

Díez Merino, L., 'Tosefta targumica a Genesis y Exodo: Biblioteca Complutense de San Bernardo, Ms. 117-Z-15', *Anuario de Filologia* 8 (1982) 137-143

Ginsburger, M., *Pseudo-Jonathan (Thargum Jonathan ben Usiel zum Pentateuch) nach der Londoner Handschrift. Brit. Mus. add. 27031*, Berlin 1903, repr. Hildesheim – New York 1971

Grossfeld, B., *Targum Neofiti 1: An Exegetical Commentary To Genesis: Including Full Rabbinic Parallels*, New-York 2000

Grossfeld, B., *The First Targum to Esther: According to the MS Paris Hebrew 110 of the Bibliothèque Nationale*, New York 1983

Grossfeld, B., *The Targum to the Five Megilloth*, New York 1973

Grossfeld, B., *The Targum Sheni to the Book of Esther: A Critical Edition Based on MS Sassoon 282 with Critical Apparatus*, New York 1994

Heide, A. van der, *The Yemenite Tradition of the Targum of Lamentations: Critical Text and Analysis of the Variant Readings*, Leiden 1981

Kasher, R., *Targumic Toseftot to the Prophets*, Jerusalem 1996 (Hebr)

Levine, E., *The Targum to the Five Megillot: Ruth, Ecclesiastes, Canticles, Lamentations, Esther: Codex Urbinati 1*, Jerusalem 1971

Levine, E., *The Aramaic Version of Ruth*, Rome 1973

Levine, E., *The Aramaic Version of Jonah*, Jerusalem 1975

Levine, E., *The Aramaic Version of Lamentations*, New York 1976

Levine, E., *The Aramaic Version of Qohelet*, New York 1978

Melamed, E.A., 'Targum Megillath Ruth', *Bar-Ilan* 1 (1963) 190-194 (Hebr)

Melamed, R.H., 'The Targum to Canticles According to Six Yemen MSS: Compared With the "Textus Receptus" (ed De Lagarde)', *JQR* 10 (1919-1920) 377-410; 11 (1920-1921) 1-20; 12 (1921-1922) 57-117

Melamed, R.H., *The Targum to Canticles According to Six Yemen MSS: Compared With the 'Textus Receptus' as Contained in De Lagarde's 'Hagiographa Chaldaice'*, Philadelphia 1921

Ploeg, J.P.M. van der – Woude, A.S. van der, *Le Targum de Job de la grotte XI de Qumrân*, Leiden 1971

Sokoloff, M., *The Targum to Job from Qumran Cave XI*, Ramat-Gan 1974

Sperber, A., *The Bible in Aramaic, based on old manuscripts and printed texts*, vol 1: *The Pentateuch According to Targum Onkelos*; vol 2: *The Former Prophets According to Targum Jonathan*; vol 3: *The Latter Prophets According to Targum Jonathan*; vol 4a: *The Hagiographa: Transition from Translation to Midrash*; Leiden 1959-68

Tal, A. (ed), *The Samaritan Targum of the Pentateuch*, vols 1-3, Tel Aviv 1980-83

Techen, G. L., *Das Targum zu den Psalmen* 1-2, Wismer 1896-1907

Targums: Translations

Drazin, I., *Targum Onkelos to Exodus: an English transl. of the text with analysis and commentary*; idem, *...to Leviticus...*; idem, *...to Numbers...*; idem, *...to Deutronomy...*; Hoboken 1982-1990

McNamara, M. *et al.* (eds), *The Aramaic Bible*, Edinburgh / Wilmington:
- vol 1A: M. McNamara, *Targum Neofiti 1: Genesis*, 1992
- vol 1B: M.J. Maher, *Targum Pseudo-Jonathan: Genesis*, 1992
- vol 2: M. McNamara, (notes by R. Hayward), *Targum Neofiti 1: Exodus*; M.J. Maher, *Targum Pseudo-Jonathan: Exodus*, 1994
- vol 3: M. McNamara, (introd and notes by R. Hayward), *Targum Neofiti 1: Leviticus*; M.J. Maher, *Targum Pseudo-Jonathan: Leviticus*, 1994
- vol 4: M. McNamara, *Targum Neofiti 1: Numbers*, 1995
- vol 5A: M. McNamara, *Targum Neofiti 1: Deuteronomy*, 1997
- vol 5B: E.G. Clarke, *Targum Pseudo-Jonathan: Deuteronomy*, with collab by S. Magder, 1998
- vol 6: B. Grossfeld, *The Targum Onqelos to Genesis*, 1988
- vol 7: B. Grossfeld, *The Targum Onqelos to Exodus*, 1988
- vol 8: B. Grossfeld, *The Targum Onqelos to Leviticus and The Targum Onqelos to Numbers*, 1988
- vol 9: B. Grossfeld, *The Targum Onqelos to Deuteronomy*, 1988
- vol 10: D.J. Harrington – A.J. Saldarini, *Targum Jonathan of the Former Prophets*, 1987
- vol 11: B. Chilton, *The Isaiah Targum*, 1987
- vol 12: R. Hayward, *The Targum of Jeremiah*, 1987
- vol 13: S.H. Levey, *The Targum of Ezekiel*, 1987
- vol 14: K.J. Cathcart – R.P. Gordon, *The Targum of the Minor Prophets*, 1989
- vol 15: C. Mangan – J.F. Healey – P.S. Knobel, *The Targum of Job / The Targum of Proverbs / The Targum of Qohelet*, 1991
- vol 16: D.M. Stec, *The Targum of Psalms*, 2004
- vol 17A: P.S. Alexander, *The Targum of Canticles*, 2003
- vol 18: B. Grossfeld, *The Two Targums of Esther*, 1991
- vol 19: D.R.G. Beattie – J. Stanley McIvor, *The Targum of Ruth – The Targum of Chronicles*, 1994

Modern Scholarly Literature

Abraham ben Elijah of Vilna, *Rav pealim*, Warsaw 1894 (Hebr)

Abramson, S., 'Arbaa inyanot be-Midrashei ha-Halakha', *Sinai* 74 (1974) 1-13

Abramson, S., *Rav Nissim Gaon – Five Works*, Jerusalem 1965 (Hebr)

Abramson, S., *Center and Periphery in the Geonic Period*, Jerusalem 1965 (Hebr)

Abramson, S., 'A New Fragment of the Mekhilta de-Rabbi Shimeon Bar Yohai', *Tarbiz* 41 (1972) 361-372 (Hebr)

Abramson, S., 'Rabbi Joseph Rosh ha-Seder', *KS* 26 (1950) 72-95 (Hebr)

Abramson, S., *Rav Nissim Gaon – Five Works*, Jerusalem 1965 (Hebr)

Abusch, R., 'Rabbi Ishmael's Miraculous Conception: Jewish Redemption History in Anti-Christian Polemic', in A.H. Becker – A. Yoshiko Reed (eds), *The Ways That Never Parted; Jews and Christians in Late Antiquity and the Early Middle Ages*, Tübingen 2003, 307-343

Afik, I., *Hazal's Perception of the Dream*, diss Bar-Ilan U 1990 (Hebr)

Aharoni, Y., *The Land of the Bible*, trans and ed A.T. Rainey, London 1979

Aharoni, Y. – Avi-Yonah, M. – Rainey, A.F. – Safrai, Z., *The Macmilllan Atlas*, Jerusalem 1993

Albani, M., 'Horoscopes in Qumran Scrolls', in P.W. Flint – J.C. Vanderkam (eds), *The Dead Sea Scrolls after Fifty Years*, Leiden 1999, 279-330

Albeck, Ch., 'Apocryphal Halakhah in the Palestinian Targums and the Aggadah', in J.L. Fishman (ed), *Jubilee Volume to B.M. Lewin*, Jerusalem 1940, 93-104 (Hebr)

Albeck, Ch., *Ha-Derashot*, see: Zunz, *Vorträge*

Albeck, Ch., 'Einleitung und Register zum Bereschit Rabba', in Theodor – Albeck, *Bereshit Rabba* 3, 1-138

Albeck, H., *Introduction to the Mishna*, Jerusalem – Tel-Aviv 1959 (Hebr)

Albeck, Ch., *Introduction to the Talmud, Babli and Yerushalmi*, Tel Aviv 1969 (Hebr)

Albeck, Ch., *Mehkarim ba-baraita ve-Tosefta ve-yahasan la-Talmud*, Jerusalem 1944 (Hebr)

Albeck, Ch., 'Midrash Vayikra Rabba', in A. Marx (ed), *Louis Ginzberg Jubilee Volume*, New York 1945, Hebrew section 25-43 (Hebr)

Albeck, Ch., 'Zu den neueren Ausgaben halachischer Midraschim', *MGWJ* 75 (1931) 401-412

Albeck, Ch., *Shisha sidrei Mishna* 1-6, Jerusalem - Tel Aviv 1952-58 and repr (Hebr)

Albeck, Ch., *Untersuchungen über die halakischen Midraschim*, Berlin 1927

Albeck, Ch., 'Die vierte Eulogie des Tischgebetes', *MGWJ* 78 (1934) 430–437

Alexander, P.[S.], 'Bavli Berakhot 55a-57b: The Talmudic Dreambook in Context', *JJS* 46 (1995), 230-248

Alexander, P.S., 'Comparing Merkavah Mysticism and Gnosticism: An Essay in Method', *JJS* 35 (1984) 1-18

Alexander, P.S., 'The Demonology of the Dead Sea Scrolls', in P.W. Flint, J.C. Vanderkam (eds), *The Dead Sea Scrolls After Fifty Years* 2, Leiden 1999, 331-353

Alexander, P.S., '3 Enoch and the Talmud', *JSJ* 18 (1987) 40-68

Alexander, P.S., '3 (Hebrew Apocalypse of) Enoch', in Charlesworth, *Old Testament Pseudepigrapha*, 223-315

Alexander, P.S., 'The Historical Setting of the Hebrew Book of Enoch', *JJS* 28 (1977) 156-180

Alexander, P.S., 'Jewish Aramaic Translations of Hebrew Scriptures', in Mulder – Sysling, *Mikra*, 217-253

Alexander, P.S., 'The Rabbinic Lists of Forbidden Targumim', *JJS* 27 (1976) 177-191

Alexander, P.S., 'Response', in Schäfer – Dan, *Gershom Scholem's Major Trends*, 79-83

Alexander, P.S., '"A Sixtieth Part of Prophecy": The Problem of Continuing Revelation in Judaism', in J. Davis – G. Harvey – W.G.E. Watson (eds), *Words Remembered, Texts Renewed – Essays in Honour of John F. A. Sawyer*, Sheffield 1995, 414-433

Alexander, P.S., 'The Targumim and the Rabbinic Rules for the Delivery of the Targum', *VTSup* 36 (1985) 14-28

Alexander, P.S., 'The Textual Tradition of Targum Lamentations', *Abr-Nahrain* 24 (1986) 1-26

Alexander, P.S., 'Textual Criticism and Rabbinic Literature: The Case of The Targum of Song of Songs', *BJRL* 75 (1993) 159-173

Alexander, P.S., 'Tradition and Originality in the Targum of Song of Songs', in Beattie – McNamara, *Aramaic Bible*, 318-339

Alexander, P.S., '"Wrestling Against Wickedness in High Places": Magic in the Worldview of The Qumran Community', in S.E. Porter – C.A. Evans (eds), *The Scrolls and the Scriptures: Qumran Fifty Years After*, London 1997, 318-337

Allony, N., *The Jewish Library in the Middle Ages: Book Lists from the Cairo Geniza*, Jerusalem 2006 (Hebr)

Allony, N., '"Midrash ha-Tora", a Book by R. Hai (b. Nahshon) Gaon', *Alei Sefer* 9 (1981) 56-62 (Hebr).

Allony, N., 'Sefer Yetsira nusah RaSa"G be-tsurat megilla mi-Genizat Kahir', *Temirin* 2 (1982) 9-29

Allony, N. – D.S. Loewinger, *List of Photocopies in the Institute* 1-3, Jerusalem 1957-1964

Alon, G., 'The Halacha in the Teaching of the Twelve Apostles (Didache)', in J.A. Draper (ed), *The Didache in Modern Research*, Leiden 1996, 165-194 (ET of 'Ha-halakha be-torat 12 ha-Shelihim', in idem, *Studies* 1, 274-294)

Alon, G., 'Ha-Yavanit be-Erets Yisrael he-yehudit', *KS* 20 (1943) 76-95, repr in idem, *Studies* 2, 248-277

Alon, G., 'Le-yishuva shel baraita ahat', in idem, *Studies* 2, 120-127

Alon, G., *Studies in Jewish History in the Times of the Second Temple, the Mishna and the Talmud* 1-2, Tel-Aviv 1957-58, repr 1967-70 (Hebr)

Althaus, H.-P., *Kleines Lexikon deutscher Wörter jiddischer Herkunft*, München 2003

Altman[n], A., 'The Gnostic Background of the Rabbinic Adam Legends', *JQR* 35 (1944-1945) 371-91

Altman[n], A., 'Shirei Kedusha be-sifrut ha-Hekhalot ha-keduma', *Melilah* 2 (1946) 1-24

Ameling, W. (ed), *Inscriptiones Judaicae Orientis* 2: *Kleinasien*, Tübingen 2004

Amir, A., 'Shimeon ben Shatah and the Sorceresses', *Sinai* 112 (1993) 144-161 (Hebr)

Anderson, G.A., 'The Interpretation of Genesis 1:1 in the Targums', *CBQ* 52 (1990) 21-29

Aptowitzer, A., 'Zur Kosmologie der Agada: Licht als Urstoff', *MGWJ* 72 (1928) 363-370

Aptowitzer, V., *Sefer Rabiyah*, 2nd ed Jerusalem 1994

Aptowitzer, V., *Das Schriftwort in der rabbinischen Literatur*, Vienna 1906-1915

Arbel, D.V., "'Seal of Resemblance, Full of Wisdom, and Perfect in Beauty": The Enoch/Metatron Narrative of 3 Enoch and Ezekiel 28', *HTR* 98 (2005) 121-142

Ashkenazi, B., *Derashot u-maamarim le-Rabbenu Bezalel Ashkenazi*, ed Y. Buchbut, Jerusalem 1996 (Hebr)

Ashur, A., *Engagement according to Documents from the Cairo Geniza*, MA thesis Tel-Aviv U 2000 (Hebr)

Assaf, S., 'The Book of Shetaroth (Formulary) of R. Hai Gaon', *Suppl Tarbiz* I/3, Jerusalem 1930 (Hebr)

Atzmon, A., *Esther Rabbah II: Towards a Critical Edition*, diss Bar-Ilan U, Ramat Gan 2005 (Hebr)

Aune, D.E., 'Magic in Early Christianity', *ANRW* II.23.2 (1980) 1507-1557

Ausubel, N., *A Treasury of Jewish Folklore*, New York 1972

Avigad, N., 'Aramaic Inscriptions from Jason's Tomb', *Atiqot* 4 (1964) 32-8 (Heb.)

Avigad, N., *Beth She'arim 3: Catacombs 12-23*, Jerusalem 1976

Avishur, Y., ' "The ways of the Amorite": The Canaanite-Babylonian Background and the Literary Structure', in C. Rabin – D. Patterson – B.-Z. Luria – Y. Avishur (eds), *Studies in the Bible and the Hebrew Language offered to Meir Wallenstein*, Jerusalem 1979, 17-47 (Hebr)

Avi-Yonah, M., *The Holy Land from the Persian Period to the Arab Conquests (536 B.C to A.D. 640)*, Grand Rapids 1966

Avi-Yonah, M., *Gazetteer of Roman Palestine*, Jerusalem 1976

Bacher, W., *Die Agada der babylonischen Amoräer*, 2nd ed Frankfurt/M 1913, repr Hildesheim 1967

Bacher, W., *Die Agada der palästinensischen Amoräer* 1-3, Strassburg 1892-99, repr Hildesheim 1965

Bacher, W., *Die Agada der Tannaiten* 1-2, Strassburg 1884-90, 2nd ed vol 1, 1903; repr Berlin 1965-66

Bacher, W., 'Anti-Karaisches in einem jungeren Midrasch', *MGWJ* 23 (1874) 266-274.

Bacher, W., *Die exegetische Terminologie der jüdischen Traditionsliteratur* 1-2, Leipzig 1899-1905, repr in one vol Darmstadt 1965 (Hebr transl A.S. Rabinowitz, *Erkhei midrash Tannaim*, Tel Aviv 1923, repr 1970; *Erkhei midrash Amoraim*, Tel Aviv 1923, repr 1970)

Bacher, W., 'The Origin of the Word Haggada (Agada)', *JQR* 4 (1892) 406-429

Bacher, W., *Die Proömien der alten jüdischen Homilie*, Leipzig 1913

Bacher, W., *Rabbanan: Die Gelehrten der Tradition*, Budapest 1914

Bacher, W., 'Eine südarabische Midraschcompilation zu Esther', *MGWJ* 41 (1897) 350-356

Bacher, W., *Tradition und Tradenten in den Schulen Palästinas und Babyloniens: Studien und Materialien zur Entstehungsgeschichte des Talmuds*, Leipzig 1914, repr Berlin 1966

Baer, Y.(I.) , 'Israel, the Christian Church and the Roman Empire from the Days of Septimus Severus to the "Edict of Toleration" of 313 C.E.', *Zion* 21 (1956) 1-49; 237 (Hebr)

Barag, D. and D. Flusser, 'The Ossuary of Yehohanah Granddaughter of the High Priest Theophilus', *IEJ* 36 (1986) 39-44

Bar-Asher, M., 'The Different Traditions of Mishnaic Hebrew', in D.M. Golomb (ed), *'Working With No Data', Semitic and Egyptian Studies Presented to Thomas O. Lambdin*, Winona Lake 1987, 1-38

Bar-Asher, M., 'Forgotten Linguistic Features in Tannaitic Language', in Bar-Asher – Dotan – Sarfatti – Tene, *Hebrew Language Studies*, 83-110 (Hebr)

Bar-Asher, M., *L'hébreu mishnique – études linguistiques*, Leuven-Paris 1999

Bar-Asher, M., 'The Historical Unity of Hebrew and Mishnaic Hebrew Research', *Mehqarim ba-Lashon*, vol 1, Hebrew University of Jerusalem 1985, 75-99 (Hebr)

Bar-Asher, M., 'An Introduction to Mishna Parma-B-Codex De Rossi 497', Jerusalem 1971 (quoted according to Bar-Asher, *Kovets maamarim* 1, 166-185) (Hebr)

Bar-Asher, M., 'La langue de la Mishna d'après les traditions des comunautés juives d'Italie', *REJ* 145 (1986) 267-278

Bar-Asher, M., 'Linguistic Studies in the Manuscripts of the Mishna', *PIASH* 7 (1986) 183-210 (Hebr)

Bar-Asher, M., 'The Place of Aramaic in Modern Hebrew', in idem, *et al.*, *Evolution and Renewal: Trends in the Development of the Hebrew Language*, Jerusalem 1996 14-76 (Hebr)

Bar-Asher, M. 'A Preliminary Study of Mishnaic Hebrew as Reflected in Codex Vatican 32 of Sifre-Bamidbar', *Te'uda* 3 (1983) 139-65 (Hebr)

Bar-Asher, M., 'Quelques phénomènes grammaticaux en hébreu mishnique', *REJ* 99 (1990) 351-367

Bar-Asher, M., 'Rare Forms in Tannaitic Hebrew', *Lešonenu* 41 (1977) 83-102 (quoted according to Bar-Asher, *Kovets maamarim* 2, 123-142) (Hebr)

Bar-Asher, M., 'The Study of Mishnaic Hebrew Grammar – Achievements, Problems and Goals', in M. Bar-Asher (ed), *PWCJS* 9, Panel Sessions *Hebrew and Aramaic*, Jerusalem 1988, 3-37 (Hebr)

Bar-Asher, M., *The Tradition of Mishnaic Hebrew in the Communities of Italy*, Jerusalem 1980 (Hebr)

Bar-Asher, M., 'On Vocalization Errors in Codex Kaufman of the Mishna', in M. Bar-Asher (ed), *Massorot*, 1 (1984) 1-17 (Hebr)

Bar-Asher, M. (ed), *Kovets maamarim bi-leshon Hazal* 1-2, Jerusalem 1972-1980 (Hebr)

Bar-Asher, M. (ed), *Studies in Mishnaic Hebrew*, ScrHier 37 (1998)

Bar-Asher, M. – Dotan, A. – Sarfatti, G.B. – Tene, D. (eds), *Hebrew Language Studies Presented to Professor Zeev Ben--Hayyim*, Jerusalem 1983

Bar-Asher, M. – Levinson, J. – Lifschitz, B. (eds), *Studies in Talmudic and Midrashic Literature: In Memory of Tirzah Lifshitz* , Jerusalem 2005

Bar-Asher, M. – Rosenthal, D. (eds), *Talmudic Studies*, Jerusalem 1993 (Hebr)

Bar-Ilan, M. 'The Character and Origin of Megillat Taanit', *Sinai* 98 (1986) 114-137 (Hebr)

Bar-Ilan, M., 'Between Magic and Religion: Sympathetic Magic in the World of the Sages of the Mishnah and the Talmud', *Review of Rabbinic Judaism* 5 (2002) 383-399

Bar-Ilan, M., 'Exorcism by Rabbis: Talmudic Sages and Magic', *Da'at* 34 (1995) 17-31 (Hebr)

Bar-Ilan, M., *Polemics between Sages and Priests towards the end of the days of the Second Temple*, diss Bar-Ilan U 1982

Bar-Ilan, M., *Sitre tefilla ve-Hekhalot*, Ramat Gan 1987

Bar-Ilan, M., 'Witches in the Bible and in the Talmud', *Approaches to Ancient Judaism* NS 5, (1993) 7-32

Barkai, G. – Shiller, E. (eds), *Christianity and Christians in the Land of Israel*, (*Ariel* 155-156) Tel Aviv 2002 (Hebr)

Baroja, J.C., *The World of the Witches*, Chicago 1965

Barr, J., 'Hebrew, Aramaic and Greek in the Hellenistic Age', in W.D. Davies – L. Finkelstein, *The Cambridge History of Judaism* 2, Cambridge 1989, 79-114

Barth, L., *An Analysis of Vatican 30*, Cincinnati – Jerusalem 1973

Barth, L., 'Is Every Medieval Manuscript a New Composition?' in M.L. Raphael (ed), *Agendas for the Study of Midrash in the Twenty-first Century*, Williamsburg VA 1999, 43-62

Barth, L., 'Pirqe Rabbi Eliezer Electronic Text Editing Project': www.usc.edu/dept/huc-la/pre-project/agendas.html

Barton, T., *Ancient Astrology*, London 1994

Basser, H.W., *Midrashic Interpretations of the Song of Moses*, New York 1984

Basser, H.W., 'On M. Kahana's Article', *Tarbiz* 59 (1990) 233-34 (Hebr)

Basser, H.W., *Pseudo-Rabad: Commentary to Sifre Deuteronomy*, Atlanta 1994

Basser, H.W., *Pseudo-Rabad: Commentary to Sifre Numbers*, Atlanta 1998

Bassfreund, J., 'Das Fragmenten-Targum zum Pentateuch', *MGWJ* 40 (1896) 1-14, 49-67, 97-109, 145-163; 396-405

Bauer H. – Leander, P., *Grammatik des Biblisch-Aramäischen*, Halle 1927

Baum-Sheridan, J., *Studien zu den westjiddischen Estherdichtungen*, Hamburg 1996

Baumann, P., *Spätantike Stifter im Heiligen Land*, Wiesbaden 1999

Baumgarten, J.M., 'The Qumran Songs Against Demons', *Tarbiz* 55 (1986) 442-445 (Hebr)

Beattie, D.R.G., 'Towards Dating the Targum of Ruth', in J.D. Martin – P.R. Davies (eds), *A Word in Season; Essays in Honour of William McKane*, Sheffield 1986, 205-221

Beattie, D.R.G. – McNamara, M.J. (eds), *The Aramaic Bible: Targums in their Historical Context*, Sheffield 1994

Beckerath, J. von, 'Astronomie und Astrologie', in W. Helck, E. Otto (eds), *Lexikon der Ägyptologie* 1, Wiesbaden 1972-92, 511-514

Beer, G., *Faksimile-Ausgabe des Mischnacodex Kaufmann*, Haag 1929, repr Jerusalem 1968

Beeri, T., 'Early Stages in the Babylonian Piyyut', *HUCA* 68 (1997) Hebr section 1-33

Ben-Arie, M., *Hebrew Codicology*, Jerusalem 1981

Benayahu, M., 'The Glosses of Rabbi Bezalel Ashkenazi and Rabbi Joseph Ashkenazi and Their Master Copy', *Asufot* 1 (1987) 47-104 (Hebr)

Benayahu, M., 'R. Ezra of Pano', in S. Israeli – N. Lamm – Y. Raphael (eds), *Jubilee Volume in Honor of Moreinu Hagaon Rabbi Joseph B. Soloveitchik*, Jerusalem and New York 1984, 786-855 (Hebr)

Benayahu, M., 'R. Samuel Ashkenazi and Other Commentators of *Midrash Rabba*', *Tarbiz* 42 (1973) 419-460 (Hebr)

Benayahu, M., '*Sefer Beit Vaad*', in idem (ed), *Studies in Memory of the Rishon Le-Zion R. Yitzhak Nissim* (vols 1-6), Jerusalem 1985, vol 4, 109-154 (Hebr)

Bendavid, A., *Biblical Hebrew and Mishnaic Hebrew*, Tel Aviv 1967 (Hebr)

Ben-Hayyim, Z., 'The Historical Unity of the Hebrew-Language and its Division into Periods', in M. Bar-Asher (ed), *Language Studies* 1, Jerusalem 1985, 3-25 (Hebr)

Ben-Hayyim, Z., *The Literary and Oral Tradition of Hebrew and Aramaic amongst the Samaritans* 1-5, Jerusalem 1957-77 (Hebr)

Ben-Hayyim, Z., 'Massoret ha-Shomronim ve-zikkata le-massoret ha-lashon shel Megillot Yam-Hamelah veli-Leshon Hazal', *Lešonenu* 22 (1958) 223-245 (quoted according to Bar-Asher, *Kovets maamarim* 1, 36-58) (Hebr)

Benoît, P. – Milik, J.T. – de Vaux, R. (eds), *Les Grottes de Murabba'at*, Texts and Plates, (DJD 2) Oxford 1961 (Aramaic and Hebrew by Milik, Greek by Benoît)

Benovitz, M., 'The Prohibitive Vow in Second Temple and Tannaitic Literature: Its Origin and Meaning', *Tarbiz* 64 (1995) 203-228 (Hebr)

Ben-Sasson, M., 'Fragments from Saadya's *Sefer Ha-edut VeHa-Shetarot*', *Shenaton ha-Mishpat ha-Ivri* 11-12 (1984-6) 135-278 (Hebr)

Ben-Shalom, I., *The School of Shammai and the Zealots' Struggle against Rome*, Jerusalem 1993 (Hebr)

Bergel, J., *Die Medizin der Talmudisten*, Leipzig 1885

Berman, J.A., 'Aggadah and Anti-Semitism: The Midrashim to Esther 3:8', *Judaism* 38 (1989) 195-196

Bet Arie, M., *Supplement of Addenda and Corrigenda to the Catalogue of Hebrew Manuscripts in the Bodleian Library*, Oxford 1994

Beyer, K., *Die aramäischen Texte vom Toten Meer*, Gottingen 1984

Biale, D., *Gershom Scholem: Kabbalah and Counter-History*, Cambridge 1979

Bickerman[n], E.J., 'The Civic Prayer of Jerusalem', *Studies in Jewish and Christian History* 2, Leiden 1980

Bickerman, E. 'Notes on the Megillath Ta'anith', *Zion* 1 (1936) 317-355 (Hebr)

Bickerman, E.J., 'The Warning Inscriptions of Herod's Temple', *JQR* 37 (1946/47) 387-405.

Bieberstein, K. – Bloedhorn, H., *Jerusalem. Grundzüge der Baugeschichte vom Chalkolithikum bis zur Frühzeit der osmanischen Herrschaft* 2-3, (Tübinger Atlas des vorderen Orients B 100) Tübingen 1994

Bietenhard, H. – Ljungman, H., *Der tannaitische Midrasch Sifre Deuteronomium*, Bern 1984

Black, M., *An Aramaic Approach to the Gospels and Acts*, 3rd ed Oxford 1967

Blank, D.R., 'Jewish Rites of Adolescence', in P. Bradshaw – L. A. Hoffman (eds), *Life Cycles in Jewish and Christian Worship*, Notre Dame 1996, 81-110

Blau, L., *Das Altjüdische Zauberwesen*, Budapest 1898

Blidstein, G., 'The Sheliach Zibbur: His Nature, Functions and History', in J. Tabory (ed), *From Qumran to Cairo: Studies in the History of Prayer*, Jerusalem 1999 (Hebr)

Bloch, P., 'Die יורדי מרכבה, die Mystiker der Gaonzeit und ihrer Einfluss auf die Liturgie', *MGWJ* 37 (1893) 18-25, 69-74, 257-266, 305-311

Bodenheimer, S., *Animal Life in the Bible Lands*, Jerusalem 1950 (Hebr)

Boerner-Klein, D. – Hollender, E., *Rabbinische Kommentare zum Buch Ester*, 1: *Der Traktat Megilla*; 2: *Die Midraschim zu Esther übersetzt*, Leiden – Boston – Köln 2000

Boffo, L., *Iscrizioni greche e latine per lo studio della Bibbia*, Brescia 1994

Bohak, G., 'Magical Means for Handling *Minim* in Rabbinic Literature', in P.J. Tomson – D. Lambers-Petry (eds), *The Image of the Judeo-Christians in Ancient Jewish and Christian Literature*, Tübingen 2003, 267-279

Bohak, G., 'Remains of Greek Words and Magical Formulas in Hekhalot Literature', *Kabbalah* 6 (2001) 121-134

Bohec, Y. Le, 'Inscriptions juives et judaïsantes de l'Afrique romaine', *Antiquités africaines* 17 (1981) 165-207

Bokser, Baruch, '*Ma'al* and Blessings over Food', *JBL* 100 (1981) 557-574

Bokser, B., *The Origins of the Seder: The Passover Rite and Early Rabbinic Judaism*, Berkeley – Los Angeles 1984

Bonsirven, J., *Textes rabbiniques des deux premières siècles chrétiens*, Rome 1955

Börner-Klein: see also Boerner-Klein

Börner-Klein, D., *Der Midrasch Sifre zu Numeri*, Stuttgart 1997

Börner-Klein, D., *Der Midrasch Sifre Zuta*, Stuttgart 2002

Bouché-Leclercq, A., *L'Astrologie grecque*, Paris 1963

Boustan, R., *From Martyr to Mystic:* the Story of the Ten Martyrs, Hekhalot Rabbati, and the Making of Merkavah Mysticism, Tübingen 2005

Bowker, J.W., *The Targums and Rabbinic Literature: An Introduction to Jewish Interpretations of Scripture*, Cambridge 1969

Boyarin, D., 'From the Hidden Light of the Geniza: Towards the Original Text of the Mekhilta d'Rabbi Ishmael', *Sidra* 2 (1986) 5-13 (Hebr)

Boyarin, D., *Intertextuality and the Reading of Midrash*, Bloomington – Indianapolis 1990

Boyarin, D., 'The Loss of Final Consonants in Babylonian Jewish Aramaic', *Afroasiatic Linguistics* 3 (1976) 103-107

Boyarin, D., 'A Review of: Yehiel Kara, Studies in the Aramaic of the Yemenite Manuscripts of the Talmud', *Lešonenu* 51 (1987) 252-256 (Hebr)

Boyarin, D., 'On the Status of the Tannaitic Midrashim', *JAOS* 112 (1992) 455-65

Boyarin, D., 'Towards the Talmudic Lexicon III', *Te'uda* 4 (1986) 115-22 (Hebr)

Boyarin, D. et al. (eds), *Atara L'Haim: Studies in the Talmud and Medieval Rabbinic Literature in Honor of Professor H.Z. Dimitrovsky*, Jerusalem 2000 (Hebr)

Braavig, J., 'Magic: Reconsidering the Grand Dichotomy', in D.R. Jordan – H. Montgomery – E. Thomassen (eds), *The World of Ancient Magic*, Bergen 1999, 21-54

Bradshaw, P. – Hoffman, L.A. (eds), *Life Cycles in Jewish and Christian* Worship, Notre Dame 1996

Bram, J.R., 'Fate and Freedom: Astrology vs. Mystery Religions', *SBLSP*, Chico 1976, 326-330

Brand, J., *Seder Tanna Debe Eliyyahu Rabba ve-Zutta, Zalman Shazar Festschrift*, Jerusalem 1973, 597-617

Brann, M., 'Entstehung und Werth der Megillath Taanit', *MGWJ* 25 (1876) 375-384, 410-418, 445-460

Brann, M. – Elbogen, I. (eds), *FS zum siebzigsten Geburtstag Israel Lewy's*, Breslau 1910

Brashear, W.M., 'The Greek Magical Papyri: an Introduction and Survey; Annotated Bibliography (1928-1994)', *ANRW* II 18.5 (1995), 3380-3684

Braude, W.G. – Kapstein, I.J., *Tanna Debe Eliyyahu: The Love of the School of Elijah*, Philadelphia 1981

Brederek, E., *Konkordanz zum Targum Onkelos*, Giessen 1906

Bregman, M., 'Circular Proems and Proems Beginning with the Formula "zo hi shen'emra beruah haq-qodesh"', *Studies in Aggadah, Targum and Jewish Liturgy in Memory of Joseph Heinemann*, Jerusalem 1981, 34-51 (Hebr)

Bregman, M., 'Edei nusah shel Midreshe Tanhuma-Yelammedenu', *PWCJS* 9:3 (1986) 49-56 (Hebr)

Bregman, M., 'Midrash Rabbah and the Medieval Collector Mentality', in *The Jewish Anthological Imagination* 1, *Prooftexts* 17 (1997) 63-76

Bregman, M., 'Pseudepigraphy in Rabbinic Literature', in E.G. Chazon – M. Stone (eds), *Pseudepigraphic Perspectives: The Apocrypha and Pseudepigrapha in Light of the Dead Sea Scrolls; Proc., Intern. Symposium of the Orion Center, etc., 12-14 January, 1997*, (STDJ 31) Leiden 1999, 27-41

Bregman, M., *The Tanhuma-Yelammedenu Literature*, diss Hebrew U, Jerusalem 1991 (Hebr)

Bregman, M., *Sifrut Tanhhuma-Yelamdenu: teur nusaheha ve-iyunim be-darkhe hithavutam*, Piscataway NJ 2003

Breuer, Y., *The Hebrew in the Babylonian Talmud according to the Manuscripts of Tractate Pesahim*, Jerusalem 2002 (Hebr)

Breuer, Y., 'The Hebrew Component in the Aramaic of the Babylonian Talmud', *Lešonenu* 62 (1999) 23-80 (Hebr)

Breuer, Y., 'On the Hebrew Dialect of the Amoraim in the Babylonian Talmud', *Mehkarim ba-lashon* 2-3 (1987) 127-153 (Hebr)

Breuer, Y., '*Rabbi* is Greater than *Rav*, *Rabban* is Greater than *Rabbi*, the Simple Name is Greater than *Rabban*', *Tarbiz* 66 (1997) 41-59 (Hebr)

Brisman, S., *History and Guide to Judaic Dictionaries and Concordances*, Hoboken NJ 2000

Brock, S., 'A Letter Attributed to Cyril of Jerusalem on the Rebuilding of the Temple', *BSOAS* 40 (1977) 267-286

Brody, H. – Wiener, M., *Mivhar ha-shira ha-ivrit*, Leipzig 1922

Brody, R., *A Hand-list of Rabbinic Manuscripts in the Cambridge Genizah Collections* 1: *Taylor-Schechter New Series*, Cambridge 1998

Broshi, M. and Qimron, E., 'A Hebrew Bill of Debt from the Period of Bar-Kokhba', *Yadin Memorial Volume* (= *Eretz Israel* 20), Jerusalem 1989, 256-261 (Hebr)

Brown, F. – Driver, S.R. – Briggs, C.A., *Enhanced Brown-Driver-Briggs Hebrew and English Lexicon*, electronic ed Oak Harbor: Logos Research Systems

Brown, P., 'Sorcery, Demons and the Rise of Christianity from Late Antiquity into the Middle Ages', in M. Douglas (ed), *Witchcraft Confessions and Accusations*, London/New York 1970, 17-45

Brown, R., 'A Literary Analysis of Selected Sections of Sifra', *PWCJS* 10:3:1 (1990) 39-46 (Hebr)

Brownlee, W.H., 'The Habakkuk Midrash and the Targum of Yonatan', *JJS* 7 (1956) 169-186

Brüll, N., 'Der kleine Sifre', in *Jubelschrift zum siebzigsten Geburtstage des Prof. Dr. H. Graetz*, Breslau 1887, 179-193

Brüll, N., 'Sifre de-Agadeta al Megillat Esther' (review), *Jahrbücher* 8 (1887) 148-154

Brumberg-Kraus, Jonathan D., ' "Not by Bread Alone...": The Ritualization of Food and Table Talk in the Passover 'Seder' and in the Last Supper', *Semeia* 86 (1999) 165-191

Brunel, P., *Companion to Literary Myths: Heroes and Archetypes*, London – New York 1996

Buber, S., *Erläuterungen der Psalmen Haggada von Jedaja Penini (Bedarschi)*, Krakau 1891

Buber, S., *Likkutim mi-Midrash Avkir*, Vienna 1883

Buber, S., *Likkutim mi-Midrash Elle ha-Devarim Zutta*, Vienna 1885

Buber, S., 'Midrash Esfa', *Knesset Yisrael* 1 (1886) 309-319

Büchler, A., 'Learning and Teaching in Open Air in Palestine', *JQR* 4 (1914) 485-491 (repr in H.Z. Dimitrovsky, *Exploring the Talmud*, New York 1976)

Büchler, A., 'The History of the Blessing "Who is good and does good" and the situation of Judaea after the war', *Maamarim lezekher Zvi Peretz Hayot*, Vienna 1933, 137-167 (Hebr)

Büchler, A., 'Der Patriarch R. Jehuda und die griechisch-römischen Städte Palästinas', *JQR* 13 (1901) 683-740

Buchner, D., 'On the Relationship between Mekhilta de-Rabbi Ishmael and Septuagint Exodus', *IOSCS Congress* 9 (1997) 403-20

Cameron, A., *Christianity and the Rhetoric of the Empire*, Berkeley 1991

Canova, R., *Iscrizioni e monumenti protocristiani del paese di Moab*, Rome 1954

Cassel, P., *Messianische Stellen des Alten Testaments* 2, Berlin 1885

Cassuto, D., 'The Israelite Epic', *Biblical and Oriental Studies* 1, Jerusalem 1973, 69-109

Cassuto, M.D., 'Birkat Kohanim', *Encyclopedia Biblica*, Jerusalem 1964, 358-359

Cassuto, U. – Klausner, J. – Gutmann, J. (eds), *Sefer Assaf*, Jerusalem 1953 (Hebr)

Catalogue of the Jack Mosseri Collection, Jerusalem 1990 (Hebr)

Catelli, I., 'Astrology and the Worship of Stars in the Bible', *ZAW* 103 (1991) 86-99

Charles, R.H. (ed), *Apocrypha of the Old Testament*, Bellingham, WA: Logos Research Systems 2004

Charlesworth, J.H., 'Jewish Interest in Astrology during the Hellenistic and Roman Period', *ANRW* II 20.2 (1987), 926-950

Charlesworth, J.H. (ed), *The Old Testament Pseudepigrapha*, Garden City NY 1983

Chazon, E.G., 'When Did They Pray? Times for Prayer in the Dead Sea Scrolls and Associated Literature', in R.A. Argall – B.A. Bow – R.A. Werline (eds), *For a Later Generation: The Transformation of Tradition in Israel, Early Judaism and Early Christianity*, FS G.W.E. Nickelsburg, Harrisburg 2000, 42-51

Chernick, M.L., 'The Formal Development of כלל ופרט וכלל', *Tarbiz* 52 (1983) 393-410 (Hebr)

Chernick, M.L., *Hermeneutical Studies in Talmudic and Midrashic Literature*, Lod 1984 (Hebr)

Chernick, M.L., 'The Use of Ribbuyim and Miutim in the Halakic Midrash of R. Ishmael', *JQR* 70 (1979) 96-116

Chilton, B.D., *Targumic Approaches to the Gospels: Essays in the Mutual Definition of Judaism and Christianity*, Lanham MD 1986

Churgin, P., 'The Halakhah in Targum Onqelos', *Horeb* 7 (1943) 103-109

Churgin, P., 'Targum Ekha', *Horeb* 5 (1939) 123-132 (Hebr)

Churgin, P., 'Targum Shir ha-Shirim', in C.D. Regensburg (ed), *Gibeath Saul: Essays Contributed in Honor of Rabbi Saul Silber*, Chicago 1935, 82-102

Cohen, A., *Everyman's Talmud*, New York 1978

Clarke, E.G., 'The Bible and Translation: the Targums', in J.C. Hurd – B.H. McLean (eds), *Origins and Method*, Sheffield 1993, 380-393

Cohen, M.S., *The Shi'ur Qomah: Liturgy and Theurgy in Pre-Kabbalistic Jewish Mysticism*, Lanham – New York – London 1983

Cohen, M.S., *Shi'ur Qomah: Texts and Recensions*, Tübingen 1985

Cohen, N., 'R. Abun and his Son Shimon', *Al Atar* 4-5 (1999) 277-278 (Hebr)

Cohen, N.G., *Philo Judaeus: His Universe of Discourse*, Frankfurt/M 1995

Cohen, S.J.D., 'Epigraphical Rabbis', *JQR* 72 (1981/2) 1-17

Collins, J.J. – Fishbane, M. (eds), *Death, Ecstasy, and Other Worldly Journeys*, Albany NJ 1995

Cook, A.B., *Zeus: A Study in Ancient Religion*, vol 1, *Zeus God of the Bright Sky*, Cambridge 1914; vol 2, *Zeus God of the Dark Sky (Thunder and Lightning)*, Cambridge 1925

Cook, E.M., *Rewriting the Bible: The Text and Language of Pseudo-Jonathan Targum*, diss Los Angeles 1986

Cooper, J.C., *Symbolic and Magical Animals, s.l.* 1992

Coronel, N., *Commentarios quinque*, Vienna 1864

Cotton, H.M., 'A Cancelled Marriage Contract from the Judaean Desert', *JRS* 84 (1994) 64-86

Cotton, H.M., 'The Rabbis and the Documents', in M. Goodman (ed), *Jews in the Graeco-Roman World*, Oxford 1998, 167-179

Cotton, H.M., 'Die Papyrusdokumente aus der judäischen Wüste und ihr Beitrag zur Erforschung der jüdischen Geschichte des 1. und 2. Jh. n. Chr.', *ZDPV* 115 (1999) 228-47

Cotton, H.M., 'The Languages of the Legal and Administrative Documents from the Judaean Desert', *ZPE* 125 (1999) 219-231

Cotton, H.M., 'Documentary Texts from the Judaean Desert: A Matter of Nomenclature', *SCI* 20 (2001) 113-9

Cotton, H.M., 'Women and Law in the Documents from the Judaean Desert', in H. Melaerts – L. Mooren (eds), *Le rôle et le statut de la femme en Égypte hellénistique, romaine et byzantine*, Paris 2002, 123-147

Cotton, H.M. – Price, J.J., 'A Bilingual Tombstone from Zo'ar (Arabia)', *ZPE* 134 (2001) 277-283

Cotton, H.M. – Cockle, W.E.H. – Millar, F.G.B., 'The Papyrology of the Roman Near East: A Survey', *JRS* 85 (1995) 214-235

Cotton, H. – Qimron, E., 'XHev/Se ar 13 of 134 or 135 C.E.: A Wife's Renunciation of Claims', *JJS* 49 (1998) 108-118

Cotton, H. – Yardeni, A. (eds), *Aramaic, Hebrew and Greek Documentary Texts from Nahal Hever and Other Sites (the Seiy l Collection II)*, (DJD 27) Oxford 1997

Cox-Miller, P., *Dreams in Late Antiquity: Studies in the Imagination of a Culture*, Princeton 1994

Cramer, F.H., *Astrology in Roman Law and Politics*, Philadelphia 1954

Crane, O.T., *The Targums of the Books of Ruth and Jonah*, New York 1886

Cross, F.M., 'The Discovery of the Samaria Papyri', *Biblical Archeologist* 26 (1963) 110-121

Cross, F.M., 'The Papyri and their Historical Implications', in P.W. & N.L. Lapp (eds), *Discoveries in the Wadi ed-Daliyeh = AASOR* 41 (1974) 17-29

Cross, F.M., 'Samaria Papyrus 1: An Aramaic Slave Conveyance of 335 BCE Found in the Wadi ed-Daliyeh', *Eretz Israel* 18 (1985) 7*-17*

Cross, F.M., 'A Report on the Samaria Papyri', *Congress Volume Jerusalem 1986, International Organization for the Study of the Old Testament*, (VT Supp 40) Leiden 1988, 17-26

Cross, F.M. – E. Eshel, 'An Ostracon from Khirbet Qumran', *IEJ* 47 (1997) 17-28

Cryer, F.H., *Divination in Ancient Israel and its Near Eastern Environment*, Sheffied 1994

Cryer, F.H., 'Magic in Ancient Syria-Palestine and in the Old Testament', in B. Ankarloo – S. Clark (eds), *Witchcraft and Magic in Europe: Biblical and Pagan Societies*, Philadelphia 2001, 97-164

Cumont, F., *Astrology and Religion among the Greeks and the Romans*, New York 1960

Dafni, A., 'Autumn Mandrake gave a Fragrance', in *Chapters on the Folklore of the Plants of Israel*, Haifa 1981 (Hebr)

Daiches, S., *Babylonian Oil Magic in the Talmud and in Later Jewish Literature*, (Jews' College Publications 5) London 1913

Dalman, G., *Aramäische Dialektproben*, Leipzig 1896; and Dalman, G., *Grammatik des jüdisch-palästinischen Aramäisch*, Leipzig 1905; repr in one vol, Darmstadt 1960

Dan, J., 'The Concept of Knowledge in the Shi'ur Qomah', in S. Stein – R. Loewe (eds), *Studies in Jewish Religious and Intellectual History Presented to A. Altmann on the Occasion of his 70th Birthday*, U of Alabama 1979, 67-73

Dan, J., 'The Princes of Thumb and Cup', *Tarbiz* 32 (1963) 359-369 (Hebr)

Dan, J. 'Three Phases of the History of the Sefer Yezira', *FJB* 21 (1994) 29

Danby, H., *The Mishnah*, Oxford 1933

Daniel-Nataf, S., *Philo of Alexandria, Writings* 1, Jerusalem 1986 (Hebr)

Danker, F.D., *A Greek-English Lexicon of the New Testament and other Christian Literature*, Chicago – London 2000

Danzig, N., *A Catalogue of Fragments of Halakhah and Midrash from the Cairo Genizah in the Elkan Nathan Adler Collection of the Library of the Jewish Theological Seminary of America*, New York – Jerusalem 1997 (Hebr)

Danzig, N., *Introduction to Halakhot Pesuqot*, New York and Jerusalem 1993 (Hebr)

Dar, Sh., Sumaqa, *A Jewish Village on the Carmel*, Oxford 1998

Daris, S., *Il lessico Latino nel Greco d'Egitto*, Barcelona 1971

Daube, D., 'Methods of Interpretation and Hellenistic Rhetoric', *HUCA* 22 (1949) 239-63

David, A. – Tabory, J. (eds), *The Italian Genizah*, Jerusalem 1998 (Hebr)

David, Y., *Formulae of the Bill of Divorce as Reflected in the Geniza and Other Sources*, MA thesis Tel-Aviv U 1991 (Hebr)

David, Y., *Divorce among the Jews as Reflected in the Geniza Documents and Other Sources*, diss Tel-Aviv U 2000 (Hebr)

Davidson, E., 'Megillat Esther be-aggadat Hazal', *Mahanayim* 104 (1966) 16-21

Davidson, I. – Assaf, S. – Joel, B.I. (eds), *Siddur R. Saadja Gaon*, Jerusalem 1941

659

Davila, J.R., 'The *Hodayot* Hymnist and the Four Who Entered Paradise', *RQ* 17 (1996) 457-478

Dawkins, R.M., 'The Modern Carnival in Thrace and the Cult of Dionysus', *JHS* 26 (1906) 191-206

Deaut, R. Le, 'The Targumim', in W.D. Damers – L. Finkelstein (eds), *The Cambridge History of Judaism* 2, Cambridge 1989, 563-590

de Lange: see Lange

Derenbourg, J., *Essai sur l'histoire et la géographie de la Palestine*, Paris 1867

Dickie, M.W., *Magic and Magicians in the Greco-Roman World*, London 2001

Díez Macho, A., *Neophyti 1: Targum Palestinense Ms de la Biblioteca Vaticana* 1-6, Madrid – Barcelona 1968-79

Díez Merino, L., 'El Targum de Ester en la Tradicion Sefardi: El Ms. De El Escorial G-1-5', *Estudios Biblicos* 45 (1987) 57-92

Díez Merino, L., 'Targum al Cantar de los Cantares (texto arameo del Codice Urbinati 1 y su traduccion)', *Anuario de Filologia* 7 (1981) 237-284

Díez Merino, L., 'Targum de Rut, Ms. De la Biblioteca Nacional (Madrid), n. 7542, de Alfonso de Zamora', *Anuario de Filologia* 12 (1986) 19-36

Dikduke sofrim, see Rabinowitz, R.N.

Dilke, O.H.M., *Greek and Roman Maps*, London 1985

Dilke, O.H.M., *Mathematics and Measurement*, Berkeley 1987

Dillon, M., *Pilgrims and Pilgrimage in Ancient Greece*, London 1997

Dinari, Y.A., *The Rabbis of Germany and Austria at the Close of the Middle Ages*, Jerusalem 1984 (Hebr)

Dittenberger, W. (ed), *Orientis Graeci Inscriptiones Selectae* 1-4, Leipzig 1903-1905

Dor, M., *Animal Life in the Times of the Bible, the Talmud and the Mishna*, Tel Aviv 1996 (Hebr)

Dothan, M., *Hammath Tiberias: Early Synagogues and the Hellenistic and Roman Remains*, Jerusalem 1983

Duling, D.C., 'Solomon, Exorcism and the Son of David', *HTR* 68 (1975) 235-252

Dunsky, S., *Midrash Rabbah Esther*, with Yiddish Translation, Explanatory Notes and Introduction, Montreal 1962

Ebstein, W., *Die Medizin im neuen Testament und im Talmud*, Stuttgart 1903

Eckart, K.G., *Untersuchungen zur Traditionsgeschichte der Mechilta [Parshat Bo]*, Berlin 1959

Efron, J., *Studies of the Hasmonean Period*, Tel Aviv 1980 (Hebr)

Ehrlich, U., *The Non-Verbal Language of Jewish Prayers*, Jerusalem 1999 (Hebr)

Ehrlich, U., 'The Earliest Versions of the Amida – The Blessing about the Temple Worship', in J. Tabory (ed), *From Qumran to Cairo: Studies in the History of Prayer*, Jerusalem 1999, 17-38 (Hebr)

Ehrlich, U., 'The Significance of the Final Three Blessings of the Amida, *Kol Peh leach Yodeh: iyyunim ... Prof. Dov Rapel*, Jerusalem 2002, 163-179 (Hebr)

Ehrlich, U., 'On the Ancient Version of the Benediction 'Builder of Jerusalem' and the Benediction of David', *Pe'amim*, 28 (1999) 16-43 (Hebr)

Ehrlich, U. – Tal, S., *Studies in Jewish Thought and Culture presented to Bracha Sack*, Beer Sheva 2004, 13-26

Eisenstein, J.D. (ed), *Bibliotheca Midrashica* (= *Otsar Midrashim*) 1-2, New York 1915, repr Bene Berak 1990

Elbaum, J., 'On the Character of the Late Midrashic Literature', *PWCJS* 9:3 (1986) 57-62 (Hebr)

Elbogen, I., *Jewish Liturgy: A Comprehensive History*, ET R.P. Scheindlin [fr. the German 1913 ed and the Hebrew ed by J. Heinemann, Tel Aviv 1972] New York 1993

Elboim, B., *Midrash Aba Gurion on Esther: Towards Criticized [sic] Edition*, MA Thesis Bar Ilan U, Ramat-Gan 2005 (Hebr)

Eldar [Adler], I., *The Hebrew Language Tradition in Medieval Ashkenaz (ca. 950-1350 C.E.)*, vol 1: *Phonology and Vocalization*, Jerusalem 1978; vol 2: *Morphology*, 1979 (Hebr)

Elias, *Ha-Mekhilta de-Rabbi Yishmael al pi otek meule min ha-Geniza*, MA thesis Hebrew U, Jerusalem 1997 (Hebr)

Elijah of Vilna, *Seder Olam Rabba*, with ann. by Elijah of Vilna, Shklov 1800

Elior, R., *The Three Temples: On the Emergence of Jewish Mysticism*, Oxford – Portland Or 2004

Elitzur, B., *Pesikta Rabbati – perek mavo*, diss Hebrew U, Jerusalem 2000

Elizur, Sh., 'An Abstract of Three or of Four', *Shana beshana* 1999, 421-428 (Hebr)

Elizur, Sh., *Betoda va-Shir*, Jerusalem 1991

Elizur, Sh., *Elazar bi-Rabbi Kilir: kedushtaot le-yom mattan Tora*, Jerusalem 2000

Elizur, Sh., 'The Enigmatic Nature of Hebrew Poetry in the Orient from its Origins until the Twelfth Century', *Peamim* 59 (1994) 14-34 (Hebr)

Elizur, Sh., *Kedusha va-shir*, Jerusalem 1988

Elizur, Sh., *Mahzorei shivatot li-sedarim ule-farashot*, Jerusalem 1993

Elizur, Sh., *Piyyutei Rabbi Pinhas ha-Kohen mi-Kafra*, Jerusalem 2003

Encyclopædia Britannica, Ultimate Reference Suite 2004 DVD, May 30, 2003

Eph'al, I. – J. Naveh, *Aramaic Ostraca of the Fourth Century B.C. from Idumaea*, Jerusalem 1996

Epstein, A., *Mikadmoniot ha-Yehudim: mehkarim u-reshimot*, Jerusalem 1957

Epstein, A., 'Das talmudische Lexicon אמוראים תנאים יחוסי und Jehuda b. Kalonymos aus Speier', *MGWJ* 1895, 398-403, 447-60, 507-513

Epstein, I. (ed), *The Babylonian Talmud* 1-7, (ET) London 1961

Epstein, J.N., 'Finkelstein L., Siphre zu Deuteronomium', *Tarbiz* 8 (1937) 375-92 (Hebr)

Epstein, J.N., *The Gaonic Commentary on the Order Toharoth*, (ed and comm.) Jerusalem and Tel Aviv 1982 (Hebr)

Epstein, J.N., *A Grammar of Babylonian Aramaic*, Jerusalem - Tel Aviv 1960 (Hebr)

Epstein, J.N., *Mavo le-nosah ha-Mishna: Nosah ha-Mishna ve-gilgulav lemi-yemei ha-Amoraim ha-rishonim ve-ad defusei R. Yomtov Lippmann Heller*, Jerusalem 1948; repr 1964; 2000 (Hebr)

Epstein, J.N., 'Mechilta and Sifre in the Works of Maimonides', *Tarbiz* 6 (1935) 343-82 (Hebr)

Epstein, J.N., 'Mishnat R. Eliezer', *HUCA* 23 (1950) 1-15 (Hebr)

Epstein, J.N., 'Perushei ha-Rivan u-perushei Vermayza', *Tarbiz* 4 (1933) 11-34, 153-192 (Hebr)

Epstein, J.N., 'A Rejoinder', *Tarbiz* 3 (1932) 232-36 (Hebr)

Epstein, J.N., 'Sifrei Zuttah Parashat Parah', *Tarbiz* 1 (1930) 46-78, repr in idem, *Studies* 2,1, 141-173 (Hebr)

Epstein, J.N., *Prolegomena ad Litteras Tannaiticas*, ed E.Z. Melamed, Jerusalem – Tel Aviv 1957 (Hebr)

Epstein, J.N., *Studies in Talmudic Literature and Semitic languages*, ed E.Z. Melamed, vols 1-2, Jerusalem 1983-1988 (Hebr)

Epstein, J.N. – Melamed, E.Z. (eds), *Mekhilta d'Rabbi Sim'on b. Jochai*, Jerusalem 1955

Eshel, E., *Belief in Demons in the Land of Israel during the Second Temple Period*, diss Hebrew U, Jerusalem 1999 (Hebr)

Eshel, E. – Kloner, A., 'An Aramaic Ostracon of an Edomite Marriage Document from Maresha, Dated 176 B.C.E.', *Tarbiz* 63 (1994) 485-502 (Hebr)

Eshel, E., – A. Kloner, 'An Aramaic ostracon of an Edomite marriage contract from Maresha, dated 176 B.C.E.', *IEJ* 46 (1996) 1-22

Eshel, H., 'Megillat Ta'anit in Light of Holidays Found in Jubilees and the Temple Scroll', in M. Bar-Asher – D. Dimant (eds), *Megillot: Mehkarim bi-Megillot Midbar Yehuda* 3, Jerusalem 2005, 253-257 (Hebr)

Falk, D.K., 'Other Evidence for Daily Prayer', in idem, *Daily, Sabbath, and Festival Prayers in the Dead Sea Scrolls*, (STDJ 27) Leiden 1998, 95-124

Falk, Z.W., *Introduction to Jewish Law of the Second Commonwealth* 1-2, Leiden 1972-78

Falk, Z.W., 'Neo-Babylonian Law in the Halakhah', *Tarbiz* 37 (1967) 39-47 (Hebr)

Fassberg, S.E., *A Grammar of the Palestinian Targum Fragments from the Cairo Genizah*, (Harvard Semitic Studies 38) Atlanta 1990

Fassberg, S.E. 'Hebraisms in the Aramaic Documents from Qumran', in T. Muraoka (ed), *Abr-Nahrain, Studies in Qumran Aramaic*, Louvain 1992, 48-69

Faur, J., 'Concerning the Term "*kore be-iggeret*"', *Alei Sefer* 15 (1989) 21-30 (Hebr)

Fauth, W., 'Lilits und Astarten in aramäischen, mandäischen und syrischen Zaubertexten', *Die Welt des Orients* 17 (1986) 66-94

Feist, M., 'Shalom in the Inscriptions and in Archaeological Discoveries', *Mahanayim* 121 (1969) 96-121 (Hebr)

Feldman, L. *Jew and Gentile in the Ancient World*, Princeton 1996

Feliks, Y., *Nature and Land in the Bible: Chapters on Biblical Ecology*, Jerusalem 1992 (Hebr)

Feliks, Y., 'Ha-Targumim (Rishon ve-Sheni) le-Esther be-yahas le-Midrash Esther Rabba A', *Talelei Orot* 6 (1995) 77-107

Fenton, P.B., 'Découverte de manuscrits hébreux anciens à la bibliotheque humaniste de Selestat', *Annuaires* (1998) 97-101

Fenton, P.B., 'A Judaeo-Arabic Commentary on the Haftarot by Hanan'el ben Semu'el(?), Abraham Maimonides Father-in-Law', in Hyman, *Maimonidean Studies*, 27-36

Ferguson, Everett, 'The Disgrace and the Glory: A Jewish Motif in Early Christianity', *Studia Patristica* 21 (1989) 86-94

Fernandes, M.P., *Midras Sifre Numeros*, Valencia 1989

Fidler, R., *Dreams Speak Falsely? Dream Theophanies in the Bible: Their Place in Ancient Israelite Faith and Traditions*, Jerusalem 2005 (Hebr)

Filipovsky, Z., *Mivhar ha-pninim u-Megillat Antiochos*, London 1851

Finkelstein, L., *Akiba, Scholar, Saint and Martyr*, New York 1936, repr 1970

Finkelstein, L., 'The Core of the Sifra: A Temple Textbook for Priests', *JQR* 80 (1989) 15-34

Finkelstein, L., '*Hashpaat Beit Shammai al Sifre Devarim* [The Influence of Beit Shammai on SifDeut]', in: Cassuto, Klausner, and Gutmann, (eds), *Sefer Assaf*, 415-426

Finkelstein, L., 'Improved Readings in the Sifre', *PAAJR* 4 (1933) 43-51

Finkelstein, L., *Mabo le-Massektot Abot ve-Abot d'Rabbi Natan (Introduction to the Treatises Abot and Abot of Rabbi Nathan)*, New York 1950

Finkelstein, L., 'Maimonides and the Tannaitic Midrashim', *JQR* 25 (1935) 469-517

Finkelstein, L., 'The Mekhilta and Its Text', *PAAJR* 5 (1933-34) 3-54

Finkelstein, L., 'Midrash, halachot ve-aggadot', repr in idem, *Sifra on Leviticus* 5, 100-119 (Hebr)

Finkelstein, L., *New Light from the Prophets*, London 1969

Finkelstein, L., 'An Old Baraita in Sifre on Deuteronomy', *Eretz-Israel* 10 (1971) 218-20

Finkelstein, L., 'The Oldest Midrash: Pre-Rabbinic Ideals and Teachings in the Passover Haggadah', *HTR* 31 (1938) 13-30

Finkelstein, L., 'Pre-Maccabean Documents in the Passover Haggadah', *HTR* 35 (1942) 41-120

Finkelstein, L., 'Prolegomena to an Edition of Sifre Deuteronomy', *PAAJR* 3 (1932) 3-42

Finkelstein, L., 'The Sources of the Tannaitic Midrashim', *JQR* 31 (1940-1941) 211-43

Finkelstein, L., 'Studies in the Tannaitic Midrashim', *PAAJR* 6 (1934-35) 189-228

Finkelstein, L., (ed), *Sifra on Leviticus*, vols 1-5, New York 1983-1992 (Hebr)

Finkelstein, L., (ed) *Sifre on Deuteronomy*, Berlin 1939 (Hebr)

Fishbane, M., *Biblical Interpretation in Ancient Israel*, Oxford 1985

Fishbane, S., ' "Most Women Engage in Sorcery": An Analysis of Sorceresses in the Babylonian Talmud', *Jewish History* 7 (1993) 27-42

Fishman, J.L. [cf Maimon, J.L.], *Hagim u-Moadim*, Jerusalem 1943

Fitzmyer, J.A., *The Genesis Apocryphon of Qumran Cave I*, 2nd ed Rome 1971

Fitzmyer, J.A., 'The So-Called Aramaic Divorce Text from Wadi Seiyal', *Eretz-Israel*, 26 (1999) 16*-22*

Fitzmyer, J.A., *A Wandering Aramean*, Ann Arbor MI 1979

Fitzmyer, J. A. – D. J. Harrington, *A Manual of Palestinian Aramaic Texts (Second Century B.C. – Second Century A.D.)*, Rome 1978

Fleischer, E., 'Annual and Triennial Reading of the Bible in the Old Synagogue', *Tarbiz* 61 (1991-92) 25-43 (repr in *Likutei Tarbiz* 6, Jerusalem 2003)

Fleischer, E., 'On the Beginnings of Obligatory Jewish Prayer', *Tarbiz* 59 (1990) 397-441 (Hebr)

Fleischer, E., 'Behinot be-tahalikh aliyyat he-haruz ba-shira ha-Ivrit ha-keduma', *Mehkerei Yerushalayim be-sifrut Ivrit* 1 (1981) 226-238

Fleischer, E., 'Compositions of Ha-Kalir for Tisha Be-Av', *HUCA* 45 (1974) 15ff

Fleischer, E., 'The Diffusion of the *Qedushshot* of the *'Amida* and the *Yozer* in the Palestinian Jewish Ritual', *Tarbiz* 38 (1969) 255-284 (Hebr)

Fleischer, E., 'Early Hebrew Liturgical Poetry in its Cultural Setting', *Moises Starosta Memorial Lectures*, First Series, Jerusalem 1993, 63-97 (Hebr)

Fleischer, E., 'An Early Siddur of the Erez Israel Rite', in Ezra Fleischer *et al.* (eds), *Me'ah She'arim: Studies in Medieval Jewish Spiritual Life in Memory of I. Twersky*, Jerusalem 2001, 21-59 (Hebr)

Fleischer, E., 'Girdle-Like Strophic Patterns in the Ancient *Piyyut'*, *Hasifrut* 2 (1970) 194-240 (Hebr)

Fleischer, E., 'Haduta-Hadutahu-Chedweta: Solving an old Riddle', *Tarbiz* 53 (1983) 71-96 (Hebr)

Fleischer, E., 'Havdalah Shivatot According to Palestinian Ritual', *Tarbiz* 37 (1967) 342-365 (Hebr)

Fleischer, E., *Hebrew Liturgical Poetry in the Middle Ages*, Jerusalem 1975 (Hebr)

Fleischer, E., 'The Influence of Choral Elements on the Formation and Development of the *Piyyut* Genres', *Yuval* 3 (1974) 18-48 (Hebr)

Fleischer, E., 'Piyyut', in *EJ* 13, 573-602

Fleischer, E., 'Remarks Concerning the Metric System of Ancient Hebrew Liturgic Poetry', *Hasifrut* 24 (1977) 70-83 (Hebr)

Fleischer, E., 'Response to Ruth Langer', *Prooftexts* 20 (2000) 381-382

Fleischer, E., 'Solving the Qiliri Riddle', *Tarbiz*, 54 (1985) 383-427 (Hebr)

Fleischer, E., 'Studies in the Problems Relating to the Liturgical Function of the Types of Early *Piyyut'*, *Tarbiz* 40 (1970) 41-63 (Hebr)

Fleischer, E., 'Terumat ha-Geniza le-heqer shirat ha-kodesh ha-Ivrit', *Te'uda* 1 (1980) 83-87

Fleischer, E., *The Yozer, its Emergence and Development*, Jerusalem 1984 (Hebr)

Flesher, P.V.M., 'Mapping the Synoptic Palestinian Targums of the Pentateuch', in Beattie – McNamara, *Aramaic Bible*, 247-253

Flesher, P.V.M. (ed), *Targum Studies 2: Targum and Peschitta*, Atlanta 1998

Flesher, P.V.M., 'The Targumim', in J. Neusner (ed), *Judaism in Late Antiquity* 1, Leiden 1995, 40-63

Flesher, P.V.M., 'Is *Targum Onqelos* a Palestinian Targum? The Evidence of Genesis 28-50', *JSP* 19 (1999) 35-79

Flesher, P.V.M. (ed), *Targum and Scripture; Studies in Aramaic Translations and Interpretation in Memory of Ernest G. Clarke*, Leiden 2002

Flint, V.I.J., *The Rise of Magic in Early Medieval Europe*, Oxford 1991

Flusser, D., *Judaism and the Origins of Christianity* (collected papers), Jerusalem 1983

Flusser, D., 'A Lost Jewish Benediction in Matthew 9:8', in idem, *Judaism*, 535-542

Flusser, D., 'Midrash ha-Tanakh ba-Berit ha-Hadasha', *Jewish Sources in Early Christianity*, Tel Aviv 1979, 305-12 (Hebr)

Flusser, D., 'The Second Blessing of the Amida and a Text from Qumran', *Tarbiz* 64 (1995) 331-335

Flusser, D., 'Some of the Precepts of the Tora from Qumran [4QMMT] and the Benediction against the Heretics', *Tarbiz* 61 (1992) 333-374

Flusser, D. (ed), *Iosippon (Josephus Gorionides)*, 1. *Text*; 2. *Introduction*, 1978-80 (Hebr)

Foerster, G., 'Synagogue Inscriptions and Their Relation to Liturgical Versions', *Cathedra* 19 (1981) 11-40 (Hebr)

Foerster, G., 'The Zodiac in Ancient Synagogues and its Place in Jewish Thought and Literature', *Eretz-Israel* 19 (1987) 225-234 (Hebr)

Ford, J.N., 'Additions and Corrections to Ninety-Nine by the Evil Eye', *Ugarit-Forschungen* 32 (2000) 711-715

Ford, J.N., ' "Ninety-Nine by the Evil Eye and One from Natural Causes": KTU2 1.96 in its Near Eastern Context', *Ugarit-Forschungen* 30 (1998) 201-278

Fox, H., 'The Circular Proem: Composition, Terminology and Antecedents', *PAAJR* 49 (1982) 1-31

Fox, H., 'Note: A Difficult Reading in Sifre Deuteronomy', *Tarbiz* 59 (1990) 229-31 (Hebr)

Fox, M., 'Nahmanides on the Status of Aggadot: Perspectives on the Disputation at Barcelona 1263', *JJS* 40 (1989) 95-109

Fraade, S.[D.], 'Interpreting Midrash 2: Midrash and Its Literary Contents', *Prooftexts* 7 (1987) 284-99

Fraade, S.D., 'Looking for Narrative Midrash at Qumran', in Stone – Chazon, *Biblical Perspectives*, 59-79

Fraade, S.D., 'Rabbinic Views on the Practice of Targum and Multilingualism in the Jewish Galilee of the Third-Sixth Centuries', in Levine, *Galilee*, 253-86

Fraade, S.D., 'Scripture, Targum and Talmud as Instruction: A Complex Textual Story from the Sifra', in Magness – Gitin, *Hesed ve-Emet*, 109-21

Fraade, S.D., 'Sifre Deuteronomy 26 (ad Deut. 3.23): How Conscious the Composition?', *HUCA* 54 (1983) 254-301

Fraade, S.D., *From Tradition to Commentary: Torah and Its Interpretation in the Midrash Sifre to Deuteronomy*, New York 1991

Fraade, S.D., 'The Turn to Commentary in Ancient Judaism: The Case of Sifre Deuteronomy', in Ochs, *Return to Scripture*, 142-171

Fraenkel, J., *The Aggadic Narrative: Harmony of Form and Content*, Tel Aviv 2001 (Hebr)

Fraenkel, J., *Darkhei ha-aggada ve-ha-midrash* 1-2, Givatayim 1991

Fraenkel, J., *Iyunim be-olamo ha-ruhani shel sippur ha-aggada*, Tel-Aviv 1981 (Hebr)

Fraenkel, J., *Midrash and Agadah* 1-3, Tel Aviv 1996

Fraenkel, S., 'Notizen', *MGWJ* 30 (1881) 82-83

Francis, F.O., 'The Baraita of the Four Sons', *JAAR* 42 (1974) 280–297 (= *PSBL* 1 (1972) 245–283)

Frankel, Z., *Darkhei ha-Mishna* (*Hodegetica zur Mischna*), Warsaw 19232 (Hebr)

Frankel, Z., *Einleitung in den Jerusalemischen Talmud*, Berlin 1923 (Hebr)

Frazer, J.G. *The Golden Bough*, London 1911-36

Freedman, H. – Simon, M., *Midrash Rabbah*, vol 1-10, London and Bournemouth 1939

Frey, J.B., *Corpus Inscriptionum Iudaicarum: Recueil des inscriptions juives qui vont du IIIe siècle avant Jésus-Christ au VIIe siècle de notre ère*, vol 1-2, Rome 1936-52; vol 1 repr w 'Prologomenon' by B. Lifshitz, New York 1975

Fried, N., 'Al Megillat Antiochos ve-hitkadshuta bi-merutsat ha-zemanim', *Sinai* 64 (1969) 108-124

Fried, N., 'Nusah ivri hadash shel Megillat Antiochus, *Tzefunot* 5 (1993) 65-74

Friedenwald, H., *The Jews and Medicine* 2, Baltimore 1944, 22f

Friedman, M.A., 'Babatha's *Ketubba* — Some Preliminary Observations', *IEJ* 46 (1996) 55-76

Friedman, M.A., 'On the Contribution of the Geniza to Talmudic Literature', *Jewish Studies* 38 (1998) 277-301 (Hebr)

Friedman, M.A., 'The "Handwriting" (כיר) of the Almighty on the Tablets of the Decalogue according to a New Passage in the Mekhilta', *Te'uda* 9 (1995) 65-73 (Hebr)

Friedman, M.A., '"An Important *Ma'ase*" – A New Fragment of *Ma'asim livne Erez Israel*', *Tarbiz* 51 (1982) 193-205 (Hebr)

Friedman, M.A., 'Israel's Response in Hosea 2:17b: "You are my Husband"', *JBL* 99 (1980) 199-204

Friedman, M.A., *Jewish Marriage in Palestine – A Cairo Geniza Study* 1-2, Tel-Aviv and New York, 1980-81

Friedman, M.A., 'On Linguistic Chronology in Rabbinic Literature', *Sidra* 1 (1985) 59-68 (Hebr)

Friedman, M.A., 'Marriage and the Family in the Talmud – Selected Chapters (from Mohar to Ketubba)', in E.E. Urbarch (ed), *Yad la-Talmud – Selected Chapters, s.l.* [Israel] 1983, 29-36, 99-100 (Hebr)

Friedman, M.A., 'Marriage as an Institution: Jewry under Islam', in D. Kraemer (ed), *The Jewish Family – Metaphor and Memory*, New York – Oxford 1989, 31-45

Friedman, M.A., 'On the New Fragment of Ma'asim Livnei Eretz Israel', *Tarbiz* 51 (1982) 662-4 (Hebr)

Friedman, M.A., 'The Phrase כיר יד and the Signing of the Second Tablets of the Decalogue in the Midrash', *Te'uda* 7 (1991) 161-189 (Hebr)

Friedman, M.A., *Polygyny in the Middle Ages – New Documents from the Cairo Geniza*, Jerusalem 1986 (Hebr)

Friedman, M.A., 'Publication of a Book by Depositing it in a Sanctuary: On the Phrase "Written and Deposited" ', *Lešonenu* 48-49 (1983) 49-52 (Hebr)

Friedman, M.A., 'On the Relationship of the Karaite and the Palestinian Rabbanite Marriage Contracts from the Geniza', *Te'uda* 15 (1999) 145-157 (Hebr)

Friedman, M.A., 'Remarriage of One's Divorcee after her Marriage to Someone Else and the Impurity of the Adulteress and Raped Wife', in S. Friedman (ed), *Saul Lieberman Memorial Volume*, New York and Jerusalem 1993, 189-232 (Hebr)

Friedman, M.A., 'The Royal Era (ὑπατειά) in Legal Documents and in the Midrash – Literary Expressions of Legal Reality', *Te'uda* 11 (1996) 205-229 (Hebr)

Friedman, M.A., 'Shenei ketaim mi-Sefer ha-Ma'asim Linei Eretz Israel', *Sinai* 74 (1973) 14-36

Friedman, M.A., 'He Writes, He Makes a Writ', *Sinai* 84 (1979) 177-179 (Hebr)

Friedman, M.A. – Lerner, M.B. (eds), *Studies in the Aggadic Midrashim = Te'uda* 12 (1996) (Hebr)

Friedmann, M., *Mechilta de-Rabbi Ismael, der älteste halachische und hagadische Midrasch zu Exodus*, Vienna 1870 (Hebr)

Friedmann, M., *Seder Eliahu Rabba und Seder Eliahu Zuta*, Vienna 1902 (Hebr)

Friedmann, M., *Sifra der alteste Midrasch zu Levitikus*, Breslau 1915 (Hebr)

Fürst, J., *Glossarium Graeco-Hebraeum oder der griechische Wörterschatz der jüdischen Midraschwerke*, Strassburg 1890

Gafni, I., 'Babylonian Rabbinic Culture', in D. Biale (ed), *Cultures of the Jews*, New York 2002, 244-250

Gafni, I., *The Jews of Babylonia in the Talmudic Era, A Social and Cultural History*, Jerusalem 1990 (Hebr)

Gafni, I.M. – Oppenheimer, A. – Schwartz, D.R. (eds), *The Jews in the Hellenistic-Roman World: Studies in Memory of Menahem Stern*, Jerusalem 1996

Gager, J.G., *Curse Tablets and Binding Spells from the Ancient World*, Oxford 1992

Garb, Y., *Manifestations of Power in Jewish Mysticism*, Jerusalem 2005 (Hebr)

Garbus, E.Z., *Sifre Zuta al Bamidbar ... in Perush Sapire Efrayim*, Jerusalem 1949 (Hebr)

García Martínez, F. – E.J.C. Tigchelaar, *The Dead Sea Scrolls Study Edition* 2, Leiden – Boston 1997-98 (CDRom edition)

García Martínez, F. – Tigchelaar, E.J.C. – Woude, A.S. van der, *Qumran Cave 11*, vol 2: *11Q2-18, 11Q20-31*, (DJD 23) Oxford 1999

Gartner, Y., 'Why did the Geonim Institute the Custom of Saying "Avoth" on the Sabbath?' *Sidra* 4 (1988) 17-32 (Hebr)

Gaster, M., 'Demetrius und Seder Olam: Ein Problem hellenistischer Literatur', in *Festskrift in anledning af professor David Simonsens 70-aarige Fodselsdag*, Copenhagen 1923, 243-252

Gaster, M., 'Eliezer Grescas and his Bet Zvul, the Bible References in Talmud and Midrash', *HUCA* 6 (1929) 277-295

Gaster, M., *The Exempla of the Rabbis*, 2nd ed New York 1968

Gaster, M., 'The Oldest Version of Midrash Megillah', in *Semitic Studies in Memory of Rev. Dr. Alexander Kohut*, Berlin 1897, 167-178, repr in idem, *Studies and Texts* 3, 44-49

Gaster, M., 'Samaritan Phylacteries and Amulets', *Proceedings of the Society of Biblical Archaeology* 37 (1915) 135-144

Gaster, M., *Studies and Texts* 1-3, London 1971

Gaster, M., trans., *The Chronicles of Jerahmeel* (or, The Hebrew Bible Historiale), prolegomenon by H. Schwarzbaum, 2nd ed New York 1971

Gauthier, P., *Les Cités grecques et leurs bienfaiteurs*, Athens 1985

Geiger, A., *Kevutsat maamarim*, [= *Ha-Karmel* 1875] Breslau 1885 (Hebr)

Geiger, A., *Lehr- und Lesebuch zur Sprache der Mischnah*, Breslau 1845

Geiger, A., *Urschrift und Ubersetzungen der Bibel*, Frankfurt/M 1928²

Geiger, J., 'The Gallos Rebellion and the Julian Affair', in Z. Baras *et al.* (eds), *Eretz Israel from the Destruction of the Second Temple to the Muslim Conquest*, Jerusalem 1982, vol 1, 208-217

Geller, M.J., 'Akkadian Medicine in the Babylonian Talmud', in D. Cohn-Sherbok (ed), *A Traditional Quest*, Sheffield 1991, 102-112

Geller, M.J., 'An Akkadian Vademecum in the Babylonian Talmud', in S. Kottek *et al.* (eds), *From Athens to Jerusalem: Medicine in Hellenized Jewish Lore and in Early Christian Literature*, Rotterdam 2000, 13-32

Genebrard, G., *Seder Olam Rabba*, with Latin translation, Basel 1580

Gertner, M., 'The Masorah and the Levites', *VT* 10 (1960) 241-272

Gertner, M., 'Terms of Scriptural Interpretation: A Study in Hebrew Semantics', *BSOAS* 25 (1962) 4-14

Geula, A., *Midrash Avkir: mevoot u-muvaot*, Master's thesis Hebrew U, Jerusalem 1998

Geula, A., 'The Riddle of the Index of Verses in MS Moscow-Ginzburg 1420/7', *Tarbiz* 70 (2001) 429-464 (Hebr)

Geula, A., 'On the Study of Midrash Yelammedenu: A Re-Examination of Attribution in Yalkut Shim'oni and its Sources', *Tarbiz* 74 (2005) 221-259 (Hebr)

Gibson, J.C.L., *Textbook of Syrian Semitic Inscriptions* 2, Oxford 1975

Gil, M., *Documents of the Jewish Pious Foundations from the Cairo Geniza*, Leiden 1976

Gilat, Y.D., 'On Fasting on the Sabbath', *Tarbiz* 52 (1982) 1-15, repr in idem, *Studies in the Development of the Halacha*, Jerusalem 1992, 109-122 (Hebr)

Gilat, Y.D., *Studies in the Development of the Halakha*, Ramat Gan 1992 (Hebr)

Gilat, Y.D., *The Teachings of R. Eliezer ben Hyrcanos and their Position in the History of the Halakha*, Tel Aviv 1968 (Hebr)

Gilat, Y.D. – Levin, C., – Rabinowitz, Z.M. (eds), *Studies in Rabbinic Literature, Bible and Jewish History Devoted to Prof. E.Z. Melamed*, Ramat Gan 1982 (Hebr)

Ginzberg, L., *A Commentary on the Palestinian Talmud* 3, New York 1941

Ginzburg, L., *Gaonica* 1, 2nd pr New York 1968

Ginzberg, L., *Ginze Schechter* 1, New York 1928 (Hebr)

Ginzberg, L., *Al ha-halakha ve-aggada*, Tel Aviv 1960

Ginzberg, L., *Genizah Studies in Memory of Doctor Solomon Schechter*, vols 1-3, New York 1928 (Hebr)

Ginzberg, L., *The Legends of the Jews*, vol 1-6, Philadelphia 1909-1928; vol 7 Index by B. Cohen, Philadelphia 1938; repr JPS 2003

Ginzberg, L., 'Yahas hakhmei Erets Yisrael ve-yahas ha-Geonim el ha-piyyut', in idem, *Ginzei Schechter* 3, 544-573

Ginzberg, L., 'Al ha-Yahas she-bein ha-Mishnah ve-ha-Mekhilta', in idem, *Al ha-halakha ve-aggada*, 66-103

Ginzberg, L. (ed), *Yerushalmi Fragments from the Genizah*, New York 1909

Ginsberg, M., *Sifra with Translation and Commentary, Dibura Denedabah*, Atlanta 1999

Girón, L., 'A Preliminary Description of the Languge of Canticles Rabba: Sample Edition', in M. Bar-Asher (ed), *Language Studies* 4 (1990) 129-160 (Hebr)

Glick, A., 'Another Fragment of the Mekhilta de-RaShBI', *Lešonenu* 48-49 (1985) 210-15 (Hebr)

Gluska, I., *Hebrew and Aramaic Contact during the Tannaitic Period: A Sociolinguistic Approach*, Tel-Aviv 1999 (Hebr)

Gluska, I., *The Influences of Aramaic on Mishnaic Hebrew*, diss Bar-Ilan U, Ramat-Gan 1987 (Hebr)

Gnuse, R., *The Dream Theophany of Samuel: Its Structure in Relation to Ancient Near Eastern Dreams and its Theological Significance*, New York 1984

Goitein, S.D., *A Mediterranean Society – The Jewish Communities of the Arab World as Portrayed in the Documents of the Cairo Geniza* 1-4, Berkeley, Los Angeles and London, 1967-1983

Goldberg, Abr., 'Beayot arikha ve-siddur Bereshit Rabba u-Vayyikra Rabba', *Mehkerei Talmud* 3 (2005) 130-152

Goldberg, Abr., 'The Dual Exegeses in *Mekhilta de-Milu'im*', *Sinai* 89 (1981) 115-118 (Hebr)

Goldberg, Abr., 'The Early and the Late Midrash', *Tarbiz* 50 (1981) 94-106 (Hebr)

Goldberg, Abr., 'Chanokh Albeck: Mavo la-Talmudim', *KS* 47 (1972) 9-19 (Hebr)

Goldberg, Abr., 'Leshonot 'davar aher' be-Midrashei ha-Halakhah', in: Gilat, et al., *Studies in Rabbinic Literature*, 99-107 (Hebr)

Goldberg, Abr., 'The Mishna – a Study Book of Halakha', in Safrai, *Literature of the Sages*, 211-262

Goldberg, Abr., 'The School of Rabbi Akiva and the School of Rabbi Ishmael in Sifre Deuteronomy, Pericopes 1-54', *Te'uda* 3 (1983) 9-16 (Hebr)

Goldberg, Arn., 'Der Peroratio [Hatima] als Kompositionsform der rabbinische Homilie' *FJB* 6 (1978) 1-22

Goldberg, Arn., 'Petiha und Hariza', *JSJ* 10 (1979) 213-218

Goldberg, Arn., 'Versuch über die hermeneutische Präsupposition und Struktur der Petiha', *FJB* 8 (1980) 1-59

Goldin, J., *The Munich Manuscript of the Mekilta*, Copenhagen 1980

Goldin, J., 'Not by Means of an Angel and not by Means of a Messenger', in J. Neusner (ed), *Religions in Antiquity, Essays in memory of E.R. Goodenoough* (Studies in the History of Religions 14) Leiden 1968, 412-424 (= J. Goldin, *Studies in Midrash and Related Literature*, Philadelphia 1988, 163-173)

Goldin, J., 'Towards a Profile of the Tanna Aqiba ben Joseph', *JAOS* 96 (1976) 38-56

Goldin, J., *The Song at the Sea: Being a Commentary on a Commentary on Two Parts*, New Haven – London 1971, repr Philadelphia 1990

Goldin, J., *Studies in Midrash and Related Literature*, Philadelphia 1988

Goldstein, J.A., 'The Syriac Bill of Sale from Dura-Europas', *JNES* 25 (1966) 1-16

Goldstein, N., 'Midrash Carticles Rabba in MS Parma 1240', *Kobez Al Yad* 9 (19), Jerusalem 1980, 1-24 (Hebr)

Goodenough, E.R., *Jewish Symbols in the Greco-Roman Period* 1-13, New York 1953-1968

Gooding, D.W. 'On The Use of the LXX for Dating Midrashic Elements in the Targum', *JTS* 25 (1974) 1-11

Gordon, B.L., 'Medicine among the Ancient Hebrews', *Annals Med. Hist.* 3rd ser. vol 4 (1942) 218-235

Goshen-Gottstein, A., *The Sinner and the Amnesiac: The Rabbinic Invention of Elisha ben Abuya and Eleazar ben Arach*, Stanford 2000

Goshen-Gottstein, M.H., 'Targum-Studies: An Overview of Recent Developments', *Textus* 16 (1991) 1-11

Gottlieb, I., 'Succession in Elephantine and Jewish Law', *JSS* 26 (1981) 193-203

Gottlieb, I.B., 'Language Understanding in Sifre Deuteronomy', diss New York U 1972

Gottlieb, I.B., 'Midrash as Philology', *JQR* 75 (1984) 132-61

Graetz, H., 'Die mystische Literatur in der gaonischen Epoche', *MGWJ* 8 (1859) 67-78, 103-118, 140-153

Grätz [Graetz], H. *Geschichte der Juden,* III/2, fifth ed Leipzig 1906

Gräz [Graetz], H., 'בית המדרש oder Sammlung Kleiner Midraschim' (review), *MGWJ* 2 (1853) 347-356

Green, W.S., 'Palestinian Holy Men: Charismatic Leadership and Rabbinic Tradition', *ANRW* II 19.2 (1979) 619-647

Greenberg, M., 'The Patterns of Prayers of Petition in the Bible', *Eretz-Israel* 16 (1982) [H.M. Orlinsky Volume] 47-55

Greenberg, M., *Biblical Prose Prayer as a Window to the Popular Religion of Israel*, U of California Press 1983

Greenberg, M., 'Nebuchadnezzar and the Parting of the Ways: Ezek. 21:26-27', *ScrHier* 33 (1991) 267-271

Greenfield, J.[C.], *Al Kanfei Yonah: Collected Studies of Jonas C. Greenfield on Semitic Philology* 1, ed by S.M. Paul *et al.*, Leiden – Jerusalem 2001

Greenfield, J.C., 'Babylonian-Aramaic Relations', in H.-J. Nissen and J. Renger (eds), *Mesopotamien und seine Nachbarn*, Berlin 1982, 471-482

Greenfield, J.C., 'The Dialects of Early Aramaic', *JNES* 37 (1978) 93-99

Greenfield, J.C., 'The Languages of Palestine, 200 B.C.E.-200 C.E.', in H.J. Paper (ed), *Jewish Languages – Theme and Variations*, Cambridge MA 1978

Greenfield, J.C., 'Prolegomenon', in H. Odeberg, *3 Enoch, or the Hebrew Book of Enoch*), 2nd ed New York 1973, xi-xlvii

Greenfield, J.C., 'Studies in the Legal Terminology of the Nabatean Funerary Inscriptions', in Kutscher *et al.*, *Yalon Memorial Volume*, 64-83 (Hebr)

Greenfield, J.C. – Sokoloff, M., 'An Astrological Text from Qumran *(4Q318)* and Reflections on Some Zodiacal Names', *RQ* 16 (1995) 507-525

Grintz, Y.M., *Sefer Yehudith, A Reconstruction of the Original Hebrew Text with Introduction, Commentary, Appendices and Indices*, Jerusalem 1957, repr 1986 (Hebr)

Groner, Z., 'From Halakhic Works of the Geonim', *Alei Sefer* 15 (1989) 31-5 (Hebr)

Gropp, D.M., 'The Samaria Papyri and the Babylonio-Aramean Symbiosis', in L.H. Schiffman (ed), *Semitic Papyrology in Context*, Leiden and Boston 2003, 23-49

Gropp, D.M., 'The Wadi Daliyeh Documents Compared to the Elephantine Documents' in L.H. Schiffman – E. Tov – J.C. VanderKam, (eds), *The Dead Sea Scrolls Fifty Years after Their Discovery*, Jerusalem 2000, 826-835

Gross, M.D., *Otsar ha-aggada meha-Mishna veha-Tosefta, ha-Talmudim veha-Midrashim ve-sifrei ha-Zohar* 1-3, Jerusalem 1993 (Hebr)

Grossfeld, B., *A Bibliography of Targum Literature*, Cincinnati 1972, 1977

Grossfeld, B., 'The Haggada in the Targum Rishon to Esther According to the Bibliothèque Nationale Paris Héb. 110', *Hebrew Studies* 23 (1982) 101-109

Grossman, A., *The Early sages of France*, Jerusalem 1995 (Hebr)

Gruenwald, I., *Apocalyptic and Merkavah Mysticism*, Leiden 1980

Gruenwald, I., *From Apocalypticism to Gnosticism*, Frankfurt/M 1988

Gruenwald, I., 'Ketaim hadashim mi-sifrut ha-Hekhalot', *Tarbiz* 38 (1969) 300-319

Gruenwald, I., 'Ha-ketav, ha-mikhtav, veha-shem ha-meforash: magia, ruhaniut, ve-mistika', in M. Oron – A. Goldreich (eds), *Massu'ot, Studies in Kabbalistic Literature and Jewish Philosophy in memory of Prof. E. Gottlieb*, Jerusalem 1992, 75-98 (Hebr)

Gruenwald, I., 'Tikkunim ve-hearot le-ketaim hadashim mi-sifrut ha-Hekhalot', *Tarbiz* 39 (1970) 216-217

Gulak, A., 'Diethemen', *Tarbiz* 1/4 (1930) 144-5 (Hebr)

Gulak, A., *Legal Documents in the Talmud*, edited and supplemented by R. Katzoff, Jerusalem 1994 (Hebr)

Gulak, A., *Otzar ha-Shetarot*, Jerusalem 1926

Gulak, A., 'The Right of Ownership of Property of a Heather Slave according to Talmudic Law', *Tarbiz* 1 (1930) 20-26

Gulak, A., 'Simfon be-erusin lefi ha-Talmud ha-Yerushalmi', *Tarbiz* 5 (1934) 126-133

Gundel, W. – Gundel, H.G., *Astrologumena: Die astrologische Literatur in der Antike und ihre Geschichte*, Wiesbaden 1966

Habermann, A.M., *Hadashim gam yeshanim*, Jerusalem 1975

Habermann, A.M., 'The Phylacteries in Antiquity', *Eretz-Israel* 3 (1954) 174-77 (Hebr)

Ha-Kohen, E., 'On the Relationship between the Midrashim on Esther and the Expansive Piyyutim of Hakalir for Purim – אספרה אל חוק and אמל ורבך', *Netuim* 7(2000) 45-74 (Hebr)

Halbertal, M., *Interpretative Revolutions in the Making: Values as Interpretive Considerations in Midrashei Halakhah*, Jerusalem 1997 (Hebr)

Halevy, A.A., *Olama shel ha-aggada*, Tel-Aviv 1972

Halevy, I., *Dorot ha-Rishonim*, Frankfurt/M 1918 (Hebr)

Halivni (Weiss), D., *Midrash, Mishnah and Gemara*, Cambridge MA – London 1986

Halivni, D., *Sources and Traditions – Source Critical Commentary: on Seder Nashim*, Tel-Aviv 1968; *on Baba Kama*, Jerusalem 1993 (Hebr)

Halperin, D.J., *Faces of the Chariot: Early Jewish Responses to Ezekiel's Vision*, Tübingen 1988

Halperin, D.J., *The Merkabah in Rabbinic Literature*, New Haven 1980

Halperin, D.J., 'A New Edition of Hekhalot Literature', *JAOS* 104 (1984) 543-552

Hammer, R., 'Neusner's Sifre to Deuteronomy', *JQR* 81 (1990) 170-74

Hammer, R., 'A Rabbinic Response to the Post Bar Kochba Era: Sifre Ha'azinu', *PAAJR* 52 (1985) 37-53

Hammer, R., 'Section 38 of Sifre Deuteronomy: An Example of the Use of Independent Sources to Create a Literary Unit', *HUCA* 50 (1979) 165-78

Hammer, R., *Sifre: A Tannaitic Commentary on the Book of Deuteronomy*, New Haven-London 1986

Hammer, Reuven, 'What Did They Bless? A Study of Mishnah Tamid 5.1", *JQR* 81 (1991) 305-324

Hammond, N.G.L. – Scullard, H.H. (eds), *Oxford Classical Dictionary*, Oxford 1970

Haneman, G., 'On the Linguistic Tradition of the Written Text in the Sifra Ms. (Rome, Codex Assemani 66)', in Kutscher *et al.*, *Yalon Memorial Volume*, 84-98 (Hebr)

Haneman, G., *A Morphology of Mishnaic Hebrew, according to Parma Manuscript (De Rossi 138)*, Tel-Aviv 1980 (Hebr)

Haran, M., 'On the Diffusion of Literacy and Schools in Ancient Israel', *Congress Volume Jerusalem 1986, International Oganization for the Study of the Old Testament*, (VT Supp 40) Leiden 1988, 81-95

Haran, M., 'Mi-mokhorat ha-shabbat', *Enziklopedia Mikra'it* (*Encyclopaedia Biblica*), vol 7, cols. 517-21 (Hebr)

Harari, Y., *Early Jewish Magic: Study, Method and Sources*, (forthcoming, Hebr)

Harari, Y., *Early Jewish Magic – Methodological and Phenomenological Studies*, diss Hebrew U 1998 (Hebr)

Harari, Y., 'How to Do Things with Words: Philosophical Theory and Magical Deeds', *Jerusalem Studies in Jewish Folklore* 19-20 (1997-98) 365-392 (Hebr)

Harari, Y., 'If You Wish to Kill a Person: Harmful Magic and Protection from it in Early Jewish Magic', *Jewish Studies* 37 (1997) 111-142 (Hebr)

Harari, Y., 'Love Charms in Early Jewish Magic', *Kabbala* 5 (2000) 247-264 (Hebr)

Harari, Y., 'Moses, the Sword, and the Sword of Moses: Between Rabbinical and Magical Traditions', *JSQ* 12 (2005) 293-329

Harari, Y., 'The Opening of the Heart: Magical Practices for Gaining Knowledge, Understanding and Good Memory in Judaism in Late Antiquity and the Early Middle Ages', in Z. Gries – H. Kreisel – B. Huss (eds), *Shefa Tal, Studies in Jewish Thought and Culture presented to Bracha Sack*, Beer Sheva 2004, 303-347 (Hebr)

Harari, Y., 'Power and Money: Economic Aspects of the Use of Magic by Jews in Ancient Times and the Early Middle Ages', *Pe'amim* 85 (2001) 14-42 (Hebr)

Harari, Y., *The Sword of Moses – A New Edition and Study*, Jerusalem 1997 (Hebr)

Harari, Y., 'What is a Magical Text? – Methodological Reflections Aimed at Redefining Early Jewish Magic', in S. Shaked (ed), *Officina Magica: Essays on the Practice of Magic in Antiquity*, Leiden 2005, 91-124

Harduf, D.M., *Biblical Proper Names*, Tel-Aviv 1964 (Hebr)

671

Harduf, D.M., *Exegesis of Biblical Proper Names in the Talmud and Midrash*, Tel-Aviv 1960 (Hebr)

Harkavi, A.E., *Ha-sarid veha-palit mi-Sefer ha-Agron ve-Sefer ha-Galui: al pi kitvei yad be-otsar ha-kesari be-Petersburg ve-shaarei kitvei yad Rav Saadya Alfiumi*, Petersburg 1891, repr Jerusalem [1969]

Harley, J.R. – Woodward, D., (eds.), *The History of Cartography*, Chicago 1987

Harris, J.M., *How Do We Know This: The Midrash and the Fragmentation of Modern Judaism*, New York 1995

Hartman, G.H. – Budick, S., *Midrash and Literature*, New Haven 1986

Harviainen, T., 'Diglossia in Jewish Eastern Aramaic', *Studia Orientalia* 55 (1984) 97-113

Hasan-Rokem, G., ' "A Dream Amounts to the Sixtieth Part of Prophecy": On Interaction between Textual Establishment and Popular Context in Dream Interpretation by the Jewish Sages', in B.Z. Kedar (ed), *Studies in the History of Popular Culture*, Jerusalem 1996, 45-54 (Hebr)

Hasan-Rokem, G., *Tales of the Neighborhood: Jewish Narrative Dialogues in Late Antiquity*, Berkeley 2003

Hasan-Rokem, G., *Web of Life: Folklore in Rabbinic Literature*, ET B. Stein, Stanford 2000

Hauptman, Judith, 'How Old is the Haggadah', *Judaism* 51/1 (2002) 9

Hayman, P., *Sefer Yesira: Edition, Translation, and Text-Critical Commentary*, Tübingen 2004

Hayman, P. 'The Temple at the Center of the Universe,' *JJS* 37 (1986), 176-182

Hayward, R., 'Major Aspects of Targumic Studies 1983-1993; a survey', *Currents in Research* 2 (1994) 107-122

Hefets ben Yatsliah, *A Volume of the Book of Precepts by Hefes b. Yasliah*, ed B. Halper, Philadelphia 1915 (Hebr)

Heichelheim, F.M., 'Roman Syria', in *An Economic Survey of Ancient Rome*, ed Tenney Frank, vol 4, Baltimore 1938

Heinemann, I., *Darkhei ha-aggada*, 2nd ed Jerusalem 1954

Heinemann, I., art. 'Midrash', in *Encyclopedia Biblica*, Jerusalem 1962, vol 4, 696 (Hebr)

Heinemann, J., *Aggadot ve-toldotehen*, Jerusalem 1974

Heinemann, J., 'Birkath Ha'zimmun and Havurah Meals', *JJS* 13 (1962) 23-39

Heinemann, J., 'Early Halakhah in the Palestinian Targumim', *JJS* 25 (1974) 114-122

Heinemann, J., 'Le-hitpathut ha-munahim ha-miktzoiyim: I. Derash', *Lešonenu* 14 (1946) 182-89 (Hebr)

Heinemann, J., *Prayer in the Talmud: Forms and Patterns*, Berlin – New York 1977; ET of *He-tefilla bi-tekufat ha-Tannaim veha-Amoraim*, Jerusalem 1964

Heinemann, J., 'The Proem in the Aggadic Midrashim: A Form-Critical Study', *ScrHier* 22 (1971) 100-122

Heinemann, J., 'Rabbinic Relations to Targum Onkelos', in *Joshua Finkel Festschrift*, New York 1974, 169-174

Heinemann, J., 'The Targum of Ex. 22:4 and the Ancient Halakhah', *Tarbiz* 38 (1968-9) 294- 296 (Hebr)

Hengel, M., *The Zealots: Investigations into the Jewish Freedom Movement in the Period from Herod I Until 70 A.D.*, ET D. Smith, Edinburgh 1989

Henshke, D., 'The *Midrash* of the Passover *Haggada*", *Sidra* 4 (1988) 3352 (Hebr)

Henshke, D., 'The Rabbis' Approach to Biblical Contradictions', *Sidra* 10 (1994) 39-55 (Hebr)

Henshke, D., 'On the Relationship between Targum Pseudo-Jonathan and the Halakhic Midrashim', *Tarbiz* 68 (1999) 187-210 (Hebr)

Henshke, D., 'Two Subjects Typifying the Tannaitic Halakhic Midrash', *Tarbiz* 65 (1996) 427-34 (Hebr)

Henshke, D., 'When is the Time of *Hakhel?*' *Tarbiz* 61 (1992) 177-194 (Hebr)

Henshke, D., 'What Should be Omitted in the Reading of the Bible: Forbidden Verses and Translations', *Kenishta* 1 (2001) 39-42 (Hebr)

Herr, M.D., 'Anti-Semitism in Imperial Rome in the Light of Rabbinic Literature', *Benjamin De Vries Memorial Volume*, Jerusalem 1968, 149-159 (Hebr)

Herr, M.D., 'The Conception of History among the Sages', *PWCJS,* 6:3 (1973) 129-142

Herr, M.D., 'Esther Rabbah', *EJ* 6 (1971) 915f

Herr, M.D., 'The Historical Significance of the Dialogues between Jewish Sages and Roman Dignitaries', *ScrHier* 22 (1971) 123-150

Herr, M.D., 'Persecution and Martyrdom in Hadrian's Days', *ScrHier* 23 (1972) 85-125

Herr, M.D., 'The Problem of War on Shabath in the Second Temple and the Talmudic Periods', *Tarbiz* 30 (1961) 242-56, 341-56 (Hebr)

Herr, M.D., 'Tanhuma Yelammedenu', in *EJ* 15 (1972) 794-796

Herr, M.D., 'Who Were the Boethusians?' *PWCJS* 7:3 (1981) 1-20 (Hebr)

Herrmann, K., 'Text und Fiktion; zur Textüberlieferung des "Shiur Qoma"', *FJB* 16 (1988) 89-142

Herskovitz, E., *Sefer ha-perushim u-fesakim le-R. Avigdor Zarfati al ha-Tora*, Jerusalem 1996

Hershkowitz, Y., 'Perush Yefe Anaf le-Midrash Kohelet', *Yeshurun* 1 (1997) 7-24; 6 (1999) 119-127; 9 (2001) 137-149

Heschel, A.J., *Theology of Ancient Judaism* (= *Tora min ha-Shamayim be-aspeklaria ha-dorot*), vols 1-2, London – New York, 1962-1965 (Hebr)

Higger, M., *Agadot Ha-Tannaim*, New York 1929

Hildesheimer, H. *Beiträge zur Geographie Palästinas*, *JRSB* 1885 (Hebr); ET H. Bar Daroma, *Studies in the Geography of Eretz Israel*, Jerusalem 1965

Himmelfarb, M., *Ascent to Heaven in Jewish and Christian Apocalypses*, New York – Oxford 1993

Himmelfarb, M., 'Heavenly Ascent and the Relationship of the Apocalypses and the *Hekhalot* Literature', *HUCA* 59 (1988) 73-100

Hirschfeld, H., *Arabic Chresthomathy*, London 1892

Hirshman, M., 'The Greek Fathers and the Aggada on Ecclesiastes: Formats of Exegesis in Late Antiquity', *HUCA* 59 (1988) 137-165

Hirshman, M., 'The Place of Aggada and Who Were the Baalei Aggada', in Sussmann – Rosenthal, *Talmudic Studies* 3/1, 190-208

Hirshman, M., 'The Preacher and his Public in Third Century Palestine', *JJS* 42 (1991) 108-114

Hirshman, M., 'The Priest's Gate and Elijah ben Menahem's Pilgrimage', *Tarbiz* 55 (1986) 217-227 (Hebr)

Hirshman, M., 'Rabbinic Universalism in the Second and Third Centuries', *HTR* 93 (2000) 101-15

Hirshman, M., ' "R. Elijah's Interpretation of the Verse Concerning Pilgrims" (Shir Rabba 2, 14, 7): Another Medieval Interpolation and Again R. Elijah', *Tarbiz* 60 (1991) 275-276 (Hebr)

Hirshman, M., *A Rivalry of Genius: Jewish and Christian Biblical Interpretation in Late Antiquity*, Albany 1996

Hirshman, M., *Tora for the Entire World*, Tel Aviv 1999 (Hebr)

Hoenig, S.B., 'Tefillat ha-Kohanim be-lishkat ha-gazit: Parasha nosefet le-inyan ha-mahloket bein ha-Perushim veha-Tsedukim', *Hegut Ivrit be-Amerika* 3 (1974) 32-43

Hoffman, L.A., 'Rituals of Birth in Judaism', in Bradshaw – Hoffman, *Life Cycles*, 32-54

Hoffman, L.A., 'Rites of Death and Mourning in Judaism', in Bradshaw – Hoffman, *Life Cycles*, 262-285

Hoffman, L.A., 'The Jewish Wedding Ceremony', in Bradshaw – Hoffman, *Life Cycles*, 129-153

Hoffman, L.A., *My People's Prayer Book*, 1: *The Sh'ma and its Blessings*, Woodstock 1997

Hoffman, L.A., *The Canonization of the Synagogue Service*, Notre Dame 1979, 7-23

Hoffmann, D., *Das Buch Leviticus übersetzt und erklärt*, Berlin 1904

Hoffmann, D., 'Zur Einleitung in die Halachischen Midraschim', *JRSB* 1888, 1-92

Hoffmann, D., 'Zur Einleitung in den Midrasch Tannaim zum Deuteronomium', *Jahrbuch der Judisch-Literarischen Gesellschaft* 6 (1909) 304-23

Hoffmann, D., '*Likutei batar Likutei me-Mekhilta le-Sefer Devarim* [Additional Collections of the *Mekhilta* on Deuteronomy]', *JRSB* 1897, 1-36 (Hebr)

Hoffmann, D., 'Likutei Mekhilta le-Sefer Devarim', in *Jubelschrift des I. Hildesheimer*, Hebrew Section, Berlin 1890, 3-32 (Hebr)

Hoffmann, D., *Mechilta de-Rabbi Simon b. Jochai zu Exodus*, Frankfurt/M 1905 (Hebr)

Hoffmann, D., *Der Midrasch Tannaim zum Deuteronomium*, Berlin 1908-1909 (Hebr)

Hoffmann, D., 'Ein Midrasch über die dreizehn Middot', in M. Freimann – M. Hildesheimer (eds), *Festschrift zum siebzigsten Geburtstage A. Berliner's*, Frankfurt/M 1903, Hebrew Section, 55-71

Hoffmann, D., 'Über eine Mechilta zu Deuteronomium', *Jubelschrift des I. Hildesheimer*, Berlin 1890, 83-93

Hopkins, S., *A Miscellany of Literary Pieces from the Cambridge Genizah Collections*, Cambridge 1978

Horbury, W., *Jews and Christians in Contact and Controversy*, Edinburgh 1999

Horgan, M.P., *Pesharim: Qumran Interpretation of Biblical Books*, Washington DC 1979

Horovitz, H.S. (ed), *Siphre d'be Rab: Siphre ad Numeros adjecto Siphre zutta cum variis lectionibus et adnotationibus*, Leipzig 1917, repr Jerusalem 1966 (Hebr)

Horovitz, H.S., *Der Sifre Zutta*, Breslau 1910

Horovitz, H.S. - Rabin, I.A. (eds), *Mechilta d'Rabbi Ismael cum variis lectionibus et adnotationibus*, Frankfurt 1931, repr Jerusalem 1970 (Hebr)

Horowitz, Ch.M., *Bet Eked Ha-Agadot*, Frankfort/M 1881

Horowitz, Ch.M., *Sammlung Kleiner Midraschim*, Berlin 1881, 47-50; 56-75 (Hebr)

Horst, P.W. van der, *Ancient Jewish Epitaphs: An Introductory Survey of a Millennium of Jewish Funerary Epigraphy*, Kampen 1991

Horst, P.W. van der, 'The Birkat ha-minim in Recent Research', in idem, *Hellenism, Judaism, Christianity: Essays on their Interaction*, Kampen 1994, 99-114

Horst, P.W. van der, 'The Greek Synagogue Prayers in the Apostolic Constitutions, book VII', in J. Tabory (ed), *From Qumran to Cairo: Studies in the History of Prayer*, Jerusalem 1999, 19-46

Horst, P.W. van der, 'Papyrus Egerton 5: Christian or Jewish?' *ZPE* 121 (1998) 173-182

Horst, P.W. van der, 'Seven Month's Children in Jewish and Christian Literature from Antiquity, *ETL* 54 (1978) 346-360

Hrushovski, B., 'The Major Systems of Hebrew Rhyme from Piyyut to Modern Times', *Hasifrut* 2 (1971) 721-749 (Hebr)

Hrushovski, B., 'Prosody, Hebrew', in *EJ* 13, 1195-1240

Hunter, E., 'Technical Tables', in Segal, *Catalogue*, 189-204

Hunter, E., 'The Typology of the Incantation Bowls: Physical Features and Decorative Aspects', in Segal, *Catalogue*, 163-188

Hunter, E., 'Who are the Demons? Iconography of Incantation Bowls', *Studi epigrafici e linguistici sul vicino Oriente antico* 15 (1998) 95-115

Hurvitz, A., *The Transition Period in Biblical Hebrew*, Jerusalem 1972 (Hebr)

Hurwitz, S., *Lilith, die erste Eva: eine Studie über dunkle Aspekte des Weiblichen*, Zürich 1980

Hutter, M., 'Asmodeus', in Toorn – Becking – Horst, *Dictionary*, 106-108

Hutter, M., 'Lilith', in Toorn – Becking – Horst, *Dictionary*, 520-521

Hyman, A., *Sefer Torah ha-ketuva veha-messura al Tora, Neviim u-Khetuvim*1-3, (1937-40) repr Tel Aviv 1979 (Hebr)

Hyman, A., *Toldoth Tannaim ve'Amoraim* 1-3, London 1910

Hyman, A. (ed), *Maimonidean Studies*, New York 1990

Hyman, A.B. (Dov), *The Sources of the Yalkut Shimeoni* 1-2, Jerusalem 1965-1974 (Hebr)

Idel, M., *Golem: Jewish Magical and Mystical Traditions on the Artificial Anthropoid*, Albany 1990

Idel, M., 'On Judaism, Jewish Mysticism, and Magic', in P. Schäfer – H.G. Kippenberg (eds), *Envisioning Magic: A Princeton Seminar and Symposium*, 195-214.

Idel, M., *Kabbalah: New Perspectives*, New Haven 1988

Idel, M., 'PaRDeS; Some Reflections on Kabbalistic Hermeneutics', in Collins – Fishbane, *Death, Ecstasy*, 249-268

Ilan, T., 'Ben Sira's Attitude to Women and its Reception by the Babylonian Talmud', *Jewish Studies* 40 (2000) 103-111 (Hebr)

Ilan, T., *Jewish Women in Greco-Roman Palestine: An Inquiry into the Image and Status*, Tübingen 1995

Ilan, T., *Lexicon of Jewish Names in Late Antiquity*, Tübingen 2002

Ilan, T., 'Notes and Observations on a Newly Published Divorce Bill from the Judaean Desert', *HTR* 89 (1996) 195-202

Ilan, T., 'The Ossuary and Sarcophagus Inscriptions', in G. Avni – Z. Greenhut (eds), *The Akeldama Tombs*, Jerusalem 1996, 57-72

Ilan, T., 'Premarital Cohabitation in Ancient Judea: The Evidence of the Babatha Archive and the Mishnah (*Ketubbot* 1.4)', *HTR* 86 (1993) 247-64

Ilan, T., 'The Provocative Approach Once Again: A Response to Adiel Schremer', *HTR* 91 (1998) 203-4

Ilan, T., 'A Witch-hunt in Ashkelon', in A. Sasson – Z. Safrai – N. Sagiv (eds), *Ashkelon, A City on the Seashore*, Ashkelon 2001, 135-146 (Hebr)

Inscriptions Reveal – Ketovot mesaprot: Yemei ha-Bayit ha-rishon veha-sheni u-tekufat ha-Mishna veha-Talmud, Miriam Tadmor *et al.* (eds), Exhibition catalogue, 2nd ed, Jerusalem 1973

Jabez, Z., *Toledot Yisrael* 1-14, Tel-Aviv 1955-63 (Hebr)

Jackson, H.M., 'The Origins and Development of *Shi'ur Qomah* Revelation in Jewish Mysticism', *JSJ* 31 (2005) 373-415

Jacobs, Louis, 'Praying for the Downfall of the Wicked', *Modern Judaism* 2/3 (1982) 297-310

Jacobson, H., 'Did Saul Lieberman Know Greek and Latin?', in Lubetski, *Saul Lieberman*, 12-23

Jaffee, M., *Tora in the Mouth*, Oxford 2001

James, W., *The Varieties of Religious Experience*, (1902) repr New York 1982

Janowitz, N., *The Poetics of Ascent: Theories of Language in a Rabbinic Ascent Text*, Albany 1989

Japhet, S., *The Ideology of the Book of Chronicles*, Jerusalem 1977 (Hebr)

Japhet, S. (ed), *Studies in Bible and Talmud*, Jerusalem 1987 (Hebr)

Jaskowicz, J. Z. *Sifre Zuta al Sefer Bamidbar*, Lodz 1929 (Hebr)

Jastrow, M., *A Dictionary of the Targumim, The Talmud Babli, Yerushalmi, and the Midrashic Literature* 1-2, London – New York 1903 and repr

Jeffers, A., *Magic and Divination in Ancient Palestine and Syria*, Leiden 1996

Jellinek, A., 'Literarische Berichte', *MGWJ* 3 (1854) 242-248

Jellinek, A. (ed), *Bet ha-Midrasch: Sammlung kleiner Midraschim* 1-6, Leipzig 1853-1878, repr Jerusalem 1938, 1967

Joel, D.H., *Der Aberglaube und die Stellung des Judenthums zu demselben*, (Jahresb. des jüd.-theol. Sem. Fraenckel'scher Stiftung) Breslau 1881-83

Joel, M., *Blicke in die Religionsgeschichte*, Breslau 1880

Jones, J.W., *The Law and Legal Theory of the Greeks: An Introduction*, Oxford 1956

Johnston, S.I., 'Charming Children: The Use of the Child in Ancient Divination', *Arethusa* 34 (2001) 97-117

Juusola, H., *Linguistic Peculiarities in the Aramaic Magic Bowl Texts*, Helsinki 1999

Kad[d]ari, M.Z. 'The Aramaic Megillat Antiochus', *Bar Ilan* 1 (1963) 81-105; 2 (1964) 178-214 (Hebr)

Kadari, M.Z. 'Be-eizo Aramit nikhteva Megillat Antiochus?' *Lešonenu* 23 (1959) 129-145

Kadari, M.Z., 'Research on Onqelos Today: The State of the Research', in B. Uffenheimer (ed), *Bible and Jewish History: Studies in Bible and Jewish History dedicated to the Memory of J. Liver*, Tel Aviv 1971, 341-374 (Hebr)

Kadari, T., 'Midrash Teshuvat Yona Ha-Navi', *Kovets al-yad* 16 (2002) 68-84

Kadari, T., *On the Redaction of Midrash Shir HaShirim Rabbah*, diss Hebrew U, Jerusalem 2004 (Hebr)

Kadushin, M., *A Conceptual Approach to the Mekilta*, New York 1969

Kafih: see Qafih

Kagan, S.R., *Jewish Medicine*, Medico-Historical Press, Boston 1952

Kahana, A., *Ha-sefarim ha-hitsoniim*, 2nd ed Tel Aviv 1955-56

Kahana, M.[I.], 'Another Page from the Mekhilta of R. Simeon b. Yohai', *Alei Sefer* 15 (1989) 5-20 (Hebr)

Kahana, M.I., 'The Biblical Text as Reflected in MS Vatican 32 of the Sifre', in Sussmann – Rosenthal, *Talmudic Studies* 1, 1-10 (Hebr)

Kahana, M.I., 'Citations of the Deuteronomy Mekhilta Ekev and Ha'azinu', *Tarbiz* 56 (1987) 19-59 (Hebr)

Kahana, M.I., 'Citations from a New Tannaitic Midrash on Deuteronomy', *PWCJS* 11 (1994) 23-30 (Hebr)

Kahana, M.I., 'The Commentary of Rabbenu Hillel to the Sifre', *KS* 63 (1990) 271-80 (Hebr)

Kahana, M.I., 'The Critical Editions of Mekhilta de-Rabbi Ishmael in the Light of the Genizah Fragments', *Tarbiz* 55 (1986) 489-524 (Hebr)

Kahana, M.I., 'The Development of the Hermeneutical Principle of *Kelal u-Ferat* in the Tannaitic Period', in Bar-Asher – Levinson – Lifshitz, *Studies*, 173-216 (Hebr)

Kahana, M.I., 'Genesis Rabba MS Vatican 60 and Parallels', *Te'uda* 11 (1996) 17-60 (Hebr)

Kahana, M.I., *The Genizah Fragments of the Halakhic Midrashim* 1, Jerusalem 2005 (Hebr)

Kahana, M.I., 'Ginzei Midrash be-sifriot Leningrad u-Moskova', *Assufot* 6 (1992) 41-70

Kahana, M.I., 'The Importance of Dwelling in the Land of Israel according to the Deuteronomy Mekhilta', *Tarbiz* 62 (1993) 501-13 (Hebr)

Kahana, M.I., 'Manuscripts Commentaries on the Sifrei', in M. Benayahu (ed), *Studies in Memory of the Rishon Le-Zion R. Yitzhak Nissim*, (vols 1-6) Jerusalem 1985, vol 2, 95-118 (Hebr)

Kahana, M.I., *Manuscripts of the Halakhic Midrashim: An Annotated Catalogue*, Jerusalem 1995 (Hebr)

Kahana, M.I., 'Marginal Annotations of the School of Rabbi Judah the Prince in Halakhic Midrashim', in Jafet, *Studies*, 69-85 (Hebr)

Kahana, M.I., 'Midrashic Fragments in the Libraries of Leningrad and Moscow', *Asufot* 6 (1992) 41-70 (Hebr)

Kahana, M.I., 'New Fragments of the Mekhilta on Deuteronomy', *Tarbiz* 54 (1985) 485-551 (Hebr)

Kahana, M.I., 'Notes to the Mekhilta', *Tarbiz* 59 (1990) 235-241 (Hebr)

Kahana, M.I., 'Pages of the Deuteronomy Mekhilta Portions Ha'azinu and Zoth Haberakha', *Tarbiz* 57 (1988) 165-201 (Hebr)

Kahana, M.I., 'Pages of Halakhic Midrashim in the Archives of Nonantola and Modena', in David – Tabory, *Italian Genizah*, 61-69 (Hebr)

Kahana, M.I., *Prolegomena to a New Edition of the Sifre on Numbers*, Jerusalem 1982 (Hebr)

Kahana, M.I., 'The Redaction of Ma'aseh Bereshit in Genesis Rabba', *Prof. J. Fraenkel Jubilee Volume* (in print) (Hebr)

Kahana, M.I., 'The Relation to the Gentile in the Mishnah and Talmud Period', *Eth Hada'at* 3 (2000) 22-36 (Hebr)

Kahana, M.I., 'Searching Examination in the Light of a New Citation of Sifre Zuta on Deuteronomy', in Boyarin, *Atara L'Haim*, 112-28 (Hebr)

Kahana, M.I., *Sifre Zuta on Deuteronomy*, Jerusalem 2002 (Hebr)

Kahana, M.I., *The Two Mekhiltot on the Amalek Portion: The Originality of the Version of the Mekhilta d'Rabbi Ishma'el with Respect to the Mekhilta of Rabbi Shim'on ben Yohay*, Jerusalem 1999 (Hebr)

Kahana, M.I., 'To Whom Was the Land Divided', in S. Schmidt (ed), *Gedenkschrift for Mordechai Wiser*, Kevutzat Yavneh 1981, 249-73 (Hebr)

Kahana, M.I., 'The Yemenite Midrashim and Their Usage of Halakhic Midrashim', *PWCJS* 1:3:1 (1990) 31-38 (Hebr)

Kahana, M.I. (ed), *Commentary of Rabbi Eliezer Nahum to Sifre*, Jerusalem 1993 (Hebr)

Kahle, P.E., *Die Masoreten des Westens*, Stuttgart 1927

Kalmin, R., *Sages, Stories, Authors, and Editors in Rabbinic Babylonia*, Atlanta 1994

Kamesar A., 'Church Fathers and Midrash', in J. Neusner – A. Avery Peck (eds), *Encyclopedia of Midrash*, Leiden 2004

Kamesar A., *Jerome, Greek Scholarship and the Hebrew Bible*, Oxford 1993

Kamesar A., 'The Narrative Aggada as seen from the Greco-Latin Perspective', *JJS* 45 (1994) 52-70

Kampffmeyer, G. 'Alte Namen im heutigen Palastina und Syrien', *ZDPV* 15 (1892) 1-33, 65-116; 16 (1893) 1-71

Kant, L., 'Jewish Inscriptions in Greek and Latin', *ANRW* II.20.2 (Berlin 1987), 671-713

Kara, Y., *Babylonian Aramaic in the Yemenite Manuscripts of the Talmud*, Jerusalem 1983 (Hebr)

Kasher, A., 'Hareka hahistori lehibura shel 'megillat antiokhus,' in B. Bar Kokhba (ed), *Ha-tekufa ha-Selevkit be-Eretz Yisrael*, Tel Aviv 1980, 85-107

Kasher, M.M., *Hagadah Shelemah*, Jerusalem 1967 (Hebr)

Kasher, M.M., *Sefer ha-Rambam ve-Mekhilta de-Rashbi*, 2nd pr Jerusalem 1980 (Hebr)

Kasher, M.M., *Torah Shelemah*, vols 1-42, 2nd pr Jerusalem 1992 (Hebr)

Kasher, M.H., *Torah Shelemah 35: Aramaic Versions of the Bible*, Jerusalem 1983 (Hebr)

Kasher, M.M., *Torah Shelemah: Megillat Esther*, Jerusalem 1994

Kasher, M.M. – Mandelbaum, J.B., *Sarei Ha-Elef* 1-2, 2nd ed Jerusalem 1978

Kasher, R., 'The Aramaic Targumim and their Sitz im Leben', *PWCJS* 9 *Bible Studies and Ancient Near East* (1988) 75-85

Kasher, R., 'The Beliefs of Synagogue *Meturgemanim* and their Audience', in Levine L.I. (ed), *Continuity and Renewal: Jews and Judaism in Byzantine-Christian Palestine*, Jerusalem 2004, 420-442 (Hebr)

Kasher, R., 'A New Targum to the Ten Commandments According to a Genizah Manuscript', *HUCA* 60 (1989) 1-17

Kasher, R., *Targumic Toseftot to the Prophets*, Jerusalem 1996 (Hebr)

Kasher, R. – Klein, M., 'New Fragments of Targum to Esther from the Cairo Genizah', *HUCA* 66 (1990) 89-124

Katsh, A.I. (ed), *Ginze Mishna: One Hundred and Fifty Nine Fragments from the Cairo Geniza in the Saltykov-Shchedrin Library in Leningrad*, Jerusalem 1970

Katz, K., *The Hebrew Language Tradition of the Community of Djerba (Tunisia), The Phonology and the Morphology of the Verb*, Jerusalem 1977 (Hebr)

Katz, S., *Mysticism and Religious Traditions*, New York 1983

Katz, S. (ed), *Mysticism and Philosophical Analysis*, New York 1978

Katzenellenbogen, I., *Das Buch Esther in der Aggada*, diss Würzburg 1933

Katzenellenbogen, M.L., *Megillat Esther ... im peirushei ha-Rishonim*, Jerusalem 2006

Katzman, T., 'Beur ha-haggadot le-Rabbi Yedaya ha-Penini', *Bet ha-Vaad*, Jerusalem 2003, 153-154.

Katzoff, R., 'Hellenistic Marriage Contracts', in M. J. Geller – J. Maehler (eds), *Legal Documents of the Hellenistic World*, London 1995, 37-445

Katzoff, R., 'Papyrus Yadin 18 Again: A Rejoinder', *JQR* 82 (1991) 171-176

Katzoff, R., 'Philo and Hillel on Violation of Betrothal in Alexandria', in Gafni – Oppenheimer – Schwartz (eds), *The Jews in the Hellenistic-Roman World*, Jerusalem 1996, 39*–57*

Katzoff, R., 'Polygamy in *P. Yadin*?', *ZPE* 109 (1995) 128-131

Katzoff, R., 'Review of D. Sperber, A Dictionary of Greek and Latin Legal Terms in Rabbinic Literature', *Dine Israel* 13-14 (1986-1988) 327-335 (Hebr)

Katzoff, R., 'Sperber's Dictionary of Greek and Latin Legal Terms in Rabbinic Literature – A Review Essay', *JSJ* 20 (1989) 195-206

Katzoff, R. – Schaps, D. (eds), *Law in the Documents of the Judaean Desert*, Leiden 2005

Kaufman, S.A., *The Akkadian Influences on Aramaic*, Chicago – London 1974

Kautzsch, E., *Grammatik des Biblisch-Aramäischen*, Leipzig 1884

Keller, A., 'Nihush ve-siman', *Barkai* 2 (1985) 50-58 (Hebr)

Kerenyi, C., *Dionysus: Archetypal Image of Indestructable Life*, transl fr the German by Ralph Manheim, Princeton NJ 1996

Kern-Ulmer, Rivka, 'The Midrashim on Hannukkah: A Survey and a Sample Analysis', *Approaches to Ancient Judaism*, NS 3, Atlanta 1993, 163-178

Kessler, E., *Bound by the Bible : Jews, Christians and the Sacrifice of Isaac*, Cambridge 2004

Kimelman, R., 'The Messiah of the Amida: A Study in Comparative Messianism', *JBL* 116 (1997) 313-324

Kimelman, R., 'The Shema' Liturgy: From Covenant Ceremony to Coronation', *Kenishta* 1 (2001) 9-105

Kipperwasser, R., *Midrashim on Kohelet: Studies in Their Redaction and Formation* 1-2, diss Bar-Ilan U, Ramat-Gan 2005

Kirschner, R., *Baraita de-Melekhet ha-Mishkan: A Critical Edition with Introduction and Translation*, Cincinnati 1992

Kister, M., 'A Common Heritage: Biblical Interpretation at Qumran and its Implications', in Stone – Chazon, *Biblical Perspectives*, 101-111

Kister, M., 'A Contribution to the Interpretation of Ben Sira', *Tarbiz* 59 (1990) 303-78 (Hebr)

Kister, M., 'Additions to the Article "Notes on the Book of Ben-Sira" ', *Lešonenu* 53 (1988) 36-53 (Hebr)

Kister, M., 'The Interpretation of Ben Sira', *Tarbiz* 59 (1980) 303-378

Kister, M., '"Ke-dat Moshe ve-Yehuda'e": Toldoteha shel nusha mishpatit-datit', in D. Boyarin *et al.* (eds), *Atara L'Haim: Studies in the Talmud and Medieval Rabbinic Literature in Honor of Professor H.Z. Dimitrovsky*, Jerusalem 2000, 202-208 (Hebr)

Kister, M., 'Mesorot aggada ve-gilguleihen', *Tarbiz* 60 (1991) 179-224

Kister, M., 'Metamorphoses of Aggadic Traditions', *Tarbiz* 60 (1991) 179-244 (Hebr)

Kister, M., 'Notes on the Book of Ben-Sira', *Lešonenu* 47 (1983) 125-146 (Hebr)

Kister, M., 'Observations on Aspects of Exegesis, Tradition, and Theology in Midrash, Pseudepigrapha, and Other Jewish Writings', in J.C. Reeves (ed), *Tracing the Threads: Studies in the Vitality of Jewish Pseudepigrapha*, Atlanta 1994, 1-34

Kister, M., 'Plucking of Grain on the Sabbath and the Jewish-Christian Debate', *Jerusalem Studies in Jewish Thought* 3 (1984) 349-66

Kister, M., *Studies in Avot de-Rabbi Nathan: Text, Redaction and Interpretation*, Jerusalem 1998 (Hebr)

Kister, M., 'Studies in 4QMiqsat Ma'ase Ha-Tora and Related Texts: Law, Theology, Language and Calendar', *Tarbiz* 68 (1999) 317-371 (Hebr)

Klein, M.L., 'Additional Targum Manuscripts', *JQR* 83 (1992) 173-177

Klein, M.L., *The Fragment-Targums of the Pentateuch* 1-2, Rome 1980

Klein, M.L., *Genizah Manuscripts of Palestinian Targum to the Pentateuch* 1-2, Cincinnati 1986

Klein, M.L., 'Nine Fragments of Palestinian Targum to the Pentateuch', *HUCA* 50 (1979) 149-164

Klein, M.L., *Targumic Manuscripts in the Cambridge Genizah Collections*, Cambridge 1992

Klein, S., *Erets Yehuda*, Tel Aviv 1939 (Hebr)

Klein, S., *Galilee*, Jerusalem 1967 (Hebr)

Klein, S., *On the History of the Study of the Land of Israel*, Jerusalem 1937 (Hebr)

Klein, S. (ed), *Sefer ha-yishuv* 1, Jerusalem 1939, repr Jerusalem 1977

Klein, S., 'Das tannaitische Grenzverzeichnis Palästinas', *HUCA* 5 (1928) 197-259; ET in H. Bar Daroma, *Studies in the Geography of Eretz Israel*, Jerusalem 1965 (Hebr)

Knohl, I., *The Sanctuary of Silence: A Study of the Priestly Strata in the Pentateuch*, Jerusalem 1992 (Hebr)

Koffmahn, E., *Die Doppelurkunden aus der Wüste Juda*, Leiden 1968

Kohut, A., *Aruch Completum* 1-8, Vienna 1926 (Hebr)

Komlosh, Y., *The Bible in the Light of the Aramaic Translations*, Tel Aviv 1973 (Hebr)

Komlosh, Y., 'A Fragment of Ps-Jonathan "Then Sang Moses"', *Sefer Zeidel*, 1962, 7-11 (Hebr)

Komlosh, Y., 'Manuscripts of the Targumim', *Sinai* Jubilee Volume (1958) 466-481 (Hebr)

Kosovsky, B., *Concordantiae Verborum quae in Mechilta D'Rabbi Ismael, Sifra und Sifre*, Jerusalem 1965-71

Kosta, M., *Insects Against Man: Introduction to Medical Entomology From an Ecological and Evolutionary Perspective*, Tel Aviv 1978 (Hebr)

Kotansky, R., 'Greek Exorcistic Amulets', in M. Meyer – P. Mirecki, *Ancient Magic and Ritual Power*, Leiden 1995, 243-277

Kotler, D., *Human Ecology in the Ancient World*, Tel-Aviv 1977 (Hebr)

Kottek, S., 'The Essenes and Medicine; A Comparative Study of Medical and Para-Medical Items with Reference to Ancient Jewish Lore', *Clio medica* 18/1-4 (1983) 81-99

Kottek, S., 'Magic and Healing in Hellenistic Jewish Writings', *FJB* 27 (2000) 1-16

Kottek, S., *Medicine and Hygiene in the Works of Flavius Josephus*, Leiden 1994

Kottek, S., 'Šabbetay Donnolo en tant que médecin: anatomie et physiologie dans *Sefer Ḥakm n* ', in G. Lacerenza (ed), *Šabbetay Donnolo, scienza e cultura ebraica nell'Italia del secolo X*, Naples 2004, 21-43

Krappe, A.H., *The Science of Folklore*, New York 1964

Krauss, S., *Additamenta ad Librum Aruch Completum Alexandri Kohut*, Vienna 1937 (Hebr)

Krauss, S., *Griechische und Lateinische Lehnwörter im Talmud, Midrasch und Targum* 1-2, Berlin 1898-99, repr Hildesheim 1964

Krauss, S., *Paras ve-Romi ba-Talmud uva-Midrashim*, Jerusalem 1948

Krebs, W., 'Lilith – Adams erste Frau', *Zeitschrift für Religions- und Geistesgeschichte* 27 (1975) 141-152

Kremers, H., 'Die Auslegung der Bibel', in idem (ed), *Juden und Christen lesen dieselbe Bibel*, Duisburg 1973

Kristianpoller, A., *Traum und Traumdeutung*, (Monumenta Talmudica 4/2.1) Vienna 1923

Kugel, J., *In Potiphar's House*, New York 1990

Kugel, J., *Traditions of the Bible*, Cambridge 1998

Kuhn, K.G. (ed), *Sifre zu Numeri*, (Tannaitische Midraschim: Übersetzung und Erklärung) Stuttgart 1954

Kuiper, G.J., *The Pseudo Jonathan Targum and Its Relationship to Targum Onkelos*, Rome 1972

Kutscher, E.Y., 'Genizah Fragments of the Mekilta of Rabbi Yishma'el', *Lešonenu* 32 (1968) 103-116 (Hebr)

Kutscher, E.Y., 'Aramaic', in *EJ* 3, 260-287

Kutscher, E.Y., *Hebrew and Aramaic Studies*, Jerusalem 1977 (Hebr)

Kutscher, E.Y., *A History of the Hebrew Language*, Leiden 1982

Kutscher, E.Y., 'The Language of the "Genesis Apocryphon": A Preliminary Study', in Ch. Rabin – Y. Yadin (eds), *Aspects of the Dead Sea Scrolls = ScrHier* 4 (1957) 1-35

Kutscher, E.Y., 'The Language of the Hebrew and Aramaic Letters of Bar Koseba and His Contemporaries. Part I: The Aramaic Letters', *Lešonenu* 25 (1961) 117-133 (Hebr)

Kutscher, E.Y., 'The Language of the Hebrew and Aramaic Letters of Bar Koseba and His Contemporaries. Part II: The Hebrew Letters', *Lešonenu* 26 (1962) 7-23 (Hebr)

Kutscher, E.Y., *The Language and Linguistic Background of the Isaiah Scroll*, Jerusalem 1959 (Hebr)

Kutscher, E.Y., 'The Present State of Research into Mishnaic Hebrew (Especially Lexicography) and its Tasks', in *Archive of the New Dictionary of Rabbinical Literature* 1, Ramat-Gan 1972, 3-28 (Hebr; English Abstract, III-X)

Kutscher, E.Y., 'Some Problems of the Lexicography of Mishnaic Hebrew and Its Comparison with Biblical Hebrew', in *Archive of the New Dictionary of Rabbinical Literature* 1, Ramat-Gan 1972, 29-82 (Hebr; English Abstract, XI-XXVII)

Kutscher, E.Y., 'Research in the Grammar of the Aramaic of the Babylonian Talmud', *Lešonenu* 26 (1962) 149-183 (Hebr)

Kutscher, E.Y., *Studies in Galilean Aramaic*, ET M. Sokoloff, Ramat Gan – Jerusalem 1976 (Hebr)

Kutscher, E.Y., 'Terms of Legal Documents in the Talmud and in Gaonic Literature', *Tarbiz* 17 (1946) 125-7; 19 (1948) 53-59, 125-8 (Hebr) (= *Hebrew and Aramaic Studies*, 417ff)

Kutscher, E.Y., *Words and Their History*, Jerusalem 1961 (Hebr)

Kutscher, E.Y. – Lieberman, S. – Kaddari, M.Z. (eds), *Henoch Yalon Memorial Volume*, Ramat Gan 1974

Kuyt, A., The 'Descent' to the Chariot: Towards a Description of the Terminology, Place, Function, and Nature of the Yeridah in Hekhalot Literature, Tübingen 1995

Lacks, S.T., 'Midrash Hallel and Merkabah Mysticism', Gratz College Annniversary Volume, Philadelphia 1971, 193-203

Lange, N.R.M. de, Origen and the Jews: Studies in Jewish Christian Relations in Third Century Palestine, Cambridge 1976

Lapin, H., Economy, Geography and Provincial History in Later Roman Empire, Tübingen 2001

Lapin, H., 'Palestinian Inscriptions and Jewish Ethnicity in late Antiquity', in E. Meyers (ed), Galilee Through the Centuries: Confluence of Cultures, Winona Lake ID 1999, 239-268

Lauterbach, J.Z., 'The Arrangement and the Division of the Mekhilta', HUCA 1 (1924) 427-66

Lauterbach, J.Z., 'Me-biurei ha-Mekhilta', in Sefer KLausner, 181-188

Lauterbach, J. Z. 'Meghillat Taanit', Jewish Encyclopaedia 8, New York-London 1904, 427-428

Lauterbach, J.Z., Mekilta De-Rabbi Ishmael: A Critical Edition on the Basis of the MSS. and Early Editions 1-3, Philadelphia 1933-1935

Lauterbach, J.Z., 'The Name of the Mekilta', JQR 11 (1920) 169-82

Laytner, A., Arguing with God – A Jewish Tradition, Northvale NJ 1990

Le Bohec: see Bohec

Le Deaut: see Deaut

Lehmann, C.M. – K. Holum, The Greek and Latin Inscriptions of Caesarea Maritima, Boston 2000

Lehmann, M.R., 'The Commentary of R. Nethanel b. Yeshaya to the Scroll of Esther', Sefer Zikkaron leha-Rav Yizhak Nissim 3, Jerusalem 1985, 341-358 (Hebr)

Lehmann, M.R., 'Studies in the Murabba'at and Nahal Hever Documents', RQ 4 (1963-4) 53-81

Leibowitz, J.O., 'History of Jewish Hospitals', Dapim Refuiyim, 11 (1952) 237-240 (Hebr)

Leibowitz, J.O., 'The Problem of Medical Licence in Hebrew Sources', Koroth 7/5-6 (1977) 360-363 (Hebr) and xlvii-liii (Engl)

Leiner, Y.M., Meir Ayin, annotations to Seder Olam Rabba (text included), Warsaw 1904

Lemaire, A., Nouvelles inscriptions araméennes d'Idumée au musée d'Israel, Paris 1996

Leonhard, C., 'Die Pesachhaggada als Spiegel religiöser Konflikte', in A. Gerhards – S. Wahle (eds), Kontinuität und Unterbrechung; Gottesdienst und Gebet in Judentum und Christentum, Paderborn 2005, 143-171

Leonhard, C., 'Die älteste Haggada, Übersetzung der Pesachhaggada nach dem palästinschen Ritus und Vorschläge zu ihrem Ursprung und ihrer Bedeutung für die Geschichte der christlichen Liturgie', Archiv für Liturgiewissenschaft, 45 (2004) 201-232

Leoni, A., Folklore and Wisdom in the Ancient World: Greece and Rome, Tel Aviv 1949 (Hebr)

Lerner, M.B., 'The Aggadic Midrashim in the Commentary of Rabbenu Hillel to Sifra, KS 64 (1992-93) 1055-1065 (Hebr)

Lerner, M.B., *The Book of Ruth in Aggadic Literature and Midrash Ruth Rabba* 1-3, introd, text, comm.; diss Hebrew U, Jerusalem 1971

Lerner, M.B., 'On the Beginnings of Liturgical Poetry: Midrashic and Talmudic Clasifications', *Sidra* 9 (1993) 13-34

Lerner, M.B. 'Collected Exempla: Studies in Aggadic Texts Published in the *Genizot* Series', *KS* 61 (1986-1987), 867-892 (Hebr).

Lerner, M.B., 'The Editio Princeps of Midrash Hamesh Megillot: Studies in the Activities of Hebrew Printers in Constantinople and Pesaro', *A.M. Habermann Memorial Volume*, Lod 1983, 289-311 (Hebr)

Lerner, M.B., 'Enquiries into the Meaning of Various Titles and Designations, I. Abba', *Te'uda* 4 (1986) 93-113 (Hebr)

Lerner, M.B. 'Al ha-Midrashim le-Aseret Ha-Dibrot', in Sussmann – Rosenthal, *Talmudic Studies* 1, 217-236

Lerner, M.B., 'Lexicon and Lectiones: A Rejoinder', *Lešonenu* 56 (1992) 363-369

Lerner, M.B., 'Mehkarim be-Midrash Mishle', in Sussman – Rosenthal, *Talmudic Studies* 3/1, 461-488

Lerner, M.B., 'A New Fragment of Midrash Eshet Hayil and the Opening Section of a Work Dealing with Twelve Women', in Bar-Asher – Levinson – Lifshitz, *Studies*, 265-292

Lerner, M.B., 'New Light on the Spanish Recension of Deuteronomy Rabba [1]: The evolution of ed. Lieberman', *Te'uda* 11 (1996) 107-145 (Hebr)

Lerner, M.B., 'New Light on the Spanish Recension of Deuteronomy Rabba [2]: On the Origin of Pericopes *Va'ethanan-Eqev*', *Tarbiz* 70 (2001) 417-427 (Hebr)

Lerner, M.B., 'Notes on the Editing of Midrash Hagadol', *Peamim* 10 (1981) 109-118 (Hebr)

Lerner, M.B., 'Notes on the Editing of Midrash Hagadol: Corrections and Additions', *Peamim* 12 (1982) 143-144 (Hebr)

Lerner, M.B., 'Novel Explanations to Some Enigmatic Passages in Sifre and Mekhilta Eqev', *Tarbiz* 57 (1988) 599-607 (Hebr)

Lerner, M.B., *Perush kadum le-Midrash Vayyikra Rabba*, Jerusalem 1995

Lerner, M.B., 'Studies in a Geniza Book List', *Te'uda* 1 (1980) 41-55

Lesses, R.M., 'Exe(o)rcising Power: Women as Sorceresses, Exorcists, and Demonesses in Babylonian Jewish Society of Late Antiquity', *JAAR* 69 (2001) 343-375

Lesses, R., *Ritual Practices to Gain Power: Angels, Incantations, and Revelation in Early Jewish Mysticism*, Harrisburg PA 1998

Levene, D., 'Calvariae Magicae: The Berlin, Philadelphia and Moussaieff Skulls', *Orientalia* (forthcoming)

Levene, D., *A Corpus of Magic Bowls: Incantation Texts in Jewish Aramaic from Late Antiquity*, London 2003

Levene, D., 'Heal O' Israel: A Pair of Duplicate Magic Bowls from the Pergamon Museum in Berlin', *JJS* 54 (2003) 116-119

Levenson, J., *The Twice Told Tale: A Poetics of the Exegetical Narrative in Rabbinic Midrash*, Jerusalem 2005 (Hebr)

Levertoff, P., *Midrash Sifre on Numbers*, London 1926

Levey, S.H., 'The Date of Targum Jonathan to the Prophets', *VT* 71 (1971) 186-196

Levi, I., 'Bari dans la Pesikta Rabbati', *REJ* 32 (1896) 278-282

Levias, C., *A Grammar of the Aramaic Idiom contained in the Babylonian Talmud*, Cincinnati 1900

Levine, D., *Communal Fasts and Rabbinic Sermons – Theory and Practice in the Talmudic Period*, Tel Aviv 2001 (Hebr)

Levine, E., 'The Targums: Their Interpretative Character and Their Place in Jewish Text Tradition', in M. Saebø (ed), *Hebrew Bible/Old Testament; the History of Its Interpretation;* vol. 1, part 1: *Antiquity*, Göttingen 1996, 323-331

Levine, H.I., *Studies in Talmudic Literature and Halakhic Midrashim*, Ramat Gan 1987 (Hebr)

Levine, L.I., *The Ancient Synagogue: The First Thousand Years*, New Haven – London 2000

Levine, L.I., *Jerusalem: Portrait of the City in the Second Temple Period (538 B.C.E. – 70 C.E.)*, Philadelphia 2002

Levine, L.I., *Judaism and Hellenism – Conflict or Confluence?* Seattle 1998

Levine, L.I., *The Rabbinic Class in Palestine during the Talmudic Period*, Jerusalem 1985

Levine, L.[I.] (ed), *The Galilee in Late Antiquity*, New York and Jerusalem 1992

Levine Katz, Y., *Midreshei Eshet Hayil*, diss Bar Ilan U, Ramat-Gan 1992

Levy, J., *Chaldäisches Wörterbuch über die Targumim* 1-2, Leipzig 1881

Levy, J., *Wörterbuch über die Talmudim und Midraschim*, Leipzig 1876-1889

Levy, Y., *Olamot nifgashim: mehkarim al maamda shel ha-Yahadut ba-olam ha-Yavani-ha-Romai*, Jerusalem 1970

Lewin, B.M., *Otsar Ha-Geonim*, Jerusalem 1932 (Hebr)

Lewin, B.M. (ed), *Ginzei kedem*, vol 1, Haifa 1922

Lewis, N. (ed), *The Documents from the Bar Kokhba Period in the Cave of Letters, Greek Papyri, (Aramaic and Nabatean Signatures and Subscriptions*, ed Y. Yadin – J.C. Greenfield, Jerusalem 1989

Lewis, N., 'The World of P. Yadin', *Bulletin of the American Society of Papyrologists* 28 (1991) 35-41

Lewis, N. – Katzoff, R. – Greenfield, J.C., 'Papyrus Yadin 18', *IEJ* 37 (1987) 229-250

Lewy, H., 'Zu dem Traumbuche des Artemidoros', *Rheinisches Museum für Philologie* nF 48 (1893) 398-419

Lewy, I., 'Ein Wort uber die "Mechilta des R. Simon",' *Jahresb. d. jüd.-theol. Sem.* Breslau 1889

Lichtenstein, H. 'Die Fastenrolle: eine Untersuchung zur jüdisch-hellenistischen Geschichte', *HUCA* 8-9 (1931-1932) 237-351 (257-316, hist. and comm.; 317-351, text)

Liddell, H.G. – Scott, R. – Jones, H.S., *A Greek-English Lexicon*, 9th ed Oxford 1940

Lieber, E., 'The Covenant which Asaf and Yohanan made with their pupils; Text & Translation', in J.O. Leibowitz (ed), *Memorial Vol. in Honor of Prof. S. Muntner*, Jerusalem 1983, 83-94

Lieberman, S., *Greek in Jewish Palestine: Studies in the Life and Manners of Jewish Palestine in the II-IV Centuries C.E.*, New York 1942, 2nd ed 1965

Lieberman, S., *Greek in Jewish Palestine / Hellenism in Jewish Palestine*, with a new introd. by D. Zlotnick, New York and Jerusalem 1994 (see also: *Yevanit ve-Yavanut*)

Lieberman, S., 'The Halakhic Inscription from the Bet-Shean Valley', *Tarbiz* 45 (1976) 54-63 (Hebr)

Lieberman, S., 'Hazanut Yannai', *Sinai* 4 (1939) 221-50

Lieberman, S., *Hellenism in Jewish Palestine: Studies in the Literary Transmission, Beliefs and Manners of Palestine in the I Century B.C E – IV Century C.E.*, New York 1950, 2nd ed 1962

Lieberman, S., 'The Knowledge of *Halakha* by the Author (or Authors) of the *Heikhaloth*', in Gruenwald, *Apocalyptic*, 241-244

Lieberman, S., 'Mekhilta de-Rabbi Yishmael ed J. Z. Lauterbach', *KS* 12 (1935) 54-65 (Hebr)

Lieberman, S., 'Persecution' (Redifat Dat Yisrael), in idem, *Studies*, 348-380 (Hebr)

Lieberman, S., 'Piska hadashah mi-Mekhilta u-perushah' (A New *Piska* from the Mekhilta and Its Meaning), *Sinai* 75 (1975) 1-3 (Hebr)

Lieberman, S., 'Roman Legal Institutions in Early Rabbinics and in the Acta Martyrum', *JQR* 35 (1944) 1-55 (repr in idem, *Texts and Studies*, 57-111)

Lieberman, S., 'Siphre zu Deuteromium ed L. Finkelstein', *KS* 14 (1938) 323-36 (Hebr)

Lieberman, S., *Siphre Zutta: The Midrash of Lydda*, New York 1968 (Hebr)

Lieberman, S., *Studies in Palestinian Talmudic Literature*, ed D. Rosenthal, Jerusalem 1991 (Hebr)

Lieberman, S., 'Tikkune Yerushalmi 5', *Tarbiz* 3 (1932) 452-457 (Hebr)

Lieberman, S., *Tosefta Ki-Fshutah: A Comprehensive Commentary on the Tosefta*, New York 1955-1988 (Hebr)

Lieberman, S., *Texts and Studies*, New York 1974

Lieberman, S., 'About Two MSS.', *KS* 13 (1937) 105-14 (Hebr)

Lieberman, S., *Yerushalmi Kiphshuto: Shabbat, Erubin, Pesahim*, Jerusalem 1934 (Hebr)

Lieberman, S., 'Yerushalmi Neziqin', Introduction and Commentary in *Yerushalmi Neziqin, edited from the Escorial Manuscript*, ed E.S. Rosenthal, Jerusalem 1983 (Hebr)

Lieberman, S., *Yevanit ve-Yavanut be-Erets Yisrael: Mehkarim be-orhot-hayim be-Erets Yisrael bi-tekufat ha-Mishna veha-Talmud*, Jerusalem 1962, repr 1984 (see also: *Greek / Hellenism*)

Liebes, Y., *Hatato shel Elisha: Arbaa she-nikhnesu la-Pardes ve-tiva shel ha-mistika ha-talmudit*, Jerusalem 1990

Liebes, Y., *Torat ha-Yetsira shel Sefer Yetsira*, Jerusalem 2000

Liebeschuetz, J.H.W., *Continuity and Change in Roman Religion*, Oxford 1979

Lifschitz, E.M., 'Ha-dikduk ha-mikrai weha-dikduk hamishnati', *Sefatenu* 1, Jerusalem-Berlin (1917) 39-42 (Hebr)

Lifshitz, B., 'Aggada and its place in the Tora shebeal peh', *Shnaton ha-mishpat ha-ivri* 22 (2003) 233-328 (Hebr)

Lifshitz, B., *Asmakhta*, Jerusalem 1988

Lifshitz, B., *Donateurs et fondateurs dans les synagogues juives: répertoire des dédicaces grecques relatives à la construction et à la réfection des synagogues*, Paris 1967

Löw, I., *Die Flora der Juden*, Vienna – Leipzig 1934

Lowe, W.H. (ed), *The Mishna on which the Palestinian Talmud Rests, from the Unique Manuscript Preserved in the University of Cambridge Library*, Cambridge 1883

Lubetski, M. (ed), *Saul Lieberman (1898-1983): Talmudic Scholar and Classicist*, Lampeter 2002

Lüderitz, G., *Corpus jüdischer Zeugnisse aus der Cyrenaika, mit einem Anhang von Joyce M. Reynolds* Wiesbaden 1983

Luger, Yehezkel, *The Weekday Amida in the Cairo Genizah*, Jerusalem 2001

Lurie, B. *Megillath Ta'anith*, w introd and notes, Jerusalem 1964 (Hebr)

MacDonald, D.W., 'Observations on the Behavior and Ecology of the Striped Hyaena in Israel,' *Israel Journal of Zoology* 27 (1978) 189-198

Mack, H., 'A Medieval Midrash on *Isaiah* Chapter I (in MS Oxford Bod. 155)', *Sidra* 13 (1997) 111-129 (Hebr)

Mack, H., 'Numbers Rabba: Its Date, Location and Circulation', *Te'uda* 11 (1996) 91-105 (Hebr)

Mack, H., *Prolegomena and Example to an Edition of Midrash Bemidbar Rabba Part 1*, diss Hebrew U, Jerusalem 1991

Mack, H., 'The Reworking of a Midrash by Printers in Istanbul in 1512', *Peamim* 52 (1992) 379-346 (Hebr)

Mack, H., 'A Sermon by Rabbi Eliahu the Elder within a Medieval *Midrash*', *Zion* 61 (1996) 209-318 (Hebr)

Mack, H., 'The Unique Character of the Zippori Synagogue Mosaic and Eretz Israel Midrashim', *Cathedra* 88 (1998) 39-56 (Hebr)

MacMullen, R., *Enemies of the Roman Order: Treason, Unrest, and Alienation in the Empire*, Cambridge MA 1967

MacMullen, R., 'The Epigraphic Habit in the Roman Empire', *AJP* 103 (1982) 233-46.

Macuch, M., 'Iranian Legal Terminology in the Babylonian Talmud in the Light of Sasanian Jurisprudence', *Irano-Judaica* 4 (1999) 91-101

Magness, J. – Gitin, S. (eds), *Hesed ve-Emet: Studies in Honor of Ernst S. Frerichs*, Atlanta 1998

Maimon (Fishman), J.L. (ed), 'Sefer Mafteah Ha-Derashot leha-Rambam', in idem, *Rabbenu Moshe b. Maimon: hayyav, sefarav, peulotav ve-deotav*, Jerusalem 1935

Maman, A., 'The Reading Tradition of the Jews of Tetouan: Phonology of Biblical and Mishnaic Hebrew', *Massorot* 1 (1984) 51-120 (Hebr)

Mandel, P., 'Between Byzantium and Islam: The Transmission of a Jewish Book in the Byzantine and Early Islamic Period', in Y. Elbaum – I. Gershoni (eds), *Transmitting Jewish Traditions: Orality, Textuality, and Cultural Diffusion*, New Haven – London 2000, 74-106

Mandel, P., 'Midrashic Exegesis and its Precedents in the Dead Sea Scrolls', *DSD* 8 (2001) 149-168

Mandel, P.D., *Midrash Lamentations Rabbati: Prolegomenon, and a Critical Edition to the Third Parasha*, diss Hebrew U, Jerusalem 1997 (Hebr)

Mandelbaum, B. (ed), *Pesikta de Rav Kahana According to an Oxford Manuscript with Variants..., Commentary and Introduction* 1-2, New York 1962

Mandell, S., 'Did Saul Lieberman Know Latin or Greek?' in J. Neusner, *Why There Never Was a 'Talmud of Caesarea': Saul Lieberman's Mistakes*, Atlanta 1995, 137-146 (Appendix One)

Mangan, C., 'Some Observations on the Dating of Targum Job', in K.J. Cathcart – J.R. Healy (eds), *Back to the Sources*, Dublin 1989, 67-78

Mann, J., 'Some Midrashic Genizah Fragments', *HUCA* 14 (1939) 303-358

Mann, J., *The Bible as Read and Preached in the Old Synagogue* 1-2, Cincinnati 1940-1966

Mann, J., 'Genizah Fragments of the Palestinian Order of Service', *HUCA* 2 (1925) 269–338, repr in idem, *Collected Articles* 3, Gedera 1971, 352–421

Mann, J., *Texts and Studies in Jewish History and Literature* 2, Cincinnati 1935, repr New York 1972

Mantel, H.D., 'The Megilat Ta'anit and the Sects', in idem (ed), *The Men of the Great Synagogue*, Tel-Aviv 1983, 213-226; = *Studies in the History of the Jewish People and the Land of Israel in Memory of Zvi Avneri*, ed by A. Gilboa *et al.*, U of Haifa 1970, 51-70 (Hebr)

Maori, Y., 'The Aramaic Targumim and Rabbinic Exegesis', *PWCJS* 9, *Bible Studies and Ancient Near East* (1985) 1-12 (Hebr)

Maori, Y., *The Peshitta Version of the Pentateuch and Early Jewish Exegetes*, Jerusalem 1995 (Hebr)

Marblestone, H., 'Lieberman φιλόλογος: Professor Saul Lieberman as Lexicographer: Hebrew, Greek, Latin', in Lubetski, *Saul Lieberman*, 24-43

Margaliot, R., *Sheelot u-teshuvot min ha-shamayim le-Rabbenu Yaakov mi-Marvis*, Jerusalem 1957 (Hebr)

Margolis, M.L., *A Manual of the Aramaic Language of the Babylonian Talmud*, (Clavis Linguarum Semiticarum 3) München 1910

Margulies [Margaliot], M.[M.], *Ha-hillukim she-bein anshei mizrah u-benei Erets Yisrael*, Jerusalem: 1937

Margulies, M.M., *Hilkhot Erets Yisrael min ha-Geniza*, Jerusalem 1973

Margulies, M.M., 'Mavo', in idem, *Wayyikra Rabbah* 5, IX-XL

Margulies, M.M., 'Mekhilta de-R. Shimeon ben Yohai hotza'at Epstein-Melamed', *KS* 31 (1956) 155-159

Margulies, M.M., 'Moadim ve-tsomot be-Erets Yisrael uva-Bavel bi-tekufat he-Geonim', *Areshet* 1 (1944) 204-216

Margulies, M.M., 'A New Document on the Fast of the Earthquake', *Tarbiz* 29 (1960) 339-344

Margulies, M.M., (ed), *Sefer ha-Razim: A Newly Recovered Book of Magic from the Talmudic Period*, Jerusalem 1966 (Hebr); ET M.A. Morgan, *Sepher ha Razim – The Book of Mysteries*, Chicago 1983

Margulies, M.M., (ed), *Wayyikra Rabbah: A Critical Edition Based on Manuscripts and Genizah Fragments with Variants and Notes* 1-5, Jerusalem 1953-60, repr in 3 vols 1972 (Hebr)

Marmorstein, A., 'Ein Fragment einer neuen Piska zum Wochenfest und der Kampf gegen das Muendliche Gesetz', *Jeschurun* 12 (1925) 34-53

Marmorstein, A., 'Jesus Sirach 51 12 ff.', *ZAW* 29 (1909) 287-293

Marmorstein, A., 'Kiddush Yerahim de-R. Pinhas', *Hazofeh Quartalis Hebraica* 5 (1921)

Marmorstein, A., 'Midrash 'Avkir', *Devir* 1 (1923) 113-144 (Hebr)

Marmorstein, A., *Midrash haserot vi-yeterot*, London 1917 (Hebr)

Marmorstein, A., *Religionsgeschichtliche Studien*, vol 1 Skotschau (?) 1910

Marmorstein, A., *Studies in Jewish Theology*, London 1950

Martines, T., *Mekilta de Rabbi Ismael; comentario rabinico al libro del Exodo*, Navarra 1995

Martines, T., *Sifre Deuteronomio: comentario al libro de Deuteronomio* 1-2, Catalonia 1989-1997

Marx, A., 'Eine Sammelhandschrift im Besitze des Herrn A. Epstein', *ZHB* 1 (1901) 54-61

Marx, A., *Seder Olam (Cap. 1-10) nach Handschriften herausgegeben, übersetzt, und erklärt*, Inaug.-Diss. Königsberg i. Pr., Berlin 1903

McNamara, M., *The New Testament and the Palestinian Targum to the Pentateuch*, Rome 1966

McNamara, M., 'Targumic Studies', *CBQ* 28 (1966) 1-19

McNamara, M., 'The Aramaic Translations: A Newly Recognized Aid for New Testament Study', *IrERec* 109 (1968) 158-165

Meir, O., *Ha-sippur ha-darshani ba-Bereishit Rabba*, Tel Aviv 1987

Meir, O., 'Responding or Asking: on the Development of the Rhetoric of Debate in Rabbinic Literature in Israel', *Sifrut* 8 (1992) 159-186; 9 (1994) 155-174 (Hebr)

Meir, O., 'The Wedding in Kings' Parables (in the Aggada)', in I. Ben-Ame – D. Noy, (eds), *Studies in Marriage Customs*, Jerusalem 1974 (Hebr)

Melam[m]ed, E.Z., *Bible Commentators* 1-2, Jerusalem 1975 (Hebr)

Melamed, E.Z., *Halachic Midrashim of the Tannaim in the Babylonian Talmud*, 2nd ed Jerusalem 1988 (Hebr)

Melamed, E.Z., *Halachic Midrashim of the Tannaim in the Palestinian Talmud*, Jerusalem 2000 (Hebr)

Melamed, E.Z., 'Horovitz-Rabin: Mechilta d'Rabbi Ismael', *Tarbiz* 6 (1935) 112-23 (Hebr)

Melamed, E.Z., *An Introduction to Talmudic Literature*, Jerusalem 1973 (Hebr)

Melamed, E.Z., *The Relationship between the Halakhic Midrashim and the Mishna and Tosefta*, Jerusalem 1967 (Hebr)

Melzer, A., *Asaph the Physician, the Man and his Book*, diss U of Wisconsin 1972

Meyer, E., 'Explaining the Epigraphic Habit in the Roman Empire: The Evidence of Epitaphs', *JRS* 80 (1990) 74-96.

Meyer, J., *Seder Olam Rabba*, text w. Latin transl. and comm., Amsterdam 1699

Milik, J.T., 'Deux Documents inédits du Désert de Juda', *Biblica* 38 (1957) 245-268

Milikowsky, Ch., 'Seder Olam and the Tosefta', *Tarbiz* 49 (1979-80) 246-263 (Hebr)

Milikowsky, Ch., 'On the Formation and Transmission of Bereshit Rabba and the Yerushalmi: Literary Questions of Redaction, Text-Criticism and Relationships', *JQR* 92 (2002) 521-567

Milikowsky, Ch., 'Further on Editing Rabbinic Texts: A Review-Essay of A Synoptic Edition of Pesiqta Rabbati Based on All Extant Manuscripts and the Editio Princeps by Rivka Ulmer', *JQR* 90 (1999) 137-149

Milikowsky, Ch., 'On Parallels and Primacy: Seder Olam and Mekhilta d'Rabbi Shimon ben Yohai on the Israelites in Egypt', *Bar-Ilan* 26-27 (1995) 221-25 (Hebr)

Milikowsky, Ch., 'The Search for the "Original Text": Studies in the Text and the Editing of Seder Olam and Vayyiqra Rabba', in Bar-Asher – Levinson – Lifshitz, *Studies*, 349-384 (Hebr)

Milikowsky, Ch., *Seder Olam: A Rabbinic Chronography*, diss Yale U 1981

Milikowsky, Ch., 'Seder 'Olam and Jewish Chronography in the Hellenistic and Roman Periods', *PAAJR* 52 (1985) 115-139

Milikowsky, Ch., 'Source Criticism', *Lešonenu* 56 (1992) 361 (Hebr)

Milikowsky, Ch., 'The *Status Quaestionis* of Research in Rabbinic Literature', *JJS* 39 (1988) 201-211

Milikowsky, Ch., 'Vayyiqra Rabba, Chapter 28, Section 1-3: Questions of Text, Redaction and Affinity to Pesiqta D'Rav Kahana', *Tarbiz* 71 (2002) 19-65 (Hebr)

Milikowsky, Ch., 'Vayyiqra Rabba Chapter 30, Sections 1 and 2: The History of its Transmission and Publication and the Presentation of a New Edition', *Bar Ilan* 30-31 (2006) 269-318 (Hebr)

Milikowsky, C. – Schlüter, M., 'Vayyiqra Rabba through History: A Project to Study its Textual Transmission', in J. Targarona – A. Saenz-Badillos (eds), *Jewish Studies at the Turn of the Twentieth Century: Proc., 6th EAJS Congress*, vol 1, Leiden 1999, 149-162

Millard, A., *Reading and Writing in the Time of Jesus*, New York 2000

Miller, S., ' "Epigraphical" Rabbis, Helios, and Psalm 19: Were the Synagogues of Archaeology and the Synagogues of the Sages One and the Same?', *JQR* 94 (2004) 27-76.

Mirsky, A., 'Mahtsavtan shel tsurot ha-piyyut', in *Yediot ha-Makhon le-heker ha-shira ha-ivrit* 7, Jerusalem 1958, 3-129

Mirsky, A., 'Midrash Tannaim le-Bereshit', *Sinai* 108 (1991) 97-128; 108 (1996) 97-115

Mirsky, A., *Midrash Tannaim li-Bereshit*, Jerusalem 2000

Mirsky, A., *Ha'Piyut: The Development of Post Biblical Poetry in Eretz Israel and the Diaspora*, Jerusalem 1990

Mirsky, A., 'Ha-shira bi-tekufat ha-Talmud', in idem, *Ha-piyyut*, 57-76

Mirsky, A., 'Sources of Prayer', in idem, *Ha'Piyut*

Mirsky, A., *Reshit ha-piyyut*, Jerusalem 1965

Mirsky, S.K., 'Le-mahuta shel Midrash Tanhuma', *Sura* 3 (1958) 93-119

Misgav, H. 'Jewish Courts of Law as Reflected in Documents from the Dead Sea', *Cathedra* 82 (1997) 17-24 (Hebr)

Misgav, H., 'Nomenclature in Ossuary Inscriptions', *Tarbiz* 66 (1996) 123-130 (Hebr)

Mishor, M., 'Ashkenazi Traditions – Toward a Method of Research', *Massorot* 3-4 (1989) 87-127 (Hebr)

Mishor, M., 'A Hebrew Letter Oxford MS. HEB D.69 (P)', *Lešonenu* 53 (1989) 215-64 (Hebr)

Mishor, M., 'Yotze she-hu "dome"', *Lešonenu* 47 (1987) 285 (Hebr)

Mishor, M., 'A New Edition of a Hebrew Letter: Oxford Ms. Heb. d. 69(p)', *Lešonenu* 54 (1989) 215-264 (Hebr)

Montgomery, J.A., *Aramaic Incantation Texts from Nippur*, Philadelphia 1913

Moor, J.C. de, 'A Bilingual Concordance to the Targum of the Prophets', in I.E. Zwiep – A. Kuyt (eds), *Dutch Studies in the Targum*, Amsterdam 1993, 104-117

Moor, J.C. de, – Houtman, A. (eds), *A Bilingual Concordance to the Targum of the Prophets*, Leiden – New York 1995-2005

Moore, G.F., *Judaism in the First Centuries of the Christian Era*, Cambridge MA 1927-30, 5th ed 1946

Morag, M., *The Hebrew Language Tradition of the Baghdadi Community: The Phonology*, (Eda ve-lashon 1) Jerusalem 1977 (Hebr)

Morag, M., *The Hebrew Language Tradition of the Yemenite Jews*, Jerusalem 1963 (Hebr)

Morag, M., 'Pa'el and Nitpa'el in Leshon Hakhamim Traditions', *Tarbiz* 26 (1957) 349-356 (quoted according to Bar-Asher, *Kovets maamarim* 1, 93-100) (Hebr)

Morag, S., *Babylonian Aramaic: The Yemenite Tradition*, Jerusalem 1988 (Hebr)

Morag, S., 'The Babylonian Aramaic Tradition of the Yemenite Jews', *Tarbiz* 30 (1961) 120-129 (Hebr)

Morag, S., 'On the Background of the Babylonian Aramaic Tradition of the Yemenite Community and Clarification of two Topics in this Tradition', in S. Morag – I. Ben-Ami (eds), *Studies in Geniza and Sepharadi Heritage*, FS S.D. Goitein, Jerusalem 1981, 137-171 (Hebr)

Morag, S., 'Some Notes on the Grammar of Babylonian Aramaic as Reflected in the Geniza Manuscripts', *Tarbiz* 42 (1972-73) 60-78 (Hebr)

Morag, S., 'On the Vocalization of the Babylonian Talmud in the Geonic period', *PWCJS* 4:2 (1968) 89-94 (Hebr)

Morag, S., *Vocalized Talmudic Manuscripts in the Cambridge Geniza Collections*, Cambridge 1988

Moreshet, M., *A Lexicon of the New Verbs in Tannaitic Hebrew*, Ramat-Gan 1980 (Hebr)

Morray-Jones, C.R.A., *A Transparent Illusion: The Dangerous Vision of Water in Hekhalot Mysticism. A Source-Critical and Tradition-Historical Inquiry*, Leiden 2002

Moulton, J.H., – Milligan, G., *The Vocabulary of the Greek Testament*, Glasgow 1930

Muffs, Y., *Studies in the Aramaic Legal Papyri from Elephantine*, Leiden 1969

Mulder, M.J. – Sysling, H. (eds), *Mikra: Text, Translation, Reading and Interpretation of the Hebrew Bible in Ancient Judaism and Early Christianity*, (CRINT II/1) Assen – Philadelphia 1988

Müller, J. 'Der Text der Fastenrolle', *MGWJ* 24 (1875) 43-48, 139-144; 81 (1937) 351-355

Müller, J. (ed), *Responsen der Lehrer des Ostens und Westens*, Berlin 1888

Muntner, S., *Introduction to the Book of Assaph the Physician*, Jerusalem 1957 (Hebr)

Musajoff, S., *Merkavah shelemah*, Jerusalem 1921

Mussies, G., 'Greek in Palestine and the Diaspora', in Safrai – Stern, *Jewish People*, 1040-64

Naeh, S., 'Did the Tannaim Interpret the Script of the Torah Differently from the Authorized Reading?', *Tarbiz* 61 (1992) 401-48 (Hebr)

Naeh, S., 'Notes to Tannaitic Hebrew Based on Codex Vat. 66 of the Sifra', in M. Bar-Asher (ed), *Language Studies* 4 (1990) 271-95 (Hebr)

Naeh, S., 'The Structure and the Division of Torat Kohanim, A: Scrolls', *Tarbiz* 66 (1997) 483-515 (Hebr)

Naeh, S., 'The Structure and the Division of *Torat Kohanim* (B): Parashot, Perakim, Halakhot', *Tarbiz* 69 (1999-2000) 59-104 (Hebr)

Naeh, S., *The Tannaic Hebrew in the Sifra according to Codex Vatican 66*, diss Hebrew U, Jerusalem 1989 (Hebr)

Naeh, S. – Shemesh, A., 'The Manna Story and the Time of Morning Prayer' (Hebrew), *Tarbiz* 64 (1995) 335-340

Nahum, Y.L., 'Midrash Megillat Esther of R. Zecharia the Physician (= *Midrash ha-Hefez*)', *Hasifat Genuzim mi-Teman*, Holon 1971, 192-201 (Hebr)

Nahum, Y.L., *Mi-yetsirot sifrutiyyot mi-Teman*, Holon 1981

Naveh, J., 'An Aramaic Consolatory Burial Inscription', *Atiqot* 14 (1980) 55-59

Naveh, J., 'Inscriptions from Ancient Synagogues', *Eretz-Israel* 20 (1989) 302-310 (Hebr)

Naveh, J., 'Seven New Epitaphs from Zoar', *Tarbiz* 69 (2000) 619-635 (Hebr)

Naveh, J., *On Sherd and Papyrus: Aramaic and Hebrew Inscriptions from the Second Temple, Mishnaic and Talmudic Periods*, Jerusalem 1992 (Hebr)

Naveh, J., *On Stone and Mosaic: The Aramaic and Hebrew Inscriptions from Ancient Synagogues*, Jerusalem 1978 (Hebr)

Naveh, J., 'Two Tombstones from Zoar in the Hecht Museum Collection – The Aramaic Inscriptions', *Michmanim* 15 (2001) 5-7 (Hebr)

Naveh, J. – Shaked, S., 'A Knot and a Break: Terms for a Receipt in Antiquity', *IEJ* 53 (2003) 111-118

Naveh, J. – Shaked, S. (eds), *Amulets and Magic Bowls*, Jerusalem 1985, 1998

Naveh, J. – Shaked, S. (eds), *Magic Spells and Formulae*, Jerusalem 1993

Nelson, W.D., *Textuality and Talmud Torah: Issues of Early Rabbinic Written and Oral Transmission of Tradition as Exemplified in the Mekhilta of Rabbi Shimon b. Yohai*, diss Hebrew Union College 1999

Nemoy, L., *The Scroll of Antiochus*, New Haven 1952

Ness, L., *Astrology and Judaism in Late Antiquity*, diss Miami U 1990

Neubauer, A., *Mediaeval Jewish Chronicles and Chronological Notes* 2, Oxford 1895

Neubauer, A., *Seder ha-Hakhamim Ve-Korot Ha-Yamim*, (Anecdota Oxoniensia, Semitic Series 1, pt. 4,6) Oxford 1893

Neubauer, A., 'Seder Olam', in idem, *Medieval Jewish Chronicles and Chronological Notes* 2, Oxford 1895, 26-67

Neuhausen, H.S., 'Targumic Citations in the Zohar', *Otzar Hayyim* 8 (1932) 181-187

Neuman, H., '*Ha-Ma'asim Livne Eretz Israel* and their Historical Background', MA thesis Hebrew U 1987 (Hebr)

Neusner, J., *The Components of the Rabbinic Documents (From the Whole to the Parts)* 2, *Esther Rabbah* 1, Atlanta Georgia 1997

Neusner, J., *Esther Rabbah I: An Analytical Translation*, Atlanta GA 1989

Neusner, J., *A History of the Jews in Babylonia* 1-5, Leiden 1965-1970

Neusner, J., 'The Phenomenon of the Rabbi in Late Antiquity', *Numen* 16 (1969) 1-20

Neusner, J., 'The Phenomenon of the Rabbi in Late Antiquity II: The Ritual of "Being a Rabbi" in Later Sassanian Babylonia', *Numen* 17 (1970) 1-18

Neusner, J., 'Rabbi and Magus in Third-Century Sasanian Babylonia', *History of Religions* 6 (1966/67) 169-178

Neusner, J., *The Judaism Behind the Texts: The Generative Premises of Rabbinic Literature* 4: *The Latest Midrashic Compilations*, Atlanta 1994

Neusner, J., *Mekhilta according to Rabbi Ishmael: An Analytical Translation*, Atlanta 1988

Neusner, J., *The Midrashic Compilations of the Sixth and Seventh Centuries* 2, Atlanta Georgia 1989

Neusner, J., *Sifra: An Analytical Translation* 1-3, Atlanta 1988

Neusner, J., 'Sifra and the Problem of the Mishnah', *Henoch* 11 (1989) 17-40

Neusner, J., 'Sifra's Critique of Mishnaic Logic', *Hebrew Studies* 29 (1988) 49-65

Neusner, J., *Sifre to Deuteronomy: An Analytical Translation*, Atlanta 1987

Neusner, J., *Sifre to Numbers: An Analytical Translation*, Atlanta 1986

Neusner, J., *The Talmud of the Land of Israel* 18: *Besah and Taanit*, Chicago 1987

Neusner, J. – Avery Peck, A., *Encyclopedia of Midrash*, 2 vols Leiden 2004

Nevo, D., *Pests in agricultural crops and their disinfestations in the Land of Israel during the Bible and Mishna period*, diss Bar Ilan U 1992

Newman, H., *Jerome and the Jews*, diss Hebrew U, Jerusalem 1997 (Hebr)

Newsom, C., *Songs of the Sabbath Sacrifice: A Critical Edition*, Atlanta 1985

Niehof, M., 'A Dream which is not Interpreted is like a Letter which is not Read', *JJS* 43 (1992) 58-84

Nitzan, B. 'Hymns from Qumran "לפחד ולבהל" Evil Ghosts (4Q, 510; 4Q, 511)', *Tarbiz* 55 (1986) 19-46 (Hebr)

Nitzan, B., *Pesher Habakkuk*, Jerusalem 1986 (Hebr)

Nitzan, B., *Qumran Prayer and Poetry*, Jerusalem 1996 (Hebr)

Noam, V., *Megillat Ta'anit: Versions, Interpretation, History, with a Critical Edition*, Jerusalem 2003 (Hebr)

Noam, V., 'The Miracle of the Cruse of Oil, The Metamorphosis of a Legend', *HUCA* 73 (2002) 191-226

Noam, V., 'From Philology to History, the Case of Megillat Ta`anit', in Teugels – Ulmer, *Recent Developments*, 53-95

Noam, V., 'The Scholion to the Megilat Ta'anit: Towards an Understanding of its Stemma', *Tarbiz* 62 (1992) 55-99 (Hebr)

Noam, V., 'The Seventeenth of Elul in Megillat Ta'anit', *Zion* 59 (1994) 433-444 (Hebr)

Noam, V., 'From Textual Criticism to Historical Reconstruction', *Cathedra* 104 (2002) 7-30 (Hebr)

Noam, V., 'Two Testimonies to the Route of Transmission of *Megilat Ta'anit* and the Source of the Hybrid Version of the Scholion', *Tarbiz* 65 (1996) 389-416 (Hebr)

Nock, A.D., 'Paul and the Magus', in idem, *Essays on Religion and the Ancient World* (select. and ed Z. Stewart), Oxford 1972, vol 1, 308-330

Notley R.S. – Safrai, Z., *Eusebius, Onomasticon*, Leiden – Boston 2005

Nowak, R.M., *Walker's Mammals of the World*, 5th ed, Johns Hopkins UP 1991

Noy, D., *Forms and Content in Folk Stories*, Jerusalem 1983 (Hebr)

Noy, D., *The Jewish Animal Tale of Oral Tradition*, Haifa 1976 (Hebr)

Noy, D., 'Yesodot humor be-Midrash Esther Rabba', *Mahanayim* 89 (1964) 46-49

Noy, D., 'Yud-bet ha-mazzalot ve-yud bet ha-shevatim', *Mahanayim* 90 (1964) 128-133

Noy, D. (ed), *Jewish Inscriptions from Western Europe* 1-2, Cambridge 1993-95

Noy, D. – Bloedhorn, H. (eds), *Inscriptiones Judaicae Orientis* 3: *Syria and Cyprus*, Tübingen 2004

Noy, D. – Horbury, W. (eds), *Jewish Inscriptions of Graeco-Roman Egypt*, Cambridge 1992

Noy, D. – Panayotov, A. – Bloedhorn, H. (eds), *Inscriptiones Judaicae Orientis* 1: *Eastern Europe*, Tübingen 2004

Ochs, P. (ed), *The Return to Scripture in Judaism and Christianity*, New York 1993

Odeberg, H., *3 Enoch, or the Hebrew Book of Enoch*, Cambridge 1928

Offer, J., 'Sidre Nevi'im u-Khetuvim', *Tarbiz* 58 (1989) 155-189 (Hebr)

Olszowy-Schlanger, J., *Karaite Marriage Documents from the Cairo Geniza*, Leiden 1998

Oppenheim, H., 'Maamar bikoret le-Sefer Tanna debe Eliyahu', *Bet Talmud* 1 (1881) 304-310

Oppenheim, L.A., 'Divination and Celestial Observation in the Last Assyrian Empire', *Centaurus* 14 (1969) 97-135

Oppenheimer, A., *Babylonia Judaica in the Talmudic Period*, Wiesbaden 1983

Orlov, A., 'Celestial Choirmaster: The Liturgical Role of Enoch-Metatron in "2 Enoch" and the Merkabah Tradition', *JSP* 14 (2004) 3-29

Orman, D., 'Jewish Inscriptions from Dabura in the Golan', *Tarbiz* 40 (1971) 399-408 (Hebr)

Park, J.S., *Conceptions of Afterlife in Jewish Inscriptions with Special Reference to Pauline Literature*, Tübingen 2000

Parker, F.R.A., 'Egyptian Astronomy, Astrology, and Calendrical Reckoning', in C.C. Gillispie (ed), *Dictionary of Scientific Biography* 1-18, New York 1970-90, vol 15, 706-727

Patai, R., *Man and Land*, Jerusalem 1952 (Hebr)

Perreau, P., 'Ein Rundschreiben Haman's', *Hebräische Bibliographie* 7 (1864) 46-47

Perrot, C., 'The Reading of the Bible in the Ancient Synagogue', in Mulder – Sysling, *Mikra*, 149-159

Petterson, O., 'Magic-Religion: Some Marginal Notes to an Old Problem', *Ethnos* 22 (1957) 109-119

Philips, C.R., 'The Sociology of Religious Knowledge in the Roman Empire to A. D. 284', *ANRW* II 16.3 (1986), 2677-2773

Pineles, Z.M., *Darka shel Tora*, Vienna 1861

Pines, S., 'The Oath of Asaph the Physician', *PIASH* 5:9 (1975)

Pines, S. 'Points of Similarity between the Exposition of the Doctrine of the Sefirot in the Sefer Yezira and a text of the Pseudo-Clementine Homilies, *PIASH* 7 (1989), 63-14

Pines, S., 'Wrath and Creatures of Wrath in Pahlavi, Jewish and New Testament Sources', in S. Shaked (ed), *Irano-Judaica: Studies Relating to Jewish Contacts with Persian Culture Throughout the Ages*, Jerusalem 1982, 76-82

Polotsky, H.J., 'The Greek Papyri from the Cave of Letters,' *IEJ* 12 (1962) 258-262

Polotsky, H.J., 'Three Greek Documents from the Family Archive of Babatha', *Eretz-Israel* 8 (1967) 47-51 (Hebr)

Porten, B., *Archives from Elephantine*, Berkeley – Los Angeles 1968

Porten, B. and Yardeni, A., *Textbook of Aramaic Documents from Ancient Egypt* 2, *Contracts*, Jerusalem 1989

Porton, G.G., *Goyim: Gentiles and Israelites in Mishna-Tosefta*, Atlanta 1988

Porton, G.G., *The Traditions of Rabbi Ishmael* 1-4, Leiden 1965-1970

Porton, G.G., *Understanding Rabbinic Midrash*, Hoboken, NJ 1985

Preuss, J., *Biblisch Talmudische Medizin: Beiträge zur Geschichte der Heilkunde und der Kultur überhaupt*, Berlin 1911, repr Westmead 1969, New York 1971, ET (updated) F. Rosner, *Biblical and Talmudic Medicine*, Northvale NJ – London 1993

Price, J.J., 'Five Inscriptions from Jaffa', *SCI* 22 (2003) 215-231

Pringsheim, F., *The Greek Law of Sale*, Weimar 1950

Puech, E., 'Ossuaires et inscriptions', *RB* 90 (1983) 481-533

Puech, E., 'A-t-on redécouvert le tombeau du grand-pretre Caiphe?', *Le monde de la Bible* 80 (1993) 42-47

Pullyen, S., *Prayer in Greek Religion*, Oxford 1997

Qafih, J., 'Leket Midrash al Esther', *Hamesh Megillot*, Jerusalem 1962, 325-326

Qafih, J., *Collected Papers* 1-2, Jerusalem 1989 (Hebr)

Quass, F., *Die Honoratiorenschicht in den Städten des griechischen Ostens*, Stuttgart 1993

Rabbinowicz, I.M., *La médecine du Thalmud*, Paris 1880

Rabin, C., 'Hebrew and Aramaic in the First Century', in Safrai – Stern, *Jewish People*, 1007-1039

Rabinovitz, Z.M., *Ginzé Midrash: The Oldest Forms of Rabbinic Midrashim According to Geniza Manuscripts*, Tel Aviv 1976 (Hebr)

Rabinovitz, Z.M., *Halakha and Aggada in the Liturgical Poetry of Yannai*, Tel Aviv 1965 (Hebr)

Rabinovitz, Z.M., *The Liturgical Poems of Rabbi Yannai* 1-2, Jerusalem 1985-87 (Hebr)

Rabinovitz, Z.M., 'A Novel Edition of Midrash Abba Gurion', see idem, *Ginzé Midrash*

Rabinowitz, H., 'Esther Rabba, Parasha 6,8-14', *Ilanot* 1 (1984) 77-86 (Hebr)

Rabinowitz, J.J., *Jewish Law – Its Influence of the Development of Legal Institutions*, New York 1956

Rabinowitz, J.J., *Studies in Legal History*, Jerusalem 1958

Rabinowitz, L.I., 'Divination, in the Talmud', in *EJ* 6, 116-118

Rabinowitz [Rabbinovicz], R.N., *Sefer dikdukei soferim: Variae lectiones in Mischnam et in Talmud Babylonicum* 1-16, Munich – Mainz – Przemysl 1866-97, repr in 2 vols New York 1976

Rahmani, L.Y., *A Catalogue of Jewish Ossuaries in the Collections of the State of Israel*, Jerusalem 1994

Rainey, A.F., 'The Toponymics of Eretz-Israel', *BASOR* 231 (1978) 1-17

Rainey, A.F. – Notley, R.S., *The Sacred Bridge* 1, Jerusalem 2005

Rajak, T., *The Jewish Dialogue with Greece and Rome*, Leiden 2002

Rapeld, M., 'Megillat Antiochus, Selected Bibliography', in D. Sperber (ed), *Minhagei Israel* 5, Jerusalem 1995, 117-120

Rappel, D., *Targum Onkelos ke-ferush la-Torah*, Tel Aviv 1985

Ratner, B., 'On the Antiquities of the Jews' (Mikadmoniyot ha-Yehudim), *Measef* 1 (1902) 91-105

Ratner, B., *Mavo leha-Seder Olam Rabba*, Vilna 1894

Ratner, B., 'Notes on Megillat Taanit', *Sokolov Jubilee Volume*, Warsaw 1904, 500-511 (Hebr)

Ratner, B., *Seder Olam Rabba; Die Grosse Weltchronik nach Handschriften und Druckwerken mit kritischen Noten und Erklärungen*, Vilna 1897

Ratner, D.B., *Ahawath Zion we-Jeruscholaim*, Traktat Megilla, Vilna 1912

Ratzaby, Y., *Teshuvot R. Yehoshua Ha-Nagid*, Jerusalem 1989

Reeg, G., *Die Geschichte von den Zehn Märtyrern: synoptische Edition mit Übersetzung und Einleitung*, Tübingen 1985

Reeg, G., *Die Ortsnamen Israels nach der rabbinischen Literatur*, Wiesbaden 1989

Reich, R., 'Ossuary inscriptions from the "Caiaphas" tomb', *Atiqot* 21 (1992) 72-87

Reichman, R., *Mishna und Sifra: Ein literarkritischer Vergleich paralleler Überlieferungen*, Tübingen 1998

Reider, D., 'On Targum Yerushalmi Ms. Neofiti', *Tarbiz* 35 (1969) 81-88 (Hebr)

Reif, S.C., *A Jewish Archive from Old Cairo: The History of Cambridge University's Genizah Collection*, Richmond 2000

Rivlin, J., *Bills and Contracts from Lucena (1020-1025 C.E.)*, Ramat-Gan 1994 (Hebr)

Rivlin, J., *Inheritance and Wills in Jewish Law*, Ramat-Gan 1999 (Hebr)

Rochberg-Halton, F., *Aspects of Babylonian Celestial Divination: The Lunar Eclipse Tablets of Enuma Anu Enlil*, (Archiv für Orientforschung 22) Horn 1988

Rochberg-Halton, F., 'Babylonian Horoscopes and their Sources', *Orientalia* 58 (1989) 102-144

Romer, F.E., *Pomponius Mela's Description of the World* 1, Ann Arbor MI 1998

Rosenfeld, B.-Z., *Lod and its Sages in the Periods of the Mishnah and Talmud*, Jerusalem 1977 (Hebr)

Rosenfeld, B.-Z., 'Rabbi Joshua ben Levi and his Wife Kyra Mega: Interpretation of Inscriptions from Beth She'arim', *Cathedra* 114 (2004) 11-36 (Hebr)

Rosenthal, A., 'The Oral Law and the Torah from Sinai: Halakhah and Practice', in Bar-Asher – Rosenthal, *Talmudic Studies* 2, 448-489 (Hebr)

Rosenthal, D., *Mishna Aboda Zara: A Critical Edition with Introduction*, Jerusalem 1980 (Hebr)

Rosenthal, D., 'The Sages' Methodical Approach to Textual Variants within the Hebrew Bible', in A. Rofe and Y. Zakovitch (eds), *I.L. Seeligmann Volume*, Jerusalem 1983, 395-417 (Hebr)

Rosenthal, E.S., 'The Teacher' (Ha-moreh), *PAAJR* 31 (1963) 1-71 (Hebr)

Rosenthal, E.S., 'The Giv'at ha-Mivtar Inscription', *Peraqim* 2 (1974) 335-373 (Hebr)

Rosenthal, E.S., 'Leshonot Sofrim', *Yuval Shay: maamarim likhvod Shemuel Yosef Agnon*, Ramat-Gan 1958, 293-324

Rosenthal, E.S., 'Notes on the Giv'at ha-Mivtar Inscription', *P'raqim* 2 (1974) 335-373 (Hebr)

Rosenthal, E.S., 'Tradition and Innovation in the Halakha of the Sages', *Tarbiz* 63 (1994) 321-374 (Hebr)

Rosenthal, E.S., 'Word Sorting and Version Studies', in Bar Asher – Rosenthal, *Talmudic Studies* 2, 13-46 (Hebr)

Rosenthal, E.S. (ed), *Yerushalmi Neziqin, Edited From the Escorial Manuscript*, with intr and comm by S. Lieberman, Jerusalem 1983 (Hebr)

Rosenthal, F., *Die aramaistische Forschung seit Th. Nöldeke's Veröffentlichungen*, Leiden 1939

Rossell, W.H., *A Handbook of Aramaic Magical Texts*, Ringwood Borough NJ 1953

Roth-Gerson, L., *The Greek Inscriptions from the Synagogues in Eretz-Israel*, Jerusalem 1987 (Hebr)

Rovner, J., 'An Early Passover Haggadah According to the Palestinian Rite', *JQR* 90 (2000) 337-396

Rovner, J., 'A New Version of the Eres Israel Haggadah Liturgy and the Evolution of the Eres Israel "Miqra' Bikkurim" Midrash', *JQR* 92 (2002) 421-453

Rovner, J., 'Two Early Witnesses to the Formation of the *Miqra Bikurim Midrash* and their Implications for the Evolution of the Haggadah Text', *HUCA* 75 (2004) 75-119

Rubenstein J., *Talmudic Stories: Narrative Art, Composition and Culture*, Baltimore 1999

Rutgers, L.V., *The Jews in Late Ancient Rome: Evidence of Cultural Interaction in the Roman Diaspora*, Leiden 1995

Ruuk, H.K. 'Feeding and Social Behavior of the Striped Hyaena (Hyaena vulgaris Desma-rest)', *East African Wildlife Journal* 14 (1976) 91-111

Rybak, S., *The Aramaic Language of Nedarim*, diss Yeshiva U 1980

Safrai, S., *Akiva ben Yosef: hayyav u-mishnato*, Jerusalem 1971

Safrai, S., 'Halakha', in idem, *Literature of the Sages*, 121-210

Safrai, S., 'Hassidic Teaching in Mishnaic Literature', *JJS* 16 (1956) 15-33, repr (expanded and corrected) in idem, *In Times of Temple* 2, 501-517 (Hebr)

Safrai, S., 'Hassidim ve-anshei maase', *Zion* 50 (1984-5) 133-154, repr in idem, *In Times of Temple* 2, 518-539

Safrai, S., 'Oral Tora', in idem, *Literature of the Sages* 1, 35-119

Safrai, S., *In Times of Temple and Mishnah: Studies in Jewish History* 1-2, (collected studies) Jerusalem 1996 (Hebr)

Safrai, S., 'Yeshu weha-tenua he-hassidit', in A. Oppenheimer – I. Gafni – D. Schwartz (eds), *The Jews in the Hellenistic-Roman World; Studies in Memory of Menahem Stern*, Jerusalem 1996, 413-436 (Hebr)

Safrai, S. (ed), *The Literature of the Sages, First Part: Oral Tora, Halakha, Mishna, Tosefta, Talmud, External Tractates*, (CRINT II/3a) Assen/Maastricht – Philadelphia 1987

Safrai, S. – Stern, M. (eds), *The Jewish People in the First Century: Historical Geography, Political History, Social, Cultural and Religious Life and Institutions*, (CRINT I/1-2) Assen – Philadelphia 1974-76

Safrai, Z., 'The Bar-Kochva Revolt and its Effect on Settlement', in A. Oppenheimer – U. Rappaport (eds.), *The Bar-Kochva Revolt*, Jerusalem 1984, 212-214 (Hebr)

Safrai, Z., *Boundaries and Administration in the Land of Israel in the Mishna and Talmud Period*, Jerusalem 1980 (Hebr)

Safrai, Z., 'Geographical Midrashim as a Historical Source', *PWCJS* 7, *Studies in the Talmud, Halacha and Midrash* (1981) 79-80 (Hebr)

Safrai, Z., *The Jewish Community in the Talmudic Period*, Jerusalem 1995

Safrai, Z., 'Marginal Notes on the Rehob Inscription', *Zion* 42 (1977) 1-22 (Hebr)

Safrai, Z., 'The Origins of Reading the Aramaic Targum in Synagogue', *Immanuel* 24-25 (1990) 187-193

Sagiv, N., *The Jewish Settlement East of the Jordan*, diss Bar Ilan U, Ramat-Gan 2003 (Hebr)

Saperstein, M., *Decoding the Rabbis: A Thirteenth-Century Commentary on the Aggadah*, Cambridge MA 1980

Sarason, R.S., 'The "Petihtot" in Leviticus Rabba: "Oral homilies" or redactional constructions?' *JJS* 33 (1982) 557-567

Sarfatti, G.B., '*Keta mitokh Mekhilta de-Rabbi Shimeon bar Yohai* [A Fragment from *Mekhilta de-Rabbi Simeon bar Yohai*]', *Lešonenu* 27-28 (1964) 176 (Hebr)

Sarfatti, G.B. – Artzi, P. – Greenfield, J.C. – Kaddari, M. (eds), *Studies in Hebrew and Semitic Languages dedicated to the Memory of Prof. Kutscher*, Ramat-Gan 1980 (Hebr)

Sassoon, D.S., *Ohel Dawid* 1-2, London 1932

Schäfer, P., 'The Aim and Purpose of Early Jewish Mysticism', in idem, *Hekhalot-Studien*, 277-295

Schäfer, P., *Geniza-Fragmente zur Hekhalot-Literatur*, Tübingen, 1984

Schäfer, P., 'Handschriften zur Hekhalot-Literatur', *FJB* 11 (1983) 113-193

Schäfer, P., 'In Heaven as It Is in Hell: The Cosmology of Seder Rabbah di-Bereshit', in R. Boustan – A.Y. Reed (eds), *Heavenly Realms and Earthly Realities in Late Antique Religions*, Cambridge 2004

Schäfer, P., *Hekhalot-Studien*, Tübingen 1988

Schäfer, P., *The Hidden and Manifest God: Some Major Themes in Early Jewish Mysticism*, Albany 1992

Schäfer, P., 'Merkavah Mysticism and Magic', in P. Schäfer – J. Dan (eds), *Gershom Scholem's Major Trends in Jewish Mysticism 50 Years After*, Tübingen 1993, 59-78

Schäfer, P., 'Once again the Status Quaestionis of Research in Rabbinic Literature: An Answer to Chaim Milikowsky', *JJS* 40 (1989) 89-94

Schäfer, P., 'Zum Problem der redaktionellen Identität von *Hekhalot Rabbati*', in idem, *Hekhalot-Studien*, 63-74

Schäfer, P., 'Research into Rabbinic Literature: An Attempt to Define the *Status Quaestionis*', *JJS* 37 (1986) 139-152

Schäfer, P., *Synopse zur Hekhalot-Literatur*, Tübingen 1981

Schäfer, P., 'Tradition and Redaction in Hekhalot Literature', *JSJ* 14 (1983) 172-181, repr in *idem, Hekhalot-Studien*, 8-16

Schäfer, P., *Übersetzung der Hekhalot-Literatur* 1-4, Tübingen 1987-95

Schäfer, P. – Shaked, S., *Magische Texte aus der Kairoer Geniza* 1-3, Tübingen 1994-99

Schechter, S., 'A Fragment of Sifre Zuta', *JQR* 6 (1894) 656-663

Schechter, S., 'Genizah Fragments', *JQR* 16 (1904) 446-452

Schechter, S., 'The Mechilta to Deuteronomy', *JQR* 16 (1904) 695-699

Schechter, S., 'Mekhilta Devarim parshat Re'eh', in Brann – Elbogen, *FS Israel Lewy*, Hebr section, 188-192

Schechter, S., 'Midrash Suta ... von Salomon Buber' (Recension), *JQR* 8 (1896) 179-184

Schechter, S., 'Notes to Canticles Zutta', in idem, *Midrash Agadath Shir Hashirim*

Schechter, S., 'Postscript', in idem, *Midrash Agadath Shir Hashirim*

Schechter, S. (ed), *Midrash Agadath Shir Hashirim*, Cambridge 1896

Schechter, S. – Taylor, C., *The Wisdom of Ben Sira*, Cambridge 1899

Schelbert, G., 'Exodus XXII 4 im palästinischen Targum', *VT* 8 (1958) 253-263

Schepansky, I., *The Takkanot of Israel*, Jerusalem 1991 (Hebr)

Schiffman, L.H., 'The Recall of Rabbi Nehunia ben ha-Qanah from Ecstasy in the "Hekhalot Rabbati"', *AJS Review* 1 (1976) 269-281

Schiffman L.H. – Swartz, M.D., *Hebrew and Aramaic Incantation Texts from the Cairo Genizah: Selected Texts from Taylor-Schechter Box K1*, Sheffield 1992

Schirmann, J., 'Hebrew Liturgical Poetry and Christian Hymnology', *JQR* 44 (1953-54) 123-161

Schlüter, M., 'Ein Auslegungsmidrasch im Midrasch Tanhuma', *FJB* 14 (1986), 71-98

Schlüter, M., 'Die Erzählung von der Rückholung des R. Nehunya ben Haqana aus der *Merkava*-Schau in ihrem redaktionellen Rahmen', *FJB* 10 (1982) 65-109

Schlüter, M., 'Midrash parshani al Bemidbar be-tokh Midrash Tanhuma', *PWCJS* 9:3 (1986) 43-47

Schmilg, J., *Über Entstehung und historischen Werth des Siegeskalenders Megillath Taanith*, Leipzig 1874

Scholem, G., 'Havdala de-Rabbi Aqiva', *Tarbiz* 50 (1981) 243-281 (Hebr)

Scholem G., 'Havdalah de-Rabbi Aqiba: A Source of the Jewish Magical Tradition from the Geonic Period', *Tarbiz* 50 (1980/81) 243-281 (Hebr)

Scholem, G., *Jewish Gnosticism, Merkavah Mysticism, and Talmudic Tradition*, 2nd ed New York 1965

Scholem, G., *Major Trends in Jewish Mysticism*, 2nd ed New York 1954

Schorr, Y.H., 'Payyetanim v-Piyyutim Shelo Nod'u', *Hechalutz* 9:2 (1873) 43-57

Schremer, A. 'The Concluding Passage of *Megilat Ta'anit* and the Nullification of its Halakhic Significance during the Talmudic Period', *Zion* 65 (2000) 411-439 (Hebr)

Schremer, A., 'Divorce in Papyrus Se'elim 13 Once Again: A Reply to Tal Ilan', *HTR* 91 (1998) 193-202

Schremer, A., 'Papyrus Se'elim 13 and the Question of Divorce Initiated by Women in Ancient Jewish *Halakha*', *Zion* 63 (1998) 377-390

Schürer, E., *A History of the Jewish People in the Age of Jesus Christ* 1-3, ET rev and ed by G. Vermes, F. Millar, M. Black and M. Goodman, Edinburgh 1973-87

Schwab, M. 'La Meghillath Taanith ou "Anniversaires Historiques" ', *Actes du onzième congrès international des orientalistes, Paris 1879*, Paris 1898, 199-259

Schwab, M., (A. Marx), 'Quelques notes sur la Meghillath Taanit', *REJ* 41 (1900) 266-268

Schwabe, M., – Lifshitz, B., *Beth She'arim* 2: *The Greek Inscriptions*, Hebr ed, Jerusalem 1967

Schwartz, A., 'Die Hauptergebnisse der wissenschaftlich-hermeneutischen Forschung', *Orientalia et Judaica* 1 (1923) 1-27

Schwartz, A., 'Die hermeneutische Quantitätsrelation in der Talmudischen Litratur', *Jahresbericht der Israelitisch-theologischen Lehranstalt*, Vienna 1916

Schwartz, J., *Jewish Settlement in Judea after the Bar-Kochba War until the Arab Conquest 135 C.E.-640 C.E.*, Jerusalem 1986 (Hebr)

Schwartz, J., Lod (Lydda), *Israel from its Origins through the Byzantine Period 5600 B.C.E.-640 C.E.*, (BAR International Series 571) Oxford 1991

Schwartz, S., *Imperialism and Jewish Society: 200 B.C.E. to 640 C.E.*, Princeton 2001

Schwarz, A.Z., *Die hebräischen Handschriften in Österreich (ausserhalb der National-bibliothek in Wien)*, Leipzig 1931

Schwarz, A.Z. – Loewinger, D.S. – Roth, E., *Die hebräischen Handschriften in Österreich* 2, New York 1973

Schwarzbaum, H., 'Prolegomenon', in Gaster, *The Chronicles of Jerahmeel*

Schwarzbaum, H., *Roots and Landscapes – Studies in Folklore*, Beer Sheva 1993 (Hebr)

Scott, J.M., *Geography in Early Judaism and Christianity: The Book of Jubilees*, Cambridge – New York 2002

Seeligmann, I.L., 'The Beginnings of the Midrash in the Book of Chronicles', *Tarbiz* 49 (1980) 14-32 (Hebr)

Segal, A., 'Hellenistic Magic: Some Questions of Definition', in R. Van den Broek – M.J. Vermaseren, *Études préliminaires aux religions orientales dans l'empire Romain*, Leiden 1981, 349-375

Segal, A.F., *Two Powers in Heaven: Early Rabbinic Reports about Christianity and Gnosticism*, Leiden 1977

Segal, E., *The Babylonian Esther Midrash: A Critical Commentary* 1-3, Atlanta GA 1994

Segal, E., 'The *Petihta* in Babylonia', *Tarbiz* 54 (1985) 177-204 (Hebr)

Segal, E., 'Human Anger and Divine Intervention in Esther', *Prooftexts* 9 (1989) 247-256

Segal, E., ' "The Same from the Beginning to End": On the Development of a Midrashic Homily', *JJS* 32 (1981) 158-165

Segal, J.B., *Catalogue of the Aramaic and Mandaic Incantation Bowls in the British Museum*, London 2000

Segal, M.H., *Dikduk leshon ha-Mishna*, Tel-Aviv 1936 (Hebr)

Segal, M.H., 'Ḥālōm – Ḥālōmōt - Ḥªlōmōt', *Lešonenu* 10 (1939-1940) 154-156 (Hebr)

Segal, M.H., 'Miscellanies: דרש, מדרש, בית מדרש', *Tarbiz* 17 (1946) 194-96 (Hebr)

Segal, M.H., *Sefer Ben Sira ha-shalem*, (1933) 2nd ed 3rd pr, Jerusalem 1972 (Hebr)

Segal, P., 'The Hebrew IOU Note from the Time of the Bar Kokhba Period', *Tarbiz* 60 (1990) 113-116 (Hebr)

Segal, P., 'The Penalty of the Warning Inscription from the Temple of Jerusalem', *IEJ* 39 (1989) 79-84

Seidel, J., '"Charming Criminals": Classification of Magic in the Babylonian Talmud', in M. Meyer – P. Mirecki (eds), *Ancient Magic and Ritual Power*, Leiden 1995, 145-166

Seidel, J., '"Release Us and We will Release You!": Rabbinic Encounters with Witches and Witchcraft', *Journal of the Association of Graduates in Near Eastern Studies* 3 (1992) 45-61

Sevenster, J.N., *Do You Know Greek? How Much Greek could the First Jewish Christians Have Known?* Leiden 1968

Shahar, Y., *Josephus Geographicus: The Classical Context of Geography in Josephus,* (TSAJ 98) Tübingen 2004

Shaked, S., 'Bagdana, King of the Demons, and other Iranian Terms in Babylonian Aramaic Magic', *Papers in honour of Mary Boyce: Acta Iranica* 24 (1985) 511-525

Shaked, S., 'Form and Purpose in Aramaic Spells: Some Jewish Themes', in idem (ed), *Officina Magica: The Working of Magic*, Leiden 2005, 1-30

Shaked, S., 'Iranian Loanwords in Middle Aramaic', *Encyclopedia Iranica* 2, London 1986, 259-261

Shaked, S. 'Jews, Christians, and Pagans in the Aramaic Incantation Bowls of the Sasanian Period', in A. Destro, M. Pesce (eds), *Religions and Cultures*, Binghamton 2002, 61-89

Shama, A., *Mekhilta de-Arayot: Introduction, Text, and Interpretive Notes*, MA thesis Hebrew U, Jerusalem 2000 (Hebr)

Shapira, A., *Midrash Aseret ha-Dibrot (A Midrash on the Ten Comandments): Text, Sources and Interpretation*, Jerusalem 2005 (Hebr)

Shapira, H., *Beit Hamidrash during the Late Second Temple Period and the Age of the Mishna*, diss Hebrew U, Jerusalem 2001 (Hebr)

Shapira, H., 'The Deposition of R. Gamliel: Between History and Legend', *Zion* 64 (1999) 5-38 (Hebr)

Sharvit, S., 'Studies in Lexicography and Grammar of Mishnaic Hebrew', in M.Z. Kaddari (ed), *Archive of the New Dictionary of Rabbinic Literature* 2, Ramat Gan 1974, 112-124 (Hebr)

Sharvit, S. 'The "Tense" System of Mishnaic Hebrew', in Sarfatti *et al.*, *Studies*, 110-125 (Hebr)

Sharvit, S., *Textual Variants and Language of the Treatise Abot*, diss Bar-Ilan U, Ramat-Gan 1976 (Hebr)

Sharvit, S., *Tractate Avoth Through the Ages*, Jerusalem 2004 (Hebr)

Shemesh, A., 'The Grace after Meals – Three Blessings or Four?' *Sidra*, 11 (1995) 153-166 (Hebr)

Shemesh, A.O., 'The Attitude of the Halacha to Irregular Plants', *Techomin* 32 (2002) 511-518 (Hebr)

Shemesh, A.O., 'The Striped Hyaena in Israel Sources – Between Legend and Reality,' *Al Ha'atar* 12 (2003) 7-28 (Hebr)

Shinan, A., 'The Aggadah of the Palestinian Targums of the Pentateuch and rabbinic Aggadah; some methodological considerations', in Beattie – McNamara, *Aramaic Bible*, 203-217

Shinan, A., *The Aggadah in the Aramaic Targums to the Pentateuch. Literary Analysis and Description* 1-2, Jerusalem 1979 (Hebr)

Shinan, A., 'The Aramaic Targum as a Mirror of Galilean Jewry', L.I. Levine (ed), *The Galilee in Late Antiquity*, New York 1992, 241-251

Shinan, A., *The Biblical Story as Reflected in its Aramaic Translations*, Tel Aviv 1993 (Hebr)

Shinan, A., *The Embroidered Targum: The Aggadah in Targum Pseudo-Jonathan of the Pentateuch*, Jerusalem 1992 (Hebr)

Shinan, A., 'Live translation; on the nature of the Aramaic Targums to the Pentateuch', *Prooftexts* 3 (1983) 41-49

Shinan, A., *Midrash Shemot Rabba : Parashiyyot 1-14*, Jerusalem-Tel Aviv 1984

Shinan, A., 'The "Palestinian" Targums - Repetitions, Internal Unity, Contradictions', *JJS* 36 (1985) 72-87

Shinan, A., ' "Targumic Additions" in Targum Pseudo-Jonathan', *Textus* 16 (1991) 139-155

Shinan, A. – Zakovitch, Y., 'Midrash in Scripture and Midrash Within Scripture', *ScrHier* 31 (1986) 259-277

Shivtiel, Y., 'Massorot ha-Temanim be-dikduk Leshon Hakhamim', in Bar-Asher, *Kovets maamarim*, vol 1, 207-251 (Hebr)

Shorey, P., 'Sirens', in *Encyclopaedia of Religion and Ethics* 9, ed J. Hastings, Edinburgh – New York 1920, 578

Shoshana, A., *Sifra on Leviticus* 1-3, Jerusalem – Cleveland 1981-88

Simon, M., *Midrash Rabbah: Esther*, translated into English, London 1939

Sirat, C., *Les Papyrus en caractères hebraïques trouvés en Egypte*, Paris 1985

Sirat, C. – Cauderlier, P. – Dukan, M. – Friedman, M.A. (eds), *La Ketouba de Cologne*, Opladen 1986

Skaist, A., 'The Background of the Talmudic Formula וקים שריר והכל', in Sarfatti *et al.*, *Studies*, XL-LIV

Skehan, P.W. – Di Lella, A.A. (trans & ed), *The Wisdom of Ben Sira*, (Anchor Bible) New York 1987

Smith, M., 'Helios in Palestine', *Erets Israel* 16 (1982) 199*-214*

Smith, M., 'Observations on Hekhalot Rabbati', in A. Altmann (ed), *Biblical and Other Studies*, Cambridge MA 1963, 142-160

Smith, W., *Dictionary of Greek and Roman Mythology* 2, London 1846

Smythe, P.A., *Babylonian Influence on the Bible and Popular Beliefs: 'Tehom and Tiamat', 'Hades and Satan': A Comparative Study of Genesis 1-2*, London 1897

Sokoloff, M., *A Dictionary of Jewish Babylonian Aramaic of the Talmudic and Geonic Periods*, Ramat Gan 2002 (Hebr)

Sokoloff, M., *A Dictionary of Jewish Palestinian Aramaic*, Ramat Gan 1990 (Hebr)

Sokoloff, M., 'The Hebrew of Bereshit Rabba According to Ms. Vat. 30', *Lešonenu* 33 (1969) 25-42; 135-149; 270-279 (Hebr)

Sokoloff, M., *The Geniza Fragments of Genesis Rabba and MS Vat. Ebr. 60 of Genesis Rabba* 1-2, diss Hebrew U, Jerusalem 1971

Sokoloff, M., *Kit'ei Bereshit Rabba min Ha-Geniza*, Jerusalem 1982

Sperber, D., *A Dictionary of Greek and Latin Legal Terms in Rabbinic Literature*, Ramat-Gan / Jerusalem 1984

Sperber, D., 'Etymological Studies in Rabbinic Hebrew', *Lešonenu* 53 (1989) 60-66 (Hebr)

Sperber, D., 'Greek and Latin Words in Rabbinic literature: Prolegomena to a New Dictionary of Classical Works in Rabbinic Literature', *Bar-Ilan* 14-15 (1977) 6-60; 16-17 (1979) 9-30

Sperber, D., '7... in jüdischen Gesetzen und Gebräuchen', in D. Tyrandellis – M. Friedländer (eds), *10+5 = Gott: Die Macht der Zeichen*, Berlin 2004, 51-52

Sperber, D., *Magic and Folklore in Rabbinic Literature*, Ramat Gan / Jerusalem 1994

Sperber, D., *Nautica Talmudica*, Ramat-Gan – Leiden 1986

Sperber, D., 'Studies in Greek and Latin Loanwords in Rabbinic Literature', *SCI* 2 (1975) 168-174

Spiegel, Sh., *The Fathers of Piyyut, Texts and Studies*, ed M. Schmelzer, New York – Jerusalem 1996 (Hebr)

Spivak, C.D., 'Medicine in Bible and Talmud', in *Jewish Encyclopaedia* 8 (1904) 409-414

Spolsky, B., 'Triglossia and Literacy in Jewish Palestine of the First Century', *International Journal of Social Languages* 42 (1983) 95-109

Stec, D.M., 'The Recent English Translation of the Targums to Job, Proverbs, and Qohelet: a Review', *JSS* 39 (1994) 161-181

Stec, D.M., *The Text of the Targum of Job: An Introduction and Critical Edition*, Leiden 1993

Stein, E., 'Die Homiletische Peroratio in Midrasch', *HUCA* 8-9 (1931-1932) 353-371

Steinsaltz, A. (ed), *Midrash ha-Gadol*, Leviticus, Jerusalem 1976

Steller, H. – Steller, R., 'Preliminary Remarks to a New Edition of Shir Hashirim Rabba', G. Sed Rajna ed., *Rashi 1040-1990, Hommage à Ephraim E. Urbach*, Paris 1993, 301-311

Stemberger, G., 'Die Datierung der Mekhilta', *Karios* 21 (1979) 81-118

Stemberger, G., *Einleitung in Talmud und Midrasch*, Munich 1992; ET M. Bockmuehl, *Introduction to the Talmud and Midrash*, 2nd pr Edinburgh – Minneapolis 1996

Stemberger, G., 'Hieronymus und die Juden seiner Zeit', in D.A. Koch – H. Lichtenberger (eds), *Begegnungen zwischen Christentum und Judentum in Antike und Mittelalter*, Göttingen 1993, 361-362

Stemberger, G., *Midrasch: Vom Umgang der Rabbinen mit der Bibel*, Munich 1989

Stemberger, G., 'Ronen Reichman: Mishna und Sifra; ein literarkritischer Vergleich paralleler Überlieferungen",' *FJB* 26 (1999) 189-197

Stemberger, G., 'Sifra-Tosefta-Yerushalmi: Zur Redaktion und frühen Rezeption von Sifra', *JSJ* 30 (1999) 271-311

Stemberger, G. – Strack, H.: see Strack – Stemberger

Stern, D., *Parables in Midrash: Narrative and Exegesis in Rabbinic Literature*, Cambridge 1991

Stern, D., *Midrash and Theory: Ancient Jewish Exegesis and Contemporary Literary Studies*, Evanston 1996

Stern, D., 'Anthological Imagination in Jewish Literature', in *The Jewish Anthological Imagination* 1 = *Prooftexts* 17 (1997) 1-7

Stern, D. – Mirsky, M.J., *Rabbinic Fantasies: Imaginative Narratives from Classical Hebrew Literature*, Philadelphia 1990

Stern, E. (ed), *The New Encyclopedia of Archeological Excavations in the Holy Land* 1, Jerusalem 1992 (Hebr)

Stern, S., *Calendar and Community: A History of the Jewish Calendar, 2nd cent. BCE – 10th cent. CE*, Oxford 2001

Stern, S., 'Figurative Art and *Halakhah* in the Mishnaic-Talmudic Period', *Zion* 61 (1996) 397-419 (Hebr)

Steudel, A., '*4Q408:* A Liturgy on Morning and Evening Prayer: Preliminary Edition', *RQ* 16 (1993) 313-334

Stone, M.E. – Chazon, E.G. (eds), *Biblical Perspectives: Early Use and Interpretation of the Bible in Light of the Dead Sea Scrolls; Proc. of the First International Symposium of the Orion Center, etc., 12-14 May 1996,* (STDJ 28) Leiden 1998

Strack, H.L., *Introduction to the Talmud and Midrash*, Philadelphia 1945, repr New York 1965

Strack, H. – Billerbeck, P., *Kommentar zum Neuen Testament aus Talmud und Midrasch* 1-4, Munich 1922-1928; vol 5-6: Indexes, J. Jeremias – K. Adolph, Munich 1961-1965

Strack, H.L. – Billerbeck, P., 'Zur altjüdischen Dämonologie', in idem – idem, *Kommentar* 4/1, 501-535

Strack, H.L. – Stemberger, G., *Einleitung in Talmud und Midrasch*, 7th ed Munich 1982

Stroumsa, G., 'Form(s) of God: Some notes on Metatron and Christ', *HTR* 76 (1983) 269-288

Stroumsa, G., 'Mystical Descents', in Collins – Fishbane, *Death, Ecstasy*, 139-154

Stuckrad, K. von, *Frömmigkeit und Wissenschaft: Astrologie in Tanach, Qumran und frührabbinischer Literatur*, Frankfurt/M 1996

Stuckrad, K. von, 'Jewish and Christian Astrology in Late Antiquity: A New Approach', *Numen* 47 (2000) 1-40

Stuckrad, K. von, *Das Ringen um die Astrologie: jüdische und christlische Beiträge zum antiken Zeitverständnis*, Berlin 2000

Sukenik, E.L., 'Coffins and Inscriptions', *Hashiloach* 42 (1924) 335-344 (Hebr)

Sussman[n], Y., 'A Halakhic Inscription from the Beth-Shean Valley', *Tarbiz* 43 (1974) 88-158 (Hebr)

Sussman, Y., 'The Inscription in the Synagogue at Rehob', *Qadmoniot* 8 (1975) 123-128 (Hebr)

Sussman, Y., 'Additional Notes to "A Halakhic Inscription from the Beth-Shean Valley"', *Tarbiz* 44 (1975) 193-195 (Hebr)

Sussman, Y., 'The Baraita of the "Boundaries of Eretz-Israel"', *Tarbiz* 45 (1976) 213-257 (Hebr)

Sussman, Y., 'A Halakhic Inscription from the Beth-Shean Valley', *Tarbiz* 43 (1974) 88-158 (Hebr)

Sussman, Y., 'The History of Halakha and the Dead Sea Scrolls: Preliminary Observations on Miqsat Maase ha-Tora (4QMMT)', *Tarbiz* 59 (1990) 11-76 (Hebr)

Sussman, Y., 'Mesoret limmud u-messoret nusah shel ha-Talmud ha-Yerushalmi: Leverur nushaoteha shel Yerushalmi Shekalim', *Research in Talmudic Literature... in Honour of... Saul Lieberman*, Jerusalem 1983, 12-76

Sussman, Y., 'Professor J.N. Epstein and the Hebrew University', in S. Katz – M. Heyd (eds), *The History of the Hebrew University of Jerusalem*, Jerusalem 1997, 476-486 (Hebr)

Sussman, Y., 'Schechter the Scholar', *Jewish Studies* 38 (1998) 213-230 (Hebr)

Sussman, Y., 'Tora she-beal pe – peshuta kemashmaa' / 'Oral Tora Literally Understood: The Power of a Y', in Sussman – Rosenthal, *Talmudic Studies* 3/1, 209-384

Sussman, Y. et al., *Talmud Yerushalmi According to Ms. Or. 4720 (Scal. 3)*, introd Y. Sussman, Ac. of the Hebr. Lang., Jerusalem 2001 (Hebr)

Sussman, Y. – Rosenthal, D. (eds), *Talmudic Studies dedicated to the memory of E.E. Urbach*, vols 1, 2, 3/1, 3/2, Jerusalem 1990-2005

Swartz, M.D., ' '*Alay le-shabbeaḥ*: A Liturgical Prayer in *Ma'aseh Merkabah*', *JQR* 77 (1986-87) 179-190

Swartz, M.D., 'The Dead Sea Scrolls and Later Jewish Magic and Mysticism', *DSD* 8 (2001) 1-12

Swartz, M.D., *Mystical Prayer in Ancient Judaism: An Analysis of Ma'aseh Merkavah*, Tübingen 1992

Swartz, M.D., *Scholastic Magic: Ritual and Revelation in Early Jewish Mysticism*, Princeton 1996

Swartz, M.D., 'The Seal of the Merkavah', in R. Valentasis (ed), *Religions of Late Antiquity in Practice*, Princeton 2000, 322-329

Syren, R., 'The Isaiah-Targum and Christian Interpretation', *SJOT* 1 (1989) 46-65

Sznol, S., 'Sefer Ha Razim – El Libro de los Secretos; Introduccion y Comentario al Vocabulario Griego', *Erytheia: Revista de estudios bizantinos y neogriegos* 10 (1989) 205-287

Tabory, J., 'On the Ancient Version of the Benediction "Builder of Jerusalem" and the Benediction of David' [Hebrew], *Pe'amim* 78 (1999) 16-43

Tabory, J., 'The Benedictions of Self-Identity and The Changing Status of Women and of Orthodoxy', *Kenishta* 1 (2001) 107-138

Tabory, J., 'The Division of Esther Rabba into *Parashiyyot*', *Te'uda* 11 (1996) 191-203 (Hebr)

Tabory, J., 'Esther Rabbah', *The Oxford Dictionary of the Jewish Religion*, New York – Oxford 1997, 236

Tabory, J., 'The Evolution of the Midrash on "The Words of the Wise are Gracious"', *Sidra* 2 (1986) 151-155 (Hebr)

Tabory, J., 'Towards a History of the Paschal Meal', *Passover and Easter: Origin and History to Modern Times* (ed Paul F. Bradshaw and Lawrence A. Hoffman; Two Liturgical Traditions vol. 5), Notre Dame ID 1999, 62-80

Tabory, J., *Jewish Festivals in the Time of the Mishnah and Talmud*, 3rd ed Jerusalem 2000

Tabory, J., *Jewish Prayer and the Yearly Cycle: A List of Articles*, suppl vol *Kiryat Sefer* 64, Jerusalem 1992-93

Tabory, J., 'Ma'amadot: A Second-Temple Non-Temple Liturgy', in E.G. Chazon (ed), *Liturgical Perspectives: Prayer and Poetry in Light of the Dead Sea Scrolls; Proc. 5th Intern. Symp. of the Orion Center, 19–23 January, 2000*, (STDJ 48) Leiden 2003, 235-261

Tabory, J., *The Passover Ritual throughout the Generations*, Tel Aviv 1996 (Hebr)

Tabory, J., 'The Place of the "Malkhuyot" Blessing in the New Year Liturgy' (Hebrew), *Tarbiz* 48 (1979) 30-34

Tabory, J., 'The Prayer Book (Siddur) as an Anthology of Judaism', *Prooftexts* 17 (1997) 115-132; repr in D. Stern (ed), *The Anthology in Jewish Literature*, Oxford 2004, 143-158

Tabory, J., 'The Prayer of the High Priest on the Day of Atonement in *Piyyut* and Prayer', in B. Bar-Tikva – E. Hazan (eds), *Piyyut in Tradition* 2, Ramat Gan 1996, 55-84 (Hebr)

Tabory, J., 'The Precursors of the Amida', in A. Gerhards *et al.* (eds), *Identität durch Gebet: Zur gemeinschaftsbildenden Funktion institutionalisierten Betens in Judentum und Christentum*, Paderborn-München-Wien-Zürich 2003, 113-125

Tabory, J., 'The Priestly Blessing – From Temple to Synagogue', *Kol Peh leach Yodeh: iyyunim ... Prof. Dov Rapel*, Jerusalem 2002, 158-162 (Hebr)

Tabory, J., 'Some Problems in Preparing a Scientific Edition of *Esther Rabbah*', *Sidra* 1 (1985) 145-152 (Hebr)

Tabory, J., 'The Proems to the Seventh Chapter [sic!] of Esther Rabba and Midrash Abba Gurion', *Jerusalem Studies in Hebrew Literature* 16 (1997) 7-18 (Hebr)

Tabory, J. 'When was the Scroll of Fasts Abrogated?', *Tarbiz* 55 2 (1986) 261-265 = idem, *Jewish Festivals in the Time of the Talmud*, Jerusalem 1995, 318-322 (Hebr)

Tabory, J., review of E. Segal, *The Babylonian Esther Midrash: A Critical Commentary*, *JQR* 88 (1997) 113-120

Tal, A., 'The Dialects of Jewish Palestinian Aramaic and the Palestinian Targum of the Pentateuch', *Sefarad* 46 (1986) 441-448

Tal, A., 'The Forms of the Infinitive in Jewish Aramaic', in Bar-Asher *et al.*, *Hebrew Language Studies*, 201-218 (Hebr)

Tal, A., *The Language of the Targum of the Former Prophets and Its Position within the Aramaic Dialects*, Tel Aviv 1975 (Hebr)

Tal, A., 'Layers in the Jewish Aramaic of Palestine: The Appended Nun as a Criterion', *Lešonenu* 43 (1979) 165-184 (Hebr)

Tal, A. (ed), *The Samaritan Targum of the Pentateuch* 1-3, Tel Aviv 1980-83

Tal, A., 'Studies in Palestinian Aramaic: The Demonstrative Pronouns', *Lešonenu* 44 (1980) 43-65 (Hebr)

Talmon, S., 'Aspects of the Textual Transmission of the Bible in the Light of Qumran Manuscripts', *Textus* 4 (1964) 95-132

Talmon, S., 'The Calendar Reckoning of the Sect from the Judean Desert', *ScrHier* 4 (1958) 162-99

Talmon, S., 'The Three Scrolls of the Law That Were Found in the Temple Court', in J.M. Grintz – J. Liver (eds), *Studies in the Bible Presented to Prof. M. H. Segal*, Jerusalem 1965, 252-64 (Hebr)

Talmud Yerushalmi According to Ms. Or. 4720 (Scal. 3), see: Sussman

Talmudic Encyclopedia, vol 1-26, ed S.J. Zevin, Jerusalem 1973-2003 (Hebr)

Talshir, D., 'The Nature of the Aramaic in Tannaitic Literature', in: M. Bar-Asher (ed), *Sugyot bi-leshon Hachamim* (summaries, workshop 'Grammar and Lexicon of Mishnaic Hebrew'), Jerusalem 1991 69-70 (Hebr)

Ta-Shema, I.M., 'Lost Books from the Medieval Period', in *Reseaches in Talmudic Literature: A Study Conference in Honor of Eightieth Birthday of Shaul Lieberman*, Jerusalem 1983, 214-222 (Hebr)

Ta-Shma, I.M., *The Early Ashkenazic Prayer: Literary and Historical Aspects*, Jerusalem 2003, 84-90

Ta-Shema, I.[M.], 'Notes to "Hymns from Qumran"', *Tarbiz* 55 (1986) 440-442 (Hebr)

Ta-Shema, I.M., 'An Unpublished Franco-German Commentary on Bereshit and Vayikra Rabba, Mekhilta and Sifre', *Tarbiz* 55 (1986) 61-75 (Hebr)

Taubenschlag, R., *The Law of Greco-Roman Egypt in the Light of the Papyri* 2, Warsaw 1955

Taylor, J.E., *Christians and the Holy Places: The Myth of Jewish-Christian Origins*, Oxford 1993

Tcherikover, V. – Fuks, A. (eds), *Corpus Papyrorum Judaicorum* 1-3, Cambridge MA 1957-64

Teicher, J.L., 'A Sixth Century Fragment of the Palestinian Targum?', *VT* 1 (1951) 125-129

Telegdi, S., 'Essai sur la phonétique des emprunts iraniens en araméen talmudique', *Journal Asiatique* 1935 177-256

Teugels, L., 'Textual Criticism of a Late Rabbinic Midrash: *Aggadat Bereshit*', in Teugels – Ulmer, *Recent Developments*, 137-153

Teugels, L. – Kern-Ulmer, R. (eds), *Recent Developments in Midrash Research: Proc., 2002 and 2003 SBL Consultation on Midrash*, (Judaism in Context 2) Piscataway NJ 2005

Theodor, J. – Albeck, Ch. (eds), *Midrash Bereshit Rabba: Critical Edition with Notes and Commentary* 1-3, 2nd ed with add corr, Jerusalem 1965

Thünen, J.H. von, *Isolated State*, ed P. Hall, Oxford 1996

Tigay, J.H., *JPS Commentary on Deuteronomy*, Varda Books 2004

Tobi, J., *Midrash ha-Gadol: The Sources and the Structure* 1-2, diss Hebrew U, Jerusalem 1993 (Hebr)

Toorn, K. van der – Becking, B. – Horst, P.W. van der (eds), *Dictionary of Dieties and Demons in the Bible*, 2nd ed Leiden 1999

Toropower, J., *Kevod ha-Levanon* 1, Paris 1863

Tov, E., *Textual Criticism of the Hebrew Bible*, Minneapolis 1992

Towner, W.S., *The Rabbinic 'Enumeration of Scriptural Examples': A Study of a Rabbinic Pattern of Discourse with Special Reference to Mekhilta d'R. Ishmael*, Leiden 1973

Trachtenberg, J., *Jewish Magic and Superstition: A Study in Folk Religion*, New York 1970

Treitel, E., 'Edei ha-nusah shel Pirke de-R. Eliezer: miyyun mukdam', research seminar paper Hebrew U, Jerusalem 2002

Tropper, A., *Wisdom, Politics and Historiography*, Oxford 2004

Tsafrir, Y. – Di Segni, L. – Green, J., *Tabula Imperi Romani, Judea Palaestina: Eretz Israel in the Hellemistic, Roman and Byzantine periods : maps and gazetteer*, Jerusalem 1994

705

Tucker, G.M., 'Witnesses and "Dates" in Israelite Contracts', *CBQ* 28 (1966) 42-45

Tur-Sinai, N., 'On the Understanding of the Aramaic Targum on the Torah', *Ha-Lashon weha-sefer, Ha-sefer* Volume, Jerusalem 1951, 94-101 (Hebr)

Tur-Sinai [Torczyner], N.H., 'Millim sheulot bi-leshonenu', *Lešonenu* 8 (1937) 99-109, 256-278 (Hebr)

Twelftree, G.H., *Jesus the Exorcist: A Contribution to the Study of the Historical Jesus*, Tübingen 1993

Ugolini, B., *Thesaurus Antiquitatum*, Venice 1752-1753

Ulmer, R., 'Creating Rabbinic Texts: Moving from a Synoptic to a Critical Edition of Pesiqta Rabbati', in Teugels – Ulmer, *Recent Developments*, 117-136

Ulmer, R., *The Evil Eye in the Bible and in Rabbinic Literature*, Hoboken 1994

Underhill, E., *Mysticism: A Study in the Nature and Development of Man's Spiritual Consciousness*, 1911, repr New York 1990

Urbach, E.E., *Arugat ha-Bosem,* Jerusalem 1963

Urbach, E.E., *Collected Writings in Jewish Studies*, Jerusalem 1999

Urbach, E.E., 'The Derasha as a Basis of the Halakha and the Problem of the Sofrim', *Tarbiz* 27 (1958) 166-182 (Hebr)

Urbach, E.E., 'History and Halakha', in Robert Hamerton-Kelly and Robin Scroggs (eds), *Jews, Greeks and Christians: Religious Cultures in Late Antiquity, Essays in Honor of W.D. Davies*, Leiden 1976, 112-128

Urbach, E.E., 'Ha-mesoret al Torat ha-Sod bi-tekufat ha-Tannaim', in E.E. Urbach – R.J. Zwi Werblowsky – Ch. Wirszubski (eds), *Studies in Mysticism and Religion Presented to Gershom G. Scholem*, Jerusalem 1967, Hebrew section, 1-28

Urbach, E.E., 'The Derasha as a Basis of the Halakha and the Problem of the Soferim', *Tarbiz* 27 (1958) 166-182, repr in idem, *World of the Sages*, 50-66 (Hebr)

Urbach, E.E., *The Halakha: Its Sources and Developments*, Givatayim 1984 (Hebr)

Urbach, E.E., 'The Place of the Ten Commandments in Ritual and Prayer', in Segal, B.Z. (ed), *The Ten Commandments*, Jerusalem 1985, 127-145 (Hebr)

Urbach, E.E., 'The Rabbinical Laws of Idolatry in the Second and Third Centuries in the Light of the Archaeological and Historical Facts', in idem, *Collected Writings*, 151-193

Urbach, E.E., *The Sages: Their Concepts and Beliefs*, ET I. Abrahams, Jerusalem 1975, repr 1979

Urbach, E.E., *Studies in Judaica*, ed M. D. Herr and J. Fraenkel, Jerusalem 1998 (Hebr)

Urbach, E.E., *The Tosafists: Their History, Writings and Methods*, 2nd ed Jerusalem 1980 (Hebr)

Urbach, E.E., *The World of the Sages – Collected Studies*, Jerusalem 1988, 2002 (Hebr)

Urbach, E.E. (ed), *Sefer Pitron Torah*, Jerusalem 1978 (facs. ed Jerusalem 1995) (Hebr)

Vargon, S., 'The Identity and Period of the Author of Ecclesiastes according to S. D. Luzzatto', *Studies in Bible and Exegesis* 5 (2000) (Hebr)

Vaux, R. de – Milik, J.T. (eds), *Qumrân Grotte 4* II. *Tefillin, Mezuzot et Targums (4Q128 – 4Q157)*, (DJD 6) Oxford 1977

Veltri, G., 'On the Influence of 'Greek Wisdom': Theoretical and Empirical Sciences in Rabbinic Literature', *JSQ* 5 (1998) 300-317

Veltri, G., *Magie und Halakha: Ansätze zu einem empirischen Wissenschaftsbegriff im spätantiken und frühmittelalterlichen Judentum*, Tübingen 1997

Veltri, G., 'The "Other" Physicians: The Amorites of the Rabbis and the Magi of Pliny', *Korot* 13 (1998-99) 37-54

Venetianer, L., *Asaf Judaeus, der älteste medizinische Schriftsteller in hebräischer Sprache*, Budapest 1915-16

Vermes, G., 'Haggadah in the Onkelos Targum ', *JSS* 8 (1963) 159-169

Vermes, G., *Post-Biblical Jewish Studies*, Leiden 1975

Vermes, G., *Scripture and Tradition in Judaism: Haggadic Studies*, Leiden 1973

Visotzky, B.L., *Fathers of the World: Essays in Rabbinic and Patristic Literatures*, Tübingen 1995

Visotzky, B.L., 'On Critical Editions of Midrash', in Teugels – Ulmer, *Recent Developments*, 155-161

Visotzky, B.L., *Midrash Mishle al pi ktav yad Vatikan Ebr 44... ve-im mavo* (etc), diss JTS, New York 1990

Visotzky, B.L., *The Midrash on Proverbs: Translated, with Annotations*, New Haven – London 1992

Vries, B. de, *Studies in the Literature of the Talmud*, Jerusalem 1968 (Hebr)

Vries, B. de, 'The Use of *Mekhilta de-Rabbi Ishmael* by the Redactor of *Mekhilta de-Rabbi Simeon ben Yohai*', in idem, *Studies*, 142-147 (Hebr)

Wacholder, B.Z., 'The Date of the Meckilta De-Rabbi Ismael', *HUCA* 39 (1968) 117-44

Wächter, L., 'Astrologie und Schicksalsglaube im rabbinischen Judentum', *Kairos* 11 (1969) 181-200

Wajsberg, E., 'The Aramaic Dialect of the Early Amoraim', *Lešonenu* 60 (1997) 95-156 (Hebr)

Wajsberg, E., 'The Difference between the Midrashic Terms 'talmud' and 'talmud lomar',' *Lešonenu* 39 (1975) 147-152 (Hebr)

Walfish, B.D., *Esther in Medieval Garb: Jewish Interpretations of the Book of Esther in the Middle Ages*, Albany 1993

Wasserstein, A., 'A Marriage Contract from the Province of Arrabia Nova: Notes on Papyrus Yadin 18', *JQR* 80 (1989) 93-130

Wasserstrom, S., 'Sefer Yesira and Early Islam: A Reappraisal', *JJTP* 3 (1993) 1-30

Weinberger, J.L., *Jewish Hymnography*, London 1998

Weinfeld, M., 'The Morning Prayers (Birkot Haschachar) in Qumran and in the Conventional Jewish Liturgy', *RQ* 13 (1988) 481-494

Weinfeld, M., *The Decalogue and the Recitation of 'Shema': The Development of the Confessions*, Tel Aviv 2001 (Hebr)

Weinstock, M.Y., *Seder Olam Rabba with commentary and annotations* 1-3, Jerusalem 1956-65

Weiss, I.H. (ed), *Sifra de-vei Rav*, Vienna 1862 (Hebr)

Weiss, I.[J.]H., *Dor Dor ve-Dorshav* (= *Zur Geschichte der jüdischen Tradition*), Vilna 1901 – New York 1924

Weiss, M., 'The Authenticity of the Explicit Discussions in Bet Shammai – Bet Hillel Disputes', *Sidra* 4 (1988) 53-66 (Hebr)

Weiss, R., *Ha-Targum ha-Arami le-Sefer Iyov*, Tel Aviv 1979

Weiss, Z. – Netzer, E., *Promise and Redemption: A Synagogue Mosaic from Sepphoris*, Jerusalem 1996

Wellhausen, J., *Die Pharisäer und die Sadducäer*, Hannover 1924

Werner, E., 'Melito of Sardis, the First Poet of Deicide', *HUCA* 37 (1966) 191-210

Wertheimer, A.J., *The Responsa of Rabbi Isaiah the Elder*, Jerusalem 1962 (Hebr)

Wertheimer, S.A., 'The Last Chapter of Pirke de-R. Eliezer', *Batei Midrashot* 1, Jerusalem 1952, 225-226, 238-243 (Hebr)

Wertheimer, S.A., *Leket Midrashim*, Jerusalem 1903

Wertheimer, S.A., *Batei Midrashot* 1-4, Jerusalem 1893-1897, 2nd ed A. Wertheimer, Jerusalem 1969

Wieder, N., 'The Habakkuk Scroll and the Targum', *JJS* 4 (1953) 14-18

Wilkinson, J., *Egeria's Travels to the Holy Land*, Jerusalem 1981

Wilkinson, J., *Jerusalem Pilgrims before the Crusades*, Jerusalem 1977

Williams, M., 'The Contribution of Jewish Inscriptions to the Study of Judaism', in W. Horbury *et al.* (eds), *The Cambridge History of Judaism* 3, Cambridge 1999, 75-93

Winter, J., *Sifra, halachischer Midrasch zu Leviticus*, Breslau 1938

Winter, J. and Wünsche, A., *Mechiltha, ein tannaitischer Midrasch zu Exodus*, Leipzig 1909

Winter, P., ΟΥ ΔΙΑ ΧΕΙΡ ΠΡΕΣΒΕΩΣ ΟΥΔΕ ΔΙΑ ΧΕΙΡ ΣΕΡΑΠΗ ΟΥΔΕ ΔΙΑ ΧΕΙΡ ΑΓΓΕΛΟΥ: Isa lxiii:9 (Gk) and the Passover Haggadah', *VT* 4 (1954) 439-441

Wise, M.O., *Thunder in Gimini*, (JSP SupSer 15) Sheffield 1994

Wolfson, E., *Through a Speculum that Shines: Vision and Imagination in Medieval Jewish Mysticism*, Princeton 1994

Wolfson, E., '*Yeridah la-Merkavah*: Typology of Ecstasy and Enthronement in Ancient Jewish Mysticismn', in R.A. Herrera (ed), *Mystics of the Book: Themes, Topics, and Typologies*, New York 1993, 13-44

Wunderbar, R.J., *Biblisch-talmudische Medizin*, Riga – Leipzig 1850-60

Wünsche, A., *Bibliothecha Rabbinica: Eine Sammlung Alter Midraschim, Neunte Lieferung: Der Midrasch zum Buche Esther*, Leipzig 1881

Yadin, Y., *Bar-Kokhba: Rediscovery of the Legendary Hero of the Last Jewish Revolt against Imperial Rome*, London and Jerusalem 1971

Yadin, Y., 'Expedition D: The Cave of Letters', *IEJ* 12 (1962) 226-257

Yadin, Y., *The Finds from the Bar-Kokhba Period in the Cave of Letters*, Jerusalem 1963

Yadin, A., *Rabbi Ishmael and the Origins of Midrash*, Philadelphia 2004

Yadin, Y., *Tefillin from Qumran*, Jerusalem 1969

Yadin, Y., 'Tefillin (Phylacteries) from Qumran (XQPhyl 1–4)', *Eretz-Israel* 9 (1969) 60-85 (W.F. Albright Volume)

Yadin, Y. (ed), *The Temple Scroll* 1-3, Jerusalem 1983

Yadin, Y. – Broshi, M. – Qimron, E., 'A Deed of Land Sale in Kefar Baru from the Period of Bar Kokhba', *Cathedra* 40 (1986) 201-213 (Hebr)

Yadin, Y. – Greenfield, J.C. – Yardeni, A. – Levine, B.A. (eds), *The Documents from the Bar Kokhba Period in the Cave of Letters, Hebrew, Aramaic and Nabatean-Aramaic Papyri*, Jerusalem 2002

Yadin, Y. – Naveh, J., *Masada I: The Aramaic and Hebrew Ostraca and Jar Inscriptions*, Jerusalem 1989

Yahalom, J., *Piyyutei Shimon ben Megas*, Jerusalem 1984 (Hebr)

Yahalom, J., *Poetic Language in the Early Piyyut*, Jerusalem 1985 (Hebr)

Yahalom, J., *Poetry and Society in Jewish Galilee of Late Antiquity*, Tel Aviv 1999 (Hebr)

Yahalom, J., 'Synagogue Inscriptions in Palestine – A Stylistic Classification', *Immanuel* 19 (1988) 47-56

Yahalom, J. and Sokoloff, M., *Jewish Palestinian Aramaic Poetry from Late Antiquity*, Jerusalem 1999 (Hebr)

Yahalom, Sh., 'R. Moshe Ha-Darshan ve-Agadat Provence Be-Mishnat Ha-Ramban', *Peamim* 94-95 (2003) 135-158

Yalon, H., *Introduction to the Vocalization of the Mishna*, Jerusalem 1964 (Hebr)

Yalon, H., *Studies in the Dead Sea Scrolls, Philological Essays (1949-1952)*, Jerusalem 1967 (Hebr)

Yalon, H., *Studies in the Hebrew Language*, Jerusalem 1971, 419-423 (Hebr)

Yardeni, A., 'A Draft of a Deed on an Ostracon from Khirbet Qumran', *IEJ* 47 (1997) 233-237

Yardeni, A., *'Nahal Se'elim' Documents*, Jerusalem 1995

Yardeni, A., 'New Jewish Aramaic Ostraca', *IEJ* 40 (1990) 130-152

Yardeni, A., *Textbook of Aramaic, Hebrew and Nabataean Documentary Texts from the Judaean Desert and Related Material* 1-2, Jerusalem 2000

Yardeni, A. – Greenfield, J.C., 'A Receipt for a Ketubba', in Gafni – Oppenheimer – Schwartz, *The Jews in the Hellenistic-Roman World*, 197-208 (Hebr)

Yaron, R., 'On Defension Clauses of some Oriental Deeds of Sale and Lease, from Mesopotamia and Egypt', *Bibliotheca Orientalis* 15 (1958) 15-22

Yaron, R., 'Gerushin be-Massada', *Ha-Uma* 3 (1965) 332-341

Yaron, R., *Gifts in Contemplation of Death in Jewish and Roman Law*, Oxford 1960

Yaron, R., *Introduction to the Law of the Aramaic Papyri*, Oxford 1961

Yaron, R., 'The Murabbaat Documents', *JJS* 11 (1960) 157-171

Yassif, E.[E.], *The Tales of Ben Sira in the Middle-Ages*, Jerusalem 1984 (Hebr)

Yassif, E., *Sippur ha-am ha-ivri: toldotav, sugav u-mashmautav*, Jerusalem 1994; ET J.S. Teitelbaum: *The Hebrew Folktale: History, Genre, Meaning*, Bloomington 1999

Yavin, S., 'The Conclusion of Prophecy', *Ha-Uma* 13 (1975) 70-79 (Hebr)

Yehuda, Z.A., 'The Two Mekhiltot on the Hebrew Slave', diss Yeshivah U, New York 1974

Yeivin, I., *The Hebrew Language Tradition as Reflected in the Babylonian Vocalization*, Jerusalem 1985 (Hebr)

Yerushalmi, M.D., *Seder Olam Rabba*, with annotations, Jerusalem 1955 (Hebr)

Yerushalmi, Y.H., *Zakhor: Jewish History and Jewish Memory*, New York 1989

Yoel, I., 'The Editio Princeps of the Antiochus Scroll', *KS* 37 (1961) 132-136 (Hebr)

York, A.D., 'The Targum in the Synagogue and in the School', *JSJ* 10 (1979) 75-86

Yuval, I.J., 'Easter and Passover as Early Jewish Christian Dialogue', in P.F. Bradshaw – L.A. Hoffman (eds), *Passover and Easter: Origin and History to Modern Times*, (Two Liturgical Traditions 5), Notre Dame ID 1999, 106-107

Yuval, I.J., 'Two Nations in Your Womb', *Perceptions of Jews and Christians*, Tel Aviv 2000 (Hebr)

Zahavy, T., *The Mishnaic Law of Blessings and Prayers*, Atlanta 1987

Zeitlin, S., *Megillat Taanit as a Source for Jewish Chronology and History in the Hellenistic and Roman Periods*, Philadelphia 1922 [= *JQR* 9 (1918-19) 71-102; 10 (1919-20) 49-80]

Zeitlin, S. 'Nennt Megillat Taanit antisaduzäische Gedenktage?' *MGJW* 81 (1937) 351-355

Zetterholm, K.H., *A Portrait of a Villain: Laban the Aramean in Rabbinic Literature*, Leuven 2002

Zucker, M., 'Two Anti-Karaite Passages', *PAAJR* 18 (1948-49) Hebrew section 1-39

Zucker, M., '*Le-Pitron Bayat 32 Middot ve'Mishnat R. Eliezer*' [For the Resolution of the Problem of the 32 Middot and '*Mishnat R. Eliezer*'] *PAAJR* 23 (1954) 1-39 (Hebr)

Zucker, M., (*Al Targum RaSa"G la-Tora*) *Rav Saadya Gaon's Translation of the Torah, Texts and Studies*, New York 1959 (Hebr)

Zucker, M., 'Teguvot li-tenuat Avalei Ziyyon ha-Karaim ba-sifrut ha-rabbanit', in *Sefer ha-Yovel le-Rabbi Hanokh Albek*, Jerusalem 1963, 378-401 (Hebr)

Zucker, M., 'Le-fitron baayat 32 Middot u-"Mishnat R. Eliezer"', *PAAJR* 13 (1954) 1-39

Zuesse, E.M. 'Divination', M. Eliade (ed in chief), *The Encyclopedia of Religion* 1-16, New York 1987, vol 4, 375-382

Zulay, M., *Ha-askola ha-paytanit shel Rav Saadiah Gaon*, Jerusalem 1964

Zulay, M., 'Li-dmutah shel leshon ha-paytanim', in idem, *Erets Israel u-fiyyuteha*, Jerusalem 1996, 415-426

Zulay, M., 'Iyyunei lashon be-fiyyutei Yannai', in idem, *Erets Israel u-fiyyuteha*, Jerusalem 1996, 451-527

Zulay, M., 'Le-toledot ha-piyyut be-Erets Yisrael', in idem, *Erets Israel u-fiyyuteha*, Jerusalem 1996, 126-197

Zulay, M., *Piyyutei Yannai*, Jerusalem–Berlin 1938

Zundel, H. *Ets Yosef, Anaf Yosef* and *Yad Yosef*, (text, comm and annot) to Seder Olam Rabba, Vilna 1845

Zunz, L., *Die gottesdienstlichen Vorträge der Juden historisch entwickelt*, Berlin 1832, 2nd ed N. Brüll Frankfort/M 1892; Hebr tr with add. notes: Ch. Albeck, *Ha-derashot be-Yisrael ve-hishtalshelutan ha-historit*, Jerusalem 1954, 3rd ed 1974

Zunz, L., *Die synagogale Poesie des Mittelalters*, Berlin 1855

Indices

Sources

Personal Names

t. Periods of Second Temple, Tannaim and Amoraim

u. Period of Geonim, Rishonim, Aharonim

755

756

Sherira Gaon, Rav   77, 404
Shimon ha-Darshan, R.   160, 187, 207, 224
Shimon of Frankfurt, R.   189, 196
Shlomo Alkabaz, R.   197, 218, 226
Shlomo b. Adret, R.   203
Shlomo ibn Gabirol   389f
Shmuel b. Hofni, R.   68, 88
Shmuel b. Nissim, R.   160, 270, 276
Shmuel ibn Sid, R.   82
Shmuel he-Hasid, R.   71, 83
Solomon ibn Adret, R.   187
Tobias b. Eliezer, R.   102, 160, 187
Yaakov b. Hananel Sekili (Sikili), R.   89, 160, 203
Yaakov Emden, R.   236
Yedaia ha-Penini of Beziers   171
Yehuda Gedalya, R.   171
Yehuda Halevi   389f
Yehuda Najar, R.   71
Yehudai Gaon, Rav   238f
Yellin, R. Arye Leib   149
Yeshaya di Trani, R.   239
Yeshua ben Yehuda   89, 103
Yishmael be-R. Yosi, R.   557
Yitshak Elijah Landau, R.   71
Yitshak Yisraeli   486, 494
Yom Tov of Sevilla, R.   203
Yosef ibn Abitur   390
Yosef ibn Haviva   203

v. Modern Period

Aberbach, M.   265
Abramson, S.   70, 72f, 75, 83, 88, 203, 377, 382, 430
Abusch, R.   401
Afik, I.   553
Aharoni, Y.   500f
Albani, M.   558
Albeck, Ch.   17, 24, 27f, 36, 39, 44, 59-65, 72, 85, 92, 94, 97, 104, 108, 110f, 123,
    131f, 134f, 141f, 146-150, 161, 163, 167, 173, 175, 177f, 180f, 183f, 186, 188, 192,
    194, 198-201, 203-205, 209, 212, 221, 228, 235, 237, 254, 292, 297, 322, 450, 588
Alexander, P.S.   244, 251f, 256, 266f, 270f, 274f, 395, 411, 417, 538, 540, 549, 553,
    557, 564
Allony, N.   159, 168, 203, 418
Alon, G.   348, 627, 629
Althaus, H.-P.   627
Altmann, A.   408
Ameling, W.   461
Amir, A.   532
Anderson, G.A.   244
Aptowitzer, V.   13, 69, 113
Arbel, D.V.   411f
Ashkenazi, B.   71

759

Compendia Rerum Iudaicarum ad Novum Testamentum

SECTION III

JEWISH TRADITIONS IN EARLY CHRISTIAN LITERATURE

Volume I
PAUL AND THE JEWISH LAW; HALAKHA IN THE LETTERS
OF THE APOSTLE TO THE GENTILES
Peter J. Tomson

Volume 2
JEWISH HISTORIOGRAPHY AND ICONOGRAPHY
IN EARLY AND MEDIEVAL CHRISTIANITY
Heinz Schreckenberg – Kurt Schubert
Translations from the German: Paul A. Cathey

Volume 3
PHILO IN EARLY CHRISTIAN LITERATURE; A SURVEY
David T. Runia

Volume 4
THE JEWISH APOCALYPTIC HERITAGE IN EARLY CHRISTIANITY
Edited by James C. VanderKam and William Adler

Volume 5
THE DIDACHE; ITS JEWISH SOURCES AND ITS PLACE
IN EARLY JUDAISM AND CHRISTIANITY
Huub van de Sandt – David Flusser

Published under the auspices of the
Foundation Compendia Rerum Iudaicarum ad Novum Testamentum
Amsterdam

CPSIA information can be obtained at www.ICGtesting.com
Printed in the USA
LVOW13*1927190314

378076LV00016B/805/P